For Reference

Not to be taken from this room

y Bernan Press
of The Rowman & Littlefield Publishing Group, Inc.
Boulevard, Suite 200, Lanham, Maryland 20706
an.com

Street, London EC2A 4NE

© 2023 by The Rowman & Littlefield Publishing Group, Inc.

636710747 (cloth) | ISBN 9781636710754 (ebook)

STATE PROFILES

THE POPULATION AND E
OF EACH U.S. STAT

Thirteenth Edition
2022

Edited by Hannah Anderson Kr

Published
An imprin
4501 Forb
www.row

86-90 Pau

Copyrigh

All rights
in any for
informati
from the
The Row
does not

ISBN 978

Bernan Press

Lanham • Boulder • New York • Londo

CONTENTS

LIST OF TABLES

The following tables are included for each state and the District of Columbia:

PREFACE

Bernan Press is pleased to present the thirteenth edition of *State Profiles*, a publication that provides a state-by-state view of the United States. Topics covered include population composition by age, sex, race, and ethnicity; marital status; migration, origin, and language; households and housing; income and poverty; health insurance; employment; educational indicators; voting; crime; and more.

The publication's primary focus is on the 50 states and the District of Columbia, each of which possesses considerable differences in economic structure and demographics and has experienced various changes over time. Changes at the national level, including the diminished importance of agriculture and manufacturing and the growing influence of global trade, have resulted in today's information-based, service-providing economy. While national trends have laid the broad framework for change, each state has been affected differently. Cyclical fluctuations have also affected states in various ways during the nationwide recessions and the subsequent recovery periods.

Beyond the market forces, local and national government policies and expenditures on items such as education, health care, energy production and conservation, national defense, and homeland security have influenced economic circumstances. This edition includes some data detailing the effects of the global COVID-19 pandemic on the economies of U.S. states.

The information provided in *State Profiles* aims to illuminate these trends. As such, the analysis and statistics are of interest not only to researchers and policy analysts but also to businesses seeking a broad basis for investments and expansion or relocation plans. The volume also profiles recent voting patterns, which will be of interest to political scientists.

DATA SELECTION

This edition of *State Profiles* generally continues the broad selection of information from previous editions.

All of the data items have been updated through 2019, 2020, and even 2021, as demographic estimates from the U.S. Census Bureau became available.

Due to the impact of the COVID-19 pandemic on data collection for the American Community Survey (ACS), the U.S. Census Bureau did not release ACS 1-year estimates for the year 2020. Therefore, we have occasionally used ACS 5-year 2020 estimates for some of the tables in this edition, which is noted in the footnotes of those tables affected.

As in the past, space constraints have influenced the amount of data presented for each state. The most meaningful and relevant data have thus been selected, analyzed, and highlighted. For most of the subjects addressed in this edition, further data are generally available from the source government agencies. Locations of sources of information are listed in notes and definitions at the end of the volume.

Although the editor has taken care to present accurate data, all statistical data are subject to a degree of error, resulting from sampling variability, erroneous reporting, and other causes. Many of the data are subject to subsequent revision by the source agencies.

The data in this book meet the publication standards of the federal agencies from which they were obtained. The responsibilities of the editor and publisher of this volume are limited to reasonable care in the reproduction and presentation of the data from the established sources.

Hannah Anderson Krog has edited the past seven editions of *State Profiles*. She previously worked as an assistant editor for Bernan Press and is now a freelance writer and editor for several reference titles. She has a B.A. in journalism from the University of Maryland.

USING THIS BOOK: ORGANIZATION AND CONTENTS

STATE PROFILES 2022 **PROVIDES:**

- Rankings of states for key demographic, economic, and social indicators
- A chapter for each state, complete with tables and figures that summarize and illustrate demographic, economic, and social characteristics
- Notes and definitions to assist with interpreting the information contained in this volume and to locate related data if desired

THE U.S. OVERVIEW. This short introduction to the demographics of the United States provides commentary on overall trends within the country.

THE STATE RANKINGS. The ranking tables that follow the national overview give state rankings by 32 characteristics, including population, demographic and age composition, income, gross domestic product, homeownership, poverty, health indicators, educational attainment, and crime rates. These rankings provide the user with a quick analysis of the performance of each state in relation to the other states.

THE STATE CHAPTERS. The state chapters are the focus of this book. Each chapter follows a standard format and contains text highlighting the key features shown in the tables and figures. Some of these tables and figures contain references to the U.S. averages for the same characteristics.

Each of the state chapters is organized as follows:

Population. This table provides data on the state's total population and average annual population growth in comparison with the national average. It also shows the major population groups by sex, age, race, and ethnicity.

Marital status. The table shows the marital status for all men and women age 15 years and over.

Housing. This table showcases data pertaining to housing, such as number of households, types of households, housing characteristics, and median gross rent, mortgage, and monthly owner cost amounts.

Migration, origin, and language. This table provides statistics on residence one year ago, year of entry, place of origin, language spoken at home, and the native-born and foreign-born populations.

Income and poverty. Median household and family income and poverty rates by sex and age are contained in this table.

Health insurance coverage. This table provides information on health insurance, by type and coverage.

Employment. These tables illustrate each state's particular economic configuration. They exhibit employment status by detailed demographic group, labor force, participation rates, employment, unemployment, average wages and salaries by industry, and employment by family type.

Education. These tables provide the user with details on educational attainment, elementary and secondary school enrollment, student/teacher ratios, per student expenditures, and higher education enrollments.

Voter participation. Information is given on voter registration and voter participation in the 2020 presidential election, categorized by sex and race/ethnicity.

Crime. This table include the number and rates of violent and property crime.

Government finance. These tables provide data on revenues and expenditures by source for each state and the District of Columbia. In addition, tax information for each state/district is included.

NOTES AND DEFINITIONS. Each chapter relies on the same standard set of federal data sources. Since the basic data sources are common to all chapters, the main body of the volume contains few footnotes. Basic data and corresponding definitions and sources are identified in the notes and definition section at the end of the volume. It provides brief descriptions, methodologies, data availability, information on calculations made by the editors, and references to additional sources of information.

INTRODUCTION

During the early 2000s, the United States experienced several economic fluctuations that had a great impact on the strength, size, and performance of its economy. The recession that began in March 2001 was concluded in a few months; however, the longer-lasting recession that began in December 2007 left a more serious impact on the country. In March 2020, the global COVID-19 pandemic reached the U.S., upending every sector of the economy. The data in this book track the impacts of these changes the United States' economy over the past two decades.

This edition of *State Profiles: The Population and Economy of Each U.S. State* creates a snapshot of the people and economy in each state and the District of Columbia. Each chapter (one per state/district) includes information on topics such as population, employment, marital status, insurance coverage, crime, government finance, housing, education, and language.

SUMMARY

The U.S. population grew 2.7 percent between 2010 and 2021. Idaho experienced the largest population growth in the nation at 21.3 percent. Other states with the largest population growth included Utah (20.8 percent), Texas (17.4 percent), Nevada (16.4 percent), Florida (15.8 percent), Colorado (15.6 percent), North Dakota (15.2 percent), Washington (15.1 percent), Arizona (13.8 percent), and South Carolina (12.2 percent). Three states' populations declined during that time period: West Virginia (–3.8 percent), Illinois (–1.2 percent), and Mississippi (–0.6 percent).

Utah had the highest percentage of population younger than 18 years old in 2021, with 28.4 percent of its population in this age group, followed by Texas at 25.3 percent. Vermont and Maine had the smallest percent of minors (18.1 percent and 18.4 percent, respectively). Maine was also the state with the highest percentage of people 65 years and older (21.7 percent), followed by Florida, which had 21.1 percent of its population in this age group. At 11.7 percent, Utah had the lowest percentage of senior residents, followed by the District of Columbia (12.8 percent) and Texas (13.1 percent).

In 2020, the median household income in the United States was $64,994. The District of Columbia had the highest median household income ($90,842), followed by Maryland ($87,063), New Jersey ($85,245), Massachusetts ($84,385), and Hawaii ($83,173). The states with the lowest median household incomes were Mississippi ($46,511), West Virginia ($48,037), Arkansas ($49,475), Louisiana ($50,800), and New Mexico ($51,243). Some correlation to the percentage of residents with a bachelor's degree or more can be inferred, as the District of Columbia, Massachusetts, Maryland, and New Jersey rank in the top five states in this category. Mississippi, West Virginia, Arkansas, and Louisiana rank in the bottom five states in this category. The unemployment rate for the United States fell from 8.1 percent in 2020 to 5.3 percent in 2021, reflecting some recovery in the U.S. job market from the effects of the COVID-19 pandemic. California had the highest percentage of unemployed residents in 2021 (7.3 percent), followed by Nevada (7.2 percent), New York (6.9 percent), and New Mexico (6.8 percent). Nebraska (2.5 percent), Utah (2.7 percent), and South Dakota (3.1 percent) had the lowest percentage of unemployed residents.

In the United States in 2020, 12.8 percent of the population lived below the poverty level. Mississippi, which had the lowest median household income, had the highest poverty rate, with 19.6 percent of its residents below the poverty level. New Hampshire had the lowest poverty rate (7.4 percent). Mississippi also had the highest rate of persons younger than 18 years of age below the poverty level (27.6 percent), followed by Louisiana (26.3 percent), New Mexico (25.6 percent), West Virginia (23.1 percent), and the District of Columbia (22.8 percent). The states with the fewest residents under 18 years of age below the poverty level included New Hampshire (8.9 percent), Utah (9.9 percent), North Dakota (11.1 percent), Colorado (11.5 percent), and Minnesota (11.6 percent).

UNITED STATES RANKING

Population, 2021		
Rank	State	Population
	United States...........................	331,893,745
1	California..................................	39,237,836
2	Texas.......................................	29,527,941
3	Florida.....................................	21,781,128
4	New York..................................	19,835,913
5	Pennsylvania............................	12,964,056
6	Illinois.....................................	12,671,469
7	Ohio..	11,780,017
8	Georgia....................................	10,799,566
9	North Carolina...........................	10,551,162
10	Michigan...................................	10,050,811
11	New Jersey...............................	9,267,130
12	Virginia....................................	8,642,274
13	Washington...............................	7,738,692
14	Arizona....................................	7,276,316
15	Massachusetts..........................	6,984,723
16	Tennessee................................	6,975,218
17	Indiana....................................	6,805,985
18	Missouri...................................	6,168,187
19	Maryland..................................	6,165,129
20	Wisconsin.................................	5,895,908
21	Colorado..................................	5,812,069
22	Minnesota.................................	5,707,390
23	South Carolina..........................	5,190,705
24	Alabama..................................	5,039,877
25	Louisiana.................................	4,624,047
26	Kentucky..................................	4,509,394
27	Oregon....................................	4,246,155
28	Oklahoma................................	3,986,639
29	Connecticut..............................	3,605,597
30	Utah..	3,337,975
31	Iowa..	3,193,079
32	Nevada....................................	3,143,991
33	Arkansas.................................	3,025,891
34	Mississippi...............................	2,949,965
35	Kansas....................................	2,934,582
36	New Mexico..............................	2,115,877
37	Nebraska.................................	1,963,692
38	Idaho......................................	1,900,923
39	West Virginia............................	1,782,959
40	Hawaii.....................................	1,441,553
41	New Hampshire..........................	1,388,992
42	Maine......................................	1,372,247
43	Montana...................................	1,104,271
44	Rhode Island............................	1,095,610
45	Delaware..................................	1,003,384
46	South Dakota............................	895,376
47	North Dakota.............................	774,948
48	Alaska.....................................	732,673
49	District of Columbia....................	670,050
50	Vermont...................................	645,570
51	Wyoming..................................	578,803

Population, Percent Change, 2010–2021		
Rank	State	Percent
	United States...........................	2.7
1	Idaho......................................	21.3
2	Utah..	20.8
3	Texas.......................................	17.4
4	Nevada....................................	16.4
5	Florida.....................................	15.8
6	Colorado..................................	15.6
7	North Dakota.............................	15.2
8	Washington...............................	15.1
9	Arizona....................................	13.8
10	South Carolina..........................	12.2
11	Delaware..................................	11.7
12	Montana...................................	11.6
13	Georgia....................................	11.5
14	District of Columbia....................	11.4
15	Oregon....................................	10.8
16	North Carolina...........................	10.7
17	South Dakota............................	10.0
18	Tennessee................................	9.9
19	Virginia....................................	8.0
20	Minnesota.................................	7.6
21	Nebraska.................................	7.5
22	Maryland..................................	6.8
23	Massachusetts..........................	6.7
24	Oklahoma................................	6.3
25	Hawaii.....................................	6.0
26	New Hampshire..........................	5.5
27	Alabama..................................	5.4
27	New Jersey...............................	5.4
29	California..................................	5.3
30	Indiana....................................	5.0
31	Iowa..	4.8
32	Rhode Island............................	4.1
33	Kentucky..................................	3.9
34	Arkansas.................................	3.8
35	Wisconsin.................................	3.7
36	Maine......................................	3.3
37	Vermont...................................	3.2
37	Alaska.....................................	3.2
39	Missouri...................................	3.0
40	Kansas....................................	2.9
41	New Mexico..............................	2.8
42	Wyoming..................................	2.7
43	New York..................................	2.4
44	Ohio..	2.1
44	Pennsylvania............................	2.1
46	Louisiana.................................	2.0
47	Michigan...................................	1.7
48	Connecticut..............................	0.9
49	Mississippi...............................	-0.6
50	Illinois.....................................	-1.2
51	West Virginia............................	-3.8

Percent Population Under 18 Years Old, 2021		
Rank	State	Percent
	United States...........................	22.2
1	Utah..	28.4
2	Texas.......................................	25.3
3	Idaho......................................	24.7
4	South Dakota............................	24.6
4	Nebraska.................................	24.6
6	Alaska.....................................	24.5
7	Oklahoma................................	24.1
8	North Dakota.............................	24.0
8	Kansas....................................	24.0
10	Mississippi...............................	23.5
11	Louisiana.................................	23.4
11	Georgia....................................	23.4
13	Indiana....................................	23.3
14	Arkansas.................................	23.2
15	Minnesota.................................	23.1
15	Iowa..	23.1
17	Wyoming..................................	22.9
18	Kentucky..................................	22.5
19	Missouri...................................	22.4
19	New Mexico..............................	22.4
19	California..................................	22.4
22	Alabama..................................	22.3
23	Nevada....................................	22.2
23	Arizona....................................	22.2
25	Illinois.....................................	22.1
25	Ohio..	22.1
25	Maryland..................................	22.1
25	Tennessee................................	22.1
29	New Jersey...............................	21.8
29	North Carolina...........................	21.8
29	Virginia....................................	21.8
32	Washington...............................	21.7
33	Wisconsin.................................	21.6
34	South Carolina..........................	21.5
35	Michigan...................................	21.4
35	Colorado..................................	21.4
37	Montana...................................	21.3
38	Hawaii.....................................	21.1
39	Delaware..................................	20.8
40	New York..................................	20.7
41	Pennsylvania............................	20.6
42	Oregon....................................	20.3
43	Connecticut..............................	20.2
44	West Virginia............................	20.1
45	Florida.....................................	19.7
46	Massachusetts..........................	19.5
47	Rhode Island............................	19.1
48	District of Columbia....................	18.8
49	New Hampshire..........................	18.5
50	Maine......................................	18.4
51	Vermont...................................	18.1

4 STATE PROFILES

Percent Population 65 Years and Over, 2021

Rank	State	Percent
	United States	16.8
1	Maine	21.7
2	Florida	21.1
3	West Virginia	20.7
4	Vermont	20.6
5	Delaware	20.1
6	Montana	19.6
6	Hawaii	19.6
8	New Hampshire	19.3
9	Pennsylvania	19.0
10	South Carolina	18.6
10	Oregon	18.6
12	New Mexico	18.5
13	Arizona	18.3
14	Rhode Island	18.1
14	Michigan	18.1
16	Connecticut	18.0
17	Wyoming	17.9
17	Wisconsin	17.9
19	Ohio	17.8
20	Iowa	17.7
21	Alabama	17.6
21	Missouri	17.6
23	New York	17.5
23	South Dakota	17.5
23	Arkansas	17.5
26	Massachusetts	17.4
27	Kentucky	17.1
28	North Carolina	17.0
28	Tennessee	17.0
30	New Jersey	16.9
31	Mississippi	16.8
32	Minnesota	16.7
32	Kansas	16.7
34	Idaho	16.6
34	Illinois	16.6
36	Nevada	16.5
36	Louisiana	16.5
38	Nebraska	16.4
38	Indiana	16.4
40	Virginia	16.3
40	Maryland	16.3
42	Washington	16.2
42	Oklahoma	16.2
44	North Dakota	16.1
45	California	15.2
46	Colorado	15.1
47	Georgia	14.7
48	Alaska	13.3
49	Texas	13.1
50	District of Columbia	12.8
51	Utah	11.7

Percent White Alone, 2021

Rank	State	Percent
	United States	78.4
1	Maine	94.2
2	Vermont	94.0
3	West Virginia	93.1
4	Idaho	92.8
4	New Hampshire	92.8
6	Wyoming	92.4
7	Utah	90.3
8	Iowa	90.1
9	Montana	88.7
10	Nebraska	87.7
10	Kentucky	87.1
12	North Dakota	86.7
13	Wisconsin	86.6
14	Colorado	86.5
15	Oregon	86.2
16	Kansas	86.0
17	Indiana	84.2
17	South Dakota	84.2
19	Rhode Island	83.1
20	Minnesota	83.0
21	Missouri	82.6
22	Arizona	82.0
23	New Mexico	81.3
24	Ohio	81.2
25	Pennsylvania	81.0
26	Massachusetts	79.8
27	Michigan	79.0
28	Connecticut	78.8
29	Arkansas	78.6
30	Tennessee	78.2
31	Texas	77.9
32	Washington	77.5
33	Florida	76.9
34	Illinois	76.3
35	Oklahoma	73.2
36	Nevada	72.8
37	New Jersey	71.1
37	California	71.1
39	North Carolina	70.1
40	New York	69.1
41	Alabama	68.9
42	Virginia	68.8
43	South Carolina	68.6
44	Delaware	68.4
45	Alaska	64.5
46	Louisiana	62.4
47	Georgia	59.4
48	Mississippi	58.8
49	Maryland	57.8
50	District of Columbia	45.9
51	Hawaii	25.3

Percent Black or African American Alone, 2021

Rank	State	Percent
	United States	14.9
1	District of Columbia	45.8
2	Mississippi	38.0
3	Louisiana	33.0
3	Georgia	33.0
5	Maryland	31.4
6	Alabama	26.8
7	South Carolina	26.7
8	Delaware	23.6
9	North Carolina	22.3
10	Virginia	20.0
11	New York	17.6
12	Florida	17.0
12	Tennessee	17.0
14	Arkansas	15.7
15	New Jersey	15.3
16	Illinois	14.7
17	Michigan	14.1
18	Ohio	13.2
18	Texas	13.2
20	Connecticut	12.7
21	Pennsylvania	12.2
22	Missouri	11.8
23	Nevada	10.6
24	Indiana	10.2
25	Massachusetts	9.3
26	Rhode Island	8.8
27	Kentucky	8.6
28	Oklahoma	7.8
29	Minnesota	7.4
30	Wisconsin	6.8
31	California	6.5
32	Kansas	6.2
33	Arizona	5.4
34	Nebraska	5.3
35	Colorado	4.7
36	Washington	4.5
37	Iowa	4.3
38	West Virginia	3.7
39	Alaska	3.6
40	North Dakota	3.5
41	New Mexico	2.7
42	South Dakota	2.5
43	Oregon	2.3
44	Hawaii	2.2
45	New Hampshire	1.9
46	Maine	1.8
47	Utah	1.5
47	Vermont	1.5
49	Wyoming	1.2
50	Idaho	0.9
51	Montana	0.6

Percent American Indian and Alaska Native Alone, 2021

Rank	State	Percent
	United States............................	2.2
1	Alaska	15.7
2	New Mexico	11.2
3	Oklahoma...................................	9.7
4	South Dakota	9.0
5	Montana.....................................	6.6
6	North Dakota	5.7
7	Arizona......................................	5.3
8	Wyoming	2.8
9	Washington................................	2.0
10	Oregon	1.9
11	Idaho...	1.7
11	Nevada	1.7
11	California	1.7
11	Colorado	1.7
15	Nebraska	1.6
15	North Carolina............................	1.6
15	Utah	1.6
18	Minnesota	1.4
19	Kansas	1.2
19	Wisconsin	1.2
19	Rhode Island	1.2
22	Arkansas	1.1
22	Texas...	1.1
24	New York....................................	1.0
25	Louisiana	0.8
26	Michigan	0.7
26	Maine...	0.7
26	Alabama	0.7
26	Delaware	0.7
26	New Jersey	0.7
26	Connecticut................................	0.7
26	Maryland	0.7
33	Mississippi.................................	0.6
33	Illinois.......................................	0.6
33	District of Columbia	0.6
33	Missouri.....................................	0.6
33	South Carolina	0.6
33	Iowa..	0.6
33	Virginia......................................	0.6
40	Georgia	0.5
40	Florida	0.5
40	Massachusetts	0.5
40	Tennessee	0.5
44	Indiana	0.4
44	Pennsylvania	0.4
44	Hawaii	0.4
44	Vermont	0.4
48	New Hampshire...........................	0.3
48	Kentucky	0.3
48	Ohio	0.3
48	West Virginia..............................	0.3

Percent Asian Alone, 2021

Rank	State	Percent
	United States............................	7.2
1	Hawaii	36.8
2	California...................................	15.9
3	New Jersey	10.3
4	Washington................................	10.0
5	New York....................................	9.3
6	Nevada	9.1
7	Massachusetts	7.5
8	Virginia......................................	7.2
9	Maryland	6.9
10	Alaska	6.6
11	Illinois.......................................	6.1
12	Texas...	5.5
13	Minnesota	5.4
14	Connecticut................................	5.1
15	Oregon	5.0
16	Georgia	4.6
17	District of Columbia	4.5
18	Delaware	4.2
19	Pennsylvania	3.9
20	Arizona......................................	3.8
21	Rhode Island	3.7
22	Colorado	3.6
23	Michigan	3.4
23	North Carolina............................	3.4
25	Kansas	3.2
25	Wisconsin	3.2
27	New Hampshire...........................	3.1
28	Florida	3.0
29	Nebraska	2.8
29	Iowa..	2.8
31	Indiana	2.7
31	Utah	2.7
31	Ohio	2.7
34	Oklahoma...................................	2.5
35	Missouri.....................................	2.2
36	Tennessee	2.0
36	Vermont	2.0
38	South Carolina	1.9
38	New Mexico	1.9
38	Louisiana	1.9
41	Arkansas	1.8
42	Kentucky	1.7
42	South Dakota	1.7
42	North Dakota	1.7
45	Idaho...	1.6
45	Alabama	1.6
47	Maine...	1.4
48	Mississippi.................................	1.1
48	Wyoming	1.1
50	Montana.....................................	1.0
51	West Virginia..............................	0.9

Percent Native Hawaiian and Other Pacific Islander Alone, 2021

Rank	State	Percent
	United States............................	0.5
1	Hawaii	10.5
2	Alaska	1.6
3	Utah	1.1
4	Nevada	0.9
5	Washington................................	0.8
6	California	0.5
6	Oregon	0.5
8	Arkansas	0.4
9	Arizona......................................	0.3
10	Oklahoma...................................	0.2
10	Idaho...	0.2
10	Colorado	0.2
10	Rhode Island	0.2
10	Iowa..	0.2
10	Missouri.....................................	0.2
10	New Mexico	0.2
10	District of Columbia	0.2
10	Texas...	0.2
19	North Carolina............................	0.1
19	New York....................................	0.1
19	Kansas	0.1
19	Georgia	0.1
19	Nebraska	0.1
19	New Jersey	0.1
19	Maryland	0.1
19	Virginia......................................	0.1
19	Florida	0.1
19	Connecticut................................	0.1
19	Delaware	0.1
19	Massachusetts	0.1
19	Alabama	0.1
19	Kentucky	0.1
19	Tennessee	0.1
19	South Dakota	0.1
19	South Carolina	0.1
19	Wyoming	0.1
19	North Dakota	0.1
19	Montana.....................................	0.1
19	Pennsylvania	0.1
19	Minnesota	0.1
19	Indiana	0.1
19	Illinois.......................................	0.1
19	Ohio	0.1
19	Mississippi.................................	0.1
19	Louisiana	0.1
19	Wisconsin	0.1
19	New Hampshire...........................	0.1
48	Michigan	Z
48	Maine...	Z
48	Vermont	Z
48	West Virginia..............................	Z

Z = Value greater than zero but less than half of the unit shown.

Percent Two or More Races, 2021

Rank	State	Percent
	United States..................	2.9
1	Hawaii	25.0
2	Alaska	7.9
3	Oklahoma..................	6.6
4	Washington...............	5.2
5	Nevada	4.9
6	California..................	4.2
6	Oregon	4.2
8	Virginia....................	3.4
9	Colorado	3.3
9	Kansas	3.3
11	Arizona.....................	3.1
11	Maryland..................	3.1
13	District of Columbia	3.0
13	Rhode Island.............	3.0
13	Montana....................	3.0
16	Delaware...................	2.9
17	Utah.........................	2.8
17	Minnesota.................	2.8
17	New York..................	2.8
20	New Mexico	2.7
20	Michigan...................	2.7
20	Massachusetts...........	2.7
20	Idaho.......................	2.7
24	Connecticut..............	2.6
24	South Dakota	2.6
24	Ohio........................	2.6
24	Missouri...................	2.6
28	North Carolina..........	2.5
29	Nebraska..................	2.4
29	North Dakota............	2.4
29	New Jersey	2.4
29	Wyoming..................	2.4
29	Georgia....................	2.4
29	Florida.....................	2.4
35	Arkansas..................	2.3
35	Indiana....................	2.3
35	Pennsylvania............	2.3
38	Illinois.....................	2.2
38	Texas.......................	2.2
38	Wisconsin.................	2.2
38	Kentucky..................	2.2
38	Tennessee.................	2.2
43	South Carolina	2.1
43	Iowa........................	2.1
43	Vermont...................	2.1
46	West Virginia............	2.0
47	Maine.......................	1.9
47	Alabama...................	1.9
49	New Hampshire..........	1.8
49	Louisiana	1.8
51	Mississippi................	1.4

Percent Hispanic or Latino,[1] 2021

Rank	State	Percent
	United States..................	18.9
1	New Mexico	50.1
2	Texas.......................	40.2
2	California..................	40.2
4	Arizona.....................	32.3
5	Nevada	29.9
6	Florida.....................	26.8
7	Colorado	22.3
8	New Jersey	21.5
9	New York..................	19.5
10	Illinois.....................	18.0
11	Connecticut..............	17.7
12	Rhode Island.............	17.1
13	Utah.........................	14.8
14	Oregon	14.0
15	Washington...............	13.7
16	Idaho.......................	13.3
17	Massachusetts...........	12.8
18	Kansas	12.7
19	Nebraska..................	12.0
20	Oklahoma..................	11.7
21	District of Columbia	11.5
22	Hawaii	11.1
22	Maryland..................	11.1
24	Wyoming..................	10.6
25	Georgia....................	10.2
25	North Carolina..........	10.2
25	Virginia....................	10.2
28	Delaware...................	10.1
29	Pennsylvania............	8.4
30	Arkansas..................	8.3
31	Indiana....................	7.7
32	Wisconsin.................	7.5
32	Alaska	7.5
34	Iowa........................	6.7
35	South Carolina	6.4
36	Tennessee.................	6.1
37	Minnesota.................	5.8
38	Michigan...................	5.6
38	Louisiana	5.6
40	Alabama...................	4.8
41	Missouri...................	4.7
42	South Dakota	4.6
43	North Dakota............	4.4
43	New Hampshire..........	4.4
45	Montana....................	4.3
45	Ohio........................	4.3
47	Kentucky..................	4.2
48	Mississippi................	3.5
49	Vermont...................	2.2
50	Maine.......................	2.0
51	West Virginia............	1.9

[1] May be of any race.

Birth Rate, 2020

Rank	State	Rate per 1,000 population
	United States..................	11.0
1	Utah.........................	14.1
2	North Dakota............	13.1
3	Alaska	13.0
4	Nebraska..................	12.5
4	Texas.......................	12.5
6	District of Columbia	12.4
7	Louisiana	12.3
7	South Dakota	12.3
9	Mississippi................	12.0
9	Oklahoma..................	12.0
11	Idaho.......................	11.8
11	Kansas	11.8
13	Alabama...................	11.7
14	Arkansas..................	11.6
14	Indiana....................	11.6
16	Kentucky..................	11.5
17	Georgia....................	11.4
17	Iowa........................	11.4
17	Tennessee.................	11.4
20	Maryland..................	11.3
20	Missouri...................	11.3
22	Hawaii	11.2
23	Minnesota.................	11.2
24	New Jersey	11.0
24	North Carolina..........	11.0
24	Ohio........................	11.0
24	Virginia....................	11.0
28	New York..................	10.8
28	Washington...............	10.8
30	California..................	10.7
30	Nevada	10.7
30	South Carolina	10.7
33	Colorado	10.6
33	Illinois.....................	10.6
35	Delaware...................	10.5
35	Wyoming..................	10.5
37	Arizona.....................	10.4
37	Michigan...................	10.4
37	New Mexico	10.4
37	Wisconsin.................	10.4
41	Pennsylvania............	10.2
42	Montana....................	10.0
43	West Virginia............	9.7
44	Florida.....................	9.6
44	Massachusetts...........	9.6
44	Rhode Island.............	9.6
47	Connecticut..............	9.4
47	Oregon	9.4
49	New Hampshire..........	8.6
50	Maine.......................	8.5
51	Vermont...................	8.2

Drug Overdose Death Rate, 2020

Rank	State	Age-adjusted rate per 100,000 population
	United States............................	28.3
1	Washington..............................	81.4
2	Kansas.....................................	49.2
3	Delaware..................................	47.3
4	North Dakota............................	47.2
5	South Dakota	45.6
6	Maine.......................................	44.6
7	Kentucky..................................	42.7
8	Oregon.....................................	42.4
9	Louisiana..................................	39.7
10	Connecticut..............................	39.1
11	New Jersey	39.0
12	Pennsylvania............................	38.2
13	Illinois......................................	36.7
14	Arizona.....................................	35.8
15	District of Columbia	35.0
16	Rhode Island............................	34.9
17	Maryland..................................	33.9
18	Utah..	32.9
19	Mississippi................................	32.1
19	New Hampshire.........................	32.1
21	New York..................................	30.9
22	Nevada.....................................	30.3
23	Massachusetts..........................	28.6
24	Idaho.......................................	28.1
25	West Virginia............................	27.7
26	Vermont...................................	26.6
27	Nebraska..................................	26.0
28	New Mexico	25.4
29	Colorado	24.9
30	Alabama...................................	22.3
31	Alaska	22.0
31	Virginia....................................	22.0
33	California..................................	21.8
34	Minnesota	21.1
35	Texas.......................................	20.5
36	Ohio..	19.4
37	Arkansas..................................	19.1
38	Michigan..................................	19.0
39	Oklahoma.................................	18.7
40	Georgia....................................	18.3
41	Florida.....................................	18.0
42	Iowa..	17.4
42	Wisconsin.................................	17.4
44	Hawaii......................................	15.9
45	Missouri...................................	15.6
45	North Carolina..........................	15.6
47	Indiana	14.3
48	Tennessee	14.1
49	Montana...................................	11.3
50	South Carolina	10.3
51	Wyoming	8.1

Voter Turnout, November 2020

Rank	State	Percent voted, population 18 years and older
	United States............................	61.3
1	District of Columbia	77.8
2	Minnesota	74.3
3	Montana...................................	72.6
4	New Hampshire.........................	72.4
5	Wisconsin.................................	71.7
6	Oregon.....................................	71.3
7	Maine.......................................	70.5
8	Mississippi................................	69.2
9	Maryland..................................	68.7
10	Iowa..	68.5
10	Ohio..	68.5
12	New Jersey	68.2
12	Pennsylvania............................	68.2
14	Vermont...................................	67.5
15	Virginia....................................	66.0
16	Kentucky..................................	65.3
16	North Dakota............................	65.3
18	Arizona.....................................	64.7
19	Missouri...................................	64.5
20	Washington..............................	64.3
21	Michigan..................................	64.1
21	Wyoming	64.1
23	Delaware..................................	63.8
24	Tennessee	63.3
25	Colorado	62.7
25	Illinois......................................	62.7
27	Alaska	62.4
28	Nebraska..................................	62.2
29	Idaho.......................................	61.6
30	Rhode Island............................	61.3
30	South Carolina	61.3
32	Georgia....................................	60.9
33	Connecticut..............................	60.5
34	Kansas.....................................	60.1
35	Hawaii......................................	59.7
35	Utah..	59.7
37	Alabama...................................	59.6
38	Louisiana..................................	59.4
39	Indiana	58.9
39	Massachusetts..........................	58.9
39	North Carolina..........................	58.9
42	New Mexico	58.3
43	South Dakota	57.7
44	New York..................................	57.0
45	Florida.....................................	56.4
46	Nevada.....................................	56.3
47	California..................................	55.7
48	Oklahoma.................................	55.5
49	Texas.......................................	55.3
49	West Virginia............................	55.3
51	Arkansas..................................	51.9

Percent of Persons 25 Years and Over with a Bachelor's Degree or More, 2020

Rank	State	Percent
	United States............................	32.9
1	District of Columbia	59.8
2	Massachusetts..........................	44.5
3	Colorado	41.6
4	Maryland..................................	40.9
5	New Jersey	40.7
6	Connecticut..............................	40.0
7	Vermont...................................	39.7
8	Virginia....................................	39.5
9	New Hampshire.........................	37.6
10	New York..................................	37.5
11	Minnesota	36.8
12	Washington..............................	36.7
13	Illinois......................................	35.5
14	Rhode Island............................	35.0
15	California..................................	34.7
15	Utah..	34.7
17	Oregon.....................................	34.4
18	Kansas.....................................	33.9
19	Hawaii......................................	33.6
20	Montana...................................	33.1
21	Delaware..................................	32.7
22	Maine.......................................	32.5
22	Nebraska..................................	32.5
24	Pennsylvania............................	32.3
25	Georgia....................................	32.2
26	North Carolina..........................	32.0
27	Wisconsin.................................	30.8
28	North Dakota............................	30.7
28	Texas.......................................	30.7
30	Florida.....................................	30.5
31	Arizona.....................................	30.3
32	Alaska	30.0
32	Michigan..................................	30.0
34	Missouri...................................	29.9
35	Iowa..	29.3
35	South Dakota	29.3
37	South Carolina	29.0
38	Ohio..	28.9
39	Idaho.......................................	28.7
40	Tennessee	28.2
40	Wyoming	28.2
42	New Mexico	28.1
43	Indiana	27.2
44	Alabama...................................	26.2
45	Oklahoma.................................	26.1
46	Nevada.....................................	25.5
47	Kentucky..................................	25.0
48	Louisiana..................................	24.9
49	Arkansas..................................	23.8
50	Mississippi................................	22.8
51	West Virginia............................	21.3

Violent Crime, 2020

Rank	State	Rate per 100,000 population
	United States...............	398.5
1	District of Columbia[1]	999.8
2	Alaska...............................	837.8
3	New Mexico.........................	778.3
4	Tennessee...........................	672.7
5	Arkansas............................	671.9
6	Louisiana............................	639.4
7	Missouri.............................	542.7
8	South Carolina....................	530.7
9	South Dakota......................	501.4
10	Arizona..............................	484.8
11	Michigan............................	478.0
12	Montana.............................	469.8
13	Nevada...............................	460.3
14	Oklahoma...........................	458.6
15	Alabama.............................	453.6
16	Texas.................................	446.5
17	California............................	442.0
18	Delaware............................	431.9
19	Illinois...............................	425.9
20	Kansas...............................	425.0
21	Colorado............................	423.1
22	North Carolina.....................	419.3
23	Georgia..............................	400.1
24	Maryland............................	399.9
25	Pennsylvania.......................	389.5
26	Florida...............................	383.6
27	New York............................	363.8
28	Indiana...............................	357.7
29	West Virginia.......................	355.9
30	Nebraska............................	334.1
31	North Dakota.......................	329.0
32	Wisconsin...........................	323.4
33	Massachusetts.....................	308.8
33	Ohio..................................	308.8
35	Iowa..................................	303.5
36	Washington.........................	293.7
37	Oregon...............................	291.9
38	Mississippi..........................	291.2
39	Minnesota...........................	277.5
40	Utah..................................	260.7
41	Kentucky............................	259.1
42	Hawaii...............................	254.2
43	Idaho.................................	242.6
44	Wyoming............................	234.2
45	Rhode Island.......................	230.8
46	Virginia..............................	208.7
47	New Jersey.........................	195.4
48	Connecticut.........................	181.6
49	Vermont.............................	173.4
50	New Hampshire....................	146.4
51	Maine.................................	108.6

[1] Includes offenses reported by the Metro Transit Police and the District of Columbia Fire and Emergency Medical Services: Arson

Property Crime, 2020

Rank	State	Rate per 100,000 population
	United States...............	1,958.2
1	District of Columbia................	3,493.0
2	Louisiana............................	2,884.4
3	New Mexico.........................	2,841.9
4	Colorado............................	2,833.8
5	Washington.........................	2,732.4
6	South Carolina....................	2,721.1
7	Oklahoma...........................	2,705.6
8	Oregon...............................	2,659.0
9	Arkansas............................	2,613.4
10	Missouri.............................	2,531.0
11	Tennessee...........................	2,492.8
12	Utah..................................	2,464.4
13	Hawaii...............................	2,411.4
14	Alaska...............................	2,260.5
15	Texas.................................	2,245.0
16	Arizona..............................	2,227.7
17	North Carolina.....................	2,226.5
18	Kansas...............................	2,199.1
19	California............................	2,138.9
20	Alabama.............................	2,136.8
21	Minnesota...........................	2,124.9
22	North Dakota.......................	2,124.1
23	Montana.............................	2,120.8
24	Mississippi..........................	2,101.6
25	Georgia..............................	2,007.4
26	Delaware............................	1,961.4
27	South Dakota......................	1,956.7
28	Nevada...............................	1,926.6
29	Nebraska............................	1,909.2
30	Ohio..................................	1,850.3
31	Indiana...............................	1,783.2
32	Kentucky............................	1,779.5
33	Florida...............................	1,769.4
34	Iowa..................................	1,698.2
35	Pennsylvania.......................	1,644.1
36	Wyoming............................	1,610.6
37	Maryland............................	1,609.8
38	Connecticut.........................	1,565.1
39	Illinois...............................	1,559.4
40	Wisconsin...........................	1,485.7
41	Virginia..............................	1,456.4
42	New York............................	1,410.7
43	West Virginia.......................	1,399.4
44	Michigan............................	1,360.9
45	Rhode Island.......................	1,245.5
46	Vermont.............................	1,217.0
47	New Jersey.........................	1,158.2
48	Maine.................................	1,156.2
49	Idaho.................................	1,111.9
50	New Hampshire....................	1,098.9
51	Massachusetts.....................	1,053.2

State & Local Government Employment, 2021 (Full-time equivalent employees)

Rank	State	State & local employees per 1,000 residents
	United States...............	49.4
1	Wyoming............................	86.3
2	District of Columbia................	75.7
3	Alaska...............................	68.7
4	Kansas...............................	67.8
5	Nebraska............................	63.6
6	North Dakota.......................	62.5
7	Mississippi..........................	60.7
8	New York............................	59.4
9	Iowa..................................	58.7
10	Vermont.............................	57.6
11	New Mexico.........................	56.7
12	Alabama.............................	56.3
13	Louisiana............................	56.1
14	West Virginia.......................	55.2
15	Arkansas............................	54.7
16	Montana.............................	53.9
17	Colorado............................	53.4
18	South Dakota......................	52.6
19	South Carolina....................	52.3
19	Minnesota...........................	52.3
21	Kentucky............................	52.1
22	Texas.................................	51.9
23	North Carolina.....................	51.8
24	Oklahoma...........................	51.4
24	Virginia..............................	51.4
26	Maine.................................	51.1
27	Hawaii...............................	50.9
28	Maryland............................	50.1
29	Missouri.............................	50.0
29	Delaware............................	50.0
31	Washington.........................	49.9
32	New Jersey.........................	49.8
33	Connecticut.........................	49.2
34	Utah..................................	49.1
35	Oregon...............................	48.9
36	New Hampshire....................	48.7
37	Ohio..................................	47.7
38	Indiana...............................	47.5
39	Tennessee...........................	47.4
40	Illinois...............................	47.3
40	Georgia..............................	47.3
42	Massachusetts.....................	47.2
43	Wisconsin...........................	47.1
44	California............................	46.7
45	Idaho.................................	45.4
46	Rhode Island.......................	42.6
47	Pennsylvania.......................	41.8
47	Michigan............................	41.8
49	Florida...............................	40.9
50	Arizona..............................	38.4
51	Nevada...............................	36.2

Unemployment Rate, 2021

Rank	State	Unemployment rate
	United States............................	5.3
1	California................................	7.3
2	Nevada....................................	7.2
3	New York.................................	6.9
4	New Mexico..............................	6.8
5	District of Columbia	6.6
6	Alaska	6.4
7	Connecticut..............................	6.3
8	New Jersey	6.3
9	Pennsylvania............................	6.3
10	Illinois	6.1
11	Michigan	5.9
12	Maryland	5.8
13	Hawaii	5.7
14	Massachusetts..........................	5.7
15	Texas	5.7
16	Mississippi	5.6
17	Rhode Island............................	5.6
18	Louisiana	5.5
19	Colorado	5.4
20	Delaware	5.3
21	Oregon	5.2
22	Washington...............................	5.2
23	Ohio	5.1
24	West Virginia............................	5.0
25	Arizona....................................	4.9
26	North Carolina..........................	4.8
27	Kentucky	4.7
28	Florida.....................................	4.6
29	Maine	4.6
30	Wyoming	4.5
31	Missouri...................................	4.4
32	Tennessee	4.3
33	Iowa	4.2
34	Arkansas	4.0
35	South Carolina	4.0
36	Georgia	3.9
37	Virginia....................................	3.9
38	Oklahoma.................................	3.8
39	Wisconsin	3.8
40	North Dakota............................	3.7
41	Idaho	3.6
42	Indiana....................................	3.6
43	New Hampshire.........................	3.5
44	Alabama	3.4
45	Minnesota	3.4
46	Montana	3.4
47	Vermont	3.4
48	Kansas	3.2
49	South Dakota	3.1
50	Utah	2.7
51	Nebraska	2.5

Average Hourly Earnings of Employees on Private Nonfarm Payrolls, 2020

Rank	State	Percent
	United States............................	29.33
1	District of Columbia	49.78
2	Massachusetts..........................	35.76
3	Washington...............................	34.52
4	California................................	34.37
5	Connecticut..............................	34.04
6	New York.................................	33.92
7	New Jersey	32.12
8	Maryland	32.00
9	Minnesota	31.68
10	Hawaii	31.24
11	Colorado	31.00
12	Alaska	30.99
13	Illinois	30.04
14	Virginia....................................	29.80
15	New Hampshire.........................	29.50
16	Rhode Island............................	28.88
17	Oregon	28.86
18	Delaware	28.66
19	Utah	28.45
20	North Dakota............................	27.61
21	Wisconsin	27.57
22	Arizona....................................	27.55
23	Michigan	27.54
24	Vermont	27.46
25	Georgia	27.38
26	Pennsylvania............................	27.28
27	Texas	27.03
28	Nebraska	27.00
29	Florida.....................................	26.92
30	Wyoming	26.64
31	North Carolina..........................	26.57
32	Missouri...................................	26.55
33	Indiana....................................	26.25
34	Maine	26.14
35	Kansas	26.06
36	Ohio	26.05
36	South Carolina	26.05
38	Nevada....................................	26.04
39	Alabama	25.82
40	Montana	25.80
41	Iowa	25.73
42	Louisiana	25.36
43	Tennessee	25.08
44	Oklahoma.................................	24.90
45	Idaho	24.79
46	West Virginia............................	24.51
47	South Dakota	24.48
48	New Mexico..............................	23.87
49	Kentucky	23.63
50	Arkansas	23.39
51	Mississippi	22.33

Per Capita Personal Income, 2021

Rank	State	Dollars
	United States............................	63,444
1	District of Columbia	96,873
2	Massachusetts..........................	82,475
3	Connecticut..............................	82,082
4	New York.................................	76,415
5	California................................	76,386
6	New Jersey	74,805
7	New Hampshire.........................	72,003
8	Washington...............................	71,889
9	Maryland	69,266
10	Colorado	69,016
11	Alaska	67,138
12	Illinois	67,095
13	Wyoming	65,627
14	North Dakota............................	65,544
15	Minnesota	65,486
16	Virginia....................................	65,408
17	South Dakota	64,720
18	Pennsylvania............................	64,054
19	Nebraska	62,095
20	Rhode Island............................	61,942
21	Florida.....................................	60,761
22	Oregon	60,676
23	Hawaii	60,389
24	Vermont	59,704
25	Texas	59,674
26	Kansas	59,324
27	Delaware	59,002
28	Wisconsin	58,564
29	Nevada....................................	58,233
30	Maine	57,159
31	Iowa	56,973
32	Montana	56,672
33	Ohio	56,483
34	Indiana....................................	56,153
35	Michigan	55,551
36	Utah	55,392
37	Georgia	55,289
38	Missouri...................................	55,159
39	North Carolina..........................	55,043
40	Tennessee	54,873
41	Louisiana	54,435
42	Arizona....................................	54,301
43	Oklahoma.................................	53,156
44	South Carolina	52,074
45	Idaho	51,379
46	Arkansas	51,148
47	Kentucky	50,699
48	New Mexico..............................	49,320
49	Alabama	48,608
50	West Virginia............................	47,817
51	Mississippi	45,438

	Real Gross Domestic Product in Chained (2012) Dollars, 2021			Real Gross Domestic Product, Percent Change, 2019–2021				Median Household Income, 2020	
Rank	State	Dollars (millions)	Rank	State	Percent	Rank	State	Dollars	
	United States..........................	19,427,287		United States............................	5.7		United States...........................	64,994	
1	California.................................	2,871,424	1	Tennessee..............................	8.6	1	District of Columbia	90,842	
2	Texas......................................	1,831,362	2	New Hampshire.......................	8.5	2	Maryland..................................	87,063	
3	New York.................................	1,491,809	3	California................................	7.8	3	New Jersey	85,245	
4	Florida....................................	1,008,694	4	Nevada...................................	7.1	4	Massachusetts.........................	84,385	
5	Illinois....................................	774,588	5	Florida....................................	6.9	5	Hawaii.....................................	83,173	
6	Pennsylvania...........................	713,691	5	Indiana...................................	6.9	6	Connecticut.............................	79,855	
7	Ohio	615,416	7	Montana..................................	6.7	7	California.................................	78,672	
8	Washington..............................	568,303	7	North Carolina.........................	6.7	8	New Hampshire........................	77,923	
9	Georgia...................................	567,940	7	Utah	6.7	9	Alaska.....................................	77,790	
10	New Jersey	561,782	7	Washington..............................	6.7	10	Washington..............................	77,006	
11	North Carolina..........................	533,090	11	Iowa.......................................	6.4	11	Virginia....................................	76,398	
12	Massachusetts.........................	530,505	11	Massachusetts.........................	6.4	12	Colorado	75,231	
13	Virginia...................................	492,626	13	Michigan.................................	6.2	13	Utah	74,197	
14	Michigan..................................	473,333	14	South Carolina.........................	5.9	14	Minnesota................................	73,382	
15	Colorado	365,918	15	Colorado	5.8	15	New York.................................	71,117	
16	Maryland..................................	364,242	15	Georgia...................................	5.8	16	Rhode Island............................	70,305	
17	Indiana....................................	352,624	15	Idaho......................................	5.8	17	Delaware.................................	69,110	
18	Minnesota................................	345,172	18	Minnesota................................	5.7	18	Illinois....................................	68,428	
19	Tennessee...............................	343,448	19	Texas......................................	5.6	19	Oregon....................................	65,667	
20	Arizona....................................	337,425	20	Rhode Island............................	5.5	20	North Dakota............................	65,315	
21	Wisconsin................................	302,782	21	Oregon....................................	5.4	21	Wyoming	65,304	
22	Missouri..................................	295,726	22	Arizona....................................	5.3	22	Texas......................................	63,826	
23	Connecticut.............................	245,783	22	Nebraska.................................	5.3	23	Pennsylvania...........................	63,627	
24	Louisiana.................................	227,735	24	Maine.....................................	5.2	24	Vermont...................................	63,477	
25	Oregon....................................	224,429	25	Arkansas.................................	5.0	25	Wisconsin................................	63,293	
26	South Carolina	220,689	25	Illinois....................................	5.0	26	Nebraska.................................	63,015	
27	Alabama..................................	204,885	25	New York.................................	5.0	27	Nevada...................................	62,043	
28	Oklahoma................................	195,073	28	New Jersey	4.9	28	Iowa.......................................	61,836	
29	Kentucky	194,340	28	South Dakota	4.9	29	Arizona....................................	61,529	
30	Utah	182,881	30	Kentucky	4.7	30	Georgia...................................	61,224	
31	Iowa.......................................	180,266	31	Hawaii.....................................	4.6	31	Kansas	61,091	
32	Kansas	162,734	31	Missouri..................................	4.6	32	South Dakota	59,896	
33	Nevada...................................	155,510	33	Mississippi..............................	4.4	33	Maine.....................................	59,489	
34	District of Columbia	125,796	33	Pennsylvania...........................	4.4	34	Michigan..................................	59,234	
35	Nebraska.................................	123,897	35	Ohio	4.3	35	Idaho......................................	58,915	
36	Arkansas.................................	120,711	36	Connecticut.............................	4.2	36	Indiana....................................	58,235	
37	Mississippi..............................	104,010	37	Alabama..................................	4.1	37	Ohio	58,116	
38	New Mexico	95,012	38	Virginia...................................	4.0	38	Florida....................................	57,703	
39	New Hampshire........................	81,932	38	West Virginia............................	4.0	39	Missouri..................................	57,290	
40	Idaho......................................	77,913	40	Kansas	3.8	40	North Carolina..........................	56,642	
41	Hawaii.....................................	73,880	40	Wisconsin................................	3.8	41	Montana..................................	56,539	
42	West Virginia............................	72,482	42	Delaware.................................	3.7	42	South Carolina	54,864	
43	Delaware.................................	64,338	43	Vermont...................................	3.5	43	Tennessee...............................	54,833	
44	Maine.....................................	61,815	44	Maryland..................................	3.2	44	Oklahoma................................	53,840	
45	North Dakota............................	55,730	45	District of Columbia	2.8	45	Kentucky	52,238	
46	Rhode Island............................	54,223	46	New Mexico	2.5	46	Alabama..................................	52,035	
47	Alaska.....................................	50,300	47	Louisiana.................................	2.4	47	New Mexico	51,243	
48	Montana..................................	49,264	48	Oklahoma................................	2.2	48	Louisiana.................................	50,800	
49	South Dakota	48,979	49	North Dakota............................	2.1	49	Arkansas.................................	49,475	
50	Wyoming	36,661	50	Wyoming	1.1	50	West Virginia............................	48,037	
51	Vermont...................................	29,654	51	Alaska	0.3	51	Mississippi..............................	46,511	

Median Family Income, 2020

Rank	State	Dollars
	United States............................	80,069
1	District of Columbia	120,337
2	Massachusetts........................	106,526
3	Maryland.................................	105,790
4	New Jersey	104,804
5	Connecticut............................	102,061
6	Hawaii	97,813
7	New Hampshire.......................	97,001
8	Virginia...................................	93,284
9	Colorado	92,752
10	Minnesota	92,692
11	Alaska	92,648
12	Washington............................	92,422
13	California................................	89,798
14	Rhode Island..........................	89,330
15	New York................................	87,270
16	North Dakota..........................	86,798
17	Illinois....................................	86,251
18	Delaware	84,825
19	Utah	84,590
20	Vermont	83,023
21	Wyoming	81,290
22	Pennsylvania..........................	80,996
23	Wisconsin	80,844
24	Oregon...................................	80,630
25	Nebraska................................	80,125
26	Iowa	79,186
27	Kansas	77,620
28	South Dakota	77,042
29	Maine	76,192
30	Texas.....................................	76,073
31	Michigan	75,470
32	Ohio	74,391
33	Georgia	74,127
34	Nevada...................................	74,077
35	Arizona...................................	73,456
36	Indiana...................................	73,265
37	Missouri.................................	72,834
38	Montana.................................	72,773
39	North Carolina........................	70,978
40	Idaho.....................................	70,885
41	Florida....................................	69,670
42	South Carolina	68,813
43	Tennessee	68,793
44	Oklahoma...............................	67,511
45	Alabama	66,772
46	Kentucky	65,893
47	Louisiana	65,427
48	New Mexico	62,611
49	Arkansas	62,067
50	West Virginia..........................	61,707
51	Mississippi.............................	58,923

Persons Below Poverty Level, 2020

Rank	State	Percent
	United States............................	12.8
1	Mississippi.............................	19.6
2	Louisiana	18.6
2	New Mexico	18.6
4	West Virginia..........................	17.1
5	Kentucky	16.6
6	Arkansas	16.1
7	Alabama	16.0
8	District of Columbia	15.5
9	Oklahoma...............................	15.3
10	South Carolina	14.7
11	Tennessee	14.6
12	Georgia	14.3
13	Texas.....................................	14.2
14	Arizona...................................	14.1
15	North Carolina........................	14.0
16	Michigan	13.7
17	New York................................	13.6
17	Ohio	13.6
19	Florida....................................	13.3
20	Missouri.................................	13.0
21	Indiana...................................	12.9
22	Montana.................................	12.8
22	Nevada...................................	12.8
22	South Dakota	12.8
25	California................................	12.6
26	Oregon...................................	12.4
27	Illinois....................................	12.0
28	Pennsylvania..........................	12.0
29	Idaho.....................................	11.9
30	Rhode Island..........................	11.6
31	Delaware	11.4
31	Kansas	11.4
33	Iowa	11.1
33	Maine	11.1
35	Wisconsin	11.0
36	Vermont	10.8
36	Wyoming	10.8
38	North Dakota..........................	10.5
39	Nebraska................................	10.4
40	Alaska	10.3
41	Washington............................	10.2
42	Virginia...................................	10.0
43	Colorado	9.8
43	Connecticut............................	9.8
43	Massachusetts........................	9.8
46	New Jersey	9.7
47	Hawaii	9.3
47	Minnesota	9.3
49	Utah	9.1
50	Maryland.................................	9.0
51	New Hampshire.......................	7.4

Persons Under 18 Years Old Below Poverty Level, 2020

Rank	State	Percent
	United States............................	17.5
1	Mississippi.............................	27.6
2	Louisiana	26.3
3	New Mexico	25.6
4	West Virginia..........................	23.1
5	District of Columbia	22.8
6	Alabama	22.7
7	Kentucky	22.2
8	Arkansas	22.0
9	South Carolina	21.2
10	Tennessee	20.8
11	Oklahoma...............................	20.7
12	Georgia	20.1
13	Arizona...................................	20.0
13	North Carolina........................	20.0
13	Texas.....................................	20.0
16	Ohio	19.1
17	Michigan	18.8
18	Florida....................................	18.7
18	New York................................	18.7
20	Indiana...................................	17.6
20	Nevada...................................	17.6
22	Missouri.................................	17.4
23	Delaware	17.2
24	California................................	16.8
25	Pennsylvania..........................	16.7
26	Illinois....................................	16.2
27	South Carolina	16.1
28	Rhode Island..........................	15.6
29	Montana.................................	15.2
30	Oregon...................................	15.0
31	Idaho.....................................	14.4
32	Wisconsin	14.2
33	Maine	14.0
34	Kansas	13.9
35	Alaska	13.8
36	Iowa	13.3
36	New Jersey	13.3
38	Virginia...................................	13.1
39	Connecticut............................	13.0
40	Washington............................	12.6
41	Vermont	12.3
41	Wyoming	12.3
43	Massachusetts........................	12.2
43	Nebraska................................	12.2
45	Hawaii	11.7
46	Maryland.................................	11.6
46	Minnesota	11.6
48	Colorado	11.5
49	North Dakota..........................	11.1
50	Utah	9.9
51	New Hampshire.......................	8.9

Per Capita Energy-Related CO_2 Emissions, 2019

Rank	State	Metric Tons of CO_2
	United States............................	15.7
1	Wyoming	101.9
2	North Dakota..........................	74.8
3	West Virginia..........................	47.6
4	Alaska	46.7
5	Louisiana	41.8
6	Montana	30.2
7	Indiana	26.2
8	Nebraska	26.1
9	Kentucky	25.8
10	Iowa	24.5
11	Texas	23.6
12	New Mexico	23.3
13	Oklahoma	22.9
14	Alabama	21.6
15	Arkansas	21.5
16	Mississippi	21.0
17	Kansas	20.8
18	Utah	19.2
19	Missouri	19.1
20	South Dakota	18.0
21	Pennsylvania	17.1
22	Ohio	16.8
23	Minnesota	16.3
23	Wisconsin	16.3
25	Illinois	16.1
26	Michigan	15.9
26	Colorado	15.9
28	Hawaii	14.5
29	Delaware	13.9
30	Tennessee	13.5
30	Nevada	13.5
30	South Carolina	13.5
33	Georgia	12.8
34	Arizona	12.7
35	Virginia	12.5
36	North Carolina	11.7
37	New Jersey	11.3
38	Idaho	11.2
39	Washington	11.1
40	Florida	10.9
41	Maine	10.7
42	Connecticut	10.3
43	New Hampshire........................	10.2
44	Oregon	9.9
45	Rhode Island	9.8
46	Vermont	9.6
47	Maryland	9.4
48	Massachusetts	9.2
49	California	9.1
50	New York..................................	8.7
51	District of Columbia	4.0

Homeownership Rate, 2021

Rank	State	Percent
	United States............................	65.5
1	West Virginia..........................	79.0
2	Maine......................................	75.9
3	Minnesota	75.6
4	New Hampshire........................	74.0
5	Vermont	73.9
6	Delaware	73.5
7	Alabama	73.4
8	South Carolina	73.2
9	Indiana	73.0
9	Michigan	73.0
11	Missouri	72.8
12	Iowa	72.1
12	Kentucky	72.1
12	Wyoming	72.1
15	Mississippi	71.3
16	South Dakota	71.1
17	Idaho	71.0
18	Pennsylvania	70.2
19	Maryland	69.7
20	Kansas	69.3
21	New Mexico	69.0
22	Louisiana	68.9
23	Utah	68.8
24	Nebraska	68.4
25	Illinois	68.3
25	Wisconsin	68.3
27	Montana	68.1
28	Virginia	68.0
29	Tennessee	67.7
30	Ohio	67.4
31	Florida	67.2
32	Oklahoma	67.0
33	Arkansas	66.1
33	Connecticut	66.1
35	Colorado	65.9
36	North Carolina	65.8
36	Oregon	65.8
38	Arizona	65.2
39	Texas	64.1
40	Alaska	64.0
40	Georgia	64.0
42	North Dakota..........................	63.5
43	Washington	63.4
44	Rhode Island	62.8
45	New Jersey	62.7
46	Massachusetts	62.0
47	Nevada	60.5
48	Hawaii	58.1
49	California	54.2
50	New York..................................	53.6
51	District of Columbia	42.3

One-Unit Detached or Attached Housing Units, Percent of Total Housing Units, 2020[1]

Rank	State	Percent
	United States............................	68.9
1	Kansas	78.8
2	Iowa	78.6
3	Indiana	78.3
4	Idaho	77.7
5	Nebraska	77.6
6	Michigan	77.2
7	Oklahoma	76.7
7	Utah	76.7
9	Pennsylvania	76.6
10	Delaware	75.9
11	Missouri	75.7
12	Ohio	75.2
13	West Virginia..........................	74.7
14	Minnesota	74.6
15	Maryland	74.1
16	Wyoming	74.0
17	Virginia	73.9
18	Montana	73.6
18	Tennessee	73.6
20	Arkansas	73.3
21	Alabama	72.6
22	South Dakota	72.3
23	Mississippi	72.2
24	Georgia	72.1
25	Kentucky	71.7
26	Colorado	71.3
27	Wisconsin	71.0
28	Louisiana	70.9
28	North Carolina	70.9
30	Arizona	70.7
31	Alaska	70.5
32	Maine	70.1
33	Vermont	69.9
34	South Carolina	69.8
35	New Mexico	69.4
36	Texas	69.3
37	Oregon	68.3
38	New Hampshire........................	68.2
39	Washington	67.5
40	Nevada	67.2
41	Hawaii	66.2
42	Illinois	66.1
43	Connecticut	66.0
44	California	65.5
45	North Dakota..........................	65.3
46	Florida	65.0
47	New Jersey	63.6
48	Rhode Island	60.1
49	Massachusetts	57.4
50	New York..................................	47.3
51	District of Columbia	36.8

[1] 2020 ACS 5-Year estimates. 1-Year estimates were not released for 2020 due to the impact of COVID-19 on data collection that year.

Percent of Population Not Covered by Private or Public Health Insurance, 2020

Rank	State	Percent
	United States..................................	8.7
1	Texas..	17.3
2	Oklahoma..................................	14.4
3	Georgia.....................................	13.0
4	Florida......................................	12.7
5	Alaska......................................	12.6
6	Mississippi................................	12.0
7	Wyoming...................................	11.4
8	Nevada.....................................	11.2
9	North Carolina............................	10.7
10	Arizona.....................................	10.6
11	Idaho.......................................	10.4
11	South Carolina............................	10.4
13	Tennessee.................................	9.7
14	South Dakota..............................	9.6
15	Alabama....................................	9.5
15	New Mexico................................	9.5
17	Missouri....................................	9.4
18	Utah..	9.0
19	Kansas.....................................	8.7
19	Louisiana...................................	8.7
21	Montana....................................	8.4
22	Arkansas...................................	8.3
23	Virginia.....................................	8.2
24	Nebraska...................................	8.1
25	Indiana.....................................	8.0
26	Colorado...................................	7.8
27	Maine......................................	7.6
27	New Jersey................................	7.6
29	California...................................	7.2
29	North Dakota..............................	7.2
31	Illinois......................................	6.8
32	Oregon.....................................	6.6
33	Ohio..	6.2
33	Washington................................	6.2
33	West Virginia..............................	6.2
36	New Hampshire...........................	6.0
37	Maryland...................................	5.9
38	Delaware...................................	5.8
39	Kentucky...................................	5.6
39	Pennsylvania..............................	5.6
41	Wisconsin..................................	5.5
42	Michigan....................................	5.4
42	New York...................................	5.4
44	Connecticut................................	5.1
45	Iowa..	4.7
46	Minnesota..................................	4.5
47	Rhode Island..............................	4.3
48	Vermont....................................	4.0
49	Hawaii......................................	3.9
50	District of Columbia......................	3.7
51	Massachusetts............................	2.7

Traffic Fatalities Per 100,000 Population, 2020

Rank	State	Rate
	United States..................................	11.7
1	Mississippi.................................	25.4
2	Wyoming...................................	22.0
3	Arkansas...................................	21.2
4	South Carolina............................	20.7
5	Montana....................................	19.6
6	New Mexico................................	18.8
7	Alabama....................................	18.6
8	Louisiana...................................	17.8
9	Tennessee.................................	17.6
10	Kentucky...................................	17.3
11	Oklahoma..................................	16.5
12	Missouri....................................	16.0
13	South Dakota..............................	15.9
14	Georgia.....................................	15.5
15	Florida......................................	15.4
16	West Virginia..............................	14.9
17	Arizona.....................................	14.7
17	North Carolina............................	14.7
19	Kansas.....................................	14.5
20	Texas.......................................	13.3
21	Indiana.....................................	13.2
22	North Dakota..............................	12.8
23	Maine......................................	12.0
23	Oregon.....................................	12.0
25	Nebraska...................................	11.9
26	Delaware...................................	11.7
27	Idaho.......................................	11.6
28	Colorado...................................	10.8
28	Michigan....................................	10.8
30	Iowa..	10.6
31	Ohio..	10.4
31	Wisconsin..................................	10.4
33	Nevada.....................................	10.2
34	Virginia.....................................	9.8
35	California...................................	9.7
36	Vermont....................................	9.6
37	Illinois......................................	9.3
38	Maryland...................................	9.2
39	Alaska......................................	8.7
39	Pennsylvania..............................	8.7
41	Utah..	8.4
42	Connecticut................................	8.2
43	New Hampshire...........................	7.5
44	Washington................................	7.3
45	Minnesota..................................	6.9
46	New Jersey................................	6.3
47	Rhode Island..............................	6.1
48	Hawaii......................................	5.9
49	District of Columbia......................	5.2
49	New York...................................	5.2
51	Massachusetts............................	4.9

ALABAMA

Facts and Figures

Location: Southeastern United States; bordered on the N by Tennessee, on the E by Georgia, on the S by Florida and the Gulf of Mexico, and on the W by Mississippi

Area: 52,420 sq. mi. (135,765 sq. km.); rank—30th

Population: 5,039,877 (2021 est.); rank—24th

Principal Cities: capital—Montgomery; largest—Birmingham

Statehood: December 14, 1819; 22nd state

U.S. Congress: 2 senators, 7 representatives

State Motto: *Audemus jura nostra defendere* ("We dare defend our rights")

State Song: "Alabama"

State Nicknames: The Yellowhammer State; The Heart of Dixie; The Cotton State

Abbreviations: AL; Ala.

State Symbols: flower—camellia; tree—Southern longleaf pine; bird—yellowhammer

At a Glance

- With an increase in population of 5.4 percent, Alabama ranked 27th among the states in growth from 2010 to 2021.

- Alabama's per capita personal income in 2021 was $48,608, ranking 49th in the nation.

- In 2021, Alabama had 56.3 full-time equivalent state and local government employees per 1,000 residents, a rate that ranked 12th in the nation.

- In 2020, 16.0 percent of Alabama residents lived below the poverty level, a percentage that ranked 7th in the nation.

- Alabama's violent crime rate in 2020 was 453.6 per 100,000 residents, compared to 398.5 for the entire nation.

- Alabama's median household income of $52,035 ranked 46th in the nation in 2020.

Table AL-1. Population by Age, Sex, Race, and Hispanic Origin

(Number, percent, except where noted.)

Sex, age, race, and Hispanic origin	2000	2010	2021	Percent change, 2010–2021
Total Population	4,447,100	4,779,736	5,039,877	5.4
Percent of total U.S. population	1.6	1.5	1.5	X
Sex				
Male	2,146,504	2,320,188	2,448,099	5.5
Female	2,300,596	2,459,548	2,591,778	5.4
Age				
Under 5 years	295,992	304,957	291,802	-4.3
5 to 19 years	960,177	971,355	957,812	-1.4
20 to 64 years	2,611,133	2,845,632	2,901,446	2.0
65 years and over	579,798	657,792	888,817	35.1
Median age (years)	35.8	37.9	39.6	4.5
Race and Hispanic Origin				
One race				
White	3,162,808	3,362,877	3,472,742	3.3
Black	1,155,930	1,259,224	1,353,084	7.5
American Indian and Alaska Native	22,430	32,903	36,007	9.4
Asian	31,346	55,240	78,140	41.5
Native Hawaiian or Other Pacific Islander	1,409	5,208	5,485	5.3
Two or more races	44,179	64,284	94,419	46.9
Hispanic (of any race)	75,830	192,498	241,168	25.3

NOTE: Population figures for 2021 are July 1 estimates. The 2000 and 2010 estimates are taken from the respective censuses.
X = Not applicable.
- = Zero or rounds to zero.

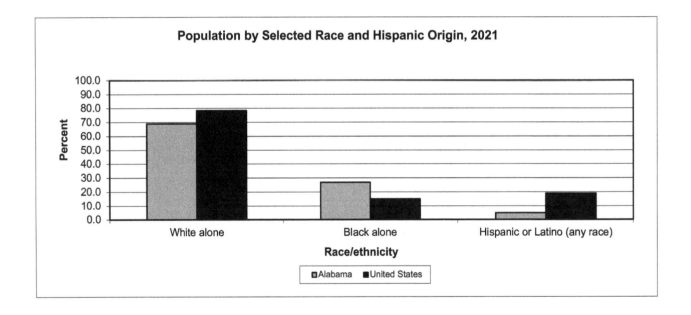

Population by Selected Race and Hispanic Origin, 2021

Table AL-2. Marital Status

(Number, percent distribution.)

Sex, age, and marital status	2000	2010	2020 [1]
Males, 15 Years and Over	1,666,798	1,844,661	1,904,931
Never married	26.7	32.5	33.7
Now married, except separated	59.0	50.6	50.2
Separated	1.8	2.5	1.8
Widowed	2.8	3.0	3.1
Divorced	9.8	11.4	11.2
Females, 15 Years and Over	1,847,401	2,004,450	2,084,343
Never married	21.4	26.1	28.2
Now married, except separated	52.5	45.9	46.0
Separated	2.5	3.1	2.4
Widowed	12.4	11.2	10.4
Divorced	11.2	13.6	13.0

[1] 2020 ACS 5-Year estimates. 1-Year estimates were not released for 2020 due to the impact of COVID-19 on data collection that year.

Table AL-3. Households and Housing Characteristics

(Number, percent, dollars.)

Item	2000	2010	2020[1]	Average annual percent change, 2010–2020
Total Households...	1,737,080	1,815,152	1,888,504	0.6
Family households	1,215,968	1,227,884	1,234,552	0.1
Married-couple family	906,916	868,946	893,948	0.4
Other family	309,052	358,938	340,604	-0.7
Male householder, no wife present...	62,586	79,308	78,016	-0.2
Female householder, no husband present...	246,466	279,630	262,588	-0.9
Nonfamily households	521,112	587,268	653,952	1.6
Householder living alone...	453,898	511,708	567,326	1.6
Householder not living alone...	67,214	75,560	86,626	2.1
Housing Characteristics				
Total housing units...	1,963,711	2,174,428	2,270,398	0.6
Occupied housing units	1,737,080	1,815,152	1,888,504	0.6
Owner occupied	1,258,705	1,272,846	1,306,505	0.4
Renter occupied	478,375	542,306	581,999	1.0
Average household size...	2.49	2.57	2.53	-0.2
Financial Characteristics				
Median gross rent of renter-occupied housing	447	667	811	3.1
Median monthly owner costs for housing units with a mortgage	816	1,130	1,196	0.8
Median value of owner-occupied housing units...	85,100	123,900	149,600	3.0

- = Zero or rounds to zero
[1] 2020 ACS 5-Year estimates. 1-Year estimates were not released for 2020 due to the impact of COVID-19 on data collection that year.

Table AL-4. Migration, Origin, and Language

(Number, percent.)

Characteristic	State	U.S.
	2016–2020[1]	2016–2020[1]
Residence 1 Year Ago		
Population 1 year and over	4,838,779	322,943,283
Same house...	86.8	86.2
Different house in the U.S...	12.8	13.2
Same county...	7.6	7.7
Different county	5.3	5.5
Same state...	3	3.2
Different state	2.3	2.3
Abroad	0.3	0.6
Place of Birth		
Native born	4,725,133	282,443,680
Male	48.3	49.4
Female	51.7	50.6
Foreign born	168,053	44,125,628
Male	49.9	48.6
Female	50.1	51.4
Foreign born; naturalized U.S. citizen...	66,928	22,456,684
Male	46.8	46.1
Female	53.2	53.9
Foreign born; not a U.S. citizen...	101,125	21,668,944
Male	51.9	51.1
Female	48.1	48.9
Entered 2010 or later	27.8	22.8
Entered 2000 to 2009	31.7	25.1
Entered before 2000...	40.5	52.1
World Region of Birth, Foreign		
Foreign-born population, excluding population born at sea	168,053	44,125,628
Europe	11.2	10.8
Asia...	32.6	31.3
Africa	4.8	5.4
Oceania	0.6	0.6
Latin America...	48.6	50.0
North America...	2.1	1.9
Language Spoken at Home and Ability to Speak English		
Population 5 years and over...	4,599,254	306,919,116
English only	94.7	78.5
Language other than English...	5.3	21.5
Speaks English less than "very well"...	2.1	8.2

[1] 2020 ACS 5-Year estimates. 1-Year estimates were not released for 2020 due to the impact of COVID-19 on data collection that year.
NA = Not available.
X = Not applicable.
- = Zero or rounds to zero.

Table AL-5. Median Income and Poverty Status, 2020[1]

(Number, percent, except as noted.)

Characteristic	State		U.S.	
	Number	Percent	Number	Percent
Median Income				
Households (dollars)..	52,035	X	64,994	X
Families (dollars)	66,772	X	80,069	X
Below Poverty Level (All People)	762,642	16.0	40,910,326	12.8
Sex				
Male	325,560	14.2	18,171,512	11.6
Female	437,082	17.7	22,738,814	14.0
Age				
Under 18 years...	244,726	22.7	12,598,699	17.5
Related children under 18 years..	241,084	22.5	12,306,532	17.2
18 to 64 years..	435,202	15.1	23,554,920	12.1
65 years and over	82,714	10.2	4,756,707	9.3

X = Not applicable.
[1] 2020 ACS 5-Year estimates. 1-Year estimates were not released for 2020 due to the impact of COVID-19 on data collection that year.

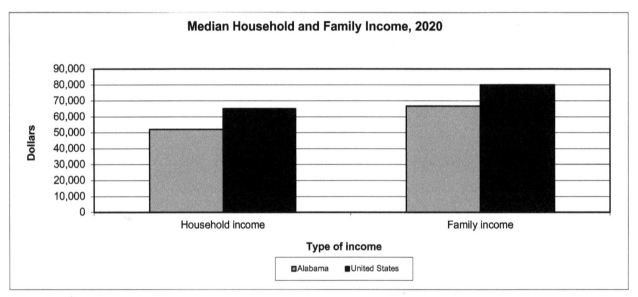

Table AL-6. Health Insurance Coverage Status for the Civilian Noninstitutionalized Population and Children Under 19 Years of Age

(Number; percent.)

Item	2011	2012	2013	2014	2015	2016	2017	2018	2019	2020 [2]
Civilian Noninstitutionalized Population	4,720,067	4,741,698	4,755,381	4,767,383	4,781,070	4,782,529	4,793,512	4,810,094	4,822,514	4,813,429
Covered by Private or Public Insurance										
Number..	4,046,103	4,109,199	4,109,946	4,188,214	4,296,799	4,347,556	4,344,586	4,328,835	4,353,613	4,357,884
Percent...	85.7	86.7	86.4	87.9	89.9	90.9	90.6	90.0	90.3	90.5
Uninsured										
Number..	673,964	632,499	645,435	579,169	484,271	434,973	448,926	481,259	468,901	455,545
Percent...	14.3	13.3	13.6	12.1	10.1	9.1	9.4	10.0	9.7	9.5
Percent in the U.S. not covered..............................	15.1	14.8	14.5	11.7	9.4	8.6	8.7	8.9	9.2	8.7
Children Under 19 Years of Age[1]	1,122,125	1,123,000	1,107,844	1,106,847	1,106,716	1,098,052	1,169,489	1,162,987	1,154,392	1,160,135
Covered by Private or Public Insurance										
Number..	1,063,064	1,077,390	1,059,663	1,064,425	1,072,948	1,071,320	1,133,440	1,122,269	1,114,232	1,123,421
Percent...	94.7	95.9	95.7	96.2	96.9	97.6	96.9	96.5	96.5	96.8
Uninsured										
Number..	59,061	45,610	48,181	42,422	33,768	26,732	36,049	40,718	40,160	36,714
Percent...	5.3	4.1	4.3	3.8	3.1	2.4	3.1	3.5	3.5	3.2
Percent in the U.S. not covered..............................	7.5	7.2	7.1	6.0	4.8	4.5	5.0	5.2	5.7	5.2

[1] Data for years prior to 2017 is for individuals under 18 years of age.
[2] 2020 ACS 5-Year estimates. 1-Year estimates were not released for 2020 due to the impact of COVID-19 on data collection that year. Data is not comparable to previous years, which are based on 1-year estimates.

Table AL-7. Employment Status by Demographic Group, 2021

(Numbers in thousands, percent.)

Characteristic	Civilian noninstitutional population	Civilian labor force		Employed		Unemployed	
		Number	Percent of population	Number	Percent of population	Number	Percent of population
Total..	3,898	2,204	56.5	2,124	54.5	80	3.6
Sex							
Male..	1,841	1,163	63.2	1,119	60.8	44	3.7
Female	2,057	1,042	50.6	1,005	48.9	37	3.5
Race, Sex, and Hispanic Origin							
White..	2,742	1,557	56.8	1,511	55.1	46	3.0
Male..	1,327	871	65.6	846	63.7	26	2.9
Female......................................	1,415	686	48.5	665	47.0	21	3.0
Black or African American..............	1,014	564	55.7	533	52.5	32	5.6
Male..	449	248	55.2	230	51.2	18	7.1
Female......................................	565	317	56.0	302	53.5	14	4.5
Hispanic or Latino ethnicity[1]	164	114	69.8	113	68.7	2	1.5
Male..	NA	NA	NA	NA	NA	NA	NA
Female......................................	NA	NA	NA	NA	NA	NA	NA
Age							
16 to 19 years..............................	NA	NA	NA	NA	NA	NA	NA
20 to 24 years..............................	299	203	67.9	191	63.8	12	6.0
25 to 34 years..............................	618	489	79.1	467	75.6	22	4.5
35 to 44 years..............................	601	486	80.8	471	78.4	15	3.0
45 to 54 years..............................	623	459	73.7	446	71.5	14	3.0
55 to 64 years..............................	644	353	54.9	344	53.4	10	2.7
65 years and over	853	134	15.7	131	15.4	3	2.2

NOTE: Data in Table 7 are from the Current Population Survey (CPS) and do not match the estimates in Table 8. See notes and definitions for further information.
[1] May be of any race.
NA = Not available.

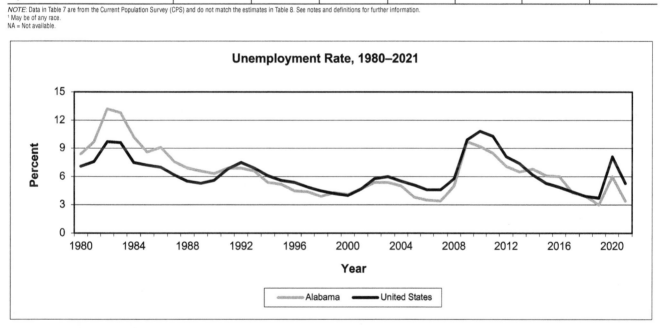

Unemployment Rate, 1980–2021

Table AL-8. Employment Status of the Civilian Noninstitutional Population Age 16 Years and Over

(Number, percent.)

Year	Civilian labor force	Civilian participation rate	Employed	Unemployed	Unemployment rate
2010..	301,893	70.1	280,953	20,940	6.9
2011..	302,932	69.3	284,273	18,659	6.2
2012..	303,748	68.4	287,110	16,638	5.5
2013..	302,201	67.4	287,792	14,409	4.8
2014..	302,865	67.3	289,694	13,171	4.3
2015..	301,608	66.8	288,894	12,714	4.2
2016..	300,546	66.6	284,439	16,107	5.4
2017..	293,802	65.9	281,164	12,638	4.3
2018..	292,781	65.7	280,909	11,872	4.1
2019..	294,380	65.8	283,377	11,003	3.7
2020..	293,722	65.3	276,739	16,983	5.8
2021..	290,404	64.1	277,372	13,032	4.5

Table AL-9. Employment and Average Wages by Industry

(Estimates are based on the 2012 North American Industry Classification System [NAICS].)

Industry	2013	2014	2015	2016	2017	2018	2019	2020
	Number of Jobs							
Wage and Salary Employment by Industry	1,979,360	1,996,182	2,024,720	2,049,658	2,072,223	2,098,185	2,127,180	2,044,978
Farm Wage and Salary Employment	7,713	5,318	7,451	7,213	9,217	7,242	7,189	6,638
Nonfarm Wage and Salary Employment	1,971,647	1,990,864	2,017,269	2,042,445	2,063,006	2,090,943	2,119,991	2,038,340
Private wage and salary employment	1,571,089	1,590,896	1,618,569	1,641,038	1,659,832	1,685,234	1,710,870	1,633,159
Forestry, fishing, and related activities	8,780	8,875	8,938	8,925	8,785	8,900	9,463	8,999
Mining	7,992	7,549	6,828	5,352	6,031	6,295	6,379	5,863
Utilities	14,382	14,293	14,437	14,170	13,735	13,774	13,303	13,025
Construction	81,656	81,857	83,802	86,254	87,258	91,361	95,784	95,115
Manufacturing	249,486	253,248	258,085	260,646	263,808	266,915	269,159	258,430
Durable goods manufacturing	159,691	165,133	169,191	170,054	171,555	173,814	175,196	168,681
Nondurable goods manufacturing	89,795	88,115	88,894	90,592	92,253	93,101	93,963	89,749
Wholesale trade	73,366	73,150	73,926	74,025	73,890	74,187	74,680	72,902
Retail trade	226,040	228,885	232,361	234,301	232,838	232,565	232,380	226,558
Transportation and warehousing	57,208	59,202	59,792	59,991	60,738	62,524	65,261	65,330
Information	22,590	21,962	21,543	20,701	20,818	21,017	21,299	19,297
Finance and insurance	73,202	74,309	74,795	75,063	76,392	75,968	76,698	77,471
Real estate and rental and leasing	22,228	22,039	22,338	22,845	23,258	23,843	24,395	23,851
Professional, scientific, and technical services	95,258	95,325	96,903	98,999	101,786	105,898	108,152	109,340
Management of companies and enterprises	15,935	15,130	15,432	16,467	16,116	15,609	16,048	15,807
Administrative and waste services	109,057	113,606	117,874	119,940	123,019	125,484	128,503	119,232
Educational services	29,535	29,599	29,691	30,392	30,294	29,692	29,759	26,637
Health care and social assistance	204,076	205,157	209,600	214,778	218,050	221,732	226,551	218,492
Arts, entertainment, and recreation	16,360	16,990	16,906	19,019	20,062	21,394	21,630	17,867
Accommodation and food services	163,776	168,368	174,090	179,626	183,518	185,807	187,940	161,758
Other services, except public administration	100,162	101,352	101,228	99,544	99,436	102,269	103,486	97,185
Government and government enterprises	400,558	399,968	398,700	401,407	403,174	405,709	409,121	405,181
	Dollars							
Average Wages and Salaries by Industry	41,599	42,653	43,632	44,160	45,308	46,718	48,169	51,313
Average Farm Wages and Salaries	19,036	23,427	22,978	19,459	14,836	19,586	14,571	14,507
Average Nonfarm Wages and Salaries	41,687	42,704	43,708	44,248	45,445	46,812	48,283	51,433
Average private wages and salaries	41,063	42,068	43,140	43,659	44,867	46,330	47,816	51,120
Forestry, fishing, and related activities	33,914	35,336	36,652	38,235	38,957	39,869	40,933	43,732
Mining	78,001	80,782	80,450	70,500	76,990	84,615	83,690	83,433
Utilities	88,364	88,427	95,522	100,657	104,422	108,312	119,165	120,954
Construction	45,537	47,811	48,728	50,520	52,222	53,941	56,168	59,149
Manufacturing	50,891	52,849	53,519	54,226	55,171	57,075	58,542	60,401
Durable goods manufacturing	53,246	55,057	55,744	56,609	57,567	59,620	61,210	62,599
Nondurable goods manufacturing	46,704	48,709	49,283	49,755	50,717	52,323	53,569	56,270
Wholesale trade	57,873	59,953	62,110	62,828	64,485	66,691	68,828	72,027
Retail trade	25,617	25,873	26,506	27,018	27,569	28,330	29,176	31,545
Transportation and warehousing	44,321	46,116	47,341	47,458	48,986	50,947	51,999	53,296
Information	51,605	53,923	55,771	57,095	58,870	60,029	62,883	69,274
Finance and insurance	65,033	67,934	71,769	71,115	73,915	77,594	79,268	84,516
Real estate and rental and leasing	38,489	40,047	41,559	42,222	43,817	44,602	47,371	49,846
Professional, scientific, and technical services	70,632	71,517	73,321	74,636	76,651	78,854	81,165	87,358
Management of companies and enterprises	83,524	85,374	87,533	91,142	102,206	103,433	105,118	102,912
Administrative and waste services	26,701	27,121	27,431	27,784	28,415	29,370	30,737	33,198
Educational services	25,272	26,112	26,888	27,323	27,378	28,135	29,074	32,843
Health care and social assistance	43,384	44,176	45,495	45,603	46,505	47,304	48,606	51,913
Arts, entertainment, and recreation	20,198	20,329	21,420	20,572	20,394	20,998	22,463	23,265
Accommodation and food services	16,295	16,593	17,043	17,542	18,027	19,014	19,794	19,649
Other services, except public administration	29,781	30,811	32,033	33,227	34,557	35,565	36,502	40,058
Government and government enterprises	44,134	45,236	46,014	46,654	47,825	48,812	50,237	52,694

Table AL-10. Employment Characteristics by Family Type

(Number, percent.)

Family type and labor force status	2018		2019		2020	
	Total	Families with own children under 18 years	Total	Families with own children under 18 years	Total	Families with own children under 18 years
All Families...	1,214,794	466,487	1,237,883	461,753	1,234,552	479,570
FAMILY TYPE AND LABOR FORCE STATUS						
Opposite-Sex Married-Couple Families............................	879,227	303,879	892,050	298,328	888,847	314,225
Both husband and wife in labor force..............................	45.7	66.0	45.4	65.7	46.3	65.8
Husband in labor force, wife not in labor force	22.5	26.9	22.9	26.9	22.9	27.3
Wife in labor force, husband not in labor force	8.6	4.1	8.7	4.8	8.6	4.6
Both husband and wife not in labor force	22.6	2.5	22.3	2.1	22.2	2.3
Other Families	335,567	162,608	345,833	163,425	340,604	164,286
Female householder, no spouse present	76.8	78.9	76.9	78.0	77.1	80.0
In labor force	46.7	62.1	49.7	63.3	48.4	63.8
Not in labor force	30.1	16.7	27.2	14.7	28.7	16.2
Male householder, no spouse present..............................	23.2	21.1	23.1	22.0	22.9	20.0
In labor force...	16.0	19.0	16.0	18.9	15.8	17.3
Not in labor force	7.2	2.1	7.1	3.1	7.1	2.7

[1] 2020 ACS 5-Year estimates. 1-Year estimates were not released for 2020 due to the impact of COVID-19 on data collection that year. Data is not comparable to previous years, which are based on 1-year estimates.

Table AL-11. School Enrollment and Educational Attainment, 2020[1]

(Number, percent.)

Item	State	U.S.
Enrollment		
Total population 3 years and over, enrolled in school	1,168,551	80,497,960
Enrolled in nursery school or preschool (percent)...	5.6	6.1
Enrolled in kindergarten (percent)...	5.2	5.0
Enrolled in elementary school, grades 1-8 (percent)...	41.5	40.4
Enrolled in high school, grades 9-12 (percent)	21.3	21.0
Enrolled in college or graduate school (percent)...	26.4	27.6
Attainment		
Total population 25 years and over	3,344,006	222,836,834
Less than ninth grade (percent)...	4	4.9
9th to 12th grade, no diploma (percent)	9.1	6.6
High school graduate, including equivalency (percent)..	30.3	26.7
Some college, no degree (percent)...	21.6	20.3
Associate's degree (percent)..	8.7	8.6
Bachelor's degree (percent)	16.3	20.2
Graduate or professional degree (percent)...	9.9	12.7
High school graduate or higher (percent)...	86.9	88.5
Bachelor's degree or higher (percent)...	26.2	32.9

[1] 2020 ACS 5-Year estimates. 1-Year estimates were not released for 2020 due to the impact of COVID-19 on data collection that year.

Table AL-12. Public School Characteristics and Educational Indicators

(Number, percent; data derived from National Center of Education Statistics.)

Item	State	U.S.
Public Elementary and Secondary Schools		
Number of regular school districts, 2018-19	140	13,452
Number of operational schools, 2019-20...	1,533	98,469
Percent charter schools	0.3	7.7
Total public school enrollment, Fall 2019..	744,235	50,796,445
Percent charter school enrollment	0.2	6.8
Student-teacher ratio, Fall 2019...	17.7	15.9
Expenditures per student (unadjusted dollars), 2018-19	10,107	13,187
Four-year adjusted cohort graduation rate (ACGR), 2018-2019[1]...	91.7	85.8
Students eligible for free or reduced-price lunch (percent), 2019-20..	55.0	52.1
English language learners (percent), Fall 2019	4.4	10.4
Students age 3 to 21 served under IDEA, part B (percent), 2020-21	13.0	14.5

Public Schools by Type, 2019-20	Number	Percent of state public schools
Total number of schools...	1,533	100.0
Special education...	81	5.3
Vocational education...	68	4.4
Alternative education..	62	4.0

[1] Adjusted Cohort Graduation Rates (ACGR) differ from Averaged Freshmen Graduation Rates (AFGR).
NA = Not available.

Table AL-13. Reported Voting and Registration of the Voting-Age Population, November 2020

(Numbers in thousands, percent.)

Item	Total population	Total citizen population	Registered			Voted		
			Total registered	Percent registered (total population)	Percent registered (total citizen population)	Total voted	Percent voted (total population)	Percent voted (total citizen population)
U.S. Total	252,274	231,593	168,308	66.7	72.7	154,628	61.3	66.8
State Total.................................	3,769	3,716	2,527	67.0	68.0	2,247	59.6	60.5
Sex								
Male	1,780	1,755	1,187	66.7	67.6	1,038	58.4	59.2
Female	1,990	1,960	1,340	67.3	68.4	1,209	60.7	61.6
Race								
White alone................................	2,657	2,619	1,860	70.0	71.0	1,647	62.0	62.9
White, non-Hispanic alone..............	2,587	2,569	1,825	70.6	71.0	1,617	62.5	63.0
Black alone.................................	973	973	590	60.6	60.6	533	54.8	54.8
Asian alone.................................	55	45	23	B	B	21	B	B
Hispanic (of any race)	79	53	35	B	B	30	B	B
White alone or in combination	2,692	2,654	1,883	69.9	70.9	1,665	61.9	62.7
Black alone or in combination............	988	988	603	61.0	61.0	543	54.9	54.9
Asian alone or in combination............	58	48	26	B	B	21	B	B
Age								
18 to 24 years.................................	431	427	218	50.6	51.1	194	44.9	45.4
25 to 34 years.................................	599	587	376	62.8	64.2	315	52.6	53.7
35 to 44 years.................................	626	608	415	66.3	68.2	365	58.3	60.0
45 to 64 years.................................	1,261	1,246	900	71.4	72.2	824	65.4	66.2
65 years and over	852	848	618	72.5	72.9	549	64.5	64.8

- = Zero or rounds to zero.
B = Base is less than 75,000 and therefore too small to show the derived measure.

Table AL-14. Crime

(Number, rate per 100,000. Data are derived from the FBI Uniform Crime Reports.)

Item	State [3]			U.S.		
	2018	2019	Percent change	2018	2019	Percent change
TOTAL POPULATION[1]	4,907,965	4,921,532	0.3	328,329,953	329,484,123	0.4
VIOLENT CRIME						
Number...	24,769	22,322	-9.9	1,250,393	1,313,105	5.0
Rate	504.7	453.6	-10.1	380.8	398.5	4.6
Murder and Nonnegligent Manslaughter						
Number...	390	471	20.8	16,669	21,570	29.4
Rate	7.9	9.6	20.4	5.1	6.5	28.9
Rape[2]						
Number...	2,119	1,608	-24.1	143,224	126,430	-11.7
Rate	43.2	32.7	-24.3	43.6	38.4	-12.0
Robbery						
Number...	3,922	2,666	-32.0	268,483	243,600	-9.3
Rate	79.9	54.2	-32.2	81.8	73.9	-9.6
Aggravated Assault						
Number...	18,338	17,577	-4.1	822,017	921,505	12.1
Rate	373.6	357.1	-4.4	250.4	279.7	11.7
PROPERTY CRIME						
Number...	128,726	105,161	-18.3	6,995,235	6,452,038	-7.8
Rate	2,622.8	2,136.8	-18.5	2,130.6	1,958.2	-8.1
Burglary						
Number...	24,805	19,660	-20.7	1,118,096	1,035,314	-7.4
Rate	505.4	399.5	-21.0	340.5	314.2	-7.7
Larceny-Theft						
Number...	91,225	74,575	-18.3	5,152,267	4,606,324	-10.6
Rate	1,858.7	1,515.3	-18.5	1,569.2	1,398.0	-10.9
Motor Vehicle Theft						
Number...	12,696	10,926	-13.9	724,872	810,400	11.8
Rate	258.7	222.0	-14.2	220.8	246.0	11.4

NOTE: Although arson data are included in the trend and clearance tables, sufficient data are not available to estimate totals for this offense. Therefore, no arson data are published in this table.
- = Zero or rounds to zero.
[1] Population figures are U.S. Census Bureau provisional estimates as of July 1, 2020.
[2] The figures shown in the rape (revised definition) column were estimated using the revised Uniform Crime Reporting (UCR) definition of rape.
[3] Limited data for 2020 were available for Alabama, Maryland and Pennsylvania.

Table AL-15. State Government Finances, 2020

(Dollar amounts in thousands, percent distribution.)

Item	Dollars	Percent distribution
Total Revenue	36,908,937	100.0
General revenue	33,149,140	89.8
Intergovernmental revenue	13,657,057	37.0
Taxes	12,044,879	32.6
General sales	2,980,152	8.1
Selective sales	2,923,709	7.9
License taxes	573,316	1.6
Individual income tax	4,274,052	11.6
Corporate income tax	754,272	2.0
Other taxes	539,378	1.5
Current charges	5,789,525	15.7
Miscellaneous general revenue	1,657,679	4.5
Utility revenue	0	-
Liquor stores revenue	422,809	1.1
Insurance trust revenue[1]	3,336,988	9.0
Total Expenditure	35,784,680	100.0
Intergovernmental expenditure	8,340,911	23.3
Direct expenditure	27,443,769	76.7
Current operation	19,559,018	54.7
Capital outlay	2,285,399	6.4
Insurance benefits and repayments	4,134,263	11.6
Assistance and subsidies	1,076,697	3.0
Interest on debt	388,392	1.1
Exhibit: Salaries and wages	5,570,751	15.6
Total Expenditure	35,784,680	100.0
General expenditure	31,250,997	87.3
Intergovernmental expenditure	8,340,911	23.3
Direct expenditure	22,910,086	64.0
General expenditure, by function:		
Education	12,882,916	36.0
Public welfare	7,953,801	22.2
Hospitals	3,367,670	9.4
Health	569,200	1.6
Highways	1,789,538	5.0
Police protection	197,231	0.6
Correction	680,743	1.9
Natural resources	273,860	0.8
Parks and recreation	29,803	0.1
Governmental administration	718,713	2.0
Interest on general debt	388,392	1.1
Other and unallocable	2,268,652	6.3
Utility expenditure	75	-
Liquor stores expenditure	399,345	1.1
Insurance trust expenditure	4,134,263	11.6
Debt at End of Fiscal Year	9,934,370	X
Cash and Security Holdings	60,243,406	X

X = Not applicable.
- = Zero or rounds to zero.
[1] Within insurance trust revenue, net earnings of state retirement systems is a calculated statistic (the item code in the data file is X08), and thus can be positive or negative. Net earnings is the sum of earnings on investments plus gains on investments minus losses on investments. The change made in 2002 for asset valuation from book to market value in accordance with Statement 34 of the Governmental Accounting Standards Board is reflected in the calculated statistics.

Table AL-16. State Government Tax Collections, 2021

(Dollars in thousands, percent.)

Item	Dollars	Percent distribution
Total Taxes	14,251,329	100.0
Property taxes	468,015	3.3
Sales and gross receipts	7,014,522	49.2
General sales and gross receipts	3,912,037	27.5
Selective sales and gross receipts	3,102,485	21.8
Alcoholic beverages	272,021	1.9
Amusements	0	-
Insurance premiums	468,162	3.3
Motor fuels	878,038	6.2
Pari-mutuels	4,112	-
Public utilities	663,891	4.7
Tobacco products	170,998	1.2
Other selective sales	645,263	4.5
Licenses	606,351	4.3
Alcoholic beverages	3,667	-
Amusements	X	-
Corporations in general	187,666	1.3
Hunting and fishing	21,506	0.2
Motor vehicle	260,114	1.8
Motor vehicle operators	43,783	0.3
Public utilities	19,815	0.1
Occupation and business, NEC	69,799	0.5
Other licenses	1	-
Income taxes	6,043,093	42.4
Individual income	4,908,837	34.4
Corporation net income	1,134,256	8.0
Other taxes	119,348	0.8
Death and gift	X	-
Documentary and stock transfer	80,496	0.6
Severance	38,852	0.3
Taxes, NEC	0	-

- = Zero or rounds to zero.
X = Not applicable.

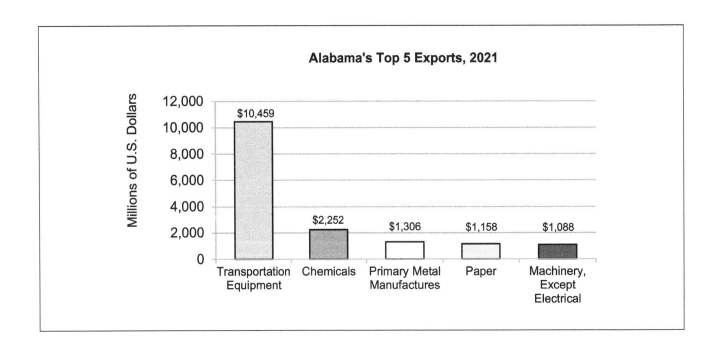

Alabama's Top 5 Exports, 2021

Category	Millions of U.S. Dollars
Transportation Equipment	$10,459
Chemicals	$2,252
Primary Metal Manufactures	$1,306
Paper	$1,158
Machinery, Except Electrical	$1,088

ALASKA

Facts and Figures

Location: Northwestern North America; bordered on the N by the Arctic Ocean, on the E by Canada, on the S by the Pacific Ocean and the Gulf of Alaska, and on the W by the Bering Sea

Area: 665,384 sq. mi. (1,717,854 sq. sq. km.); rank—1st

Population: 732,673 (2021 est.); rank—48th

Principal Cities: capital—Juneau; largest—Anchorage

Statehood: January 3, 1959; 49th state

U.S. Congress: 2 senators, 1 representative

State Motto: North to the Future

State Song: "Alaska's Flag"

State Nicknames: The Last Frontier; The Land of the Midnight Sun

Abbreviations: AK

State Symbols: flower—forget-me-not; tree—Sitka spruce; bird—willow ptarmigan

At a Glance

- With an increase in population of 3.2 percent, Alaska ranked 37th among the states for growth from 2010 to 2021.

- Alaska's 2020 violent crime rate ranked 2nd in the nation at 837.8 per 100,000 population, and the property crime rate (2,260.5 per 100,000 population) ranked 14th.

- Alaska was the state with the 3rd highest birth rate in 2020, at 13.0 births per 1,000 population.

- In 2020, 10.3 percent of Alaskans lived below the poverty level, a percent that ranked 40th in the nation.

- Of all the states, Alaska had the 6th highest percentage of residents under 18 years old (24.5 percent) and the 4th lowest percentage of residents age 65 and over (13.3 percent) in 2021.

Table AK-1. Population by Age, Sex, Race, and Hispanic Origin

(Number, percent, except where noted.)

Sex, age, race, and Hispanic origin	2000	2010	2021	Percent change, 2010–2021
Total Population..	626,932	710,231	732,673	3.2
Percent of total U.S. population	0.2	0.2	0.2	X
Sex				
Male..	324,112	369,628	384,204	3.9
Female..	302,820	340,603	348,469	2.3
Age				
Under 5 years..	47,591	53,996	48,111	-10.9
5 to 19 years..	160,526	153,844	147,886	-3.9
20 to 64 years..	383,116	447,453	439,013	-1.9
65 years and over	35,699	54,938	97,663	77.8
Median age (years)	32.4	33.8	35.6	5.3
Race and Hispanic Origin				
One race				
White	434,534	483,873	472,939	-2.3
Black	21,787	24,441	26,689	9.2
American Indian and Alaska Native	98,043	106,268	114,947	8.2
Asian	25,116	38,882	48,278	24.2
Native Hawaiian or Other Pacific Islander	3,309	7,622	11,921	56.4
Two or more races	34,146	49,105	57,899	17.9
Hispanic (of any race)	25,852	44,490	54,732	23.0

NOTE: Population figures for 2021 are July 1 estimates. The 2000 and 2010 estimates are taken from the respective censuses.
- = Zero or rounds to zero.
X = Not applicable.

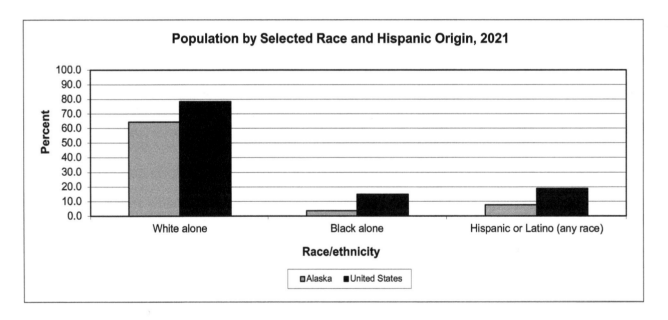

Population by Selected Race and Hispanic Origin, 2021

Table AK-2. Marital Status

(Number, percent distribution.)

Sex, age, and marital status	2000	2010	2020 [1]
Males, 15 Years and Over	243,024	290,598	305,350
Never married	32.5	35.5	38.0
Now married, except separated...	53.6	49.7	48.2
Separated..	1.7	1.7	1.6
Widowed..	1.4	1.8	2.2
Divorced..	10.8	11.4	9.9
Females, 15 Years and Over	225,837	267,563	277,118
Never married	24.1	27.3	28.8
Now married, except separated...	55.6	50.2	50.2
Separated..	2.3	2.6	1.9
Widowed..	5.6	6.1	6.0
Divorced..	12.5	13.7	13.0

[1] 2020 ACS 5-Year estimates. 1-Year estimates were not released for 2020 due to the impact of COVID-19 on data collection that year.

Table AK-3. Households and Housing Characteristics

(Number, percent, dollars.)

Item	2000	2010	2020 [1]	Average annual percent change, 2010–2020
Total Households..	221,600	254,610	255,173	-
Family households...	152,337	170,859	167,815	-0.3
Married-couple family...	116,318	127,969	127,312	-0.1
Other family..	36,019	42,890	40,503	-0.8
Male householder, no wife present................................	12,082	14,211	14,293	0.1
Female householder, no husband present......................	23,937	28,679	26,210	-1.2
Nonfamily households..	69,263	83,751	87,358	0.6
Householder living alone..	52,060	63,698	67,033	0.7
Householder not living alone..	17,203	20,053	20,325	0.2
Housing Characteristics				
Total housing units..	260,978	307,065	318,370	0.5
Occupied housing units	221,600	254,610	255,173	-
Owner occupied...	138,509	162,785	165,376	0.2
Renter occupied...	83,091	91,825	89,797	-0.3
Average household size..	2.74	2.70	2.78	0.4
Financial Characteristics				
Median gross rent of renter-occupied housing	720	981	1,240	3.8
Median monthly owner costs for housing units with a mortgage	1,315	1,772	1,937	1.3
Median value of owner-occupied housing units................	144,200	241,400	275,600	2.0

- = Zero or rounds to zero.
[1] 2020 ACS 5-Year estimates. 1-Year estimates were not released for 2020 due to the impact of COVID-19 on data collection that year.

Table AK-4. Migration, Origin, and Language

(Number, percent.)

Characteristic	State 2016-2020 [1]	U.S. 2016-2020 [1]
Residence 1 Year Ago		
Population 1 year and over	727,126	322,943,283
Same house	82.7	86.2
Different house in the U.S.	16.6	13.2
Same county	9.7	7.7
Different county	6.9	5.5
Same state	2.7	3.2
Different state	4.2	2.3
Abroad	0.8	0.6
Place of Birth		
Native born	679,648	282,443,680
Male	52.7	49.4
Female	47.3	50.6
Foreign born	57,342	44,125,628
Male	46.1	48.6
Female	53.9	51.4
Foreign born; naturalized U.S. citizen...	33,555	22,456,684
Male	45.6	46.1
Female	54.4	53.9
Foreign born; not a U.S. citizen...	23,787	21,668,944
Male	46.9	51.1
Female	53.1	48.9
Entered 2010 or later	27.1	22.8
Entered 2000 to 2009	23.5	25.1
Entered before 2000..	49.4	52.1
World Region of Birth, Foreign		
Foreign-born population, excluding population born at sea	57,342	44,125,628
Europe	12.5	10.8
Asia	56.0	31.3
Africa	4.3	5.4
Oceania	5.4	0.6
Latin America	17.2	50.0
North America...	4.7	1.9
Language Spoken at Home and Ability to Speak English		
Population 5 years and over..	684,688	306,919,116
English only	84.2	78.5
Language other than English...	15.8	21.5
Speaks English less than "very well"...	4.6	8.2

[1] 2020 ACS 5-Year estimates. 1-Year estimates were not released for 2020 due to the impact of COVID-19 on data collection that year.
NA = Not available.
X = Not applicable.
- = Zero or rounds to zero.

Table AK-5. Median Income and Poverty Status, 2020[1]

(Number, percent, except as noted.)

Characteristic	State		U.S.	
	Number	Percent	Number	Percent
Median Income				
Households (dollars)	77,790	X	64,994	X
Families (dollars)	92,648	X	80,069	X
Below Poverty Level (All People)	74,369	10.3	40,910,326	12.8
Sex				
Male	35,939	9.7	18,171,512	11.6
Female	38,430	11.1	22,738,814	14.0
Age				
Under 18 years	24,864	13.8	12,598,699	17.5
Related children under 18 years	23,902	13.4	12,306,532	17.2
18 to 64 years	43,911	9.7	23,554,920	12.1
65 years and over	5,594	6.5	4,756,707	9.3

X = Not applicable.
[1] 2020 ACS 5-Year estimates. 1-Year estimates were not released for 2020 due to the impact of COVID-19 on data collection that year.

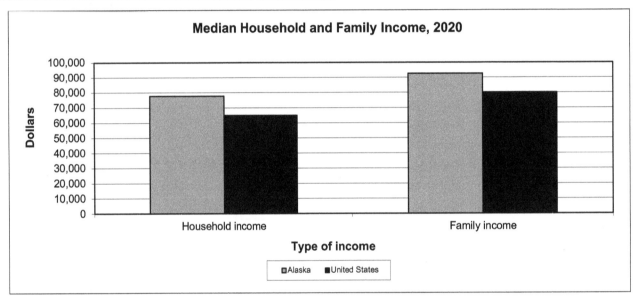

Table AK-6. Health Insurance Coverage Status for the Civilian Noninstitutionalized Population and Children Under 19 Years of Age

(Number; percent.)

Item	2011	2012	2013	2014	2015	2016	2017	2018	2019	2020 [2]
Civilian Noninstitutionalized Population	699272	708946	712248	711541	713,082	718,419	716,178	713,033	705,772	711,104
Covered by Private or Public Insurance										
Number	558,612	563,658	580,262	589,105	607,116	617,791	618,382	622,905	619,585	621,339
Percent	79.9	79.5	81.5	82.8	85.1	86.0	86.3	87.4	87.8	87.4
Uninsured										
Number	140,660	145,288	131,986	122,436	105,966	100,628	97,796	90,128	86,187	89,765
Percent	20.1	20.5	18.5	17.2	14.9	14.0	13.7	12.6	12.2	12.6
Percent in the U.S. not covered	15.1	14.8	14.5	11.7	9.4	8.6	8.7	8.9	9.2	8.7
Children Under 19 Years of Age[1]	187,708	187,072	187,885	186,245	185,917	186,839	194,383	192,588	190,002	191,841
Covered by Private or Public Insurance										
Number	165,599	161,115	166,043	164,993	166,252	168,245	175,661	174,413	172,143	173,561
Percent	88.2	86.1	88.4	88.6	89.4	90.0	90.4	90.6	90.6	90.5
Uninsured										
Number	22,109	25,957	21,842	21,252	19,665	18,594	18,722	18,175	17,859	18,280
Percent	11.8	13.9	11.6	11.4	10.6	10.0	9.6	9.4	9.4	9.5
Percent in the U.S. not covered	7.5	7.2	7.1	6.0	4.8	4.5	5.0	5.2	5.7	5.2

[1] Data for years prior to 2017 are for individuals under 18 years of age.
[2] 2020 ACS 5-Year estimates. 1-Year estimates were not released for 2020 due to the impact of COVID-19 on data collection that year. Data is not comparable to previous years, which are based on 1-year estimates.

Table AK-7. Employment Status by Demographic Group, 2021

(Numbers in thousands, percent.)

Characteristic	Civilian noninstitutional population	Civilian labor force		Employed		Unemployed	
		Number	Percent of population	Number	Percent of population	Number	Percent of population
Total...	544	352	64.7	328	60.3	24	6.8
Sex							
Male...................................	278	186	67.0	173	62.1	14	7.4
Female.................................	266	166	62.2	156	58.4	10	6.1
Race, Sex, and Hispanic Origin							
White	370	243	65.8	231	62.6	12	4.9
Male...................................	189	131	69.3	124	65.8	7	5.0
Female.................................	181	112	62.2	107	59.2	5	4.8
Black or African American...........	NA	NA	NA	NA	NA	NA	NA
Male...................................	NA	NA	NA	NA	NA	NA	NA
Female.................................	NA	NA	NA	NA	NA	NA	NA
Hispanic or Latino ethnicity[1]	30	23	76.5	21	70.8	2	7.5
Male...................................	NA	NA	NA	NA	NA	NA	NA
Female.................................	NA	NA	NA	NA	NA	NA	NA
Age							
16 to 19 years	35	14	39	12	34	2	12
20 to 24 years	41	31	74.5	27	66.4	3	10.8
25 to 34 years	107	83	78.0	77	72.5	6	7.1
35 to 44 years	94	75	80.4	71	75.5	5	6.0
45 to 54 years	80	66	82.6	62	77.9	4	5.9
55 to 64 years	92	60	65.1	57	61.7	3	5.2
65 years and over	97	24	24.7	22	23.0	2	6.7

NOTE: Data in Table 7 are from the Current Population Survey (CPS) and do not match the estimates in Table 8. See notes and definitions for further information.
[1] May be of any race.
NA = Not available.

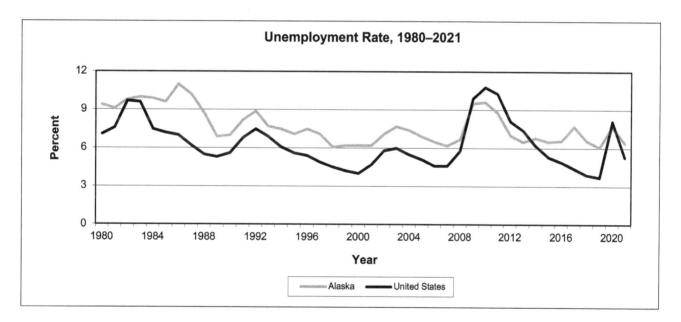

Unemployment Rate, 1980–2021

Table AK-8. Employment Status of the Civilian Noninstitutional Population Age 16 Years and Over

(Number, percent.)

Year	Civilian labor force	Civilian participation rate	Employed	Unemployed	Unemployment rate
2010........................	361,707	69.8	332,185	29,522	8.2
2011........................	364,599	69.0	336,312	28,287	7.8
2012........................	364,153	68.1	337,834	26,319	7.2
2013........................	363,544	67.5	338,104	25,440	7.0
2014........................	364,281	67.4	339,704	24,577	6.7
2015........................	362,425	66.8	339,604	22,821	6.3
2016........................	362,017	66.2	338,193	23,824	6.6
2017........................	360,589	66.0	337,108	23,481	6.5
2018........................	355,452	65.1	334,241	21,211	6.0
2019........................	352,883	64.8	333,541	19,342	5.5
2020........................	346,883	63.7	318,279	28,604	8.2
2021........................	354,936	65	332,266	22,670	6.4

Table AK-9. Employment and Average Wages by Industry

(Estimates are based on the 2012 North American Industry Classification System [NAICS].)

Industry	2013	2014	2015	2016	2017	2018	2019	2020
	Number of Jobs							
Wage and Salary Employment by Industry......................	365,773	366,038	367,546	361,040	356,627	356,145	358,567	332,120
Farm Wage and Salary Employment.............................	426	509	465	435	434	722	532	494
Nonfarm Wage and Salary Employment.........................	365,347	365,529	367,081	360,605	356,193	355,423	358,035	331,626
Private wage and salary employment..................................	258,297	260,470	262,338	256,968	253,093	252,664	255,664	230,671
Forestry, fishing, and related activities.............................	659	672	703	651	583	568	621	(D)
Mining..	17,014	17,602	17,041	14,190	12,790	12,422	13,083	11,025
Utilities...	2,135	2,112	2,138	2,122	2,118	2,197	2,203	2,294
Construction	16,840	17,546	18,154	16,682	15,550	16,219	16,790	16,222
Manufacturing...	14,463	14,436	14,083	13,609	13,236	12,641	13,077	(D)
Durable goods manufacturing.......................................	2,254	2,074	2,143	2,014	1,900	1,858	1,945	(D)
Nondurable goods manufacturing..................................	12,209	12,362	11,940	11,595	11,336	10,783	11,132	9,932
Wholesale trade	6,645	6,534	6,570	6,460	6,383	6,479	6,603	6,204
Retail trade...	36,168	37,029	37,684	37,332	36,628	36,095	35,809	33,677
Transportation and warehousing.....................................	19,619	19,596	19,855	19,899	19,852	20,113	20,414	17,172
Information	6,156	6,250	6,320	6,289	5,974	5,612	5,339	4,882
Finance and insurance	7,411	7,323	7,357	7,388	7,312	7,239	7,107	6,888
Real estate and rental and leasing....................................	4,957	4,927	4,920	4,827	4,786	4,685	4,807	4,231
Professional, scientific, and technical services	15,208	14,915	14,774	13,631	13,321	13,052	13,208	12,674
Management of companies and enterprises........................	3,058	3,002	3,139	2,914	2,866	2,819	2,797	2,648
Administrative and waste services	12,159	12,287	12,320	12,144	11,870	11,677	11,856	10,927
Educational services	3,304	3,306	3,345	3,313	3,408	3,292	3,283	2,792
Health care and social assistance....................................	44,636	44,203	44,637	46,076	47,029	47,741	48,214	47,072
Arts, entertainment, and recreation..................................	4,908	4,956	4,816	5,016	5,178	5,160	5,146	3,376
Accommodation and food services....................................	29,005	29,518	30,357	30,546	30,472	30,656	31,317	23,381
Other services, except public administration......................	13,952	14,256	14,125	13,879	13,737	13,997	13,990	12,808
Government and government enterprises.............................	107,050	105,059	104,743	103,637	103,100	102,759	102,371	100,955
	Dollars							
Average Wages and Salaries by Industry	54,540	56,348	57,716	56,711	57,052	59,070	60,840	64,844
Average Farm Wages and Salaries	38,577	32,921	33,882	38,538	38,265	26,378	35,539	37,439
Average Nonfarm Wages and Salaries	54,558	56,381	57,746	56,733	57,074	59,136	60,877	64,885
Average private wages and salaries..................................	53,463	55,541	57,074	55,369	55,545	57,829	59,864	64,349
Forestry, fishing, and related activities.............................	63,178	63,138	60,889	60,724	65,909	67,553	73,137	(D)
Mining..	130,678	137,379	141,022	136,045	136,274	147,476	148,663	164,097
Utilities...	88,145	88,411	93,208	91,065	92,863	97,426	99,338	104,163
Construction	77,234	81,766	83,982	80,225	77,491	81,738	84,016	85,123
Manufacturing...	45,120	45,479	50,904	51,400	53,008	55,390	56,880	(D)
Durable goods manufacturing.......................................	58,428	59,770	63,117	59,193	60,685	62,867	61,854	(D)
Nondurable goods manufacturing..................................	42,663	43,082	48,711	50,047	51,722	54,102	56,011	59,661
Wholesale trade	56,181	57,680	60,033	59,921	60,143	62,557	64,998	66,146
Retail trade...	31,633	32,446	32,980	32,953	33,527	34,364	35,404	38,146
Transportation and warehousing.....................................	64,335	65,986	66,491	66,503	68,266	71,030	73,438	84,508
Information	63,542	65,864	68,366	66,399	67,627	68,869	71,911	78,686
Finance and insurance	63,365	65,869	68,484	69,305	71,567	72,893	76,117	82,302
Real estate and rental and leasing....................................	42,502	44,035	45,346	46,528	46,369	48,703	50,632	54,720
Professional, scientific, and technical services	74,261	77,040	77,669	74,230	73,807	75,392	78,574	80,198
Management of companies and enterprises........................	81,416	87,345	87,860	88,688	91,782	92,308	100,671	104,932
Administrative and waste services	44,403	46,328	47,849	48,012	48,361	49,311	50,796	54,951
Educational services	29,697	29,120	29,303	29,840	30,899	32,537	34,249	39,944
Health care and social assistance....................................	48,887	50,405	52,809	53,355	54,841	57,320	59,426	62,879
Arts, entertainment, and recreation..................................	23,471	24,264	25,258	25,513	25,739	26,733	27,706	28,541
Accommodation and food services....................................	25,329	26,737	27,572	27,767	28,255	29,583	30,291	28,997
Other services, except public administration......................	36,105	37,296	38,423	39,303	40,625	41,141	41,934	46,248
Government and government enterprises.............................	57,200	58,463	59,431	60,116	60,829	62,350	63,406	66,110

(D) = Not shown to avoid disclosure of confidential information; estimates are included in higher-level totals.

Table AK-10. Employment Characteristics by Family Type

(Number, percent.)

Family type and labor force status	2018		2019		2020 [1]	
	Total	Families with own children under 18 years	Total	Families with own children under 18 years	Total	Families with own children under 18 years
All Families..	167,527	76,718	163,134	72,677	167,815	77,719
FAMILY TYPE AND LABOR FORCE STATUS						
Opposite-Sex Married-Couple Families...........................	127,824	55,431	124,608	51,781	126,464	54,897
Both husband and wife in labor force........................	54.1	65.6	51.1	59.3	54.6	64.1
Husband in labor force, wife not in labor force	21.3	27.0	24.1	32.7	21.9	28.3
Wife in labor force, husband not in labor force	9.6	6.5	8.2	5.3	8.8	5.7
Both husband and wife not in labor force........................	14.4	0.7	15.9	2.1	14.7	1.9
Other Families	39,703	21,287	38,526	20,896	40,503	22,692
Female householder, no spouse present	60.7	64.7	66.9	66.5	64.7	65.6
In labor force	44.8	53.6	48.3	55.1	47.2	54.2
Not in labor force	15.8	11.1	18.7	11.4	17.5	11.3
Male householder, no spouse present........................	39.3	35.3	33.1	33.5	35.3	34.4
In labor force	28.1	29.2	25.9	30.9	26.5	30.0
Not in labor force	11.2	6.1	7.2	2.6	8.8	4.5

[1] 2020 ACS 5-Year estimates. 1-Year estimates were not released for 2020 due to the impact of COVID-19 on data collection that year. Data is not comparable to previous years, which are based on 1-year estimates.

Table AK-11. School Enrollment and Educational Attainment, 2020[1]

(Number, percent.)

Item	State	U.S.
Enrollment		
Total population 3 years and over, enrolled in school	180,787	80,497,960
Enrolled in nursery school or preschool (percent)...	5.6	6.1
Enrolled in kindergarten (percent)..	5.3	5.0
Enrolled in elementary school, grades 1-8 (percent)..	44.0	40.4
Enrolled in high school, grades 9-12 (percent)	21.6	21.0
Enrolled in college or graduate school (percent)...	23.4	27.6
Attainment		
Total population 25 years and over	483,436	222,836,834
Less than ninth grade (percent)..	2.4	4.9
9th to 12th grade, no diploma (percent)	4.5	6.6
High school graduate, including equivalency (percent).....................................	28.4	26.7
Some college, no degree (percent)..	26	20.3
Associate's degree (percent)..	8.7	8.6
Bachelor's degree (percent)...	18.7	20.2
Graduate or professional degree (percent)...	11.3	12.7
High school graduate or higher (percent)	93.1	88.5
Bachelor's degree or higher (percent)..	30	32.9

[1] 2020 ACS 5-Year estimates. 1-Year estimates were not released for 2020 due to the impact of COVID-19 on data collection that year.

Table AK-12. Public School Characteristics and Educational Indicators

(Number, percent; data derived from National Center of Education Statistics.)

Item	State	U.S.
Public Elementary and Secondary Schools		
Number of regular school districts, 2018-19	53	13,452
Number of operational schools, 2019-20...	506	98,469
Percent charter schools	5.7	7.7
Total public school enrollment, Fall 2019..	132,017	50,796,445
Percent charter school enrollment	5.3	6.8
Student-teacher ratio, Fall 2019	17.6	15.9
Expenditures per student (unadjusted dollars), 2018-19	18,393	13,187
Four-year adjusted cohort graduation rate (ACGR), 2018-2019[1]...............................	80.4	85.8
Students eligible for free or reduced-price lunch (percent), 2019-20...........................	42.9	52.1
English language learners (percent), Fall 2019	12.0	10.4
Students age 3 to 21 served under IDEA, part B (percent), 2020-21	14.6	14.5

Public Schools by Type, 2019-20	Number	Percent of state public schools
Total number of schools...	506	100.0
Special education...	4	0.8
Vocational education..	3	0.6
Alternative education..	21	4.2

[1] Adjusted Cohort Graduation Rates (ACGR) differ from Averaged Freshmen Graduation Rates (AFGR).

Table AK-13. Reported Voting and Registration of the Voting-Age Population, November 2020

(Numbers in thousands, percent.)

Item	Total population	Total citizen population	Registered			Voted		
			Total registered	Percent registered (total population)	Percent registered (total citizen population)	Total voted	Percent voted (total population)	Percent voted (total citizen population)
U.S. Total	252,274	231,593	168,308	66.7	72.7	154,628	61.3	66.8
State Total................................	528	516	383	72.6	74.2	330	62.4	63.8
Sex								
Male	269	264	195	72.6	74.1	165	61.4	62.6
Female	259	253	188	72.5	74.3	165	63.5	65.1
Race								
White alone................................	345	343	265	76.7	77.3	243	70.3	70.9
White, non-Hispanic alone	325	323	251	77.2	77.5	230	70.6	71.0
Black alone	17	16	11	B	B	8	B	B
Asian alone	35	27	18	B	B	17	B	B
Hispanic (of any race)	28	27	21	B	B	17	B	B
White alone or in combination	375	372	287	76.6	77.1	259	69.2	69.7
Black alone or in combination	18	17	12	B	B	8	B	B
Asian alone or in combination............	43	35	24	B	B	22	B	B
Age								
18 to 24 years	60	59	38	B	B	29	B	B
25 to 34 years	97	94	59	60.7	63.1	41	41.9	43.6
35 to 44 years	102	99	74	72.5	75.1	62	60.5	62.6
45 to 64 years	177	174	141	79.8	80.9	131	73.9	75.0
65 years and over	92	91	71	77.0	77.7	67	73.0	73.6

B = Base is less than 75,000 and therefore too small to show the derived measure.

Table AK-14. Crime

(Number, rate per 100,000. Data are derived from the FBI Uniform Crime Reports.)

Item	State			U.S.		
	2018	2019	Percent change	2018	2019	Percent change
TOTAL POPULATION[1]	733,603	731,158	-0.3	328,329,953	329,484,123	0.4
VIOLENT CRIME						
Number..	6,346	6,126	-3.5	1,250,393	1,313,105	5.0
Rate	865.0	837.8	-3.1	380.8	398.5	4.6
Murder and Nonnegligent Manslaughter						
Number..	69	49	-29.0	16,669	21,570	29.4
Rate	9.4	6.7	-28.7	5.1	6.5	28.9
Rape[2]						
Number..	1,102	1,132	2.7	143,224	126,430	-11.7
Rate	150.2	154.8	3.1	43.6	38.4	-12.0
Robbery						
Number..	826	712	-13.8	268,483	243,600	-9.3
Rate	112.6	97.4	-13.5	81.8	73.9	-9.6
Aggravated Assault						
Number..	4,349	4,233	-2.7	822,017	921,505	12.1
Rate	592.8	578.9	-2.3	250.4	279.7	11.7
PROPERTY CRIME						
Number..	21,293	16,528	-22.4	6,995,235	6,452,038	-7.8
Rate	2,902.5	2,260.5	-22.1	2,130.6	1,958.2	-8.1
Burglary						
Number..	3,558	2,775	-22.0	1,118,096	1,035,314	-7.4
Rate	485.0	379.5	-21.7	340.5	314.2	-7.7
Larceny-Theft						
Number..	15,118	11,784	-22.1	5,152,267	4,606,324	-10.6
Rate	2,060.8	1,611.7	-21.8	1,569.2	1,398.0	-10.9
Motor Vehicle Theft						
Number..	2,617	1,969	-24.8	724,872	810,400	11.8
Rate	356.7	269.3	-24.5	220.8	246.0	11.4

NOTE: Although arson data are included in the trend and clearance tables, sufficient data are not available to estimate totals for this offense. Therefore, no arson data are published in this table.
- = Zero or rounds to zero.
[1] Population figures are U.S. Census Bureau provisional estimates as of July 1, 2020.
[2] The figures shown in the rape (revised definition) column were estimated using the revised Uniform Crime Reporting (UCR) definition of rape.

Table AK-15. State Government Finances, 2020

(Dollar amounts in thousands, percent distribution.)

Item	Dollars	Percent distribution
Total Revenue	10,421,195	100.0
General revenue	8,807,327	84.5
Intergovernmental revenue	4,476,466	43.0
Taxes	1,318,156	12.6
General sales	0	-
Selective sales	268,355	2.6
License taxes	152,187	1.5
Individual income tax	0	-
Corporate income tax	162,611	1.6
Other taxes	735,003	7.1
Current charges	679,953	6.5
Miscellaneous general revenue	2,332,752	22.4
Utility revenue	21,361	0.2
Liquor stores revenue	0	-
Insurance trust revenue[1]	1,592,507	15.3
Total Expenditure	12,027,170	100.0
Intergovernmental expenditure	2,261,190	18.8
Direct expenditure	9,765,980	81.2
Current operation	6,513,426	54.2
Capital outlay	1,230,132	10.2
Insurance benefits and repayments	1,647,251	13.7
Assistance and subsidies	175,501	1.5
Interest on debt	199,670	1.7
Exhibit: Salaries and wages	1,736,111	14.4
Total Expenditure	12,027,170	100.0
General expenditure	10,249,231	85.2
Intergovernmental expenditure	2,261,190	18.8
Direct expenditure	7,988,041	66.4
General expenditure, by function:		
Education	2,401,342	20.0
Public welfare	2,900,484	24.1
Hospitals	37,777	0.3
Health	273,675	2.3
Highways	1,137,474	9.5
Police protection	166,912	1.4
Correction	340,256	2.8
Natural resources	483,726	4.0
Parks and recreation	12,772	0.1
Governmental administration	672,897	5.6
Interest on general debt	198,843	1.7
Other and unallocable	1,602,395	13.3
Utility expenditure	130,688	1.3
Liquor stores expenditure	0	-
Insurance trust expenditure	1,647,251	13.7
Debt at End of Fiscal Year	5,849,366	X
Cash and Security Holdings	95,082,807	X

X = Not applicable.
- = Zero or rounds to zero.
[1] Within insurance trust revenue, net earnings of state retirement systems is a calculated statistic (the item code in the data file is X08), and thus can be positive or negative. Net earnings is the sum of earnings on investments plus gains on investments minus losses on investments. The change made in 2002 for asset valuation from book to market value in accordance with Statement 34 of the Governmental Accounting Standards Board is reflected in the calculated statistics.

Table AK-16. State Government Tax Collections, 2021

(Dollars in thousands, percent.)

Item	Dollars	Percent distribution
Total Taxes	1,053,400	100.0
Property taxes	120,028	11.4
Sales and gross receipts	267,842	25.4
General sales and gross receipts	X	-
Selective sales and gross receipts	267,842	25.4
Alcoholic beverages	41,126	3.9
Amusements	15480	1.5
Insurance premiums	61,558	5.8
Motor fuels	44,754	4.2
Pari-mutuels	X	-
Public utilities	4,361	0.4
Tobacco products	61,181	5.8
Other selective sales	39,382	3.7
Licenses	153,176	14.5
Alcoholic beverages	1,279	0.1
Amusements	X	-
Corporations in general	X	-
Hunting and fishing	32,968	3.1
Motor vehicle	36,472	3.5
Motor vehicle operators	X	-
Public utilities	7,835	0.7
Occupation and business, NEC	74,622	7.1
Other licenses	0	-
Income taxes	124,987	11.9
Individual income	X	-
Corporation net income	124,987	11.9
Other taxes	387,367	36.8
Death and gift	X	-
Documentary and stock transfer	X	-
Severance	387,367	36.8
Taxes, NEC	X	-

X = Not applicable.
- = Zero or rounds to zero.

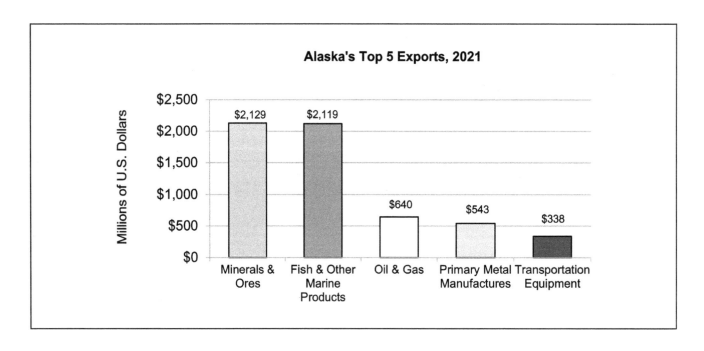

Alaska's Top 5 Exports, 2021

Export	Millions of U.S. Dollars
Minerals & Ores	$2,129
Fish & Other Marine Products	$2,119
Oil & Gas	$640
Primary Metal Manufactures	$543
Transportation Equipment	$338

ARIZONA

Facts and Figures

Location: Southwestern United States; bordered on the North by Utah, on the East by New Mexico, on the South by Mexico, and on the West by Nevada and California; Arizona is one of the Four Corner states—at its NE corner it touches Colorado, New Mexico, and Utah

Area: 113,990 sq, mi. (295,254 sq. km.); rank—6th

Population: 7,276,316 (2021 est.); rank—14th

Principal Cities: capital—Phoenix; largest—Phoenix

Statehood: February 14, 1912; 48th state

U.S. Congress: 2 senators, 9 representatives

State Motto: *Ditat Deus* ("God enriches")

State Song: "Arizona"

State Nickname: The Grand Canyon State

Abbreviations: AZ; Ariz.

State Symbols: flower—saguaro cactus blossom; tree—paloverde; bird—cactus wren

At a Glance

- With a 13.8 percent increase in population from 2010 to 2021, Arizona ranked 9th among the states for growth.

- In 2021, 18.3 percent of Arizonans were age 65 and older, the 13th highest percent in the nation.

- Arizona's median household income in 2020 was $61,529, compared to the national median household income of $64,994.

- In 2020, 14.1 percent of Arizonans lived below the poverty level, a percentage that ranked 14th in the country.

- Arizona's violent crime rate in 2020 was 484.8 per 100,000 population, ranking 10th in the nation.

Table AZ-1. Population by Age, Sex, Race, and Hispanic Origin

(Number, percent, except where noted.)

Sex, age, race, and Hispanic origin	2000	2010	2021	Percent change, 2010–2021
Total Population...	5,130,632	6,392,017	7,276,316	13.8
Percent of total U.S. population	1.8	2.1	2.2	X
Sex				
Male..	2,561,057	3,175,823	3,633,714	14.4
Female	2,569,575	3,216,814	3,642,602	13.2
Age				
Under 5 years...	382,386	455,715	401,856	-11.8
5 to 19 years..	1,135,802	1,363,926	1,405,673	3.1
20 to 64 years...	2,944,605	3,690,545	4,135,741	12.1
65 years and over..	667,839	881,831	1,333,046	51.2
Median age (years)	34.2	35.9	38.6	7.5
Race and Hispanic Origin				
One race				
White	3,873,611	5,418,483	5,969,037	10.2
Black	158,873	280,905	395,177	40.7
American Indian and Alaska Native	255,879	335,278	384,338	14.6
Asian...	92,236	188,456	277,804	47.4
Native Hawaiian or Other Pacific Islander	6,733	16,112	20,869	29.5
Two or more races..	146,526	152,783	229,091	49.9
Hispanic (of any race)...	1,295,617	1,943,466	2,351,122	21.0

NOTE: Population figures for 2021 are July 1 estimates. The 2000 and 2010 estimates are taken from the respective censuses.
- = Zero or rounds to zero.
X = Not applicable.

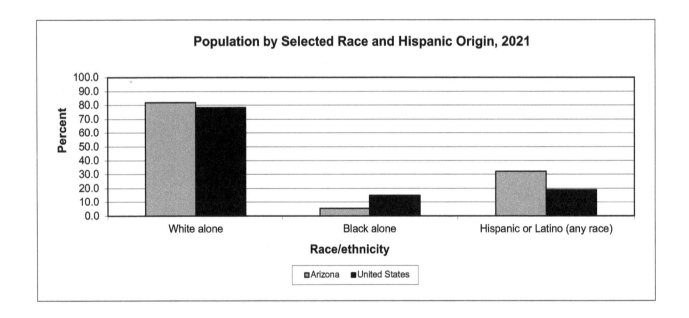

Population by Selected Race and Hispanic Origin, 2021

Legend: ☐ Arizona ■ United States

Table AZ-2. Marital Status

(Number, percent distribution.)

Sex, age, race, and Hispanic origin	2000	2010	2020 [1]
Males, 15 Years and Over	1,966,032	2,492,590	2,872,044
Never married	29.6	35.3	36.9
Now married, except separated...	56.4	50.1	48.2
Separated...	1.6	1.4	1.3
Widowed...	2.6	2.5	2.7
Divorced...	9.8	10.7	10.8
Females, 15 Years and Over	2,013,304	2,559,409	2,943,328
Never married	22.5	28.0	30.0
Now married, except separated...	53.6	48.0	46.1
Separated...	2.1	2.2	2.0
Widowed...	9.4	8.3	8.2
Divorced...	12.3	13.5	13.6

[1] 2020 ACS 5-Year estimates. 1-Year estimates were not released for 2020 due to the impact of COVID-19 on data collection that year.

Table AZ-3. Households and Housing Characteristics

(Number, percent, dollars.)

Item	2000	2010	2020 [1]	Average annual percent change, 2010–2020
Total Households...	1,901,327	2,334,050	2,643,430	1.9
Family households	1,287,367	1,548,428	1,720,736	1.6
Married-couple family	986,303	1,134,229	1,256,731	1.5
Other family	310,064	414,199	464,005	1.7
Male householder, no wife present..	90,283	123,772	144,505	2.4
Female householder, no husband present.............................	210,781	290,427	319,500	1.4
Nonfamily households	613,960	785,622	922,694	2.5
Householder living alone..	472,006	621,291	726,205	2.4
Householder not living alone..	141,954	164,331	196,489	2.8
Housing Characteristics				
Total housing units...	2,189,189	2,846,738	3,040,595	1.0
Occupied housing units...	1,901,327	2,334,050	2,643,430	1.9
Owner occupied	1,293,556	1,522,938	1,727,176	1.9
Renter occupied...	607,771	811,112	916,254	1.9
Average household size..	2.64	2.69	2.65	-0.2
Financial Characteristics				
Median gross rent of renter-occupied housing	619	844	1,097	4.3
Median monthly owner costs for housing units with a mortgage	1,039	1,442	1,464	0.2
Median value of owner-occupied housing units.........................	121,300	168,800	242,000	6.2

[1] 2020 ACS 5-Year estimates. 1-Year estimates were not released for 2020 due to the impact of COVID-19 on data collection that year.

Table AZ-4. Migration, Origin, and Language

(Number, percent.)

Characteristic	State 2016-2020 [1]	U.S. 2016-2020 [1]
Residence 1 Year Ago		
Population 1 year and over	7,093,842	322,943,283
Same house	83	86.2
Different house in the U.S..	16.3	13.2
Same county	10.8	7.7
Different county	5.5	5.5
Same state	1.8	3.2
Different state	3.8	2.3
Abroad	0.6	0.6
Place of Birth		
Native born	6,226,453	282,443,680
Male	50.0	49.4
Female	50.0	50.6
Foreign born	947,611	44,125,628
Male	47.8	48.6
Female	52.2	51.4
Foreign born; naturalized U.S. citizen..	428,788	22,456,684
Male...	45.1	46.1
Female	54.9	53.9
Foreign born; not a U.S. citizen..	518,823	21,668,944
Male...	50.0	51.1
Female	50.0	48.9
Entered 2010 or later	20.3	22.8
Entered 2000 to 2009	23.4	25.1
Entered before 2000..	56.3	52.1
World Region of Birth, Foreign		
Foreign-born population, excluding population born at sea	947,611	44,125,628
Europe	9.4	10.8
Asia	20.8	31.3
Africa	3.5	5.4
Oceania	0.6	0.6
Latin America	61.1	50.0
North America...	4.7	1.9
Language Spoken at Home and Ability to Speak English		
Population 5 years and over..	6,742,840	306,919,116
English only	73.3	78.5
Language other than English..	26.7	21.5
Speaks English less than "very well"..	8.3	8.2

[1] 2020 ACS 5-Year estimates. 1-Year estimates were not released for 2020 due to the impact of COVID-19 on data collection that year.
NA = Not available.
X = Not applicable.
- = Zero or rounds to zero.

Table AZ-5. Median Income and Poverty Status, 2020[1]

(Number, percent, except as noted.)

Characteristic	State		U.S.	
	Number	Percent	Number	Percent
Median Income				
Households (dollars)...	61,529	X	64,994	X
Families (dollars)	73,456	X	80,069	X
Below Poverty Level (All People)	990,528	14.1	40,910,326	12.8
Sex				
Male	456,524	13.2	18,171,512	11.6
Female	534,004	15.0	22,738,814	14.0
Age				
Under 18 years..	321,919	20.0	12,598,699	17.5
Related children under 18 years..	315,060	19.7	12,306,532	17.2
18 to 64 years	557,717	13.4	23,554,920	12.1
65 years and over	110,892	8.9	4,756,707	9.3

X = Not applicable.
[1] 2020 ACS 5-Year estimates. 1-Year estimates were not released for 2020 due to the impact of COVID-19 on data collection that year.

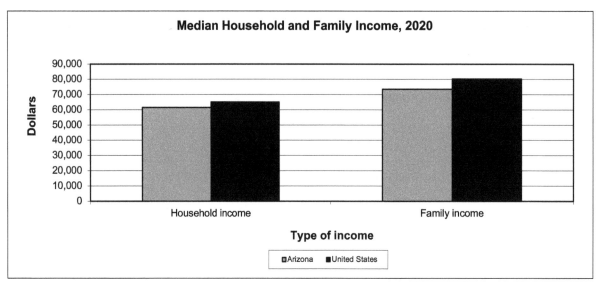

Median Household and Family Income, 2020

Table AZ-6. Health Insurance Coverage Status for the Civilian Noninstitutionalized Population and Children Under 19 Years of Age

(Number, percent.)

Item	2011	2012	2013	2014	2015	2016	2017	2018	2019	2020 [2]
Civilian Noninstitutionalized Population	6,378,280	6,443,654	6,521,226	6,623,074	6,719,354	6,824,645	6,908,121	7,064,799	7,165,904	7,065,326
Covered by Private or Public Insurance										
Number..	5,283,270	5,312,695	5,403,040	5,719,746	5,991,378	6,143,407	6,213,331	6,314,822	6,357,261	6,317,548
Percent..	82.8	82.4	82.9	86.4	89.2	90.0	89.9	89.4	88.7	89.4
Uninsured										
Number..	1,095,010	1,130,959	1,118,186	903,328	727,976	681,238	694,790	749,977	808,643	747,778
Percent..	17.2	17.6	17.1	13.6	10.8	10.0	10.1	10.6	11.3	10.6
Percent in the U.S. not covered..................................	15.1	14.8	14.5	11.7	9.4	8.6	8.7	8.9	9.2	8.7
Children Under 19 Years of Age[1]	1,621,830	1,617,380	1,613,505	1,620,576	1,619,393	1,629,040	1,729,440	1,745,643	1,744,282	1,739,980
Covered by Private or Public Insurance										
Number..	1,413,411	1,403,418	1,421,745	1,458,722	1,485,146	1,509,594	1,596,296	1,599,359	1,582,952	1,591,384
Percent..	87.1	86.8	88.1	90.0	91.7	92.7	92.3	91.6	90.8	91.5
Uninsured										
Number..	208,419	213,962	191,760	161,854	134,247	119,446	133,144	146,284	161,330	148,596
Percent..	12.9	13.2	11.9	10.0	8.3	7.3	7.7	8.4	9.2	8.5
Percent in the U.S. not covered..................................	7.5	7.2	7.1	6.0	4.8	4.5	5.0	5.2	5.7	5.2

[1] Data for years prior to 2017 are for individuals under 18 years of age.
[2] 2020 ACS 5-Year estimates. 1-Year estimates were not released for 2020 due to the impact of COVID-19 on data collection that year. Data is not comparable to previous years, which are based on 1-year estimates.

Table AZ-7. Employment Status by Demographic Group, 2021

(Numbers in thousands, percent.)

Characteristic	Civilian noninstitutional population	Civilian labor force		Employed		Unemployed	
		Number	Percent of population	Number	Percent of population	Number	Percent of population
Total..	5,993	3,686	61.5	3,497	58.3	190	5.1
Sex							
Male..	2,923	2,015	68.9	1,918	65.6	97	4.8
Female	3,070	1,671	54.4	1,578	51.4	93	5.6
Race, Sex, and Hispanic Origin							
White..	5,111	3,068	60.0	2,913	57.0	155	5.0
Male......................................	2,499	1,680	67.2	1,599	64.0	81	4.8
Female	2,612	1,388	53.1	1,314	50.3	74	5.3
Black or African American...............	315	213	67.7	197	62.6	16	7.6
Male......................................	150	117	77.8	110	73.1	7	6.1
Female	NA	NA	NA	NA	NA	NA	NA
Hispanic or Latino ethnicity[1]	1,823	1,197	65.7	1,128	61.9	68	5.7
Male......................................	876	681	77.7	645	73.7	35	5.2
Female	947	516	54.5	483	51.0	33	6.4
Age							
16 to 19 years.............................	323	115	35.5	103	32.0	11	10.0
20 to 24 years.............................	562	414	73.7	381	67.8	33	8.0
25 to 34 years.............................	1,043	873	83.7	824	79.0	49	5.6
35 to 44 years.............................	879	701	79.8	674	76.6	28	3.9
45 to 54 years.............................	933	757	81.2	722	77.4	35	4.7
55 to 64 years.............................	912	623	68.3	600	65.8	23	3.8
65 years and over	1,342	203	15.1	193	14.4	10	4.9

NOTE: Data in Table 7 are from the Current Population Survey (CPS) and do not match the estimates in Table 8. See notes and definitions for further information.
[1] May be of any race.
NA = Not available.

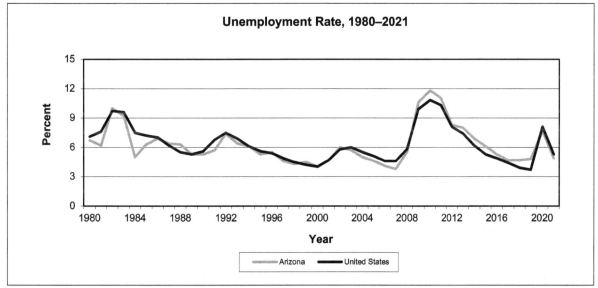

Table AZ-8. Employment Status of the Civilian Noninstitutional Population Age 16 Years and Over

(Number, percent.)

Year	Civilian labor force	Civilian participation rate	Employed	Unemployed	Unemployment rate
2010..	3,096,316	63.2	2,777,404	318,912	10.3
2011..	3,051,937	62.0	2,763,761	288,176	9.4
2012..	3,054,343	61.0	2,799,634	254,709	8.3
2013..	3,064,554	60.3	2,825,341	239,213	7.8
2014..	3,118,441	60.2	2,906,193	212,248	6.8
2015..	3,184,445	60.4	2,990,545	193,900	6.1
2016..	3,253,468	60.4	3,075,851	177,617	5.5
2017..	3,240,111	60.7	3,079,700	160,411	5.0
2018..	3,328,189	61.2	3,168,469	159,720	4.8
2019..	3,432,476	62	3,265,925	166,551	4.9
2020..	3,456,852	61.2	3,191,100	265,752	7.7
2021..	3,518,425	61.1	3,346,319	172,106	4.9

Table AZ-9. Employment and Average Wages by Industry

(Estimates are based on the 2012 North American Industry Classification System [NAICS].)

Industry	2013	2014	2015	2016	2017	2018	2019	2020
	Number of Jobs							
Wage and Salary Employment by Industry.....................	2,617,500	2,669,755	2,745,697	2,816,903	2,881,141	2,962,324	3,048,198	2,967,485
Farm Wage and Salary Employment..............................	13,949	12,360	13,584	15,203	13,219	12,815	11,943	12,465
Nonfarm Wage and Salary Employment..........................	2,603,551	2,657,395	2,732,113	2,801,700	2,867,922	2,949,509	3,036,255	2,955,020
Private wage and salary employment....................................	2,159,150	2,212,261	2,287,470	2,355,879	2,419,272	2,498,275	2,577,461	2,504,186
Forestry, fishing, and related activities.................................	11,957	12,121	13,224	12,882	12,039	11,899	11,920	10,518
Mining...	12,616	12,303	11,732	11,298	11,723	13,045	13,235	12,139
Utilities...	11,934	11,952	12,086	12,369	12,263	12,133	12,270	11,929
Construction..	126,937	128,148	130,978	138,537	149,183	162,200	175,209	178,258
Manufacturing..	153,985	155,073	156,499	158,462	162,538	168,357	176,131	175,519
Durable goods manufacturing.......................................	121,335	121,607	121,099	121,163	123,367	127,221	134,012	134,542
Nondurable goods manufacturing..................................	32,650	33,466	35,400	37,299	39,171	41,136	42,119	40,977
Wholesale trade	99,388	95,608	95,529	96,386	97,539	99,292	100,288	99,962
Retail trade..	301,687	314,829	324,208	330,485	334,074	329,685	329,237	322,918
Transportation and warehousing.......................................	73,148	75,613	79,808	82,963	86,701	99,677	107,486	119,158
Information..	41,815	43,379	45,202	45,360	45,378	47,398	49,088	45,537
Finance and insurance	135,835	140,603	149,899	156,893	166,474	171,875	180,650	186,857
Real estate and rental and leasing....................................	48,084	48,500	49,184	50,665	51,882	55,129	57,432	56,087
Professional, scientific, and technical services......................	128,475	131,733	134,738	142,187	146,242	154,946	160,480	161,257
Management of companies and enterprises.........................	28,756	29,699	31,356	31,768	31,486	28,942	30,462	32,418
Administrative and waste services....................................	220,661	225,827	235,195	242,520	245,555	250,321	257,243	241,359
Educational services	56,136	57,639	59,936	60,523	61,316	60,591	61,634	61,024
Health care and social assistance.....................................	319,520	325,901	340,468	355,341	368,137	381,576	397,103	396,359
Arts, entertainment, and recreation..................................	35,646	38,940	40,121	41,359	43,786	45,318	46,409	34,597
Accommodation and food services...................................	241,506	249,539	260,870	269,978	278,135	283,126	286,001	242,856
Other services, except public administration........................	111,064	114,854	116,437	115,903	114,821	122,765	125,183	115,434
Government and government enterprises	444,401	445,134	444,643	445,821	448,650	451,234	458,794	450,834
	Dollars							
Average Wages and Salaries by Industry	46,838	47,847	48,814	49,431	51,157	53,004	54,824	59,370
Average Farm Wages and Salaries	35,429	38,593	29,719	30,742	35,559	36,382	27,949	35,670
Average Nonfarm Wages and Salaries	46,899	47,890	48,909	49,533	51,229	53,076	54,929	59,470
Average private wages and salaries.....................................	46,909	47,957	48,946	49,567	51,329	53,210	55,155	59,845
Forestry, fishing, and related activities.................................	24,102	25,956	25,729	28,279	30,220	31,799	32,411	37,350
Mining...	78,991	79,193	81,501	77,261	80,503	85,963	85,693	88,146
Utilities...	97,516	102,398	101,069	104,607	108,747	112,071	112,130	117,008
Construction..	48,410	49,560	50,311	51,698	54,383	56,946	59,498	64,040
Manufacturing..	70,908	72,639	74,039	74,250	75,498	78,223	80,959	84,545
Durable goods manufacturing.......................................	78,198	80,185	82,147	82,699	84,259	87,486	89,693	93,326
Nondurable goods manufacturing..................................	43,818	45,218	46,300	46,804	47,907	49,576	53,171	55,715
Wholesale trade	68,749	72,278	74,866	76,105	78,597	80,777	82,917	87,803
Retail trade..	30,349	31,166	31,982	32,412	33,484	34,980	36,176	40,410
Transportation and warehousing.......................................	50,494	50,818	52,807	53,029	54,720	53,791	53,662	52,999
Information..	63,180	66,659	67,826	71,256	73,319	77,702	79,892	93,485
Finance and insurance	69,575	71,053	73,097	74,341	75,933	79,199	82,961	91,914
Real estate and rental and leasing....................................	46,637	48,586	50,253	51,405	52,749	55,304	57,770	62,509
Professional, scientific, and technical services	74,380	74,841	76,601	76,313	77,800	79,019	81,224	85,085
Management of companies and enterprises.........................	85,738	92,256	89,998	88,594	95,516	93,517	99,682	102,964
Administrative and waste services....................................	34,833	35,935	37,106	37,722	39,262	41,296	42,701	46,103
Educational services	40,992	41,316	41,513	41,371	41,939	43,649	43,767	49,206
Health care and social assistance.....................................	49,494	50,265	51,047	51,300	52,877	54,100	55,545	59,256
Arts, entertainment, and recreation..................................	36,419	39,381	39,069	40,522	41,770	43,090	44,736	50,001
Accommodation and food services...................................	21,326	21,953	22,624	22,957	24,399	25,998	26,850	26,697
Other services, except public administration........................	30,719	31,995	32,893	34,053	36,335	36,813	38,298	41,418
Government and government enterprises.............................	46,850	47,557	48,721	49,354	50,694	52,335	53,660	57,386

Table AZ-10. Employment Characteristics by Family Type

(Number, percent.)

Family type and labor force status	2018 Total	2018 Families with own children under 18 years	2019 Total	2019 Families with own children under 18 years	2020[1] Total	2020[1] Families with own children under 18 years
All Families	1,713,006	699,523	1,740,704	680,442	1,720,736	702,307
FAMILY TYPE AND LABOR FORCE STATUS						
Opposite-Sex Married-Couple Families	1,247,270	459,431	1,272,331	453,075	1,242,857	461,475
Both husband and wife in labor force	43	59.2	43.4	61.1	44.0	61.5
Husband in labor force, wife not in labor force	23	34.0	22.6	32.1	23.0	32.4
Wife in labor force, husband not in labor force	7.9	4.1	7.8	4.2	7.8	4.1
Both husband and wife not in labor force	25	2.2	25.0	2.0	25.1	2.0
Other Families	465,736	240,092	468,373	227,367	464,005	238,578
Female householder, no spouse present	67.4	67.8	68.4	68.8	68.9	70.8
In labor force	48.6	57.0	48.4	57.3	49.3	59.0
Not in labor force	18.8	10.8	20.0	11.6	19.6	11.8
Male householder, no spouse present	32.6	32.2	31.6	31.2	31.1	29.2
In labor force	26.2	29.4	24.4	27.3	25.0	26.6
Not in labor force	6.4	2.9	7.2	3.9	6.1	2.6

[1] 2020 ACS 5-Year estimates. 1-Year estimates were not released for 2020 due to the impact of COVID-19 on data collection that year. Data is not comparable to previous years, which are based on 1-year estimates.

Table AZ-11. School Enrollment and Educational Attainment, 2020[1]

(Number, percent.)

Item	State	U.S.
Enrollment		
Total population 3 years and over, enrolled in school	1,760,360	80,497,960
Enrolled in nursery school or preschool (percent)	4.8	6.1
Enrolled in kindergarten (percent)	4.9	5.0
Enrolled in elementary school, grades 1-8 (percent)	42.0	40.4
Enrolled in high school, grades 9-12 (percent)	21.5	21.0
Enrolled in college or graduate school (percent)	26.8	27.6
Attainment		
Total population 25 years and over	4,846,056	222,836,834
Less than ninth grade (percent)	5.1	4.9
9th to 12th grade, no diploma (percent)	7.0	6.6
High school graduate, including equivalency (percent)	23.8	26.7
Some college, no degree (percent)	24.9	20.3
Associate's degree (percent)	8.9	8.6
Bachelor's degree (percent)	18.8	20.2
Graduate or professional degree (percent)	11.5	12.7
High school graduate or higher (percent)	87.9	88.5
Bachelor's degree or higher (percent)	30.3	32.9

[1] 2020 ACS 5-Year estimates. 1-Year estimates were not released for 2020 due to the impact of COVID-19 on data collection that year.

Table AZ-12. Public School Characteristics and Educational Indicators

(Number, percent; data derived from National Center of Education Statistics.)

Item	State	U.S.
Public Elementary and Secondary Schools		
Number of regular school districts, 2018-19	226	13,452
Number of operational schools, 2019-20	2,325	98,469
Percent charter schools	24.0	7.7
Total public school enrollment, Fall 2019	1,152,586	50,796,445
Percent charter school enrollment	18.7	6.8
Student-teacher ratio, Fall 2019	23.6	15.9
Expenditures per student (unadjusted dollars), 2018-19	8,773	13,187
Four-year adjusted cohort graduation rate (ACGR), 2018-2019[1]	77.8	85.8
Students eligible for free or reduced-price lunch (percent), 2019-20	51.2	52.1
English language learners (percent), Fall 2019	6.6	10.4
Students age 3 to 21 served under IDEA, part B (percent), 2020-21	13.0	14.5

Public Schools by Type, 2019-20	Number	Percent of state public schools
Total number of schools	2,325	100.0
Special education	29	1.2
Vocational education	271	11.7
Alternative education	161	6.9

[1] Adjusted Cohort Graduation Rates (ACGR) differ from Averaged Freshmen Graduation Rates (AFGR).

Table AZ-13. Reported Voting and Registration of the Voting-Age Population, November 2020

(Numbers in thousands, percent.)

Item	Total population	Total citizen population	Registered			Voted		
			Total registered	Percent registered (total population)	Percent registered (total citizen population)	Total voted	Percent voted (total population)	Percent voted (total citizen population)
U.S. Total	252,274	231,593	168,308	66.7	72.7	154,628	61.3	66.8
State Total..............................	5,638	5,075	3,878	68.8	76.4	3,649	64.7	71.9
Sex								
Male	2,739	2,465	1,784	65.1	72.4	1,653	60.4	67.1
Female	2,899	2,610	2,095	72.3	80.3	1,996	68.9	76.5
Race								
White alone................................	4,840	4,365	3,328	68.8	76.3	3,152	65.1	72.2
White, non-Hispanic alone	3,140	3,096	2,480	79.0	80.1	2,385	76.0	77.0
Black alone................................	279	259	205	73.3	79.2	179	63.9	69.1
Asian alone	206	158	111	53.8	70.2	107	52.0	67.9
Hispanic (of any race)	1,800	1,340	895	49.7	66.8	814	45.2	60.8
White alone or in combination	4,966	4,472	3,422	68.9	76.5	3,242	65.3	72.5
Black alone or in combination...........	344	323	266	77.3	82.2	235	68.3	72.7
Asian alone or in combination...........	226	177	130	57.8	73.5	127	56.2	71.5
Age								
18 to 24 years................................	653	629	371	56.7	59.0	327	50.1	52.0
25 to 34 years................................	941	850	619	65.8	72.9	579	61.6	68.2
35 to 44 years................................	929	756	565	60.8	74.6	509	54.8	67.3
45 to 64 years................................	1,833	1,627	1,301	70.9	79.9	1,242	67.8	76.4
65 years and over	1,282	1,213	1,023	79.8	84.4	992	77.4	81.8

Table AZ-14. Crime

(Number, rate per 100,000. Data are derived from the FBI Uniform Crime Reports.)

Item	State			U.S.		
	2019	2020	Percent change	2019	2020	Percent change
TOTAL POPULATION[1]	7,291,843	7,421,401	1.8	328,329,953	329,484,123	0.4
VIOLENT CRIME						
Number..	32,603	35,980	10.4	1,250,393	1,313,105	5.0
Rate	447.1	484.8	8.4	380.8	398.5	4.6
Murder and Nonnegligent Manslaughter						
Number..	397	513	29.2	16,669	21,570	29.4
Rate	5.4	6.9	27.0	5.1	6.5	28.9
Rape[2]						
Number..	3,650	3,263	-10.6	143,224	126,430	-11.7
Rate	50.1	44.0	-12.2	43.6	38.4	-12.0
Robbery						
Number..	6,305	6,211	-1.5	268,483	243,600	-9.3
Rate	86.5	83.7	-3.2	81.8	73.9	-9.6
Aggravated Assault						
Number..	22,251	25,993	16.8	822,017	921,505	12.1
Rate	305.1	350.2	14.8	250.4	279.7	11.7
PROPERTY CRIME						
Number..	177,628	165,323	-6.9	6,995,235	6,452,038	-7.8
Rate	2,436.0	2,227.7	-8.6	2,130.6	1,958.2	-8.1
Burglary						
Number..	29,170	24,488	-16.1	1,118,096	1,035,314	-7.4
Rate	400.0	330.0	-17.5	340.5	314.2	-7.7
Larceny-Theft						
Number..	130,427	122,898	-5.8	5,152,267	4,606,324	-10.6
Rate	1,788.7	1,656.0	-7.4	1,569.2	1,398.0	-10.9
Motor Vehicle Theft						
Number..	18,031	17,937	-0.5	724,872	810,400	11.8
Rate	247.3	241.7	-2.3	220.8	246.0	11.4

NOTE: Although arson data are included in the trend and clearance tables, sufficient data are not available to estimate totals for this offense. Therefore, no arson data are published in this table.
- = Zero or rounds to zero.
[1] Population figures are U.S. Census Bureau provisional estimates as of July 1, 2020.
[2] The figures shown in the rape (revised definition) column were estimated using the revised Uniform Crime Reporting (UCR) definition of rape.

Table AZ-15. State Government Finances, 2020

(Dollar amounts in thousands, percent distribution.)

Item	Dollars	Percent distribution
Total Revenue	50,547,601	100.0
General revenue	44,620,559	88.3
Intergovernmental revenue	21,167,549	41.9
Taxes	17,653,813	34.9
General sales	8861931	17.5
Selective sales	2,026,515	4.0
License taxes	584,022	1.2
Individual income tax	4530410	9.0
Corporate income tax	523,062	1.0
Other taxes	1,127,873	2.2
Current charges	3,341,708	6.6
Miscellaneous general revenue	2,457,489	4.9
Utility revenue	22,014	-
Liquor stores revenue	0	-
Insurance trust revenue[1]	5,905,028	11.7
Total Expenditure	47,169,591	100.0
Intergovernmental expenditure	9,908,651	21.0
Direct expenditure	37,260,940	79.0
Current operation	25,898,280	54.9
Capital outlay	1,688,656	3.6
Insurance benefits and repayments	5,731,363	12.2
Assistance and subsidies	3,296,999	7.0
Interest on debt	645,642	1.4
Exhibit: Salaries and wages	4,539,658	9.6
Total Expenditure	47,169,591	100.0
General expenditure	41,412,030	87.8
Intergovernmental expenditure	9,908,651	21.0
Direct expenditure	31,503,379	66.8
General expenditure, by function:		
Education	14,439,887	30.6
Public welfare	17,456,354	37.0
Hospitals	491	-
Health	643,206	1.4
Highways	2,394,996	5.1
Police protection	319,460	0.7
Correction	1,171,455	2.5
Natural resources	346,098	0.7
Parks and recreation	93,652	0.2
Governmental administration	739,255	1.6
Interest on general debt	644,456	1.4
Other and unallocable	3,104,122	6.6
Utility expenditure	31,211	0.1
Liquor stores expenditure	0	-
Insurance trust expenditure	5,731,363	12.2
Debt at End of Fiscal Year	12,946,749	X
Cash and Security Holdings	77,490,317	X

X = Not applicable.

- = Zero or rounds to zero.

[1] Within insurance trust revenue, net earnings of state retirement systems is a calculated statistic (the item code in the data file is X08), and thus can be positive or negative. Net earnings is the sum of earnings on investments plus gains on investments minus losses on investments. The change made in 2002 for asset valuation from book to market value in accordance with Statement 34 of the Governmental Accounting Standards Board is reflected in the calculated statistics.

Table AZ-16. State Government Tax Collections, 2021

(Dollars in thousands, percent.)

Item	Dollars	Percent distribution
Total Taxes	20,817,605	100.0
Property taxes	1,266,990	6.1
Sales and gross receipts	11,290,897	54.2
General sales and gross receipts	9,184,958	44.1
Selective sales and gross receipts	2,105,939	10.1
Alcoholic beverages	89,138	0.4
Amusements	258	-
Insurance premiums	680,245	3.3
Motor fuels	844,828	4.1
Pari-mutuels	109	-
Public utilities	22,226	0.1
Tobacco products	294,155	1.4
Other selective sales	174,980	0.8
Licenses	618,052	3.0
Alcoholic beverages	9,679	-
Amusements	0	-
Corporations in general	28,484	0.1
Hunting and fishing	42,209	0.2
Motor vehicle	293,109	1.4
Motor vehicle operators	35,777	0.2
Public utilities	30	-
Occupation and business, NEC	206,430	1.0
Other licenses	2334	-
Income taxes	7,438,706	35.7
Individual income	6,532,753	31.4
Corporation net income	905,953	4.4
Other taxes	202,960	1.0
Death and gift	0	-
Documentary and stock transfer	19,160	0.1
Severance	35,610	0.2
Taxes, NEC	148190	0.7

- = Zero or rounds to zero.
X = Not applicable.

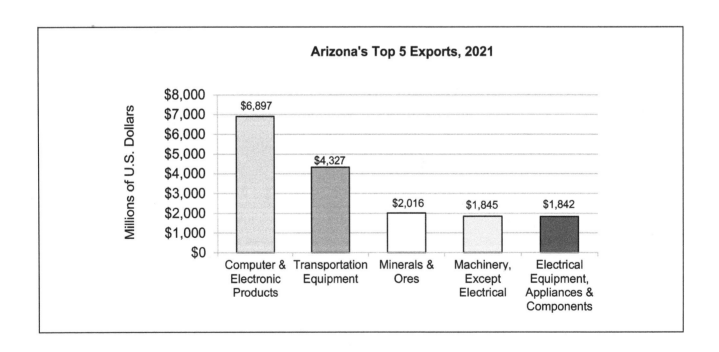

ARKANSAS

Facts and Figures

Location: South central United States; bordered on the N by Missouri, on the E by Tennessee and Mississippi, on the S by Louisiana, and on the W by Oklahoma and Texas

Area: 53,178 sq. mi. (137,733 sq. km.); rank—29th

Population: 3,025,891 (2021 est.); rank—33rd

Principal Cities: capital—Little Rock; largest—Little Rock

Statehood: June 15, 1836; 25th state

U.S. Congress: 2 senators, 4 representatives

State Motto: *Regnat populus* ("The people rule")

State Song: "Arkansas"

State Nicknames: The Natural State; The Land of Opportunity

Abbreviations: AR; Ark.

State Symbols: flower—apple blossom; tree—pine; bird—mockingbird

At a Glance

- With an increase in population of 3.8 percent, Arkansas ranked 34th among the states in growth from 2010 to 2021.

- In 2020, 23.8 percent of Arkansas residents had a bachelor's degree or higher, the 3rd lowest percent in the nation.

- Arkansas's median household income in 2020 was $49,475, and 16.1 percent of the population lived below the poverty level.

- Arkansas had the lowest voter turnout among the states in the November 2020 election, with just 51.9 percent of the population casting votes.

- Arkansas' property crime rate in 2020 was 2,613.4 per 100,000 population, which ranked 9th in the nation.

Table AR-1. Population by Age, Sex, Race, and Hispanic Origin

(Number, percent, except where noted.)

Sex, age, race, and Hispanic origin	2000	2010	2021	Percent change, 2010–2021
Total Population..	2,673,400	2,915,918	3,025,891	3.8
Percent of total U.S. population	0.9	0.9	0.9	X
Sex				
Male..	1,304,693	1,431,637	1,493,178	4.3
Female	1,368,707	1,484,281	1,532,713	3.3
Age				
Under 5 years..	181,585	197,689	181,560	-8.2
5 to 19 years..	578,924	598,241	599,830	0.3
20 to 64 years..	1,538,872	1,700,007	1,716,400	1.0
65 years and over..	374,019	419,981	528,101	25.7
Median age (years)	36.0	37.4	38.6	3.2
Race and Hispanic Origin				
One race				
White..	2,138,598	2,342,403	2,379,596	1.6
Black..	418,950	454,021	475,018	4.6
American Indian and Alaska Native..	17,808	26,134	32,625	24.8
Asian..	20,220	37,537	54,457	45.1
Native Hawaiian or Other Pacific Islander	1,068	6,685	13,196	97.4
Two or more races..	35,744	49,138	70,999	44.5
Hispanic (of any race)..	86,866	191,535	251,277	31.2

NOTE: Population figures for 2021 are July 1 estimates. The 2000 and 2010 estimates are taken from the respective censuses.
- = Zero or rounds to zero.
X = Not applicable.

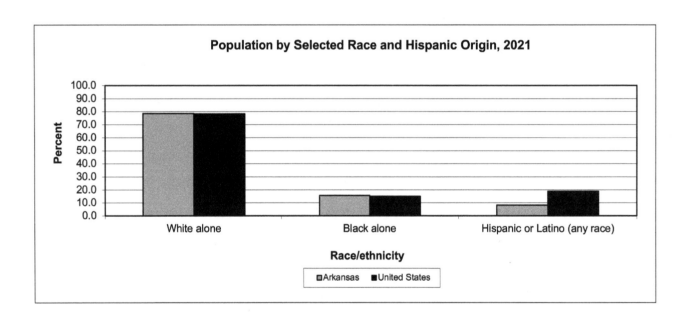

Population by Selected Race and Hispanic Origin, 2021

Race/ethnicity

□ Arkansas   ■ United States

Table AR-2. Marital Status

(Number, percent distribution.)

Sex, age, race, and Hispanic origin	2000	2010	2020 [1]
Males, 15 Years and Over	1,015,594	1,128,804	1,179,728
Never married	24.2	29.5	31.3
Now married, except separated..	61.0	53.3	51.6
Separated..	1.6	2.2	2.0
Widowed..	2.7	3.1	3.3
Divorced..	10.4	12.0	11.9
Females, 15 Years and Over	1,096,069	1,200,974	1,249,078
Never married	18.4	23.5	25.3
Now married, except separated..	55.7	48.8	47.9
Separated..	2.2	2.9	2.4
Widowed..	12.2	11.2	10.4
Divorced..	11.6	13.6	14.0

[1] 2020 ACS 5-Year estimates. 1-Year estimates were not released for 2020 due to the impact of COVID-19 on data collection that year.

Table AR-3. Households and Housing Characteristics

(Number, percent, dollars.)

Item	2000	2010	2020 [1]	Average annual percent change, 2010–2020
Total Households...	1,042,696	1,114,902	1,170,544	0.7
Family households	732,261	761,361	770,111	0.2
Married-couple family	566,401	554,946	564,299	0.2
Other family	165,860	206,415	205,812	-
Male householder, no wife present....................................	39,299	51,620	52,540	0.3
Female householder, no husband present............................	126,561	154,795	153,272	-0.1
Nonfamily households	310,435	353,541	400,433	1.9
Householder living alone..	266,585	302,127	335,974	1.6
Householder not living alone...	43,850	51,414	64,459	3.6
Housing Characteristics				
Total housing units..	1,173,043	1,317,818	1,379,778	0.7
Occupied housing units	1,042,696	1,114,902	1,170,544	0.7
Owner occupied	723,535	751,568	770,477	0.4
Renter occupied	319,161	363,334	400,067	1.4
Average household size...	2.49	2.55	2.50	-0.3
Financial Characteristics				
Median gross rent of renter-occupied housing	453	638	760	2.7
Median monthly owner costs for housing units with a mortgage	737	987	1,103	1.7
Median value of owner-occupied housing units	72,800	106,300	133,600	3.7

- = Zero or rounds to zero.
[1] 2020 ACS 5-Year estimates. 1-Year estimates were not released for 2020 due to the impact of COVID-19 on data collection that year.

Table AR-4. Migration, Origin, and Language

(Number, percent.)

Characteristic	State 2016-2020 [1]	U.S. 2016-2020 [1]
Residence 1 Year Ago		
Population 1 year and over	2,977,936	322,943,283
Same house	85.4	86.2
Different house in the U.S.	14.3	13.2
Same county	8.2	7.7
Different county	6.1	5.5
Same state	3.7	3.2
Different state	2.3	2.3
Abroad	0.3	0.6
Place of Birth		
Native born	2,863,731	282,443,680
Male	48.9	49.4
Female	51.1	50.6
Foreign born	148,142	44,125,628
Male	51.9	48.6
Female	48.1	51.4
Foreign born; naturalized U.S. citizen..	50,024	22,456,684
Male	48.5	46.1
Female	51.5	53.9
Foreign born; not a U.S. citizen	98,118	21,668,944
Male	53.6	51.1
Female	46.4	48.9
Entered 2010 or later	26.0	22.8
Entered 2000 to 2009	28.7	25.1
Entered before 2000..	45.3	52.1
World Region of Birth, Foreign		
Foreign-born population, excluding population born at sea	148,142	44,125,628
Europe	6.9	10.8
Asia..	23.5	31.3
Africa	2.9	5.4
Oceania	4.7	0.6
Latin America...	60.5	50.0
North America..	1.5	1.9
Language Spoken at Home and Ability to Speak English		
Population 5 years and over..	2,823,428	306,919,116
English only	92.4	78.5
Language other than English...	7.6	21.5
Speaks English less than "very well"...	3.2	8.2

[1] 2020 ACS 5-Year estimates. 1-Year estimates were not released for 2020 due to the impact of COVID-19 on data collection that year.
NA = Not available.
X = Not applicable.
- = Zero or rounds to zero.

Table AR-5. Median Income and Poverty Status, 2020[1]

(Number, percent, except as noted.)

Characteristic	State		U.S.	
	Number	Percent	Number	Percent
Median Income				
Households (dollars)..	49,475	X	64,994	X
Families (dollars)	62,067	X	80,069	X
Below Poverty Level (All People)	470,190	16.1	40,910,326	12.8
Sex				
Male	206,639	14.5	18,171,512	11.6
Female	263,551	17.6	22,738,814	14.0
Age				
Under 18 years..	151,653	22.0	12,598,699	17.5
Related children under 18 years.....................................	148,712	21.7	12,306,532	17.2
18 to 64 years..	270,179	15.5	23,554,920	12.1
65 years and over	48,358	9.8	4,756,707	9.3

X = Not applicable.
[1] 2020 ACS 5-Year estimates. 1-Year estimates were not released for 2020 due to the impact of COVID-19 on data collection that year.

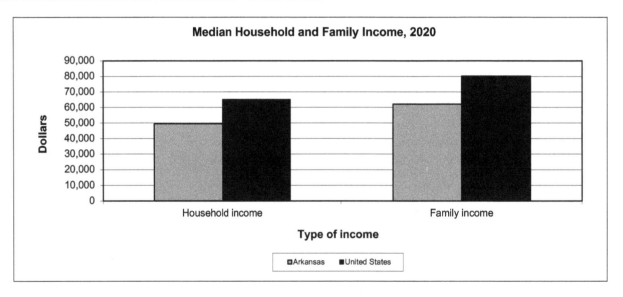

Table AR-6. Health Insurance Coverage Status for the Civilian Noninstitutionalized Population and Children Under 19 Years of Age

(Number, percent.)

Item	2011	2012	2013	2014	2015	2016	2017	2018	2019	2020 [2]
Civilian Noninstitutionalized Population	2,885,212	2,896,297	2,907,014	2,914,376	2,924,307	2,934,272	2,949,305	2,960,503	2,962,596	2,957,271
Covered by Private or Public Insurance										
Number...	2,392,902	2,419,987	2,442,064	2,571,205	2,646,760	2,702,497	2,717,503	2,716,918	2,691,626	2,711,291
Percent..	82.9	83.6	84.0	88.2	90.5	92.1	92.1	91.8	90.9	91.7
Uninsured										
Number...	492,310	476,310	464,950	343,171	277,547	231,775	231,802	243,585	270,970	245,980
Percent..	17.1	16.4	16.0	11.8	9.5	7.9	7.9	8.2	9.1	8.3
Percent in the U.S. not covered................................	15.1	14.8	14.5	11.7	9.4	8.6	8.7	8.9	9.2	8.7
Children Under 19 Years of Age[1]	708,888	709,407	709,125	703,811	703,701	705,155	751,794	746,754	740,911	742,460
Covered by Private or Public Insurance										
Number...	668,938	667,257	669,866	669,732	669,147	679,612	718,394	713,039	697,516	707,613
Percent..	94.4	94.1	94.5	95.2	95.1	96.4	95.6	95.5	94.1	95.3
Uninsured										
Number...	39,950	42,150	39,259	34,079	34,554	25,543	33,400	33,715	43,395	34,847
Percent..	5.6	5.9	5.5	4.8	4.9	3.6	4.4	4.5	5.9	4.7
Percent in the U.S. not covered................................	7.5	7.2	7.1	6.0	4.8	4.5	5.0	5.2	5.7	5.2

[1] Data for years prior to 2017 are for individuals under 18 years of age.
[2] 2020 ACS 5-Year estimates. 1-Year estimates were not released for 2020 due to the impact of COVID-19 on data collection that year. Data is not comparable to previous years, which are based on 1-year estimates.

Table AR-7. Employment Status by Demographic Group, 2021

(Numbers in thousands, percent.)

Characteristic	Civilian noninstitutional population	Civilian labor force		Employed		Unemployed	
		Number	Percent of population	Number	Percent of population	Number	Percent of population
Total..	2,372	1,353	57.0	1,297	54.7	56	4.1
Sex							
Male..	1,140	713	62.6	683	59.9	30	4.2
Female	1,232	640	51.9	614	49.9	25	3.9
Race, Sex, and Hispanic Origin							
White...	1,907	1,081	56.7	1,042	54.6	39	3.6
Male..	927	579	62.4	555	59.9	24	4.1
Female	980	502	51.2	487	49.7	15	3.0
Black or African American..................	349	196	56.3	183	52.5	13	6.8
Male..	156	91	58.4	86	54.9	6	6.1
Female	193	105	54.5	97	50.5	8	7.4
Hispanic or Latino ethnicity[1]	173	122	70.5	118	68.2	4	3.4
Male..	92	76	82.3	73	79.6	2	3.2
Female	NA	NA	NA	NA	NA	NA	NA
Age							
16 to 19 years...............................	NA	NA	NA	NA	NA	NA	NA
20 to 24 years...............................	201	146	72.5	136	67.7	10	6.7
25 to 34 years...............................	415	331	79.8	318	76.6	13	4.0
35 to 44 years...............................	342	269	78.7	258	75.5	11	4.0
45 to 54 years...............................	339	257	75.7	247	72.9	10	3.7
55 to 64 years...............................	374	203	54.3	197	52.7	6	2.9
65 years and over	554	92	16.6	91	16.4	1	1.0

NOTE: Data in Table 7 are from the Current Population Survey (CPS) and do not match the estimates in Table 8. See notes and definitions for further information.
[1] May be of any race.

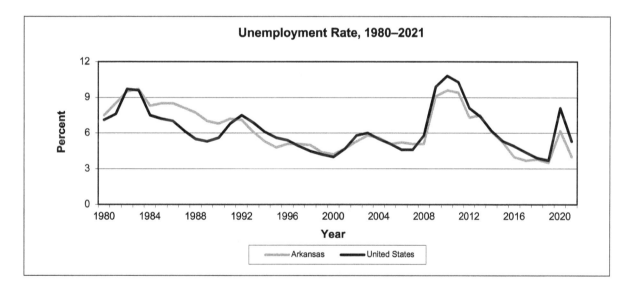

Table AR-8. Employment Status of the Civilian Noninstitutional Population Age 16 Years and Over

(Number, percent.)

Year	Civilian labor force	Civilian participation rate	Employed	Unemployed	Unemployment rate
2010..	1,353,635	60.6	1,247,059	106,576	7.9
2011..	1,357,819	60.2	1,250,431	107,388	7.9
2012..	1,349,888	59.5	1,251,883	98,005	7.3
2013..	1,331,609	58.5	1,237,609	94,000	7.1
2014..	1,327,959	58.1	1,249,766	78,193	5.9
2015..	1,339,301	58.3	1,272,785	66,516	5.0
2016..	1,343,891	58.1	1,290,430	53,461	4.0
2017..	1,348,088	58.3	1,297,854	50,234	3.7
2018..	1,351,686	58.2	1,302,629	49,057	3.6
2019..	1,365,790	58.6	1,318,465	47,325	3.5
2020..	1,356,579	57.9	1,274,070	82,509	6.1
2021..	1,332,620	56.5	1,278,984	53,636	4.0

Table AR-9. Employment and Average Wages by Industry

(Estimates are based on the 2012 North American Industry Classification System [NAICS].)

Industry	2013	2014	2015	2016	2017	2018	2019	2020
	Number of Jobs							
Wage and Salary Employment by Industry.........................	1,231,398	1,243,481	1,264,491	1,279,315	1,286,301	1,296,707	1,304,362	1,263,189
Farm Wage and Salary Employment...............................	11,167	11,319	12,578	15,485	15,067	13,815	14,156	18,686
Nonfarm Wage and Salary Employment.........................	1,220,231	1,232,162	1,251,913	1,263,830	1,271,234	1,282,892	1,290,206	1,244,503
Private wage and salary employment.................................	986,315	999,839	1,021,012	1,035,525	1,044,980	1,056,345	1,064,676	1,022,447
Forestry, fishing, and related activities..............................	8,079	8,138	8,120	8,195	8,196	8,140	8,297	8,063
Mining...	7,537	6,714	5,858	4,135	3,789	3,808	3,782	3,465
Utilities..	8,089	7,903	7,950	7,706	7,707	7,802	7,818	7,871
Construction...	46,679	47,269	50,481	51,554	52,333	52,061	53,780	54,455
Manufacturing..	152,137	153,246	155,035	154,876	157,462	160,671	162,316	155,046
Durable goods manufacturing.....................................	75,364	76,254	75,951	74,259	74,645	76,214	77,289	72,491
Nondurable goods manufacturing................................	76,773	76,992	79,084	80,617	82,817	84,457	85,027	82,555
Wholesale trade...	46,484	46,707	47,396	46,424	47,076	47,460	47,650	46,413
Retail trade..	133,986	136,980	141,322	143,065	141,373	140,050	137,531	135,937
Transportation and warehousing.....................................	53,905	54,971	56,785	56,652	56,385	58,102	60,292	58,059
Information	15,365	14,848	13,342	13,244	12,778	10,911	10,964	11,498
Finance and insurance	37,086	37,058	37,458	38,441	38,804	39,731	41,078	41,691
Real estate and rental and leasing.................................	13,436	13,133	13,346	13,520	13,616	13,971	14,350	14,004
Professional, scientific, and technical services	40,199	40,942	41,710	42,877	43,163	44,429	45,345	43,053
Management of companies and enterprises......................	31,441	32,432	33,440	35,078	35,131	34,814	33,781	33,605
Administrative and waste services	57,965	61,160	64,396	65,246	66,703	68,362	67,546	63,434
Educational services	16,431	16,627	16,465	16,776	16,946	16,737	16,799	15,876
Health care and social assistance..................................	160,095	160,455	163,297	169,383	174,015	176,721	177,956	171,687
Arts, entertainment, and recreation................................	10,109	10,772	10,774	11,237	11,418	11,633	11,932	10,378
Accommodation and food services..................................	95,373	97,670	101,521	104,760	106,011	107,493	109,390	96,738
Other services, except public administration....................	51,919	52,814	52,316	52,356	52,074	53,449	54,069	51,174
Government and government enterprises.....................................	233,916	232,323	230,901	228,305	226,254	226,547	225,530	222,056
	Dollars							
Average Wages and Salaries by Industry	39,629	40,580	41,444	42,102	43,490	44,593	46,071	49,011
Average Farm Wages and Salaries	25,708	21,544	22,574	19,813	16,662	18,506	21,241	12,278
Average Nonfarm Wages and Salaries	39,756	40,755	41,634	42,375	43,807	44,874	46,343	49,562
Average private wages and salaries.................................	39,858	40,952	41,856	42,561	44,064	45,146	46,706	50,169
Forestry, fishing, and related activities..............................	33,106	34,564	36,158	38,048	38,546	39,967	41,576	43,522
Mining...	69,133	71,749	70,983	66,626	65,906	67,654	66,901	68,326
Utilities..	79,100	82,651	83,731	86,407	89,436	92,725	94,963	101,275
Construction	41,657	43,247	45,023	46,673	48,195	48,937	50,493	53,201
Manufacturing..	44,366	45,927	46,431	47,187	48,695	49,961	51,173	53,699
Durable goods manufacturing.....................................	46,744	48,254	48,503	49,290	51,779	53,008	54,334	56,226
Nondurable goods manufacturing................................	42,032	43,622	44,441	45,251	45,915	47,213	48,299	51,479
Wholesale trade	62,357	63,998	66,635	67,785	69,617	70,482	72,934	77,213
Retail trade..	25,296	25,794	26,288	27,250	28,023	28,608	29,489	31,839
Transportation and warehousing.....................................	46,273	47,698	48,328	47,359	49,090	50,769	51,837	54,296
Information	51,181	53,498	55,713	56,971	58,904	56,034	60,116	72,117
Finance and insurance	57,838	59,968	61,981	63,509	64,980	67,493	69,536	74,839
Real estate and rental and leasing.................................	34,677	35,968	37,085	37,755	39,084	40,398	41,721	44,615
Professional, scientific, and technical services	57,064	58,294	59,877	60,534	62,596	64,678	65,102	68,648
Management of companies and enterprises......................	103,322	105,737	107,812	106,958	117,489	118,485	129,802	135,728
Administrative and waste services	26,920	27,610	28,070	29,188	30,142	31,734	32,884	36,119
Educational services	27,383	27,896	28,608	29,578	29,619	30,988	31,315	35,101
Health care and social assistance..................................	39,143	40,340	41,522	42,367	43,305	44,298	45,862	49,595
Arts, entertainment, and recreation................................	21,049	21,391	22,325	22,977	23,611	24,247	24,974	28,031
Accommodation and food services..................................	15,844	16,294	16,769	17,406	18,145	18,879	19,652	19,722
Other services, except public administration....................	28,252	29,357	30,718	31,793	32,971	34,110	35,163	38,515
Government and government enterprises.............................	39,328	39,907	40,652	41,533	42,625	43,604	44,630	46,766

Table AR-10. Employment Characteristics by Family Type

(Number, percent.)

Family type and labor force status	2018		2019		2020 [1]	
	Total	Families with own children under 18 years	Total	Families with own children under 18 years	Total	Families with own children under 18 years
All Families...	769,134	318,421	755,305	306,648	770,111	321,021
FAMILY TYPE AND LABOR FORCE STATUS						
Opposite-Sex Married-Couple Families............................	553,461	201,529	553,179	199,570	560,691	210,523
Both husband and wife in labor force...	47.0	67.2	47.5	64.0	47.8	65.9
Husband in labor force, wife not in labor force	21.3	25.5	21.0	27.3	21.3	26.4
Wife in labor force, husband not in labor force	9.0	5.1	9.2	5.8	9.2	5.5
Both husband and wife not in labor force....................................	22	1.9	21.6	2.4	21.7	2.2
Other Families	215,673	116,892	202,126	107,078	205,812	109,895
Female householder, no spouse present	73.3	76.2	74.4	76.0	74.5	76.8
In labor force...	47.8	60.9	49.7	62.6	49.4	61.9
Not in labor force	25.5	15.3	24.7	13.5	25.1	14.9
Male householder, no spouse present...	26.7	23.8	25.6	24.0	25.5	23.2
In labor force...	19.2	20.9	18.4	20.8	18.2	20.2
Not in labor force	7.5	2.9	7.1	3.2	7.3	3.0

[1] 2020 ACS 5-Year estimates. 1-Year estimates were not released for 2020 due to the impact of COVID-19 on data collection that year. Data is not comparable to previous years, which are based on 1-year estimates.

Table AR-11. School Enrollment and Educational Attainment, 2020[1]

(Number, percent.)

Item	State	U.S.
Enrollment		
Total population 3 years and over, enrolled in school	725,947	80,497,960
Enrolled in nursery school or preschool (percent)..	6.8	6.1
Enrolled in kindergarten (percent)..	5.4	5.0
Enrolled in elementary school, grades 1-8 (percent).....................................	42.9	40.4
Enrolled in high school, grades 9-12 (percent)...	21.3	21.0
Enrolled in college or graduate school (percent)...	23.7	27.6
Attainment		
Total population 25 years and over	2,026,722	222,836,834
Less than ninth grade (percent)...	4.7	4.9
9th to 12th grade, no diploma (percent)...	8.1	6.6
High school graduate, including equivalency (percent)...................................	33.9	26.7
Some college, no degree (percent)...	22	20.3
Associate's degree (percent)...	7.5	8.6
Bachelor's degree (percent)...	15.2	20.2
Graduate or professional degree (percent)...	8.6	12.7
High school graduate or higher (percent)	87.2	88.5
Bachelor's degree or higher (percent)...	23.8	32.9

[1] 2020 ACS 5-Year estimates. 1-Year estimates were not released for 2020 due to the impact of COVID-19 on data collection that year.

Table AR-12. Public School Characteristics and Educational Indicators

(Number, percent; data derived from National Center of Education Statistics.)

Item	State	U.S.
Public Elementary and Secondary Schools		
Number of regular school districts, 2018-19	234	13,452
Number of operational schools, 2019-20..	1,075	98,469
Percent charter schools	7.7	7.7
Total public school enrollment, Fall 2019..	496,927	50,796,445
Percent charter school enrollment	6.9	6.8
Student-teacher ratio, Fall 2019	12.9	15.9
Expenditures per student (unadjusted dollars), 2018-19	10,412	13,187
Four-year adjusted cohort graduation rate (ACGR), 2018-2019[1]............................	87.6	85.8
Students eligible for free or reduced-price lunch (percent), 2019-20........................	65.5	52.1
English language learners (percent), Fall 2019	8.2	10.4
Students age 3 to 21 served under IDEA, part B (percent), 2020-21	15.5	14.5

Public Schools by Type, 2019-20	Number	Percent of state public schools
Total number of schools...	1,075	100.0
Special education..	2	0.2
Vocational education...	22	2.0
Alternative education..	3	0.3

[1] Adjusted Cohort Graduation Rates (ACGR) differ from Averaged Freshmen Graduation Rates (AFGR).

Table AR-13. Reported Voting and Registration of the Voting-Age Population, November 2020

(Numbers in thousands, percent.)

Item	Total population	Total citizen population	Registered			Voted		
			Total registered	Percent registered (total population)	Percent registered (total citizen population)	Total voted	Percent voted (total population)	Percent voted (total citizen population)
U.S. Total	252,274	231,593	168,308	66.7	72.7	154,628	61.3	66.8
State Total....................................	2,283	2,195	1,361	59.6	62.0	1,186	51.9	54.0
Sex								
Male	1,101	1,057	641	58.2	60.6	546	49.6	51.6
Female	1,182	1,138	720	60.9	63.3	640	54.1	56.2
Race								
White alone.................................	1,867	1,808	1,139	61.0	63.0	1,014	54.3	56.1
White, non-Hispanic alone.................	1,744	1,733	1,111	63.7	64.1	988	56.7	57.0
Black alone..................................	336	325	186	55.3	57.1	146	43.3	44.7
Asian alone	24	18	14	B	B	11	B	B
Hispanic (of any race).....................	134	83	30	22.6	36.4	29	21.4	34.6
White alone or in combination.............	1,900	1,841	1,153	60.7	62.6	1,023	53.8	55.5
Black alone or in combination.............	348	337	193	55.4	57.2	148	42.7	44.1
Asian alone or in combination.............	25	19	16	B	B	12	B	B
Age								
18 to 24 years..............................	263	261	127	48.3	48.7	84	32.1	32.3
25 to 34 years..............................	420	389	217	51.7	55.8	176	41.8	45.1
35 to 44 years..............................	341	319	201	58.8	63.0	179	52.6	56.3
45 to 64 years..............................	706	680	446	63.2	65.7	401	56.8	59.0
65 years and over	553	547	370	66.9	67.7	346	62.5	63.2

B = Base is less than 75,000 and therefore too small to show the derived measure.

Table AR-14. Crime

(Number, rate per 100,000. Data are derived from the FBI Uniform Crime Reports.)

Item	State			U.S.		
	2019	2020	Percent change	2019	2020	Percent change
TOTAL POPULATION[1]	3,020,985	3,030,522	0.3	328,329,953	329,484,123	0.4
VIOLENT CRIME						
Number..	17,547	20,363	16.0	1,250,393	1,313,105	5.0
Rate	580.8	671.9	15.7	380.8	398.5	4.6
Murder and Nonnegligent Manslaughter						
Number..	237	321	35.4	16,669	21,570	29.4
Rate	7.8	10.6	35.0	5.1	6.5	28.9
Rape[2]						
Number..	2,420	2,226	-8.0	143,224	126,430	-11.7
Rate	80.1	73.5	-8.3	43.6	38.4	-12.0
Robbery						
Number..	1,576	1,577	0.1	268,483	243,600	-9.3
Rate	52.2	52.0	-0.3	81.8	73.9	-9.6
Aggravated Assault						
Number..	13,314	16,239	22.0	822,017	921,505	12.1
Rate	440.7	535.8	21.6	250.4	279.7	11.7
PROPERTY CRIME						
Number..	86,029	79,200	-7.9	6,995,235	6,452,038	-7.8
Rate	2,847.7	2,613.4	-8.2	2,130.6	1,958.2	-8.1
Burglary						
Number..	17,706	15,854	-10.5	1,118,096	1,035,314	-7.4
Rate	586.1	523.1	-10.7	340.5	314.2	-7.7
Larceny-Theft						
Number..	60,843	55,413	-8.9	5,152,267	4,606,324	-10.6
Rate	2,014.0	1,828.5	-9.2	1,569.2	1,398.0	-10.9
Motor Vehicle Theft						
Number..	7,480	7,933	6.1	724,872	810,400	11.8
Rate	247.6	261.8	5.7	220.8	246.0	11.4

NOTE: Although arson data are included in the trend and clearance tables, sufficient data are not available to estimate totals for this offense. Therefore, no arson data are published in this table.
- = Zero or rounds to zero.
[1] Population figures are U.S. Census Bureau provisional estimates as of July 1, 2020.
[2] The figures shown in the rape (revised definition) column were estimated using the revised Uniform Crime Reporting (UCR) definition of rape.

Table AR-15. State Government Finances, 2020

(Dollar amounts in thousands, percent distribution.)

Item	Dollars	Percent distribution
Total Revenue	28,572,105	100.0
General revenue	23,601,069	82.6
Intergovernmental revenue	9,364,650	32.8
Taxes	10,255,155	35.9
General sales	3691920	12.9
Selective sales	1,445,663	5.1
License taxes	391,409	1.4
Individual income tax	2914939	10.2
Corporate income tax	469,029	1.6
Other taxes	1,342,195	4.7
Current charges	2,815,913	9.9
Miscellaneous general revenue	1,165,351	4.1
Utility revenue	0	-
Liquor stores revenue	0	-
Insurance trust revenue[1]	4,971,036	17.4
Total Expenditure	23,639,954	100.0
Intergovernmental expenditure	5,864,447	24.8
Direct expenditure	17,775,507	75.2
Current operation	13,636,209	57.7
Capital outlay	1,193,210	5.0
Insurance benefits and repayments	2,229,779	9.4
Assistance and subsidies	529,113	2.2
Interest on debt	187,196	0.8
Exhibit: Salaries and wages	3,411,505	14.4
Total Expenditure	23,639,954	100.0
General expenditure	21,410,175	90.6
Intergovernmental expenditure	5,864,447	24.8
Direct expenditure	15,545,728	65.8
General expenditure, by function:		
Education	8,116,662	34.3
Public welfare	7,353,581	31.1
Hospitals	1,333,233	5.6
Health	176,990	0.7
Highways	1,596,808	6.8
Police protection	106,515	0.5
Correction	350,773	1.5
Natural resources	254,219	1.1
Parks and recreation	78,428	0.3
Governmental administration	757,847	3.2
Interest on general debt	187,196	0.8
Other and unallocable	1,068,873	4.5
Utility expenditure	2,590	-
Liquor stores expenditure	0	-
Insurance trust expenditure	2,229,779	9.4
Debt at End of Fiscal Year	7,565,411	X
Cash and Security Holdings	45,091,855	X

X = Not applicable.
- = Zero or rounds to zero.
[1] Within insurance trust revenue, net earnings of state retirement systems is a calculated statistic (the item code in the data file is X08), and thus can be positive or negative. Net earnings is the sum of earnings on investments plus gains on investments minus losses on investments. The change made in 2002 for asset valuation from book to market value in accordance with Statement 34 of the Governmental Accounting Standards Board is reflected in the calculated statistics.

Table AR-16. State Government Tax Collections, 2021

(Dollars in thousands, percent.)

Item	Dollars	Percent distribution
Total Taxes	11,726,678	100.0
Property taxes	1,308,040	11.2
Sales and gross receipts	5,752,828	49.1
General sales and gross receipts	4,187,473	35.7
Selective sales and gross receipts	1,565,355	13.3
Alcoholic beverages	68,024	0.6
Amusements	70993	0.6
Insurance premiums	310,009	2.6
Motor fuels	588,223	5.0
Pari-mutuels	1,670	-
Public utilities	X	
Tobacco products	233,224	2.0
Other selective sales	293,212	2.5
Licenses	423,851	3.6
Alcoholic beverages	5,858	-
Amusements	1131	-
Corporations in general	32,373	0.3
Hunting and fishing	30,622	0.3
Motor vehicle	178,731	1.5
Motor vehicle operators	19,739	0.2
Public utilities	9,135	0.1
Occupation and business, NEC	145,326	1.2
Other licenses	936	-
Income taxes	4,085,598	34.8
Individual income	3,467,141	29.6
Corporation net income	618,457	5.3
Other taxes	156,361	1.3
Death and gift	0	-
Documentary and stock transfer	67,983	0.6
Severance	33,004	0.3
Taxes, NEC	55374	0.5

- = Zero or rounds to zero.
X = Not applicable.

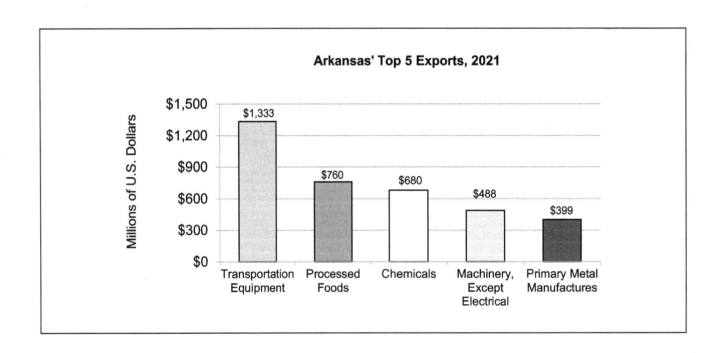

Arkansas' Top 5 Exports, 2021

CALIFORNIA

Facts and Figures

Location: Western United States; bordered on the N by Oregon, on the E by Nevada and Arizona, on the S by Mexico, and on the W by the Pacific Ocean

Area: 163,694 sq. mi. (423,970 sq. km.); rank—3rd

Population: 39,237,836 (2021 est.); rank—1st

Principal Cities: capital—Sacramento; largest—Los Angeles

Statehood: September 9, 1850; 31st state

U.S. Congress: 2 senators, 53 representatives

State Motto: *Eureka* ("I have found it")

State Song: "I Love You, California"

State Nickname: The Golden State

Abbreviations: CA; Calif.

State Symbols: flower—California poppy; tree—redwood; bird—California valley quail

At a Glance

- With an increase in population of 5.3 percent, California ranked 29th among the states in growth from 2010 to 2021.

- In 2020, California's median household income was $78,672, and 12.6 percent of the population lived below the poverty level.

- California's violent crime rate in 2020 was 442.0 per 100,000 population, compared to 398.5 for the entire nation.

- In 2021, California's unemployment rate of 7.3 percent was the highest in the nation.

- Approximately 15.9 percent of Californians self-identified their race as "Asian Alone" in 2021, which was the 2nd highest percent in the country.

Table CA-1. Population by Age, Sex, Race, and Hispanic Origin

(Number, percent, except where noted.)

Sex, age, race, and Hispanic origin	2000	2010	2021	Percent change, 2010–2021
Total population	33,871,648	37,253,956	39,237,836	5.3
Percent of total U.S. population	12.0	12.1	11.8	X
Sex				
Male	16,874,892	18,517,830	19,617,190	5.9
Female	16,996,756	18,736,126	19,620,646	4.7
Age				
Under 5 years	2,486,981	2,531,333	2,217,145	-12.4
5 to 19 years	7,747,590	7,920,709	7,572,552	-4.4
20 to 64 years	20,041,419	22,555,400	23,491,047	4.1
65 years and over	3,595,658	4,246,514	5,957,092	40.3
Median age (years)	33.3	35.2	37.6	6.8
Race and Hispanic origin				
One race				
White	20,170,059	27,636,403	27,902,177	1.0
Black	2,263,882	2,486,549	2,548,114	2.5
American Indian and Alaska Native	333,346	622,107	675,009	8.5
Asian	3,697,513	5,038,123	6,250,368	24.1
Native Hawaiian or Other Pacific Islander	116,961	181,431	204,990	13.0
Two or more races	1,607,646	1,289,343	1,657,178	28.5
Hispanic (of any race)	10,966,556	14,440,187	15,754,605	9.1

NOTE: Population figures for 2021 are July 1 estimates. The 2000 and 2010 estimates are taken from the respective censuses.
- = Zero or rounds to zero.
X = Not applicable.

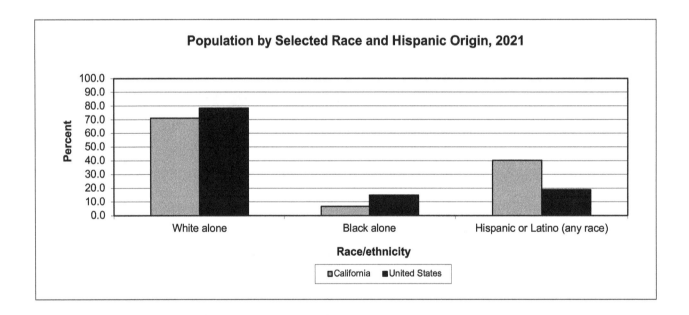

Population by Selected Race and Hispanic Origin, 2021

Table CA-2. Marital Status

(Number, percent distribution.)

Sex, age, race, and Hispanic origin	2000	2010	2020 [1]
Males, 15 Years and Over	12,844,669	14,662,335	15,759,027
Never married	33.8	39.8	40.6
Now married, except separated	54.1	48.2	48.2
Separated	2.0	1.9	1.6
Widowed	2.2	2.1	2.1
Divorced	7.9	8.0	7.5
Females, 15 Years and Over	13,231,494	15,043,190	16,148,824
Never married	26.5	32.3	33.7
Now married, except separated	50.7	45.7	45.5
Separated	2.9	2.7	2.3
Widowed	8.9	8.1	7.6
Divorced	11.0	11.2	10.8

[1] 2020 ACS 5-Year estimates. 1-Year estimates were not released for 2020 due to the impact of COVID-19 on data collection that year.

Table CA-3. Households and Housing Characteristics

(Number, percent, dollars.)

Item	2000	2010	2020 [1]	Average annual percent change, 2010–2020
Total Households............................	11,502,870	12,406,475	13,103,114	0.8
Family households	7,920,049	8,507,856	8,986,666	0.8
Married-couple family	5,877,084	6,082,566	6,510,580	1.0
Other family	2,042,965	2,425,290	2,476,086	0.3
Male householder, no wife present............................	594,455	736,626	782,812	0.9
Female householder, no husband present............................	1,448,510	1,688,664	1,693,274	-
Nonfamily households	3,582,821	3,898,619	4,116,448	0.8
Householder living alone............................	2,708,308	3,001,307	3,114,819	0.5
Householder not living alone............................	874,513	897,312	1,001,629	1.7
Housing Characteristics				
Total housing units	12,214,549	13,682,976	14,210,945	0.6
Occupied housing units	11,502,870	12,406,475	13,103,114	0.8
Owner occupied............................	6,546,334	6,903,175	7,241,318	0.7
Renter occupied............................	4,956,536	5,503,300	5,861,796	0.9
Average household size............................	2.87	2.94	2.94	-
Financial Characteristics				
Median gross rent of renter-occupied housing	747	1,163	1,586	5.2
Median monthly owner costs for housing units with a mortgage	1,478	2,242	2,422	1.1
Median value of owner-occupied housing units............................	211,500	370,900	538,500	6.5

- = Zero or rounds to zero.
[1] 2020 ACS 5-Year estimates. 1-Year estimates were not released for 2020 due to the impact of COVID-19 on data collection that year.

Table CA-4. Migration, Origin, and Language

(Number, percent.)

Characteristic	State 2016-2020 [1]	U.S. 2016-2020 [1]
Residence 1 Year Ago		
Population 1 year and over	38,921,662	322,943,283
Same house............................	87.6	86.2
Different house in the U.S.	11.7	13.2
Same county	7.7	7.7
Different county	4.0	5.5
Same state	2.8	3.2
Different state	1.3	2.3
Abroad	0.7	0.6
Place of Birth		
Native born	28,882,205	282,443,680
Male	50.3	49.4
Female	49.7	50.6
Foreign born	10,463,818	44,125,628
Male	48.2	48.6
Female	51.8	51.4
Foreign born; naturalized U.S. citizen............................	5,533,693	22,456,684
Male	45.9	46.1
Female	54.1	53.9
Foreign born; not a U.S. citizen............................	4,930,125	21,668,944
Male	50.7	51.1
Female	49.3	48.9
Entered 2010 or later	16.6	22.8
Entered 2000 to 2009	21.9	25.1
Entered before 2000............................	61.5	52.1
World Region of Birth, Foreign		
Foreign-born population, excluding population born at sea	10,463,818	44,125,628
Europe	6.5	10.8
Asia	39.9	31.3
Africa	2.0	5.4
Oceania	0.8	0.6
Latin America............................	49.5	50.0
North America............................	1.2	1.9
Language Spoken at Home and Ability to Speak English		
Population 5 years and over............................	36,936,941	306,919,116
English only	56.1	78.5
Language other than English............................	43.9	21.5
Speaks English less than "very well"............................	17.4	8.2

[1] 2020 ACS 5-Year estimates. 1-Year estimates were not released for 2020 due to the impact of COVID-19 on data collection that year.
NA = Not available.
X = Not applicable.
- = Zero or rounds to zero.

Table CA-5. Median Income and Poverty Status, 2020[1]

(Number, percent, except as noted.)

Characteristic	State		U.S.	
	Number	Percent	Number	Percent
Median Income				
Households (dollars)..	78,672	X	64,994	X
Families (dollars)	89,798	X	80,069	X
Below Poverty Level (All People)	4,853,434	12.6	40,910,326	12.8
Sex				
Male	2,194,991	11.5	18,171,512	11.6
Female	2,658,443	13.6	22,738,814	14.0
Age				
Under 18 years...	1,480,649	16.8	12,598,699	17.5
Related children under 18 years..	1,446,109	16.5	12,306,532	17.2
18 to 64 years	2,800,246	11.6	23,554,920	12.1
65 years and over	572,539	10.3	4,756,707	9.3

X = Not applicable.
[1] 2020 ACS 5-Year estimates. 1-Year estimates were not released for 2020 due to the impact of COVID-19 on data collection that year.

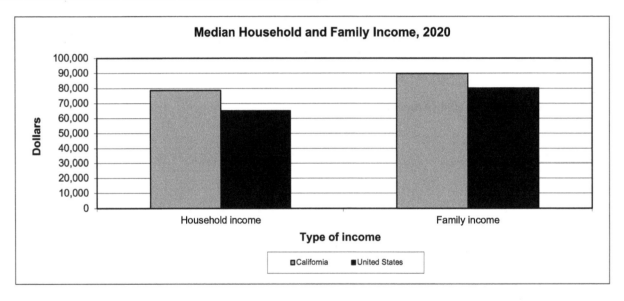

Table CA-6. Health Insurance Coverage Status for the Civilian Noninstitutionalized Population and Children Under 19 Years of Age

(Number, percent.)

Item	2011	2012	2013	2014	2015	2016	2017	2018	2019	2020[2]
Civilian Noninstitutionalized Population	37,161,789	37,524,274	37,831,553	38,297,457	38,649,621	38,763,815	39,046,835	39,062,465	38,997,581	38,838,726
Covered by Private or Public Insurance										
Number...	30,436,185	30,814,688	31,331,374	33,530,746	35,332,356	35,919,912	36,250,246	36,236,845	35,995,584	36,032,553
Percent..	81.9	82.1	82.8	87.6	91.4	92.7	92.8	92.8	92.3	92.8
Uninsured										
Number...	6,725,604	6,709,586	6,500,179	4,766,711	3,317,265	2,843,903	2,796,589	2,825,620	3,001,997	2,806,173
Percent..	18.1	17.9	17.2	12.4	8.6	7.3	7.2	7.2	7.7	7.2
Percent in the U.S. not covered...................................	15.1	14.8	14.5	11.7	9.4	8.6	8.7	8.9	9.2	8.7
Children Under 19 Years of Age[1]	9,252,466	9,223,488	9,157,955	9,135,133	9,103,139	9,079,778	9,567,473	9,514,348	9,405,057	9,465,391
Covered by Private or Public Insurance										
Number...	8,507,669	8,493,396	8,484,747	8,638,043	8,800,771	8,811,963	9,266,841	9,215,649	9,071,023	9,157,036
Percent..	92.0	92.1	92.6	94.6	96.7	97.1	96.9	96.9	96.4	96.7
Uninsured										
Number...	744,797	730,092	673,208	497,090	302,368	267,815	300,632	298,699	334,034	308,355
Percent..	8.0	7.9	7.4	5.4	3.3	2.9	3.1	3.1	3.6	3.3
Percent in the U.S. not covered...................................	7.5	7.2	7.1	6.0	4.8	4.5	5.0	5.2	5.7	5.2

[1] Data for years prior to 2017 are for individuals under 18 years of age.
[2] 2020 ACS 5-Year estimates. 1-Year estimates were not released for 2020 due to the impact of COVID-19 on data collection that year. Data is not comparable to previous years, which are based on 1-year estimates.

Table CA-7. Employment Status by Demographic Group, 2021

(Numbers in thousands, percent.)

Characteristic	Civilian noninstitutional population	Civilian labor force		Employed		Unemployed	
		Number	Percent of population	Number	Percent of population	Number	Percent of population
Total..	31,102	19,014	61.1	17,646	56.7	1,368	7.2
Sex							
Male..	15,222	10,322	67.8	9,586	63.0	736	7.1
Female...	15,879	8,692	54.7	8,060	50.8	632	7.3
Race, Sex, and Hispanic Origin							
White	22,325	13,669	61.2	12,737	57.1	932	6.8
Male..	11,078	7,589	68.5	7,088	64.0	501	6.6
Female...	11,247	6,080	54.1	5,648	50.2	431	7.1
Black or African American....................	1,978	1,187	60.0	1,045	52.8	142	12.0
Male..	947	596	62.9	521	55.0	76	12.7
Female...	1,031	591	57.3	524	50.9	67	11.2
Hispanic or Latino ethnicity[1]	11,481	7,306	63.6	6,725	58.6	581	7.9
Male..	5,696	4,155	72.9	3,841	67.4	314	7.6
Female...	5,784	3,150	54.5	2,884	49.9	266	8.4
Age							
16 to 19 years..................................	2,006	597	29.7	504	25.1	93	15.6
20 to 24 years..................................	2,558	1,687	66.0	1,498	58.6	189	11.2
25 to 34 years..................................	5,682	4,456	78.4	4,141	72.9	315	7.1
35 to 44 years..................................	5,279	4,244	80.4	3,982	75.4	263	6.2
45 to 54 years..................................	4,750	3,768	79.3	3,548	74.7	219	5.8
55 to 64 years..................................	4,767	3,078	64.6	2,881	60.4	197	6.4
65 years and over..............................	6,061	1,184	19.5	1,092	18.0	92	7.8

NOTE: Data in Table 7 are from the Current Population Survey (CPS) and do not match the estimates in Table 8. See notes and definitions for further information.
[1] May be of any race.

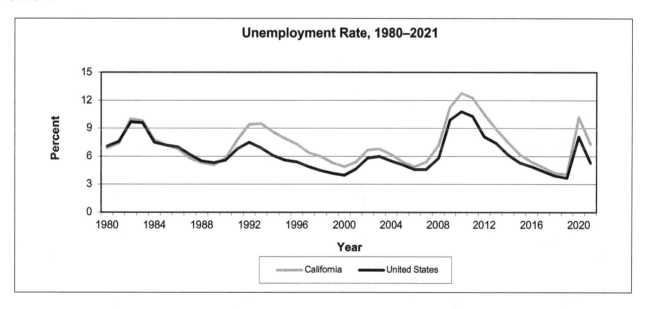

Table CA-8. Employment Status of the Civilian Noninstitutional Population Age 16 Years and Over

(Number, percent.)

Year	Civilian labor force	Civilian participation rate	Employed	Unemployed	Unemployment rate
2010..	18,370,536	64.4	16,078,454	2,292,082	12.5
2011..	18,406,756	63.6	16,220,602	2,186,154	11.9
2012..	18,484,881	63.1	16,541,039	1,943,842	10.5
2013..	18,565,408	62.7	16,887,864	1,677,544	9.0
2014..	18,676,692	62.3	17,264,518	1,412,174	7.6
2015..	18,824,141	62.2	17,647,409	1,176,732	6.3
2016..	19,012,017	62.2	17,965,407	1,046,610	5.5
2017..	19,185,366	62.3	18,258,064	927,302	4.8
2018..	19,289,507	62.3	18,468,143	821,364	4.3
2019..	19,409,413	62.5	18,612,607	796,806	4.1
2020..	18,931,116	60.9	16,996,666	1,934,450	10.2
2021..	18,923,194	61	17,541,944	1,381,250	7.3

Table CA-9. Employment and Average Wages by Industry

(Estimates are based on the 2012 North American Industry Classification System [NAICS].)

Industry	2013	2014	2015	2016	2017	2018	2019	2020
	Number of Jobs							
Wage and Salary Employment by Industry.........................	16,212,158	16,693,308	17,184,799	17,601,469	17,908,517	18,295,976	18,598,619	17,291,678
Farm Wage and Salary Employment...............................	165,674	180,221	179,440	176,653	172,128	177,621	180,956	174,153
Nonfarm Wage and Salary Employment...........................	16,046,484	16,513,087	17,005,359	17,424,816	17,736,389	18,118,355	18,417,663	17,117,525
Private wage and salary employment....................................	13,445,494	13,874,518	14,311,872	14,675,233	14,955,488	15,306,818	15,580,053	14,381,887
Forestry, fishing, and related activities....................................	212,185	216,078	221,675	227,847	229,704	232,947	237,462	223,852
Mining..	27,880	28,616	26,194	22,024	19,497	20,207	20,261	17,404
Utilities...	58,934	57,870	57,551	58,632	58,396	56,510	56,399	58,477
Construction..	653,646	689,301	749,682	794,232	828,950	881,131	906,056	876,730
Manufacturing...	1,252,668	1,271,835	1,294,100	1,304,558	1,313,515	1,321,645	1,323,833	1,264,613
Durable goods manufacturing..	779,778	793,945	811,294	817,927	824,782	844,834	848,865	819,188
Nondurable goods manufacturing.....................................	472,890	477,890	482,806	486,631	488,733	476,811	474,968	445,425
Wholesale trade	701,188	714,838	722,323	723,793	726,800	703,551	696,584	647,455
Retail trade...	1,612,398	1,640,400	1,672,856	1,689,860	1,701,741	1,698,297	1,670,585	1,537,355
Transportation and warehousing..	445,100	466,636	499,896	531,662	572,178	608,153	650,546	676,643
Information...	446,949	460,552	488,581	523,574	530,963	526,707	551,184	527,740
Finance and insurance	552,430	556,165	566,857	580,509	587,953	583,215	585,265	584,424
Real estate and rental and leasing	265,164	269,110	277,188	283,083	289,013	302,571	311,961	290,955
Professional, scientific, and technical services	1,151,705	1,184,133	1,217,060	1,229,180	1,239,785	1,297,540	1,343,604	1,313,870
Management of companies and enterprises.........................	219,138	221,154	225,551	227,375	232,202	253,366	255,536	243,862
Administrative and waste services.....................................	988,951	1,033,800	1,066,852	1,094,415	1,110,782	1,137,078	1,141,532	1,059,665
Educational services	368,637	382,035	389,083	396,083	404,030	420,236	430,484	397,621
Health care and social assistance.....................................	1,982,932	2,043,669	2,128,175	2,216,053	2,294,651	2,364,338	2,441,279	2,390,694
Arts, entertainment, and recreation...................................	271,186	286,999	292,053	304,940	312,929	322,060	334,905	212,296
Accommodation and food services....................................	1,412,324	1,484,742	1,546,596	1,605,211	1,648,514	1,681,785	1,712,688	1,284,315
Other services, except public administration........................	822,079	866,585	869,599	862,202	853,885	895,481	909,889	773,916
Government and government enterprises.................................	2,600,990	2,638,569	2,693,487	2,749,583	2,780,901	2,811,537	2,837,610	2,735,638
	Dollars							
Average Wages and Salaries by Industry	57,605	59,412	62,099	63,389	66,308	68,790	71,678	79,368
Average Farm Wages and Salaries	33,195	28,480	28,742	28,763	36,215	29,971	37,078	36,857
Average Nonfarm Wages and Salaries	57,857	59,750	62,451	63,740	66,600	69,171	72,018	79,800
Average private wages and salaries.....................................	57,663	59,607	62,447	63,668	66,744	69,382	72,319	80,754
Forestry, fishing, and related activities....................................	25,739	26,635	28,554	30,769	31,560	32,752	34,567	37,777
Mining..	135,880	138,799	138,043	135,635	123,937	125,358	125,791	119,877
Utilities...	117,333	118,239	127,775	127,185	134,138	135,776	142,746	149,568
Construction..	59,058	60,303	63,126	65,313	68,477	70,965	74,239	77,756
Manufacturing...	79,505	83,083	85,683	88,883	94,066	97,447	100,059	111,862
Durable goods manufacturing..	90,367	95,085	97,536	102,554	109,955	114,098	116,527	130,897
Nondurable goods manufacturing.....................................	61,593	63,144	65,766	65,906	67,253	67,945	70,627	76,853
Wholesale trade	70,517	73,481	77,371	77,302	80,533	80,221	83,058	88,618
Retail trade...	33,511	34,297	35,809	35,632	36,627	37,774	39,281	43,418
Transportation and warehousing..	51,889	52,784	54,206	56,792	58,508	62,099	69,451	66,272
Information...	134,254	138,154	147,503	149,199	170,295	190,366	193,382	220,711
Finance and insurance	103,204	109,870	114,562	117,344	124,158	128,440	134,918	147,726
Real estate and rental and leasing	57,127	60,432	63,881	65,138	68,984	70,206	74,262	78,998
Professional, scientific, and technical services	98,970	105,281	113,039	113,017	118,157	123,628	129,037	143,107
Management of companies and enterprises.........................	113,055	121,048	126,291	130,292	131,384	138,046	138,887	154,395
Administrative and waste services.....................................	40,034	40,736	42,688	43,755	46,016	46,732	49,338	54,004
Educational services	44,049	45,536	46,688	47,300	47,979	49,230	49,749	56,243
Health care and social assistance.....................................	47,359	47,956	49,614	50,456	51,587	52,957	54,683	58,383
Arts, entertainment, and recreation...................................	55,940	57,359	58,589	59,729	61,765	63,981	66,146	81,649
Accommodation and food services....................................	22,907	23,712	24,922	26,344	27,335	29,119	30,910	32,543
Other services, except public administration........................	31,859	32,521	34,052	35,424	37,965	38,069	39,158	43,591
Government and government enterprises.................................	58,856	60,498	62,471	64,124	65,824	68,018	70,365	74,787

Table CA-10. Employment Characteristics by Family Type

(Number, percent.)

Family type and labor force status	2018 Total	2018 Families with own children under 18 years	2019 Total	2019 Families with own children under 18 years	2020 [1] Total	2020 [1] Families with own children under 18 years
All Families..............................	8,934,621	3,824,279	8,972,643	3,807,571	8,986,666	3,894,122
FAMILY TYPE AND LABOR FORCE STATUS						
Opposite-Sex Married-Couple Families............................	6,458,423	2,719,648	6,490,186	2,713,223	6,427,608	2,768,180
Both husband and wife in labor force........................	49.6	62.0	49.6	62.0	50.5	62.1
Husband in labor force, wife not in labor force	25.0	32.0	24.8	32.2	25.2	32.1
Wife in labor force, husband not in labor force	7.5	3.7	7.3	3.8	7.6	4.0
Both husband and wife not in labor force.......................	16.6	1.7	16.9	1.6	16.6	1.8
Other Families	2,476,198	1,104,631	2,482,457	1,094,348	2,476,086	1,112,876
Female householder, no spouse present	68.1	70.6	68.0	70.8	68.4	70.5
In labor force	47.0	56.8	47.5	58.6	47.3	57.2
Not in labor force	21.0	13.7	20.5	12.3	21.1	13.3
Male householder, no spouse present........................	31.9	29.4	32.0	29.2	31.6	29.5
In labor force......................	25.7	27.1	25.7	26.8	25.3	27.1
Not in labor force	6.2	2.3	6.4	2.4	6.3	2.4

[1] 2020 ACS 5-Year estimates. 1-Year estimates were not released for 2020 due to the impact of COVID-19 on data collection that year. Data is not comparable to previous years, which are based on 1-year estimates.

Table CA-11. School Enrollment and Educational Attainment, 2020[1]

(Number, percent.)

Item	State	U.S.
Enrollment		
Total population 3 years and over, enrolled in school	10,331,447	80,497,960
Enrolled in nursery school or preschool (percent)	5.7	6.1
Enrolled in kindergarten (percent)	4.9	5.0
Enrolled in elementary school, grades 1-8 (percent)...	37.9	40.4
Enrolled in high school, grades 9-12 (percent)..	20.5	21.0
Enrolled in college or graduate school (percent)...	30.9	27.6
Attainment		
Total population 25 years and over	26,665,143	222,836,834
Less than ninth grade (percent)	8.9	4.9
9th to 12th grade, no diploma (percent)	7.2	6.6
High school graduate, including equivalency (percent)...	20.4	26.7
Some college, no degree (percent)..	20.9	20.3
Associate's degree (percent)..	8.0	8.6
Bachelor's degree (percent)	21.6	20.2
Graduate or professional degree (percent)...	13.1	12.7
High school graduate or higher (percent)...	83.9	88.5
Bachelor's degree or higher (percent)..	34.7	32.9

[1] 2020 ACS 5-Year estimates. 1-Year estimates were not released for 2020 due to the impact of COVID-19 on data collection that year.

Table CA-12. Public School Characteristics and Educational Indicators

(Number, percent; data derived from National Center of Education Statistics.)

Item	State	U.S.
Public Elementary and Secondary Schools		
Number of regular school districts, 2018-19	995	13,452
Number of operational schools, 2019-20..	10,374	98,469
Percent charter schools	12.7	7.7
Total public school enrollment, Fall 2019...	6,249,005	50,796,445
Percent charter school enrollment...	11.0	6.8
Student-teacher ratio, Fall 2019..	23.0	15.9
Expenditures per student (unadjusted dollars), 2018-19	13,641	13,187
Four-year adjusted cohort graduation rate (ACGR), 2018-2019[1]...	84.5	85.8
Students eligible for free or reduced-price lunch (percent), 2019-20..	59.4	52.1
English language learners (percent), Fall 2019...	18.6	10.4
Students age 3 to 21 served under IDEA, part B (percent), 2020-21	12.8	14.5

Public Schools by Type, 2019-20	Number	Percent of state public schools
Total number of schools..	10,374	100.0
Special education...	156	1.5
Vocational education...	66	0.6
Alternative education..	1053	10.2

[1] Adjusted Cohort Graduation Rates (ACGR) differ from Averaged Freshmen Graduation Rates (AFGR).

Table CA-13. Reported Voting and Registration of the Voting-Age Population, November 2020

(Numbers in thousands, percent.)

Item	Total population	Total citizen population	Registered			Voted		
			Total registered	Percent registered (total population)	Percent registered (total citizen population)	Total voted	Percent voted (total population)	Percent voted (total citizen population)
U.S. Total	252,274	231,593	168,308	66.7	72.7	154,628	61.3	66.8
State Total.................................	30,342	25,946	18,001	59.3	69.4	16,893	55.7	65.1
Sex								
Male	14,786	12,580	8,549	57.8	68.0	8,012	54.2	63.7
Female	15,556	13,366	9,452	60.8	70.7	8,882	57.1	66.5
Race								
White alone...........................	21,941	18,971	13,508	61.6	71.2	12,628	57.6	66.6
White, non-Hispanic alone	12,090	11,685	9,133	75.5	78.2	8,711	72.1	74.6
Black alone...........................	1,947	1,834	1,249	64.1	68.1	1,173	60.3	64.0
Asian alone	5,072	3,958	2,491	49.1	62.9	2,370	46.7	59.9
Hispanic (of any race)	11,165	8,305	5,014	44.9	60.4	4,539	40.7	54.6
White alone or in combination.......	22,586	19,549	13,924	61.6	71.2	13,024	57.7	66.6
Black alone or in combination.............	2,139	2,021	1,371	64.1	67.8	1,295	60.5	64.1
Asian alone or in combination..............	5,405	4,250	2,665	49.3	62.7	2,529	46.8	59.5
Age								
18 to 24 years..................................	3,685	3,334	1,974	53.6	59.2	1,786	48.5	53.6
25 to 34 years..................................	5,953	4,957	3,261	54.8	65.8	2,976	50.0	60.0
35 to 44 years..................................	5,090	4,016	2,759	54.2	68.7	2,554	50.2	63.6
45 to 64 years..................................	9,499	7,973	5,820	61.3	73.0	5,534	58.3	69.4
65 years and over	6,117	5,666	4,187	68.4	73.9	4,044	66.1	71.4

Table CA-14. Crime

(Number, rate per 100,000. Data are derived from the FBI Uniform Crime Reports.)

Item	State			U.S.		
	2019	2020	Percent change	2019	2020	Percent change
TOTAL POPULATION[1]	39,437,610	39,368,078	-0.2	328,329,953	329,484,123	0.4
VIOLENT CRIME						
Number..	174,341	174,026	-0.2	1,250,393	1,313,105	5.0
Rate...	442.1	442.0	*	380.8	398.5	4.6
Murder and Nonnegligent Manslaughter						
Number..	1,690	2,203	30.4	16,669	21,570	29.4
Rate...	4.3	5.6	30.6	5.1	6.5	28.9
Rape[2]						
Number..	14,801	13,449	-9.1	143,224	126,430	-11.7
Rate	37.5	34.2	-9.0	43.6	38.4	-12.0
Robbery						
Number..	52,306	44,728	-14.5	268,483	243,600	-9.3
Rate...	132.6	113.6	-14.3	81.8	73.9	-9.6
Aggravated Assault						
Number..	105,544	113,646	7.7	822,017	921,505	12.1
Rate...	267.6	288.7	7.9	250.4	279.7	11.7
PROPERTY CRIME						
Number..	921,177	842,054	-8.6	6,995,235	6,452,038	-7.8
Rate...	2,335.8	2,138.9	-8.4	2,130.6	1,958.2	-8.1
Burglary						
Number..	152,551	145,529	-4.6	1,118,096	1,035,314	-7.4
Rate...	386.8	369.7	-4.4	340.5	314.2	-7.7
Larceny-Theft						
Number..	626,865	528,202	-15.7	5,152,267	4,606,324	-10.6
Rate...	1,589.5	1,341.7	-15.6	1,569.2	1,398.0	-10.9
Motor Vehicle Theft						
Number..	141,761	168,323	18.7	724,872	810,400	11.8
Rate...	359.5	427.6	18.9	220.8	246.0	11.4

NOTE: Although arson data are included in the trend and clearance tables, sufficient data are not available to estimate totals for this offense. Therefore, no arson data are published in this table.
- = Zero or rounds to zero.
[1] Population figures are U.S. Census Bureau provisional estimates as of July 1, 2020.
[2] The figures shown in the rape (revised definition) column were estimated using the revised Uniform Crime Reporting (UCR) definition of rape.

Table CA-15. State Government Finances, 2020

(Dollar amounts in thousands, percent distribution.)

Item	Dollars	Percent distribution
Total Revenue	413,372,904	100.0
General revenue	315,857,426	76.4
Intergovernmental revenue	101,431,529	24.5
Taxes	171,964,222	41.6
General sales	43650233	10.6
Selective sales	18,902,795	4.6
License taxes	12,007,345	2.9
Individual income tax	84412243	20.4
Corporate income tax	9,817,957	2.4
Other taxes	3,173,649	0.8
Current charges	33,480,392	8.1
Miscellaneous general revenue	8,981,283	2.2
Utility revenue	910,435	0.2
Liquor stores revenue	0	-
Insurance trust revenue[1]	96,605,043	23.4
Total Expenditure	422,065,764	100.0
Intergovernmental expenditure	116,458,649	27.6
Direct expenditure	305,607,115	72.4
Current operation	210,053,557	49.8
Capital outlay	12,449,565	2.9
Insurance benefits and repayments	70,634,566	16.7
Assistance and subsidies	6,967,470	1.7
Interest on debt	5,501,957	1.3
Exhibit: Salaries and wages	39,250,294	9.3
Total Expenditure	422,065,764	100.0
General expenditure	350,334,968	83.0
Intergovernmental expenditure	116,458,649	27.6
Direct expenditure	233,876,319	55.4
General expenditure, by function:		
Education	109,368,146	25.9
Public welfare	147,236,699	34.9
Hospitals	16,277,563	3.9
Health	10,435,030	2.5
Highways	18,874,021	4.5
Police protection	2,295,791	0.5
Correction	9,982,003	2.4
Natural resources	7,935,091	1.9
Parks and recreation	1,158,690	0.3
Governmental administration	7,283,302	1.7
Interest on general debt	5,418,957	1.3
Other and unallocable	12,529,706	3.0
Utility expenditure	1,902,074	0.5
Liquor stores expenditure	0	-
Insurance trust expenditure	70,634,566	16.7
Debt at End of Fiscal Year	144,041,214	X
Cash and Security Holdings	876,253,017	X

X = Not applicable.
- = Zero or rounds to zero.
[1] Within insurance trust revenue, net earnings of state retirement systems is a calculated statistic (the item code in the data file is X08), and thus can be positive or negative. Net earnings is the sum of earnings on investments plus gains on investments minus losses on investments. The change made in 2002 for asset valuation from book to market value in accordance with Statement 34 of the Governmental Accounting Standards Board is reflected in the calculated statistics.

Table CA-16. State Government Tax Collections, 2021

(Dollars in thousands, percent.)

Item	Dollars	Percent distribution
Total Taxes	248,188,154	100.0
Property taxes	3,151,488	1.3
Sales and gross receipts	61,191,853	24.7
General sales and gross receipts	41,973,959	16.9
Selective sales and gross receipts	19,217,894	7.7
Alcoholic beverages	411,969	0.2
Amusements	X	-
Insurance premiums	3,116,772	1.3
Motor fuels	7,659,320	3.1
Pari-mutuels	18,974	-
Public utilities	652,621	0.3
Tobacco products	1,969,795	0.8
Other selective sales	5,388,443	2.2
Licenses	11,292,132	4.5
Alcoholic beverages	92,549	-
Amusements	22219	-
Corporations in general	87,904	-
Hunting and fishing	119,279	-
Motor vehicle	5,225,872	2.1
Motor vehicle operators	385,767	0.2
Public utilities	513,607	0.2
Occupation and business, NEC	4,840,571	2.0
Other licenses	4,364	-
Income taxes	172,421,856	69.5
Individual income	146,324,579	59.0
Corporation net income	26,097,277	10.5
Other taxes	130,825	0.1
Death and gift	77	-
Documentary and stock transfer	X	-
Severance	130,748	0.1
Taxes, NEC	0	0.0

- = Zero or rounds to zero.
X = Not applicable.

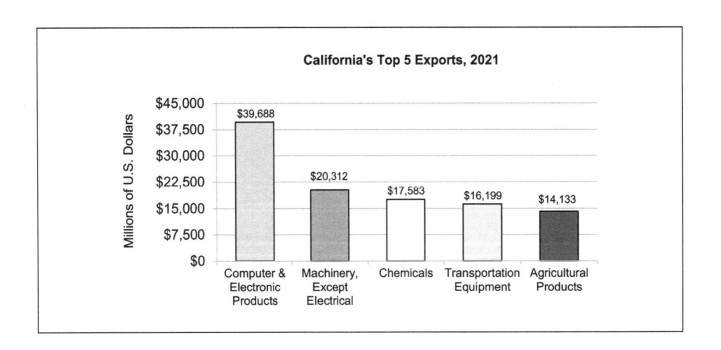

California's Top 5 Exports, 2021

Facts and Figures

Location: Western United States; bordered on the N by Wyoming and Nebraska, on the E by Nebraska and Kansas, on the S by Oklahoma and New Mexico, and on the W by Utah; Colorado is one of the Four Corner states—at its SW corner it touches Arizona, New Mexico, and Utah

Area: 104,093 sq. mi. (269,601 sq. km.); rank—8th

Population: 5,812,069 (2021 est.); rank—21st

Principal Cities: capital—Denver; largest—Denver

Statehood: August 1, 1876; 38th state

U.S. Congress: 2 senators, 7 representatives

State Motto: *Nil sine numine* ("Nothing without providence")

State Songs: "Where the Columbines Grow"; "Rocky Mountain High"

State Nicknames: The Centennial State; Colorful Colorado

Abbreviations: CO; Colo.

State Symbols: flower—Rocky Mountain columbine; tree—Colorado blue spruce; bird—lark bunting

At a Glance

- With an increase in population of 15.6 percent, Colorado ranked 5th among the states in growth from 2010 to 2021.

- In 2020, 7.8 percent of Coloradans did not have health insurance, compared to 8.7 percent of the total U.S. population.

- At a rate of 24.9 per 100,000 residents, the 2020 drug overdose death rate in Colorado was lower than the national average of 28.3 deaths per 100,000 ranking, 29th in the nation.

- In Colorado, 9.8 percent of the total population lived below the poverty level in 2020, compared to the nationwide poverty rate of 12.8 percent. Colorado's childhood poverty rate was 11.5 percent, which was the 4th lowest rate in the country.

Table CO-1. Population by Age, Sex, Race, and Hispanic Origin

(Number, percent, except where noted.)

Sex, age, race, and Hispanic origin	2000	2010	2021	Percent change, 2010–2021
Total Population..	4,301,261	5,029,196	5,812,069	15.6
Percent of total U.S. population	1.5	1.6	1.8	X
Sex				
Male..	2,165,983	2,520,662	2,944,650	16.8
Female...	2,135,278	2,508,534	2,867,419	14.3
Age				
Under 5 years...	297,505	343,960	313,160	-9.0
5 to 19 years...	927,163	1,020,732	1,079,959	5.8
20 to 64 years..	2,660,520	3,114,879	3,539,297	13.6
65 years and over...	416,073	549,625	879,653	60.0
Median age (years)..	34.3	36.1	37.5	3.9
Race and Hispanic Origin				
One race				
White	3,560,005	4,450,623	5,027,045	13.0
Black	165,063	214,919	271,768	26.5
American Indian and Alaska Native................................	44,241	78,144	97,711	25.0
Asian..	95,213	144,819	208,878	44.2
Native Hawaiian or Other Pacific Islander	4,621	8,420	12,760	51.5
Two or more races	122,187	132,271	193,907	46.6
Hispanic (of any race)...	735,601	1,078,225	1,293,214	19.9

NOTE: Population figures for 2021 are July 1 estimates. The 2000 and 2010 estimates are taken from the respective censuses.
- = Zero or rounds to zero.
X = Not applicable.

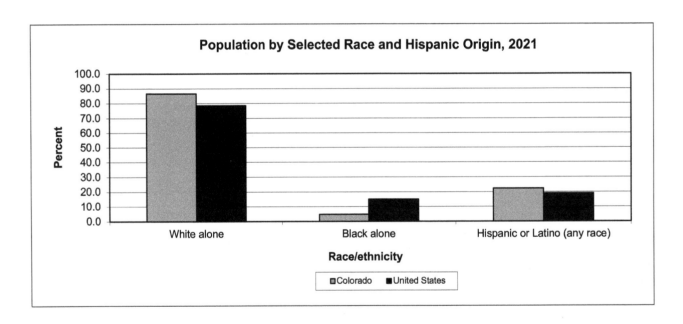

Table CO-2. Marital Status

(Number, percent distribution.)

Sex, age, race, and Hispanic origin	2000	2010	2020 [1]
Males, 15 Years and Over	1,694,635	2,004,303	2,328,666
Never married	30.5	34.4	36.2
Now married, except separated...	56.6	51.7	50.0
Separated..	1.4	1.6	1.2
Widowed..	1.9	2.0	2.1
Divorced..	9.6	10.3	10.5
Females, 15 Years and Over	1,690,734	2,017,425	2,312,613
Never married	23.4	26.9	29.0
Now married, except separated...	54.7	50.8	49.6
Separated..	1.8	2.0	1.5
Widowed..	7.6	7.0	6.6
Divorced..	12.5	13.3	13.3

[1] 2020 ACS 5-Year estimates. 1-Year estimates were not released for 2020 due to the impact of COVID-19 on data collection that year.

Table CO-3. Households and Housing Characteristics

(Number, percent, dollars.)

Item	2000	2010	2020 [1]	Average annual percent change, 2010–2020
Total Households...	1,658,238	1,960,585	2,137,402	1.3
Family households	1,084,461	1,258,885	1,358,903	1.1
Married-couple family	858,671	959,624	1,069,666	1.6
Other family	225,790	299,261	289,237	-0.5
Male householder, no wife present....................	66,811	90,518	95,610	0.8
Female householder, no husband present..........	158,979	208,743	193,627	-1.0
Nonfamily households	573,777	701,700	778,499	1.6
Householder living alone..................................	435,778	555,080	591,783	0.9
Householder not living alone............................	137,999	146,620	186,716	3.9
Housing Characteristics				
Total housing units...	1,808,037	2,214,262	2,361,372	0.9
Occupied housing units	1,658,238	1,960,585	2,137,402	1.3
Owner occupied	1,116,173	1,292,792	1,415,324	1.4
Renter occupied	542,101	667,793	722,078	1.2
Average household size.....................................	2.53	2.52	2.60	0.5
Financial Characteristics				
Median gross rent of renter-occupied housing	671	863	1,335	7.8
Median monthly owner costs for housing units with a mortgage	1,197	1,590	1,808	2.0
Median value of owner-occupied housing units............	166,600	236,600	369,900	8.0

[1] 2020 ACS 5-Year estimates. 1-Year estimates were not released for 2020 due to the impact of COVID-19 on data collection that year.

Table CO-4. Migration, Origin, and Language

(Number, percent.)

Characteristic	State 2016-2020 [1]	U.S. 2016-2020 [1]
Residence 1 Year Ago		
Population 1 year and over	5,625,572	322,943,283
Same house	82.4	86.2
Different house in the U.S.	17.0	13.2
Same county	8.0	7.7
Different county	9.0	5.5
Same state	5.0	3.2
Different state	4.0	2.3
Abroad	0.6	0.6
Place of Birth		
Native born	5,145,412	282,443,680
Male	50.5	49.4
Female	49.5	50.6
Foreign born	539,514	44,125,628
Male	48.9	48.6
Female	51.1	51.4
Foreign born; naturalized U.S. citizen..	242,460	22,456,684
Male	45.3	46.1
Female	54.7	53.9
Foreign born; not a U.S. citizen...	297,054	21,668,944
Male	51.8	51.1
Female	48.2	48.9
Entered 2010 or later	22.9	22.8
Entered 2000 to 2009	27.7	25.1
Entered before 2000...	49.4	52.1
World Region of Birth, Foreign		
Foreign-born population, excluding population born at sea	539,514	44,125,628
Europe	13.1	10.8
Asia	25.4	31.3
Africa	7.0	5.4
Oceania	1.1	0.6
Latin America..	50.6	50.0
North America	2.7	1.9
Language Spoken at Home and Ability to Speak English		
Population 5 years and over..	5,353,987	306,919,116
English only	83.6	78.5
Language other than English..	16.4	21.5
Speaks English less than "very well"..	5.6	8.2

[1] 2020 ACS 5-Year estimates. 1-Year estimates were not released for 2020 due to the impact of COVID-19 on data collection that year.
NA = Not available.
X = Not applicable.
- = Zero or rounds to zero.

Table CO-5. Median Income and Poverty Status, 2020[1]

(Number, percent, except as noted.)

Characteristic	State Number	State Percent	U.S. Number	U.S. Percent
Median Income				
Households (dollars)...	75,231	X	64,994	X
Families (dollars)	92,752	X	80,069	X
Below Poverty Level (All People)	544,232	9.8	40,910,326	12.8
Sex				
Male	249,599	9.0	18,171,512	11.6
Female	294,633	10.6	22,738,814	14.0
Age				
Under 18 years...	143,390	11.5	12,598,699	17.5
Related children under 18 years.......................................	138,734	11.2	12,306,532	17.2
18 to 64 years..	341,947	9.7	23,554,920	12.1
65 years and over	58,895	7.4	4,756,707	9.3

X = Not applicable.
[1] 2020 ACS 5-Year estimates. 1-Year estimates were not released for 2020 due to the impact of COVID-19 on data collection that year.

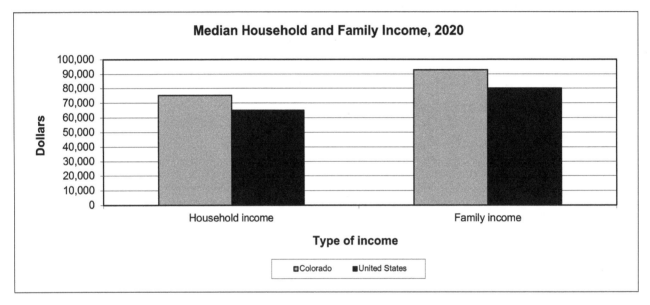

Median Household and Family Income, 2020

Table CO-6. Health Insurance Coverage Status for the Civilian Noninstitutionalized Population and Children Under 19 Years of Age

(Number, percent.)

Item	2011	2012	2013	2014	2015	2016	2017	2018	2019	2020 [2]
Civilian Noninstitutionalized Population	5,024,885	5,094,766	5,173,272	5,266,022	5,367,335	5,447,760	5,514,070	5,604,105	5,664,199	5,588,760
Covered by Private or Public Insurance										
Number..	4,265,266	4,343,522	4,444,084	4,723,411	4,934,713	5,038,017	5,099,993	5,182,461	5,210,724	5,152,499
Percent..	84.9	85.3	85.9	89.7	91.9	92.5	92.5	92.5	92.0	92.2
Uninsured										
Number..	759,619	751,244	729,188	542,611	432,622	409,743	414,077	421,644	453,475	436,261
Percent..	15.1	14.7	14.1	10.3	8.1	7.5	7.5	7.5	8.0	7.8
Percent in the U.S. not covered..............................	15.1	14.8	14.5	11.7	9.4	8.6	8.7	8.9	9.2	8.7
Children Under 19 Years of Age[1]	1,226,828	1,229,008	1,239,191	1,245,432	1,254,800	1,258,167	1,334,235	1,345,058	1,331,001	1,331,681
Covered by Private or Public Insurance										
Number..	1,111,102	1,120,313	1,137,042	1,175,348	1,202,377	1,207,518	1,276,752	1,282,826	1,258,445	1,267,329
Percent..	90.6	91.2	91.8	94.4	95.8	96.0	95.7	95.4	94.5	95.2
Uninsured										
Number..	115,726	108,695	102,149	70,084	52,423	50,649	57,483	62,232	72,556	64,352
Percent..	9.4	8.8	8.2	5.6	4.2	4.0	4.3	4.6	5.5	4.8
Percent in the U.S. not covered..............................	7.5	7.2	7.1	6.0	4.8	4.5	5.0	5.2	5.7	5.2

[1] Data for years prior to 2017 are for individuals under 18 years of age.
[2] 2020 ACS 5-Year estimates. 1-Year estimates were not released for 2020 due to the impact of COVID-19 on data collection that year. Data is not comparable to previous years, which are based on 1-year estimates.

Table CO-7. Employment Status by Demographic Group, 2021

(Numbers in thousands, percent.)

Characteristic	Civilian noninstitutional population	Civilian labor force		Employed		Unemployed	
		Number	Percent of population	Number	Percent of population	Number	Percent of population
Total..	4,670	3,160	67.7	3,000	64.2	160	5.1
Sex							
Male..	2,320	1,712	73.8	1,621	69.9	92	5.3
Female...	2,350	1,448	61.6	1,379	58.7	69	4.8
Race, Sex, and Hispanic Origin							
White	4,093	2,754	67.3	2,632	64.3	121	4.4
Male..	2,020	1,491	73.8	1,423	70.4	69	4.6
Female..	2,073	1,262	60.9	1,210	58.4	52	4.1
Black or African American........................	174	111	64.1	93	53.3	19	16.8
Male..	NA	NA	NA	NA	NA	NA	NA
Female..	NA	NA	NA	NA	NA	NA	NA
Hispanic or Latino ethnicity[1]	818	563	68.9	526	64.3	38	6.7
Male..	403	324	80.4	302	74.9	22	6.8
Female..	416	240	57.7	224	53.9	16	6.5
Age							
16 to 19 years..	297	133	45	118	40	15	11
20 to 24 years..	381	288	75.6	263	69.1	25	8.5
25 to 34 years..	869	759	87.4	719	82.7	41	5.4
35 to 44 years..	827	690	83.5	656	79.3	34	4.9
45 to 54 years..	720	623	86.5	604	83.9	19	3.0
55 to 64 years..	702	484	69.0	462	65.8	22	4.6
65 years and over...................................	875	184	21.0	179	20.4	5	2.7

NOTE: Data in Table 7 are from the Current Population Survey (CPS) and do not match the estimates in Table 8. See notes and definitions for further information.
[1] May be of any race.
NA = Not available.

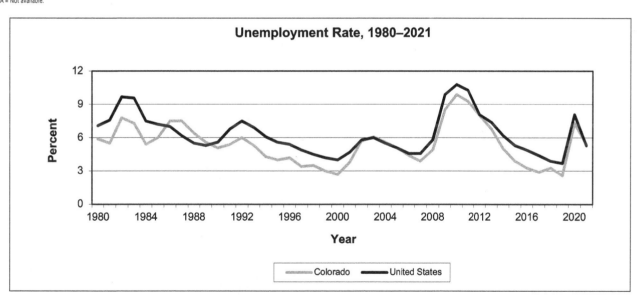

Unemployment Rate, 1980–2021

Table CO-8. Employment Status of the Civilian Noninstitutional Population Age 16 Years and Over

(Number, percent.)

Year	Civilian labor force	Civilian participation rate	Employed	Unemployed	Unemployment rate
2010..	2,715,723	70.2	2,466,996	248,727	9.2
2011..	2,730,262	69.6	2,493,472	236,790	8.7
2012..	2,749,192	68.8	2,529,785	219,407	8.0
2013..	2,766,140	68.0	2,579,568	186,572	6.7
2014..	2,800,666	67.6	2,661,070	139,596	5.0
2015..	2,825,761	66.7	2,719,997	105,764	3.7
2016..	2,894,157	67.0	2,803,504	90,653	3.1
2017..	2,963,790	67.7	2,885,980	77,810	2.6
2018..	3,049,640	68.5	2,957,690	91,950	3.0
2019..	3,100,598	68.6	3,019,934	80,664	2.6
2020..	3,087,271	67.4	2,874,857	212,414	6.9
2021..	3,156,110	68.2	2,986,711	169,399	5.4

Table CO-9. Employment and Average Wages by Industry

(Estimates are based on the 2012 North American Industry Classification System [NAICS].)

Industry	2013	2014	2015	2016	2017	2018	2019	2020
	Dollars							
Wage and Salary Employment by Industry.........................	2,507,504	2,593,887	2,670,453	2,726,685	2,784,085	2,852,274	2,916,438	2,781,124
Farm Wage and Salary Employment................................	12,747	11,976	11,633	12,285	14,783	12,934	12,965	13,700
Nonfarm Wage and Salary Employment..........................	2,494,757	2,581,911	2,658,820	2,714,400	2,769,302	2,839,340	2,903,473	2,767,424
Private wage and salary employment................................	2,029,421	2,111,086	2,180,679	2,227,860	2,276,555	2,339,140	2,392,647	2,262,877
Forestry, fishing, and related activities................................	6,374	6,409	6,495	6,562	6,819	6,898	7,174	6,817
Mining..	30,308	33,706	30,394	23,467	25,450	28,067	28,583	21,487
Utilities...	7,842	8,148	8,209	8,235	8,078	8,042	8,172	8,308
Construction..	131,178	145,844	152,503	159,077	167,337	177,343	183,371	179,203
Manufacturing..	132,880	136,558	141,021	142,505	144,217	147,446	150,378	146,685
Durable goods manufacturing....................................	86,041	88,226	90,250	89,998	90,372	92,253	94,243	91,653
Nondurable goods manufacturing..............................	46,839	48,332	50,771	52,507	53,845	55,193	56,135	55,032
Wholesale trade	97,108	100,328	103,721	105,320	107,159	108,744	110,688	108,267
Retail trade..	251,142	256,824	264,890	270,865	272,508	275,075	274,370	264,149
Transportation and warehousing................................	66,343	69,499	71,547	71,747	76,057	80,841	87,081	89,994
Information	69,965	70,263	70,896	71,819	71,692	75,111	76,388	74,924
Finance and insurance	107,600	108,811	111,546	114,229	117,228	118,922	120,090	121,413
Real estate and rental and leasing.............................	43,882	45,165	47,843	49,637	51,414	53,541	56,156	53,858
Professional, scientific, and technical services	190,421	198,200	206,260	211,670	217,294	226,649	237,425	241,258
Management of companies and enterprises........................	34,657	35,483	36,532	36,902	39,048	40,861	42,406	42,010
Administrative and waste services	149,934	155,233	158,618	159,784	159,123	159,790	163,153	150,648
Educational services	45,384	47,937	49,513	51,541	52,255	53,536	54,714	50,489
Health care and social assistance..............................	254,277	264,876	278,667	290,427	296,680	302,528	307,992	301,847
Arts, entertainment, and recreation............................	47,882	50,692	51,295	53,627	56,534	57,917	60,020	45,342
Accommodation and food services.............................	243,327	252,399	263,057	272,071	278,945	284,078	287,685	229,038
Other services, except public administration....................	118,917	124,706	127,672	128,375	128,717	133,751	136,801	127,140
Government and government enterprises	465,336	470,825	478,141	486,540	492,747	500,200	510,826	504,547
	Dollars							
Average Wages and Salaries by Industry	51,654	53,428	54,855	55,370	57,603	59,715	62,435	67,285
Average Farm Wages and Salaries	39,764	40,852	35,594	39,020	32,613	38,974	27,836	35,088
Average Nonfarm Wages and Salaries	51,714	53,486	54,939	55,444	57,736	59,809	62,589	67,444
Average private wages and salaries................................	52,348	54,236	55,709	56,096	58,590	60,662	63,662	68,941
Forestry, fishing, and related activities........................	26,161	27,564	29,364	30,278	31,656	32,594	35,467	37,267
Mining..	109,884	113,727	115,767	115,853	118,670	122,675	126,428	141,280
Utilities...	90,929	93,431	96,785	99,390	103,508	108,570	114,540	120,028
Construction..	51,964	54,558	56,260	58,235	60,346	63,339	65,481	69,319
Manufacturing..	64,234	67,036	68,409	68,151	71,315	72,610	75,852	79,466
Durable goods manufacturing....................................	71,178	73,717	76,079	76,279	81,167	82,053	85,845	89,547
Nondurable goods manufacturing..............................	51,478	54,841	54,776	54,218	54,778	56,828	59,075	62,675
Wholesale trade	75,681	78,930	80,926	81,393	84,954	87,431	92,256	97,197
Retail trade..	29,322	30,248	31,248	31,739	32,732	33,600	34,955	38,495
Transportation and warehousing................................	52,144	54,509	55,752	56,478	59,225	59,834	61,773	61,985
Information	92,101	97,812	96,212	97,571	102,935	102,862	111,470	126,091
Finance and insurance	81,359	84,937	89,862	91,805	94,354	98,129	103,625	113,525
Real estate and rental and leasing.............................	50,535	51,946	54,434	56,279	58,544	60,835	62,674	67,267
Professional, scientific, and technical services	86,365	88,599	90,251	91,729	94,929	99,166	104,471	107,739
Management of companies and enterprises........................	127,658	136,932	145,522	131,163	151,767	139,317	151,858	156,070
Administrative and waste services	35,887	37,137	38,891	40,050	42,401	45,374	47,161	50,224
Educational services	35,715	35,525	36,042	36,304	36,687	38,453	38,807	45,416
Health care and social assistance..............................	47,365	48,225	49,540	50,098	51,116	52,600	54,093	57,810
Arts, entertainment, and recreation............................	35,788	36,906	39,520	40,065	40,151	42,245	42,758	47,602
Accommodation and food services.............................	21,678	22,479	23,385	24,106	25,429	27,365	28,802	28,424
Other services, except public administration....................	35,168	35,861	37,392	38,704	40,419	41,612	42,906	47,108
Government and government enterprises	48,949	50,124	51,429	52,460	53,795	55,822	57,562	60,733

Table CO-10. Employment Characteristics by Family Type

(Number, percent.)

Family type and labor force status	2018 Total	2018 Families with own children under 18 years	2019 Total	2019 Families with own children under 18 years	2020 [1] Total	2020 [1] Families with own children under 18 years
All Families...	1,372,705	596,622	1,421,844	595,144	1,358,903	589,228
FAMILY TYPE AND LABOR FORCE STATUS						
Opposite-Sex Married-Couple Families.............................	1,068,185	437,625	1,116,767	443,303	1,058,010	434,625
Both husband and wife in labor force..................................	54.3	66.5	53.9	66.8	54.7	67.0
Husband in labor force, wife not in labor force	22.0	28.8	21.7	27.9	22.0	28.0
Wife in labor force, husband not in labor force	6.8	3.1	7.2	3.6	7.2	3.7
Both husband and wife not in labor force.................................	15.8	1.2	16.0	1.1	16.1	1.3
Other Families	304,520	158,997	305,077	151,841	289,237	152,275
Female householder, no spouse present	67.6	69.3	66.0	67.8	66.9	68.1
In labor force..	51.5	61.8	49.3	59.1	50.7	59.5
Not in labor force	16.1	7.5	16.6	8.7	16.3	8.6
Male householder, no spouse present...........................	32.4	30.7	34.0	32.2	33.1	31.9
In labor force..	26.5	28.5	28.7	30.5	27.5	29.8
Not in labor force	5.9	2.2	5.3	1.7	5.5	2.0

[1] 2020 ACS 5-Year estimates. 1-Year estimates were not released for 2020 due to the impact of COVID-19 on data collection that year. Data is not comparable to previous years, which are based on 1-year estimates.

Table CO-11. School Enrollment and Educational Attainment, 2020[1]

(Number, percent.)

Item	State	U.S.
Enrollment		
Total population 3 years and over, enrolled in school	1,388,732	80,497,960
Enrolled in nursery school or preschool (percent)...................	6.1	6.1
Enrolled in kindergarten (percent)...................................	4.8	5.0
Enrolled in elementary school, grades 1-8 (percent).................	40.8	40.4
Enrolled in high school, grades 9-12 (percent)......................	20.9	21.0
Enrolled in college or graduate school (percent)....................	27.4	27.6
Attainment		
Total population 25 years and over	3,900,754	222,836,834
Less than ninth grade (percent).....................................	3.3	4.9
9th to 12th grade, no diploma (percent).............................	4.6	6.6
High school graduate, including equivalency (percent)...............	21.2	26.7
Some college, no degree (percent)...................................	20.8	20.3
Associate's degree (percent)..	8.5	8.6
Bachelor's degree (percent)...	26.0	20.2
Graduate or professional degree (percent)...........................	15.6	12.7
High school graduate or higher (percent)............................	92.1	88.5
Bachelor's degree or higher (percent)...............................	41.6	32.9

[1] 2020 ACS 5-Year estimates. 1-Year estimates were not released for 2020 due to the impact of COVID-19 on data collection that year.

Table CO-12. Public School Characteristics and Educational Indicators

(Number, percent; data derived from National Center of Education Statistics.)

Item	State	U.S.
Public Elementary and Secondary Schools		
Number of regular school districts, 2018-19................................	178	13,452
Number of operational schools, 2019-20....................................	1,920	98,469
Percent charter schools	13.6	7.7
Total public school enrollment, Fall 2019.................................	913,223	50,796,445
Percent charter school enrollment	13.9	6.8
Student-teacher ratio, Fall 2019...	16.9	15.9
Expenditures per student (unadjusted dollars), 2018-19	11,072	13,187
Four-year adjusted cohort graduation rate (ACGR), 2018-2019[1]............	81.1	85.8
Students eligible for free or reduced-price lunch (percent), 2019-20......	40.7	52.1
English language learners (percent), Fall 2019	11.0	10.4
Students age 3 to 21 served under IDEA, part B (percent), 2020-21	12.1	14.5

Public Schools by Type, 2019-20	Number	Percent of state public schools
Total number of schools..	1,920	100.0
Special education..	5	0.3
Vocational education...	7	0.4
Alternative education..	113	5.9

[1] Adjusted Cohort Graduation Rates (ACGR) differ from Averaged Freshmen Graduation Rates (AFGR).

Table CO-13. Reported Voting and Registration of the Voting-Age Population, November 2020

(Numbers in thousands, percent.)

Item	Total population	Total citizen population	Registered			Voted		
			Total registered	Percent registered (total population)	Percent registered (total citizen population)	Total voted	Percent voted (total population)	Percent voted (total citizen population)
U.S. Total	252,274	231,593	168,308	66.7	72.7	154,628	61.3	66.8
State Total............................	4,525	4,200	2,993	66.2	71.3	2,837	62.7	67.6
Sex								
Male	2,254	2,076	1,452	64.4	70.0	1,355	60.1	65.3
Female	2,271	2,124	1,541	67.9	72.6	1,482	65.3	69.8
Race								
White alone............................	4,001	3,751	2,733	68.3	72.9	2,606	65.1	69.5
White, non-Hispanic alone	3,267	3,220	2,396	73.3	74.4	2,316	70.9	71.9
Black alone	186	181	102	54.5	56.0	96	51.6	53.1
Asian alone	152	115	57	37.7	49.9	50	32.7	43.2
Hispanic (of any race).................	854	618	374	43.8	60.5	315	37.0	51.1
White alone or in combination	4,123	3,858	2,801	67.9	72.6	2,658	64.5	68.9
Black alone or in combination	203	198	118	58.3	59.7	113	55.6	57.0
Asian alone or in combination..........	171	135	72	42.2	53.8	65	37.7	48.1
Age								
18 to 24 years.........................	528	481	293	55.6	60.9	257	48.6	53.3
25 to 34 years.........................	996	942	653	65.6	69.3	608	61.1	64.6
35 to 44 years.........................	717	629	442	61.7	70.3	420	58.5	66.7
45 to 64 years.........................	1,432	1,302	956	66.8	73.4	922	64.4	70.8
65 years and over	852	845	648	76.0	76.7	631	74.1	74.7

Table CO-14. Crime

(Number, rate per 100,000. Data are derived from the FBI Uniform Crime Reports.)

Item	State			U.S.		
	2019	2020	Percent change	2019	2020	Percent change
TOTAL POPULATION [1]	5,758,486	5,807,719	0.9	328,329,953	329,484,123	0.4
VIOLENT CRIME						
Number..	22,149	24,570	10.9	1,250,393	1,313,105	5.0
Rate	384.6	423.1	10.0	380.8	398.5	4.6
Murder and Nonnegligent Manslaughter						
Number..	229	294	28.4	16,669	21,570	29.4
Rate	4.0	5.1	27.3	5.1	6.5	28.9
Rape [2]						
Number..	4,087	3,652	-10.6	143,224	126,430	-11.7
Rate	71.0	62.9	-11.4	43.6	38.4	-12.0
Robbery						
Number..	3,716	3,964	6.7	268,483	243,600	-9.3
Rate	64.5	68.3	5.8	81.8	73.9	-9.6
Aggravated Assault						
Number..	14,117	16,660	18.0	822,017	921,505	12.1
Rate	245.2	286.9	17.0	250.4	279.7	11.7
PROPERTY CRIME						
Number..	150,564	164,582	9.3	6,995,235	6,452,038	-7.8
Rate	2,614.6	2,833.8	8.4	2,130.6	1,958.2	-8.1
Burglary						
Number..	20,266	23,246	14.7	1,118,096	1,035,314	-7.4
Rate	351.9	400.3	13.7	340.5	314.2	-7.7
Larceny-Theft						
Number..	108,575	110,884	2.1	5,152,267	4,606,324	-10.6
Rate	1,885.5	1,909.3	1.3	1,569.2	1,398.0	-10.9
Motor Vehicle Theft						
Number..	21,723	30,452	40.2	724,872	810,400	11.8
Rate	377.2	524.3	39.0	220.8	246.0	11.4

NOTE: Although arson data are included in the trend and clearance tables, sufficient data are not available to estimate totals for this offense. Therefore, no arson data are published in this table.
- = Zero or rounds to zero.
[1] Population figures are U.S. Census Bureau provisional estimates as of July 1, 2020.
[2] The figures shown in the rape (revised definition) column were estimated using the revised Uniform Crime Reporting (UCR) definition of rape.

Table CO-15. State Government Finances, 2020

(Dollar amounts in thousands, percent distribution.)

Item	Dollars	Percent distribution
Total Revenue	48,052,010	100.0
General revenue	33,681,316	70.1
Intergovernmental revenue	11,565,606	24.1
Taxes	15,074,484	31.4
General sales	3400110	7.1
Selective sales	2,611,871	5.4
License taxes	678,829	1.4
Individual income tax	7539184	15.7
Corporate income tax	696,612	1.4
Other taxes	147,878	0.3
Current charges	4,759,744	9.9
Miscellaneous general revenue	2,281,482	4.7
Utility revenue	0	-
Liquor stores revenue	0	-
Insurance trust revenue[1]	14,370,694	29.9
Total Expenditure	42,343,873	100.0
Intergovernmental expenditure	8,411,215	19.9
Direct expenditure	33,932,658	80.1
Current operation	22,106,131	52.2
Capital outlay	2,021,107	4.8
Insurance benefits and repayments	7,884,296	18.6
Assistance and subsidies	1,057,490	2.5
Interest on debt	863,634	2.0
Exhibit: Salaries and wages	6,445,260	15.2
Total Expenditure	42,343,873	100.0
General expenditure	34,448,041	81.4
Intergovernmental expenditure	8,411,215	19.9
Direct expenditure	26,036,826	61.5
General expenditure, by function:		
Education	13,542,537	32.0
Public welfare	10,863,186	25.7
Hospitals	1,374,781	3.2
Health	531,548	1.3
Highways	2,209,160	5.2
Police protection	302,950	0.7
Correction	1,205,771	2.8
Natural resources	389,848	0.9
Parks and recreation	119,977	0.3
Governmental administration	1,646,695	3.9
Interest on general debt	855,015	2.0
Other and unallocable	1,352,953	3.2
Utility expenditure	12,270	-
Liquor stores expenditure	0	-
Insurance trust expenditure	7,884,296	18.6
Debt at End of Fiscal Year	20,127,071	X
Cash and Security Holdings	94,585,765	X

X = Not applicable.
- = Zero or rounds to zero.
[1] Within insurance trust revenue, net earnings of state retirement systems is a calculated statistic (the item code in the data file is X08), and thus can be positive or negative. Net earnings is the sum of earnings on investments plus gains on investments minus losses on investments. The change made in 2002 for asset valuation from book to market value in accordance with Statement 34 of the Governmental Accounting Standards Board is reflected in the calculated statistics.

Table CO-16. State Government Tax Collections, 2021

(Dollars in thousands, percent.)

Item	Dollars	Percent distribution
Total Taxes	18,817,848	100.0
Property taxes	X	-
Sales and gross receipts	6,572,936	34.9
General sales and gross receipts	3,660,590	19.5
Selective sales and gross receipts	2,912,346	15.5
Alcoholic beverages	53,433	0.3
Amusements	115624	0.6
Insurance premiums	347,690	1.8
Motor fuels	618,724	3.3
Pari-mutuels	306	-
Public utilities	X	-
Tobacco products	227,872	1.2
Other selective sales	1,548,697	8.2
Licenses	720,335	3.8
Alcoholic beverages	6,138	0.0
Amusements	960	-
Corporations in general	25,975	0.1
Hunting and fishing	115,697	0.6
Motor vehicle	458,464	2.4
Motor vehicle operators	44,038	0.2
Public utilities	15,084	0.1
Occupation and business, NEC	53,943	0.3
Other licenses	36	-
Income taxes	11,524,577	61.2
Individual income	10,246,531	54.5
Corporation net income	1,278,046	6.8
Other taxes	0	-
Death and gift	X	-
Documentary and stock transfer	X	-
Severance	0	0.0
Taxes, NEC	0	-

X = Not applicable.
- = Zero or rounds to zero.

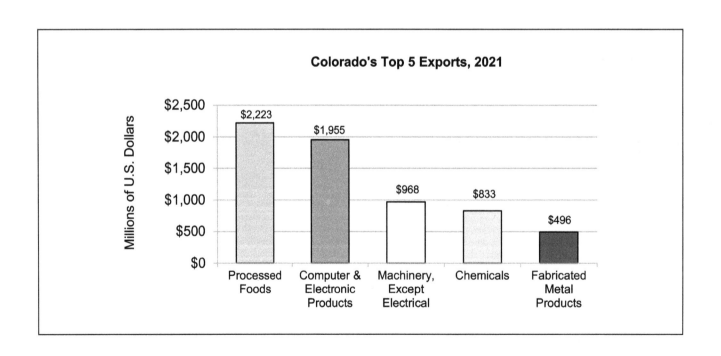

CONNECTICUT

Facts and Figures

Location: Northeastern United States; bordered on the N by Massachusetts, on the E by Rhode Island, on the S by Long Island Sound, and on the W by New York

Area: 5,543 sq. mi. (14,357); rank—48th

Population: 3,605,597 (2021 est.); rank—29th

Principal Cities: capital—Hartford; largest—Bridgeport

Statehood: January 9, 1788; 5th state

U.S. Congress: 2 senators, 5 representatives

State Motto: *Qui transtulit sustinet* ("He who transplanted still sustains")

State Song: "Yankee Doodle"

State Nicknames: The Constitution State; The Nutmeg State

Abbreviations: CT; Conn.

State Symbols: flower—mountain laurel; tree—white oak; bird—American robin

At a Glance

- Connecticut experienced a 0.9 percent increase in population between 2010 and 2021, which ranked 48th in the country.

- Connecticut's median household income in 2020 was $79,855, compared to the national median household income of $64,994.

- In 2020, 40.0 percent of Connecticut residents age 25 and older had a bachelor's degree or higher, which was the 6th highest percent in the country.

- Connecticut's per capita personal income in 2021 was $82,082, ranking 3rd in the nation.

- Connecticut's violent crime rate in 2020 was 181.6 incidences per 100,000 population (the fourth lowest in the country), and its property crime rate was 1,565.1 incidences per 100,000 population. These were lower than the national violent and property crime rates of 398.5 and 1,958.2 incidences per 100,000.

Table CT-1. Population by Age, Sex, Race, and Hispanic Origin

(Number, percent, except where noted.)

Sex, age, race, and Hispanic origin	2000	2010	2021	Percent change, 2010–2021
Total Population..	3,405,565	3,574,097	3,605,597	0.9
Percent of total U.S. population	1.2	1.2	1.1	X
Sex				
Male..	1,649,319	1,739,614	1,769,587	1.7
Female..	1,756,246	1,834,483	1,836,010	0.1
Age				
Under 5 years..	233,344	202,106	178,211	-11.8
5 to 19 years...	702,358	713,670	652,810	-8.5
20 to 64 years...	2,009,680	2,151,762	2,125,341	-1.2
65 years and over..	470,183	506,559	649,235	28.2
Median age (years)	37.4	40.0	41.1	2.8
Race and Hispanic Origin				
One race				
White...	2,780,355	2,950,820	2,842,528	-3.7
Black...	309,843	392,131	457,331	16.6
American Indian and Alaska Native	9,639	16,734	24,184	44.5
Asian...	82,313	140,516	182,469	29.9
Native Hawaiian or Other Pacific Islander	1,366	3,491	4,184	19.9
Two or more races	74,848	70,405	94,901	34.8
Hispanic (of any race)	320,323	498,638	637,112	27.8

NOTE: Population figures for 2021 are July 1 estimates. The 2000 and 2010 estimates are taken from the respective censuses.
- = Zero or rounds to zero.
X = Not applicable.

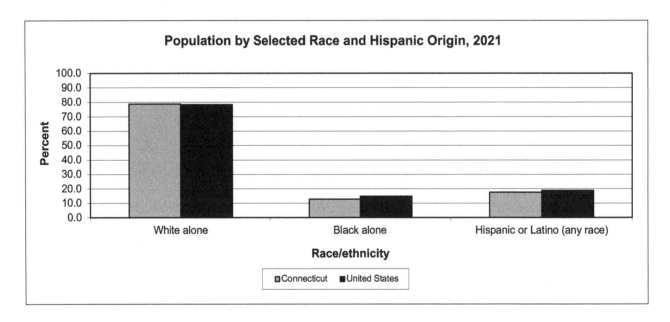

Population by Selected Race and Hispanic Origin, 2021

Table CT-2. Marital Status

(Number, percent distribution.)

Sex, age, race, and Hispanic origin	2000	2010	2020 [1]
Males, 15 Years and Over	1,284,881	1,399,329	1,437,152
Never married	30.0	36.3	37.8
Now married, except separated..	58.0	50.6	49.9
Separated..	1.3	1.1	1.1
Widowed..	2.7	2.7	2.5
Divorced..	7.9	9.3	8.7
Females, 15 Years and Over	1,411,369	1,512,492	1,536,720
Never married	24.5	29.9	31.9
Now married, except separated..	52.3	46.5	45.8
Separated..	1.8	1.8	1.4
Widowed..	10.8	9.3	8.6
Divorced..	10.5	12.5	12.2

[1] 2020 ACS 5-Year estimates. 1-Year estimates were not released for 2020 due to the impact of COVID-19 on data collection that year.

Table CT-3. Households and Housing Characteristics

(Number, percent, dollars.)

Item	2000	2010	2020 [1]	Average annual percent change, 2010–2020
Total Households	1,301,670	1,358,809	1,385,437	0.3
Family households	881,170	890,770	902,996	0.2
Married-couple family	676,467	656,629	664,429	0.2
Other family	204,703	234,141	238,567	0.3
Male householder, no wife present	47,292	58,325	65,241	1.7
Female householder, no husband present	157,411	175,816	173,326	-0.2
Nonfamily households	420,500	468,039	482,441	0.4
Householder living alone	334,224	384,382	394,346	0.4
Householder not living alone	76,276	83,657	88,095	0.8
Housing Characteristics				
Total housing units	1,385,975	1,488,215	1,521,199	0.3
Occupied housing units	1,301,670	1,358,809	1,385,437	0.3
Owner occupied	869,729	923,617	915,408	-0.1
Renter occupied	431,941	435,192	470,029	1.1
Average household size	2.53	2.55	2.50	-0.3
Financial Characteristics				
Median gross rent of renter-occupied housing	681	992	1,201	3.0
Median monthly owner costs for housing units with a mortgage	1,426	2,068	2,127	0.4
Median value of owner-occupied housing units	166,900	288,800	279,700	-0.5

[1] 2020 ACS 5-Year estimates. 1-Year estimates were not released for 2020 due to the impact of COVID-19 on data collection that year.

Table CT-4. Migration, Origin, and Language

(Number, percent.)

Characteristic	State 2016-2020 [1]	U.S. 2016-2020 [1]
Residence 1 Year Ago		
Population 1 year and over	3,537,717	322,943,283
Same house	88.3	86.2
Different house in the U.S.	11.0	13.2
Same county	6.7	7.7
Different county	4.3	5.5
Same state	1.9	3.2
Different state	2.4	2.3
Abroad	0.7	0.6
Place of Birth		
Native born	3,049,165	282,443,680
Male	48.9	49.4
Female	51.1	50.6
Foreign born	521,384	44,125,628
Male	47.8	48.6
Female	52.2	51.4
Foreign born; naturalized U.S. citizen	279,853	22,456,684
Male	44.9	46.1
Female	55.1	53.9
Foreign born; not a U.S. citizen	241,531	21,668,944
Male	51.1	51.1
Female	48.9	48.9
Entered 2010 or later	23.5	22.8
Entered 2000 to 2009	25.6	25.1
Entered before 2000	50.9	52.1
World Region of Birth, Foreign		
Foreign-born population, excluding population born at sea	521,384	44,125,628
Europe	23.1	10.8
Asia	24.3	31.3
Africa	4.9	5.4
Oceania	0.3	0.6
Latin America	44.9	50.0
North America	2.4	1.9
Language Spoken at Home and Ability to Speak English		
Population 5 years and over	3,387,841	306,919,116
English only	77.9	78.5
Language other than English	22.1	21.5
Speaks English less than "very well"	8.1	8.2

[1] 2020 ACS 5-Year estimates. 1-Year estimates were not released for 2020 due to the impact of COVID-19 on data collection that year.
NA = Not available.
X = Not applicable.
- = Zero or rounds to zero.

Table CT-5. Median Income and Poverty Status, 2020[1]

(Number, percent, except as noted.)

Characteristic	State Number	State Percent	U.S. Number	U.S. Percent
Median Income				
Households (dollars)..	79,855	X	64,994	X
Families (dollars)	102,061	X	80,069	X
Below Poverty Level (All People)	339,156	9.8	40,910,326	12.8
Sex				
Male	147,174	8.7	18,171,512	11.6
Female	191,982	10.8	22,738,814	14.0
Age				
Under 18 years...	94,665	13.0	12,598,699	17.5
Related children under 18 years...	92,237	12.7	12,306,532	17.2
18 to 64 years..	201,850	9.4	23,554,920	12.1
65 years and over	42,641	7.2	4,756,707	9.3

X = Not applicable.
[1] 2020 ACS 5-Year estimates. 1-Year estimates were not released for 2020 due to the impact of COVID-19 on data collection that year.

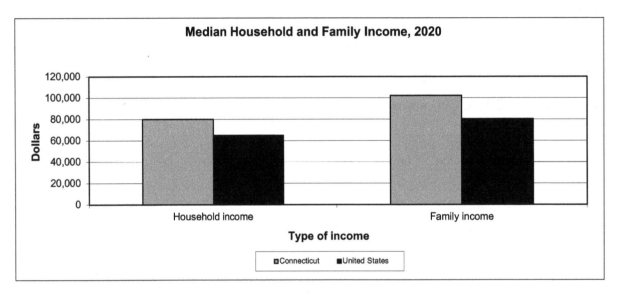

Table CT-6. Health Insurance Coverage Status for the Civilian Noninstitutionalized Population and Children Under 19 Years of Age

(Number, percent.)

Item	2011	2012	2013	2014	2015	2016	2017	2018	2019	2020 [2]
Civilian Noninstitutionalized Population	3,522,709	3,534,619	3,541,409	3,541,282	3,537,983	3,525,154	3,536,522	3,523,842	3,514,562	3,520,172
Covered by Private or Public Insurance										
Number..	3,213,764	3,212,647	3,208,906	3,295,883	3,327,461	3,352,940	3,342,726	3,336,919	3,307,378	3,341,106
Percent...	91.2	90.9	90.6	93.1	94.0	95.1	94.5	94.7	94.1	94.9
Uninsured										
Number..	308,945	321,972	332,503	245,399	210,522	172,214	193,796	186,923	207,184	179,066
Percent...	8.8	9.1	9.4	6.9	6.0	4.9	5.5	5.3	5.9	5.1
Percent in the U.S. not covered................................	15.1	14.8	14.5	11.7	9.4	8.6	8.7	8.9	9.2	8.7
Children Under 19 Years of Age[1]	802,350	791,825	784,159	774,021	761,921	751,459	792,881	788,981	773,214	786,563
Covered by Private or Public Insurance										
Number..	778,973	761,897	750,504	745,151	736,821	730,592	768,525	768,609	746,313	764,094
Percent...	97.1	96.2	95.7	96.3	96.7	97.2	96.9	97.4	96.5	97.1
Uninsured										
Number..	23,377	29,928	33,655	28,870	25,100	20,867	24,356	20,372	26,901	22,469
Percent...	2.9	3.8	4.3	3.7	3.3	2.8	3.1	2.6	3.5	2.9
Percent in the U.S. not covered................................	7.5	7.2	7.1	6.0	4.8	4.5	5.0	5.2	5.7	5.2

[1] Data for years prior to 2017 are for individuals under 18 years of age.
[2] 2020 ACS 5-Year estimates. 1-Year estimates were not released for 2020 due to the impact of COVID-19 on data collection that year. Data is not comparable to previous years, which are based on 1-year estimates.

Table CT-7. Employment Status by Demographic Group, 2021

(Numbers in thousands, percent.)

Characteristic	Civilian noninstitutional population	Civilian labor force		Employed		Unemployed	
		Number	Percent of population	Number	Percent of population	Number	Percent of population
Total..	2,877	1,834	63.7	1,716	59.7	117	6.4
Sex							
Male...	1,385	965	69.7	901	65.1	64	6.6
Female...	1,492	869	58.2	815	54.6	54	6.2
Race, Sex, and Hispanic Origin							
White	2,287	1,448	63.3	1,354	59.2	93	6.4
Male...	1,112	770	69.2	719	64.6	51	6.7
Female...	1,175	678	57.7	636	54.1	42	6.2
Black or African American....................	337	224	66.5	209	62.0	15	6.7
Male...	156	109	70.0	102	65.4	7	6.7
Female...	181	115	63.4	107	59.1	8	6.8
Hispanic or Latino ethnicity[1]	443	303	68.3	277	62.6	25	8.4
Male...	213	163	76.6	153	72.0	10	6.1
Female...	230	140	60.6	124	53.8	16	11.1
Age							
16 to 19 years...................................	183	62	33.7	53	28.8	9	14.3
20 to 24 years...................................	205	138	67.2	122	59.6	16	11.3
25 to 34 years...................................	468	392	83.8	362	77.3	30	7.7
35 to 44 years...................................	428	354	82.7	337	78.8	17	4.8
45 to 54 years...................................	417	353	84.7	341	81.8	12	3.4
55 to 64 years...................................	514	374	72.7	352	68.4	22	5.9
65 years and over..............................	662	161	24.3	149	22.6	12	7.1

NOTE: Data in Table 7 are from the Current Population Survey (CPS) and do not match the estimates in Table 8. See notes and definitions for further information.
[1] May be of any race.

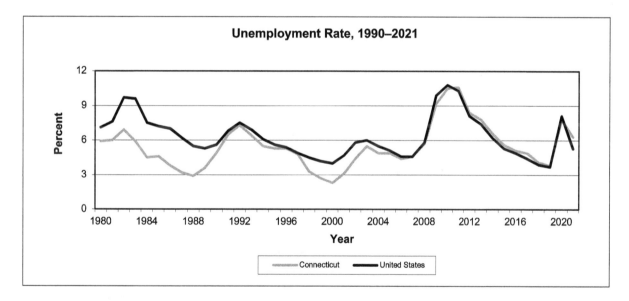

Unemployment Rate, 1990–2021

Connecticut — United States

Table CT-8. Employment Status of the Civilian Noninstitutional Population Age 16 Years and Over

(Number, percent.)

Year	Civilian labor force	Civilian participation rate	Employed	Unemployed	Unemployment rate
2010...	1,911,289	68.3	1,728,121	183,168	9.6
2011...	1,914,449	67.7	1,741,971	172,478	9.0
2012...	1,887,545	66.3	1,729,687	157,858	8.4
2013...	1,867,378	65.4	1,718,834	148,544	8.0
2014...	1,889,102	65.9	1,764,118	124,984	6.6
2015...	1,892,087	65.9	1,785,788	106,299	5.6
2016...	1,893,200	65.9	1,801,390	91,810	4.8
2017...	1,923,711	66.3	1,838,833	84,878	4.4
2018...	1,931,495	66.4	1,855,969	75,526	3.9
2019...	1,950,349	66.9	1,881,688	68,661	3.5
2020...	1,897,782	65.1	1,749,954	147,828	7.8
2021...	1,855,923	63.4	1,739,815	116,108	6.3

Table CT-9. Employment and Average Wages by Industry

(Estimates are based on the 2012 North American Industry Classification System [NAICS].)

Industry	2013	2014	2015	2016	2017	2018	2019	2020
	Dollars							
Wage and Salary Employment by Industry......................	1,717,324	1,730,733	1,740,318	1,744,009	1,745,197	1,752,016	1,750,171	1,628,139
Farm Wage and Salary Employment...............................	5,456	5,478	5,457	5,093	5,082	4,554	4,588	4,382
Nonfarm Wage and Salary Employment..........................	1,711,868	1,725,255	1,734,861	1,738,916	1,740,115	1,747,462	1,745,583	1,623,757
Private wage and salary employment..........................	1,450,184	1,464,155	1,474,568	1,480,847	1,485,960	1,494,933	1,492,909	1,385,842
Forestry, fishing, and related activities.....................	677	701	699	665	640	625	638	(D)
Mining..	543	547	553	556	539	525	518	(D)
Utilities...	6,042	5,943	5,613	5,624	5,333	5,177	5,161	5,095
Construction...	55,067	57,247	59,404	60,582	59,702	60,165	61,097	58,325
Manufacturing...	164,028	159,808	159,090	156,561	158,977	160,594	162,030	153,961
Durable goods manufacturing................................	127,615	124,431	123,740	122,910	124,503	126,263	127,367	121,575
Nondurable goods manufacturing..........................	36,413	35,377	35,350	33,651	34,474	34,331	34,663	32,386
Wholesale trade	63,406	63,318	62,765	62,774	62,813	61,792	59,912	56,166
Retail trade...	185,017	186,160	186,038	185,905	184,782	182,205	176,859	161,782
Transportation and warehousing................................	42,425	43,729	45,324	46,057	47,477	50,153	52,906	56,409
Information	32,093	32,073	32,462	32,412	31,604	31,752	31,514	29,255
Finance and insurance	114,260	111,566	112,247	111,681	110,578	108,108	106,772	104,831
Real estate and rental and leasing.........................	19,468	19,550	20,255	20,355	20,197	20,499	20,675	19,321
Professional, scientific, and technical services	91,038	95,986	96,505	97,601	97,079	97,199	96,642	93,521
Management of companies and enterprises.........................	30,693	31,893	32,936	32,956	32,344	33,663	33,031	31,705
Administrative and waste services..............................	85,619	86,270	88,780	88,997	90,347	91,722	90,541	82,815
Educational services	67,406	69,227	69,664	70,996	72,567	74,318	75,773	73,668
Health care and social assistance...........................	261,725	263,880	265,909	268,872	270,919	272,427	274,854	267,352
Arts, entertainment, and recreation..........................	26,156	27,197	27,025	27,802	28,861	28,993	29,056	20,300
Accommodation and food services............................	122,065	124,573	125,095	127,212	128,884	129,890	129,688	98,212
Other services, except public administration.........................	82,456	84,487	84,204	83,239	82,317	85,126	85,242	72,026
Government and government enterprises.................................	261,684	261,100	260,293	258,069	254,155	252,529	252,674	237,915
	Dollars							
Average Wages and Salaries by Industry	61,406	62,975	64,569	64,903	65,748	66,798	68,768	73,783
Average Farm Wages and Salaries	27,295	28,804	23,619	29,043	26,415	25,216	19,874	20,209
Average Nonfarm Wages and Salaries	61,515	63,084	64,698	65,008	65,863	66,906	68,896	73,927
Average private wages and salaries..........................	62,768	64,319	65,835	66,145	66,938	67,949	70,154	75,271
Forestry, fishing, and related activities.....................	25,866	26,502	28,070	30,146	29,830	31,029	31,201	(D)
Mining..	64,799	70,247	71,329	71,847	76,534	75,309	77,736	(D)
Utilities...	110,980	111,297	116,881	112,092	124,289	131,257	135,157	138,584
Construction...	59,402	61,080	64,270	66,586	68,656	69,762	72,364	75,609
Manufacturing...	81,583	81,393	80,712	79,460	81,880	82,441	85,031	87,747
Durable goods manufacturing................................	81,638	82,095	81,069	81,468	83,623	84,963	87,708	89,773
Nondurable goods manufacturing..........................	81,387	78,927	79,465	72,127	75,585	73,169	75,191	80,141
Wholesale trade	85,972	87,743	92,686	93,605	94,572	95,480	97,718	103,255
Retail trade...	31,555	32,092	33,016	33,264	33,529	34,622	35,876	39,188
Transportation and warehousing................................	47,007	47,790	48,688	48,832	48,587	48,974	49,833	49,439
Information	89,129	92,966	99,237	102,355	103,193	110,701	120,452	138,941
Finance and insurance	150,126	159,068	163,498	163,344	166,847	169,581	171,827	180,808
Real estate and rental and leasing.........................	64,018	65,776	69,524	70,679	66,303	70,319	72,627	76,503
Professional, scientific, and technical services	92,642	95,867	99,005	101,154	103,410	105,266	110,903	114,903
Management of companies and enterprises.........................	161,131	163,472	162,487	163,349	154,205	151,398	159,995	153,877
Administrative and waste services..............................	40,821	43,014	44,072	44,064	45,640	46,153	47,486	51,473
Educational services	51,044	52,516	53,340	52,998	54,359	54,566	56,871	59,712
Health care and social assistance...........................	48,564	49,835	50,277	50,890	51,493	52,733	54,660	58,210
Arts, entertainment, and recreation..........................	29,226	30,081	31,216	31,386	31,777	32,957	33,659	39,751
Accommodation and food services............................	21,382	22,063	23,102	23,922	24,574	25,680	26,413	26,027
Other services, except public administration.........................	32,806	33,578	34,657	35,312	36,517	37,307	38,224	41,639
Government and government enterprises.................................	54,569	56,160	58,257	58,482	59,577	60,734	61,468	66,098

(D) = Not shown to avoid disclosure of confidential information; estimates are included in higher-level totals.

Table CT-10. Employment Characteristics by Family Type

(Number, percent.)

Family type and labor force status	2018		2019		2020 [1]	
	Total	Families with own children under 18 years	Total	Families with own children under 18 years	Total	Families with own children under 18 years
All Families..........................	891,935	370,384	885,911	346,517	902,996	372,439
FAMILY TYPE AND LABOR FORCE STATUS						
Opposite-Sex Married-Couple Families...........................	650,317	248,465	649,536	237,151	657,447	254,720
Both husband and wife in labor force..............................	55.8	72.2	56.0	72.8	56.7	72.6
Husband in labor force, wife not in labor force	19.3	22.7	19.1	21.8	19.5	22.7
Wife in labor force, husband not in labor force	7.6	3.4	7.4	3.6	7.7	3.6
Both husband and wife not in labor force.........................	16.0	1.2	16.5	1.3	16.1	1.2
Other Families	241,618	121,919	236,375	109,366	238,567	116,424
Female householder, no spouse present	72.3	74.5	72.1	74.8	72.7	76.2
In labor force..........................	53.7	64.4	52.5	65.4	53.5	65.6
Not in labor force......................	18.6	10.1	19.7	9.3	19.2	10.6
Male householder, no spouse present...........................	27.7	25.5	27.9	25.2	27.3	23.8
In labor force..........................	22.6	24.4	21.9	23.4	22.0	22.1
Not in labor force	5.1	1.1	5.9	1.9	5.4	1.7

[1] 2020 ACS 5-Year estimates. 1-Year estimates were not released for 2020 due to the impact of COVID-19 on data collection that year. Data is not comparable to previous years, which are based on 1-year estimates.

Table CT-11. School Enrollment and Educational Attainment, 2020[1]

(Number, percent.)

Item	State	U.S.
Enrollment		
Total population 3 years and over, enrolled in school	888,200	80,497,960
Enrolled in nursery school or preschool (percent)..	5.9	6.1
Enrolled in kindergarten (percent)..	4.5	5.0
Enrolled in elementary school, grades 1-8 (percent)...	37.3	40.4
Enrolled in high school, grades 9-12 (percent)..	21.8	21.0
Enrolled in college or graduate school (percent)..	30.4	27.6
Attainment		
Total population 25 years and over	2,489,205	222,836,834
Less than ninth grade (percent)..	4	4.9
9th to 12th grade, no diploma (percent)..	5.1	6.6
High school graduate, including equivalency (percent)...	26.3	26.7
Some college, no degree (percent)..	16.8	20.3
Associate's degree (percent)...	7.8	8.6
Bachelor's degree (percent)..	22.2	20.2
Graduate or professional degree (percent)..	17.9	12.7
High school graduate or higher (percent)...	90.9	88.5
Bachelor's degree or higher (percent)..	40	32.9

[1] 2020 ACS 5-Year estimates. 1-Year estimates were not released for 2020 due to the impact of COVID-19 on data collection that year.

Table CT-12. Public School Characteristics and Educational Indicators

(Number, percent; data derived from National Center of Education Statistics.)

Item	State	U.S.
Public Elementary and Secondary Schools		
Number of regular school districts, 2018-19	169	13,452
Number of operational schools, 2019-20	1,004	98,469
Percent charter schools	2.2	7.7
Total public school enrollment, Fall 2019..	523,690	50,796,445
Percent charter school enrollment	2.1	6.8
Student-teacher ratio, Fall 2019	12.4	15.9
Expenditures per student (unadjusted dollars), 2018-19	21,140	13,187
Four-year adjusted cohort graduation rate (ACGR), 2018-2019[1].................................	88.5	85.8
Students eligible for free or reduced-price lunch (percent), 2019-20............................	42.7	52.1
English language learners (percent), Fall 2019	8.3	10.4
Students age 3 to 21 served under IDEA, part B (percent), 2020-21	16.5	14.5

Public Schools by Type, 2019-20	Number	Percent of state public schools
Total number of schools..	1,004	100.0
Special education...	2	0.2
Vocational education..	17	1.7
Alternative education...	3	0.3

[1] Adjusted Cohort Graduation Rates (ACGR) differ from Averaged Freshmen Graduation Rates (AFGR).

Table CT-13. Reported Voting and Registration of the Voting-Age Population, November 2020

(Numbers in thousands, percent.)

Item	Total population	Total citizen population	Registered			Voted		
			Total registered	Percent registered (total population)	Percent registered (total citizen population)	Total voted	Percent voted (total population)	Percent voted (total citizen population)
U.S. Total	252,274	231,593	168,308	66.7	72.7	154,628	61.3	66.8
State Total..................................	2,777	2,524	1,850	66.6	73.3	1,681	60.5	66.6
Sex								
Male	1,333	1,204	843	63.2	70.0	767	57.5	63.7
Female	1,444	1,320	1,008	69.8	76.3	915	63.4	69.3
Race								
White alone...............................	2,197	2,043	1,543	70.2	75.5	1,392	63.4	68.1
White, non-Hispanic alone	1,841	1,788	1,381	75.0	77.3	1,270	69.0	71.0
Black alone................................	323	282	192	59.5	68.3	184	56.8	65.2
Asian alone	216	158	96	44.4	60.5	90	41.6	56.6
Hispanic (of any race)	461	347	235	51.0	67.8	196	42.4	56.4
White alone or in combination	2,211	2,058	1,548	70.0	75.2	1,395	63.1	67.8
Black alone or in combination.........	326	285	195	59.9	68.6	184	56.3	64.5
Asian alone or in combination.........	216	158	96	44.4	60.5	90	41.6	56.6
Age								
18 to 24 years...........................	281	271	163	58.0	60.1	141	50.1	51.9
25 to 34 years...........................	442	372	259	58.5	69.5	225	50.9	60.5
35 to 44 years...........................	456	366	245	53.7	66.9	228	49.9	62.2
45 to 64 years...........................	994	942	726	73.1	77.1	660	66.4	70.0
65 years and over	603	573	457	75.8	79.8	428	70.9	74.7

Table CT-14. Crime

(Number, rate per 100,000. Data are derived from the FBI Uniform Crime Reports.)

Item	State			U.S.		
	2019	2020	Percent change	2019	2020	Percent change
TOTAL POPULATION[1]	3,566,022	3,557,006	-0.3	328,329,953	329,484,123	0.4
VIOLENT CRIME						
Number..	6,583	6,459	-1.9	1,250,393	1,313,105	5.0
Rate...	184.6	181.6	-1.6	380.8	398.5	4.6
Murder and Nonnegligent Manslaughter						
Number..	107	140	30.8	16,669	21,570	29.4
Rate...	3.0	3.9	31.2	5.1	6.5	28.9
Rape[2]						
Number..	797	594	-25.5	143,224	126,430	-11.7
Rate...	22.3	16.7	-25.3	43.6	38.4	-12.0
Robbery						
Number..	1,942	2,033	4.7	268,483	243,600	-9.3
Rate...	54.5	57.2	5.0	81.8	73.9	-9.6
Aggravated Assault						
Number..	3,737	3,692	-1.2	822,017	921,505	12.1
Rate...	104.8	103.8	-1.0	250.4	279.7	11.7
PROPERTY CRIME						
Number..	51,076	55,670	9.0	6,995,235	6,452,038	-7.8
Rate...	1,432.3	1,565.1	9.3	2,130.6	1,958.2	-8.1
Burglary						
Number..	6,468	6,656	2.9	1,118,096	1,035,314	-7.4
Rate...	181.4	187.1	3.2	340.5	314.2	-7.7
Larceny-Theft						
Number..	38,616	40,592	5.1	5,152,267	4,606,324	-10.6
Rate...	1,082.9	1,141.2	5.4	1,569.2	1,398.0	-10.9
Motor Vehicle Theft						
Number..	5,992	8,422	40.6	724,872	810,400	11.8
Rate...	168.0	236.8	40.9	220.8	246.0	11.4

NOTE: Although arson data are included in the trend and clearance tables, sufficient data are not available to estimate totals for this offense. Therefore, no arson data are published in this table.
- = Zero or rounds to zero.
[1] Population figures are U.S. Census Bureau provisional estimates as of July 1, 2020.
[2] The figures shown in the rape (revised definition) column were estimated using the revised Uniform Crime Reporting (UCR) definition of rape.

Table CT-15. State Government Finances, 2020

(Dollar amounts in thousands, percent distribution.)

Item	Dollars	Percent distribution
Total Revenue	39,645,784	100.0
General revenue	32,781,055	82.7
Intergovernmental revenue	10,344,239	26.1
Taxes	18,400,534	46.4
General sales	4581615	11.6
Selective sales	2,886,836	7.3
License taxes	370,415	0.9
Individual income tax	8177456	20.6
Corporate income tax	2,062,263	5.2
Other taxes	321,949	0.8
Current charges	2,414,604	6.1
Miscellaneous general revenue	1,621,678	4.1
Utility revenue	57,833	0.1
Liquor stores revenue	0	-
Insurance trust revenue[1]	6,806,896	17.2
Total Expenditure	30,844,260	100.0
Intergovernmental expenditure	6,304,877	20.4
Direct expenditure	24,539,383	79.6
Current operation	14,529,319	47.1
Capital outlay	1,652,923	5.4
Insurance benefits and repayments	6,092,556	19.8
Assistance and subsidies	541,396	1.8
Interest on debt	1,723,189	5.6
Exhibit: Salaries and wages	4,539,350	14.7
Total Expenditure	30,844,260	100.0
General expenditure	24,155,008	78.3
Intergovernmental expenditure	6,304,877	20.4
Direct expenditure	17,850,131	57.9
General expenditure, by function:		
Education	7,743,089	25.1
Public welfare	4,941,524	16.0
Hospitals	1,620,595	5.3
Health	1,025,837	3.3
Highways	1,614,522	5.2
Police protection	281,769	0.9
Correction	716,415	2.3
Natural resources	220,453	0.7
Parks and recreation	42,481	0.1
Governmental administration	1,562,461	5.1
Interest on general debt	1,723,189	5.6
Other and unallocable	2,623,216	8.5
Utility expenditure	598,618	1.5
Liquor stores expenditure	0	-
Insurance trust expenditure	6,092,556	19.8
Debt at End of Fiscal Year	41,363,053	X
Cash and Security Holdings	55,486,780	X

X = Not applicable.
- = Zero or rounds to zero.
[1] Within insurance trust revenue, net earnings of state retirement systems is a calculated statistic (the item code in the data file is X08), and thus can be positive or negative. Net earnings is the sum of earnings on investments plus gains on investments minus losses on investments. The change made in 2002 for asset valuation from book to market value in accordance with Statement 34 of the Governmental Accounting Standards Board is reflected in the calculated statistics.

Table CT-16. State Government Tax Collections, 2021

(Dollars in thousands, percent.)

Item	Dollars	Percent distribution
Total Taxes	22,066,648	100.0
Property taxes	X	-
Sales and gross receipts	8,148,270	36.9
General sales and gross receipts	5,252,683	23.8
Selective sales and gross receipts	2,895,587	13.1
Alcoholic beverages	79,109	0.4
Amusements	222943	1.0
Insurance premiums	181,373	0.8
Motor fuels	469,851	2.1
Pari-mutuels	11,738	0.1
Public utilities	256,751	1.2
Tobacco products	322,806	1.5
Other selective sales	1,351,016	6.1
Licenses	387,836	1.8
Alcoholic beverages	9,091	-
Amusements	229	-
Corporations in general	33,456	0.2
Hunting and fishing	6,062	-
Motor vehicle	223,255	1.0
Motor vehicle operators	51,650	0.2
Public utilities	X	-
Occupation and business, NEC	59,187	0.3
Other licenses	4906	-
Income taxes	12,866,247	58.3
Individual income	10,259,183	46.5
Corporation net income	2,607,064	11.8
Other taxes	664,295	3.0
Death and gift	285779	1.3
Documentary and stock transfer	378,209	1.7
Severance	X	-
Taxes, NEC	307	-

- = Zero or rounds to zero.
X = Not applicable.

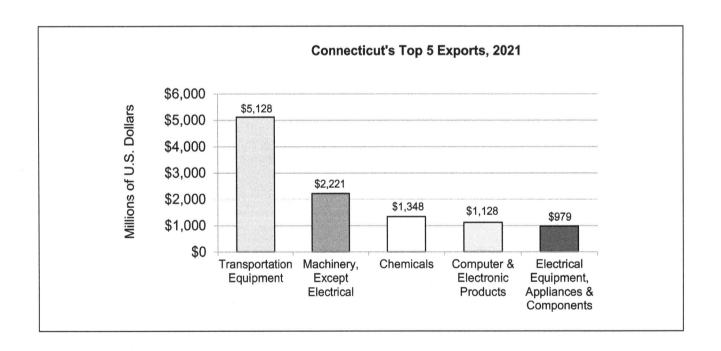

Connecticut's Top 5 Exports, 2021

DELAWARE

Facts and Figures

Location: Northeastern United States; bordered on the N by Pennsylvania, on the E by New Jersey, and on the S and W by Maryland

Area: 2,488 sq. mi. (6,447 sq. km.); rank — 49th

Population: 1,003,384 (2021 est.); rank — 45th

Principal Cities: capital — Dover; largest — Wilmington

Statehood: December 7, 1787; 1st state

U.S. Congress: 2 senators, 1 representative

State Motto: Liberty and Independence

State Song: "Our Delaware"

State Nickname: The First State

Abbreviations: DE; Del.

State Symbols: flower — peach blossom; tree — American holly; bird — blue hen chicken

At a Glance

- With an increase in population of 11.7 percent, Delaware ranked 11th among the states in growth from 2010 to 2021.

- In 2020, 5.8 percent of Delawareans did not have health insurance, compared to 8.7 percent of the total U.S. population.

- Delaware's violent crime rate in 2020 was 431.9 per 100,000 population, compared to 398.5 for the entire nation.

- Delaware's homeownership rate ranked 6th in the nation in 2021, with 73.5 percent of homes being occupied by the owner.

- In 2020, 11.4 percent of Delawareans lived below the poverty level, compared to 12.8 percent of the total U.S. population.

Table DE-1. Population by Age, Sex, Race, and Hispanic Origin

(Number, percent, except where noted.)

Sex, age, race, and Hispanic origin	2000	2010	2021	Percent change, 2010–2021
Total Population..	783,600	897,934	1,003,384	11.7
Percent of total U.S. population	0.3	0.3	0.3	X
Sex				
Male..	380,541	434,939	487,336	12.0
Female..	403,059	462,995	516,048	11.5
Age				
Under 5 years...	51,531	55,886	53,501	-4.3
5 to 19 years...	166,719	177,917	180,745	1.6
20 to 64 years...	463,624	648,387	567,492	-12.5
65 years and over..	101,726	129,277	201,646	56.0
Median age (years)	36.0	38.8	41.6	7.2
Race and Hispanic Origin				
One race				
White..	584,773	645,770	686,599	6.3
Black..	150,666	196,281	236,621	20.6
American Indian and Alaska Native	2,731	5,929	7,124	20.2
Asian..	16,259	29,342	42,419	44.6
Native Hawaiian or Other Pacific Islander	283	690	1,163	68.6
Two or more races..	13,033	19,922	29,458	47.9
Hispanic (of any race).......................................	37,277	76,137	101,213	32.9

NOTE: Population figures for 2021 are July 1 estimates. The 2000 and 2010 estimates are taken from the respective censuses.
- = Zero or rounds to zero.
X = Not applicable.

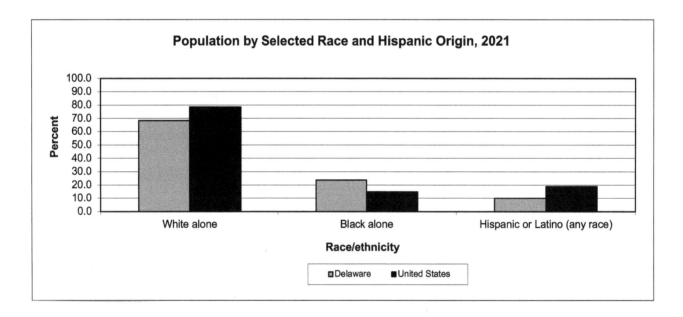

Population by Selected Race and Hispanic Origin, 2021

Legend: □ Delaware   ■ United States

Table DE-2. Marital Status

(Number, percent distribution.)

Sex, age, race, and Hispanic origin	2000	2010	2020 [1]
Males, 15 Years and Over	296,619	350,025	382,040
Never married	29.4	35.3	35.9
Now married, except separated.................................	57.4	50.4	50.8
Separated..	1.8	1.9	1.3
Widowed..	2.8	2.9	2.7
Divorced...	8.7	9.4	9.3
Females, 15 Years and Over	324,042	380,618	416,455
Never married	25.3	30.8	31.1
Now married, except separated.................................	50.9	45.3	45.1
Separated..	2.2	2.0	1.9
Widowed..	10.7	9.8	9.1
Divorced...	10.9	12.1	12.8

[1] 2020 ACS 5-Year estimates. 1-Year estimates were not released for 2020 due to the impact of COVID-19 on data collection that year.

Table DE-3. Households and Housing Characteristics

(Number, percent, dollars.)

Item	2000	2010	2020 [1]	Average annual percent change, 2010–2020
Total Households	298,736	328,765	370,953	1.8
Family households	204,590	221,233	243,012	1.4
Married-couple family	153,136	161,575	178,030	1.5
Other family	51,454	59,658	64,982	1.3
Male householder, no wife present	12,468	14,124	17,737	3.7
Female householder, no husband present	38,986	45,534	47,245	0.5
Nonfamily households	94,146	107,532	127,941	2.7
Householder living alone	74,639	86,990	104,384	2.9
Householder not living alone	19,507	20,542	23,557	2.1
Housing Characteristics				
Total housing units	343,072	406,489	438,438	1.1
Occupied housing units	298,736	328,765	370,953	1.8
Owner occupied	216,038	239,884	264,915	1.5
Renter occupied	86,698	88,881	106,038	2.8
Average household size	2.54	2.66	2.54	-0.6
Financial Characteristics				
Median gross rent of renter-occupied housing	639	952	1,150	3.0
Median monthly owner costs for housing units with a mortgage	1,101	1,569	1,591	0.2
Median value of owner-occupied housing units	130,400	243,600	258,300	0.9

[1] 2020 ACS 5-Year estimates. 1-Year estimates were not released for 2020 due to the impact of COVID-19 on data collection that year.

Table DE-4. Migration, Origin, and Language

(Number, percent.)

Characteristic	State 2016-2020 [1]	U.S. 2016-2020 [1]
Residence 1 Year Ago		
Population 1 year and over	958,478	322,943,283
Same house	88.0	86.2
Different house in the U.S.	11.6	13.2
Same county	6.7	7.7
Different county	4.9	5.5
Same state	1.1	3.2
Different state	3.8	2.3
Abroad	0.4	0.6
Place of Birth		
Native born	876,546	282,443,680
Male	48.3	49.4
Female	51.7	50.6
Foreign born	91,133	44,125,628
Male	48.5	48.6
Female	51.5	51.4
Foreign born; naturalized U.S. citizen	46,928	22,456,684
Male	45.8	46.1
Female	54.2	53.9
Foreign born; not a U.S. citizen	44,205	21,668,944
Male	51.5	51.1
Female	48.5	48.9
Entered 2010 or later	25.5	22.8
Entered 2000 to 2009	31.3	25.1
Entered before 2000	43.2	52.1
World Region of Birth, Foreign		
Foreign-born population, excluding population born at sea	91,133	44,125,628
Europe	10.2	10.8
Asia	34.1	31.3
Africa	11.3	5.4
Oceania	0.2	0.6
Latin America	42.8	50.0
North America	1.4	1.9
Language Spoken at Home and Ability to Speak English		
Population 5 years and over	912,905	306,919,116
English only	86.6	78.5
Language other than English	13.4	21.5
Speaks English less than "very well"	4.7	8.2

[1] 2020 ACS 5-Year estimates. 1-Year estimates were not released for 2020 due to the impact of COVID-19 on data collection that year.
NA = Not available.
X = Not applicable.
- = Zero or rounds to zero.

Table DE-5. Median Income and Poverty Status, 2020[1]

(Number, percent, except as noted.)

Characteristic	State		U.S.	
	Number	Percent	Number	Percent
Median Income				
Households (dollars)...	69,110	X	64,994	X
Families (dollars)	84,825	X	80,069	X
Below Poverty Level (All People)	107,641	11.4	40,910,326	12.0
Sex				
Male	45,776	10.1	18,171,512	11.6
Female	61,865	12.7	22,738,814	14.0
Age				
Under 18 years...	34,390	17.2	12,598,699	17.5
Related children under 18 years...	33,468	16.8	12,306,532	17.2
18 to 64 years..	61,671	10.9	23,554,920	12.1
65 years and over	11,580	6.5	4,756,707	9.3

X = Not applicable.
[1] 2020 ACS 5-Year estimates. 1-Year estimates were not released for 2020 due to the impact of COVID-19 on data collection that year.

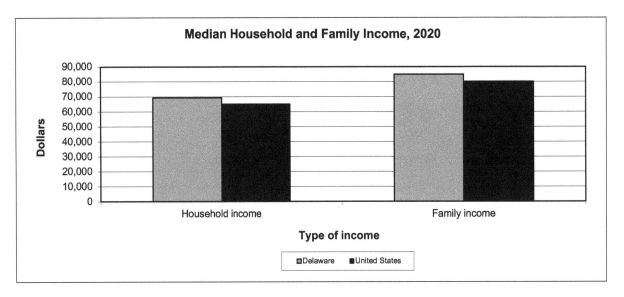

Median Household and Family Income, 2020

Table DE-6. Health Insurance Coverage Status for the Civilian Noninstitutionalized Population and Children Under 19 Years of Age

(Number, percent.)

Item	2011	2012	2013	2014	2015	2016	2017	2018	2019	2020 [2]
Civilian Noninstitutionalized Population	892132	902.915	911.502	920,930	931,203	937,935	947,259	952,211	956,378	951,930
Covered by Private or Public Insurance										
Number..	808,137	823,021	828,218	849,333	876,705	884,796	896,016	898,249	893,608	896,359
Percent...	90.6	91.2	90.9	92.2	94.1	94.3	94.6	94.3	93.4	94.2
Uninsured										
Number..	83,995	79,894	83,284	71,597	54,498	53,139	51,243	53,962	62,770	55,571
Percent...	9.4	8.8	9.1	7.8	5.9	5.7	5.4	5.7	6.6	5.8
Percent in the U.S. not covered...................................	15.1	14.8	14.5	11.7	9.4	8.6	8.7	8.9	9.2	8.7
Children Under 19 Years of Age[1]	204,295	204,494	203,339	203,414	203,771	203,704	218,473	215,130	215,399	217,221
Covered by Private or Public Insurance										
Number..	194,916	197,329	194,251	191,762	197,686	197,461	210,828	207,292	205,017	208,934
Percent...	95.4	96.5	95.5	94.3	97.0	96.9	96.5	96.4	95.2	96.2
Uninsured										
Number..	9,379	7,165	9,088	11,652	6,085	6,243	7,645	7,838	10,382	8,287
Percent...	4.6	3.5	4.5	5.7	3.0	3.1	3.5	3.6	4.8	3.8
Percent in the U.S. not covered...................................	7.5	7.2	7.1	6.0	4.8	4.5	5.0	5.2	5.7	5.2

[1] Data for years prior to 2017 are for individuals under 18 years of age.
[2] 2020 ACS 5-Year estimates. 1-Year estimates were not released for 2020 due to the impact of COVID-19 on data collection that year. Data is not comparable to previous years, which are based on 1-year estimates.

Table DE-7. Employment Status by Demographic Group, 2021

(Numbers in thousands, percent.)

Characteristic	Civilian noninstitutional population	Civilian labor force		Employed		Unemployed	
		Number	Percent of population	Number	Percent of population	Number	Percent of population
Total...	801	489	61.1	462	57.7	27	5.5
Sex							
Male..	379	251	66.1	237	62.4	14	5.5
Female	422	239	56.6	225	53.5	13	5.5
Race, Sex, and Hispanic Origin							
White	563	332	58.8	317	56.3	15	4.4
Male..	269	174	64.6	166	61.6	8	4.7
Female	294	158	53.6	151	51.4	6	4.1
Black or African American...................	178	116	65.5	106	59.9	10	8.5
Male..	80	53	66.2	48	60.2	5	9.0
Female	98	64	64.9	58	59.8	5	8.0
Hispanic or Latino ethnicity[1]	69	48	69.3	46	65.9	2	4.8
Male..	35	27	77.7	26	75.1	1	3.3
Female	34	21	60.8	19	56.6	1	6.8
Age							
16 to 19 years.................................	NA	NA	NA	NA	NA	NA	NA
20 to 24 years.................................	59	46	77.5	42	70.3	4	9.4
25 to 34 years.................................	122	103	83.9	96	78.4	7	6.7
35 to 44 years.................................	124	106	85.3	101	81.8	4	4.2
45 to 54 years.................................	107	90	83.5	85	79.2	5	5.2
55 to 64 years.................................	142	94	66.5	91	64.3	3	3.4
65 years and over	205	35	17.1	34	16.4	1	3.7

NOTE: Data in Table 7 are from the Current Population Survey (CPS) and do not match the estimates in Table 8. See notes and definitions for further information.
[1] May be of any race.
NA = Not Available

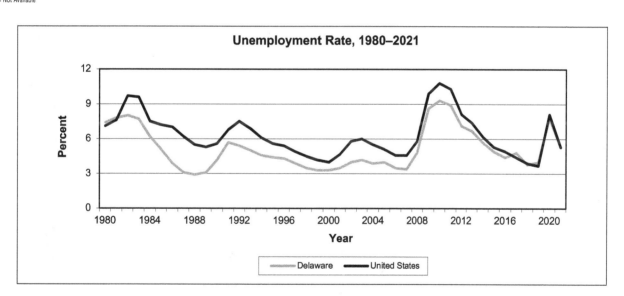

Table DE-8. Employment Status of the Civilian Noninstitutional Population Age 16 Years and Over

(Number, percent.)

Year	Civilian labor force	Civilian participation rate	Employed	Unemployed	Unemployment rate
2010...	436,196	62.2	398,388	37,808	8.7
2011...	443,971	62.4	410,229	33,742	7.6
2012...	445,962	62.0	414,489	31,473	7.1
2013...	443,551	61.0	414,215	29,336	6.6
2014...	452,712	61.4	427,400	25,312	5.6
2015...	462,752	62.0	440,555	22,197	4.8
2016...	468,808	62.1	447,640	21,168	4.5
2017...	475,214	62.2	453,949	21,265	4.5
2018...	480,154	62.1	462,143	18,011	3.8
2019...	484,845	61.9	466,856	17,989	3.7
2020...	485,813	61.2	449,114	36,699	7.6
2021...	496,430	61.7	469,875	26,555	5.3

Table DE-9. Employment and Average Wages by Industry

(Estimates are based on the 2012 North American Industry Classification System [NAICS].)

Industry	2013	2014	2015	2016	2017	2018	2019	2020
	Number of Jobs							
Wage and Salary Employment by Industry........................	441,311	450,681	459,075	464,150	466,853	472,585	478,205	452,189
Farm Wage and Salary Employment...............................	1,672	1,797	1,740	2,100	2,022	1,549	1,423	1,198
Nonfarm Wage and Salary Employment..........................	439,639	448,884	457,335	462,050	464,831	471,036	476,782	450,991
Private wage and salary employment.......................................	365,494	374,768	384,132	388,238	390,629	396,869	401,749	376,787
Forestry, fishing, and related activities.............................	(D)	(D)	(D)	(D)	(D)	(D)	(D)	526
Mining..	(D)	(D)	(D)	(D)	(D)	(D)	(D)	70
Utilities..	2,086	2,148	2,158	2,156	2,194	2,124	2,073	2,058
Construction	20,104	20,893	21,283	21,484	22,274	22,717	23,450	22,955
Manufacturing...	25,379	25,713	27,070	25,749	25,777	27,090	27,313	25,582
Durable goods manufacturing...	9,428	9,198	9,370	9,325	9,321	9,557	9,838	9,312
Nondurable goods manufacturing..................................	15,951	16,515	17,700	16,424	16,456	17,533	17,475	16,270
Wholesale trade	12,254	12,028	11,850	11,915	10,901	10,770	11,023	10,873
Retail trade..	51,840	52,732	53,335	54,029	53,774	53,581	52,164	48,177
Transportation and warehousing.....................................	11,680	12,910	14,433	14,703	14,371	14,460	15,788	16,692
Information	5,259	4,893	4,724	4,614	4,557	4,064	3,907	3,617
Finance and insurance	39,224	40,628	42,034	42,412	43,259	43,170	43,639	43,119
Real estate and rental and leasing...................................	5,619	5,359	5,455	5,581	5,552	5,549	5,763	5,716
Professional, scientific, and technical services	28,704	29,138	28,700	25,828	25,930	27,002	26,298	25,566
Management of companies and enterprises.........................	5,968	5,498	4,888	8,654	8,305	7,652	8,038	8,429
Administrative and waste services	23,886	25,469	26,699	27,155	28,027	29,188	29,754	28,353
Educational services	6,734	6,951	6,807	6,814	6,850	6,809	6,928	6,096
Health care and social assistance......................................	61,952	64,096	66,848	68,691	69,809	71,586	72,969	70,615
Arts, entertainment, and recreation...................................	9,730	10,261	10,202	10,020	10,247	9,307	10,047	7,656
Accommodation and food services....................................	36,328	37,252	38,776	39,780	40,191	42,746	43,334	33,938
Other services, except public administration........................	18,082	18,132	18,171	17,968	17,987	18,380	18,631	16,749
Government and government enterprises.................................	74,145	74,116	73,203	73,812	74,202	74,167	75,033	74,204
	Dollars							
Average Wages and Salaries by Industry	51,204	52,400	53,319	53,090	55,134	56,270	57,944	61,689
Average Farm Wages and Salaries	25,308	24,949	21,048	20,014	18,864	23,626	20,421	23,558
Average Nonfarm Wages and Salaries	51,302	52,510	53,442	53,241	55,292	56,378	58,056	61,791
Average private wages and salaries..	51,925	53,225	54,024	53,664	55,837	56,828	58,566	62,538
Forestry, fishing, and related activities.............................	(D)	(D)	(D)	(D)	(D)	(D)	(D)	37,561
Mining..	(D)	(D)	(D)	(D)	(D)	(D)	(D)	58,886
Utilities..	98,745	104,323	106,632	108,019	112,877	114,365	120,205	124,236
Construction	53,046	53,826	55,137	56,708	59,142	59,809	62,496	64,953
Manufacturing...	57,904	59,590	64,072	59,925	62,019	64,163	66,193	67,968
Durable goods manufacturing...	68,272	70,859	71,350	69,125	71,670	73,423	74,171	74,586
Nondurable goods manufacturing..................................	51,775	53,313	60,219	54,702	56,552	59,116	61,702	64,180
Wholesale trade	79,102	83,268	79,874	80,225	72,552	74,382	76,004	80,608
Retail trade..	26,439	27,181	28,290	28,453	28,844	29,597	30,784	33,732
Transportation and warehousing.....................................	45,486	46,350	46,374	45,770	47,972	50,251	50,656	50,513
Information	61,110	62,356	63,640	64,959	64,658	65,758	69,948	78,944
Finance and insurance	89,500	91,004	91,800	92,870	97,349	100,827	102,625	108,659
Real estate and rental and leasing...................................	42,687	44,534	46,197	47,648	49,847	52,304	55,445	59,119
Professional, scientific, and technical services	94,591	100,162	107,091	93,242	101,410	100,675	106,895	112,065
Management of companies and enterprises.........................	143,251	143,788	115,525	128,572	154,953	152,781	153,030	140,371
Administrative and waste services	33,748	35,343	36,623	37,228	39,067	41,829	42,491	45,790
Educational services	39,156	41,294	41,321	40,943	40,990	41,766	41,780	47,574
Health care and social assistance......................................	49,862	50,998	51,986	52,299	53,505	54,174	55,679	57,711
Arts, entertainment, and recreation...................................	27,721	27,057	27,177	27,852	27,891	27,011	26,877	29,274
Accommodation and food services....................................	18,917	19,488	20,220	20,872	21,212	22,574	23,694	22,892
Other services, except public administration........................	32,571	33,288	34,261	35,257	35,979	36,870	38,227	41,081
Government and government enterprises.................................	48,233	48,890	50,389	51,015	52,421	53,968	55,326	57,993

(D) = Not shown to avoid disclosure of confidential information; estimates are included in higher-level totals.

Table DE-10. Employment Characteristics by Family Type

(Number, percent.)

Family type and labor force status	2018		2019		2020 [1]	
	Total	Families with own children under 18 years	Total	Families with own children under 18 years	Total	Families with own children under 18 years
All Families...	238,399	89,176	242,584	86,583	243,012	90,822
FAMILY TYPE AND LABOR FORCE STATUS						
Opposite-Sex Married-Couple Families........................	173,834	56,840	177,794	54,679	175,257	57,394
Both husband and wife in labor force..................................	48.3	72.8	47.2	71.9	49.2	70.4
Husband in labor force, wife not in labor force	18.4	22.9	18.8	23.2	19.6	25.0
Wife in labor force, husband not in labor force	8.1	3.3	8.3	3.4	8.0	3.1
Both husband and wife not in labor force...........................	23.5	0.5	23.9	1.2	23.2	1.4
Other Families	64,565	32,336	64,790	31,904	64,982	33,166
Female householder, no spouse present	71.8	73.1	69.4	69.7	72.7	74.0
In labor force..	50.2	61.5	50.2	58.8	53.2	64.9
Not in labor force	21.6	11.6	19.2	10.9	19.5	9.1
Male householder, no spouse present.................................	28.2	26.9	30.6	30.3	27.3	26.0
In labor force..	23.1	25.1	24.7	28.2	21.5	24.2
Not in labor force	5.1	1.8	5.9	2.1	5.8	1.8

[1] 2020 ACS 5-Year estimates. 1-Year estimates were not released for 2020 due to the impact of COVID-19 on data collection that year. Data is not comparable to previous years, which are based on 1-year estimates.

Table DE-11. School Enrollment and Educational Attainment, 2020[1]

(Number, percent.)

Item	State	U.S.
Enrollment		
Total population 3 years and over, enrolled in school	225,882	80,497,960
Enrolled in nursery school or preschool (percent)	5.9	6.1
Enrolled in kindergarten (percent)...	4.7	5.0
Enrolled in elementary school, grades 1-8 (percent)..	40.3	40.4
Enrolled in high school, grades 9-12 (percent)...	20.6	21.0
Enrolled in college or graduate school (percent)..	28.5	27.6
Attainment		
Total population 25 years and over	679,870	222,836,834
Less than ninth grade (percent)	3.3	4.9
9th to 12th grade, no diploma (percent)	6.1	6.6
High school graduate, including equivalency (percent)..	31	26.7
Some college, no degree (percent)	18.9	20.3
Associate's degree (percent)...	8.0	8.6
Bachelor's degree (percent)	19.0	20.2
Graduate or professional degree (percent)...	13.7	12.7
High school graduate or higher (percent)	90.6	88.5
Bachelor's degree or higher (percent)...	32.7	32.9

[1] 2020 ACS 5-Year estimates. 1-Year estimates were not released for 2020 due to the impact of COVID-19 on data collection that year.

Table DE-12. Public School Characteristics and Educational Indicators

(Number, percent; data derived from National Center of Education Statistics.)

Item	State	U.S.
Public Elementary and Secondary Schools		
Number of regular school districts, 2018-19..	19	13,452
Number of operational schools, 2019-20..	222	98,469
Percent charter schools	9.9	7.7
Total public school enrollment, Fall 2019...	139,930	50,796,445
Percent charter school enrollment	11.7	6.8
Student-teacher ratio, Fall 2019..	14.4	15.9
Expenditures per student (unadjusted dollars), 2018-19	15,929	13,187
Four-year adjusted cohort graduation rate (ACGR), 2018-2019[1]...	89.0	85.8
Students eligible for free or reduced-price lunch (percent), 2019-20..	28.3	52.1
English language learners (percent), Fall 2019	11.1	10.4
Students age 3 to 21 served under IDEA, part B (percent), 2020-21	17.9	14.5

Public Schools by Type, 2019-20	Number	Percent of state public schools
Total number of schools..	222	100.0
Special education	19	8.6
Vocational education	6	2.7
Alternative education..	5	2.3

[1] Adjusted Cohort Graduation Rates (ACGR) differ from Averaged Freshmen Graduation Rates (AFGR).

Table DE-13. Reported Voting and Registration of the Voting-Age Population, November 2020

(Numbers in thousands, percent.)

Item	Total population	Total citizen population	Registered			Voted		
			Total registered	Percent registered (total population)	Percent registered (total citizen population)	Total voted	Percent voted (total population)	Percent voted (total citizen population)
U.S. Total	252,274	231,593	168,308	66.7	72.7	154,628	61.3	66.8
State Total..................................	766	722	542	70.8	75.1	489	63.8	67.7
Sex								
Male	361	339	247	68.3	72.8	223	61.6	65.7
Female	404	383	296	73.1	77.2	266	65.8	69.5
Race								
White alone...............................	540	519	392	72.6	75.5	348	64.4	67.0
White, non-Hispanic alone	495	490	378	76.3	77.1	335	67.8	68.4
Black alone	172	164	114	66.6	69.8	106	61.7	64.7
Asian alone	31	21	18	B	B	18	B	B
Hispanic (of any race).....................	57	37	22	B	B	20	B	B
White alone or in combination........	554	531	404	73.0	76.1	359	64.8	67.6
Black alone or in combination.............	181	171	121	67.2	70.9	112	62.0	65.3
Asian alone or in combination.............	36	26	23	B	B	23	B	B
Age								
18 to 24 years.............................	84	81	54	64.9	67.2	43	51.8	53.6
25 to 34 years.............................	119	104	71	59.7	68.5	58	49.0	56.2
35 to 44 years.............................	113	102	79	69.9	77.6	71	62.8	69.7
45 to 64 years.............................	257	245	183	71.4	74.7	168	65.6	68.6
65 years and over	192	189	154	79.9	81.4	147	76.4	77.8

B = Base is less than 75,000 and therefore too small to show the derived measure.

Table DE-14. Crime

(Number, rate per 100,000. Data are derived from the FBI Uniform Crime Reports.)

Item	State			U.S.		
	2019	2020	Percent change	2019	2020	Percent change
TOTAL POPULATION[1]	976,668	986,809	1.0	328,329,953	329,484,123	0.4
VIOLENT CRIME						
Number..	4,128	4,262	3.2	1,250,393	1,313,105	5.0
Rate..	422.7	431.9	2.2	380.8	398.5	4.6
Murder and Nonnegligent Manslaughter						
Number..	47	73	55.3	16,669	21,570	29.4
Rate..	4.8	7.4	53.7	5.1	6.5	28.9
Rape[2]						
Number..	329	261	-20.7	143,224	126,430	-11.7
Rate..	33.7	26.4	-21.5	43.6	38.4	-12.0
Robbery						
Number..	789	700	-11.3	268,483	243,600	-9.3
Rate..	80.8	70.9	-12.2	81.8	73.9	-9.6
Aggravated Assault						
Number..	2,963	3,228	8.9	822,017	921,505	12.1
Rate..	303.4	327.1	7.8	250.4	279.7	11.7
PROPERTY CRIME						
Number..	21,932	19,355	-11.7	6,995,235	6,452,038	-7.8
Rate..	2,245.6	1,961.4	-12.7	2,130.6	1,958.2	-8.1
Burglary						
Number..	2,984	2,508	-16.0	1,118,096	1,035,314	-7.4
Rate..	305.5	254.2	-16.8	340.5	314.2	-7.7
Larceny-Theft						
Number..	17,343	15,182	-12.5	5,152,267	4,606,324	-10.6
Rate..	1,775.7	1,538.5	-13.4	1,569.2	1,398.0	-10.9
Motor Vehicle Theft						
Number..	1,605	1,665	3.7	724,872	810,400	11.8
Rate..	164.3	168.7	2.7	220.8	246.0	11.4

NOTE: Although arson data are included in the trend and clearance tables, sufficient data are not available to estimate totals for this offense. Therefore, no arson data are published in this table.
- = Zero or rounds to zero.
[1] Population figures are U.S. Census Bureau provisional estimates as of July 1, 2020.
[2] The figures shown in the rape (revised definition) column were estimated using the revised Uniform Crime Reporting (UCR) definition of rape.

Table DE-15. State Government Finances, 2020

(Dollar amounts in thousands, percent distribution.)

Item	Dollars	Percent distribution
Total Revenue	12,605,385	100.0
General revenue	11,110,002	88.1
Intergovernmental revenue	4,309,043	34.2
Taxes	4,554,943	36.1
General sales	0	-
Selective sales	585,504	4.6
License taxes	1,851,086	14.7
Individual income tax	1685848	13.4
Corporate income tax	244,913	1.9
Other taxes	187,592	1.5
Current charges	1,089,628	8.6
Miscellaneous general revenue	1,156,388	9.2
Utility revenue	17,549	0.1
Liquor stores revenue	0	-
Insurance trust revenue[1]	1,477,834	11.7
Total Expenditure	11,273,304	100.0
Intergovernmental expenditure	2,015,484	17.9
Direct expenditure	9,257,820	82.1
Current operation	6,748,363	59.9
Capital outlay	914,896	8.1
Insurance benefits and repayments	954,394	8.5
Assistance and subsidies	401,682	3.6
Interest on debt	238,485	2.1
Exhibit: Salaries and wages	1,625,290	14.4
Total Expenditure	11,273,304	100.0
General expenditure	10,139,134	89.9
Intergovernmental expenditure	2,015,484	17.9
Direct expenditure	8,123,650	72.1
General expenditure, by function:		
Education	3,989,561	35.4
Public welfare	2,822,193	25.0
Hospitals	79,929	0.7
Health	483,562	4.3
Highways	567,258	5.0
Police protection	161,586	1.4
Correction	362,801	3.2
Natural resources	78,848	0.7
Parks and recreation	64,400	0.6
Governmental administration	609,154	5.4
Interest on general debt	238,485	2.1
Other and unallocable	658,181	5.8
Utility expenditure	179,910	1.4
Liquor stores expenditure	0	-
Insurance trust expenditure	954,394	8.5
Debt at End of Fiscal Year	5,068,699	X
Cash and Security Holdings	19,015,141	X

X = Not applicable.
- = Zero or rounds to zero.
[1] Within insurance trust revenue, net earnings of state retirement systems is a calculated statistic (the item code in the data file is X08), and thus can be positive or negative. Net earnings is the sum of earnings on investments plus gains on investments minus losses on investments. The change made in 2002 for asset valuation from book to market value in accordance with Statement 34 of the Governmental Accounting Standards Board is reflected in the calculated statistics.

Table DE-16. State Government Tax Collections, 2021

(Dollars in thousands, percent.)

Item	Dollars	Percent distribution
Total Taxes	5,395,712	100.0
Property taxes	X	-
Sales and gross receipts	587,923	10.9
General sales and gross receipts	X	-
Selective sales and gross receipts	587,923	10.9
Alcoholic beverages	32,719	0.6
Amusements	X	-
Insurance premiums	123,324	2.3
Motor fuels	124,842	2.3
Pari-mutuels	39	-
Public utilities	45,518	0.8
Tobacco products	115,700	2.1
Other selective sales	145,781	2.7
Licenses	2,076,828	38.5
Alcoholic beverages	1,693	-
Amusements	333	-
Corporations in general	1,822,622	33.8
Hunting and fishing	4,492	0.1
Motor vehicle	62,180	1.2
Motor vehicle operators	8,379	0.2
Public utilities	550	-
Occupation and business, NEC	161,821	3.0
Other licenses	14758	0.3
Income taxes	2,483,094	46.0
Individual income	2,148,289	39.8
Corporation net income	334,805	6.2
Other taxes	247,867	4.6
Death and gift	2	-
Documentary and stock transfer	246,549	4.6
Severance	2	-
Taxes, NEC	1314	-

X = Not applicable.
- = Zero or rounds to zero.

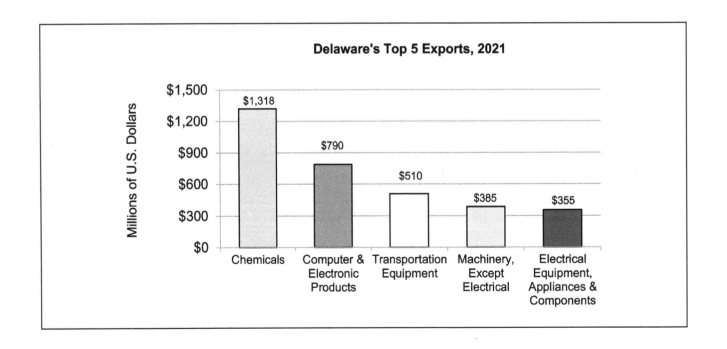

Delaware's Top 5 Exports, 2021

DISTRICT OF COLUMBIA

Facts and Figures

Location: South Atlantic United States; bordered on the SE, NE, and NW by Maryland and on the SW by Virginia

Area: 68 sq. mi.

Population: 670,050 (2021 est.); rank—49th

Official Motto: Justitia omnibus ("Justice for All")

U.S. Congress: 1 delegate

Abbreviation: D.C.

Symbols: flower—American beauty rose; tree—scarlet oak; bird—wood thrush

At a Glance

- The District of Columbia saw an increase in population of 11.4 percent from 2010 to 2021, but its population decreased 2.9 percent from the year 2020 to 2021.

- In 2021, the District of Columbia had the 4th lowest percentage of people under 18 years of age (18.8 percent). It also had the 2nd lowest percentage of people 65 years and older (12.8 percent).

- The violent crime rate in the District of Columbia was the highest in the nation, at 999.8 per 100,000 population in 2020. This was more than twice the national violent crime rate of 398.5 per 100,000. The District of Columbia also had the highest property crime rate in the country (3,493.0 per 100,000 population).

- The District of Columbia had the highest median household income in the United States ($90,842) and ranked 8th for the percent of residents below the poverty level (15.5 percent) in 2020. It ranked 5th for percent of children under 18 years of age in poverty (22.8 percent).

Table DC-1. Population by Age, Sex, Race, and Hispanic Origin

(Number, percent, except where noted.)

Sex, age, race, and Hispanic origin	2000	2010	2021	Percent change, 2010–2021
Total Population...	572,059	601,723	670,050	11.4
Percent of total U.S. population	0.2	0.2	0.2	X
Sex				
Male...	269,366	284,222	318,904	12.2
Female..	302,693	317,501	351,146	10.6
Age				
Under 5 years..	32,536	32,613	40,759	25.0
5 to 19 years...	103,270	91,107	104,951	15.2
20 to 64 years..	366,355	409,194	438,502	7.2
65 years and over	69,898	68,809	85,838	24.7
Median age (years)...	34.8	33.8	34.9	3.3
Race and Hispanic Origin				
One race				
White	176,101	251,265	307,274	22.3
Black..	343,312	310,379	306,925	-1.1
American Indian and Alaska Native	1,713	3,264	4,067	24.6
Asian..	15,189	21,705	30,342	39.8
Native Hawaiian or Other Pacific Islander	348	770	1,063	38.1
Two or more races	13,446	14,340	20,379	42.1
Hispanic (of any race)..	44,953	57,833	76,919	33.0

NOTE: Population figures for 2021 are July 1 estimates. The 2000 and 2010 estimates are taken from the respective censuses.
- = Zero or rounds to zero.
X = Not applicable.

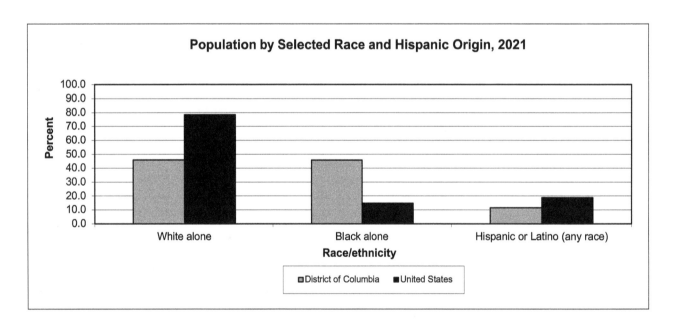

Table DC-2. Marital Status

(Number, percent distribution.)

Sex, age, race, and Hispanic origin	2000	2010	2020 [1]
Males, 15 Years and Over	219,706	243,152	277,237
Never married	51.2	58.9	58.0
Now married, except separated..............................	32.8	28.2	32.1
Separated..	3.9	2.4	1.7
Widowed...	3.4	2.1	1.4
Divorced...	8.7	8.4	6.8
Females, 15 Years and Over	254,711	277,203	314,312
Never married	46.0	55.8	56.2
Now married, except separated..............................	27.5	22.8	26.5
Separated..	4.4	3.1	2.0
Widowed...	11.6	7.5	5.9
Divorced...	10.6	10.8	9.5

[1] 2020 ACS 5-Year estimates. 1-Year estimates were not released for 2020 due to the impact of COVID-19 on data collection that year.

Table DC-3. Households and Housing Characteristics

(Number, percent, dollars.)

Item	2000	2010	2020 [1]	Average annual percent change, 2010–2020
Total Households...	248,338	252,388	288,307	2.0
Family households	114,166	101,519	123,496	3.1
Married-couple family	56,631	57,275	75,305	4.5
Other family	57,535	44,244	48,191	1.3
Male householder, no wife present.................................	10,503	8,740	9,808	1.7
Female householder, no husband present.......................	47,032	35,504	38,383	1.2
Nonfamily households	134,172	150,869	164,811	1.3
Householder living alone..	108,744	121,036	130,042	1.1
Householder not living alone..	25,428	29,833	34,769	2.4
Housing Characteristics				
Total housing units...	274,845	296,836	319,192	1.1
Occupied housing units	248,338	252,388	288,307	2.0
Owner occupied	101,214	107,193	122,648	2.1
Renter occupied	147,124	145,195	165,659	2.0
Average household size...	2.16	2.24	2.30	0.4
Financial Characteristics				
Median gross rent of renter-occupied housing	618	1,198	1,607	4.9
Median monthly owner costs for housing units with a mortgage	1,291	2,297	2,676	2.4
Median value of owner-occupied housing units.......................	157,200	426,900	618,100	6.4

[1] 2020 ACS 5-Year estimates. 1-Year estimates were not released for 2020 due to the impact of COVID-19 on data collection that year.

Table DC-4. Migration, Origin, and Language

(Number, percent.)

Characteristic	State 2016-2020 [1]	U.S. 2016-2020 [1]
Residence 1 Year Ago		
Population 1 year and over	693,253	322,943,283
Same house	80.7	86.2
Different house in the U.S.	17.9	13.2
Same county	9.7	7.7
Different county	8.2	5.5
Same state	-	3.2
Different state	8.2	2.3
Abroad	1.5	0.6
Place of Birth		
Native born	607,781	282,443,680
Male	47.5	49.4
Female	52.5	50.6
Foreign born	94,193	44,125,628
Male	47.5	48.6
Female	52.5	51.4
Foreign born; naturalized U.S. citizen..	42,945	22,456,684
Male	43.6	46.1
Female	56.4	53.9
Foreign born; not a U.S. citizen..	51,248	21,668,944
Male	50.8	51.1
Female	49.2	48.9
Entered 2010 or later	30.7	22.8
Entered 2000 to 2009	27.4	25.1
Entered before 2000..	41.8	52.1
World Region of Birth, Foreign		
Foreign-born population, excluding population born at sea	94,193	44,125,628
Europe	17.8	10.8
Asia..	22.1	31.3
Africa...	14.9	5.4
Oceania	0.9	0.6
Latin America...	41.9	50.0
North America...	2.4	1.9
Language Spoken at Home and Ability to Speak English		
Population 5 years and over..	657,061	306,919,116
English only	82.8	78.5
Language other than English..	17.2	21.5
Speaks English less than "very well"...	5.7	8.2

[1] 2020 ACS 5-Year estimates. 1-Year estimates were not released for 2020 due to the impact of COVID-19 on data collection that year.
NA = Not available.
X = Not applicable.
- = Zero or rounds to zero.

Table DC-5. Median Income and Poverty Status, 2020[1]

(Number, percent, except as noted.)

Characteristic	State		U.S.	
	Number	Percent	Number	Percent
Median Income				
Households (dollars)..	90,842	X	64,994	X
Families (dollars)	120,337	X	80,069	X
Below Poverty Level (All People)	103,391	15.5	40,910,326	12.8
Sex				
Male	45,274	14.3	18,171,512	11.6
Female	58,117	16.5	22,738,814	14.0
Age				
Under 18 years...	28,347	22.8	12,598,699	17.5
Related children under 18 years...	28,055	22.7	12,306,532	17.2
18 to 64 years..	63,622	13.8	23,554,920	12.1
65 years and over	11,422	13.7	4,756,707	9.3

X = Not applicable.
[1] 2020 ACS 5-Year estimates. 1-Year estimates were not released for 2020 due to the impact of COVID-19 on data collection that year.

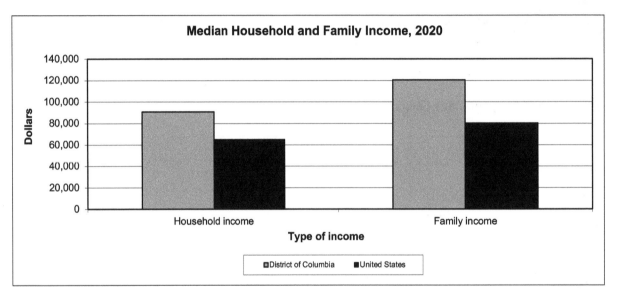

Median Household and Family Income, 2020

Table DC-6. Health Insurance Coverage Status for the Civilian Noninstitutionalized Population and Children Under 19 Years of Age

(Number, percent.)

Item	2011	2012	2013	2014	2015	2016	2017	2018	2019	2020 [2]
Civilian Noninstitutionalized Population	608,165	621,380	635,833	647,966	660,682	670,985	683,808	692,817	696,599	692,059
Covered by Private or Public Insurance										
Number...	566,158	584,526	593,538	613,778	635,702	644,639	657,797	670,920	672,093	666,771
Percent...	93.1	94.1	93.3	94.7	96.2	96.1	96.2	96.8	96.5	96.3
Uninsured										
Number...	42,007	36,854	42,295	34,188	24,980	26,346	26,011	21,897	24,506	25,288
Percent...	6.9	5.9	6.7	5.3	3.8	3.9	3.8	3.2	3.5	3.7
Percent in the U.S. not covered..............................	15.1	14.8	14.5	11.7	9.4	8.6	8.7	8.9	9.2	8.7
Children Under 19 Years of Age[1]	105,312	109,182	111,287	114,834	117,415	120,313	133,635	137,437	138,489	136,567
Covered by Private or Public Insurance										
Number...	101,179	107,312	108,657	112,449	115,609	116,572	132,060	135,008	135,665	133,898
Percent...	96.1	98.3	97.6	97.9	98.5	96.9	98.8	98.2	98.0	98.0
Uninsured										
Number...	4,133	1,870	2,630	2,385	1,806	3,741	1,575	2,429	2,824	2,669
Percent...	3.9	1.7	2.4	2.1	1.5	3.1	1.2	1.8	2.0	2.0
Percent in the U.S. not covered..............................	7.5	7.2	7.1	6.0	4.8	4.5	5.0	5.2	5.7	5.2

[1] Data for years prior to 2017 are for individuals under 18 years of age.
[2] 2020 ACS 5-Year estimates. 1-Year estimates were not released for 2020 due to the impact of COVID-19 on data collection that year. Data is not comparable to previous years, which are based on 1-year estimates.

Table DC-7. Employment Status by Demographic Group, 2021

(Numbers in thousands, percent.)

Characteristic	Civilian noninstitutional population	Civilian labor force		Employed		Unemployed	
		Number	Percent of population	Number	Percent of population	Number	Percent of population
Total..	585	405	69.2	380	65.0	25	6.1
Sex							
Male..	271	199	73.3	188	69.1	11	5.6
Female...	314	206	65.8	193	61.5	14	6.6
Race, Sex, and Hispanic Origin							
White...	283	228	80.5	221	78.0	7	3.1
Male...	140	118	84.0	115	81.6	3	2.8
Female..	143	110	77.1	106	74.5	4	3.3
Black or African American....................	255	143	56.2	127	49.7	17	11.6
Male...	111	66	59.1	58	52.4	7	11.3
Female..	144	78	53.9	69	47.5	9	11.9
Hispanic or Latino ethnicity[1]...............	55	39	71.1	36	65.8	3	7.5
Male...	25	19	73.8	17	68.3	1	7.4
Female..	30	20	68.8	19	63.6	2	7.6
Age							
16 to 19 years..................................	NA	NA	NA	NA	NA	NA	NA
20 to 24 years..................................	53	37	69.2	33	62.0	4	10.1
25 to 34 years..................................	159	138	86.6	130	81.8	8	5.6
35 to 44 years..................................	121	104	86.4	100	82.6	5	4.3
45 to 54 years..................................	70	56	80.5	53	75.9	3	5.7
55 to 64 years..................................	68	43	63.6	40	59.0	3	7.2
65 years and over..............................	93	22	23.5	21	22.1	1	6.0

NOTE: Data in Table 7 are from the Current Population Survey (CPS) and do not match the estimates in Table 8. See notes and definitions for further information.
[1] May be of any race.
NA = Not available.

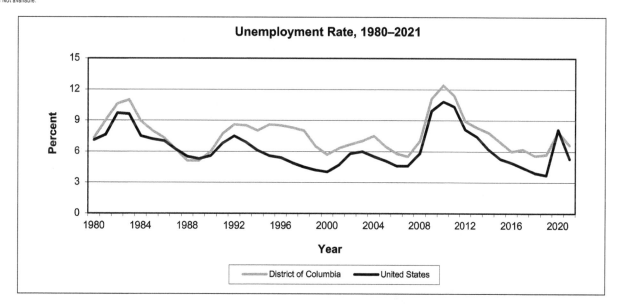

Table DC-8. Employment Status of the Civilian Noninstitutional Population Age 16 Years and Over

(Number, percent.)

Year	Civilian labor force	Civilian participation rate	Employed	Unemployed	Unemployment rate
2010..	346,707	68.9	312,132	34,575	10.0
2011..	352,193	68.1	316,372	35,821	10.2
2012..	365,176	69.1	332,412	32,764	9.0
2013..	374,199	69.4	342,609	31,590	8.4
2014..	379,678	69.3	350,415	29,263	7.7
2015..	388,446	69.7	361,556	26,890	6.9
2016..	395,124	69.9	370,553	24,571	6.2
2017..	393,326	70.5	369,388	23,938	6.1
2018..	396,039	70.5	373,772	22,267	5.6
2019..	400,577	71.1	379,016	21,561	5.4
2020..	389,384	69.2	358,370	31,014	8.0
2021..	381,673	69.8	356,578	25,095	6.6

Table DC-9. Employment and Average Wages by Industry

(Estimates are based on the 2012 North American Industry Classification System [NAICS].)

Industry	2013	2014	2015	2016	2017	2018	2019	2020
					Number of Jobs			
Wage and Salary Employment by Industry........................	758,641	767,130	775,658	788,013	793,524	801,650	806,196	754,454
Farm Wage and Salary Employment.............................	0	0	0	0	0	0	0	0
Nonfarm Wage and Salary Employment.........................	758,641	767,130	775,658	788,013	793,524	801,650	806,196	754,454
Private wage and salary employment...	505,628	515,390	527,234	537,330	543,372	552,662	557,885	503,967
Forestry, fishing, and related activities	0	0	0	0	0	0	0	0
Mining..	0	0	0	0	0	0	0	0
Utilities..	1,891	1,920	2,004	1,998	2,028	2,037	1,988	(D)
Construction	14,450	14,679	15,019	15,762	(D)	15,981	15,187	15,377
Manufacturing...	1,008	1,031	1,104	1,218	(D)	1,337	1,331	(D)
Durable goods manufacturing.......................................	441	418	456	542	(D)	512	487	(D)
Nondurable goods manufacturing.................................	567	613	648	676	(D)	825	844	648
Wholesale trade	4,868	4,934	4,874	5,035	4,948	4,866	5,136	4,942
Retail trade..	20,212	21,465	22,636	23,084	23,489	23,243	23,237	20,167
Transportation and warehousing......................................	3,780	3,938	4,435	4,397	4,643	4,775	4,361	3,415
Information...	17,059	17,245	17,190	17,058	17,853	19,204	20,009	19,802
Finance and insurance	14,818	15,137	15,157	14,986	15,142	15,295	15,309	15,024
Real estate and rental and leasing	11,057	11,988	12,280	12,609	12,708	12,846	13,245	12,961
Professional, scientific, and technical services	108,658	109,564	113,169	115,828	117,328	119,770	121,879	122,476
Management of companies and enterprises........................	2,046	2,157	2,148	2,434	2,770	2,619	2,739	2,865
Administrative and waste services	46,399	46,928	48,013	48,184	47,528	46,808	47,437	42,660
Educational services	55,898	56,763	56,811	57,552	56,729	55,484	55,016	51,586
Health care and social assistance...................................	64,578	65,113	66,150	68,204	68,973	70,230	70,349	67,874
Arts, entertainment, and recreation.................................	6,994	7,501	7,757	8,397	9,156	9,579	10,072	6,400
Accommodation and food services...................................	61,256	62,993	65,735	66,657	68,005	70,567	71,969	41,219
Other services, except public administration........................	70,656	72,034	72,752	73,927	75,133	78,021	78,621	74,203
Government and government enterprises............................	253,013	251,740	248,424	250,683	250,152	248,988	248,311	250,487
					Dollars			
Average Wages and Salaries by Industry	81,981	84,301	87,230	88,771	91,720	95,266	97,321	106,107
Average Farm Wages and Salaries	0	0	0	0	0	0	0	0
Average Nonfarm Wages and Salaries	81,981	84,301	87,230	88,771	91,720	95,266	97,321	106,107
Average private wages and salaries..................................	76,130	78,350	81,005	82,164	85,094	88,336	90,973	101,744
Forestry, fishing, and related activities..............................	0	0	0	0	0	0	0	0
Mining..	0	0	0	0	0	0	0	0
Utilities..	98,332	98,384	103,130	107,138	112,671	130,476	121,342	(D)
Construction	62,917	65,118	63,558	63,956	(D)	71,819	73,546	77,243
Manufacturing..	109,943	95,381	95,827	93,412	(D)	93,049	89,545	(D)
Durable goods manufacturing.......................................	83,778	82,557	91,037	96,915	(D)	120,020	116,008	(D)
Nondurable goods manufacturing.................................	130,295	104,126	99,198	90,604	(D)	76,312	74,276	88,514
Wholesale trade	116,530	120,472	121,059	117,984	123,920	124,883	138,833	154,289
Retail trade..	33,264	33,259	33,784	35,894	36,001	37,909	38,660	42,685
Transportation and warehousing......................................	73,687	76,131	75,677	78,164	75,769	74,468	78,546	94,768
Information...	122,427	120,673	121,514	126,473	131,082	133,919	139,011	166,723
Finance and insurance	148,745	156,450	167,244	171,256	179,061	185,860	189,697	195,835
Real estate and rental and leasing	80,027	94,266	94,226	94,846	104,188	107,756	110,924	112,653
Professional, scientific, and technical services	122,637	126,655	128,788	131,857	135,788	141,229	144,522	152,415
Management of companies and enterprises........................	219,007	232,866	297,382	222,637	215,427	248,596	253,012	280,397
Administrative and waste services	48,390	49,074	51,283	50,649	52,521	53,081	54,872	61,316
Educational services	47,291	48,006	50,042	50,840	52,272	55,282	56,746	62,452
Health care and social assistance...................................	57,758	60,404	62,661	62,653	63,999	65,385	67,561	72,246
Arts, entertainment, and recreation.................................	54,688	57,353	82,527	76,579	86,288	89,625	87,546	89,616
Accommodation and food services...................................	33,531	34,457	35,685	36,833	37,848	39,425	41,008	37,521
Other services, except public administration........................	81,565	83,422	86,877	88,936	90,897	93,416	96,012	104,495
Government and government enterprises............................	93,673	96,486	100,441	102,932	106,114	110,648	111,583	114,885

(D) = Not shown to avoid disclosure of confidential information; estimates are included in higher-level totals.

Table DC-10. Employment Characteristics by Family Type

(Number, percent.)

Family type and labor force status	2018		2019		2020 [1]	
	Total	Families with own children under 18 years	Total	Families with own children under 18 years	Total	Families with own children under 18 years
All Families...	121,529	50,501	124,978	47,438	123,496	50,882
FAMILY TYPE AND LABOR FORCE STATUS						
Opposite-Sex Married-Couple Families.............................	73,009	26,405	78,331	25,730	70,719	27,992
Both husband and wife in labor force................................	64.7	81.3	63.1	76.7	66.8	79.4
Husband in labor force, wife not in labor force	11.5	14.2	13.6	15.7	14.0	17.0
Wife in labor force, husband not in labor force........................	6.7	1.9	7.2	3.9	7.8	2.2
Both husband and wife not in labor force.............................	11.3	0.9	10.6	1.3	11.5	1.3
Other Families	48,520	24,096	46,647	21,708	48,191	22,389
Female householder, no spouse present	79.0	81.5	81.7	82.5	79.6	82.7
In labor force..	50.8	67.7	54.4	74.8	51.6	67.4
Not in labor force..	28.2	13.7	27.3	7.7	28.1	15.3
Male householder, no spouse present.................................	21.0	18.5	18.3	17.5	20.4	17.3
In labor force..	16.3	15.7	13.3	14.9	16.3	14.9
Not in labor force..	4.7	2.8	4.9	2.6	4.1	2.4

[1] 2020 ACS 5-Year estimates. 1-Year estimates were not released for 2020 due to the impact of COVID-19 on data collection that year. Data is not comparable to previous years, which are based on 1-year estimates.

Table DC-11. School Enrollment and Educational Attainment, 2020[1]

(Number, percent.)

Item	District	U.S.
Enrollment		
Total population 3 years and over, enrolled in school	168,035	80,497,960
Enrolled in nursery school or preschool (percent)..	8.9	6.1
Enrolled in kindergarten (percent)..	5.0	5.0
Enrolled in elementary school, grades 1-8 (percent)...	29.9	40.4
Enrolled in high school, grades 9-12 (percent)...	13.5	21.0
Enrolled in college or graduate school (percent)..	42.7	27.6
Attainment		
Total population 25 years and over	501,986	222,836,834
Less than ninth grade (percent)...	3.3	4.9
9th to 12th grade, no diploma (percent)...	4.8	6.6
High school graduate, including equivalency (percent)..	16.6	26.7
Some college, no degree (percent)	12.6	20.3
Associate's degree (percent)...	2.9	8.6
Bachelor's degree (percent)	25.3	20.2
Graduate or professional degree (percent)...	34.5	12.7
High school graduate or higher (percent)	91.9	88.5
Bachelor's degree or higher (percent)...	59.8	32.9

[1] 2020 ACS 5-Year estimates. 1-Year estimates were not released for 2020 due to the impact of COVID-19 on data collection that year.

Table DC-12. Public School Characteristics and Educational Indicators

(Number, percent; data derived from National Center of Education Statistics.)

Item	State	U.S.
Public Elementary and Secondary Schools		
Number of regular school districts, 2018-19	1	13,452
Number of operational schools, 2019-20..	230	98,469
Percent charter schools	49.6	7.7
Total public school enrollment, Fall 2019...	89,878	50,796,445
Percent charter school enrollment	43.3	6.8
Student-teacher ratio, Fall 2019..	12.1	15.9
Expenditures per student (unadjusted dollars), 2018-19	22,831	13,187
Four-year adjusted cohort graduation rate (ACGR), 2018-2019[1]...................................	68.9	85.8
Students eligible for free or reduced-price lunch (percent), 2019-20.............................	76.4	52.1
English language learners (percent), Fall 2019	12.3	10.4
Students age 3 to 21 served under IDEA, part B (percent), 2020-21	16.7	14.5

Public Schools by Type, 2019-20	Number	Percent of district public schools
Total number of schools..	230	100.0
Special education..	2	0.9
Vocational education...	0	-
Alternative education..	6	2.6

[1] Adjusted Cohort Graduation Rates (ACGR) differ from Averaged Freshmen Graduation Rates (AFGR).
- = Zero or rounds to zero.

Table DC-13. Reported Voting and Registration of the Voting-Age Population, November 2020

(Numbers in thousands, percent.)

Item	Total population	Total citizen population	Registered			Voted		
			Total registered	Percent registered (total population)	Percent registered (total citizen population)	Total voted	Percent voted (total population)	Percent voted (total citizen population)
U.S. Total	252,274	231,593	168,308	66.7	72.7	154,628	61.3	66.8
State Total....................	576	534	464	80.5	86.9	448	77.8	84.0
Sex								
Male	264	245	209	79.0	85.1	200	75.7	81.5
Female	312	288	255	81.7	88.4	248	79.5	86.0
Race								
White alone......................	278	253	229	82.5	90.5	223	80.3	88.1
White, non-Hispanic alone	243	232	213	87.5	91.5	206	84.9	88.8
Black alone....................	251	243	202	80.4	83.2	193	76.7	79.3
Asian alone	36	27	25	B	B	25	B	B
Hispanic (of any race)	50	32	26	B	B	26	B	B
White alone or in combination	285	259	234	82.3	90.4	228	80.2	88.0
Black alone or in combination	256	248	207	80.6	83.3	197	76.9	79.5
Asian alone or in combination............	40	30	27	B	B	27	B	B
Age								
18 to 24 years......................	63	56	48	B	B	47	B	B
25 to 34 years......................	159	148	132	83.1	89.1	127	80.1	85.9
35 to 44 years......................	126	115	100	79.1	86.5	95	75.5	82.6
45 to 64 years......................	136	124	108	79.9	87.1	106	78.4	85.4
65 years and over	93	89	76	81.3	84.6	72	78.0	81.1

B = Base is less than 75,000 and therefore too small to show the derived measure.

Table DC-14. Crime

(Number, rate per 100,000. Data are derived from the FBI Uniform Crime Reports.)

Item	District [1]			U.S.		
	2019	2020	Percent change	2019	2020	Percent change
TOTAL POPULATION[2]	708,253	712,816	0.6	328,329,953	329,484,123	0.4
VIOLENT CRIME						
Number........................	7,403	7,127	-3.7	1,250,393	1,313,105	5.0
Rate..........................	1045.2	999.8	-4.3	380.8	398.5	4.6
Murder and Nonnegligent Manslaughter						
Number........................	166	201	21.1	16,669	21,570	29.4
Rate	23.4	28.2	20.3	5.1	6.5	28.9
Rape[3]						
Number........................	345	311	-9.9	143,224	126,430	-11.7
Rate	48.7	43.6	-10.4	43.6	38.4	-12.0
Robbery						
Number........................	2,714	2,373	-12.6	268,483	243,600	-9.3
Rate	383.2	332.9	-13.1	81.8	73.9	-9.6
Aggravated Assault						
Number........................	4,178	4,242	1.5	822,017	921,505	12.1
Rate	589.9	595.1	0.9	250.4	279.7	11.7
PROPERTY CRIME						
Number........................	30,819	24,899	-19.2	6,995,235	6,452,038	-7.8
Rate	4,351.4	3,493.0	-19.7	2,130.6	1,958.2	-8.1
Burglary						
Number........................	1,843	1,964	6.6	1,118,096	1,035,314	-7.4
Rate	260.2	275.5	5.9	340.5	314.2	-7.7
Larceny-Theft						
Number........................	26,643	19,536	-26.7	5,152,267	4,606,324	-10.6
Rate	3,761.8	2,740.7	-27.1	1,569.2	1,398.0	-10.9
Motor Vehicle Theft						
Number........................	2,333	3,399	45.7	724,872	810,400	11.8
Rate	329.4	476.8	44.8	220.8	246.0	11.4

NOTE: Although arson data are included in the trend and clearance tables, sufficient data are not available to estimate totals for this offense. Therefore, no arson data are published in this table.
- = Zero or rounds to zero.
[1] Includes offenses reported by the Metro Transit Police and the District of Columbia Fire and Emergency Medical Services: Arson
[2] Population figures are U.S. Census Bureau provisional estimates as of July 1, 2020.
[3] The figures shown in the rape (revised definition) column were estimated using the revised Uniform Crime Reporting (UCR) definition of rape.

Table DC-15. Local Government Finances, 2019

(Dollar amounts in thousands, percent distribution.)

Item	Dollars	Percent distribution
Total Revenue	16,482,979	100.0
General revenue	14,471,965	87.8
Intergovernmental revenue	4,076,224	24.7
Taxes	8,560,621	51.9
Property	2,800,884	17.0
Sales and gross receipts	2,023,319	12.3
Individual income tax	2,299,326	13.9
Corporate income tax	642,656	3.9
Motor vehicle license	45,973	0.3
Other taxes	748,463	4.5
Current charges	840,889	5.1
Miscellaneous general revenue	994,231	6.0
Utility revenue	944,896	5.7
Liquor stores revenue	0	-
Insurance trust revenue[1]	1,066,118	6.5
Total Expenditure	20,172,049	100.0
Intergovernmental expenditure	0	-
Direct expenditure	20,172,049	100.0
Current operation	14,295,789	70.9
Capital outlay	4,038,963	20.0
Assistance and subsidies	550,125	2.7
Interest on debt	688,160	3.4
Insurance benefits and repayments	599,012	3.0
Exhibit: Salaries and wages	4,680,296	23.2
Direct Expenditure	20,172,049	100.0
Direct expenditure by function:		
Direct general expenditure	14,919,860	74.0
Education	3,113,274	15.4
Public welfare	4,093,259	20.3
Hospitals	293,380	1.5
Health	670,833	3.3
Highways	610,896	3.0
Police protection	657,169	3.3
Correction	257,240	1.3
Natural resources	101,345	0.5
Parks and recreation	444,302	2.2
Governmental administration	892,237	4.4
Interest on general debt	616,004	3.1
Other and unallocable	624,578	3.1
Utility expenditure	4,653,177	23.1
Liquor stores expenditure	0	-
Insurance trust expenditure	599,012	3.0
Debt at End of Fiscal Year	4,886,222	X
Cash and Security Holdings	16,064,488	X

Note: At the time of publication, the Census Bureau had not yet released 2020 finance data for the District of Columbia.
X = Not applicable.
- = Zero or rounds to zero.
[1] Within insurance trust revenue, net earnings of state retirement systems is a calculated statistic (the item code in the data file is X08), and thus can be positive or negative. Net earnings is the sum of earnings on investments plus gains on investments minus losses on investments. The change made in 2002 for asset valuation from book to market value in accordance with Statement 34 of the Governmental Accounting Standards Board is reflected in the calculated statistics.

Table DC-16. District Government Tax Collections, 2021

(Dollars in thousands, percent.)

Item	Dollars	Percent distribution
Total Taxes	8,980,395	100.0
Property taxes	2,994,580	33.3
Sales and gross receipts	1,646,672	18.3
General sales and gross receipts	1,201,346	13.4
Selective sales and gross receipts	445,326	5.0
Alcoholic beverages	6,197	0.1
Amusements	2141	-
Insurance premiums	133,546	1.5
Motor fuels	23,638	0.3
Pari-mutuels	X	-
Public utilities	167,152	1.9
Tobacco products	22,185	0.2
Other selective sales	90,467	1.0
Licenses	183,696	2.0
Alcoholic beverages	6,186	0.1
Amusements	1429	-
Corporations in general	37,014	0.4
Hunting and fishing	87	-
Motor vehicle	34,843	0.4
Motor vehicle operators	5,784	0.1
Public utilities	X	-
Occupation and business, NEC	47,612	0.5
Other licenses	50741	0.6
Income taxes	3,506,270	39.0
Individual income	2,643,213	29.4
Corporation net income	863,057	9.6
Other taxes	649,177	7.2
Death and gift	31,742	0.4
Documentary and stock transfer	553,515	6.2
Severance	X	-
Taxes, NEC	63,920	0.7

X = Not applicable.
- = Zero or rounds to zero.

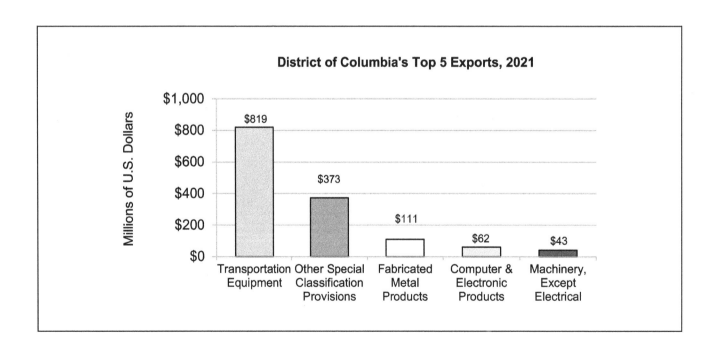

Facts and Figures

Location: Southeastern United States; bordered on the N by Georgia and Alabama, on the E by the Atlantic Ocean, on the S by the Straits of Florida, and on the W by Alabama and the Gulf of Mexico

Area: 65,757 sq. mi. (170,304 sq. km.); rank—22nd

Population: 21,781,128 (2021 est.); rank—3rd

Principal Cities: capital—Tallahassee; largest—Jacksonville

Statehood: March 3, 1845; 27th state

U.S. Congress: 2 senators, 27 representatives

State Motto: In God We Trust

State Song: "The Swanee River (Old Folks at Home)"

State Nickname: The Sunshine State

Abbreviations: FL; Fla.

State Symbols: flower—orange blossom; tree—Sabal palm (cabbage palm); bird—mockingbird

At a Glance

- With an increase in population of 15.8 percent, Florida ranked 14th among the states in growth from 2010 to 2021.

- Florida's violent crime rate in 2020 was 383.6 incidences per 100,000 population, compared to 398.5 for the entire nation.

- In 2021, Florida was the state with the 2nd largest percentage of its population in the 65 and older age group (21.1 percent).

- Florida ranked 6th among the states for the highest percent of Hispanic or Latino residents (26.8 percent) in 2021. Hispanic or Latino residents may be of any race.

- In 2020, 12.7 percent of all Florida residents were uninsured, the 4th highest percent in the nation.

Table FL-1. Population by Age, Sex, Race, and Hispanic Origin

(Number, percent, except where noted.)

Sex, age, race, and Hispanic origin	2000	2010	2021	Percent change, 2010–2021
Total Population..	15,982,378	18,801,310	21,781,128	15.8
Percent of total U.S. population	5.7	6.1	6.6	X
Sex				
Male..	7,797,715	9,189,355	10,710,357	16.6
Female...	8,184,663	9,611,955	11,070,771	15.2
Age				
Under 5 years..	945,823	1,073,506	1,103,794	2.8
5 to 19 years...	3,102,809	3,439,484	3,660,974	6.4
20 to 64 years...	9,126,149	11,034,718	12,417,974	12.5
65 years and over	2,807,597	3,259,602	4,598,386	41.1
Median age (years)	38.7	40.7	42.7	4.9
Race and Hispanic Origin				
One race				
White	12,465,029	14,808,867	16,749,416	13.1
Black..	2,335,505	3,078,067	3,710,894	20.6
American Indian and Alaska Native	53,541	89,119	117,401	31.7
Asian..	266,256	474,199	663,832	40.0
Native Hawaiian or Other Pacific Islander	8,625	18,790	26,678	42.0
Two or more races	376,315	332,268	512,907	54.4
Hispanic (of any race)..	2,682,715	4,301,853	5,830,908	35.5

NOTE: Population figures for 2021 are July 1 estimates. The 2000 and 2010 estimates are taken from the respective censuses.
- = Zero or rounds to zero.
X = Not applicable.

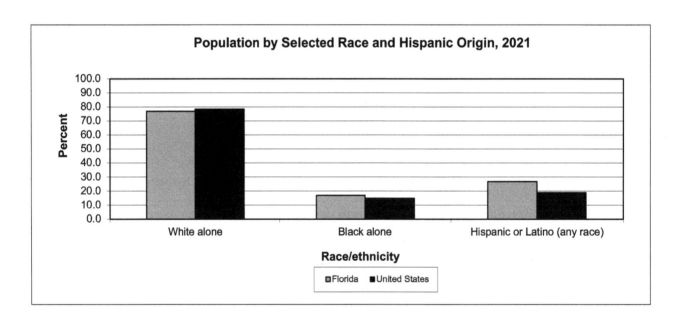

Table FL-2. Marital Status

(Number, percent distribution.)

Sex, age, race, and Hispanic origin	2000	2010	2020 [1]
Males, 15 Years and Over	6,232,987	7,534,535	8,593,468
Never married	27.3	33.9	34.9
Now married, except separated..	56.9	49.3	48.7
Separated...	2.1	2.2	1.8
Widowed...	3.2	3.2	3.2
Divorced...	10.5	11.5	11.3
Females, 15 Years and Over	6,714,003	8,021,290	9,135,489
Never married	20.5	26.6	28.4
Now married, except separated..	51.9	45.1	44.5
Separated...	2.7	3.0	2.3
Widowed...	12.3	10.8	10.2
Divorced...	12.7	14.5	14.6

[1] 2020 ACS 5-Year estimates. 1-Year estimates were not released for 2020 due to the impact of COVID-19 on data collection that year.

Table FL-3. Households and Housing Characteristics

(Number, percent, dollars.)

Item	2000	2010	2020 [1]	Average annual percent change, 2010–2020
Total Households..	6,337,929	7,035,068	7,931,313	1.8
Family households	4,210,760	4,556,930	5,118,059	1.8
Married-couple family	3,192,266	3,307,884	3,721,358	1.8
Other family	1,018,494	1,249,046	1,396,701	1.7
Male householder, no wife present.........................	259,924	313,305	392,029	3.6
Female householder, no husband present................	759,000	935,741	1,004,672	1.1
Nonfamily households	2,127,169	2,478,138	2,813,254	1.9
Householder living alone.....................................	1,687,303	2,013,028	2,267,320	1.8
Householder not living alone................................	439,886	465,110	545,934	2.5
Housing Characteristics				
Total housing units..	7,302,947	8,994,091	9,562,324	0.9
Occupied housing units	6,337,929	7,035,068	7,931,313	1.8
Owner occupied	4,441,799	4,794,130	5,250,878	1.4
Renter occupied	1,896,130	2,240,938	2,680,435	2.8
Average household size..	2.46	2.62	2.62	-
Financial Characteristics				
Median gross rent of renter-occupied housing	641	947	1,218	4.1
Median monthly owner costs for housing units with a mortgage	1,004	1,505	1,539	0.3
Median value of owner-occupied housing units...........................	105,500	164,200	232,000	5.9

- = Zero or rounds to zero
[1] 2020 ACS 5-Year estimates. 1-Year estimates were not released for 2020 due to the impact of COVID-19 on data collection that year.

Table FL-4. Migration, Origin, and Language

(Number, percent.)

Characteristic	State 2016-2020 [1]	U.S. 2016-2020 [1]
Residence 1 Year Ago		
Population 1 year and over..	21,005,410	322,943,283
Same house..	84.9	86.2
Different house in the U.S..	14.1	13.2
Same county..	8.1	7.7
Different county	6.0	5.5
Same state...	3.1	3.2
Different state	2.8	2.3
Abroad	1.0	0.6
Place of Birth		
Native born	16,806,638	282,443,680
Male	49.3	49.4
Female	50.7	50.6
Foreign born	4,410,286	44,125,628
Male	47.2	48.6
Female	52.8	51.4
Foreign born; naturalized U.S. citizen...........................	2,521,185	22,456,684
Male	44.6	46.1
Female	55.4	53.9
Foreign born; not a U.S. citizen..................................	1,889,101	21,668,944
Male	50.6	51.1
Female	49.4	48.9
Entered 2010 or later	25.1	22.8
Entered 2000 to 2009	24.8	25.1
Entered before 2000...	50.1	52.1
World Region of Birth, Foreign		
Foreign-born population, excluding population born at sea	4,410,286	44,125,628
Europe	9.4	10.8
Asia...	10.7	31.3
Africa	1.8	5.4
Oceania	0.2	0.6
Latin America...	75.3	50.0
North America..	2.6	1.9
Language Spoken at Home and Ability to Speak English		
Population 5 years and over..	20,083,534	306,919,116
English only	70.6	78.5
Language other than English.......................................	29.4	21.5
Speaks English less than "very well".........................	11.8	8.2

[1] 2020 ACS 5-Year estimates. 1-Year estimates were not released for 2020 due to the impact of COVID-19 on data collection that year.
NA = Not available.
X = Not applicable.
- = Zero or rounds to zero.

Table FL-5. Median Income and Poverty Status, 2020[1]

(Number, percent, except as noted.)

Characteristic	State		U.S.	
	Number	Percent	Number	Percent
Median Income				
Households (dollars)	57,703	X	64,994	X
Families (dollars)	69,670	X	80,069	X
Below Poverty Level (All People)	2,772,939	13.3	40,910,326	12.8
Sex				
Male	1,239,481	12.3	18,171,512	11.6
Female	1,533,458	14.3	22,738,814	14.0
Age				
Under 18 years	773,801	18.7	12,598,699	17.5
Related children under 18 years	755,962	18.3	12,306,532	17.2
18 to 64 years	1,549,183	12.5	23,554,920	12.1
65 years and over	449,955	10.5	4,756,707	9.3

X = Not applicable.
[1] 2020 ACS 5-Year estimates. 1-Year estimates were not released for 2020 due to the impact of COVID-19 on data collection that year.

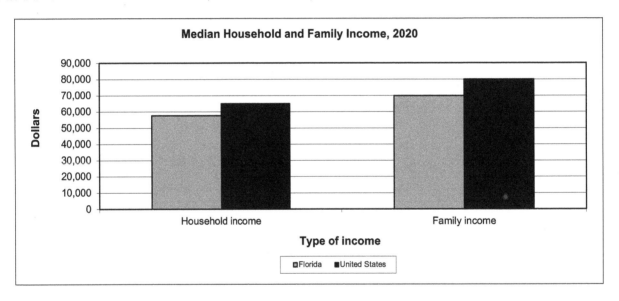

Table FL-6. Health Insurance Coverage Status for the Civilian Noninstitutionalized Population and Children Under 19 Years of Age

(Number, percent.)

Item	2011	2012	2013	2014	2015	2016	2017	2018	2019	2020[2]
Civilian Noninstitutionalized Population	18,752,294	19,011,070	19,245,127	19,583,357	19,960,169	20,294,479	20,678,704	20,996,007	21,156,770	20,897,188
Covered by Private or Public Insurance										
Number	14,840,913	15,195,230	15,392,164	16,338,196	17,298,620	17,750,232	18,002,557	18,267,522	18,372,422	18,250,257
Percent	79.1	79.9	80.0	83.4	86.7	87.5	87.1	87.0	86.8	87.3
Uninsured										
Number	3,911,381	3,815,840	3,852,963	3,245,161	2,661,549	2,544,247	2,676,147	2,728,485	2,784,348	2,646,931
Percent	20.9	20.1	20.0	16.6	13.3	12.5	12.9	13.0	13.2	12.7
Percent in the U.S. not covered	15.1	14.8	14.5	11.7	9.4	8.6	8.7	8.9	9.2	8.7
Children Under 19 Years of Age[1]	3,986,946	3,991,143	4,019,835	4,046,150	4,093,401	4,136,345	4,450,443	4,488,358	4,479,868	4,455,752
Covered by Private or Public Insurance										
Number	3,511,834	3,554,977	3,574,800	3,668,163	3,809,595	3,879,598	4,125,583	4,149,314	4,137,189	4,134,956
Percent	88.1	89.1	88.9	90.7	93.1	93.8	92.7	92.4	92.4	92.8
Uninsured										
Number	475,112	436,166	445,035	377,987	283,806	256,747	324,860	339,044	342,679	320,796
Percent	11.9	10.9	11.1	9.3	6.9	6.2	7.3	7.6	7.6	7.2
Percent in the U.S. not covered	7.5	7.2	7.1	6.0	4.8	4.5	5.0	5.2	5.7	5.2

[1] Data for years prior to 2017 are for individuals under 18 years of age.
[2] 2020 ACS 5-Year estimates. 1-Year estimates were not released for 2020 due to the impact of COVID-19 on data collection that year. Data is not comparable to previous years, which are based on 1-year estimates.

Table FL-7. Employment Status by Demographic Group, 2021

(Numbers in thousands, percent.)

Characteristic	Civilian noninstitutional population	Civilian labor force		Employed		Unemployed	
		Number	Percent of population	Number	Percent of population	Number	Percent of population
Total..	17,844	10,406	58.3	9,935	55.7	471	4.5
Sex							
Male	8,562	5,524	64.5	5,279	61.7	245	4.4
Female	9,283	4,882	52.6	4,655	50.2	226	4.6
Race, Sex, and Hispanic Origin							
White	14,111	8,094	57.4	7,760	55.0	333	4.1
Male..	6,852	4,406	64.3	4,234	61.8	172	3.9
Female......................................	7,258	3,688	50.8	3,527	48.6	161	4.4
Black or African American................	2,799	1,718	61.4	1,610	57.5	108	6.3
Male..	1,295	843	65.1	785	60.6	58	6.9
Female......................................	1,504	875	58.2	825	54.9	50	5.7
Hispanic or Latino ethnicity[1]	4,960	3,152	63.6	2,981	60.1	171	5.4
Male..	2,402	1,757	73.1	1,674	69.7	83	4.7
Female......................................	2,558	1,395	54.6	1,307	51.1	88	6.3
Age							
16 to 19 years...............................	916	274	29.9	242	26.5	32	11.6
20 to 24 years...............................	1,180	837	70.9	778	66.0	58	6.9
25 to 34 years...............................	2,751	2,258	82.1	2,149	78.1	109	4.8
35 to 44 years...............................	2,683	2,169	80.8	2,075	77.3	94	4.3
45 to 54 years...............................	2,745	2,159	78.7	2,075	75.6	84	3.9
55 to 64 years...............................	3,066	1,959	63.9	1,887	61.6	72	3.7
65 years and over	4,504	751	16.7	728	16.2	23	3.1

NOTE: Data in Table 7 are from the Current Population Survey (CPS) and do not match the estimates in Table 8. See notes and definitions for further information.
[1] May be of any race.

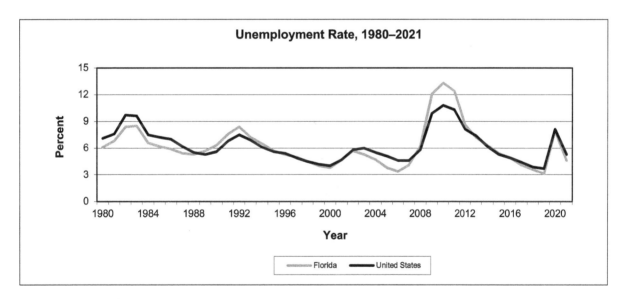

Unemployment Rate, 1980–2021

Table FL-8. Employment Status of the Civilian Noninstitutional Population Age 16 Years and Over

(Number, percent.)

Year	Civilian labor force	Civilian participation rate	Employed	Unemployed	Unemployment rate
2010..	9,147,107	61.2	8,155,401	991,706	10.8
2011..	9,260,348	60.9	8,334,119	926,229	10.0
2012..	9,335,727	60.5	8,529,063	806,664	8.6
2013..	9,414,664	60.1	8,706,060	708,604	7.5
2014..	9,546,407	59.9	8,931,440	614,967	6.4
2015..	9,639,737	59.3	9,106,772	532,965	5.5
2016..	9,841,301	59.2	9,360,237	481,064	4.9
2017..	9,972,990	59.3	9,544,892	428,098	4.3
2018..	10,107,191	59.2	9,734,029	373,162	3.7
2019..	10,259,198	59.4	9,928,235	330,963	3.2
2020..	10,094,878	57.7	9,267,151	827,727	8.2
2021..	10,312,768	58.3	9,843,057	469,711	4.6

Table FL-9. Employment and Average Wages by Industry

(Estimates are based on the 2012 North American Industry Classification System [NAICS].)

Industry	2013	2014	2015	2016	2017	2018	2019	2020
	Number of Jobs							
Wage and Salary Employment by Industry.........................	7,935,168	8,192,310	8,472,417	8,736,178	8,917,106	9,147,156	9,338,828	8,901,285
Farm Wage and Salary Employment................................	44,639	48,772	42,091	40,153	41,185	39,342	39,774	42,061
Nonfarm Wage and Salary Employment.........................	7,890,529	8,143,538	8,430,326	8,696,025	8,875,921	9,107,814	9,299,054	8,859,224
Private wage and salary employment...........................	6,727,155	6,985,325	7,264,806	7,518,605	7,689,525	7,912,192	8,094,459	7,661,648
Forestry, fishing, and related activities...........................	44,342	45,168	45,084	44,502	44,302	44,463	44,615	42,578
Mining..	3,958	4,101	4,086	4,168	4,072	4,135	4,045	3,720
Utilities..	22,301	21,994	22,482	22,870	23,027	23,305	22,581	22,821
Construction...	375,700	406,888	442,777	486,257	516,274	554,468	577,952	576,307
Manufacturing...	322,368	331,796	342,989	355,287	363,807	372,181	384,440	377,185
Durable goods manufacturing..............................	214,950	222,982	233,236	240,649	246,969	254,171	262,761	258,893
Nondurable goods manufacturing.........................	107,418	108,814	109,753	114,638	116,838	118,010	121,679	118,292
Wholesale trade	323,244	329,238	336,379	341,302	345,243	347,116	354,252	345,192
Retail trade..	1,012,294	1,048,918	1,089,637	1,109,347	1,122,391	1,138,600	1,118,374	1,063,850
Transportation and warehousing.............................	227,419	236,636	247,659	258,231	267,916	282,822	326,492	328,246
Information	134,306	136,999	136,522	137,186	138,289	139,102	139,040	130,504
Finance and insurance.......................................	355,260	362,719	373,924	382,421	398,315	409,407	420,619	434,018
Real estate and rental and leasing.........................	169,643	173,664	181,370	184,489	186,498	193,336	201,926	193,550
Professional, scientific, and technical services	472,286	490,220	512,240	533,897	550,970	577,093	600,412	607,907
Management of companies and enterprises.................	91,063	94,208	96,989	100,512	103,655	108,063	115,441	111,698
Administrative and waste services..........................	562,736	589,521	623,558	659,953	678,097	691,590	686,516	649,709
Educational services	150,980	157,364	160,664	163,712	168,159	172,397	176,363	164,313
Health care and social assistance..........................	989,336	1,012,894	1,050,710	1,089,556	1,113,358	1,139,554	1,170,050	1,147,720
Arts, entertainment, and recreation........................	199,627	214,735	218,786	226,725	232,269	237,128	244,864	190,449
Accommodation and food services.........................	843,316	880,179	921,201	955,848	975,798	999,692	1,021,751	827,270
Other services, except public administration................	426,976	448,083	457,749	462,342	457,085	477,740	484,726	444,611
Government and government enterprises......................	1,163,374	1,158,213	1,165,520	1,177,420	1,186,396	1,195,622	1,204,595	1,197,576
	Dollars							
Average Wages and Salaries by Industry	45,143	46,225	47,674	48,463	49,906	51,674	53,292	57,360
Average Farm Wages and Salaries	27,609	23,125	23,223	28,468	25,060	28,199	30,986	32,381
Average Nonfarm Wages and Salaries	45,242	46,363	47,796	48,555	50,021	51,775	53,387	57,479
Average private wages and salaries..........................	44,622	45,764	47,262	48,007	49,506	51,319	52,990	57,253
Forestry, fishing, and related activities....................	24,570	25,086	26,977	28,353	29,273	30,518	32,006	34,803
Mining..	64,248	66,302	67,422	68,235	71,827	73,848	73,663	77,419
Utilities...	88,022	92,404	95,342	100,224	104,623	106,348	103,449	111,784
Construction...	43,177	44,725	46,835	48,240	50,231	52,368	53,988	57,079
Manufacturing...	56,251	57,716	59,611	59,927	61,537	64,029	66,165	69,099
Durable goods manufacturing..............................	59,406	60,813	62,234	62,727	65,002	67,710	69,654	72,679
Nondurable goods manufacturing.........................	49,938	51,370	54,036	54,050	54,214	56,099	58,630	61,262
Wholesale trade	68,366	70,252	72,746	73,188	75,809	79,280	81,956	85,836
Retail trade..	29,157	29,809	30,765	31,067	31,819	32,833	33,947	37,189
Transportation and warehousing.............................	50,619	52,104	53,956	54,211	55,791	57,004	56,034	57,002
Information	70,725	72,998	76,092	79,632	82,763	83,685	88,808	96,389
Finance and insurance.......................................	75,465	79,152	81,777	83,081	86,374	89,740	91,914	99,491
Real estate and rental and leasing.........................	44,274	46,655	48,658	49,090	50,948	52,785	53,525	57,307
Professional, scientific, and technical services	69,649	71,547	73,655	75,571	77,110	79,999	82,706	87,326
Management of companies and enterprises.................	101,672	104,365	107,054	106,511	114,612	115,661	118,479	123,660
Administrative and waste services..........................	34,654	35,356	36,550	37,422	38,271	39,898	41,491	44,678
Educational services	37,951	38,711	39,170	39,757	39,045	39,812	40,327	45,290
Health care and social assistance..........................	48,221	49,229	50,874	51,147	52,237	53,815	55,076	58,386
Arts, entertainment, and recreation........................	38,147	38,860	40,840	41,769	42,900	44,423	45,328	50,347
Accommodation and food services.........................	22,984	23,595	24,264	24,726	25,245	26,689	27,442	26,626
Other services, except public administration................	31,585	32,436	33,747	34,762	36,175	37,182	38,375	41,893
Government and government enterprises......................	48,826	49,977	51,123	52,059	53,362	54,798	56,060	58,921

Table FL-10. Employment Characteristics by Family Type

(Number, percent.)

Family type and labor force status	2018 Total	2018 Families with own children under 18 years	2019 Total	2019 Families with own children under 18 years	2020[1] Total	2020[1] Families with own children under 18 years
All Families	5,026,515	1,789,492	5,083,272	1,772,760	5,118,059	1,863,076
FAMILY TYPE AND LABOR FORCE STATUS						
Opposite-Sex Married-Couple Families	3,638,058	1,150,292	3,670,205	1,132,833	3,674,806	1,202,544
Both husband and wife in labor force	43.9	64.8	45.1	67.7	45.1	66.1
Husband in labor force, wife not in labor force	20.6	28.2	19.3	25.6	20.4	27.1
Wife in labor force, husband not in labor force	8.1	4.5	8.0	4.6	8.3	4.6
Both husband and wife not in labor force	26.1	2.1	26.3	1.7	26.2	2.2
Other Families	1,388,457	639,200	1,413,067	639,927	1,396,701	654,262
Female householder, no spouse present	72.0	75.3	71.3	73.8	71.9	74.1
In labor force	50.3	64.0	49.7	63.1	50.4	63.1
Not in labor force	21.7	11.3	21.7	10.7	21.5	11.0
Male householder, no spouse present	28.0	24.7	28.7	26.2	28.1	25.9
In labor force	21.0	22.6	21.9	24.3	21.5	23.7
Not in labor force	7.0	2.1	6.7	1.9	6.5	2.2

[1] 2020 ACS 5-Year estimates. 1-Year estimates were not released for 2020 due to the impact of COVID-19 on data collection that year. Data is not comparable to previous years, which are based on 1-year estimates.

Table FL-11. School Enrollment and Educational Attainment, 2020[1]

(Number, percent.)

Item	State	U.S.
Enrollment		
Total population 3 years and over, enrolled in school	4,774,888	80,497,960
Enrolled in nursery school or preschool (percent)	6.2	6.1
Enrolled in kindergarten (percent)	4.8	5.0
Enrolled in elementary school, grades 1-8 (percent)	39.5	40.4
Enrolled in high school, grades 9-12 (percent)	20.7	21.0
Enrolled in college or graduate school (percent)	28.8	27.6
Attainment		
Total population 25 years and over	15,255,326	222,836,834
Less than ninth grade (percent)	4.6	4.9
9th to 12th grade, no diploma (percent)	6.9	6.6
High school graduate, including equivalency (percent)	28.2	26.7
Some college, no degree (percent)	19.8	20.3
Associate's degree (percent)	10.0	8.6
Bachelor's degree (percent)	19.3	20.2
Graduate or professional degree (percent)	11.3	12.7
High school graduate or higher (percent)	88.5	88.5
Bachelor's degree or higher (percent)	30.5	32.9

[1] 2020 ACS 5-Year estimates. 1-Year estimates were not released for 2020 due to the impact of COVID-19 on data collection that year.

Table FL-12. Public School Characteristics and Educational Indicators

(Number, percent; data derived from National Center of Education Statistics.)

Item	State	U.S.
Public Elementary and Secondary Schools		
Number of regular school districts, 2018-19	67	13,452
Number of operational schools, 2019-20	4,192	98,469
Percent charter schools	16.1	7.7
Total public school enrollment, Fall 2019	2,858,461	50,796,445
Percent charter school enrollment	11.5	6.8
Student-teacher ratio, Fall 2019	17.2	15.9
Expenditures per student (unadjusted dollars), 2018-19	9,986	13,187
Four-year adjusted cohort graduation rate (ACGR), 2018-2019[1]	87.2	85.8
Students eligible for free or reduced-price lunch (percent), 2019-20	53.9	52.1
English language learners (percent), Fall 2019	10.0	10.4
Students age 3 to 21 served under IDEA, part B (percent), 2020-21	14.7	14.5

Public Schools by Type, 2019-20	Number	Percent of state public schools
Total number of schools	4,192	100.0
Special education	158	3.8
Vocational education	36	0.9
Alternative education	387	9.2

[1] Adjusted Cohort Graduation Rates (ACGR) differ from Averaged Freshmen Graduation Rates (AFGR).

Table FL-13. Reported Voting and Registration of the Voting-Age Population, November 2020

(Numbers in thousands, percent.)

Item	Total population	Total citizen population	Registered			Voted		
			Total registered	Percent registered (total population)	Percent registered (total citizen population)	Total voted	Percent voted (total population)	Percent voted (total citizen population)
U.S. Total	252,274	231,593	168,308	66.7	72.7	154,628	61.3	66.8
State Total..	17,244	15,645	10,495	60.9	67.1	9,720	56.4	62.1
Sex								
Male	8,263	7,523	4,965	60.1	66.0	4,563	55.2	60.7
Female	8,982	8,121	5,530	61.6	68.1	5,157	57.4	63.5
Race								
White alone......................................	13,675	12,515	8,468	61.9	67.7	7,887	57.7	63.0
White, non-Hispanic alone	9,553	9,374	6,676	69.9	71.2	6,260	65.5	66.8
Black alone......................................	2,652	2,344	1,533	57.8	65.4	1,375	51.8	58.7
Asian alone	585	462	260	44.5	56.4	257	43.9	55.6
Hispanic (of any race)	4,439	3,394	1,992	44.9	58.7	1,789	40.3	52.7
White alone or in combination	13,843	12,675	8,569	61.9	67.6	7,982	57.7	63.0
Black alone or in combination	2,819	2,504	1,624	57.6	64.9	1,460	51.8	58.3
Asian alone or in combination...........	591	467	266	45.0	56.9	263	44.4	56.2
Age								
18 to 24 years	1,556	1,391	775	49.8	55.7	648	41.6	46.6
25 to 34 years	2,713	2,397	1,476	54.4	61.6	1,302	48.0	54.3
35 to 44 years	2,732	2,336	1,514	55.4	64.8	1,370	50.1	58.6
45 to 64 years	5,776	5,253	3,520	60.9	67.0	3,325	57.6	63.3
65 years and over	4,468	4,267	3,210	71.9	75.2	3,076	68.8	72.1

Table FL-14. Crime

(Number, rate per 100,000. Data are derived from the FBI Uniform Crime Reports.)

Item	State			U.S.		
	2019	2020	Percent change	2019	2020	Percent change
TOTAL POPULATION[1]	21,492,056	21,733,312	1.1	328,329,953	329,484,123	0.4
VIOLENT CRIME						
Number..	81,291	83,368	2.6	1,250,393	1,313,105	5.0
Rate	378.2	383.6	1.4	380.8	398.5	4.6
Murder and Nonnegligent Manslaughter						
Number..	1,122	1,290	15.0	16,669	21,570	29.4
Rate	5.2	5.9	13.7	5.1	6.5	28.9
Rape[2]						
Number..	8,463	7,686	-9.2	143,224	126,430	-11.7
Rate	39.4	35.4	-10.2	43.6	38.4	-12.0
Robbery						
Number..	16,234	13,521	-16.7	268,483	243,600	-9.3
Rate	75.5	62.2	-17.6	81.8	73.9	-9.6
Aggravated Assault						
Number..	55,472	60,871	9.7	822,017	921,505	12.1
Rate	258.1	280.1	8.5	250.4	279.7	11.7
PROPERTY CRIME						
Number..	460,966	384,556	-16.6	6,995,235	6,452,038	-7.8
Rate	2,144.8	1,769.4	-17.5	2,130.6	1,958.2	-8.1
Burglary						
Number..	63,338	52,293	-17.4	1,118,096	1,035,314	-7.4
Rate	294.7	240.6	-18.4	340.5	314.2	-7.7
Larceny-Theft						
Number..	358,537	293,992	-18.0	5,152,267	4,606,324	-10.6
Rate	1,668.2	1,352.7	-18.9	1,569.2	1,398.0	-10.9
Motor Vehicle Theft						
Number..	39,091	38,271	-2.1	724,872	810,400	11.8
Rate	181.9	176.1	-3.2	220.8	246.0	11.4

NOTE: Although arson data are included in the trend and clearance tables, sufficient data are not available to estimate totals for this offense. Therefore, no arson data are published in this table.
- = Zero or rounds to zero.
[1] Population figures are U.S. Census Bureau provisional estimates as of July 1, 2020.
[2] The figures shown in the rape (revised definition) column were estimated using the revised Uniform Crime Reporting (UCR) definition of rape.

Table FL-15. State Government Finances, 2020

(Dollar amounts in thousands, percent distribution.)

Item	Dollars	Percent distribution
Total Revenue	110,295,047	100.0
General revenue	100,055,957	90.7
Intergovernmental revenue	36,791,015	33.4
Taxes	43,117,933	39.1
General sales	26960208	24.4
Selective sales	8,207,278	7.4
License taxes	2,122,244	1.9
Individual income tax	0	-
Corporate income tax	2,481,710	2.3
Other taxes	3,346,493	3.0
Current charges	8,647,581	7.8
Miscellaneous general revenue	11,499,428	10.4
Utility revenue	26,063	-
Liquor stores revenue		-
Insurance trust revenue[1]	10,213,027	9.3
	0	
Total Expenditure	107,659,776	100.0
Intergovernmental expenditure	19,365,020	18.0
Direct expenditure	88,294,756	82.0
Current operation	63,200,759	58.7
Capital outlay	8,059,274	7.5
Insurance benefits and repayments	13,216,603	12.3
Assistance and subsidies	3,113,704	2.9
Interest on debt	704,416	0.7
Exhibit: Salaries and wages	10,103,091	9.4
Total Expenditure	107,659,776	100.0
General expenditure	94,202,036	87.5
Intergovernmental expenditure	19,365,020	18.0
Direct expenditure	74,837,016	69.5
General expenditure, by function:		
Education	31,001,305	28.8
Public welfare	29,385,477	27.3
Hospitals	1,650,805	1.5
Health	5,642,856	5.2
Highways	9,022,205	8.4
Police protection	651,734	0.6
Correction	2,946,503	2.7
Natural resources	1,803,413	1.7
Parks and recreation	178,381	0.2
Governmental administration	2,646,571	2.5
Interest on general debt	704,416	0.7
Other and unallocable	8,243,958	7.7
Utility expenditure	307,412	0.3
Liquor stores expenditure	0	-
Insurance trust expenditure	13,216,603	12.3
Debt at End of Fiscal Year	25,012,950	X
Cash and Security Holdings	257,167,242	X

X = Not applicable.
- = Zero or rounds to zero.
[1] Within insurance trust revenue, net earnings of state retirement systems is a calculated statistic (the item code in the data file is X08), and thus can be positive or negative. Net earnings is the sum of earnings on investments plus gains on investments minus losses on investments. The change made in 2002 for asset valuation from book to market value in accordance with Statement 34 of the Governmental Accounting Standards Board is reflected in the calculated statistics.

Table FL-16. State Government Tax Collections, 2021

(Dollars in thousands, percent.)

Item	Dollars	Percent distribution
Total Taxes	49,314,384	100.0
Property taxes	X	-
Sales and gross receipts	38,522,113	78.1
General sales and gross receipts	29,873,668	60.6
Selective sales and gross receipts	8,648,445	17.5
Alcoholic beverages	338,642	0.7
Amusements	168200	0.3
Insurance premiums	1,491,831	3.0
Motor fuels	2,873,845	5.8
Pari-mutuels	7,184	-
Public utilities	1,682,256	3.4
Tobacco products	1,100,091	2.2
Other selective sales	986,396	2.0
Licenses	2,509,455	5.1
Alcoholic beverages	4,346	-
Amusements	15,000	-
Corporations in general	535,900	1.1
Hunting and fishing	17,083	-
Motor vehicle	1,523,039	3.1
Motor vehicle operators	218,600	0.4
Public utilities	24,090	-
Occupation and business, NEC	159,607	0.3
Other licenses	11,790	-
Income taxes	3,407,190	6.9
Individual income	X	-
Corporation net income	3,407,190	6.9
Other taxes	4,875,626	9.9
Death and gift	X	-
Documentary and stock transfer	4,846,085	9.8
Severance	29,541	0.1
Taxes, NEC	0	-

X = Not applicable.
- = Zero or rounds to zero.

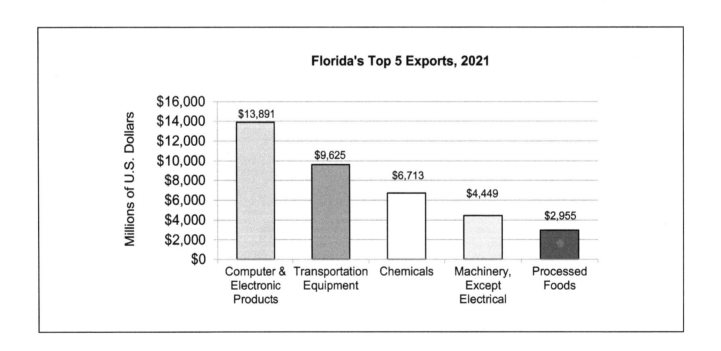

Florida's Top 5 Exports, 2021

Millions of U.S. Dollars

- Computer & Electronic Products: $13,891
- Transportation Equipment: $9,625
- Chemicals: $6,713
- Machinery, Except Electrical: $4,449
- Processed Foods: $2,955

GEORGIA

Facts and Figures

Location: Southeastern United States; bordered on the N by Tennessee and North Carolina, on the E by South Carolina and the Atlantic Ocean, on the S by Florida, and on the W by Florida and Alabama

Area: 59,425 sq. mi. (153,909 sq. km.); rank—21st

Population: 10,799,566 (2021 est.); rank—8th

Principal Cities: capital—Atlanta; largest—Atlanta

Statehood: January 2, 1788; 4th state

U.S. Congress: 2 senators, 14 representatives

State Motto: Wisdom, Justice, and Moderation

State Song: "Georgia on My Mind"

State Nicknames: The Empire State of the South; The Peach State

Abbreviations: GA; Ga.

State Symbols: flower—Cherokee rose; tree—live oak; bird—brown thrasher

At a Glance

- With an increase in population of 11.5 percent, Georgia ranked 13th among the states in growth from 2010 to 2021.

- Georgia's median household income in 2020 was $61,224, and 14.3 percent of the state's population lived below the poverty level.

- In 2020, 13.0 percent of Georgians did not have health insurance, which was the 3rd highest percent among the states.

- Georgia's violent crime rate was 400.1 per 100,000 population, compared to 398.5 for the U.S. as a whole in 2020.

- The property crime rate in Georgia in 2020 was 2,007.4 per 100,000 population, a rate that ranked 25th among the states.

Table GA-1. Population by Age, Sex, Race, and Hispanic Origin

(Number, percent, except where noted.)

Sex, age, race, and Hispanic origin	2000	2010	2021	Percent change, 2010–2021
Total Population..	8,186,453	9,687,653	10,799,566	11.5
Percent of total U.S. population	2.9	3.1	3.3	X
Sex				
Male...	4,027,113	4,729,171	5,269,761	11.4
Female...	4,159,340	4,958,482	5,529,805	11.5
Age				
Under 5 years..	595,150	686,785	633,315	-7.8
5 to 19 years...	1,819,620	2,094,844	2,188,145	4.5
20 to 64 years...	4,986,408	5,873,989	6,394,035	8.9
65 years and over....................................	785,275	1,032,035	1,584,071	53.5
Median age (years)	33.4	35.3	37.5	6.2
Race and Hispanic Origin				
One race				
White..	5,327,281	6,144,931	6,418,207	4.4
Black..	2,349,542	2,993,927	3,558,724	18.9
American Indian and Alaska Native	21,737	48,599	59,144	21.7
Asian..	173,170	323,459	493,398	52.5
Native Hawaiian or Other Pacific Islander	4,246	10,454	14,864	42.2
Two or more races.....................................	114,188	166,283	255,229	53.5
Hispanic (of any race)...............................	435,227	911,863	1,104,836	21.2

NOTE: Population figures for 2021 are July 1 estimates. The 2000 and 2010 estimates are taken from the respective censuses.
- = Zero or rounds to zero.
X = Not applicable.

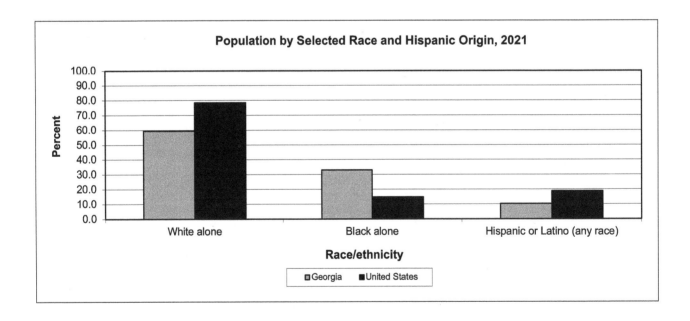

Population by Selected Race and Hispanic Origin, 2021

Table GA-2. Marital Status

(Number, percent distribution.)

Sex, age, race, and Hispanic origin	2000	2010	2020 [1]
Males, 15 Years and Over	3,092,736	3,683,258	4,059,104
Never married	30.4	35.4	37.1
Now married, except separated.................................	56.5	50.5	49.1
Separated..	2.0	2.1	1.8
Widowed..	2.1	2.2	2.4
Divorced...	9.0	9.9	9.6
Females, 15 Years and Over	3,273,889	3,954,542	4,388,000
Never married	24.4	29.7	32.0
Now married, except separated.................................	51.5	46.1	44.7
Separated..	2.7	2.9	2.5
Widowed..	9.8	8.6	8.2
Divorced...	11.6	12.7	12.6

[1] 2020 ACS 5-Year estimates. 1-Year estimates were not released for 2020 due to the impact of COVID-19 on data collection that year.

Table GA-3. Households and Housing Characteristics

(Number, percent, dollars.)

Item	2000	2010	2020 [1]	Average annual percent change, 2010–2020
Total Households..	3,006,369	3,482,420	3,830,264	1.4
Family households	2,111,647	2,385,969	2,565,233	1.1
Married-couple family	1,548,800	1,688,896	1,813,793	1.1
Other family	562,847	697,073	751,440	1.1
Male householder, no wife present..........................	127,437	161,001	179,970	1.7
Female householder, no husband present...................	435,410	536,072	571,470	0.9
Nonfamily households	894,722	1,096,451	1,265,031	2.2
Householder living alone...	710,523	921,005	1,046,237	1.9
Householder not living alone..	184,199	175,446	218,794	3.5
Housing Characteristics				
Total housing units	3,281,737	4,091,482	4,329,675	0.8
Occupied housing units	3,006,369	3,482,420	3,830,264	1.4
Owner occupied	2,029,154	2,304,165	2,453,159	0.9
Renter occupied	977,215	1,178,255	1,377,105	2.4
Average household size..	2.65	2.72	2.68	-0.2
Financial Characteristics				
Median gross rent of renter-occupied housing	613	819	1,042	3.9
Median monthly owner costs for housing units with a mortgage	1,039	1,390	1,449	0.6
Median value of owner-occupied housing units...................	111,200	156,200	190,200	3.1

[1] 2020 ACS 5-Year estimates. 1-Year estimates were not released for 2020 due to the impact of COVID-19 on data collection that year.

Table GA-4. Migration, Origin, and Language

(Number, percent.)

Characteristic	State 2016-2020 [1]	U.S. 2016-2020 [1]
Residence 1 Year Ago		
Population 1 year and over	10,394,332	322,943,283
Same house	85.5	86.2
Different house in the U.S..	14.0	13.2
Same county	6.6	7.7
Different county	7.4	5.5
Same state	4.7	3.2
Different state	2.7	2.3
Abroad	0.5	0.6
Place of Birth		
Native born	9,448,552	282,443,680
Male	48.4	49.4
Female	51.6	50.6
Foreign born	1,068,027	44,125,628
Male	50.2	48.6
Female	49.8	51.4
Foreign born; naturalized U.S. citizen...	485,195	22,456,684
Male	47.3	46.1
Female	52.7	53.9
Foreign born; not a U.S. citizen..	582,832	21,668,944
Male	52.6	51.1
Female	47.4	48.9
Entered 2010 or later	25.4	22.8
Entered 2000 to 2009	29.3	25.1
Entered before 2000..	45.3	52.1
World Region of Birth, Foreign		
Foreign-born population, excluding population born at sea	1,068,027	44,125,628
Europe	8.5	10.8
Asia	31.3	31.3
Africa	10.0	5.4
Oceania	0.4	0.6
Latin America	48.1	50.0
North America	1.8	1.9
Language Spoken at Home and Ability to Speak English		
Population 5 years and over...	9,864,494	306,919,116
English only	86.0	78.5
Language other than English..	14.0	21.5
Speaks English less than "very well"...	5.4	8.2

[1] 2020 ACS 5-Year estimates. 1-Year estimates were not released for 2020 due to the impact of COVID-19 on data collection that year.
NA = Not available.
X = Not applicable.
- = Zero or rounds to zero.

Table GA-5. Median Income and Poverty Status, 2020[1]

(Number, percent, except as noted.)

Characteristic	State		U.S.	
	Number	Percent	Number	Percent
Median Income				
Households (dollars)...	61,224	X	64,994	X
Families (dollars)	74,127	X	80,069	X
Below Poverty Level (All People)	1,461,572	14.3	40,910,326	12.8
Sex				
Male	637,626	12.9	18,171,512	11.6
Female	823,946	15.5	22,738,814	14.0
Age				
Under 18 years...	495,477	20.1	12,598,699	17.5
Related children under 18 years..	486,699	19.8	12,306,532	17.2
18 to 64 years..	821,046	12.9	23,554,920	12.1
65 years and over	145,049	10.1	4,756,707	9.3

X = Not applicable.
[1] 2020 ACS 5-Year estimates. 1-Year estimates were not released for 2020 due to the impact of COVID-19 on data collection that year.

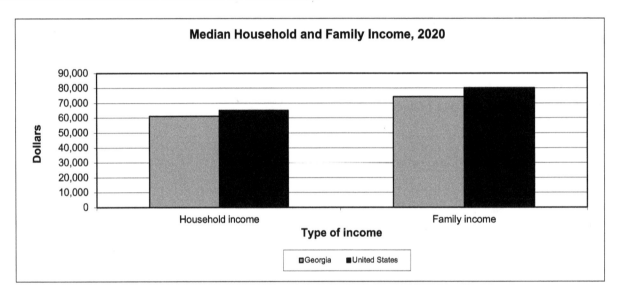

Table GA-6. Health Insurance Coverage Status for the Civilian Noninstitutionalized Population and Children Under 19 Years of Age

(Number, percent.)

Item	2011	2012	2013	2014	2015	2016	2017	2018	2019	2020[2]
Civilian Noninstitutionalized Population	9,619,740	9,719,411	9,800,887	9,906,878	10,024,056	10,120,788	10,241,594	10,334,958	10,420,412	10,321,846
Covered by Private or Public Insurance										
Number..	7,736,982	7,927,092	7,954,582	8,338,497	8,635,656	8,811,215	8,866,418	8,923,775	9,022,589	8,976,552
Percent..	80.4	81.6	81.2	84.2	86.1	87.1	86.6	86.3	86.6	87.0
Uninsured										
Number..	1,882,758	1,792,319	1,846,305	1,568,381	1,388,400	1,309,573	1,375,176	1,411,183	1,397,823	1,345,294
Percent..	19.6	18.4	18.8	15.8	13.9	12.9	13.4	13.7	13.4	13.0
Percent in the U.S. not covered................................	15.1	14.8	14.5	11.7	9.4	8.6	8.7	8.9	9.2	8.7
Children Under 19 Years of Age[1]	2,484,715	2,492,161	2,487,079	2,488,247	2,499,334	2,506,326	2,670,877	2,670,578	2,661,991	2,658,741
Covered by Private or Public Insurance										
Number..	2,248,147	2,272,200	2,249,028	2,299,212	2,333,101	2,343,554	2,471,248	2,453,288	2,464,855	2,462,470
Percent..	90.5	91.2	90.4	92.4	93.3	93.5	92.5	91.9	92.6	92.6
Uninsured										
Number..	236,568	219,961	238,051	189,035	166,233	162,772	199,629	217,290	197,136	196,271
Percent..	9.5	8.8	9.6	7.6	6.7	6.5	7.5	8.1	7.4	7.4
Percent in the U.S. not covered................................	7.5	7.2	7.1	6.0	4.8	4.5	5.0	5.2	5.7	5.2

[1] Data for years prior to 2017 are for individuals under 18 years of age.
[2] 2020 ACS 5-Year estimates. 1-Year estimates were not released for 2020 due to the impact of COVID-19 on data collection that year. Data is not comparable to previous years, which are based on 1-year estimates.

Table GA-7. Employment Status by Demographic Group, 2021

(Numbers in thousands, percent.)

Characteristic	Civilian noninstitutional population	Civilian labor force		Employed		Unemployed	
		Number	Percent of population	Number	Percent of population	Number	Percent of population
Total...	8,383	5,186	61.9	4,977	59.4	209	4.0
Sex							
Male..	3,959	2,695	68.1	2,589	65.4	107	4.0
Female.....................................	4,424	2,491	56.3	2,389	54.0	102	4.1
Race, Sex, and Hispanic Origin							
White.......................................	5,104	3,075	60.2	2,978	58.3	97	3.1
Male....................................	2,486	1,712	68.9	1,658	66.7	55	3.2
Female.................................	2,619	1,363	52.0	1,320	50.4	42	3.1
Black or African American................	2,691	1,698	63.1	1,598	59.4	100	5.9
Male....................................	1,196	770	64.4	724	60.5	46	6.0
Female.................................	1,494	928	62.1	874	58.5	54	5.8
Hispanic or Latino ethnicity[1]	857	596	69.6	581	67.8	16	2.6
Male....................................	457	365	79.9	356	77.9	9	2.4
Female.................................	400	232	57.9	225	56.2	7	3.0
Age							
16 to 19 years...........................	NA	NA	NA	NA	NA	NA	NA
20 to 24 years...........................	680	462	68.0	430	63.2	33	7.0
25 to 34 years...........................	1,506	1,238	82.2	1,191	79.1	48	3.8
35 to 44 years...........................	1,357	1,102	81.2	1,069	78.8	33	3.0
45 to 54 years...........................	1,411	1,122	79.5	1,084	76.8	38	3.4
55 to 64 years...........................	1,265	815	64.4	791	62.5	24	3.0
65 years and over.......................	1,603	279	17.4	264	16.5	15	5.2

NOTE: Data in Table 7 are from the Current Population Survey (CPS) and do not match the estimates in Table 8. See notes and definitions for further information.
[1] May be of any race.

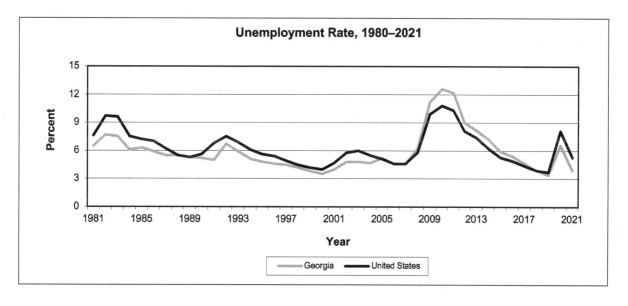

Unemployment Rate, 1980–2021

Table GA-8. Employment Status of the Civilian Noninstitutional Population Age 16 Years and Over

(Number, percent.)

Year	Civilian labor force	Civilian participation rate	Employed	Unemployed	Unemployment rate
2010..	4,709,781	64.3	4,207,266	502,515	10.7
2011..	4,739,281	64.2	4,258,833	480,448	10.1
2012..	4,770,618	63.8	4,339,369	431,249	9.0
2013..	4,750,046	62.8	4,363,292	386,754	8.1
2014..	4,745,859	62.0	4,407,067	338,792	7.1
2015..	4,734,088	61.0	4,446,515	287,573	6.1
2016..	4,921,814	62.4	4,653,740	268,074	5.4
2017..	5,107,889	63.9	4,864,813	243,076	4.8
2018..	5,121,172	63.2	4,915,713	205,459	4.0
2019..	5,152,944	62.8	4,967,503	185,441	3.6
2020..	5,079,555	61.2	4,751,105	328,450	6.5
2021..	5,186,969	61.9	4,983,732	203,237	3.9

Table GA-9. Employment and Average Wages by Industry

(Estimates are based on the 2012 North American Industry Classification System [NAICS].)

Industry	2013	2014	2015	2016	2017	2018	2019	2020
	Number of Jobs							
Wage and Salary Employment by Industry.........................	4,199,911	4,319,374	4,438,480	4,551,906	4,641,076	4,722,305	4,804,775	4,609,427
Farm Wage and Salary Employment...............................	15,251	16,194	15,830	19,165	22,342	16,454	16,331	21,110
Nonfarm Wage and Salary Employment..........................	4,184,660	4,303,180	4,422,650	4,532,741	4,618,734	4,705,851	4,788,444	4,588,317
Private wage and salary employment...	3,413,979	3,538,369	3,655,461	3,762,412	3,842,545	3,926,305	4,003,960	3,810,531
Forestry, fishing, and related activities....................................	15,075	15,296	15,945	16,024	15,497	15,528	15,591	15,141
Mining...	4,728	4,851	4,839	5,056	5,175	5,226	5,318	5,239
Utilities...	19,862	19,784	20,081	20,117	19,628	19,124	19,396	19,702
Construction..	149,968	160,672	170,197	181,116	187,242	200,754	209,453	206,897
Manufacturing...	358,221	367,979	377,861	388,287	398,346	408,690	405,694	385,322
Durable goods manufacturing..	171,753	177,266	182,689	187,999	193,741	201,501	202,826	192,596
Nondurable goods manufacturing......................................	186,468	190,713	195,172	200,288	204,605	207,189	202,868	192,726
Wholesale trade	205,696	211,049	218,267	220,140	221,978	216,205	218,646	209,389
Retail trade..	456,754	470,363	487,904	495,594	500,521	499,093	497,879	482,226
Transportation and warehousing......................................	170,113	177,721	186,180	195,626	204,878	215,522	214,453	218,592
Information	102,998	107,159	106,459	111,825	116,656	114,633	116,238	109,348
Finance and insurance	166,267	171,889	175,162	178,824	182,621	184,691	188,488	192,434
Real estate and rental and leasing	58,430	60,375	63,838	65,293	67,025	70,859	74,348	71,802
Professional, scientific, and technical services	240,337	253,845	262,918	263,526	272,074	279,367	285,638	285,087
Management of companies and enterprises........................	59,654	62,511	66,017	68,431	68,370	73,717	91,058	88,631
Administrative and waste services.....................................	290,869	306,243	314,679	326,336	334,688	342,532	348,454	327,069
Educational services	82,140	83,138	83,652	86,476	88,034	88,754	90,646	86,093
Health care and social assistance.....................................	429,181	436,674	452,427	470,611	478,321	491,239	506,906	491,769
Arts, entertainment, and recreation..................................	43,002	45,308	47,015	50,133	52,343	54,879	57,223	44,342
Accommodation and food services....................................	370,739	386,845	402,836	418,930	428,991	437,586	446,117	374,762
Other services, except public administration........................	189,945	196,667	199,184	200,067	200,157	207,906	212,414	196,686
Government and government enterprises.....................................	770,681	764,811	767,189	770,329	776,189	779,546	784,484	777,786
	Dollars							
Average Wages and Salaries by Industry	47,794	49,111	50,474	51,557	53,035	54,611	56,292	59,735
Average Farm Wages and Salaries	20,665	23,633	22,913	19,254	14,500	19,603	19,654	15,005
Average Nonfarm Wages and Salaries	47,892	49,207	50,572	51,694	53,221	54,733	56,417	59,941
Average private wages and salaries..	48,777	50,085	51,472	52,661	54,193	55,702	57,459	61,333
Forestry, fishing, and related activities....................................	33,463	34,282	35,229	37,054	37,234	38,221	39,926	43,473
Mining...	61,195	63,247	66,017	70,118	71,195	71,780	72,077	72,187
Utilities...	85,496	86,958	92,943	98,948	100,514	105,143	110,117	114,944
Construction	49,807	51,770	53,933	56,808	59,240	62,038	64,716	67,313
Manufacturing...	55,955	57,070	57,906	58,598	59,861	61,534	60,416	62,521
Durable goods manufacturing..	58,519	59,990	60,915	61,134	62,112	64,117	65,542	66,631
Nondurable goods manufacturing......................................	53,593	54,356	55,089	56,217	57,729	59,021	55,291	58,415
Wholesale trade	72,490	73,984	75,963	77,316	78,791	78,805	81,638	84,571
Retail trade..	28,274	28,843	30,268	30,699	31,407	32,358	33,288	35,964
Transportation and warehousing......................................	56,416	58,889	59,733	62,536	62,881	63,125	59,622	60,002
Information	85,827	89,003	88,600	92,509	98,349	98,984	103,280	111,752
Finance and insurance	81,700	84,165	87,955	89,532	93,267	96,986	99,955	106,766
Real estate and rental and leasing	51,897	53,684	55,099	57,553	58,964	62,518	63,253	66,816
Professional, scientific, and technical services	77,425	79,297	82,387	85,929	86,474	88,676	91,924	96,576
Management of companies and enterprises........................	99,236	106,149	110,283	107,215	115,838	122,329	133,180	138,863
Administrative and waste services.....................................	35,734	36,367	37,775	38,479	39,730	40,742	42,581	45,564
Educational services	43,326	44,515	45,027	45,784	46,431	48,737	50,055	55,157
Health care and social assistance.....................................	47,593	48,411	49,960	50,823	51,945	53,419	55,166	58,601
Arts, entertainment, and recreation..................................	35,605	36,602	36,978	36,253	38,858	38,760	39,708	45,303
Accommodation and food services....................................	19,682	20,197	19,876	20,332	21,041	22,096	22,770	21,996
Other services, except public administration........................	31,088	31,744	33,016	34,093	35,444	36,216	37,404	41,196
Government and government enterprises.....................................	43,974	45,143	46,287	46,969	48,411	49,854	51,101	53,119

Table GA-10. Employment Characteristics by Family Type

(Number, percent.)

Family type and labor force status	2018		2019		2020 [1]	
	Total	Families with own children under 18 years	Total	Families with own children under 18 years	Total	Families with own children under 18 years
All Families..........................	2,537,406	1,089,403	2,555,440	1,072,198	2,565,233	1,114,023
FAMILY TYPE AND LABOR FORCE STATUS						
Opposite-Sex Married-Couple Families...........................	1,783,375	708,193	1,802,484	704,892	1,796,279	729,626
Both husband and wife in labor force................	51.1	66.2	50.6	66.0	51.6	65.9
Husband in labor force, wife not in labor force	22.6	27.5	22.7	27.4	23.1	28.1
Wife in labor force, husband not in labor force	7.1	3.9	8.1	4.5	7.9	4.3
Both husband and wife not in labor force........	18.1	1.9	17.7	1.6	17.5	1.6
Other Families	754,031	381,210	752,956	367,306	751,440	380,718
Female householder, no spouse present	75.7	78.9	75.4	79.5	76.0	79.1
In labor force................	54.0	67.1	53.5	68.4	54.0	67.3
Not in labor force..................	21.7	11.8	22.0	11.2	22.0	11.7
Male householder, no spouse present................	24.3	21.1	24.6	20.5	24.0	20.9
In labor force..................	18.6	19.4	18.8	19.0	18.1	18.9
Not in labor force.................	5.7	1.7	5.8	1.5	5.8	2.0

[1] 2020 ACS 5-Year estimates. 1-Year estimates were not released for 2020 due to the impact of COVID-19 on data collection that year. Data is not comparable to previous years, which are based on 1-year estimates.

Table GA-11. School Enrollment and Educational Attainment, 2020[1]

(Number, percent.)

Item	State	U.S.
Enrollment		
Total population 3 years and over, enrolled in school	2,743,653	80,497,960
Enrolled in nursery school or preschool (percent)............................	6.3	6.1
Enrolled in kindergarten (percent)............................	5.0	5.0
Enrolled in elementary school, grades 1-8 (percent)............................	41.2	40.4
Enrolled in high school, grades 9-12 (percent)	21.6	21.0
Enrolled in college or graduate school (percent)............................	25.9	27.6
Attainment		
Total population 25 years and over	6,996,425	222,836,834
Less than ninth grade (percent)	4.5	4.9
9th to 12th grade, no diploma (percent)	7.7	6.6
High school graduate, including equivalency (percent)	27.5	26.7
Some college, no degree (percent)	20.2	20.3
Associate's degree (percent)............................	8.0	8.6
Bachelor's degree (percent)	19.7	20.2
Graduate or professional degree (percent)............................	12.5	12.7
High school graduate or higher (percent)	87.9	88.5
Bachelor's degree or higher (percent)	32.2	32.9

[1] 2020 ACS 5-Year estimates. 1-Year estimates were not released for 2020 due to the impact of COVID-19 on data collection that year.

Table GA-12. Public School Characteristics and Educational Indicators

(Number, percent; data derived from National Center of Education Statistics.)

Item	State	U.S.
Public Elementary and Secondary Schools		
Number of regular school districts, 2018-19	180	13,452
Number of operational schools, 2019-20............................	2,304	98,469
Percent charter schools	3.9	7.7
Total public school enrollment, Fall 2019............................	1,769,657	50,796,445
Percent charter school enrollment	3.7	6.8
Student-teacher ratio, Fall 2019............................	15.0	15.9
Expenditures per student (unadjusted dollars), 2018-19	11,203	13,187
Four-year adjusted cohort graduation rate (ACGR), 2018-2019[1]............................	82.0	85.8
Students eligible for free or reduced-price lunch (percent), 2019-20............................	59.7	52.1
English language learners (percent), Fall 2019	7.5	10.4
Students age 3 to 21 served under IDEA, part B (percent), 2020-21	12.9	14.5

Public Schools by Type, 2019-20	Number	Percent of state public schools
Total number of schools............................	2,304	100.0
Special education............................	12	0.5
Vocational education............................	0	-
Alternative education............................	31	1.3

[1] Adjusted Cohort Graduation Rates (ACGR) differ from Averaged Freshmen Graduation Rates (AFGR).
- = Zero or rounds to zero.

Table GA-13. Reported Voting and Registration of the Voting-Age Population, November 2020

(Numbers in thousands, percent.)

Item	Total population	Total citizen population	Registered			Voted		
			Total registered	Percent registered (total population)	Percent registered (total citizen population)	Total voted	Percent voted (total population)	Percent voted (total citizen population)
U.S. Total	252,274	231,593	168,308	66.7	72.7	154,628	61.3	66.8
State Total.................................	8,032	7,400	5,233	65.2	70.7	4,888	60.9	66.1
Sex								
Male	3,765	3,461	2,354	62.5	68.0	2,180	57.9	63.0
Female	4,267	3,938	2,880	67.5	73.1	2,707	63.5	68.7
Race								
White alone..............................	4,785	4,521	3,297	68.9	72.9	3,079	64.3	68.1
White, non-Hispanic alone	4,239	4,194	3,152	74.3	75.1	2,947	69.5	70.3
Black alone..............................	2,569	2,513	1,721	67.0	68.5	1,608	62.6	64.0
Asian alone	389	217	124	31.8	56.9	116	29.8	53.3
Hispanic (of any race).................	739	403	192	25.9	47.6	178	24.1	44.2
White alone or in combination	4,857	4,593	3,351	69.0	73.0	3,127	64.4	68.1
Black alone or in combination........	2,702	2,597	1,776	65.7	68.4	1,657	61.3	63.8
Asian alone or in combination.......	398	226	133	33.3	58.7	125	31.4	55.2
Age								
18 to 24 years..........................	990	925	556	56.1	60.1	489	49.4	52.9
25 to 34 years..........................	1,496	1,354	913	61.0	67.4	794	53.1	58.6
35 to 44 years..........................	1,287	1,083	723	56.2	66.8	690	53.6	63.7
45 to 64 years..........................	2,634	2,454	1,854	70.4	75.6	1,783	67.7	72.6
65 years and over	1,625	1,584	1,187	73.1	75.0	1,132	69.6	71.4

Table GA-14. Crime

(Number, rate per 100,000. Data are derived from the FBI Uniform Crime Reports.)

Item	State			U.S.		
	2019	2020	Percent change	2019	2020	Percent change
TOTAL POPULATION[1]	10,628,020	10,710,017	0.8	328,329,953	329,484,123	0.4
VIOLENT CRIME						
Number..........................	34,666	42,850	23.6	1,250,393	1,313,105	5.0
Rate..............................	326.2	400.1	22.7	380.8	398.5	4.6
Murder and Nonnegligent Manslaughter						
Number..........................	605	943	55.9	16,669	21,570	29.4
Rate..............................	5.7	8.8	54.7	5.1	6.5	28.9
Rape[2]						
Number..........................	3,005	3,420	13.8	143,224	126,430	-11.7
Rate..............................	28.3	31.9	12.9	43.6	38.4	-12.0
Robbery						
Number..........................	7,488	7,016	-6.3	268,483	243,600	-9.3
Rate..............................	70.5	65.5	-7.0	81.8	73.9	-9.6
Aggravated Assault						
Number..........................	23,568	31,471	33.5	822,017	921,505	12.1
Rate..............................	221.8	293.8	32.5	250.4	279.7	11.7
PROPERTY CRIME						
Number..........................	294,817	214,988	-27.1	6,995,235	6,452,038	-7.8
Rate..............................	2,774.0	2,007.4	-27.6	2,130.6	1,958.2	-8.1
Burglary						
Number..........................	37,476	31,139	-16.9	1,118,096	1,035,314	-7.4
Rate..............................	352.6	290.7	-17.5	340.5	314.2	-7.7
Larceny-Theft						
Number..........................	234,850	158,343	-32.6	5,152,267	4,606,324	-10.6
Rate..............................	2,209.7	1,478.5	-33.1	1,569.2	1,398.0	-10.9
Motor Vehicle Theft						
Number..........................	22,491	25,506	13.4	724,872	810,400	11.8
Rate..............................	211.6	238.2	12.5	220.8	246.0	11.4

NOTE: Although arson data are included in the trend and clearance tables, sufficient data are not available to estimate totals for this offense. Therefore, no arson data are published in this table.
- = Zero or rounds to zero.
[1] Population figures are U.S. Census Bureau provisional estimates as of July 1, 2020.
[2] The figures shown in the rape (revised definition) column were estimated using the revised Uniform Crime Reporting (UCR) definition of rape.

Table GA-15. State Government Finances, 2020

(Dollar amounts in thousands, percent distribution.)

Item	Dollars	Percent distribution
Total Revenue	61,196,004	100.0
General revenue	47,953,015	78.4
Intergovernmental revenue	17,799,647	29.1
Taxes	23,608,597	38.6
General sales	6163508	10.1
Selective sales	3,375,043	5.5
License taxes	719,188	1.2
Individual income tax	11704328	19.1
Corporate income tax	984,087	1.6
Other taxes	662,443	1.1
Current charges	3,910,100	6.4
Miscellaneous general revenue	2,634,671	4.3
Utility revenue	0	-
Liquor stores revenue	0	-
Insurance trust revenue[1]	13,242,989	21.6
Total Expenditure	60,621,037	100.0
Intergovernmental expenditure	14,859,079	24.5
Direct expenditure	45,761,958	75.5
Current operation	28,752,378	47.4
Capital outlay	3,392,425	5.6
Insurance benefits and repayments	11,465,618	18.9
Assistance and subsidies	1,576,644	2.6
Interest on debt	574,893	0.9
Exhibit: Salaries and wages	7,111,154	11.7
Total Expenditure	60,621,037	100.0
General expenditure	49,118,656	81.0
Intergovernmental expenditure	14,859,079	24.5
Direct expenditure	34,259,577	56.5
General expenditure, by function:		
Education	22,182,975	36.6
Public welfare	14,153,903	23.3
Hospitals	1,535,403	2.5
Health	1,851,613	3.1
Highways	3,248,160	5.4
Police protection	499,930	0.8
Correction	1,316,910	2.2
Natural resources	584,481	1.0
Parks and recreation	203,968	0.3
Governmental administration	1,192,574	2.0
Interest on general debt	574,893	0.9
Other and unallocable	1,736,898	2.9
Utility expenditure	36,763	0.1
Liquor stores expenditure	0	-
Insurance trust expenditure	11,465,618	18.9
Debt at End of Fiscal Year	14,115,682	X
Cash and Security Holdings	124,948,728	X

X = Not applicable.
- = Zero or rounds to zero.
[1] Within insurance trust revenue, net earnings of state retirement systems is a calculated statistic (the item code in the data file is X08), and thus can be positive or negative. Net earnings is the sum of earnings on investments plus gains on investments minus losses on investments. The change made in 2002 for asset valuation from book to market value in accordance with Statement 34 of the Governmental Accounting Standards Board is reflected in the calculated statistics.

Table GA-16. State Government Tax Collections, 2021

(Dollars in thousands, percent.)

Item	Dollars	Percent distribution
Total Taxes	27,850,996	100.0
Property taxes	732,325	2.6
Sales and gross receipts	10,257,930	36.8
General sales and gross receipts	6,948,296	24.9
Selective sales and gross receipts	3,309,634	11.9
Alcoholic beverages	227,872	0.8
Amusements	X	-
Insurance premiums	538,106	1.9
Motor fuels	1,781,682	6.4
Pari-mutuels	X	-
Public utilities	X	-
Tobacco products	242,897	0.9
Other selective sales	519,077	1.9
Licenses	750,136	2.7
Alcoholic beverages	4,363	-
Amusements	X	-
Corporations in general	66,937	0.2
Hunting and fishing	35,899	0.1
Motor vehicle	406,893	1.5
Motor vehicle operators	117,993	0.4
Public utilities	X	-
Occupation and business, NEC	85,652	0.3
Other licenses	32,399	0.1
Income taxes	15,971,641	57.3
Individual income	14,220,906	51.1
Corporation net income	1,750,735	6.3
Other taxes	138,964	0.5
Death and gift	0	-
Documentary and stock transfer	0	-
Severance	X	-
Taxes, NEC	138,964	0.5

X = Not applicable.
- = Zero or rounds to zero.

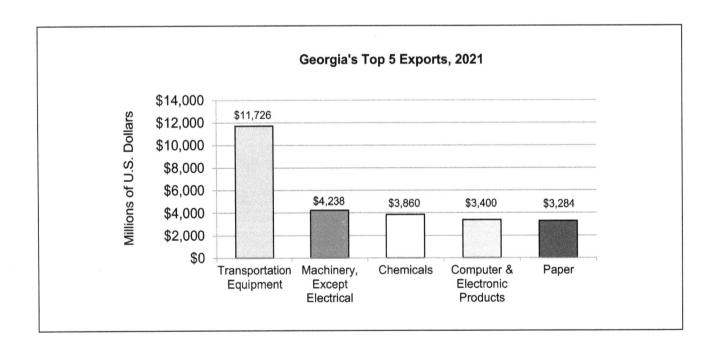

Georgia's Top 5 Exports, 2021

Export	Millions of U.S. Dollars
Transportation Equipment	$11,726
Machinery, Except Electrical	$4,238
Chemicals	$3,860
Computer & Electronic Products	$3,400
Paper	$3,284

Facts and Figures

Location: North Pacific Ocean

Area: 10,931 sq. mi. (28,311 sq. km.); rank—43rd

Population: 1,441,553 (2021 est.); rank—40th

Principal Cities: capital—Honolulu; largest—Honolulu

Statehood: August 21, 1959; 50th state

U.S. Congress: 2 senators, 2 representatives

State Motto: *Ua mau ke ea o ka'ina i ka pono* ("The life of the land is perpetuated in righteousness")

State Song: "Hawai'i Pono' (Hawaii's Own)"

State Nickname: The Aloha State

Abbreviations: HI

State Symbols: flower—native yellow hibiscus; tree—kukui (candlenut tree); bird—nene (Hawaiian goose)

At a Glance

- With an increase in population of 6.0 percent, Hawaii ranked 25th among the states in growth from 2010 to 2021.

- In 2020, 3.9 percent of Hawaiians did not have health insurance, compared to 8.7 percent of the total U.S. population, a rate that was the 3rd lowest in the country.

- Hawaii had the 13th highest property crime rate in the country in 2020, with 2,411.4 incidents per 100,000 population.

- Hawaii had 50.9 state and local government employees per 1,000 residents in 2021, compared to the national average of 49.4 employees per 1,000 residents.

- Hawaii had the largest percent of Asian Alone residents in 2021, with 36.8 percent of its residents self-identifying as Asian.

Table HI-1. Population by Age, Sex, Race, and Hispanic Origin

(Number, percent, except where noted.)

Sex, age, race, and Hispanic origin	2000	2010	2021	Percent change, 2010–2021
Total Population...	1,211,537	1,360,301	1,441,553	6.0
Percent of total U.S. population	0.4	0.4	0.4	X
Sex				
Male..	563,891	681,243	725,333	6.5
Female..	544,338	679,058	716,220	5.5
Age				
Under 5 years..	78,163	87,407	82,785	-5.3
5 to 19 years..	249,088	250,894	252,128	0.5
20 to 64 years...	723,685	826,868	824,336	-0.3
65 years and over	160,601	195,138	282,304	44.7
Median age (years)	36.2	38.6	40.2	4.1
Race and Hispanic Origin				
One race				
White	294,102	349,051	364,116	4.3
Black..	22,003	22,473	31,000	37.9
American Indian and Alaska Native	3,535	4,960	5,698	14.9
Asian..	503,868	531,633	529,888	-0.3
Native Hawaiian or Other Pacific Islander	113,539	138,292	150,726	9.0
Two or more races	259,343	313,892	360,125	14.7
Hispanic (of any race).....................................	87,699	133,342	160,134	20.1

NOTE: Population figures for 2021 are July 1 estimates. The 2000 and 2010 estimates are taken from the respective censuses.
- = Zero or rounds to zero.
X = Not applicable.

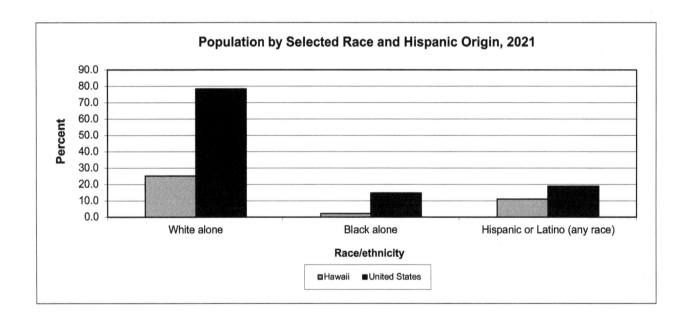

Table HI-2. Marital Status

(Number, percent distribution.)

Sex, age, race, and Hispanic origin	2000	2010	2020 [1]
Males, 15 Years and Over..	481,768	554,154	580,276
Never married	34.6	37.8	37.7
Now married, except separated..	53.7	49.1	50.5
Separated...	1.4	1.2	1.2
Widowed...	2.2	2.7	2.6
Divorced...	8.1	9.2	8.0
Females, 15 Years and Over..	484,107	556,915	583,832
Never married	25.9	28.7	29.4
Now married, except separated..	52.5	48.5	49.0
Separated...	1.7	1.8	1.4
Widowed...	9.8	10.1	9.9
Divorced...	10.0	11.0	10.2

[1] 2020 ACS 5-Year estimates. 1-Year estimates were not released for 2020 due to the impact of COVID-19 on data collection that year.

Table HI-3. Households and Housing Characteristics

(Number, percent, dollars.)

Item	2000	2010	2020 [1]	Average annual percent change, 2010–2020
Total Households..	403,240	445,812	467,932	0.7
Family households	287,068	303,075	324,482	1.0
Married-couple family	216,077	224,402	239,548	1.0
Other family	70,991	78,673	84,934	1.1
Male householder, no wife present............................	21,068	24,247	27,029	1.6
Female householder, no husband present....................	49,923	54,426	57,905	0.9
Nonfamily households	116,172	142,737	143,450	0.1
Householder living alone..	88,153	108,872	113,636	0.6
Householder not living alone..................................	28,019	33,865	29,814	-1.7
Housing Characteristics				
Total housing units...	460,542	519,992	546,571	0.7
Occupied housing units	403,240	445,812	467,932	0.7
Owner occupied	227,888	258,533	282,037	1.3
Renter occupied	175,352	187,279	185,895	-0.1
Average household size...	2.92	2.96	2.94	-0.1
Financial Characteristics				
Median gross rent of renter-occupied housing	779	1,291	1,651	4.0
Median monthly owner costs for housing units with a mortgage	1,636	2,240	2,443	1.3
Median value of owner-occupied housing units.............	272,700	525,400	636,400	3.0

[1] 2020 ACS 5-Year estimates. 1-Year estimates were not released for 2020 due to the impact of COVID-19 on data collection that year.

Table HI-4. Migration, Origin, and Language

(Number, percent.)

Characteristic	State 2016-2020 [1]	U.S. 2016-2020 [1]
Residence 1 Year Ago		
Population 1 year and over	1,402,177	322,943,283
Same house	86.8	86.2
Different house in the U.S.	12.1	13.2
Same county	7.8	7.7
Different county	4.3	5.5
Same state	0.7	3.2
Different state	3.6	2.3
Abroad	1.1	0.6
Place of Birth		
Native born	1,160,402	282,443,680
Male	51.9	49.4
Female	48.1	50.6
Foreign born	259,672	44,125,628
Male	42.2	48.6
Female	57.8	51.4
Foreign born; naturalized U.S. citizen..	152,550	22,456,684
Male	41.7	46.1
Female	58.3	53.9
Foreign born; not a U.S. citizen..	107,122	21,668,944
Male	43.0	51.1
Female	57.0	48.9
Entered 2010 or later	21.7	22.8
Entered 2000 to 2009	21.3	25.1
Entered before 2000...	57.0	52.1
World Region of Birth, Foreign		
Foreign-born population, excluding population born at sea	259,672	44,125,628
Europe	4.6	10.8
Asia	77.5	31.3
Africa	0.6	5.4
Oceania	10.8	0.6
Latin America...	4.7	50.0
North America	1.8	1.9
Language Spoken at Home and Ability to Speak English		
Population 5 years and over..	1,331,895	306,919,116
English only	73.9	78.5
Language other than English...	26.1	21.5
Speaks English less than "very well"...	11.4	8.2

[1] 2020 ACS 5-Year estimates. 1-Year estimates were not released for 2020 due to the impact of COVID-19 on data collection that year.
NA = Not available.
X = Not applicable.
- = Zero or rounds to zero.

Table HI-5. Median Income and Poverty Status, 2020[1]

(Number, percent, except as noted.)

Characteristic	State		U.S.	
	Number	Percent	Number	Percent
Median Income				
Households (dollars)..	83,173	X	64,994	X
Families (dollars)	97,813	X	80,069	X
Below Poverty Level (All People)	127,971	9.3	40,910,326	12.8
Sex				
Male	58,550	8.5	18,171,512	11.6
Female	69,421	10.0	22,738,814	14.0
Age				
Under 18 years...	34,575	11.7	12,598,699	17.5
Related children under 18 years.............................	32,902	11.2	12,306,532	17.2
18 to 64 years..	72,100	8.7	23,554,920	12.1
65 years and over	21,296	8.3	4,756,707	9.3

X = Not applicable.
[1] 2020 ACS 5-Year estimates. 1-Year estimates were not released for 2020 due to the impact of COVID-19 on data collection that year.

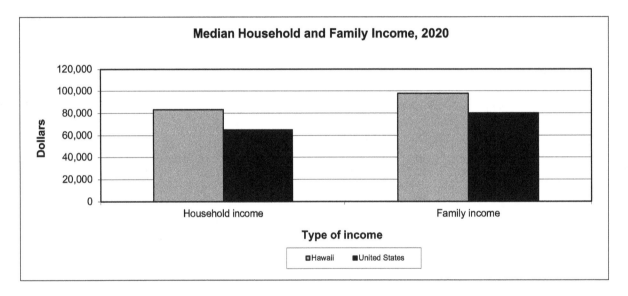

Table HI-6. Health Insurance Coverage Status for the Civilian Noninstitutionalized Population and Children Under 19 Years of Age

(Number, percent.)

Item	2011	2012	2013	2014	2015	2016	2017	2018	2019	2020 [2]
Civilian Noninstitutionalized Population	1,326,065	1,341,708	1,345,168	1,367,770	1,375,062	1,378,730	1,373,202	1,368,549	1,358,715	1,365,172
Covered by Private or Public Insurance										
Number...	1,231,666	1,249,370	1,254,413	1,295,659	1,320,531	1,330,057	1,320,375	1,312,750	1,302,236	1,312,365
Percent..	92.9	93.1	93.3	94.7	96.0	96.5	96.2	95.9	95.8	96.1
Uninsured										
Number...	94,399	92,338	90,755	72,111	54,531	48,673	52,827	55,799	56,479	52,807
Percent..	7.1	6.9	6.7	5.3	4.0	3.5	3.8	4.1	4.2	3.9
Percent in the U.S. not covered..................................	15.1	14.8	14.5	11.7	9.4	8.6	8.7	8.9	9.2	8.7
Children Under 19 Years of Age[1]	304,077	302,565	306,848	308,018	310,995	307,561	320,949	318,909	315,053	317,280
Covered by Private or Public Insurance										
Number...	293,097	292,102	297,513	298,466	305,950	300,664	313,911	310,599	306,230	308,771
Percent..	96.4	96.5	97.0	96.9	98.4	97.8	97.8	97.4	97.2	97.3
Uninsured										
Number...	10,980	10,463	9,335	9,552	5,045	6,897	7,038	8,310	8,823	8,509
Percent..	3.6	3.5	3.0	3.1	1.6	2.2	2.2	2.6	2.8	2.7
Percent in the U.S. not covered..................................	7.5	7.2	7.1	6.0	4.8	4.5	5.0	5.2	5.7	5.2

[1] Data for years prior to 2017 are for individuals under 18 years of age.
[2] 2020 ACS 5-Year estimates. 1-Year estimates were not released for 2020 due to the impact of COVID-19 on data collection that year. Data is not comparable to previous years, which are based on 1-year estimates.

Table HI-7. Employment Status by Demographic Group, 2021

(Numbers in thousands, percent.)

Characteristic	Civilian noninstitutional population	Civilian labor force		Employed		Unemployed	
		Number	Percent of population	Number	Percent of population	Number	Percent of population
Total..	1,080	645	59.7	605	56.0	40	6.1
Sex							
Male...	521	339	65.0	317	60.9	21	6.3
Female	559	306	54.7	288	51.5	18	5.9
Race, Sex, and Hispanic Origin							
White	249	149	60.0	139	55.7	11	7.1
Male	129	83	64.7	78	60.5	5	6.4
Female	120	66	55.0	61	50.5	5	8.1
Black or African American....................	NA	NA	NA	NA	NA	NA	NA
Male	NA	NA	NA	NA	NA	NA	NA
Female	NA	NA	NA	NA	NA	NA	NA
Hispanic or Latino ethnicity[1]	80	55	68.7	51	63.1	5	8.1
Male	42	32	75	30	70	2	7
Female	38	23	62	21	56	2	10
Age							
16 to 19 years	NA	NA	NA	NA	NA	NA	NA
20 to 24 years	69	47	68.5	43	61.9	5	10.0
25 to 34 years	164	130	79.5	124	75.4	7	5.1
35 to 44 years	169	137	81.0	129	76.5	8	5.6
45 to 54 years	165	138	83.4	129	78.0	9	6.5
55 to 64 years	171	114	67.0	107	62.6	7	6.5
65 years and over	273	60	22.1	58	21.3	2	3.5

NOTE: Data in Table 7 are from the Current Population Survey (CPS) and do not match the estimates in Table 8. See notes and definitions for further information.
[1] May be of any race.
NA = Not available.

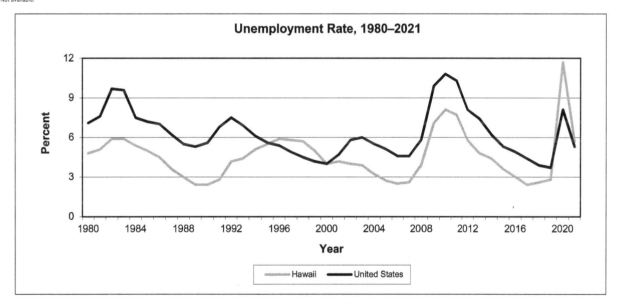

Table HI-8. Employment Status of the Civilian Noninstitutional Population Age 16 Years and Over

(Number, percent.)

Year	Civilian labor force	Civilian participation rate	Employed	Unemployed	Unemployment rate
2010..	648,549	63.0	604,210	44,339	6.8
2011..	660,634	62.6	615,470	45,164	6.8
2012..	650,415	61.0	611,985	38,430	5.9
2013..	650,978	60.6	620,005	30,973	4.8
2014..	664,014	61.5	635,913	28,101	4.2
2015..	670,594	61.7	647,616	22,978	3.4
2016..	679,121	62.1	659,557	19,564	2.9
2017..	695,303	62.0	679,865	15,438	2.2
2018..	691,982	61.6	675,681	16,301	2.4
2019..	684,690	60.9	667,914	16,776	2.5
2020..	662,491	59	582,979	79,512	12.0
2021..	668,413	59.8	630,187	38,226	5.7

Table HI-9. Employment and Average Wages by Industry

(Estimates are based on the 2012 North American Industry Classification System [NAICS].)

Industry	2013	2014	2015	2016	2017	2018	2019	2020
	Number of Jobs							
Wage and Salary Employment by Industry.........................	693,539	702,977	715,201	722,186	727,610	732,550	730,842	626,110
Farm Wage and Salary Employment................................	6,168	7,376	6,734	6,294	6,281	6,568	4,843	4,489
Nonfarm Wage and Salary Employment...........................	687,371	695,601	708,467	715,892	721,329	725,982	725,999	621,621
Private wage and salary employment............................	504,592	512,575	522,855	532,367	538,955	544,437	543,150	450,068
Forestry, fishing, and related activities.....................	1,518	1,532	1,574	1,534	1,517	1,490	1,545	1,467
Mining..	255	252	279	232	237	220	231	238
Utilities..	3,771	3,808	3,827	3,772	3,785	3,800	3,714	3,673
Construction..	31,569	32,592	35,572	38,592	36,747	36,833	37,868	37,008
Manufacturing...	13,588	13,934	14,097	14,130	14,281	14,210	14,013	11,978
Durable goods manufacturing..........................	3,632	3,600	3,699	3,728	3,853	3,783	3,773	3,415
Nondurable goods manufacturing.....................	9,956	10,334	10,398	10,402	10,428	10,427	10,240	8,563
Wholesale trade...	17,819	17,778	18,085	17,902	18,001	17,887	18,367	16,501
Retail trade...	70,183	70,323	71,285	71,115	71,669	72,365	71,774	61,829
Transportation and warehousing.........................	25,967	26,659	27,442	28,075	29,333	29,907	30,702	23,992
Information	8,792	8,482	8,724	8,829	9,039	9,144	8,688	7,273
Finance and insurance	15,762	15,671	15,962	16,168	16,344	16,342	17,032	16,990
Real estate and rental and leasing.....................	12,031	12,197	12,213	12,542	12,691	13,092	13,659	11,157
Professional, scientific, and technical services	24,584	24,554	24,763	24,638	24,549	25,034	25,088	24,112
Management of companies and enterprises............	8,255	8,377	8,507	8,720	8,886	8,968	9,185	8,297
Administrative and waste services	47,612	49,794	50,888	50,865	49,380	49,449	40,528	34,481
Educational services	16,101	15,805	15,566	15,791	16,051	16,509	16,555	13,679
Health care and social assistance.......................	64,960	65,709	67,839	69,307	70,974	72,271	73,955	71,619
Arts, entertainment, and recreation....................	12,097	12,398	11,860	12,243	12,882	13,257	14,029	8,285
Accommodation and food services.....................	99,657	101,678	103,306	106,668	110,982	111,324	113,276	69,876
Other services, except public administration..........	30,071	31,032	31,066	31,244	31,607	32,335	32,941	27,613
Government and government enterprises	182,779	183,026	185,612	183,525	182,374	181,545	182,849	171,553
	Dollars							
Average Wages and Salaries by Industry	45,440	46,681	48,332	49,584	50,968	52,274	54,143	58,281
Average Farm Wages and Salaries	38,569	32,882	33,869	38,552	38,271	26,393	35,534	37,502
Average Nonfarm Wages and Salaries	45,501	46,828	48,470	49,681	51,078	52,508	54,267	58,431
Average private wages and salaries...........................	42,376	43,490	45,347	46,621	48,169	49,615	51,431	55,667
Forestry, fishing, and related activities.....................	24,211	24,690	26,890	29,399	29,452	30,386	32,248	33,373
Mining..	88,325	93,694	96,878	94,345	86,181	93,150	100,905	99,660
Utilities..	92,306	94,486	99,620	97,875	102,023	106,175	107,839	106,568
Construction..	65,056	66,496	70,603	72,552	73,834	75,674	77,018	80,491
Manufacturing...	40,692	41,272	42,871	44,634	45,428	46,924	46,559	49,122
Durable goods manufacturing..........................	50,854	53,247	55,157	57,387	57,994	60,160	61,170	64,718
Nondurable goods manufacturing.....................	36,986	37,101	38,500	40,064	40,785	42,123	41,176	42,903
Wholesale trade...	52,573	54,246	55,790	57,552	60,247	59,738	61,865	63,720
Retail trade...	28,805	29,668	30,302	31,310	32,202	33,215	34,092	36,564
Transportation and warehousing.........................	46,390	48,239	50,711	52,924	56,569	56,529	57,571	63,298
Information	58,677	61,975	63,566	62,027	62,255	69,510	67,470	73,321
Finance and insurance	64,472	65,693	69,119	71,270	74,809	76,093	79,718	87,999
Real estate and rental and leasing.....................	46,221	46,937	49,914	51,520	55,526	56,240	56,858	62,825
Professional, scientific, and technical services	66,764	68,333	69,889	71,154	74,432	75,894	78,331	84,638
Management of companies and enterprises............	82,657	84,358	86,738	87,986	88,437	90,474	94,274	95,827
Administrative and waste services	31,048	31,586	32,928	34,415	35,500	36,652	38,091	41,752
Educational services	34,625	34,911	35,627	35,237	36,045	36,259	37,358	44,482
Health care and social assistance.......................	48,295	49,759	51,504	52,256	54,016	55,775	58,186	62,435
Arts, entertainment, and recreation....................	28,622	30,001	30,141	29,660	32,452	34,407	35,448	39,151
Accommodation and food services.....................	32,598	33,759	35,234	36,416	37,749	39,578	41,192	36,356
Other services, except public administration..........	34,110	34,818	36,223	37,368	38,602	40,065	41,322	44,992
Government and government enterprises	54,129	56,176	57,266	58,557	59,676	61,183	62,691	65,682

Table HI-10. Employment Characteristics by Family Type

(Number, percent.)

Family type and labor force status	2018 Total	2018 Families with own children under 18 years	2019 Total	2019 Families with own children under 18 years	2020 [1] Total	2020 [1] Families with own children under 18 years
All Families	316,849	116,964	316,206	110,403	324,482	118,089
FAMILY TYPE AND LABOR FORCE STATUS						
Opposite-Sex Married-Couple Families	235,162	86,726	232,024	80,229	236,910	85,444
Both husband and wife in labor force	53.5	69.0	50.9	67.3	52.7	68.1
Husband in labor force, wife not in labor force	18.5	23.9	19.4	25.4	19.2	25.1
Wife in labor force, husband not in labor force	8.3	4.7	9.6	4.8	9.5	4.9
Both husband and wife not in labor force	18.6	1.6	19.3	1.9	18.6	1.9
Other Families	81,687	30,238	84,182	30,174	84,934	32,250
Female householder, no spouse present	71.7	75.3	69.2	71.8	68.2	69.0
In labor force	43.4	61.2	44.1	59.1	43.0	58.0
Not in labor force	28.2	14.1	25.1	12.7	25.2	11.1
Male householder, no spouse present	28.3	24.7	30.8	28.2	31.8	31.0
In labor force	20.4	22.7	22.8	24.8	22.9	27.3
Not in labor force	7.9	2.1	7.9	3.4	8.9	3.7

[1] 2020 ACS 5-Year estimates. 1-Year estimates were not released for 2020 due to the impact of COVID-19 on data collection that year. Data is not comparable to previous years, which are based on 1-year estimates.

Table HI-11. School Enrollment and Educational Attainment, 2020[1]

(Number, percent.)

Item	State	U.S.
Enrollment		
Total population 3 years and over, enrolled in school	318,529	80,497,960
Enrolled in nursery school or preschool (percent)	6.9	6.1
Enrolled in kindergarten (percent)	5.1	5.0
Enrolled in elementary school, grades 1-8 (percent)	39.9	40.4
Enrolled in high school, grades 9-12 (percent)	19.2	21.0
Enrolled in college or graduate school (percent)	28.8	27.6
Attainment		
Total population 25 years and over	996,423	222,836,834
Less than ninth grade (percent)	3.5	4.9
9th to 12th grade, no diploma (percent)	4.1	6.6
High school graduate, including equivalency (percent)	27.3	26.7
Some college, no degree (percent)	20.8	20.3
Associate's degree (percent)	10.9	8.6
Bachelor's degree (percent)	21.9	20.2
Graduate or professional degree (percent)	11.6	12.7
High school graduate or higher (percent)	92.5	88.5
Bachelor's degree or higher (percent)	33.6	32.9

[1] 2020 ACS 5-Year estimates. 1-Year estimates were not released for 2020 due to the impact of COVID-19 on data collection that year.

Table HI-12. Public School Characteristics and Educational Indicators

(Number, percent; data derived from National Center of Education Statistics.)

Item	State	U.S.
Public Elementary and Secondary Schools		
Number of regular school districts, 2018-19	1	13,452
Number of operational schools, 2019-20	293	98,469
Percent charter schools	12.6	7.7
Total public school enrollment, Fall 2019	181,088	50,796,445
Percent charter school enrollment	6.6	6.8
Student-teacher ratio, Fall 2019	14.8	15.9
Expenditures per student (unadjusted dollars), 2018-19	16,132	13,187
Four-year adjusted cohort graduation rate (ACGR), 2018-2019[1]	85.2	85.8
Students eligible for free or reduced-price lunch (percent), 2019-20	45.5	52.1
English language learners (percent), Fall 2019	9.9	10.4
Students age 3 to 21 served under IDEA, part B (percent), 2020-21	11.3	14.5

Public Schools by Type, 2019-20	Number	Percent of state public schools
Total number of schools	293	100.0
Special education	1	0.3
Vocational education	0	-
Alternative education	1	0.3

[1] Adjusted Cohort Graduation Rates (ACGR) differ from Averaged Freshmen Graduation Rates (AFGR).
- = Zero or rounds to zero.

Table HI-13. Reported Voting and Registration of the Voting-Age Population, November 2020

(Numbers in thousands, percent.)

Item	Total population	Total citizen population	Registered			Voted		
			Total registered	Percent registered (total population)	Percent registered (total citizen population)	Total voted	Percent voted (total population)	Percent voted (total citizen population)
U.S. Total	252,274	231,593	168,308	66.7	72.7	154,628	61.3	66.8
State Total...	1,056	980	673	63.8	68.7	630	59.7	64.3
Sex								
Male	509	481	333	65.4	69.3	313	61.5	65.2
Female	546	499	340	62.3	68.2	317	57.9	63.5
Race								
White alone...	261	246	184	70.5	74.8	175	67.0	71.1
White, non-Hispanic alone	228	218	165	72.4	75.6	159	69.5	72.7
Black alone...	18	18	15	B	B	11	B	B
Asian alone	489	436	291	59.5	66.7	268	54.8	61.4
Hispanic (of any race)	71	66	35	B	B	30	B	B
White alone or in combination	374	359	260	69.6	72.5	248	66.4	69.2
Black alone or in combination	25	25	15	B	B	11	B	B
Asian alone or in combination...........................	613	561	377	61.4	67.2	351	57.3	62.7
Age								
18 to 24 years	107	93	46	43.4	49.6	41	38.8	44.4
25 to 34 years	170	156	88	51.9	56.7	80	47.3	51.7
35 to 44 years	170	156	110	65.0	70.5	103	60.4	65.6
45 to 64 years	332	311	244	73.5	78.3	230	69.4	73.9
65 years and over	278	263	185	66.5	70.2	175	63.2	66.6

B = Base is less than 75,000 and therefore too small to show the derived measure.

Table HI-14. Crime

(Number, rate per 100,000. Data are derived from the FBI Uniform Crime Reports.)

Item	State			U.S.		
	2019	2020	Percent change	2019	2020	Percent change
TOTAL POPULATION[1]	1,415,615	1,407,006	-0.6	328,329,953	329,484,123	0.4
VIOLENT CRIME						
Number..	3,745	3,576	-4.5	1,250,393	1,313,105	5.0
Rate	264.5	254.2	-3.9	380.8	398.5	4.6
Murder and Nonnegligent Manslaughter						
Number..	37	41	10.8	16,669	21,570	29.4
Rate	2.6	2.9	11.5	5.1	6.5	28.9
Rape[2]						
Number..	625	569	-9.0	143,224	126,430	-11.7
Rate	44.2	40.4	-8.4	43.6	38.4	-12.0
Robbery						
Number..	1,079	867	-19.6	268,483	243,600	-9.3
Rate	76.2	61.6	-19.2	81.8	73.9	-9.6
Aggravated Assault						
Number..	2,004	2,099	4.7	822,017	921,505	12.1
Rate	141.6	149.2	5.4	250.4	279.7	11.7
PROPERTY CRIME						
Number..	40,617	33,928	-16.5	6,995,235	6,452,038	-7.8
Rate	2,869.2	2,411.4	-16.0	2,130.6	1,958.2	-8.1
Burglary						
Number..	5,534	4,630	-16.3	1,118,096	1,035,314	-7.4
Rate	390.9	329.1	-15.8	340.5	314.2	-7.7
Larceny-Theft						
Number..	29,878	23,954	-19.8	5,152,267	4,606,324	-10.6
Rate	2,110.6	1,702.5	-19.3	1,569.2	1,398.0	-10.9
Motor Vehicle Theft						
Number..	5,205	5,344	2.7	724,872	810,400	11.8
Rate	367.7	379.8	3.3	220.8	246.0	11.4

NOTE: Although arson data are included in the trend and clearance tables, sufficient data are not available to estimate totals for this offense. Therefore, no arson data are published in this table.
- = Zero or rounds to zero.
[1] Population figures are U.S. Census Bureau provisional estimates as of July 1, 2020.
[2] The figures shown in the rape (revised definition) column were estimated using the revised Uniform Crime Reporting (UCR) definition of rape.

Table HI-15. State Government Finances, 2020

(Dollar amounts in thousands, percent distribution.)

Item	Dollars	Percent distribution
Total Revenue	18,322,618	100.0
General revenue	15,498,108	84.6
Intergovernmental revenue	4,205,193	23.0
Taxes	7,707,502	42.1
General sales	3697191	20.2
Selective sales	1,226,778	6.7
License taxes	274,200	1.5
Individual income tax	2359093	12.9
Corporate income tax	43,679	0.2
Other taxes	106,561	0.6
Current charges	1,680,940	9.2
Miscellaneous general revenue	1,904,473	10.4
Utility revenue	0	-
Liquor stores revenue	0	-
Insurance trust revenue[1]	2,824,510	15.4
Total Expenditure	14,539,887	100.0
Intergovernmental expenditure	323,474	2.2
Direct expenditure	14,216,413	97.8
Current operation	11,003,573	75.7
Capital outlay	1,174,815	8.1
Insurance benefits and repayments	1,797,387	12.4
Assistance and subsidies	123,158	0.8
Interest on debt	117,480	0.8
Exhibit: Salaries and wages	3,557,469	24.5
Total Expenditure	14,539,887	100.0
General expenditure	12,742,500	87.6
Intergovernmental expenditure	323,474	2.2
Direct expenditure	12,419,026	85.4
General expenditure, by function:		
Education	3,718,401	25.6
Public welfare	2,991,694	20.6
Hospitals	539,245	3.7
Health	740,311	5.1
Highways	528,814	3.6
Police protection	53,022	0.4
Correction	234,183	1.6
Natural resources	158,616	1.1
Parks and recreation	63,537	0.4
Governmental administration	686,027	4.7
Interest on general debt	117,480	0.8
Other and unallocable	2,894,138	19.9
Utility expenditure	0	-
Liquor stores expenditure	0	-
Insurance trust expenditure	1,797,387	12.4
Debt at End of Fiscal Year	9,430,284	X
Cash and Security Holdings	29,531,338	X

X = Not applicable.
- = Zero or rounds to zero.
[1] Within insurance trust revenue, net earnings of state retirement systems is a calculated statistic (the item code in the data file is X08), and thus can be positive or negative. Net earnings is the sum of earnings on investments plus gains on investments minus losses on investments. The change made in 2002 for asset valuation from book to market value in accordance with Statement 34 of the Governmental Accounting Standards Board is reflected in the calculated statistics.

Table HI-16. State Government Tax Collections, 2021

(Dollars in thousands, percent.)

Item	Dollars	Percent distribution
Total Taxes	8,046,691	100.0
Property taxes	X	-
Sales and gross receipts	4,147,624	51.5
General sales and gross receipts	3,296,268	41.0
Selective sales and gross receipts	851,356	10.6
Alcoholic beverages	45,178	0.6
Amusements	X	-
Insurance premiums	191,516	2.4
Motor fuels	70,796	0.9
Pari-mutuels	X	-
Public utilities	125,221	1.6
Tobacco products	108,529	1.3
Other selective sales	310,116	3.9
Licenses	258,953	3.2
Alcoholic beverages	X	-
Amusements	X	-
Corporations in general	2,203	-
Hunting and fishing	615	-
Motor vehicle	177,165	2.2
Motor vehicle operators	327	-
Public utilities	17,224	0.2
Occupation and business, NEC	49,591	0.6
Other licenses	11,828	0.1
Income taxes	3,546,116	44.1
Individual income	3,354,690	41.7
Corporation net income	191,426	2.4
Other taxes	93,998	1.2
Death and gift	31,275	0.4
Documentary and stock transfer	62,723	0.8
Severance	X	-
Taxes, NEC	0	-

X = Not applicable.
- = Zero or rounds to zero.

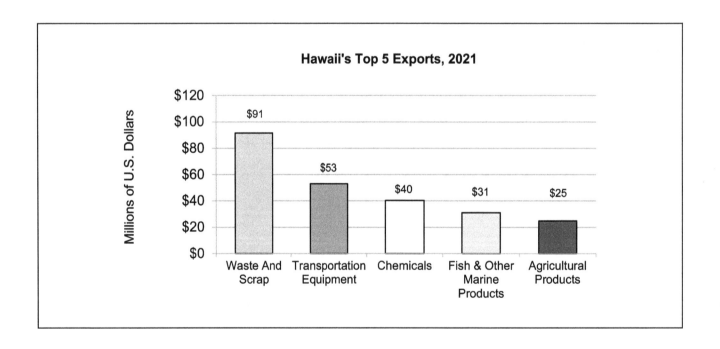

Hawaii's Top 5 Exports, 2021

Export	Millions of U.S. Dollars
Waste And Scrap	$91
Transportation Equipment	$53
Chemicals	$40
Fish & Other Marine Products	$31
Agricultural Products	$25

Facts and Figures

Location: Northwestern United States; bordered on the N by Canada, on the E by Montana and Wyoming, on the S by Nevada and Utah, and on the W by Washington and Oregon

Area: 83,568 sq. mi. (216,446 sq. km.); rank—14th

Population: 1,900,923 (2021 est.); rank—38th

Principal Cities: capital—Boise; largest—Boise

Statehood: July 3, 1890; 43rd state

U.S. Congress: 2 senators, 2 representatives

State Motto: *Esto perpetua* ("Let it be perpetual")

State Song: "Here We Have Idaho"

State Nickname: The Gem State

Abbreviations: ID

State Symbols: flower—syringa (mock orange); tree—Western white pine; bird—mountain bluebird

At a Glance

- With an increase in population of 21.3 percent, Idaho ranked 1st among the states in growth from 2010 to 2021.

- With 1,111.9 incidences per 100,000 population, Idaho had the 2nd lowest property crime rate in the country in 2020.

- Idaho's violent crime rate in 2020 was 242.6 per 100,000 population, compared to 398.5 for the entire nation.

- With 24.7 percent of its population under age 18, Idaho ranked 3rd among the states for the highest percent of minors in 2021.

- Idaho's unemployment rate ranked 41st in the nation in 2021, with 3.6 percent of the population unemployed, compared to 5.3 percent of the entire country.

Table ID-1. Population by Age, Sex, Race, and Hispanic Origin

(Number, percent, except where noted.)

Sex, age, race, and Hispanic origin	2000	2010	2021	Percent change, 2010–2021
Total Population...	1,293,953	1,567,582	1,900,923	21.3
Percent of total U.S. population	0.5	0.5	0.6	X
Sex				
Male...	648,660	785,324	958,616	22.1
Female...	645,293	782,258	942,307	20.5
Age				
Under 5 years..	97,643	121,772	114,324	-6.1
5 to 19 years..	316,222	353,509	404,485	14.4
20 to 64 years.......................................	734,172	897,633	1,066,658	18.8
65 years and over....................................	145,916	194,668	315,456	62.0
Median age (years)	33.2	34.6	37.4	8.1
Race and Hispanic Origin				
One race				
White	1,177,304	1,476,097	1,764,099	19.5
Black	5,456	10,950	17,786	62.4
American Indian and Alaska Native	17,645	25,782	33,064	28.2
Asian	11,889	20,034	30,778	53.6
Native Hawaiian or Other Pacific Islander	1,308	2,786	4,355	56.3
Two or more races	25,609	31,933	50,841	59.2
Hispanic (of any race)................................	101,690	182,424	251,919	38.1

NOTE: Population figures for 2021 are July 1 estimates. The 2000 and 2010 estimates are taken from the respective censuses.
- = Zero or rounds to zero.
X = Not applicable.

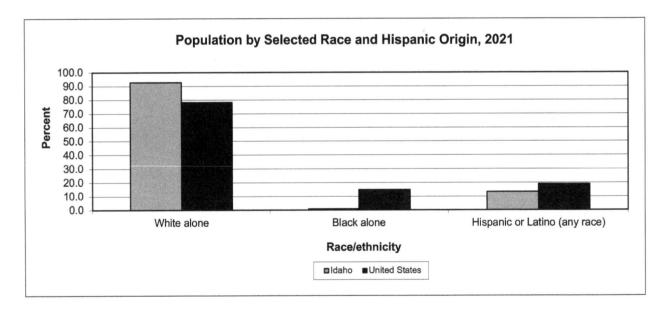

Population by Selected Race and Hispanic Origin, 2021

□ Idaho   ■ United States

Table ID-2. Marital Status

(Number, percent distribution.)

Sex, age, race, and Hispanic origin	2000	2010	2020 [1]
Males, 15 Years and Over	493,045	602,308	691,244
Never married	26.1	28.3	30.2
Now married, except separated..........................	61.0	57.0	55.2
Separated...	1.0	1.4	1.0
Widowed..	2.1	2.4	2.4
Divorced..	9.9	10.9	11.3
Females, 15 Years and Over	498,579	608,900	695,362
Never married	19.6	22.4	23.8
Now married, except separated..........................	59.0	55.3	54.6
Separated...	1.3	1.6	1.2
Widowed..	8.6	7.6	7.6
Divorced..	11.4	13.1	12.8

[1] 2020 ACS 5-Year estimates. 1-Year estimates were not released for 2020 due to the impact of COVID-19 on data collection that year.

Table ID-3. Households and Housing Characteristics

(Number, percent, dollars.)

Item	2000	2010	2020 [1]	Average annual percent change, 2010–2020
Total Households..	469,645	576,709	649,299	1.8
Family households..	333,588	401,806	441,391	1.4
Married-couple family..	276,511	322,129	356,168	1.5
Other family...	59,077	79,677	85,223	1.0
Male householder, no wife present.............................	18,228	23,583	28,881	3.2
Female householder, no husband present.....................	40,849	56,094	56,342	0.1
Nonfamily households	134,057	174,903	207,908	2.7
Householder living alone...	105,175	139,909	166,745	2.7
Householder not living alone..	28,882	34,994	41,163	2.5
Housing Characteristics				
Total housing units...	527,824	668,634	737,411	1.5
Occupied housing units	469,645	576,709	649,299	1.8
Owner occupied...	339,960	401,532	459,428	2.1
Renter occupied...	129,685	175,177	189,871	1.2
Average household size...	2.69	2.67	2.66	-0.1
Financial Characteristics				
Median gross rent of renter-occupied housing	515	683	887	4.3
Median monthly owner costs for housing units with a mortgage	887	1,187	1,312	1.5
Median value of owner-occupied housing units......................	106,300	165,100	235,600	6.1

[1] 2020 ACS 5-Year estimates. 1-Year estimates were not released for 2020 due to the impact of COVID-19 on data collection that year.

Table ID-4. Migration, Origin, and Language

(Number, percent.)

Characteristic	State 2016-2020 [1]	U.S. 2016-2020 [1]
Residence 1 Year Ago		
Population 1 year and over	1,733,958	322,943,283
Same house	83.2	86.2
Different house in the U.S.	16.4	13.2
Same county	8.8	7.7
Different county	7.6	5.5
Same state	3.2	3.2
Different state	4.3	2.3
Abroad	0.4	0.6
Place of Birth		
Native born	1,651,346	282,443,680
Male	50.2	49.4
Female	49.8	50.6
Foreign born	103,021	44,125,628
Male	49.2	48.6
Female	50.8	51.4
Foreign born; naturalized U.S. citizen...	44,198	22,456,684
Male	44.7	46.1
Female	55.3	53.9
Foreign born; not a U.S. citizen...	58,823	21,668,944
Male	52.7	51.1
Female	47.3	48.9
Entered 2010 or later	21.7	22.8
Entered 2000 to 2009	28.2	25.1
Entered before 2000..	50.1	52.1
World Region of Birth, Foreign		
Foreign-born population, excluding population born at sea	103,021	44,125,628
Europe	13.6	10.8
Asia	19.5	31.3
Africa	2.9	5.4
Oceania	0.9	0.6
Latin America	58.1	50.0
North America	4.9	1.9
Language Spoken at Home and Ability to Speak English		
Population 5 years and over..	1,640,035	306,919,116
English only	89.2	78.5
Language other than English...	10.8	21.5
Speaks English less than "very well"..	3.8	8.2

[1] 2020 ACS 5-Year estimates. 1-Year estimates were not released for 2020 due to the impact of COVID-19 on data collection that year.
NA = Not available.
X = Not applicable.
- = Zero or rounds to zero.

Table ID-5. Median Income and Poverty Status, 2020[1]

(Number, percent, except as noted.)

Characteristic	State		U.S.	
	Number	Percent	Number	Percent
Median Income				
Households (dollars)..	58,915	X	64,994	X
Families (dollars)	70,885	X	80,069	X
Below Poverty Level (All People)	205,676	11.9	40,910,326	12.8
Sex				
Male	93,429	10.9	18,171,512	11.6
Female	112,247	13.0	22,738,814	14.0
Age				
Under 18 years...	63,003	14.4	12,598,699	17.5
Related children under 18 years..................................	60,968	14.0	12,306,532	17.2
18 to 64 years..	121,078	12.0	23,554,920	12.1
65 years and over	21,595	7.9	4,756,707	9.3

X = Not applicable.
[1] 2020 ACS 5-Year estimates. 1-Year estimates were not released for 2020 due to the impact of COVID-19 on data collection that year.

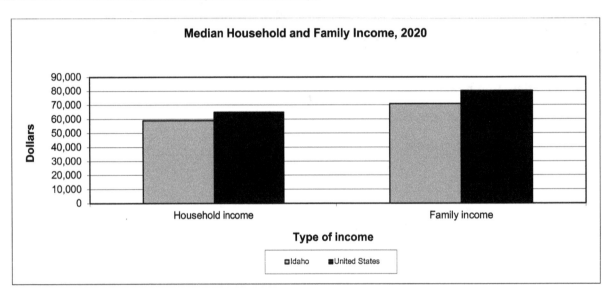

Median Household and Family Income, 2020

□ Idaho   ■ United States

Table ID-6. Health Insurance Coverage Status for the Civilian Noninstitutionalized Population and Children Under 19 Years of Age

(Number, percent.)

Item	2011	2012	2013	2014	2015	2016	2017	2018	2019	2020 [2]
Civilian Noninstitutionalized Population	1,565,645	1,575,682	1,592,172	1,612,889	1,632,247	1,662,867	1,695,273	1,733,484	1,764,911	1,732,106
Covered by Private or Public Insurance										
Number..	1,306,551	1,320,939	1,334,697	1,394,182	1,451,902	1,494,757	1,523,260	1,540,864	1,573,716	1,552,616
Percent...	83.5	83.8	83.8	86.4	89.0	89.9	89.9	88.9	89.2	89.6
Uninsured										
Number..	259,094	254,743	257,475	218,707	180,345	168,110	172,013	192,620	191,195	179,490
Percent...	16.5	16.2	16.2	13.6	11.0	10.1	10.1	11.1	10.8	10.4
Percent in the U.S. not covered................................	15.1	14.8	14.5	11.7	9.4	8.6	8.7	8.9	9.2	8.7
Children Under 19 Years of Age[1]	427,064	423,926	425,948	430,662	431,339	435,630	471,739	471,103	474,852	469,258
Covered by Private or Public Insurance										
Number..	388,096	387,897	387,931	396,885	406,497	415,147	450,102	442,305	451,283	444,561
Percent...	90.9	91.5	91.1	92.2	94.2	95.3	95.4	93.9	95.0	94.7
Uninsured										
Number..	38,968	36,029	38,017	33,777	24,842	20,483	21,637	28,798	23,569	24,697
Percent...	9.1	8.5	8.9	7.8	5.8	4.7	4.6	6.1	5.0	5.3
Percent in the U.S. not covered................................	7.5	7.2	7.1	6.0	4.8	4.5	5.0	5.2	5.7	5.2

[1] Data for years prior to 2017 are for individuals under 18 years of age.
[2] 2020 ACS 5-Year estimates. 1-Year estimates were not released for 2020 due to the impact of COVID-19 on data collection that year. Data is not comparable to previous years, which are based on 1-year estimates.

Table ID-7. Employment Status by Demographic Group, 2021

(Numbers in thousands, percent.)

Characteristic	Civilian noninstitutional population	Civilian labor force		Employed		Unemployed	
		Number	Percent of population	Number	Percent of population	Number	Percent of population
Total...	1,444	909	63.0	875	60.6	34	3.7
Sex							
Male..	714	505	70.7	485	67.9	20	3.9
Female...	730	404	55.4	390	53.4	14	3.6
Race, Sex, and Hispanic Origin							
White...	1,363	854	62.7	823	60.4	31	3.7
Male...	675	476	70.6	458	67.9	18	3.8
Female......................................	688	378	54.9	364	52.9	13	3.5
Black or African American.................	NA	NA	NA	NA	NA	NA	NA
Male...	NA	NA	NA	NA	NA	NA	NA
Female......................................	NA	NA	NA	NA	NA	NA	NA
Hispanic or Latino ethnicity[1]............	184	134	72.9	129	70.1	5	3.8
Male...	95	78	81.9	75	78.7	3	3.9
Female......................................	89	56	63.3	54	61.1	2	3.7
Age							
16 to 19 years...............................	94	45	48	41	44	4	9
20 to 24 years...............................	138	112	81.0	105	76.1	7	6.1
25 to 34 years...............................	244	198	81.2	191	78.1	8	3.9
35 to 44 years...............................	221	183	82.9	178	80.5	5	2.8
45 to 54 years...............................	217	179	82.7	176	81.0	4	2.1
55 to 64 years...............................	215	136	63.6	132	61.5	5	3.4
65 years and over...........................	316	55	17.4	53	16.9	2	3.1

NOTE: Data in Table 7 are from the Current Population Survey (CPS) and do not match the estimates in Table 8. See notes and definitions for further information.
[1] May be of any race.
NA = Not available.

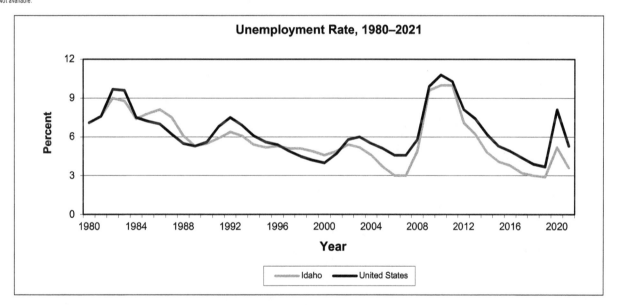

Unemployment Rate, 1980–2021

Table ID-8. Employment Status of the Civilian Noninstitutional Population Age 16 Years and Over

(Number, percent.)

Year	Civilian labor force	Civilian participation rate	Employed	Unemployed	Unemployment rate
2010..	762,147	65.4	695,265	66,882	8.8
2011..	764,205	64.8	701,660	62,545	8.2
2012..	772,112	64.7	714,969	57,143	7.4
2013..	777,606	64.3	724,545	53,061	6.8
2014..	776,937	63.3	742,805	34,132	4.4
2015..	795,014	63.8	764,121	30,893	3.9
2016..	812,921	63.8	783,180	29,741	3.7
2017..	839,776	63.9	812,875	26,901	3.2
2018..	862,513	64.1	837,514	24,999	2.9
2019..	889,194	64.4	862,864	26,330	3.0
2020..	897,739	63.2	848,741	48,998	5.5
2021..	917,056	62.5	884,328	32,728	3.6

Table ID-9. Employment and Average Wages by Industry

(Estimates are based on the 2012 North American Industry Classification System [NAICS].)

Industry	2013	2014	2015	2016	2017	2018	2019	2020
	Number of Jobs							
Wage and Salary Employment by Industry..........................	667,781	685,278	703,568	726,463	748,265	772,994	796,965	792,781
Farm Wage and Salary Employment.................................	16,382	17,623	17,001	17,215	19,927	18,627	19,608	18,283
Nonfarm Wage and Salary Employment.............................	651,399	667,655	686,567	709,248	728,338	754,367	777,357	774,498
Private wage and salary employment..	524,718	540,229	557,474	578,017	595,200	619,224	640,325	639,878
Forestry, fishing, and related activities..............................	8,168	8,381	8,669	8,502	8,412	8,504	8,631	8,605
Mining..	2,548	2,417	2,322	2,364	2,178	2,217	2,290	2,488
Utilities..	2,806	2,912	3,013	3,010	2,983	3,012	2,944	2,966
Construction...	32,611	34,682	37,071	40,444	43,723	47,934	51,904	54,754
Manufacturing...	59,236	59,928	61,656	63,840	66,166	67,819	68,448	67,736
Durable goods manufacturing..............................	34,027	34,482	35,615	36,847	37,811	39,325	39,315	38,508
Nondurable goods manufacturing..........................	25,209	25,446	26,041	26,993	28,355	28,494	29,133	29,228
Wholesale trade	28,270	28,721	28,728	28,476	28,783	29,442	30,669	30,955
Retail trade...	78,526	80,215	83,374	85,021	86,158	87,041	87,547	87,642
Transportation and warehousing...................................	18,744	19,520	20,481	20,570	21,109	22,248	23,254	23,932
Information	9,236	9,221	9,187	9,001	8,960	8,797	8,809	7,355
Finance and insurance	21,748	22,246	22,870	23,766	24,698	25,836	26,368	27,445
Real estate and rental and leasing................................	6,830	6,925	7,281	7,390	7,819	8,277	8,814	9,006
Professional, scientific, and technical services	31,241	32,732	34,369	35,433	36,228	38,193	40,452	42,231
Management of companies and enterprises.....................	5,435	5,479	5,538	5,302	5,832	6,793	7,106	7,246
Administrative and waste services................................	39,807	40,258	39,886	44,552	46,743	47,334	47,354	48,346
Educational services	11,201	11,482	11,994	12,077	12,150	13,571	14,009	15,761
Health care and social assistance.................................	80,845	83,485	86,519	89,123	90,422	94,124	98,774	99,873
Arts, entertainment, and recreation..............................	9,336	9,990	9,684	10,373	11,113	12,349	12,867	11,488
Accommodation and food services................................	53,652	56,054	58,519	61,884	64,414	67,090	70,199	63,815
Other services, except public administration......................	24,478	25,581	26,313	26,889	27,309	28,643	29,886	28,234
Government and government enterprises...............................	126,681	127,426	129,093	131,231	133,138	135,143	137,032	134,620
	Dollars							
Average Wages and Salaries by Industry	37,817	38,886	39,610	40,488	42,022	43,700	44,731	48,224
Average Farm Wages and Salaries	38,875	36,986	30,600	34,986	30,398	36,423	24,772	35,388
Average Nonfarm Wages and Salaries	37,791	38,936	39,833	40,621	42,341	43,879	45,234	48,527
Average private wages and salaries......................................	37,973	39,248	40,072	40,897	42,708	44,286	45,652	49,090
Forestry, fishing, and related activities..............................	29,061	30,530	31,918	33,602	34,944	36,384	36,983	39,583
Mining..	76,004	76,496	71,394	72,985	72,739	71,729	74,831	75,061
Utilities..	78,927	81,030	83,034	83,414	87,769	90,700	92,477	98,019
Construction	39,813	40,059	40,859	42,485	43,691	45,202	47,099	49,554
Manufacturing...	54,776	60,062	57,217	56,983	63,310	65,822	64,366	67,565
Durable goods manufacturing..............................	62,222	69,867	63,801	63,429	73,275	76,071	72,941	76,430
Nondurable goods manufacturing..........................	44,725	46,776	48,214	48,184	50,023	51,677	52,793	55,884
Wholesale trade	50,886	53,289	56,868	58,131	60,051	62,558	65,835	70,046
Retail trade...	27,644	28,755	29,828	30,673	31,508	31,855	32,535	35,480
Transportation and warehousing...................................	41,186	42,278	43,129	43,367	45,122	46,566	48,462	49,871
Information	46,882	48,206	48,946	51,110	53,068	54,879	58,310	67,150
Finance and insurance	53,870	55,761	58,075	60,895	62,298	64,747	68,803	79,181
Real estate and rental and leasing................................	31,973	33,981	34,640	34,647	36,383	38,630	40,681	45,101
Professional, scientific, and technical services	59,102	59,336	61,457	60,824	63,902	65,989	69,389	74,854
Management of companies and enterprises.....................	87,249	78,953	78,142	81,546	85,748	93,754	102,049	109,852
Administrative and waste services................................	27,074	27,832	29,584	32,197	34,791	36,954	38,541	42,034
Educational services	27,204	27,426	28,293	27,745	28,234	27,800	29,465	29,260
Health care and social assistance.................................	38,617	39,640	41,028	42,382	42,486	43,706	45,000	47,149
Arts, entertainment, and recreation..............................	19,479	19,864	20,702	21,393	21,799	23,287	24,551	25,941
Accommodation and food services................................	16,026	16,618	17,175	17,809	18,494	19,614	20,121	20,012
Other services, except public administration......................	26,896	27,565	28,517	29,643	31,227	32,260	33,284	36,283
Government and government enterprises...............................	37,037	37,617	38,804	39,407	40,696	42,015	43,284	45,854

Table ID-10. Employment Characteristics by Family Type

(Number, percent.)

Family type and labor force status	2018		2019		2020 [1]	
	Total	Families with own children under 18 years	Total	Families with own children under 18 years	Total	Families with own children under 18 years
All Families..	437,765	185,628	448,979	189,358	441,391	190,133
FAMILY TYPE AND LABOR FORCE STATUS						
Opposite-Sex Married-Couple Families............................	348,814	137,001	357,453	144,669	354,311	142,579
Both husband and wife in labor force....................	47.5	60.6	48.9	63.0	48.8	62.1
Husband in labor force, wife not in labor force	24.2	33.7	23.3	31.6	23.9	32.4
Wife in labor force, husband not in labor force	7.6	4.1	7.7	3.6	7.1	3.6
Both husband and wife not in labor force....................	20.2	1.2	19.7	1.5	20.2	1.8
Other Families	88,951	48,627	91,526	44,689	85,223	47,132
Female householder, no spouse present	67.8	70.3	66.3	68.6	66.1	67.3
In labor force........................	50.8	61.4	47.4	61.0	48.4	57.7
Not in labor force........................	17.0	8.8	19.0	7.6	17.7	9.6
Male householder, no spouse present........................	32.2	29.7	33.7	31.4	33.9	32.7
In labor force........................	24.9	28.0	25.4	29.0	27.1	30.0
Not in labor force........................	7.3	1.8	8.3	2.4	6.8	2.7

[1] 2020 ACS 5-Year estimates. 1-Year estimates were not released for 2020 due to the impact of COVID-19 on data collection that year. Data is not comparable to previous years, which are based on 1-year estimates.

Table ID-11. School Enrollment and Educational Attainment, 2020[1]

(Number, percent.)

Item	State	U.S.
Enrollment		
Total population 3 years and over, enrolled in school	456,826	80,497,960
Enrolled in nursery school or preschool (percent)........................	5.2	6.1
Enrolled in kindergarten (percent)........................	5.2	5.0
Enrolled in elementary school, grades 1-8 (percent)........................	43.7	40.4
Enrolled in high school, grades 9-12 (percent)	22.1	21.0
Enrolled in college or graduate school (percent)........................	23.9	27.6
Attainment		
Total population 25 years and over	1,145,344	222,836,834
Less than ninth grade (percent)........................	3.1	4.9
9th to 12th grade, no diploma (percent)........................	5.6	6.6
High school graduate, including equivalency (percent)........................	26.7	26.7
Some college, no degree (percent)........................	26.1	20.3
Associate's degree (percent)........................	9.8	8.6
Bachelor's degree (percent)........................	19.3	20.2
Graduate or professional degree (percent)........................	9.4	12.7
High school graduate or higher (percent)	91.3	88.5
Bachelor's degree or higher (percent)........................	28.7	32.9

[1] 2020 ACS 5-Year estimates. 1-Year estimates were not released for 2020 due to the impact of COVID-19 on data collection that year.

Table ID-12. Public School Characteristics and Educational Indicators

(Number, percent; data derived from National Center of Education Statistics.)

Item	State	U.S.
Public Elementary and Secondary Schools		
Number of regular school districts, 2018-19	115	13,452
Number of operational schools, 2019-20........................	751	98,469
Percent charter schools	9.1	7.7
Total public school enrollment, Fall 2019........................	311,096	50,796,445
Percent charter school enrollment	7.8	6.8
Student-teacher ratio, Fall 2019........................	18.1	15.9
Expenditures per student (unadjusted dollars), 2018-19	8,043	13,187
Four-year adjusted cohort graduation rate (ACGR), 2018-2019[1]........................	80.8	85.8
Students eligible for free or reduced-price lunch (percent), 2019-20........................	37.1	52.1
English language learners (percent), Fall 2019	6.9	10.4
Students age 3 to 21 served under IDEA, part B (percent), 2020-21	11.5	14.5

Public Schools by Type, 2019-20	Number	Percent of state public schools
Total number of schools........................	751	100.0
Special education........................	10	1.3
Vocational education........................	13	1.7
Alternative education........................	74	9.9

[1] Adjusted Cohort Graduation Rates (ACGR) differ from Averaged Freshmen Graduation Rates (AFGR).

Table ID-13. Reported Voting and Registration of the Voting-Age Population, November 2020

(Numbers in thousands, percent.)

Item	Total population	Total citizen population	Registered			Voted		
			Total registered	Percent registered (total population)	Percent registered (total citizen population)	Total voted	Percent voted (total population)	Percent voted (total citizen population)
U.S. Total	252,274	231,593	168,308	66.7	72.7	154,628	61.3	66.8
State Total	1,370	1,299	900	65.7	69.3	843	61.6	64.9
Sex								
Male	679	643	434	63.9	67.5	410	60.4	63.8
Female	691	656	466	67.5	71.1	433	62.7	66.0
Race								
White alone	1,279	1,227	857	67.0	69.8	806	63.0	65.6
White, non-Hispanic alone	1,130	1,119	800	70.8	71.5	755	66.8	67.5
Black alone	10	7	5	B	B	4	B	B
Asian alone	22	12	7	B	B	5	B	B
Hispanic (of any race)	166	119	63	38.1	53.2	55	33.1	46.3
White alone or in combination	1,303	1,252	873	67.0	69.8	822	63.0	65.6
Black alone or In combination	16	13	8	B	B	7	B	B
Asian alone or in combination	22	12	7	B	B	5	B	B
Age								
18 to 24 years	182	177	102	55.8	57.6	95	52.1	53.9
25 to 34 years	253	235	151	59.8	64.5	140	55.4	59.7
35 to 44 years	203	185	132	65.0	71.3	123	60.4	66.2
45 to 64 years	418	398	278	66.6	69.9	262	62.7	65.8
65 years and over	313	304	237	75.7	77.9	223	71.3	73.4

B = Base is less than 75,000 and therefore too small to show the derived measure.

Table ID-14. Crime

(Number, rate per 100,000. Data are derived from the FBI Uniform Crime Reports.)

Item	State			U.S.		
	2019	2020	Percent change	2019	2020	Percent change
TOTAL POPULATION[1]	1,789,060	1,826,913	2.1	328,329,953	329,484,123	0.4
VIOLENT CRIME						
Number	4,162	4,432	6.5	1,250,393	1,313,105	5.0
Rate	232.6	242.6	4.3	380.8	398.5	4.6
Murder and Nonnegligent Manslaughter						
Number	28	41	46.4	16,669	21,570	29.4
Rate	1.6	2.2	43.4	5.1	6.5	28.9
Rape[2]						
Number	918	832	-9.4	143,224	126,430	-11.7
Rate	51.3	45.5	-11.2	43.6	38.4	-12.0
Robbery						
Number	161	174	8.1	268,483	243,600	-9.3
Rate	9.0	9.5	5.8	81.8	73.9	-9.6
Aggravated Assault						
Number	3,055	3,385	10.8	822,017	921,505	12.1
Rate	170.8	185.3	8.5	250.4	279.7	11.7
PROPERTY CRIME						
Number	22,244	20,313	-8.7	6,995,235	6,452,038	-7.8
Rate	1,243.3	1,111.9	-10.6	2,130.6	1,958.2	-8.1
Burglary						
Number	4,045	3,731	-7.8	1,118,096	1,035,314	-7.4
Rate	226.1	204.2	-9.7	340.5	314.2	-7.7
Larceny-Theft						
Number	16,591	14,815	-10.7	5,152,267	4,606,324	-10.6
Rate	927.4	810.9	-12.6	1,569.2	1,398.0	-10.9
Motor Vehicle Theft						
Number	1,608	1,767	9.9	724,872	810,400	11.8
Rate	89.9	96.7	7.6	220.8	246.0	11.4

NOTE: Although arson data are included in the trend and clearance tables, sufficient data are not available to estimate totals for this offense. Therefore, no arson data are published in this table.
- = Zero or rounds to zero.
[1] Population figures are U.S. Census Bureau provisional estimates as of July 1, 2020.
[2] The figures shown in the rape (revised definition) column were estimated using the revised Uniform Crime Reporting (UCR) definition of rape.

Table ID-15. State Government Finances, 2020

(Dollar amounts in thousands, percent distribution.)

Item	Dollars	Percent distribution
Total Revenue	13,347,821	100.0
General revenue	11,512,708	86.3
Intergovernmental revenue	4,729,640	35.4
Taxes	5,279,821	39.6
General sales	2099543	15.7
Selective sales	615,285	4.6
License taxes	399,784	3.0
Individual income tax	1913459	14.3
Corporate income tax	245,969	1.8
Other taxes	5,781	0.0
Current charges	918,787	6.9
Miscellaneous general revenue	584,460	4.4
Utility revenue	0	-
Liquor stores revenue	206226	1.5
Insurance trust revenue[1]	1,628,887	12.2
Total Expenditure	12,089,281	100.0
Intergovernmental expenditure	2,840,768	23.5
Direct expenditure	9,248,513	76.5
Current operation	6,430,914	53.2
Capital outlay	976,268	8.1
Insurance benefits and repayments	1,462,589	12.1
Assistance and subsidies	212,976	1.8
Interest on debt	165,766	1.4
Exhibit: Salaries and wages	1,629,096	13.5
Total Expenditure	12,089,281	100.0
General expenditure	10,466,621	86.6
Intergovernmental expenditure	2,840,768	23.5
Direct expenditure	7,625,853	63.1
General expenditure, by function:		
Education	3,692,736	30.5
Public welfare	3,243,957	26.8
Hospitals	55,387	0.5
Health	170,952	1.4
Highways	966,815	8.0
Police protection	77,568	0.6
Correction	347,271	2.9
Natural resources	266,286	2.2
Parks and recreation	44,419	0.4
Governmental administration	589,467	4.9
Interest on general debt	165,766	1.4
Other and unallocable	795,091	6.6
Utility expenditure	2,619	-
Liquor stores expenditure	160,071	1.3
Insurance trust expenditure	1,462,589	12.1
Debt at End of Fiscal Year	3,348,042	X
Cash and Security Holdings	29,361,905	X

X = Not applicable.
- = Zero or rounds to zero.
[1] Within insurance trust revenue, net earnings of state retirement systems is a calculated statistic (the item code in the data file is X08), and thus can be positive or negative. Net earnings is the sum of earnings on investments plus gains on investments minus losses on investments. The change made in 2002 for asset valuation from book to market value in accordance with Statement 34 of the Governmental Accounting Standards Board is reflected in the calculated statistics.

Table ID-16. State Government Tax Collections, 2021

(Dollars in thousands, percent.)

Item	Dollars	Percent distribution
Total Taxes	6,472,467	100.0
Property taxes	X	-
Sales and gross receipts	3,180,226	49.1
General sales and gross receipts	2,516,997	38.9
Selective sales and gross receipts	663,229	10.2
Alcoholic beverages	10,980	0.2
Amusements	X	-
Insurance premiums	118,439	1.8
Motor fuels	405,050	6.3
Pari-mutuels	1,524	-
Public utilities	1,961	-
Tobacco products	48,796	0.8
Other selective sales	76,479	1.2
Licenses	473,872	7.3
Alcoholic beverages	1,766	-
Amusements	241	-
Corporations in general	5,381	0.1
Hunting and fishing	59,845	0.9
Motor vehicle	232,064	3.6
Motor vehicle operators	12,261	0.2
Public utilities	63,214	1.0
Occupation and business, NEC	94,829	1.5
Other licenses	4,271	0.1
Income taxes	2,809,422	43.4
Individual income	2,457,943	38.0
Corporation net income	351,479	5.4
Other taxes	8,947	0.1
Death and gift	X	-
Documentary and stock transfer	X	-
Severance	5,870	0.1
Taxes, NEC	3,077	-

X = Not applicable.
- = Zero or rounds to zero.

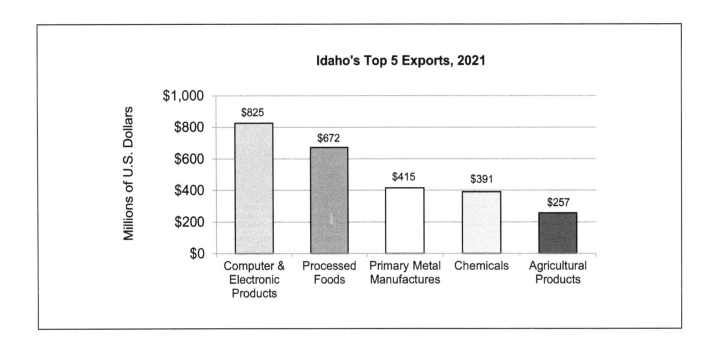

Idaho's Top 5 Exports, 2021

ILLINOIS

Facts and Figures

Location: North central United States; bordered on the N by Wisconsin, on the E by Lake Michigan and Indiana, on the S by Kentucky, and on the W by Iowa and Missouri

Area: 57,913 sq. mi. (149,998 sq. km.); rank—25th

Population: 12,671,469 (2021 est.); rank—6th

Principal Cities: capital—Springfield; largest—Chicago

Statehood: December 3, 1818; 21st state

U.S. Congress: 2 senators, 18 representatives

State Motto: State Sovereignty, National Union

State Song: "Illinois"

State Nicknames: The Prairie State; The Land of Lincoln

Abbreviations: IL; Ill.

State Symbols: flower—native violet; tree—white oak; bird—cardinal

At a Glance

- Illinois was one of three states that experienced a population decline between 2010 and 2021, with a decrease in population of 1.2 percent.

- In 2021, Illinois employed 47.3 state and local government employees per 1,000 residents, which ranked 40th in the country.

- Illinois had the 5th highest real GDP among the states in 2021 at $775 billion (in chained 2012 dollars).

- Illinois ranked 18th for median household income in 2020, with an income of $68,428.

- In 2020, 6.8 percent of Illinois residents did not have health insurance, compared to 8.7 percent of the entire U.S. population.

Table IL-1. Population by Age, Sex, Race, and Hispanic Origin

(Number, percent, except where noted.)

Sex, age, race, and Hispanic origin	2000	2010	2021	Percent change, 2010–2021
Total Population...	12,419,293	12,830,632	12,671,469	-1.2
Percent of total U.S. population	4.4	4.2	3.8	X
Sex				
Male..	6,080,336	6,292,276	6,265,082	-0.4
Female	6,338,957	6,538,356	6,406,387	-2.0
Age				
Under 5 years...	876,549	835,557	706,621	-15.4
5 to 19 years..	2,728,957	2,660,945	2,422,672	-9.0
20 to 64 years..	7,313,762	7,724,917	7,440,714	-3.7
65 years and over	1,500,025	1,609,213	2,101,462	30.6
Median age (years)......................................	34.7	36.6	39.0	6.6
Race and Hispanic Origin				
One race				
White	9,125,471	10,030,587	9,668,380	-3.6
Black...	1,878,875	1,903,458	1,866,607	-1.9
American Indian and Alaska Native	31,006	73,486	79,517	8.2
Asian	423,603	604,399	771,000	27.6
Native Hawaiian or Other Pacific Islander	4,610	7,436	8,708	17.1
Two or more races	235,016	210,906	277,257	31.5
Hispanic (of any race)....................................	1,530,262	2,073,054	2,282,133	10.1

NOTE: Population figures for 2021 are July 1 estimates. The 2000 and 2010 estimates are taken from the respective censuses.
- = Zero or rounds to zero.
X = Not applicable.

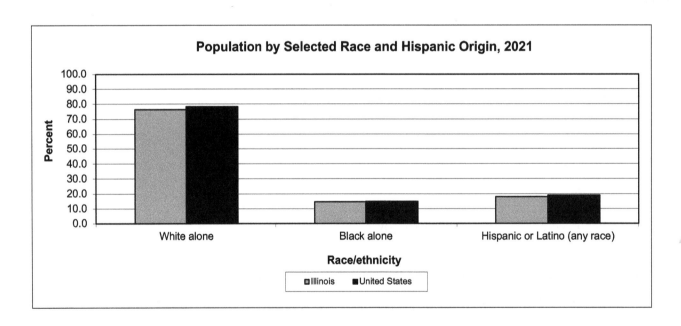

Table IL-2. Marital Status

(Number, percent distribution.)

Sex, age, race, and Hispanic origin	2000	2010	2020 [1]
Males, 15 Years and Over	4,685,982	4,977,964	5,045,488
Never married	31.9	37.2	38.1
Now married, except separated..	56.1	50.0	49.4
Separated...	1.6	1.4	1.4
Widowed...	2.5	2.6	2.7
Divorced...	7.9	8.8	8.4
Females, 15 Years and Over	5,021,855	5,289,803	5,316,575
Never married	26.1	31.1	32.4
Now married, except separated..	51.3	46.3	46.2
Separated...	2.0	2.1	1.7
Widowed...	10.7	9.5	8.7
Divorced...	9.9	11.0	10.9

[1] 2020 ACS 5-Year estimates. 1-Year estimates were not released for 2020 due to the impact of COVID-19 on data collection that year.

Table IL-3. Households and Housing Characteristics

(Number, percent, dollars.)

Item	2000	2010	2020 [1]	Average annual percent change, 2010–2020
Total Households.................................	4,591,779	4,752,857	4,884,061	0.4
Family households	3,105,513	3,133,813	3,116,415	-0.1
Married-couple family	2,353,892	2,301,009	2,301,114	-
Other family	751,621	832,804	815,301	-0.3
Male householder, no wife present...........	187,903	220,197	224,181	0.3
Female householder, no husband present.....	563,718	612,607	591,120	-0.5
Nonfamily households	1,486,266	1,619,044	1,767,646	1.3
Householder living alone.......................	1,229,807	1,340,394	1,457,411	1.2
Householder not living alone...................	256,459	278,650	310,235	1.6
Housing Characteristics				
Total housing units..............................	4,885,615	5,297,077	5,373,385	0.2
Occupied housing units	4,591,779	4,752,857	4,884,061	0.4
Owner occupied	3,088,884	3,219,338	3,237,778	0.1
Renter occupied	1,502,895	1,533,519	1,646,283	1.1
Average household size...........................	2.63	2.64	2.54	-0.5
Financial Characteristics				
Median gross rent of renter-occupied housing	605	848	1,038	3.2
Median monthly owner costs for housing units with a mortgage	1,198	1,655	1,709	0.5
Median value of owner-occupied housing units.........	130,800	191,800	202,100	0.8

- = Zero or rounds to zero.
[1] 2020 ACS 5-Year estimates. 1-Year estimates were not released for 2020 due to the impact of COVID-19 on data collection that year.

Table IL-4. Migration, Origin, and Language

(Number, percent.)

Characteristic	State	U.S.
	2016-2020 [1]	2016-2020 [1]
Residence 1 Year Ago		
Population 1 year and over	12,574,010	322,943,283
Same house	87.5	86.2
Different house in the U.S.	12.0	13.2
Same county	7.8	7.7
Different county	4.2	5.5
Same state	2.6	3.2
Different state	1.6	2.3
Abroad	0.5	0.6
Place of Birth		
Native born	10,943,097	282,443,680
Male	49.0	49.4
Female	51.0	50.6
Foreign born	1,773,067	44,125,628
Male	49.6	48.6
Female	50.4	51.4
Foreign born; naturalized U.S. citizen....................	923,500	22,456,684
Male	47.8	46.1
Female	52.2	53.9
Foreign born; not a U.S. citizen..........................	849,567	21,668,944
Male	51.6	51.1
Female	48.4	48.9
Entered 2010 or later	18.8	22.8
Entered 2000 to 2009	24.7	25.1
Entered before 2000.......................................	56.4	52.1
World Region of Birth, Foreign		
Foreign-born population, excluding population born at sea	1,773,067	44,125,628
Europe	20.4	10.8
Asia	31.0	31.3
Africa	4.1	5.4
Oceania	0.2	0.6
Latin America..	43.3	50.0
North America..	1.1	1.9
Language Spoken at Home and Ability to Speak English		
Population 5 years and over..................................	11,960,646	306,919,116
English only	77.0	78.5
Language other than English...............................	23.0	21.5
Speaks English less than "very well".....................	8.4	8.2

[1] 2020 ACS 5-Year estimates. 1-Year estimates were not released for 2020 due to the impact of COVID-19 on data collection that year.
NA = Not available.
X = Not applicable.
- = Zero or rounds to zero.

Table IL-5. Median Income and Poverty Status, 2020[1]

(Number, percent, except as noted.)

Characteristic	State		U.S.	
	Number	Percent	Number	Percent
Median Income				
Households (dollars)...	68,428	X	64,994	X
Families (dollars)	86,251	X	80,069	X
Below Poverty Level (All People)	1,488,670	12.0	40,910,326	12.8
Sex				
Male	654,596	10.8	18,171,512	11.6
Female	834,074	13.1	22,738,814	14.0
Age				
Under 18 years..	454,654	16.2	12,598,699	17.5
Related children under 18 years...	444,689	15.9	12,306,532	17.2
18 to 64 years..	864,994	11.3	23,554,920	12.1
65 years and over	169,022	8.8	4,756,707	9.3

X = Not applicable.
[1] 2020 ACS 5-Year estimates. 1-Year estimates were not released for 2020 due to the impact of COVID-19 on data collection that year.

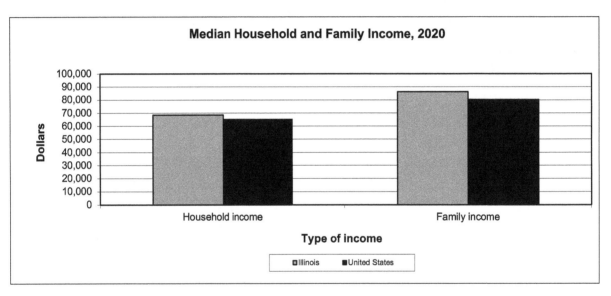

Table IL-6. Health Insurance Coverage Status for the Civilian Noninstitutionalized Population and Children Under 19 Years of Age

(Number, percent.)

Item	2011	2012	2013	2014	2015	2016	2017	2018	2019	2020[2]
Civilian Noninstitutionalized Population	12,688,006	12,698,371	12,704,616	12,702,393	12,679,860	12,620,388	12,620,126	12,563,908	12,488,377	12,536,614
Covered by Private or Public Insurance										
Number...	11,028,731	11,075,906	11,086,412	11,464,467	11,779,571	11,803,786	11,760,869	11,689,300	11,565,086	11,682,181
Percent...	86.9	87.2	87.3	90.3	92.9	93.5	93.2	93.0	92.6	93.2
Uninsured										
Number...	1,659,275	1,622,465	1,618,204	1,237,926	900,289	816,602	859,257	874,608	923,291	854,433
Percent...	13.1	12.8	12.7	9.7	7.1	6.5	6.8	7.0	7.4	6.8
Percent in the U.S. not covered..................................	15.1	14.8	14.5	11.7	9.4	8.6	8.7	8.9	9.2	8.7
Children Under 19 Years of Age[1]	3,091,887	3,059,055	3,017,960	2,980,902	2,956,262	2,919,863	3,069,418	3,027,744	2,981,525	3,023,805
Covered by Private or Public Insurance										
Number...	2,978,576	2,957,589	2,892,609	2,881,400	2,880,990	2,848,544	2,980,069	2,925,278	2,861,486	2,929,145
Percent...	96.3	96.7	95.8	96.7	97.5	97.6	97.1	96.6	96.0	96.9
Uninsured										
Number...	113,311	101,466	125,351	99,502	75,272	71,319	89,349	102,466	120,039	94,660
Percent...	3.7	3.3	4.2	3.3	2.5	2.4	2.9	3.4	4.0	3.1
Percent in the U.S. not covered..................................	7.5	7.2	7.1	6.0	4.8	4.5	5.0	5.2	5.7	5.2

[1] Data for years prior to 2017 are for individuals under 18 years of age.
[2] 2020 ACS 5-Year estimates. 1-Year estimates were not released for 2020 due to the impact of COVID-19 on data collection that year. Data is not comparable to previous years, which are based on 1-year estimates.

Table IL-7. Employment Status by Demographic Group, 2021

(Numbers in thousands, percent.)

Characteristic	Civilian noninstitutional population	Civilian labor force		Employed		Unemployed	
		Number	Percent of population	Number	Percent of population	Number	Percent of population
Total...	9,913	6,282	63.4	5,907	59.6	375	6.0
Sex							
Male...	4,797	3,291	68.6	3,087	64.4	204	6.2
Female...	5,116	2,991	58.5	2,820	55.1	171	5.7
Race, Sex, and Hispanic Origin							
White...	7,691	4,965	64.6	4,710	61.2	254	5.1
Male...	3,746	2,645	70.6	2,500	66.7	145	5.5
Female.....................................	3,945	2,319	58.8	2,210	56.0	110	4.7
Black or African American................	1,394	761	54.6	668	47.9	93	12.3
Male...	619	329	53.1	285	46.0	44	13.4
Female.....................................	774	432	55.8	383	49.4	49	11.4
Hispanic or Latino ethnicity[1]...........	1,584	1,124	71.0	1,047	66.1	77	6.9
Male...	804	648	80.6	603	74.9	45	7.0
Female.....................................	779	477	61.1	445	57.1	32	6.7
Age							
16 to 19 years..............................	634	231	36.4	196	31.0	35	15.0
20 to 24 years..............................	725	519	71.5	466	64.3	53	10.1
25 to 34 years..............................	1,715	1,430	83.4	1,354	78.9	77	5.4
35 to 44 years..............................	1,639	1,386	84.5	1,326	80.9	60	4.3
45 to 54 years..............................	1,525	1,263	82.8	1,204	78.9	59	4.7
55 to 64 years..............................	1,608	1,085	67.5	1,023	63.6	63	5.8
65 years and over..........................	2,066	368	17.8	339	16.4	30	8.0

NOTE: Data in Table 7 are from the Current Population Survey (CPS) and do not match the estimates in Table 8. See notes and definitions for further information.
[1] May be of any race.

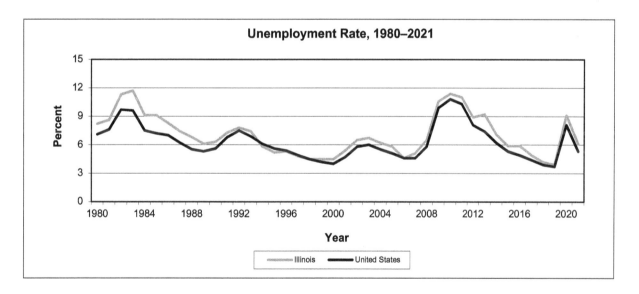

Table IL-8. Employment Status of the Civilian Noninstitutional Population Age 16 Years and Over

(Number, percent.)

Year	Civilian labor force	Civilian participation rate	Employed	Unemployed	Unemployment rate
2010.........................	6,612,433	66.8	5,918,202	694,231	10.5
2011.........................	6,567,531	66.0	5,925,787	641,744	9.8
2012.........................	6,583,689	65.9	5,989,454	594,235	9.0
2013.........................	6,556,593	65.4	5,961,201	595,392	9.1
2014.........................	6,516,372	64.8	6,049,059	467,313	7.2
2015.........................	6,511,797	64.8	6,119,934	391,863	6.0
2016.........................	6,559,038	65.3	6,172,672	386,366	5.9
2017.........................	6,562,291	64.7	6,237,933	324,358	4.9
2018.........................	6,568,208	64.8	6,281,764	286,444	4.4
2019.........................	6,568,815	64.9	6,308,535	260,280	4.0
2020.........................	6,366,716	63	5,781,084	585,632	9.2
2021.........................	6,318,915	62.9	5,935,974	382,941	6.1

Table IL-9. Employment and Average Wages by Industry

(Estimates are based on the 2012 North American Industry Classification System [NAICS].)

Industry	2013	2014	2015	2016	2017	2018	2019	2020
	Number of Jobs							
Wage and Salary Employment by Industry.........................	5,965,073	6,044,058	6,139,569	6,176,576	6,210,786	6,253,799	6,280,415	5,848,155
Farm Wage and Salary Employment................................	12,653	11,710	14,743	14,215	13,744	14,744	12,981	13,142
Nonfarm Wage and Salary Employment...........................	5,952,420	6,032,348	6,124,826	6,162,361	6,197,042	6,239,055	6,267,434	5,835,013
Private wage and salary employment..................................	5,075,143	5,157,446	5,248,161	5,289,354	5,325,125	5,370,287	5,392,079	4,997,414
Forestry, fishing, and related activities..................................	4,798	5,916	5,539	5,506	5,545	5,421	5,351	5,155
Mining..	9,651	9,862	9,281	7,991	7,767	7,797	8,191	6,745
Utilities..	23,795	24,015	24,175	24,342	24,498	24,641	24,494	23,813
Construction..	196,717	206,988	219,298	224,264	225,044	231,364	233,367	221,949
Manufacturing...	580,224	580,285	581,803	575,079	577,022	586,446	586,569	555,273
Durable goods manufacturing...............................	350,844	349,987	348,363	338,173	337,375	345,359	344,430	321,779
Nondurable goods manufacturing...........................	229,380	230,298	233,440	236,906	239,647	241,087	242,139	233,494
Wholesale trade	300,062	301,268	302,974	303,421	307,063	295,398	295,891	282,552
Retail trade..	603,470	608,907	619,278	621,993	616,295	605,535	591,070	559,034
Transportation and warehousing................................	244,418	250,953	260,188	263,092	267,560	289,241	299,376	296,690
Information	98,983	99,409	101,208	99,945	96,901	94,355	95,003	87,577
Finance and insurance	293,581	292,392	301,046	300,797	303,359	306,556	315,110	316,319
Real estate and rental and leasing..............................	75,399	76,273	78,867	80,978	83,064	84,356	86,138	80,693
Professional, scientific, and technical services	378,991	390,558	405,693	413,069	414,877	421,084	425,811	415,114
Management of companies and enterprises.....................	103,688	103,279	94,810	94,766	97,166	92,884	87,035	83,633
Administrative and waste services	412,263	428,116	429,444	431,272	437,045	441,746	441,695	399,707
Educational services	167,053	167,562	167,399	171,459	172,250	169,081	167,768	157,405
Health care and social assistance..............................	730,629	739,200	756,950	767,222	773,274	783,569	790,579	759,858
Arts, entertainment, and recreation.............................	80,840	84,554	85,565	89,245	92,370	94,104	95,974	65,226
Accommodation and food services.............................	469,073	477,469	495,937	511,854	521,878	527,246	531,167	400,813
Other services, except public administration.....................	301,508	310,440	308,706	303,059	302,147	309,463	311,490	279,858
Government and government enterprises.....................	877,277	874,902	876,665	873,007	871,917	868,768	875,355	837,599
	Dollars							
Average Wages and Salaries by Industry	53,662	55,135	57,019	57,568	59,191	61,225	62,877	67,399
Average Farm Wages and Salaries	30,784	35,797	31,985	33,559	28,697	28,950	31,220	32,827
Average Nonfarm Wages and Salaries	53,711	55,173	57,080	57,623	59,258	61,301	62,943	67,477
Average private wages and salaries..............................	54,054	55,691	57,765	58,368	60,081	62,138	63,838	68,547
Forestry, fishing, and related activities..........................	27,490	30,293	32,704	34,104	36,287	38,363	40,081	43,239
Mining..	70,867	74,133	75,785	77,109	76,964	79,016	81,085	79,743
Utilities..	106,958	112,947	115,566	119,109	121,534	121,579	128,755	131,329
Construction	62,917	65,709	68,753	70,235	71,990	73,042	74,875	77,759
Manufacturing...	65,364	67,867	70,429	70,639	72,453	74,183	75,089	77,174
Durable goods manufacturing...............................	65,704	67,130	68,518	70,030	71,696	73,417	74,616	74,802
Nondurable goods manufacturing...........................	64,844	68,987	73,281	71,508	73,518	75,279	75,762	80,444
Wholesale trade	75,651	77,996	80,382	80,954	82,827	86,594	89,269	92,063
Retail trade..	28,858	29,240	30,427	30,769	31,820	32,851	34,396	37,434
Transportation and warehousing................................	52,970	54,647	56,069	56,608	58,339	58,586	59,517	58,829
Information	77,539	79,721	82,940	84,910	87,456	93,689	99,227	112,905
Finance and insurance	99,778	105,553	110,729	112,954	117,580	122,748	125,929	134,844
Real estate and rental and leasing..............................	58,407	60,964	64,986	66,051	67,422	71,181	74,201	76,912
Professional, scientific, and technical services	89,210	91,935	95,726	96,237	98,477	102,516	104,071	109,643
Management of companies and enterprises.....................	123,511	124,603	129,845	127,623	130,002	135,520	137,584	141,982
Administrative and waste services	35,253	36,660	38,853	39,585	41,630	43,316	45,473	49,267
Educational services	44,224	45,434	46,491	46,500	47,462	49,382	50,990	54,753
Health care and social assistance..............................	46,442	47,377	48,431	49,375	50,726	52,370	53,287	56,900
Arts, entertainment, and recreation.............................	36,956	36,316	38,594	39,220	39,405	40,560	41,421	46,793
Accommodation and food services.............................	21,168	21,616	22,573	23,148	23,865	25,204	26,161	24,773
Other services, except public administration.....................	35,984	37,582	38,926	40,012	41,637	42,665	43,916	48,234
Government and government enterprises.............................	51,725	52,120	52,979	53,109	54,235	56,126	57,429	61,095

Table IL-10. Employment Characteristics by Family Type

(Number, percent.)

Family type and labor force status	2018 Total	2018 Families with own children under 18 years	2019 Total	2019 Families with own children under 18 years	2020 [1] Total	2020 [1] Families with own children under 18 years
All Families..	3,119,101	1,318,366	3,059,067	1,272,523	3,116,415	1,323,108
FAMILY TYPE AND LABOR FORCE STATUS						
Opposite-Sex Married-Couple Families.............................	2,293,091	906,420	2,251,401	873,220	2,281,604	910,040
Both husband and wife in labor force..................................	54.3	70.2	53.6	69.8	54.5	69.8
Husband in labor force, wife not in labor force	20.2	25.0	20.5	25.9	20.7	25.7
Wife in labor force, husband not in labor force	7.5	3.4	7.7	3.0	7.6	3.4
Both husband and wife not in labor force................................	17.1	1.0	17.3	0.9	17.1	1.1
Other Families	826,010	411,946	807,666	399,303	815,301	409,602
Female householder, no spouse present	72.5	75.5	71.7	75.2	72.5	75.6
In labor force..	52.2	64.8	51.9	65.0	52.9	65.5
Not in labor force	20.3	10.7	19.8	10.2	19.6	10.1
Male householder, no spouse present................................	27.5	24.5	28.3	24.8	27.5	24.4
In labor force..	21.8	22.5	22.4	23.0	21.9	22.5
Not in labor force	5.7	2.0	6.0	1.9	5.6	1.9

[1] 2020 ACS 5-Year estimates. 1-Year estimates were not released for 2020 due to the impact of COVID-19 on data collection that year. Data is not comparable to previous years, which are based on 1-year estimates.

Table IL-11. School Enrollment and Educational Attainment, 2020[1]

(Number, percent.)

Item	State	U.S.
Enrollment		
Total population 3 years and over, enrolled in school	3,166,891	80,497,960
Enrolled in nursery school or preschool (percent)...........................	6.8	6.1
Enrolled in kindergarten (percent)..	4.7	5.0
Enrolled in elementary school, grades 1-8 (percent).......................	40.1	40.4
Enrolled in high school, grades 9-12 (percent).............................	21.3	21.0
Enrolled in college or graduate school (percent)...........................	27.1	27.6
Attainment		
Total population 25 years and over	8,686,700	222,836,834
Less than ninth grade (percent)	4.6	4.9
9th to 12th grade, no diploma (percent).....................................	5.7	6.6
High school graduate, including equivalency (percent)......................	25.6	26.7
Some college, no degree (percent)..	20.4	20.3
Associate's degree (percent)..	8.1	8.6
Bachelor's degree (percent)	21.6	20.2
Graduate or professional degree (percent).................................	13.9	12.7
High school graduate or higher (percent)	89.7	88.5
Bachelor's degree or higher (percent)......................................	35.5	32.9

[1] 2020 ACS 5-Year estimates. 1-Year estimates were not released for 2020 due to the impact of COVID-19 on data collection that year.

Table IL-12. Public School Characteristics and Educational Indicators

(Number, percent; data derived from National Center of Education Statistics.)

Item	State	U.S.
Public Elementary and Secondary Schools		
Number of regular school districts, 2018-19	892	13,452
Number of operational schools, 2019-20....................................	4,351	98,469
Percent charter schools	3.2	7.7
Total public school enrollment, Fall 2019...................................	1,943,117	50,796,445
Percent charter school enrollment	3.3	6.8
Student-teacher ratio, Fall 2019..	14.6	15.9
Expenditures per student (unadjusted dollars), 2018-19	16,281	13,187
Four-year adjusted cohort graduation rate (ACGR), 2018-2019[1]...........	86.2	85.8
Students eligible for free or reduced-price lunch (percent), 2019-20.......	48.4	52.1
English language learners (percent), Fall 2019	12.3	10.4
Students age 3 to 21 served under IDEA, part B (percent), 2020-21	15.4	14.5

Public Schools by Type, 2019-20	Number	Percent of state public schools
Total number of schools..	4,351	100.0
Special education...	217	5.0
Vocational education...	0	-
Alternative education...	141	3.2

[1] Adjusted Cohort Graduation Rates (ACGR) differ from Averaged Freshmen Graduation Rates (AFGR).
- = Zero or rounds to zero.

Table IL-13. Reported Voting and Registration of the Voting-Age Population, November 2020

(Numbers in thousands, percent.)

Item	Total population	Total citizen population	Registered			Voted		
			Total registered	Percent registered (total population)	Percent registered (total citizen population)	Total voted	Percent voted (total population)	Percent voted (total citizen population)
U.S. Total	252,274	231,593	168,308	66.7	72.7	154,628	61.3	66.8
State Total...	9,658	8,860	6,590	68.2	74.4	6,058	62.7	68.4
Sex								
Male	4,671	4,281	3,098	66.3	72.4	2,876	61.6	67.2
Female	4,987	4,579	3,492	70.0	76.3	3,182	63.8	69.5
Race								
White alone..................................	7,551	7,015	5,303	70.2	75.6	4,849	64.2	69.1
White, non-Hispanic alone.................	6,218	6,075	4,826	77.6	79.4	4,429	71.2	72.9
Black alone..................................	1,335	1,270	861	64.5	67.8	811	60.7	63.8
Asian alone	643	452	331	51.5	73.3	313	48.7	69.3
Hispanic (of any race)......................	1,421	1,016	532	37.4	52.4	475	33.4	46.8
White alone or in combination	7,600	7,064	5,331	70.1	75.5	4,873	64.1	69.0
Black alone or in combination	1,382	1,317	895	64.8	67.9	839	60.7	63.7
Asian alone or in combination.............	652	461	340	52.2	73.8	322	49.4	09.9
Age								
18 to 24 years..............................	1,135	1,060	664	58.5	62.7	583	51.4	55.0
25 to 34 years..............................	1,703	1,525	1,010	59.3	66.2	892	52.4	58.5
35 to 44 years..............................	1,598	1,418	1,069	66.9	75.4	985	61.7	69.5
45 to 64 years..............................	3,196	2,937	2,310	72.3	78.7	2,153	67.4	73.3
65 years and over	2,027	1,920	1,537	75.8	80.0	1,444	71.2	75.2

Table IL-14. Crime

(Number, rate per 100,000. Data are derived from the FBI Uniform Crime Reports.)

Item	State			U.S.		
	2019	2020	Percent change	2019	2020	Percent change
TOTAL POPULATION[1]	12,667,017	12,587,530	-0.6	328,329,953	329,484,123	0.4
VIOLENT CRIME						
Number..	52,601	53,612	1.9	1,250,393	1,313,105	5.0
Rate	415.3	425.9	2.6	380.8	398.5	4.6
Murder and Nonnegligent Manslaughter						
Number..	851	1,151	35.3	16,669	21,570	29.4
Rate	6.7	9.1	36.1	5.1	6.5	28.9
Rape[2]						
Number..	6,161	5,090	-17.4	143,224	126,430	-11.7
Rate	48.6	40.4	-16.9	43.6	38.4	-12.0
Robbery						
Number..	12,660	12,261	-3.2	268,483	243,600	-9.3
Rate	99.9	97.4	-2.5	81.8	73.9	-9.6
Aggravated Assault						
Number..	32,929	35,110	6.6	822,017	921,505	12.1
Rate	260.0	278.9	7.3	250.4	279.7	11.7
PROPERTY CRIME						
Number..	235,033	196,287	-16.5	6,995,235	6,452,038	-7.8
Rate	1,855.5	1,559.4	-16.0	2,130.6	1,958.2	-8.1
Burglary						
Number..	34,789	31,020	-10.8	1,118,096	1,035,314	-7.4
Rate	274.6	246.4	-10.3	340.5	314.2	-7.7
Larceny-Theft						
Number..	181,225	143,935	-20.6	5,152,267	4,606,324	-10.6
Rate	1,430.7	1,143.5	-20.1	1,569.2	1,398.0	-10.9
Motor Vehicle Theft						
Number..	19,019	21,332	12.2	724,872	810,400	11.8
Rate	150.1	169.5	12.9	220.8	246.0	11.4

NOTE: Although arson data are included in the trend and clearance tables, sufficient data are not available to estimate totals for this offense. Therefore, no arson data are published in this table.
- = Zero or rounds to zero.
[1] Population figures are U.S. Census Bureau provisional estimates as of July 1, 2020.
[2] The figures shown in the rape (revised definition) column were estimated using the revised Uniform Crime Reporting (UCR) definition of rape.

Table IL-15. State Government Finances, 2020

(Dollar amounts in thousands, percent distribution.)

Item	Dollars	Percent distribution
Total Revenue	106,590,791	100.0
General revenue	82,822,225	77.7
Intergovernmental revenue	26,816,787	25.2
Taxes	45,284,625	42.5
General sales	11861155	11.1
Selective sales	8,788,858	8.2
License taxes	2,748,276	2.6
Individual income tax	17956356	16.8
Corporate income tax	3,491,688	3.3
Other taxes	438,292	0.4
Current charges	5,408,892	5.1
Miscellaneous general revenue	5,311,921	5.0
Utility revenue	0	-
Liquor stores revenue	0	-
Insurance trust revenue[1]	23,768,566	22.3
Total Expenditure	99,227,849	100.0
Intergovernmental expenditure	23,265,509	23.4
Direct expenditure	75,962,340	76.6
Current operation	47,379,604	47.7
Capital outlay	4,851,947	4.9
Insurance benefits and repayments	18,105,015	18.2
Assistance and subsidies	1,566,541	1.6
Interest on debt	4,059,233	4.1
Exhibit: Salaries and wages	9,326,997	9.4
Total Expenditure	99,227,849	100.0
General expenditure	81,110,888	81.7
Intergovernmental expenditure	23,265,509	23.4
Direct expenditure	57,845,379	58.3
General expenditure, by function:		
Education	19,483,743	19.6
Public welfare	30,277,477	30.5
Hospitals	962,408	1.0
Health	1,369,313	1.4
Highways	6,014,519	6.1
Police protection	559,198	0.6
Correction	1,635,544	1.6
Natural resources	255,808	0.3
Parks and recreation	298,437	0.3
Governmental administration	2,009,325	2.0
Interest on general debt	4,059,233	4.1
Other and unallocable	13,138,463	13.2
Utility expenditure	978,926	1.0
Liquor stores expenditure	0	-
Insurance trust expenditure	18,105,015	18.2
Debt at End of Fiscal Year	64,854,111	X
Cash and Security Holdings	187,063,749	X

X = Not applicable.
- = Zero or rounds to zero.
[1] Within insurance trust revenue, net earnings of state retirement systems is a calculated statistic (the item code in the data file is X08), and thus can be positive or negative. Net earnings is the sum of earnings on investments plus gains on investments minus losses on investments. The change made in 2002 for asset valuation from book to market value in accordance with Statement 34 of the Governmental Accounting Standards Board is reflected in the calculated statistics.

Table IL-16. State Government Tax Collections, 2021

(Dollars in thousands, percent.)

Item	Dollars	Percent distribution
Total Taxes	55,531,962	100.0
Property taxes	59,589	0.1
Sales and gross receipts	23,486,335	42.3
General sales and gross receipts	13,429,355	24.2
Selective sales and gross receipts	10,056,980	18.1
Alcoholic beverages	312,101	0.6
Amusements	881,505	1.6
Insurance premiums	513,239	0.9
Motor fuels	2,383,666	4.3
Pari-mutuels	7,811	-
Public utilities	1,276,429	2.3
Tobacco products	917,043	1.7
Other selective sales	3,765,186	6.8
Licenses	3,818,851	6.9
Alcoholic beverages	16,706	-
Amusements	73,270	0.1
Corporations in general	401,332	0.7
Hunting and fishing	39,783	0.1
Motor vehicle	2,443,924	4.4
Motor vehicle operators	209,309	0.4
Public utilities	12,897	-
Occupation and business, NEC	589,448	1.1
Other licenses	32,182	0.1
Income taxes	27,600,197	49.7
Individual income	21,870,696	39.4
Corporation net income	5,729,501	10.3
Other taxes	566,990	1.0
Death and gift	478,611	0.9
Documentary and stock transfer	88,379	0.2
Severance	X	-
Taxes, NEC	0	-

X = Not applicable.
- = Zero or rounds to zero.

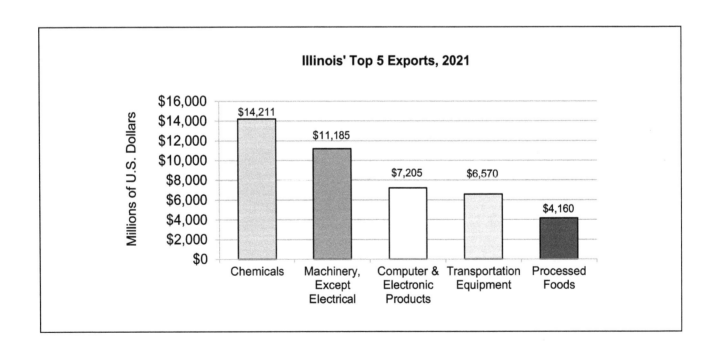

Facts and Figures

Location: East north central United States; bordered on the N by Michigan and Lake Michigan, on the E by Ohio, on the S by Kentucky, and on the W by Illinois

Area: 36,418 sq. mi. (94,321 sq. km.); rank—38th

Population: 6,805,985 (2021 est.); rank—17th

Principal Cities: capital—Indianapolis; largest—Indianapolis

Statehood: December 11, 1816; 19th state

U.S. Congress: 2 senators, 9 representatives

State Motto: The Crossroads of America

State Song: "On the Banks of the Wabash, Far Away"

State Nickname: The Hoosier State

Abbreviations: IN; Ind.

State Symbols: flower—peony; tree—tulip tree; bird—cardinal

At a Glance

- With an increase in population of 5.0 percent, Indiana ranked 30th among the states in growth from 2010 to 2021.

- Indiana's violent crime rate in 2020 was 357.7 per 100,000 population, compared to 398.5 for the entire nation.

- The property crime rate in Indiana in 2020 was 1,783.2 per 100,000 population, ranking 31st in the nation.

- The median household income in Indiana in 2020 was $58,235, compared to the nationwide median of $64,994.

- Approximately 12.9 percent of all Indianans and 17.6 percent of children under 18 years of age in Indiana lived in poverty in 2020, percentages that ranked 21st and 20th in the nation, respectively.

Table IN-1. Population by Age, Sex, Race, and Hispanic Origin

(Number, percent, except where noted.)

Sex, age, race, and Hispanic origin	2000	2010	2021	Percent change, 2010–2021
Total Population..	6,080,485	6,483,802	6,805,985	5.0
Percent of total U.S. population	2.2	2.1	2.1	X
Sex				
Male..	2,982,474	3,189,737	3,377,670	5.9
Female	3,098,011	3,294,065	3,428,315	4.1
Age				
Under 5 years..	423,215	434,075	408,309	-5.9
5 to 19 years..	1,340,171	1,372,507	1,363,199	-0.7
20 to 64 years..	3,564,268	3,836,112	3,919,789	2.2
65 years and over..	752,831	841,108	1,114,688	32.5
Median age (years)	35.2	37.0	38.1	3.0
Race and Hispanic Origin				
One race				
White	5,320,022	5,638,833	5,732,894	1.7
Black..	510,034	603,797	695,117	15.1
American Indian and Alaska Native	15,815	24,487	30,234	23.5
Asian	59,126	105,535	184,780	75.1
Native Hawaiian or Other Pacific Islander	2,005	3,532	5,007	41.8
Two or more races	75,072	107,010	157,953	46.0
Hispanic (of any race)..	214,536	403,234	522,944	29.7

NOTE: Population figures for 2021 are July 1 estimates. The 2000 and 2010 estimates are taken from the respective censuses.
- = Zero or rounds to zero.
X = Not applicable.

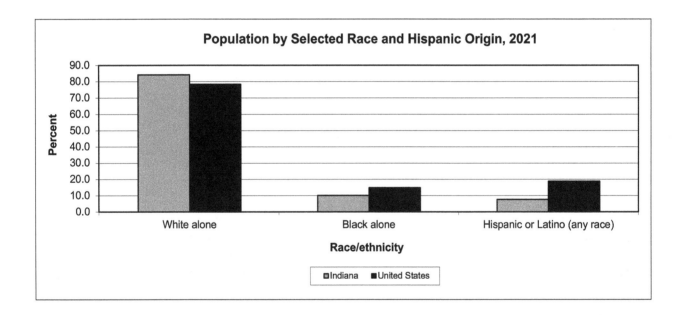

Population by Selected Race and Hispanic Origin, 2021

Legend: □ Indiana ■ United States

X-axis (Race/ethnicity): White alone, Black alone, Hispanic or Latino (any race)
Y-axis: Percent (0.0 to 90.0)

Table IN-2. Marital Status

(Number, percent distribution.)

Sex, age, race, and Hispanic origin	2000	2010	2020 [1]
Males, 15 Years and Over	2,308,917	2,513,953	2,635,151
Never married	27.9	32.6	34.6
Now married, except separated..	58.5	52.3	50.2
Separated..	1.3	1.1	1.2
Widowed..	2.4	2.5	2.7
Divorced..	10.0	11.4	11.3
Females, 15 Years and Over	2,462,123	2,644,068	2,762,876
Never married	22.0	26.7	28.6
Now married, except separated..	54.3	49.1	47.8
Separated..	1.5	1.8	1.5
Widowed..	10.6	9.2	8.9
Divorced..	11.6	13.2	13.3

[1] 2020 ACS 5-Year estimates. 1-Year estimates were not released for 2020 due to the impact of COVID-19 on data collection that year.

Table IN-3. Households and Housing Characteristics

(Number, percent, dollars.)

Item	2000	2010	2020 [1]	Average annual percent change, 2010–2020
Total Households	2,336,306	2,470,905	2,602,770	0.8
Family households	1,602,501	1,656,386	1,679,392	0.2
Married-couple family	1,251,458	1,236,518	1,252,150	0.2
Other family	351,043	419,868	427,242	0.3
Male householder, no wife present	91,671	110,663	127,125	2.1
Female householder, no husband present	259,372	309,205	300,117	-0.4
Nonfamily households	733,805	814,519	923,378	1.9
Householder living alone	605,428	678,460	755,193	1.6
Householder not living alone	128,377	136,059	168,185	3.4
Housing Characteristics				
Total housing units	2,532,319	2,797,172	2,903,720	0.5
Occupied housing units	2,336,306	2,470,905	2,602,770	0.8
Owner occupied	1,669,192	1,736,751	1,808,293	0.6
Renter occupied	667,144	734,154	794,477	1.2
Average household size	2.53	2.55	2.50	-0.3
Financial Characteristics				
Median gross rent of renter-occupied housing	521	683	844	3.4
Median monthly owner costs for housing units with a mortgage	869	1,090	1,155	0.9
Median value of owner-occupied housing units	94,300	123,300	148,900	3.0

[1] 2020 ACS 5-Year estimates. 1-Year estimates were not released for 2020 due to the impact of COVID-19 on data collection that year.

Table IN-4. Migration, Origin, and Language

(Number, percent.)

Characteristic	State 2016-2020 [1]	U.S. 2016-2020 [1]
Residence 1 Year Ago		
Population 1 year and over	6,622,838	322,943,283
Same house	85.7	86.2
Different house in the U.S.	13.9	13.2
Same county	8.0	7.7
Different county	5.9	5.5
Same state	3.7	3.2
Different state	2.2	2.3
Abroad	0.4	0.6
Place of Birth		
Native born	6,341,055	282,443,680
Male	49.2	49.4
Female	50.8	50.6
Foreign born	355,838	44,125,628
Male	51.6	48.6
Female	48.4	51.4
Foreign born; naturalized U.S. citizen	143,614	22,456,684
Male	48.9	46.1
Female	51.1	53.9
Foreign born; not a U.S. citizen	212,224	21,668,944
Male	53.3	51.1
Female	46.7	48.9
Entered 2010 or later	32.3	22.8
Entered 2000 to 2009	29.9	25.1
Entered before 2000	37.8	52.1
World Region of Birth, Foreign		
Foreign-born population, excluding population born at sea	355,838	44,125,628
Europe	11.1	10.8
Asia	36.3	31.3
Africa	8.8	5.4
Oceania	0.4	0.6
Latin America	41.4	50.0
North America	2.0	1.9
Language Spoken at Home and Ability to Speak English		
Population 5 years and over	6,278,766	306,919,116
English only	91.2	78.5
Language other than English	8.8	21.5
Speaks English less than "very well"	3.2	8.2

[1] 2020 ACS 5-Year estimates. 1-Year estimates were not released for 2020 due to the impact of COVID-19 on data collection that year.
NA = Not available.
X = Not applicable.
- = Zero or rounds to zero.

Table IN-5. Median Income and Poverty Status, 2020[1]

(Number, percent, except as noted.)

Characteristic	State Number	State Percent	U.S. Number	U.S. Percent
Median Income				
Households (dollars)...	58,235	X	64,994	X
Families (dollars)	73,265	X	80,069	X
Below Poverty Level (All People)	838,149	12.9	40,910,326	12.8
Sex				
Male	372,593	11.7	18,171,512	11.6
Female	465,556	14.1	22,738,814	14.0
Age				
Under 18 years..	269,559	17.6	12,598,699	17.5
Related children under 18 years................................	261,939	17.2	12,306,532	17.2
18 to 64 years..	493,101	12.5	23,554,920	12.1
65 years and over..	75,489	7.4	4,756,707	9.3

X = Not applicable.
[1] 2020 ACS 5-Year estimates. 1-Year estimates were not released for 2020 due to the impact of COVID-19 on data collection that year.

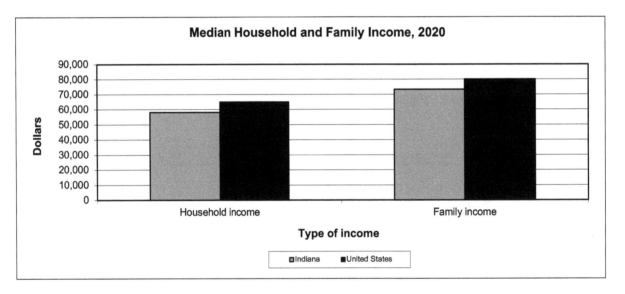

Table IN-6. Health Insurance Coverage Status for the Civilian Noninstitutionalized Population and Children Under 19 Years of Age

(Number, percent.)

Item	2011	2012	2013	2014	2015	2016	2017	2018	2019	2020 [2]
Civilian Noninstitutionalized Population	6,417,644	6,437,142	6,471,551	6,498,029	6,520,267	6,534,914	6,568,434	6,592,504	6,631,529	6,597,701
Covered by Private or Public Insurance										
Number...	5,486,815	5,517,276	5,568,640	5,722,145	5,892,506	6,004,551	6,032,035	6,047,381	6,053,093	6,069,525
Percent...	85.5	85.7	86.0	88.1	90.4	91.9	91.8	91.7	91.3	92.0
Uninsured										
Number...	930,829	919,866	902,911	775,884	627,761	530,363	536,399	545,123	578,436	528,176
Percent...	14.5	14.3	14.0	11.9	9.6	8.1	8.2	8.3	8.7	8.0
Percent in the U.S. not covered............................	15.1	14.8	14.5	11.7	9.4	8.6	8.7	8.9	9.2	8.7
Children Under 19 Years of Age[1]	1,593,636	1,585,435	1,584,015	1,579,992	1,576,006	1,573,925	1,670,417	1,660,376	1,663,849	1,664,343
Covered by Private or Public Insurance										
Number...	1,464,911	1,451,515	1,454,011	1,466,497	1,469,681	1,481,775	1,564,632	1,551,382	1,545,066	1,559,331
Percent...	91.9	91.6	91.8	92.8	93.3	94.1	93.7	93.4	92.9	93.7
Uninsured										
Number...	128,725	133,920	130,004	113,495	106,325	92,150	105,785	108,994	118,783	105,012
Percent...	8.1	8.4	8.2	7.2	6.7	5.9	6.3	6.6	7.1	6.3
Percent in the U.S. not covered............................	7.5	7.2	7.1	6.0	4.8	4.5	5.0	5.2	5.7	5.2

[1] Data for years prior to 2017 are for individuals under 18 years of age.
[2] 2020 ACS 5-Year estimates. 1-Year estimates were not released for 2020 due to the impact of COVID-19 on data collection that year. Data is not comparable to previous years, which are based on 1-year estimates.

Table IN-7. Employment Status by Demographic Group, 2021

(Numbers in thousands, percent.)

Characteristic	Civilian noninstitutional population	Civilian labor force		Employed		Unemployed	
		Number	Percent of population	Number	Percent of population	Number	Percent of population
Total...	5,297	3,306	62.4	3,182	60.1	124	3.8
Sex							
Male..............................	2,569	1,790	69.7	1,719	66.9	71	4.0
Female...........................	2,728	1,516	55.6	1,463	53.6	53	3.5
Race, Sex, and Hispanic Origin							
White..................................	4,543	2,823	62.1	2,731	60.1	92	3.3
Male..............................	2,222	1,539	69.3	1,487	66.9	52	3.4
Female...........................	2,321	1,284	55.3	1,244	53.6	40	3.1
Black or African American..........................	479	304	63.5	278	58.0	26	8.6
Male..............................	218	158	72.6	143	65.6	15	9.6
Female...........................	261	146	55.9	135	51.7	11	7.5
Hispanic or Latino ethnicity[1]	337	229	68.0	221	65.6	8	3.5
Male..............................	185	145	78.2	140	75.5	5	3.4
Female...........................	NA	NA	NA	NA	NA	NA	NA
Age							
16 to 19 years........................	355	156	44.0	144	40.7	12	7.6
20 to 24 years........................	424	314	74.0	290	68.4	24	7.6
25 to 34 years........................	882	721	81.7	698	79.2	22	3.1
35 to 44 years........................	863	715	82.8	684	79.3	31	4.3
45 to 54 years........................	841	670	79.6	651	77.4	19	2.8
55 to 64 years........................	816	513	62.9	499	61.2	15	2.9
65 years and over	1,118	218	19.5	215	19.3	2	1.1

NOTE: Data in Table 7 are from the Current Population Survey (CPS) and do not match the estimates in Table 8. See notes and definitions for further information.
[1] May be of any race.

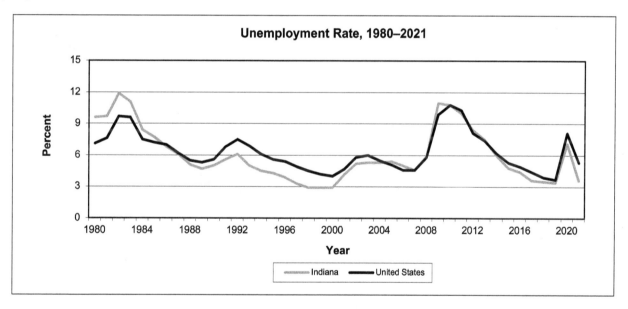

Unemployment Rate, 1980–2021

Table IN-8. Employment Status of the Civilian Noninstitutional Population Age 16 Years and Over

(Number, percent.)

Year	Civilian labor force	Civilian participation rate	Employed	Unemployed	Unemployment rate
2010..	3,175,885	64.0	2,854,843	321,042	10.1
2011..	3,189,011	63.7	2,904,397	284,614	8.9
2012..	3,172,556	63.0	2,911,925	260,631	8.2
2013..	3,193,683	63.1	2,953,672	240,011	7.5
2014..	3,228,524	63.4	3,036,685	191,839	5.9
2015..	3,266,392	63.8	3,109,791	156,601	4.8
2016..	3,331,821	64.7	3,186,420	145,401	4.4
2017..	3,333,693	64.2	3,217,049	116,644	3.5
2018..	3,385,707	64.8	3,270,727	114,980	3.4
2019..	3,393,763	64.5	3,282,443	111,320	3.3
2020..	3,322,829	62.8	3,083,159	239,670	7.2
2021..	3,321,548	62.5	3,203,166	118,382	3.6

Table IN-9. Employment and Average Wages by Industry

(Estimates are based on the 2012 North American Industry Classification System [NAICS].)

Industry	2013	2014	2015	2016	2017	2018	2019	2020
	Number of Jobs							
Wage and Salary Employment by Industry	3,009,962	3,054,388	3,104,469	3,150,896	3,185,079	3,226,669	3,250,655	3,089,435
Farm Wage and Salary Employment	12,374	11,533	10,443	10,556	12,285	14,713	12,954	11,675
Nonfarm Wage and Salary Employment	2,997,588	3,042,855	3,094,026	3,140,340	3,172,794	3,211,956	3,237,701	3,077,760
Private wage and salary employment	2,554,567	2,599,475	2,650,738	2,694,913	2,728,126	2,763,464	2,789,547	2,636,045
Forestry, fishing, and related activities	3,464	4,115	3,997	4,124	4,082	4,099	4,438	(D)
Mining	6,686	6,876	6,511	5,900	5,749	5,946	5,780	(D)
Utilities	14,176	14,131	13,984	13,782	13,796	13,940	13,805	13,844
Construction	126,643	126,078	130,349	135,007	141,283	144,386	149,318	147,538
Manufacturing	492,421	507,857	519,217	522,988	534,745	542,076	541,085	504,843
Durable goods manufacturing	352,175	363,607	373,274	375,482	384,838	392,110	389,033	358,087
Nondurable goods manufacturing	140,246	144,250	145,943	147,506	149,907	149,966	152,052	146,756
Wholesale trade	117,483	118,184	119,785	118,612	119,705	121,125	123,632	119,491
Retail trade	318,444	320,938	326,942	334,474	335,031	323,554	319,098	307,639
Transportation and warehousing	120,990	124,819	125,909	129,155	129,575	142,219	146,783	151,017
Information	35,780	35,616	33,673	32,752	31,528	29,365	28,647	26,060
Finance and insurance	97,777	99,242	101,191	102,928	103,924	104,887	106,928	107,622
Real estate and rental and leasing	33,231	33,324	33,906	35,123	35,450	36,754	37,824	35,932
Professional, scientific, and technical services	102,737	105,982	110,404	113,407	115,596	120,231	123,473	124,560
Management of companies and enterprises	31,072	32,149	33,353	34,601	34,425	34,370	34,873	34,065
Administrative and waste services	175,934	185,014	188,620	187,984	189,081	190,591	189,623	171,096
Educational services	66,107	66,540	67,741	68,557	68,623	71,331	72,349	63,732
Health care and social assistance	374,683	374,814	383,901	397,702	406,602	413,532	421,303	409,988
Arts, entertainment, and recreation	41,626	41,968	41,120	42,036	42,842	43,329	43,922	33,956
Accommodation and food services	250,452	254,236	261,550	266,700	267,348	269,167	272,104	232,069
Other services, except public administration	144,861	147,592	148,505	149,081	148,741	152,562	154,562	143,243
Government and government enterprises	443,021	443,380	443,288	445,427	444,668	448,492	448,154	441,715
	Dollars							
Average Wages and Salaries by Industry	42,370	43,306	44,675	45,264	46,897	48,293	49,525	52,635
Average Farm Wages and Salaries	31,286	35,447	32,159	32,835	29,055	29,777	27,763	28,930
Average Nonfarm Wages and Salaries	42,416	43,336	44,717	45,306	46,966	48,378	49,612	52,725
Average private wages and salaries	42,975	43,969	45,426	45,968	47,720	49,208	50,399	53,745
Forestry, fishing, and related activities	24,396	29,100	30,843	33,179	33,525	35,114	37,448	(D)
Mining	68,309	70,368	69,950	68,931	72,557	72,360	78,262	(D)
Utilities	88,376	90,448	94,778	94,861	96,836	100,913	104,486	105,911
Construction	54,396	53,371	54,650	55,692	57,983	59,342	60,957	63,727
Manufacturing	58,049	59,489	60,997	61,016	63,016	64,695	65,424	67,383
Durable goods manufacturing	57,395	58,775	60,495	60,308	62,335	64,294	64,799	65,860
Nondurable goods manufacturing	59,693	61,289	62,282	62,817	64,763	65,744	67,025	71,100
Wholesale trade	59,601	62,019	64,345	65,951	67,765	70,433	71,254	74,856
Retail trade	25,502	26,193	27,217	27,645	28,542	29,160	30,126	32,890
Transportation and warehousing	44,013	45,507	47,211	47,009	48,645	49,633	50,695	52,092
Information	55,509	56,579	58,084	58,733	61,370	62,542	64,655	70,040
Finance and insurance	63,148	65,697	68,542	68,568	71,403	74,665	77,284	81,904
Real estate and rental and leasing	39,005	41,596	42,902	43,488	45,251	47,112	48,308	52,731
Professional, scientific, and technical services	62,986	62,616	64,875	66,661	68,955	71,045	72,119	76,731
Management of companies and enterprises	88,129	90,730	94,601	97,003	101,034	103,320	104,492	108,909
Administrative and waste services	29,162	29,571	30,392	31,466	33,129	34,363	35,678	38,985
Educational services	31,467	32,192	32,735	32,878	33,646	33,313	34,177	38,258
Health care and social assistance	43,893	44,893	46,549	47,232	49,008	50,056	51,537	55,250
Arts, entertainment, and recreation	33,366	33,707	35,054	35,368	36,379	37,887	39,380	42,544
Accommodation and food services	16,199	16,536	17,214	17,695	18,404	19,539	20,051	19,980
Other services, except public administration	29,674	30,655	31,865	32,698	33,895	34,888	35,817	39,407
Government and government enterprises	39,191	39,624	40,482	41,302	42,339	43,263	44,712	46,633

(D) = Not shown to avoid disclosure of confidential information; estimates are included in higher-level totals.

Table IN-10. Employment Characteristics by Family Type

(Number, percent.)

Family type and labor force status	2018		2019		2020 [1]	
	Total	Families with own children under 18 years	Total	Families with own children under 18 years	Total	Families with own children under 18 years
All Families..	1,683,176	709,918	1,639,230	683,069	1,679,392	716,930
FAMILY TYPE AND LABOR FORCE STATUS						
Opposite-Sex Married-Couple Families............................	1,248,277	467,344	1,221,373	449,915	1,242,485	473,369
Both husband and wife in labor force...	52.4	68.7	53.1	70.4	53.4	69.4
Husband in labor force, wife not in labor force	21.0	25.9	20.4	24.8	20.8	25.6
Wife in labor force, husband not in labor force	7.4	3.5	7.3	3.1	7.6	3.6
Both husband and wife not in labor force....................................	18.3	1.5	18.3	1.2	18.3	1.5
Other Families	434,899	242,574	417,857	233,154	427,242	241,496
Female householder, no spouse present	70.1	71.2	68.6	70.7	70.2	72.0
In labor force..	50.9	60.4	49.6	60.6	50.2	60.5
Not in labor force...	19.2	10.8	19.0	10.1	20.0	11.4
Male householder, no spouse present..	29.9	28.8	31.4	29.3	29.8	28.0
In labor force..	23.8	26.6	24.4	26.5	23.4	25.3
Not in labor force...	6.1	2.2	7.0	2.8	6.4	2.7

[1] 2020 ACS 5-Year estimates. 1-Year estimates were not released for 2020 due to the impact of COVID-19 on data collection that year. Data is not comparable to previous years, which are based on 1-year estimates.

Table IN-11. School Enrollment and Educational Attainment, 2020[1]

(Number, percent.)

Item	State	U.S.
Enrollment		
Total population 3 years and over, enrolled in school	1,654,841	80,497,960
Enrolled in nursery school or preschool (percent)...	6.1	6.1
Enrolled in kindergarten (percent)..	5.1	5.0
Enrolled in elementary school, grades 1-8 (percent)...	42.1	40.4
Enrolled in high school, grades 9-12 (percent)	21.5	21.0
Enrolled in college or graduate school (percent)..	25.2	27.6
Attainment		
Total population 25 years and over	4,466,180	222,836,834
Less than ninth grade (percent)	3.6	4.9
9th to 12th grade, no diploma (percent)	7.1	6.6
High school graduate, including equivalency (percent)..	33.2	26.7
Some college, no degree (percent)	20.1	20.3
Associate's degree (percent)...	8.9	8.6
Bachelor's degree (percent)	17.3	20.2
Graduate or professional degree (percent)...	9.9	12.7
High school graduate or higher (percent)	89.3	88.5
Bachelor's degree or higher (percent)	27.2	32.9

[1] 2020 ACS 5-Year estimates. 1-Year estimates were not released for 2020 due to the impact of COVID-19 on data collection that year.

Table IN-12. Public School Characteristics and Educational Indicators

(Number, percent; data derived from National Center of Education Statistics.)

Item	State	U.S.
Public Elementary and Secondary Schools		
Number of regular school districts, 2018-19	294	13,452
Number of operational schools, 2019-20..	1,912	98,469
Percent charter schools	5.3	7.7
Total public school enrollment, Fall 2019...	1,051,411	50,796,445
Percent charter school enrollment	4.3	6.8
Student-teacher ratio, Fall 2019...	17.0	15.9
Expenditures per student (unadjusted dollars), 2018-19	10,252	13,187
Four-year adjusted cohort graduation rate (ACGR), 2018-2019[1]...	87.2	85.8
Students eligible for free or reduced-price lunch (percent), 2019-20..	48.4	52.1
English language learners (percent), Fall 2019	6.6	10.4
Students age 3 to 21 served under IDEA, part B (percent), 2020-21	17.5	14.5

Public Schools by Type, 2019-20	Number	Percent of state public schools
Total number of schools..	1,912	100.0
Special education	21	1.1
Vocational education	30	1.6
Alternative education	7	0.4

[1] Adjusted Cohort Graduation Rates (ACGR) differ from Averaged Freshmen Graduation Rates (AFGR).

Table IN-13. Reported Voting and Registration of the Voting-Age Population, November 2020

(Numbers in thousands, percent.)

Item	Total population	Total citizen population	Registered			Voted		
			Total registered	Percent registered (total population)	Percent registered (total citizen population)	Total voted	Percent voted (total population)	Percent voted (total citizen population)
U.S. Total	252,274	231,593	168,308	66.7	72.7	154,628	61.3	66.8
State Total..	5,096	4,921	3,412	67.0	69.3	3,002	58.9	61.0
Sex								
Male	2,463	2,375	1,632	66.2	68.7	1,408	57.2	59.3
Female	2,633	2,546	1,781	67.6	69.9	1,594	60.5	62.6
Race								
White alone.......................................	4,318	4,219	2,967	68.7	70.3	2,601	60.2	61.7
White, non-Hispanic alone	4,122	4,107	2,904	70.5	70.7	2,546	61.8	62.0
Black alone..	473	467	306	64.7	65.5	281	59.5	60.2
Asian alone	178	114	76	42.5	66.1	68	38.5	59.9
Hispanic (of any race)	225	135	72	32.1	53.5	60	26.4	44.0
White alone or in combination	4,420	4,315	3,010	68.1	69.8	2,632	59.5	61.0
Black alone or in combination..........................	532	520	333	62.7	64.2	299	56.3	57.6
Asian alone or in combination..........................	189	125	76	40.0	60.3	68	36.3	54.7
Age								
18 to 24 years......................................	587	571	276	47.0	48.3	221	37.7	38.8
25 to 34 years......................................	799	760	493	61.7	64.8	401	50.2	52.8
35 to 44 years......................................	946	888	611	64.5	68.8	515	54.4	58.0
45 to 64 years......................................	1,642	1,609	1,155	70.3	71.8	1,045	63.6	64.9
65 years and over	1,121	1,092	878	78.3	80.4	820	73.2	75.1

B = Base is less than 75,000 and therefore too small to show the derived measure.

Table IN-14. Crime

(Number, rate per 100,000. Data are derived from the FBI Uniform Crime Reports.)

Item	State			U.S.		
	2019	2020	Percent change	2019	2020	Percent change
TOTAL POPULATION[1]	6,731,010	6,754,953	0.4	328,329,953	329,484,123	0.4
VIOLENT CRIME						
Number..	25,006	24,161	-3.4	1,250,393	1,313,105	5.0
Rate	371.5	357.7	-3.7	380.8	398.5	4.6
Murder and Nonnegligent Manslaughter						
Number..	373	505	35.4	16,669	21,570	29.4
Rate	5.5	7.5	34.9	5.1	6.5	28.9
Rape[2]						
Number..	2,553	2,348	-8.0	143,224	126,430	-11.7
Rate	37.9	34.8	-8.4	43.6	38.4	-12.0
Robbery						
Number..	5,335	4,215	-21.0	268,483	243,600	-9.3
Rate	79.3	62.4	-21.3	81.8	73.9	-9.6
Aggravated Assault						
Number..	16,745	17,093	2.1	822,017	921,505	12.1
Rate	248.8	253.0	1.7	250.4	279.7	11.7
PROPERTY CRIME						
Number..	131,097	120,453	-8.1	6,995,235	6,452,038	-7.8
Rate	1,947.7	1,783.2	-8.4	2,130.6	1,958.2	-8.1
Burglary						
Number..	21,586	18,938	-12.3	1,118,096	1,035,314	-7.4
Rate	320.7	280.4	-12.6	340.5	314.2	-7.7
Larceny-Theft						
Number..	95,745	86,080	-10.1	5,152,267	4,606,324	-10.6
Rate	1,422.4	1,274.3	-10.4	1,569.2	1,398.0	-10.9
Motor Vehicle Theft						
Number..	13,766	15,435	12.1	724,872	810,400	11.8
Rate	204.5	228.5	11.7	220.8	246.0	11.4

NOTE: Although arson data are included in the trend and clearance tables, sufficient data are not available to estimate totals for this offense. Therefore, no arson data are published in this table.
- = Zero or rounds to zero.
[1] Population figures are U.S. Census Bureau provisional estimates as of July 1, 2020.
[2] The figures shown in the rape (revised definition) column were estimated using the revised Uniform Crime Reporting (UCR) definition of rape.

Table IN-15. State Government Finances, 2020

(Dollar amounts in thousands, percent distribution.)

Item	Dollars	Percent distribution
Total Revenue	52,343,959	100.0
General revenue	48,685,285	93.0
Intergovernmental revenue	19,471,529	37.2
Taxes	22,374,096	42.7
General sales	8233400	15.7
Selective sales	4,273,135	8.2
License taxes	792,545	1.5
Individual income tax	8303278	15.9
Corporate income tax	756,866	1.4
Other taxes	14,872	-
Current charges	4,020,104	7.7
Miscellaneous general revenue	2,819,556	5.4
Utility revenue	0	-
Liquor stores revenue	0	-
Insurance trust revenue[1]	3,658,674	7.0
Total Expenditure	47,085,289	100.0
Intergovernmental expenditure	10,700,023	22.7
Direct expenditure	36,385,266	77.3
Current operation	27,183,974	57.7
Capital outlay	2,817,643	6.0
Insurance benefits and repayments	3,881,786	8.2
Assistance and subsidies	1,496,515	3.2
Interest on debt	1,005,348	2.1
Exhibit: Salaries and wages	5,142,970	10.9
Total Expenditure	47,085,289	100.0
General expenditure	43,203,503	91.8
Intergovernmental expenditure	10,700,023	22.7
Direct expenditure	32,503,480	69.0
General expenditure, by function:		
Education	16,797,733	35.7
Public welfare	16,824,507	35.7
Hospitals	150,669	0.3
Health	624,163	1.3
Highways	3,338,670	7.1
Police protection	279,636	0.6
Correction	767,223	1.6
Natural resources	442,181	0.9
Parks and recreation	73,329	0.2
Governmental administration	897,866	1.9
Interest on general debt	1,005,348	2.1
Other and unallocable	1,808,090	3.8
Utility expenditure	97,487	0.2
Liquor stores expenditure	0	-
Insurance trust expenditure	3,881,786	8.2
Debt at End of Fiscal Year	23,841,296	X
Cash and Security Holdings	70,030,489	X

X = Not applicable.
- = Zero or rounds to zero.
[1] Within insurance trust revenue, net earnings of state retirement systems is a calculated statistic (the item code in the data file is X08), and thus can be positive or negative. Net earnings is the sum of earnings on investments plus gains on investments minus losses on investments. The change made in 2002 for asset valuation from book to market value in accordance with Statement 34 of the Governmental Accounting Standards Board is reflected in the calculated statistics.

Table IN-16. State Government Tax Collections, 2021

(Dollars in thousands, percent.)

Item	Dollars	Percent distribution
Total Taxes	26,645,852	100.0
Property taxes	13,876	0.1
Sales and gross receipts	13,847,723	52.0
General sales and gross receipts	9,282,907	34.8
Selective sales and gross receipts	4,564,816	17.1
Alcoholic beverages	58,542	0.2
Amusements	608,043	2.3
Insurance premiums	234,753	0.9
Motor fuels	1,545,597	5.8
Pari-mutuels	1,589	-
Public utilities	207,932	0.8
Tobacco products	410,363	1.5
Other selective sales	1,497,997	5.6
Licenses	819,109	3.1
Alcoholic beverages	16,012	0.1
Amusements	5,925	-
Corporations in general	11,810	-
Hunting and fishing	21,565	0.1
Motor vehicle	351,739	1.3
Motor vehicle operators	278,503	1.0
Public utilities	X	-
Occupation and business, NEC	47,155	0.2
Other licenses	86,400	0.3
Income taxes	11,964,087	44.9
Individual income	10,578,929	39.7
Corporation net income	1,385,158	5.2
Other taxes	1,057	-
Death and gift	289	-
Documentary and stock transfer	X	-
Severance	768	-
Taxes, NEC	0	-

- = Zero or rounds to zero.
X = Not applicable.

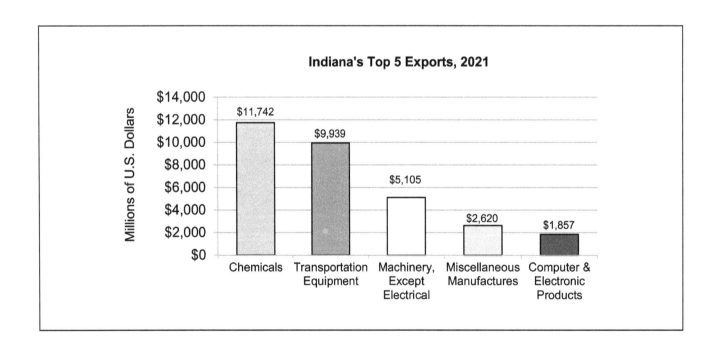

Facts and Figures

Location: North central United States; bordered on the N by Minnesota, on the E by Wisconsin and Illinois, on the S by Missouri, and on the W by Nebraska and South Dakota

Area: 56,272 sq. mi. (145,743 sq. km.); rank—26th

Population: 3,193,079 (2021 est.); rank—31st

Principal Cities: capital—Des Moines; largest—Des Moines

Statehood: December 28, 1846; 29th state

U.S. Congress: 2 senators, 4 representatives

State Motto: Our Liberties We Prize and Our Rights We Will Maintain

State Song: "The Song of Iowa"

State Nickname: The Hawkeye State

Abbreviations: IA; Ia.

State Symbols: flower—wild prairie rose; tree—oak; bird—Eastern goldfinch

At a Glance

- With an increase in population of 4.8 percent, Iowa ranked 31st among the states in growth from 2010 to 2021.

- In 2020, Iowa's median household income was $61,836, and 11.1 percent of the population lived below the poverty level.

- Compared to 8.7 percent of the total U.S. population, 4.7 percent of Iowans did not have health insurance in 2020, which was the 7th lowest percent in the country.

- Iowa's violent crime rate in 2020 was 303.5 per 100,000 population, compared to the rate of 398.5 for the U.S. as a whole.

- Iowa had the 2nd highest percent of single-family homes in 2020, with 78.6 percent of housing units being one-unit attached or detached homes.

Table IA-1. Population by Age, Sex, Race, and Hispanic Origin

(Number, percent, except where noted.)

Sex, age, race, and Hispanic origin	2000	2010	2021	Percent change, 2010–2021
Total Population......................	2,926,324	3,046,355	3,193,079	4.8
Percent of total U.S. population	1.0	1.0	1.0	X
Sex				
Male....................................	1,435,515	1,508,319	1,601,384	6.2
Female..................................	1,490,809	1,538,036	1,591,695	3.5
Age				
Under 5 years............................	188,413	202,123	189,056	-6.5
5 to 19 years............................	639,570	618,387	637,839	3.1
20 to 64 years...........................	1,662,128	1,772,957	1,800,911	1.6
65 years and over........................	436,213	452,888	565,273	24.8
Median age (years)	36.6	38.1	38.6	1.3
Race and Hispanic Origin				
One race				
White	2,748,640	2,839,615	2,875,490	1.3
Black...................................	61,853	91,695	137,863	50.3
American Indian and Alaska Native.........	8,989	13,563	18,190	34.1
Asian...................................	36,635	54,232	88,093	62.4
Native Hawaiian or Other Pacific Islander .	1,009	2,419	6,324	161.4
Two or more races........................	31,778	44,831	67,119	49.7
Hispanic (of any race)...................	82,473	156,932	215,119	37.1

NOTE: Population figures for 2021 are July 1 estimates. The 2000 and 2010 estimates are taken from the respective censuses.
- = Zero or rounds to zero.
X = Not applicable.

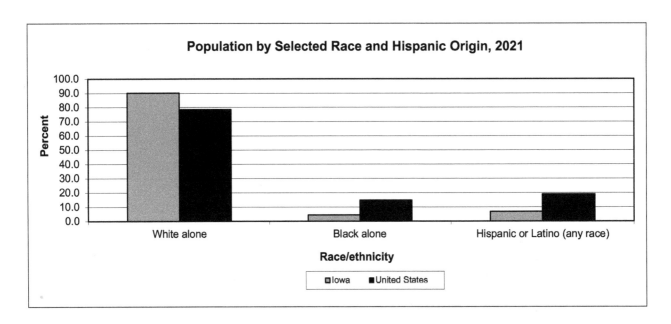

Population by Selected Race and Hispanic Origin, 2021

Legend: □ Iowa ■ United States

Race/ethnicity: White alone, Black alone, Hispanic or Latino (any race)

Table IA-2. Marital Status

(Number, percent distribution.)

Sex, age, race, and Hispanic origin	2000	2010	2020 [1]
Males, 15 Years and Over............................	1,126,566	1,199,509	1,256,179
Never married	28.2	31.3	33.8
Now married, except separated...........................	59.8	55.2	52.5
Separated...	0.9	1.1	1.0
Widowed...	2.5	2.6	2.8
Divorced..	8.5	9.7	9.9
Females, 15 Years and Over..........................	1,198,297	1,250,612	1,288,199
Never married	21.8	24.7	26.7
Now married, except separated...........................	55.8	52.4	51.3
Separated...	1.1	1.5	1.2
Widowed...	11.6	10.2	9.1
Divorced..	9.6	11.2	11.6

[1] 2020 ACS 5-Year estimates. 1-Year estimates were not released for 2020 due to the impact of COVID-19 on data collection that year.

Table IA-3. Households and Housing Characteristics

(Number, percent, dollars.)

Item	2000	2010	2020 [1]	Average annual percent change, 2010–2020
Total Households.............................	1,149,276	1,223,439	1,273,941	0.6
Family households.............................	769,684	793,768	800,738	0.1
Married-couple family.............................	633,254	633,602	631,258	-0.1
Other family.............................	136,430	160,166	169,480	0.8
Male householder, no wife present.............................	38,160	46,829	53,911	2.2
Female householder, no husband present.............................	98,270	113,337	115,569	0.3
Nonfamily households.............................	379,592	429,671	473,203	1.4
Householder living alone.............................	313,083	349,736	379,248	1.2
Householder not living alone.............................	66,509	79,935	93,955	2.5
Housing Characteristics				
Total housing units.............................	1,232,511	1,337,563	1,407,819	0.8
Occupied housing units.............................	1,149,276	1,223,439	1,273,941	0.6
Owner occupied.............................	831,419	885,284	906,967	0.3
Renter occupied.............................	317,857	338,155	366,974	1.2
Average household size.............................	2.46	2.41	2.40	-0.1
Financial Characteristics				
Median gross rent of renter-occupied housing.............................	470	629	806	4.0
Median monthly owner costs for housing units with a mortgage.............................	829	1,140	1,279	1.7
Median value of owner-occupied housing units.............................	82,500	123,400	153,900	3.5

[1] 2020 ACS 5-Year estimates. 1-Year estimates were not released for 2020 due to the impact of COVID-19 on data collection that year.

Table IA-4. Migration, Origin, and Language

(Number, percent.)

Characteristic	State 2016-2020 [1]	U.S. 2016-2020 [1]
Residence 1 Year Ago		
Population 1 year and over.............................	3,113,551	322,943,283
Same house.............................	85.6	86.2
Different house in the U.S.............................	14.0	13.2
Same county.............................	8.0	7.7
Different county.............................	6.0	5.5
Same state.............................	3.6	3.2
Different state.............................	2.4	2.3
Abroad.............................	0.4	0.6
Place of Birth		
Native born.............................	2,979,686	282,443,680
Male.............................	49.5	49.4
Female.............................	50.5	50.6
Foreign born.............................	170,325	44,125,628
Male.............................	51.9	48.6
Female.............................	48.1	51.4
Foreign born; naturalized U.S. citizen.............................	69,832	22,456,684
Male.............................	48.9	46.1
Female.............................	51.1	53.9
Foreign born; not a U.S. citizen.............................	100,493	21,668,944
Male.............................	53.9	51.1
Female.............................	46.1	48.9
Entered 2010 or later.............................	35.5	22.8
Entered 2000 to 2009.............................	28.7	25.1
Entered before 2000.............................	35.7	52.1
World Region of Birth, Foreign		
Foreign-born population, excluding population born at sea.............................	170,325	44,125,628
Europe.............................	10.5	10.8
Asia.............................	37.0	31.3
Africa.............................	14.4	5.4
Oceania.............................	1.0	0.6
Latin America.............................	35.4	50.0
North America.............................	1.7	1.9
Language Spoken at Home and Ability to Speak English		
Population 5 years and over.............................	2,954,549	306,919,116
English only.............................	91.6	78.5
Language other than English.............................	8.4	21.5
Speaks English less than "very well".............................	3.4	8.2

[1] 2020 ACS 5-Year estimates. 1-Year estimates were not released for 2020 due to the impact of COVID-19 on data collection that year.
NA = Not available.
X = Not applicable.
- = Zero or rounds to zero.

Table IA-5. Median Income and Poverty Status, 2020[1]

(Number, percent, except as noted.)

Characteristic	State		U.S.	
	Number	Percent	Number	Percent
Median Income				
Households (dollars)...	61,836	X	64,994	X
Families (dollars)	79,186	X	80,069	X
Below Poverty Level (All People)	339,090	11.1	40,910,326	12.8
Sex				
Male	150,447	10.0	18,171,512	11.6
Female	188,643	12.3	22,738,814	14.0
Age				
Under 18 years...	95,105	13.3	12,598,699	17.5
Related children under 18 years......................................	91,802	12.9	12,306,532	17.2
18 to 64 years..	207,738	11.4	23,554,920	12.1
65 years and over	36,247	7.0	4,756,707	9.3

X = Not applicable.
[1] 2020 ACS 5-Year estimates. 1-Year estimates were not released for 2020 due to the impact of COVID-19 on data collection that year.

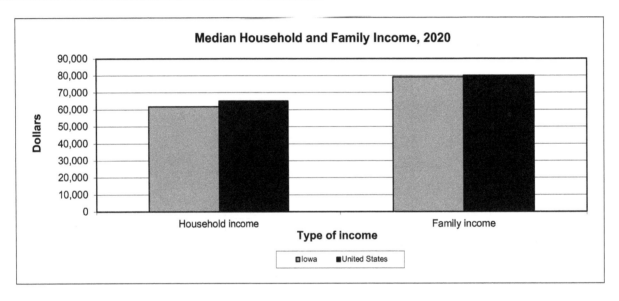

Table IA-6. Health Insurance Coverage Status for the Civilian Noninstitutionalized Population and Children Under 19 Years of Age

(Number, percent.)

Item	2011	2012	2013	2014	2015	2016	2017	2018	2019	2020[2]
Civilian Noninstitutionalized Population	3,017,465	3,028,864	3,045,284	3,062,900	3,080,411	3,091,437	3,102,179	3,113,029	3,111,914	3,106,492
Covered by Private or Public Insurance										
Number..	2,747,975	2,774,589	2,797,567	2,874,015	2,925,441	2,959,825	2,956,162	2,965,990	2,955,852	2,960,859
Percent...	91.1	91.6	91.9	93.8	95.0	95.7	95.3	95.3	95.0	95.3
Uninsured										
Number..	269,490	254,275	247,717	188,885	154,970	131,612	146,017	147,039	156,062	145,633
Percent...	8.9	8.4	8.1	6.2	5.0	4.3	4.7	4.7	5.0	4.7
Percent in the U.S. not covered...............................	15.1	14.8	14.5	11.7	9.4	8.6	8.7	8.9	9.2	8.7
Children Under 19 Years of Age[1]	721,561	720,427	721,264	723,351	726,495	724,997	775,929	780,762	765,322	770,491
Covered by Private or Public Insurance										
Number..	689,820	691,735	691,509	700,117	700,899	706,555	751,885	759,740	742,971	749,201
Percent...	95.6	96.0	95.9	96.8	96.5	97.5	96.9	97.3	97.1	97.2
Uninsured										
Number..	31,741	28,692	29,755	23,234	25,596	18,442	24,044	21,022	22,351	21,290
Percent...	4.4	4.0	4.1	3.2	3.5	2.5	3.1	2.7	2.9	2.8
Percent in the U.S. not covered...............................	7.5	7.2	7.1	6.0	4.8	4.5	5.0	5.2	5.7	5.2

[1] Data for years prior to 2017 are for individuals under 18 years of age.
[2] 2020 ACS 5-Year estimates. 1-Year estimates were not released for 2020 due to the impact of COVID-19 on data collection that year. Data is not comparable to previous years, which are based on 1-year estimates.

Table IA-7. Employment Status by Demographic Group, 2021

(Numbers in thousands, percent.)

Characteristic	Civilian noninstitutional population	Civilian labor force		Employed		Unemployed	
		Number	Percent of population	Number	Percent of population	Number	Percent of population
Total...	2,484	1,668	67.1	1,605	64.6	63	3.8
Sex							
Male...	1,227	883	71.9	849	69.1	34	3.9
Female.....................................	1,257	785	62.5	756	60.2	29	3.7
Race, Sex, and Hispanic Origin							
White..	2,277	1,527	67.1	1,476	64.8	51	3.3
Male.....................................	1,121	801	71.5	773	69.0	28	3.5
Female..................................	1,156	726	62.8	703	60.9	22	3.1
Black or African American............	NA	NA	NA	NA	NA	NA	NA
Male.....................................	NA	NA	NA	NA	NA	NA	NA
Female..................................	NA	NA	NA	NA	NA	NA	NA
Hispanic or Latino ethnicity[1]........	127	94	73.9	89	70.2	5	4.9
Male.....................................	NA	NA	NA	NA	NA	NA	NA
Female..................................	NA	NA	NA	NA	NA	NA	NA
Age							
16 to 19 years..........................	NA	NA	NA	NA	NA	NA	NA
20 to 24 years..........................	225	178	79.2	165	73.6	13	7.1
25 to 34 years..........................	421	364	86.4	353	83.8	11	3.1
35 to 44 years..........................	380	343	90.2	331	87.1	12	3.5
45 to 54 years..........................	351	294	83.6	284	80.8	10	3.4
55 to 64 years..........................	408	295	72.2	286	70.2	9	2.9
65 years and over.....................	554	129	23.3	126	22.7	3	2.5

NOTE: Data in Table 7 are from the Current Population Survey (CPS) and do not match the estimates in Table 8. See notes and definitions for further information.
[1] May be of any race.
NA = Not available

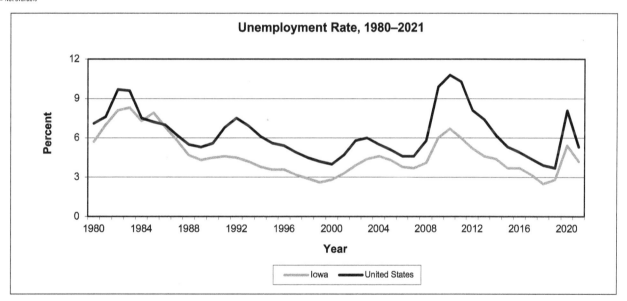

Table IA-8. Employment Status of the Civilian Noninstitutional Population Age 16 Years and Over

(Number, percent.)

Year	Civilian labor force	Civilian participation rate	Employed	Unemployed	Unemployment rate
2010..	1,674,411	71.0	1,571,960	102,451	6.1
2011..	1,670,056	70.3	1,575,767	94,289	5.6
2012..	1,660,180	69.5	1,576,236	83,944	5.1
2013..	1,676,565	69.7	1,597,139	79,426	4.7
2014..	1,698,718	70.2	1,626,676	72,042	4.2
2015..	1,700,549	69.9	1,637,467	63,082	3.7
2016..	1,703,164	69.7	1,642,152	61,012	3.6
2017..	1,697,495	68.9	1,645,660	51,835	3.1
2018..	1,714,951	69.3	1,671,631	43,320	2.5
2019..	1,749,620	70.3	1,704,063	45,557	2.6
2020..	1,682,257	67.4	1,595,824	86,433	5.1
2021..	1,676,075	66.9	1,605,206	70,869	4.2

Table IA-9. Employment and Average Wages by Industry

(Estimates are based on the 2012 North American Industry Classification System [NAICS].)

Industry	2013	2014	2015	2016	2017	2018	2019	2020
	Number of Jobs							
Wage and Salary Employment by Industry......................	1,592,602	1,607,246	1,626,375	1,632,862	1,630,848	1,638,255	1,644,686	1,569,147
Farm Wage and Salary Employment...............................	19,233	14,833	19,160	18,686	16,838	16,937	19,397	19,861
Nonfarm Wage and Salary Employment........................	1,573,369	1,592,413	1,607,215	1,614,176	1,614,010	1,621,318	1,625,289	1,549,286
Private wage and salary employment...........................	1,306,151	1,324,779	1,339,726	1,345,784	1,344,056	1,350,506	1,353,331	1,284,713
Forestry, fishing, and related activities........................	8,507	7,618	7,516	7,536	7,560	7,597	7,640	7,429
Mining...	2,228	2,166	2,218	2,185	2,319	2,434	2,394	2,231
Utilities..	6,456	6,483	6,576	6,467	6,424	6,397	6,205	6,048
Construction..	69,595	76,100	80,228	82,845	77,897	79,063	79,966	78,436
Manufacturing...	214,678	217,229	216,587	214,043	216,231	222,841	226,358	216,894
Durable goods manufacturing...............................	128,846	130,959	129,087	124,756	123,658	128,010	130,431	122,032
Nondurable goods manufacturing..........................	85,832	86,270	87,500	89,287	92,573	94,831	95,927	94,862
Wholesale trade	69,595	69,307	67,995	67,051	66,789	66,363	66,470	65,092
Retail trade..	177,330	178,004	181,529	183,744	182,861	180,115	176,283	169,434
Transportation and warehousing.............................	59,378	60,184	61,221	60,391	60,944	61,988	63,866	62,682
Information	26,152	25,715	24,997	22,635	21,916	22,016	21,329	19,152
Finance and insurance	94,033	94,402	95,725	98,235	99,336	99,312	100,858	101,191
Real estate and rental and leasing............................	13,756	14,192	14,529	14,629	14,835	15,161	15,320	14,791
Professional, scientific, and technical services	46,939	48,713	49,874	52,159	52,940	54,082	53,227	52,842
Management of companies and enterprises.....................	16,590	18,215	19,227	19,069	19,177	19,602	20,670	21,024
Administrative and waste services.............................	69,515	70,349	70,442	68,255	67,838	67,825	66,320	61,886
Educational services	40,730	40,632	40,515	41,968	42,206	38,399	37,906	34,930
Health care and social assistance............................	185,875	187,465	189,647	192,604	193,817	194,415	194,458	186,920
Arts, entertainment, and recreation...........................	18,683	19,168	18,999	20,958	20,780	21,238	21,874	16,728
Accommodation and food services...........................	118,582	119,711	121,618	122,631	123,249	123,423	123,259	102,734
Other services, except public administration..................	67,529	69,126	70,283	68,379	66,937	68,235	68,928	64,269
Government and government enterprises.....................	267,218	267,634	267,489	268,392	269,954	270,812	271,958	264,573
	Dollars							
Average Wages and Salaries by Industry	40,185	41,763	43,053	43,898	45,186	46,636	47,711	50,963
Average Farm Wages and Salaries	30,150	46,445	30,060	30,621	42,389	37,398	33,538	27,375
Average Nonfarm Wages and Salaries	40,308	41,720	43,208	44,052	45,215	46,732	47,880	51,265
Average private wages and salaries............................	40,235	41,730	43,269	44,086	45,292	46,937	48,147	51,666
Forestry, fishing, and related activities............................	26,895	29,698	30,753	31,868	32,863	34,447	35,845	38,347
Mining..	46,947	51,767	54,337	57,509	58,119	58,483	60,698	60,731
Utilities..	80,939	86,365	86,924	88,081	91,440	94,397	96,968	102,697
Construction	48,520	51,967	54,959	58,064	55,428	57,442	58,954	61,809
Manufacturing...	52,891	54,389	55,915	56,038	58,605	60,248	60,176	63,083
Durable goods manufacturing...............................	55,992	57,375	58,761	58,312	61,859	63,755	62,760	65,174
Nondurable goods manufacturing..........................	48,236	49,854	51,717	52,861	54,258	55,514	56,662	60,394
Wholesale trade	57,035	58,796	60,250	61,105	63,237	65,782	66,985	69,803
Retail trade..	23,903	24,595	25,212	25,820	26,526	27,266	27,929	30,361
Transportation and warehousing.............................	42,306	44,646	45,973	45,679	47,242	49,149	49,193	51,537
Information	49,005	50,756	52,858	53,842	55,937	58,539	60,526	66,810
Finance and insurance	65,911	68,254	71,512	72,359	75,272	77,801	80,261	84,995
Real estate and rental and leasing............................	41,119	42,772	44,782	44,589	45,680	46,763	48,181	51,829
Professional, scientific, and technical services	58,913	60,423	62,962	64,378	66,684	68,212	70,871	75,301
Management of companies and enterprises.....................	75,656	77,926	81,841	02,341	83,123	84,202	87,713	95,779
Administrative and waste services.............................	27,730	28,546	29,634	30,970	32,308	34,031	35,649	38,647
Educational services	24,130	24,755	24,740	26,212	26,242	28,871	29,398	31,512
Health care and social assistance............................	38,397	39,437	41,349	41,944	42,701	43,644	45,018	47,789
Arts, entertainment, and recreation...........................	18,928	19,642	20,242	19,494	19,791	20,324	20,898	22,514
Accommodation and food services...........................	15,631	16,179	16,755	17,547	18,113	19,018	19,449	19,025
Other services, except public administration..................	28,516	29,461	30,625	32,619	33,421	34,369	36,097	38,750
Government and government enterprises.............................	40,663	41,667	42,903	43,878	44,830	45,712	46,552	49,316

Table IA-10. Employment Characteristics by Family Type

(Number, percent.)

Family type and labor force status	2018 Total	2018 Families with own children under 18 years	2019 Total	2019 Families with own children under 18 years	2020 [1] Total	2020 [1] Families with own children under 18 years
All Families..	800,329	344,949	808,802	343,739	800,738	349,346
FAMILY TYPE AND LABOR FORCE STATUS						
Opposite-Sex Married-Couple Families............................	622,142	234,450	628,853	237,254	627,590	241,897
Both husband and wife in labor force..................................	57.6	78.3	57.7	78.9	58.4	78.4
Husband in labor force, wife not in labor force........................	16.8	18.0	15.7	16.8	16.6	17.8
Wife in labor force, husband not in labor force........................	7.1	2.5	7.1	2.9	7.0	2.7
Both husband and wife not in labor force..............................	17.8	1.0	19.0	1.1	18.1	1.1
Other Families	178,187	110,499	179,949	106,485	169,480	106,733
Female householder, no spouse present.....................................	67.9	69.6	68.4	71.0	68.2	70.0
In labor force....................................	52.2	60.8	52.8	62.0	53.1	60.9
Not in labor force	15.7	8.8	15.6	9.0	15.0	9.1
Male householder, no spouse present............................	32.1	30.4	31.6	29.0	31.8	30.0
In labor force....................................	27.3	28.6	26.2	27.2	26.8	28.0
Not in labor force	4.8	1.8	5.4	1.8	5.0	2.0

[1] 2020 ACS 5-Year estimates. 1-Year estimates were not released for 2020 due to the impact of COVID-19 on data collection that year. Data is not comparable to previous years, which are based on 1-year estimates.

Table IA-11. School Enrollment and Educational Attainment, 2020[1]

(Number, percent.)

Item	State	U.S.
Enrollment		
Total population 3 years and over, enrolled in school	785,736	80,497,960
Enrolled in nursery school or preschool (percent)................................	6.7	6.1
Enrolled in kindergarten (percent)...	5.4	5.0
Enrolled in elementary school, grades 1-8 (percent)............................	40.8	40.4
Enrolled in high school, grades 9-12 (percent)...................................	20.2	21.0
Enrolled in college or graduate school (percent)................................	26.9	27.6
Attainment		
Total population 25 years and over	2,104,864	222,836,834
Less than ninth grade (percent)...	2.9	4.9
9th to 12th grade, no diploma (percent)...	4.6	6.6
High school graduate, including equivalency (percent)..........................	30.8	26.7
Some college, no degree (percent)..	20.6	20.3
Associate's degree (percent)..	11.8	8.6
Bachelor's degree (percent)	19.7	20.2
Graduate or professional degree (percent).......................................	9.6	12.7
High school graduate or higher (percent)	92.5	88.5
Bachelor's degree or higher (percent)...	29.3	32.9

[1] 2020 ACS 5-Year estimates. 1-Year estimates were not released for 2020 due to the impact of COVID-19 on data collection that year.

Table IA-12. Public School Characteristics and Educational Indicators

(Number, percent; data derived from National Center of Education Statistics.)

Item	State	U.S.
Public Elementary and Secondary Schools		
Number of regular school districts, 2018-19	330	13,452
Number of operational schools, 2019-20...	1,310	98,469
Percent charter schools	0.2	7.7
Total public school enrollment, Fall 2019..	517,324	50,796,445
Percent charter school enrollment	#	6.8
Student-teacher ratio, Fall 2019..	14.5	15.9
Expenditures per student (unadjusted dollars), 2018-19	11,933	13,187
Four-year adjusted cohort graduation rate (ACGR), 2018-2019[1]..............	91.6	85.8
Students eligible for free or reduced-price lunch (percent), 2019-20............	42.0	52.1
English language learners (percent), Fall 2019	6.5	10.4
Students age 3 to 21 served under IDEA, part B (percent), 2020-21	13.7	14.5

Public Schools by Type, 2019-20	Number	Percent of state public schools
Total number of schools..	1,310	100.0
Special education	2	0.2
Vocational education...	0	-
Alternative education..	17	1.3

[1] Adjusted Cohort Graduation Rates (ACGR) differ from Averaged Freshmen Graduation Rates (AFGR).
- = Zero or rounds to zero.

Table IA-13. Reported Voting and Registration of the Voting-Age Population, November 2020

(Numbers in thousands, percent.)

Item	Total population	Total citizen population	Registered			Voted		
			Total registered	Percent registered (total population)	Percent registered (total citizen population)	Total voted	Percent voted (total population)	Percent voted (total citizen population)
U.S. Total	252,274	231,593	168,308	66.7	72.7	154,628	61.3	66.8
State Total...	2,361	2,293	1,742	73.8	76.0	1,618	68.5	70.5
Sex								
Male	1,167	1,133	853	73.2	75.3	785	67.3	69.2
Female	1,194	1,160	888	74.4	76.6	833	69.7	71.8
Race								
White alone.........................	2,160	2,125	1,630	75.4	76.7	1,521	70.4	71.5
White, non-Hispanic alone	2,068	2,050	1,603	77.5	78.2	1,496	72.3	73.0
Black alone........................	95	87	55	58.6	63.5	40	42.6	46.2
Asian alone	77	52	36	B	B	36	B	B
Hispanic (of any race)	108	90	42	39.1	46.8	40	37.0	44.2
White alone or in combination	2,176	2,141	1,645	75.6	76.9	1,536	70.6	71.8
Black alone or in combination	110	103	71	64.4	69.0	56	50.7	54.2
Asian alone or in combination........................	80	55	39	B	B	39	B	B
Age								
18 to 24 years...................	260	248	169	65.2	68.3	157	60.5	63.3
25 to 34 years...................	377	356	248	65.7	69.5	223	59.2	62.7
35 to 44 years...................	412	395	307	74.5	77.8	276	66.8	69.8
45 to 64 years...................	722	707	545	75.4	77.0	511	70.7	72.3
65 years and over	590	587	473	80.2	80.5	451	76.5	76.8

B = Base is less than 75,000 and therefore too small to show the derived measure.

Table IA-14. Crime

(Number, rate per 100,000. Data are derived from the FBI Uniform Crime Reports.)

Item	State			U.S.		
	2019	2020	Percent change	2019	2020	Percent change
TOTAL POPULATION[1]	3,159,596	3,163,561	0.1	328,329,953	329,484,123	0.4
VIOLENT CRIME						
Number........................	9,086	9,601	5.7	1,250,393	1,313,105	5.0
Rate	287.6	303.5	5.5	380.8	398.5	4.6
Murder and Nonnegligent Manslaughter						
Number........................	70	111	58.6	16,669	21,570	29.4
Rate	2.2	3.5	58.4	5.1	6.5	28.9
Rape[2]						
Number........................	1,365	1,289	-5.6	143,224	126,430	-11.7
Rate	43.2	40.7	-5.7	43.6	38.4	-12.0
Robbery						
Number........................	919	943	2.6	268,483	243,600	-9.3
Rate	29.1	29.8	2.5	81.8	73.9	-9.6
Aggravated Assault						
Number........................	6,732	7,258	7.8	822,017	921,505	12.1
Rate	213.1	229.4	7.7	250.4	279.7	11.7
PROPERTY CRIME						
Number........................	58,446	53,725	-8.1	6,995,235	6,452,038	-7.8
Rate	1,849.8	1,698.2	-8.2	2,130.6	1,958.2	-8.1
Burglary						
Number........................	12,406	11,739	-5.4	1,118,096	1,035,314	-7.4
Rate	392.6	371.1	-5.5	340.5	314.2	-7.7
Larceny-Theft						
Number........................	40,479	35,751	-11.7	5,152,267	4,606,324	-10.6
Rate	1,281.1	1,130.1	-11.8	1,569.2	1,398.0	-10.9
Motor Vehicle Theft						
Number........................	5,561	6,235	12.1	724,872	810,400	11.8
Rate	176.0	197.1	12.0	220.8	246.0	11.4

NOTE: Although arson data are included in the trend and clearance tables, sufficient data are not available to estimate totals for this offense. Therefore, no arson data are published in this table.
- = Zero or rounds to zero.
[1] Population figures are U.S. Census Bureau provisional estimates as of July 1, 2020.
[2] The figures shown in the rape (revised definition) column were estimated using the revised Uniform Crime Reporting (UCR) definition of rape.

Table IA-15. State Government Finances, 2020

(Dollar amounts in thousands, percent distribution.)

Item	Dollars	Percent distribution
Total Revenue	32,304,217	100.0
General revenue	28,450,692	88.1
Intergovernmental revenue	8,563,372	26.5
Taxes	10,661,437	33.0
General sales	3546984	11.0
Selective sales	1,411,159	4.4
License taxes	1,021,357	3.2
Individual income tax	3960027	12.3
Corporate income tax	620,486	1.9
Other taxes	101,424	0.3
Current charges	4,122,170	12.8
Miscellaneous general revenue	5,103,713	15.8
Utility revenue	0	-
Liquor stores revenue	367375	1.1
Insurance trust revenue[1]	3,486,150	10.8
Total Expenditure	25,727,333	100.0
Intergovernmental expenditure	5,632,619	21.9
Direct expenditure	20,094,714	78.1
Current operation	14,579,478	56.7
Capital outlay	1,819,854	7.1
Insurance benefits and repayments	2,787,609	10.8
Assistance and subsidies	681,009	2.6
Interest on debt	226,764	0.9
Exhibit: Salaries and wages	3,745,847	14.6
Total Expenditure	25,727,333	100.0
General expenditure	22,682,247	88.2
Intergovernmental expenditure	5,632,619	21.9
Direct expenditure	17,049,628	66.3
General expenditure, by function:		
Education	7,437,403	28.9
Public welfare	7,288,721	28.3
Hospitals	2,451,170	9.5
Health	238,286	0.9
Highways	2,379,359	9.2
Police protection	114,687	0.4
Correction	305,974	1.2
Natural resources	450,902	1.8
Parks and recreation	31,123	0.1
Governmental administration	657,134	2.6
Interest on general debt	226,764	0.9
Other and unallocable	1,025,634	4.0
Utility expenditure	57,536	0.2
Liquor stores expenditure	257477	1.0
Insurance trust expenditure	2,787,609	10.8
Debt at End of Fiscal Year	6,250,299	X
Cash and Security Holdings	53,732,625	X

X = Not applicable.
- = Zero or rounds to zero.
[1] Within insurance trust revenue, net earnings of state retirement systems is a calculated statistic (the item code in the data file is X08), and thus can be positive or negative. Net earnings is the sum of earnings on investments plus gains on investments minus losses on investments. The change made in 2002 for asset valuation from book to market value in accordance with Statement 34 of the Governmental Accounting Standards Board is reflected in the calculated statistics.

Table IA-16. State Government Tax Collections, 2021

(Dollars in thousands, percent.)

Item	Dollars	Percent distribution
Total Taxes	11,816,502	100.0
Property taxes	2,024	-
Sales and gross receipts	5,522,117	46.7
General sales and gross receipts	4,002,493	33.9
Selective sales and gross receipts	1,519,624	12.9
Alcoholic beverages	29,798	0.3
Amusements	339,345	2.9
Insurance premiums	143,752	1.2
Motor fuels	673,571	5.7
Pari-mutuels	3,870	-
Public utilities	78,826	0.7
Tobacco products	200,579	1.7
Other selective sales	49,883	0.4
Licenses	1,101,447	9.3
Alcoholic beverages	18,664	0.2
Amusements	27,920	0.2
Corporations in general	64,639	0.5
Hunting and fishing	35,549	0.3
Motor vehicle	760,540	6.4
Motor vehicle operators	21,978	0.2
Public utilities	10,791	0.1
Occupation and business, NEC	160,355	1.4
Other licenses	1,011	-
Income taxes	5,060,175	42.8
Individual income	4,266,534	36.1
Corporation net income	793,641	6.7
Other taxes	130,739	1.1
Death and gift	100,141	0.8
Documentary and stock transfer	30,598	0.3
Severance	X	-
Taxes, NEC	0	-

X = Not applicable.
- = Zero or rounds to zero.

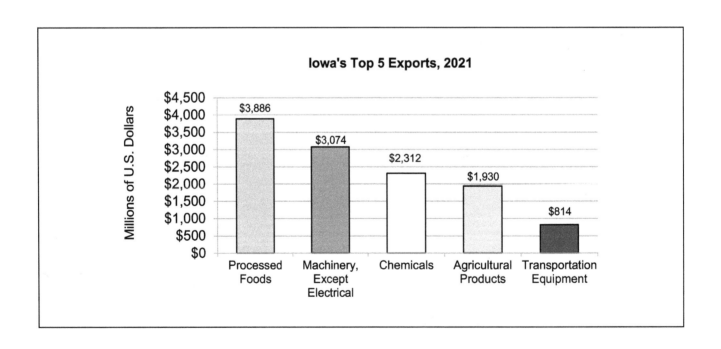

Iowa's Top 5 Exports, 2021

Export	Millions of U.S. Dollars
Processed Foods	$3,886
Machinery, Except Electrical	$3,074
Chemicals	$2,312
Agricultural Products	$1,930
Transportation Equipment	$814

KANSAS

Facts and Figures

Location: Central United States; bordered on the N by Nebraska, on the E by Missouri, on the S by Oklahoma, and on the W by Colorado

Area: 82,277 sq. mi. (213,096 sq. km.); rank—15th

Population: 3,193,079 (2021 est.); rank—35th

Principal Cities: capital—Topeka; largest—Wichita

Statehood: January 29, 1861; 34th state

U.S. Congress: 2 senators, 4 representatives

State Motto: *Ad astra per aspera* ("To the stars through difficulties")

State Song: "Home on the Range"

State Nicknames: The Sunflower State; The Jayhawk State

Abbreviations: KS; Kan.; Kans.

State Symbols: flower—wild native sunflower; tree—cottonwood; bird—Western meadowlark

At a Glance

- With an increase in population of 4.8 percent, Kansas ranked 40th among the states in growth from 2010 to 2021.

- In 2020, 8.7 percent of Kansans did not have health insurance, which was the same percent as the overall U.S. population.

- Kansans younger than 18 years old comprised 24.0 percent of the state's population in 2021, which was the 8th highest percentage in the United States.

- Kansas's unemployment rate was 3.2 percent in 2021, the 4th lowest percent in the country.

- In 2020, Kansas had the second highest drug overdose death rate in the country, with 49.2 deaths per 100,000 population.

Table KS-1. Population by Age, Sex, Race, and Hispanic Origin

(Number, percent, except where noted.)

Sex, age, race, and Hispanic origin	2000	2010	2021	Percent change, 2010–2021
Total Population...	2,688,418	2,853,118	2,934,582	2.9
Percent of total U.S. population	1.0	0.9	0.9	X
Sex				
Male..	1,328,474	1,415,408	1,470,491	3.9
Female..	1,359,944	1,437,710	1,464,091	1.8
Age				
Under 5 years...	188,708	205,492	178,147	-13.3
5 to 19 years..	609,710	605,152	606,974	0.3
20 to 64 years..	1,533,771	1,666,358	1,659,823	-0.4
65 years and over..	356,229	376,116	489,638	30.2
Median age (years)	35.2	36.0	37.4	3.9
Race and Hispanic Origin				
One race				
White	2,313,944	2,501,057	2,522,698	0.9
Black..	154,198	173,298	181,676	4.8
American Indian and Alaska Native	24,936	33,044	36,318	9.9
Asian..	46,806	69,628	94,163	35.2
Native Hawaiian or Other Pacific Islander	1,313	2,864	4,083	42.6
Two or more races	56,496	73,227	95,644	30.6
Hispanic (of any race)...	188,252	311,460	374,093	20.1

NOTE: Population figures for 2021 are July 1 estimates. The 2000 and 2010 estimates are taken from the respective censuses.
- = Zero or rounds to zero.
X = Not applicable.

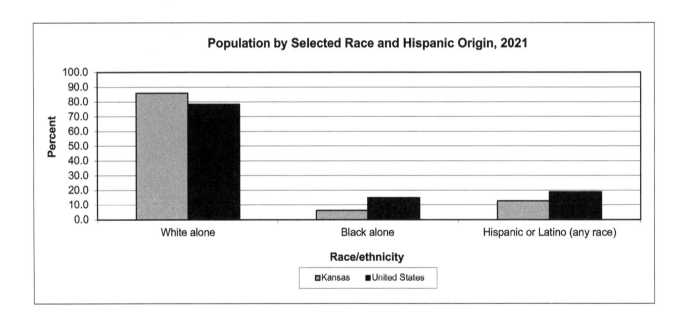

Population by Selected Race and Hispanic Origin, 2021

Table KS-2. Marital Status

(Number, percent distribution.)

Sex, age, race, and Hispanic origin	2000	2010	2020 [1]
Males, 15 Years and Over	1,025,114	1,106,102	1,151,163
Never married	27.4	31.6	33.0
Now married, except separated...	59.9	53.9	53.0
Separated...	1.1	1.4	1.1
Widowed..	2.3	2.6	2.7
Divorced..	9.2	10.5	10.2
Females, 15 Years and Over	1,075,542	1,145,453	1,174,433
Never married	20.8	25.1	26.0
Now married, except separated...	56.4	51.4	51.5
Separated...	1.3	1.7	1.5
Widowed..	10.6	9.2	8.7
Divorced..	10.9	12.6	12.3

[1] 2020 ACS 5-Year estimates. 1-Year estimates were not released for 2020 due to the impact of COVID-19 on data collection that year.

Table KS-3. Households and Housing Characteristics

(Number, percent, dollars.)

Item	2000	2010	2020 [1]	Average annual percent change, 2010–2020
Total Households...	1,037,891	1,101,658	1,141,985	0.5
Family households	701,547	721,592	737,611	0.3
Married-couple family	567,924	559,199	576,150	0.4
Other family	133,623	162,393	161,461	-0.1
Male householder, no wife present....................	36,962	46,692	49,728	0.9
Female householder, no husband present....................	96,661	115,701	111,733	-0.5
Nonfamily households	336,344	380,066	404,374	0.9
Householder living alone................................	280,387	313,390	332,412	0.9
Householder not living alone............................	55,957	66,676	71,962	1.1
Housing Characteristics				
Total housing units....................................	1,131,200	1,234,037	1,280,376	0.5
Occupied housing units................................	1,037,891	1,101,658	1,141,985	0.5
Owner occupied	718,703	749,907	756,309	0.1
Renter occupied	319,188	351,751	385,676	1.4
Average household size.................................	2.51	2.52	2.48	-0.2
Financial Characteristics				
Median gross rent of renter-occupied housing	498	682	863	3.8
Median monthly owner costs for housing units with a mortgage	888	1,239	1,400	1.9
Median value of owner-occupied housing units....................	83,500	127,300	157,600	3.4

[1] 2020 ACS 5-Year estimates. 1-Year estimates were not released for 2020 due to the impact of COVID-19 on data collection that year.

Table KS-4. Migration, Origin, and Language

(Number, percent.)

	State	U.S.
Characteristic	2016-2020 [1]	2016-2020 [1]
Residence 1 Year Ago		
Population 1 year and over	2,877,400	322,943,283
Same house	84.1	86.2
Different house in the U.S.	15.5	13.2
Same county	8.9	7.7
Different county	6.6	5.5
Same state	3.5	3.2
Different state	3.1	2.3
Abroad	0.4	0.6
Place of Birth		
Native born	2,708,590	282,443,680
Male	49.8	49.4
Female	50.2	50.6
Foreign born	204,029	44,125,628
Male	51.1	48.6
Female	48.9	51.4
Foreign born; naturalized U.S. citizen....................	84,390	22,456,684
Male	48.9	46.1
Female	51.1	53.9
Foreign born; not a U.S. citizen....................	119,639	21,668,944
Male	52.6	51.1
Female	47.4	48.9
Entered 2010 or later	26.4	22.8
Entered 2000 to 2009	29.3	25.1
Entered before 2000....................	44.3	52.1
World Region of Birth, Foreign		
Foreign-born population, excluding population born at sea	204,029	44,125,628
Europe	6.7	10.8
Asia....................	33.1	31.3
Africa	6.0	5.4
Oceania	0.5	0.6
Latin America....................	52.2	50.0
North America	1.4	1.9
Language Spoken at Home and Ability to Speak English		
Population 5 years and over....................	2,723,766	306,919,116
English only	88.3	78.5
Language other than English....................	11.7	21.5
Speaks English less than "very well"....................	4.5	8.2

[1] 2020 ACS 5-Year estimates. 1-Year estimates were not released for 2020 due to the impact of COVID-19 on data collection that year.
NA = Not available.
X = Not applicable.
- = Zero or rounds to zero.

Table KS-5. Median Income and Poverty Status, 2020[1]

(Number, percent, except as noted.)

Characteristic	State		U.S.	
	Number	Percent	Number	Percent
Median Income				
Households (dollars)..	61,091	X	64,994	X
Families (dollars)	77,620	X	80,069	X
Below Poverty Level (All People)	323,644	11.4	40,910,326	12.8
Sex				
Male	142,224	10.1	18,171,512	11.6
Female	181,420	12.7	22,738,814	14.0
Age				
Under 18 years...	96,696	13.9	12,598,699	17.5
Related children under 18 years.......................................	93,562	13.6	12,306,532	17.2
18 to 64 years	192,813	11.4	23,554,920	12.1
65 years and over	34,135	7.7	4,756,707	9.3

X = Not applicable.
[1] 2020 ACS 5-Year estimates. 1-Year estimates were not released for 2020 due to the impact of COVID-19 on data collection that year.

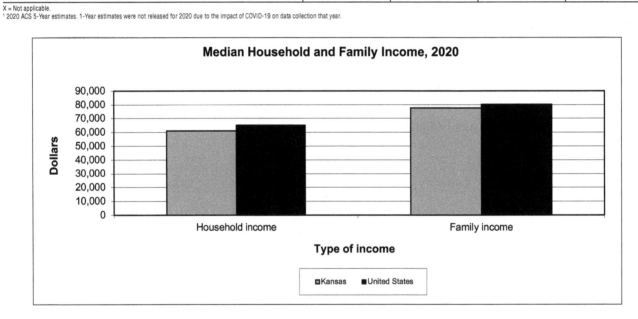

Table KS-6. Health Insurance Coverage Status for the Civilian Noninstitutionalized Population and Children Under 19 Years of Age

(Number, percent.)

Item	2011	2012	2013	2014	2015	2016	2017	2018	2019	2020 [2]
Civilian Noninstitutionalized Population	2,813,530	2,825,416	2,836,733	2,845,414	2,850,159	2,850,862	2,855,454	2,854,774	2,851,831	2,853,649
Covered by Private or Public Insurance										
Number..	2,458,900	2,469,852	2,488,636	2,553,940	2,589,651	2,601,888	2,606,062	2,604,419	2,589,439	2,604,426
Percent..	87.4	87.4	87.7	89.8	90.9	91.3	91.3	91.2	90.8	91.3
Uninsured										
Number..	354,630	355,564	348,097	291,474	260,508	248,974	249,392	250,355	262,392	249,223
Percent..	12.6	12.6	12.3	10.2	9.1	8.7	8.7	8.8	9.2	8.7
Percent in the U.S. not covered.................................	15.1	14.8	14.5	11.7	9.4	8.6	8.7	8.9	9.2	8.7
Children Under 19 Years of Age[1]	721,211	719,917	718,934	720,908	718,994	713,102	755,441	746,787	739,651	745,240
Covered by Private or Public Insurance										
Number..	674,866	672,059	674,804	681,497	682,459	682,190	715,965	708,650	696,615	706,959
Percent..	93.6	93.4	93.9	94.5	94.9	95.7	94.8	94.9	94.2	94.9
Uninsured										
Number..	46,345	47,858	44,130	39,411	36,535	30,912	39,476	38,137	43,036	38,281
Percent..	6.4	6.6	6.1	5.5	5.1	4.3	5.2	5.1	5.8	5.1
Percent in the U.S. not covered.................................	7.5	7.2	7.1	6.0	4.8	4.5	5.0	5.2	5.7	5.2

[1] Data for years prior to 2017 are for individuals under 18 years of age.
[2] 2020 ACS 5-Year estimates. 1-Year estimates were not released for 2020 due to the impact of COVID-19 on data collection that year. Data is not comparable to previous years, which are based on 1-year estimates.

Table KS-7. Employment Status by Demographic Group, 2021

(Numbers in thousands, percent.)

Characteristic	Civilian noninstitutional population	Civilian labor force		Employed		Unemployed	
		Number	Percent of population	Number	Percent of population	Number	Percent of population
Total...	2,240	1,485	66.3	1,436	64.1	49	3.3
Sex							
Male...	1,096	780	71.2	753	68.7	27	3.4
Female..	1,144	705	61.6	683	59.7	23	3.2
Race, Sex, and Hispanic Origin							
White..	1,965	1,299	66.1	1,258	64.0	41	3.1
Male...	958	682	71.1	658	68.7	23	3.4
Female...	1,007	617	61.3	600	59.6	17	2.8
Black or African American.....................	NA	NA	NA	NA	NA	NA	NA
Male...	NA	NA	NA	NA	NA	NA	NA
Female...	NA	NA	NA	NA	NA	NA	NA
Hispanic or Latino ethnicity[1]	218	159	73.0	153	70.3	6	3.6
Male...	105	88	83.5	85	80.7	3	3.4
Female...	NA	NA	NA	NA	NA	NA	NA
Age							
16 to 19 years..................................	NA	NA	NA	NA	NA	NA	NA
20 to 24 years..................................	179	135	75.4	128	71.6	7	5.1
25 to 34 years..................................	415	358	86.4	346	83.5	12	3.4
35 to 44 years..................................	346	294	85.0	285	82.5	9	3.0
45 to 54 years..................................	326	273	83.8	269	82.4	5	1.7
55 to 64 years..................................	351	242	69.1	235	67.1	7	2.8
65 years and over	483	115	23.8	112	23.3	2	2.1

NOTE: Data in Table 7 are from the Current Population Survey (CPS) and do not match the estimates in Table 8. See notes and definitions for further information.
[1] May be of any race.

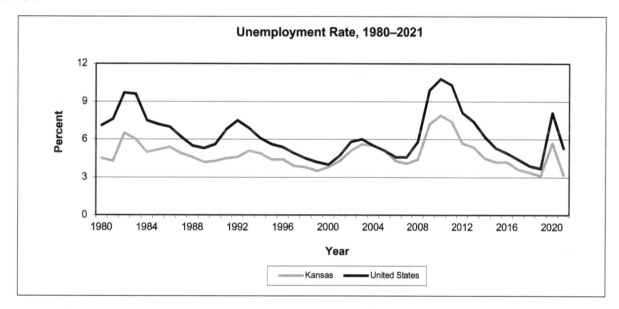

Unemployment Rate, 1980–2021

Table KS-8. Employment Status of the Civilian Noninstitutional Population Age 16 Years and Over

(Number, percent.)

Year	Civilian labor force	Civilian participation rate	Employed	Unemployed	Unemployment rate
2010..	1,500,463	69.8	1,396,172	104,291	7.0
2011..	1,498,000	69.3	1,402,198	95,802	6.4
2012..	1,490,808	68.6	1,405,638	85,170	5.7
2013..	1,489,395	68.2	1,410,470	78,925	5.3
2014..	1,494,203	68.1	1,426,892	67,311	4.5
2015..	1,493,782	67.8	1,431,533	62,249	4.2
2016..	1,491,961	67.4	1,431,920	60,041	4.0
2017..	1,488,346	66.8	1,434,516	53,830	3.6
2018..	1,488,027	66.6	1,439,329	48,698	3.3
2019..	1,497,517	66.8	1,450,705	46,812	3.1
2020..	1,493,706	66.4	1,408,965	84,741	5.7
2021..	1,495,665	66.3	1,447,323	48,342	3.2

Table KS-9. Employment and Average Wages by Industry

(Estimates are based on the 2012 North American Industry Classification System [NAICS].)

Industry	2013	2014	2015	2016	2017	2018	2019	2020
	\multicolumn{8}{c}{Number of Jobs}							
Wage and Salary Employment by Industry.......................	1,447,857	1,471,209	1,481,464	1,480,741	1,479,026	1,497,980	1,509,013	1,445,399
Farm Wage and Salary Employment...............................	9,329	11,907	12,622	13,057	12,209	12,664	12,696	14,273
Nonfarm Wage and Salary Employment..........................	1,438,528	1,459,302	1,468,842	1,467,684	1,466,817	1,485,316	1,496,317	1,431,126
Private wage and salary employment.......................................	1,140,839	1,162,817	1,173,655	1,176,547	1,176,479	1,187,744	1,196,770	1,138,543
Forestry, fishing, and related activities..................................	4,760	4,873	4,946	4,972	4,844	5,016	5,124	4,934
Mining..	10,397	10,397	8,453	6,803	6,703	6,723	6,729	5,805
Utilities..	7,752	7,779	6,751	6,677	6,557	6,363	6,221	6,263
Construction..	58,356	61,255	62,557	62,853	61,666	62,662	65,229	64,711
Manufacturing...	163,196	162,639	161,550	160,402	161,240	164,708	166,848	158,814
Durable goods manufacturing..	100,573	98,917	98,142	95,852	94,849	97,762	99,771	92,078
Nondurable goods manufacturing......................................	62,623	63,722	63,408	64,550	66,391	66,946	67,077	66,736
Wholesale trade..	60,109	61,612	60,459	60,006	60,251	59,748	58,602	56,220
Retail trade..	145,275	147,386	149,623	151,142	148,429	146,802	143,161	137,658
Transportation and warehousing...	48,598	49,893	50,656	52,515	55,652	58,631	62,114	62,425
Information...	27,560	27,822	21,004	20,589	19,304	18,658	18,258	16,725
Finance and insurance	61,395	62,461	63,930	63,287	64,110	62,801	64,174	64,391
Real estate and rental and leasing.......................................	14,233	14,708	15,414	15,638	15,578	16,251	16,401	15,663
Professional, scientific, and technical services	66,717	67,723	70,277	73,532	73,923	74,885	74,898	73,767
Management of companies and enterprises...........................	15,197	18,627	27,605	24,459	25,001	25,610	27,520	22,661
Administrative and waste services..	81,323	83,957	82,181	81,524	79,596	80,140	77,950	73,546
Educational services	20,496	21,013	21,120	20,862	21,170	21,263	21,382	19,461
Health care and social assistance..	170,780	172,158	177,433	180,201	180,522	183,142	185,958	183,893
Arts, entertainment, and recreation......................................	16,038	16,638	16,432	17,015	17,241	17,519	17,310	13,407
Accommodation and food services.......................................	105,974	107,159	110,080	111,220	112,067	112,698	113,431	98,139
Other services, except public administration.........................	62,683	64,717	63,184	62,850	62,625	64,124	65,460	60,060
Government and government enterprises.................................	297,689	296,485	295,187	291,137	290,338	297,572	299,547	292,583
	\multicolumn{8}{c}{Dollars}							
Average Wages and Salaries by Industry	42,734	43,805	45,013	45,361	46,413	47,756	49,218	52,441
Average Farm Wages and Salaries	40,813	40,727	35,122	39,385	36,632	36,446	40,872	30,248
Average Nonfarm Wages and Salaries	42,746	43,830	45,097	45,414	46,494	47,852	49,289	52,662
Average private wages and salaries.......................................	43,570	44,747	46,113	46,215	47,413	48,983	50,479	54,515
Forestry, fishing, and related activities..................................	25,020	25,900	27,664	29,592	29,970	31,012	33,104	35,507
Mining..	56,352	59,869	56,546	56,131	55,936	59,427	59,929	58,882
Utilities..	88,168	89,266	91,013	93,697	95,824	102,435	103,040	109,642
Construction	48,738	50,537	51,819	52,538	53,775	55,739	58,022	60,235
Manufacturing...	54,585	55,328	56,996	57,782	59,548	61,311	61,750	65,308
Durable goods manufacturing..	58,731	59,423	60,941	61,125	62,178	63,869	64,477	66,700
Nondurable goods manufacturing......................................	47,927	48,971	50,890	52,817	55,791	57,576	57,694	63,388
Wholesale trade	63,096	65,377	66,424	67,079	69,026	72,211	74,781	77,669
Retail trade..	25,643	26,073	27,013	27,461	27,880	28,512	29,284	31,615
Transportation and warehousing...	48,361	49,923	50,841	49,755	50,404	51,711	52,802	54,793
Information...	69,737	73,230	62,757	63,733	63,392	65,711	68,919	76,646
Finance and insurance	66,714	69,665	71,941	74,125	75,414	77,463	78,899	86,213
Real estate and rental and leasing.......................................	36,996	38,449	40,661	41,516	42,101	43,205	44,941	48,545
Professional, scientific, and technical services	63,647	65,809	68,735	69,406	70,123	71,579	73,515	78,093
Management of companies and enterprises...........................	93,022	94,652	105,172	99,034	103,795	107,480	114,219	137,799
Administrative and waste services..	37,320	36,741	36,928	37,215	38,426	40,820	42,195	44,663
Educational services	29,199	29,754	30,428	29,731	30,055	31,101	31,549	34,836
Health care and social assistance..	40,844	41,531	42,671	42,265	43,473	44,728	46,055	50,986
Arts, entertainment, and recreation......................................	20,977	20,862	21,623	21,620	21,948	23,202	24,044	25,877
Accommodation and food services.......................................	16,084	16,695	17,271	17,783	18,388	19,231	19,760	19,560
Other services, except public administration.........................	29,410	30,345	32,065	32,862	34,125	35,017	36,087	39,508
Government and government enterprises.................................	39,588	40,232	41,060	42,181	42,771	43,339	44,533	45,454

Table KS-10. Employment Characteristics by Family Type

(Number, percent.)

Family type and labor force status	2018		2019		2020 [1]	
	Total	Families with own children under 18 years	Total	Families with own children under 18 years	Total	Families with own children under 18 years
All Families..	726,748	323,524	733,489	317,647	737,611	324,122
FAMILY TYPE AND LABOR FORCE STATUS						
Opposite-Sex Married-Couple Families............................	570,740	231,960	571,620	223,616	572,332	228,772
Both husband and wife in labor force..	55.5	71.4	55.8	72.7	56.1	71.4
Husband in labor force, wife not in labor force	20.2	23.8	19.9	23.0	20.4	24.5
Wife in labor force, husband not in labor force	6.9	2.9	7.3	2.9	7.2	3.0
Both husband and wife not in labor force..................................	16.6	1.3	16.4	1.1	16.3	1.1
Other Families	156,008	91,564	161,869	94,031	161,461	94,512
Female householder, no spouse present.......................................	70.0	72.1	68.3	70.7	69.2	71.2
In labor force...	52.8	62.1	50.9	60.5	52.7	62.3
Not in labor force	17.2	10.0	17.4	10.2	16.5	8.9
Male householder, no spouse present..	30.0	27.9	31.7	29.3	30.8	28.8
In labor force...	23.9	25.1	25.6	27.5	25.5	26.9
Not in labor force	6.1	2.7	6.1	1.9	5.3	1.9

[1] 2020 ACS 5-Year estimates. 1-Year estimates were not released for 2020 due to the impact of COVID-19 on data collection that year. Data is not comparable to previous years, which are based on 1-year estimates.

Table KS-11. School Enrollment and Educational Attainment, 2020[1]

(Number, percent.)

Item	State	U.S.
Enrollment		
Total population 3 years and over, enrolled in school	758,270	80,497,960
Enrolled in nursery school or preschool (percent)...	6.8	6.1
Enrolled in kindergarten (percent)...	4.8	5.0
Enrolled in elementary school, grades 1-8 (percent)...	41.2	40.4
Enrolled in high school, grades 9-12 (percent)...	20.6	21.0
Enrolled in college or graduate school (percent)..	26.5	27.6
Attainment		
Total population 25 years and over	1,911,990	222,836,834
Less than ninth grade (percent)...	3.5	4.9
9th to 12th grade, no diploma (percent)...	5.2	6.6
High school graduate, including equivalency (percent)..	25.8	26.7
Some college, no degree (percent)...	22.8	20.3
Associate's degree (percent)...	8.8	8.6
Bachelor's degree (percent)...	21.5	20.2
Graduate or professional degree (percent)...	12.5	12.7
High school graduate or higher (percent)...	91.4	88.5
Bachelor's degree or higher (percent)..	33.9	32.9

[1] 2020 ACS 5-Year estimates. 1-Year estimates were not released for 2020 due to the impact of COVID-19 on data collection that year.

Table KS-12. Public School Characteristics and Educational Indicators

(Number, percent; data derived from National Center of Education Statistics.)

Item	State	U.S.
Public Elementary and Secondary Schools		
Number of regular school districts, 2018-19	286	13,452
Number of operational schools, 2019-20..	1,311	98,469
Percent charter schools	0.7	7.7
Total public school enrollment, Fall 2019..	497,963	50,796,445
Percent charter school enrollment	0.6	6.8
Student-teacher ratio, Fall 2019	13.6	15.9
Expenditures per student (unadjusted dollars), 2018-19	11,328	13,187
Four-year adjusted cohort graduation rate (ACGR), 2018-2019[1]...	87.2	85.8
Students eligible for free or reduced-price lunch (percent), 2019-20..	46.6	52.1
English language learners (percent), Fall 2019	9.0	10.4
Students age 3 to 21 served under IDEA, part B (percent), 2020-21	15.8	14.5

Public Schools by Type, 2019-20	Number	Percent of state public schools
Total number of schools..	1,311	100.0
Special education	4	0.3
Vocational education	0	-
Alternative education..	1	0.1

[1] Adjusted Cohort Graduation Rates (ACGR) differ from Averaged Freshmen Graduation Rates (AFGR).
- = Zero or rounds to zero.

Table KS-13. Reported Voting and Registration of the Voting-Age Population, November 2020

(Numbers in thousands, percent.)

Item	Total population	Total citizen population	Registered			Voted		
			Total registered	Percent registered (total population)	Percent registered (total citizen population)	Total voted	Percent voted (total population)	Percent voted (total citizen population)
U.S. Total	252,274	231,593	168,308	66.7	72.7	154,628	61.3	66.8
State Total	2,157	1,975	1,398	64.8	70.8	1,297	60.1	65.7
Sex								
Male	1,057	969	667	63.1	68.9	621	58.7	64.0
Female	1,101	1,006	731	66.4	72.7	676	61.4	67.2
Race								
White alone	1,867	1,749	1,263	67.7	72.2	1,181	63.3	67.5
White, non-Hispanic alone	1,566	1,556	1,171	74.8	75.3	1,099	70.2	70.7
Black alone	106	97	69	65.4	71.4	59	55.8	61.0
Asian alone	86	54	13	B	B	11	B	B
Hispanic (of any race)	317	210	108	34.1	51.5	96	30.1	45.5
White alone or in combination	1,916	1,798	1,298	67.7	72.2	1,216	63.5	67.6
Black alone or in combination	121	112	82	67.9	73.3	72	59.6	64.3
Asian alone or in combination	87	55	14	B	B	12	B	B
Age								
18 to 24 years	264	240	149	56.5	62.3	128	48.4	53.4
25 to 34 years	392	331	210	53.5	63.5	191	48.7	57.8
35 to 44 years	343	304	221	64.4	72.6	204	59.4	67.0
45 to 64 years	659	607	424	64.4	69.9	392	59.5	64.6
65 years and over	499	493	394	78.9	79.9	382	76.5	77.5

B = Base is less than 75,000 and therefore too small to show the derived measure.

Table KS-14. Crime

(Number, rate per 100,000. Data are derived from the FBI Uniform Crime Reports.)

Item	State			U.S.		
	2019	2020	Percent change	2019	2020	Percent change
TOTAL POPULATION[1]	2,912,635	2,913,805	-	328,329,953	329,484,123	0.4
VIOLENT CRIME						
Number	11,811	12,385	4.9	1,250,393	1,313,105	5.0
Rate	405.5	425.0	4.8	380.8	398.5	4.6
Murder and Nonnegligent Manslaughter						
Number	95	100	5.3	16,669	21,570	29.4
Rate	3.3	3.4	5.2	5.1	6.5	28.9
Rape[2]						
Number	1,500	1,263	-15.8	143,224	126,430	-11.7
Rate	51.5	43.3	-15.8	43.6	38.4	-12.0
Robbery						
Number	1,157	928	-19.8	268,483	243,600	-9.3
Rate	39.7	31.8	-19.8	81.8	73.9	-9.6
Aggravated Assault						
Number	9,059	10,094	11.4	822,017	921,505	12.1
Rate	311.0	346.4	11.4	250.4	279.7	11.7
PROPERTY CRIME						
Number	66,306	64,077	-3.4	6,995,235	6,452,038	-7.8
Rate	2,276.5	2,199.1	-3.4	2,130.6	1,958.2	-8.1
Burglary						
Number	9,996	9,655	-3.4	1,118,096	1,035,314	-7.4
Rate	343.2	331.4	-3.5	340.5	314.2	-7.7
Larceny-Theft						
Number	49,420	47,193	-4.5	5,152,267	4,606,324	-10.6
Rate	1,696.7	1,619.6	-4.5	1,569.2	1,398.0	-10.9
Motor Vehicle Theft						
Number	6,890	7,229	4.9	724,872	810,400	11.8
Rate	236.6	248.1	4.9	220.8	246.0	11.4

NOTE: Although arson data are included in the trend and clearance tables, sufficient data are not available to estimate totals for this offense. Therefore, no arson data are published in this table.
- = Zero or rounds to zero.
[1] Population figures are U.S. Census Bureau provisional estimates as of July 1, 2020.
[2] The figures shown in the rape (revised definition) column were estimated using the revised Uniform Crime Reporting (UCR) definition of rape.

Table KS-15. State Government Finances, 2020

(Dollar amounts in thousands, percent distribution.)

Item	Dollars	Percent distribution
Total Revenue	23,717,200	100.0
General revenue	21,544,596	90.8
Intergovernmental revenue	6,025,448	25.4
Taxes	9,659,846	40.7
General sales	3414591	14.4
Selective sales	1,183,598	5.0
License taxes	432,005	1.8
Individual income tax	3380030	14.3
Corporate income tax	433,931	1.8
Other taxes	815,691	3.4
Current charges	4,531,444	19.1
Miscellaneous general revenue	1,327,858	5.6
Utility revenue	0	-
Liquor stores revenue	0	-
Insurance trust revenue[1]	2,172,604	9.2
Total Expenditure	22,681,589	100.0
Intergovernmental expenditure	5,992,889	26.4
Direct expenditure	16,688,700	73.6
Current operation	12,925,595	57.0
Capital outlay	909,228	4.0
Insurance benefits and repayments	2,412,603	10.6
Assistance and subsidies	249,936	1.1
Interest on debt	191,338	0.8
Exhibit: Salaries and wages	3,303,478	14.6
Total Expenditure	22,681,589	100.0
General expenditure	20,268,986	89.4
Intergovernmental expenditure	5,992,889	26.4
Direct expenditure	14,276,097	62.9
General expenditure, by function:		
Education	8,454,006	37.3
Public welfare	5,132,430	22.6
Hospitals	2,963,749	13.1
Health	443,442	2.0
Highways	1,102,026	4.9
Police protection	121,802	0.5
Correction	397,306	1.8
Natural resources	236,132	1.0
Parks and recreation	44,743	0.2
Governmental administration	568,551	2.5
Interest on general debt	191,338	0.8
Other and unallocable	597,624	2.6
Utility expenditure	0	-
Liquor stores expenditure	0	-
Insurance trust expenditure	2,412,603	10.6
Debt at End of Fiscal Year	6,928,288	X
Cash and Security Holdings	27,961,546	X

X = Not applicable.
- = Zero or rounds to zero.
[1] Within insurance trust revenue, net earnings of state retirement systems is a calculated statistic (the item code in the data file is X08), and thus can be positive or negative. Net earnings is the sum of earnings on investments plus gains on investments minus losses on investments. The change made in 2002 for asset valuation from book to market value in accordance with Statement 34 of the Governmental Accounting Standards Board is reflected in the calculated statistics.

Table KS-16. State Government Tax Collections, 2021

(Dollars in thousands, percent.)

Item	Dollars	Percent distribution
Total Taxes	11,615,757	100.0
Property taxes	815,701	7.0
Sales and gross receipts	4,970,129	42.8
General sales and gross receipts	3,767,434	32.4
Selective sales and gross receipts	1,202,695	10.4
Alcoholic beverages	148,735	1.3
Amusements	256	-
Insurance premiums	450,742	3.9
Motor fuels	445,472	3.8
Pari-mutuels	X	-
Public utilities	312	-
Tobacco products	123,410	1.1
Other selective sales	33,768	0.3
Licenses	457,796	3.9
Alcoholic beverages	3,089	-
Amusements	9,213	0.1
Corporations in general	32,099	0.3
Hunting and fishing	31,951	0.3
Motor vehicle	243,334	2.1
Motor vehicle operators	28,775	0.2
Public utilities	5,313	-
Occupation and business, NEC	100,883	0.9
Other licenses	3,139	-
Income taxes	5,344,578	46.0
Individual income	4,617,143	39.7
Corporation net income	727,435	6.3
Other taxes	27,553	0.2
Death and gift	0	-
Documentary and stock transfer	0	-
Severance	27,553	0.2
Taxes, NEC	0	-

- = Zero or rounds to zero.

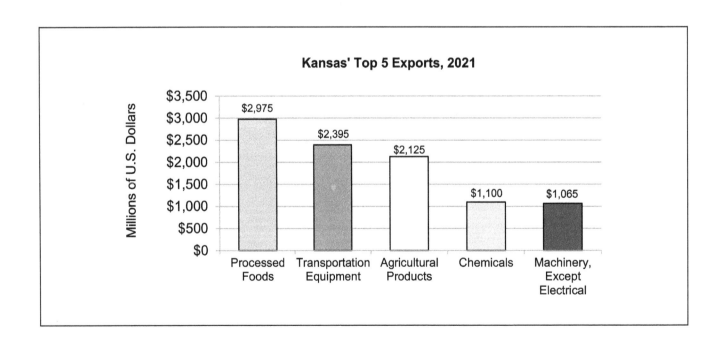

Kansas' Top 5 Exports, 2021

Facts and Figures

Location: East central United States; bordered on the N by Illinois, Indiana, and Ohio, on the E by West Virginia and Virginia, on the S by Tennessee, and on the W by Missouri and Illinois

Area: 40,409 sq. mi. (104,659 sq. km.); rank—37th

Population: 4,509,394 (2021 est.); rank—26th

Principal Cities: capital—Frankfort; largest—Lexington

Statehood: June 1, 1792; 15th state

U.S. Congress: 2 senators, 6 representatives

State Motto: United We Stand, Divided We Fall

State Song: "My Old Kentucky Home"

State Nickname: The Bluegrass State

Abbreviations: KY; Ky.

State Symbols: flower—goldenrod; tree—tulip poplar; bird—cardinal

At a Glance

- With an increase in population of 3.9 percent, Kentucky ranked 33rd among the states in growth from 2010 to 2021.

- Kentucky ranked 7th in the nation for drug overdose deaths in 2020, with 42.7 deaths per 100,000 population.

- In 2020, Kentucky's median household income was $52,238, the 7th lowest in the country. The state's poverty level was 16.6 percent, the 5th highest in the country.

- The property crime rate in Kentucky in 2020 was 1,779.5 per 100,000 population, compared to the U.S. rate of 1,958.2 per 100,000 population.

- In 2020, 5.6 percent of Kentucky residents did not have health insurance, compared to 8.7 percent of all U.S. residents.

Table KY-1. Population by Age, Sex, Race, and Hispanic Origin

(Number, percent, except where noted.)

Sex, age, race, and Hispanic origin	2000	2010	2021	Percent change, 2010–2021
Total Population..	4,041,769	4,339,367	4,509,394	3.9
Percent of total U.S. population	1.4	1.4	1.4	X
Sex				
Male..	1,975,368	2,134,952	2,233,889	4.6
Female..	2,066,401	2,204,425	2,275,505	3.2
Age				
Under 5 years...	265,901	282,367	265,121	-6.1
5 to 19 years..	847,743	863,837	866,353	0.3
20 to 64 years..	2,423,332	2,614,936	2,607,660	-0.3
65 years and over	504,793	578,227	770,260	33.2
Median age (years)...	35.9	38.1	39.2	2.9
Race and Hispanic Origin				
One race				
White	3,640,889	3,864,193	3,926,400	1.6
Black..	295,994	342,804	389,241	13.5
American Indian and Alaska Native	8,610	12,105	14,029	15.9
Asian..	29,744	50,177	76,900	53.3
Native Hawaiian or Other Pacific Islander	1,460	3,199	4,819	50.6
Two or more races	42,443	66,889	98,005	46.5
Hispanic (of any race)...	59,939	138,618	187,984	35.6

NOTE: Population figures for 2021 are July 1 estimates. The 2000 and 2010 estimates are taken from the respective censuses.
- = Zero or rounds to zero.
X = Not applicable.

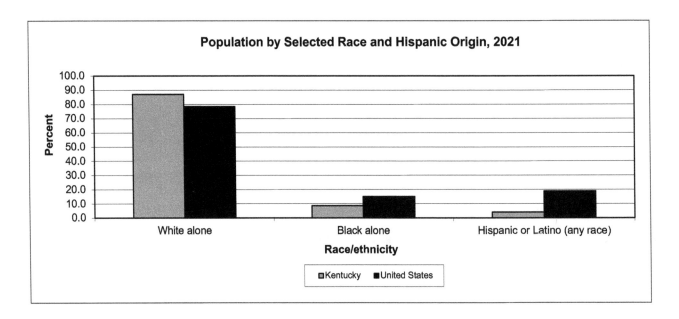

Population by Selected Race and Hispanic Origin, 2021

Legend: ▢ Kentucky ■ United States

Table KY-2. Marital Status

(Number, percent distribution.)

Sex, age, race, and Hispanic origin	2000	2010	2020 [1]
Males, 15 Years and Over	1,551,174	1,702,020	1,768,458
Never married	25.9	30.8	32.3
Now married, except separated..	59.9	52.0	50.9
Separated..	1.5	2.1	1.7
Widowed..	2.6	2.8	3.2
Divorced..	10.2	12.3	11.9
Females, 15 Years and Over	1,665,993	1,794,164	1,857,337
Never married	19.7	24.2	25.8
Now married, except separated..	55.0	48.9	47.9
Separated..	2.1	2.6	2.2
Widowed..	11.5	10.6	10.0
Divorced..	11.8	13.7	14.1

[1] 2020 ACS 5-Year estimates. 1-Year estimates were not released for 2020 due to the impact of COVID-19 on data collection that year.

Table KY-3. Households and Housing Characteristics

(Number, percent, dollars.)

Item	2000	2010	2020 [1]	Average annual percent change, 2010–2020
Total Households...	1,590,647	1,684,348	1,748,053	0.5
Family households	1,104,398	1,126,685	1,139,116	0.2
Married-couple family................................	857,944	833,872	839,220	0.1
Other family	246,454	292,813	299,896	0.3
Male householder, no wife present................	58,497	76,832	86,535	1.8
Female householder, no husband present.......	187,957	215,981	213,361	-0.2
Nonfamily households	486,249	557,663	608,937	1.3
Householder living alone..............................	414,095	470,103	502,100	1.0
Householder not living alone........................	72,154	87,560	106,837	3.1
Housing Characteristics				
Total housing units..	1,750,927	1,928,617	1,994,554	0.5
Occupied housing units	1,590,647	1,684,348	1,748,053	0.5
Owner occupied	1,125,397	1,156,292	1,181,021	0.3
Renter occupied	465,250	528,056	567,032	1.1
Average household size....................................	2.47	2.51	2.48	-0.2
Financial Characteristics				
Median gross rent of renter-occupied housing	445	613	783	4.0
Median monthly owner costs for housing units with a mortgage	816	1,072	1,191	1.6
Median value of owner-occupied housing units.......................	86,700	121,600	147,100	3.0

[1] 2020 ACS 5-Year estimates. 1-Year estimates were not released for 2020 due to the impact of COVID-19 on data collection that year.

Table KY-4. Migration, Origin, and Language

(Number, percent.)

Characteristic	State 2016-2020 [1]	U.S. 2016-2020 [1]
Residence 1 Year Ago		
Population 1 year and over	4,411,553	322,943,283
Same house	85.5	86.2
Different house in the U.S.	14.2	13.2
Same county	8.1	7.7
Different county	6.1	5.5
Same state	3.7	3.2
Different state	2.4	2.3
Abroad	0.3	0.6
Place of Birth		
Native born	4,285,629	282,443,680
Male	49.1	49.4
Female	50.9	50.6
Foreign born	176,323	44,125,628
Male	52.1	48.6
Female	47.9	51.4
Foreign born; naturalized U.S. citizen..	71,451	22,456,684
Male	49.3	46.1
Female	50.7	53.9
Foreign born; not a U.S. citizen...	104,872	21,668,944
Male	54.0	51.1
Female	46.0	48.9
Entered 2010 or later	38.2	22.8
Entered 2000 to 2009	32.1	25.1
Entered before 2000...	29.7	52.1
World Region of Birth, Foreign		
Foreign-born population, excluding population born at sea	176,323	44,125,628
Europe	12.9	10.8
Asia..	35.0	31.3
Africa	12.1	5.4
Oceania	0.8	0.6
Latin America...	36.8	50.0
North America..	2.5	1.9
Language Spoken at Home and Ability to Speak English		
Population 5 years and over...	4,188,377	306,919,116
English only	94.3	78.5
Language other than English..	5.7	21.5
Speaks English less than "very well"...	2.3	8.2

[1] 2020 ACS 5-Year estimates. 1-Year estimates were not released for 2020 due to the impact of COVID-19 on data collection that year.
NA = Not available.
X = Not applicable.
- = Zero or rounds to zero.

Table KY-5. Median Income and Poverty Status, 2020[1]

(Number, percent, except as noted.)

Characteristic	State		U.S.	
	Number	Percent	Number	Percent
Median Income				
Households (dollars)..	52,238	X	64,994	X
Families (dollars)	65,893	X	80,069	X
Below Poverty Level (All People)	717,895	16.6	40,910,326	12.8
Sex				
Male	316,903	15.0	18,171,512	11.6
Female	400,992	18.2	22,738,814	14.0
Age				
Under 18 years..	218,023	22.2	12,598,699	17.5
Related children under 18 years..	212,304	21.7	12,306,532	17.2
18 to 64 years...	421,831	16.0	23,554,920	12.1
65 years and over	78,041	11.0	4,756,707	9.3

X = Not applicable.
[1] 2020 ACS 5-Year estimates. 1-Year estimates were not released for 2020 due to the impact of COVID-19 on data collection that year.

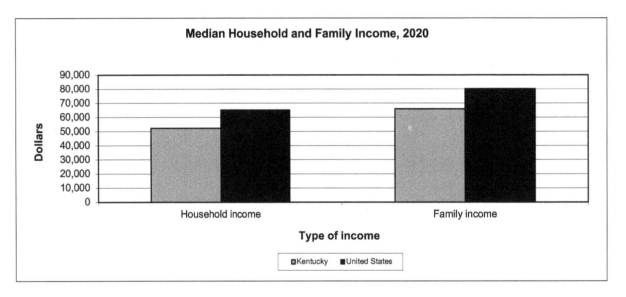

Median Household and Family Income, 2020

Table KY-6. Health Insurance Coverage Status for the Civilian Noninstitutionalized Population and Children Under 19 Years of Age

(Number, percent.)

Item	2011	2012	2013	2014	2015	2016	2017	2018	2019	2020 [2]
Civilian Noninstitutionalized Population	4,284,357	4,292,718	4,312,100	4,328,524	4,342,711	4,354,380	4,370,940	4,388,204	4,384,896	4,379,339
Covered by Private or Public Insurance										
Number..	3,665,899	3,697,258	3,695,652	3,962,462	4,081,243	4,131,030	4,135,713	4,140,563	4,102,333	4,133,261
Percent...	85.6	86.1	85.7	91.5	94.0	94.9	94.6	94.4	93.6	94.4
Uninsured										
Number..	618,458	595,460	616,448	366,062	261,468	223,350	235,227	247,641	282,563	246,078
Percent...	14.4	13.9	14.3	8.5	6.0	5.1	5.4	5.6	6.4	5.6
Percent in the U.S. not covered.................................	15.1	14.8	14.5	11.7	9.4	8.6	8.7	8.9	9.2	8.7
Children Under 19 Years of Age[1]	1,022,948	1,016,026	1,012,120	1,012,771	1,008,187	1,009,986	1,078,842	1,066,094	1,058,586	1,065,464
Covered by Private or Public Insurance										
Number..	960,504	959,668	952,590	969,473	965,380	977,991	1,037,936	1,026,070	1,013,495	1,024,009
Percent...	93.9	94.5	94.1	95.7	95.8	96.8	96.2	96.2	95.7	96.1
Uninsured										
Number..	62,444	56,358	59,530	43,298	42,807	31,995	40,906	40,024	45,091	41,455
Percent...	6.1	5.5	5.9	4.3	4.2	3.2	3.8	3.8	4.3	3.9
Percent in the U.S. not covered.................................	7.5	7.2	7.1	6.0	4.8	4.5	5.0	5.2	5.7	5.2

[1] Data for years prior to 2017 are for individuals under 18 years of age.
[2] 2020 ACS 5-Year estimates. 1-Year estimates were not released for 2020 due to the impact of COVID-19 on data collection that year. Data is not comparable to previous years, which are based on 1-year estimates.

Table KY-7. Employment Status by Demographic Group, 2021

(Numbers in thousands, percent.)

Characteristic	Civilian noninstitutional population	Civilian labor force		Employed		Unemployed	
		Number	Percent of population	Number	Percent of population	Number	Percent of population
Total..	3,518	2,016	57.3	1,921	54.6	95	4.7
Sex							
Male..	1,699	1,076	63.4	1,025	60.3	51	4.7
Female.......................................	1,819	940	51.7	896	49.3	43	4.6
Race, Sex, and Hispanic Origin							
White...	3,106	1,774	57.1	1,695	54.6	79	4.5
Male..	1,511	951	63.0	907	60.1	44	4.6
Female.....................................	1,596	823	51.6	787	49.3	36	4.3
Black or African American..................	270	155	57.3	145	53.8	9	6.0
Male..	NA	NA	NA	NA	NA	NA	NA
Female.....................................	NA	NA	NA	NA	NA	NA	NA
Hispanic or Latino ethnicity[1]	170	120	70	115	68	4	4
Male..	NA	NA	NA	NA	NA	NA	NA
Female.....................................	NA	NA	NA	NA	NA	NA	NA
Age							
16 to 19 years..............................	NA	NA	NA	NA	NA	NA	NA
20 to 24 years..............................	277	198	71.4	177	63.9	21	10.6
25 to 34 years..............................	572	440	76.8	417	72.9	23	5.1
35 to 44 years..............................	535	437	81.8	423	79.0	15	3.4
45 to 54 years..............................	513	394	76.8	380	74.0	14	3.5
55 to 64 years..............................	619	333	53.9	322	52.0	11	3.4
65 years and over	764	123	16.1	119	15.5	4	3.2

NOTE: Data in Table 7 are from the Current Population Survey (CPS) and do not match the estimates in Table 8. See notes and definitions for further information.
[1] May be of any race.
NA = Not available.

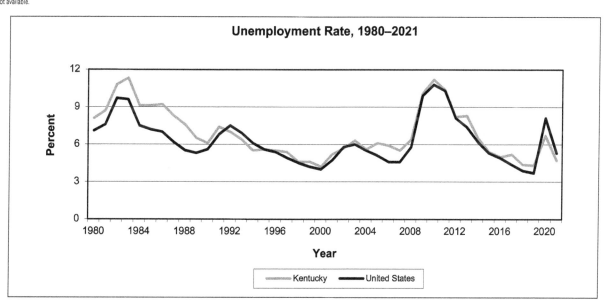

Unemployment Rate, 1980–2021

Table KY-8. Employment Status of the Civilian Noninstitutional Population Age 16 Years and Over

(Number, percent.)

Year	Civilian labor force	Civilian participation rate	Employed	Unemployed	Unemployment rate
2010..	2,065,023	61.6	1,852,302	212,721	10.3
2011..	2,061,500	61.1	1,868,168	193,332	9.4
2012..	2,060,084	60.8	1,891,109	168,975	8.2
2013..	2,055,895	60.3	1,892,777	163,118	7.9
2014..	2,006,518	58.5	1,877,551	128,967	6.4
2015..	1,979,641	57.5	1,876,009	103,632	5.2
2016..	2,015,645	58.3	1,914,479	101,166	5.0
2017..	2,053,398	58.8	1,955,234	98,164	4.8
2018..	2,054,913	58.7	1,968,398	86,515	4.2
2019..	2,070,409	58.9	1,986,171	84,238	4.1
2020..	2,016,802	57.2	1,886,999	129,803	6.4
2021..	2,036,942	57.6	1,941,737	95,205	4.7

Table KY-9. Employment and Average Wages by Industry

(Estimates are based on the 2012 North American Industry Classification System [NAICS].)

Industry	2013	2014	2015	2016	2017	2018	2019	2020
	Number of Jobs							
Wage and Salary Employment by Industry..........................	1,923,075	1,948,724	1,978,345	1,996,627	2,011,592	2,024,711	2,039,331	1,934,420
Farm Wage and Salary Employment.................................	13,643	14,615	16,632	13,699	15,865	15,398	15,100	15,098
Nonfarm Wage and Salary Employment..........................	1,909,432	1,934,109	1,961,713	1,982,928	1,995,727	2,009,313	2,024,231	1,919,322
Private wage and salary employment..........................	1,542,028	1,571,828	1,604,398	1,629,710	1,642,284	1,655,129	1,670,245	1,576,247
Forestry, fishing, and related activities......................	7,399	7,494	7,642	7,676	7,522	7,659	7,952	7,779
Mining..	17,194	16,239	13,697	10,269	9,970	10,036	9,794	7,213
Utilities..	6,512	6,624	6,569	6,630	6,689	6,782	6,764	6,730
Construction...	69,877	74,634	77,693	78,754	79,214	79,817	82,385	79,719
Manufacturing...	229,642	235,105	241,530	247,875	250,363	251,511	252,812	236,054
Durable goods manufacturing...........................	143,824	149,467	155,815	161,255	162,396	163,632	164,081	150,667
Nondurable goods manufacturing.....................	85,818	85,638	85,715	86,620	87,967	87,879	88,731	85,387
Wholesale trade	74,302	74,692	74,963	76,045	76,620	75,193	76,175	72,837
Retail trade..	204,656	206,292	211,056	215,557	216,755	215,650	211,666	203,439
Transportation and warehousing..........................	86,629	91,110	96,076	100,709	103,806	108,015	112,499	115,553
Information	26,325	26,348	25,234	22,753	22,723	21,980	21,676	20,178
Finance and insurance	73,708	74,966	76,865	77,606	78,109	77,644	77,985	77,932
Real estate and rental and leasing......................	18,609	18,477	18,904	19,521	19,817	20,091	21,123	20,042
Professional, scientific, and technical services	69,913	72,136	73,925	75,209	74,403	76,922	77,634	77,441
Management of companies and enterprises............	20,570	20,674	19,975	20,917	20,127	20,135	20,011	20,150
Administrative and waste services	111,610	119,005	122,984	122,011	120,656	121,679	119,797	111,750
Educational services	32,093	32,688	32,355	31,982	32,246	30,799	31,320	28,247
Health care and social assistance.......................	233,506	231,575	236,804	242,165	246,350	251,536	256,361	248,840
Arts, entertainment, and recreation.....................	20,232	20,657	21,259	22,144	23,239	23,596	24,399	18,801
Accommodation and food services......................	160,199	162,843	167,682	172,860	175,063	175,632	178,719	148,416
Other services, except public administration..........	78,972	80,269	79,185	79,027	78,612	80,552	81,173	75,126
Government and government enterprises...................	367,404	362,281	357,315	353,218	353,443	354,184	353,986	343,075
	Dollars							
Average Wages and Salaries by Industry	40,706	41,801	43,129	43,894	44,855	46,049	47,371	50,235
Average Farm Wages and Salaries	23,254	22,251	16,509	23,002	18,025	19,390	15,202	15,152
Average Nonfarm Wages and Salaries	40,830	41,948	43,355	44,038	45,068	46,253	47,611	50,511
Average private wages and salaries...........................	40,487	41,710	43,154	43,888	44,971	46,226	47,718	50,786
Forestry, fishing, and related activities......................	27,654	28,264	29,557	31,139	32,106	33,059	35,072	37,909
Mining..	68,374	68,621	68,432	66,123	70,065	71,299	71,493	69,301
Utilities..	76,422	79,771	82,316	82,806	84,902	88,371	90,299	93,857
Construction...	47,383	49,895	51,655	51,748	53,167	53,964	55,599	58,544
Manufacturing...	53,287	55,076	56,727	57,098	58,153	59,256	61,176	62,863
Durable goods manufacturing...........................	54,819	56,307	58,260	58,546	59,528	59,859	62,354	62,956
Nondurable goods manufacturing.....................	50,720	52,927	53,940	54,404	55,615	58,134	58,997	62,700
Wholesale trade	55,076	57,413	60,114	60,932	62,489	64,977	66,938	69,944
Retail trade..	24,817	25,140	26,006	26,702	27,199	27,829	28,890	31,284
Transportation and warehousing..........................	49,502	50,633	52,110	51,977	53,637	55,120	56,149	58,175
Information	46,387	48,989	48,963	52,807	54,778	54,652	58,579	63,164
Finance and insurance	60,937	63,905	66,598	68,434	71,541	74,641	76,775	82,204
Real estate and rental and leasing......................	35,431	37,190	38,383	39,440	40,079	41,684	44,619	47,628
Professional, scientific, and technical services	56,276	57,921	60,464	61,523	62,967	64,403	66,765	70,564
Management of companies and enterprises............	91,138	91,845	97,259	100,861	102,759	103,048	109,604	108,043
Administrative and waste services	26,771	27,252	28,340	29,978	31,059	32,286	33,743	36,439
Educational services	25,076	24,816	25,708	25,813	26,209	28,719	29,119	32,656
Health care and social assistance.......................	43,444	44,570	46,584	47,347	48,077	49,073	49,991	52,862
Arts, entertainment, and recreation.....................	22,471	23,848	23,492	23,118	23,447	24,686	25,505	30,561
Accommodation and food services......................	16,181	16,848	17,412	17,968	18,617	19,519	20,095	19,694
Other services, except public administration..........	30,094	30,997	32,279	33,146	34,407	35,546	36,634	40,116
Government and government enterprises...................	42,271	42,985	44,256	44,728	45,520	46,377	47,109	49,248

Table KY-10. Employment Characteristics by Family Type

(Number, percent.)

Family type and labor force status	2018 Total	2018 Families with own children under 18 years	2019 Total	2019 Families with own children under 18 years	2020[1] Total	2020[1] Families with own children under 18 years
All Families..	1,138,927	465,327	1,129,276	458,870	1,139,116	467,621
FAMILY TYPE AND LABOR FORCE STATUS						
Married-Couple Families...	837,979	310,489	830,268	300,337	832,608	309,219
Both husband and wife in labor force....................................	48.0	68.4	47.6	68.1	49.0	68.6
Husband in labor force, wife not in labor force	19.6	23.3	19.8	23.4	19.8	23.4
Wife in labor force, husband not in labor force	9.2	4.5	9.7	5.1	9.2	4.9
Both husband and wife not in labor force................................	22.3	3.1	22.2	3.2	22.1	3.1
Other Families	300,948	154,838	299,008	158,533	299,896	156,848
Female householder, no spouse present	72.2	73.9	69.7	69.6	71.1	72.1
In labor force...	44.2	56.9	43.2	54.7	45.4	57.4
Not in labor force	28.0	17.0	26.6	14.9	25.8	14.7
Male householder, no spouse present....................................	27.8	26.1	30.3	30.4	28.9	27.9
In labor force...	20.7	23.3	21.7	26.2	20.8	24.3
Not in labor force	7.1	2.8	8.5	4.2	8.0	3.6

[1] 2020 ACS 5-Year estimates. 1-Year estimates were not released for 2020 due to the impact of COVID-19 on data collection that year. Data is not comparable to previous years, which are based on 1-year estimates.

Table KY-11. School Enrollment and Educational Attainment, 2020[1]

(Number, percent.)

Item	State	U.S.
Enrollment		
Total population 3 years and over, enrolled in school	1,043,315	80,497,960
Enrolled in nursery school or preschool (percent)...	6.1	6.1
Enrolled in kindergarten (percent)...	4.8	5.0
Enrolled in elementary school, grades 1-8 (percent)..	42.8	40.4
Enrolled in high school, grades 9-12 (percent)..	21.2	21.0
Enrolled in college or graduate school (percent)..	25.1	27.6
Attainment		
Total population 25 years and over	3,034,491	222,836,834
Less than ninth grade (percent)..	5	4.9
9th to 12th grade, no diploma (percent)	7.8	6.6
High school graduate, including equivalency (percent)..	32.6	26.7
Some college, no degree (percent)..	20.9	20.3
Associate's degree (percent)...	8.6	8.6
Bachelor's degree (percent)	14.8	20.2
Graduate or professional degree (percent)...	10.3	12.7
High school graduate or higher (percent)	87.2	88.5
Bachelor's degree or higher (percent)..	25	32.9

[1] 2020 ACS 5-Year estimates. 1-Year estimates were not released for 2020 due to the impact of COVID-19 on data collection that year.

Table KY-12. Public School Characteristics and Educational Indicators

(Number, percent; data derived from National Center of Education Statistics.)

Item	State	U.S.
Public Elementary and Secondary Schools		
Number of regular school districts, 2018-19	173	13,452
Number of operational schools, 2019-20..	1,535	98,469
Percent charter schools	0.0	7.7
Total public school enrollment, Fall 2019...	691,996	50,796,445
Percent charter school enrollment	0.0	6.8
Student-teacher ratio, Fall 2019	16.4	15.9
Expenditures per student (unadjusted dollars), 2018-19	11,280	13,187
Four-year adjusted cohort graduation rate (ACGR), 2018-2019[1]..	90.6	85.8
Students eligible for free or reduced-price lunch (percent), 2019-20..	55.7	52.1
English language learners (percent), Fall 2019	4.3	10.4
Students age 3 to 21 served under IDEA, part B (percent), 2020-21	16.1	14.5

Public Schools by Type, 2019-20	Number	Percent of state public schools
Total number of schools..	1,535	100.0
Special education...	10	0.7
Vocational education..	126	8.2
Alternative education...	188	12.2

[1] Adjusted Cohort Graduation Rates (ACGR) differ from Averaged Freshmen Graduation Rates (AFGR).
- = Zero or rounds to zero.

Table KY-13. Reported Voting and Registration of the Voting-Age Population, November 2020

(Numbers in thousands, percent.)

Item	Total population	Total citizen population	Registered			Voted		
			Total registered	Percent registered (total population)	Percent registered (total citizen population)	Total voted	Percent voted (total population)	Percent voted (total citizen population)
U.S. Total	252,274	231,593	168,308	66.7	72.7	154,628	61.3	66.8
State Total	3,384	3,227	2,450	72.4	75.9	2,210	65.3	68.5
Sex								
Male	1,616	1,524	1,159	71.7	76.0	1,057	65.4	69.4
Female	1,768	1,703	1,291	73.0	75.8	1,153	65.2	67.7
Race								
White alone	2,994	2,888	2,194	73.3	76.0	1,997	66.7	69.1
White, non-Hispanic alone	2,845	2,831	2,165	76.1	76.5	1,971	69.3	69.6
Black alone	259	224	167	64.5	74.6	140	54.0	62.5
Asian alone	46	31	24	B	B	24	B	B
Hispanic (of any race)	163	60	30	B	B	26	B	B
White alone or in combination	3,063	2,957	2,243	73.2	75.8	2,035	66.4	68.8
Black alone or in combination	306	271	198	64.7	73.0	161	52.5	59.3
Asian alone or in combination	49	35	24	B	B	24	B	B
Age								
18 to 24 years	281	265	172	61.3	65.2	157	55.8	59.3
25 to 34 years	570	498	330	57.8	66.2	271	47.4	54.3
35 to 44 years	640	606	479	74.8	79.0	439	68.6	72.5
45 to 64 years	1,141	1,111	874	76.6	78.7	787	68.9	70.8
65 years and over	751	748	595	79.2	79.5	557	74.1	74.4

B = Base is less than 75,000 and therefore too small to show the derived measure.

Table KY-14. Crime

(Number, rate per 100,000. Data are derived from the FBI Uniform Crime Reports.)

Item	State			U.S.		
	2019	2020	Percent change	2019	2020	Percent change
TOTAL POPULATION[1]	4,472,345	4,477,251	0.1	328,329,953	329,484,123	0.4
VIOLENT CRIME						
Number	9,872	11,600	17.5	1,250,393	1,313,105	5.0
Rate	220.7	259.1	17.4	380.8	398.5	4.6
Murder and Nonnegligent Manslaughter						
Number	229	323	41.0	16,669	21,570	29.4
Rate	5.1	7.2	40.9	5.1	6.5	28.9
Rape[2]						
Number	1,673	1,371	-18.1	143,224	126,430	-11.7
Rate	37.4	30.6	-18.1	43.6	38.4	-12.0
Robbery						
Number	2,162	2,369	9.6	268,483	243,600	-9.3
Rate	48.3	52.9	9.5	81.8	73.9	-9.6
Aggravated Assault						
Number	5,808	7,537	29.8	822,017	921,505	12.1
Rate	129.9	168.3	29.6	250.4	279.7	11.7
PROPERTY CRIME						
Number	85,387	79,673	-6.7	6,995,235	6,452,038	-7.8
Rate	1,909.2	1,779.5	-6.8	2,130.6	1,958.2	-8.1
Burglary						
Number	15,567	15,407	-1.0	1,118,096	1,035,314	-7.4
Rate	348.1	344.1	-1.1	340.5	314.2	-7.7
Larceny-Theft						
Number	59,535	52,769	-11.4	5,152,267	4,606,324	-10.6
Rate	1,331.2	1,178.6	-11.5	1,569.2	1,398.0	-10.9
Motor Vehicle Theft						
Number	10,285	11,497	11.8	724,872	810,400	11.8
Rate	230.0	256.8	11.7	220.8	246.0	11.4

NOTE: Although arson data are included in the trend and clearance tables, sufficient data are not available to estimate totals for this offense. Therefore, no arson data are published in this table.
- = Zero or rounds to zero.
[1] Population figures are U.S. Census Bureau provisional estimates as of July 1, 2020.
[2] The figures shown in the rape (revised definition) column were estimated using the revised Uniform Crime Reporting (UCR) definition of rape.

Table KY-15. State Government Finances, 2020

(Dollar amounts in thousands, percent distribution.)

Item	Dollars	Percent distribution
Total Revenue	40,266,198	100.0
General revenue	34,688,206	86.1
Intergovernmental revenue	15,452,881	38.4
Taxes	13,370,578	33.2
General sales	4191324	10.4
Selective sales	2,347,873	5.8
License taxes	545,074	1.4
Individual income tax	4831399	12.0
Corporate income tax	639,200	1.6
Other taxes	815,708	2.0
Current charges	4,498,586	11.2
Miscellaneous general revenue	1,366,161	3.4
Utility revenue	0	-
Liquor stores revenue	0	-
Insurance trust revenue[1]	5,577,992	13.9
Total Expenditure	38,446,209	100.0
Intergovernmental expenditure	4,910,271	12.8
Direct expenditure	33,535,938	87.2
Current operation	23,680,254	61.6
Capital outlay	2,007,179	5.2
Insurance benefits and repayments	5,958,347	15.5
Assistance and subsidies	1,291,211	3.4
Interest on debt	598,947	1.6
Exhibit: Salaries and wages	4,459,202	11.6
Total Expenditure	38,446,209	100.0
General expenditure	32,453,716	84.4
Intergovernmental expenditure	4,910,271	12.8
Direct expenditure	27,543,445	71.6
General expenditure, by function:		
Education	9,961,316	25.9
Public welfare	13,355,991	34.7
Hospitals	2,274,374	5.9
Health	468,778	1.2
Highways	1,999,646	5.2
Police protection	225,929	0.6
Correction	640,239	1.7
Natural resources	411,959	1.1
Parks and recreation	107,085	0.3
Governmental administration	1,108,497	2.9
Interest on general debt	598,947	1.6
Other and unallocable	1,194,887	3.1
Utility expenditure	72,828	0.2
Liquor stores expenditure	0	-
Insurance trust expenditure	5,958,347	15.5
Debt at End of Fiscal Year	14,634,789	X
Cash and Security Holdings	51,596,302	X

X = Not applicable.
- = Zero or rounds to zero.
[1] Within insurance trust revenue, net earnings of state retirement systems is a calculated statistic (the item code in the data file is X08), and thus can be positive or negative. Net earnings is the sum of earnings on investments plus gains on investments minus losses on investments. The change made in 2002 for asset valuation from book to market value in accordance with Statement 34 of the Governmental Accounting Standards Board is reflected in the calculated statistics.

Table KY-16. State Government Tax Collections, 2021

(Dollars in thousands, percent.)

Item	Dollars	Percent distribution
Total Taxes	14,617,202	100.0
Property taxes	707,461	4.8
Sales and gross receipts	7,088,138	48.5
General sales and gross receipts	4,558,439	31.2
Selective sales and gross receipts	2,529,699	17.3
Alcoholic beverages	174,267	1.2
Amusements	22	-
Insurance premiums	187,041	1.3
Motor fuels	699,875	4.8
Pari-mutuels	31,596	0.2
Public utilities	81,185	0.6
Tobacco products	420,634	2.9
Other selective sales	935,079	6.4
Licenses	533,047	3.6
Alcoholic beverages	225	-
Amusements	243	-
Corporations in general	116,242	0.8
Hunting and fishing	31,326	0.2
Motor vehicle	223,193	1.5
Motor vehicle operators	23,037	0.2
Public utilities	X	-
Occupation and business, NEC	136,386	0.9
Other licenses	2,395	-
Income taxes	6,138,893	42.0
Individual income	5,212,818	35.7
Corporation net income	926,075	6.3
Other taxes	149,663	1.0
Death and gift	61,625	0.4
Documentary and stock transfer	3,592	-
Severance	84,446	0.6
Taxes, NEC	0	-

- = Zero or rounds to zero.
X = Not applicable.

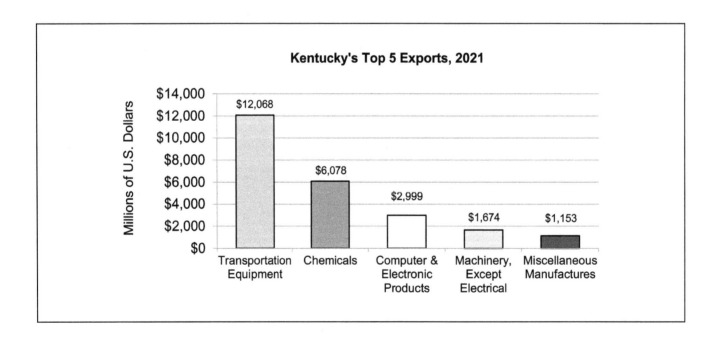

Kentucky's Top 5 Exports, 2021

Category	Millions of U.S. Dollars
Transportation Equipment	$12,068
Chemicals	$6,078
Computer & Electronic Products	$2,999
Machinery, Except Electrical	$1,674
Miscellaneous Manufactures	$1,153

LOUISIANA

Facts and Figures

Location: South central United States; bordered on the N by Arkansas, on the E by Mississippi, on the S by the Gulf of Mexico, and on the W by Texas

Area: 51,840 sq. mi. (134,264 sq. km.); rank—31st

Population: 4,624,047 (2021 est.); rank—25th

Principal Cities: capital—Baton Rouge; largest—New Orleans

Statehood: April 30, 1812; 18th state

U.S. Congress: 2 senators, 6 representatives

State Motto: Union, Justice, Confidence

State Song: "Give Me Louisiana"

State Nicknames: The Pelican State; The Bayou State

Abbreviations: LA; La.

State Symbols: flower—magnolia; tree—bald cypress; bird—Eastern brown pelican

At a Glance

- With an increase in population of 2.0 percent, Louisiana ranked 46th in population growth from 2010 to 2021.

- Louisiana's median household income in 2020 was $50,800, the 4th lowest in the country, and 18.6 percent of the population lived below the poverty level, which was the 2nd highest poverty rate among the states.

- In 2021, Louisiana had the 3rd highest percent of residents who self-identified as "Black or African-American Alone," with 33.0 percent of residents in this category.

- In 2020, 8.7 percent of Louisiana's population did not have health insurance, the same rate as the total U.S. population.

- Louisiana ranked 5th among the states for per capita energy-related CO_2 emissions in 2019, releasing 41.8 metric tons of CO_2 per person.

Table LA-1. Population by Age, Sex, Race, and Hispanic Origin

(Number, percent, except where noted.)

Sex, age, race, and Hispanic origin	2000	2010	2021	Percent change, 2010–2021
Total Population..	4,468,976	4,533,372	4,624,047	2.0
Percent of total U.S. population	1.6	1.5	1.4	X
Sex				
Male..	2,162,903	2,219,292	2,265,191	2.1
Female...	2,306,073	2,314,080	2,358,856	1.9
Age				
Under 5 years...	317,392	314,260	285,149	-9.3
5 to 19 years...	1,050,637	939,977	910,759	-3.1
20 to 64 years...	2,584,018	2,721,278	2,666,329	-2.0
65 years and over..	516,929	557,857	761,810	36.6
Median age (years)	34.0	35.8	38.0	6.1
Race and Hispanic Origin				
One race				
White...	2,856,161	2,902,875	2,886,564	-0.6
Black..	1,451,944	1,462,969	1,524,944	4.2
American Indian and Alaska Native	25,477	33,037	37,772	14.3
Asian..	54,758	71,829	86,989	21.1
Native Hawaiian or Other Pacific Islander	1,240	2,500	3,008	16.2
Two or more races...	48,265	60,074	84,770	41.1
Hispanic (of any race)..	107,738	200,653	258,338	28.7

NOTE: Population figures for 2021 are July 1 estimates. The 2000 and 2010 estimates are taken from the respective censuses.
- = Zero or rounds to zero.
X = Not applicable.

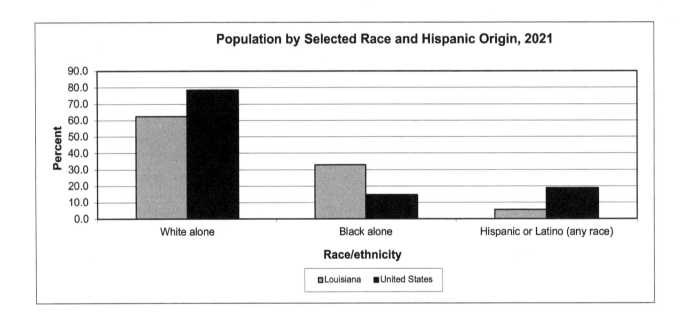

Population by Selected Race and Hispanic Origin, 2021

□ Louisiana   ■ United States

Table LA-2. Marital Status

(Number, percent distribution.)

Sex, age, race, and Hispanic origin	2000	2010	2020 [1]
Males, 15 Years and Over	1,648,133	1,751,556	1,810,945
Never married	31.2	37.0	38.7
Now married, except separated..	54.5	47.2	46.0
Separated..	2.2	2.2	2.2
Widowed..	2.8	2.8	2.8
Divorced..	9.2	10.8	10.3
Females, 15 Years and Over	1,828,247	1,861,490	1,937,452
Never married	26.3	30.8	33.1
Now married, except separated..	48.2	42.6	41.6
Separated..	2.9	3.2	2.6
Widowed..	11.5	10.1	9.9
Divorced..	11.1	13.3	12.8

[1] 2020 ACS 5-Year estimates. 1-Year estimates were not released for 2020 due to the impact of COVID-19 on data collection that year.

Table LA-3. Households and Housing Characteristics

(Number, percent, dollars.)

Item	2000	2010	2020 [1]	Average annual percent change, 2010–2020
Total Households	1,656,053	1,689,822	1,751,956	0.5
Family households	1,156,438	1,129,117	1,116,752	-0.2
Married-couple family	809,498	753,423	759,939	0.1
Other family	346,940	375,694	356,813	-0.7
Male householder, no wife present	71,865	79,560	85,758	1.1
Female householder, no husband present	275,075	296,134	271,055	-1.2
Nonfamily households	499,615	560,705	635,204	1.9
Householder living alone	419,200	468,853	538,083	2.1
Householder not living alone	80,415	91,852	97,121	0.8
Housing Characteristics				
Total housing units	1,847,181	1,967,947	2,074,664	0.8
Occupied housing units	1,656,053	1,689,822	1,751,956	0.5
Owner occupied	1,125,135	1,141,504	1,167,628	0.3
Renter occupied	530,918	548,318	584,328	0.9
Average household size	2.62	2.61	2.59	-0.1
Financial Characteristics				
Median gross rent of renter-occupied housing	466	736	876	2.7
Median monthly owner costs for housing units with a mortgage	816	1,163	1,310	1.8
Median value of owner-occupied housing units	85,000	137,500	168,100	3.2

[1] 2020 ACS 5-Year estimates. 1-Year estimates were not released for 2020 due to the impact of COVID-19 on data collection that year.

Table LA-4. Migration, Origin, and Language

(Number, percent.)

Characteristic	State 2016-2020 [1]	U.S. 2016-2020 [1]
Residence 1 Year Ago		
Population 1 year and over	4,607,350	322,943,283
Same house	87.4	86.2
Different house in the U.S.	12.2	13.2
Same county	7.3	7.7
Different county	4.9	5.5
Same state	3.2	3.2
Different state	1.7	2.3
Abroad	0.3	0.6
Place of Birth		
Native born	4,471,575	282,443,680
Male	48.7	49.4
Female	51.3	50.6
Foreign born	193,041	44,125,628
Male	52.1	48.6
Female	47.9	51.4
Foreign born; naturalized U.S. citizen	79,911	22,456,684
Male	46.9	46.1
Female	53.1	53.9
Foreign born; not a U.S. citizen	113,130	21,668,944
Male	55.8	51.1
Female	44.2	48.9
Entered 2010 or later	32.8	22.8
Entered 2000 to 2009	26.5	25.1
Entered before 2000	40.7	52.1
World Region of Birth, Foreign		
Foreign-born population, excluding population born at sea	193,041	44,125,628
Europe	8.3	10.8
Asia	31.2	31.3
Africa	4.5	5.4
Oceania	0.4	0.6
Latin America	54.1	50.0
North America	1.5	1.9
Language Spoken at Home and Ability to Speak English		
Population 5 years and over	4,359,716	306,919,116
English only	92.2	78.5
Language other than English	7.8	21.5
Speaks English less than "very well"	2.9	8.2

[1] 2020 ACS 5-Year estimates. 1-Year estimates were not released for 2020 due to the impact of COVID-19 on data collection that year.
NA = Not available.
X = Not applicable.
- = Zero or rounds to zero.

Table LA-5. Median Income and Poverty Status, 2020[1]

(Number, percent, except as noted.)

Characteristic	State Number	State Percent	U.S. Number	U.S. Percent
Median Income				
Households (dollars)...	50,800	X	64,994	X
Families (dollars)	65,427	X	80,069	X
Below Poverty Level (All People)	845,230	18.6	40,910,326	12.8
Sex				
Male	365,843	16.7	18,171,512	11.6
Female	479,387	20.4	22,738,814	14.0
Age				
Under 18 years..	284,760	26.3	12,598,699	17.5
Related children under 18 years..	281,769	26.1	12,306,532	17.2
18 to 64 years	477,610	17.4	23,554,920	12.1
65 years and over	82,860	11.9	4,756,707	9.3

X = Not applicable.
[1] 2020 ACS 5-Year estimates. 1-Year estimates were not released for 2020 due to the impact of COVID-19 on data collection that year.

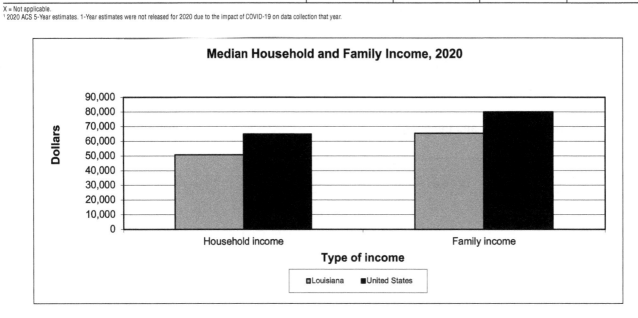

Median Household and Family Income, 2020

□ Louisiana   ■ United States

Table LA-6. Health Insurance Coverage Status for the Civilian Noninstitutionalized Population and Children Under 19 Years of Age

(Number, percent.)

Item	2011	2012	2013	2014	2015	2016	2017	2018	2019	2020[2]
Civilian Noninstitutionalized Population	4,473,068	4,498,884	4,522,910	4,547,572	4,567,431	4,577,182	4,580,258	4,556,078	4,539,690	4,556,953
Covered by Private or Public Insurance										
Number...	3,689,053	3,739,257	3,771,587	3,875,819	4,021,800	4,107,350	4,197,609	4,192,716	4,135,437	4,161,694
Percent..	82.5	83.1	83.4	85.2	88.1	89.7	91.6	92.0	91.1	91.3
Uninsured										
Number...	784,015	759,627	751,323	671,753	545,631	469,832	382,649	363,362	404,253	395,259
Percent..	17.5	16.9	16.6	14.8	11.9	10.3	8.4	8.0	8.9	8.7
Percent in the U.S. not covered...................................	15.1	14.8	14.5	11.7	9.4	8.6	8.7	8.9	9.2	8.7
Children Under 19 Years of Age[1]	1,117,293	1,117,427	1,110,977	1,112,618	1,114,678	1,115,457	1,175,200	1,160,494	1,148,751	1,154,339
Covered by Private or Public Insurance										
Number...	1,052,658	1,058,356	1,047,665	1,055,087	1,074,755	1,081,831	1,139,133	1,121,290	1,098,713	1,111,075
Percent..	94.2	94.7	94.3	94.8	96.4	97.0	96.9	96.6	95.6	96.3
Uninsured										
Number...	64,635	59,071	63,312	57,531	39,923	33,626	36,067	39,204	50,038	43,264
Percent..	5.8	5.3	5.7	5.2	3.6	3.0	3.1	3.4	4.4	3.7
Percent in the U.S. not covered...................................	7.5	7.2	7.1	6.0	4.8	4.5	5.0	5.2	5.7	5.2

[1] Data for years prior to 2017 are for individuals under 18 years of age.
[2] 2020 ACS 5-Year estimates. 1-Year estimates were not released for 2020 due to the impact of COVID-19 on data collection that year. Data is not comparable to previous years, which are based on 1-year estimates.

Table LA-7. Employment Status by Demographic Group, 2021

(Numbers in thousands, percent.)

Characteristic	Civilian noninstitutional population	Civilian labor force		Employed		Unemployed	
		Number	Percent of population	Number	Percent of population	Number	Percent of population
Total..	3,575	2,061	57.7	1,950	54.5	112	5.4
Sex							
Male..	1,689	1,068	63.2	1,001	59.3	67	6.3
Female	1,886	993	52.6	949	50.3	44	4.5
Race, Sex, and Hispanic Origin							
White...	2,300	1,332	57.9	1,280	55.7	52	3.9
Male......................................	1,118	728	65.1	696	62.3	32	4.3
Female...................................	1,182	604	51.1	584	49.4	21	3.4
Black or African American................	1,127	634	56.2	577	51.2	57	9.0
Male......................................	502	290	57.8	255	50.9	35	12.0
Female...................................	625	344	55.0	322	51.4	22	6.5
Hispanic or Latino ethnicity[1]	206	141	68.4	132	64.0	9	6.5
Male......................................	105	86	81.7	80	75.8	6	7.2
Female...................................	101	55	54.5	52	51.6	3	5.4
Age							
16 to 19 years.............................	253	71	28.1	63	24.8	8	11.6
20 to 24 years.............................	278	181	65.3	165	59.5	16	9.0
25 to 34 years.............................	623	493	79.2	460	73.8	33	6.8
35 to 44 years.............................	553	433	78.4	412	74.5	21	4.9
45 to 54 years.............................	506	388	76.6	375	74.0	13	3.4
55 to 64 years.............................	602	348	57.8	336	55.8	12	3.3
65 years and over........................	761	147	19.3	139	18.3	8	5.2

NOTE: Data in Table 7 are from the Current Population Survey (CPS) and do not match the estimates in Table 8. See notes and definitions for further information.
[1] May be of any race.

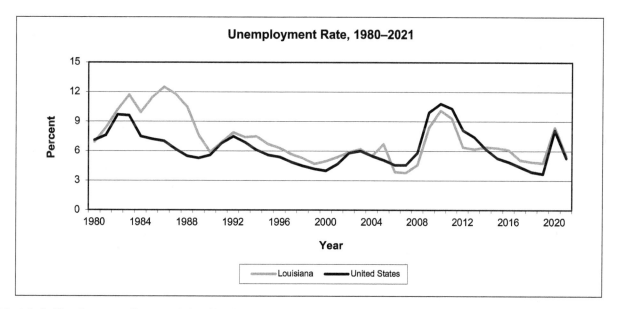

Table LA-8. Employment Status of the Civilian Noninstitutional Population Age 16 Years and Over

(Number, percent.)

Year	Civilian labor force	Civilian participation rate	Employed	Unemployed	Unemployment rate
2010..........	2,084,462	60.6	1,927,720	156,742	7.5
2011..........	2,080,525	59.8	1,926,038	154,487	7.4
2012..........	2,089,644	59.7	1,948,630	141,014	6.7
2013..........	2,101,974	59.6	1,966,755	135,219	6.4
2014..........	2,141,519	60.4	2,007,668	133,851	6.3
2015..........	2,150,050	60.3	2,015,081	134,969	6.3
2016..........	2,123,690	59.3	1,994,639	129,051	6.1
2017..........	2,108,485	58.8	2,000,487	107,998	5.1
2018..........	2,112,495	58.9	2,010,719	101,776	4.8
2019..........	2,108,410	58.8	2,010,405	98,005	4.6
2020..........	2,062,175	57.6	1,882,665	179,510	8.7
2021..........	2,062,492	57.8	1,949,403	113,089	5.5

Table LA-9. Employment and Average Wages by Industry

(Estimates are based on the 2012 North American Industry Classification System [NAICS].)

Industry	2013	2014	2015	2016	2017	2018	2019	2020
	Number of Jobs							
Wage and Salary Employment by Industry..........................	2,038,049	2,066,426	2,074,947	2,048,289	2,044,106	2,063,260	2,062,866	1,912,917
Farm Wage and Salary Employment................................	6,545	6,186	8,839	7,889	8,873	8,844	9,063	7,213
Nonfarm Wage and Salary Employment.............................	2,031,504	2,060,240	2,066,108	2,040,400	2,035,233	2,054,416	2,053,803	1,905,704
Private wage and salary employment...	1,653,425	1,694,081	1,703,916	1,680,979	1,677,702	1,694,401	1,694,786	1,556,485
Forestry, fishing, and related activities..................................	7,169	7,301	7,323	7,371	7,079	7,166	7,365	7,050
Mining...	51,242	50,921	44,887	35,578	32,369	34,137	34,740	28,769
Utilities..	9,155	8,838	8,606	8,442	8,487	8,692	8,605	8,677
Construction	134,785	142,781	144,369	143,671	150,707	155,783	145,480	124,582
Manufacturing...	144,069	147,286	143,922	135,936	134,813	135,589	137,786	131,541
Durable goods manufacturing..	74,639	77,252	73,206	65,135	63,599	63,603	65,419	60,815
Nondurable goods manufacturing......................................	69,430	70,034	70,716	70,801	71,214	71,986	72,367	70,726
Wholesale trade	73,614	73,774	72,620	70,785	69,877	69,792	69,308	65,603
Retail trade...	225,750	228,572	234,486	236,483	233,064	228,940	224,611	214,958
Transportation and warehousing......................................	77,132	80,813	80,318	74,609	73,039	75,994	78,915	74,392
Information..	26,672	26,099	26,756	23,668	22,917	22,865	22,454	18,705
Finance and insurance	60,698	61,150	60,897	61,030	61,345	60,319	60,174	59,609
Real estate and rental and leasing....................................	33,379	32,488	31,900	30,773	30,020	30,677	31,304	28,626
Professional, scientific, and technical services	87,145	89,156	89,874	87,375	87,347	88,764	90,506	87,266
Management of companies and enterprises............................	25,286	25,220	23,716	23,372	23,543	22,468	22,305	20,903
Administrative and waste services....................................	96,677	100,015	101,498	100,804	100,190	103,574	104,629	97,711
Educational services	42,757	43,269	44,070	44,700	44,975	44,030	45,291	42,420
Health care and social assistance....................................	248,617	256,461	261,494	267,282	269,971	271,972	275,917	268,049
Arts, entertainment, and recreation..................................	29,844	31,221	30,565	29,819	30,004	29,371	29,693	22,200
Accommodation and food services....................................	184,631	191,715	199,015	203,324	204,593	208,453	208,820	167,513
Other services, except public administration..........................	94,803	97,001	97,600	95,957	93,362	95,815	96,883	87,911
Government and government enterprises...............................	378,079	366,159	362,192	359,421	357,531	360,015	359,017	349,219
	Dollars							
Average Wages and Salaries by Industry	44,852	46,186	46,833	46,684	47,645	49,294	50,427	53,218
Average Farm Wages and Salaries	24,975	20,814	21,564	19,807	17,157	18,455	13,103	15,363
Average Nonfarm Wages and Salaries	44,916	46,262	46,941	46,788	47,778	49,426	50,592	53,361
Average private wages and salaries...	45,292	46,801	47,441	47,117	48,140	49,847	51,047	53,882
Forestry, fishing, and related activities..................................	35,416	36,254	36,193	38,268	39,337	42,069	42,208	44,619
Mining...	90,699	95,698	95,943	94,793	93,516	97,341	101,280	102,098
Utilities..	80,347	84,563	87,825	88,130	91,684	94,704	97,217	105,912
Construction	53,505	56,620	58,684	60,537	62,713	64,860	66,009	66,612
Manufacturing...	66,506	69,388	71,444	72,816	74,772	78,083	79,805	80,647
Durable goods manufacturing..	58,508	60,885	60,902	60,435	62,618	64,798	65,801	65,357
Nondurable goods manufacturing......................................	75,104	78,768	82,357	84,207	85,627	89,821	92,464	93,795
Wholesale trade	61,105	63,252	64,206	63,641	65,421	67,820	70,352	73,259
Retail trade...	27,072	27,388	27,991	28,197	28,823	29,400	30,140	32,516
Transportation and warehousing......................................	62,046	64,640	63,532	60,855	60,990	61,391	62,589	65,116
Information..	49,788	52,546	53,560	55,040	57,467	60,621	63,098	68,913
Finance and insurance	61,991	65,880	66,183	67,369	69,275	72,864	73,622	81,155
Real estate and rental and leasing....................................	49,093	50,114	49,381	47,632	48,999	51,241	52,623	53,747
Professional, scientific, and technical services	66,830	68,199	69,956	68,919	70,296	72,344	73,798	75,814
Management of companies and enterprises............................	79,415	70,501	81,133	83,247	86,760	87,023	87,651	93,238
Administrative and waste services....................................	35,421	36,807	38,452	37,464	38,200	39,848	40,827	43,272
Educational services	34,687	34,902	35,099	36,045	36,065	38,837	39,217	45,104
Health care and social assistance....................................	39,877	41,189	42,843	43,304	43,977	45,020	46,531	50,304
Arts, entertainment, and recreation..................................	34,699	34,571	36,219	37,456	38,079	41,238	42,821	47,713
Accommodation and food services....................................	19,868	20,380	20,944	21,063	21,532	22,390	22,697	21,752
Other services, except public administration..........................	31,370	32,111	33,273	34,236	35,510	36,562	37,552	40,838
Government and government enterprises...............................	43,275	43,770	44,586	45,249	46,079	47,446	48,442	51,039

Table LA-10. Employment Characteristics by Family Type

(Number, percent.)

Family type and labor force status	2018		2019		2020 [1]	
	Total	Families with own children under 18 years	Total	Families with own children under 18 years	Total	Families with own children under 18 years
All Families...	1,104,847	459,211	1,113,831	457,978	1,116,752	469,595
FAMILY TYPE AND LABOR FORCE STATUS						
Opposite-Sex Married-Couple Families...............................	748,604	274,123	737,222	263,834	753,924	280,608
Both husband and wife in labor force...............................	48.0	68.5	47.3	68.5	48.0	67.5
Husband in labor force, wife not in labor force	22.2	24.8	23.0	25.6	22.9	25.9
Wife in labor force, husband not in labor force	8.4	4.3	8.2	3.8	8.4	4.5
Both husband and wife not in labor force.............................	20.6	1.8	20.8	1.7	20.6	2.1
Other Families	356,243	185,088	376,609	194,144	356,813	187,494
Female householder, no spouse present	75.2	77.8	75.7	78.6	76.0	77.7
In labor force..	49.5	62.8	48.9	62.0	49.9	62.4
Not in labor force..	25.7	15.0	26.8	16.6	26.0	15.3
Male householder, no spouse present..................................	24.8	22.2	24.3	21.4	24.0	22.3
In labor force..	17.4	19.1	16.5	18.7	16.9	18.7
Not in labor force..	7.4	3.1	7.8	2.7	7.2	3.6

[1] 2020 ACS 5-Year estimates. 1-Year estimates were not released for 2020 due to the impact of COVID-19 on data collection that year. Data is not comparable to previous years, which are based on 1-year estimates.

Table LA-11. School Enrollment and Educational Attainment, 2020[1]

(Number, percent.)

Item	State	U.S.
Enrollment		
Total population 3 years and over, enrolled in school	1,145,889	80,497,960
Enrolled in nursery school or preschool (percent)...	6.8	6.1
Enrolled in kindergarten (percent)...	5.1	5.0
Enrolled in elementary school, grades 1-8 (percent)..	43.0	40.4
Enrolled in high school, grades 9-12 (percent)	21.1	21.0
Enrolled in college or graduate school (percent)...	24	27.6
Attainment		
Total population 25 years and over	3,139,520	222,836,834
Less than ninth grade (percent)..	4.7	4.9
9th to 12th grade, no diploma (percent)...	9.5	6.6
High school graduate, including equivalency (percent)...	33.3	26.7
Some college, no degree (percent)	21.2	20.3
Associate's degree (percent)..	6.5	8.6
Bachelor's degree (percent)	15.9	20.2
Graduate or professional degree (percent)..	8.9	12.7
High school graduate or higher (percent)	85.9	88.5
Bachelor's degree or higher (percent)...	24.9	32.9

[1] 2020 ACS 5-Year estimates. 1-Year estimates were not released for 2020 due to the impact of COVID-19 on data collection that year.

Table LA-12. Public School Characteristics and Educational Indicators

(Number, percent; data derived from National Center of Education Statistics.)

Item	State	U.S.
Public Elementary and Secondary Schools		
Number of regular school districts, 2018-19	71	13,452
Number of operational schools, 2019-20	1,363	98,469
Percent charter schools	10.7	7.7
Total public school enrollment, Fall 2019...	710,439	50,796,445
Percent charter school enrollment	12.2	6.8
Student-teacher ratio, Fall 2019..	18.4	15.9
Expenditures per student (unadjusted dollars), 2018-19	11,920	13,187
Four-year adjusted cohort graduation rate (ACGR), 2018-2019[1]...	80.1	85.8
Students eligible for free or reduced-price lunch (percent), 2019-20...	56.8	52.1
English language learners (percent), Fall 2019..	4.3	10.4
Students age 3 to 21 served under IDEA, part B (percent), 2020-21	12.5	14.5

Public Schools by Type, 2019-20	Number	Percent of state public schools
Total number of schools..	1,363	100.0
Special education..	29	2.1
Vocational education..	10	0.7
Alternative education...	6	0.4

[1] Adjusted Cohort Graduation Rates (ACGR) differ from Averaged Freshmen Graduation Rates (AFGR).

Table LA-13. Reported Voting and Registration of the Voting-Age Population, November 2020

(Numbers in thousands, percent.)

Item	Total population	Total citizen population	Registered			Voted		
			Total registered	Percent registered (total population)	Percent registered (total citizen population)	Total voted	Percent voted (total population)	Percent voted (total citizen population)
U.S. Total	252,274	231,593	168,308	66.7	72.7	154,628	61.3	66.8
State Total..	3,438	3,299	2,286	66.5	69.3	2,041	59.4	61.9
Sex								
Male	1,618	1,557	1,073	66.3	68.9	959	59.3	61.6
Female	1,820	1,742	1,214	66.7	69.7	1,082	59.5	62.1
Race								
White alone..	2,212	2,120	1,486	67.2	70.1	1,362	61.6	64.2
White, non-Hispanic alone	2,048	2,022	1,426	69.6	70.5	1,309	63.9	64.7
Black alone...	1,068	1,048	720	67.5	68.7	607	56.9	57.9
Asian alone	84	57	23	B	B	23	B	B
Hispanic (of any race)............................	210	131	84	40.0	64.3	72	34.3	55.1
White alone or in combination................	2,261	2,169	1,524	67.4	70.3	1,396	61.8	64.4
Black alone or in combination....................	1,092	1,072	737	67.5	68.8	624	57.2	58.2
Asian alone or in combination....................	90	63	29	B	B	26	B	B
Age								
18 to 24 years......................................	389	370	207	53.1	55.9	173	44.5	46.9
25 to 34 years......................................	598	563	358	59.8	63.6	290	48.5	51.5
35 to 44 years......................................	587	563	391	66.7	69.5	356	60.7	63.2
45 to 64 years......................................	1,089	1,043	744	68.3	71.3	688	63.1	65.9
65 years and over	775	760	586	75.7	77.1	535	69.0	70.4

B = Base is less than 75,000 and therefore too small to show the derived measure.

Table LA-14. Crime

(Number, rate per 100,000. Data are derived from the FBI Uniform Crime Reports.)

Item	State			U.S.		
	2019	2020	Percent change	2019	2020	Percent change
TOTAL POPULATION[1]	4,658,285	4,645,318	-0.3	328,329,953	329,484,123	0.4
VIOLENT CRIME						
Number..	26,072	29,704	13.9	1,250,393	1,313,105	5.0
Rate	559.7	639.4	14.2	380.8	398.5	4.6
Murder and Nonnegligent Manslaughter						
Number..	547	734	34.2	16,669	21,570	29.4
Rate	11.7	15.8	34.6	5.1	6.5	28.9
Rape[2]						
Number..	2,282	2,136	-6.4	143,224	126,430	-11.7
Rate	49.0	46.0	-6.1	43.6	38.4	-12.0
Robbery						
Number..	4,129	3,747	-9.3	268,483	243,600	-9.3
Rate	88.6	80.7	-9.0	81.8	73.9	-9.6
Aggravated Assault						
Number..	19,114	23,087	20.8	822,017	921,505	12.1
Rate	410.3	497.0	21.1	250.4	279.7	11.7
PROPERTY CRIME						
Number..	148,429	133,989	-9.7	6,995,235	6,452,038	-7.8
Rate	3,186.3	2,884.4	-9.5	2,130.6	1,958.2	-8.1
Burglary						
Number..	27,440	23,698	-13.6	1,118,096	1,035,314	-7.4
Rate	589.1	510.1	-13.4	340.5	314.2	-7.7
Larceny-Theft						
Number..	110,123	97,891	-11.1	5,152,267	4,606,324	-10.6
Rate	2,364.0	2,107.3	-10.9	1,569.2	1,398.0	-10.9
Motor Vehicle Theft						
Number..	10,866	12,400	14.1	724,872	810,400	11.8
Rate	233.3	266.9	14.4	220.8	246.0	11.4

NOTE: Although arson data are included in the trend and clearance tables, sufficient data are not available to estimate totals for this offense. Therefore, no arson data are published in this table.
- = Zero or rounds to zero.
[1] Population figures are U.S. Census Bureau provisional estimates as of July 1, 2020.
[2] The figures shown in the rape (revised definition) column were estimated using the revised Uniform Crime Reporting (UCR) definition of rape.

Table LA-15. State Government Finances, 2020

(Dollar amounts in thousands, percent distribution.)

Item	Dollars	Percent distribution
Total Revenue	38,268,818	100.0
General revenue	32,997,848	86.2
Intergovernmental revenue	17,246,644	45.1
Taxes	11,381,008	29.7
General sales	3571559	9.3
Selective sales	2,488,126	6.5
License taxes	417,186	1.1
Individual income tax	3916190	10.2
Corporate income tax	450,449	1.2
Other taxes	537,498	1.4
Current charges	2,123,927	5.6
Miscellaneous general revenue	2,246,269	5.9
Utility revenue	13,165	-
Liquor stores revenue	0	-
Insurance trust revenue[1]	5,257,805	13.7
Total Expenditure	39,438,561	100.0
Intergovernmental expenditure	6,836,549	17.3
Direct expenditure	32,602,012	82.7
Current operation	22,597,595	57.3
Capital outlay	2,089,246	5.3
Insurance benefits and repayments	6,269,348	15.9
Assistance and subsidies	816,813	2.1
Interest on debt	829,010	2.1
Exhibit: Salaries and wages	4,388,813	11.1
Total Expenditure	39,438,561	100.0
General expenditure	33,158,940	84.1
Intergovernmental expenditure	6,836,549	17.3
Direct expenditure	26,322,391	66.7
General expenditure, by function:		
Education	10,311,736	26.1
Public welfare	13,534,847	34.3
Hospitals	363,538	0.9
Health	498,519	1.3
Highways	1,574,443	4.0
Police protection	380,770	1.0
Correction	732,432	1.9
Natural resources	812,306	2.1
Parks and recreation	362,771	0.9
Governmental administration	792,970	2.0
Interest on general debt	829,010	2.1
Other and unallocable	2,878,563	7.3
Utility expenditure	10,273	-
Liquor stores expenditure	0	-
Insurance trust expenditure	6,269,348	15.9
Debt at End of Fiscal Year	16,858,298	X
Cash and Security Holdings	71,118,439	X

X = Not applicable.
- = Zero or rounds to zero.
[1] Within insurance trust revenue, net earnings of state retirement systems is a calculated statistic (the item code in the data file is X08), and thus can be positive or negative. Net earnings is the sum of earnings on investments plus gains on investments minus losses on investments. The change made in 2002 for asset valuation from book to market value in accordance with Statement 34 of the Governmental Accounting Standards Board is reflected in the calculated statistics.

Table LA-16. State Government Tax Collections, 2021

(Dollars in thousands, percent.)

Item	Dollars	Percent distribution
Total Taxes	12,257,234	100.0
Property taxes	103,750	0.8
Sales and gross receipts	6,853,513	55.9
General sales and gross receipts	4,048,616	33.0
Selective sales and gross receipts	2,804,897	22.9
Alcoholic beverages	79,279	0.6
Amusements	686,865	5.6
Insurance premiums	1,004,261	8.2
Motor fuels	639,727	5.2
Pari-mutuels	5,535	-
Public utilities	9,250	0.1
Tobacco products	268,752	2.2
Other selective sales	111,228	0.9
Licenses	477,174	3.9
Alcoholic beverages	0	-
Amusements	X	-
Corporations in general	237,606	1.9
Hunting and fishing	30,818	0.3
Motor vehicle	85,059	0.7
Motor vehicle operators	5,619	
Public utilities	6,119	0.0
Occupation and business, NEC	107,217	0.9
Other licenses	4,736	-
Income taxes	4,520,855	36.9
Individual income	3,933,108	32.1
Corporation net income	587,747	4.8
Other taxes	301,942	2.5
Death and gift	0	-
Documentary and stock transfer	X	-
Severance	301,942	2.5
Taxes, NEC	X	-

- = Zero or rounds to zero.
X = Not applicable.

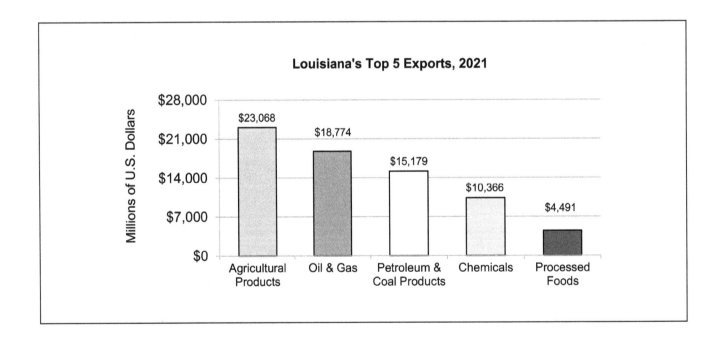

Louisiana's Top 5 Exports, 2021

MAINE

Facts and Figures

Location: Northeast corner of the United States; bordered on the N and E by New Brunswick, Canada; on the S by the Atlantic Ocean; on the W by New Hampshire; and on the NW by Quebec, Canada

Area: 35,385 sq. mi. (91,646 sq. km.); rank—39th

Population: 1,372,247 (2021 est.); rank—42nd

Principal Cities: capital—Augusta; largest—Portland

Statehood: March 15, 1820; 23rd state

U.S. Congress: 2 senators, 2 representatives

State Motto: *Dirigo* ("I lead")

State Song: "State of Maine Song"

State Nickname: The Pine Tree State

Abbreviations: ME; Me.

State Symbols: flower—white pinecone and tassel; tree—Eastern white pine; bird—chickadee

At a Glance

- With a population that grew 3.3 percent, Maine ranked 36th among the states in growth from 2010 to 2021.

- Maine had the highest percent of residents who self-identified as "White alone" in 2021, with 94.2 percent of its residents in this category.

- Maine was the state with the 2nd lowest percent of its population who identified as "Hispanic or Latino" in 2021, with just 2.0 percent of residents in this category.

- With 21.7 percent of its population in the 65 and older age group, Maine was state with the most people in this category in 2021.

- Maine's drug overdose rate of 44.6 per 100,000 population was the 6th highest among the states in 2020.

Table ME-1. Population by Age, Sex, Race, and Hispanic Origin

(Number, percent, except where noted.)

Sex, age, race, and Hispanic origin	2000	2010	2021	Percent change, 2010–2021
Total Population..	1,274,923	1,328,361	1,372,247	3.3
Percent of total U.S. population	0.5	0.4	0.4	X
Sex				
Male..	620,309	650,056	676,493	4.1
Female...	654,614	678,305	695,754	2.6
Age				
Under 5 years...	70,726	69,520	62,340	-10.3
5 to 19 years..	264,729	241,439	221,551	-8.2
20 to 64 years..	756,036	806,322	791,191	-1.9
65 years and over	183,402	211,080	297,165	40.8
Median age (years)	38.6	42.7	44.7	4.7
Race and Hispanic Origin				
One race				
White	1,236,014	1,269,764	1,292,011	1.8
Black...	6,760	16,269	24,915	53.1
American Indian and Alaska Native	7,098	8,771	9,808	11.8
Asian..	9,111	13,783	18,786	36.3
Native Hawaiian or Other Pacific Islander	382	377	556	47.5
Two or more races	12,647	19,397	26,171	34.9
Hispanic (of any race)...	9,360	18,261	27,037	48.1

NOTE: Population figures for 2021 are July 1 estimates. The 2000 and 2010 estimates are taken from the respective censuses.
- = Zero or rounds to zero.
X = Not applicable.

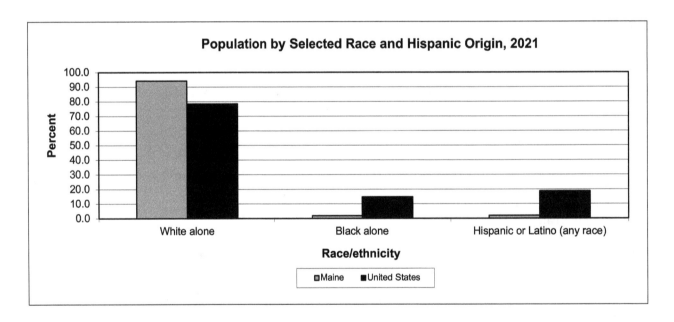

Table ME-2. Marital Status

(Number, percent distribution.)

Sex, age, race, and Hispanic origin	2000	2010	2020 [1]
Males, 15 Years and Over	494,217	534,474	550,845
Never married	26.8	31.0	31.2
Now married, except separated...	58.8	52.5	52.1
Separated..	1.1	1.2	0.8
Widowed...	2.8	2.9	3.0
Divorced...	10.5	12.5	12.8
Females, 15 Years and Over	534,606	570,281	584,733
Never married	21.2	24.2	25.2
Now married, except separated...	54.1	49.3	49.4
Separated..	1.3	1.6	1.1
Widowed...	11.0	9.9	9.4
Divorced...	12.4	15.0	14.9

[1] 2020 ACS 5-Year estimates. 1-Year estimates were not released for 2020 due to the impact of COVID-19 on data collection that year.

Table ME-3. Households and Housing Characteristics

(Number, percent, dollars.)

Item	2000	2010	2020 [1]	Average annual percent change, 2010–2020
Total Households..	518,200	545,417	569,551	0.6
Family households..	340,685	345,328	349,955	0.2
Married-couple family.......................................	272,152	266,670	275,146	0.5
Other family..	68,533	78,658	74,809	-0.7
Male householder, no wife present.....................	19,511	23,620	23,837	0.1
Female householder, no husband present............	49,022	55,038	50,972	-1.1
Nonfamily households...	177,515	200,089	219,596	1.4
Householder living alone....................................	139,969	155,623	169,560	1.3
Householder not living alone..............................	37,546	44,466	50,036	1.8
Housing Characteristics				
Total housing units..	651,901	722,217	746,793	0.5
Occupied housing units......................................	518,200	545,417	569,551	0.6
Owner occupied..	370,905	396,395	414,939	0.7
Renter occupied...	147,295	149,022	154,612	0.5
Average household size.......................................	2.39	2.37	2.29	-0.5
Financial Characteristics				
Median gross rent of renter-occupied housing	497	707	873	3.4
Median monthly owner costs for housing units with a mortgage	923	1,289	1,404	1.3
Median value of owner-occupied housing units.............	98,700	179,100	198,000	1.5

[1] 2020 ACS 5-Year estimates. 1-Year estimates were not released for 2020 due to the impact of COVID-19 on data collection that year.

Table ME-4. Migration, Origin, and Language

(Number, percent.)

Characteristic	State 2016-2020 [1]	U.S. 2016-2020 [1]
Residence 1 Year Ago		
Population 1 year and over	1,328,222	322,943,283
Same house	87.1	86.2
Different house in the U.S.	12.6	13.2
Same county	7.1	7.7
Different county	5.5	5.5
Same state	2.9	3.2
Different state	2.6	2.3
Abroad	0.3	0.6
Place of Birth		
Native born	1,292,686	282,443,680
Male	49.1	49.4
Female	50.9	50.6
Foreign born	48,139	44,125,628
Male	45.5	48.6
Female	54.5	51.4
Foreign born; naturalized U.S. citizen......................................	26,408	22,456,684
Male	42.4	46.1
Female	57.6	53.9
Foreign born; not a U.S. citizen...	21,731	21,668,944
Male	49.1	51.1
Female	50.9	48.9
Entered 2010 or later	28.0	22.8
Entered 2000 to 2009	19.2	25.1
Entered before 2000..	52.8	52.1
World Region of Birth, Foreign		
Foreign-born population, excluding population born at sea	48,139	44,125,628
Europe	23.0	10.8
Asia..	28.5	31.3
Africa	16.4	5.4
Oceania	1.3	0.6
Latin America...	10.9	50.0
North America	19.9	1.9
Language Spoken at Home and Ability to Speak English		
Population 5 years and over..	1,276,837	306,919,116
English only	94.0	78.5
Language other than English...	6.0	21.5
Speaks English less than "very well"......................................	1.4	8.2

[1] 2020 ACS 5-Year estimates. 1-Year estimates were not released for 2020 due to the impact of COVID-19 on data collection that year.
NA = Not available.
X = Not applicable.
- = Zero or rounds to zero.

Table ME-5. Median Income and Poverty Status, 2020[1]

(Number, percent, except as noted.)

Characteristic	State Number	State Percent	U.S. Number	U.S. Percent
Median Income				
Households (dollars)............................	59,489	X	64,994	X
Families (dollars)	76,192	X	80,069	X
Below Poverty Level (All People)	144,384	11.1	40,910,326	12.8
Sex				
Male	64,177	10.1	18,171,512	11.6
Female	80,207	12.0	22,738,814	14.0
Age				
Under 18 years............................	34,067	14.0	12,598,699	17.5
Related children under 18 years............................	32,382	13.4	12,306,532	17.2
18 to 64 years............................	87,428	11.0	23,554,920	12.1
65 years and over	22,889	8.5	4,756,707	9.3

X = Not applicable.
[1] 2020 ACS 5-Year estimates. 1-Year estimates were not released for 2020 due to the impact of COVID-19 on data collection that year.

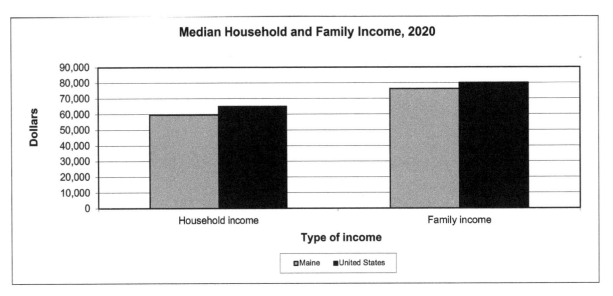

Median Household and Family Income, 2020

Table ME-6. Health Insurance Coverage Status for the Civilian Noninstitutionalized Population and Children Under 19 Years of Age

(Number, percent.)

Item	2011	2012	2013	2014	2015	2016	2017	2018	2019	2020[2]
Civilian Noninstitutionalized Population	1,314,121	1,315,703	1,314,191	1,315,996	1,314,849	1,317,148	1,321,649	1,323,289	1,327,623	1,325,025
Covered by Private or Public Insurance										
Number............................	1,173,956	1,180,994	1,167,176	1,182,465	1,204,341	1,211,175	1,214,582	1,217,102	1,221,086	1,223,980
Percent............................	89.3	89.8	88.8	89.9	91.6	92.0	91.9	92.0	92.0	92.4
Uninsured										
Number............................	140,165	134,709	147,015	133,531	110,508	105,973	107,067	106,187	106,537	101,045
Percent............................	10.7	10.2	11.2	10.1	8.4	8.0	8.1	8.0	8.0	7.6
Percent in the U.S. not covered............................	15.1	14.8	14.5	11.7	9.4	8.6	8.7	8.9	9.2	8.7
Children Under 19 Years of Age[1]	269,901	265,495	259,827	257,390	255,319	254,723	271,746	264,131	261,737	266,859
Covered by Private or Public Insurance										
Number............................	255,736	253,255	244,441	241,098	240,871	243,104	258,321	249,619	247,074	253,589
Percent............................	94.8	95.4	94.1	93.7	94.3	95.4	95.1	94.5	94.4	95.0
Uninsured										
Number............................	14,165	12,240	15,386	16,292	14,448	11,619	13,425	14,512	14,663	13,270
Percent............................	5.2	4.6	5.9	6.3	5.7	4.6	4.9	5.5	5.6	5.0
Percent in the U.S. not covered............................	7.5	7.2	7.1	6.0	4.8	4.5	5.0	5.2	5.7	5.2

[1] Data for years prior to 2017 are for individuals under 18 years of age.
[2] 2020 ACS 5-Year estimates. 1-Year estimates were not released for 2020 due to the impact of COVID-19 on data collection that year. Data is not comparable to previous years, which are based on 1-year estimates.

Table ME-7. Employment Status by Demographic Group, 2021

(Numbers in thousands, percent.)

Characteristic	Civilian noninstitutional population	Civilian labor force		Employed		Unemployed	
		Number	Percent of population	Number	Percent of population	Number	Percent of population
Total..	1,123	680	60.5	649	57.8	31	4.5
Sex							
Male.......................................	545	347	63.6	331	60.8	15	4.4
Female....................................	578	333	57.6	318	54.9	16	4.7
Race, Sex, and Hispanic Origin							
White......................................	1,070	645	60.3	616	57.6	29	4.5
Male....................................	520	330	63.5	316	60.9	14	4.2
Female.................................	551	315	57.2	300	54.5	15	4.7
Black or African American............	NA	NA	NA	NA	NA	NA	NA
Male....................................	NA	NA	NA	NA	NA	NA	NA
Female.................................	NA	NA	NA	NA	NA	NA	NA
Hispanic or Latino ethnicity[1]......	NA	NA	NA	NA	NA	NA	NA
Male....................................	NA	NA	NA	NA	NA	NA	NA
Female.................................	NA	NA	NA	NA	NA	NA	NA
Age							
16 to 19 years...........................	NA	NA	NA	NA	NA	NA	NA
20 to 24 years...........................	69	52	76	48	70	4	8
25 to 34 years...........................	157	131	83.5	124	79.4	7	5.0
35 to 44 years...........................	172	145	84.0	137	79.8	7	5.0
45 to 54 years...........................	149	120	80.1	117	78.4	3	2.2
55 to 64 years...........................	209	140	67.0	133	63.9	7	4.7
65 years and over......................	310	62	20.1	61	19.6	2	2.7

NOTE: Data in Table 7 are from the Current Population Survey (CPS) and do not match the estimates in Table 8. See notes and definitions for further information.
[1] May be of any race.
NA = Not available.

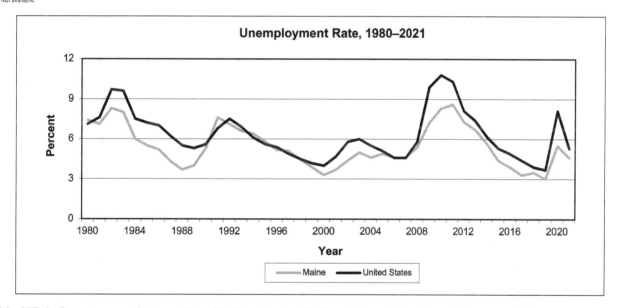

Unemployment Rate, 1980–2021

Table ME-8. Employment Status of the Civilian Noninstitutional Population Age 16 Years and Over

(Number, percent.)

Year	Civilian labor force	Civilian participation rate	Employed	Unemployed	Unemployment rate
2010..........................	697,832	65.0	638,984	58,848	8.4
2011..........................	698,979	64.8	644,967	54,012	7.7
2012..........................	700,730	64.7	650,315	50,415	7.2
2013..........................	704,240	64.9	657,058	47,182	6.7
2014..........................	698,035	64.1	659,008	39,027	5.6
2015..........................	687,859	63.0	657,550	30,309	4.4
2016..........................	693,917	63.4	667,723	26,194	3.8
2017..........................	703,871	63.6	680,164	23,707	3.4
2018..........................	703,138	63.2	681,334	21,804	3.1
2019..........................	701,631	62.7	682,271	19,360	2.8
2020..........................	675,231	59.9	641,262	33,969	5.0
2021..........................	681,884	59.9	650,334	31,550	4.6

Table ME-9. Employment and Average Wages by Industry

(Estimates are based on the 2012 North American Industry Classification System [NAICS].)

Industry	2013	2014	2015	2016	2017	2018	2019	2020
	Number of Jobs							
Wage and Salary Employment by Industry	615,236	619,376	624,837	632,306	637,895	645,481	651,621	612,484
Farm Wage and Salary Employment	4,150	4,166	4,151	3,875	3,867	3,563	3,589	3,429
Nonfarm Wage and Salary Employment	611,086	615,210	620,686	628,431	634,028	641,918	648,032	609,055
Private wage and salary employment	504,103	508,479	514,553	521,322	526,706	534,164	539,265	504,329
Forestry, fishing, and related activities	4,098	4,150	4,240	4,080	4,173	4,221	4,227	4,087
Mining	187	190	191	211	209	230	214	228
Utilities	1,619	1,551	1,630	1,647	1,669	1,632	1,628	1,612
Construction	26,227	26,613	27,220	28,095	28,994	30,070	30,757	31,075
Manufacturing	50,423	50,253	50,700	50,744	51,059	52,013	53,284	50,326
Durable goods manufacturing	27,255	27,769	28,159	28,490	28,695	29,447	30,146	28,390
Nondurable goods manufacturing	23,168	22,484	22,541	22,254	22,364	22,566	23,138	21,936
Wholesale trade	19,666	19,815	20,120	20,027	19,693	19,576	19,727	18,876
Retail trade	81,883	82,192	82,224	82,522	82,039	81,746	80,993	76,460
Transportation and warehousing	16,031	16,578	16,584	16,987	17,579	17,026	17,222	16,163
Information	7,641	7,453	7,595	7,710	7,366	7,417	7,163	6,403
Finance and insurance	24,993	23,683	23,984	24,024	24,270	24,539	25,258	25,343
Real estate and rental and leasing	6,601	6,550	6,517	6,736	6,756	7,088	7,213	6,924
Professional, scientific, and technical services	24,814	25,004	25,341	25,527	26,019	27,609	28,416	28,446
Management of companies and enterprises	7,428	9,091	9,124	9,984	10,484	11,191	12,129	12,035
Administrative and waste services	28,301	29,666	30,492	30,824	30,685	31,173	29,734	28,802
Educational services	15,043	15,339	15,703	16,406	16,750	17,614	17,915	17,169
Health care and social assistance	102,287	102,230	103,776	104,899	106,554	106,444	107,747	104,789
Arts, entertainment, and recreation	8,879	8,594	8,747	9,148	9,384	9,685	10,037	7,450
Accommodation and food services	54,182	55,013	55,712	56,993	58,499	59,368	60,004	44,865
Other services, except public administration	23,800	24,514	24,653	24,758	24,524	25,522	25,597	23,276
Government and government enterprises	106,983	106,731	106,133	107,109	107,322	107,754	108,767	104,726
	Dollars							
Average Wages and Salaries by Industry	40,466	41,622	42,896	43,715	45,053	46,514	48,315	52,718
Average Farm Wages and Salaries	27,296	28,810	23,619	29,036	26,405	25,219	19,879	20,208
Average Nonfarm Wages and Salaries	40,555	41,709	43,025	43,806	45,167	46,632	48,472	52,901
Average private wages and salaries	40,266	41,481	42,792	43,586	44,989	46,469	48,347	53,197
Forestry, fishing, and related activities	40,456	42,281	44,051	44,496	47,475	49,575	50,123	49,790
Mining	55,807	58,853	59,550	58,867	61,407	58,635	61,696	63,434
Utilities	79,952	87,721	82,707	83,565	91,798	91,738	92,041	101,532
Construction	44,581	45,895	46,668	47,453	48,840	50,578	52,626	56,665
Manufacturing	53,348	54,619	55,913	55,856	57,467	57,941	59,194	63,876
Durable goods manufacturing	53,401	54,578	56,096	56,135	57,058	57,790	58,474	61,176
Nondurable goods manufacturing	53,285	54,669	55,684	55,500	57,992	58,138	60,133	67,370
Wholesale trade	56,996	59,646	62,620	63,598	65,400	68,414	70,235	75,082
Retail trade	25,897	26,691	27,567	28,042	28,984	29,987	31,341	34,963
Transportation and warehousing	40,707	42,107	43,350	43,183	43,805	45,068	46,474	50,313
Information	47,606	47,964	49,867	53,244	54,814	56,727	59,621	66,759
Finance and insurance	66,306	68,723	70,446	71,553	75,841	78,593	80,556	86,357
Real estate and rental and leasing	37,690	39,041	40,832	41,897	43,063	44,293	45,566	50,023
Professional, scientific, and technical services	60,997	63,727	66,422	68,131	70,484	72,671	75,644	81,843
Management of companies and enterprises	75,334	74,508	76,518	79,648	79,996	83,176	87,272	92,136
Administrative and waste services	33,479	34,423	35,872	36,926	37,732	38,356	39,985	43,864
Educational services	35,338	36,647	37,438	37,335	38,057	37,530	38,631	40,499
Health care and social assistance	43,364	44,540	45,798	46,556	47,676	49,372	51,469	55,763
Arts, entertainment, and recreation	26,339	26,737	27,027	28,177	28,616	29,393	30,116	34,724
Accommodation and food services	19,662	20,553	21,471	22,489	23,731	25,276	26,396	26,994
Other services, except public administration	28,690	29,414	30,528	31,576	32,844	33,676	34,710	38,522
Government and government enterprises	41,916	42,794	44,153	44,875	46,041	47,440	49,094	51,476

Table ME-10. Employment Characteristics by Family Type

(Number, percent.)

Family type and labor force status	2018		2019		2020 [1]	
	Total	Families with own children under 18 years	Total	Families with own children under 18 years	Total	Families with own children under 18 years
All Families..	342,542	123,657	342,894	124,352	349,955	129,627
FAMILY TYPE AND LABOR FORCE STATUS						
Opposite-Sex Married-Couple Families............................	267,015	83,003	268,258	82,161	271,707	86,932
Both husband and wife in labor force..............................	51.6	73.0	51.5	74.8	52.6	74.9
Husband in labor force, wife not in labor force	17.3	20.6	16.9	19.5	16.9	19.0
Wife in labor force, husband not in labor force	8.8	4.3	8.7	3.1	9.1	4.3
Both husband and wife not in labor force..........................	20.9	1.4	21.4	1.3	21.5	1.8
Other Families	75,527	40,654	74,636	42,191	74,809	41,929
Female householder, no spouse present	67.8	70.9	69.1	68.7	68.1	68.0
In labor force...	48.1	57.8	47.0	55.8	47.2	55.5
Not in labor force	19.8	13.1	22.0	12.8	20.9	12.5
Male householder, no spouse present..............................	32.2	29.1	30.9	31.3	31.9	32.0
In labor force...	24.2	24.3	24.2	28.7	24.8	28.3
Not in labor force	7.9	4.8	6.8	2.7	7.1	3.7

[1] 2020 ACS 5-Year estimates. 1-Year estimates were not released for 2020 due to the impact of COVID-19 on data collection that year. Data is not comparable to previous years, which are based on 1-year estimates.

Table ME-11. School Enrollment and Educational Attainment, 2020[1]

(Number, percent.)

Item	State	U.S.
Enrollment		
Total population 3 years and over, enrolled in school	278,782	80,497,960
Enrolled in nursery school or preschool (percent)..	5.7	6.1
Enrolled in kindergarten (percent)..	4.6	5.0
Enrolled in elementary school, grades 1-8 (percent)..	39.8	40.4
Enrolled in high school, grades 9-12 (percent)..	21.6	21.0
Enrolled in college or graduate school (percent)..	28.2	27.6
Attainment		
Total population 25 years and over	982,385	222,836,834
Less than ninth grade (percent)..	2.3	4.9
9th to 12th grade, no diploma (percent)..	4.5	6.6
High school graduate, including equivalency (percent)..	31.3	26.7
Some college, no degree (percent)..	19.2	20.3
Associate's degree (percent)..	10.2	8.6
Bachelor's degree (percent)..	20.3	20.2
Graduate or professional degree (percent)..	12.2	12.7
High school graduate or higher (percent)..	93.2	88.5
Bachelor's degree or higher (percent)..	32.5	32.9

[1] 2020 ACS 5-Year estimates. 1-Year estimates were not released for 2020 due to the impact of COVID-19 on data collection that year.

Table ME-12. Public School Characteristics and Educational Indicators

(Number, percent; data derived from National Center of Education Statistics.)

Item	State	U.S.
Public Elementary and Secondary Schools		
Number of regular school districts, 2018-19	256	13,452
Number of operational schools, 2019-20..	594	98,469
Percent charter schools	2.0	7.7
Total public school enrollment, Fall 2019..	180,291	50,796,445
Percent charter school enrollment	1.4	6.8
Student-teacher ratio, Fall 2019..	12.2	15.9
Expenditures per student (unadjusted dollars), 2018-19	15,686	13,187
Four-year adjusted cohort graduation rate (ACGR), 2018-2019[1]..	87.4	85.8
Students eligible for free or reduced-price lunch (percent), 2019-20..	42.0	52.1
English language learners (percent), Fall 2019	3.1	10.4
Students age 3 to 21 served under IDEA, part B (percent), 2020-21	20.0	14.5

Public Schools by Type, 2019-20	Number	Percent of state public schools
Total number of schools..	594	100.0
Special education..	1	0.2
Vocational education..	27	4.5
Alternative education..	0	-

[1] Adjusted Cohort Graduation Rates (ACGR) differ from Averaged Freshmen Graduation Rates (AFGR).
- = Zero or rounds to zero.

Table ME-13. Reported Voting and Registration of the Voting-Age Population, November 2020

(Numbers in thousands, percent.)

Item	Total population	Total citizen population	Registered			Voted		
			Total registered	Percent registered (total population)	Percent registered (total citizen population)	Total voted	Percent voted (total population)	Percent voted (total citizen population)
U.S. Total	252,274	231,593	168,308	66.7	72.7	154,628	61.3	66.8
State Total	1,087	1,075	832	76.5	77.4	766	70.5	71.3
Sex								
Male	523	515	383	73.2	74.3	351	67.2	68.2
Female	564	560	449	79.5	80.2	415	73.5	74.1
Race								
White alone	1,036	1,031	803	77.5	77.9	739	71.3	71.7
White, non-Hispanic alone	1,027	1,022	798	77.7	78.1	734	71.5	71.8
Black alone	13	8	4	B	B	4	B	B
Asian alone	10	7	6	B	B	6	B	B
Hispanic (of any race)	11	11	7	B	B	7	B	B
White alone or in combination	1,058	1,053	818	77.3	77.7	752	71.1	71.4
Black alone or in combination	15	10	6	B	B	6	D	B
Asian alone or in combination	18	15	12	B	B	12	B	B
Age								
18 to 24 years	93	90	60	64.6	66.4	57	61.4	63.1
25 to 34 years	158	157	116	73.3	74.1	102	64.3	65.0
35 to 44 years	170	170	136	79.8	79.8	120	70.8	70.8
45 to 64 years	367	361	285	77.7	78.8	263	71.7	72.7
65 years and over	300	296	236	78.6	79.5	224	74.9	75.7

B = Base is less than 75,000 and therefore too small to show the derived measure.

Table ME-14. Crime

(Number, rate per 100,000. Data are derived from the FBI Uniform Crime Reports.)

Item	State			U.S.		
	2019	2020	Percent change	2019	2020	Percent change
TOTAL POPULATION[1]	1,345,770	1,350,141	0.3	328,329,953	329,484,123	0.4
VIOLENT CRIME						
Number	1,562	1,466	-6.1	1,250,393	1,313,105	5.0
Rate	116.1	108.6	-6.4	380.8	398.5	4.6
Murder and Nonnegligent Manslaughter						
Number	22	22	0.0	16,669	21,570	29.4
Rate	1.6	1.6	-0.3	5.1	6.5	28.9
Rape[2]						
Number	520	486	-6.5	143,224	126,430	-11.7
Rate	38.6	36.0	-6.8	43.6	38.4	-12.0
Robbery						
Number	192	170	-11.5	268,483	243,600	-9.3
Rate	14.3	12.6	-11.7	81.8	73.9	-9.6
Aggravated Assault						
Number	828	788	-4.8	822,017	921,505	12.1
Rate	61.5	58.4	-5.1	250.4	279.7	11.7
PROPERTY CRIME						
Number	16,791	15,610	-7.0	6,995,235	6,452,038	-7.8
Rate	1,247.7	1,156.2	-7.3	2,130.6	1,958.2	-8.1
Burglary						
Number	2,360	2,009	-14.9	1,118,096	1,035,314	-7.4
Rate	175.4	148.8	-15.1	340.5	314.2	-7.7
Larceny-Theft						
Number	13,705	12,739	-7.0	5,152,267	4,606,324	-10.6
Rate	1,018.4	943.5	-7.3	1,569.2	1,398.0	-10.9
Motor Vehicle Theft						
Number	726	862	18.7	724,872	810,400	11.8
Rate	53.9	63.8	18.3	220.8	246.0	11.4

NOTE: Although arson data are included in the trend and clearance tables, sufficient data are not available to estimate totals for this offense. Therefore, no arson data are published in this table.
- = Zero or rounds to zero.
[1] Population figures are U.S. Census Bureau provisional estimates as of July 1, 2020.
[2] The figures shown in the rape (revised definition) column were estimated using the revised Uniform Crime Reporting (UCR) definition of rape.

Table ME-15. State Government Finances, 2020

(Dollar amounts in thousands, percent distribution.)

Item	Dollars	Percent distribution
Total Revenue	12,707,247	100.0
General revenue	11,041,709	86.9
Intergovernmental revenue	4,777,882	37.6
Taxes	4,851,219	38.2
General sales	1666718	13.1
Selective sales	735,015	5.8
License taxes	284,666	2.2
Individual income tax	1843459	14.5
Corporate income tax	216,131	1.7
Other taxes	105,230	0.8
Current charges	923,572	7.3
Miscellaneous general revenue	489,036	3.8
Utility revenue	8,620	0.1
Liquor stores revenue	218520	1.7
Insurance trust revenue[1]	1,438,398	11.3
Total Expenditure	10,954,376	100.0
Intergovernmental expenditure	1,522,381	13.9
Direct expenditure	9,431,995	86.1
Current operation	7,053,279	64.4
Capital outlay	484,053	4.4
Insurance benefits and repayments	1,502,729	13.7
Assistance and subsidies	207,517	1.9
Interest on debt	184,417	1.7
Exhibit: Salaries and wages	1,143,472	10.4
Total Expenditure	10,954,376	100.0
General expenditure	9,280,336	84.7
Intergovernmental expenditure	1,522,381	13.9
Direct expenditure	7,757,955	70.8
General expenditure, by function:		
Education	2,358,441	21.5
Public welfare	3,874,009	35.4
Hospitals	105,846	1.0
Health	221,213	2.0
Highways	908,248	8.3
Police protection	96,906	0.9
Correction	170,292	1.6
Natural resources	153,897	1.4
Parks and recreation	8,851	0.1
Governmental administration	522,920	4.8
Interest on general debt	184,417	1.7
Other and unallocable	635,736	5.8
Utility expenditure	26,522	0.2
Liquor stores expenditure	144789	1.1
Insurance trust expenditure	1,502,729	13.7
Debt at End of Fiscal Year	5,151,077	X
Cash and Security Holdings	23,745,748	X

X = Not applicable.
- = Zero or rounds to zero.
[1] Within insurance trust revenue, net earnings of state retirement systems is a calculated statistic (the item code in the data file is X08), and thus can be positive or negative. Net earnings is the sum of earnings on investments plus gains on investments minus losses on investments. The change made in 2002 for asset valuation from book to market value in accordance with Statement 34 of the Governmental Accounting Standards Board is reflected in the calculated statistics.

Table ME-16. State Government Tax Collections, 2021

(Dollars in thousands, percent.)

Item	Dollars	Percent distribution
Total Taxes	5,452,250	100.0
Property taxes	44,636	0.8
Sales and gross receipts	2,629,517	48.2
General sales and gross receipts	1,909,696	35.0
Selective sales and gross receipts	719,821	13.2
Alcoholic beverages	18,461	0.3
Amusements	43,368	0.8
Insurance premiums	101,947	1.9
Motor fuels	231,938	4.3
Pari-mutuels	1,141	-
Public utilities	21,732	0.4
Tobacco products	144,593	2.7
Other selective sales	156,641	2.9
Licenses	325,922	6.0
Alcoholic beverages	8,499	0.2
Amusements	404	-
Corporations in general	15,039	0.3
Hunting and fishing	19,749	0.4
Motor vehicle	126,182	2.3
Motor vehicle operators	13,178	0.2
Public utilities	X	-
Occupation and business, NEC	130,503	2.4
Other licenses	12,368	0.2
Income taxes	2,359,590	43.3
Individual income	2,075,273	38.1
Corporation net income	284,317	5.2
Other taxes	92,585	1.7
Death and gift	40,399	0.7
Documentary and stock transfer	52,186	1.0
Severance	X	-
Taxes, NEC	0	-

X = Not applicable.
- = Zero or rounds to zero.

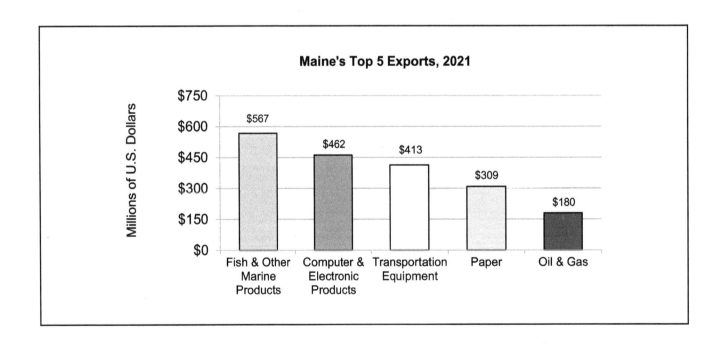

Maine's Top 5 Exports, 2021

MARYLAND

Facts and Figures

Location: Eastern United States; bordered on the N by Pennsylvania, on the E by Delaware and the Atlantic Ocean, and on the S and W by Virginia and West Virginia

Area: 12,407 sq. mi. (32,133 sq. km.); rank—42nd

Population: 6,165,129 (2021 est.); rank—19th

Principal Cities: capital—Annapolis; largest—Baltimore

Statehood: April 28, 1788; 7th state

U.S. Congress: 2 senators, 8 representatives

State Motto: *Fatti maschii parole femine* ("Manly deeds, womanly words")

State Song: "Maryland, My Maryland"

State Nicknames: The Old Line State; The Free State

Abbreviations: MD; Md.

State Symbols: flower—black-eyed susan; tree—white oak; bird—Baltimore oriole

At a Glance

- With an increase in population of 6.8 percent, Maryland ranked 22nd among the states in growth from 2010 to 2021.

- Maryland's 2020 median household income of $87,063 was the 2nd highest in the country, and its poverty rate of 9.0 percent was the 2nd lowest among the states.

- Approximately 31.4 percent of Marylanders self-identified their race as "Black or African American alone" in 2021, which was the 5th highest percentage in the country.

- Maryland's violent crime rate in 2020 was 399.9 per 100,000 population, compared to 398.5 for the entire nation.

- In 2020, 5.9 percent of all Marylanders were uninsured, compared to the national average of 8.7 percent uninsured.

Table MD-1. Population by Age, Sex, Race, and Hispanic Origin

(Number, percent, except where noted.)

Sex, age, race, and Hispanic origin	2000	2010	2021	Percent change, 2010–2021
Total Population	5,296,486	5,773,552	6,165,129	6.8
Percent of total U.S. population	1.9	1.9	1.9	X
Sex				
Male	2,557,794	2,791,762	3,002,424	7.5
Female	2,738,692	2,981,790	3,162,705	6.1
Age				
Under 5 years	353,393	364,488	354,588	-2.7
5 to 19 years	1,139,572	1,152,138	1,164,643	1.1
20 to 64 years	3,204,214	3,549,284	3,642,741	2.6
65 years and over	599,307	707,642	1,003,157	41.8
Median age (years)	36.0	38.0	39.3	3.4
Race and Hispanic Origin				
One race				
White	3,391,308	3,542,379	3,560,883	0.5
Black	1,477,411	1,731,513	1,937,665	11.9
American Indian and Alaska Native	15,423	30,885	40,213	30.2
Asian	210,929	326,655	427,264	30.8
Native Hawaiian or Other Pacific Islander	2,303	5,391	7,676	42.4
Two or more races	103,587	137,729	191,428	39.0
Hispanic (of any race)	227,916	493,811	684,437	38.6

NOTE: Population figures for 2021 are July 1 estimates. The 2000 and 2010 estimates are taken from the respective censuses.
- = Zero or rounds to zero.
X = Not applicable.

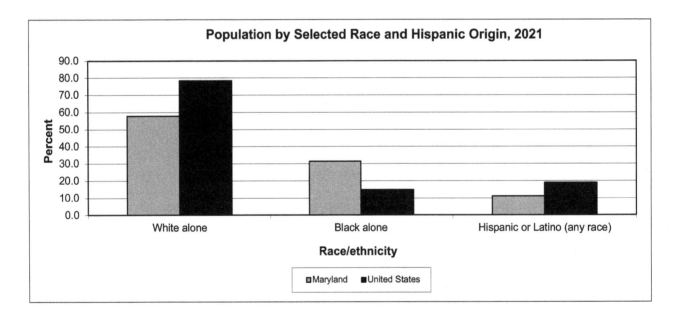

Table MD-2. Marital Status

(Number, percent distribution.)

Sex, age, race, and Hispanic origin	2000	2010	2020 [1]
Males, 15 Years and Over	1,972,921	2,232,162	2,357,559
Never married	31.0	36.8	37.8
Now married, except separated	56.3	50.2	49.8
Separated	2.8	2.3	1.8
Widowed	2.5	2.7	2.5
Divorced	7.4	8.0	8.2
Females, 15 Years and Over	2,186,715	2,442,021	2,566,982
Never married	26.8	32.2	33.1
Now married, except separated	49.7	45.3	44.8
Separated	3.4	2.9	2.1
Widowed	10.1	9.0	8.5
Divorced	10.1	10.7	11.5

[1] 2020 ACS 5-Year estimates. 1-Year estimates were not released for 2020 due to the impact of COVID-19 on data collection that year.

Table MD-3. Households and Housing Characteristics

(Number, percent, dollars.)

Item	2000	2010	2020 [1]	Average annual percent change, 2010–2020
Total Households..	1,980,859	2,127,439	2,230,527	0.7
Family households...	1,359,318	1,431,958	1,479,378	0.5
Married-couple family..	994,549	1,022,613	1,062,391	0.6
Other family...	364,789	409,345	416,987	0.3
Male householder, no wife present.................................	84,893	104,112	105,003	0.1
Female householder, no husband present.........................	279,876	305,233	311,984	0.3
Nonfamily households..	621,541	695,481	751,149	1.1
Householder living alone..	495,459	570,388	613,024	1.1
Householder not living alone...	126,082	125,093	138,125	1.5
Housing Characteristics				
Total housing units..	2,145,283	2,380,605	2,459,650	0.5
Occupied housing units...	1,980,859	2,127,439	2,230,527	0.7
Owner occupied..	1,341,751	1,426,267	1,495,828	0.7
Renter occupied...	639,108	701,172	734,699	0.7
Average household size...	2.61	2.65	2.64	-0.1
Financial Characteristics				
Median gross rent of renter-occupied housing	689	1,131	1,415	3.6
Median monthly owner costs for housing units with a mortgage	1,296	2,016	2,038	0.2
Median value of owner-occupied housing units.....................	146,000	301,400	325,400	1.1

[1] 2020 ACS 5-Year estimates. 1-Year estimates were not released for 2020 due to the impact of COVID-19 on data collection that year.

Table MD-4. Migration, Origin, and Language

(Number, percent.)

Characteristic	State	U.S.
	2016-2020 [1]	2016-2020 [1]
Residence 1 Year Ago		
Population 1 year and over	5,971,717	322,943,283
Same house...	86.8	86.2
Different house in the U.S...	12.5	13.2
Same county..	6.8	7.7
Different county	5.6	5.5
Same state..	3.0	3.2
Different state..	2.7	2.3
Abroad..	0.7	0.6
Place of Birth		
Native born	5,121,557	282,443,680
Male..	48.5	49.4
Female...	51.5	50.6
Foreign born	916,067	44,125,628
Male	48.1	48.6
Female...	51.9	51.4
Foreign born; naturalized U.S. citizen...	487,295	22,456,684
Male..	46.0	46.1
Female...	54.0	53.9
Foreign born; not a U.S. citizen...	428,772	21,668,944
Male..	50.4	51.1
Female...	49.6	48.9
Entered 2010 or later	24.9	22.8
Entered 2000 to 2009	29.6	25.1
Entered before 2000..	45.5	52.1
World Region of Birth, Foreign		
Foreign-born population, excluding population born at sea	916,067	44,125,628
Europe..	9.0	10.8
Asia...	32.4	31.3
Africa...	18.3	5.4
Oceania..	0.3	0.6
Latin America...	39.0	50.0
North America...	1.0	1.9
Language Spoken at Home and Ability to Speak English		
Population 5 years and over..	5,674,006	306,919,116
English only...	81.0	78.5
Language other than English...	19.0	21.5
Speaks English less than "very well"..	7.0	8.2

[1] 2020 ACS 5-Year estimates. 1-Year estimates were not released for 2020 due to the impact of COVID-19 on data collection that year.
NA = Not available.
X = Not applicable.
- = Zero or rounds to zero.

Table MD-5. Median Income and Poverty Status, 2020[1]

(Number, percent, except as noted.)

Characteristic	State Number	State Percent	U.S. Number	U.S. Percent
Median Income				
Households (dollars)...	87,063	X	64,994	X
Families (dollars)	105,790	X	80,069	X
Below Poverty Level (All People)	531,553	9.0	40,910,326	12.8
Sex				
Male	229,901	8.1	18,171,512	11.6
Female	301,652	9.9	22,738,814	14.0
Age				
Under 18 years..	153,356	11.6	12,598,699	17.5
Related children under 18 years..	148,796	11.3	12,306,532	17.2
18 to 64 years...	306,634	8.4	23,554,920	12.1
65 years and over	71,563	7.9	4,756,707	9.3

X = Not applicable.
[1] 2020 ACS 5-Year estimates. 1-Year estimates were not released for 2020 due to the impact of COVID-19 on data collection that year.

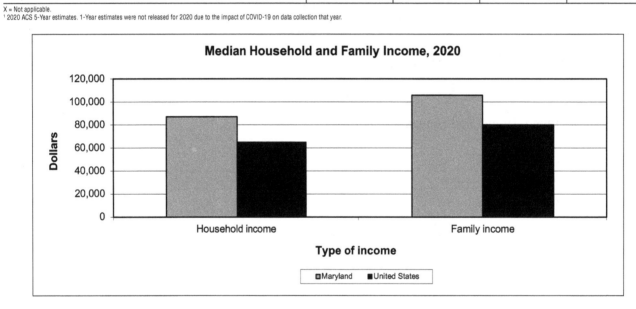

Median Household and Family Income, 2020

☐ Maryland ■ United States

Table MD-6. Health Insurance Coverage Status for the Civilian Noninstitutionalized Population and Children Under 19 Years of Age

(Number, percent.)

Item	2011	2012	2013	2014	2015	2016	2017	2018	2019	2020[2]
Civilian Noninstitutionalized Population	5,736,588	5,788,196	5,834,039	5,885,847	5,908,522	5,918,535	5,957,871	5,943,064	5,945,846	5,938,200
Covered by Private or Public Insurance										
Number..	5,138,144	5,190,642	5,240,861	5,422,579	5,519,323	5,555,356	5,592,274	5,586,356	5,589,015	5,586,014
Percent...	89.6	89.7	89.8	92.1	93.4	93.9	93.9	94.0	94.0	94.1
Uninsured										
Number..	598,444	597,554	593,178	463,268	389,199	363,179	365,597	356,708	356,831	352,186
Percent...	10.4	10.3	10.2	7.9	6.6	6.1	6.1	6.0	6.0	5.9
Percent in the U.S. not covered.................	15.1	14.8	14.5	11.7	9.4	8.6	8.7	8.9	9.2	8.7
Children Under 19 Years of Age[1]	1,344,498	1,341,118	1,343,118	1,349,767	1,346,154	1,344,588	1,419,540	1,420,111	1,410,735	1,417,908
Covered by Private or Public Insurance										
Number..	1,283,012	1,289,667	1,283,833	1,307,172	1,293,887	1,299,633	1,365,464	1,373,341	1,362,953	1,368,443
Percent...	95.4	96.2	95.6	96.8	96.1	96.7	96.2	96.7	96.6	96.5
Uninsured										
Number..	61,486	51,451	59,285	42,595	52,267	44,955	54,076	46,770	47,782	49,465
Percent...	4.6	3.8	4.4	3.2	3.9	3.3	3.8	3.3	3.4	3.5
Percent in the U.S. not covered.................	7.5	7.2	7.1	6.0	4.8	4.5	5.0	5.2	5.7	5.2

[1] Data for years prior to 2017 are for individuals under 18 years of age.
[2] 2020 ACS 5-Year estimates. 1-Year estimates were not released for 2020 due to the impact of COVID-19 on data collection that year. Data is not comparable to previous years, which are based on 1-year estimates.

Table MD-7. Employment Status by Demographic Group, 2021

(Numbers in thousands, percent.)

Characteristic	Civilian noninstitutional population	Civilian labor force		Employed		Unemployed	
		Number	Percent of population	Number	Percent of population	Number	Percent of population
Total...	4,773	3,135	65.7	2,960	62.0	175	5.6
Sex							
Male...	2,258	1,620	71.7	1,527	67.6	93	5.7
Female...	2,515	1,515	60.2	1,433	57.0	83	5.4
Race, Sex, and Hispanic Origin							
White...	2,742	1,776	64.8	1,690	61.6	85	4.8
Male..	1,343	976	72.6	931	69.3	45	4.6
Female..	1,399	800	57.2	759	54.3	41	5.1
Black or African American....................	1,473	990	67.2	918	62.3	72	7.3
Male..	659	456	69.1	419	63.5	37	8.1
Female..	814	534	65.6	499	61.4	35	6.5
Hispanic or Latino ethnicity[1]...............	378	271	71.7	257	68.0	14	5.1
Male..	201	168	83.3	163	81.3	4	2.4
Female..	177	104	58.5	94	52.9	10	9.5
Age							
16 to 19 years...................................	NA	NA	NA	NA	NA	NA	NA
20 to 24 years...................................	393	283	72.0	243	61.9	40	14.1
25 to 34 years...................................	779	630	80.9	580	74.4	51	8.0
35 to 44 years...................................	781	666	85.3	639	81.7	28	4.2
45 to 54 years...................................	707	602	85.1	580	82.1	21	3.5
55 to 64 years...................................	861	625	72.6	608	70.6	17	2.7
65 years and over..............................	982	230	23.4	222	22.6	8	3.3

NOTE: Data in Table 7 are from the Current Population Survey (CPS) and do not match the estimates in Table 8. See notes and definitions for further information.
[1] May be of any race.

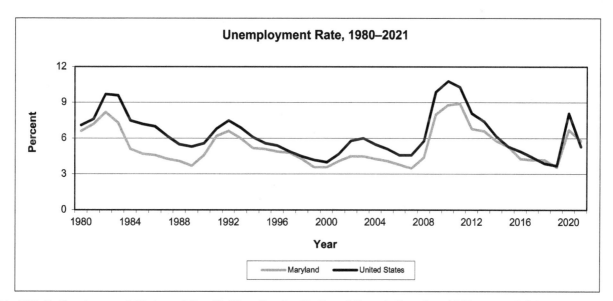

Unemployment Rate, 1980–2021

Table MD-8. Employment Status of the Civilian Noninstitutional Population Age 16 Years and Over

(Number, percent.)

Year	Civilian labor force	Civilian participation rate	Employed	Unemployed	Unemployment rate
2010..............................	3,078,368	68.6	2,836,945	241,423	7.8
2011..............................	3,097,300	68.0	2,870,857	226,443	7.3
2012..............................	3,120,947	67.8	2,906,518	214,429	6.9
2013..............................	3,128,908	67.4	2,924,626	204,282	6.5
2014..............................	3,125,017	66.9	2,945,911	179,106	5.7
2015..............................	3,139,988	66.8	2,983,083	156,905	5.0
2016..............................	3,155,918	66.9	3,020,827	135,091	4.3
2017..............................	3,243,896	67.6	3,114,580	129,316	4.0
2018..............................	3,261,068	67.6	3,142,323	118,745	3.6
2019..............................	3,326,497	68.6	3,212,155	114,342	3.4
2020..............................	3,227,527	66.4	3,012,106	215,421	6.7
2021..............................	3,175,550	65.3	2,992,228	183,322	5.8

Table MD-9. Employment and Average Wages by Industry

(Estimates are based on the 2012 North American Industry Classification System [NAICS].)

Industry	2013	2014	2015	2016	2017	2018	2019	2020
	Number of Jobs							
Wage and Salary Employment by Industry	2,702,351	2,727,672	2,767,425	2,804,311	2,828,811	2,859,504	2,880,591	2,689,103
Farm Wage and Salary Employment	5,973	6,416	6,214	7,499	7,224	7,046	6,467	5,450
Nonfarm Wage and Salary Employment	2,696,378	2,721,256	2,761,211	2,796,812	2,821,587	2,852,458	2,874,124	2,683,653
Private wage and salary employment	2,127,875	2,154,238	2,194,027	2,229,746	2,252,674	2,280,274	2,301,259	2,122,910
Forestry, fishing, and related activities	2,012	2,049	2,148	2,180	2,143	2,099	2,193	1,935
Mining	1,340	1,260	1,297	1,165	1,147	1,115	1,128	1,114
Utilities	9,781	9,738	9,579	9,836	9,760	9,729	9,633	9,669
Construction	150,016	153,215	158,344	165,045	165,951	167,025	169,933	164,284
Manufacturing	106,376	103,372	103,588	103,395	106,654	109,795	112,356	108,662
Durable goods manufacturing	56,308	53,737	54,416	53,950	55,618	57,992	58,413	56,650
Nondurable goods manufacturing	50,068	49,635	49,172	49,445	51,036	51,803	53,943	52,012
Wholesale trade	86,166	85,221	86,291	86,195	86,660	85,555	86,778	81,735
Retail trade	286,362	288,620	291,328	291,889	289,803	286,043	280,400	257,358
Transportation and warehousing	69,178	71,829	77,313	78,919	81,963	87,154	92,841	99,112
Information	39,537	38,977	38,457	38,667	37,633	36,233	35,689	33,049
Finance and insurance	99,368	98,448	99,469	100,123	98,738	98,129	96,011	94,413
Real estate and rental and leasing	44,037	44,236	45,492	45,800	48,103	47,675	47,319	43,697
Professional, scientific, and technical services	237,217	241,058	243,808	248,333	248,745	254,090	260,349	258,310
Management of companies and enterprises	25,906	25,570	25,198	26,278	26,043	27,429	28,666	27,640
Administrative and waste services	156,609	159,631	164,658	171,021	171,937	174,381	175,998	159,609
Educational services	71,879	73,895	74,754	77,105	79,593	83,226	84,123	77,452
Health care and social assistance	345,961	349,793	359,018	366,468	373,141	380,290	385,588	362,440
Arts, entertainment, and recreation	42,270	45,412	45,917	46,235	47,084	48,202	45,850	30,977
Accommodation and food services	213,420	217,225	223,139	228,047	235,163	235,748	238,666	181,742
Other services, except public administration	140,440	144,689	144,229	143,045	142,413	146,356	147,738	129,712
Government and government enterprises	568,503	567,018	567,184	567,066	568,913	572,184	572,865	560,743
	Dollars							
Average Wages and Salaries by Industry	55,555	56,911	58,701	59,587	61,133	62,831	64,626	70,446
Average Farm Wages and Salaries	25,305	24,960	21,052	20,019	18,860	23,620	20,434	23,549
Average Nonfarm Wages and Salaries	55,622	56,987	58,786	59,693	61,242	62,928	64,726	70,541
Average private wages and salaries	53,220	54,484	56,173	57,088	58,632	60,248	61,942	67,853
Forestry, fishing, and related activities	28,744	29,364	30,863	32,305	33,701	34,323	35,944	38,153
Mining	60,106	62,669	61,487	68,482	71,257	70,505	72,529	71,979
Utilities	115,067	114,555	122,170	123,671	129,820	130,278	134,708	133,563
Construction	57,115	59,213	61,090	63,514	66,103	67,092	68,921	71,894
Manufacturing	70,972	72,408	75,452	75,788	79,280	80,629	81,286	87,904
Durable goods manufacturing	78,362	78,132	80,302	82,117	84,914	85,464	88,342	93,505
Nondurable goods manufacturing	62,661	66,210	70,084	68,883	73,140	75,217	73,644	81,803
Wholesale trade	75,204	77,533	79,704	79,625	80,876	83,508	84,582	89,759
Retail trade	29,502	30,137	31,544	31,935	32,526	33,523	34,597	38,097
Transportation and warehousing	50,614	53,256	54,576	54,904	54,494	54,809	52,736	53,480
Information	83,111	85,334	86,578	90,327	90,499	95,389	101,228	113,754
Finance and insurance	93,248	96,713	100,457	103,524	106,609	110,903	116,411	129,924
Real estate and rental and leasing	58,010	60,650	62,817	63,249	65,219	66,813	67,479	73,715
Professional, scientific, and technical services	90,280	92,647	94,261	95,588	97,803	100,999	105,131	110,775
Management of companies and enterprises	107,487	111,217	116,537	112,929	123,799	126,010	128,106	126,604
Administrative and waste services	39,506	40,229	42,003	42,838	44,869	45,440	46,282	51,061
Educational services	47,722	49,286	50,578	50,678	51,205	52,500	52,807	57,846
Health care and social assistance	49,977	51,012	52,786	53,166	54,291	55,420	56,701	61,165
Arts, entertainment, and recreation	32,623	33,114	34,714	36,461	37,046	36,477	36,391	44,052
Accommodation and food services	21,283	21,879	22,668	23,458	24,789	26,183	27,203	26,979
Other services, except public administration	37,724	38,414	39,904	41,073	42,745	44,080	45,128	49,102
Government and government enterprises	64,615	66,494	68,891	69,937	71,575	73,608	75,909	80,719

Table MD-10. Employment Characteristics by Family Type

(Number, percent.)

Family type and labor force status	2018		2019		2020 [1]	
	Total	Families with own children under 18 years	Total	Families with own children under 18 years	Total	Families with own children under 18 years
All Families..	1,472,372	616,144	1,462,070	608,132	1,479,378	626,188
FAMILY TYPE AND LABOR FORCE STATUS						
Opposite-Sex Married-Couple Families.............................	1,069,433	424,341	1,051,319	418,663	1,051,014	425,831
Both husband and wife in labor force....................	57.4	74.0	57.9	74.7	58.7	74.4
Husband in labor force, wife not in labor force	18.7	21.0	18.0	20.5	19.0	21.5
Wife in labor force, husband not in labor force	7.5	3.4	7.9	3.1	7.5	3.2
Both husband and wife not in labor force....................	15.2	0.8	15.2	0.9	14.8	0.9
Other Families	402,939	191,803	410,751	189,469	416,987	197,563
Female householder, no spouse present	74.8	75.6	74.0	74.8	74.8	75.2
In labor force....................................	55.5	66.5	54.8	65.4	55.8	66.1
Not in labor force	19.2	9.1	19.2	9.4	19.0	9.1
Male householder, no spouse present........................	25.2	24.4	26.0	25.2	25.2	24.8
In labor force....................................	20.6	23.1	21.4	24.4	20.8	23.6
Not in labor force	4.6	1.3	4.6	0.8	4.4	1.2

[1] 2020 ACS 5-Year estimates. 1-Year estimates were not released for 2020 due to the impact of COVID-19 on data collection that year. Data is not comparable to previous years, which are based on 1-year estimates.

Table MD-11. School Enrollment and Educational Attainment, 2020[1]

(Number, percent.)

Item	State	U.S.
Enrollment		
Total population 3 years and over, enrolled in school	1,520,676	80,497,960
Enrolled in nursery school or preschool (percent)......................	6.3	6.1
Enrolled in kindergarten (percent)......................	4.7	5.0
Enrolled in elementary school, grades 1-8 (percent)......................	39.1	40.4
Enrolled in high school, grades 9-12 (percent)......................	20.3	21.0
Enrolled in college or graduate school (percent)......................	29.6	27.6
Attainment		
Total population 25 years and over	4,164,698	222,836,834
Less than ninth grade (percent)......................	3.9	4.9
9th to 12th grade, no diploma (percent)......................	5.6	6.6
High school graduate, including equivalency (percent)......................	24.2	26.7
Some college, no degree (percent)......................	18.7	20.3
Associate's degree (percent)......................	6.8	8.6
Bachelor's degree (percent)......................	21.8	20.2
Graduate or professional degree (percent)......................	19.1	12.7
High school graduate or higher (percent)......................	90.6	88.5
Bachelor's degree or higher (percent)......................	40.9	32.9

[1] 2020 ACS 5-Year estimates. 1-Year estimates were not released for 2020 due to the impact of COVID-19 on data collection that year.

Table MD-12. Public School Characteristics and Educational Indicators

(Number, percent; data derived from National Center of Education Statistics.)

Item	State	U.S.
Public Elementary and Secondary Schools		
Number of regular school districts, 2018-19......................	24	13,452
Number of operational schools, 2019-20......................	1,420	98,469
Percent charter schools	3.2	7.7
Total public school enrollment, Fall 2019......................	909,404	50,796,445
Percent charter school enrollment	2.5	6.8
Student-teacher ratio, Fall 2019......................	14.8	15.9
Expenditures per student (unadjusted dollars), 2018-19......................	15,576	13,187
Four-year adjusted cohort graduation rate (ACGR), 2018-2019[1]......................	86.9	85.8
Students eligible for free or reduced-price lunch (percent), 2019-20......................	42.0	52.1
English language learners (percent), Fall 2019......................	10.6	10.4
Students age 3 to 21 served under IDEA, part B (percent), 2020-21	12.6	14.5

Public Schools by Type, 2019-20	Number	Percent of state public schools
Total number of schools......................	1,420	100.0
Special education......................	36	2.5
Vocational education......................	26	1.8
Alternative education......................	46	3.2

[1] Adjusted Cohort Graduation Rates (ACGR) differ from Averaged Freshmen Graduation Rates (AFGR).

Table MD-13. Reported Voting and Registration of the Voting-Age Population, November 2020

(Numbers in thousands, percent.)

Item	Total population	Total citizen population	Registered			Voted		
			Total registered	Percent registered (total population)	Percent registered (total citizen population)	Total voted	Percent voted (total population)	Percent voted (total citizen population)
U.S. Total	252,274	231,593	168,308	66.7	72.7	154,628	61.3	66.8
State Total	4,606	4,303	3,383	73.4	78.6	3,166	68.7	73.6
Sex								
Male	2,199	2,052	1,517	69.0	73.9	1,430	65.0	69.7
Female	2,407	2,251	1,865	77.5	82.9	1,737	72.2	77.2
Race								
White alone	2,757	2,650	2,069	75.0	78.1	1,917	69.5	72.3
White, non-Hispanic alone	2,487	2,469	1,934	77.8	78.3	1,786	71.8	72.3
Black alone	1,421	1,289	1,022	71.9	79.3	971	68.3	75.3
Asian alone	302	239	166	55.0	69.7	153	50.6	64.1
Hispanic (of any race)	323	195	150	46.2	76.7	145	44.9	74.4
White alone or in combination	2,840	2,732	2,151	75.7	78.7	1,999	70.4	73.2
Black alone or in combination	1,482	1,350	1,083	73.1	80.2	1,032	69.6	76.4
Asian alone or in combination	337	273	201	59.7	73.5	187	55.6	68.6
Age								
18 to 24 years	573	530	413	72.0	77.8	375	65.4	70.7
25 to 34 years	754	684	517	68.6	75.6	460	61.0	67.3
35 to 44 years	726	655	534	73.5	81.5	498	68.6	76.0
45 to 64 years	1,542	1,447	1,125	72.9	77.7	1,080	70.0	74.6
65 years and over	1,010	986	794	78.6	80.5	753	74.5	76.4

Table MD-14. Crime

(Number, rate per 100,000. Data are derived from the FBI Uniform Crime Reports.)

Item	State [3]			U.S.		
	2019	2020	Percent change	2019	2020	Percent change
TOTAL POPULATION[1]	6,054,954	6,055,802	-	328,329,953	329,484,123	0.4
VIOLENT CRIME						
Number	27,511	24,215	-12.0	1,250,393	1,313,105	5.0
Rate	454.4	399.9	-12.0	380.8	398.5	4.6
Murder and Nonnegligent Manslaughter						
Number	545	553	1.5	16,669	21,570	29.4
Rate	9.0	9.1	1.5	5.1	6.5	28.9
Rape[2]						
Number	1,944	1,732	-10.9	143,224	126,430	-11.7
Rate	32.1	28.6	-10.9	43.6	38.4	-12.0
Robbery						
Number	9,215	7,174	-22.1	268,483	243,600	-9.3
Rate	152.2	118.5	-22.2	81.8	73.9	-9.6
Aggravated Assault						
Number	15,807	14,756	-6.6	822,017	921,505	12.1
Rate	261.1	243.7	-6.7	250.4	279.7	11.7
PROPERTY CRIME						
Number	118,091	97,487	-17.4	6,995,235	6,452,038	-7.8
Rate	1,950.3	1,609.8	-17.5	2,130.6	1,958.2	-8.1
Burglary						
Number	16,872	15,261	-9.5	1,118,096	1,035,314	-7.4
Rate	278.6	252.0	-9.6	340.5	314.2	-7.7
Larceny-Theft						
Number	89,938	71,757	-20.2	5,152,267	4,606,324	-10.6
Rate	1,485.4	1,184.9	-20.2	1,569.2	1,398.0	-10.9
Motor Vehicle Theft						
Number	11,281	10,469	-7.2	724,872	810,400	11.8
Rate	186.3	172.9	-7.2	220.8	246.0	11.4

NOTE: Although arson data are included in the trend and clearance tables, sufficient data are not available to estimate totals for this offense. Therefore, no arson data are published in this table.
- = Zero or rounds to zero.
[1] Population figures are U.S. Census Bureau provisional estimates as of July 1, 2020.
[2] The figures shown in the rape (revised definition) column were estimated using the revised Uniform Crime Reporting (UCR) definition of rape.
[3] Limited data for 2020 were available for Alabama, Maryland and Pennsylvania.

Table MD-15. State Government Finances, 2020

(Dollar amounts in thousands, percent distribution.)

Item	Dollars	Percent distribution
Total Revenue	52,422,740	100.0
General revenue	46,348,276	88.4
Intergovernmental revenue	15,700,504	29.9
Taxes	23,882,883	45.6
General sales	4936660	9.4
Selective sales	4,574,124	8.7
License taxes	800,356	1.5
Individual income tax	10698876	20.4
Corporate income tax	1,325,456	2.5
Other taxes	1,547,411	3.0
Current charges	4,242,448	8.1
Miscellaneous general revenue	2,522,441	4.8
Utility revenue	101,950	0.2
Liquor stores revenue	0	-
Insurance trust revenue[1]	5,972,514	11.4
Total Expenditure	53,537,920	100.0
Intergovernmental expenditure	10,468,957	19.6
Direct expenditure	43,068,963	80.4
Current operation	29,920,455	55.9
Capital outlay	3,618,201	6.8
Insurance benefits and repayments	6,311,897	11.8
Assistance and subsidies	1,878,715	3.5
Interest on debt	1,339,695	2.5
Exhibit: Salaries and wages	6,585,732	12.3
Total Expenditure	53,537,920	100.0
General expenditure	45,038,148	84.1
Intergovernmental expenditure	10,468,957	19.6
Direct expenditure	34,569,191	64.6
General expenditure, by function:		
Education	14,351,358	26.8
Public welfare	14,727,597	27.5
Hospitals	374,843	0.7
Health	3,710,759	6.9
Highways	2,640,718	4.9
Police protection	779,508	1.5
Correction	1,568,895	2.9
Natural resources	526,803	1.0
Parks and recreation	290,379	0.5
Governmental administration	1,775,016	3.3
Interest on general debt	1,339,695	2.5
Other and unallocable	2,749,223	5.1
Utility expenditure	2,307,476	4.4
Liquor stores expenditure	0	-
Insurance trust expenditure	6,311,897	11.8
Debt at End of Fiscal Year	29,359,300	X
Cash and Security Holdings	79,203,439	X

X = Not applicable.
- = Zero or rounds to zero.
[1] Within insurance trust revenue, net earnings of state retirement systems is a calculated statistic (the item code in the data file is X08), and thus can be positive or negative. Net earnings is the sum of earnings on investments plus gains on investments minus losses on investments. The change made in 2002 for asset valuation from book to market value in accordance with Statement 34 of the Governmental Accounting Standards Board is reflected in the calculated statistics.

Table MD-16. State Government Tax Collections, 2021

(Dollars in thousands, percent.)

Item	Dollars	Percent distribution
Total Taxes	25,220,541	100.0
Property taxes	893,215	3.5
Sales and gross receipts	10,587,203	42.0
General sales and gross receipts	5,458,909	21.6
Selective sales and gross receipts	5,128,294	20.3
Alcoholic beverages	38,941	0.2
Amusements	1,034,508	4.1
Insurance premiums	757,839	3.0
Motor fuels	1,025,338	4.1
Pari-mutuels	1,119	-
Public utilities	144,260	0.6
Tobacco products	388,243	1.5
Other selective sales	1,738,046	6.9
Licenses	969,440	3.8
Alcoholic beverages	849	-
Amusements	1,342	-
Corporations in general	168,085	0.7
Hunting and fishing	19,157	0.1
Motor vehicle	520,688	2.1
Motor vehicle operators	23,715	0.1
Public utilities	X	-
Occupation and business, NEC	233,561	0.9
Other licenses	2,043	-
Income taxes	12,026,945	47.7
Individual income	10,186,240	40.4
Corporation net income	1,840,705	7.3
Other taxes	743,738	2.9
Death and gift	240,585	1.0
Documentary and stock transfer	269,373	1.1
Severance	X	-
Taxes, NEC	233,780	0.9

X = Not applicable.
- = Zero or rounds to zero.

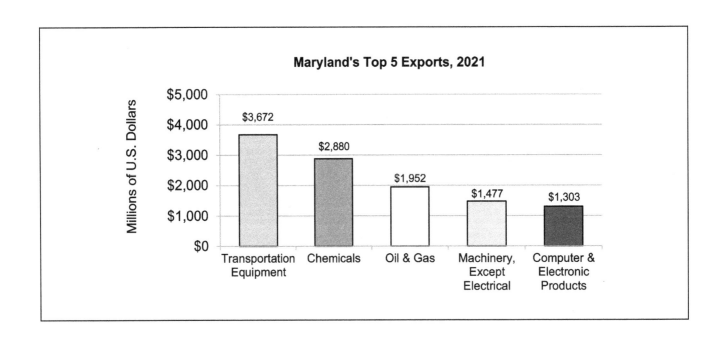

Maryland's Top 5 Exports, 2021

MASSACHUSETTS

Facts and Figures

Location: Northeastern United States; bordered on the N by Vermont and New Hampshire, on the E by the Atlantic Ocean, on the S by Connecticut and Rhode Island, and on the W by New York

Area: 10,555 sq. mi. (27,336 sq. km.); rank—44th

Population: 6,984,723 (2021 est.); rank—15th

Principal Cities: capital—Boston; largest—Boston

Statehood: February 6, 1788; 6th state

U.S. Congress: 2 senators, 9 representatives

State Motto: *Ense petit placidam sub libertate quietem* ("By the sword we seek peace, but peace only under liberty")

State Song: "All Hail to Massachusetts"

State Nickname: The Bay State

Abbreviations: MA; Mass.

State Symbols: flower—mayflower; tree—American elm; bird—chickadee

At a Glance

- With an increase in population of 6.7 percent, Massachusetts ranked 23rd among the states in growth from 2010 to 2021.

- Massachusetts's median household income in 2020 was $84,385, the 4th highest in the country.

- Approximately 9.8 percent of Massachusetts' population lived below the poverty level in 2020, compared to 12.8 percent of the entire U.S. population.

- Massachusetts's violent crime rate in 2020 was 308.8 per 100,000 population, compared to 398.5 for the entire nation.

- Massachusetts had the 2nd highest percent of people age 25 years and older with a bachelor's degree or more in 2020 (44.5 percent).

Table MA-1. Population by Age, Sex, Race, and Hispanic Origin

(Number, percent, except where noted.)

Sex, age, race, and Hispanic origin	2000	2010	2021	Percent change, 2010–2021
Total Population..	6,349,097	6,547,629	6,984,723	6.7
Percent of total U.S. population	2.3	2.1	2.1	X
Sex				
Male...	3,058,816	3,166,628	3,412,092	7.8
Female..	3,290,281	3,381,001	3,572,631	5.7
Age				
Under 5 years..	397,268	367,087	346,922	-5.5
5 to 19 years...	1,277,845	1,254,056	1,222,478	-2.5
20 to 64 years...	3,813,822	4,023,762	4,200,630	4.4
65 years and over...	860,162	902,724	1,214,693	34.6
Median age (years)	36.5	39.1	39.9	2.0
Race and Hispanic Origin				
One race				
White..	5,367,286	5,524,937	5,576,809	0.9
Black..	343,454	504,365	650,915	29.1
American Indian and Alaska Native	15,015	29,944	37,002	23.6
Asian..	238,124	359,673	525,188	46.0
Native Hawaiian or Other Pacific Islander	2,489	5,971	7,812	30.8
Two or more races	146,005	122,739	186,997	52.4
Hispanic (of any race)	428,729	656,888	897,349	36.6

NOTE: Population figures for 2021 are July 1 estimates. The 2000 and 2010 estimates are taken from the respective censuses.
- = Zero or rounds to zero.
X = Not applicable.

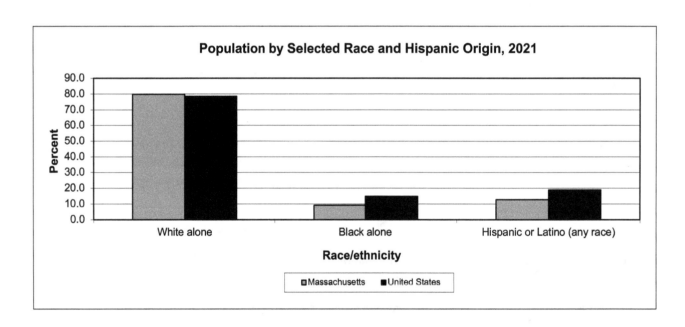

Population by Selected Race and Hispanic Origin, 2021

Table MA-2. Marital Status

(Number, percent distribution.)

Sex, age, race, and Hispanic origin	2000	2010	2020[1]
Males, 15 Years and Over	2,412,349	2,579,221	2,766,209
Never married	33.9	38.7	39.5
Now married, except separated..	54.7	49.1	48.7
Separated...	1.6	1.6	1.3
Widowed...	2.7	2.7	2.4
Divorced...	7.0	8.0	8.1
Females, 15 Years and Over	2,679,020	2,819,768	2,991,503
Never married	28.5	33.2	34.6
Now married, except separated..	48.9	44.1	44.6
Separated...	2.3	2.4	1.9
Widowed...	10.8	9.1	8.1
Divorced...	9.5	11.1	10.7

[1] 2020 ACS 5-Year estimates. 1-Year estimates were not released for 2020 due to the impact of COVID-19 on data collection that year.

Table MA-3. Households and Housing Characteristics

(Number, percent, dollars.)

Item	2000	2010	2020 [1]	Average annual percent change, 2010–2020
Total Households..	2,443,580	2,520,419	2,646,980	0.7
Family households..	1,576,696	1,590,257	1,673,992	0.8
Married-couple family..................................	1,197,917	1,166,204	1,240,714	0.9
Other family..	378,779	424,053	433,278	0.3
Male householder, no wife present..............	88,835	100,400	114,876	2.1
Female householder, no husband present......	289,944	323,653	318,402	-0.2
Nonfamily households.......................................	866,884	930,162	972,988	0.7
Householder living alone................................	684,345	736,320	751,536	0.3
Householder not living alone..........................	182,539	193,842	221,452	2.0
Housing Characteristics				
Total housing units..	2,621,989	2,808,727	2,913,009	0.5
Occupied housing units....................................	2,443,580	2,520,419	2,646,980	0.7
Owner occupied...	1,508,052	1,568,382	1,654,892	0.8
Renter occupied..	935,528	952,037	992,088	0.6
Average household size....................................	2.51	2.51	2.50	-0.1
Financial Characteristics				
Median gross rent of renter-occupied housing	684	1,009	1,336	4.6
Median monthly owner costs for housing units with a mortgage	1,353	2,036	2,268	1.6
Median value of owner-occupied housing units........	185,700	334,100	398,800	2.8

[1] 2020 ACS 5-Year estimates. 1-Year estimates were not released for 2020 due to the impact of COVID-19 on data collection that year.

Table MA-4. Migration, Origin, and Language

(Number, percent.)

Characteristic	State 2016-2020 [1]	U.S. 2016-2020 [1]
Residence 1 Year Ago		
Population 1 year and over..	6,806,326	322,943,283
Same house..	87.4	86.2
Different house in the U.S...	11.6	13.2
Same county..	6.6	7.7
Different county...	5.0	5.5
Same state..	2.9	3.2
Different state...	2.2	2.3
Abroad..	0.9	0.6
Place of Birth		
Native born..	5,714,094	282,443,680
Male	48.6	49.4
Female	51.4	50.6
Foreign born..	1,158,909	44,125,628
Male	48.0	48.6
Female	52.0	51.4
Foreign born; naturalized U.S. citizen............................	627,843	22,456,684
Male	45.7	46.1
Female	54.3	53.9
Foreign born; not a U.S. citizen....................................	531,066	21,668,944
Male	50.8	51.1
Female	49.2	48.9
Entered 2010 or later	29.4	22.8
Entered 2000 to 2009	24.5	25.1
Entered before 2000...	46.2	52.1
World Region of Birth, Foreign		
Foreign-born population, excluding population born at sea	1,158,909	44,125,628
Europe	20.0	10.8
Asia..	31.1	31.3
Africa	9.3	5.4
Oceania	0.3	0.6
Latin America..	36.7	50.0
North America...	2.5	1.9
Language Spoken at Home and Ability to Speak English		
Population 5 years and over..	6,514,973	306,919,116
English only	76.1	78.5
Language other than English...	23.9	21.5
Speaks English less than "very well"..........................	9.2	8.2

[1] 2020 ACS 5-Year estimates. 1-Year estimates were not released for 2020 due to the impact of COVID-19 on data collection that year.
NA = Not available.
X = Not applicable.
- = Zero or rounds to zero.

Table MA-5. Median Income and Poverty Status, 2020[1]

(Number, percent, except as noted.)

Characteristic	State		U.S.	
	Number	Percent	Number	Percent
Median Income				
Households (dollars)..........	84,385	X	64,994	X
Families (dollars)	106,526	X	80,069	X
Below Poverty Level (All People)	653,454	9.8	40,910,326	12.8
Sex				
Male	283,099	8.8	18,171,512	11.6
Female	370,355	10.8	22,738,814	14.0
Age				
Under 18 years..........	164,081	12.2	12,598,699	17.5
Related children under 18 years..........	159,073	11.9	12,306,532	17.2
18 to 64 years..........	391,040	9.3	23,554,920	12.1
65 years and over	98,333	8.9	4,756,707	9.3

X = Not applicable.
[1] 2020 ACS 5-Year estimates. 1-Year estimates were not released for 2020 due to the impact of COVID-19 on data collection that year.

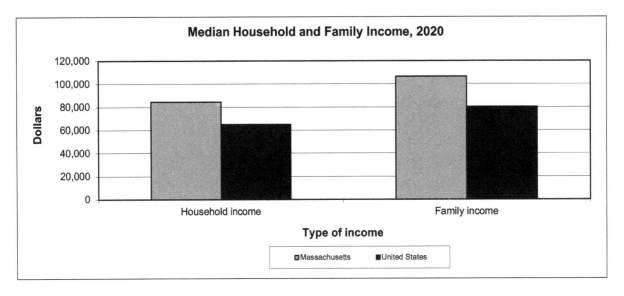

Table MA-6. Health Insurance Coverage Status for the Civilian Noninstitutionalized Population and Children Under 19 Years of Age

(Number, percent.)

Item	2011	2012	2013	2014	2015	2016	2017	2018	2019	2020 [2]
Civilian Noninstitutionalized Population	6,507,596	6,566,851	6,613,654	6,668,348	6,718,090	6,736,017	6,785,622	6,830,796	6,820,969	6,800,682
Covered by Private or Public Insurance										
Number..........	6,230,656	6,312,556	6,366,988	6,449,626	6,528,817	6,564,958	6,595,821	6,641,889	6,616,890	6,614,995
Percent..........	95.7	96.1	96.3	96.7	97.2	97.5	97.2	97.2	97.0	97.3
Uninsured										
Number..........	276,940	254,295	246,666	218,722	189,273	171,059	189,801	188,907	204,079	185,687
Percent..........	4.3	3.9	3.7	3.3	2.8	2.5	2.8	2.8	3.0	2.7
Percent in the U.S. not covered..........	15.1	14.8	14.5	11.7	9.4	8.6	8.7	8.9	9.2	8.7
Children Under 19 Years of Age[1]	1,401,873	1,397,972	1,389,165	1,387,398	1,383,924	1,375,244	1,478,961	1,470,670	1,446,247	1,464,881
Covered by Private or Public Insurance										
Number..........	1,377,774	1,377,766	1,368,086	1,366,087	1,368,039	1,362,535	1,457,076	1,452,714	1,424,224	1,443,612
Percent..........	98.3	98.6	98.5	98.5	98.9	99.1	98.5	98.8	98.5	98.5
Uninsured										
Number..........	24,099	20,206	21,079	21,311	15,885	12,709	21,885	17,956	22,023	21,269
Percent..........	1.7	1.4	1.5	1.5	1.1	0.9	1.5	1.2	1.5	1.5
Percent in the U.S. not covered..........	7.5	7.2	7.1	6.0	4.8	4.5	5.0	5.2	5.7	5.2

[1] Data for years prior to 2017 are for individuals under 18 years of age.
[2] 2020 ACS 5-Year estimates. 1-Year estimates were not released for 2020 due to the impact of COVID-19 on data collection that year. Data is not comparable to previous years, which are based on 1-year estimates.

Table MA-7. Employment Status by Demographic Group, 2021

(Numbers in thousands, percent.)

Characteristic	Civilian noninstitutional population	Civilian labor force		Employed		Unemployed	
		Number	Percent of population	Number	Percent of population	Number	Percent of population
Total...	5,643	3,679	65.2	3,466	61.4	212	5.8
Sex							
Male..	2,705	1,888	69.8	1,768	65.4	120	6.4
Female	2,938	1,790	60.9	1,698	57.8	92	5.1
Race, Sex, and Hispanic Origin							
White	4,508	2,905	64.4	2,756	61.1	149	5.1
Male......................................	2,167	1,495	69.0	1,412	65.2	83	5.5
Female	2,340	1,410	60.3	1,344	57.4	66	4.7
Black or African American..............	488	324	66.4	295	60.4	29	9.1
Male......................................	233	160	68.9	145	62.2	16	9.8
Female	255	164	64.1	150	58.8	14	8.3
Hispanic or Latino ethnicity[1]	708	459	64.8	412	58.2	46	10.1
Male......................................	334	239	71.4	213	63.8	26	10.8
Female	373	220	58.8	199	53.3	21	9.4
Age							
16 to 19 years............................	327	124	37.9	107	32.6	18	14.1
20 to 24 years............................	431	299	69.4	267	61.9	32	10.8
25 to 34 years............................	1,004	856	85.2	802	79.9	54	6.3
35 to 44 years............................	904	774	85.7	741	82.0	33	4.2
45 to 54 years............................	831	702	84.4	670	80.6	32	4.5
55 to 64 years............................	935	657	70.2	627	67.0	30	4.6
65 years and over	1,211	267	22.1	253	20.9	14	5.2

NOTE: Data in Table 7 are from the Current Population Survey (CPS) and do not match the estimates in Table 8. See notes and definitions for further information.
[1] May be of any race.

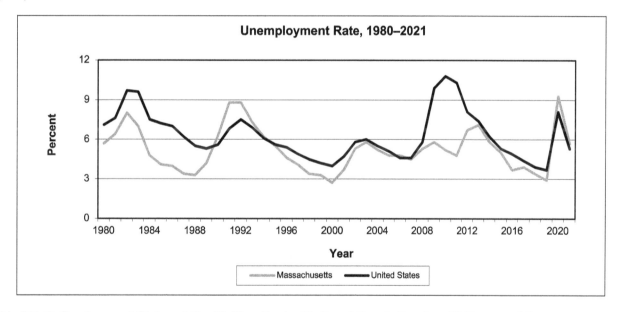

Unemployment Rate, 1980–2021

Table MA-8. Employment Status of the Civilian Noninstitutional Population Age 16 Years and Over

(Number, percent.)

Year	Civilian labor force	Civilian participation rate	Employed	Unemployed	Unemployment rate
2010..	3,479,304	66.2	3,198,617	280,687	8.1
2011..	3,484,135	65.8	3,232,458	251,677	7.2
2012..	3,506,457	65.5	3,271,256	235,201	6.7
2013..	3,516,689	65.0	3,283,144	233,545	6.6
2014..	3,569,557	65.4	3,364,853	204,704	5.7
2015..	3,589,409	65.2	3,417,296	172,113	4.8
2016..	3,617,498	65.3	3,472,327	145,171	4.0
2017..	3,724,520	65.9	3,582,389	142,131	3.8
2018..	3,809,873	66.9	3,678,445	131,428	3.4
2019..	3,831,947	66.9	3,714,547	117,400	3.1
2020..	3,741,684	65.2	3,390,249	351,435	9.4
2021..	3,750,870	65.5	3,535,478	215,392	5.7

Table MA-9. Employment and Average Wages by Industry

(Estimates are based on the 2012 North American Industry Classification System [NAICS].)

Industry	2013	2014	2015	2016	2017	2018	2019	2020
	Number of Jobs							
Wage and Salary Employment by Industry........................	3,474,851	3,541,525	3,610,422	3,674,544	3,719,842	3,777,588	3,822,709	3,509,394
Farm Wage and Salary Employment..............................	5,066	5,086	5,067	4,729	4,718	4,205	4,237	4,046
Nonfarm Wage and Salary Employment.........................	3,469,785	3,536,439	3,605,355	3,669,815	3,715,124	3,773,383	3,818,472	3,505,348
Private wage and salary employment..	3,014,049	3,074,997	3,144,958	3,206,294	3,252,372	3,307,550	3,350,193	3,053,905
Forestry, fishing, and related activities....................................	3,794	3,804	4,241	4,283	4,411	4,165	4,300	4,160
Mining...	886	931	984	995	998	985	968	910
Utilities..	10,056	10,683	10,478	10,750	11,345	10,949	11,496	11,615
Construction...	125,756	132,057	142,509	150,148	155,526	162,367	166,697	156,137
Manufacturing..	250,877	250,705	249,312	245,917	244,876	245,219	244,379	230,060
Durable goods manufacturing...	163,559	162,504	161,249	158,703	157,566	157,912	158,025	150,742
Nondurable goods manufacturing......................................	87,318	88,201	88,063	87,214	87,310	87,307	86,354	79,318
Wholesale trade	123,945	124,461	124,366	125,948	126,080	124,786	124,156	116,544
Retail trade..	349,842	351,989	355,737	357,947	357,605	356,956	354,322	320,742
Transportation and warehousing...	77,461	80,756	83,769	86,032	89,712	92,247	94,553	84,678
Information...	86,170	86,286	88,393	89,427	91,898	91,844	92,985	89,354
Finance and insurance	170,688	171,493	173,584	175,885	176,642	176,477	177,614	175,505
Real estate and rental and leasing......................................	42,976	43,688	44,862	46,241	47,264	48,751	50,225	46,201
Professional, scientific, and technical services	276,156	285,445	296,561	307,409	316,886	330,228	347,078	349,038
Management of companies and enterprises..........................	64,315	63,553	65,262	65,663	67,545	74,210	74,188	69,797
Administrative and waste services	169,291	173,016	178,042	181,947	184,767	186,805	187,467	168,659
Educational services	194,122	196,028	200,043	202,199	205,229	215,866	217,298	209,891
Health care and social assistance...	570,887	587,124	606,592	625,701	634,959	636,246	648,054	609,963
Arts, entertainment, and recreation......................................	52,768	56,126	57,355	60,112	61,901	64,225	64,271	40,945
Accommodation and food services..	283,856	289,644	295,598	304,429	309,789	314,140	317,429	223,660
Other services, except public administration..........................	160,203	167,208	167,270	165,261	164,939	171,084	172,713	146,046
Government and government enterprises.................................	455,736	461,442	460,397	463,521	462,752	465,833	468,279	451,443
	Dollars							
Average Wages and Salaries by Industry	60,418	62,668	65,208	65,995	68,455	70,935	73,694	81,315
Average Farm Wages and Salaries	27,291	28,801	23,615	29,038	26,415	25,215	19,870	20,209
Average Nonfarm Wages and Salaries	60,467	62,717	65,267	66,043	68,508	70,986	73,754	81,385
Average private wages and salaries..	61,220	63,557	66,096	66,932	69,487	72,037	74,912	83,175
Forestry, fishing, and related activities..................................	53,924	51,466	50,127	52,105	54,212	57,207	58,856	57,556
Mining...	58,369	62,006	65,063	68,340	68,096	69,002	76,028	82,134
Utilities..	107,734	110,017	111,654	111,359	125,368	131,119	137,228	139,365
Construction...	66,425	68,657	71,081	72,698	75,377	78,838	81,480	84,946
Manufacturing..	79,816	83,375	86,138	86,358	88,088	88,594	89,701	96,071
Durable goods manufacturing...	88,676	91,978	92,882	96,440	98,467	97,879	100,471	105,430
Nondurable goods manufacturing......................................	63,220	67,525	73,790	68,013	69,358	71,799	69,992	78,285
Wholesale trade	84,447	88,341	91,561	93,483	97,610	98,742	102,177	110,336
Retail trade..	28,920	30,072	31,369	32,368	33,531	34,947	36,993	40,870
Transportation and warehousing...	46,717	48,371	50,048	50,924	51,593	53,419	55,219	60,565
Information...	97,443	103,276	107,910	110,437	114,193	123,204	128,183	146,754
Finance and insurance	126,306	136,261	144,057	143,052	150,147	160,379	163,478	173,848
Real estate and rental and leasing......................................	69,829	72,759	73,244	74,656	76,834	79,672	83,285	92,048
Professional, scientific, and technical services	110,270	113,987	118,817	121,441	128,560	134,807	141,224	152,958
Management of companies and enterprises..........................	118,770	126,648	140,155	130,775	131,718	135,075	139,077	145,743
Administrative and waste services	41,119	42,262	44,277	45,426	47,122	49,181	53,011	56,529
Educational services	47,248	48,623	49,361	50,544	51,947	50,959	52,283	55,852
Health care and social assistance...	51,640	52,548	53,537	54,033	55,205	55,780	57,218	61,661
Arts, entertainment, and recreation......................................	38,513	38,551	39,923	40,817	42,075	43,852	45,590	50,147
Accommodation and food services..	23,134	23,978	25,130	26,266	27,426	28,787	30,694	29,572
Other services, except public administration..........................	33,343	34,127	35,356	36,731	37,845	39,121	40,673	45,478
Government and government enterprises.............................	55,481	57,114	59,603	59,895	61,634	63,523	65,463	69,277

Table MA-10. Employment Characteristics by Family Type

(Number, percent.)

Family type and labor force status	2018		2019		2020 [1]	
	Total	Families with own children under 18 years	Total	Families with own children under 18 years	Total	Families with own children under 18 years
All Families..	1,644,205	680,839	1,665,005	668,195	1,673,992	690,194
FAMILY TYPE AND LABOR FORCE STATUS						
Opposite-Sex Married-Couple Families............................	1,225,244	481,740	1,238,203	468,989	1,221,968	479,354
Both husband and wife in labor force..	58.2	74.4	58.3	75.2	59.1	75.3
Husband in labor force, wife not in labor force	17.3	19.9	17.0	19.8	17.4	19.9
Wife in labor force, husband not in labor force.........................	7.6	3.6	7.9	3.1	7.9	3.4
Both husband and wife not in labor force..................................	15.5	1.3	15.3	1.1	15.6	1.4
Other Families	418,961	199,099	426,802	199,206	433,278	206,681
Female householder, no spouse present	73.9	78.8	71.3	76.0	73.5	77.4
In labor force...	52.5	64.8	49.4	63.6	52.4	64.3
Not in labor force..	21.4	14.0	21.8	12.5	21.1	13.1
Male householder, no spouse present...	26.1	21.2	28.7	24.0	26.5	22.6
In labor force...	20.1	19.4	23.2	22.2	20.8	20.7
Not in labor force..	6.0	1.8	5.5	1.8	5.7	1.9

[1] 2020 ACS 5-Year estimates. 1-Year estimates were not released for 2020 due to the impact of COVID-19 on data collection that year. Data is not comparable to previous years, which are based on 1-year estimates.

Table MA-11. School Enrollment and Educational Attainment, 2020[1]

(Number, percent.)

Item	State	U.S.
Enrollment		
Total population 3 years and over, enrolled in school	1,702,976	80,497,960
Enrolled in nursery school or preschool (percent)..	6.2	6.1
Enrolled in kindergarten (percent)..	4.4	5.0
Enrolled in elementary school, grades 1-8 (percent)..	35.3	40.4
Enrolled in high school, grades 9-12 (percent)...	19.8	21.0
Enrolled in college or graduate school (percent)...	34.3	27.6
Attainment		
Total population 25 years and over	4,815,331	222,836,834
Less than ninth grade (percent)...	4.2	4.9
9th to 12th grade, no diploma (percent)...	4.7	6.6
High school graduate, including equivalency (percent)...	23.5	26.7
Some college, no degree (percent)...	15.3	20.3
Associate's degree (percent)..	7.7	8.6
Bachelor's degree (percent)..	24.5	20.2
Graduate or professional degree (percent)...	20.0	12.7
High school graduate or higher (percent)	91.1	88.5
Bachelor's degree or higher (percent)..	44.5	32.9

[1] 2020 ACS 5-Year estimates. 1-Year estimates were not released for 2020 due to the impact of COVID-19 on data collection that year.

Table MA-12. Public School Characteristics and Educational Indicators

(Number, percent; data derived from National Center of Education Statistics.)

Item	State	U.S.
Public Elementary and Secondary Schools		
Number of regular school districts, 2018-19	324	13,452
Number of operational schools, 2019-20...	1,847	98,469
Percent charter schools	4.4	7.7
Total public school enrollment, Fall 2019	959,394	50,796,445
Percent charter school enrollment	5.1	6.8
Student-teacher ratio, Fall 2019...	12.8	15.9
Expenditures per student (unadjusted dollars), 2018-19	19,196	13,187
Four-year adjusted cohort graduation rate (ACGR), 2018-2019[1]..	88.0	85.8
Students eligible for free or reduced-price lunch (percent), 2019-20..	32.8	52.1
English language learners (percent), Fall 2019	10.6	10.4
Students age 3 to 21 served under IDEA, part B (percent), 2020-21	19.0	14.5

Public Schools by Type, 2019-20	Number	Percent of state public schools
Total number of schools...	1,847	100.0
Special education..	11	0.6
Vocational education...	36	1.9
Alternative education..	24	1.3

[1] Adjusted Cohort Graduation Rates (ACGR) differ from Averaged Freshmen Graduation Rates (AFGR).

Table MA-13. Reported Voting and Registration of the Voting-Age Population, November 2020

(Numbers in thousands, percent.)

Item	Total population	Total citizen population	Registered			Voted		
			Total registered	Percent registered (total population)	Percent registered (total citizen population)	Total voted	Percent voted (total population)	Percent voted (total citizen population)
U.S. Total	252,274	231,593	168,308	66.7	72.7	154,628	61.3	66.8
State Total....................................	5,514	4,897	3,546	64.3	72.4	3,249	58.9	66.3
Sex								
Male	2,642	2,311	1,656	62.7	71.6	1,505	57.0	65.1
Female	2,872	2,586	1,891	65.8	73.1	1,744	60.7	67.4
Race								
White alone.................................	4,429	4,140	3,174	71.7	76.7	2,936	66.3	70.9
White, non-Hispanic alone..................	3,953	3,799	2,949	74.6	77.6	2,749	69.6	72.4
Black alone..................................	489	390	165	33.6	42.2	142	29.0	36.4
Asian alone..................................	415	244	139	33.5	57.1	109	26.3	44.9
Hispanic (of any race)......................	636	449	271	42.6	60.4	227	35.8	50.7
White alone or in combination..............	4,597	4,251	3,233	70.3	76.1	2,988	65.0	70.3
Black alone or in combination..............	640	484	211	32.9	43.5	181	28.3	37.4
Asian alone or in combination..............	433	262	157	36.3	60.1	128	29.4	48.7
Age								
18 to 24 years...............................	562	469	303	54.0	64.7	259	46.1	55.2
25 to 34 years...............................	1,142	939	647	56.7	68.9	566	49.6	60.3
35 to 44 years...............................	830	696	492	59.2	70.6	433	52.2	62.2
45 to 64 years...............................	1,845	1,713	1,247	67.6	72.8	1,171	63.4	68.3
65 years and over...........................	1,135	1,081	857	75.5	79.2	820	72.2	75.8

Table MA-14. Crime

(Number, rate per 100,000. Data are derived from the FBI Uniform Crime Reports.)

Item	State			U.S.		
	2019	2020	Percent change	2019	2020	Percent change
TOTAL POPULATION[1]	6,894,883	6,893,574	-	328,329,953	329,484,123	0.4
VIOLENT CRIME						
Number..	22,662	21,288	-6.1	1,250,393	1,313,105	5.0
Rate	328.7	308.8	-6.0	380.8	398.5	4.6
Murder and Nonnegligent Manslaughter						
Number..	153	160	4.6	16,669	21,570	29.4
Rate	2.2	2.3	4.6	5.1	6.5	28.9
Rape[2]						
Number..	2,244	1,851	-17.5	143,224	126,430	-11.7
Rate	32.5	26.9	-17.5	43.6	38.4	-12.0
Robbery						
Number..	3,625	3,015	-16.8	268,483	243,600	-9.3
Rate	52.6	43.7	-16.8	81.8	73.9	-9.6
Aggravated Assault						
Number..	16,640	16,262	-2.3	822,017	921,505	12.1
Rate	241.3	235.9	-2.3	250.4	279.7	11.7
PROPERTY CRIME						
Number..	81,399	72,602	-10.8	6,995,235	6,452,038	-7.8
Rate	1,180.6	1,053.2	-10.8	2,130.6	1,958.2	-8.1
Burglary						
Number..	12,323	10,323	-16.2	1,118,096	1,035,314	-7.4
Rate	178.7	149.7	-16.2	340.5	314.2	-7.7
Larceny-Theft						
Number..	62,944	55,444	-11.9	5,152,267	4,606,324	-10.6
Rate	912.9	804.3	-11.9	1,569.2	1,398.0	-10.9
Motor Vehicle Theft						
Number..	6,132	6,835	11.5	724,872	810,400	11.8
Rate	88.9	99.2	11.5	220.8	246.0	11.4

NOTE: Although arson data are included in the trend and clearance tables, sufficient data are not available to estimate totals for this offense. Therefore, no arson data are published in this table.
- = Zero or rounds to zero.
[1] Population figures are U.S. Census Bureau provisional estimates as of July 1, 2020.
[2] The figures shown in the rape (revised definition) column were estimated using the revised Uniform Crime Reporting (UCR) definition of rape.

Table MA-15. State Government Finances, 2020

(Dollar amounts in thousands, percent distribution.)

Item	Dollars	Percent distribution
Total Revenue	75,908,038	100.0
General revenue	64,555,984	85.0
Intergovernmental revenue	21,483,876	28.3
Taxes	31,630,313	41.7
General sales	6815727	9.0
Selective sales	2,673,926	3.5
License taxes	1,130,025	1.5
Individual income tax	17414713	22.9
Corporate income tax	2,532,411	3.3
Other taxes	1,063,511	1.4
Current charges	5,858,797	7.7
Miscellaneous general revenue	5,582,998	7.4
Utility revenue	835,865	1.1
Liquor stores revenue	0	-
Insurance trust revenue[1]	10,516,189	13.9
Total Expenditure	78,292,385	100.0
Intergovernmental expenditure	10,419,877	13.3
Direct expenditure	67,872,508	86.7
Current operation	45,654,182	58.3
Capital outlay	5,248,965	6.7
Insurance benefits and repayments	12,827,971	16.4
Assistance and subsidies	1,185,114	1.5
Interest on debt	2,956,276	3.8
Exhibit: Salaries and wages	8,210,454	10.5
Total Expenditure	78,292,385	100.0
General expenditure	61,279,171	78.3
Intergovernmental expenditure	10,419,877	13.3
Direct expenditure	50,859,294	65.0
General expenditure, by function:		
Education	13,908,983	17.8
Public welfare	25,868,091	33.0
Hospitals	752,154	1.0
Health	1,864,680	2.4
Highways	2,509,240	3.2
Police protection	674,259	0.9
Correction	1,687,537	2.2
Natural resources	288,493	0.4
Parks and recreation	188,258	0.2
Governmental administration	2,571,476	3.3
Interest on general debt	2,670,586	3.4
Other and unallocable	8,077,703	10.3
Utility expenditure	4,198,076	5.5
Liquor stores expenditure	0	-
Insurance trust expenditure	12,827,971	16.4
Debt at End of Fiscal Year	77,321,138	X
Cash and Security Holdings	107,910,003	X

X = Not applicable.
- = Zero or rounds to zero.
[1] Within insurance trust revenue, net earnings of state retirement systems is a calculated statistic (the item code in the data file is X08), and thus can be positive or negative. Net earnings is the sum of earnings on investments plus gains on investments minus losses on investments. The change made in 2002 for asset valuation from book to market value in accordance with Statement 34 of the Governmental Accounting Standards Board is reflected in the calculated statistics.

Table MA-16. State Government Tax Collections, 2021

(Dollars in thousands, percent.)

Item	Dollars	Percent distribution
Total Taxes	36,336,125	100.0
Property taxes	10,368	-
Sales and gross receipts	10,427,871	28.7
General sales and gross receipts	7,785,108	21.4
Selective sales and gross receipts	2,642,763	7.3
Alcoholic beverages	93,206	0.3
Amusements	224,641	0.6
Insurance premiums	537,405	1.5
Motor fuels	662,932	1.8
Pari-mutuels	1,117	-
Public utilities	X	-
Tobacco products	398,214	1.1
Other selective sales	725,248	2.0
Licenses	1,274,252	3.5
Alcoholic beverages	4,091	-
Amusements	11,396	-
Corporations in general	27,548	0.1
Hunting and fishing	6,337	-
Motor vehicle	472,172	1.3
Motor vehicle operators	86,081	0.2
Public utilities	X	-
Occupation and business, NEC	351,358	1.0
Other licenses	315,269	0.9
Income taxes	23,356,481	64.3
Individual income	19,683,486	54.2
Corporation net income	3,672,995	10.1
Other taxes	1,267,153	3.5
Death and gift	787,764	2.2
Documentary and stock transfer	479,389	1.3
Severance	X	-
Taxes, NEC	0	-

X = Not applicable.
- = Zero or rounds to zero.

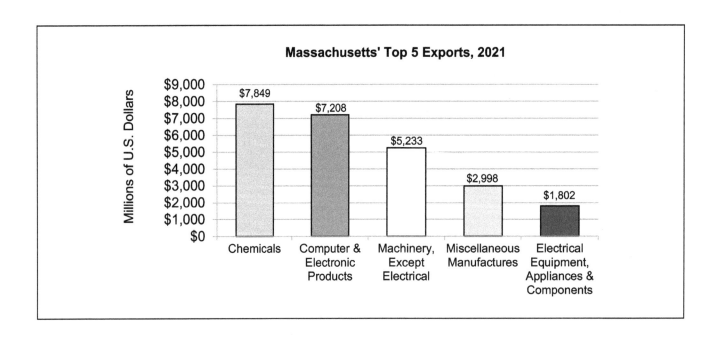

Massachusetts' Top 5 Exports, 2021

MICHIGAN

Facts and Figures

Location: East north central United States; bordered on the N by Lake Superior, on the E by Ontario, Canada, and Lakes Huron and Erie, on the S by Indiana and Ohio, and on the W by Wisconsin and Lake Michigan

Area: 96,716 sq. mi. (250,494 sq. km.); rank—11th

Population: 10,050,811 (2021 est.); rank—10th

Principal Cities: capital—Lansing; largest—Detroit

Statehood: January 26, 1837; 26th state

U.S. Congress: 2 senators, 14 representatives

State Motto: *Si quaeris peninsulam amoenam, circumspice* ("If you seek a pleasant peninsula, look about you")

State Song: "Michigan, My Michigan"

State Nicknames: The Wolverine State; The Great Lakes State

Abbreviations: MI; Mich.

State Symbols: flower—apple blossom; tree—Eastern white pine; bird—robin

At a Glance

- With an increase in population of 1.7 percent, Michigan ranked 47th among the states in growth from 2010 to 2021.

- In 2020, 5.4 percent of Michiganders did not have health insurance, compared to 8.7 percent of the total U.S. population.

- Michigan's violent crime rate in 2020 was 478.0 per 100,000 population, compared to the U.S. rate of 398.5 per 100,000 population.

- Approximately 13.7 percent of Michigan residents lived below the poverty level in 2020, compared to the national poverty rate of 12.8 percent.

- Michigan's unemployment rate of 5.9 percent ranked 11th in the nation in 2021.

Table MI-1. Population by Age, Sex, Race, and Hispanic Origin

(Number, percent, except where noted.)

Sex, age, race, and Hispanic origin	2000	2010	2021	Percent change, 2010–2021
Total Population..	9,938,444	9,883,640	10,050,811	1.7
Percent of total U.S. population	3.5	3.2	3.0	X
Sex				
Male..	4,873,095	4,848,114	4,980,579	2.7
Female..	5,065,349	5,035,526	5,070,232	0.7
Age				
Under 5 years..	672,005	596,286	548,355	-8.0
5 to 19 years...	2,212,060	2,052,599	1,863,420	-9.2
20 to 64 years...	5,835,361	5,873,225	5,816,254	-1.0
65 years and over..	1,219,018	1,361,530	1,822,782	33.9
Median age (years)	35.5	38.9	40.1	3.1
Race and Hispanic Origin				
One race				
White..	7,966,053	7,949,497	7,935,511	-0.2
Black...	1,412,742	1,416,067	1,419,656	0.3
American Indian and Alaska Native	58,479	68,396	75,117	9.8
Asian...	176,510	243,062	343,402	41.3
Native Hawaiian or Other Pacific Islander	2,692	3,442	4,493	30.5
Two or more races..	192,416	203,176	272,632	34.2
Hispanic (of any race)...	323,877	459,751	561,587	22.2

NOTE: Population figures for 2021 are July 1 estimates. The 2000 and 2010 estimates are taken from the respective censuses.
- = Zero or rounds to zero.
X = Not applicable.

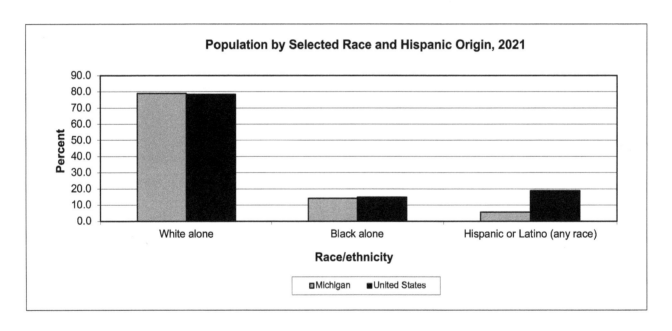

Table MI-2. Marital Status

(Number, percent distribution.)

Sex, age, race, and Hispanic origin	2000	2010	2020 [1]
Males, 15 Years and Over	3,761,881	3,875,107	4,003,560
Never married	30.8	34.9	36.4
Now married, except separated...	56.1	50.5	49.2
Separated..	1.3	1.3	1.0
Widowed..	2.5	2.7	2.8
Divorced..	9.3	10.6	10.6
Females, 15 Years and Over	4,013,722	4,099,384	4,196,226
Never married	25.0	29.0	30.2
Now married, except separated...	51.8	47.2	47.0
Separated..	1.6	1.6	1.3
Widowed..	10.4	9.7	8.9
Divorced..	11.2	12.5	12.6

[1] 2020 ACS 5-Year estimates. 1-Year estimates were not released for 2020 due to the impact of COVID-19 on data collection that year.

Table MI-3. Households and Housing Characteristics

(Number, percent, dollars.)

Item	2000	2010	2020 [1]	Average annual percent change, 2010–2020
Total Households...	3,785,661	3,806,621	3,980,408	0.7
Family households	2,575,699	2,508,780	2,526,437	0.1
Married-couple family	1,947,610	1,845,094	1,865,163	0.2
Other family	627,989	663,686	661,274	-0.1
Male householder, no wife present..........................	154,187	168,337	190,513	1.9
Female householder, no husband present	473,802	495,349	470,761	-0.7
Nonfamily households	1,209,962	1,297,841	1,453,971	1.7
Householder living alone..	993,607	1,090,126	1,189,594	1.3
Householder not living alone....................................	216,335	207,715	264,377	3.9
Housing Characteristics				
Total housing units..	4,234,279	4,531,231	4,611,913	0.3
Occupied housing units	3,785,661	3,806,621	3,980,408	0.7
Owner occupied	2,793,124	2,769,474	2,855,485	0.4
Renter occupied	992,537	1,037,147	1,124,923	1.2
Average household size..	2.56	2.53	2.45	-0.5
Financial Characteristics				
Median gross rent of renter-occupied housing	546	730	892	3.2
Median monthly owner costs for housing units with a mortgage	972	1,288	1,312	0.3
Median value of owner-occupied housing units............	115,600	123,300	162,600	4.6

[1] 2020 ACS 5-Year estimates. 1-Year estimates were not released for 2020 due to the impact of COVID-19 on data collection that year.

Table MI-4. Migration, Origin, and Language

(Number, percent.)

Characteristic	State 2016-2020 [1]	U.S. 2016-2020 [1]
Residence 1 Year Ago		
Population 1 year and over	9,865,836	322,943,283
Same house	86.6	86.2
Different house in the U.S.	12.9	13.2
Same county	7.8	7.7
Different county	5.1	5.5
Same state	3.7	3.2
Different state	1.4	2.3
Abroad..	0.4	0.6
Place of Birth		
Native born	9,287,260	282,443,680
Male	49.2	49.4
Female	50.8	50.6
Foreign born	686,647	44,125,628
Male	50.0	48.6
Female	50.0	51.4
Foreign born; naturalized U.S. citizen......................................	369,210	22,456,684
Male	48.0	46.1
Female	52.0	53.9
Foreign born; not a U.S. citizen..	317,437	21,668,944
Male	52.4	51.1
Female	47.6	48.9
Entered 2010 or later	30.2	22.8
Entered 2000 to 2009	23.2	25.1
Entered before 2000...	46.6	52.1
World Region of Birth, Foreign		
Foreign-born population, excluding population born at sea	686,647	44,125,628
Europe	18.9	10.8
Asia..	51.4	31.3
Africa...	5.3	5.4
Oceania	0.4	0.6
Latin America...	18.6	50.0
North America..	5.4	1.9
Language Spoken at Home and Ability to Speak English		
Population 5 years and over..	9,405,581	306,919,116
English only	90.3	78.5
Language other than English..	9.7	21.5
Speaks English less than "very well"......................................	3.4	8.2

[1] 2020 ACS 5-Year estimates. 1-Year estimates were not released for 2020 due to the impact of COVID-19 on data collection that year.
NA = Not available.
X = Not applicable.
- = Zero or rounds to zero.

Table MI-5. Median Income and Poverty Status, 2020[1]

(Number, percent, except as noted.)

Characteristic	State		U.S.	
	Number	Percent	Number	Percent
Median Income				
Households (dollars)	59,234	X	64,994	X
Families (dollars)	75,470	X	80,069	X
Below Poverty Level (All People)	1,337,256	13.7	40,910,326	12.8
Sex				
Male	601,304	12.6	18,171,512	11.6
Female	735,952	14.8	22,738,814	14.0
Age				
Under 18 years	398,119	18.8	12,598,699	17.5
Related children under 18 years	388,133	18.4	12,306,532	17.2
18 to 64 years	797,515	13.4	23,554,920	12.1
65 years and over	141,622	8.5	4,756,707	9.3

X = Not applicable.
[1] 2020 ACS 5-Year estimates. 1-Year estimates were not released for 2020 due to the impact of COVID-19 on data collection that year.

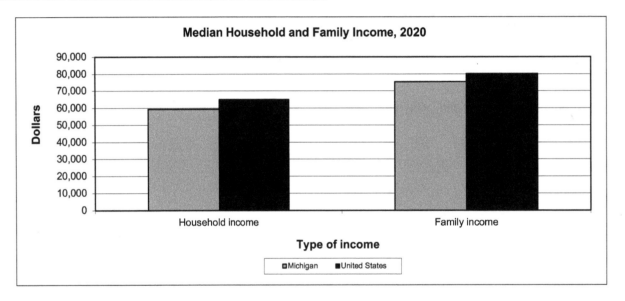

Table MI-6. Health Insurance Coverage Status for the Civilian Noninstitutionalized Population and Children Under 19 Years of Age

(Number, percent.)

Item	2011	2012	2013	2014	2015	2016	2017	2018	2019	2020[2]
Civilian Noninstitutionalized Population	9,762,306	9,772,550	9,784,451	9,798,621	9,810,800	9,818,099	9,853,156	9,888,529	9,879,486	9,866,076
Covered by Private or Public Insurance										
Number	8,612,395	8,658,229	8,712,930	8,961,893	9,214,158	9,291,109	9,343,617	9,353,978	9,308,346	9,337,676
Percent	88.2	88.6	89.0	91.5	93.9	94.6	94.8	94.6	94.2	94.6
Uninsured										
Number	1,149,911	1,114,321	1,071,521	836,728	596,642	526,990	509,539	534,551	571,140	528,400
Percent	11.8	11.4	11.0	8.5	6.1	5.4	5.2	5.4	5.8	5.4
Percent in the U.S. not covered	15.1	14.8	14.5	11.7	9.4	8.6	8.7	8.9	9.2	8.7
Children Under 19 Years of Age[1]	2,289,531	2,263,671	2,240,003	2,219,940	2,204,443	2,187,554	2,312,692	2,295,104	2,280,491	2,293,655
Covered by Private or Public Insurance										
Number	2,195,721	2,173,626	2,150,062	2,136,686	2,136,367	2,124,318	2,243,515	2,217,245	2,202,527	2,222,672
Percent	95.9	96.0	96.0	96.2	96.9	97.1	97.0	96.6	96.6	96.9
Uninsured										
Number	93,810	90,045	89,941	83,254	68,076	63,236	69,177	77,859	77,964	70,983
Percent	4.1	4.0	4.0	3.8	3.1	2.9	3.0	3.4	3.4	3.1
Percent in the U.S. not covered	7.5	7.2	7.1	6.0	4.8	4.5	5.0	5.2	5.7	5.2

[1] Data for years prior to 2017 are for individuals under 18 years of age.
[2] 2020 ACS 5-Year estimates. 1-Year estimates were not released for 2020 due to the impact of COVID-19 on data collection that year. Data is not comparable to previous years, which are based on 1-year estimates.

Table MI-7. Employment Status by Demographic Group, 2021

(Numbers in thousands, percent.)

Characteristic	Civilian noninstitutional population	Civilian labor force		Employed		Unemployed	
		Number	Percent of population	Number	Percent of population	Number	Percent of population
Total...	7,994	4,701	58.8	4,433	55.5	268	5.7
Sex							
Male..	3,881	2,476	63.8	2,321	59.8	155	6.3
Female..	4,113	2,225	54.1	2,112	51.3	113	5.1
Race, Sex, and Hispanic Origin							
White...	6,484	3,816	58.8	3,632	56.0	185	4.8
Male..	3,165	2,027	64.0	1,915	60.5	112	5.5
Female..	3,320	1,789	53.9	1,717	51.7	73	4.1
Black or African American..................	1,059	600	56.7	534	50.5	66	11.0
Male..	479	276	57.7	247	51.6	29	10.5
Female..	580	324	55.9	287	49.5	37	11.4
Hispanic or Latino ethnicity[1]	368	239	65.1	222	60.4	17	7.1
Male..	178	141	79.0	129	72.4	12	8.3
Female..	190	99	52.0	93	49.2	5	5.4
Age							
16 to 19 years...................................	507	197	38.9	171	33.8	26	13.1
20 to 24 years...................................	619	456	73.6	405	65.4	51	11.2
25 to 34 years...................................	1,312	1,052	80.1	984	75.0	67	6.4
35 to 44 years...................................	1,177	945	80.3	902	76.6	43	4.6
45 to 54 years...................................	1,250	995	79.6	953	76.2	42	4.2
55 to 64 years...................................	1,296	740	57.1	715	55.1	26	3.5
65 years and over	1,833	316	17.2	303	16.5	12	3.9

NOTE: Data in Table 7 are from the Current Population Survey (CPS) and do not match the estimates in Table 8. See notes and definitions for further information.
[1] May be of any race.

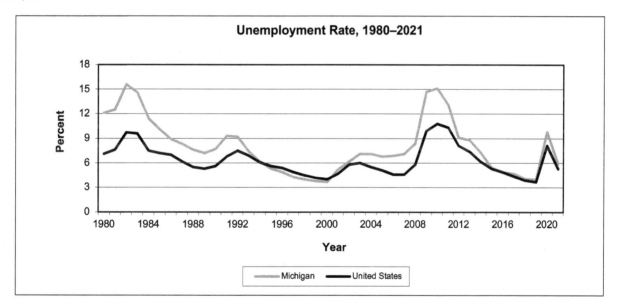

Unemployment Rate, 1980–2021

Table MI-8. Employment Status of the Civilian Noninstitutional Population Age 16 Years and Over

(Number, percent.)

Year	Civilian labor force	Civilian participation rate	Employed	Unemployed	Unemployment rate
2010..	4,754,799	61.4	4,173,946	580,853	12.2
2011..	4,668,979	60.2	4,201,785	467,194	10.0
2012..	4,685,462	60.1	4,261,963	423,499	9.0
2013..	4,736,919	60.5	4,323,410	413,509	8.7
2014..	4,759,720	60.6	4,416,017	343,703	7.2
2015..	4,760,207	60.4	4,501,816	258,391	5.4
2016..	4,848,638	61.2	4,606,948	241,690	5.0
2017..	4,911,247	61.4	4,685,853	225,394	4.6
2018..	4,940,313	61.5	4,734,158	206,155	4.2
2019..	4,969,294	61.7	4,766,050	203,244	4.1
2020..	4,846,013	60.1	4,361,873	484,140	10.0
2021..	4,776,110	59.2	4,495,651	280,459	5.9

Table MI-9. Employment and Average Wages by Industry

(Estimates are based on the 2012 North American Industry Classification System [NAICS].)

Industry	2013	2014	2015	2016	2017	2018	2019	2020
	Number of Jobs							
Wage and Salary Employment by Industry......................	4,179,314	4,254,464	4,326,978	4,403,195	4,450,757	4,498,209	4,521,246	4,129,357
Farm Wage and Salary Employment.............................	21,907	22,981	25,200	23,888	19,689	22,033	23,806	20,933
Nonfarm Wage and Salary Employment.........................	4,157,407	4,231,483	4,301,778	4,379,307	4,431,068	4,476,176	4,497,440	4,108,424
Private wage and salary employment.......................................	3,546,556	3,625,384	3,697,754	3,770,111	3,817,777	3,861,690	3,878,971	3,517,406
Forestry, fishing, and related activities.................................	8,019	8,841	8,733	8,844	8,774	8,770	8,918	8,594
Mining...	6,488	6,647	6,001	5,442	5,440	5,543	5,539	4,893
Utilities..	19,365	19,771	19,886	20,128	20,221	20,340	20,633	20,468
Construction...	137,048	145,189	151,927	158,918	165,982	173,005	177,608	168,814
Manufacturing..	547,814	569,317	587,225	601,514	616,940	629,372	627,651	556,876
Durable goods manufacturing..	412,355	429,988	444,244	453,043	465,504	476,156	473,943	416,250
Nondurable goods manufacturing.....................................	135,459	139,329	142,981	148,471	151,436	153,216	153,708	140,626
Wholesale trade	164,489	168,267	170,394	172,668	173,444	172,294	172,243	161,720
Retail trade..	458,347	463,520	470,246	475,776	477,144	473,605	467,660	432,489
Transportation and warehousing.......................................	106,356	111,706	116,778	118,748	123,588	130,262	140,253	140,742
Information..	57,915	60,548	59,398	59,691	56,720	56,371	55,491	50,725
Finance and insurance	147,348	148,015	149,836	153,793	157,815	158,255	163,827	167,971
Real estate and rental and leasing....................................	50,570	51,416	52,223	53,548	55,161	56,269	57,771	53,025
Professional, scientific, and technical services	270,738	278,920	289,045	297,902	295,285	301,141	303,083	291,288
Management of companies and enterprises.........................	54,692	55,222	56,447	58,820	66,206	68,545	70,613	70,772
Administrative and waste services....................................	288,980	290,280	294,446	293,249	290,334	294,671	287,917	244,237
Educational services	79,001	80,199	79,975	77,807	78,560	74,562	74,779	65,438
Health care and social assistance.....................................	561,965	564,568	575,466	590,800	597,455	603,606	605,688	573,696
Arts, entertainment, and recreation...................................	48,629	50,633	50,767	52,477	54,146	54,218	54,537	36,604
Accommodation and food services....................................	351,819	358,738	364,933	375,190	380,854	381,785	383,594	290,892
Other services, except public administration........................	186,973	193,587	194,028	194,796	193,708	199,076	201,166	178,162
Government and government enterprises.............................	610,851	606,099	604,024	609,196	613,291	614,486	618,469	591,018
	Dollars							
Average Wages and Salaries by Industry	46,641	47,998	49,580	50,526	52,069	53,474	54,594	58,761
Average Farm Wages and Salaries	31,235	35,035	31,790	38,290	37,907	36,137	33,770	29,903
Average Nonfarm Wages and Salaries	46,723	48,069	49,684	50,592	52,132	53,559	54,704	58,908
Average private wages and salaries....................................	46,688	48,099	49,830	50,794	52,421	53,838	54,977	59,417
Forestry, fishing, and related activities.................................	27,178	27,683	29,663	31,352	32,479	33,679	35,011	37,662
Mining...	73,367	77,103	75,619	73,910	75,506	81,515	82,033	81,370
Utilities..	104,105	109,025	112,220	112,552	117,090	120,606	122,994	130,248
Construction	53,620	55,588	57,317	59,088	61,529	62,382	63,563	67,559
Manufacturing..	62,522	63,557	65,106	65,174	66,205	67,543	68,450	70,875
Durable goods manufacturing..	64,898	65,872	67,441	67,389	68,333	69,651	70,662	72,505
Nondurable goods manufacturing.....................................	55,290	56,412	57,851	58,417	59,662	60,992	61,627	66,052
Wholesale trade	67,328	69,917	71,148	72,291	73,923	76,263	77,361	80,911
Retail trade..	26,508	27,351	28,511	29,225	30,108	31,122	32,083	35,361
Transportation and warehousing.......................................	50,567	52,009	53,215	54,242	55,121	56,744	57,072	58,480
Information..	64,329	65,440	67,887	69,531	70,832	73,578	77,470	88,679
Finance and insurance	68,194	70,864	73,988	75,787	77,812	80,011	82,354	89,762
Real estate and rental and leasing....................................	38,258	39,689	42,286	43,734	45,355	48,000	49,116	55,306
Professional, scientific, and technical services	75,935	77,809	80,717	82,247	86,365	87,805	89,077	92,611
Management of companies and enterprises.........................	110,684	119,947	122,438	124,357	132,243	128,099	126,525	127,527
Administrative and waste services....................................	31,712	32,443	33,934	34,730	35,934	36,776	37,753	42,043
Educational services	29,963	30,854	31,474	32,628	33,123	35,195	35,171	39,114
Health care and social assistance.....................................	45,527	46,451	48,168	48,775	49,479	50,779	51,984	55,230
Arts, entertainment, and recreation...................................	32,587	32,998	33,896	35,378	36,358	36,438	36,980	42,972
Accommodation and food services....................................	17,073	17,584	18,576	19,244	20,117	21,438	21,954	21,503
Other services, except public administration........................	30,172	31,225	32,649	33,645	34,729	35,808	36,689	40,808
Government and government enterprises.............................	46,924	47,887	48,791	49,343	50,335	51,804	52,990	55,880

Table MI-10. Employment Characteristics by Family Type

(Number, percent.)

Family type and labor force status	2018		2019		2020 [1]	
	Total	Families with own children under 18 years	Total	Families with own children under 18 years	Total	Families with own children under 18 years
All Families..	2,520,001	1,005,419	2,496,550	977,424	2,526,437	1,017,313
FAMILY TYPE AND LABOR FORCE STATUS						
Married-Couple Families..........................	1,849,470	660,363	1,825,191	643,620	1,852,632	674,027
Both husband and wife in labor force...................	48.7	67.1	48.8	68.5	49.3	67.5
Husband in labor force, wife not in labor force........	20.5	26.7	20.3	25.5	20.4	26.2
Wife in labor force, husband not in labor force.........	8.2	4.2	8.0	4.0	8.6	4.5
Both husband and wife not in labor force...............	21.7	1.7	22.3	1.7	21.8	1.8
Other Families	670,531	345,056	671,359	333,804	661,274	341,132
Female householder, no spouse present	70.8	72.6	70.0	71.6	71.2	73.2
In labor force...	48.0	60.4	47.8	60.7	48.9	60.6
Not in labor force..	22.9	12.2	22.2	10.9	22.3	12.7
Male householder, no spouse present...................	29.2	27.4	30.0	28.4	28.8	26.8
In labor force...	21.5	24.2	22.5	25.5	21.4	23.8
Not in labor force..	7.6	3.2	7.5	2.9	7.4	3.0

[1] 2020 ACS 5-Year estimates. 1-Year estimates were not released for 2020 due to the impact of COVID-19 on data collection that year. Data is not comparable to previous years, which are based on 1-year estimates.

Table MI-11. School Enrollment and Educational Attainment, 2020[1]

(Number, percent.)

Item	State	U.S.
Enrollment		
Total population 3 years and over, enrolled in school	2,400,867	80,497,960
Enrolled in nursery school or preschool (percent)...................	5.9	6.1
Enrolled in kindergarten (percent).................................	5.0	5.0
Enrolled in elementary school, grades 1-8 (percent)................	39.3	40.4
Enrolled in high school, grades 9-12 (percent)	21.7	21.0
Enrolled in college or graduate school (percent)	28.2	27.6
Attainment		
Total population 25 years and over	6,853,674	222,836,834
Less than ninth grade (percent)	2.7	4.9
9th to 12th grade, no diploma (percent)	6.0	6.6
High school graduate, including equivalency (percent)...............	28.5	26.7
Some college, no degree (percent)	23.2	20.3
Associate's degree (percent).......................................	9.6	8.6
Bachelor's degree (percent)	18.3	20.2
Graduate or professional degree (percent)..........................	11.7	12.7
High school graduate or higher (percent)..........................	91.3	88.5
Bachelor's degree or higher (percent)..............................	30.0	32.9

[1] 2020 ACS 5-Year estimates. 1-Year estimates were not released for 2020 due to the impact of COVID-19 on data collection that year.

Table MI-12. Public School Characteristics and Educational Indicators

(Number, percent; data derived from National Center of Education Statistics.)

Item	State	U.S.
Public Elementary and Secondary Schools		
Number of regular school districts, 2018-19	537	13,452
Number of operational schools, 2019-20...........................	3,550	98,469
Percent charter schools	10.4	7.7
Total public school enrollment, Fall 2019.........................	1,495,925	50,796,445
Percent charter school enrollment	10.1	6.8
Student-teacher ratio, Fall 2019...................................	17.6	15.9
Expenditures per student (unadjusted dollars), 2018-19	12,052	13,187
Four-year adjusted cohort graduation rate (ACGR), 2018-2019[1]	81.4	85.8
Students eligible for free or reduced-price lunch (percent), 2019-20....	50.5	52.1
English language learners (percent), Fall 2019	6.5	10.4
Students age 3 to 21 served under IDEA, part B (percent), 2020-21	13.5	14.5

Public Schools by Type, 2019-20	Number	Percent of state public schools
Total number of schools...	3,550	100.0
Special education...	188	5.3
Vocational education..	46	1.3
Alternative education...	360	10.1

[1] Adjusted Cohort Graduation Rates (ACGR) differ from Averaged Freshmen Graduation Rates (AFGR).

Table MI-13. Reported Voting and Registration of the Voting-Age Population, November 2020

(Numbers in thousands, percent.)

Item	Total population	Total citizen population	Registered			Voted		
			Total registered	Percent registered (total population)	Percent registered (total citizen population)	Total voted	Percent voted (total population)	Percent voted (total citizen population)
U.S. Total	252,274	231,593	168,308	66.7	72.7	154,628	61.3	66.8
State Total..........................	7,790	7,467	5,513	70.8	73.8	4,994	64.1	66.9
Sex								
Male	3,795	3,616	2,648	69.8	73.2	2,378	62.7	65.8
Female	3,995	3,851	2,865	71.7	74.4	2,616	65.5	67.9
Race								
White alone..........................	6,269	6,118	4,568	72.9	74.7	4,144	66.1	67.7
White, non-Hispanic alone..........................	5,922	5,865	4,408	74.4	75.2	3,997	67.5	68.2
Black alone..........................	1,021	984	713	69.8	72.4	628	61.5	63.8
Asian alone..........................	281	145	72	25.7	49.6	65	23.3	45.1
Hispanic (of any race)..........................	406	302	178	43.9	58.9	165	40.7	54.7
White alone or in combination	6,374	6,223	4,649	72.9	74.7	4,225	66.3	67.9
Black alone or in combination..........................	1,091	1,054	773	70.9	73.3	684	62.7	64.9
Asian alone or in combination..........................	309	173	90	29.3	52.1	84	27.1	48.3
Age								
18 to 24 years	932	887	546	58.5	61.5	469	50.3	52.9
25 to 34 years	1,344	1,257	910	67.8	72.4	777	57.8	61.8
35 to 44 years	1,130	1,063	764	67.6	71.8	666	58.9	62.6
45 to 64 years	2,663	2,547	1,969	74.0	77.3	1,798	67.5	70.6
65 years and over	1,721	1,713	1,324	76.9	77.3	1,284	74.6	75.0

Table MI-14. Crime

(Number, rate per 100,000. Data are derived from the FBI Uniform Crime Reports.)

Item	State			U.S.		
	2019	2020	Percent change	2019	2020	Percent change
TOTAL POPULATION[1]	9,984,795	9,966,555	-0.2	328,329,953	329,484,123	0.4
VIOLENT CRIME						
Number..........................	43,793	47,641	8.8	1,250,393	1,313,105	5.0
Rate..........................	438.6	478.0	9.0	380.8	398.5	4.6
Murder and Nonnegligent Manslaughter						
Number..........................	576	754	30.9	16,669	21,570	29.4
Rate	5.8	7.6	31.1	5.1	6.5	28.9
Rape[2]						
Number..........................	7,356	6,065	-17.6	143,224	126,430	-11.7
Rate	73.7	60.9	-17.4	43.6	38.4	-12.0
Robbery						
Number..........................	5,352	4,438	-17.1	268,483	243,600	-9.3
Rate	53.6	44.5	-16.9	81.8	73.9	-9.6
Aggravated Assault						
Number..........................	30,509	36,384	19.3	822,017	921,505	12.1
Rate	305.6	365.1	19.5	250.4	279.7	11.7
PROPERTY CRIME						
Number..........................	158,317	135,633	-14.3	6,995,235	6,452,038	-7.8
Rate	1,585.6	1,360.9	-14.2	2,130.6	1,958.2	-8.1
Burglary						
Number..........................	28,574	23,231	-18.7	1,118,096	1,035,314	-7.4
Rate	286.2	233.1	-18.6	340.5	314.2	-7.7
Larceny-Theft						
Number..........................	111,900	94,017	-16.0	5,152,267	4,606,324	-10.6
Rate	1,120.7	943.3	-15.8	1,569.2	1,398.0	-10.9
Motor Vehicle Theft						
Number..........................	17,843	18,385	3.0	724,872	810,400	11.8
Rate	178.7	184.5	3.2	220.8	246.0	11.4

NOTE: Although arson data are included in the trend and clearance tables, sufficient data are not available to estimate totals for this offense. Therefore, no arson data are published in this table.
- = Zero or rounds to zero.
[1] Population figures are U.S. Census Bureau provisional estimates as of July 1, 2020.
[2] The figures shown in the rape (revised definition) column were estimated using the revised Uniform Crime Reporting (UCR) definition of rape.

Table MI-15. State Government Finances, 2020

(Dollar amounts in thousands, percent distribution.)

Item	Dollars	Percent distribution
Total Revenue	80,951,679	100.0
General revenue	69,206,513	85.5
Intergovernmental revenue	26,752,326	33.0
Taxes	28,061,998	34.7
General sales	9223410	11.4
Selective sales	4,185,759	5.2
License taxes	2,017,443	2.5
Individual income tax	9029493	11.2
Corporate income tax	812,842	1.0
Other taxes	2,793,051	3.5
Current charges	10,279,667	12.7
Miscellaneous general revenue	4,112,522	5.1
Utility revenue	46	-
Liquor stores revenue	1252015	1.5
Insurance trust revenue[1]	10,493,105	13.0
Total Expenditure	86,678,501	100.0
Intergovernmental expenditure	24,755,359	28.6
Direct expenditure	61,923,142	71.4
Current operation	42,856,187	49.4
Capital outlay	2,870,198	3.3
Insurance benefits and repayments	13,072,126	15.1
Assistance and subsidies	1,837,794	2.1
Interest on debt	1,286,837	1.5
Exhibit: Salaries and wages	10,859,310	12.5
Total Expenditure	86,678,501	100.0
General expenditure	72,598,568	83.8
Intergovernmental expenditure	24,755,359	28.6
Direct expenditure	47,843,209	55.2
General expenditure, by function:		
Education	28,376,278	32.7
Public welfare	21,575,730	24.9
Hospitals	5,258,723	6.1
Health	2,330,758	2.7
Highways	4,144,785	4.8
Police protection	595,699	0.7
Correction	1,944,633	2.2
Natural resources	435,487	0.5
Parks and recreation	164,693	0.2
Governmental administration	1,290,522	1.5
Interest on general debt	1,286,837	1.5
Other and unallocable	4,441,547	5.1
Utility expenditure	366,401	0.4
Liquor stores expenditure	1007671	1.2
Insurance trust expenditure	13,072,126	15.1
Debt at End of Fiscal Year	34,402,762	X
Cash and Security Holdings	120,905,870	X

X = Not applicable.
- = Zero or rounds to zero.
[1] Within insurance trust revenue, net earnings of state retirement systems is a calculated statistic (the item code in the data file is X08), and thus can be positive or negative. Net earnings is the sum of earnings on investments plus gains on investments minus losses on investments. The change made in 2002 for asset valuation from book to market value in accordance with Statement 34 of the Governmental Accounting Standards Board is reflected in the calculated statistics.

Table MI-16. State Government Tax Collections, 2021

(Dollars in thousands, percent.)

Item	Dollars	Percent distribution
Total Taxes	34,431,625	100.0
Property taxes	2,396,416	7.0
Sales and gross receipts	15,925,763	46.3
General sales and gross receipts	11,190,298	32.5
Selective sales and gross receipts	4,735,465	13.8
Alcoholic beverages	235,383	0.7
Amusements	157,621	0.5
Insurance premiums	349,170	1.0
Motor fuels	1,336,795	3.9
Pari-mutuels	2,656	-
Public utilities	38,425	0.1
Tobacco products	886,370	2.6
Other selective sales	1,729,045	5.0
Licenses	2,178,822	6.3
Alcoholic beverages	20,572	0.1
Amusements	X	-
Corporations in general	33,845	0.1
Hunting and fishing	76,709	0.2
Motor vehicle	1,455,962	4.2
Motor vehicle operators	66,802	0.2
Public utilities	37,098	0.1
Occupation and business, NEC	268,448	0.8
Other licenses	219,386	0.6
Income taxes	13,495,663	39.2
Individual income	11,999,165	34.8
Corporation net income	1,496,498	4.3
Other taxes	434,961	1.3
Death and gift	0	-
Documentary and stock transfer	411,412	1.2
Severance	23,549	0.1
Taxes, NEC	0	-

- = Zero or rounds to zero.
X = Not applicable.

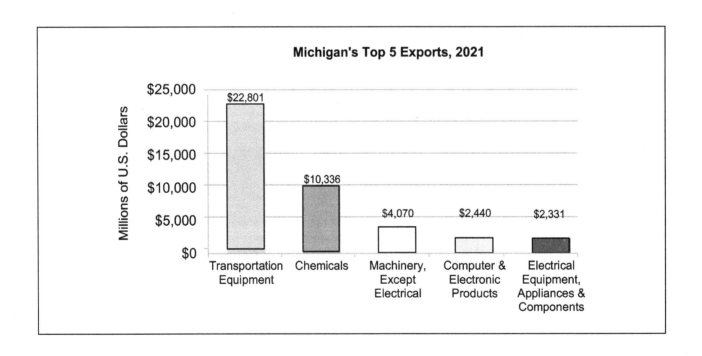

Michigan's Top 5 Exports, 2021

MINNESOTA

Facts and Figures

Location: North central United States; bordered on the N by Canada (Manitoba and Ontario), on the E by Lake Superior and Wisconsin, on the S by Iowa, and on the W by North Dakota and South Dakota

Area: 86,939 sq. mi. (225,171 sq. km.); rank—12th

Population: 5,707,390 (2021 est.); rank—22nd

Principal Cities: capital—St. Paul; largest—Minneapolis

Statehood: May 11, 1858; 32nd state

U.S. Congress: 2 senators, 8 representatives

State Motto: *L'Etoile du Nord* ("The Star of the North")

State Song: "Hail! Minnesota"

State Nicknames: The North Star State; The Land of 10,000 Lakes; The Gopher State

Abbreviations: MN; Minn.

State Symbols: flower—showy (pink and white) lady's slipper; tree—red (Norway) pine; bird—loon

At a Glance

- With an increase in population of 7.6 percent, Minnesota ranked 20th among the states in growth from 2010 to 2021.

- Minnesota had the 2nd highest voter turnout for the November 2020 election, with 74.3 percent of the voting-age population casting votes.

- The unemployment rate in Minnesota in 2021 was 3.4 percent, compared to the national unemployment rate of 5.3 percent.

- Minnesota's median household income was $73,382 in 2020, which ranked 14th among the states.

- In 2020, 9.3 percent of all Minnesotans and 11.6 percent of children in Minnesota lived below the poverty level, compared to 12.8 percent of the entire U.S. population and 17.5 percent of all U.S. children.

Table MN-1. Population by Age, Sex, Race, and Hispanic Origin

(Number, percent, except where noted.)

Sex, age, race, and Hispanic origin	2000	2010	2021	Percent change, 2010–2021
Total Population...	4,919,479	5,303,925	5,707,390	7.6
Percent of total U.S. population	1.7	1.7	1.7	X
Sex				
Male...	2,435,631	2,632,132	2,860,413	8.7
Female...	2,483,848	2,671,793	2,846,977	6.6
Age				
Under 5 years...	329,594	355,504	337,504	-5.1
5 to 19 years...	1,105,251	1,075,707	1,123,901	4.5
20 to 64 years...	2,890,368	3,189,593	3,290,302	3.2
65 years and over	594,266	683,121	955,683	39.9
Median age (years)	35.4	37.4	38.7	3.5
Race and Hispanic Origin				
One race				
White	4,400,282	4,623,461	4,735,626	2.4
Black...	171,731	280,949	423,656	50.8
American Indian and Alaska Native	54,967	67,325	79,214	17.7
Asian...	141,968	217,792	306,706	40.8
Native Hawaiian or Other Pacific Islander	1,979	2,958	4,914	66.1
Two or more races	82,742	111,440	157,274	41.1
Hispanic (of any race)...	143,382	264,432	333,474	26.1

NOTE: Population figures for 2021 are July 1 estimates. The 2000 and 2010 estimates are taken from the respective censuses.
- = Zero or rounds to zero.
X = Not applicable.

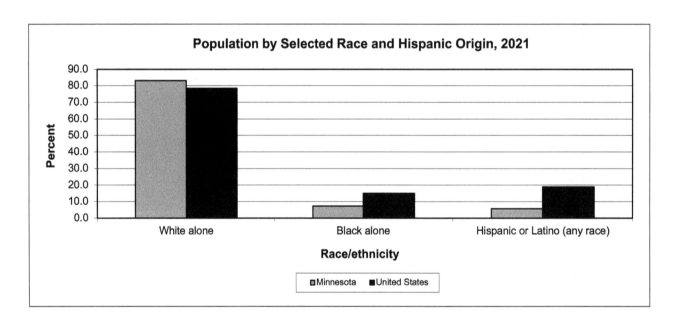

Table MN-2. Marital Status

(Number, percent distribution.)

Sex, age, race, and Hispanic origin	2000	2010	2020 [1]
Males, 15 Years and Over	1,889,936	2,090,940	2,236,068
Never married	31.3	34.6	35.4
Now married, except separated...	57.7	53.5	52.3
Separated...	0.9	0.9	0.8
Widowed...	2.1	2.2	2.3
Divorced...	8.0	8.7	9.2
Females, 15 Years and Over	1,967,819	2,155,042	2,282,073
Never married	25.0	28.2	29.1
Now married, except separated...	55.0	51.5	51.1
Separated...	1.2	1.2	1.1
Widowed...	9.4	8.4	7.5
Divorced...	9.5	10.7	11.2

[1] 2020 ACS 5-Year estimates. 1-Year estimates were not released for 2020 due to the impact of COVID-19 on data collection that year.

Table MN-3. Households and Housing Characteristics

(Number, percent, dollars.)

Item	2000	2010	2020 [1]	Average annual percent change, 2010–2020
Total Households...........................	1,895,127	2,091,548	2,207,988	0.8
Family households...........................	1,255,141	1,353,758	1,404,798	0.5
Married-couple family...........................	1,018,245	1,069,000	1,110,550	0.6
Other family...........................	236,986	284,758	294,248	0.5
Male householder, no wife present...........................	68,114	87,757	95,422	1.2
Female householder, no husband present...........................	168,782	197,001	198,826	0.1
Nonfamily households...........................	639,986	737,790	803,190	1.3
Householder living alone...........................	509,468	591,124	635,930	1.1
Householder not living alone...........................	130,518	146,666	167,260	2.0
Housing Characteristics				
Total housing units...........................	2,065,946	2,348,242	2,458,030	0.7
Occupied housing units...........................	1,895,127	2,091,548	2,207,988	0.8
Owner occupied...........................	1,412,865	1,527,328	1,588,611	0.6
Renter occupied...........................	482,262	564,220	619,377	1.4
Average household size...........................	2.52	2.47	2.48	0.1
Financial Characteristics				
Median gross rent of renter-occupied housing...........................	566	764	1,010	4.6
Median monthly owner costs for housing units with a mortgage...........................	1,044	1,503	1,606	1.0
Median value of owner-occupied housing units...........................	122,400	194,300	235,700	3.0

[1] 2020 ACS 5-Year estimates. 1-Year estimates were not released for 2020 due to the impact of COVID-19 on data collection that year.

Table MN-4. Migration, Origin, and Language

(Number, percent.)

Characteristic	State 2016-2020 [1]	U.S. 2016-2020 [1]
Residence 1 Year Ago		
Population 1 year and over...........................	5,535,623	322,943,283
Same house...........................	86.3	86.2
Different house in the U.S...........................	13.3	13.2
Same county...........................	6.8	7.7
Different county...........................	6.4	5.5
Same state...........................	4.5	3.2
Different state...........................	1.9	2.3
Abroad...........................	0.4	0.6
Place of Birth		
Native born...........................	5,129,479	282,443,680
Male...........................	49.8	49.4
Female...........................	50.2	50.6
Foreign born...........................	470,687	44,125,628
Male...........................	49.7	48.6
Female...........................	50.3	51.4
Foreign born; naturalized U.S. citizen...........................	257,167	22,456,684
Male...........................	47.7	46.1
Female...........................	52.3	53.9
Foreign born; not a U.S. citizen...........................	213,520	21,668,944
Male...........................	52.0	51.1
Female...........................	48.0	48.9
Entered 2010 or later...........................	28.5	22.8
Entered 2000 to 2009...........................	30.0	25.1
Entered before 2000...........................	41.5	52.1
World Region of Birth, Foreign		
Foreign-born population, excluding population born at sea...........................	470,687	44,125,628
Europe...........................	9.7	10.8
Asia...........................	37.1	31.3
Africa...........................	26.6	5.4
Oceania...........................	0.4	0.6
Latin America...........................	23.6	50.0
North America...........................	2.5	1.9
Language Spoken at Home and Ability to Speak English		
Population 5 years and over...........................	5,249,062	306,919,116
English only...........................	88.1	78.5
Language other than English...........................	11.9	21.5
Speaks English less than "very well"...........................	4.5	8.2

[1] 2020 ACS 5-Year estimates. 1-Year estimates were not released for 2020 due to the impact of COVID-19 on data collection that year.
NA = Not available.
X = Not applicable.
- = Zero or rounds to zero.

Table MN-5. Median Income and Poverty Status, 2020[1]

(Number, percent, except as noted.)

Characteristic	State Number	State Percent	U.S. Number	U.S. Percent
Median Income				
Households (dollars)	73,382	X	64,994	X
Families (dollars)	92,692	X	80,069	X
Below Poverty Level (All People)	511,185	9.3	40,910,326	12.8
Sex				
Male	230,592	8.5	18,171,512	11.6
Female	280,593	10.2	22,738,814	14.0
Age				
Under 18 years	147,958	11.6	12,598,699	17.5
Related children under 18 years	142,629	11.2	12,306,532	17.2
18 to 64 years	301,979	9.0	23,554,920	12.1
65 years and over	61,248	7.1	4,756,707	9.3

X = Not applicable.
[1] 2020 ACS 5-Year estimates. 1-Year estimates were not released for 2020 due to the impact of COVID-19 on data collection that year.

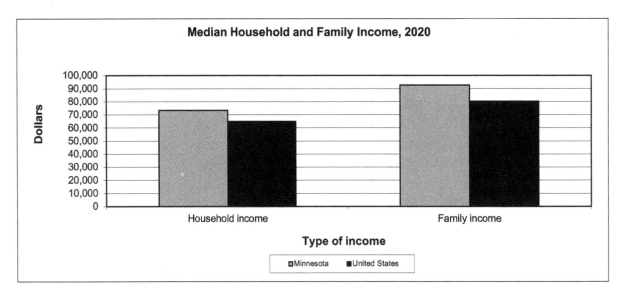

Median Household and Family Income, 2020

Table MN-6. Health Insurance Coverage Status for the Civilian Noninstitutionalized Population and Children Under 19 Years of Age

(Number, percent.)

Item	2011	2012	2013	2014	2015	2016	2017	2018	2019	2020[2]
Civilian Noninstitutionalized Population	5,286,728	5,319,783	5,362,681	5,398,211	5,431,894	5,462,438	5,519,199	5,553,564	5,580,828	5,541,421
Covered by Private or Public Insurance										
Number	4,819,295	4,895,121	4,922,902	5,080,954	5,186,786	5,237,492	5,276,690	5,309,185	5,308,216	5,289,521
Percent	91.2	92.0	91.8	94.1	95.5	95.9	95.6	95.6	95.1	95.5
Uninsured										
Number	467,433	424,662	439,779	317,257	245,108	224,946	242,509	244,379	272,612	251,900
Percent	8.8	8.0	8.2	5.9	4.5	4.1	4.4	4.4	4.9	4.5
Percent in the U.S. not covered	15.1	14.8	14.5	11.7	9.4	8.6	8.7	8.9	9.2	8.7
Children Under 19 Years of Age[1]	1,276,035	1,275,509	1,280,236	1,280,791	1,280,978	1,286,323	1,372,988	1,376,114	1,378,383	1,374,076
Covered by Private or Public Insurance										
Number	1,196,211	1,207,024	1,208,254	1,231,774	1,241,570	1,243,038	1,325,783	1,330,920	1,335,996	1,328,225
Percent	93.7	94.6	94.4	96.2	96.9	96.6	96.6	96.7	96.9	96.7
Uninsured										
Number	79,824	68,485	71,982	49,017	39,408	43,285	47,205	45,194	42,387	45,851
Percent	6.3	5.4	5.6	3.8	3.1	3.4	3.4	3.3	3.1	3.3
Percent in the U.S. not covered	7.5	7.2	7.1	6.0	4.8	4.5	5.0	5.2	5.7	5.2

[1] Data for years prior to 2017 are for individuals under 18 years of age.
[2] 2020 ACS 5-Year estimates. 1-Year estimates were not released for 2020 due to the impact of COVID-19 on data collection that year. Data is not comparable to previous years, which are based on 1-year estimates.

Table MN-7. Employment Status by Demographic Group, 2021

(Numbers in thousands, percent.)

Characteristic	Civilian noninstitutional population	Civilian labor force		Employed		Unemployed	
		Number	Percent of population	Number	Percent of population	Number	Percent of population
Total..	4,467	3,022	67.6	2,907	65.1	115	3.8
Sex							
Male...	2,212	1,587	71.8	1,529	69.1	58	3.7
Female..	2,256	1,435	63.6	1,378	61.1	57	4.0
Race, Sex, and Hispanic Origin							
White..	3,800	2,587	68.1	2,495	65.7	92	3.6
Male...	1,873	1,361	72.7	1,312	70.1	49	3.6
Female......................................	1,927	1,226	63.6	1,183	61.4	43	3.5
Black or African American.................	251	167	66.4	156	62.3	10	6.2
Male...	NA	NA	NA	NA	NA	NA	NA
Female......................................	NA	NA	NA	NA	NA	NA	NA
Hispanic or Latino ethnicity[1]............	191	150	78.3	143	74.6	7	4.7
Male...	NA	NA	NA	NA	NA	NA	NA
Female......................................	NA	NA	NA	NA	NA	NA	NA
Age							
16 to 19 years...............................	279	149	53.5	141	50.6	8	5.4
20 to 24 years...............................	336	254	75.5	230	68.4	24	9.4
25 to 34 years...............................	732	639	87.3	618	84.4	22	3.4
35 to 44 years...............................	786	668	85.0	648	82.5	20	3.0
45 to 54 years...............................	694	582	83.8	567	81.6	15	2.6
55 to 64 years...............................	730	516	70.8	495	67.8	21	4.1
65 years and over...........................	911	214	23.5	208	22.8	6	2.6

NOTE: Data in Table 7 are from the Current Population Survey (CPS) and do not match the estimates in Table 8. See notes and definitions for further information.
[1] May be of any race.
NA = Not available.

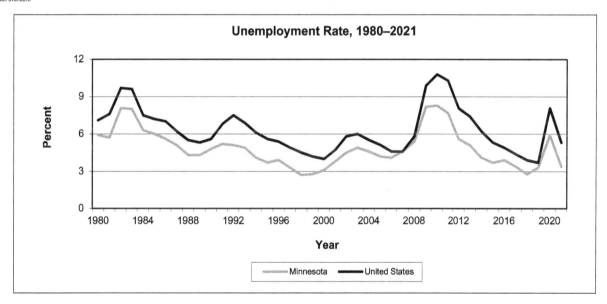

Table MN-8. Employment Status of the Civilian Noninstitutional Population Age 16 Years and Over

(Number, percent.)

Year	Civilian labor force	Civilian participation rate	Employed	Unemployed	Unemployment rate
2010..	2,940,696	71.5	2,722,623	218,073	7.4
2011..	2,952,527	71.1	2,760,400	192,127	6.5
2012..	2,949,770	70.5	2,783,181	166,589	5.6
2013..	2,961,729	70.2	2,812,453	149,276	5.0
2014..	2,979,798	70.1	2,852,488	127,310	4.3
2015..	3,005,414	70.2	2,891,673	113,741	3.8
2016..	3,023,110	70.0	2,906,348	116,762	3.9
2017..	3,071,006	70.1	2,963,830	107,176	3.5
2018..	3,085,627	69.8	2,989,055	96,572	3.1
2019..	3,129,844	70.3	3,021,984	107,860	3.4
2020..	3,122,981	69.7	2,925,515	197,466	6.3
2021..	3,021,360	67.2	2,918,393	102,967	3.4

Table MN-9. Employment and Average Wages by Industry

(Estimates are based on the 2012 North American Industry Classification System [NAICS].)

Industry	2013	2014	2015	2016	2017	2018	2019	2020
	Number of Jobs							
Wage and Salary Employment by Industry......................	2,833,384	2,873,671	2,923,387	2,956,259	2,993,016	3,019,075	3,038,946	2,841,249
Farm Wage and Salary Employment.............................	15,781	14,250	17,516	15,629	14,372	14,899	16,097	17,463
Nonfarm Wage and Salary Employment........................	2,817,603	2,859,421	2,905,871	2,940,630	2,978,644	3,004,176	3,022,849	2,823,786
Private wage and salary employment.......................................	2,400,023	2,439,900	2,484,119	2,517,643	2,549,805	2,576,194	2,593,210	2,413,080
Forestry, fishing, and related activities...............................	5,931	6,024	6,349	6,319	6,394	6,296	6,452	6,311
Mining..	6,219	6,370	6,164	5,364	5,735	5,887	5,825	5,462
Utilities..	13,012	12,863	12,787	12,506	12,365	12,302	12,053	11,890
Construction..	103,303	110,288	118,035	118,934	122,517	124,553	130,104	126,858
Manufacturing...	307,551	312,306	317,562	317,743	319,342	322,096	324,247	309,365
Durable goods manufacturing..	195,244	198,796	202,763	201,568	201,543	204,715	208,254	198,913
Nondurable goods manufacturing..................................	112,307	113,510	114,799	116,175	117,799	117,381	115,993	110,452
Wholesale trade	131,002	132,434	133,441	132,365	132,904	131,331	128,820	125,208
Retail trade..	288,449	290,302	295,140	300,057	300,353	300,447	294,975	277,871
Transportation and warehousing.......................................	81,017	84,145	86,677	89,201	93,829	95,511	97,465	91,781
Information	53,354	52,715	51,801	50,471	50,343	49,178	46,989	43,188
Finance and insurance	144,250	142,018	145,230	144,212	148,179	150,236	155,402	154,557
Real estate and rental and leasing....................................	40,541	39,814	40,067	35,163	35,368	36,111	36,526	34,939
Professional, scientific, and technical services	136,866	142,057	146,753	159,537	160,647	164,258	160,961	155,489
Management of companies and enterprises........................	77,025	78,753	78,193	78,539	80,109	81,307	89,205	87,020
Administrative and waste services	133,859	134,589	135,137	136,995	134,942	135,367	135,633	121,051
Educational services	71,353	71,779	73,374	73,845	74,390	73,882	73,699	66,893
Health care and social assistance.....................................	421,144	428,762	437,733	451,246	462,523	473,365	477,388	464,973
Arts, entertainment, and recreation...................................	39,821	41,508	42,073	43,559	45,825	46,854	48,374	32,908
Accommodation and food services....................................	211,853	215,110	218,979	223,638	226,752	227,871	228,975	173,620
Other services, except public administration......................	133,473	138,063	138,624	137,949	137,288	139,342	140,117	123,696
Government and government enterprises.................................	417,580	419,521	421,752	422,987	428,839	427,982	429,639	410,706
	Dollars							
Average Wages and Salaries by Industry	49,258	50,759	52,611	53,460	55,310	57,238	58,857	63,051
Average Farm Wages and Salaries	31,962	35,874	32,212	39,843	38,819	36,808	41,997	33,627
Average Nonfarm Wages and Salaries	49,355	50,833	52,734	53,533	55,389	57,339	58,947	63,233
Average private wages and salaries....................................	50,105	51,602	53,601	54,303	56,365	58,202	59,847	64,265
Forestry, fishing, and related activities.............................	28,965	29,394	30,746	32,471	33,376	34,507	35,419	37,874
Mining..	84,167	85,443	79,646	78,727	84,829	92,388	92,372	86,741
Utilities..	97,246	99,314	102,120	104,112	107,561	112,602	117,417	122,667
Construction	57,332	58,950	61,519	63,271	65,467	67,256	69,733	72,848
Manufacturing...	59,555	61,096	63,256	63,760	65,731	67,115	68,085	70,890
Durable goods manufacturing..	64,219	65,804	67,881	68,161	70,303	71,744	72,215	74,404
Nondurable goods manufacturing..................................	51,447	52,850	55,087	56,125	57,908	59,041	60,668	64,561
Wholesale trade	75,995	76,985	79,117	78,961	83,308	84,437	85,073	89,404
Retail trade..	25,970	27,215	28,235	28,815	29,513	30,757	31,512	34,008
Transportation and warehousing.......................................	48,374	50,238	51,247	52,538	53,053	54,819	56,415	58,535
Information	66,769	69,447	72,050	72,019	75,483	78,945	83,810	92,290
Finance and insurance	88,624	92,787	96,809	95,689	100,079	105,596	107,379	114,894
Real estate and rental and leasing....................................	53,617	55,046	58,217	50,221	51,800	52,619	54,738	58,186
Professional, scientific, and technical services	81,015	83,875	85,984	90,119	91,695	94,630	97,647	102,560
Management of companies and enterprises........................	112,836	115,301	120,493	119,059	125,055	127,264	129,420	131,752
Administrative and waste services	32,271	33,895	35,996	38,245	41,339	40,780	42,605	46,631
Educational services	30,140	30,746	30,931	31,215	31,695	33,221	33,945	37,718
Health care and social assistance.....................................	44,937	45,851	48,030	49,005	50,481	52,318	53,453	55,797
Arts, entertainment, and recreation...................................	32,284	32,425	34,035	34,692	35,635	38,862	39,439	46,788
Accommodation and food services....................................	17,493	18,240	19,426	20,382	21,342	22,551	23,257	21,922
Other services, except public administration......................	29,991	30,973	32,240	33,063	34,938	35,844	37,073	41,000
Government and government enterprises.................................	45,044	46,364	47,629	48,950	49,589	52,149	53,514	57,168

Table MN-10. Employment Characteristics by Family Type

(Number, percent.)

Family type and labor force status	2018 Total	2018 Families with own children under 18 years	2019 Total	2019 Families with own children under 18 years	2020[1] Total	2020[1] Families with own children under 18 years
All Families...	1,396,827	605,560	1,401,623	601,811	1,404,798	619,373
FAMILY TYPE AND LABOR FORCE STATUS						
Opposite-Sex Married-Couple Families.............................	1,103,111	436,012	1,100,581	427,830	1,100,940	441,327
Both husband and wife in labor force................................	59.6	78.4	59.7	78.8	60.2	78.3
Husband in labor force, wife not in labor force	15.0	17.5	15.0	17.5	15.4	17.6
Wife in labor force, husband not in labor force	6.9	2.9	7.1	2.8	7.2	3.2
Both husband and wife not in labor force................	17.6	0.8	17.4	0.6	17.2	0.9
Other Families	293,716	169,548	301,042	173,981	294,248	175,827
Female householder, no spouse present	67.2	69.6	65.2	67.2	67.6	69.9
In labor force...	53.2	62.6	51.1	59.6	53.4	61.7
Not in labor force	14.0	7.0	14.1	7.6	14.1	8.1
Male householder, no spouse present...........................	32.8	30.4	34.8	32.8	32.4	30.1
In labor force...	27.9	28.2	29.5	30.1	27.9	28.3
Not in labor force	4.9	2.2	5.2	2.7	4.6	1.9

[1] 2020 ACS 5-Year estimates. 1-Year estimates were not released for 2020 due to the impact of COVID-19 on data collection that year. Data is not comparable to previous years, which are based on 1-year estimates.

Table MN-11. School Enrollment and Educational Attainment, 2020[1]

(Number, percent.)

Item	State	U.S.
Enrollment		
Total population 3 years and over, enrolled in school	1,392,298	80,497,960
Enrolled in nursery school or preschool (percent)	6.7	6.1
Enrolled in kindergarten (percent)...	5.2	5.0
Enrolled in elementary school, grades 1-8 (percent).................................	41.4	40.4
Enrolled in high school, grades 9-12 (percent).................................	21.2	21.0
Enrolled in college or graduate school (percent).................................	25.6	27.6
Attainment		
Total population 25 years and over	3,802,438	222,836,834
Less than ninth grade (percent)	2.8	4.9
9th to 12th grade, no diploma (percent)	3.9	6.6
High school graduate, including equivalency (percent).................................	24.2	26.7
Some college, no degree (percent)...	20.8	20.3
Associate's degree (percent)...	11.6	8.6
Bachelor's degree (percent)...	24.2	20.2
Graduate or professional degree (percent).................................	12.6	12.7
High school graduate or higher (percent)	93.4	88.5
Bachelor's degree or higher (percent).................................	36.8	32.9

[1] 2020 ACS 5-Year estimates. 1-Year estimates were not released for 2020 due to the impact of COVID-19 on data collection that year.

Table MN-12. Public School Characteristics and Educational Indicators

(Number, percent; data derived from National Center of Education Statistics.)

Item	State	U.S.
Public Elementary and Secondary Schools		
Number of regular school districts, 2018-19	331	13,452
Number of operational schools, 2019-20...	2,545	98,469
Percent charter schools	9.6	7.7
Total public school enrollment, Fall 2019...	893,203	50,796,445
Percent charter school enrollment	7.0	6.8
Student-teacher ratio, Fall 2019...	16.1	15.9
Expenditures per student (unadjusted dollars), 2018-19	13,297	13,187
Four-year adjusted cohort graduation rate (ACGR), 2018-2019[1].................................	83.7	85.8
Students eligible for free or reduced-price lunch (percent), 2019-20.................................	35.8	52.1
English language learners (percent), Fall 2019	8.6	10.4
Students age 3 to 21 served under IDEA, part B (percent), 2020-21	16.6	14.5

Public Schools by Type, 2019-20	Number	Percent of state public schools
Total number of schools...	2,545	100.0
Special education...	331	13.0
Vocational education...	7	0.3
Alternative education...	471	18.5

[1] Adjusted Cohort Graduation Rates (ACGR) differ from Averaged Freshmen Graduation Rates (AFGR).

Table MN-13. Reported Voting and Registration of the Voting-Age Population, November 2020

(Numbers in thousands, percent.)

Item	Total population	Total citizen population	Registered			Voted		
			Total registered	Percent registered (total population)	Percent registered (total citizen population)	Total voted	Percent voted (total population)	Percent voted (total citizen population)
U.S. Total	252,274	231,593	168,308	66.7	72.7	154,628	61.3	66.8
State Total................................	4,339	4,142	3,436	79.2	82.9	3,225	74.3	77.9
Sex								
Male	2,149	2,051	1,690	78.6	82.4	1,575	73.3	76.8
Female	2,190	2,091	1,746	79.7	83.5	1,649	75.3	78.9
Race								
White alone................................	3,744	3,678	3,086	82.4	83.9	2,918	77.9	79.3
White, non-Hispanic alone	3,573	3,555	2,990	83.7	84.1	2,840	79.5	79.9
Black alone................................	260	197	139	53.5	70.5	130	50.2	66.1
Asian alone	179	115	91	51.2	79.4	74	41.3	64.0
Hispanic (of any race)	209	156	116	55.8	74.7	98	46.8	62.7
White alone or in combination	3,816	3,750	3,146	82.5	83.9	2,979	78.1	79.4
Black alone or in combination	299	236	170	56.9	72.0	161	54.0	68.3
Asian alone or in combination..........................	191	127	104	54.3	81.4	86	45.1	67.5
Age								
18 to 24 years	440	430	317	72.0	73.8	297	67.5	69.2
25 to 34 years	787	772	595	75.6	77.1	541	68.7	70.0
35 to 44 years	771	672	539	69.9	80.2	503	65.3	74.9
45 to 64 years	1,431	1,379	1,199	83.8	86.9	1,134	79.2	82.2
65 years and over	909	889	785	86.4	88.4	749	82.5	84.3

B = Base is less than 75,000 and therefore too small to show the derived measure.

Table MN-14. Crime

(Number, rate per 100,000. Data are derived from the FBI Uniform Crime Reports.)

Item	State [1]			U.S.		
	2019	2020	Percent change	2019	2020	Percent change
TOTAL POPULATION[1]	5,640,053	5,657,342	0.3	328,329,953	329,484,123	0.4
VIOLENT CRIME						
Number................................	13,395	15,698	17.2	1,250,393	1,313,105	5.0
Rate	237.5	277.5	16.8	380.8	398.5	4.6
Murder and Nonnegligent Manslaughter						
Number................................	127	190	49.6	16,669	21,570	29.4
Rate	2.3	3.4	49.1	5.1	6.5	28.9
Rape[2]						
Number................................	2,499	2,211	-11.5	143,224	126,430	-11.7
Rate	44.3	39.1	-11.8	43.6	38.4	-12.0
Robbery						
Number................................	3,155	3,877	22.9	268,483	243,600	-9.3
Rate	55.9	68.5	22.5	81.8	73.9	-9.6
Aggravated Assault						
Number................................	7,614	9,420	23.7	822,017	921,505	12.1
Rate	135.0	166.5	23.3	250.4	279.7	11.7
PROPERTY CRIME						
Number................................	117,971	120,212	1.9	6,995,235	6,452,038	-7.8
Rate	2,091.7	2,124.9	1.6	2,130.6	1,958.2	-8.1
Burglary						
Number................................	16,026	17,370	8.4	1,118,096	1,035,314	-7.4
Rate	284.1	307.0	8.1	340.5	314.2	-7.7
Larceny-Theft						
Number................................	90,685	88,696	-2.2	5,152,267	4,606,324	-10.6
Rate	1,607.9	1,567.8	-2.5	1,569.2	1,398.0	-10.9
Motor Vehicle Theft						
Number................................	11,260	14,146	25.6	724,872	810,400	11.8
Rate	199.6	250.0	25.2	220.8	246.0	11.4

NOTE: Although arson data are included in the trend and clearance tables, sufficient data are not available to estimate totals for this offense. Therefore, no arson data are published in this table.
- = Zero or rounds to zero.
[1] Population figures are U.S. Census Bureau provisional estimates as of July 1, 2020.
[2] The figures shown in the rape (revised definition) column were estimated using the revised Uniform Crime Reporting (UCR) definition of rape.

Table MN-15. State Government Finances, 2020

(Dollar amounts in thousands, percent distribution.)

Item	Dollars	Percent distribution
Total Revenue	57,362,323	100.0
General revenue	46,917,950	81.8
Intergovernmental revenue	14,775,582	25.8
Taxes	26,790,884	46.7
General sales	6435200	11.2
Selective sales	4,917,702	8.6
License taxes	1,578,328	2.8
Individual income tax	10923158	19.0
Corporate income tax	1,604,450	2.8
Other taxes	1,332,046	2.3
Current charges	2,877,353	5.0
Miscellaneous general revenue	2,474,131	4.3
Utility revenue	104,464	0.2
Liquor stores revenue	0	-
Insurance trust revenue[1]	10,339,909	18.0
Total Expenditure	55,575,289	100.0
Intergovernmental expenditure	15,514,183	27.9
Direct expenditure	40,061,106	72.1
Current operation	28,331,412	51.0
Capital outlay	1,959,075	3.5
Insurance benefits and repayments	7,815,653	14.1
Assistance and subsidies	1,345,735	2.4
Interest on debt	609,231	1.1
Exhibit: Salaries and wages	6,216,687	11.2
Total Expenditure	55,575,289	100.0
General expenditure	47,216,223	85.0
Intergovernmental expenditure	15,514,183	27.9
Direct expenditure	31,702,040	57.0
General expenditure, by function:		
Education	17,040,188	30.7
Public welfare	17,079,921	30.7
Hospitals	389,391	0.7
Health	1,160,613	2.1
Highways	3,307,878	6.0
Police protection	571,284	1.0
Correction	618,445	1.1
Natural resources	731,651	1.3
Parks and recreation	317,300	0.6
Governmental administration	2,058,681	3.7
Interest on general debt	609,231	1.1
Other and unallocable	3,010,814	5.4
Utility expenditure	654,090	1.1
Liquor stores expenditure	0	-
Insurance trust expenditure	7,815,653	14.1
Debt at End of Fiscal Year	17,400,637	X
Cash and Security Holdings	96,659,127	X

X = Not applicable.
- = Zero or rounds to zero.
[1] Within insurance trust revenue, net earnings of state retirement systems is a calculated statistic (the item code in the data file is X08), and thus can be positive or negative. Net earnings is the sum of earnings on investments plus gains on investments minus losses on investments. The change made in 2002 for asset valuation from book to market value in accordance with Statement 34 of the Governmental Accounting Standards Board is reflected in the calculated statistics.

Table MN-16. State Government Tax Collections, 2021

(Dollars in thousands, percent.)

Item	Dollars	Percent distribution
Total Taxes	31,793,412	100.0
Property taxes	809,160	2.5
Sales and gross receipts	11,204,458	35.2
General sales and gross receipts	6,698,560	21.1
Selective sales and gross receipts	4,505,898	14.2
Alcoholic beverages	101,472	0.3
Amusements	132,221	0.4
Insurance premiums	650,137	2.0
Motor fuels	844,730	2.7
Pari-mutuels	2,463	-
Public utilities	95,402	0.3
Tobacco products	626,480	2.0
Other selective sales	2,052,993	6.5
Licenses	1,505,670	4.7
Alcoholic beverages	3,070	-
Amusements	5,575	-
Corporations in general	16,055	0.1
Hunting and fishing	110,681	0.3
Motor vehicle	945,653	3.0
Motor vehicle operators	59,219	0.2
Public utilities	7,570	-
Occupation and business, NEC	271,262	0.9
Other licenses	86,585	0.3
Income taxes	17,593,996	55.3
Individual income	15,170,613	47.7
Corporation net income	2,423,383	7.6
Other taxes	680,128	2.1
Death and gift	204,646	0.6
Documentary and stock transfer	410,830	1.3
Severance	64,652	0.2
Taxes, NEC	0	-

- = Zero or rounds to zero.

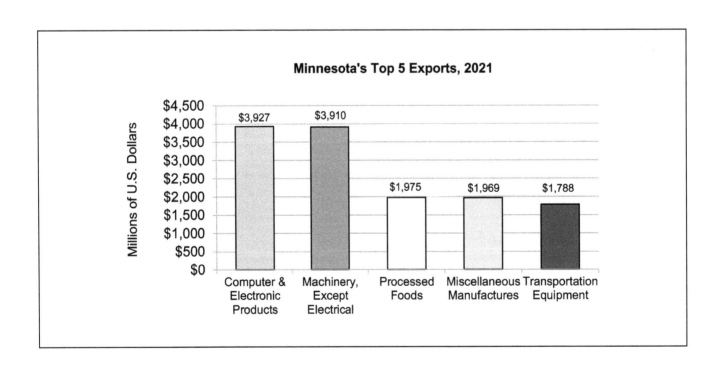

Minnesota's Top 5 Exports, 2021

Export	Millions of U.S. Dollars
Computer & Electronic Products	$3,927
Machinery, Except Electrical	$3,910
Processed Foods	$1,975
Miscellaneous Manufactures	$1,969
Transportation Equipment	$1,788

Facts and Figures

Location: South central United States; bordered on the N by Tennessee, on the E by Alabama, on the S by Louisiana and the Gulf of Mexico, and on the W by Arkansas and Louisiana

Area: 48,430 sq. mi. (125,434 sq. km.); rank—32nd

Population: 2,949,965 (2021 est.); rank—34th

Principal Cities: capital—Jackson; largest—Jackson

Statehood: December 10, 1817; 20th state

U.S. Congress: 2 senators, 4 representatives

State Motto: *Virtute et armis* ("By valor and arms")

State Song: "Go, Mississippi"

State Nicknames: The Magnolia State; The Hospitality State

Abbreviations: MS; Miss.

State Symbols: flower—magnolia blossom; tree—Southern magnolia; bird—mockingbird

At a Glance

- With a 0.6 percent decrease in population, Mississippi was one of three states that experienced a population decline from 2010 to 2021.

- In 2020, Mississippi had the lowest median household income in the country ($46,511) and the highest percent of population living the below the poverty level (19.6 percent).

- In 2020, 12.0 percent of Mississippians did not have health insurance, compared to 8.7 percent of the total U.S. population.

- Mississippi had the highest traffic fatality rate in 2020, with 25.4 deaths per 100,000 population.

- In 2020, 22.8 percent of Mississippians age 25 years and older had a bachelor's degree or higher, which was the 2nd lowest percentage among states.

Table MS-1. Population by Age, Sex, Race, and Hispanic Origin

(Number, percent, except where noted.)

Sex, age, race, and Hispanic origin	2000	2010	2021	Percent change, 2010–2021
Total Population..	2,844,658	2,967,297	2,949,965	-0.6
Percent of total U.S. population	1.0	1.0	0.9	X
Sex				
Male..	1,373,554	1,441,240	1,435,336	-0.4
Female	1,471,104	1,526,057	1,514,629	-0.7
Age				
Under 5 years..	204,364	210,956	176,891	-16.1
5 to 19 years...	668,850	638,539	595,041	-6.8
20 to 64 years...	1,627,921	1,737,395	1,683,789	-3.1
65 years and over	343,523	380,407	494,244	29.9
Median age (years)	33.8	36.0	38.4	6.7
Race and Hispanic Origin				
One race				
White	1,746,099	1,789,391	1,733,991	-3.1
Black	1,033,809	1,103,101	1,119,623	1.5
American Indian and Alaska Native	11,652	16,837	18,851	12.0
Asian	18,626	26,477	33,467	26.4
Native Hawaiian or Other Pacific Islander	667	1,700	1,957	15.1
Two or more races..	20,021	29,791	42,076	41.2
Hispanic (of any race)...	39,569	85,107	102,936	20.9

NOTE: Population figures for 2021 are July 1 estimates. The 2000 and 2010 estimates are taken from the respective censuses.
- = Zero or rounds to zero.
X = Not applicable.

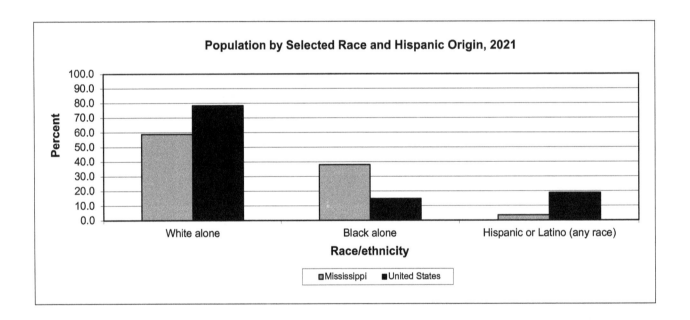

Table MS-2. Marital Status

(Number, percent distribution.)

Sex, age, race, and Hispanic origin	2000	2010	2020 [1]
Males, 15 Years and Over	1,046,252	1,121,265	1,144,925
Never married	30.6	34.9	36.5
Now married, except separated......................................	54.6	48.3	47.2
Separated..	2.4	2.5	2.3
Widowed..	2.9	2.7	3.4
Divorced...	9.5	11.7	10.7
Females, 15 Years and Over	1,157,363	1,224,423	1,251,448
Never married	25.1	29.8	31.3
Now married, except separated......................................	48.6	43.8	42.9
Separated..	3.2	3.4	3.1
Widowed..	12.5	10.8	10.5
Divorced...	10.6	12.3	12.2

[1] 2020 ACS 5-Year estimates. 1-Year estimates were not released for 2020 due to the impact of COVID-19 on data collection that year.

Table MS-3. Households and Housing Characteristics

(Number, percent, dollars.)

Item	2000	2010	2020 [1]	Average annual percent change, 2010–2020
Total Households..	1,046,434	1,079,999	1,116,649	0.5
Family households	747,159	746,115	740,489	-0.1
Married-couple family	520,884	501,571	499,635	-0.1
Other family	226,315	244,544	240,854	-0.2
Male householder, no wife present..................................	45,610	51,400	50,593	-0.2
Female householder, no husband present........................	180,705	193,144	190,261	-0.2
Nonfamily households	299,275	333,884	376,160	1.8
Householder living alone...	257,708	293,185	326,514	1.6
Householder not living alone...	41,567	40,699	49,646	3.1
Housing Characteristics				
Total housing units..	1,161,953	1,276,441	1,330,867	0.6
Occupied housing units	1,046,434	1,079,999	1,116,649	0.5
Owner occupied	756,967	753,374	767,972	0.3
Renter occupied	289,467	326,625	348,677	1.0
Average household size..	2.63	2.66	2.59	-0.4
Financial Characteristics				
Median gross rent of renter-occupied housing	439	672	789	2.5
Median monthly owner costs for housing units with a mortgage	762	1,043	1,161	1.6
Median value of owner-occupied housing units................	71,400	100,100	125,500	3.6

[1] 2020 ACS 5-Year estimates. 1-Year estimates were not released for 2020 due to the impact of COVID-19 on data collection that year.

Table MS-4. Migration, Origin, and Language

(Number, percent.)

Characteristic	State 2016-2020 [1]	U.S. 2016-2020 [1]
Residence 1 Year Ago		
Population 1 year and over	2,946,605	322,943,283
Same house	87.5	86.2
Different house in the U.S.	12.3	13.2
Same county	6.7	7.7
Different county	5.6	5.5
Same state	3.4	3.2
Different state	2.2	2.3
Abroad	0.2	0.6
Place of Birth		
Native born	2,912,624	282,443,680
Male	48.3	49.4
Female	51.7	50.6
Foreign born	69,211	44,125,628
Male	52.0	48.6
Female	48.0	51.4
Foreign born; naturalized U.S. citizen...	29,012	22,456,684
Male	46.8	46.1
Female	53.2	53.9
Foreign born; not a U.S. citizen...	40,199	21,668,944
Male	55.7	51.1
Female	44.3	48.9
Entered 2010 or later	33.0	22.8
Entered 2000 to 2009	25.7	25.1
Entered before 2000..	41.2	52.1
World Region of Birth, Foreign		
Foreign-born population, excluding population born at sea	69,211	44,125,628
Europe	10.1	10.8
Asia..	33.4	31.3
Africa...	4.8	5.4
Oceania	0.8	0.6
Latin America..	49.0	50.0
North America..	1.9	1.9
Language Spoken at Home and Ability to Speak English		
Population 5 years and over..	2,796,561	306,919,116
English only	96.0	78.5
Language other than English..	4.0	21.5
Speaks English less than "very well"..	1.6	8.2

[1] 2020 ACS 5-Year estimates. 1-Year estimates were not released for 2020 due to the impact of COVID-19 on data collection that year.
NA = Not available.
X = Not applicable.
- = Zero or rounds to zero.

Table MS-5. Median Income and Poverty Status, 2020[1]

(Number, percent, except as noted.)

Characteristic	State		U.S.	
	Number	Percent	Number	Percent
Median Income				
Households (dollars)...	46,511	X	64,994	X
Families (dollars)	58,923	X	80,069	X
Below Poverty Level (All People)	564,439	19.6	40,910,326	12.8
Sex				
Male	241,674	17.5	18,171,512	11.6
Female	322,765	21.5	22,738,814	14.0
Age				
Under 18 years...	191,339	27.6	12,598,699	17.5
Related children under 18 years..	188,939	27.3	12,306,532	17.2
18 to 64 years	314,225	18.2	23,554,920	12.1
65 years and over	58,875	12.8	4,756,707	9.3

X = Not applicable.
[1] 2020 ACS 5-Year estimates. 1-Year estimates were not released for 2020 due to the impact of COVID-19 on data collection that year.

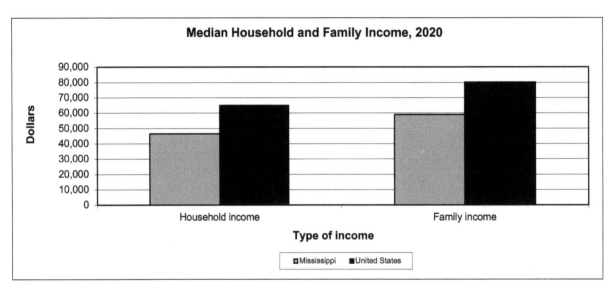

Table MS-6. Health Insurance Coverage Status for the Civilian Noninstitutionalized Population and Children Under 19 Years of Age

(Number, percent.)

Item	2011	2012	2013	2014	2015	2016	2017	2018	2019	2020[2]
Civilian Noninstitutionalized Population	2,911,811	2,918,405	2,925,211	2,927,088	2,927,568	2,924,168	2,920,808	2,919,673	2,904,609	2,912,057
Covered by Private or Public Insurance										
Number..	2,395,398	2,420,895	2,425,362	2,502,958	2,555,983	2,577,987	2,569,054	2,565,522	2,527,737	2,562,055
Percent...	82.3	83.0	82.9	85.5	87.3	88.2	88.0	87.9	87.0	88.0
Uninsured										
Number..	516,413	497,510	499,849	424,130	371,585	346,181	351,754	354,151	376,872	350,002
Percent...	17.7	17.0	17.1	14.5	12.7	11.8	12.0	12.1	13.0	12.0
Percent in the U.S. not covered..........................	15.1	14.8	14.5	11.7	9.4	8.6	8.7	8.9	9.2	8.7
Children Under 19 Years of Age[1]	749,572	745,603	734,075	729,802	725,664	721,108	763,456	756,077	744,641	749,257
Covered by Private or Public Insurance										
Number..	688,589	690,862	677,926	690,970	696,297	688,518	726,463	720,648	698,928	710,968
Percent...	91.9	92.7	92.4	94.7	96.0	95.5	95.2	95.3	93.9	94.9
Uninsured										
Number..	60,983	54,741	56,149	38,832	29,367	32,590	36,993	35,429	45,713	38,289
Percent...	8.1	7.3	7.6	5.3	4.0	4.5	4.8	4.7	6.1	5.1
Percent in the U.S. not covered..........................	7.5	7.2	7.1	6.0	4.8	4.5	5.0	5.2	5.7	5.2

[1] Data for years prior to 2017 are for individuals under 18 years of age.
[2] 2020 ACS 5-Year estimates. 1-Year estimates were not released for 2020 due to the impact of COVID-19 on data collection that year. Data is not comparable to previous years, which are based on 1-year estimates.

Table MS-7. Employment Status by Demographic Group, 2021

(Numbers in thousands, percent.)

Characteristic	Civilian noninstitutional population	Civilian labor force		Employed		Unemployed	
		Number	Percent of population	Number	Percent of population	Number	Percent of population
Total..	2,286	1,253	54.8	1,184	51.8	68	5.5
Sex							
Male..	1,072	640	59.7	601	56.1	39	6.0
Female	1,214	613	50.5	583	48.0	30	4.9
Race, Sex, and Hispanic Origin							
White	1,393	763	54.8	734	52.7	29	3.8
Male..	673	413	61.3	394	58.6	18	4.4
Female	720	350	48.7	340	47.2	11	3.0
Black or African American...............	838	458	54.7	421	50.2	37	8.1
Male..	374	210	56.1	190	50.8	20	9.4
Female	464	248	53.6	231	49.8	18	7.1
Hispanic or Latino ethnicity[1]	NA	NA	NA	NA	NA	NA	NA
Male..	NA	NA	NA	NA	NA	NA	NA
Female	NA	NA	NA	NA	NA	NA	NA
Age							
16 to 19 years	NA	NA	NA	NA	NA	NA	NA
20 to 24 years	165	98	59.5	85	51.6	13	13.2
25 to 34 years	390	296	76.1	276	70.9	20	6.7
35 to 44 years	359	276	76.7	262	72.9	14	5.0
45 to 54 years	346	260	75.1	252	72.6	9	3.3
55 to 64 years	383	208	54.3	203	53.0	5	2.5
65 years and over	493	73	14.8	71	14.4	2	2.7

NOTE: Data in Table 7 are from the Current Population Survey (CPS) and do not match the estimates in Table 8. See notes and definitions for further information.
[1] May be of any race.
NA = Not available.

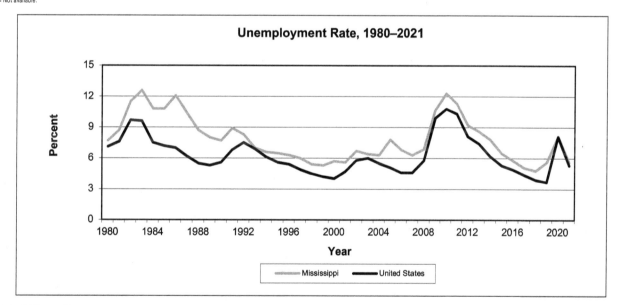

Unemployment Rate, 1980–2021

Table MS-8. Employment Status of the Civilian Noninstitutional Population Age 16 Years and Over

(Number, percent.)

Year	Civilian labor force	Civilian participation rate	Employed	Unemployed	Unemployment rate
2010..	1,309,128	58.8	1,176,938	132,190	10.1
2011..	1,345,990	60.0	1,214,638	131,352	9.8
2012..	1,330,450	59.0	1,213,245	117,205	8.8
2013..	1,273,057	56.2	1,164,832	108,225	8.5
2014..	1,243,934	54.7	1,149,277	94,657	7.6
2015..	1,260,015	55.3	1,178,018	81,997	6.5
2016..	1,271,836	55.7	1,196,241	75,595	5.9
2017..	1,272,685	55.7	1,206,102	66,583	5.2
2018..	1,268,435	55.6	1,205,737	62,698	4.9
2019..	1,277,143	56	1,207,543	69,600	5.4
2020..	1,243,515	54.6	1,145,211	98,304	7.9
2021..	1,254,239	55	1,184,401	69,838	5.6

Table MS-9. Employment and Average Wages by Industry

(Estimates are based on the 2012 North American Industry Classification System [NAICS].)

Industry	2013	2014	2015	2016	2017	2018	2019	2020
	Number of Jobs							
Wage and Salary Employment by Industry........................	1,179,070	1,194,211	1,202,135	1,209,425	1,214,455	1,217,171	1,223,735	1,174,858
Farm Wage and Salary Employment...............................	6,941	12,119	9,375	8,367	9,411	9,162	9,388	7,471
Nonfarm Wage and Salary Employment..........................	1,172,129	1,182,092	1,192,760	1,201,058	1,205,044	1,208,009	1,214,347	1,167,387
Private wage and salary employment..	895,338	906,128	918,425	927,828	933,189	938,213	943,012	899,342
Forestry, fishing, and related activities............................	7,820	7,883	7,956	8,133	7,925	8,217	8,298	7,826
Mining...	6,181	6,254	5,053	3,840	4,062	3,975	3,838	3,078
Utilities...	7,870	7,826	7,870	7,942	8,058	7,896	7,748	7,727
Construction...	52,593	50,321	47,193	45,577	44,493	44,985	45,622	44,988
Manufacturing...	136,980	139,717	141,925	143,245	144,164	144,907	146,919	139,607
Durable goods manufacturing....................................	90,651	93,638	94,756	94,960	95,211	95,437	96,879	90,687
Nondurable goods manufacturing...............................	46,329	46,079	47,169	48,285	48,953	49,470	50,040	48,920
Wholesale trade	34,274	34,202	34,673	34,443	34,920	34,260	34,570	33,584
Retail trade..	134,447	136,557	139,036	141,604	141,263	139,303	136,665	133,911
Transportation and warehousing....................................	40,983	42,729	44,834	46,905	48,292	50,525	52,758	53,952
Information..	12,806	13,246	13,622	12,143	11,579	10,968	10,690	9,625
Finance and insurance	33,492	33,162	33,233	33,380	33,517	33,489	33,873	33,542
Real estate and rental and leasing.................................	11,734	11,679	11,756	11,781	11,823	11,896	12,011	11,415
Professional, scientific, and technical services	30,863	31,226	31,088	30,949	31,390	31,657	31,668	32,402
Management of companies and enterprises........................	10,777	10,658	10,611	11,055	11,017	11,493	11,237	11,073
Administrative and waste services..................................	57,901	60,368	63,962	66,616	66,079	67,481	66,276	65,063
Educational services	19,868	19,651	19,368	18,769	19,094	18,423	18,355	16,018
Health care and social assistance..................................	123,653	124,814	127,523	129,870	132,735	134,585	136,796	130,396
Arts, entertainment, and recreation................................	11,588	11,562	11,413	11,572	9,780	9,742	9,932	8,269
Accommodation and food services.................................	113,061	115,149	118,393	122,156	125,560	125,755	127,032	110,762
Other services, except public administration......................	48,447	49,124	48,916	47,848	47,438	48,656	48,724	46,104
Government and government enterprises.................................	276,791	275,964	274,335	273,230	271,855	269,796	271,335	268,045
	Dollars							
Average Wages and Salaries by Industry	37,468	37,993	38,553	39,118	39,825	40,904	41,800	44,448
Average Farm Wages and Salaries	24,977	20,815	21,563	19,807	17,156	18,454	13,300	15,364
Average Nonfarm Wages and Salaries	37,542	38,169	38,687	39,252	40,002	41,074	42,020	44,634
Average private wages and salaries..................................	37,286	37,953	38,369	38,778	39,557	40,623	41,534	44,366
Forestry, fishing, and related activities............................	32,599	33,883	35,655	36,681	37,378	39,368	41,157	43,874
Mining...	75,693	78,592	78,763	76,571	75,657	76,448	80,940	86,281
Utilities...	71,797	73,931	77,768	79,649	81,758	84,902	86,149	93,230
Construction	46,684	47,288	47,198	48,655	49,772	51,302	51,898	54,901
Manufacturing...	45,847	47,644	48,334	49,256	50,376	51,382	52,171	54,328
Durable goods manufacturing....................................	47,286	49,077	49,515	50,790	52,063	52,712	53,243	55,214
Nondurable goods manufacturing...............................	43,031	44,732	45,963	46,239	47,095	48,818	50,096	52,685
Wholesale trade	53,067	54,638	56,191	57,121	59,080	61,180	62,767	65,678
Retail trade..	25,035	25,352	25,866	26,212	26,539	27,076	27,764	30,202
Transportation and warehousing....................................	43,631	44,378	45,444	44,486	45,661	46,979	48,190	50,625
Information..	46,406	47,748	46,180	49,525	50,490	51,491	51,820	57,279
Finance and insurance	54,719	55,916	57,529	58,760	60,371	62,741	64,225	68,953
Real estate and rental and leasing.................................	33,502	34,837	35,615	35,607	36,758	37,755	39,090	42,570
Professional, scientific, and technical services	55,784	55,970	57,826	59,015	59,463	60,708	61,153	63,439
Management of companies and enterprises........................	80,302	82,985	84,889	83,167	87,488	88,719	89,495	98,721
Administrative and waste services..................................	27,641	27,745	27,822	27,891	28,005	28,234	29,353	30,771
Educational services	28,563	28,893	28,131	29,306	29,244	29,997	30,266	35,162
Health care and social assistance..................................	40,630	41,006	41,532	41,904	42,486	43,712	44,644	48,014
Arts, entertainment, and recreation................................	23,868	23,540	24,256	24,112	21,757	22,556	22,776	24,590
Accommodation and food services.................................	18,787	18,920	18,869	19,190	19,671	20,535	20,855	20,509
Other services, except public administration......................	28,641	29,567	30,401	31,647	32,748	33,311	34,562	37,629
Government and government enterprises.................................	38,370	38,877	39,748	40,862	41,532	42,645	43,707	45,533

Table MS-10. Employment Characteristics by Family Type

(Number, percent.)

Family type and labor force status	2018 Total	2018 Families with own children under 18 years	2019 Total	2019 Families with own children under 18 years	2020[1] Total	2020[1] Families with own children under 18 years
All Families........................	727,948	298,013	718,382	281,962	740,489	302,379
FAMILY TYPE AND LABOR FORCE STATUS						
Opposite-Sex Married-Couple Families....................	491,760	182,169	481,478	166,838	496,679	181,657
Both husband and wife in labor force....................	47.8	68.4	46.9	66.9	48.6	68.9
Husband in labor force, wife not in labor force	20.8	24.3	21.7	26.9	21.1	24.6
Wife in labor force, husband not in labor force	9.0	5.3	8.7	4.2	9.1	4.7
Both husband and wife not in labor force....................	21.8	1.6	22.1	1.8	21.2	1.9
Other Families	236,188	115,844	236,904	115,124	240,854	120,355
Female householder, no spouse present	80.4	85.0	78.2	83.3	79.0	82.0
In labor force....................	50.4	67.3	49.8	66.5	50.9	65.7
Not in labor force....................	29.9	17.6	28.4	16.8	28.0	16.3
Male householder, no spouse present....................	19.6	15.0	21.8	16.7	21.0	18.0
In labor force....................	13.2	13.6	14.1	14.8	14.2	15.8
Not in labor force....................	6.4	1.5	7.8	1.9	6.8	2.2

[1] 2020 ACS 5-Year estimates. 1-Year estimates were not released for 2020 due to the impact of COVID-19 on data collection that year. Data is not comparable to previous years, which are based on 1-year estimates.

Table MS-11. School Enrollment and Educational Attainment, 2020[1]

(Number, percent.)

Item	State	U.S.
Enrollment		
Total population 3 years and over, enrolled in school	754,722	80,497,960
Enrolled in nursery school or preschool (percent)....................	6.4	6.1
Enrolled in kindergarten (percent)....................	5.2	5.0
Enrolled in elementary school, grades 1-8 (percent)....................	42.6	40.4
Enrolled in high school, grades 9-12 (percent)....................	20.9	21.0
Enrolled in college or graduate school (percent)....................	25	27.6
Attainment		
Total population 25 years and over	1,983,112	222,836,834
Less than ninth grade (percent)....................	4.7	4.9
9th to 12th grade, no diploma (percent)....................	10.0	6.6
High school graduate, including equivalency (percent)....................	30.1	26.7
Some college, no degree (percent)	22.2	20.3
Associate's degree (percent)....................	10.2	8.6
Bachelor's degree (percent)....................	13.8	20.2
Graduate or professional degree (percent)....................	8.9	12.7
High school graduate or higher (percent)....................	85.3	88.5
Bachelor's degree or higher (percent)....................	22.8	32.9

[1] 2020 ACS 5-Year estimates. 1-Year estimates were not released for 2020 due to the impact of COVID-19 on data collection that year.

Table MS-12. Public School Characteristics and Educational Indicators

(Number, percent; data derived from National Center of Education Statistics.)

Item	State	U.S.
Public Elementary and Secondary Schools		
Number of regular school districts, 2018-19	141	13,452
Number of operational schools, 2019-20....................	1,047	98,469
Percent charter schools	0.6	7.7
Total public school enrollment, Fall 2019....................	466,002	50,796,445
Percent charter school enrollment	0.5	6.8
Student-teacher ratio, Fall 2019....................	14.8	15.9
Expenditures per student (unadjusted dollars), 2018-19	9,253	13,187
Four-year adjusted cohort graduation rate (ACGR), 2018-2019[1]....................	85.0	85.8
Students eligible for free or reduced-price lunch (percent), 2019-20....................	74.8	52.1
English language learners (percent), Fall 2019	2.5	10.4
Students age 3 to 21 served under IDEA, part B (percent), 2020-21	15.2	14.5

Public Schools by Type, 2019-20	Number	Percent of state public schools
Total number of schools....................	1,047	100.0
Special education....................	2	0.2
Vocational education....................	92	8.8
Alternative education....................	68	6.5

[1] Adjusted Cohort Graduation Rates (ACGR) differ from Averaged Freshmen Graduation Rates (AFGR).

Table MS-13. Reported Voting and Registration of the Voting-Age Population, November 2020

(Numbers in thousands, percent.)

Item	Total population	Total citizen population	Registered			Voted		
			Total registered	Percent registered (total population)	Percent registered (total citizen population)	Total voted	Percent voted (total population)	Percent voted (total citizen population)
U.S. Total	252,274	231,593	168,308	66.7	72.7	154,628	61.3	66.8
State Total	2,212	2,177	1,749	79.1	80.4	1,531	69.2	70.3
Sex								
Male	1,029	1,015	792	76.9	78.0	680	66.1	67.0
Female	1,182	1,162	957	81.0	82.4	850	71.9	73.2
Race								
White alone	1,350	1,337	1,054	78.1	78.8	921	68.3	68.9
White, non-Hispanic alone	1,300	1,295	1,026	78.9	79.2	904	69.5	69.8
Black alone	792	787	654	82.5	83.1	573	72.3	72.8
Asian alone	37	20	9	B	B	8	B	B
Hispanic (of any race)	67	53	34	B	B	23	B	B
White alone or in combination	1,375	1,363	1,079	78.5	79.2	942	68.5	69.1
Black alone or in combination	805	799	666	82.8	83.4	582	72.4	72.9
Asian alone or in combination	41	24	13	B	B	11	B	B
Age								
18 to 24 years	249	249	154	61.9	61.9	105	42.3	42.3
25 to 34 years	376	365	288	76.5	78.8	250	66.3	68.3
35 to 44 years	366	354	288	78.8	81.3	249	68.2	70.4
45 to 64 years	734	723	611	83.2	84.4	562	76.5	77.7
65 years and over	486	485	408	84.0	84.2	365	75.0	75.2

B = Base is less than 75,000 and therefore too small to show the derived measure.
- = Zero or rounds to zero.

Table MS-14. Crime

(Number, rate per 100,000. Data are derived from the FBI Uniform Crime Reports.)

Item	State			U.S.		
	2019	2020	Percent change	2019	2020	Percent change
TOTAL POPULATION[1]	2,978,227	2,966,786	-0.4	328,329,953	329,484,123	0.4
VIOLENT CRIME						
Number	7,779	8,638	11.0	1,250,393	1,313,105	5.0
Rate	261.2	291.2	11.5	380.8	398.5	4.6
Murder and Nonnegligent Manslaughter						
Number	298	315	5.7	16,669	21,570	29.4
Rate	10.0	10.6	6.1	5.1	6.5	28.9
Rape[2]						
Number	924	1,148	24.2	143,224	126,430	-11.7
Rate	31.0	38.7	24.7	43.6	38.4	-12.0
Robbery						
Number	1,620	1,419	-12.4	268,483	243,600	-9.3
Rate	54.4	47.8	-12.1	81.8	73.9	-9.6
Aggravated Assault						
Number	4,937	5,756	16.6	822,017	921,505	12.1
Rate	165.8	194.0	17.0	250.4	279.7	11.7
PROPERTY CRIME						
Number	69,727	62,351	-10.6	6,995,235	6,452,038	-7.8
Rate	2,341.2	2,101.6	-10.2	2,130.6	1,958.2	-8.1
Burglary						
Number	18,341	14,488	-21.0	1,118,096	1,035,314	-7.4
Rate	615.8	488.3	-20.7	340.5	314.2	-7.7
Larceny-Theft						
Number	45,665	41,780	-8.5	5,152,267	4,606,324	-10.6
Rate	1,533.3	1,408.3	-8.2	1,569.2	1,398.0	-10.9
Motor Vehicle Theft						
Number	5,721	6,083	6.3	724,872	810,400	11.8
Rate	192.1	205.0	6.7	220.8	246.0	11.4

NOTE: Although arson data are included in the trend and clearance tables, sufficient data are not available to estimate totals for this offense. Therefore, no arson data are published in this table.
- = Zero or rounds to zero.
[1] Population figures are U.S. Census Bureau provisional estimates as of July 1, 2020.
[2] This state's agencies submitted rape data according to the legacy UCR definition of rape.

Table MS-15. State Government Finances, 2020

(Dollar amounts in thousands, percent distribution.)

Item	Dollars	Percent distribution
Total Revenue	24,807,766	100.0
General revenue	21,508,967	86.7
Intergovernmental revenue	10,176,952	41.0
Taxes	8,099,990	32.7
General sales	3808624	15.4
Selective sales	1,455,674	5.9
License taxes	487,110	2.0
Individual income tax	1861263	7.5
Corporate income tax	421,425	1.7
Other taxes	65,894	0.3
Current charges	2,444,125	9.9
Miscellaneous general revenue	787,900	3.2
Utility revenue	0	-
Liquor stores revenue	427617	1.7
Insurance trust revenue[1]	2,871,182	11.6
Total Expenditure	23,853,431	100.0
Intergovernmental expenditure	5,515,459	23.1
Direct expenditure	18,337,972	76.9
Current operation	13,177,510	55.2
Capital outlay	990,017	4.2
Insurance benefits and repayments	3,417,868	14.3
Assistance and subsidies	464,420	1.9
Interest on debt	288,157	1.2
Exhibit: Salaries and wages	2,814,659	11.8
Total Expenditure	23,853,431	100.0
General expenditure	20,007,946	83.9
Intergovernmental expenditure	5,515,459	23.1
Direct expenditure	14,492,487	60.8
General expenditure, by function:		
Education	6,066,845	25.4
Public welfare	6,963,205	29.2
Hospitals	1,690,916	7.1
Health	470,126	2.0
Highways	1,127,802	4.7
Police protection	161,754	0.7
Correction	341,702	1.4
Natural resources	305,623	1.3
Parks and recreation	36,888	0.2
Governmental administration	532,830	2.2
Interest on general debt	288,157	1.2
Other and unallocable	1,919,903	8.0
Utility expenditure	0	-
Liquor stores expenditure	427617	1.8
Insurance trust expenditure	3,417,868	14.3
Debt at End of Fiscal Year	7,288,707	X
Cash and Security Holdings	39,566,312	X

X = Not applicable.
= Zero or rounds to zero.
[1] Within insurance trust revenue, net earnings of state retirement systems is a calculated statistic (the item code in the data file is X08), and thus can be positive or negative. Net earnings is the sum of earnings on investments plus gains on investments minus losses on investments. The change made in 2002 for asset valuation from book to market value in accordance with Statement 34 of the Governmental Accounting Standards Board is reflected in the calculated statistics.

Table MS-16. State Government Tax Collections, 2021

(Dollars in thousands, percent.)

Item	Dollars	Percent distribution
Total Taxes	9,353,158	100.0
Property taxes	29,885	0.3
Sales and gross receipts	5,657,362	60.5
General sales and gross receipts	4,230,391	45.2
Selective sales and gross receipts	1,426,971	15.3
Alcoholic beverages	45,761	0.5
Amusements	114,778	1.2
Insurance premiums	397,786	4.3
Motor fuels	449,814	4.8
Pari-mutuels	X	-
Public utilities	1,874	-
Tobacco products	140,868	1.5
Other selective sales	276,090	3.0
Licenses	570,447	6.1
Alcoholic beverages	1,347	-
Amusements	18,108	0.2
Corporations in general	213,898	2.3
Hunting and fishing	3,072	-
Motor vehicle	169,938	1.8
Motor vehicle operators	19,466	0.2
Public utilities	6,605	0.1
Occupation and business, NEC	78,063	0.8
Other licenses	59,950	0.6
Income taxes	3,065,829	32.8
Individual income	2,515,630	26.9
Corporation net income	550,199	5.9
Other taxes	29,635	0.3
Death and gift	0	-
Documentary and stock transfer	X	-
Severance	29,635	0.3
Taxes, NEC	0	-

- = Zero or rounds to zero.
X = Not applicable.

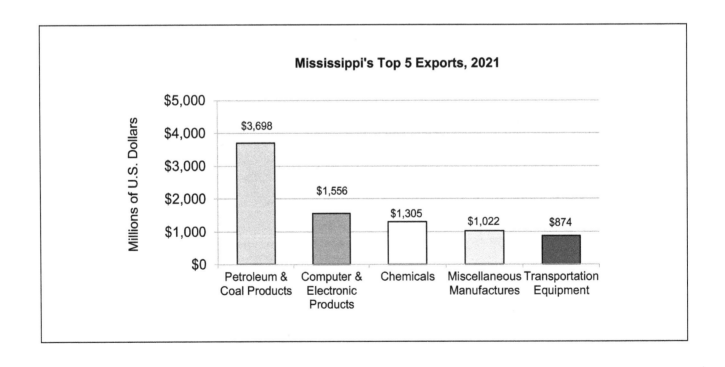

MISSOURI

Facts and Figures

Location: Central United States; bordered on the N by Iowa, on the E by Illinois, Kentucky, and Tennessee, on the S by Arkansas, and on the W by Oklahoma, Kansas, and Nebraska

Area: 69,704 sq. mi. (180,533 sq. km.); rank—21st

Population: 6,168,187 (2021 est.); rank—18th

Principal Cities: capital—Jefferson City; largest—Kansas City

Statehood: August 10, 1821; 24th state

U.S. Congress: 2 senators, 8 representatives

State Motto: *Salus populi suprema lex esto* ("The welfare of the people shall be the supreme law")

State Song: "Missouri Waltz"

State Nickname: The Show Me State

Abbreviations: MO; Mo

State Symbols: flower—hawthorn; tree—flowering dogwood; bird—Eastern bluebird

At a Glance

- With an increase in population of 3.0 percent, Missouri ranked 39th among the states in growth from 2010 to 2021.

- In 2020, 9.4 percent of Missourians did not have health insurance, compared to the national average of 8.7 percent.

- Missouri's violent crime rate was 542.7 per 100,000 population in 2020, compared to the U.S. rate of 398.5 per 100,000 population.

- Missouri's median household income of $57,290 ranked 39th in the country in 2020.

- In Missouri in 2020, 13.0 percent of residents lived below the poverty level, which was slightly above the national average of 12.8 percent; 17.4 percent of Missouri children lived in poverty, which was slightly lower than the national average of 17.5 percent.

Table MO-1. Population by Age, Sex, Race, and Hispanic Origin

(Number, percent, except where noted.)

Sex, age, race, and Hispanic origin	2000	2010	2021	Percent change, 2010–2021
Total Population..	5,595,211	5,988,927	6,168,187	3.0
Percent of total U.S. population	2.0	1.9	1.9	X
Sex				
Male..	2,720,177	2,933,477	3,044,665	3.8
Female..	2,875,034	3,055,450	3,123,522	2.2
Age				
Under 5 years..	269,898	390,237	360,045	-7.7
5 to 19 years..	1,224,274	1,211,174	1,180,248	-2.6
20 to 64 years..	3,245,660	3,549,222	3,544,127	-0.1
65 years and over	755,379	838,294	1,083,767	29.3
Median age (years)...	36.1	37.9	39.1	3.2
Race and Hispanic Origin				
One race				
White	4,748,083	5,038,407	5,095,927	1.1
Black..	629,391	700,178	727,065	3.8
American Indian and Alaska Native	25,076	30,595	37,409	22.3
Asian..	61,595	100,213	138,565	38.3
Native Hawaiian or Other Pacific Islander	3,178	7,178	10,836	51.0
Two or more races	82,061	112,356	158,385	41.0
Hispanic (of any race)...	118,592	223,421	287,125	28.5

NOTE: Population figures for 2021 are July 1 estimates. The 2000 and 2010 estimates are taken from the respective censuses.
- = Zero or rounds to zero.
X = Not applicable.

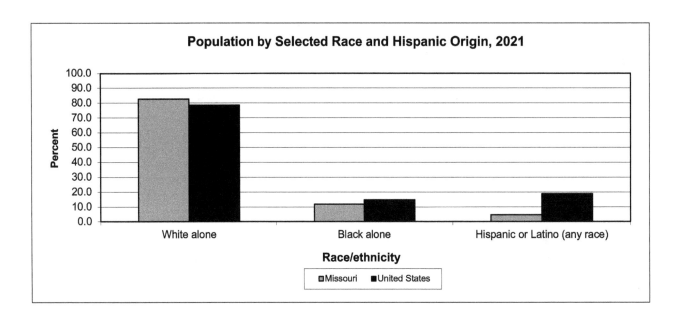

Table MO-2. Marital Status

(Number, percent distribution.)

Sex, age, race, and Hispanic origin	2000	2010	2020 [1]
Males, 15 Years and Over	2,114,280	2,332,888	2,418,811
Never married	27.8	32.1	33.5
Now married, except separated..	58.0	52.5	50.8
Separated...	1.6	1.7	1.6
Widowed...	2.6	2.6	2.9
Divorced...	10.0	11.0	11.1
Females, 15 Years and Over	2,300,111	2,492,198	2,562,608
Never married	22.1	26.8	27.4
Now married, except separated..	53.1	48.2	48.1
Separated...	2.0	2.2	1.9
Widowed...	11.3	10.0	9.4
Divorced...	11.5	12.8	13.2

[1] 2020 ACS 5-Year estimates. 1-Year estimates were not released for 2020 due to the impact of COVID-19 on data collection that year.

Table MO-3. Households and Housing Characteristics

(Number, percent, dollars.)

Item	2000	2010	2020 [1]	Average annual percent change, 2010–2020
Total Households..	2,194,594	2,350,628	2,440,212	0.5
Family households	1,476,516	1,524,078	1,551,056	0.3
Married-couple family	1,140,866	1,146,501	1,165,218	0.2
Other family	335,650	377,577	385,838	0.3
Male householder, no wife present................................	81,890	99,807	108,611	1.3
Female householder, no husband present......................	253,760	277,770	277,227	-
Nonfamily households	718,078	826,550	889,156	1.1
Householder living alone..	599,808	689,361	727,063	0.8
Householder not living alone..	118,270	137,189	162,093	2.6
Housing Characteristics				
Total housing units...	2,442,017	2,714,017	2,804,664	0.5
Occupied housing units	2,194,594	2,350,628	2,440,212	0.5
Owner occupied	1,542,149	1,621,371	1,637,374	0.1
Renter occupied	652,445	729,257	802,838	1.4
Average household size..	2.48	2.48	2.44	-0.2
Financial Characteristics				
Median gross rent of renter-occupied housing	484	682	843	3.4
Median monthly owner costs for housing units with a mortgage	861	1,182	1,287	1.3
Median value of owner-occupied housing units...................	89,900	139,000	163,600	2.5

- = Zero or rounds to zero
[1] 2020 ACS 5-Year estimates. 1-Year estimates were not released for 2020 due to the impact of COVID-19 on data collection that year.

Table MO-4. Migration, Origin, and Language

(Number, percent.)

Characteristic	State 2016-2020 [1]	U.S. 2016-2020 [1]
Residence 1 Year Ago		
Population 1 year and over	6,052,441	322,943,283
Same house	85.5	86.2
Different house in the U.S.	14.1	13.2
Same county	7.7	7.7
Different county	6.4	5.5
Same state	3.9	3.2
Different state	2.5	2.3
Abroad	0.4	0.6
Place of Birth		
Native born	5,867,824	282,443,680
Male	49.1	49.4
Female	50.9	50.6
Foreign born	256,336	44,125,628
Male	48.8	48.6
Female	51.2	51.4
Foreign born; naturalized U.S. citizen...	128,880	22,456,684
Male	46.5	46.1
Female	53.5	53.9
Foreign born; not a U.S. citizen..	127,456	21,668,944
Male	51.1	51.1
Female	48.9	48.9
Entered 2010 or later	29.6	22.8
Entered 2000 to 2009	27.7	25.1
Entered before 2000..	42.7	52.1
World Region of Birth, Foreign		
Foreign-born population, excluding population born at sea	256,336	44,125,628
Europe	18.4	10.8
Asia..	39.8	31.3
Africa	9.7	5.4
Oceania	1.5	0.6
Latin America	28.6	50.0
North America	2.1	1.9
Language Spoken at Home and Ability to Speak English		
Population 5 years and over..	5,753,114	306,919,116
English only	93.7	78.5
Language other than English..	6.3	21.5
Speaks English less than "very well"..	2.2	8.2

[1] 2020 ACS 5-Year estimates. 1-Year estimates were not released for 2020 due to the impact of COVID-19 on data collection that year.
NA = Not available.
X = Not applicable.
- = Zero or rounds to zero.

Table MO-5. Median Income and Poverty Status, 2020[1]

(Number, percent, except as noted.)

Characteristic	State Number	State Percent	U.S. Number	U.S. Percent
Median Income				
Households (dollars)...	57,290	X	64,994	X
Families (dollars)	72,834	X	80,069	X
Below Poverty Level (All People)	772,992	13.0	40,910,326	12.8
Sex				
Male	343,547	11.8	18,171,512	11.6
Female	429,445	14.1	22,738,814	14.0
Age				
Under 18 years..	233,927	17.4	12,598,699	17.5
Related children under 18 years..................................	226,170	16.9	12,306,532	17.2
18 to 64 years...	452,917	12.6	23,554,920	12.1
65 years and over	86,148	8.6	4,756,707	9.3

X = Not applicable.
[1] 2020 ACS 5-Year estimates. 1-Year estimates were not released for 2020 due to the impact of COVID-19 on data collection that year.

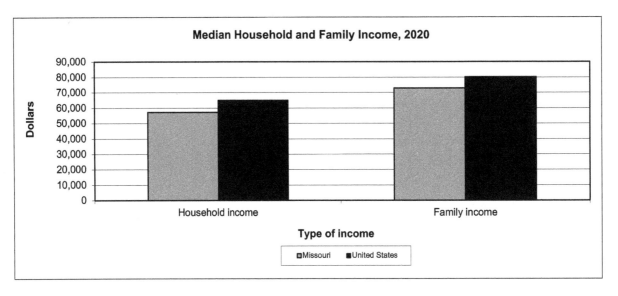

Table MO-6. Health Insurance Coverage Status for the Civilian Noninstitutionalized Population and Children Under 19 Years of Age

(Number, percent.)

Item	2011	2012	2013	2014	2015	2016	2017	2018	2019	2020[2]
Civilian Noninstitutionalized Population	5,898,968	5,908,769	5,930,677	5,950,606	5,969,392	5,977,199	6,000,326	6,014,742	6,020,665	6,011,968
Covered by Private or Public Insurance										
Number..	5,091,554	5,107,389	5,157,844	5,256,728	5,386,284	5,445,276	5,452,055	5,448,415	5,416,963	5,446,869
Percent...	86.3	86.4	87.0	88.3	90.2	91.1	90.9	90.6	90.0	90.6
Uninsured										
Number..	807,414	801,380	772,833	693,878	583,108	531,923	548,271	566,327	603,702	565,099
Percent...	13.7	13.6	13.0	11.7	9.8	8.9	9.1	9.4	10.0	9.4
Percent in the U.S. not covered..	15.1	14.8	14.5	11.7	9.4	8.6	8.7	8.9	9.2	8.7
Children Under 19 Years of Age[1]	1,409,255	1,399,674	1,394,588	1,387,561	1,387,714	1,386,471	1,464,725	1,453,042	1,446,554	1,454,835
Covered by Private or Public Insurance										
Number..	1,314,321	1,301,641	1,297,042	1,287,589	1,308,016	1,324,598	1,390,219	1,370,509	1,351,868	1,370,412
Percent...	93.3	93.0	93.0	92.8	94.3	95.5	94.9	94.3	93.5	94.2
Uninsured										
Number..	94,934	98,033	97,546	99,972	79,698	61,873	74,506	82,533	94,686	84,423
Percent...	6.7	7.0	7.0	7.2	5.7	4.5	5.1	5.7	6.5	5.8
Percent in the U.S. not covered..	7.5	7.2	7.1	6.0	4.8	4.5	5.0	5.2	5.7	5.2

[1] Data for years prior to 2017 are for individuals under 18 years of age.
[2] 2020 ACS 5-Year estimates. 1-Year estimates were not released for 2020 due to the impact of COVID-19 on data collection that year. Data is not comparable to previous years, which are based on 1-year estimates.

Table MO-7. Employment Status by Demographic Group, 2021

(Numbers in thousands, percent.)

Characteristic	Civilian noninstitutional population	Civilian labor force		Employed		Unemployed	
		Number	Percent of population	Number	Percent of population	Number	Percent of population
Total...	4,854	3,053	62.9	2,923	60.2	131	4.3
Sex							
Male..	2,343	1,580	67.4	1,505	64.2	75	4.7
Female..	2,510	1,473	58.7	1,418	56.5	56	3.8
Race, Sex, and Hispanic Origin							
White..	4,090	2,573	62.9	2,482	60.7	91	3.5
Male..	1,998	1,355	67.8	1,302	65.2	53	3.9
Female..	2,092	1,218	58.2	1,180	56.4	38	3.1
Black or African American........................	532	321	60.4	293	55.0	29	9.0
Male..	241	151	62.8	136	56.4	15	10.2
Female..	291	170	58.4	157	53.8	14	7.9
Hispanic or Latino ethnicity[1]	203	150	73.5	143	70.5	6	4.1
Male..	NA	NA	NA	NA	NA	NA	NA
Female..	NA	NA	NA	NA	NA	NA	NA
Age							
16 to 19 years......................................	NA	NA	NA	NA	NA	NA	NA
20 to 24 years......................................	400	305	76.3	284	71.1	21	6.8
25 to 34 years......................................	805	684	84.9	656	81.4	28	4.1
35 to 44 years......................................	776	662	85.3	640	82.5	22	3.4
45 to 54 years......................................	683	579	84.7	558	81.7	20	3.5
55 to 64 years......................................	817	510	62.4	490	60.0	20	3.9
65 years and over..................................	1,093	203	18.6	196	18.0	6	3.2

NOTE: Data in Table 7 are from the Current Population Survey (CPS) and do not match the estimates in Table 8. See notes and definitions for further information.
[1] May be of any race.

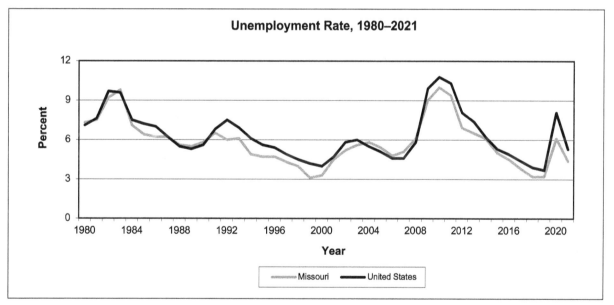

Unemployment Rate, 1980–2021

Table MO-8. Employment Status of the Civilian Noninstitutional Population Age 16 Years and Over

(Number, percent.)

Year	Civilian labor force	Civilian participation rate	Employed	Unemployed	Unemployment rate
2010..	3,043,249	65.7	2,753,910	289,339	9.5
2011..	3,032,960	65.2	2,770,662	262,298	8.6
2012..	3,004,347	64.3	2,789,025	215,322	7.2
2013..	3,011,198	64.2	2,807,115	204,083	6.8
2014..	3,035,599	64.4	2,848,571	187,028	6.2
2015..	3,057,859	64.6	2,901,467	156,392	5.1
2016..	3,072,904	64.6	2,933,457	139,447	4.5
2017..	3,053,526	63.9	2,939,306	114,220	3.7
2018..	3,045,865	63.6	2,949,910	95,955	3.2
2019..	3,072,073	63.8	2,976,643	95,430	3.1
2020..	3,037,162	62.9	2,853,353	183,809	6.1
2021..	3,062,449	63.1	2,928,368	134,081	4.4

Table MO-9. Employment and Average Wages by Industry

(Estimates are based on the 2012 North American Industry Classification System [NAICS].)

Industry	2013	2014	2015	2016	2017	2018	2019	2020
	Number of Jobs							
Wage and Salary Employment by Industry	2,808,712	2,834,816	2,886,985	2,925,546	2,948,639	2,971,173	2,993,332	2,856,984
Farm Wage and Salary Employment	8,666	7,131	9,971	10,251	7,000	7,363	8,433	9,106
Nonfarm Wage and Salary Employment	2,800,046	2,827,685	2,877,014	2,915,295	2,941,639	2,963,810	2,984,899	2,847,878
Private wage and salary employment	2,324,189	2,355,073	2,406,070	2,444,246	2,470,258	2,491,968	2,512,272	2,387,134
Forestry, fishing, and related activities	5,420	5,511	5,563	5,548	5,555	5,775	6,059	5,912
Mining	3,947	3,896	3,924	3,874	4,045	4,143	4,156	4,101
Utilities	12,119	11,960	11,859	11,696	11,721	11,761	11,847	11,671
Construction	110,818	112,846	117,327	123,585	125,925	125,564	129,527	129,490
Manufacturing	252,924	256,197	261,529	263,424	266,025	273,273	277,301	266,647
Durable goods manufacturing	147,852	152,374	157,248	158,166	158,627	164,214	167,575	159,695
Nondurable goods manufacturing	105,072	103,823	104,281	105,258	107,398	109,059	109,726	106,952
Wholesale trade	119,023	121,339	120,887	120,876	121,688	121,566	124,031	120,484
Retail trade	304,040	307,128	313,852	317,778	315,670	313,444	306,455	293,447
Transportation and warehousing	91,333	93,645	97,436	97,739	99,446	100,736	104,668	103,800
Information	52,592	52,327	50,237	49,421	48,280	47,637	46,729	43,666
Finance and insurance	127,897	127,945	128,619	130,039	134,287	133,889	136,704	139,198
Real estate and rental and leasing	35,063	35,433	36,487	37,286	37,875	38,109	39,884	38,080
Professional, scientific, and technical services	133,669	137,240	147,236	154,149	160,098	163,591	163,611	162,584
Management of companies and enterprises	63,607	66,114	65,571	65,139	65,320	65,541	65,284	62,053
Administrative and waste services	151,796	155,217	159,788	161,260	158,683	159,185	156,050	143,464
Educational services	66,460	66,661	67,075	67,722	68,420	71,943	72,174	71,881
Health care and social assistance	381,487	382,244	392,708	401,488	411,141	415,593	423,366	411,550
Arts, entertainment, and recreation	43,333	44,674	41,793	42,888	41,938	42,590	43,548	32,836
Accommodation and food services	238,999	243,763	252,424	258,390	263,189	264,819	267,112	222,601
Other services, except public administration	129,662	130,933	131,755	131,944	130,952	132,809	133,766	123,669
Government and government enterprises	475,857	472,612	470,944	471,049	471,381	471,842	472,627	460,744
	Dollars							
Average Wages and Salaries by Industry	44,066	45,342	46,609	47,193	48,525	50,203	51,644	55,076
Average Farm Wages and Salaries	30,512	48,171	28,872	30,824	41,151	38,446	36,160	31,186
Average Nonfarm Wages and Salaries	44,108	45,334	46,671	47,250	48,543	50,232	51,688	55,152
Average private wages and salaries	44,707	46,008	47,384	47,959	49,290	51,089	52,629	56,329
Forestry, fishing, and related activities	26,656	27,280	28,299	30,393	32,143	32,924	34,200	36,958
Mining	68,204	69,599	69,625	66,847	69,193	68,581	73,091	73,570
Utilities	85,825	89,324	91,273	94,222	98,147	98,479	103,602	107,857
Construction	51,649	53,441	55,396	57,009	58,802	60,496	62,778	65,853
Manufacturing	54,661	56,945	58,403	58,309	59,247	60,567	61,941	64,312
Durable goods manufacturing	57,330	59,918	60,666	60,625	61,818	63,544	65,039	66,006
Nondurable goods manufacturing	50,905	52,580	54,990	54,828	55,450	56,084	57,211	61,781
Wholesale trade	62,175	64,575	66,392	67,400	69,105	72,340	73,007	76,999
Retail trade	26,418	26,916	27,918	28,370	29,096	29,784	30,640	33,540
Transportation and warehousing	47,024	48,232	49,109	49,582	50,545	51,695	52,276	53,845
Information	70,516	71,213	74,871	75,881	76,091	84,311	88,453	92,351
Finance and insurance	69,348	71,785	75,164	77,124	79,329	83,838	86,604	93,624
Real estate and rental and leasing	39,113	40,598	42,984	43,107	44,272	46,442	48,569	52,294
Professional, scientific, and technical services	71,063	72,691	76,146	76,178	78,016	79,273	82,791	86,698
Management of companies and enterprises	97,530	102,956	101,218	100,100	104,518	112,963	112,088	114,084
Administrative and waste services	32,893	33,927	34,429	35,530	37,246	38,617	40,383	44,411
Educational services	35,034	36,057	36,151	36,371	36,764	36,333	36,962	38,440
Health care and social assistance	42,710	43,102	44,536	45,155	46,096	47,591	49,015	52,224
Arts, entertainment, and recreation	40,037	39,973	42,390	41,782	40,560	40,599	41,437	43,213
Accommodation and food services	17,555	18,114	18,959	19,477	20,339	21,536	22,201	21,982
Other services, except public administration	30,700	31,653	32,865	33,987	35,224	36,453	37,584	41,489
Government and government enterprises	41,185	41,980	43,028	43,572	44,626	45,702	46,685	49,055

Table MO-10. Employment Characteristics by Family Type

(Number, percent.)

Family type and labor force status	2018 Total	2018 Families with own children under 18 years	2019 Total	2019 Families with own children under 18 years	2020[1] Total	2020[1] Families with own children under 18 years
All Families...	1,550,876	624,752	1,546,045	627,679	1,551,056	640,224
FAMILY TYPE AND LABOR FORCE STATUS						
Opposite-Sex Married-Couple Families............................	1,159,502	414,668	1,160,554	420,287	1,155,339	429,636
Both husband and wife in labor force.................................	51.7	71.4	52.3	72.5	52.5	71.9
Husband in labor force, wife not in labor force	18.7	23.2	18.2	21.7	19.1	22.8
Wife in labor force, husband not in labor force	8.1	3.0	8.2	4.1	8.2	3.6
Both husband and wife not in labor force................................	20.5	1.7	20.4	1.3	20.2	1.6
Other Families	391,374	210,084	385,491	207,392	385,838	208,153
Female householder, no spouse present	72.0	73.5	71.1	70.6	71.9	72.5
In labor force..	50.3	62.0	51.0	60.3	51.4	62.0
Not in labor force	21.7	11.5	20.1	10.2	20.4	10.5
Male householder, no spouse present...........................	28.0	26.5	28.9	29.4	28.1	27.5
In labor force..	21.3	24.6	21.9	26.4	21.9	25.2
Not in labor force	6.7	1.9	7.0	3.0	6.3	2.4

[1] 2020 ACS 5-Year estimates. 1-Year estimates were not released for 2020 due to the impact of COVID-19 on data collection that year. Data is not comparable to previous years, which are based on 1-year estimates.

Table MO-11. School Enrollment and Educational Attainment, 2020[1]

(Number, percent.)

Item	State	U.S.
Enrollment		
Total population 3 years and over, enrolled in school	1,459,812	80,497,960
Enrolled in nursery school or preschool (percent)........................	6.6	6.1
Enrolled in kindergarten (percent)....................................	5.0	5.0
Enrolled in elementary school, grades 1-8 (percent)........................	41.6	40.4
Enrolled in high school, grades 9-12 (percent)............................	21.1	21.0
Enrolled in college or graduate school (percent)........................	25.6	27.6
Attainment		
Total population 25 years and over	4,176,792	222,836,834
Less than ninth grade (percent)......................................	2.9	4.9
9th to 12th grade, no diploma (percent)................................	6.5	6.6
High school graduate, including equivalency (percent)........................	30.5	26.7
Some college, no degree (percent)...................................	22	20.3
Associate's degree (percent)..	8.1	8.6
Bachelor's degree (percent)...	18.4	20.2
Graduate or professional degree (percent)............................	11.5	12.7
High school graduate or higher (percent)	90.6	88.5
Bachelor's degree or higher (percent)................................	29.9	32.9

[1] 2020 ACS 5-Year estimates. 1-Year estimates were not released for 2020 due to the impact of COVID-19 on data collection that year.

Table MO-12. Public School Characteristics and Educational Indicators

(Number, percent; data derived from National Center of Education Statistics.)

Item	State	U.S.
Public Elementary and Secondary Schools		
Number of regular school districts, 2018-19	518	13,452
Number of operational schools, 2019-20	2,431	98,469
Percent charter schools	2.9	7.7
Total public school enrollment, Fall 2019	910,466	50,796,445
Percent charter school enrollment	2.7	6.8
Student-teacher ratio, Fall 2019	13.2	15.9
Expenditures per student (unadjusted dollars), 2018-19	11,349	13,187
Four-year adjusted cohort graduation rate (ACGR), 2018-2019[1]	89.7	85.8
Students eligible for free or reduced-price lunch (percent), 2019-20........................	50.0	52.1
English language learners (percent), Fall 2019	3.9	10.4
Students age 3 to 21 served under IDEA, part B (percent), 2020-21	14.3	14.5

Public Schools by Type, 2019-20	Number	Percent of state public schools
Total number of schools..	2,431	100.0
Special education..	48	2.0
Vocational education..	62	2.6
Alternative education..	60	2.5

[1] Adjusted Cohort Graduation Rates (ACGR) differ from Averaged Freshmen Graduation Rates (AFGR).

Table MO-13. Reported Voting and Registration of the Voting-Age Population, November 2020

(Numbers in thousands, percent.)

Item	Total population	Total citizen population	Registered			Voted		
			Total registered	Percent registered (total population)	Percent registered (total citizen population)	Total voted	Percent voted (total population)	Percent voted (total citizen population)
U.S. Total	252,274	231,593	168,308	66.7	72.7	154,628	61.3	66.8
State Total..............................	4,637	4,475	3,388	73.1	75.7	2,990	64.5	66.8
Sex								
Male	2,205	2,136	1,556	70.5	72.9	1,361	61.7	63.7
Female	2,432	2,340	1,832	75.3	78.3	1,629	67.0	69.6
Race								
White alone.............................	3,871	3,812	2,935	75.8	77.0	2,576	66.5	67.6
White, non-Hispanic alone...........	3,687	3,664	2,816	76.4	76.8	2,488	67.5	67.9
Black alone.............................	518	507	373	72.1	73.6	351	67.8	69.2
Asian alone	138	64	38	B	B	38	B	B
Hispanic (of any race)................	232	178	127	54.8	71.3	95	40.9	53.3
White alone or in combination	3,941	3,873	2,963	75.2	76.5	2,588	65.7	66.8
Black alone or in combination	552	533	381	69.0	71.4	351	63.6	65.8
Asian alone or in combination.........	146	72	46	B	B	46	B	B
Age								
18 to 24 years...........................	587	563	382	65.0	67.7	313	53.3	55.5
25 to 34 years...........................	716	697	474	66.2	68.1	418	58.3	60.0
35 to 44 years...........................	743	682	465	62.7	68.3	368	49.5	53.9
45 to 64 years...........................	1,596	1,542	1,222	76.6	79.3	1,124	70.5	72.9
65 years and over	995	992	844	84.9	85.1	768	77.2	77.4

B = Base is less than 75,000 and therefore too small to show the derived measure.

Table MO-14. Crime

(Number, rate per 100,000. Data are derived from the FBI Uniform Crime Reports.)

Item	State			U.S.		
	2019	2020	Percent change	2019	2020	Percent change
TOTAL POPULATION[1]	6,140,475	6,151,548	0.2	328,329,953	329,484,123	0.4
VIOLENT CRIME						
Number..	30,680	33,385	8.8	1,250,393	1,313,105	5.0
Rate..	499.6	542.7	8.6	380.8	398.5	4.6
Murder and Nonnegligent Manslaughter						
Number..	576	723	25.5	16,669	21,570	29.4
Rate..	9.4	11.8	25.3	5.1	6.5	28.9
Rape[2]						
Number..	3,019	2,661	-11.9	143,224	126,430	-11.7
Rate..	49.2	43.3	-12.0	43.6	38.4	-12.0
Robbery						
Number..	4,995	4,575	-8.4	268,483	243,600	-9.3
Rate..	81.3	74.4	-8.6	81.8	73.9	-9.6
Aggravated Assault						
Number..	22,090	25,426	15.1	822,017	921,505	12.1
Rate..	359.7	413.3	14.9	250.4	279.7	11.7
PROPERTY CRIME						
Number..	163,223	155,698	-4.6	6,995,235	6,452,038	-7.8
Rate..	2,658.1	2,531.0	-4.8	2,130.6	1,958.2	-8.1
Burglary						
Number..	26,617	23,300	-12.5	1,118,096	1,035,314	-7.4
Rate..	433.5	378.8	-12.6	340.5	314.2	-7.7
Larceny-Theft						
Number..	115,324	108,209	-6.2	5,152,267	4,606,324	-10.6
Rate..	1,878.1	1,759.1	-6.3	1,569.2	1,398.0	-10.9
Motor Vehicle Theft						
Number..	21,282	24,189	13.7	724,872	810,400	11.8
Rate..	346.6	393.2	13.5	220.8	246.0	11.4

NOTE: Although arson data are included in the trend and clearance tables, sufficient data are not available to estimate totals for this offense. Therefore, no arson data are published in this table.
- = Zero or rounds to zero.
[1] Population figures are U.S. Census Bureau provisional estimates as of July 1, 2020.
[2] The figures shown in the rape (revised definition) column were estimated using the revised Uniform Crime Reporting (UCR) definition of rape.

Table MO-15. State Government Finances, 2020

(Dollar amounts in thousands, percent distribution.)

Item	Dollars	Percent distribution
Total Revenue	40,228,153	100.0
General revenue	33,907,178	84.3
Intergovernmental revenue	15,416,108	38.3
Taxes	12,409,761	30.8
General sales	3793379	9.4
Selective sales	1,665,376	4.1
License taxes	634,725	1.6
Individual income tax	5901668	14.7
Corporate income tax	364,460	0.9
Other taxes	50,153	0.1
Current charges	3,179,218	7.9
Miscellaneous general revenue	2,902,091	7.2
Utility revenue	0	-
Liquor stores revenue	0	-
Insurance trust revenue[1]	6,320,975	15.7
Total Expenditure	38,460,163	100.0
Intergovernmental expenditure	6,829,296	17.8
Direct expenditure	31,630,867	82.2
Current operation	22,408,854	58.3
Capital outlay	1,607,220	4.2
Insurance benefits and repayments	6,011,248	15.6
Assistance and subsidies	784,567	2.0
Interest on debt	818,978	2.1
Exhibit: Salaries and wages	4,169,605	10.8
Total Expenditure	38,460,163	100.0
General expenditure	32,442,976	84.4
Intergovernmental expenditure	6,829,296	17.8
Direct expenditure	25,613,680	66.6
General expenditure, by function:		
Education	10,324,021	26.8
Public welfare	10,215,706	26.6
Hospitals	2,706,653	7.0
Health	2,123,217	5.5
Highways	1,600,096	4.2
Police protection	258,232	0.7
Correction	800,745	2.1
Natural resources	398,134	1.0
Parks and recreation	43,751	0.1
Governmental administration	906,713	2.4
Interest on general debt	818,978	2.1
Other and unallocable	2,153,457	5.6
Utility expenditure	51,831	0.1
Liquor stores expenditure	0	-
Insurance trust expenditure	6,011,248	15.6
Debt at End of Fiscal Year	18,969,986	X
Cash and Security Holdings	101,918,726	X

X = Not applicable.
- = Zero or rounds to zero.
[1] Within insurance trust revenue, net earnings of state retirement systems is a calculated statistic (the item code in the data file is X08), and thus can be positive or negative. Net earnings is the sum of earnings on investments plus gains on investments minus losses on investments. The change made in 2002 for asset valuation from book to market value in accordance with Statement 34 of the Governmental Accounting Standards Board is reflected in the calculated statistics.

Table MO-16. State Government Tax Collections, 2021

(Dollars in thousands, percent.)

Item	Dollars	Percent distribution
Total Taxes	15,091,423	100.0
Property taxes	37,418	0.2
Sales and gross receipts	5,945,293	39.4
General sales and gross receipts	4,119,671	27.3
Selective sales and gross receipts	1,825,622	12.1
Alcoholic beverages	46,316	0.3
Amusements	354,428	2.3
Insurance premiums	447,949	3.0
Motor fuels	696,002	4.6
Pari-mutuels	X	-
Public utilities	X	-
Tobacco products	99,418	0.7
Other selective sales	181,509	1.2
Licenses	691,696	4.6
Alcoholic beverages	6,509	-
Amusements	20	-
Corporations in general	0	-
Hunting and fishing	41,203	0.3
Motor vehicle	334,238	2.2
Motor vehicle operators	17,234	0.1
Public utilities	19,056	0.1
Occupation and business, NEC	183,559	1.2
Other licenses	89,877	0.6
Income taxes	8,402,368	55.7
Individual income	7,715,511	51.1
Corporation net income	686,857	4.6
Other taxes	14,648	0.1
Death and gift	3	-
Documentary and stock transfer	14,599	0.1
Severance	0	-
Taxes, NEC	46	-

- = Zero or rounds to zero.
X = Not applicable.

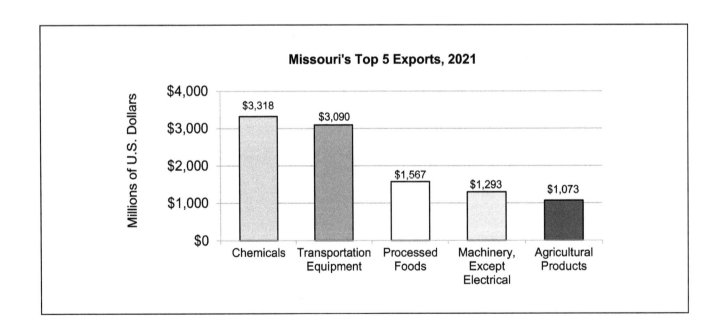

MONTANA

Facts and Figures

Location: Northwestern United States; bordered on the N by Canada (British Columbia, Alberta, and Saskatchewan), on the E by North Dakota and South Dakota, on the S by Idaho and Wyoming, and on the W by Idaho

Area: 147,042 sq. mi. (380,838 sq. km.); rank—4th

Population: 1,104,271 (2021 est.); rank—43rd

Principal Cities: capital—Helena; largest—Billings

Statehood: November 8, 1889; 41st state

U.S. Congress: 2 senators, 1 representative

State Motto: *Oro y plata* ("Gold and silver")

State Song: "Montana"

State Nicknames: The Treasure State; Big Sky Country

Abbreviations: MT; Mont.

State Symbols: flower—bitterroot; tree—ponderosa pine; bird—Western meadowlark

At a Glance

- With an increase in population of 11.6 percent, Montana ranked 12th among the states in growth from 2010 to 2021.

- The median household income in Montana in 2020 was $56,539 compared to the national median household income of $64,994.

- In 2021, 19.6 percent of Montana residents were in the 65 and older age group, a percentage that ranked 6th in the country.

- Approximately 0.6 percent of Montana residents self-identified as "Black or African-American alone" in 2021, which was the lowest percentage among all the states.

Table MT-1. Population by Age, Sex, Race, and Hispanic Origin

(Number, percent, except where noted.)

Sex, age, race, and Hispanic origin	2000	2010	2021	Percent change, 2010–2021
Total Population..	902,195	989,415	1,104,271	11.6
Percent of total U.S. population	0.3	0.3	0.3	X
Sex				
Male...	449,480	496,667	559,270	12.6
Female	452,715	492,748	545,001	10.6
Age				
Under 5 years...	54,869	62,423	58,251	-6.7
5 to 19 years..	202,571	188,613	203,300	7.8
20 to 64 years..	523,806	591,637	626,297	5.9
65 years and over...	120,949	146,742	216,423	47.5
Median age (years)	37.5	39.8	40.1	0.8
Race and Hispanic Origin				
One race				
White..	817,229	891,529	980,015	9.9
Black..	2,692	4,215	6,894	63.6
American Indian and Alaska Native	56,068	63,495	72,551	14.3
Asian..	4,691	6,379	11,153	74.8
Native Hawaiian or Other Pacific Islander	470	734	997	35.8
Two or more races..	15,730	23,063	32,661	41.6
Hispanic (of any race)...	18,081	31,018	48,014	54.8

NOTE: Population figures for 2021 are July 1 estimates. The 2000 and 2010 estimates are taken from the respective censuses.
- = Zero or rounds to zero.
X = Not applicable.

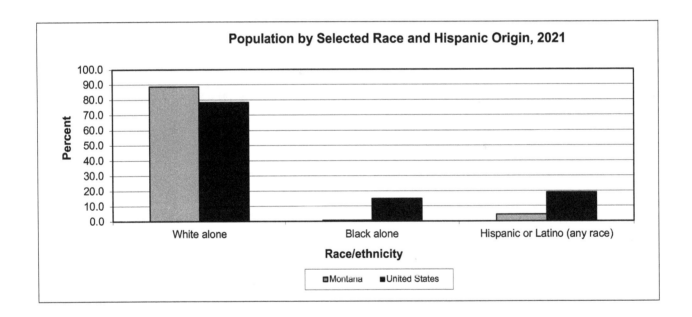

Table MT-2. Marital Status

(Number, percent distribution.)

Sex, age, race, and Hispanic origin	2000	2010	2020 [1]
Males, 15 Years and Over	353,801	404,179	436,214
Never married	27.7	30.5	32.4
Now married, except separated..	58.3	53.4	51.9
Separated...	1.2	1.5	1.1
Widowed...	2.6	2.3	2.9
Divorced...	10.2	12.4	11.8
Females, 15 Years and Over	362,114	403,766	435,265
Never married	20.4	23.5	24.9
Now married, except separated..	56.3	52.9	52.1
Separated...	1.3	1.6	1.2
Widowed...	10.4	9.7	8.6
Divorced...	11.6	12.3	13.1

[1] 2020 ACS 5-Year estimates. 1-Year estimates were not released for 2020 due to the impact of COVID-19 on data collection that year.

Table MT-3. Households and Housing Characteristics

(Number, percent, dollars.)

Item	2000	2010	2020 [1]	Average annual percent change, 2010–2020
Total Households	358,667	402,747	436,048	1.2
Family households	237,407	255,199	267,258	0.7
Married-couple family	192,067	203,500	215,085	0.8
Other family	45,340	51,699	52,173	0.1
Male householder, no wife present	13,324	16,926	18,558	1.4
Female householder, no husband present	32,016	34,773	33,615	-0.5
Nonfamily households	121,260	147,548	168,790	2.1
Householder living alone	98,422	119,762	134,377	1.7
Householder not living alone	22,838	27,786	34,413	3.4
Housing Characteristics				
Total housing units	412,633	483,006	514,956	0.9
Occupied housing units	358,667	402,747	436,048	1.2
Owner occupied	247,723	280,633	298,728	0.9
Renter occupied	110,944	122,114	137,320	1.8
Average household size	2.45	2.39	2.37	-0.1
Financial Characteristics				
Median gross rent of renter-occupied housing	447	642	836	4.3
Median monthly owner costs for housing units with a mortgage	863	1,217	1,456	2.8
Median value of owner-occupied housing units	99,500	181,200	244,900	5.0

[1] 2020 ACS 5-Year estimates. 1-Year estimates were not released for 2020 due to the impact of COVID-19 on data collection that year.

Table MT-4. Migration, Origin, and Language

(Number, percent.)

Characteristic	State 2016-2020[1]	U.S. 2016-2020[1]
Residence 1 Year Ago		
Population 1 year and over	1,050,375	322,943,283
Same house	84.5	86.2
Different house in the U.S.	15.2	13.2
Same county	8.1	7.7
Different county	7.1	5.5
Same state	3.4	3.2
Different state	3.7	2.3
Abroad	0.3	0.6
Place of Birth		
Native born	1,038,384	282,443,680
Male	50.5	49.4
Female	49.5	50.6
Foreign born	23,321	44,125,628
Male	42.3	48.6
Female	57.7	51.4
Foreign born; naturalized U.S. citizen	13,421	22,456,684
Male	38.8	46.1
Female	61.2	53.9
Foreign born; not a U.S. citizen	9,900	21,668,944
Male	47.1	51.1
Female	52.9	48.9
Entered 2010 or later	24.8	22.8
Entered 2000 to 2009	19.5	25.1
Entered before 2000	55.7	52.1
World Region of Birth, Foreign		
Foreign-born population, excluding population born at sea	23,321	44,125,628
Europe	32.2	10.8
Asia	30.2	31.3
Africa	4.0	5.4
Oceania	1.2	0.6
Latin America	16.8	50.0
North America	15.5	1.9
Language Spoken at Home and Ability to Speak English		
Population 5 years and over	1,000,367	306,919,116
English only	96.0	78.5
Language other than English	4.0	21.5
Speaks English less than "very well"	0.8	8.2

[1] 2020 ACS 5-Year estimates. 1-Year estimates were not released for 2020 due to the impact of COVID-19 on data collection that year.
NA = Not available.
X = Not applicable.
- = Zero or rounds to zero.

Table MT-5. Median Income and Poverty Status, 2020[1]

(Number, percent, except as noted.)

Characteristic	State		U.S.	
	Number	Percent	Number	Percent
Median Income				
Households (dollars)...	56,539	X	64,994	X
Families (dollars)	72,773	X	80,069	X
Below Poverty Level (All People)	132,476	12.8	40,910,326	12.8
Sex				
Male	62,992	12.1	18,171,512	11.6
Female	69,484	13.5	22,738,814	14.0
Age				
Under 18 years...	33,815	15.2	12,598,699	17.5
Related children under 18 years..	32,577	14.7	12,306,532	17.2
18 to 64 years..	81,518	13.1	23,554,920	12.1
65 years and over	17,143	8.9	4,756,707	9.3

X = Not applicable.
[1] 2020 ACS 5-Year estimates. 1-Year estimates were not released for 2020 due to the impact of COVID-19 on data collection that year.

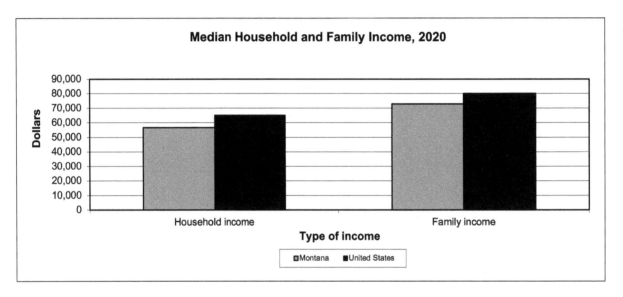

Table MT-6. Health Insurance Coverage Status for the Civilian Noninstitutionalized Population and Children Under 19 Years of Age

(Number, percent.)

Item	2011	2012	2013	2014	2015	2016	2017	2018	2019	2020[2]
Civilian Noninstitutionalized Population	983,214	989,823	999,390	1,008,116	1,017,458	1,027,510	1,036,245	1,047,075	1,053,646	1,046,670
Covered by Private or Public Insurance										
Number..	803,639	811,411	834,842	864,795	898,949	944,094	948,536	961,046	966,505	958,813
Percent..	81.7	82.0	83.5	85.8	88.4	91.9	91.5	91.8	91.7	91.6
Uninsured										
Number..	179,575	178,412	164,548	143,321	118,509	83,416	87,709	86,029	87,141	87,857
Percent..	18.3	18.0	16.5	14.2	11.6	8.1	8.5	8.2	8.3	8.4
Percent in the U.S. not covered................................	15.1	14.8	14.5	11.7	9.4	8.6	8.7	8.9	9.2	8.7
Children Under 19 Years of Age[1]	222,102	219,198	223,043	224,051	225,169	227,631	240,764	244,049	241,743	240,362
Covered by Private or Public Insurance										
Number..	196,540	194,796	200,548	205,630	208,050	217,003	226,900	229,132	226,709	226,050
Percent..	88.5	88.9	89.9	91.8	92.4	95.3	94.2	93.9	93.8	94.0
Uninsured										
Number..	25,562	24,402	22,495	18,421	17,119	10,628	13,864	14,917	15,034	14,312
Percent..	11.5	11.1	10.1	8.2	7.6	4.7	5.8	6.1	6.2	6.0
Percent in the U.S. not covered................................	7.5	7.2	7.1	6.0	4.8	4.5	5.0	5.2	5.7	5.2

[1] Data for years prior to 2017 are for individuals under 18 years of age.
[2] 2020 ACS 5-Year estimates. 1-Year estimates were not released for 2020 due to the impact of COVID-19 on data collection that year. Data is not comparable to previous years, which are based on 1-year estimates.

Table MT-7. Employment Status by Demographic Group, 2021

(Numbers in thousands, percent.)

Characteristic	Civilian noninstitutional population	Civilian labor force		Employed		Unemployed	
		Number	Percent of population	Number	Percent of population	Number	Percent of population
Total..	872	549	63.0	531	60.9	18	3.3
Sex							
Male..	434	286	65.9	276	63.4	11	3.7
Female	437	263	60.1	255	58.4	7	2.8
Race, Sex, and Hispanic Origin							
White	808	508	62.8	492	60.9	16	3.1
Male..	402	265	65.8	255	63.5	10	3.6
Female	406	243	59.9	237	58.3	6	2.6
Black or African American...................	NA	NA	NA	NA	NA	NA	NA
Male..	NA	NA	NA	NA	NA	NA	NA
Female	NA	NA	NA	NA	NA	NA	NA
Hispanic or Latino ethnicity[1]	NA	NA	NA	NA	NA	NA	NA
Male..	NA	NA	NA	NA	NA	NA	NA
Female	NA	NA	NA	NA	NA	NA	NA
Age							
16 to 19 years................................	NA	NA	NA	NA	NA	NA	NA
20 to 24 years................................	62	49	79.2	46	74.4	3	6.3
25 to 34 years................................	138	118	86.0	114	83.1	4	3.2
35 to 44 years................................	143	126	88.5	123	86.4	3	2.4
45 to 54 years................................	112	91	81.3	89	78.9	3	3.0
55 to 64 years................................	138	91	65.8	89	64.1	2	2.5
65 years and over	229	48	21.1	47	20.5	1	2.9

NOTE: Data in Table 7 are from the Current Population Survey (CPS) and do not match the estimates in Table 8. See notes and definitions for further information.
[1] May be of any race.
NA = Not available.

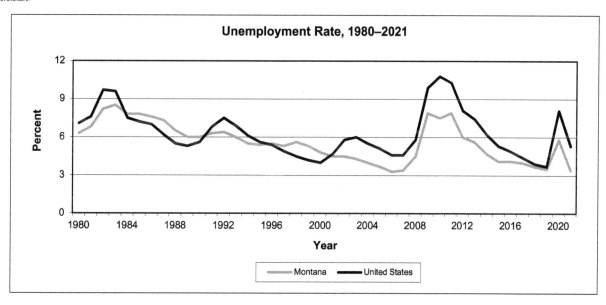

Unemployment Rate, 1980–2021

Table MT-8. Employment Status of the Civilian Noninstitutional Population Age 16 Years and Over

(Number, percent.)

Year	Civilian labor force	Civilian participation rate	Employed	Unemployed	Unemployment rate
2010..	500,895	64.4	464,808	36,087	7.2
2011..	501,065	63.9	467,786	33,279	6.6
2012..	506,441	64.0	477,056	29,385	5.8
2013..	511,199	64.0	483,798	27,401	5.4
2014..	512,613	63.5	488,738	23,875	4.7
2015..	517,901	63.6	495,725	22,176	4.3
2016..	521,736	63.3	499,266	22,470	4.3
2017..	528,441	63.2	506,871	21,570	4.1
2018..	533,821	63.1	513,858	19,963	3.7
2019..	542,279	63.5	522,898	19,381	3.6
2020..	542,917	62.7	511,616	31,301	5.8
2021..	549,743	62.3	531,202	18,541	3.4

Table MT-9. Employment and Average Wages by Industry

(Estimates are based on the 2012 North American Industry Classification System [NAICS].)

Industry	2013	2014	2015	2016	2017	2018	2019	2020
	Number of Jobs							
Wage and Salary Employment by Industry	466,811	470,408	479,194	484,003	489,276	494,412	501,103	486,849
Farm Wage and Salary Employment	6,618	6,407	6,867	6,954	8,049	6,741	7,096	6,617
Nonfarm Wage and Salary Employment	460,193	464,001	472,327	477,049	481,227	487,671	494,007	480,232
Private wage and salary employment	365,084	368,689	376,987	380,970	385,073	392,247	397,872	384,777
Forestry, fishing, and related activities	3,573	3,663	3,809	3,850	3,882	3,921	4,025	3,973
Mining	8,833	8,527	7,560	6,377	6,322	6,655	6,725	6,232
Utilities	3,179	3,157	3,080	3,029	2,874	2,826	2,823	2,793
Construction	24,728	25,585	27,160	27,736	28,405	29,809	30,672	31,639
Manufacturing	18,355	18,909	19,131	19,513	19,921	20,581	20,991	20,454
Durable goods manufacturing	11,115	11,567	11,714	11,778	11,925	11,958	12,238	11,995
Nondurable goods manufacturing	7,240	7,342	7,417	7,735	7,996	8,623	8,753	8,459
Wholesale trade	17,126	17,000	17,621	17,378	17,268	17,252	17,260	16,973
Retail trade	56,388	57,657	59,101	59,697	59,453	59,488	58,721	57,721
Transportation and warehousing	15,111	15,491	15,610	15,252	15,218	15,644	15,883	15,360
Information	6,907	6,420	6,377	6,334	6,408	6,351	6,219	5,807
Finance and insurance	15,945	16,059	16,196	16,209	16,324	16,496	17,504	17,584
Real estate and rental and leasing	5,389	5,375	5,699	5,685	6,007	6,188	6,372	6,227
Professional, scientific, and technical services	20,203	20,296	21,004	21,774	22,127	22,747	23,384	23,749
Management of companies and enterprises	1,973	1,962	2,067	2,074	2,079	2,068	2,071	2,046
Administrative and waste services	17,732	17,304	17,545	16,943	17,124	17,966	18,361	18,161
Educational services	5,935	6,064	6,066	6,004	6,138	6,525	6,699	5,838
Health care and social assistance	63,365	63,958	65,115	67,420	69,089	69,492	70,563	69,698
Arts, entertainment, and recreation	11,280	11,535	11,596	11,876	11,941	12,324	12,627	11,027
Accommodation and food services	49,009	49,326	51,399	52,932	53,548	54,228	54,899	48,425
Other services, except public administration	20,053	20,401	20,851	20,887	20,945	21,686	22,073	21,070
Government and government enterprises	95,109	95,312	95,340	96,079	96,154	95,424	96,135	95,455
	Dollars							
Average Wages and Salaries by Industry	37,741	39,059	40,143	40,885	42,133	43,643	44,905	48,342
Average Farm Wages and Salaries	38,873	38,757	30,604	34,987	30,401	36,426	24,774	35,388
Average Nonfarm Wages and Salaries	37,725	39,063	40,282	40,971	42,329	43,743	45,194	48,520
Average private wages and salaries	37,106	38,558	39,768	40,303	41,712	43,193	44,753	48,242
Forestry, fishing, and related activities	29,412	31,018	33,383	35,761	37,654	38,378	38,776	43,885
Mining	83,422	88,252	87,576	88,061	87,727	90,951	92,178	89,613
Utilities	78,666	81,114	87,486	86,271	88,971	87,855	92,876	100,346
Construction	44,794	46,108	47,823	48,673	50,355	52,981	53,970	55,890
Manufacturing	43,690	45,742	47,243	47,751	48,811	50,262	51,743	54,292
Durable goods manufacturing	42,902	44,078	45,719	46,455	47,771	49,478	50,292	53,685
Nondurable goods manufacturing	44,901	48,363	49,649	49,724	50,362	51,349	53,770	55,153
Wholesale trade	50,785	53,237	54,828	55,004	56,941	59,147	61,435	65,398
Retail trade	25,851	26,867	27,695	28,327	29,254	29,991	31,339	33,923
Transportation and warehousing	49,651	51,891	51,640	51,166	52,802	55,181	56,964	59,722
Information	44,055	45,667	48,405	50,183	51,874	54,524	56,601	65,700
Finance and insurance	55,555	57,632	60,144	61,507	64,932	67,673	69,269	76,184
Real estate and rental and leasing	30,464	32,246	34,492	34,976	35,784	38,318	39,563	43,506
Professional, scientific, and technical services	54,412	57,893	59,350	59,324	61,327	63,219	66,667	73,076
Management of companies and enterprises	73,095	71,993	75,761	75,235	76,186	78,471	81,898	89,043
Administrative and waste services	28,766	30,153	32,095	33,560	34,415	35,431	35,989	39,116
Educational services	22,048	22,756	23,552	24,347	24,793	24,803	25,097	29,763
Health care and social assistance	41,061	42,133	44,380	45,445	47,345	48,711	50,497	53,832
Arts, entertainment, and recreation	21,069	22,631	23,280	23,988	25,163	25,685	25,923	28,936
Accommodation and food services	17,300	18,179	18,862	19,437	20,211	21,284	22,115	21,753
Other services, except public administration	26,994	27,976	28,968	30,204	31,470	32,389	33,628	36,393
Government and government enterprises	40,102	41,016	42,311	43,616	44,801	46,005	47,019	49,643

Table MT-10. Employment Characteristics by Family Type

(Number, percent.)

Family type and labor force status	2018 Total	2018 Families with own children under 18 years	2019 Total	2019 Families with own children under 18 years	2020[1] Total	2020[1] Families with own children under 18 years
All Families..	265,643	104,454	269,009	99,398	267,258	103,839
FAMILY TYPE AND LABOR FORCE STATUS						
Opposite-Sex Married-Couple Families............................	213,173	73,196	213,679	67,092	213,825	74,254
Both husband and wife in labor force..................................	50.4	71.7	48.9	68.4	51.5	70.4
Husband in labor force, wife not in labor force	18.4	22.2	19.2	25.1	18.6	23.9
Wife in labor force, husband not in labor force	9.4	4.1	8.2	4.7	8.4	4.1
Both husband and wife not in labor force..............................	21.3	1.5	23.2	1.6	21.5	1.6
Other Families	52,470	31,258	55,330	32,306	52,173	29,249
Female householder, no spouse present	66.0	65.3	64.2	66.5	64.4	65.3
In labor force..	47.2	54.2	48.5	58.6	45.9	55.5
Not in labor force	18.8	11.1	15.8	7.8	18.6	9.7
Male householder, no spouse present............................	34.0	34.7	35.8	33.5	35.6	34.7
In labor force..	26.6	30.2	27.2	30.1	27.6	30.8
Not in labor force	7.3	4.6	8.6	3.5	8.0	3.9

[1] 2020 ACS 5-Year estimates. 1-Year estimates were not released for 2020 due to the impact of COVID-19 on data collection that year. Data is not comparable to previous years, which are based on 1-year estimates.

Table MT-11. School Enrollment and Educational Attainment, 2020[1]

(Number, percent.)

Item	State	U.S.
Enrollment		
Total population 3 years and over, enrolled in school	238,528	80,497,960
Enrolled in nursery school or preschool (percent)	5.9	6.1
Enrolled in kindergarten (percent)...........................	5.5	5.0
Enrolled in elementary school, grades 1-8 (percent)........................	42.7	40.4
Enrolled in high school, grades 9-12 (percent)........................	20.1	21.0
Enrolled in college or graduate school (percent)........................	25.8	27.6
Attainment		
Total population 25 years and over	734,688	222,836,834
Less than ninth grade (percent)	1.7	4.9
9th to 12th grade, no diploma (percent)	4.3	6.6
High school graduate, including equivalency (percent)........................	28.1	26.7
Some college, no degree (percent)	23.3	20.3
Associate's degree (percent)........................	9.4	8.6
Bachelor's degree (percent)	22.2	20.2
Graduate or professional degree (percent)........................	10.9	12.7
High school graduate or higher (percent)	94.0	88.5
Bachelor's degree or higher (percent)	33.1	32.9

[1] 2020 ACS 5-Year estimates. 1-Year estimates were not released for 2020 due to the impact of COVID-19 on data collection that year.

Table MT-12. Public School Characteristics and Educational Indicators

(Number, percent; data derived from National Center of Education Statistics.)

Item	State	U.S.
Public Elementary and Secondary Schools		
Number of regular school districts, 2018-19	401	13,452
Number of operational schools, 2019-20........................	826	98,469
Percent charter schools	-	7.7
Total public school enrollment, Fall 2019........................	149,917	50,796,445
Percent charter school enrollment	-	6.8
Student-teacher ratio, Fall 2019........................	14.0	15.9
Expenditures per student (unadjusted dollars), 2018-19	11,984	13,187
Four-year adjusted cohort graduation rate (ACGR), 2018-2019[1]........................	86.6	85.8
Students eligible for free or reduced-price lunch (percent), 2019-20........................	40.2	52.1
English language learners (percent), Fall 2019	2.4	10.4
Students age 3 to 21 served under IDEA, part B (percent), 2020-21	13.1	14.5

Public Schools by Type, 2019-20	Number	Percent of state public schools
Total number of schools........................	826	100.0
Special education........................	2	0.2
Vocational education........................	0	-
Alternative education........................	2	0.2

[1] Adjusted Cohort Graduation Rates (ACGR) differ from Averaged Freshmen Graduation Rates (AFGR).
- = Zero or rounds to zero.

Table MT-13. Reported Voting and Registration of the Voting-Age Population, November 2020

(Numbers in thousands, percent.)

Item	Total population	Total citizen population	Registered				Voted		
			Total registered	Percent registered (total population)	Percent registered (total citizen population)		Total voted	Percent voted (total population)	Percent voted (total citizen population)
U.S. Total	252,274	231,593	168,308	66.7	72.7		154,628	61.3	66.8
State Total..	836	827	641	76.6	77.5		607	72.6	73.5
Sex									
Male	415	411	322	77.8	78.4		299	72.0	72.5
Female	422	415	318	75.5	76.7		309	73.2	74.4
Race									
White alone.................................	772	765	597	77.3	78.0		572	74.0	74.7
White, non-Hispanic alone	757	751	584	77.2	77.8		560	74.0	74.6
Black alone.................................	4	4	2	B	B		2	B	B
Asian alone	10	7	4	B	B		4	B	B
Hispanic (of any race)	20	19	15	B	B		14	B	B
White alone or in combination	791	784	609	77.0	77.7		582	73.6	74.3
Black alone or in combination.................	6	6	4	B	B		3	B	B
Asian alone or in combination.................	13	10	5	B	B		5	B	B
Age									
18 to 24 years................................	107	104	69	65.0	66.6		60	56.2	57.6
25 to 34 years................................	128	126	89	69.4	70.3		83	65.2	66.1
35 to 44 years................................	128	127	105	82.4	82.7		97	75.6	75.9
45 to 64 years................................	253	251	201	79.3	79.9		193	76.2	76.9
65 years and over	221	218	177	80.0	81.1		175	78.9	80.0

- = Zero or rounds to zero.
B = Base is less than 75,000 and therefore too small to show the derived measure.

Table MT-14. Crime

(Number, rate per 100,000. Data are derived from the FBI Uniform Crime Reports.)

Item	State			U.S.		
	2019	2020	Percent change	2019	2020	Percent change
TOTAL POPULATION[1]	1,070,123	1,080,577	1.0	328,329,953	329,484,123	0.4
VIOLENT CRIME						
Number..	4,472	5,077	13.5	1,250,393	1,313,105	5.0
Rate	417.9	469.8	12.4	380.8	398.5	4.6
Murder and Nonnegligent Manslaughter						
Number..	32	54	68.8	16,669	21,570	29.4
Rate	3.0	5.0	67.1	5.1	6.5	28.9
Rape[2]						
Number..	679	598	-11.9	143,224	126,430	-11.7
Rate	63.5	55.3	-12.8	43.6	38.4	-12.0
Robbery						
Number..	209	279	33.5	268,483	243,600	-9.3
Rate	19.5	25.8	32.2	81.8	73.9	-9.6
Aggravated Assault						
Number..	3,552	4,146	16.7	822,017	921,505	12.1
Rate	331.9	383.7	15.6	250.4	279.7	11.7
PROPERTY CRIME						
Number..	23,929	22,917	-4.2	6,995,235	6,452,038	-7.8
Rate	2,236.1	2,120.8	-5.2	2,130.6	1,958.2	-8.1
Burglary						
Number..	2,968	2,919	-1.7	1,118,096	1,035,314	-7.4
Rate	277.4	270.1	-2.6	340.5	314.2	-7.7
Larceny-Theft						
Number..	18,547	17,322	-6.6	5,152,267	4,606,324	-10.6
Rate	1,733.2	1,603.0	-7.5	1,569.2	1,398.0	-10.9
Motor Vehicle Theft						
Number..	2,414	2,676	10.9	724,872	810,400	11.8
Rate	225.6	247.6	9.8	220.8	246.0	11.4

NOTE: Although arson data are included in the trend and clearance tables, sufficient data are not available to estimate totals for this offense. Therefore, no arson data are published in this table.
- = Zero or rounds to zero.
[1] Population figures are U.S. Census Bureau provisional estimates as of July 1, 2020.
[2] The figures shown in the rape (revised definition) column were estimated using the revised Uniform Crime Reporting (UCR) definition of rape.

Table MT-15. State Government Finances, 2020

(Dollar amounts in thousands, percent distribution.)

Item	Dollars	Percent distribution
Total Revenue	9,101,812	100.0
General revenue	7,704,984	84.7
Intergovernmental revenue	3,589,366	39.4
Taxes	3,168,411	34.8
General sales	0	-
Selective sales	678,835	7.5
License taxes	453,759	5.0
Individual income tax	1338737	14.7
Corporate income tax	186,297	2.0
Other taxes	510,783	5.6
Current charges	541,859	6.0
Miscellaneous general revenue	405,348	4.5
Utility revenue	0	-
Liquor stores revenue	116632	1.3
Insurance trust revenue[1]	1,280,196	14.1
Total Expenditure	8,601,582	100.0
Intergovernmental expenditure	1,170,127	13.6
Direct expenditure	7,431,455	86.4
Current operation	5,321,754	61.9
Capital outlay	586,863	6.8
Insurance benefits and repayments	1,301,065	15.1
Assistance and subsidies	108,443	1.3
Interest on debt	113,330	1.3
Exhibit: Salaries and wages	1,183,888	13.8
Total Expenditure	8,601,582	100.0
General expenditure	7,186,266	83.5
Intergovernmental expenditure	1,170,127	13.6
Direct expenditure	6,016,139	69.9
General expenditure, by function:		
Education	1,957,575	22.8
Public welfare	2,419,051	28.1
Hospitals	64,389	0.7
Health	180,700	2.1
Highways	814,831	9.5
Police protection	70,842	0.8
Correction	227,850	2.6
Natural resources	294,466	3.4
Parks and recreation	18,235	0.2
Governmental administration	484,800	5.6
Interest on general debt	113,330	1.3
Other and unallocable	469,083	5.5
Utility expenditure	17,377	0.2
Liquor stores expenditure	98322	1.1
Insurance trust expenditure	1,301,065	15.1
Debt at End of Fiscal Year	2,725,873	X
Cash and Security Holdings	22,857,411	X

X = Not applicable.
- = Zero or rounds to zero.
[1] Within insurance trust revenue, net earnings of state retirement systems is a calculated statistic (the item code in the data file is X08), and thus can be positive or negative. Net earnings is the sum of earnings on investments plus gains on investments minus losses on investments. The change made in 2002 for asset valuation from book to market value in accordance with Statement 34 of the Governmental Accounting Standards Board is reflected in the calculated statistics.

Table MT-16. State Government Tax Collections, 2021

(Dollars in thousands, percent.)

Item	Dollars	Percent distribution
Total Taxes	3,880,366	100.0
Property taxes	334,759	8.6
Sales and gross receipts	768,499	19.8
General sales and gross receipts	X	-
Selective sales and gross receipts	768,499	19.8
Alcoholic beverages	46,484	1.2
Amusements	116,507	3.0
Insurance premiums	138,905	3.6
Motor fuels	274,353	7.1
Pari-mutuels	104	-
Public utilities	41,015	1.1
Tobacco products	73,677	1.9
Other selective sales	77,454	2.0
Licenses	481,678	12.4
Alcoholic beverages	4,235	0.1
Amusements	4,770	0.1
Corporations in general	7,279	0.2
Hunting and fishing	76,370	2.0
Motor vehicle	188,314	4.9
Motor vehicle operators	7,947	0.2
Public utilities	10	-
Occupation and business, NEC	176,809	4.6
Other licenses	15,944	0.4
Income taxes	2,157,888	55.6
Individual income	1,889,444	48.7
Corporation net income	268,444	6.9
Other taxes	137,542	3.5
Death and gift	X	-
Documentary and stock transfer	X	-
Severance	130,998	3.4
Taxes, NEC	6,544	0.2

X = Not applicable.
- = Zero or rounds to zero.

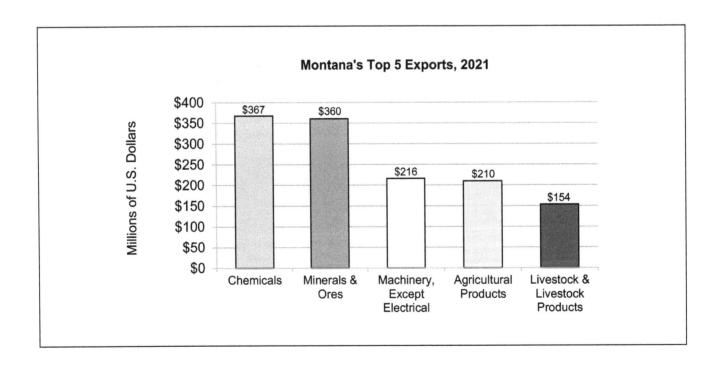

Montana's Top 5 Exports, 2021

Export	Millions of U.S. Dollars
Chemicals	$367
Minerals & Ores	$360
Machinery, Except Electrical	$216
Agricultural Products	$210
Livestock & Livestock Products	$154

Facts and Figures

Location: Central United States; bordered on the N by South Dakota, on the E by Iowa and Missouri, on the S by Kansas and Colorado, and on the W by Wyoming

Area: 77,354 sq. mi. (200,345 sq. km.); rank—16th

Population: 1,963,692 (2021 est.); rank—37th

Principal Cities: capital—Lincoln; largest—Omaha

Statehood: March 1, 1867; 37th state

U.S. Congress: 2 senators, 3 representatives

State Motto: Equality Before the Law

State Song: "Beautiful Nebraska"

State Nickname: The Cornhusker State

Abbreviations: NE; Nebr.; Neb.

State Symbols: flower—goldenrod; tree—cottonwood; bird—Western meadowlark

At a Glance

- With an increase in population of 7.5 percent, Nebraska ranked 21st among the states in growth from 2010 to 2021.

- In 2020, 8.1 percent of Nebraskans did not have health insurance, which was lower than the national average of 8.7 percent.

- The birth rate in Nebraska in 2020 was 12.5 births per 1,000 population, the 4th highest in the country.

- Nebraska ranked 39th for the percent of children in poverty, with 10.4 percent of persons under 18 years old below the poverty level.

- The state's violent crime rate in 2020 was 334.1 per 100,000 population, compared to the national rate of 398.5 per 100,000 population.

Table NE-1. Population by Age, Sex, Race, and Hispanic Origin

(Number, percent, except where noted.)

Sex, age, race, and Hispanic origin	2000	2010	2021	Percent change, 2010–2021
Total Population...	1,711,263	1,826,341	1,963,692	7.5
Percent of total U.S. population	0.6	0.6	0.6	X
Sex				
Male...	843,351	906,296	986,792	8.9
Female...	867,912	920,045	976,900	6.2
Age				
Under 5 years..	117,048	131,908	125,790	-4.6
5 to 19 years..	387,288	380,564	412,443	8.4
20 to 64 years...	974,732	1,067,192	1,103,569	3.4
65 years and over	232,195	246,677	321,890	30.5
Median age (years)	35.3	36.2	37.1	2.5
Race and Hispanic Origin				
One race				
White	1,533,261	1,649,264	1,721,884	4.4
Black..	68,541	85,971	104,653	21.7
American Indian and Alaska Native	14,896	23,418	31,809	35.8
Asian..	21,931	33,322	54,620	63.9
Native Hawaiian or Other Pacific Islander	836	2,061	2,637	27.9
Two or more races	23,953	32,305	48,089	48.9
Hispanic (of any race)..	94,425	173,058	235,669	36.2

NOTE: Population figures for 2021 are July 1 estimates. The 2000 and 2010 estimates are taken from the respective censuses.
- = Zero or rounds to zero.
X = Not applicable.

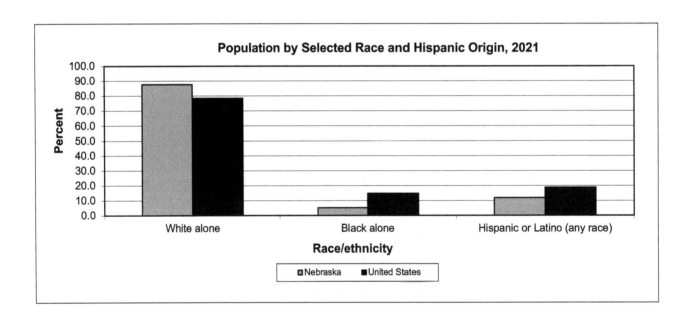

Table NE-2. Marital Status

(Number, percent distribution.)

Sex, age, race, and Hispanic origin	2000	2010	2020 [1]
Males, 15 Years and Over	654,559	708,783	756,101
Never married	29.2	32.4	33.8
Now married, except separated..	59.1	54.0	53.5
Separated...	1.0	1.4	0.9
Widowed...	2.4	2.3	2.5
Divorced..	8.3	9.9	9.2
Females, 15 Years and Over	687,863	735,744	770,706
Never married	22.5	25.3	27.3
Now married, except separated..	55.7	52.7	51.9
Separated...	1.3	1.5	1.2
Widowed...	10.8	9.5	8.6
Divorced..	9.7	10.9	11.1

[1] 2020 ACS 5-Year estimates. 1-Year estimates were not released for 2020 due to the impact of COVID-19 on data collection that year.

Table NE-3. Households and Housing Characteristics

(Number, percent, dollars.)

Item	2000	2010	2020 [1]	Average annual percent change, 2010–2020
Total Households	666,184	719,304	766,663	0.9
Family households	443,411	468,407	488,849	0.6
Married-couple family	360,996	368,023	383,188	0.6
Other family	82,415	100,384	105,661	0.8
Male householder, no wife present	22,072	31,177	33,987	1.3
Female householder, no husband present	60,343	69,207	71,674	0.5
Nonfamily households	222,773	250,897	277,814	1.5
Householder living alone	183,550	205,263	225,695	1.4
Householder not living alone	39,223	45,634	52,119	2.0
Housing Characteristics				
Total housing units	722,668	797,677	844,248	0.8
Occupied housing units	666,184	719,304	766,663	0.9
Owner occupied	449,317	484,649	507,291	0.7
Renter occupied	216,867	234,655	259,372	1.5
Average household size	2.49	2.47	2.44	-0.2
Financial Characteristics				
Median gross rent of renter-occupied housing	491	669	857	4.0
Median monthly owner costs for housing units with a mortgage	895	1,218	1,412	2.3
Median value of owner-occupied housing units	88,000	127,600	164,000	4.1

[1] 2020 ACS 5-Year estimates. 1-Year estimates were not released for 2020 due to the impact of COVID-19 on data collection that year.

Table NE-4. Migration, Origin, and Language

(Number, percent.)

Characteristic	State 2016-2020 [1]	U.S. 2016-2020 [1]
Residence 1 Year Ago		
Population 1 year and over	1,899,820	322,943,283
Same house	84.7	86.2
Different house in the U.S.	14.8	13.2
Same county	8.6	7.7
Different county	6.2	5.5
Same state	3.7	3.2
Different state	2.5	2.3
Abroad	0.5	0.6
Place of Birth		
Native born	1,781,210	282,443,680
Male	49.7	49.4
Female	50.3	50.6
Foreign born	142,616	44,125,628
Male	52.4	48.6
Female	47.6	51.4
Foreign born; naturalized U.S. citizen	56,117	22,456,684
Male	50.7	46.1
Female	49.3	53.9
Foreign born; not a U.S. citizen	86,499	21,668,944
Male	53.5	51.1
Female	46.5	48.9
Entered 2010 or later	33.3	22.8
Entered 2000 to 2009	30.1	25.1
Entered before 2000	36.6	52.1
World Region of Birth, Foreign		
Foreign-born population, excluding population born at sea	142,616	44,125,628
Europe	6.8	10.8
Asia	29.1	31.3
Africa	9.9	5.4
Oceania	0.3	0.6
Latin America	52.7	50.0
North America	1.2	1.9
Language Spoken at Home and Ability to Speak English		
Population 5 years and over	1,793,084	306,919,116
English only	88.2	78.5
Language other than English	11.8	21.5
Speaks English less than "very well"	5.2	8.2

[1] 2020 ACS 5-Year estimates. 1-Year estimates were not released for 2020 due to the impact of COVID-19 on data collection that year.
NA = Not available.
X = Not applicable.
- = Zero or rounds to zero.

Table NE-5. Median Income and Poverty Status, 2020[1]

(Number, percent, except as noted.)

Characteristic	State		U.S.	
	Number	Percent	Number	Percent
Median Income				
Households (dollars)...	63,015	X	64,994	X
Families (dollars)	80,125	X	80,069	X
Below Poverty Level (All People)	193,820	10.4	40,910,326	12.8
Sex				
Male	86,238	9.3	18,171,512	11.6
Female	107,582	11.5	22,738,814	14.0
Age				
Under 18 years...	56,828	12.2	12,598,699	17.5
Related children under 18 years...	54,589	11.8	12,306,532	17.2
18 to 64 years	114,278	10.3	23,554,920	12.1
65 years and over	22,714	7.8	4,756,707	9.3

X = Not applicable.
[1] 2020 ACS 5-Year estimates. 1-Year estimates were not released for 2020 due to the impact of COVID-19 on data collection that year.

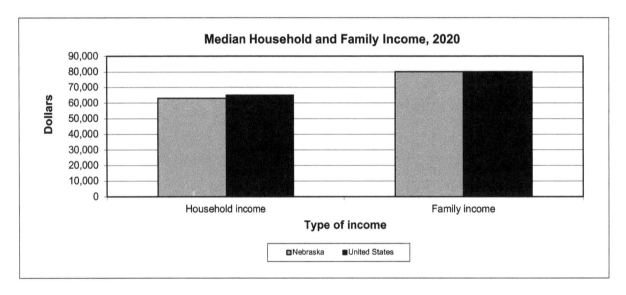

Table NE-6. Health Insurance Coverage Status for the Civilian Noninstitutionalized Population and Children Under 19 Years of Age

(Number, percent.)

Item	2011	2012	2013	2014	2015	2016	2017	2018	2019	2020 [2]
Civilian Noninstitutionalized Population	1,814,388	1,826,832	1,840,659	1,853,684	1,866,488	1,877,654	1,891,453	1,900,165	1,904,211	1,894,327
Covered by Private or Public Insurance										
Number...	1,607,294	1,621,225	1,632,081	1,674,478	1,712,699	1,717,091	1,734,669	1,742,553	1,746,288	1,740,040
Percent..	88.6	88.7	88.7	90.3	91.8	91.4	91.7	91.7	91.7	91.9
Uninsured										
Number...	207,094	205,607	208,578	179,206	153,789	160,563	156,784	157,612	157,923	154,287
Percent..	11.4	11.3	11.3	9.7	8.2	8.6	8.3	8.3	8.3	8.1
Percent in the U.S. not covered.........................	15.1	14.8	14.5	11.7	9.4	8.6	8.7	8.9	9.2	8.7
Children Under 19 Years of Age[1]	459,191	461,309	462,637	466,590	469,243	472,689	500,004	501,129	502,094	500,238
Covered by Private or Public Insurance										
Number...	432,299	433,503	437,258	441,795	444,513	448,982	474,289	474,901	473,700	474,029
Percent..	94.1	94.0	94.5	94.7	94.7	95.0	94.9	94.8	94.3	94.8
Uninsured										
Number...	26,892	27,806	25,379	24,795	24,730	23,707	25,715	26,228	28,394	26,209
Percent..	5.9	6.0	5.5	5.3	5.3	5.0	5.1	5.2	5.7	5.2
Percent in the U.S. not covered.........................	7.5	7.2	7.1	6.0	4.8	4.5	5.0	5.2	5.7	5.2

[1] Data for years prior to 2017 are for individuals under 18 years of age.
[2] 2020 ACS 5-Year estimates. 1-Year estimates were not released for 2020 due to the impact of COVID-19 on data collection that year. Data is not comparable to previous years, which are based on 1-year estimates.

Table NE-7. Employment Status by Demographic Group, 2021

(Numbers in thousands, percent.)

Characteristic	Civilian noninstitutional population	Civilian labor force		Employed		Unemployed	
		Number	Percent of population	Number	Percent of population	Number	Percent of population
Total...	1,493	1,040	69.7	1,011	67.7	29	2.8
Sex							
Male..	737	551	74.7	537	72.8	14	2.5
Female	756	490	64.8	475	62.7	15	3.1
Race, Sex, and Hispanic Origin							
White	1,335	928	69.5	905	67.8	23	2.4
Male.....................................	658	490	74.5	480	72.9	10	2.1
Female	677	438	64.7	425	62.8	12	2.8
Black or African American...........	NA	NA	NA	NA	NA	NA	NA
Male.....................................	NA	NA	NA	NA	NA	NA	NA
Female	NA	NA	NA	NA	NA	NA	NA
Hispanic or Latino ethnicity[1]	147	107	72.5	102	69.0	5	4.9
Male.....................................	NA	NA	NA	NA	NA	NA	NA
Female	NA	NA	NA	NA	NA	NA	NA
Age							
16 to 19 years..........................	NA	NA	NA	NA	NA	NA	NA
20 to 24 years..........................	123	101	81.9	96	78.2	5	4.6
25 to 34 years..........................	266	236	88.9	229	86.2	7	3.0
35 to 44 years..........................	240	208	86.7	205	85.3	3	1.6
45 to 54 years..........................	220	188	85.5	184	83.7	4	2.1
55 to 64 years..........................	239	184	77.2	181	75.8	3	1.8
65 years and over......................	303	76	25.1	74	24.5	2	2.2

NOTE: Data in Table 7 are from the Current Population Survey (CPS) and do not match the estimates in Table 8. See notes and definitions for further information.
[1] May be of any race.
NA = Not available.

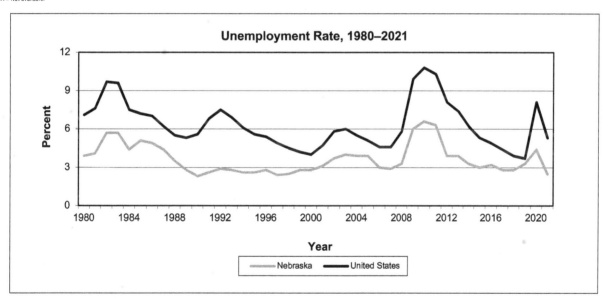

Unemployment Rate, 1980–2021

Table NE-8. Employment Status of the Civilian Noninstitutional Population Age 16 Years and Over

(Number, percent.)

Year	Civilian labor force	Civilian participation rate	Employed	Unemployed	Unemployment rate
2010...	992,009	71.6	945,195	46,814	4.7
2011...	1,003,635	71.7	959,325	44,310	4.4
2012...	1,012,807	71.8	973,448	39,359	3.9
2013...	1,014,830	71.4	977,464	37,366	3.7
2014...	1,012,727	70.8	979,728	32,999	3.3
2015...	1,011,666	70.2	981,326	30,340	3.0
2016...	1,016,062	70.0	984,966	31,096	3.1
2017...	1,023,163	69.4	992,740	30,423	3.0
2018...	1,034,214	69.7	1,004,261	29,953	2.9
2019...	1,048,820	70.2	1,016,904	31,916	3.0
2020...	1,044,541	69.5	1,001,426	43,115	4.1
2021...	1,049,033	69.5	1,022,662	26,371	2.5

Table NE-9. Employment and Average Wages by Industry

(Estimates are based on the 2012 North American Industry Classification System [NAICS].)

Industry	2013	2014	2015	2016	2017	2018	2019	2020
	Number of Jobs							
Wage and Salary Employment by Industry.........................	1,000,260	1,013,641	1,030,768	1,036,447	1,040,572	1,048,136	1,052,893	1,015,211
Farm Wage and Salary Employment................................	12,277	12,168	16,089	14,485	15,416	16,600	16,644	16,226
Nonfarm Wage and Salary Employment...........................	987,983	1,001,473	1,014,679	1,021,962	1,025,156	1,031,536	1,036,249	998,985
Private wage and salary employment...	814,673	827,481	840,079	846,330	849,342	855,798	860,545	826,027
Forestry, fishing, and related activities...................................	6,089	6,009	5,629	5,935	5,895	5,893	5,794	5,542
Mining..	1,042	1,133	1,066	982	1,044	1,081	1,025	970
Utilities..	1,290	1,264	1,081	1,072	1,090	1,070	1,082	1,014
Construction	45,389	47,336	50,140	51,812	52,402	53,557	55,054	56,530
Manufacturing..	96,556	97,553	97,417	96,952	98,181	99,859	100,022	97,508
Durable goods manufacturing..	44,995	45,916	45,416	44,055	43,982	44,748	45,202	43,195
Nondurable goods manufacturing.......................................	51,561	51,637	52,001	52,897	54,199	55,111	54,820	54,313
Wholesale trade	42,126	43,089	42,490	42,021	41,258	40,345	40,251	40,049
Retail trade..	107,151	108,732	110,649	111,143	109,938	108,667	106,055	102,104
Transportation and warehousing.......................................	52,199	52,871	53,998	51,282	50,974	51,896	52,980	50,315
Information..	17,220	17,068	17,581	18,515	18,224	17,652	17,188	16,169
Finance and insurance	55,716	56,626	57,200	58,296	59,214	59,152	60,444	60,173
Real estate and rental and leasing....................................	9,208	9,269	9,605	9,828	10,059	10,408	10,769	10,586
Professional, scientific, and technical services	44,362	44,353	44,885	44,306	45,234	45,956	46,390	47,238
Management of companies and enterprises.........................	19,340	20,410	22,127	21,451	21,638	21,812	21,672	21,261
Administrative and waste services	46,686	48,908	50,543	52,286	51,371	52,208	52,770	49,521
Educational services	18,192	18,393	18,736	18,806	18,916	18,953	19,295	17,962
Health care and social assistance....................................	122,094	122,955	123,890	127,301	128,331	129,829	130,720	126,752
Arts, entertainment, and recreation...................................	13,376	13,996	14,280	14,418	14,951	15,172	15,545	12,021
Accommodation and food services....................................	72,910	73,748	74,629	76,602	77,491	78,028	78,931	68,122
Other services, except public administration........................	43,727	43,768	44,133	43,322	43,131	44,260	44,558	42,190
Government and government enterprises.................................	173,310	173,992	174,600	175,632	175,814	175,738	175,704	172,958
	Dollars							
Average Wages and Salaries by Industry	41,505	42,842	44,387	45,205	46,540	48,102	49,701	53,256
Average Farm Wages and Salaries	39,781	41,575	35,024	37,944	36,458	36,743	35,439	29,270
Average Nonfarm Wages and Salaries	41,527	42,857	44,535	45,308	46,692	48,285	49,930	53,646
Average private wages and salaries....................................	41,050	42,463	44,215	44,963	46,406	48,082	49,794	53,800
Forestry, fishing, and related activities................................	25,367	26,665	28,705	29,078	29,900	30,590	33,448	37,804
Mining..	52,361	53,190	54,466	56,775	55,635	58,622	60,506	63,949
Utilities..	86,069	111,415	108,917	97,390	100,708	116,661	137,373	134,714
Construction	44,169	46,649	48,319	49,264	50,577	52,776	54,857	57,784
Manufacturing..	45,685	47,428	48,627	49,341	51,502	53,840	55,001	59,010
Durable goods manufacturing..	48,850	50,525	51,226	51,690	54,307	56,070	56,616	59,290
Nondurable goods manufacturing.......................................	42,923	44,674	46,357	47,385	49,226	52,030	53,669	58,787
Wholesale trade	56,263	58,760	60,528	61,600	63,149	65,648	68,409	71,097
Retail trade..	25,153	25,664	26,526	27,528	28,349	29,164	30,313	32,811
Transportation and warehousing.......................................	52,183	55,065	56,732	56,582	58,875	60,366	61,414	64,204
Information..	56,486	57,571	60,021	62,532	63,741	67,027	69,608	79,504
Finance and insurance	61,257	62,849	65,635	67,233	70,110	74,312	76,768	83,395
Real estate and rental and leasing....................................	37,370	39,145	40,540	42,149	42,300	43,838	45,255	48,023
Professional, scientific, and technical services	60,872	62,021	64,690	66,513	68,473	70,800	73,272	76,778
Management of companies and enterprises.........................	92,162	95,500	100,137	96,435	97,150	89,540	91,255	100,556
Administrative and waste services	32,392	34,211	36,077	37,227	39,015	40,142	42,199	44,571
Educational services	30,577	29,690	30,322	31,358	31,732	32,934	33,553	35,746
Health care and social assistance....................................	40,959	41,594	44,045	45,098	46,216	48,642	50,804	54,201
Arts, entertainment, and recreation...................................	18,863	19,227	19,496	20,154	20,578	21,115	21,809	25,044
Accommodation and food services....................................	15,506	16,169	17,072	17,899	18,437	19,420	19,869	19,670
Other services, except public administration........................	28,640	29,881	30,758	32,064	33,175	34,199	35,430	39,023
Government and government enterprises.............................	43,767	44,733	46,075	46,971	48,071	49,276	50,596	52,912

Table NE-10. Employment Characteristics by Family Type

(Number, percent.)

Family type and labor force status	2018 Total	2018 Families with own children under 18 years	2019 Total	2019 Families with own children under 18 years	2020 [1] Total	2020 [1] Families with own children under 18 years
All Families...	485,628	220,353	493,013	221,206	488,849	222,321
FAMILY TYPE AND LABOR FORCE STATUS						
Opposite-Sex Married-Couple Families............................	379,801	155,599	388,538	161,340	380,736	157,958
Both husband and wife in labor force..................................	59.0	75.2	61.5	80.0	60.6	76.4
Husband in labor force, wife not in labor force	18.5	20.6	16.3	17.1	17.6	19.9
Wife in labor force, husband not in labor force	6.8	3.0	6.3	2.3	6.6	3.1
Both husband and wife not in labor force.............................	14.9	0.8	15.3	0.4	15.2	0.7
Other Families	105,827	64,754	104,475	59,866	105,661	63,905
Female householder, no spouse present	67.5	70.7	67.4	70.7	67.8	70.3
In labor force..	54.0	64.1	52.0	61.9	53.7	63.0
Not in labor force	13.5	6.5	15.3	8.8	14.2	7.3
Male householder, no spouse present................................	32.5	29.3	32.6	29.3	32.2	29.7
In labor force..	26.6	25.9	28.7	28.6	27.2	27.5
Not in labor force	5.9	3.4	4.0	0.8	4.9	2.2

[1] 2020 ACS 5-Year estimates. 1-Year estimates were not released for 2020 due to the impact of COVID-19 on data collection that year. Data is not comparable to previous years, which are based on 1-year estimates.

Table NE-11. School Enrollment and Educational Attainment, 2020[1]

(Number, percent.)

Item	State	U.S.
Enrollment		
Total population 3 years and over, enrolled in school	505,631	80,497,960
Enrolled in nursery school or preschool (percent)........................	6.7	6.1
Enrolled in kindergarten (percent)..	5.2	5.0
Enrolled in elementary school, grades 1-8 (percent)......................	40.9	40.4
Enrolled in high school, grades 9-12 (percent)..............................	20.5	21.0
Enrolled in college or graduate school (percent)...........................	26.8	27.6
Attainment		
Total population 25 years and over	1,259,540	222,836,834
Less than ninth grade (percent)	3.8	4.9
9th to 12th grade, no diploma (percent)	4.6	6.6
High school graduate, including equivalency (percent)....................	25.7	26.7
Some college, no degree (percent)	22.7	20.3
Associate's degree (percent)...	10.7	8.6
Bachelor's degree (percent)	21.4	20.2
Graduate or professional degree (percent).................................	11.1	12.7
High school graduate or higher (percent)	91.6	88.5
Bachelor's degree or higher (percent).....................................	32.5	32.9

[1] 2020 ACS 5-Year estimates. 1-Year estimates were not released for 2020 due to the impact of COVID-19 on data collection that year.

Table NE-12. Public School Characteristics and Educational Indicators

(Number, percent; data derived from National Center of Education Statistics.)

Item	State	U.S.
Public Elementary and Secondary Schools		
Number of regular school districts, 2018-19	244	13,452
Number of operational schools, 2019-20......................................	1,082	98,469
Percent charter schools	-	7.7
Total public school enrollment, Fall 2019....................................	330,018	50,796,445
Percent charter school enrollment	-	6.8
Student-teacher ratio, Fall 2019..	13.7	15.9
Expenditures per student (unadjusted dollars), 2018-19	12,746	13,187
Four-year adjusted cohort graduation rate (ACGR), 2018-2019[1]..........	88.4	85.8
Students eligible for free or reduced-price lunch (percent), 2019-20........	45.6	52.1
English language learners (percent), Fall 2019	7.4	10.4
Students age 3 to 21 served under IDEA, part B (percent), 2020-21	16.0	14.5

Public Schools by Type, 2019-20	Number	Percent of state public schools
Total number of schools..	1,082	100.0
Special education...	27	2.5
Vocational education...	0	-
Alternative education...	51	4.7

[1] Adjusted Cohort Graduation Rates (ACGR) differ from Averaged Freshmen Graduation Rates (AFGR).
- = Zero or rounds to zero.

Table NE-13. Reported Voting and Registration of the Voting-Age Population, November 2020

(Numbers in thousands, percent.)

Item	Total population	Total citizen population	Registered			Voted		
			Total registered	Percent registered (total population)	Percent registered (total citizen population)	Total voted	Percent voted (total population)	Percent voted (total citizen population)
U.S. Total	252,274	231,593	168,308	66.7	72.7	154,628	61.3	66.8
State Total.......................................	1,435	1,369	971	67.7	70.9	892	62.2	65.2
Sex								
Male	708	674	464	65.6	68.9	421	59.6	62.5
Female	728	695	507	69.7	73.0	471	64.7	67.8
Race								
White alone......................................	1,301	1,255	903	69.4	71.9	826	63.5	65.8
White, non-Hispanic alone	1,205	1,202	877	72.7	72.9	801	66.5	66.6
Black alone......................................	80	71	45	B	B	44	B	B
Asian alone	26	17	9	B	B	9	B	B
Hispanic (of any race)	98	55	28	B	B	27	B	B
White alone or in combination	1,307	1,261	907	69.4	71.9	830	63.5	65.8
Black alone or in combination	82	73	47	B	B	46	B	B
Asian alone or in combination..................	26	17	9	B	B	9	B	B
Age								
18 to 24 years	123	117	59	47.5	50.1	49	40.1	42.3
25 to 34 years	301	281	190	63.0	67.6	168	55.7	59.8
35 to 44 years	246	217	147	59.6	67.6	138	55.9	63.3
45 to 64 years	465	457	338	72.7	74.0	311	66.9	68.2
65 years and over	299	297	238	79.5	80.0	226	75.5	76.0

B = Base is less than 75,000 and therefore too small to show the derived measure.

Table NE-14. Crime

(Number, rate per 100,000. Data are derived from the FBI Uniform Crime Reports.)

Item	State			U.S.		
	2019	2020	Percent change	2019	2020	Percent change
TOTAL POPULATION[1]	1,932,571	1,937,552	0.3	328,329,953	329,484,123	0.4
VIOLENT CRIME						
Number..	5,887	6,473	10.0	1,250,393	1,313,105	5.0
Rate	304.6	334.1	9.7	380.8	398.5	4.6
Murder and Nonnegligent Manslaughter						
Number..	45	69	53.3	16,669	21,570	29.4
Rate	2.3	3.6	52.9	5.1	6.5	28.9
Rape[2]						
Number..	1,284	1,163	-9.4	143,224	126,430	-11.7
Rate	66.4	60.0	-9.7	43.6	38.4	-12.0
Robbery						
Number..	795	799	0.5	268,483	243,600	-9.3
Rate	41.1	41.2	0.2	81.8	73.9	-9.6
Aggravated Assault						
Number..	3,763	4,442	18.0	822,017	921,505	12.1
Rate	194.7	229.3	17.7	250.4	279.7	11.7
PROPERTY CRIME						
Number..	39,553	36,991	-6.5	6,995,235	6,452,038	-7.8
Rate	2,046.7	1,909.2	-6.7	2,130.6	1,958.2	-8.1
Burglary						
Number..	4,763	4,455	-6.5	1,118,096	1,035,314	-7.4
Rate	246.5	229.9	-6.7	340.5	314.2	-7.7
Larceny-Theft						
Number..	29,817	27,488	-7.8	5,152,267	4,606,324	-10.6
Rate	1,542.9	1,418.7	-8.0	1,569.2	1,398.0	-10.9
Motor Vehicle Theft						
Number..	4,973	5,048	1.5	724,872	810,400	11.8
Rate	257.3	260.5	1.2	220.8	246.0	11.4

NOTE: Although arson data are included in the trend and clearance tables, sufficient data are not available to estimate totals for this offense. Therefore, no arson data are published in this table.
- = Zero or rounds to zero.
[1] Population figures are U.S. Census Bureau provisional estimates as of July 1, 2020.
[2] The figures shown in the rape (revised definition) column were estimated using the revised Uniform Crime Reporting (UCR) definition of rape.

Table NE-15. State Government Finances, 2020

(Dollar amounts in thousands, percent distribution.)

Item	Dollars	Percent distribution
Total Revenue	13,796,416	100.0
General revenue	12,382,146	89.7
Intergovernmental revenue	4,710,119	34.1
Taxes	5,857,227	42.5
General sales	2169821	15.7
Selective sales	642,834	4.7
License taxes	186,656	1.4
Individual income tax	2445647	17.7
Corporate income tax	391,164	2.8
Other taxes	21,105	0.2
Current charges	1,082,181	7.8
Miscellaneous general revenue	732,619	5.3
Utility revenue	0	-
Liquor stores revenue	0	-
Insurance trust revenue[1]	1,414,270	10.3
Total Expenditure	12,047,912	100.0
Intergovernmental expenditure	2,881,587	23.9
Direct expenditure	9,166,325	76.1
Current operation	7,004,331	58.1
Capital outlay	834,858	6.9
Insurance benefits and repayments	1,002,240	8.3
Assistance and subsidies	264,743	2.2
Interest on debt	60,153	0.5
Exhibit: Salaries and wages	1,980,604	16.4
Total Expenditure	12,047,912	100.0
General expenditure	11,045,672	91.7
Intergovernmental expenditure	2,881,587	23.9
Direct expenditure	8,164,085	67.8
General expenditure, by function:		
Education	4,103,087	34.1
Public welfare	2,840,216	23.6
Hospitals	197,423	1.6
Health	302,477	2.5
Highways	976,431	8.1
Police protection	98,322	0.8
Correction	431,928	3.6
Natural resources	223,039	1.9
Parks and recreation	52,147	0.4
Governmental administration	345,015	2.9
Interest on general debt	60,153	0.5
Other and unallocable	1,387,452	11.5
Utility expenditure	0	-
Liquor stores expenditure	0	-
Insurance trust expenditure	1,002,240	8.3
Debt at End of Fiscal Year	2,585,834	X
Cash and Security Holdings	28,076,771	X

X = Not applicable.
- = Zero or rounds to zero.
[1] Within insurance trust revenue, net earnings of state retirement systems is a calculated statistic (the item code in the data file is X08), and thus can be positive or negative. Net earnings is the sum of earnings on investments plus gains on investments minus losses on investments. The change made in 2002 for asset valuation from book to market value in accordance with Statement 34 of the Governmental Accounting Standards Board is reflected in the calculated statistics.

Table NE-16. State Government Tax Collections, 2021

(Dollars in thousands, percent.)

Item	Dollars	Percent distribution
Total Taxes	6,960,988	100.0
Property taxes	123	-
Sales and gross receipts	3,040,622	43.7
General sales and gross receipts	2,382,381	34.2
Selective sales and gross receipts	658,241	9.5
Alcoholic beverages	35,338	0.5
Amusements	6,180	0.1
Insurance premiums	69,558	1.0
Motor fuels	415,141	6.0
Pari-mutuels	180	-
Public utilities	53,973	0.8
Tobacco products	55,790	0.8
Other selective sales	22,081	0.3
Licenses	194,771	2.8
Alcoholic beverages	1,016	-
Amusements	432	-
Corporations in general	6,988	0.1
Hunting and fishing	19,575	0.3
Motor vehicle	117,972	1.7
Motor vehicle operators	11,523	0.2
Public utilities	X	-
Occupation and business, NEC	35,995	0.5
Other licenses	1,270	-
Income taxes	3,701,819	53.2
Individual income	3,130,599	45.0
Corporation net income	571,220	8.2
Other taxes	23,653	0.3
Death and gift	X	-
Documentary and stock transfer	21,139	0.3
Severance	2,514	-
Taxes, NEC	0	-

- = Zero or rounds to zero.
X = Not applicable.

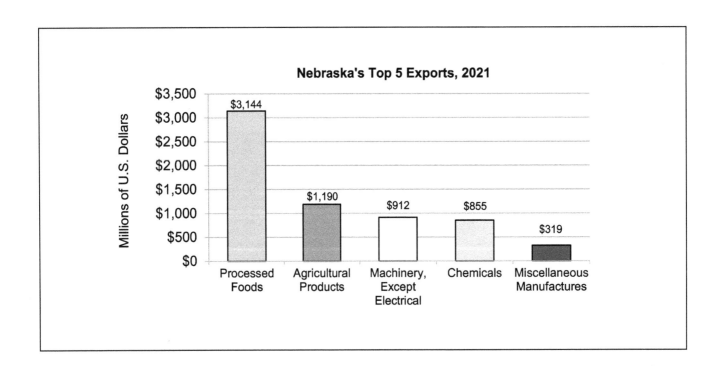

Nebraska's Top 5 Exports, 2021

NEVADA

Facts and Figures

Location: Western United States; bordered on the N by Oregon and Idaho, on the E by Utah and Arizona, on the S by Arizona and California, and on the W by California

Area: 110,561 sq. mi. (286,351 sq. km.); rank—7th

Population: 3,143,991 (2021 est.); rank—32nd

Principal Cities: capital—Carson City; largest—Las Vegas

Statehood: October 31, 1864; 36th state

U.S. Congress: 2 senators, 4 representatives

State Motto: All for Our Country

State Song: "Home Means Nevada"

State Nicknames: The Silver State; The Sagebrush State

Abbreviations: NV; Nev.

State Symbols: flower—sagebrush; tree—single-leaf piñon and bristlecone pine; bird—mountain bluebird

At a Glance

- With an increase in population of 16.4 percent, Nevada ranked 4th among the states in growth from 2010 to 2021.

- Approximately 29.9 percent of Nevadans self-identified their ethnicity as "Hispanic or Latino" in 2021, the 5th highest percentage in the country.

- In 2021, Nevada had the 2nd highest unemployment rate in the country, with 7.2 percent of residents unemployed, compared to 5.3 percent of the whole nation.

- Nevada's violent crime rate in 2020 was 460.3 per 100,000 population, which ranked 13th among the states. The national violent crime rate was 398.5 per 100,000 population.

Table NV-1. Population by Age, Sex, Race, and Hispanic Origin

(Number, percent, except where noted.)

Sex, age, race, and Hispanic origin	2000	2010	2021	Percent change, 2010–2021
Total Population..	1,998,257	2,700,551	3,143,991	16.4
Percent of total U.S. population	0.7	0.9	0.9	X
Sex				
Male..	1,018,051	1,363,616	1,584,097	16.2
Female...	980,206	1,336,935	1,559,894	16.7
Age				
Under 5 years..	145,817	187,478	178,077	-5.0
5 to 19 years...	415,684	548,850	588,635	7.2
20 to 64 years...	1,217,827	1,639,864	1,858,812	13.4
65 years and over..	218,929	324,359	518,467	59.8
Median age (years)	35.0	36.3	38.7	6.6
Race and Hispanic Origin				
One race				
White..	1,501,886	2,106,494	2,287,445	8.6
Black...	135,477	231,224	334,455	44.6
American Indian and Alaska Native	26,420	42,965	54,145	26.0
Asian...	90,266	203,478	285,911	40.5
Native Hawaiian or Other Pacific Islander	8,426	19,307	27,165	40.7
Two or more races...	76,428	97,083	154,870	59.5
Hispanic (of any race).......................................	393,970	741,200	940,757	26.9

NOTE: Population figures for 2021 are July 1 estimates. The 2000 and 2010 estimates are taken from the respective censuses.
- = Zero or rounds to zero.
X = Not applicable.

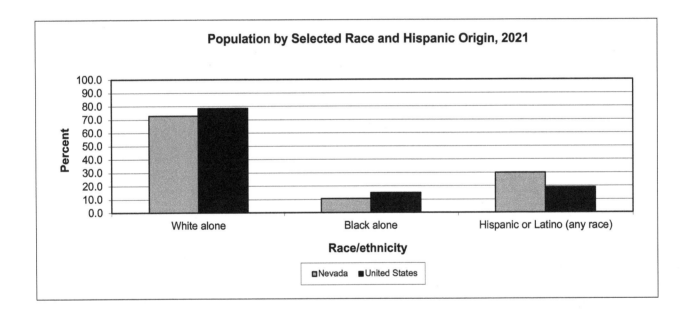

Population by Selected Race and Hispanic Origin, 2021

□ Nevada ■ United States

Table NV-2. Marital Status

(Number, percent distribution.)

Sex, age, race, and Hispanic origin	2000	2010	2020 [1]
Males, 15 Years and Over	792,317	1,081,514	1,227,637
Never married	28.8	35.0	37.0
Now married, except separated...	53.8	47.6	46.3
Separated..	2.0	2.0	1.7
Widowed..	2.5	2.9	2.5
Divorced..	12.9	12.5	12.4
Females, 15 Years and Over	771,263	1,069,123	1,229,893
Never married	20.9	27.2	29.4
Now married, except separated...	53.1	47.2	45.1
Separated..	2.7	2.8	2.4
Widowed..	8.6	8.0	7.9
Divorced..	14.7	14.8	15.2

[1] 2020 ACS 5-Year estimates. 1-Year estimates were not released for 2020 due to the impact of COVID-19 on data collection that year.

Table NV-3. Households and Housing Characteristics

(Number, percent, dollars.)

Item	2000	2010	2020 [1]	Average annual percent change, 2010–2020
Total Households..	751,165	989,811	1,130,011	2.0
Family households	498,333	639,686	720,213	1.8
Married-couple family	373,201	452,361	501,828	1.6
Other family	125,132	187,325	218,385	2.4
Male householder, no wife present..........	41,650	63,327	71,659	1.9
Female householder, no husband present....	83,482	123,998	146,726	2.6
Nonfamily households	252,832	350,125	409,798	2.4
Householder living alone	186,745	266,232	318,983	2.8
Householder not living alone	66,087	83,893	90,815	1.2
Housing Characteristics				
Total housing units..................................	827,457	1,175,070	1,268,533	1.1
Occupied housing units	751,165	989,811	1,130,011	2.0
Owner occupied	457,247	565,869	644,864	2.0
Renter occupied	293,918	423,942	485,147	2.1
Average household size.............................	2.62	2.7	2.65	-0.3
Financial Characteristics				
Median gross rent of renter-occupied housing	699	952	1,159	3.1
Median monthly owner costs for housing units with a mortgage	1,190	1,638	1,574	-0.6
Median value of owner-occupied housing units..........	142,000	174,800	290,200	9.4

[1] 2020 ACS 5-Year estimates. 1-Year estimates were not released for 2020 due to the impact of COVID-19 on data collection that year.

Table NV-4. Migration, Origin, and Language

(Number, percent.)

Characteristic	State 2016-2020 [1]	U.S. 2016-2020 [1]
Residence 1 Year Ago		
Population 1 year and over	2,997,824	322,943,283
Same house	83.0	86.2
Different house in the U.S.	16.5	13.2
Same county	11.2	7.7
Different county	5.2	5.5
Same state	0.9	3.2
Different state	4.3	2.3
Abroad	0.5	0.6
Place of Birth		
Native born	2,442,473	282,443,680
Male	50.8	49.4
Female	49.2	50.6
Foreign born	587,808	44,125,628
Male	47.4	48.6
Female	52.6	51.4
Foreign born; naturalized U.S. citizen.............	298,127	22,456,684
Male	45.5	46.1
Female	54.5	53.9
Foreign born; not a U.S. citizen..................	289,681	21,668,944
Male	49.3	51.1
Female	50.7	48.9
Entered 2010 or later	17.6	22.8
Entered 2000 to 2009	26.1	25.1
Entered before 2000..............................	56.2	52.1
World Region of Birth, Foreign		
Foreign-born population, excluding population born at sea	587,808	44,125,628
Europe	7.4	10.8
Asia..	31.4	31.3
Africa..	3.7	5.4
Oceania	0.6	0.6
Latin America.................................	55.0	50.0
North America.................................	1.9	1.9
Language Spoken at Home and Ability to Speak English		
Population 5 years and over........................	2,846,140	306,919,116
English only	69.8	78.5
Language other than English....................	30.2	21.5
Speaks English less than "very well"..........	11.3	8.2

[1] 2020 ACS 5-Year estimates. 1-Year estimates were not released for 2020 due to the impact of COVID-19 on data collection that year.
NA = Not available.
X = Not applicable.
- = Zero or rounds to zero.

Table NV-5. Median Income and Poverty Status, 2020[1]

(Number, percent, except as noted.)

Characteristic	State		U.S.	
	Number	Percent	Number	Percent
Median Income				
Households (dollars)...	62,043	X	64,994	X
Families (dollars)	74,077	X	80,069	X
Below Poverty Level (All People)	381,695	12.8	40,910,326	12.8
Sex				
Male	173,998	11.7	18,171,512	11.6
Female	207,697	13.9	22,738,814	14.0
Age				
Under 18 years..	119,005	17.6	12,598,699	17.5
Related children under 18 years...	115,729	17.2	12,306,532	17.2
18 to 64 years	219,087	11.9	23,554,920	12.1
65 years and over	43,603	9.2	4,756,707	9.3

X = Not applicable.
[1] 2020 ACS 5-Year estimates. 1-Year estimates were not released for 2020 due to the impact of COVID-19 on data collection that year.

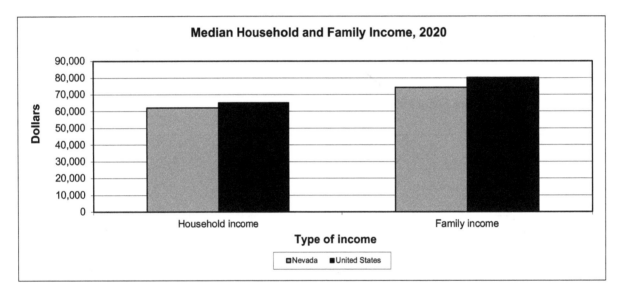

Median Household and Family Income, 2020

(Chart: Dollars by Type of income — Household income, Family income. Legend: Nevada, United States.)

Table NV-6. Health Insurance Coverage Status for the Civilian Noninstitutionalized Population and Children Under 19 Years of Age

(Number, percent.)

Item	2011	2012	2013	2014	2015	2016	2017	2018	2019	2020 [2]
Civilian Noninstitutionalized Population	2,686,989	2,723,965	2,757,207	2,805,532	2,855,974	2,905,767	2,962,236	2,998,585	3,043,419	2,993,632
Covered by Private or Public Insurance										
Number..	2,098,195	2,120,540	2,187,128	2,378,879	2,505,290	2,575,349	2,629,612	2,662,394	2,695,788	2,659,502
Percent...	78.1	77.8	79.3	84.8	87.7	88.6	88.8	88.8	88.6	88.8
Uninsured										
Number..	588,794	603,425	570,079	426,653	350,684	330,418	332,624	336,191	347,631	334,130
Percent...	21.9	22.2	20.7	15.2	12.3	11.4	11.2	11.2	11.4	11.2
Percent in the U.S. not covered..	15.1	14.8	14.5	11.7	9.4	8.6	8.7	8.9	9.2	8.7
Children Under 19 Years of Age[1]	662,359	663,481	661,097	661,634	667,602	676,435	718,836	721,982	724,678	720,745
Covered by Private or Public Insurance										
Number..	554,955	553,334	562,588	597,902	617,152	630,576	661,283	664,442	666,692	665,384
Percent...	83.8	83.4	85.1	90.4	92.4	93.2	92.0	92.0	92.0	92.3
Uninsured										
Number..	107,404	110,147	98,509	63,732	50,450	45,859	57,553	57,540	57,986	55,361
Percent...	16.2	16.6	14.9	9.6	7.6	6.8	8.0	8.0	8.0	7.7
Percent in the U.S. not covered..	7.5	7.2	7.1	6.0	4.8	4.5	5.0	5.2	5.7	5.2

[1] Data for years prior to 2017 are for individuals under 18 years of age.
[2] 2020 ACS 5-Year estimates. 1-Year estimates were not released for 2020 due to the impact of COVID-19 on data collection that year. Data is not comparable to previous years, which are based on 1-year estimates.

Table NV-7. Employment Status by Demographic Group, 2021

(Numbers in thousands, percent.)

Characteristic	Civilian noninstitutional population	Civilian labor force		Employed		Unemployed	
		Number	Percent of population	Number	Percent of population	Number	Percent of population
Total..	2,526	1,523	60.3	1,406	55.7	117	7.7
Sex							
Male..	1,250	825	66.0	762	61.0	63	7.7
Female.......................................	1,277	698	54.7	644	50.5	54	7.7
Race, Sex, and Hispanic Origin							
White...	1,833	1,084	59.2	1,012	55.2	72	6.6
Male.......................................	918	607	66.2	566	61.6	42	6.9
Female....................................	916	477	52.1	447	48.8	30	6.4
Black or African American...............	252	161	63.8	136	54.1	25	15.3
Male.......................................	119	76	64.1	67	55.9	10	12.8
Female....................................	133	85	63.6	70	52.5	15	17.5
Hispanic or Latino ethnicity[1]	633	427	67.5	399	63.0	28	6.6
Male.......................................	314	241	76.6	227	72.1	14	5.9
Female....................................	319	187	58.5	173	54.1	14	7.5
Age							
16 to 19 years.............................	161	60	37.4	54	33.8	6	9.5
20 to 24 years.............................	186	140	75.2	126	67.7	14	9.9
25 to 34 years.............................	465	374	80.5	346	74.3	29	7.6
35 to 44 years.............................	393	315	80.1	291	74.1	23	7.4
45 to 54 years.............................	387	296	76.4	275	70.9	21	7.2
55 to 64 years.............................	362	224	61.7	205	56.5	19	8.5
65 years and over.........................	573	115	20.1	110	19.3	5	4.3

NOTE: Data in Table 7 are from the Current Population Survey (CPS) and do not match the estimates in Table 8. See notes and definitions for further information.
[1] May be of any race.

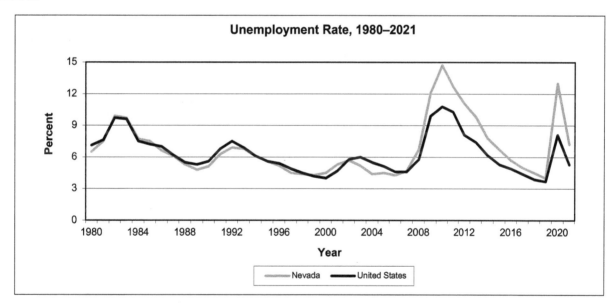

Table NV-8. Employment Status of the Civilian Noninstitutional Population Age 16 Years and Over

(Number, percent.)

Year	Civilian labor force	Civilian participation rate	Employed	Unemployed	Unemployment rate
2010..	1,358,860	65.9	1,171,879	186,981	13.8
2011..	1,360,791	65.0	1,179,653	181,138	13.3
2012..	1,366,208	64.4	1,207,733	158,475	11.6
2013..	1,370,727	63.6	1,234,021	136,706	10.0
2014..	1,380,084	63.0	1,267,424	112,660	8.2
2015..	1,396,761	62.5	1,301,094	95,667	6.8
2016..	1,414,233	62.0	1,332,390	81,843	5.8
2017..	1,444,262	62.6	1,372,022	72,240	5.0
2018..	1,492,831	63.3	1,427,371	65,460	4.4
2019..	1,541,772	64	1,479,777	61,995	4.0
2020..	1,502,848	61.2	1,299,640	203,208	13.5
2021..	1,504,761	60.5	1,395,939	108,822	7.2

Table NV-9. Employment and Average Wages by Industry

(Estimates are based on the 2012 North American Industry Classification System [NAICS].)

Industry	2013	2014	2015	2016	2017	2018	2019	2020
					Number of Jobs			
Wage and Salary Employment by Industry	1,207,788	1,251,274	1,292,456	1,329,421	1,371,359	1,419,789	1,458,453	1,317,100
Farm Wage and Salary Employment	2,245	2,109	2,049	2,164	2,603	2,121	2,126	2,247
Nonfarm Wage and Salary Employment	1,205,543	1,249,165	1,290,407	1,327,257	1,368,756	1,417,668	1,456,327	1,314,853
Private wage and salary employment	1,038,884	1,081,124	1,121,731	1,156,181	1,193,494	1,239,981	1,276,146	1,137,861
Forestry, fishing, and related activities	699	707	719	700	701	740	719	705
Mining	15,314	14,382	14,174	13,681	14,208	14,576	14,708	14,855
Utilities	3,967	3,884	3,962	4,068	4,094	4,089	4,088	4,091
Construction	58,397	64,752	71,996	77,697	85,110	91,358	98,298	96,620
Manufacturing	40,618	41,555	42,157	43,570	47,829	55,505	59,475	56,237
Durable goods manufacturing	25,653	25,800	26,121	26,827	30,175	36,804	40,177	37,754
Nondurable goods manufacturing	14,965	15,755	16,036	16,743	17,654	18,701	19,298	18,483
Wholesale trade	33,087	34,105	34,600	34,727	36,305	37,398	38,778	36,575
Retail trade	136,214	140,762	144,244	145,018	146,844	149,099	149,608	141,751
Transportation and warehousing	50,543	53,705	57,727	60,242	63,774	66,867	71,631	75,054
Information	12,834	13,727	13,934	14,801	14,805	15,674	15,924	13,433
Finance and insurance	33,047	33,420	34,592	35,972	37,272	38,253	39,781	40,769
Real estate and rental and leasing	23,195	23,939	25,681	26,386	26,800	28,094	28,669	25,744
Professional, scientific, and technical services	49,416	50,786	52,762	54,782	56,657	60,235	62,315	61,449
Management of companies and enterprises	20,230	20,909	22,638	24,016	25,319	26,868	27,459	24,528
Administrative and waste services	81,323	85,369	92,745	98,446	101,020	105,349	108,130	95,763
Educational services	9,984	10,509	10,642	11,015	11,429	12,312	13,433	12,791
Health care and social assistance	100,435	104,345	109,657	115,611	120,868	127,337	132,538	131,452
Arts, entertainment, and recreation	27,424	28,927	28,979	30,571	31,876	33,661	34,968	26,178
Accommodation and food services	297,984	308,993	313,804	316,293	319,533	320,676	322,762	233,157
Other services, except public administration	44,173	46,348	46,718	48,585	49,050	51,890	52,862	46,709
Government and government enterprises	166,659	168,041	168,676	171,076	175,262	177,687	180,181	176,992
					Dollars			
Average Wages and Salaries by Industry	45,473	46,109	47,113	48,331	49,316	51,222	52,473	56,368
Average Farm Wages and Salaries	39,763	40,856	35,590	39,012	32,620	38,983	27,843	35,090
Average Nonfarm Wages and Salaries	45,483	46,118	47,131	48,346	49,348	51,240	52,509	56,404
Average private wages and salaries	44,581	45,206	46,204	47,459	48,439	50,393	51,613	55,509
Forestry, fishing, and related activities	34,887	35,950	34,978	34,819	35,665	37,828	38,961	38,702
Mining	87,105	88,539	92,025	93,753	94,809	97,406	102,277	102,954
Utilities	107,058	103,117	106,040	106,302	108,021	111,328	113,703	116,986
Construction	51,424	52,620	53,287	55,375	58,144	61,211	64,582	68,217
Manufacturing	53,722	54,809	55,581	54,849	56,591	58,650	59,570	67,148
Durable goods manufacturing	60,387	61,833	62,200	60,834	63,007	64,471	64,732	74,477
Nondurable goods manufacturing	42,295	43,307	44,799	45,260	45,625	47,196	48,824	52,178
Wholesale trade	65,555	67,763	70,536	71,324	75,419	77,627	77,431	82,462
Retail trade	29,158	29,575	29,951	30,484	31,317	32,174	33,345	36,498
Transportation and warehousing	51,400	52,110	53,037	50,946	51,427	51,908	51,722	51,709
Information	58,537	59,454	61,440	62,446	65,834	70,383	73,286	88,614
Finance and insurance	65,330	67,013	71,723	72,278	74,901	78,542	82,905	94,190
Real estate and rental and leasing	42,074	43,620	46,815	47,385	48,945	50,618	52,672	55,488
Professional, scientific, and technical services	70,305	71,397	72,256	73,481	74,571	75,644	78,721	82,770
Management of companies and enterprises	121,210	120,702	114,037	130,468	123,383	138,029	126,520	140,219
Administrative and waste services	29,657	30,274	31,341	31,766	32,851	34,468	36,039	38,567
Educational services	37,472	37,533	38,453	39,003	39,420	42,419	40,778	49,091
Health care and social assistance	50,551	51,255	52,504	53,106	54,111	55,031	55,785	58,823
Arts, entertainment, and recreation	34,269	35,955	37,027	50,390	38,694	39,503	40,685	51,598
Accommodation and food services	35,497	35,906	36,402	36,775	37,563	38,587	39,311	36,146
Other services, except public administration	32,045	32,461	33,688	34,388	35,731	36,727	37,418	40,073
Government and government enterprises	51,104	51,989	53,295	54,345	55,537	57,150	58,854	62,158

Table NV-10. Employment Characteristics by Family Type

(Number, percent.)

Family type and labor force status	2018		2019		2020 [1]	
	Total	Families with own children under 18 years	Total	Families with own children under 18 years	Total	Families with own children under 18 years
All Families..	706,638	290,072	723,755	293,612	720,213	302,429
FAMILY TYPE AND LABOR FORCE STATUS						
Opposite-Sex Married-Couple Families............................	489,381	180,673	506,470	188,766	495,482	191,193
Both husband and wife in labor force................................	47.3	63.5	47.7	63.2	48.2	63.0
Husband in labor force, wife not in labor force	22.8	31.1	22.3	30.5	22.9	30.8
Wife in labor force, husband not in labor force	8.2	3.7	7.4	3.8	8.2	4.2
Both husband and wife not in labor force................................	20.7	1.4	21.3	2.0	20.7	2.1
Other Families	217,257	109,399	217,285	104,846	218,385	109,916
Female householder, no spouse present	63.8	66.5	67.5	70.1	67.2	70.1
In labor force..	47.1	56.2	49.1	59.5	49.4	59.7
Not in labor force	16.7	10.3	18.5	10.7	17.8	10.3
Male householder, no spouse present....................................	36.2	33.5	32.5	29.9	32.8	29.9
In labor force..	30.5	30.6	26.1	27.6	26.7	27.7
Not in labor force	5.8	2.8	6.3	2.3	6.1	2.2

[1] 2020 ACS 5-Year estimates. 1-Year estimates were not released for 2020 due to the impact of COVID-19 on data collection that year. Data is not comparable to previous years, which are based on 1-year estimates.

Table NV-11. School Enrollment and Educational Attainment, 2020[1]

(Number, percent.)

Item	State	U.S.
Enrollment		
Total population 3 years and over, enrolled in school	697,235	80,497,960
Enrolled in nursery school or preschool (percent)............................	5.0	6.1
Enrolled in kindergarten (percent)............................	5.0	5.0
Enrolled in elementary school, grades 1-8 (percent)............................	44.0	40.4
Enrolled in high school, grades 9-12 (percent)............................	22.3	21.0
Enrolled in college or graduate school (percent)............................	23.7	27.6
Attainment		
Total population 25 years and over	2,093,820	222,836,834
Less than ninth grade (percent)............................	5.3	4.9
9th to 12th grade, no diploma (percent)............................	7.7	6.6
High school graduate, including equivalency (percent)............................	27.9	26.7
Some college, no degree (percent)............................	25.1	20.3
Associate's degree (percent)............................	8.4	8.6
Bachelor's degree (percent)............................	16.6	20.2
Graduate or professional degree (percent)............................	8.8	12.7
High school graduate or higher (percent)............................	86.9	88.5
Bachelor's degree or higher (percent)............................	25.5	32.9

[1] 2020 ACS 5-Year estimates. 1-Year estimates were not released for 2020 due to the impact of COVID-19 on data collection that year.

Table NV-12. Public School Characteristics and Educational Indicators

(Number, percent; data derived from National Center of Education Statistics.)

Item	State	U.S.
Public Elementary and Secondary Schools		
Number of regular school districts, 2018-19	18	13,452
Number of operational schools, 2019-20............................	708	98,469
Percent charter schools	11.0	7.7
Total public school enrollment, Fall 2019............................	496,934	50,796,445
Percent charter school enrollment	11.3	6.8
Student-teacher ratio, Fall 2019............................	19.5	15.9
Expenditures per student (unadjusted dollars), 2018-19	9,126	13,187
Four-year adjusted cohort graduation rate (ACGR), 2018-2019[1]............................	84.1	85.8
Students eligible for free or reduced-price lunch (percent), 2019-20............................	64.6	52.1
English language learners (percent), Fall 2019	14.5	10.4
Students age 3 to 21 served under IDEA, part B (percent), 2020-21	12.9	14.5

Public Schools by Type, 2019-20	Number	Percent of state public schools
Total number of schools..	708	100.0
Special education	13	1.8
Vocational education..	0	-
Alternative education..	32	4.5

[1] Adjusted Cohort Graduation Rates (ACGR) differ from Averaged Freshmen Graduation Rates (AFGR).
- = Zero or rounds to zero.

Table NV-13. Reported Voting and Registration of the Voting-Age Population, November 2020

(Numbers in thousands, percent.)

Item	Total population	Total citizen population	Registered			Voted		
			Total registered	Percent registered (total population)	Percent registered (total citizen population)	Total voted	Percent voted (total population)	Percent voted (total citizen population)
U.S. Total	252,274	231,593	168,308	66.7	72.7	154,628	61.3	66.8
State Total..	2,402	2,198	1,455	60.6	66.2	1,351	56.3	61.5
Sex								
Male	1,192	1,088	698	58.6	64.1	649	54.5	59.7
Female	1,210	1,110	757	62.6	68.2	702	58.0	63.2
Race								
White alone......................................	1,691	1,561	1,072	63.4	68.6	1,013	59.9	64.9
White, non-Hispanic alone	1,211	1,187	868	71.7	73.1	827	68.3	69.7
Black alone.......................................	233	232	155	66.5	66.8	136	58.2	58.5
Asian alone	230	195	136	59.0	69.7	134	58.4	68.9
Hispanic (of any race)	654	515	268	41.0	52.0	239	36.6	46.4
White alone or in combination	1,815	1,652	1,113	61.4	67.4	1,050	57.9	63.6
Black alone or in combination.............	259	258	167	64.6	64.9	146	56.3	56.6
Asian alone or in combination.............	252	217	146	57.8	67.2	144	57.2	66.5
Age								
18 to 24 years...................................	284	262	110	38.7	41.9	96	33.9	36.7
25 to 34 years...................................	463	415	275	59.4	66.2	236	51.1	57.0
35 to 44 years...................................	352	310	193	54.8	62.2	176	50.0	56.7
45 to 64 years...................................	804	734	505	62.8	68.8	481	59.8	65.5
65 years and over	500	477	373	74.5	78.1	363	72.4	76.0

Table NV-14. Crime

(Number, rate per 100,000. Data are derived from the FBI Uniform Crime Reports.)

Item	State			U.S.		
	2019	2020	Percent change	2019	2020	Percent change
TOTAL POPULATION[1]	3,090,771	3,138,259	1.5	328,329,953	329,484,123	0.4
VIOLENT CRIME						
Number..	15,334	14,445	-5.8	1,250,393	1,313,105	5.0
Rate	496.1	460.3	-7.2	380.8	398.5	4.6
Murder and Nonnegligent Manslaughter						
Number..	144	180	25.0	16,669	21,570	29.4
Rate	4.7	5.7	23.1	5.1	6.5	28.9
Rape[2]						
Number..	2,155	1,851	-14.1	143,224	126,430	-11.7
Rate	69.7	59.0	-15.4	43.6	38.4	-12.0
Robbery						
Number..	3,289	2,785	-15.3	268,483	243,600	-9.3
Rate	106.4	88.7	-16.6	81.8	73.9	-9.6
Aggravated Assault						
Number..	9,746	9,629	-1.2	822,017	921,505	12.1
Rate	315.3	306.8	-2.7	250.4	279.7	11.7
PROPERTY CRIME						
Number..	72,028	60,462	-16.1	6,995,235	6,452,038	-7.8
Rate	2,330.4	1,926.6	-17.3	2,130.6	1,958.2	-8.1
Burglary						
Number..	15,630	11,574	-26.0	1,118,096	1,035,314	-7.4
Rate	505.7	368.8	-27.1	340.5	314.2	-7.7
Larceny-Theft						
Number..	45,127	38,332	-15.1	5,152,267	4,606,324	-10.6
Rate	1,460.1	1,221.4	-16.3	1,569.2	1,398.0	-10.9
Motor Vehicle Theft						
Number..	11,271	10,556	-6.3	724,872	810,400	11.8
Rate	364.7	336.4	-7.8	220.8	246.0	11.4

NOTE: Although arson data are included in the trend and clearance tables, sufficient data are not available to estimate totals for this offense. Therefore, no arson data are published in this table.
- = Zero or rounds to zero.
[1] Population figures are U.S. Census Bureau provisional estimates as of July 1, 2020.
[2] The figures shown in the rape (revised definition) column were estimated using the revised Uniform Crime Reporting (UCR) definition of rape.

Table NV-15. State Government Finances, 2020

(Dollar amounts in thousands, percent distribution.)

Item	Dollars	Percent distribution
Total Revenue	22,025,771	100.0
General revenue	16,801,419	76.3
Intergovernmental revenue	5,757,789	26.1
Taxes	9,452,840	42.9
General sales	5479823	24.9
Selective sales	2,115,103	9.6
License taxes	637,899	2.9
Individual income tax	0	-
Corporate income tax	0	-
Other taxes	1,220,015	5.5
Current charges	923,856	4.2
Miscellaneous general revenue	666,934	3.0
Utility revenue	52,404	0.2
Liquor stores revenue	0	-
Insurance trust revenue[1]	5,171,948	23.5
Total Expenditure	20,144,167	100.0
Intergovernmental expenditure	5,028,198	25.0
Direct expenditure	15,115,969	75.0
Current operation	8,639,784	42.9
Capital outlay	980,747	4.9
Insurance benefits and repayments	4,664,638	23.2
Assistance and subsidies	670,959	3.3
Interest on debt	159,841	0.8
Exhibit: Salaries and wages	2,013,283	10.0
Total Expenditure	20,144,167	100.0
General expenditure	15,433,292	76.6
Intergovernmental expenditure	5,028,198	25.0
Direct expenditure	10,405,094	51.7
General expenditure, by function:		
Education	5,872,018	29.1
Public welfare	4,380,579	21.7
Hospitals	305,128	1.5
Health	315,717	1.6
Highways	974,884	4.8
Police protection	100,761	0.5
Correction	355,541	1.8
Natural resources	158,276	0.8
Parks and recreation	39,142	0.2
Governmental administration	472,265	2.3
Interest on general debt	159,841	0.8
Other and unallocable	2,269,166	11.3
Utility expenditure	49,056	0.2
Liquor stores expenditure	0	-
Insurance trust expenditure	4,664,638	23.2
Debt at End of Fiscal Year	3,652,724	X
Cash and Security Holdings	54,297,717	X

X = Not applicable.
- = Zero or rounds to zero.
[1] Within insurance trust revenue, net earnings of state retirement systems is a calculated statistic (the item code in the data file is X08), and thus can be positive or negative. Net earnings is the sum of earnings on investments plus gains on investments minus losses on investments. The change made in 2002 for asset valuation from book to market value in accordance with Statement 34 of the Governmental Accounting Standards Board is reflected in the calculated statistics.

Table NV-16. State Government Tax Collections, 2021

(Dollars in thousands, percent.)

Item	Dollars	Percent distribution
Total Taxes	10,416,344	100.0
Property taxes	386,450	3.7
Sales and gross receipts	8,392,630	80.6
General sales and gross receipts	6,179,597	59.3
Selective sales and gross receipts	2,213,033	21.2
Alcoholic beverages	44,690	0.4
Amusements	764,287	7.3
Insurance premiums	489,269	4.7
Motor fuels	351,627	3.4
Pari-mutuels	0	-
Public utilities	37,518	0.4
Tobacco products	185,039	1.8
Other selective sales	340,603	3.3
Licenses	623,260	6.0
Alcoholic beverages	X	-
Amusements	36,886	0.4
Corporations in general	87,976	0.8
Hunting and fishing	14,066	0.1
Motor vehicle	209,528	2.0
Motor vehicle operators	30,163	0.3
Public utilities	X	-
Occupation and business, NEC	236,364	2.3
Other licenses	8,277	0.1
Income taxes	X	-
Individual income	X	-
Corporation net income	X	-
Other taxes	1,014,004	9.7
Death and gift	X	-
Documentary and stock transfer	144,312	1.4
Severance	278,504	2.7
Taxes, NEC	591,188	5.7

X = Not applicable.
- = Zero or rounds to zero.

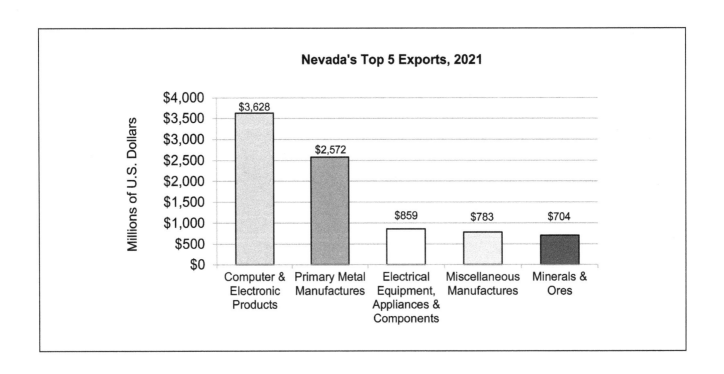

Nevada's Top 5 Exports, 2021

Export	Millions of U.S. Dollars
Computer & Electronic Products	$3,628
Primary Metal Manufactures	$2,572
Electrical Equipment, Appliances & Components	$859
Miscellaneous Manufactures	$783
Minerals & Ores	$704

Facts and Figures

Location: Northeastern United States; bordered on the N by Canada (Quebec), on the E by Maine, on the SE by the Atlantic Ocean, on the S by Massachusetts, and on the W by Vermont

Area: 9,350 sq. mi. (24,216 sq. km.); rank—46th

Population: 1,388,992 (2021 est.); rank—41st

Principal Cities: capital—Concord; largest—Manchester

Statehood: June 21, 1788; 9th state

U.S. Congress: 2 senators, 2 representatives

State Motto: Live Free or Die

State Song: "Old New Hampshire"

State Nickname: The Granite State

Abbreviations: NH; N.H.

State Symbols: flower—purple lilac; tree—white birch; bird—purple finch

At a Glance

- With an increase in population of 5.5 percent, New Hampshire ranked 26th among the states in growth from 2010 to 2021.

- New Hampshire's violent crime rate in 2020 was 146.4 per 100,000 population, the 2nd lowest in the country, compared to a rate of 398.5 for the entire nation.

- The state's property crime rate, 1,098.9 per 100,000 population, was the 2nd lowest in the country in 2020.

- New Hampshire had the 4th highest homeownership rate in 2021, with 74.0 percent of homes being owner-occupied.

- New Hampshire had the 3rd lowest birth rate in the country in 2020, with 8.6 births per 1,000 population.

Table NH-1. Population by Age, Sex, Race, and Hispanic Origin

(Number, percent, except where noted.)

Sex, age, race, and Hispanic origin	2000	2010	2021	Percent change, 2010–2021
Total Population...	1,235,786	1,316,470	1,388,992	5.5
Percent of total U.S. population	0.4	0.4	0.4	X
Sex				
Male...	607,687	649,394	693,132	6.7
Female...	628,099	667,076	695,860	4.3
Age				
Under 5 years..	75,685	69,806	62,292	-10.8
5 to 19 years..	268,480	255,996	230,214	-10.1
20 to 64 years...	743,651	812,400	828,965	2.0
65 years and over	147,970	178,268	267,521	50.1
Median age (years)...	37.1	41.1	43.0	4.6
Race and Hispanic Origin				
One race				
White	1,186,851	1,248,321	1,288,649	3.2
Black..	9,035	16,365	26,779	63.6
American Indian and Alaska Native	2,964	3,530	4,341	23.0
Asian..	15,931	28,933	42,912	48.3
Native Hawaiian or Other Pacific Islander	371	532	747	40.4
Two or more races	13,214	18,789	25,564	36.1
Hispanic (of any race)	20,489	38,688	60,873	57.3

NOTE: Population figures for 2021 are July 1 estimates. The 2000 and 2010 estimates are taken from the respective censuses.
- = Zero or rounds to zero.
X = Not applicable.

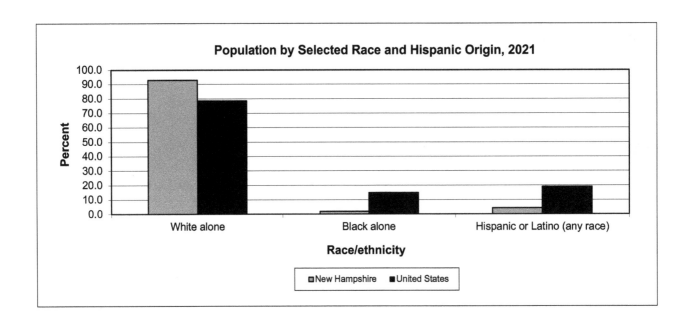

Population by Selected Race and Hispanic Origin, 2021

Legend: ☐ New Hampshire ■ United States

X-axis: Race/ethnicity — White alone, Black alone, Hispanic or Latino (any race)
Y-axis: Percent

Table NH-2. Marital Status

(Number, percent distribution.)

Sex, age, race, and Hispanic origin	2000	2010	2020 [1]
Males, 15 Years and Over	476,409	529,439	564,580
Never married	27.7	30.5	33.0
Now married, except separated...	59.1	54.7	52.7
Separated..	1.2	1.3	1.1
Widowed..	2.4	2.6	2.6
Divorced...	9.6	10.9	10.7
Females, 15 Years and Over	502,232	555,698	581,229
Never married	22.3	25.4	26.3
Now married, except separated...	55.7	51.4	50.9
Separated..	1.5	1.3	1.2
Widowed..	9.2	8.6	8.4
Divorced...	11.3	13.4	13.3

[1] 2020 ACS 5-Year estimates. 1-Year estimates were not released for 2020 due to the impact of COVID-19 on data collection that year.

Table NH-3. Households and Housing Characteristics

(Number, percent, dollars.)

Item	2000	2010	2020 [1]	Average annual percent change, 2010–2020
Total Households..	474,606	515,431	539,116	0.7
Family households	323,651	344,057	351,445	0.3
Married-couple family	262,438	274,195	281,607	0.4
Other family	61,213	69,862	69,838	-
Male householder, no wife present........................	18,261	22,205	23,684	1.0
Female householder, no husband present................	42,952	47,657	46,154	-0.5
Nonfamily households	150,955	171,374	187,671	1.4
Householder living alone	116,014	130,327	143,739	1.5
Householder not living alone	34,941	41,047	43,932	1.0
Housing Characteristics				
Total housing units..	547,024	614,996	638,611	0.5
Occupied housing units	474,606	515,431	539,116	0.7
Owner occupied	330,700	369,448	383,839	0.6
Renter occupied	143,906	145,983	155,277	0.9
Average household size.......................................	2.53	2.48	2.44	-0.2
Financial Characteristics				
Median gross rent of renter-occupied housing	646	951	1,145	2.9
Median monthly owner costs for housing units with a mortgage	1,226	1,853	1,967	0.9
Median value of owner-occupied housing units	133,300	243,000	272,300	1.7

- = Zero or rounds to zero.
[1] 2020 ACS 5-Year estimates. 1-Year estimates were not released for 2020 due to the impact of COVID-19 on data collection that year.

Table NH-4. Migration, Origin, and Language

(Number, percent.)

Characteristic	State 2016-2020 [1]	U.S. 2016-2020 [1]
Residence 1 Year Ago		
Population 1 year and over	1,343,840	322,943,283
Same house	86.4	86.2
Different house in the U.S.	13.1	13.2
Same county	6.8	7.7
Different county	6.4	5.5
Same state	2.5	3.2
Different state	3.9	2.3
Abroad	0.5	0.6
Place of Birth		
Native born	1,272,622	282,443,680
Male	49.6	49.4
Female	50.4	50.6
Foreign born	82,622	44,125,628
Male	48.7	48.6
Female	51.3	51.4
Foreign born; naturalized U.S. citizen..	47,022	22,456,684
Male	45.8	46.1
Female	54.2	53.9
Foreign born; not a U.S. citizen..	35,600	21,668,944
Male	52.6	51.1
Female	47.4	48.9
Entered 2010 or later	26.7	22.8
Entered 2000 to 2009	23.6	25.1
Entered before 2000...	49.7	52.1
World Region of Birth, Foreign		
Foreign-born population, excluding population born at sea	82,622	44,125,628
Europe	24.0	10.8
Asia...	36.8	31.3
Africa	7.6	5.4
Oceania	0.6	0.6
Latin America...	20.7	50.0
North America..	10.3	1.9
Language Spoken at Home and Ability to Speak English		
Population 5 years and over...	1,291,567	306,919,116
English only	91.9	78.5
Language other than English...	8.1	21.5
Speaks English less than "very well"...	2.5	8.2

[1] 2020 ACS 5-Year estimates. 1-Year estimates were not released for 2020 due to the impact of COVID-19 on data collection that year.
NA = Not available.
X = Not applicable.
- = Zero or rounds to zero.

Table NH-5. Median Income and Poverty Status, 2020[1]

(Number, percent, except as noted.)

Characteristic	State Number	State Percent	U.S. Number	U.S. Percent
Median Income				
Households (dollars)..	77,923	X	64,994	X
Families (dollars)	97,001	X	80,069	X
Below Poverty Level (All People)	97,418	7.4	40,910,326	12.8
Sex				
Male	42,476	6.5	18,171,512	11.6
Female	54,942	8.3	22,738,814	14.0
Age				
Under 18 years...	22,509	8.9	12,598,699	17.5
Related children under 18 years..	21,142	8.4	12,306,532	17.2
18 to 64 years...	60,487	7.3	23,554,920	12.1
65 years and over	14,422	6.1	4,756,707	9.3

X = Not applicable.
[1] 2020 ACS 5-Year estimates. 1-Year estimates were not released for 2020 due to the impact of COVID-19 on data collection that year.

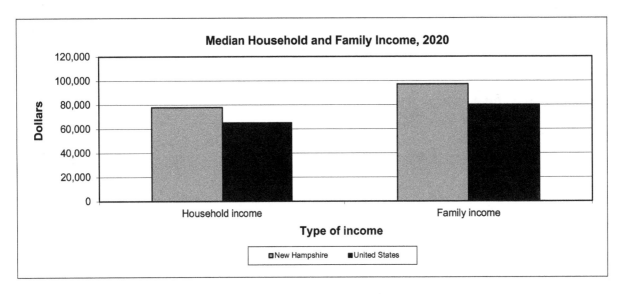

Table NH-6. Health Insurance Coverage Status for the Civilian Noninstitutionalized Population and Children Under 19 Years of Age

(Number, percent.)

Item	2011	2012	2013	2014	2015	2016	2017	2018	2019	2020[2]
Civilian Noninstitutionalized Population	1,303,868	1,306,026	1,308,658	1,311,921	1,314,249	1,316,467	1,325,016	1,339,549	1,343,337	1,338,372
Covered by Private or Public Insurance										
Number..	1,166,946	1,167,184	1,168,406	1,191,465	1,230,861	1,238,790	1,247,957	1,262,538	1,259,313	1,258,301
Percent...	89.5	89.4	89.3	90.8	93.7	94.1	94.2	94.3	93.7	94.0
Uninsured										
Number..	136,922	138,842	140,252	120,456	83,388	77,677	77,059	77,011	84,024	80,071
Percent...	10.5	10.6	10.7	9.2	6.3	5.9	5.8	5.7	6.3	6.0
Percent in the U.S. not covered...	15.1	14.8	14.5	11.7	9.4	8.6	8.7	8.9	9.2	8.7
Children Under 19 Years of Age[1]	279,210	274,563	270,642	266,833	262,932	259,410	275,977	279,907	276,888	276,273
Covered by Private or Public Insurance										
Number..	269,018	263,665	260,381	255,132	255,940	252,563	269,639	272,651	266,712	268,397
Percent...	96.3	96.0	96.2	95.6	97.3	97.4	97.7	97.4	96.3	97.1
Uninsured										
Number..	10,192	10,898	10,261	11,701	6,992	6,847	6,338	7,256	10,176	7,876
Percent...	3.7	4.0	3.8	4.4	2.7	2.6	2.3	2.6	3.7	2.9
Percent in the U.S. not covered...	7.5	7.2	7.1	6.0	4.8	4.5	5.0	5.2	5.7	5.2

[1] Data for years prior to 2017 are for individuals under 18 years of age.
[2] 2020 ACS 5-Year estimates. 1-Year estimates were not released for 2020 due to the impact of COVID-19 on data collection that year. Data is not comparable to previous years, which are based on 1-year estimates.

Table NH-7. Employment Status by Demographic Group, 2021

(Numbers in thousands, percent.)

Characteristic	Civilian noninstitutional population	Civilian labor force		Employed		Unemployed	
		Number	Percent of population	Number	Percent of population	Number	Percent of population
Total..	1,137	734	64.6	707	62.2	27	3.7
Sex							
Male..	559	388	69.4	371	66.4	17	4.3
Female.....................................	577	346	59.9	335	58.1	11	3.1
Race, Sex, and Hispanic Origin							
White.......................................	1,063	681	64.1	656	61.7	25	3.6
Male..	523	359	68.5	344	65.7	15	4.1
Female.....................................	540	322	59.7	312	57.9	10	3.1
Black or African American................	NA	NA	NA	NA	NA	NA	NA
Male..	NA	NA	NA	NA	NA	NA	NA
Female.....................................	NA	NA	NA	NA	NA	NA	NA
Hispanic or Latino ethnicity[1]..........	NA	NA	NA	NA	NA	NA	NA
Male..	NA	NA	NA	NA	NA	NA	NA
Female.....................................	NA	NA	NA	NA	NA	NA	NA
Age							
16 to 19 years............................	70	35	50.5	33	47.5	2	6.0
20 to 24 years............................	71	57	79.9	52	73.6	5	8.0
25 to 34 years............................	181	154	85.5	148	82.0	6	4.0
35 to 44 years............................	166	145	87.4	141	84.7	4	3.0
45 to 54 years............................	149	128	86.0	126	84.4	3	2.0
55 to 64 years............................	210	151	71.9	145	69.3	6	3.8
65 years and over........................	291	64	22.0	62	21.3	2	3.1

NOTE: Data in Table 7 are from the Current Population Survey (CPS) and do not match the estimates in Table 8. See notes and definitions for further information.
[1] May be of any race.
NA = Not available.

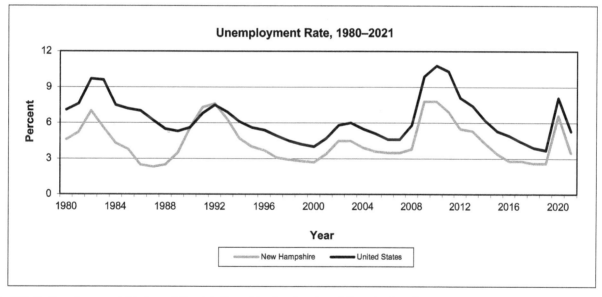

Unemployment Rate, 1980–2021

Table NH-8. Employment Status of the Civilian Noninstitutional Population Age 16 Years and Over

(Number, percent.)

Year	Civilian labor force	Civilian participation rate	Employed	Unemployed	Unemployment rate
2010............................	739,340	70.0	694,132	45,208	6.1
2011............................	736,785	69.5	696,591	40,194	5.5
2012............................	740,796	69.3	700,448	40,348	5.4
2013............................	743,036	69.1	704,023	39,013	5.3
2014............................	743,756	68.6	711,740	32,016	4.3
2015............................	746,317	68.5	720,832	25,485	3.4
2016............................	752,478	68.5	731,002	21,476	2.9
2017............................	758,133	68.1	736,918	21,215	2.8
2018............................	767,629	68.5	747,415	20,214	2.6
2019............................	776,471	68.7	756,267	20,204	2.6
2020............................	759,770	66.7	708,566	51,204	6.7
2021............................	755,422	65.6	728,940	26,482	3.5

Table NH-9. Employment and Average Wages by Industry

(Estimates are based on the 2012 North American Industry Classification System [NAICS].)

Industry	2013	2014	2015	2016	2017	2018	2019	2020
	Number of Jobs							
Wage and Salary Employment by Industry..........................	647,086	655,565	666,446	676,434	682,227	688,974	695,650	653,928
Farm Wage and Salary Employment...............................	1,658	1,664	1,658	1,548	1,544	1,311	1,320	1,261
Nonfarm Wage and Salary Employment..........................	645,428	653,901	664,788	674,886	680,683	687,663	694,330	652,667
Private wage and salary employment..............................	550,738	558,847	569,930	580,407	586,304	593,359	599,865	561,837
Forestry, fishing, and related activities.....................	786	825	820	803	769	783	805	775
Mining...	531	532	526	556	548	565	549	579
Utilities..	2,481	2,320	2,182	2,129	2,090	2,032	2,002	2,002
Construction	23,142	23,787	24,864	26,118	27,100	27,554	28,515	28,618
Manufacturing..	66,076	66,598	67,273	68,179	69,179	70,685	71,574	67,415
Durable goods manufacturing..........................	49,886	49,950	50,169	50,801	51,455	52,679	53,488	50,586
Nondurable goods manufacturing.....................	16,190	16,648	17,104	17,378	17,724	18,006	18,086	16,829
Wholesale trade	26,869	27,214	27,681	27,896	28,127	28,168	28,288	27,524
Retail trade..	95,469	95,065	95,615	96,650	96,216	95,321	94,823	89,603
Transportation and warehousing..........................	12,561	13,008	13,483	14,322	14,617	14,921	15,374	15,347
Information	11,927	12,044	12,285	12,532	12,579	12,365	12,349	11,753
Finance and insurance	29,174	29,418	30,159	30,841	28,467	27,983	28,207	28,406
Real estate and rental and leasing.......................	6,921	6,932	6,809	7,021	7,164	7,317	7,249	6,784
Professional, scientific, and technical services	31,989	32,687	33,719	34,252	37,797	38,230	39,123	39,420
Management of companies and enterprises.............	8,187	8,191	8,646	8,906	8,956	9,163	9,270	9,005
Administrative and waste services	30,690	33,191	34,843	35,172	35,585	36,097	35,736	33,892
Educational services	22,870	23,362	24,540	25,391	25,666	27,007	27,164	25,854
Health care and social assistance........................	86,746	87,429	89,129	91,116	92,308	93,656	95,319	90,753
Arts, entertainment, and recreation......................	11,382	11,389	11,450	11,797	12,012	12,524	13,077	9,558
Accommodation and food services	55,213	56,218	57,446	58,473	59,259	60,024	60,691	48,182
Other services, except public administration...........	27,724	28,637	28,460	28,253	27,865	28,964	29,750	26,367
Government and government enterprises....................	94,690	95,054	94,858	94,479	94,379	94,304	94,465	90,830
	Dollars							
Average Wages and Salaries by Industry	48,253	50,382	51,727	52,767	54,319	55,941	57,787	63,653
Average Farm Wages and Salaries	27,287	28,806	23,616	29,029	26,413	25,207	19,877	20,210
Average Nonfarm Wages and Salaries	48,307	50,437	51,797	52,821	54,383	55,999	57,859	63,737
Average private wages and salaries.............................	49,224	51,549	52,890	53,957	55,589	57,217	59,203	65,421
Forestry, fishing, and related activities.................	40,710	45,013	47,511	44,724	47,568	45,442	46,884	48,665
Mining...	53,339	54,147	57,757	58,453	63,111	63,193	66,811	72,570
Utilities..	94,651	102,353	103,231	103,327	111,422	116,766	110,781	123,795
Construction	52,968	54,208	57,292	58,909	61,595	62,715	64,838	68,922
Manufacturing..	64,629	66,253	66,915	68,346	70,454	71,795	73,412	77,894
Durable goods manufacturing..........................	67,986	69,827	70,096	71,524	73,725	75,441	77,453	82,123
Nondurable goods manufacturing.....................	54,286	55,530	57,585	59,056	60,958	61,129	61,462	65,184
Wholesale trade	82,161	84,863	90,571	89,896	91,618	93,917	97,218	105,764
Retail trade...	28,483	29,670	30,752	31,013	31,676	32,874	34,029	37,885
Transportation and warehousing..........................	40,002	40,888	43,020	43,336	44,760	46,847	48,640	50,168
Information	78,946	91,493	82,669	85,312	88,097	93,685	97,288	107,338
Finance and insurance	85,901	94,523	94,655	100,186	100,414	104,989	110,077	119,710
Real estate and rental and leasing.......................	46,136	47,654	50,873	52,139	53,369	55,082	59,383	64,375
Professional, scientific, and technical services	80,187	84,859	86,971	88,698	93,886	97,735	100,730	108,935
Management of companies and enterprises.............	89,768	106,453	106,548	103,648	109,439	102,205	106,391	111,176
Administrative and waste services	42,388	43,547	45,242	46,226	47,577	49,753	51,821	57,880
Educational services	42,825	44,025	45,157	45,049	44,804	44,778	46,116	51,358
Health care and social assistance........................	49,101	50,368	51,841	52,995	54,534	56,248	58,251	63,781
Arts, entertainment, and recreation......................	23,153	24,347	24,508	24,324	25,126	26,261	26,787	30,559
Accommodation and food services	20,134	20,897	21,783	22,693	23,517	24,909	25,814	26,107
Other services, except public administration...........	32,724	33,261	34,714	35,607	36,457	37,654	38,718	41,998
Government and government enterprises....................	42,971	43,902	45,227	45,843	46,890	48,336	49,326	53,317

Table NH-10. Employment Characteristics by Family Type

(Number, percent.)

Family type and labor force status	2018		2019		2020 [1]	
	Total	Families with own children under 18 years	Total	Families with own children under 18 years	Total	Families with own children under 18 years
All Families..	341,752	124,135	346,413	126,375	351,445	133,128
FAMILY TYPE AND LABOR FORCE STATUS						
Opposite-Sex Married-Couple Families............................	274,309	88,224	273,682	90,194	278,389	94,874
Both husband and wife in labor force......................................	55.5	74.6	54.9	75.7	56.3	75.2
Husband in labor force, wife not in labor force..........................	18.5	20.3	17.1	18.2	17.8	20.1
Wife in labor force, husband not in labor force..........................	7.2	2.7	7.9	3.9	8.1	3.6
Both husband and wife not in labor force..................................	17.5	1.1	18.7	1.1	17.8	1.1
Other Families	67,443	35,911	72,731	36.181	69,838	37,469
Female householder, no spouse present...................................	67.1	68.5	65.6	67.5	66.1	67.2
In labor force...	46.9	56.0	48.6	56.9	48.1	55.7
Not in labor force...	20.2	12.5	17.0	10.6	18.0	11.5
Male householder, no spouse present......................................	32.9	31.5	34.4	32.5	33.9	32.8
In labor force...	26.3	29.3	27.6	30.5	27.7	30.1
Not in labor force...	6.6	2.1	6.8	2.0	6.2	2.7

[1] 2020 ACS 5-Year estimates. 1-Year estimates were not released for 2020 due to the impact of COVID-19 on data collection that year. Data is not comparable to previous years, which are based on 1-year estimates.

Table NH-11. School Enrollment and Educational Attainment, 2020[1]

(Number, percent.)

Item	State	U.S.
Enrollment		
Total population 3 years and over, enrolled in school	301,741	80,497,960
Enrolled in nursery school or preschool (percent)	6.0	6.1
Enrolled in kindergarten (percent)...	4.5	5.0
Enrolled in elementary school, grades 1-8 (percent)...	38.7	40.4
Enrolled in high school, grades 9-12 (percent)	21.1	21.0
Enrolled in college or graduate school (percent)...	29.6	27.6
Attainment		
Total population 25 years and over	971,162	222,836,834
Less than ninth grade (percent)..	2.2	4.9
9th to 12th grade, no diploma (percent)	4.5	6.6
High school graduate, including equivalency (percent)...	27.3	26.7
Some college, no degree (percent)...	18.0	20.3
Associate's degree (percent)...	10.4	8.6
Bachelor's degree (percent)..	23.0	20.2
Graduate or professional degree (percent)..	14.5	12.7
High school graduate or higher (percent)	93.3	88.5
Bachelor's degree or higher (percent)...	37.6	32.9

[1] 2020 ACS 5-Year estimates. 1-Year estimates were not released for 2020 due to the impact of COVID-19 on data collection that year.

Table NH-12. Public School Characteristics and Educational Indicators

(Number, percent; data derived from National Center of Education Statistics.)

Item	State	U.S.
Public Elementary and Secondary Schools		
Number of regular school districts, 2018-19	180	13,452
Number of operational schools, 2019-20..	496	98,469
Percent charter schools	8.1	7.7
Total public school enrollment, Fall 2019...	177,351	50,796,445
Percent charter school enrollment	2.4	6.8
Student-teacher ratio, Fall 2019...	12.1	15.9
Expenditures per student (unadjusted dollars), 2018-19	17,457	13,187
Four-year adjusted cohort graduation rate (ACGR), 2018-2019[1]..	88.4	85.8
Students eligible for free or reduced-price lunch (percent), 2019-20...................................	24.7	52.1
English language learners (percent), Fall 2019	2.8	10.4
Students age 3 to 21 served under IDEA, part B (percent), 2020-21	17.3	14.5
Public Schools by Type, 2019-20...	Number	Percent of state public schools
Total number of schools...	496	100.0
Special education	0	-
Vocational education...	0	-
Alternative education..	0	-

[1] Adjusted Cohort Graduation Rates (ACGR) differ from Averaged Freshmen Graduation Rates (AFGR).
- = Zero or rounds to zero.

Table NH-13. Reported Voting and Registration of the Voting-Age Population, November 2020

(Numbers in thousands, percent.)

Item	Total population	Total citizen population	Registered			Voted		
			Total registered	Percent registered (total population)	Percent registered (total citizen population)	Total voted	Percent voted (total population)	Percent voted (total citizen population)
U.S. Total	252,274	231,593	168,308	66.7	72.7	154,628	61.3	66.8
State Total..	1,101	1,077	843	76.6	78.3	797	72.4	74.0
Sex								
Male	542	531	401	74.1	75.5	375	69.2	70.5
Female	559	546	442	78.9	80.9	423	75.5	77.4
Race								
White alone..	1,030	1,015	813	78.9	80.0	771	74.8	75.9
White, non-Hispanic alone	1,000	993	799	79.8	80.5	758	75.8	76.4
Black alone..	20	20	4	B	B	4	B	B
Asian alone	27	17	9	B	B	8	B	B
Hispanic (of any race)	38	31	19	B	B	14	B	B
White alone or in combination	1,045	1,030	823	78.8	79.9	782	74.8	75.9
Black alone or in combination	32	32	14	B	B	14	B	B
Asian alone or in combination............	27	17	9	B	B	8	B	B
Age								
18 to 24 years.....................................	110	108	74	67.7	69.1	67	61.1	62.3
25 to 34 years.....................................	176	166	123	69.6	73.8	111	63.0	66.7
35 to 44 years.....................................	167	163	126	75.8	77.3	118	70.9	72.4
45 to 64 years.....................................	383	375	289	75.4	77.0	278	72.7	74.2
65 years and over	265	264	231	87.1	87.3	223	84.0	84.2

B = Base is less than 75,000 and therefore too small to show the derived measure.

Table NH-14. Crime

(Number, rate per 100,000. Data are derived from the FBI Uniform Crime Reports.)

Item	State			U.S.		
	2019	2020	Percent change	2019	2020	Percent change
TOTAL POPULATION[1]	1,360,783	1,366,275	0.4	328,329,953	329,484,123	0.4
VIOLENT CRIME						
Number..	2,152	2,000	-7.1	1,250,393	1,313,105	5.0
Rate...	158.1	146.4	-7.4	380.8	398.5	4.6
Murder and Nonnegligent Manslaughter						
Number..	33	12	-63.6	16,669	21,570	29.4
Rate...	2.4	0.9	-63.8	5.1	6.5	28.9
Rape[2]						
Number..	606	542	-10.6	143,224	126,430	-11.7
Rate...	44.5	39.7	-10.9	43.6	38.4	-12.0
Robbery						
Number..	327	280	-14.4	268,483	243,600	-9.3
Rate...	24.0	20.5	-14.7	81.8	73.9	-9.6
Aggravated Assault						
Number..	1,186	1,166	-1.7	822,017	921,505	12.1
Rate...	87.2	85.3	-2.1	250.4	279.7	11.7
PROPERTY CRIME						
Number..	16,552	15,014	-9.3	6,995,235	6,452,038	-7.8
Rate...	1,216.4	1,098.9	-9.7	2,130.6	1,958.2	-8.1
Burglary						
Number..	1,783	1,412	-20.8	1,118,096	1,035,314	-7.4
Rate...	131.0	103.3	-21.1	340.5	314.2	-7.7
Larceny-Theft						
Number..	13,826	12,558	-9.2	5,152,267	4,606,324	-10.6
Rate...	1,016.0	919.1	-9.5	1,569.2	1,398.0	-10.9
Motor Vehicle Theft						
Number..	943	1,044	10.7	724,872	810,400	11.8
Rate...	69.3	76.4	10.3	220.8	246.0	11.4

NOTE: Although arson data are included in the trend and clearance tables, sufficient data are not available to estimate totals for this offense. Therefore, no arson data are published in this table.
- = Zero or rounds to zero.
[1] Population figures are U.S. Census Bureau provisional estimates as of July 1, 2020.
[2] The figures shown in the rape (revised definition) column were estimated using the revised Uniform Crime Reporting (UCR) definition of rape.

Table NH-15. State Government Finances, 2020

(Dollar amounts in thousands, percent distribution.)

Item	Dollars	Percent distribution
Total Revenue	10,405,292	100.0
General revenue	8,790,162	84.5
Intergovernmental revenue	4,168,181	40.1
Taxes	2,858,212	27.5
General sales	0	-
Selective sales	973,219	9.4
License taxes	420,669	4.0
Individual income tax	122631	1.2
Corporate income tax	780,672	7.5
Other taxes	561,021	5.4
Current charges	863,276	8.3
Miscellaneous general revenue	900,493	8.7
Utility revenue	0	-
Liquor stores revenue	740244	7.1
Insurance trust revenue[1]	874,886	8.4
Total Expenditure	9,974,933	100.0
Intergovernmental expenditure	1,864,712	18.7
Direct expenditure	8,110,221	81.3
Current operation	5,953,327	59.7
Capital outlay	476,827	4.8
Insurance benefits and repayments	1,093,582	11.0
Assistance and subsidies	273,237	2.7
Interest on debt	313,248	3.1
Exhibit: Salaries and wages	1,184,964	11.9
Total Expenditure	9,974,933	100.0
General expenditure	8,278,697	83.0
Intergovernmental expenditure	1,864,712	18.7
Direct expenditure	6,413,985	64.3
General expenditure, by function:		
Education	2,391,447	24.0
Public welfare	2,751,393	27.6
Hospitals	67,498	0.7
Health	133,474	1.3
Highways	554,747	5.6
Police protection	74,204	0.7
Correction	136,305	1.4
Natural resources	47,284	0.5
Parks and recreation	27,853	0.3
Governmental administration	749,734	7.5
Interest on general debt	313,248	3.1
Other and unallocable	1,024,280	10.3
Utility expenditure	6,786	0.1
Liquor stores expenditure	596,059	6.0
Insurance trust expenditure	1,093,582	11.0
Debt at End of Fiscal Year	7,543,417	X
Cash and Security Holdings	16,749,363	X

X = Not applicable.
- = Zero or rounds to zero.
[1] Within insurance trust revenue, net earnings of state retirement systems is a calculated statistic (the item code in the data file is X08), and thus can be positive or negative. Net earnings is the sum of earnings on investments plus gains on investments minus losses on investments. The change made in 2002 for asset valuation from book to market value in accordance with Statement 34 of the Governmental Accounting Standards Board is reflected in the calculated statistics.

Table NH-16. State Government Tax Collections, 2021

(Dollars in thousands, percent.)

Item	Dollars	Percent distribution
Total Taxes	3,213,039	100.0
Property taxes	401,407	12.5
Sales and gross receipts	977,640	30.4
General sales and gross receipts	X	-
Selective sales and gross receipts	977,640	30.4
Alcoholic beverages	13,701	0.4
Amusements	17,936	0.6
Insurance premiums	138,900	4.3
Motor fuels	117,200	3.6
Pari-mutuels	566	-
Public utilities	38,200	1.2
Tobacco products	251,000	7.8
Other selective sales	400,137	12.5
Licenses	472,669	14.7
Alcoholic beverages	19,030	0.6
Amusements	325	-
Corporations in general	80,162	2.5
Hunting and fishing	12,900	0.4
Motor vehicle	94,400	2.9
Motor vehicle operators	10,200	0.3
Public utilities	26,485	0.8
Occupation and business, NEC	226,668	7.1
Other licenses	2,499	0.1
Income taxes	1,158,623	36.1
Individual income	148,648	4.6
Corporation net income	1,009,975	31.4
Other taxes	202,700	6.3
Death and gift	X	-
Documentary and stock transfer	202,700	6.3
Severance	X	-
Taxes, NEC	0	-

X = Not applicable.
- = Zero or rounds to zero.

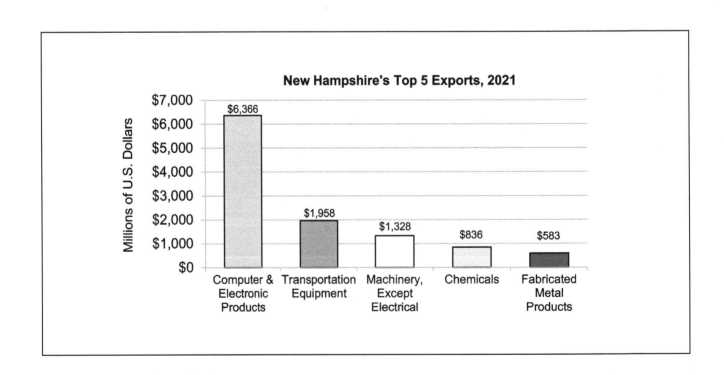

NEW JERSEY

Facts and Figures

Location: Middle Atlantic region of the United States; bordered on the N and NE by New York, on the E by the Atlantic Ocean, on the S by Delaware Bay, and on the W by Delaware and Pennsylvania

Area: 8,721 sq. mi. (22,588 sq. km.); rank—47th

Population: 9,267,130 (2021 est.); rank—11th

Principal Cities: capital—Trenton; largest—Newark

Statehood: December 18, 1787; 3rd state

U.S. Congress: 2 senators, 12 representatives

State Motto: Liberty and Prosperity

State Song: None

State Nickname: The Garden State

Abbreviations: NJ; N.J.

State Symbols: flower—common meadow violet; tree—red oak; bird—Eastern goldfinch

At a Glance

- With an increase in population of 5.4 percent, New Jersey ranked 27th among the states in growth from 2010 to 2021.

- New Jersey's median household income was $85,245 in 2020, the 3rd highest in the country.

- In 2020, 9.7 percent of the New Jersey's population lived below the poverty level, compared to 12.8 percent of the entire U.S. population.

- New Jersey's property crime rate of 1,158.2 incidents per 100,000 population, was the 5th lowest rate in the country in 2020.

- Approximately 40.7 percent of New Jersey residents had a bachelor's degree or more in 2020, the 5th highest percentage in the country.

Table NJ-1. Population by Age, Sex, Race, and Hispanic Origin

(Number, percent, except where noted.)

Sex, age, race, and Hispanic origin	2000	2010	2021	Percent change, 2010–2021
Total Population...	8,414,350	8,791,894	9,267,130	5.4
Percent of total U.S. population	3.0	2.8	2.8	X
Sex				
Male..	4,082,813	4,279,600	4,561,942	6.6
Female...	4,331,357	4,512,294	4,705,188	4.3
Age				
Under 5 years...	563,785	541,020	519,195	-4.0
5 to 19 years..	1,720,332	1,750,184	1,723,729	-1.5
20 to 64 years..	5,017,107	5,314,697	5,458,289	2.7
65 years and over..	1,113,136	1,185,993	1,565,917	32.0
Median age (years)	36.7	39.0	40.3	3.3
Race and Hispanic Origin				
One race				
White..	6,104,705	6,546,498	6,593,546	0.7
Black..	1,141,821	1,282,005	1,419,801	10.7
American Indian and Alaska Native	19,492	49,907	64,812	29.9
Asian..	480,276	746,212	957,387	28.3
Native Hawaiian or Other Pacific Islander	3,329	7,731	11,683	51.1
Two or more races...	13,755	159,541	219,901	37.8
Hispanic (of any race)..	1,117,191	1,606,006	1,991,638	24.0

NOTE: Population figures for 2021 are July 1 estimates. The 2000 and 2010 estimates are taken from the respective censuses.
- = Zero or rounds to zero.
X = Not applicable.

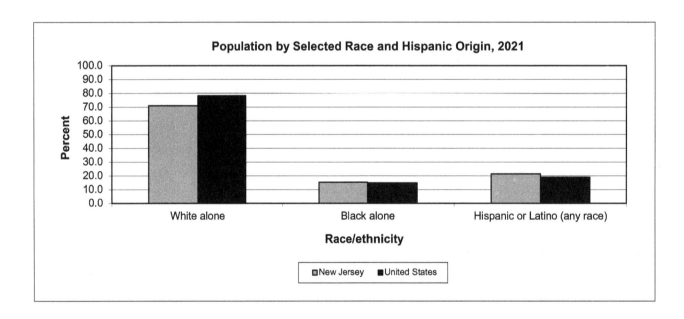

Table NJ-2. Marital Status

(Number, percent distribution.)

Sex, age, race, and Hispanic origin	2000	2010	2020 [1]
Males, 15 Years and Over	3,176,413	3,419,050	3,519,140
Never married	31.1	36.4	36.8
Now married, except separated..	57.7	52.1	52.2
Separated...	2.0	1.8	1.5
Widowed...	2.9	2.6	2.5
Divorced...	6.2	7.1	6.9
Females, 15 Years and Over	3,478,920	3,690,673	3,755,973
Never married	25.3	30.2	31.3
Now married, except separated..	51.8	47.6	47.5
Separated...	2.7	2.2	2.1
Widowed...	11.5	10.2	9.0
Divorced...	8.7	9.8	10.2

[1] 2020 ACS 5-Year estimates. 1-Year estimates were not released for 2020 due to the impact of COVID-19 on data collection that year.

Table NJ-3. Households and Housing Characteristics

(Number, percent, dollars.)

Item	2000	2010	2020 [1]	Average annual percent change, 2010–2020
Total Households	3,064,645	3,172,421	3,272,054	0.4
Family households	2,154,539	2,185,732	2,247,306	0.4
Married-couple family	1,638,322	1,614,230	1,669,437	0.5
Other family	516,217	571,502	577,869	0.2
Male householder, no wife present	129,205	154,036	158,332	0.4
Female householder, no husband present	387,012	417,466	419,537	0.1
Nonfamily households	910,106	986,689	1,024,748	0.6
Householder living alone	751,287	827,294	851,817	0.4
Householder not living alone	158,819	159,395	172,931	1.2
Housing Characteristics				
Total housing units	3,310,275	3,554,909	3,628,732	0.3
Occupied housing units	3,064,645	3,172,421	3,272,054	0.4
Owner occupied	2,012,473	2,106,728	2,094,427	-0.1
Renter occupied	1,053,172	1,065,693	1,177,627	1.5
Average household size	2.68	2.72	2.66	-0.3
Financial Characteristics				
Median gross rent of renter-occupied housing	751	1,114	1,368	3.3
Median monthly owner costs for housing units with a mortgage	1,560	2,370	2,476	0.6
Median value of owner-occupied housing units	170,800	339,200	343,500	0.2

[1] 2020 ACS 5-Year estimates. 1-Year estimates were not released for 2020 due to the impact of COVID-19 on data collection that year.

Table NJ-4. Migration, Origin, and Language

(Number, percent.)

Characteristic	State 2016-2020 [1]	U.S. 2016-2020 [1]
Residence 1 Year Ago		
Population 1 year and over	8,793,299	322,943,283
Same house	89.7	86.2
Different house in the U.S.	9.6	13.2
Same county	5.3	7.7
Different county	4.3	5.5
Same state	2.6	3.2
Different state	1.7	2.3
Abroad	0.7	0.6
Place of Birth		
Native born	6,872,546	282,443,680
Male	49.0	49.4
Female	51.0	50.6
Foreign born	2,012,872	44,125,628
Male	48.5	48.6
Female	51.5	51.4
Foreign born; naturalized U.S. citizen	1,153,765	22,456,684
Male	47.1	46.1
Female	52.9	53.9
Foreign born; not a U.S. citizen	859,107	21,668,944
Male	50.2	51.1
Female	49.8	48.9
Entered 2010 or later	22.6	22.8
Entered 2000 to 2009	25.7	25.1
Entered before 2000	51.7	52.1
World Region of Birth, Foreign		
Foreign-born population, excluding population born at sea	2,012,872	44,125,628
Europe	14.6	10.8
Asia	32.5	31.3
Africa	5.9	5.4
Oceania	0.1	0.6
Latin America	45.9	50.0
North America	0.8	1.9
Language Spoken at Home and Ability to Speak English		
Population 5 years and over	8,367,069	306,919,116
English only	68.4	78.5
Language other than English	31.6	21.5
Speaks English less than "very well"	12.1	8.2

[1] 2020 ACS 5-Year estimates. 1-Year estimates were not released for 2020 due to the impact of COVID-19 on data collection that year.
NA = Not available.
X = Not applicable.
- = Zero or rounds to zero.

Table NJ-5. Median Income and Poverty Status, 2020[1]

(Number, percent, except as noted.)

Characteristic	State		U.S.	
	Number	Percent	Number	Percent
Median Income				
Households (dollars)..	85,245	X	64,994	X
Families (dollars)	104,804	X	80,069	X
Below Poverty Level (All People)	842,704	9.7	40,910,326	12.8
Sex				
Male	367,044	8.7	18,171,512	11.6
Female	475,660	10.6	22,738,814	14.0
Age				
Under 18 years...	257,552	13.3	12,598,699	17.5
Related children under 18 years.......................................	252,263	13.1	12,306,532	17.2
18 to 64 years..	466,647	8.7	23,554,920	12.1
65 years and over	118,505	8.4	4,756,707	9.3

X = Not applicable.
[1] 2020 ACS 5-Year estimates. 1-Year estimates were not released for 2020 due to the impact of COVID-19 on data collection that year.

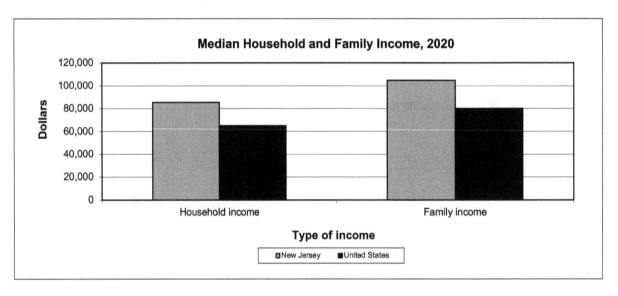

Table NJ-6. Health Insurance Coverage Status for the Civilian Noninstitutionalized Population and Children Under 19 Years of Age

(Number, percent.)

Item	2011	2012	2013	2014	2015	2016	2017	2018	2019	2020[2]
Civilian Noninstitutionalized Population	8,712,982	8,756,542	8,791,652	8,830,969	8,850,415	8,837,578	8,902,432	8,803,988	8,775,976	8,780,160
Covered by Private or Public Insurance										
Number..	7,573,878	7,643,733	7,631,358	7,865,558	8,079,219	8,132,608	8,214,364	8,148,988	8,083,635	8,117,243
Percent...	86.9	87.3	86.8	89.1	91.3	92.0	92.3	92.6	92.1	92.4
Uninsured										
Number..	1,139,104	1,112,809	1,160,294	965,411	771,196	704,970	688,068	655,000	692,341	662,917
Percent...	13.1	12.7	13.2	10.9	8.7	8.0	7.7	7.4	7.9	7.6
Percent in the U.S. not covered......................................	15.1	14.8	14.5	11.7	9.4	8.6	8.7	8.9	9.2	8.7
Children Under 19 Years of Age[1]	2,038,167	2,024,150	2,017,712	2,007,362	1,993,774	1,979,948	2,093,669	2,059,124	2,041,577	2,059,449
Covered by Private or Public Insurance										
Number..	1,933,002	1,921,334	1,905,595	1,915,520	1,919,180	1,909,909	2,015,469	1,979,363	1,953,456	1,978,171
Percent...	94.8	94.9	94.4	95.4	96.3	96.5	96.3	96.1	95.7	96.1
Uninsured										
Number..	105,165	102,816	112,117	91,842	74,594	70,039	78,200	79,761	88,121	81,278
Percent...	5.2	5.1	5.6	4.6	3.7	3.5	3.7	3.9	4.3	3.9
Percent in the U.S. not covered......................................	7.5	7.2	7.1	6.0	4.8	4.5	5.0	5.2	5.7	5.2

[1] 2017 data is for individuals under 19 years of age.
[2] 2020 ACS 5-Year estimates. 1-Year estimates were not released for 2020 due to the impact of COVID-19 on data collection that year. Data is not comparable to previous years, which are based on 1-year estimates.

Table NJ-7. Employment Status by Demographic Group, 2021

(Numbers in thousands, percent.)

Characteristic	Civilian noninstitutional population	Civilian labor force		Employed		Unemployed	
		Number	Percent of population	Number	Percent of population	Number	Percent of population
Total...	7,069	4,448	62.9	4,167	59.0	281	6.3
Sex							
Male..	3,408	2,379	69.8	2,236	65.6	143	6.0
Female.....................................	3,661	2,069	56.5	1,932	52.8	138	6.7
Race, Sex, and Hispanic Origin							
White......................................	5,028	3,115	61.9	2,944	58.5	171	5.5
Male......................................	2,447	1,673	68.4	1,584	64.7	90	5.4
Female...................................	2,581	1,442	55.9	1,360	52.7	81	5.6
Black or African American............	1,027	667	64.9	603	58.7	64	9.6
Male......................................	470	332	70.8	303	64.5	30	8.9
Female...................................	558	335	60.0	300	53.8	35	10.3
Hispanic or Latino ethnicity[1].........	1,262	834	66.1	775	61.4	59	7.1
Male......................................	635	474	74.7	444	70.0	30	6.4
Female...................................	627	360	57.4	331	52.8	29	8.0
Age							
16 to 19 years...........................	425	132	31.1	110	25.9	22	16.7
20 to 24 years...........................	497	315	63.4	284	57.1	31	10.0
25 to 34 years...........................	1,196	979	81.8	902	75.4	77	7.8
35 to 44 years...........................	1,093	922	84.3	872	79.7	50	5.4
45 to 54 years...........................	1,108	939	84.8	895	80.7	45	4.8
55 to 64 years...........................	1,194	835	69.9	796	66.7	39	4.6
65 years and over.......................	1,555	326	21.0	309	19.9	17	5.2

NOTE: Data in Table 7 are from the Current Population Survey (CPS) and do not match the estimates in Table 8. See notes and definitions for further information.
[1] May be of any race.

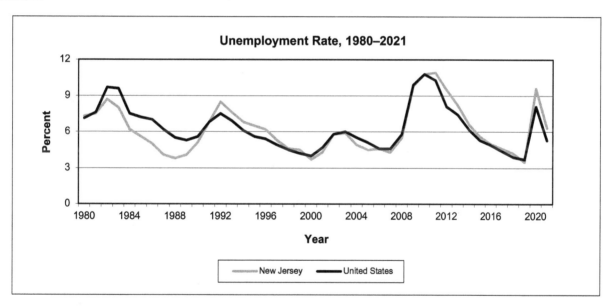

Table NJ-8. Employment Status of the Civilian Noninstitutional Population Age 16 Years and Over

(Number, percent.)

Year	Civilian labor force	Civilian participation rate	Employed	Unemployed	Unemployment rate
2010...	4,559,778	66.5	4,118,982	440,796	9.7
2011...	4,561,786	66.0	4,134,708	427,078	9.4
2012...	4,576,286	65.9	4,147,221	429,065	9.4
2013...	4,528,019	64.9	4,147,661	380,358	8.4
2014...	4,493,894	64.2	4,191,318	302,576	6.7
2015...	4,494,606	64.1	4,237,876	256,730	5.7
2016...	4,492,821	63.9	4,271,201	221,620	4.9
2017...	4,614,953	63.5	4,406,151	208,802	4.5
2018...	4,609,773	63	4,426,617	183,156	4.0
2019...	4,686,701	63.8	4,528,168	158,533	3.4
2020...	4,642,945	62.9	4,203,278	439,667	9.5
2021...	4,661,087	63.1	4,365,397	295,690	6.3

Table NJ-9. Employment and Average Wages by Industry

(Estimates are based on the 2012 North American Industry Classification System [NAICS].)

Industry	2013	2014	2015	2016	2017	2018	2019	2020
	Number of Jobs							
Wage and Salary Employment by Industry	3,978,040	4,010,203	4,061,862	4,123,132	4,174,996	4,221,213	4,261,715	3,920,973
Farm Wage and Salary Employment	8,892	9,552	9,252	11,166	10,756	8,865	8,136	6,858
Nonfarm Wage and Salary Employment	3,969,148	4,000,651	4,052,610	4,111,966	4,164,240	4,212,348	4,253,579	3,914,115
Private wage and salary employment	3,350,612	3,383,679	3,439,130	3,501,160	3,553,573	3,600,236	3,640,015	3,325,678
Forestry, fishing, and related activities	2,893	3,522	3,785	4,251	4,089	3,998	3,968	3,703
Mining	1,317	1,412	1,388	1,323	1,290	1,339	1,375	1,366
Utilities	13,671	13,659	14,208	14,174	14,180	15,273	14,707	13,955
Construction	141,334	144,904	151,919	157,215	159,593	161,771	164,232	155,785
Manufacturing	242,972	242,371	238,039	242,349	244,530	247,076	251,399	237,941
Durable goods manufacturing	110,875	108,906	109,329	110,017	111,336	115,301	116,705	109,608
Nondurable goods manufacturing	132,097	133,465	128,710	132,332	133,194	131,775	134,694	128,333
Wholesale trade	213,833	215,024	217,519	217,139	218,755	216,669	215,659	202,471
Retail trade	451,587	457,378	464,351	464,953	466,095	460,592	453,438	411,624
Transportation and warehousing	150,825	153,622	161,009	172,195	187,858	196,745	206,332	205,626
Information	75,223	75,507	74,437	73,264	70,987	69,894	67,979	68,241
Finance and insurance	191,144	184,597	189,520	191,194	196,766	197,633	198,746	196,938
Real estate and rental and leasing	55,522	55,509	56,949	58,483	59,759	61,267	63,335	57,779
Professional, scientific, and technical services	285,212	289,737	297,578	303,202	301,219	305,236	308,129	301,684
Management of companies and enterprises	83,332	79,003	79,991	80,733	83,389	84,378	86,624	84,694
Administrative and waste services	262,429	268,683	274,765	282,029	287,238	290,126	291,910	265,249
Educational services	96,875	97,744	99,396	101,924	103,260	103,689	105,743	94,964
Health care and social assistance	532,091	540,275	551,789	563,699	576,097	587,851	600,776	558,923
Arts, entertainment, and recreation	57,866	61,268	62,579	65,376	67,672	69,602	71,006	46,139
Accommodation and food services	297,127	298,823	299,157	306,793	310,914	320,871	325,669	240,082
Other services, except public administration	195,359	200,641	200,751	200,864	199,882	206,226	208,988	178,514
Government and government enterprises	618,536	616,972	613,480	610,806	610,667	612,112	613,564	588,437
	Dollars							
Average Wages and Salaries by Industry	58,811	59,968	61,775	62,270	63,563	65,241	66,868	73,234
Average Farm Wages and Salaries	25,309	24,962	21,052	20,018	18,860	23,621	20,436	23,546
Average Nonfarm Wages and Salaries	58,886	60,052	61,868	62,385	63,679	65,329	66,956	73,321
Average private wages and salaries	58,655	59,820	61,751	62,261	63,578	65,211	66,896	73,758
Forestry, fishing, and related activities	27,753	27,435	28,011	31,280	32,914	35,199	37,204	40,096
Mining	72,156	71,305	77,421	76,745	81,604	81,420	87,079	88,197
Utilities	107,123	113,032	116,156	118,690	120,284	123,274	122,246	130,481
Construction	63,792	64,990	67,612	68,730	71,115	72,667	74,653	78,020
Manufacturing	77,266	79,949	77,057	78,574	78,771	80,105	81,634	86,252
Durable goods manufacturing	69,681	72,136	73,705	75,390	77,739	80,331	79,752	82,808
Nondurable goods manufacturing	83,632	86,323	79,904	81,221	79,635	79,907	83,264	89,194
Wholesale trade	82,350	85,235	87,506	87,065	87,457	88,736	90,458	94,679
Retail trade	30,964	31,707	32,929	33,262	33,914	34,646	36,312	39,875
Transportation and warehousing	51,625	52,541	54,213	54,506	53,957	54,862	55,568	56,288
Information	96,253	98,928	102,954	105,041	108,470	114,617	117,566	130,535
Finance and insurance	110,969	115,946	120,813	122,880	127,795	131,150	134,595	145,190
Real estate and rental and leasing	58,614	60,365	63,656	62,872	64,042	67,046	67,407	74,053
Professional, scientific, and technical services	97,658	100,182	106,531	106,327	108,951	111,912	115,701	124,930
Management of companies and enterprises	150,461	151,816	159,410	160,244	167,189	170,595	174,833	183,214
Administrative and waste services	39,168	39,740	40,821	41,479	43,688	45,134	46,729	51,305
Educational services	40,078	41,313	42,341	42,787	42,811	44,493	44,870	50,693
Health care and social assistance	48,534	49,511	50,971	51,576	52,245	53,516	55,269	60,265
Arts, entertainment, and recreation	37,077	36,288	37,064	37,444	37,360	40,570	41,312	51,784
Accommodation and food services	23,733	24,517	24,651	25,262	25,681	27,469	27,201	26,845
Other services, except public administration	32,981	33,480	34,653	35,317	36,433	37,440	38,408	41,700
Government and government enterprises	60,135	61,322	62,526	63,094	64,267	66,020	67,313	70,855

Table NJ-10. Employment Characteristics by Family Type

(Number, percent.)

Family type and labor force status	2018		2019		2020 [1]	
	Total	Families with own children under 18 years	Total	Families with own children under 18 years	Total	Families with own children under 18 years
All Families....................................	2,231,636	933,310	2,241,555	931,496	2,247,306	959,366
FAMILY TYPE AND LABOR FORCE STATUS						
Opposite-Sex Married-Couple Families..........................	1,663,794	683,287	1,667,463	680,701	1,655,629	696,311
Both husband and wife in labor force................................	55.0	69.2	54.7	69.6	55.7	69.5
Husband in labor force, wife not in labor force	21.7	26.1	21.4	25.6	21.7	25.7
Wife in labor force, husband not in labor force	7.2	3.6	7.7	3.5	7.6	3.7
Both husband and wife not in labor force.............................	15.2	0.8	15.3	1.0	15.0	1.0
Other Families	567,842	250,023	574,092	250,795	577,869	260,423
Female householder, no spouse present	72.1	74.7	71.3	74.6	72.6	75.4
In labor force	52.9	63.4	52.3	65.0	52.8	64.6
Not in labor force	19.2	11.4	19.0	9.5	19.8	10.8
Male householder, no spouse present.............................	27.9	25.3	28.7	25.4	27.4	24.6
In labor force	23.0	24.2	23.2	23.9	21.9	23.0
Not in labor force	4.9	1.0	5.5	1.5	5.5	1.6

[1] 2020 ACS 5-Year estimates. 1-Year estimates were not released for 2020 due to the impact of COVID-19 on data collection that year. Data is not comparable to previous years, which are based on 1-year estimates.

Table NJ-11. School Enrollment and Educational Attainment, 2020[1]

(Number, percent.)

Item	State	U.S.
Enrollment		
Total population 3 years and over, enrolled in school	2,192,185	80,497,960
Enrolled in nursery school or preschool (percent)...	7.4	6.1
Enrolled in kindergarten (percent)...	5.1	5.0
Enrolled in elementary school, grades 1-8 (percent)..	39.6	40.4
Enrolled in high school, grades 9-12 (percent)...	21.1	21.0
Enrolled in college or graduate school (percent)...	26.9	27.6
Attainment		
Total population 25 years and over	6,169,501	222,836,834
Less than ninth grade (percent)	4.7	4.9
9th to 12th grade, no diploma (percent)	5.1	6.6
High school graduate, including equivalency (percent)..	26.7	26.7
Some college, no degree (percent)	16.1	20.3
Associate's degree (percent)...	6.6	8.6
Bachelor's degree (percent)..	24.8	20.2
Graduate or professional degree (percent)...	15.9	12.7
High school graduate or higher (percent)	90.3	88.5
Bachelor's degree or higher (percent)..	40.7	32.9

[1] 2020 ACS 5-Year estimates. 1-Year estimates were not released for 2020 due to the impact of COVID-19 on data collection that year.

Table NJ-12. Public School Characteristics and Educational Indicators

(Number, percent; data derived from National Center of Education Statistics.)

Item	State	U.S.
Public Elementary and Secondary Schools		
Number of regular school districts, 2018-19	564	13,452
Number of operational schools, 2019-20...	2,565	98,469
Percent charter schools	3.4	7.7
Total public school enrollment, Fall 2019...	1,411,917	50,796,445
Percent charter school enrollment	4.0	6.8
Student-teacher ratio, Fall 2019	12.1	15.9
Expenditures per student (unadjusted dollars), 2018-19	21,331	13,187
Four-year adjusted cohort graduation rate (ACGR), 2018-2019[1].................................	90.6	85.8
Students eligible for free or reduced-price lunch (percent), 2019-20............................	38.2	52.1
English language learners (percent), Fall 2019	7.3	10.4
Students age 3 to 21 served under IDEA, part B (percent), 2020-21	17.3	14.5

Public Schools by Type, 2019-20	Number	Percent of state public schools
Total number of schools..	2,565	100.0
Special education	61	2.4
Vocational education	70	2.7
Alternative education..	70	2.7

[1] Adjusted Cohort Graduation Rates (ACGR) differ from Averaged Freshmen Graduation Rates (AFGR).

Table NJ-13. Reported Voting and Registration of the Voting-Age Population, November 2020

(Numbers in thousands, percent.)

Item	Total population	Total citizen population	Registered			Voted		
			Total registered	Percent registered (total population)	Percent registered (total citizen population)	Total voted	Percent voted (total population)	Percent voted (total citizen population)
U.S. Total	252,274	231,593	168,308	66.7	72.7	154,628	61.3	66.8
State Total.......................................	6,801	5,921	5,008	73.6	84.6	4,638	68.2	78.3
Sex								
Male	3,281	2,814	2,366	72.1	84.1	2,193	66.8	77.9
Female	3,520	3,107	2,642	75.0	85.0	2,445	69.5	78.7
Race								
White alone..............................	4,900	4,462	3,826	78.1	85.7	3,543	72.3	79.4
White, non-Hispanic alone	3,755	3,636	3,134	83.5	86.2	2,950	78.6	81.1
Black alone..............................	994	850	658	66.2	77.5	606	60.9	71.3
Asian alone	810	524	443	54.7	84.5	408	50.4	77.9
Hispanic (of any race)	1,347	996	817	60.7	82.0	719	53.4	72.1
White alone or in combination	4,971	4,520	3,884	78.1	85.9	3,602	72.5	79.7
Black alone or in combination.....................	1,064	907	716	67.2	78.9	663	62.3	73.1
Asian alone or in combination.....................	816	530	449	55.1	84.7	414	50.8	78.1
Age								
18 to 24 years.............................	783	706	613	78.3	86.9	532	67.9	75.3
25 to 34 years.............................	1,125	885	708	62.9	79.9	619	55.0	69.9
35 to 44 years.............................	1,032	813	678	65.7	83.4	624	60.5	76.8
45 to 64 years.............................	2,408	2,134	1,807	75.1	84.7	1,720	71.4	80.6
65 years and over	1,453	1,383	1,202	82.7	86.9	1,143	78.6	82.6

Table NJ-14. Crime

(Number, rate per 100,000. Data are derived from the FBI Uniform Crime Reports.)

Item	State			U.S.		
	2019	2020	Percent change	2019	2020	Percent change
TOTAL POPULATION¹	8,891,258	8,882,371	-0.1	328,329,953	329,484,123	0.4
VIOLENT CRIME						
Number..	18,382	17,353	-5.6	1,250,393	1,313,105	5.0
Rate	206.7	195.4	-5.5	380.8	398.5	4.6
Murder and Nonnegligent Manslaughter						
Number..	263	329	25.1	16,669	21,570	29.4
Rate	3.0	3.7	25.2	5.1	6.5	28.9
Rape²						
Number..	1,537	1,277	-16.9	143,224	126,430	-11.7
Rate	17.3	14.4	-16.8	43.6	38.4	-12.0
Robbery						
Number..	5,730	4,384	-23.5	268,483	243,600	-9.3
Rate	64.4	49.4	-23.4	81.8	73.9	-9.6
Aggravated Assault						
Number..	10,852	11,363	4.7	822,017	921,505	12.1
Rate	122.1	127.9	4.8	250.4	279.7	11.7
PROPERTY CRIME						
Number..	118,637	102,875	-13.3	6,995,235	6,452,038	-7.8
Rate	1,334.3	1,158.2	-13.2	2,130.6	1,958.2	-8.1
Burglary						
Number..	16,399	12,983	-20.8	1,118,096	1,035,314	-7.4
Rate	184.4	146.2	-20.8	340.5	314.2	-7.7
Larceny-Theft						
Number..	91,902	79,614	-13.4	5,152,267	4,606,324	-10.6
Rate	1,033.6	896.3	-13.3	1,569.2	1,398.0	-10.9
Motor Vehicle Theft						
Number..	10,336	10,278	-0.6	724,872	810,400	11.8
Rate	116.2	115.7	-0.5	220.8	246.0	11.4

NOTE: Although arson data are included in the trend and clearance tables, sufficient data are not available to estimate totals for this offense. Therefore, no arson data are published in this table.
- = Zero or rounds to zero.
¹ Population figures are U.S. Census Bureau provisional estimates as of July 1, 2020.
² The figures shown in the rape (revised definition) column were estimated using the revised Uniform Crime Reporting (UCR) definition of rape.

Table NJ-15. State Government Finances, 2020

(Dollar amounts in thousands, percent distribution.)

Item	Dollars	Percent distribution
Total Revenue	84,759,151	100.0
General revenue	70,460,446	83.1
Intergovernmental revenue	20,120,548	23.7
Taxes	37,927,482	44.7
General sales	11068018	13.1
Selective sales	5,203,731	6.1
License taxes	1,691,586	2.0
Individual income tax	15412766	18.2
Corporate income tax	3,565,191	4.2
Other taxes	986,190	1.2
Current charges	6,734,836	7.9
Miscellaneous general revenue	5,677,580	6.7
Utility revenue	861,125	1.0
Liquor stores revenue	0	-
Insurance trust revenue[1]	13,437,580	15.9
Total Expenditure	85,380,041	100.0
Intergovernmental expenditure	16,100,829	18.9
Direct expenditure	69,279,212	81.1
Current operation	43,023,526	50.4
Capital outlay	4,319,978	5.1
Insurance benefits and repayments	17,511,294	20.5
Assistance and subsidies	1,979,844	2.3
Interest on debt	2,444,570	2.9
Exhibit: Salaries and wages	10,871,635	12.7
Total Expenditure	85,380,041	100.0
General expenditure	64,446,556	75.5
Intergovernmental expenditure	16,100,829	18.9
Direct expenditure	48,345,727	56.6
General expenditure, by function:		
Education	23,772,452	27.8
Public welfare	20,571,291	24.1
Hospitals	2,690,742	3.2
Health	1,884,079	2.2
Highways	3,331,477	3.9
Police protection	961,848	1.1
Correction	1,565,763	1.8
Natural resources	593,375	0.7
Parks and recreation	159,468	0.2
Governmental administration	2,195,945	2.6
Interest on general debt	2,443,850	2.9
Other and unallocable	4,092,474	4.8
Utility expenditure	3,422,191	4.0
Liquor stores expenditure	0	-
Insurance trust expenditure	17,511,294	20.5
Debt at End of Fiscal Year	64,058,342	X
Cash and Security Holdings	124,057,662	X

X = Not applicable.
- = Zero or rounds to zero.
[1] Within insurance trust revenue, net earnings of state retirement systems is a calculated statistic (the item code in the data file is X08), and thus can be positive or negative. Net earnings is the sum of earnings on investments plus gains on investments minus losses on investments. The change made in 2002 for asset valuation from book to market value in accordance with Statement 34 of the Governmental Accounting Standards Board is reflected in the calculated statistics.

Table NJ-16. State Government Tax Collections, 2021

(Dollars in thousands, percent.)

Item	Dollars	Percent distribution
Total Taxes	43,683,029	100.0
Property taxes	5,166	-
Sales and gross receipts	17,871,986	40.9
General sales and gross receipts	12,803,267	29.3
Selective sales and gross receipts	5,068,719	11.6
Alcoholic beverages	174,692	0.4
Amusements	308,883	0.7
Insurance premiums	639,103	1.5
Motor fuels	386,173	0.9
Pari-mutuels	X	-
Public utilities	935,252	2.1
Tobacco products	601,614	1.4
Other selective sales	2,023,002	4.6
Licenses	1,986,338	4.5
Alcoholic beverages	4,662	-
Amusements	60,072	0.1
Corporations in general	517,923	1.2
Hunting and fishing	15,989	-
Motor vehicle	681,061	1.6
Motor vehicle operators	60,487	0.1
Public utilities	21,565	-
Occupation and business, NEC	622,514	1.4
Other licenses	2,065	-
Income taxes	22,793,255	52.2
Individual income	16,833,495	38.5
Corporation net income	5,959,760	13.6
Other taxes	1,026,284	2.3
Death and gift	530,341	1.2
Documentary and stock transfer	495,943	1.1
Severance	X	-
Taxes, NEC	0	-

X = Not applicable.
- = Zero or rounds to zero.

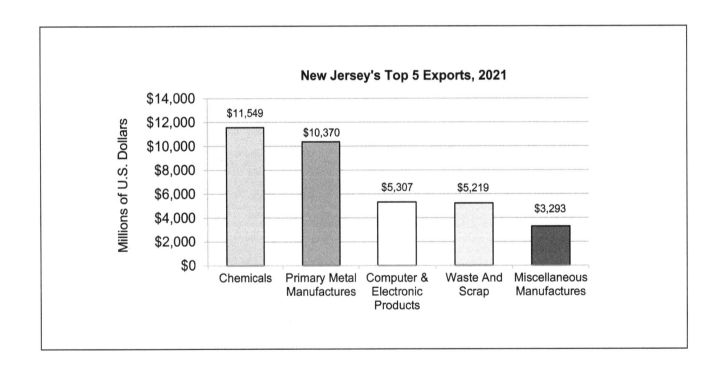

New Jersey's Top 5 Exports, 2021

(bar chart, Millions of U.S. Dollars)
- Chemicals: $11,549
- Primary Metal Manufactures: $10,370
- Computer & Electronic Products: $5,307
- Waste And Scrap: $5,219
- Miscellaneous Manufactures: $3,293

NEW MEXICO

Facts and Figures

Location: Southwestern United States; bordered on the N by Colorado, on the E by Oklahoma and Texas, on the S by Texas and Mexico, and on the W by Arizona; New Mexico is one of the Four Corner states—at its NW corner it touches Arizona, Colorado, and Utah

Area: 121,590 sq. mi. (314,915 sq. km.); rank—5th

Population: 2,115,877 (2021 est.); rank—36th

Principal Cities: capital—Santa Fe; largest—Albuquerque

Statehood: January 6, 1912; 47th state

U.S. Congress: 2 senators, 3 representatives

State Motto: *Crescit eundo* ("It grows as it goes")

State Song: "O, Fair New Mexico"

State Nickname: The Land of Enchantment

Abbreviations: NM; N. Mex.

State Symbols: flower—yucca; tree—piñon; bird—roadrunner

At a Glance

- With an increase in population of 2.8 percent, New Mexico ranked 41st among the states in growth from 2010 to 2021.

- In 2020, New Mexico's violent crime rate of 778.3 per 100,000 population was the 3rd highest rate in the country, and its property crime rate of 2,841.9 per 100,000 population, was also the 3rd highest in the country.

- New Mexico had the 3rd highest percentage of residents living below the poverty level in 2020 (18.6 percent).

- In 2021, New Mexico's household income was $51,243, which ranked 47th among the states, compared to the national average of $64,994.

- With approximately 50.1 percent of its residents self-identifying as "Hispanic or Latino," New Mexico was the state with the highest percentage of this population in 2021.

Table NM-1. Population by Age, Sex, Race, and Hispanic Origin

(Number, percent, except where noted.)

Sex, age, race, and Hispanic origin	2000	2010	2021	Percent change, 2010–2021
Total Population...	1,819,046	2,059,179	2,115,877	2.8
Percent of total U.S. population	0.6	0.7	0.6	X
Sex				
Male..	894,317	1,017,421	1,052,697	3.5
Female..	924,729	1,041,758	1,063,180	2.1
Age				
Under 5 years..	130,628	144,981	115,008	-20.7
5 to 19 years...	434,231	434,860	414,588	-4.7
20 to 64 years...	1,041,962	1,207,083	1,194,335	-1.1
65 years and over..	212,225	272,255	391,946	44.0
Median age (years)..	34.6	36.7	38.8	5.7
Race and Hispanic origin				
One race				
White..	1,214,253	1,720,992	1,720,615	-
Black...	34,343	49,006	57,350	17.0
American Indian and Alaska Native	173,483	208,890	236,809	13.4
Asian...	19,255	31,253	39,851	27.5
Native Hawaiian or Other Pacific Islander	1,503	3,132	3,528	12.6
Two or more races...	66,327	45,906	57,724	25.7
Hispanic (of any race)...	765,386	973,088	1,059,242	8.9

NOTE: Population figures for 2021 are July 1 estimates. The 2000 and 2010 estimates are taken from the respective censuses.
- = Zero or rounds to zero.
X = Not applicable.

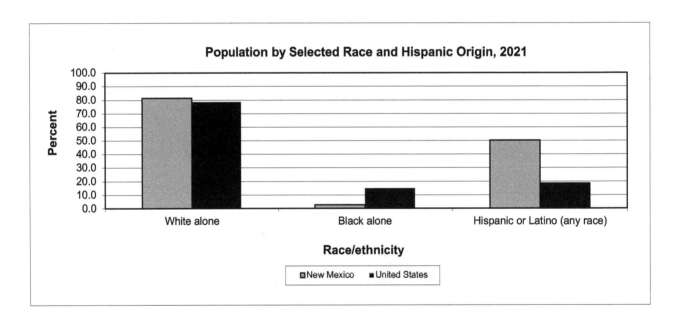

Table NM-2. Marital Status

(Number, percent distribution.)

Sex, age, race, and Hispanic origin	2000	2010	2020 [1]
Males, 15 Years and Over	677,967	801,901	834,171
Never married	30.5	35.4	38.9
Now married, except separated..	55.0	48.4	44.9
Separated..	1.6	1.6	1.5
Widowed..	2.6	2.6	2.9
Divorced..	10.4	11.9	11.8
Females, 15 Years and Over	720,529	833,357	863,052
Never married	24.7	29.9	31.7
Now married, except separated..	51.2	45.0	42.9
Separated..	2.0	2.6	1.8
Widowed..	9.4	8.5	8.8
Divorced..	12.8	14.1	14.8

[1] 2020 ACS 5-Year estimates. 1-Year estimates were not released for 2020 due to the impact of COVID-19 on data collection that year.

Table NM-3. Households and Housing Characteristics

(Number, percent, dollars.)

Item	2000	2010	2020 [1]	Average annual percent change, 2010–2020
Total Households...	677,971	765,183	792,755	0.5
Family households	466,515	501,092	496,734	-0.1
Married-couple family	341,818	349,344	340,736	-0.4
Other family	124,697	151,748	155,998	0.4
Male householder, no wife present................................	35,075	49,041	47,576	-0.4
Female householder, no husband present.......................	89,622	102,707	108,422	0.8
Nonfamily households	211,456	264,091	296,021	1.7
Householder living alone	172,181	216,704	246,025	1.9
Householder not living alone	39,275	47,387	49,996	0.8
Housing Characteristics				
Total housing units..	780,579	902,242	943,568	0.7
Occupied housing units	677,971	765,183	792,755	0.5
Owner occupied	474,445	519,864	539,082	0.5
Renter occupied	203,526	245,319	253,673	0.5
Average household size...	2.63	2.64	2.59	-0.3
Financial Characteristics				
Median gross rent of renter-occupied housing	503	699	857	3.2
Median monthly owner costs for housing units with a mortgage	929	1,202	1,293	1.1
Median value of owner-occupied housing units.........................	108,100	161,200	175,700	1.3

[1] 2020 ACS 5-Year estimates. 1-Year estimates were not released for 2020 due to the impact of COVID-19 on data collection that year.

Table NM-4. Migration, Origin, and Language

(Number, percent.)

Characteristic	State 2016-2020 [1]	U.S. 2016-2020 [1]
Residence 1 Year Ago		
Population 1 year and over	2,075,584	322,943,283
Same house	87.0	86.2
Different house in the U.S.	12.5	13.2
Same county	7.3	7.7
Different county	5.2	5.5
Same state	2.3	3.2
Different state	2.9	2.3
Abroad	0.5	0.6
Place of Birth		
Native born	1,903,798	282,443,680
Male	49.6	49.4
Female	50.4	50.6
Foreign born	193,223	44,125,628
Male	48.2	48.6
Female	51.8	51.4
Foreign born; naturalized U.S. citizen...	83,060	22,456,684
Male	43.9	46.1
Female	56.1	53.9
Foreign born; not a U.S. citizen...	110,163	21,668,944
Male	51.4	51.1
Female	48.6	48.9
Entered 2010 or later	18.4	22.8
Entered 2000 to 2009	24.1	25.1
Entered before 2000..	57.5	52.1
World Region of Birth, Foreign		
Foreign-born population, excluding population born at sea	193,223	44,125,628
Europe	7.6	10.8
Asia..	14.4	31.3
Africa	2.5	5.4
Oceania	0.3	0.6
Latin America...	74.1	50.0
North America	1.2	1.9
Language Spoken at Home and Ability to Speak English		
Population 5 years and over...	1,974,028	306,919,116
English only	66.5	78.5
Language other than English...	33.5	21.5
Speaks English less than "very well"...	8.6	8.2

[1] 2020 ACS 5-Year estimates. 1-Year estimates were not released for 2020 due to the impact of COVID-19 on data collection that year.
NA = Not available.
X = Not applicable.
- = Zero or rounds to zero.

Table NM-5. Median Income and Poverty Status, 2020[1]

(Number, percent, except as noted.)

Characteristic	State		U.S.	
	Number	Percent	Number	Percent
Median Income				
Households (dollars)	51,243	X	64,994	X
Families (dollars)	62,611	X	80,069	X
Below Poverty Level (All People)	381,026	18.6	40,910,326	12.8
Sex				
Male	174,937	17.4	18,171,512	11.6
Female	206,089	19.7	22,738,814	14.0
Age				
Under 18 years	121,373	25.6	12,598,699	17.5
Related children under 18 years	119,244	25.2	12,306,532	17.2
18 to 64 years	214,901	17.6	23,554,920	12.1
65 years and over	44,752	12.4	4,756,707	9.3

X = Not applicable.
[1] 2020 ACS 5-Year estimates. 1-Year estimates were not released for 2020 due to the impact of COVID-19 on data collection that year.

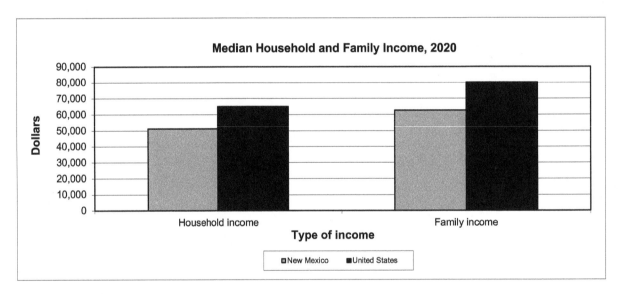

Table NM-6. Health Insurance Coverage Status for the Civilian Noninstitutionalized Population and Children Under 19 Years of Age

(Number, percent.)

Item	2011	2012	2013	2014	2015	2016	2017	2018	2019	2020[2]
Civilian Noninstitutionalized Population	2,047,242	2,051,805	2,051,900	2,050,369	2,050,178	2,046,001	2,054,301	2,060,718	2,058,918	2,060,539
Covered by Private or Public Insurance										
Number	1,641,058	1,673,819	1,669,460	1,752,620	1,826,147	1,858,312	1,867,305	1,864,468	1,853,762	1,865,643
Percent	80.2	81.6	81.4	85.5	89.1	90.8	90.9	90.5	90.0	90.5
Uninsured										
Number	406,184	377,986	382,440	297,749	224,031	187,689	186,996	196,250	205,156	194,896
Percent	19.8	18.4	18.6	14.5	10.9	9.2	9.1	9.5	10.0	9.5
Percent in the U.S. not covered	15.1	14.8	14.5	11.7	9.4	8.6	8.7	8.9	9.2	8.7
Children Under 19 Years of Age[1]	516,787	515,341	506,951	498,680	498,415	488,598	522,820	510,645	501,566	510,571
Covered by Private or Public Insurance										
Number	469,318	473,906	463,846	462,278	475,997	462,513	496,366	483,836	472,729	481,630
Percent	90.8	92.0	91.5	92.7	95.5	94.7	94.9	94.7	94.3	94.3
Uninsured										
Number	47,469	41,435	43,105	36,402	22,418	26,085	26,454	26,809	28,837	28,941
Percent	9.2	8.0	8.5	7.3	4.5	5.3	5.1	5.3	5.7	5.7
Percent in the U.S. not covered	7.5	7.2	7.1	6.0	4.8	4.5	5.0	5.2	5.7	5.2

[1] Data for years prior to 2017 are for individuals under 18 years of age.
[2] 2020 ACS 5-Year estimates. 1-Year estimates were not released for 2020 due to the impact of COVID-19 on data collection that year. Data is not comparable to previous years, which are based on 1-year estimates.

Table NM-7. Employment Status by Demographic Group, 2021

(Numbers in thousands, percent.)

Characteristic	Civilian noninstitutional population	Civilian labor force		Employed		Unemployed	
		Number	Percent of population	Number	Percent of population	Number	Percent of population
Total..................................	1,664	936	56.3	873	52.5	63	6.7
Sex							
Male....................................	807	499	61.8	461	57.2	37	7.4
Female	857	438	51.1	412	48.1	26	5.9
Race, Sex, and Hispanic Origin							
White....................................	1,345	750	55.8	705	52.4	46	6.1
Male..................................	656	405	61.8	378	57.6	27	6.6
Female	689	345	50.1	326	47.4	19	5.4
Black or African American...............	NA	NA	NA	NA	NA	NA	NA
Male..................................	NA	NA	NA	NA	NA	NA	NA
Female	NA	NA	NA	NA	NA	NA	NA
Hispanic or Latino ethnicity[1]	679	398	58.6	368	54.2	30	7.4
Male..................................	325	212	65.4	195	60.0	18	8.3
Female	354	186	52.3	174	49.0	12	6.4
Age							
16 to 19 years........................	111	35	32	31	28	5	13
20 to 24 years........................	144	104	72.5	93	64.6	11	10.8
25 to 34 years........................	262	197	75.4	182	69.6	15	7.6
35 to 44 years........................	256	204	79.9	192	75.0	12	6.1
45 to 54 years........................	225	172	76.3	163	72.2	9	5.4
55 to 64 years........................	266	158	59.5	151	56.7	8	4.7
65 years and over....................	401	65	16.3	62	15.5	3	4.7

NOTE: Data in Table 7 are from the Current Population Survey (CPS) and do not match the estimates in Table 8. See notes and definitions for further information.
[1] May be of any race.
NA = Not available.

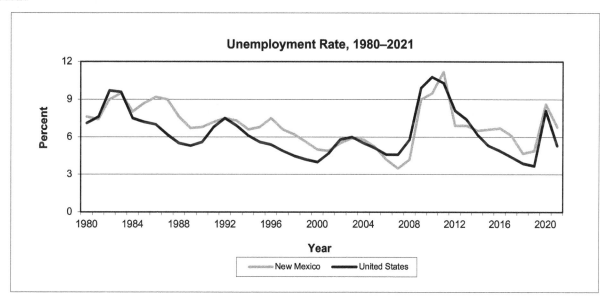

Table NM-8. Employment Status of the Civilian Noninstitutional Population Age 16 Years and Over

(Number, percent.)

Year	Civilian labor force	Civilian participation rate	Employed	Unemployed	Unemployment rate
2010..	928,862	59.5	856,602	72,260	7.8
2011..	925,108	58.4	858,165	66,943	7.2
2012..	928,762	58.3	863,937	64,825	7.0
2013..	929,410	58.1	865,207	64,203	6.9
2014..	931,950	58.1	870,570	61,380	6.6
2015..	938,300	58.3	876,206	62,094	6.6
2016..	944,245	58.4	880,515	63,730	6.7
2017..	948,581	58.3	890,988	57,593	6.1
2018..	950,366	58.1	903,757	46,609	4.9
2019..	963,804	58.6	916,149	47,655	4.9
2020..	935,706	56.5	860,105	75,601	8.1
2021..	943,356	56.7	879,329	64,027	6.8

Table NM-9. Employment and Average Wages by Industry

(Estimates are based on the 2012 North American Industry Classification System [NAICS].)

Industry	2013	2014	2015	2016	2017	2018	2019	2020
	Number of Jobs							
Wage and Salary Employment by Industry.........................	846,495	852,348	860,023	861,222	862,272	876,083	889,967	834,033
Farm Wage and Salary Employment...............................	7,661	6,789	7,461	8,350	7,261	7,435	6,929	7,233
Nonfarm Wage and Salary Employment..........................	838,834	845,559	852,562	852,872	855,011	868,648	883,038	826,800
Private wage and salary employment..........................	627,979	636,207	643,993	644,350	648,726	662,478	675,090	625,136
Forestry, fishing, and related activities......................	3,029	3,369	3,534	3,617	3,549	3,491	3,447	3,228
Mining..	25,846	27,679	25,328	19,693	20,925	24,446	25,824	19,860
Utilities..	4,446	4,418	4,384	4,441	4,353	4,316	4,215	4,155
Construction..	43,387	43,838	44,627	44,365	46,562	48,374	51,257	49,745
Manufacturing..	29,109	28,019	27,818	26,847	26,412	27,159	28,502	27,243
Durable goods manufacturing..............................	18,293	17,293	16,880	15,621	15,040	15,325	15,840	14,987
Nondurable goods manufacturing..........................	10,816	10,726	10,938	11,226	11,372	11,834	12,662	12,256
Wholesale trade	21,669	21,716	21,544	21,516	21,174	21,082	21,449	20,266
Retail trade..	92,659	93,371	94,387	93,999	91,813	92,021	90,296	87,133
Transportation and warehousing............................	19,283	19,851	20,275	19,509	19,754	21,106	21,517	20,944
Information	13,085	12,564	12,735	13,063	12,421	12,012	11,171	9,082
Finance and insurance	22,277	22,870	23,173	23,476	23,978	24,089	24,648	24,271
Real estate and rental and leasing.........................	10,112	10,159	10,267	10,224	10,145	10,506	10,961	10,340
Professional, scientific, and technical services	52,576	53,006	53,958	54,674	56,148	57,747	60,274	60,603
Management of companies and enterprises................	5,081	5,055	5,177	5,312	5,383	5,649	5,821	5,565
Administrative and waste services.........................	41,829	41,799	41,424	41,813	43,432	44,273	45,914	42,138
Educational services	10,306	10,253	10,138	10,081	10,065	9,582	9,841	8,707
Health care and social assistance..........................	108,216	109,707	114,570	119,340	119,784	120,863	122,135	119,181
Arts, entertainment, and recreation........................	9,060	9,169	9,521	9,563	10,010	10,204	10,976	7,218
Accommodation and food services.........................	79,848	82,358	84,357	86,510	86,874	88,158	88,944	72,030
Other services, except public administration..............	36,161	37,006	36,776	36,307	35,944	37,400	37,898	33,427
Government and government enterprises...................	210,855	209,352	208,569	208,522	206,285	206,170	207,948	201,664
	Dollars							
Average Wages and Salaries by Industry	41,828	42,950	43,538	43,653	44,725	46,371	48,095	51,426
Average Farm Wages and Salaries	35,430	38,591	29,719	30,742	35,556	36,383	27,950	35,665
Average Nonfarm Wages and Salaries	41,886	42,985	43,659	43,779	44,803	46,456	48,253	51,564
Average private wages and salaries........................	40,898	41,997	42,577	42,447	43,539	45,299	47,149	50,169
Forestry, fishing, and related activities....................	23,514	23,532	24,613	26,570	27,785	30,333	32,850	35,248
Mining..	74,164	77,569	76,469	75,594	77,618	81,149	85,289	84,314
Utilities..	76,907	79,459	81,273	82,243	82,452	84,434	88,230	92,308
Construction	42,269	43,427	44,347	45,205	47,223	50,195	52,893	54,389
Manufacturing..	57,088	58,810	59,086	57,418	55,153	54,955	57,506	60,599
Durable goods manufacturing..............................	64,144	66,134	65,449	65,920	61,552	61,758	65,247	68,682
Nondurable goods manufacturing..........................	45,155	47,000	49,267	45,588	46,691	46,145	47,822	50,714
Wholesale trade	51,574	53,311	54,299	53,913	55,373	57,262	60,449	62,425
Retail trade..	27,157	27,909	28,790	29,056	29,748	30,583	30,903	32,853
Transportation and warehousing............................	49,737	52,104	52,244	50,140	52,760	56,039	57,489	57,993
Information	47,519	49,723	52,678	53,210	53,172	55,207	59,797	64,966
Finance and insurance	58,651	59,661	61,931	61,721	62,793	65,289	67,009	72,142
Real estate and rental and leasing.........................	36,786	37,863	38,619	38,090	39,900	41,420	43,172	45,484
Professional, scientific, and technical services	72,446	75,202	76,772	78,775	80,140	82,073	84,244	89,565
Management of companies and enterprises................	66,510	69,820	70,353	67,972	70,062	71,853	76,079	85,918
Administrative and waste services.........................	34,677	34,620	35,212	35,218	36,290	37,606	39,571	43,301
Educational services	32,683	32,897	33,245	34,494	34,873	37,043	37,487	42,842
Health care and social assistance..........................	40,160	40,641	41,234	41,353	42,132	43,150	44,307	46,608
Arts, entertainment, and recreation........................	22,728	24,008	24,311	23,914	24,675	26,168	28,029	32,072
Accommodation and food services.........................	18,320	18,880	19,255	19,726	20,185	21,318	22,148	21,296
Other services, except public administration..............	28,066	28,672	29,503	30,087	31,700	32,961	33,777	37,596
Government and government enterprises...................	44,832	45,989	47,001	47,894	48,779	50,175	51,838	55,887

Table NM-10. Employment Characteristics by Family Type

(Number, percent.)

Family type and labor force status	2018		2019		2020 [1]	
	Total	Families with own children under 18 years	Total	Families with own children under 18 years	Total	Families with own children under 18 years
All Families....................................	495,378	191,502	496,961	198,891	496,734	199,483
FAMILY TYPE AND LABOR FORCE STATUS						
Opposite-Sex Married-Couple Families............................	344,252	115,210	331,505	114,145	336,492	117,177
Both husband and wife in labor force.......................	40.9	58.3	41.3	60.0	42.5	59.7
Husband in labor force, wife not in labor force	22.6	32.8	23.5	30.2	23.3	30.9
Wife in labor force, husband not in labor force	9.5	5.6	9.1	6.9	9.7	6.4
Both husband and wife not in labor force.....................	25.5	2.7	24.7	2.6	24.5	3.0
Other Families	151,126	76,292	165,456	84,746	155,998	81,426
Female householder, no spouse present	70.1	71.2	70.5	71.7	69.5	70.4
In labor force...	45.5	55.5	49.2	59.4	47.0	56.6
Not in labor force	24.7	15.7	21.3	12.3	22.5	13.8
Male householder, no spouse present........................	29.9	28.8	29.5	28.3	30.5	29.6
In labor force...	22.1	25.9	22.2	25.2	22.8	25.9
Not in labor force	7.7	2.9	7.3	3.1	7.7	3.7

[1] 2020 ACS 5-Year estimates. 1-Year estimates were not released for 2020 due to the impact of COVID-19 on data collection that year. Data is not comparable to previous years, which are based on 1-year estimates.

Table NM-11. School Enrollment and Educational Attainment, 2020[1]

(Number, percent.)

Item	State	U.S.
Enrollment		
Total population 3 years and over, enrolled in school	526,666	80,497,960
Enrolled in nursery school or preschool (percent)	5.5	6.1
Enrolled in kindergarten (percent)..	4.7	5.0
Enrolled in elementary school, grades 1-8 (percent)..	42.3	40.4
Enrolled in high school, grades 9-12 (percent)...	20.7	21.0
Enrolled in college or graduate school (percent)...	26.8	27.6
Attainment		
Total population 25 years and over	1,415,298	222,836,834
Less than ninth grade (percent)	5.6	4.9
9th to 12th grade, no diploma (percent)	7.9	6.6
High school graduate, including equivalency (percent)...	26.2	26.7
Some college, no degree (percent)	23.4	20.3
Associate's degree (percent)..	8.8	8.6
Bachelor's degree (percent)...	15.8	20.2
Graduate or professional degree (percent)...	12.3	12.7
High school graduate or higher (percent)..	86.5	88.5
Bachelor's degree or higher (percent)...	28.1	32.9

[1] 2020 ACS 5-Year estimates. 1-Year estimates were not released for 2020 due to the impact of COVID-19 on data collection that year.

Table NM-12. Public School Characteristics and Educational Indicators

(Number, percent; data derived from National Center of Education Statistics.)

Item	State	U.S.
Public Elementary and Secondary Schools		
Number of regular school districts, 2018-19	89	13,452
Number of operational schools, 2019-20...	884	98,469
Percent charter schools	11.0	7.7
Total public school enrollment, Fall 2019...	331,206	50,796,445
Percent charter school enrollment	8.1	6.8
Student-teacher ratio, Fall 2019	15.2	15.9
Expenditures per student (unadjusted dollars), 2018-19	10,466	13,187
Four-year adjusted cohort graduation rate (ACGR), 2018-2019[1]...	75.1	85.8
Students eligible for free or reduced-price lunch (percent), 2019-20.......................................	71.9	52.1
English language learners (percent), Fall 2019	16.5	10.4
Students age 3 to 21 served under IDEA, part B (percent), 2020-21	17.0	14.5

Public Schools by Type, 2019-20	Number	Percent of state public schools
Total number of schools..	884	100.0
Special education...	9	1.0
Vocational education..	0	-
Alternative education...	45	5.1

[1] Adjusted Cohort Graduation Rates (ACGR) differ from Averaged Freshmen Graduation Rates (AFGR).
- = Zero or rounds to zero.

Table NM-13. Reported Voting and Registration of the Voting-Age Population, November 2020

(Numbers in thousands, percent.)

Item	Total population	Total citizen population	Registered			Voted		
			Total registered	Percent registered (total population)	Percent registered (total citizen population)	Total voted	Percent voted (total population)	Percent voted (total citizen population)
U.S. Total	252,274	231,593	168,308	66.7	72.7	154,628	61.3	66.8
State Total	1,610	1,498	1,028	63.9	68.6	938	58.3	62.6
Sex								
Male	784	732	495	63.1	67.6	450	57.4	61.4
Female	826	766	533	64.5	69.5	488	59.2	63.7
Race								
White alone...	1,340	1,249	881	65.7	70.5	812	60.6	65.0
White, non-Hispanic alone	745	741	578	77.5	78.0	542	72.7	73.1
Black alone..	34	32	24	B	B	21	B	B
Asian alone	28	15	12	B	B	12	B	B
Hispanic (of any race)	636	539	323	50.7	59.9	290	45.6	53.8
White alone or in combination	1,384	1,288	911	65.8	70.7	840	60.7	65.2
Black alone or in combination	46	44	34	B	B	29	B	B
Asian alone or in combination.................	38	25	22	B	B	22	B	B
Age								
18 to 24 years...	184	177	88	48.0	49.9	76	41.3	42.9
25 to 34 years...	284	269	175	61.7	65.2	143	50.3	53.1
35 to 44 years...	254	231	144	56.6	62.2	132	52.2	57.3
45 to 64 years...	504	455	329	65.4	72.4	312	62.0	68.7
65 years and over	384	366	291	75.8	79.5	274	71.4	74.9

B = Base is less than 75,000 and therefore too small to show the derived measure.

Table NM-14. Crime

(Number, rate per 100,000. Data are derived from the FBI Uniform Crime Reports.)

Item	State			U.S.		
	2019	2020	Percent change	2019	2020	Percent change
TOTAL POPULATION[1]	2,099,634	2,106,319	0.3	328,329,953	329,484,123	0.4
VIOLENT CRIME						
Number..	17,302	16,393	-5.3	1,250,393	1,313,105	5.0
Rate	824.0	778.3	-5.6	380.8	398.5	4.6
Murder and Nonnegligent Manslaughter						
Number..	185	164	-11.4	16,669	21,570	29.4
Rate	8.8	7.8	-11.6	5.1	6.5	28.9
Rape[2]						
Number..	1,355	1,170	-13.7	143,224	126,430	-11.7
Rate	64.5	55.5	-13.9	43.6	38.4	-12.0
Robbery						
Number..	2,477	2,086	-15.8	268,483	243,600	-9.3
Rate	118.0	99.0	-16.1	81.8	73.9	-9.6
Aggravated Assault						
Number..	13,285	12,973	-2.3	822,017	921,505	12.1
Rate	632.7	615.9	-2.7	250.4	279.7	11.7
PROPERTY CRIME						
Number..	66,744	59,859	-10.3	6,995,235	6,452,038	-7.8
Rate	3,178.8	2,841.9	-10.6	2,130.6	1,958.2	-8.1
Burglary						
Number..	14,640	13,665	-6.7	1,118,096	1,035,314	-7.4
Rate	697.3	648.8	-7.0	340.5	314.2	-7.7
Larceny-Theft						
Number..	42,749	37,188	-13.0	5,152,267	4,606,324	-10.6
Rate	2,036.0	1,765.5	-13.3	1,569.2	1,398.0	-10.9
Motor Vehicle Theft						
Number..	9,355	9,006	-3.7	724,872	810,400	11.8
Rate	445.6	427.6	-4.0	220.8	246.0	11.4

NOTE: Although arson data are included in the trend and clearance tables, sufficient data are not available to estimate totals for this offense. Therefore, no arson data are published in this table.
- = Zero or rounds to zero.
[1] Population figures are U.S. Census Bureau provisional estimates as of July 1, 2020.
[2] The figures shown in the rape (revised definition) column were estimated using the revised Uniform Crime Reporting (UCR) definition of rape.

Table NM-15. State Government Finances, 2020

(Dollar amounts in thousands, percent distribution.)

Item	Dollars	Percent distribution
Total Revenue	22,755,305	100.0
General revenue	21,251,467	93.4
Intergovernmental revenue	8,882,573	39.0
Taxes	7,150,005	31.4
General sales	3103765	13.6
Selective sales	831,241	3.7
License taxes	332,374	1.5
Individual income tax	1227926	5.4
Corporate income tax	95,556	0.4
Other taxes	1,559,143	6.9
Current charges	1,958,509	8.6
Miscellaneous general revenue	3,260,380	14.3
Utility revenue	0	-
Liquor stores revenue	0	-
Insurance trust revenue[1]	1,503,838	6.6
Total Expenditure	24,001,546	100.0
Intergovernmental expenditure	5,923,813	24.7
Direct expenditure	18,077,733	75.3
Current operation	13,599,004	56.7
Capital outlay	813,717	3.4
Insurance benefits and repayments	2,971,966	12.4
Assistance and subsidies	270,094	1.1
Interest on debt	422,952	1.8
Exhibit: Salaries and wages	2,762,679	11.5
Total Expenditure	24,001,546	100.0
General expenditure	21,027,260	87.6
Intergovernmental expenditure	5,923,813	24.7
Direct expenditure	15,103,447	62.9
General expenditure, by function:		
Education	5,939,530	24.7
Public welfare	7,267,765	30.3
Hospitals	1,355,781	5.6
Health	479,366	2.0
Highways	864,067	3.6
Police protection	163,397	0.7
Correction	528,264	2.2
Natural resources	234,458	1.0
Parks and recreation	55,541	0.2
Governmental administration	626,132	2.6
Interest on general debt	422,952	1.8
Other and unallocable	2,979,970	12.4
Utility expenditure	18,152	0.1
Liquor stores expenditure	0	-
Insurance trust expenditure	2,971,966	12.4
Debt at End of Fiscal Year	7,267,902	X
Cash and Security Holdings	66,411,901	X

X = Not applicable.
- = Zero or rounds to zero.
[1] Within insurance trust revenue, net earnings of state retirement systems is a calculated statistic (the item code in the data file is X08), and thus can be positive or negative. Net earnings is the sum of earnings on investments plus gains on investments minus losses on investments. The change made in 2002 for asset valuation from book to market value in accordance with Statement 34 of the Governmental Accounting Standards Board is reflected in the calculated statistics.

Table NM-16. State Government Tax Collections, 2021

(Dollars in thousands, percent.)

Item	Dollars	Percent distribution
Total Taxes	7,471,575	100.0
Property taxes	91,813	1.2
Sales and gross receipts	3,822,575	51.2
General sales and gross receipts	2,971,970	39.8
Selective sales and gross receipts	850,605	11.4
Alcoholic beverages	24,359	0.3
Amusements	68,021	0.9
Insurance premiums	235,054	3.1
Motor fuels	230,303	3.1
Pari-mutuels	842	-
Public utilities	34,757	0.5
Tobacco products	95,230	1.3
Other selective sales	162,039	2.2
Licenses	343,487	4.6
Alcoholic beverages	0	-
Amusements	2,364	-
Corporations in general	42,949	0.6
Hunting and fishing	27,382	0.4
Motor vehicle	213,998	2.9
Motor vehicle operators	5,004	0.1
Public utilities	1,800	-
Occupation and business, NEC	49,990	0.7
Other licenses	0	-
Income taxes	1,351,634	18.1
Individual income	1,198,906	16.0
Corporation net income	152,728	2.0
Other taxes	1,862,066	24.9
Death and gift	X	-
Documentary and stock transfer	X	-
Severance	1,804,377	24.1
Taxes, NEC	57,689	-

- = Zero or rounds to zero.

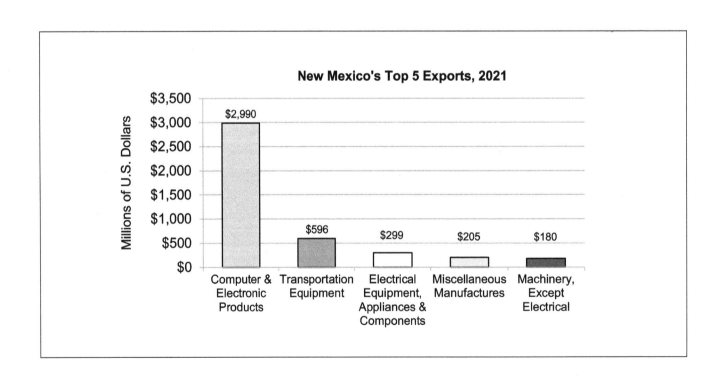

New Mexico's Top 5 Exports, 2021

NEW YORK

Facts and Figures

Location: Northeastern United States; bordered on the N by Canada (Ontario and Quebec) and Lake Ontario; on the E by Vermont, Massachusetts, and Connecticut; on the S by New Jersey and Pennsylvania; and on the W by Pennsylvania, Lake Erie, Canada (Ontario), and Lake Ontario

Area: 54,556 sq. mi. (141,299 sq. km.); rank—27th

Population: 19,835,913 (2021 est.); rank—4th

Principal Cities: capital—Albany; largest—New York City

Statehood: July 26, 1788; 11th state

U.S. Congress: 2 senators, 27 representatives

State Motto: *Excelsior* ("Ever upward")

State Song: "I Love New York"

State Nickname: The Empire State

Abbreviations: NY; N.Y.

State Symbols: flower—rose; tree—sugar maple; bird—bluebird

At a Glance

- With an increase in population of 2.4 percent, New York ranked 43rd for population growth from 2010 to 2021.

- In 2020, 5.4 percent of New Yorkers did not have health insurance, compared to 8.7 percent of the total U.S. population.

- New York had the 2nd lowest homeownership rate in 2021, with 53.6 percent of homes being owner-occupied.

- New York ranked 42nd among the states for property crime in 2020, with 1,410.7 incidences per 100,000 population, compared to the national average of 1,958.2 incidences per 100,000 population.

- New York had the 3rd highest GDP of all states in 2021 ($1.5 trillion).

Table NY-1. Population by Age, Sex, Race, and Hispanic Origin

(Number, percent, except where noted.)

Sex, age, race, and Hispanic origin	2000	2010	2021	Percent change, 2010–2021
Total Population.....................................	18,976,457	19,378,102	19,835,913	2.4
Percent of total U.S. population	6.7	6.3	6.0	X
Sex				
Male..	9,146,748	9,377,147	9,695,302	3.4
Female..	9,829,709	10,000,955	10,140,611	1.4
Age				
Under 5 years..	1,239,417	1,155,822	1,099,062	-4.9
5 to 19 years..	3,971,834	3,741,689	3,511,816	-6.1
20 to 64 years.......................................	11,316,854	11,862,648	11,747,314	-1.0
65 years and over....................................	2,448,352	2,617,943	3,477,721	32.8
Median age (years)	35.9	38.0	39.7	4.5
Race and Hispanic Origin				
One race				
White	12,893,689	13,901,661	13,711,327	-1.4
Black	3,014,385	3,378,047	3,499,231	3.6
American Indian and Alaska Native	82,461	183,046	204,766	11.9
Asian	1,044,976	1,481,555	1,845,668	24.6
Native Hawaiian or Other Pacific Islander	8,818	24,000	28,858	20.2
Two or more races	590,182	409,793	546,063	33.3
Hispanic (of any race)	2,867,583	3,564,228	3,868,268	8.5

NOTE: Population figures for 2021 are July 1 estimates. The 2000 and 2010 estimates are taken from the respective censuses.
- = Zero or rounds to zero.
X = Not applicable.

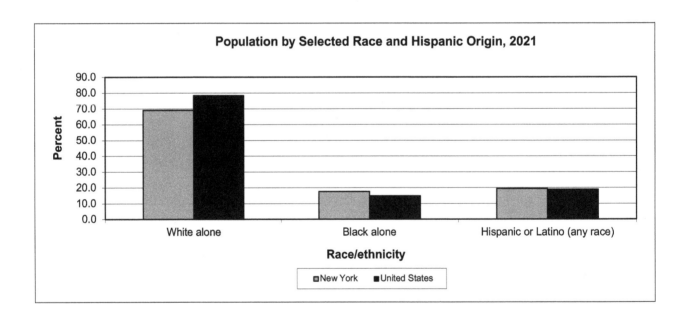

Table NY-2. Marital Status

(Number, percent distribution.)

Sex, age, race, and Hispanic origin	2000	2010	2020 [1]
Males, 15 Years and Over	7,125,715	7,586,733	7,747,167
Never married	34.7	40.5	40.5
Now married, except separated	53.3	47.6	47.8
Separated	2.7	2.2	1.8
Widowed	2.8	2.6	2.6
Divorced	6.5	7.2	7.3
Females, 15 Years and Over	7,932,161	8,283,542	8,389,718
Never married	29.0	34.8	35.4
Now married, except separated	47.1	42.8	42.8
Separated	3.7	3.1	2.7
Widowed	11.2	9.6	8.9
Divorced	8.9	9.7	10.2

[1] 2020 ACS 5-Year estimates. 1-Year estimates were not released for 2020 due to the impact of COVID-19 on data collection that year.

Table NY-3. Households and Housing Characteristics

(Number, percent, dollars.)

Item	2000	2010	2020 [1]	Average annual percent change, 2010–2020
Total Households................................	7,056,860	7,196,427	7,417,224	0.4
Family households	4,639,387	4,632,676	4,670,153	0.1
Married-couple family	3,289,514	3,210,895	3,259,898	0.2
Other family	1,349,873	1,421,781	1,410,255	-0.1
Male householder, no wife present................................	311,697	355,236	370,639	0.6
Female householder, no husband present	1,038,176	1,066,545	1,039,616	-0.4
Nonfamily households	2,417,473	2,563,751	2,747,071	1.0
Householder living alone................................	1,982,742	2,089,816	2,208,809	0.8
Householder not living alone................................	434,731	473,935	538,262	1.9
Housing Characteristics				
Total housing units................................	7,679,301	8,108,211	8,362,971	0.4
Occupied housing units	7,056,860	7,196,427	7,417,224	0.4
Owner occupied	3,739,166	3,904,123	4,014,516	0.4
Renter occupied	3,317,694	3,292,304	3,402,708	0.5
Average household size................................	2.61	2.61	2.55	-0.3
Financial Characteristics				
Median gross rent of renter-occupied housing	627	1,020	1,315	4.1
Median monthly owner costs for housing units with a mortgage	1,357	1,963	2,174	1.5
Median value of owner-occupied housing units................................	148,700	296,500	325,000	1.4

[1] 2020 ACS 5-Year estimates. 1-Year estimates were not released for 2020 due to the impact of COVID-19 on data collection that year.

Table NY-4. Migration, Origin, and Language

(Number, percent.)

Characteristic	State 2016-2020 [1]	U.S. 2016-2020 [1]
Residence 1 Year Ago		
Population 1 year and over	19,299,541	322,943,283
Same house	89.6	86.2
Different house in the U.S.	9.7	13.2
Same county	5.8	7.7
Different county	3.9	5.5
Same state	2.6	3.2
Different state	1.3	2.3
Abroad	0.7	0.6
Place of Birth		
Native born	15,142,682	282,443,680
Male	49.0	49.4
Female	51.0	50.6
Foreign born	4,372,167	44,125,628
Male	47.1	48.6
Female	52.9	51.4
Foreign born; naturalized U.S. citizen................................	2,551,469	22,456,684
Male	44.9	46.1
Female	55.1	53.9
Foreign born; not a U.S. citizen................................	1,820,698	21,668,944
Male	50.2	51.1
Female	49.8	48.9
Entered 2010 or later	21.2	22.8
Entered 2000 to 2009	23.4	25.1
Entered before 2000................................	55.5	52.1
World Region of Birth, Foreign		
Foreign-born population, excluding population born at sea	4,372,167	44,125,628
Europe	15.9	10.8
Asia	29.5	31.3
Africa	4.7	5.4
Oceania	0.4	0.6
Latin America................................	48.3	50.0
North America	1.3	1.9
Language Spoken at Home and Ability to Speak English		
Population 5 years and over................................	18,374,180	306,919,116
English only	69.7	78.5
Language other than English................................	30.3	21.5
Speaks English less than "very well"................................	13.1	8.2

[1] 2020 ACS 5-Year estimates. 1-Year estimates were not released for 2020 due to the impact of COVID-19 on data collection that year.
NA = Not available.
X = Not applicable.
- = Zero or rounds to zero.

Table NY-5. Median Income and Poverty Status, 2020[1]

(Number, percent, except as noted.)

Characteristic	State		U.S.	
	Number	Percent	Number	Percent
Median Income				
Households (dollars)..	71,117	X	64,994	X
Families (dollars)	87,270	X	80,069	X
Below Poverty Level (All People)	2,581,048	13.6	40,910,326	12.8
Sex				
Male	1,131,023	12.3	18,171,512	11.6
Female	1,450,025	14.8	22,738,814	14.0
Age				
Under 18 years...	746,203	18.7	12,598,699	17.5
Related children under 18 years......................	729,637	18.3	12,306,532	17.2
18 to 64 years...	1,475,003	12.4	23,554,920	12.1
65 years and over	359,842	11.5	4,756,707	9.3

X = Not applicable.
[1] 2020 ACS 5-Year estimates. 1-Year estimates were not released for 2020 due to the impact of COVID-19 on data collection that year.

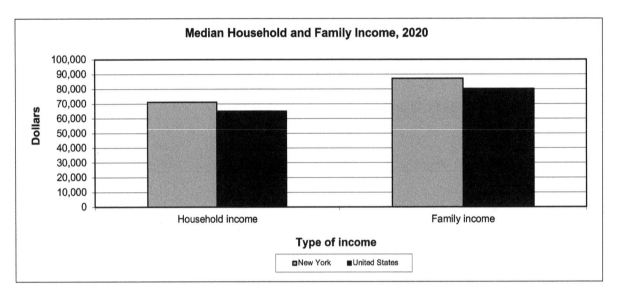

Table NY-6. Health Insurance Coverage Status for the Civilian Noninstitutionalized Population and Children Under 19 Years of Age

(Number, percent.)

Item	2011	2012	2013	2014	2015	2016	2017	2018	2019	2020 [2]
Civilian Noninstitutionalized Population	19,208,419	19,316,728	19,400,069	19,499,548	19,556,452	19,505,596	19,608,066	19,302,636	19,212,803	19,276,809
Covered by Private or Public Insurance										
Number..	17,013,070	17,213,819	17,330,548	17,802,989	18,175,904	18,322,902	18,495,124	18,261,403	18,206,275	18,239,538
Percent..	88.6	89.1	89.3	91.3	92.9	93.9	94.3	94.6	94.8	94.6
Uninsured										
Number..	2,195,349	2,102,909	2,069,521	1,696,559	1,380,548	1,182,694	1,112,942	1,041,233	1,006,528	1,037,271
Percent..	11.4	10.9	10.7	8.7	7.1	6.1	5.7	5.4	5.2	5.4
Percent in the U.S. not covered...........................	15.1	14.8	14.5	11.7	9.4	8.6	8.7	8.9	9.2	8.7
Children Under 19 Years of Age[1]	4,270,110	4,252,821	4,230,975	4,217,078	4,204,378	4,170,786	4,403,144	4,306,394	4,264,419	4,310,934
Covered by Private or Public Insurance										
Number..	4,089,276	4,085,154	4,060,192	4,079,553	4,100,735	4,069,720	4,285,641	4,199,013	4,163,624	4,202,562
Percent..	95.8	96.1	96.0	96.7	97.5	97.6	97.3	97.5	97.6	97.5
Uninsured										
Number..	180,834	167,667	170,783	137,525	103,643	101,066	117,503	107,381	100,795	108,372
Percent..	4.2	3.9	4.0	3.3	2.5	2.4	2.7	2.5	2.4	2.5
Percent in the U.S. not covered...........................	7.5	7.2	7.1	6.0	4.8	4.5	5.0	5.2	5.7	5.2

[1] Data for years prior to 2017 are for individuals under 18 years of age.
[2] 2020 ACS 5-Year estimates. 1-Year estimates were not released for 2020 due to the impact of COVID-19 on data collection that year. Data is not comparable to previous years, which are based on 1-year estimates.

Table NY-7. Employment Status by Demographic Group, 2021

(Numbers in thousands, percent.)

Characteristic	Civilian noninstitutional population	Civilian labor force		Employed		Unemployed	
		Number	Percent of population	Number	Percent of population	Number	Percent of population
Total...	15,475	9,176	59.3	8,533	55.1	643	7.0
Sex							
Male..	7,393	4,807	65.0	4,461	60.3	346	7.2
Female.......................................	8,082	4,369	54.1	4,072	50.4	297	6.8
Race, Sex, and Hispanic Origin							
White	10,890	6,508	59.8	6,117	56.2	391	6.0
Male......................................	5,267	3,469	65.9	3,267	62.0	202	5.8
Female...................................	5,623	3,040	54.1	2,851	50.7	189	6.2
Black or African American............	2,639	1,492	56.5	1,341	50.8	151	10.1
Male......................................	1,188	712	60.0	627	52.8	86	12.0
Female...................................	1,451	779	53.7	714	49.2	65	8.3
Hispanic or Latino ethnicity[1]	2,735	1,712	62.6	1,550	56.7	162	9.5
Male......................................	1,306	915	70.1	821	62.9	94	10.3
Female...................................	1,429	796	55.7	729	51.0	68	8.5
Age							
16 to 19 years............................	979	262	26.8	220	22.5	42	16.1
20 to 24 years............................	1,228	761	62.0	667	54.3	94	12.3
25 to 34 years............................	2,671	2,201	82.4	2,031	76.0	169	7.7
35 to 44 years............................	2,382	1,920	80.6	1,811	76.0	110	5.7
45 to 54 years............................	2,222	1,753	78.9	1,654	74.4	100	5.7
55 to 64 years............................	2,571	1,631	63.4	1,536	59.8	95	5.8
65 years and over........................	3,422	648	18.9	614	17.9	34	5.2

NOTE: Data in Table 7 are from the Current Population Survey (CPS) and do not match the estimates in Table 8. See notes and definitions for further information.
[1] May be of any race.

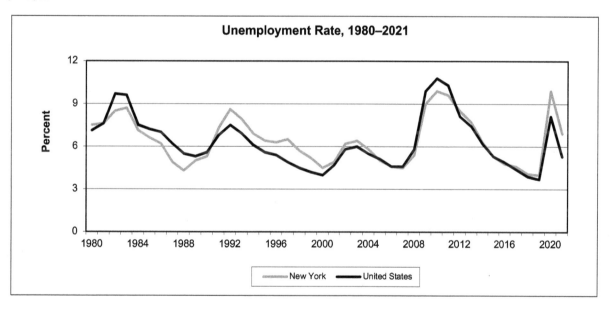

Unemployment Rate, 1980–2021

New York — United States

Table NY-8. Employment Status of the Civilian Noninstitutional Population Age 16 Years and Over

(Number, percent.)

Year	Civilian labor force	Civilian participation rate	Employed	Unemployed	Unemployment rate
2010..	9,630,297	62.6	8,790,607	839,690	8.7
2011..	9,537,752	61.6	8,741,662	796,090	8.3
2012..	9,602,599	61.7	8,775,083	827,516	8.6
2013..	9,632,949	61.6	8,880,792	752,157	7.8
2014..	9,523,567	60.7	8,925,328	598,239	6.3
2015..	9,536,519	60.7	9,035,989	500,530	5.2
2016..	9,527,021	60.6	9,062,866	464,155	4.9
2017..	9,838,170	60.8	9,382,750	455,420	4.6
2018..	9,842,263	60.7	9,440,487	401,776	4.1
2019..	9,880,211	60.8	9,502,625	377,586	3.8
2020..	9,575,032	59.1	8,631,276	943,756	9.9
2021..	9,441,458	59	8,786,280	655,178	6.9

Table NY-9. Employment and Average Wages by Industry

(Estimates are based on the 2012 North American Industry Classification System [NAICS].)

Industry	2013	2014	2015	2016	2017	2018	2019	2020
	Number of Jobs							
Wage and Salary Employment by Industry	9,051,229	9,221,011	9,385,967	9,510,338	9,623,705	9,794,133	9,914,379	8,934,657
Farm Wage and Salary Employment	22,515	22,608	22,524	21,022	20,976	21,562	21,723	20,749
Nonfarm Wage and Salary Employment	9,028,714	9,198,403	9,363,443	9,489,316	9,602,729	9,772,571	9,892,656	8,913,908
Private wage and salary employment	7,570,669	7,744,644	7,910,686	8,034,010	8,143,784	8,273,806	8,388,177	7,450,235
Forestry, fishing, and related activities	5,286	5,545	5,743	5,671	5,756	5,814	5,889	5,640
Mining	4,408	4,621	4,655	4,437	4,400	4,729	4,706	4,514
Utilities	36,174	37,697	38,330	37,643	38,082	37,718	37,132	36,301
Construction	335,998	351,440	370,582	386,441	395,718	409,981	416,147	371,865
Manufacturing	456,627	453,410	455,253	451,155	446,646	442,898	439,018	401,447
Durable goods manufacturing	266,755	265,267	266,133	262,446	257,245	256,394	254,315	232,196
Nondurable goods manufacturing	189,872	188,143	189,120	188,709	189,401	186,504	184,703	169,251
Wholesale trade	337,768	339,723	342,648	340,359	340,199	331,662	328,292	296,571
Retail trade	933,745	948,836	952,897	951,509	945,365	939,712	923,136	809,211
Transportation and warehousing	231,778	240,732	250,266	253,715	259,523	266,297	277,126	245,093
Information	261,361	265,665	267,490	268,216	271,047	276,659	279,065	269,156
Finance and insurance	511,596	520,750	528,371	530,540	533,040	536,169	544,593	538,711
Real estate and rental and leasing	186,984	189,128	195,425	199,673	203,192	207,406	209,490	196,273
Professional, scientific, and technical services	618,757	634,744	656,986	669,050	680,032	684,215	693,668	670,005
Management of companies and enterprises	138,822	142,417	143,255	142,857	144,343	144,831	145,877	132,061
Administrative and waste services	454,728	461,331	475,662	490,507	502,584	523,618	544,106	453,747
Educational services	381,614	390,058	406,604	413,045	416,976	416,079	420,824	383,042
Health care and social assistance	1,366,068	1,396,266	1,426,030	1,479,629	1,524,164	1,585,007	1,651,157	1,571,103
Arts, entertainment, and recreation	157,103	165,446	165,806	170,018	174,218	181,199	182,509	114,004
Accommodation and food services	687,430	714,197	737,033	754,615	778,692	785,232	785,487	527,677
Other services, except public administration	464,422	482,638	487,650	484,930	479,807	494,580	499,955	423,814
Government and government enterprises	1,458,045	1,453,759	1,452,757	1,455,306	1,458,945	1,498,765	1,504,479	1,463,673
	Dollars							
Average Wages and Salaries by Industry	62,417	65,173	66,820	67,348	69,947	72,320	74,667	82,070
Average Farm Wages and Salaries	26,969	28,804	23,616	29,039	26,412	25,548	19,415	20,209
Average Nonfarm Wages and Salaries	62,505	65,262	66,924	67,433	70,043	72,423	74,789	82,214
Average private wages and salaries	63,762	66,683	68,318	68,716	71,491	73,155	75,634	84,027
Forestry, fishing, and related activities	29,643	30,350	32,417	33,621	34,478	35,522	36,487	38,882
Mining	60,322	65,188	64,937	63,561	65,455	68,331	70,528	71,632
Utilities	106,103	107,817	110,484	114,262	120,084	123,702	126,527	132,948
Construction	63,422	65,249	67,511	70,104	71,465	73,251	75,611	78,189
Manufacturing	61,176	62,072	65,497	64,161	65,874	67,612	69,123	73,053
Durable goods manufacturing	66,333	66,870	70,323	69,343	71,240	73,533	75,526	78,660
Nondurable goods manufacturing	53,931	55,309	58,706	56,953	58,586	59,472	60,308	65,361
Wholesale trade	76,834	79,573	82,993	82,573	84,342	86,380	88,565	94,392
Retail trade	31,466	32,476	33,432	33,865	35,141	36,560	38,490	41,886
Transportation and warehousing	48,279	49,219	50,011	51,322	52,371	53,685	54,435	56,389
Information	102,514	110,359	115,022	120,004	119,384	129,862	135,908	154,344
Finance and insurance	197,264	216,989	213,880	211,239	231,098	226,449	230,884	247,356
Real estate and rental and leasing	60,063	63,839	66,736	69,376	71,824	74,278	76,724	81,817
Professional, scientific, and technical services	97,939	102,994	106,116	108,546	111,438	114,712	119,934	129,420
Management of companies and enterprises	142,752	143,631	149,070	140,474	147,583	151,249	155,389	164,490
Administrative and waste services	44,024	44,937	48,456	47,720	50,535	53,700	58,526	63,562
Educational services	44,855	46,228	49,656	51,080	52,438	54,779	55,328	62,229
Health care and social assistance	46,586	47,473	48,117	48,508	49,679	51,236	52,444	56,400
Arts, entertainment, and recreation	48,726	51,339	54,150	55,126	56,447	57,984	61,069	72,285
Accommodation and food services	26,627	27,726	28,247	29,729	31,109	33,212	34,995	32,356
Other services, except public administration	35,738	36,408	37,993	39,222	41,018	42,352	43,466	48,720
Government and government enterprises	55,979	57,690	59,338	60,346	61,955	68,383	70,074	72,987

Table NY-10. Employment Characteristics by Family Type

(Number, percent.)

Family type and labor force status	2018 Total	2018 Families with own children under 18 years	2019 Total	2019 Families with own children under 18 years	2020 [1] Total	2020 [1] Families with own children under 18 years
All Families..	4,632,936	1,868,562	4,636,356	1,839,198	4,670,153	1,899,744
FAMILY TYPE AND LABOR FORCE STATUS						
Opposite-Sex Married-Couple Families...........................	3,243,513	1,258,831	3,222,615	1,236,787	3,218,990	1,275,301
Both husband and wife in labor force..........................	51.9	67.7	52.6	68.8	52.8	67.9
Husband in labor force, wife not in labor force	20.2	25.4	19.7	24.5	20.5	25.4
Wife in labor force, husband not in labor force	8.6	4.7	8.8	4.6	8.7	4.8
Both husband and wife not in labor force.........................	18.1	1.7	17.7	1.5	18.0	1.9
Other Families	1,389,423	609,731	1,413,741	602,411	1,410,255	616,846
Female householder, no spouse present	74.0	77.5	73.0	76.9	73.7	77.2
In labor force..	49.6	63.1	49.1	62.1	49.3	62.2
Not in labor force	24.5	14.5	23.9	14.8	24.5	15.1
Male householder, no spouse present...........................	26.0	22.5	27.0	23.1	26.3	22.8
In labor force..	19.7	20.2	20.2	20.7	20.0	20.3
Not in labor force	6.3	2.2	6.8	2.4	6.3	2.4

[1] 2020 ACS 5-Year estimates. 1-Year estimates were not released for 2020 due to the impact of COVID-19 on data collection that year. Data is not comparable to previous years, which are based on 1-year estimates.

Table NY-11. School Enrollment and Educational Attainment, 2020[1]

(Number, percent.)

Item	State	U.S.
Enrollment		
Total population 3 years and over, enrolled in school	4,656,339	80,497,960
Enrolled in nursery school or preschool (percent)..	6.4	6.1
Enrolled in kindergarten (percent)..	4.8	5.0
Enrolled in elementary school, grades 1-8 (percent)..	38.2	40.4
Enrolled in high school, grades 9-12 (percent)..	20.3	21.0
Enrolled in college or graduate school (percent)..	30.4	27.6
Attainment		
Total population 25 years and over	13,649,157	222,836,834
Less than ninth grade (percent)..	6	4.9
9th to 12th grade, no diploma (percent)..	6.8	6.6
High school graduate, including equivalency (percent)..	25.5	26.7
Some college, no degree (percent)..	15.5	20.3
Associate's degree (percent)..	8.9	8.6
Bachelor's degree (percent)..	20.9	20.2
Graduate or professional degree (percent)..	16.5	12.7
High school graduate or higher (percent)..	87.2	88.5
Bachelor's degree or higher (percent)..	37.5	32.9

[1] 2020 ACS 5-Year estimates. 1-Year estimates were not released for 2020 due to the impact of COVID-19 on data collection that year.

Table NY-12. Public School Characteristics and Educational Indicators

(Number, percent; data derived from National Center of Education Statistics.)

Item	State	U.S.
Public Elementary and Secondary Schools		
Number of regular school districts, 2018-19	689	13,452
Number of operational schools, 2019-20..	4,819	98,469
Percent charter schools	6.6	7.7
Total public school enrollment, Fall 2019..	2,692,589	50,796,445
Percent charter school enrollment	6.0	6.8
Student-teacher ratio, Fall 2019..	12.4	15.9
Expenditures per student (unadjusted dollars), 2018-19	24,882	13,187
Four-year adjusted cohort graduation rate (ACGR), 2018-2019[1]..	82.8	85.8
Students eligible for free or reduced-price lunch (percent), 2019-20..	56.1	52.1
English language learners (percent), Fall 2019	8.9	10.4
Students age 3 to 21 served under IDEA, part B (percent), 2020-21	20.5	14.5

Public Schools by Type, 2019-20	Number	Percent of state public schools
Total number of schools..	4,819	100.0
Special education..	135	2.8
Vocational education..	49	1.0
Alternative education..	39	0.8

[1] Adjusted Cohort Graduation Rates (ACGR) differ from Averaged Freshmen Graduation Rates (AFGR).

Table NY-13. Reported Voting and Registration of the Voting-Age Population, November 2020

(Numbers in thousands, percent.)

Item	Total population	Total citizen population	Registered			Voted		
			Total registered	Percent registered (total population)	Percent registered (total citizen population)	Total voted	Percent voted (total population)	Percent voted (total citizen population)
U.S. Total	252,274	231,593	168,308	66.7	72.7	154,628	61.3	66.8
State Total	15,105	13,298	9,370	62.0	70.5	8,609	57.0	64.7
Sex								
Male	7,164	6,216	4,309	60.1	69.3	3,936	54.9	63.3
Female	7,941	7,082	5,061	63.7	71.5	4,673	58.8	66.0
Race								
White alone	10,551	9,556	6,933	65.7	72.5	6,443	61.1	67.4
White, non-Hispanic alone	8,764	8,365	6,188	70.6	74.0	5,775	65.9	69.0
Black alone.......................................	2,554	2,329	1,598	62.6	68.6	1,459	57.1	62.7
Asian alone	1,533	1,019	593	38.7	58.2	528	34.5	51.9
Hispanic (of any race)	2,330	1,608	991	42.5	61.6	883	37.9	54.9
White alone or in combination	10,786	9,748	7,086	65.7	72.7	6,543	60.7	67.1
Black alone or in combination	2,722	2,464	1,694	62.2	68.7	1,523	55.9	61.8
Asian alone or in combination	1,630	1,096	665	40.8	60.7	568	34.9	51.9
Age								
18 to 24 years....................................	1,613	1,461	816	50.6	55.9	698	43.3	47.8
25 to 34 years....................................	2,568	2,171	1,463	57.0	67.4	1,371	53.4	63.2
35 to 44 years....................................	2,677	2,191	1,563	58.4	71.3	1,457	54.4	66.5
45 to 64 years....................................	4,737	4,197	3,085	65.1	73.5	2,856	60.3	68.0
65 years and over	3,511	3,279	2,442	69.6	74.5	2,226	63.4	67.9

Table NY-14. Crime

(Number, rate per 100,000. Data are derived from the FBI Uniform Crime Reports.)

Item	State			U.S.		
	2019	2020	Percent change	2019	2020	Percent change
TOTAL POPULATION[1]	19,463,131	19,336,776	-0.6	328,329,953	329,484,123	0.4
VIOLENT CRIME						
Number..	70,260	70,339	0.1	1,250,393	1,313,105	5.0
Rate	361.0	363.8	0.8	380.8	398.5	4.6
Murder and Nonnegligent Manslaughter						
Number..	565	808	43.0	16,669	21,570	29.4
Rate	2.9	4.2	43.9	5.1	6.5	28.9
Rape[2]						
Number..	6,642	5,468	-17.7	143,224	126,430	-11.7
Rate	34.1	28.3	-17.1	43.6	38.4	-12.0
Robbery						
Number..	18,165	17,525	-3.5	268,483	243,600	-9.3
Rate	93.3	90.6	-2.9	81.8	73.9	-9.6
Aggravated Assault						
Number..	44,888	46,538	3.7	822,017	921,505	12.1
Rate	230.6	240.7	4.4	250.4	279.7	11.7
PROPERTY CRIME						
Number..	269,787	272,788	1.1	6,995,235	6,452,038	-7.8
Rate	1,386.1	1,410.7	1.8	2,130.6	1,958.2	-8.1
Burglary						
Number..	28,065	32,003	14.0	1,118,096	1,035,314	-7.4
Rate	144.2	165.5	14.8	340.5	314.2	-7.7
Larceny-Theft						
Number..	228,672	221,129	-3.3	5,152,267	4,606,324	-10.6
Rate	1,174.9	1,143.6	-2.7	1,569.2	1,398.0	-10.9
Motor Vehicle Theft						
Number..	13,050	19,656	50.6	724,872	810,400	11.8
Rate	67.0	101.7	51.6	220.8	246.0	11.4

NOTE: Although arson data are included in the trend and clearance tables, sufficient data are not available to estimate totals for this offense. Therefore, no arson data are published in this table.
- = Zero or rounds to zero.
[1] Population figures are U.S. Census Bureau provisional estimates as of July 1, 2020.
[2] The figures shown in the rape (revised definition) column were estimated using the revised Uniform Crime Reporting (UCR) definition of rape.

Table NY-15. State Government Finances, 2020

(Dollar amounts in thousands, percent distribution.)

Item	Dollars	Percent distribution
Total Revenue	211,059,104	100.0
General revenue	188,170,305	89.2
Intergovernmental revenue	70,868,703	33.6
Taxes	92,720,854	43.9
General sales	15965689	7.6
Selective sales	12,422,589	5.9
License taxes	1,823,176	0.9
Individual income tax	53659401	25.4
Corporate income tax	4,824,289	2.3
Other taxes	4,025,710	1.9
Current charges	11,691,754	5.5
Miscellaneous general revenue	12,888,994	6.1
Utility revenue	8,011,373	3.8
Liquor stores revenue	0	-
Insurance trust revenue[1]	14,877,426	7.0
Total Expenditure	227,367,234	100.0
Intergovernmental expenditure	64,784,080	28.5
Direct expenditure	162,583,154	71.5
Current operation	114,412,000	50.3
Capital outlay	12,864,864	5.7
Insurance benefits and repayments	26,863,853	11.8
Assistance and subsidies	2,348,495	1.0
Interest on debt	6,093,942	2.7
Exhibit: Salaries and wages	19,080,318	8.4
Total Expenditure	227,367,234	100.0
General expenditure	182,907,296	80.4
Intergovernmental expenditure	64,784,080	28.5
Direct expenditure	118,123,216	52.0
General expenditure, by function:		
Education	49,556,575	21.8
Public welfare	79,153,989	34.8
Hospitals	6,482,900	2.9
Health	10,691,998	4.7
Highways	5,682,677	2.5
Police protection	1,144,777	0.5
Correction	3,512,233	1.5
Natural resources	632,170	0.3
Parks and recreation	828,307	0.4
Governmental administration	6,544,521	2.9
Interest on general debt	4,308,781	1.9
Other and unallocable	10,803,463	4.8
Utility expenditure	20,961,743	9.9
Liquor stores expenditure	0	-
Insurance trust expenditure	26,863,853	11.8
Debt at End of Fiscal Year	156,004,196	X
Cash and Security Holdings	462,018,709	X

X = Not applicable.
- = Zero or rounds to zero.
[1] Within insurance trust revenue, net earnings of state retirement systems is a calculated statistic (the item code in the data file is X08), and thus can be positive or negative. Net earnings is the sum of earnings on investments plus gains on investments minus losses on investments. The change made in 2002 for asset valuation from book to market value in accordance with Statement 34 of the Governmental Accounting Standards Board is reflected in the calculated statistics.

Table NY-16. State Government Tax Collections, 2021

(Dollars in thousands, percent.)

Item	Dollars	Percent distribution
Total Taxes	93,503,736	100.0
Property taxes	X	-
Sales and gross receipts	27,164,353	29.1
General sales and gross receipts	15,612,861	16.7
Selective sales and gross receipts	11,551,492	12.4
Alcoholic beverages	271,087	0.3
Amusements	76	-
Insurance premiums	2,078,985	2.2
Motor fuels	1,465,180	1.6
Pari-mutuels	13,939	-
Public utilities	792,610	0.8
Tobacco products	1,006,782	1.1
Other selective sales	5,922,833	6.3
Licenses	1,793,375	1.9
Alcoholic beverages	55,626	0.1
Amusements	X	-
Corporations in general	879	-
Hunting and fishing	40,184	-
Motor vehicle	1,419,382	1.5
Motor vehicle operators	134,842	0.1
Public utilities	20,818	-
Occupation and business, NEC	120,914	0.1
Other licenses	730	-
Income taxes	59,950,819	64.1
Individual income	54,996,670	58.8
Corporation net income	4,954,149	5.3
Other taxes	4,595,189	4.9
Death and gift	1,537,437	1.6
Documentary and stock transfer	1,387,474	1.5
Severance	X	-
Taxes, NEC	1,670,278	1.8

X = Not applicable.
- = Zero or rounds to zero.

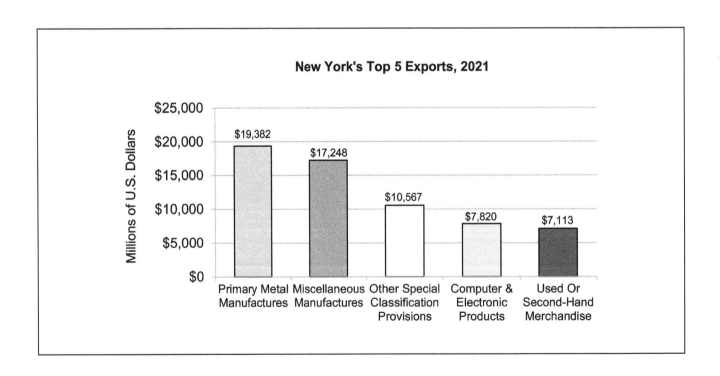

New York's Top 5 Exports, 2021

Facts and Figures

Location: Southeastern United States; bordered on the N by Virginia, on the E by the Atlantic Ocean, on the S by South Carolina and Georgia, and on the W by Tennessee

Area: 53,819 sq. mi. (139,389 sq. km.); rank—28th

Population: 10,551,162 (2021 est.); rank—9th

Principal Cities: capital—Raleigh; largest—Charlotte

Statehood: November 21, 1789; 12th state

U.S. Congress: 2 senators, 13 representatives

State Motto: *Esse quam videri* ("To be rather than to seem")

State Song: "The Old North State"

State Nicknames: The Tar Heel State; The Old North State

Abbreviations: NC; N.C.

State Symbols: flower—flowering dogwood; tree—pine; bird—cardinal

At a Glance

- With an increase in population of 10.7 percent, North Carolina ranked 16th among the states in growth from 2010 to 2021.

- North Carolina's median household income of $56,642 ranked 40th among all states in 2020, and 14.0 percent of the population lived below the poverty level, a percent which ranked 15th in the country.

- In 2020, 10.7 percent of North Carolinians did not have health insurance, compared to 8.7 percent of the entire U.S. population.

- North Carolina had the 6th lowest drug overdose rate in the country in 2020, with 15.6 drug-overdose deaths per 100,000 population.

- North Carolina's unemployment rate of 4.8 percent ranked 26th in the nation in 2021 and was lower than the national average of 5.3 percent.

Table NC-1. Population by Age, Sex, Race, and Hispanic Origin

(Number, percent, except where noted.)

Sex, age, race, and Hispanic origin	2000	2010	2021	Percent change, 2010–2021
Total Population..	8,049,313	9,535,483	10,551,162	10.7
Percent of total U.S. population	2.9	3.1	3.2	X
Sex				
Male..	3,942,695	4,645,492	5,156,255	11.0
Female...	4,106,618	4,889,991	5,394,907	10.3
Age				
Under 5 years..	539,509	632,040	589,463	-6.7
5 to 19 years...	1,653,851	1,926,640	2,000,109	3.8
20 to 64 years...	4,886,905	5,742,724	6,168,276	7.4
65 years and over..	969,048	1,234,079	1,793,314	45.3
Median age (years)	35.3	37.4	39.3	5.1
Race and Hispanic Origin				
One race				
White	5,804,656	6,898,296	7,392,234	7.2
Black..	1,737,545	2,088,362	2,349,731	12.5
American Indian and Alaska Native	99,551	147,566	168,957	14.5
Asian	113,689	215,952	358,902	66.2
Native Hawaiian or Other Pacific Islander	3,983	10,309	15,452	49.9
Two or more races	103,260	174,998	265,886	51.9
Hispanic (of any race).......................................	378,963	830,172	1,078,224	29.9

NOTE: Population figures for 2021 are July 1 estimates. The 2000 and 2010 estimates are taken from the respective censuses.
- = Zero or rounds to zero.
X = Not applicable.

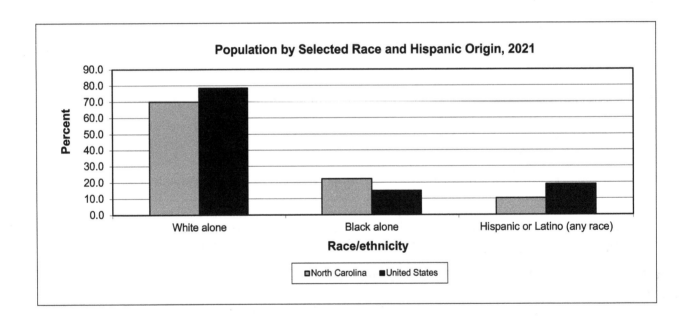

Table NC-2. Marital Status

(Number, percent distribution.)

Sex, age, race, and Hispanic origin	2000	2010	2020 [1]
Males, 15 Years and Over	3,092,380	3,678,950	4,081,467
Never married	28.2	33.3	35.0
Now married, except separated............................	58.7	51.8	50.9
Separated..	2.7	2.9	2.3
Widowed..	2.4	2.5	2.7
Divorced..	8.1	9.6	9.2
Females, 15 Years and Over	3,301,327	3,975,748	4,403,180
Never married	22.0	27.3	29.3
Now married, except separated............................	53.9	47.3	46.5
Separated..	3.3	3.5	2.7
Widowed..	10.9	9.8	9.2
Divorced..	9.9	12.1	12.2

[1] 2020 ACS 5-Year estimates. 1-Year estimates were not released for 2020 due to the impact of COVID-19 on data collection that year.

Table NC-3. Households and Housing Characteristics

(Number, percent, dollars.)

Item	2000	2010	2020 [1]	Average annual percent change, 2010–2020
Total Households..	3,132,012	3,670,859	4,031,592	1.4
Family households..	2,158,869	2,441,916	2,625,055	1.1
Married-couple family...	1,645,346	1,770,863	1,931,039	1.3
Other family...	513,523	671,053	694,016	0.5
Male householder, no wife present............................	123,526	159,752	179,599	1.8
Female householder, no husband present....................	389,997	511,301	514,417	0.1
Nonfamily households	973,144	1,228,943	1,406,537	2.1
Householder living alone...	795,271	1,022,017	1,158,923	1.9
Householder not living alone......................................	177,873	206,926	247,614	2.8
Housing Characteristics				
Total housing units..	3,523,944	4,333,479	4,687,122	1.2
Occupied housing units..	3,132,012	3,670,859	4,031,592	1.4
Owner occupied...	2,172,355	2,465,551	2,649,849	1.1
Renter occupied..	959,658	1,205,308	1,381,743	2.1
Average household size..	2.49	2.53	2.51	-0.1
Financial Characteristics				
Median gross rent of renter-occupied housing	548	731	932	3.9
Median monthly owner costs for housing units with a mortgage	985	1,250	1,328	0.9
Median value of owner-occupied housing units...................	108,300	154,200	182,100	2.6

[1] 2020 ACS 5-Year estimates. 1-Year estimates were not released for 2020 due to the impact of COVID-19 on data collection that year.

Table NC-4. Migration, Origin, and Language

(Number, percent.)

	State	U.S.
Characteristic	2016-2020 [1]	2016-2020 [1]
Residence 1 Year Ago		
Population 1 year and over	10,273,903	322,943,283
Same house	85.4	86.2
Different house in the U.S.	14.1	13.2
Same county	7.2	7.7
Different county	6.8	5.5
Same state	3.7	3.2
Different state	3.1	2.3
Abroad	0.5	0.6
Place of Birth		
Native born	9,553,625	282,443,680
Male	48.5	49.4
Female	51.5	50.6
Foreign born	832,602	44,125,628
Male	50.1	48.6
Female	49.9	51.4
Foreign born; naturalized U.S. citizen...	337,899	22,456,684
Male	47.0	46.1
Female	53.0	53.9
Foreign born; not a U.S. citizen..	494,703	21,668,944
Male	52.3	51.1
Female	47.7	48.9
Entered 2010 or later	26.5	22.8
Entered 2000 to 2009	30.0	25.1
Entered before 2000..	43.4	52.1
World Region of Birth, Foreign		
Foreign-born population, excluding population born at sea	832,602	44,125,628
Europe	10.6	10.8
Asia	28.5	31.3
Africa	7.9	5.4
Oceania	0.4	0.6
Latin America...	50.3	50.0
North America...	2.3	1.9
Language Spoken at Home and Ability to Speak English		
Population 5 years and over...	9,780,928	306,919,116
English only	88.2	78.5
Language other than English..	11.8	21.5
Speaks English less than "very well"..	4.4	8.2

[1] 2020 ACS 5-Year estimates. 1-Year estimates were not released for 2020 due to the impact of COVID-19 on data collection that year.
NA = Not available.
X = Not applicable.
- = Zero or rounds to zero.

Table NC-5. Median Income and Poverty Status, 2020[1]

(Number, percent, except as noted.)

Characteristic	State		U.S.	
	Number	Percent	Number	Percent
Median Income				
Households (dollars)...	56,642	X	64,994	X
Families (dollars)	70,978	X	80,069	X
Below Poverty Level (All People)	1,411,939	14.0	40,910,326	12.8
Sex				
Male	613,309	12.6	18,171,512	11.6
Female	798,630	15.3	22,738,814	14.0
Age				
Under 18 years..	452,423	20.0	12,598,699	17.5
Related children under 18 years...........................	442,627	19.7	12,306,532	17.2
18 to 64 years..	807,496	13.0	23,554,920	12.1
65 years and over	152,020	9.2	4,756,707	9.3

X = Not applicable.
[1] 2020 ACS 5-Year estimates. 1-Year estimates were not released for 2020 due to the impact of COVID-19 on data collection that year.

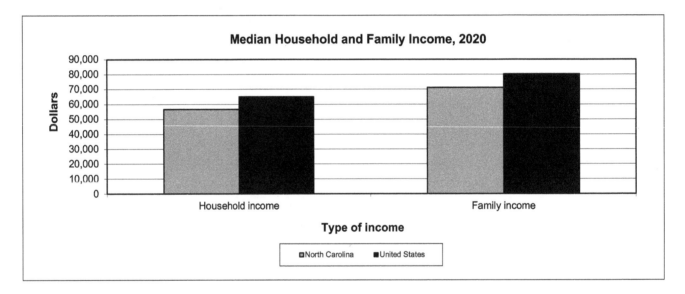

Table NC-6. Health Insurance Coverage Status for the Civilian Noninstitutionalized Population and Children Under 19 Years of Age

(Number, percent.)

Item	2011	2012	2013	2014	2015	2016	2017	2018	2019	2020 [2]
Civilian Noninstitutionalized Population	9,461,018	9,552,529	9,645,320	9,752,148	9,855,612	9,957,830	10,070,781	10,183,721	10,281,062	10,178,084
Covered by Private or Public Insurance										
Number..	7,916,111	7,970,289	8,136,322	8,476,094	8,752,825	8,919,431	8,994,798	9,091,675	9,123,782	9,093,981
Percent..	83.7	83.4	84.4	86.9	88.8	89.6	89.3	89.3	88.7	89.3
Uninsured										
Number..	1,544,907	1,582,240	1,508,998	1,276,054	1,102,787	1,038,399	1,075,983	1,092,046	1,157,280	1,084,103
Percent..	16.3	16.6	15.6	13.1	11.2	10.4	10.7	10.7	11.3	10.7
Percent in the U.S. not covered................................	15.1	14.8	14.5	11.7	9.4	8.6	8.7	8.9	9.2	8.7
Children Under 19 Years of Age[1]	2,286,872	2,281,544	2,280,549	2,286,665	2,283,011	2,292,483	2,450,911	2,446,320	2,454,735	2,446,253
Covered by Private or Public Insurance										
Number..	2,112,300	2,108,583	2,136,355	2,167,587	2,183,693	2,190,251	2,332,345	2,316,258	2,313,207	2,316,476
Percent..	92.4	92.4	93.7	94.8	95.6	95.5	95.2	94.7	94.2	94.7
Uninsured										
Number..	174,572	172,961	144,194	119,078	99,318	102,232	118,566	130,062	141,528	129,777
Percent..	7.6	7.6	6.3	5.2	4.4	4.5	4.8	5.3	5.8	5.3
Percent in the U.S. not covered................................	7.5	7.2	7.1	6.0	4.8	4.5	5.0	5.2	5.7	5.2

[1] Data for years prior to 2017 are for individuals under 18 years of age.
[2] 2020 ACS 5-Year estimates. 1-Year estimates were not released for 2020 due to the impact of COVID-19 on data collection that year. Data is not comparable to previous years, which are based on 1-year estimates.

Table NC-7. Employment Status by Demographic Group, 2021

(Numbers in thousands, percent.)

Characteristic	Civilian noninstitutional population	Civilian labor force		Employed		Unemployed	
		Number	Percent of population	Number	Percent of population	Number	Percent of population
Total..	8,460	5,024	59.4	4,795	56.7	229	4.6
Sex							
Male...	4,002	2,614	65.3	2,490	62.2	125	4.8
Female	4,457	2,410	54.1	2,305	51.7	105	4.4
Race, Sex, and Hispanic Origin							
White...	6,020	3,598	59.8	3,465	57.6	134	3.7
Male..	2,896	1,935	66.8	1,859	64.2	76	3.9
Female	3,124	1,663	53.3	1,605	51.4	58	3.5
Black or African American...................	1,829	1,055	57.7	974	53.2	82	7.7
Male..	821	473	57.6	432	52.6	41	8.6
Female	1,008	583	57.8	541	53.7	41	7.1
Hispanic or Latino ethnicity[1]	813	569	70.0	538	66.1	32	5.6
Male..	425	352	82.9	335	78.9	17	4.7
Female	388	218	56.0	203	52.2	15	6.9
Age							
16 to 19 years...............................	495	185	37.4	168	33.9	17	9.3
20 to 24 years...............................	691	464	67.1	431	62.3	33	7.1
25 to 34 years...............................	1,333	1,077	80.7	1,008	75.6	68	6.3
35 to 44 years...............................	1,377	1,092	79.3	1,049	76.2	43	3.9
45 to 54 years...............................	1,261	1,016	80.6	984	78.1	32	3.1
55 to 64 years...............................	1,356	819	60.4	798	58.8	21	2.6
65 years and over...........................	1,946	373	19.1	358	18.4	15	4.1

NOTE: Data in Table 7 are from the Current Population Survey (CPS) and do not match the estimates in Table 8. See notes and definitions for further information.
[1] May be of any race.

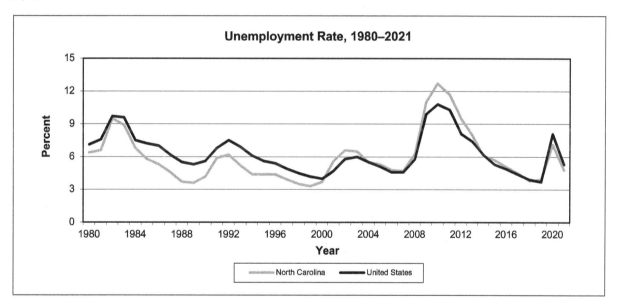

Table NC-8. Employment Status of the Civilian Noninstitutional Population Age 16 Years and Over

(Number, percent.)

Year	Civilian labor force	Civilian participation rate	Employed	Unemployed	Unemployment rate
2010................	4,633,695	63.5	4,135,783	497,912	10.7
2011................	4,657,873	62.8	4,180,071	477,802	10.3
2012................	4,720,203	62.9	4,271,383	448,820	9.5
2013................	4,701,391	61.9	4,336,379	365,012	7.8
2014................	4,698,287	61.1	4,410,647	287,640	6.1
2015................	4,763,821	61.1	4,493,882	269,939	5.7
2016................	4,844,851	61.2	4,598,456	246,395	5.1
2017................	4,865,900	61.3	4,646,212	219,688	4.5
2018................	4,915,963	61.2	4,719,018	196,945	4.0
2019................	4,999,810	61.5	4,808,270	191,540	3.8
2020................	4,848,893	59	4,505,462	343,431	7.1
2021................	4,959,672	59.6	4,721,198	238,474	4.8

Table NC-9. Employment and Average Wages by Industry

(Estimates are based on the 2012 North American Industry Classification System [NAICS].)

Industry	2013	2014	2015	2016	2017	2018	2019	2020
	Number of Jobs							
Wage and Salary Employment by Industry......................	4,298,323	4,380,948	4,494,854	4,588,883	4,657,504	4,735,868	4,826,288	4,643,484
Farm Wage and Salary Employment.............................	22,628	24,334	27,259	27,288	24,799	22,325	24,197	25,175
Nonfarm Wage and Salary Employment.........................	4,275,695	4,356,614	4,467,595	4,561,595	4,632,705	4,713,543	4,802,091	4,618,309
Private wage and salary employment..	3,416,337	3,504,358	3,615,821	3,706,737	3,772,330	3,852,963	3,936,723	3,770,160
Forestry, fishing, and related activities..............................	14,418	14,797	15,007	14,982	14,941	15,115	15,134	14,402
Mining..	2,935	2,812	2,769	2,759	2,927	3,123	3,111	3,137
Utilities..	12,460	13,645	14,045	13,947	13,908	14,518	14,243	14,287
Construction	178,220	183,470	194,223	205,634	213,525	225,986	237,270	234,963
Manufacturing..	443,466	450,002	461,737	464,990	468,299	474,813	477,526	452,825
Durable goods manufacturing............................	236,315	240,409	248,749	251,268	253,040	258,753	260,601	244,111
Nondurable goods manufacturing.......................	207,151	209,593	212,988	213,722	215,259	216,060	216,925	208,714
Wholesale trade	174,576	177,372	179,489	183,563	185,843	182,885	187,957	183,148
Retail trade...	463,568	474,567	487,154	498,286	501,478	503,496	504,709	492,334
Transportation and warehousing..................................	111,380	115,817	121,641	124,544	131,328	137,339	146,232	162,387
Information	69,843	72,592	76,099	78,813	78,879	80,071	75,991	73,430
Finance and insurance	156,921	161,047	166,284	171,484	177,742	183,622	196,677	205,743
Real estate and rental and leasing.............................	51,121	53,022	55,797	57,884	59,438	61,556	63,290	61,624
Professional, scientific, and technical services	201,402	209,216	220,955	230,394	240,886	256,916	266,365	269,324
Management of companies and enterprises.......................	77,928	80,496	81,975	83,966	82,884	83,890	84,917	82,585
Administrative and waste services..............................	272,584	284,228	290,402	295,206	295,877	298,872	302,393	289,773
Educational services	92,330	94,565	106,701	108,158	108,113	107,269	109,422	101,245
Health care and social assistance................................	472,305	476,081	483,927	493,711	504,272	515,733	525,329	509,578
Arts, entertainment, and recreation..............................	60,800	63,327	63,774	69,711	71,940	73,598	75,744	56,235
Accommodation and food services..............................	372,376	383,833	398,078	413,711	424,934	432,020	442,594	367,422
Other services, except public administration........................	187,704	193,469	195,764	194,994	195,116	202,141	207,819	195,718
Government and government enterprises.................................	859,358	852,256	851,774	854,858	860,375	860,580	865,368	848,149
	Dollars							
Average Wages and Salaries by Industry	44,731	45,865	47,351	48,252	49,867	51,835	53,438	57,014
Average Farm Wages and Salaries	25,355	22,765	20,045	24,658	27,103	23,164	26,996	25,643
Average Nonfarm Wages and Salaries	44,833	45,994	47,518	48,393	49,989	51,971	53,572	57,185
Average private wages and salaries..........................	44,799	46,075	47,572	48,405	50,176	52,167	53,811	57,858
Forestry, fishing, and related activities..............................	30,256	31,408	32,608	34,004	34,706	35,458	37,054	39,306
Mining..	48,175	50,326	56,308	60,957	65,152	63,321	67,833	67,236
Utilities..	93,365	91,011	91,068	96,026	96,315	99,403	101,541	103,494
Construction	44,768	46,445	48,536	50,959	53,273	55,488	57,884	60,174
Manufacturing..	56,286	57,017	58,344	58,478	60,219	61,781	63,076	65,414
Durable goods manufacturing............................	61,197	61,058	62,228	62,627	64,650	66,599	68,151	69,551
Nondurable goods manufacturing.......................	50,685	52,383	53,808	53,600	55,011	56,010	56,978	60,575
Wholesale trade	65,968	68,455	70,456	70,933	74,187	76,064	78,455	83,593
Retail trade...	26,866	27,342	27,921	28,399	28,954	29,788	30,985	33,646
Transportation and warehousing..................................	45,604	47,291	48,211	48,331	49,747	51,556	51,748	50,758
Information	72,322	76,075	78,498	80,443	82,712	86,533	89,340	98,728
Finance and insurance	82,818	86,739	90,658	91,746	96,770	101,530	103,801	110,988
Real estate and rental and leasing.............................	43,613	45,190	47,057	48,371	49,963	52,255	54,037	57,431
Professional, scientific, and technical services	71,333	73,882	76,181	78,250	80,836	86,101	86,653	91,275
Management of companies and enterprises.......................	97,339	102,849	108,409	106,492	111,064	111,853	116,531	122,601
Administrative and waste services..............................	32,736	33,621	34,362	35,691	37,419	38,462	40,668	43,557
Educational services	37,250	38,039	41,100	41,409	40,792	44,241	45,254	50,283
Health care and social assistance................................	43,303	44,129	45,329	46,263	48,072	49,444	51,223	54,389
Arts, entertainment, and recreation..............................	31,959	33,031	34,239	33,160	33,543	34,459	34,938	39,797
Accommodation and food services..............................	17,630	18,068	18,565	19,138	19,828	20,936	21,652	21,377
Other services, except public administration........................	30,726	31,167	32,386	33,945	35,277	36,321	37,656	41,641
Government and government enterprises.................................	44,968	45,657	47,291	48,341	49,167	51,093	52,482	54,191

Table NC-10. Employment Characteristics by Family Type

(Number, percent.)

Family type and labor force status	2018 Total	2018 Families with own children under 18 years	2019 Total	2019 Families with own children under 18 years	2020[1] Total	2020[1] Families with own children under 18 years
All Families..	2,622,295	1,065,985	2,630,365	1,073,988	2,625,055	1,084,168
FAMILY TYPE AND LABOR FORCE STATUS						
Opposite-Sex Married-Couple Families............................	1,920,236	707,580	1,926,079	701,522	1,915,378	719,449
Both husband and wife in labor force.....................................	49.8	66.7	49.8	67.5	50.1	66.7
Husband in labor force, wife not in labor force	21.5	27.4	21.2	26.5	21.7	27.6
Wife in labor force, husband not in labor force	8.0	4.0	7.9	4.0	8.3	4.2
Both husband and wife not in labor force..............................	19.9	1.5	20.2	1.5	19.9	1.5
Other Families	702,059	358,405	704,286	372,466	694,016	361,595
Female householder, no spouse present	74.5	76.8	74.0	75.6	74.1	76.0
In labor force..	51.2	63.1	51.7	63.5	51.2	63.5
Not in labor force...	23.3	13.6	22.3	12.1	22.9	12.5
Male householder, no spouse present..................................	25.5	23.2	26.0	24.4	25.9	24.0
In labor force..	20.0	21.2	19.9	22.2	19.8	22.0
Not in labor force...	5.5	2.0	6.1	2.2	6.1	2.1

[1] 2020 ACS 5-Year estimates. 1-Year estimates were not released for 2020 due to the impact of COVID-19 on data collection that year. Data is not comparable to previous years, which are based on 1-year estimates.

Table NC-11. School Enrollment and Educational Attainment, 2020[1]

(Number, percent.)

Item	State	U.S.
Enrollment		
Total population 3 years and over, enrolled in school	2,521,615	80,497,960
Enrolled in nursery school or preschool (percent)...	5.5	6.1
Enrolled in kindergarten (percent)..	4.9	5.0
Enrolled in elementary school, grades 1-8 (percent)...	40.6	40.4
Enrolled in high school, grades 9-12 (percent)	21.1	21.0
Enrolled in college or graduate school (percent)..	27.8	27.6
Attainment		
Total population 25 years and over	7,096,773	222,836,834
Less than ninth grade (percent)..	4.3	4.9
9th to 12th grade, no diploma (percent)...	7.2	6.6
High school graduate, including equivalency (percent)...	25.5	26.7
Some college, no degree (percent)..	21.1	20.3
Associate's degree (percent)..	9.9	8.6
Bachelor's degree (percent)	20.4	20.2
Graduate or professional degree (percent)...	11.6	12.7
High school graduate or higher (percent)	88.5	88.5
Bachelor's degree or higher (percent)..	32.0	32.9

[1] 2020 ACS 5-Year estimates. 1-Year estimates were not released for 2020 due to the impact of COVID-19 on data collection that year.

Table NC-12. Public School Characteristics and Educational Indicators

(Number, percent; data derived from National Center of Education Statistics.)

Item	State	U.S.
Public Elementary and Secondary Schools		
Number of regular school districts, 2018-19	120	13,452
Number of operational schools, 2019-20...	2,664	98,469
Percent charter schools	7.4	7.7
Total public school enrollment, Fall 2019...	1,560,350	50,796,445
Percent charter school enrollment	7.5	6.8
Student-teacher ratio, Fall 2019...	15.5	15.9
Expenditures per student (unadjusted dollars), 2018-19	9,799	13,187
Four-year adjusted cohort graduation rate (ACGR), 2018-2019[1]..	86.5	85.8
Students eligible for free or reduced-price lunch (percent), 2019-20...	57.8	52.1
English language learners (percent), Fall 2019	8.0	10.4
Students age 3 to 21 served under IDEA, part B (percent), 2020-21	12.8	14.5

Public Schools by Type, 2019-20	Number	Percent of state public schools
Total number of schools..	2,664	100.0
Special education..	25	0.9
Vocational education..	8	0.3
Alternative education...	76	2.9

[1] Adjusted Cohort Graduation Rates (ACGR) differ from Averaged Freshmen Graduation Rates (AFGR).

Table NC-13. Reported Voting and Registration of the Voting-Age Population, November 2020

(Numbers in thousands, percent.)

Item	Total population	Total citizen population	Registered				Voted		
			Total registered	Percent registered (total population)	Percent registered (total citizen population)		Total voted	Percent voted (total population)	Percent voted (total citizen population)
U.S. Total	252,274	231,593	168,308	66.7	72.7		154,628	61.3	66.8
State Total..	8,113	7,391	5,161	63.6	69.8		4,780	58.9	64.7
Sex									
Male	3,854	3,464	2,377	61.7	68.6		2,185	56.7	63.1
Female	4,259	3,928	2,783	65.3	70.9		2,595	60.9	66.1
Race									
White alone.......................................	5,775	5,194	3,638	63.0	70.0		3,379	58.5	65.0
White, non-Hispanic alone	4,859	4,765	3,418	70.4	71.7		3,173	65.3	66.6
Black alone.......................................	1,752	1,707	1,166	66.6	68.3		1,083	61.8	63.4
Asian alone	317	221	168	53.1	76.4		156	49.3	70.9
Hispanic (of any race)	989	492	267	27.0	54.3		240	24.2	48.8
White alone or in combination	5,894	5,313	3,725	63.2	70.1		3,449	58.5	64.9
Black alone or in combination	1,802	1,757	1,209	67.1	68.8		1,118	62.0	63.6
Asian alone or in combination..................	344	247	182	52.9	73.5		170	49.4	68.6
Age									
18 to 24 years	872	820	465	53.3	56.7		404	46.4	49.3
25 to 34 years	1,412	1,259	809	57.3	64.2		706	50.0	56.0
35 to 44 years	1,315	1,068	705	53.6	66.0		637	48.4	59.6
45 to 64 years	2,524	2,303	1,699	67.3	73.8		1,638	64.9	71.1
65 years and over	1,992	1,941	1,483	74.5	76.4		1,396	70.1	71.9

Table NC-14. Crime

(Number, rate per 100,000. Data are derived from the FBI Uniform Crime Reports.)

Item	State			U.S.		
	2019	2020	Percent change	2019	2020	Percent change
TOTAL POPULATION[1]	10,501,384	10,600,823	0.9	328,329,953	329,484,123	0.4
VIOLENT CRIME						
Number..	39,773	44,451	11.8	1,250,393	1,313,105	5.0
Rate	378.7	419.3	10.7	380.8	398.5	4.6
Murder and Nonnegligent Manslaughter						
Number..	653	852	30.5	16,669	21,570	29.4
Rate	6.2	8.0	29.3	5.1	6.5	28.9
Rape[2]						
Number..	3,364	2,922	-13.1	143,224	126,430	-11.7
Rate	32.0	27.6	-14.0	43.6	38.4	-12.0
Robbery						
Number..	7,700	7,340	-4.7	268,483	243,600	-9.3
Rate	73.3	69.2	-5.6	81.8	73.9	-9.6
Aggravated Assault						
Number..	28,056	33,337	18.8	822,017	921,505	12.1
Rate	267.2	314.5	17.7	250.4	279.7	11.7
PROPERTY CRIME						
Number..	251,135	236,026	-6.0	6,995,235	6,452,038	-7.8
Rate	2,391.4	2,226.5	-6.9	2,130.6	1,958.2	-8.1
Burglary						
Number..	54,033	49,952	-7.6	1,118,096	1,035,314	-7.4
Rate	514.5	471.2	-8.4	340.5	314.2	-7.7
Larceny-Theft						
Number..	178,332	165,554	-7.2	5,152,267	4,606,324	-10.6
Rate	1,698.2	1,561.7	-8.0	1,569.2	1,398.0	-10.9
Motor Vehicle Theft						
Number..	18,770	20,520	9.3	724,872	810,400	11.8
Rate	178.7	193.6	8.3	220.8	246.0	11.4

NOTE: Although arson data are included in the trend and clearance tables, sufficient data are not available to estimate totals for this offense. Therefore, no arson data are published in this table.
- = Zero or rounds to zero.
[1] Population figures are U.S. Census Bureau provisional estimates as of July 1, 2020.
[2] This state's agencies submitted rape data according to the legacy UCR definition of rape. Use caution when comparing this data to data from states using the revised UCR definition of rape.

Table NC-15. State Government Finances, 2020

(Dollar amounts in thousands, percent distribution.)

Item	Dollars	Percent distribution
Total Revenue	71,813,539	100.0
General revenue	60,496,994	84.2
Intergovernmental revenue	22,059,811	30.7
Taxes	28,303,127	39.4
General sales	8473886	11.8
Selective sales	4,365,724	6.1
License taxes	2,197,546	3.1
Individual income tax	12505906	17.4
Corporate income tax	662,343	0.9
Other taxes	97,722	0.1
Current charges	6,626,550	9.2
Miscellaneous general revenue	3,507,506	4.9
Utility revenue	645	-
Liquor stores revenue	0	-
Insurance trust revenue[1]	11,315,900	15.8
Total Expenditure	67,814,753	100.0
Intergovernmental expenditure	16,321,124	24.1
Direct expenditure	51,493,629	75.9
Current operation	35,880,539	52.9
Capital outlay	5,275,596	7.8
Insurance benefits and repayments	7,987,649	11.8
Assistance and subsidies	1,680,314	2.5
Interest on debt	669,531	1.0
Exhibit: Salaries and wages	9,308,746	13.7
Total Expenditure	67,814,753	100.0
General expenditure	59,783,928	88.2
Intergovernmental expenditure	16,321,124	24.1
Direct expenditure	43,462,804	64.1
General expenditure, by function:		
Education	23,336,771	34.4
Public welfare	16,975,901	25.0
Hospitals	2,717,254	4.0
Health	1,801,459	2.7
Highways	5,465,051	8.1
Police protection	657,033	1.0
Correction	1,486,104	2.2
Natural resources	748,811	1.1
Parks and recreation	225,455	0.3
Governmental administration	2,374,205	3.5
Interest on general debt	669,531	1.0
Other and unallocable	2,968,296	4.4
Utility expenditure	147,956	0.2
Liquor stores expenditure	0	-
Insurance trust expenditure	7,987,649	11.8
Debt at End of Fiscal Year	15,098,522	X
Cash and Security Holdings	145,701,868	X

X = Not applicable.
- = Zero or rounds to zero.
[1] Within insurance trust revenue, net earnings of state retirement systems is a calculated statistic (the item code in the data file is X08), and thus can be positive or negative. Net earnings is the sum of earnings on investments plus gains on investments minus losses on investments. The change made in 2002 for asset valuation from book to market value in accordance with Statement 34 of the Governmental Accounting Standards Board is reflected in the calculated statistics.

Table NC-16. State Government Tax Collections, 2021

(Dollars in thousands, percent.)

Item	Dollars	Percent distribution
Total Taxes	34,711,694	100.0
Property taxes	X	-
Sales and gross receipts	14,568,180	42.0
General sales and gross receipts	9,717,598	28.0
Selective sales and gross receipts	4,850,582	14.0
Alcoholic beverages	533,809	1.5
Amusements	16	-
Insurance premiums	725,207	2.1
Motor fuels	2,113,248	6.1
Pari-mutuels	X	-
Public utilities	233	-
Tobacco products	307,357	0.9
Other selective sales	1,170,712	3.4
Licenses	2,596,969	7.5
Alcoholic beverages	5,306	-
Amusements	176	-
Corporations in general	990,019	2.9
Hunting and fishing	39,595	0.1
Motor vehicle	994,556	2.9
Motor vehicle operators	119,437	0.3
Public utilities	18,331	0.1
Occupation and business, NEC	379,170	1.1
Other licenses	50,379	0.1
Income taxes	17,423,701	50.2
Individual income	15,908,051	45.8
Corporation net income	1,515,650	4.4
Other taxes	122,844	0.4
Death and gift	35	-
Documentary and stock transfer	121,008	0.3
Severance	1,801	-
Taxes, NEC	0	-

X = Not applicable.
- = Zero or rounds to zero.

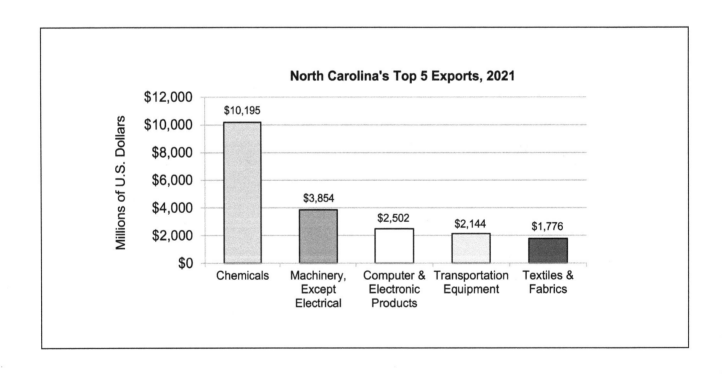

NORTH DAKOTA

Facts and Figures

Location: North central United States; bordered on the N by Canada (Manitoba and Saskatchewan), on the E by Minnesota, on the S by South Dakota, and on the W by Montana

Area: 70,700 sq. mi. (183,112 sq. km.); rank—19th

Population: 774,948 (2021 est.); rank—47th

Principal Cities: capital—Bismarck; largest—Fargo

Statehood: November 2, 1889; 39th state

U.S. Congress: 2 senators, 1 representative

State Motto: Liberty and Union, Now and Forever, One and Inseparable

State Song: "North Dakota Hymn"

State Nicknames: The Peace Garden State; The Flickertail State; The Rough Rider State

Abbreviations: ND; N.D.; N. Dak.

State Symbols: flower—wild prairie rose; tree—American elm; bird—Western meadowlark

At a Glance

- With an increase in population of 15.2 percent, North Dakota ranked 7th for population growth between 2010 and 2021.

- In 2020, 7.2 percent of North Dakotans did not have health insurance, compared to 8.7 percent of the total U.S. population.

- North Dakota had the 2nd highest birth rate in the country in 2020 (13.1 births per 1,000 population).

- In 2021, 3.7 percent of North Dakotans were unemployed, a percentage that ranked 40th in the country.

- North Dakota had the 3rd lowest childhood poverty rate in 2020, with 11.1 percent of children under 18 years old living in poverty. The national average was 17.5 percent.

Table ND-1. Population by Age, Sex, Race, and Hispanic Origin

(Number, percent, except where noted.)

Sex, age, race, and Hispanic origin	2000	2010	2021	Percent change, 2010–2021
Total Population...	642,200	672,591	774,948	15.2
Percent of total U.S. population	0.2	0.2	0.2	X
Sex				
Male..	320,524	339,864	398,409	17.2
Female...	321,676	332,727	376,539	13.2
Age				
Under 5 years..	39,400	44,595	51,390	15.2
5 to 19 years...	144,064	127,340	155,888	22.4
20 to 64 years...	364,258	403,179	443,029	9.9
65 years and over..	94,478	97,477	124,641	27.9
Median age (years)	36.2	37.0	35.7	-3.5
Race and Hispanic Origin				
One race				
White	593,181	609,136	671,664	10.3
Black	3,916	8,248	27,157	229.3
American Indian and Alaska Native	31,329	36,948	43,905	18.8
Asian	3,606	7,032	12,869	83.0
Native Hawaiian or Other Pacific Islander	230	334	713	113.5
Two or more races	7,398	10,893	18,640	71.1
Hispanic (of any race)	7,786	14,407	34,335	138.3

NOTE: Population figures for 2021 are July 1 estimates. The 2000 and 2010 estimates are taken from the respective censuses.
- = Zero or rounds to zero.
X = Not applicable.

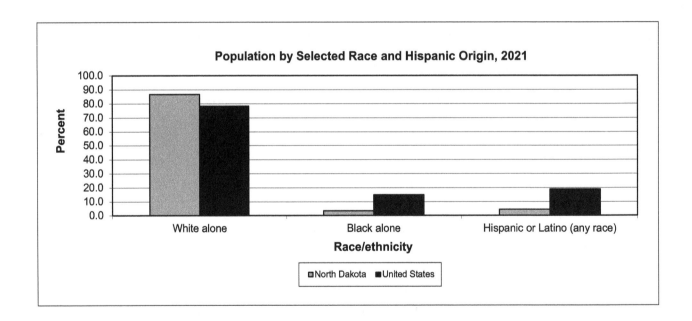

Table ND-2. Marital Status

(Number, percent distribution.)

Sex, age, race, and Hispanic origin	2000	2010	2020 [1]
Males, 15 Years and Over	253,900	278,276	311,222
Never married	32.0	35.8	36.3
Now married, except separated..	57.5	53.1	51.7
Separated...	0.6	0.6	0.8
Widowed...	2.5	2.1	2.5
Divorced...	7.3	8.4	8.7
Females, 15 Years and Over	258,381	271,462	297,556
Never married	23.2	26.6	27.0
Now married, except separated..	56.0	52.5	53.2
Separated...	0.8	0.7	0.9
Widowed...	11.7	10.1	8.8
Divorced...	8.2	10.2	10.0

[1] 2020 ACS 5-Year estimates. 1-Year estimates were not released for 2020 due to the impact of COVID-19 on data collection that year.

Table ND-3. Households and Housing Characteristics

(Number, percent, dollars.)

Item	2000	2010	2020 [1]	Average annual percent change, 2010–2020
Total Households..	257,252	280,412	320,873	2.1
Family households	166,150	171,945	189,465	1.5
Married-couple family	137,433	140,277	152,651	1.3
Other family	28,717	31,668	36,814	2.3
Male householder, no wife present..........................	8,569	8,846	12,803	6.4
Female householder, no husband present	20,148	22,822	24,011	0.7
Nonfamily households	91,002	108,467	131,408	3.0
Householder living alone..	75,420	87,883	104,366	2.7
Householder not living alone......................................	15,582	20,584	27,042	4.5
Housing Characteristics				
Total housing units..	289,677	318,099	376,597	2.6
Occupied housing units	257,252	280,412	320,873	2.1
Owner occupied	171,299	187,673	200,671	1.0
Renter occupied	85,853	92,739	120,202	4.2
Average household size..	2.41	2.32	2.29	-0.2
Financial Characteristics				
Median gross rent of renter-occupied housing	412	583	828	6.0
Median monthly owner costs for housing units with a mortgage	818	1,133	1,457	4.1
Median value of owner-occupied housing units.................	74,400	123,000	199,900	8.9

[1] 2020 ACS 5-Year estimates. 1-Year estimates were not released for 2020 due to the impact of COVID-19 on data collection that year.

Table ND-4. Migration, Origin, and Language

(Number, percent.)

Characteristic	State 2016-2020 [1]	U.S. 2016-2020 [1]
Residence 1 Year Ago		
Population 1 year and over	749,583	322,943,283
Same house	82.5	86.2
Different house in the U.S.	16.9	13.2
Same county	8.9	7.7
Different county	8.1	5.5
Same state	3.6	3.2
Different state	4.5	2.3
Abroad	0.6	0.6
Place of Birth		
Native born	728,005	282,443,680
Male	51.2	49.4
Female	48.8	50.6
Foreign born	32,389	44,125,628
Male	50.8	48.6
Female	49.2	51.4
Foreign born; naturalized U.S. citizen...	13,001	22,456,684
Male	51.1	46.1
Female	48.9	53.9
Foreign born; not a U.S. citizen...	19,388	21,668,944
Male	50.7	51.1
Female	49.3	48.9
Entered 2010 or later	43.8	22.8
Entered 2000 to 2009	31.1	25.1
Entered before 2000..	25.1	52.1
World Region of Birth, Foreign		
Foreign-born population, excluding population born at sea	32,389	44,125,628
Europe	9.2	10.8
Asia	33.4	31.3
Africa	32.5	5.4
Oceania	0.6	0.6
Latin America..	16.3	50.0
North America...	8.0	1.9
Language Spoken at Home and Ability to Speak English		
Population 5 years and over..	706,986	306,919,116
English only	94.0	78.5
Language other than English..	6.0	21.5
Speaks English less than "very well"...	1.9	8.2

[1] 2020 ACS 5-Year estimates. 1-Year estimates were not released for 2020 due to the impact of COVID-19 on data collection that year.
NA = Not available.
X = Not applicable.
- = Zero or rounds to zero.

Table ND-5. Median Income and Poverty Status, 2020[1]

(Number, percent, except as noted.)

Characteristic	State		U.S.	
	Number	Percent	Number	Percent
Median Income				
Households (dollars)..	65,315	X	64,994	X
Families (dollars)	86,798	X	80,069	X
Below Poverty Level (All People)	77,491	10.5	40,910,326	12.8
Sex				
Male	36,426	9.7	18,171,512	11.6
Female	41,065	11.4	22,738,814	14.0
Age				
Under 18 years..	19,459	11.1	12,598,699	17.5
Related children under 18 years...	18,809	10.8	12,306,532	17.2
18 to 64 years...	48,252	10.7	23,554,920	12.1
65 years and over..	9,780	8.9	4,756,707	9.3

X = Not applicable.
[1] 2020 ACS 5-Year estimates. 1-Year estimates were not released for 2020 due to the impact of COVID-19 on data collection that year.

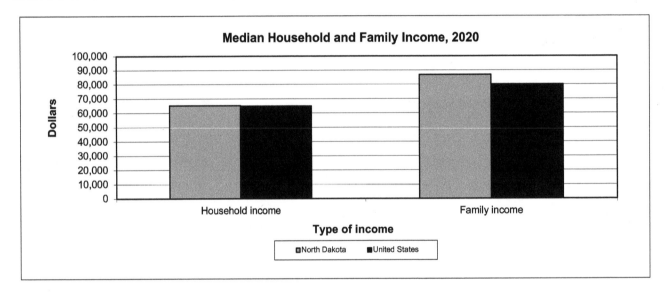

Table ND-6. Health Insurance Coverage Status for the Civilian Noninstitutionalized Population and Children Under 19 Years of Age

(Number, percent.)

Item	2011	2012	2013	2014	2015	2016	2017	2018	2019	2020 [2]
Civilian Noninstitutionalized Population	669425	684776	708,181	724,451	740,547	741,486	738,177	743,793	744,172	743,105
Covered by Private or Public Insurance										
Number................................	603,977	616,252	634,882	667,553	683,096	689,348	682,595	689,858	692,848	689,270
Percent................................	90.2	90.0	89.6	92.1	92.2	93.0	92.5	92.7	93.1	92.8
Uninsured										
Number................................	65,448	68,524	73,299	56,898	57,451	52,138	55,582	53,935	51,324	53,835
Percent................................	9.8	10.0	10.4	7.9	7.8	7.0	7.5	7.3	6.9	7.2
Percent in the U.S. not covered...................	15.1	14.8	14.5	11.7	9.4	8.6	8.7	8.9	9.2	8.7
Children Under 19 Years of Age[1]	150853	153705	160,430	167,191	170,994	174,130	183,593	185,726	187,129	188,147
Covered by Private or Public Insurance										
Number................................	141,238	143,156	147,705	155,649	157,564	160,506	169,775	174,551	172,595	174,405
Percent................................	93.6	93.1	92.1	93.1	92.1	92.2	92.5	94.0	92.2	92.7
Uninsured										
Number................................	9,615	10,549	12,725	11,542	13,430	13,624	13,818	11,175	14,534	13,742
Percent................................	6.4	6.9	7.9	6.9	7.9	7.8	7.5	6.0	7.8	7.3
Percent in the U.S. not covered...................	7.5	7.2	7.1	6.0	4.8	4.5	5.0	5.2	5.7	5.2

[1] Data for years prior to 2017 are for individuals under 18 years of age.
[2] 2020 ACS 5-Year estimates. 1-Year estimates were not released for 2020 due to the impact of COVID-19 on data collection that year. Data is not comparable to previous years, which are based on 1-year estimates.

Table ND-7. Employment Status by Demographic Group, 2021

(Numbers in thousands, percent.)

Characteristic	Civilian noninstitutional population	Civilian labor force		Employed		Unemployed	
		Number	Percent of population	Number	Percent of population	Number	Percent of population
Total..	587	402	68.5	388	66.2	13	3.3
Sex							
Male	298	220	73.8	212	71.1	8	3.6
Female	288	181	62.9	176	61.1	5	2.9
Race, Sex, and Hispanic Origin							
White	523	359	68.7	349	66.7	10	2.8
Male......................................	267	198	74.1	192	71.8	6	3.2
Female	256	161	63.0	157	61.5	4	2.4
Black or African American..............	NA	NA	NA	NA	NA	NA	NA
Male......................................	NA	NA	NA	NA	NA	NA	NA
Female	NA	NA	NA	NA	NA	NA	NA
Hispanic or Latino ethnicity[1]	NA	NA	NA	NA	NA	NA	NA
Male......................................	NA	NA	NA	NA	NA	NA	NA
Female	NA	NA	NA	NA	NA	NA	NA
Age							
16 to 19 years...........................	36	18	51	17	48	1	7
20 to 24 years...........................	58	45	77.9	43	74.3	2	4.7
25 to 34 years...........................	117	103	87.7	99	84.8	3	3.2
35 to 44 years...........................	90	81	89.9	79	87.5	2	2.6
45 to 54 years...........................	71	62	87.3	60	84.4	2	3.4
55 to 64 years...........................	91	65	71.4	63	69.0	2	3.4
65 years and over.......................	124	28	22.7	28	22.5	*	1.1

NOTE: Data in Table 7 are from the Current Population Survey (CPS) and do not match the estimates in Table 8. See notes and definitions for further information.
[1] May be of any race.
NA = Not available.
* = Fewer than 500 people.

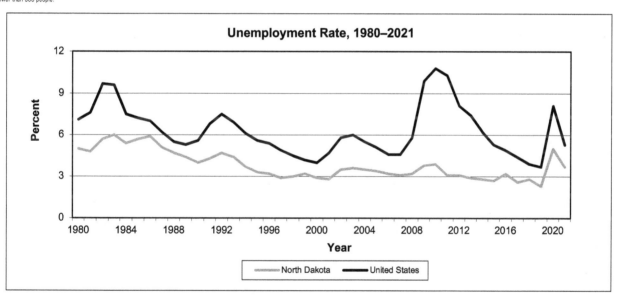

Unemployment Rate, 1980–2021

Table ND-8. Employment Status of the Civilian Noninstitutional Population Age 16 Years and Over

(Number, percent.)

Year	Civilian labor force	Civilian participation rate	Employed	Unemployed	Unemployment rate
2010..	379,062	72.8	365,041	14,021	3.7
2011..	387,383	72.6	374,434	12,949	3.3
2012..	395,490	72.6	383,888	11,602	2.9
2013..	401,518	71.9	389,928	11,590	2.9
2014..	409,503	71.8	398,783	10,720	2.6
2015..	410,764	70.8	399,296	11,468	2.8
2016..	411,778	70.9	399,001	12,777	3.1
2017..	415,765	70.7	404,901	10,864	2.6
2018..	412,764	70	403,002	9,762	2.4
2019..	415,169	70	406,304	8,865	2.1
2020..	411,550	69.2	390,504	21,046	5.1
2021..	406,187	68.5	391,255	14,932	3.7

Table ND-9. Employment and Average Wages by Industry

(Estimates are based on the 2012 North American Industry Classification System [NAICS].)

Industry	2013	2014	2015	2016	2017	2018	2019	2020
	Number of Jobs							
Wage and Salary Employment by Industry	463,244	480,665	471,312	450,659	447,667	451,269	456,960	430,442
Farm Wage and Salary Employment	6,599	7,292	5,149	4,849	5,223	5,393	5,407	6,632
Nonfarm Wage and Salary Employment	456,645	473,373	466,163	445,810	442,444	445,876	451,553	423,810
Private wage and salary employment	370,521	387,500	378,606	356,734	353,855	357,448	362,543	336,497
Forestry, fishing, and related activities	2,593	2,612	2,598	2,632	2,626	2,666	2,734	2,684
Mining	25,960	29,598	23,038	15,189	17,705	20,660	21,272	15,049
Utilities	3,593	3,702	3,831	3,843	3,781	3,669	3,446	3,325
Construction	33,205	35,617	34,940	31,876	27,381	26,637	28,646	26,001
Manufacturing	25,429	25,968	25,449	24,574	24,704	25,923	26,490	25,279
Durable goods manufacturing	17,232	17,655	17,089	16,197	16,273	17,392	17,803	16,557
Nondurable goods manufacturing	8,197	8,313	8,360	8,377	8,431	8,531	8,687	8,722
Wholesale trade	26,515	27,406	26,773	24,524	24,034	23,966	24,342	23,171
Retail trade	49,357	50,890	51,048	49,465	48,024	47,205	45,936	44,074
Transportation and warehousing	22,511	24,662	22,747	18,326	18,506	19,047	19,795	18,041
Information	6,820	6,844	6,622	6,638	6,510	6,219	6,097	5,780
Finance and insurance	17,925	18,521	18,843	18,880	18,863	18,809	18,918	18,734
Real estate and rental and leasing	5,203	5,821	5,732	5,194	5,296	5,430	5,568	5,117
Professional, scientific, and technical services	15,679	16,841	17,192	16,484	16,029	16,103	16,400	16,061
Management of companies and enterprises	5,133	5,291	5,338	5,258	5,318	5,287	3,581	3,821
Administrative and waste services	13,567	14,311	13,816	12,921	13,170	13,418	13,108	11,990
Educational services	4,184	4,129	4,303	4,451	4,540	4,331	4,507	4,001
Health care and social assistance	55,797	56,098	57,435	59,200	59,940	60,300	63,801	62,515
Arts, entertainment, and recreation	4,176	4,399	4,354	4,545	4,651	5,793	5,711	4,860
Accommodation and food services	35,227	36,365	36,292	34,988	34,913	34,840	34,969	29,647
Other services, except public administration	17,647	18,425	18,255	17,746	17,864	17,145	17,222	16,347
Government and government enterprises	86,124	85,873	87,557	89,076	88,589	88,428	89,010	87,313
	Dollars							
Average Wages and Salaries by Industry	46,835	49,904	49,718	48,041	49,441	51,448	53,246	54,327
Average Farm Wages and Salaries	38,992	40,004	33,785	38,597	38,163	36,002	45,309	33,614
Average Nonfarm Wages and Salaries	46,948	50,057	49,894	48,144	49,574	51,635	53,341	54,651
Average private wages and salaries	48,582	51,953	51,522	49,258	50,780	53,154	55,036	56,022
Forestry, fishing, and related activities	27,145	28,243	29,958	31,852	32,727	32,967	34,762	38,386
Mining	97,066	103,875	100,835	95,404	100,871	106,477	108,669	106,709
Utilities	86,453	90,554	95,223	96,277	100,355	106,186	110,372	112,378
Construction	60,161	64,853	64,917	64,240	63,000	64,549	68,106	66,695
Manufacturing	48,063	49,760	51,187	51,039	52,601	53,886	55,179	57,696
Durable goods manufacturing	48,610	49,960	50,765	50,302	51,550	53,266	54,339	56,087
Nondurable goods manufacturing	46,914	49,335	52,050	52,463	54,631	55,148	56,901	60,751
Wholesale trade	65,247	68,068	66,617	62,722	65,070	68,066	70,280	71,145
Retail trade	28,344	29,706	30,809	30,288	30,633	31,134	32,075	34,140
Transportation and warehousing	64,029	68,577	66,695	61,650	64,608	66,830	69,692	67,548
Information	55,749	58,339	59,769	63,207	65,083	70,251	71,521	79,637
Finance and insurance	54,116	56,343	59,359	60,735	63,069	66,354	69,208	73,818
Real estate and rental and leasing	53,425	59,749	56,583	48,343	50,454	53,095	54,575	53,174
Professional, scientific, and technical services	67,253	71,693	69,698	67,564	69,903	72,892	75,592	76,888
Management of companies and enterprises	69,950	76,662	81,419	77,015	80,856	85,712	102,504	99,830
Administrative and waste services	31,949	34,061	34,947	36,590	37,986	38,948	38,611	40,199
Educational services	22,498	23,699	23,625	22,600	22,835	24,755	25,753	29,275
Health care and social assistance	44,554	46,553	49,318	49,461	50,531	51,928	53,067	55,732
Arts, entertainment, and recreation	17,346	17,591	18,437	18,079	18,366	18,679	20,120	20,766
Accommodation and food services	18,478	19,564	19,773	19,660	19,801	20,799	21,355	20,818
Other services, except public administration	30,083	31,954	33,434	33,443	34,799	37,227	38,554	41,059
Government and government enterprises	39,921	41,498	42,850	43,683	44,759	45,496	46,439	49,370

Table ND-10. Employment Characteristics by Family Type

(Number, percent.)

Family type and labor force status	2018		2019		2020 [1]	
	Total	Families with own children under 18 years	Total	Families with own children under 18 years	Total	Families with own children under 18 years
All Families..	187,919	82,024	189,509	86,211	189,465	84,213
FAMILY TYPE AND LABOR FORCE STATUS						
Opposite-Sex Married-Couple Families..........................	149,349	57,655	151,995	63,023	151,905	60,266
Both husband and wife in labor force.................	59.6	76.3	61.3	78.7	60.7	77.7
Husband in labor force, wife not in labor force	18.6	21.4	16.2	17.3	16.8	18.9
Wife in labor force, husband not in labor force.........	6.0	1.9	5.7	2.1	6.6	2.4
Both husband and wife not in labor force........	15.3	0.4	16.4	1.9	15.9	1.0
Other Families	38,570	24,369	37,514	23,188	36,814	23,683
Female householder, no spouse present	66.2	68.9	65.1	65.6	65.2	66.5
In labor force..	52.8	60.6	50.3	55.5	51.8	57.7
Not in labor force	13.4	8.2	14.7	10.1	13.4	8.8
Male householder, no spouse present........................	33.8	31.1	34.9	34.4	34.8	33.5
In labor force..	29.2	29.9	29.8	31.8	30.3	31.1
Not in labor force	4.7	1.2	5.1	2.6	4.5	2.4

[1] 2020 ACS 5-Year estimates. 1-Year estimates were not released for 2020 due to the impact of COVID-19 on data collection that year. Data is not comparable to previous years, which are based on 1-year estimates.

Table ND-11. School Enrollment and Educational Attainment, 2020[1]

(Number, percent.)

Item	State	U.S.
Enrollment		
Total population 3 years and over, enrolled in school	185,329	80,497,960
Enrolled in nursery school or preschool (percent)..	5.5	6.1
Enrolled in kindergarten (percent)..	5.1	5.0
Enrolled in elementary school, grades 1-8 (percent)..	41.2	40.4
Enrolled in high school, grades 9-12 (percent)..	17.9	21.0
Enrolled in college or graduate school (percent)..	30.3	27.6
Attainment		
Total population 25 years and over	497,525	222,836,834
Less than ninth grade (percent)...	2.7	4.9
9th to 12th grade, no diploma (percent)..	4.2	6.6
High school graduate, including equivalency (percent)..	26.1	26.7
Some college, no degree (percent)...	22.2	20.3
Associate's degree (percent)...	14.1	8.6
Bachelor's degree (percent)	22.1	20.2
Graduate or professional degree (percent)...	8.6	12.7
High school graduate or higher (percent)	93.1	88.5
Bachelor's degree or higher (percent)...	30.7	32.9

[1] 2020 ACS 5-Year estimates. 1-Year estimates were not released for 2020 due to the impact of COVID-19 on data collection that year.

Table ND-12. Public School Characteristics and Educational Indicators

(Number, percent; data derived from National Center of Education Statistics.)

Item	State	U.S.
Public Elementary and Secondary Schools		
Number of regular school districts, 2018-19	174	13,452
Number of operational schools, 2019-20...	477	98,469
Percent charter schools	0.0	7.7
Total public school enrollment, Fall 2019	116,185	50,796,445
Percent charter school enrollment	0.0	6.8
Student-teacher ratio, Fall 2019	12.5	15.9
Expenditures per student (unadjusted dollars), 2018-19	14,033	13,187
Four-year adjusted cohort graduation rate (ACGR), 2018-2019[1]............................	88.3	85.8
Students eligible for free or reduced-price lunch (percent), 2019-20.........................	30.2	52.1
English language learners (percent), Fall 2019	3.7	10.4
Students age 3 to 21 served under IDEA, part B (percent), 2020-21	14.3	14.5

Public Schools by Type, 2019-20	Number	Percent of state public schools
Total number of schools...	477	100.0
Special education	0	-
Vocational education...	0	-
Alternative education..	0	-

[1] Adjusted Cohort Graduation Rates (ACGR) differ from Averaged Freshmen Graduation Rates (AFGR).
NA = Not available.
- = Zero or rounds to zero.

Table ND-13. Reported Voting and Registration of the Voting-Age Population, November 2020

(Numbers in thousands, percent.)

Item	Total population	Total citizen population	Registered			Voted		
			Total registered	Percent registered (total population)	Percent registered (total citizen population)	Total voted	Percent voted (total population)	Percent voted (total citizen population)
U.S. Total	252,274	231,593	168,308	66.7	72.7	154,628	61.3	66.8
State Total........................	571	556	429	75.2	77.3	373	65.3	67.1
Sex								
Male	289	283	217	75.1	76.7	188	64.9	66.3
Female	282	273	212	75.3	77.8	185	65.7	67.9
Race								
White alone.........................	503	495	393	78.2	79.3	352	70.0	71.0
White, non-Hispanic alone..................	489	487	388	79.3	79.7	348	71.1	71.5
Black alone.........................	13	8	2	B	B	2	B	B
Asian alone	10	7	3	B	B	3	B	B
Hispanic (of any race)....................	16	11	6	B	B	5	B	B
White alone or in combination	512	505	400	78.2	79.3	356	69.5	70.5
Black alone or in combination..................	15	10	4	B	B	2	B	B
Asian alone or in combination..................	12	8	4	B	B	3	B	B
Age								
18 to 24 years	68	64	42	B	B	30	B	B
25 to 34 years	120	114	82	68.2	71.7	69	56.9	59.9
35 to 44 years	96	93	74	76.4	79.0	63	65.7	67.9
45 to 64 years	175	173	143	81.4	82.3	129	73.7	74.6
65 years and over	111	111	89	80.6	80.9	82	73.9	74.2

- = Zero or rounds to zero.
B = Base is less than 75,000 and therefore too small to show the derived measure.

Table ND-14. Crime

(Number, rate per 100,000. Data are derived from the FBI Uniform Crime Reports.)

Item	State			U.S.		
	2019	2020	Percent change	2019	2020	Percent change
TOTAL POPULATION[1]..	763,724	765,309	0.2	328,329,953	329,484,123	0.4
VIOLENT CRIME						
Number.........................	2,302	2,518	9.4	1,250,393	1,313,105	5.0
Rate.........................	301.4	329.0	9.2	380.8	398.5	4.6
Murder and Nonnegligent Manslaughter						
Number.........................	25	32	28.0	16,669	21,570	29.4
Rate.........................	3.3	4.2	27.7	5.1	6.5	28.9
Rape[2]						
Number.........................	464	396	-14.7	143,224	126,430	-11.7
Rate.........................	60.8	51.7	-14.8	43.6	38.4	-12.0
Robbery						
Number.........................	184	151	-17.9	268,483	243,600	-9.3
Rate.........................	24.1	19.7	-18.1	81.8	73.9	-9.6
Aggravated Assault						
Number.........................	1,629	1,939	19.0	822,017	921,505	12.1
Rate.........................	213.3	253.4	18.8	250.4	279.7	11.7
PROPERTY CRIME						
Number.........................	15,270	16,256	6.5	6,995,235	6,452,038	-7.8
Rate.........................	1,999.4	2,124.1	6.2	2,130.6	1,958.2	-8.1
Burglary						
Number.........................	2,646	3,196	20.8	1,118,096	1,035,314	-7.4
Rate.........................	346.5	417.6	20.5	340.5	314.2	-7.7
Larceny-Theft						
Number.........................	10,785	10,986	1.9	5,152,267	4,606,324	-10.6
Rate.........................	1,412.2	1,435.5	1.7	1,569.2	1,398.0	-10.9
Motor Vehicle Theft						
Number.........................	1,839	2,074	12.8	724,872	810,400	11.8
Rate.........................	240.8	271.0	12.5	220.8	246.0	11.4

NOTE: Although arson data are included in the trend and clearance tables, sufficient data are not available to estimate totals for this offense. Therefore, no arson data are published in this table.
- = Zero or rounds to zero.
[1] Population figures are U.S. Census Bureau provisional estimates as of July 1, 2020.
[2] The figures shown in the rape (revised definition) column were estimated using the revised Uniform Crime Reporting (UCR) definition of rape.

Table ND-15. State Government Finances, 2020

(Dollar amounts in thousands, percent distribution.)

Item	Dollars	Percent distribution
Total Revenue	10,214,386	100.0
General revenue	9,227,536	90.3
Intergovernmental revenue	3,205,434	31.4
Taxes	4,336,232	42.5
General sales	1067967	10.5
Selective sales	496,993	4.9
License taxes	220,690	2.2
Individual income tax	376864	3.7
Corporate income tax	81,490	0.8
Other taxes	2,092,228	20.5
Current charges	744,035	7.3
Miscellaneous general revenue	941,835	9.2
Utility revenue	0	-
Liquor stores revenue	0	-
Insurance trust revenue[1]	986,850	9.7
Total Expenditure	7,936,307	100.0
Intergovernmental expenditure	2,105,424	26.5
Direct expenditure	5,830,883	73.5
Current operation	4,083,187	51.4
Capital outlay	677,689	8.5
Insurance benefits and repayments	806,660	10.2
Assistance and subsidies	134,677	1.7
Interest on debt	128,670	1.6
Exhibit: Salaries and wages	1,097,853	13.8
Total Expenditure	7,936,307	100.0
General expenditure	7,080,876	89.2
Intergovernmental expenditure	2,105,424	26.5
Direct expenditure	4,975,452	62.7
General expenditure, by function:		
Education	2,460,335	31.0
Public welfare	1,679,815	21.2
Hospitals	52,862	0.7
Health	126,119	1.6
Highways	753,989	9.5
Police protection	39,643	0.5
Correction	118,873	1.5
Natural resources	219,072	2.8
Parks and recreation	24,990	0.3
Governmental administration	226,983	2.9
Interest on general debt	128,670	1.6
Other and unallocable	1,117,533	14.1
Utility expenditure	166,433	1.6
Liquor stores expenditure	0	-
Insurance trust expenditure	806,660	10.2
Debt at End of Fiscal Year	3,017,509	X
Cash and Security Holdings	35,778,235	X

X = Not applicable.
- = Zero or rounds to zero.
[1] Within insurance trust revenue, net earnings of state retirement systems is a calculated statistic (the item code in the data file is X08), and thus can be positive or negative. Net earnings is the sum of earnings on investments plus gains on investments minus losses on investments. The change made in 2002 for asset valuation from book to market value in accordance with Statement 34 of the Governmental Accounting Standards Board is reflected in the calculated statistics.

Table ND-16. State Government Tax Collections, 2021

(Dollars in thousands, percent.)

Item	Dollars	Percent distribution
Total Taxes	3,908,672	100.0
Property taxes	5,207	0.1
Sales and gross receipts	1,426,888	36.5
General sales and gross receipts	919,915	23.5
Selective sales and gross receipts	506,973	13.0
Alcoholic beverages	9,612	0.2
Amusements	19,616	0.5
Insurance premiums	59,178	1.5
Motor fuels	173,157	4.4
Pari-mutuels	1,663	-
Public utilities	53,465	1.4
Tobacco products	26,108	0.7
Other selective sales	164,174	4.2
Licenses	210,333	5.4
Alcoholic beverages	424	-
Amusements	2,195	0.1
Corporations in general	X	-
Hunting and fishing	18,508	0.5
Motor vehicle	117,646	3.0
Motor vehicle operators	5,386	0.1
Public utilities	4	-
Occupation and business, NEC	66,170	1.7
Other licenses	0	
Income taxes	604,162	15.5
Individual income	448,704	11.5
Corporation net income	155,458	4.0
Other taxes	1,662,082	42.5
Death and gift	X	-
Documentary and stock transfer	X	-
Severance	1,662,082	42.5
Taxes, NEC	X	-

- = Zero or rounds to zero.
X = Not applicable.

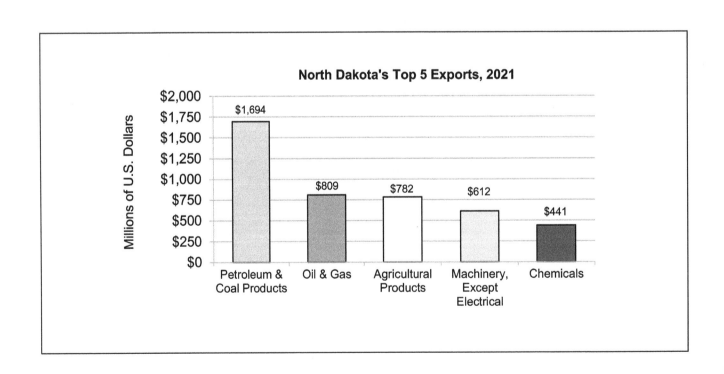

OHIO

Facts and Figures

Location: East north central United States; bordered on the N by Michigan and Lake Erie, on the E by Pennsylvania and West Virginia, on the S by West Virginia and Kentucky, and on the W by Indiana

Area: 44,825 sq. mi. (116,096 sq. km.); rank—34th

Population: 11,780,017 (2021 est.); rank—7th

Principal Cities: capital—Columbus; largest—Columbus

Statehood: March 1, 1803; 17th state

U.S. Congress: 2 senators, 16 representatives

State Motto: With God, All Things Are Possible

State Song: "Beautiful Ohio"

State Nickname: The Buckeye State

Abbreviations: OH

State Symbols: flower—scarlet carnation; tree—Ohio buckeye; bird—cardinal

At a Glance

- With an increase in population of 2.1 percent, Ohio ranked 44th among the states in growth from 2010 to 2021.

- Ohio's violent crime rate in 2020 was 308.8 per 100,000 population, compared to 398.5 for the entire nation.

- In 2020, 6.2 percent of Ohioans did not have health insurance, compared to 8.7 percent of the entire U.S. population.

- Ohio's real GDP of $615 billion ranked 7th in the nation in 2021.

- Ohio had 47.7 full-time equivalent state and local government employees per 1,000 residents in 2021, compared to the national average of 49.4 employees per 1,000 residents.

Table OH-1. Population by Age, Sex, Race, and Hispanic Origin

(Number, percent, except where noted.)

Sex, age, race, and Hispanic origin	2000	2010	2021	Percent change, 2010–2021
Total Population...	11,353,140	11,536,504	11,780,017	2.1
Percent of total U.S. population	4.0	3.7	3.5	X
Sex				
Male..	5,512,262	5,632,156	5,812,198	3.2
Female..	5,840,878	5,904,348	5,967,819	1.1
Age				
Under 5 years...	754,930	720,856	673,707	-6.5
5 to 19 years..	2,461,025	2,346,270	2,234,984	-4.7
20 to 64 years..	6,629,428	6,847,363	6,772,327	-1.1
65 years and over...	1,507,757	1,622,015	2,098,999	29.4
Median age (years)	36.2	38.8	39.6	2.1
Race and Hispanic Origin				
One race				
White...	9,645,453	9,664,524	9,560,342	-1.1
Black..	1,301,307	1,426,861	1,560,246	9.3
American Indian and Alaska Native	24,486	29,674	35,442	19.4
Asian...	132,633	196,693	312,896	59.1
Native Hawaiian or Other Pacific Islander	2,749	5,336	8,043	50.7
Two or more races	157,885	213,416	303,048	42.0
Hispanic (of any race)...	217,123	375,004	508,643	35.6

NOTE: Population figures for 2021 are July 1 estimates. The 2000 and 2010 estimates are taken from the respective censuses.
- = Zero or rounds to zero.
X = Not applicable.

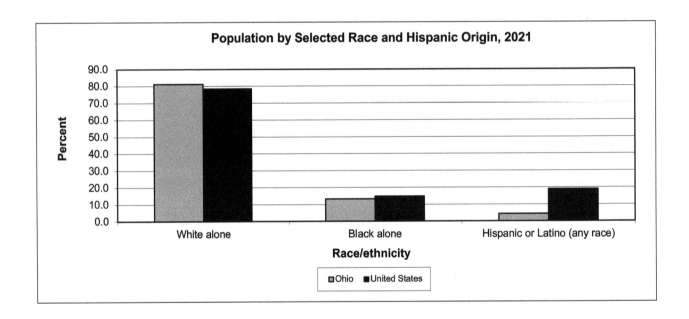

Table OH-2. Marital Status

(Number, percent distribution.)

Sex, age, race, and Hispanic origin	2000	2010	2020 [1]
Males, 15 Years and Over	4,281,736	4,487,900	4,627,531
Never married	29.2	33.5	35.8
Now married, except separated...	57.0	51.2	48.9
Separated...	1.4	1.7	1.4
Widowed...	2.7	2.9	3.1
Divorced...	9.7	10.8	10.8
Females, 15 Years and Over	4,670,985	4,809,613	4,907,751
Never married	23.5	27.9	29.7
Now married, except separated...	52.1	46.9	46.1
Separated...	1.7	2.1	1.8
Widowed...	11.1	10.1	9.4
Divorced...	11.5	12.9	13.1

[1] 2020 ACS 5-Year estimates. 1-Year estimates were not released for 2020 due to the impact of COVID-19 on data collection that year.

Table OH-3. Households and Housing Characteristics

(Number, percent, dollars.)

Item	2000	2010	2020 [1]	Average annual percent change, 2010–2020
Total Households..	4,445,773	4,525,066	4,717,226	0.6
Family households	2,993,023	2,960,107	2,952,151	-
Married-couple family	2,285,798	2,169,003	2,145,605	-0.2
Other family	707,225	791,104	806,546	0.3
Male householder, no wife present.............................	170,347	196,130	225,763	2.2
Female householder, no husband present....................	536,878	594,974	580,783	-0.3
Nonfamily households	1,452,750	1,564,959	1,765,075	1.8
Householder living alone..	1,215,614	1,315,321	1,457,645	1.5
Householder not living alone..	237,136	249,638	307,430	3.3
Housing Characteristics				
Total housing units...	4,783,051	5,128,113	5,217,090	0.2
Occupied housing units	4,445,773	4,525,066	4,717,226	0.6
Owner occupied	3,072,522	3,095,197	3,128,172	0.2
Renter occupied	1,373,251	1,429,869	1,589,054	1.6
Average household size...	2.49	2.48	2.41	-0.4
Financial Characteristics				
Median gross rent of renter-occupied housing	515	685	825	2.9
Median monthly owner costs for housing units with a mortgage	983	1,246	1,286	0.5
Median value of owner-occupied housing units.................	103,700	134,400	151,400	1.8

[1] 2020 ACS 5-Year estimates. 1-Year estimates were not released for 2020 due to the impact of COVID-19 on data collection that year.

Table OH-4. Migration, Origin, and Language

(Number, percent.)

Characteristic	State 2016-2020 [1]	U.S. 2016-2020 [1]
Residence 1 Year Ago		
Population 1 year and over	11,540,882	322,943,283
Same house	86.0	86.2
Different house in the U.S.	13.6	13.2
Same county	8.6	7.7
Different county	5.1	5.5
Same state	3.4	3.2
Different state	1.7	2.3
Abroad	0.4	0.6
Place of Birth		
Native born	11,132,571	282,443,680
Male	49.0	49.4
Female	51.0	50.6
Foreign born	542,704	44,125,628
Male	49.6	48.6
Female	50.4	51.4
Foreign born; naturalized U.S. citizen...	287,390	22,456,684
Male	47.0	46.1
Female	53.0	53.9
Foreign born; not a U.S. citizen...	255,314	21,668,944
Male	52.6	51.1
Female	47.4	48.9
Entered 2010 or later	33.6	22.8
Entered 2000 to 2009	25.7	25.1
Entered before 2000..	40.7	52.1
World Region of Birth, Foreign		
Foreign-born population, excluding population born at sea	542,704	44,125,628
Europe	18.8	10.8
Asia	43.4	31.3
Africa	15.0	5.4
Oceania	0.6	0.6
Latin America	19.5	50.0
North America	2.7	1.9
Language Spoken at Home and Ability to Speak English		
Population 5 years and over...	10,982,292	306,919,116
English only	92.8	78.5
Language other than English..	7.2	21.5
Speaks English less than "very well".......................................	2.5	8.2

[1] 2020 ACS 5-Year estimates. 1-Year estimates were not released for 2020 due to the impact of COVID-19 on data collection that year.
NA = Not available.
X = Not applicable.
- = Zero or rounds to zero.

Table OH-5. Median Income and Poverty Status, 2020[1]

(Number, percent, except as noted.)

Characteristic	State		U.S.	
	Number	Percent	Number	Percent
Median Income				
Households (dollars)	58,116	X	64,994	X
Families (dollars)	74,391	X	80,069	X
Below Poverty Level (All People)	1,546,011	13.6	40,910,326	12.8
Sex				
Male	685,678	12.4	18,171,512	11.6
Female	860,333	14.8	22,738,814	14.0
Age				
Under 18 years	486,835	19.1	12,598,699	17.5
Related children under 18 years	475,109	18.8	12,306,532	17.2
18 to 64 years	900,767	13.1	23,554,920	12.1
65 years and over	158,409	8.2	4,756,707	9.3

X = Not applicable.
[1] 2020 ACS 5-Year estimates. 1-Year estimates were not released for 2020 due to the impact of COVID-19 on data collection that year.

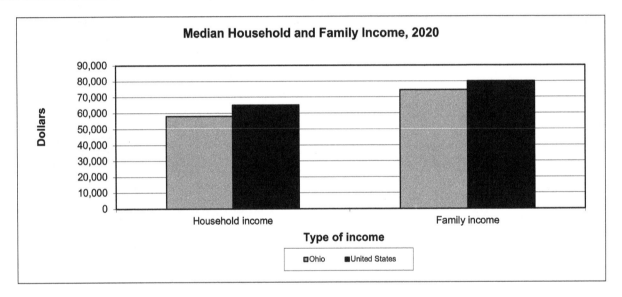

Table OH-6. Health Insurance Coverage Status for the Civilian Noninstitutionalized Population and Children Under 19 Years of Age

(Number, percent.)

Item	2011	2012	2013	2014	2015	2016	2017	2018	2019	2020 [2]
Civilian Noninstitutionalized Population	11,369,102	11,371,766	11,398,298	11,420,809	11,442,029	11,439,848	11,485,078	11,517,226	11,514,951	11,501,751
Covered by Private or Public Insurance										
Number	10,014,671	10,067,519	10,140,742	10,465,604	10,695,753	10,796,120	10,799,064	10,773,321	10,757,189	10,793,219
Percent	88.1	88.5	89.0	91.6	93.5	94.4	94.0	93.5	93.4	93.8
Uninsured										
Number	1,354,431	1,304,247	1,257,556	955,205	746,276	643,728	686,014	743,905	757,762	708,532
Percent	11.9	11.5	11.0	8.4	6.5	5.6	6.0	6.5	6.6	6.2
Percent in the U.S. not covered	15.1	14.8	14.5	11.7	9.4	8.6	8.7	8.9	9.2	8.7
Children Under 19 Years of Age[1]	2,688,340	2,656,700	2,644,952	2,631,481	2,626,771	2,605,997	2,759,296	2,748,263	2,736,050	2,747,909
Covered by Private or Public Insurance										
Number	2,531,138	2,516,034	2,503,584	2,505,342	2,511,790	2,511,444	2,633,901	2,615,696	2,605,021	2,625,949
Percent	94.2	94.7	94.7	95.2	95.6	96.4	95.5	95.2	95.2	95.6
Uninsured										
Number	157,202	140,666	141,368	126,139	114,981	94,553	125,395	132,567	131,029	121,960
Percent	5.8	5.3	5.3	4.8	4.4	3.6	4.5	4.8	4.8	4.4
Percent in the U.S. not covered	7.5	7.2	7.1	6.0	4.8	4.5	5.0	5.2	5.7	5.2

[1] Data for years prior to 2017 are for individuals under 18 years of age.
[2] 2020 ACS 5-Year estimates. 1-Year estimates were not released for 2020 due to the impact of COVID-19 on data collection that year. Data is not comparable to previous years, which are based on 1-year estimates.

Table OH-7. Employment Status by Demographic Group, 2021

(Numbers in thousands, percent.)

Characteristic	Civilian noninstitutional population	Civilian labor force		Employed		Unemployed	
		Number	Percent of population	Number	Percent of population	Number	Percent of population
Total...	9,266	5,683	61.3	5,400	58.3	283	5.0
Sex							
Male..	4,480	2,973	66.3	2,824	63.0	149	5.0
Female...	4,785	2,710	56.6	2,576	53.8	135	5.0
Race, Sex, and Hispanic Origin							
White..	7,662	4,696	61.3	4,500	58.7	196	4.2
Male..	3,736	2,471	66.1	2,364	63.3	107	4.3
Female...	3,927	2,225	56.7	2,136	54.4	89	4.0
Black or African American......................	1,139	691	60.6	621	54.5	70	10.1
Male..	522	341	65.4	306	58.7	35	10.3
Female...	618	350	56.6	315	51.0	35	9.9
Hispanic or Latino ethnicity[1]..................	372	247	66.4	236	63.5	11	4.3
Male..	178	140	78.6	137	77.0	3	2.0
Female...	NA	NA	NA	NA	NA	NA	NA
Age							
16 to 19 years.....................................	601	278	46.2	250	41.6	28	9.9
20 to 24 years.....................................	751	580	77.2	535	71.3	44	7.7
25 to 34 years.....................................	1,575	1,307	83.0	1,233	78.3	74	5.6
35 to 44 years.....................................	1,330	1,101	82.8	1,051	79.0	50	4.6
45 to 54 years.....................................	1,241	989	79.7	943	76.0	46	4.7
55 to 64 years.....................................	1,610	1,058	65.7	1,032	64.1	26	2.4
65 years and over..................................	2,159	371	17.2	356	16.5	16	4.2

NOTE: Data in Table 7 are from the Current Population Survey (CPS) and do not match the estimates in Table 8. See notes and definitions for further information.
[1] May be of any race.

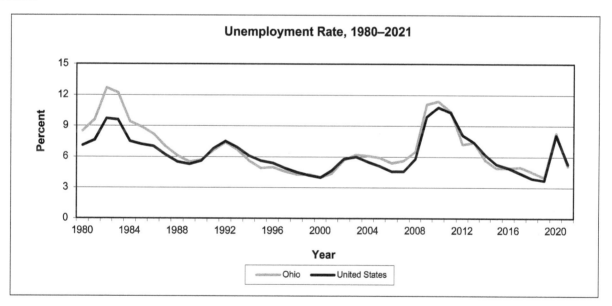

Table OH-8. Employment Status of the Civilian Noninstitutional Population Age 16 Years and Over

(Number, percent.)

Year	Civilian labor force	Civilian participation rate	Employed	Unemployed	Unemployment rate
2010...............................	5,871,473	65.5	5,267,304	604,169	10.3
2011...............................	5,773,480	64.2	5,263,728	509,752	8.8
2012...............................	5,712,475	63.3	5,290,392	422,083	7.4
2013...............................	5,706,777	63.0	5,281,459	425,318	7.5
2014...............................	5,713,176	62.8	5,381,787	331,389	5.8
2015...............................	5,710,776	62.6	5,427,850	282,926	5.0
2016...............................	5,754,480	62.8	5,464,097	290,383	5.0
2017...............................	5,818,975	63.0	5,529,479	289,496	5.0
2018...............................	5,815,549	62.7	5,553,767	261,782	4.5
2019...............................	5,871,248	63.1	5,626,326	244,922	4.2
2020...............................	5,734,179	61.5	5,263,034	471,145	8.2
2021...............................	5,736,882	61.5	5,441,879	295,003	5.1

Table OH-9. Employment and Average Wages by Industry

(Estimates are based on the 2012 North American Industry Classification System [NAICS].)

Industry	2013	2014	2015	2016	2017	2018	2019	2020
	Number of Jobs							
Wage and Salary Employment by Industry.........................	5,369,126	5,442,337	5,521,571	5,583,348	5,625,472	5,666,700	5,701,013	5,374,037
Farm Wage and Salary Employment................................	16,061	12,576	18,013	20,092	17,618	17,754	15,631	17,244
Nonfarm Wage and Salary Employment............................	5,353,065	5,429,761	5,503,558	5,563,256	5,607,854	5,648,946	5,685,382	5,356,793
Private wage and salary employment..	4,557,727	4,635,030	4,709,574	4,762,380	4,801,924	4,841,846	4,871,552	4,569,543
Forestry, fishing, and related activities.....................................	5,090	5,236	5,411	5,425	5,394	5,551	5,665	5,449
Mining..	12,142	14,398	13,722	11,019	11,100	11,806	11,531	8,972
Utilities..	18,799	18,217	19,208	19,228	19,112	19,126	18,681	18,425
Construction..	190,957	200,442	205,508	211,088	222,156	225,978	231,878	224,229
Manufacturing...	663,411	675,230	686,582	685,684	687,099	699,221	701,252	653,656
Durable goods manufacturing..	449,332	459,947	467,557	462,738	462,182	471,607	473,264	433,853
Nondurable goods manufacturing.....................................	214,079	215,283	219,025	222,946	224,917	227,614	227,988	219,803
Wholesale trade	228,843	233,781	237,114	236,645	237,338	235,786	238,166	226,445
Retail trade...	566,414	569,189	574,164	579,110	580,148	568,134	558,974	535,158
Transportation and warehousing..	175,879	181,930	191,299	193,718	196,132	208,200	219,442	230,854
Information...	75,412	72,722	71,803	71,809	71,652	70,931	69,364	63,901
Finance and insurance..	220,295	220,267	224,716	230,399	237,204	242,032	240,841	240,858
Real estate and rental and leasing......................................	60,785	61,905	63,623	64,309	64,798	65,741	67,711	64,259
Professional, scientific, and technical services	246,344	250,318	252,930	259,046	260,183	265,252	270,535	264,319
Management of companies and enterprises............................	132,404	137,524	138,957	138,015	141,689	140,553	141,245	138,232
Administrative and waste services.......................................	313,758	324,531	328,336	330,050	326,695	328,093	327,607	299,399
Educational services	113,618	114,519	115,911	117,368	119,075	113,646	114,455	101,949
Health care and social assistance.......................................	770,026	775,945	790,032	806,728	812,228	820,479	827,863	794,552
Arts, entertainment, and recreation....................................	74,169	77,706	78,010	79,434	81,053	83,232	84,703	63,098
Accommodation and food services......................................	446,771	453,318	464,355	475,727	482,971	487,308	489,346	407,180
Other services, except public administration..........................	242,610	247,852	247,893	247,578	245,897	250,777	252,293	228,608
Government and government enterprises	795,338	794,731	793,984	800,876	805,930	807,100	813,830	787,250
	Dollars							
Average Wages and Salaries by Industry	45,523	46,865	47,936	48,494	49,988	51,570	53,122	56,657
Average Farm Wages and Salaries	30,162	34,633	31,486	32,229	27,750	28,775	32,989	23,552
Average Nonfarm Wages and Salaries	45,569	46,893	47,990	48,553	50,058	51,642	53,177	56,764
Average private wages and salaries......................................	45,411	46,849	47,895	48,437	49,971	51,548	53,126	56,783
Forestry, fishing, and related activities................................	27,839	29,101	29,728	31,554	33,020	33,817	34,963	37,922
Mining..	65,213	71,149	69,419	69,963	72,797	74,963	76,176	75,936
Utilities..	90,582	93,300	96,641	96,947	100,997	105,544	106,965	110,914
Construction..	52,933	54,960	56,790	57,951	61,761	62,189	63,365	66,046
Manufacturing...	57,644	59,483	60,150	60,692	61,994	63,622	65,019	67,054
Durable goods manufacturing..	58,735	60,535	60,776	61,260	62,760	64,302	65,194	66,114
Nondurable goods manufacturing.....................................	55,353	57,237	58,813	59,514	60,420	62,211	64,656	68,908
Wholesale trade	64,668	66,543	68,357	68,783	71,094	73,808	75,584	78,676
Retail trade...	26,671	27,348	28,094	28,287	29,061	29,895	30,949	33,577
Transportation and warehousing..	47,838	49,270	50,337	50,348	52,012	53,574	53,991	54,584
Information...	63,631	64,904	66,919	68,299	70,192	72,324	74,985	82,493
Finance and insurance..	69,375	72,291	74,433	75,574	78,797	82,021	85,461	92,170
Real estate and rental and leasing......................................	42,401	44,426	45,920	46,855	48,418	50,032	51,887	54,825
Professional, scientific, and technical services	68,714	70,598	72,618	73,905	74,954	77,061	79,528	83,737
Management of companies and enterprises............................	104,995	108,850	106,428	108,894	109,831	112,698	118,227	124,945
Administrative and waste services.......................................	32,301	33,125	34,287	34,111	35,617	36,663	38,088	41,156
Educational services	30,892	31,175	31,544	31,868	32,054	33,690	34,626	38,301
Health care and social assistance.......................................	43,656	44,722	45,995	46,520	47,825	49,058	50,483	53,956
Arts, entertainment, and recreation....................................	32,078	34,110	35,066	35,583	37,444	38,206	39,027	43,991
Accommodation and food services......................................	16,727	17,289	17,867	18,351	18,844	19,868	20,563	20,060
Other services, except public administration..........................	29,115	30,080	31,320	32,394	34,299	35,465	36,392	39,692
Government and government enterprises.............................	46,480	47,153	48,553	49,242	50,576	52,206	53,482	56,654

Table OH-10. Employment Characteristics by Family Type

(Number, percent.)

Family type and labor force status	2018		2019		2020 [1]	
	Total	Families with own children under 18 years	Total	Families with own children under 18 years	Total	Families with own children under 18 years
All Families..	2,924,244	1,197,950	2,942,581	1,191,572	2,952,151	1,221,667
FAMILY TYPE AND LABOR FORCE STATUS						
Opposite-Sex Married-Couple Families...........................	2,112,567	752,951	2,126,672	755,544	2,129,907	777,751
Both husband and wife in labor force...........................	51.6	71.1	51.6	70.3	52.4	70.7
Husband in labor force, wife not in labor force	19.3	23.4	19.9	23.8	19.7	23.8
Wife in labor force, husband not in labor force	8.4	3.8	8.3	4.3	8.3	4.1
Both husband and wife not in labor force........................	19.8	1.3	19.5	1.1	19.6	1.4
Other Families	811,677	444,999	815,909	436,028	806,546	440,429
Female householder, no spouse present	72.0	74.0	71.6	74.2	72.0	73.6
In labor force..	50.7	62.1	50.1	62.1	50.5	61.5
Not in labor force	21.3	11.9	21.5	12.1	21.5	12.1
Male householder, no spouse present........................	28.0	26.0	28.4	25.8	28.0	26.4
In labor force..	21.7	23.3	21.4	23.0	21.7	23.7
Not in labor force	6.4	2.7	7.0	2.8	6.3	2.6

[1] 2020 ACS 5-Year estimates. 1-Year estimates were not released for 2020 due to the impact of COVID-19 on data collection that year. Data is not comparable to previous years, which are based on 1-year estimates.

Table OH-11. School Enrollment and Educational Attainment, 2020[1]

(Number, percent.)

Item	State	U.S.
Enrollment		
Total population 3 years and over, enrolled in school	2,771,293	80,497,960
Enrolled in nursery school or preschool (percent)	6.1	6.1
Enrolled in kindergarten (percent)...	4.9	5.0
Enrolled in elementary school, grades 1-8 (percent)...	41.3	40.4
Enrolled in high school, grades 9-12 (percent)...	21.6	21.0
Enrolled in college or graduate school (percent)..	26.1	27.6
Attainment		
Total population 25 years and over	8,014,966	222,836,834
Less than ninth grade (percent)..	2.7	4.9
9th to 12th grade, no diploma (percent)..	6.5	6.6
High school graduate, including equivalency (percent)...	32.8	26.7
Some college, no degree (percent)...	20.3	20.3
Associate's degree (percent)...	8.8	8.6
Bachelor's degree (percent)	17.9	20.2
Graduate or professional degree (percent)..	10.9	12.7
High school graduate or higher (percent)..	90.8	88.5
Bachelor's degree or higher (percent)..	28.9	32.9

[1] 2020 ACS 5-Year estimates. 1-Year estimates were not released for 2020 due to the impact of COVID-19 on data collection that year.

Table OH-12. Public School Characteristics and Educational Indicators

(Number, percent; data derived from National Center of Education Statistics.)

Item	State	U.S.
Public Elementary and Secondary Schools		
Number of regular school districts, 2018-19	619	13,452
Number of operational schools, 2019-20...	3,536	98,469
Percent charter schools	8.9	7.7
Total public school enrollment, Fall 2019..	1,689,867	50,796,445
Percent charter school enrollment...	6.3	6.8
Student-teacher ratio, Fall 2019..	15.9	15.9
Expenditures per student (unadjusted dollars), 2018-19	13,433	13,187
Four-year adjusted cohort graduation rate (ACGR), 2018-2019[1]..	82.0	85.8
Students eligible for free or reduced-price lunch (percent), 2019-20..	45.5	52.1
English language learners (percent), Fall 2019	3.6	10.4
Students age 3 to 21 served under IDEA, part B (percent), 2020-21	16.5	14.5

Public Schools by Type, 2019-20	Number	Percent of state public schools
Total number of schools..	3,536	100.0
Special education	13	0.4
Vocational education	73	2.1
Alternative education..	0	-

[1] Adjusted Cohort Graduation Rates (ACGR) differ from Averaged Freshmen Graduation Rates (AFGR).
- = Zero or rounds to zero.

Table OH-13. Reported Voting and Registration of the Voting-Age Population, November 2020

(Numbers in thousands, percent.)

Item	Total population	Total citizen population	Registered			Voted		
			Total registered	Percent registered (total population)	Percent registered (total citizen population)	Total voted	Percent voted (total population)	Percent voted (total citizen population)
U.S. Total	252,274	231,593	168,308	66.7	72.7	154,628	61.3	66.8
State Total	8,951	8,740	6,733	75.2	77.0	6,128	68.5	70.1
Sex								
Male	4,311	4,211	3,219	74.7	76.4	2,913	67.6	69.2
Female	4,640	4,529	3,514	75.7	77.6	3,216	69.3	71.0
Race								
White alone..........................	7,416	7,300	5,724	77.2	78.4	5,223	70.4	71.5
White, non-Hispanic alone	7,095	7,064	5,535	78.0	78.4	5,077	71.6	71.9
Black alone..........................	1,069	1,042	758	70.9	72.8	678	63.4	65.1
Asian alone	234	167	101	43.2	60.6	96	41.0	57.5
Hispanic (of any race)	383	299	226	59.0	75.8	175	45.7	58.7
White alone or in combination	7,592	7,476	5,844	77.0	78.2	5,324	70.1	71.2
Black alone or in combination	1,181	1,153	831	70.4	72.1	738	62.5	64.0
Asian alone or in combination	260	192	126	48.7	65.8	121	46.7	63.1
Age								
18 to 24 years.......................	1,072	1,049	635	59.2	60.6	556	51.8	53.0
25 to 34 years.......................	1,551	1,465	1,077	69.5	73.5	898	57.9	61.3
35 to 44 years.......................	1,307	1,245	958	73.3	77.0	839	64.2	67.4
45 to 64 years.......................	2,978	2,952	2,348	78.8	79.5	2,186	73.4	74.1
65 years and over	2,042	2,030	1,715	84.0	84.5	1,650	80.8	81.3

Table OH-14. Crime

(Number, rate per 100,000. Data are derived from the FBI Uniform Crime Reports.)

Item	State			U.S.		
	2019	2020	Percent change	2019	2020	Percent change
TOTAL POPULATION[1]	11,696,507	11,693,217	-	328,329,953	329,484,123	0.4
VIOLENT CRIME						
Number..............................	34,618	36,104	4.3	1,250,393	1,313,105	5.0
Rate	296.0	308.8	4.3	380.8	398.5	4.6
Murder and Nonnegligent Manslaughter						
Number..............................	584	820	40.4	16,669	21,570	29.4
Rate	5.0	7.0	40.5	5.1	6.5	28.9
Rape[2]						
Number..............................	5,850	5,052	-13.6	143,224	126,430	-11.7
Rate	50.0	43.2	-13.6	43.6	38.4	-12.0
Robbery						
Number..............................	8,861	7,826	-11.7	268,483	243,600	-9.3
Rate	75.8	66.9	-11.7	81.8	73.9	-9.6
Aggravated Assault						
Number..............................	19,323	22,406	16.0	822,017	921,505	12.1
Rate	165.2	191.6	16.0	250.4	279.7	11.7
PROPERTY CRIME						
Number..............................	240,540	216,363	-10.1	6,995,235	6,452,038	-7.8
Rate	2,056.5	1,850.3	-10.0	2,130.6	1,958.2	-8.1
Burglary						
Number..............................	44,232	37,279	-15.7	1,118,096	1,035,314	-7.4
Rate	378.2	318.8	-15.7	340.5	314.2	-7.7
Larceny-Theft						
Number..............................	177,610	159,007	-10.5	5,152,267	4,606,324	-10.6
Rate	1,518.5	1,359.8	-10.4	1,569.2	1,398.0	-10.9
Motor Vehicle Theft						
Number..............................	18,698	20,077	7.4	724,872	810,400	11.8
Rate	159.9	171.7	7.4	220.8	246.0	11.4

NOTE: Although arson data are included in the trend and clearance tables, sufficient data are not available to estimate totals for this offense. Therefore, no arson data are published in this table.
- = Zero or rounds to zero.
[1] Population figures are U.S. Census Bureau provisional estimates as of July 1, 2020.
[2] The figures shown in the rape (revised definition) column were estimated using the revised Uniform Crime Reporting (UCR) definition of rape.

Table OH-15. State Government Finances, 2020

(Dollar amounts in thousands, percent distribution.)

Item	Dollars	Percent distribution
Total Revenue	110,823,653	100.0
General revenue	77,467,752	69.9
Intergovernmental revenue	30,768,979	27.8
Taxes	30,581,546	27.6
General sales	12864718	11.6
Selective sales	7,187,367	6.5
License taxes	2,174,077	2.0
Individual income tax	8284983	7.5
Corporate income tax	3,683	-
Other taxes	66,718	0.1
Current charges	9,782,330	8.8
Miscellaneous general revenue	6,334,897	5.7
Utility revenue	0	-
Liquor stores revenue	1433432	1.3
Insurance trust revenue[1]	31,922,469	28.8
Total Expenditure	97,458,562	100.0
Intergovernmental expenditure	19,306,173	19.8
Direct expenditure	78,152,389	80.2
Current operation	49,520,949	50.8
Capital outlay	4,760,493	4.9
Insurance benefits and repayments	20,680,593	21.2
Assistance and subsidies	2,279,828	2.3
Interest on debt	910,526	0.9
Exhibit: Salaries and wages	8,590,603	8.8
Total Expenditure	97,458,562	100.0
General expenditure	75,625,181	77.6
Intergovernmental expenditure	19,306,173	19.8
Direct expenditure	56,319,008	57.8
General expenditure, by function:		
Education	23,760,710	24.4
Public welfare	30,493,929	31.3
Hospitals	4,510,466	4.6
Health	2,192,912	2.3
Highways	4,703,351	4.8
Police protection	546,016	0.6
Correction	1,920,139	2.0
Natural resources	386,947	0.4
Parks and recreation	114,339	0.1
Governmental administration	2,287,087	2.3
Interest on general debt	910,526	0.9
Other and unallocable	3,627,992	3.7
Utility expenditure	45,546	-
Liquor stores expenditure	1152783	1.2
Insurance trust expenditure	20,680,593	21.2
Debt at End of Fiscal Year	30,412,376	X
Cash and Security Holdings	269,976,955	X

X = Not applicable.
- = Zero or rounds to zero.

[1] Within insurance trust revenue, net earnings of state retirement systems is a calculated statistic (the item code in the data file is X08), and thus can be positive or negative. Net earnings is the sum of earnings on investments plus gains on investments minus losses on investments. The change made in 2002 for asset valuation from book to market value in accordance with Statement 34 of the Governmental Accounting Standards Board is reflected in the calculated statistics.

Table OH-16. State Government Tax Collections, 2021

(Dollars in thousands, percent.)

Item	Dollars	Percent distribution
Total Taxes	34,909,388	100.0
Property taxes	X	-
Sales and gross receipts	22,148,518	63.4
General sales and gross receipts	14,393,197	41.2
Selective sales and gross receipts	7,755,321	22.2
Alcoholic beverages	118,746	0.3
Amusements	219,979	0.6
Insurance premiums	666,671	1.9
Motor fuels	2,524,431	7.2
Pari-mutuels	3,690	-
Public utilities	1,036,909	3.0
Tobacco products	928,292	2.7
Other selective sales	2,256,603	6.5
Licenses	2,029,060	5.8
Alcoholic beverages	52,218	0.1
Amusements	29,865	0.1
Corporations in general	277,431	0.8
Hunting and fishing	48,625	0.1
Motor vehicle	504,197	1.4
Motor vehicle operators	83,059	0.2
Public utilities	3,013	-
Occupation and business, NEC	893,836	2.6
Other licenses	136,816	0.4
Income taxes	10,668,765	30.6
Individual income	10,662,810	30.5
Corporation net income	5,955	-
Other taxes	63,045	0.2
Death and gift	62	-
Documentary and stock transfer	X	-
Severance	62,983	0.2
Taxes, NEC	0	-

X = Not applicable.
- = Zero or rounds to zero.

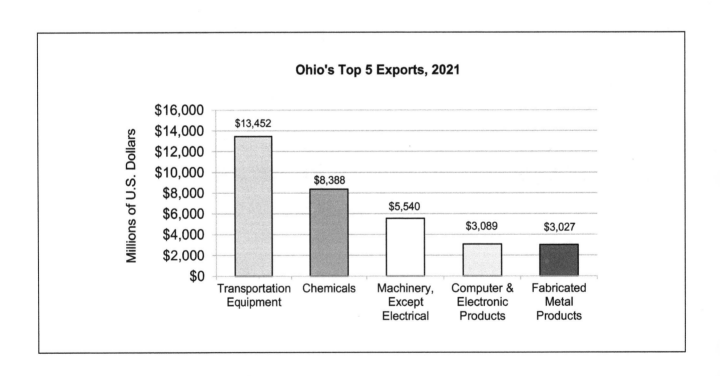

Ohio's Top 5 Exports, 2021

OKLAHOMA

Facts and Figures

Location: West south central United States; bordered on the N by Colorado and Kansas, on the E by Missouri and Arkansas, on the S by Texas, and on the W by Texas and New Mexico

Area: 69,898 sq. mi. (181,036 sq. km.); rank — 20th

Population: 3,986,639 (2021 est.); rank — 28th

Principal Cities: capital — Oklahoma City; largest — Oklahoma City

Statehood: November 16, 1907; 46th state

U.S. Congress: 2 senators, 5 representatives

State Motto: *Labor omnia vincit* ("Labor conquers all things")

State Song: "Oklahoma!"

State Nickname: The Sooner State

Abbreviations: OK; Okla.

State Symbols: flower — mistletoe; tree — redbud; bird — scissor-tailed flycatcher

At a Glance

- With an increase in population of 6.3 percent, Oklahoma ranked 24th among the states in growth from 2010 to 2021.

- Oklahoma's median household income in 2020 was $53,840, and 15.3 percent of the population lived below the poverty level.

- In 2020, 14.4 percent of Oklahomans did not have health insurance, making it the state with the 2nd highest percent of uninsured residents.

- Oklahoma's violent crime rate in 2020 was 458.6 per 100,000 population, compared to 398.5 for the entire nation.

- Its 2020 property crime rate of 2,705.6 incidences per 100,000 residents made Oklahoma the state with the 7th highest property crime rate in the country.

Table OK-1. Population by Age, Sex, Race, and Hispanic Origin

(Number, percent, except where noted.)

Sex, age, race, and Hispanic origin	2000	2010	2021	Percent change, 2010–2021
Total Population..	3,450,654	3,751,351	3,986,639	6.3
Percent of total U.S. population	1.2	1.2	1.2	X
Sex				
Male..	1,695,895	1,856,977	1,984,300	6.9
Female...	1,754,759	1,894,374	2,002,339	5.7
Age				
Under 5 years..	236,353	264,126	246,369	-6.7
5 to 19 years..	765,927	777,484	821,872	5.7
20 to 64 years..	1,992,424	2,203,027	2,273,687	3.2
65 years and over...	455,950	506,714	644,711	27.2
Median age (years)	35.5	36.2	37.1	2.5
Race and Hispanic Origin				
One race				
White...	2,628,434	2,851,510	2,917,360	2.3
Black...	260,968	284,332	312,869	10.0
American Indian and Alaska Native.............................	273,230	335,664	386,610	15.2
Asian...	46,767	67,126	98,311	46.5
Native Hawaiian or Other Pacific Islander	2,372	5,354	9,597	79.2
Two or more races..	155,985	207,365	261,892	26.3
Hispanic (of any race)...	179,304	351,542	467,249	32.9

NOTE: Population figures for 2021 are July 1 estimates. The 2000 and 2010 estimates are taken from the respective censuses.
- = Zero or rounds to zero.
X = Not applicable.

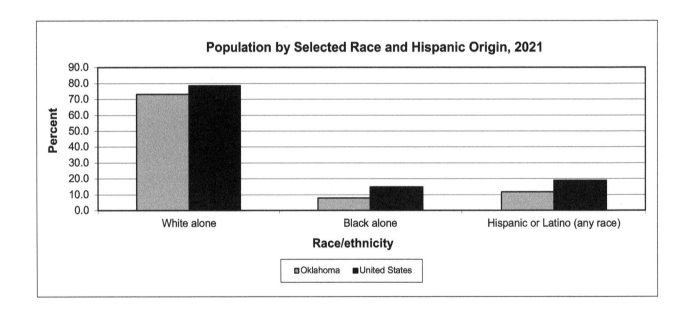

Table OK-2. Marital Status

(Number, percent distribution.)

Sex, age, race, and Hispanic origin	2000	2010	2020 [1]
Males, 15 Years and Over	1,318,729	1,457,860	1,549,444
Never married	25.8	30.7	33.0
Now married, except separated..	59.5	52.2	50.1
Separated..	1.6	1.8	1.7
Widowed..	2.5	3.0	3.1
Divorced..	10.6	12.3	12.0
Females, 15 Years and Over	1,398,823	1,521,546	1,602,110
Never married	19.1	23.8	25.8
Now married, except separated..	55.3	49.7	47.8
Separated..	1.9	2.7	2.3
Widowed..	11.1	10.1	9.9
Divorced..	12.5	13.7	14.1

[1] 2020 ACS 5-Year estimates. 1-Year estimates were not released for 2020 due to the impact of COVID-19 on data collection that year.

Table OK-3. Households and Housing Characteristics

(Number, percent, dollars.)

Item	2000	2010	2020 [1]	Average annual percent change, 2010–2020
Total Households..	1,342,293	1,432,959	1,493,569	0.6
Family households	921,750	954,622	975,207	0.3
Married-couple family	717,611	709,256	717,880	0.2
Other family	204,139	245,366	257,327	0.7
Male householder, no wife present..........................	51,564	62,855	75,128	2.8
Female householder, no husband present	152,575	182,511	182,199	-
Nonfamily households	420,543	478,337	518,362	1.2
Householder living alone....................................	358,560	400,840	432,660	1.1
Householder not living alone................................	61,983	77,497	85,702	1.5
Housing Characteristics				
Total housing units...	1,514,400	1,666,205	1,740,972	0.6
Occupied housing units	1,342,293	1,432,959	1,493,569	0.6
Owner occupied	918,259	971,378	986,555	0.2
Renter occupied	424,034	461,581	507,014	1.4
Average household size...	2.49	2.55	2.57	0.1
Financial Characteristics				
Median gross rent of renter-occupied housing	456	659	818	3.4
Median monthly owner costs for housing units with a mortgage	764	1,089	1,246	2.1
Median value of owner-occupied housing units.................	70,700	111,400	142,400	4.0

- = Zero or rounds to zero.
[1] 2020 ACS 5-Year estimates. 1-Year estimates were not released for 2020 due to the impact of COVID-19 on data collection that year.

Table OK-4. Migration, Origin, and Language

(Number, percent.)

Characteristic	State 2016-2020 [1]	U.S. 2016-2020 [1]
Residence 1 Year Ago		
Population 1 year and over	3,901,202	322,943,283
Same house	83.8	86.2
Different house in the U.S.	15.8	13.2
Same county	9.1	7.7
Different county	6.7	5.5
Same state	4.0	3.2
Different state	2.7	2.3
Abroad	0.4	0.6
Place of Birth		
Native born	3,711,530	282,443,680
Male	49.4	49.4
Female	50.6	50.6
Foreign born	237,812	44,125,628
Male	51.7	48.6
Female	48.3	51.4
Foreign born; naturalized U.S. citizen...	89,297	22,456,684
Male	48.8	46.1
Female	51.2	53.9
Foreign born; not a U.S. citizen...	148,515	21,668,944
Male	53.4	51.1
Female	46.6	48.9
Entered 2010 or later	26.7	22.8
Entered 2000 to 2009	29.7	25.1
Entered before 2000..	43.6	52.1
World Region of Birth, Foreign		
Foreign-born population, excluding population born at sea	237,812	44,125,628
Europe	6.9	10.8
Asia	27.8	31.3
Africa	4.9	5.4
Oceania	1.6	0.6
Latin America	56.7	50.0
North America	1.9	1.9
Language Spoken at Home and Ability to Speak English		
Population 5 years and over..	3,690,339	306,919,116
English only	89.4	78.5
Language other than English..	10.6	21.5
Speaks English less than "very well"..	3.9	8.2

[1] 2020 ACS 5-Year estimates. 1-Year estimates were not released for 2020 due to the impact of COVID-19 on data collection that year.
NA = Not available.
X = Not applicable.
- = Zero or rounds to zero.

Table OK-5. Median Income and Poverty Status, 2020[1]

(Number, percent, except as noted.)

Characteristic	State		U.S.	
	Number	Percent	Number	Percent
Median Income				
Households (dollars)...	53,840	X	64,994	X
Families (dollars)	67,511	X	80,069	X
Below Poverty Level (All People)	585,520	15.3	40,910,326	12.8
Sex				
Male	263,585	14.0	18,171,512	11.6
Female	321,935	16.5	22,738,814	14.0
Age				
Under 18 years..	194,537	20.7	12,598,699	17.5
Related children under 18 years...	190,708	20.4	12,306,532	17.2
18 to 64 years	338,642	14.8	23,554,920	12.1
65 years and over	52,341	8.7	4,756,707	9.3

X = Not applicable.
[1] 2020 ACS 5-Year estimates. 1-Year estimates were not released for 2020 due to the impact of COVID-19 on data collection that year.

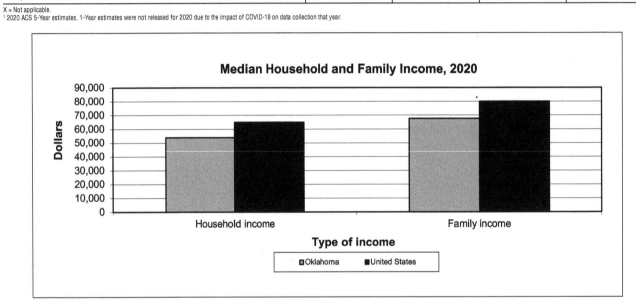

Table OK-6. Health Insurance Coverage Status for the Civilian Noninstitutionalized Population and Children Under 19 Years of Age

(Number, percent.)

Item	2011	2012	2013	2014	2015	2016	2017	2018	2019	2020 [2]
Civilian Noninstitutionalized Population	3,710,368	3,733,058	3,770,254	3,797,966	3,830,329	3,845,697	3,851,302	3,861,581	3,871,658	3,867,023
Covered by Private or Public Insurance										
Number..	3,016,823	3,047,982	3,104,481	3,214,454	3,297,820	3,316,039	3,305,819	3,313,265	3,318,823	3,310,379
Percent...	81.3	81.6	82.3	84.6	86.1	86.2	85.8	85.8	85.7	85.6
Uninsured										
Number..	693,545	685,076	665,773	583,512	532,509	529,658	545,483	548,316	552,835	556,644
Percent...	18.7	18.4	17.7	15.4	13.9	13.8	14.2	14.2	14.3	14.4
Percent in the U.S. not covered....................................	15.1	14.8	14.5	11.7	9.4	8.6	8.7	8.9	9.2	8.7
Children Under 19 Years of Age[1]	933,893	934,617	946,133	950,123	958,418	959,850	1,018,753	1,011,428	1,005,168	1,007,665
Covered by Private or Public Insurance										
Number..	834,509	840,408	851,091	867,872	887,310	889,761	936,357	928,012	918,889	921,784
Percent...	89.4	89.9	90.0	91.3	92.6	92.7	91.9	91.8	91.4	91.5
Uninsured										
Number..	99,384	94,209	95,042	82,251	71,108	70,089	82,396	83,416	86,279	85,881
Percent...	10.6	10.1	10.0	8.7	7.4	7.3	8.1	8.2	8.6	8.5
Percent in the U.S. not covered....................................	7.5	7.2	7.1	6.0	4.8	4.5	5.0	5.2	5.7	5.2

[1] Data for years prior to 2017 are for individuals under 18 years of age.
[2] 2020 ACS 5-Year estimates. 1-Year estimates were not released for 2020 due to the impact of COVID-19 on data collection that year. Data is not comparable to previous years, which are based on 1-year estimates.

Table OK-7. Employment Status by Demographic Group, 2021

(Numbers in thousands, percent.)

Characteristic	Civilian noninstitutional population	Civilian labor force		Employed		Unemployed	
		Number	Percent of population	Number	Percent of population	Number	Percent of population
Total..	3,074	1,867	60.7	1,792	58.3	75	4.0
Sex							
Male..	1,488	1,002	67.4	958	64.4	44	4.4
Female.......................................	1,586	864	54.5	833	52.5	31	3.6
Race, Sex, and Hispanic Origin							
White	2,320	1,399	60.3	1,348	58.1	51	3.6
Male..	1,149	768	66.9	739	64.3	29	3.8
Female.......................................	1,171	631	53.9	610	52.1	22	3.4
Black or African American...............	221	146	66.1	138	62.6	8	5.3
Male..	NA	NA	NA	NA	NA	NA	NA
Female.......................................	NA	NA	NA	NA	NA	NA	NA
Hispanic or Latino ethnicity[1]	370	250	67.7	237	64.2	13	5.2
Male..	193	154	79.8	147	76.2	7	4.6
Female.......................................	177	96	54.5	90	51.1	6	6.2
Age							
16 to 19 years.............................	NA	NA	NA	NA	NA	NA	NA
20 to 24 years.............................	254	189	74.3	180	70.6	9	5.0
25 to 34 years.............................	521	409	78.5	389	74.5	21	5.0
35 to 44 years.............................	505	404	80.0	389	77.0	15	3.7
45 to 54 years.............................	480	373	77.8	361	75.1	13	3.4
55 to 64 years.............................	458	280	61.1	272	59.4	8	2.8
65 years and over.........................	641	126	19.7	123	19.2	3	2.5

NOTE: Data in Table 7 are from the Current Population Survey (CPS) and do not match the estimates in Table 8. See notes and definitions for further information.
[1] May be of any race.

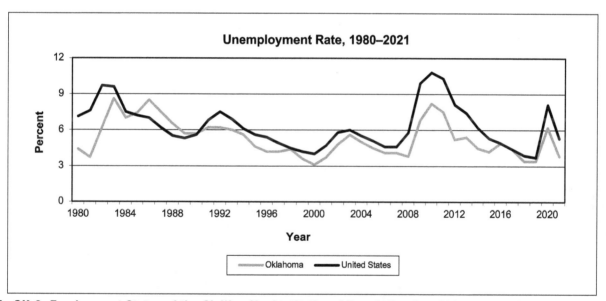

Table OK-8. Employment Status of the Civilian Noninstitutional Population Age 16 Years and Over

(Number, percent.)

Year	Civilian labor force	Civilian participation rate	Employed	Unemployed	Unemployment rate
2010..	1,765,708	62.3	1,650,502	115,206	6.5
2011..	1,767,056	61.6	1,668,235	98,821	5.6
2012..	1,794,901	62.0	1,703,624	91,277	5.1
2013..	1,799,525	61.6	1,707,220	92,305	5.1
2014..	1,797,769	61.0	1,719,826	77,943	4.3
2015..	1,829,046	61.5	1,750,501	78,545	4.3
2016..	1,828,055	61.1	1,743,225	84,830	4.6
2017..	1,826,272	61.1	1,752,733	73,539	4.0
2018..	1,833,020	61.2	1,773,125	59,895	3.3
2019..	1,840,199	61	1,782,686	57,513	3.1
2020..	1,835,861	60.5	1,721,525	114,336	6.2
2021..	1,854,234	60.6	1,783,080	71,154	3.8

Table OK-9. Employment and Average Wages by Industry

(Estimates are based on the 2012 North American Industry Classification System [NAICS].)

Industry	2013	2014	2015	2016	2017	2018	2019	2020
	Number of Jobs							
Wage and Salary Employment by Industry	1,679,717	1,699,657	1,705,980	1,688,995	1,693,826	1,719,591	1,736,582	1,667,511
Farm Wage and Salary Employment	11,398	9,773	5,799	7,400	6,980	6,274	5,742	10,688
Nonfarm Wage and Salary Employment	1,668,319	1,689,884	1,700,181	1,681,595	1,686,846	1,713,317	1,730,840	1,656,823
Private wage and salary employment	1,297,705	1,320,453	1,328,465	1,310,569	1,317,325	1,345,938	1,357,061	1,287,279
Forestry, fishing, and related activities	4,329	4,451	4,554	4,675	4,688	4,842	4,805	4,836
Mining	59,645	61,379	53,544	43,902	47,518	52,667	47,982	31,183
Utilities	11,722	12,021	12,094	11,495	10,717	10,750	10,892	9,534
Construction	76,914	77,541	79,330	79,335	79,109	82,237	84,754	80,716
Manufacturing	139,052	142,097	139,486	131,205	130,697	140,266	140,993	131,456
Durable goods manufacturing	96,163	98,877	96,557	87,858	87,629	96,768	97,215	88,284
Nondurable goods manufacturing	42,889	43,220	42,929	43,347	43,068	43,498	43,778	43,172
Wholesale trade	62,252	63,623	60,478	58,589	58,546	57,909	58,270	55,289
Retail trade	176,169	179,677	184,473	184,893	180,201	179,331	177,708	177,420
Transportation and warehousing	46,603	47,723	52,146	52,916	55,285	53,410	56,920	63,030
Information	21,846	21,733	21,142	21,130	20,449	19,848	19,612	18,245
Finance and insurance	58,798	59,776	60,256	60,074	60,371	60,155	60,708	59,846
Real estate and rental and leasing	22,561	20,971	21,015	20,693	20,899	21,681	22,112	20,507
Professional, scientific, and technical services	67,529	68,275	69,874	69,739	70,392	73,503	75,709	74,005
Management of companies and enterprises	16,599	18,678	18,689	18,096	18,744	19,158	20,101	20,543
Administrative and waste services	96,232	98,508	98,290	94,569	97,596	100,015	100,095	92,017
Educational services	21,509	21,887	22,086	22,581	22,122	22,900	22,908	21,185
Health care and social assistance	188,054	188,083	191,840	194,774	195,501	196,243	199,131	195,801
Arts, entertainment, and recreation	14,760	15,353	16,159	17,216	17,517	17,728	18,502	16,043
Accommodation and food services	137,499	141,445	146,142	148,705	151,052	154,890	156,722	141,472
Other services, except public administration	75,632	77,232	76,867	75,982	75,921	78,405	79,137	74,151
Government and government enterprises	370,614	369,431	371,716	371,026	369,521	367,379	373,779	369,544
	Dollars							
Average Wages and Salaries by Industry	43,044	44,454	45,083	44,716	45,997	47,679	48,982	50,533
Average Farm Wages and Salaries	24,925	32,314	33,121	28,820	32,319	30,607	42,197	20,629
Average Nonfarm Wages and Salaries	43,168	44,524	45,124	44,785	46,054	47,741	49,004	50,726
Average private wages and salaries	43,660	45,118	45,652	45,026	46,476	48,114	49,236	50,762
Forestry, fishing, and related activities	24,693	26,285	27,597	29,672	31,600	32,802	32,350	34,327
Mining	94,831	96,610	103,110	97,233	102,268	103,908	102,921	109,738
Utilities	96,380	114,337	99,909	98,566	101,112	100,643	115,355	103,648
Construction	46,824	47,990	49,707	50,617	51,569	53,811	55,475	56,313
Manufacturing	53,174	55,245	55,690	55,496	57,433	60,734	62,156	63,361
Durable goods manufacturing	55,321	57,406	57,313	57,033	59,098	62,871	64,174	65,150
Nondurable goods manufacturing	48,359	50,301	52,041	52,381	54,045	55,978	57,675	59,702
Wholesale trade	55,673	58,056	59,204	58,784	60,973	63,899	65,259	66,597
Retail trade	27,354	27,905	28,383	28,633	29,245	30,174	31,050	33,010
Transportation and warehousing	55,642	57,678	56,858	54,282	57,628	54,658	54,541	53,233
Information	55,031	56,547	57,110	58,111	60,274	61,421	62,845	66,634
Finance and insurance	56,767	60,089	60,659	61,995	64,273	66,485	68,568	73,171
Real estate and rental and leasing	42,098	42,818	43,248	42,238	43,685	45,145	46,158	47,910
Professional, scientific, and technical services	60,954	62,141	63,030	63,172	64,447	66,362	68,260	70,780
Management of companies and enterprises	88,731	82,009	88,985	86,988	86,885	87,303	97,730	104,823
Administrative and waste services	33,411	34,634	35,925	35,762	36,986	38,511	39,508	42,405
Educational services	31,270	32,413	31,178	31,981	32,160	32,462	32,795	38,928
Health care and social assistance	42,020	43,465	45,045	45,546	46,175	47,733	48,946	51,342
Arts, entertainment, and recreation	31,302	33,707	35,225	36,303	35,955	37,115	36,754	37,226
Accommodation and food services	16,989	17,538	17,873	18,173	18,558	19,403	19,796	19,729
Other services, except public administration	29,422	30,243	31,461	32,294	33,563	34,403	35,297	38,627
Government and government enterprises	41,445	42,402	43,236	43,934	44,552	46,376	48,162	50,600

Table OK-10. Employment Characteristics by Family Type

(Number, percent.)

Family type and labor force status	2018		2019		2020 [1]	
	Total	Families with own children under 18 years	Total	Families with own children under 18 years	Total	Families with own children under 18 years
All Families...	983,307	430,348	975,754	414,106	975,207	422,118
FAMILY TYPE AND LABOR FORCE STATUS						
Opposite-Sex Married-Couple Families............................	716,290	280,832	713,636	273,587	712,079	279,925
Both husband and wife in labor force..........................	47.6	64.0	49.1	64.4	48.9	64.3
Husband in labor force, wife not in labor force	23.9	29.0	23.3	28.9	23.4	28.7
Wife in labor force, husband not in labor force	8.1	4.3	7.9	4.1	8.1	4.4
Both husband and wife not in labor force	19.4	1.9	19.0	2.0	19.6	2.6
Other Families	267,017	149,516	262,118	140,519	257,327	140,573
Female householder, no spouse present	70.4	72.3	69.7	70.7	70.8	71.8
In labor force...	47.2	57.7	46.9	58.4	47.5	58.1
Not in labor force	23.1	14.7	22.8	12.4	23.3	13.7
Male householder, no spouse present.........................	29.6	27.7	30.3	29.3	29.2	28.2
In labor force...	23.0	25.0	23.6	26.8	22.3	25.1
Not in labor force	6.6	2.7	6.8	2.5	6.9	3.1

[1] 2020 ACS 5-Year estimates. 1-Year estimates were not released for 2020 due to the impact of COVID-19 on data collection that year. Data is not comparable to previous years, which are based on 1-year estimates.

Table OK-11. School Enrollment and Educational Attainment, 2020[1]

(Number, percent.)

Item	State	U.S.
Enrollment		
Total population 3 years and over, enrolled in school	992,436	80,497,960
Enrolled in nursery school or preschool (percent).................	6.4	6.1
Enrolled in kindergarten (percent)................................	5.5	5.0
Enrolled in elementary school, grades 1-8 (percent)...............	43.3	40.4
Enrolled in high school, grades 9-12 (percent)...................	20.8	21.0
Enrolled in college or graduate school (percent).................	24	27.6
Attainment		
Total population 25 years and over	2,611,680	222,836,834
Less than ninth grade (percent).................................	3.9	4.9
9th to 12th grade, no diploma (percent)	7.6	6.6
High school graduate, including equivalency (percent).............	31.1	26.7
Some college, no degree (percent)	23.1	20.3
Associate's degree (percent)	8.2	8.6
Bachelor's degree (percent)	17.2	20.2
Graduate or professional degree (percent).......................	9.0	12.7
High school graduate or higher (percent)........................	88.6	88.5
Bachelor's degree or higher (percent)...........................	26.1	32.9

[1] 2020 ACS 5-Year estimates. 1-Year estimates were not released for 2020 due to the impact of COVID-19 on data collection that year.

Table OK-12. Public School Characteristics and Educational Indicators

(Number, percent; data derived from National Center of Education Statistics.)

Item	State	U.S.
Public Elementary and Secondary Schools		
Number of regular school districts, 2018-19	512	13,452
Number of operational schools, 2019-20..........................	1,794	98,469
Percent charter schools	3.6	7.7
Total public school enrollment, Fall 2019.......................	703,719	50,796,445
Percent charter school enrollment	6.5	6.8
Student-teacher ratio, Fall 2019................................	16.2	15.9
Expenditures per student (unadjusted dollars), 2018-19	9,203	13,187
Four-year adjusted cohort graduation rate (ACGR), 2018-2019[1]....	84.9	85.8
Students eligible for free or reduced-price lunch (percent), 2019-20....	59.1	52.1
English language learners (percent), Fall 2019	9.1	10.4
Students age 3 to 21 served under IDEA, part B (percent), 2020-21	16.6	14.5

Public Schools by Type, 2019-20	Number	Percent of state public schools
Total number of schools..	1,794	100.0
Special education	4	0.2
Vocational education..	0	-
Alternative education...	5	0.3

[1] Adjusted Cohort Graduation Rates (ACGR) differ from Averaged Freshmen Graduation Rates (AFGR).
- = Zero or rounds to zero.

Table OK-13. Reported Voting and Registration of the Voting-Age Population, November 2020

(Numbers in thousands, percent.)

Item	Total population	Total citizen population	Registered			Voted		
			Total registered	Percent registered (total population)	Percent registered (total citizen population)	Total voted	Percent voted (total population)	Percent voted (total citizen population)
U.S. Total	252,274	231,593	168,308	66.7	72.7	154,628	61.3	66.8
State Total...........................	2,942	2,800	1,884	64.0	67.3	1,631	55.5	58.3
Sex								
Male	1,434	1,367	856	59.7	62.6	741	51.7	54.2
Female	1,508	1,433	1,028	68.2	71.7	890	59.0	62.1
Race								
White alone..........................	2,289	2,175	1,537	67.1	70.6	1,347	58.9	62.0
White, non-Hispanic alone	1,977	1,962	1,442	73.0	73.5	1,276	64.6	65.0
Black alone...........................	231	218	123	53.3	56.4	108	46.8	49.5
Asian alone	26	19	4	B	B	4	B	B
Hispanic (of any race)............	348	248	106	30.6	42.8	75	21.6	30.3
White alone or in combination	2,402	2,288	1,588	66.1	69.4	1,382	57.6	60.4
Black alone or in combination......	255	242	130	50.9	53.6	113	44.3	46.6
Asian alone or in combination......	43	36	9	B	B	4	B	B
Age								
18 to 24 years.......................	343	333	150	43.7	44.9	102	29.7	30.5
25 to 34 years.......................	481	431	260	54.1	60.4	212	44.1	49.2
35 to 44 years.......................	550	501	314	57.1	62.6	258	47.0	51.5
45 to 64 years.......................	950	917	677	71.2	73.8	624	65.7	68.1
65 years and over	618	618	484	78.3	78.3	435	70.3	70.3

B = Base is less than 75,000 and therefore too small to show the derived measure.

Table OK-14. Crime

(Number, rate per 100,000. Data are derived from the FBI Uniform Crime Reports.)

Item	State			U.S.		
	2019	2020	Percent change	2019	2020	Percent change
TOTAL POPULATION[1]	3,960,676	3,980,783	0.5	328,329,953	329,484,123	0.4
VIOLENT CRIME						
Number...	17,279	18,255	5.6	1,250,393	1,313,105	5.0
Rate	436.3	458.6	5.1	380.8	398.5	4.6
Murder and Nonnegligent Manslaughter						
Number...	275	296	7.6	16,669	21,570	29.4
Rate	6.9	7.4	7.1	5.1	6.5	28.9
Rape[2]						
Number...	2,363	2,102	-11.0	143,224	126,430	-11.7
Rate	59.7	52.8	-11.5	43.6	38.4	-12.0
Robbery						
Number...	2,383	2,351	-1.3	268,483	243,600	-9.3
Rate	60.2	59.1	-1.8	81.8	73.9	-9.6
Aggravated Assault						
Number...	12,258	13,506	10.2	822,017	921,505	12.1
Rate	309.5	339.3	9.6	250.4	279.7	11.7
PROPERTY CRIME						
Number...	113,504	107,705	-5.1	6,995,235	6,452,038	-7.8
Rate	2,865.8	2,705.6	-5.6	2,130.6	1,958.2	-8.1
Burglary						
Number...	26,820	24,415	-9.0	1,118,096	1,035,314	-7.4
Rate	677.2	613.3	-9.4	340.5	314.2	-7.7
Larceny-Theft						
Number...	73,199	68,243	-6.8	5,152,267	4,606,324	-10.6
Rate	1,848.1	1,714.3	-7.2	1,569.2	1,398.0	-10.9
Motor Vehicle Theft						
Number...	13,485	15,047	11.6	724,872	810,400	11.8
Rate	340.5	378.0	11.0	220.8	246.0	11.4

NOTE: Although arson data are included in the trend and clearance tables, sufficient data are not available to estimate totals for this offense. Therefore, no arson data are published in this table.
- = Zero or rounds to zero.
[1] Population figures are U.S. Census Bureau provisional estimates as of July 1, 2020.
[2] The figures shown in the rape (revised definition) column were estimated using the revised Uniform Crime Reporting (UCR) definition of rape.

Table OK-15. State Government Finances, 2020

(Dollar amounts in thousands, percent distribution.)

Item	Dollars	Percent distribution
Total Revenue	29,666,928	100.0
General revenue	25,549,490	86.1
Intergovernmental revenue	9,515,148	32.1
Taxes	10,172,986	34.3
General sales	2960531	10.0
Selective sales	1,651,445	5.6
License taxes	1,043,794	3.5
Individual income tax	3364947	11.3
Corporate income tax	301,574	1.0
Other taxes	850,695	2.9
Current charges	3,128,368	10.5
Miscellaneous general revenue	2,732,988	9.2
Utility revenue	626,936	2.1
Liquor stores revenue	0	-
Insurance trust revenue[1]	3,490,502	11.8
Total Expenditure	26,962,382	100.0
Intergovernmental expenditure	4,908,378	18.2
Direct expenditure	22,054,004	81.8
Current operation	15,246,224	56.5
Capital outlay	2,462,764	9.1
Insurance benefits and repayments	3,328,374	12.3
Assistance and subsidies	709,177	2.6
Interest on debt	307,465	1.1
Exhibit: Salaries and wages	3,695,458	13.7
Total Expenditure	26,962,382	100.0
General expenditure	22,929,584	85.0
Intergovernmental expenditure	4,908,378	18.2
Direct expenditure	18,021,206	66.8
General expenditure, by function:		
Education	8,723,645	32.4
Public welfare	7,154,673	26.5
Hospitals	307,341	1.1
Health	1,001,721	3.7
Highways	2,508,606	9.3
Police protection	197,184	0.7
Correction	659,222	2.4
Natural resources	240,551	0.9
Parks and recreation	83,813	0.3
Governmental administration	769,882	2.9
Interest on general debt	228,430	0.8
Other and unallocable	938,905	3.5
Utility expenditure	738,648	2.5
Liquor stores expenditure	0	-
Insurance trust expenditure	3,328,374	12.3
Debt at End of Fiscal Year	7,804,816	X
Cash and Security Holdings	52,536,034	X

X = Not applicable.
- = Zero or rounds to zero.
[1] Within insurance trust revenue, net earnings of state retirement systems is a calculated statistic (the item code in the data file is X08), and thus can be positive or negative. Net earnings is the sum of earnings on investments plus gains on investments minus losses on investments. The change made in 2002 for asset valuation from book to market value in accordance with Statement 34 of the Governmental Accounting Standards Board is reflected in the calculated statistics.

Table OK-16. State Government Tax Collections, 2021

(Dollars in thousands, percent.)

Item	Dollars	Percent distribution
Total Taxes	11,299,244	100.0
Property taxes	X	-
Sales and gross receipts	4,975,670	44.0
General sales and gross receipts	3,116,195	27.6
Selective sales and gross receipts	1,859,475	16.5
Alcoholic beverages	146,821	1.3
Amusements	22,652	0.2
Insurance premiums	448,883	4.0
Motor fuels	571,408	5.1
Pari-mutuels	1,088	-
Public utilities	47,701	0.4
Tobacco products	463,457	4.1
Other selective sales	157,465	1.4
Licenses	1,085,111	9.6
Alcoholic beverages	46	-
Amusements	165,847	1.5
Corporations in general	55,849	0.5
Hunting and fishing	27,249	0.2
Motor vehicle	812,747	7.2
Motor vehicle operators	21,471	0.2
Public utilities	6	-
Occupation and business, NEC	836	-
Other licenses	1,060	-
Income taxes	4,368,893	38.7
Individual income	3,767,669	33.3
Corporation net income	601,224	5.3
Other taxes	869,570	7.7
Death and gift	5	-
Documentary and stock transfer	27,171	0.2
Severance	754,292	6.7
Taxes, NEC	88,102	0.8

X = Not applicable.
- = Zero or rounds to zero.

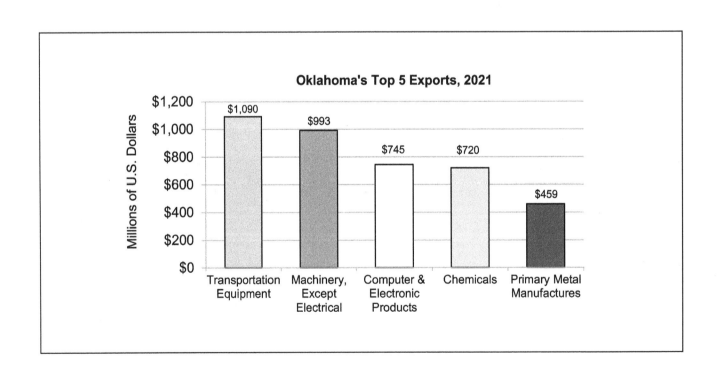

OREGON

Facts and Figures

Location: Northwestern United States; bordered on the N by Washington, on the E by Idaho, on the S by Nevada and California, and on the W by the Pacific Ocean

Area: 98,381 sq. mi. (254,805 sq. km.); rank—9th

Population: 4,246,155 (2021 est.); rank—27th

Principal Cities: capital—Salem; largest—Portland

Statehood: February 14, 1859; 33rd state

U.S. Congress: 2 senators, 5 representatives

State Motto: She Flies With Her Own Wings

State Song: "Oregon, My Oregon"

State Nickname: The Beaver State

Abbreviations: OR; Oreg.

State Symbols: flower—Oregon grape; tree—Douglas fir; bird—Western meadowlark

At a Glance

- With an increase in population of 10.8 percent, Oregon ranked 15th among the states in growth from 2010 to 2021.

- In 2020, 6.6 percent of Oregonians did not have health insurance, compared to 8.7 percent of the total U.S. population.

- Oregon's violent crime rate in 2020 was 291.9 per 100,000 population, compared to 398.5 for the entire nation.

- The homeownership rate in Oregon in 2021 was 65.8 percent, compared to the national homeownership rate of 65.5 percent.

- The median household income in Oregon was $65,667 in 2020, compared to the national median of $64,994. Oregon's the poverty rate was 12.4 percent, which ranked 26th in the nation.

Table OR-1. Population by Age, Sex, Race, and Hispanic Origin

(Number, percent, except where noted.)

Sex, age, race, and Hispanic origin	2000	2010	2021	Percent change, 2010–2021
Total Population..	3,421,399	3,831,074	4,246,155	10.8
Percent of total U.S. population	1.2	1.2	1.3	X
Sex				
Male..	1,696,550	1,896,002	2,116,838	11.6
Female..	1,724,849	1,935,072	2,129,317	10.0
Age				
Under 5 years..	223,005	237,556	212,784	-10.4
5 to 19 years...	720,999	734,627	746,602	1.6
20 to 64 years..	2,039,218	2,325,358	2,498,390	7.4
65 years and over	438,177	533,533	788,379	47.8
Median age (years)	36.3	38.4	40.0	4.2
Race and Hispanic Origin				
One race				
White	2,961,623	3,403,252	3,659,596	7.5
Black	55,662	74,414	96,520	29.7
American Indian and Alaska Native	45,211	66,784	80,314	20.3
Asian...	101,350	145,009	210,456	45.1
Native Hawaiian or Other Pacific Islander	7,976	14,649	20,379	39.1
Two or more races	104,745	126,966	178,890	40.9
Hispanic (of any race)..	275,314	467,030	596,517	27.7

NOTE: Population figures for 2021 are July 1 estimates. The 2000 and 2010 estimates are taken from the respective censuses.
- = Zero or rounds to zero.
X = Not applicable.

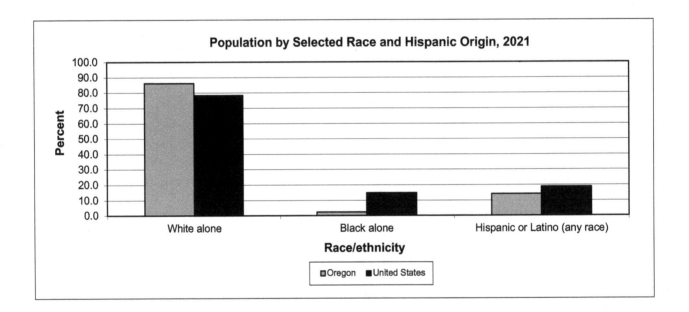

Population by Selected Race and Hispanic Origin, 2021

Legend: □ Oregon ■ United States

Table OR-2. Marital Status

(Number, percent distribution.)

Sex, age, race, and Hispanic origin	2000	2010	2020 [1]
Males, 15 Years and Over	1,336,805	1,533,177	1,702,013
Never married	28.5	32.6	34.6
Now married, except separated..	57.1	51.4	50.4
Separated..	1.5	1.6	1.2
Widowed..	2.4	2.7	2.5
Divorced..	10.6	11.8	11.3
Females, 15 Years and Over	1,385,329	1,588,428	1,755,593
Never married	21.9	25.8	27.9
Now married, except separated..	53.9	48.9	48.5
Separated..	1.9	1.9	1.6
Widowed..	9.6	8.5	7.8
Divorced..	12.7	14.9	14.1

[1] 2020 ACS 5-Year estimates. 1-Year estimates were not released for 2020 due to the impact of COVID-19 on data collection that year.

Table OR-3. Households and Housing Characteristics

(Number, percent, dollars.)

Item	2000	2010	2020 [1]	Average annual percent change, 2010–2020
Total Households...	1,333,723	1,507,137	1,642,579	1.3
Family households	877,671	963,362	1,034,877	1.1
Married-couple family	692,532	733,095	793,578	1.2
Other family	185,139	230,267	241,299	0.7
Male householder, no wife present............................	54,357	65,972	75,309	2.0
Female householder, no husband present....................	130,782	164,295	165,990	0.1
Nonfamily households	456,032	543,775	607,702	1.7
Householder living alone..	347,624	416,500	449,272	1.1
Householder not living alone.....................................	108,428	127,275	158,430	3.5
Housing Characteristics				
Total housing units	1,452,709	1,676,476	1,788,855	1.0
Occupied housing units	1,333,723	1,507,137	1,642,579	1.3
Owner occupied	856,951	942,674	1,031,006	1.3
Renter occupied	476,772	564,463	611,573	1.2
Average household size...	2.51	2.49	2.49	-
Financial Characteristics				
Median gross rent of renter-occupied housing	620	816	1,173	6.3
Median monthly owner costs for housing units with a mortgage	1,125	1,577	1,741	1.5
Median value of owner-occupied housing units..............	152,100	244,500	336,700	5.4

- = Zero or rounds to zero.
[1] 2020 ACS 5-Year estimates. 1-Year estimates were not released for 2020 due to the impact of COVID-19 on data collection that year.

Table OR-4. Migration, Origin, and Language

(Number, percent.)

Characteristic	State 2016-2020 [1]	U.S. 2016-2020 [1]
Residence 1 Year Ago		
Population 1 year and over	4,135,390	322,943,283
Same house	83.4	86.2
Different house in the U.S.	16.0	13.2
Same county	9.1	7.7
Different county	7.0	5.5
Same state	3.6	3.2
Different state	3.4	2.3
Abroad	0.5	0.6
Place of Birth		
Native born	3,766,479	282,443,680
Male	49.7	49.4
Female	50.3	50.6
Foreign born	409,867	44,125,628
Male	48.9	48.6
Female	51.1	51.4
Foreign born; naturalized U.S. citizen..	192,385	22,456,684
Male	45.6	46.1
Female	54.4	53.9
Foreign born; not a U.S. citizen..	217,482	21,668,944
Male	51.7	51.1
Female	48.3	48.9
Entered 2010 or later	22.0	22.8
Entered 2000 to 2009	24.6	25.1
Entered before 2000...	53.4	52.1
World Region of Birth, Foreign		
Foreign-born population, excluding population born at sea	409,867	44,125,628
Europe	15.3	10.8
Asia	33.7	31.3
Africa	3.9	5.4
Oceania	2.0	0.6
Latin America	41.5	50.0
North America	3.6	1.9
Language Spoken at Home and Ability to Speak English		
Population 5 years and over..	3,948,032	306,919,116
English only	84.7	78.5
Language other than English..	15.3	21.5
Speaks English less than "very well"...	5.5	8.2

[1] 2020 ACS 5-Year estimates. 1-Year estimates were not released for 2020 due to the impact of COVID-19 on data collection that year.
NA = Not available.
X = Not applicable.
- = Zero or rounds to zero.

Table OR-5. Median Income and Poverty Status, 2020[1]

(Number, percent, except as noted.)

Characteristic	State		U.S.	
	Number	Percent	Number	Percent
Median Income				
Households (dollars)..	65,667	X	64,994	X
Families (dollars)	80,630	X	80,069	X
Below Poverty Level (All People)	506,558	12.4	40,910,326	12.8
Sex				
Male	230,958	11.4	18,171,512	11.6
Female	275,600	13.3	22,738,814	14.0
Age				
Under 18 years...	127,349	15.0	12,598,699	17.5
Related children under 18 years..	121,718	14.5	12,306,532	17.2
18 to 64 years..	321,063	12.7	23,554,920	12.1
65 years and over	58,146	8.0	4,756,707	9.3

X = Not applicable.
[1] 2020 ACS 5-Year estimates. 1-Year estimates were not released for 2020 due to the impact of COVID-19 on data collection that year.

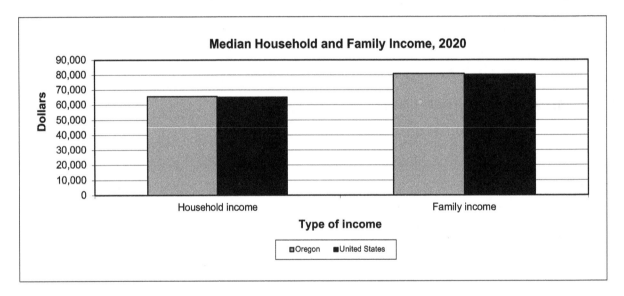

Table OR-6. Health Insurance Coverage Status for the Civilian Noninstitutionalized Population and Children Under 19 Years of Age

(Number, percent.)

Item	2011	2012	2013	2014	2015	2016	2017	2018	2019	2020[2]
Civilian Noninstitutionalized Population	3,832,640	3,860,452	3,893,092	3,931,306	3,991,133	4,054,353	4,102,901	4,151,076	4,175,002	4,135,531
Covered by Private or Public Insurance										
Number..	3,230,263	3,284,443	3,322,210	3,548,645	3,710,870	3,801,587	3,822,085	3,857,969	3,875,582	3,861,117
Percent..	84.3	85.1	85.3	90.3	93.0	93.8	93.2	92.9	92.8	93.4
Uninsured										
Number..	602,377	576,009	570,882	382,661	280,263	252,766	280,816	293,107	299,420	274,414
Percent..	15.7	14.9	14.7	9.7	7.0	6.2	6.8	7.1	7.2	6.6
Percent in the U.S. not covered...........................	15.1	14.8	14.5	11.7	9.4	8.6	8.7	8.9	9.2	8.7
Children Under 19 Years of Age[1]	861,059	859,846	858,259	857,084	859,408	866,585	928,115	924,284	914,386	918,429
Covered by Private or Public Insurance										
Number..	798,172	805,216	808,087	818,051	828,340	837,985	895,141	891,393	876,871	886,179
Percent..	92.7	93.6	94.2	95.4	96.4	96.7	96.4	96.4	95.9	96.5
Uninsured										
Number..	62,887	54,630	50,172	39,033	31,068	28,600	32,974	32,891	37,515	32,250
Percent..	7.3	6.4	5.8	4.6	3.6	3.3	3.6	3.6	4.1	3.5
Percent in the U.S. not covered...........................	7.5	7.2	7.1	6.0	4.8	4.5	5.0	5.2	5.7	5.2

[1] Data for years prior to 2017 are for individuals under 18 years of age.
[2] 2020 ACS 5-Year estimates. 1-Year estimates were not released for 2020 due to the impact of COVID-19 on data collection that year. Data is not comparable to previous years, which are based on 1-year estimates.

Table OR-7. Employment Status by Demographic Group, 2021

(Numbers in thousands, percent.)

Characteristic	Civilian noninstitutional population	Civilian labor force		Employed		Unemployed	
		Number	Percent of population	Number	Percent of population	Number	Percent of population
Total..................................	3,471	2,159	62.2	2,047	59.0	112	5.2
Sex							
Male..................................	1,697	1,138	67.1	1,077	63.5	61	5.4
Female...............................	1,774	1,021	57.5	970	54.7	51	5.0
Race, Sex, and Hispanic Origin							
White.................................	3,072	1,878	61.1	1,788	58.2	90	4.8
Male..................................	1,499	993	66.3	948	63.2	46	4.6
Female...............................	1,574	884	56.2	841	53.4	44	5.0
Black or African American...........	80	54	67.9	46	57.8	8	14.8
Male..................................	NA	NA	NA	NA	NA	NA	NA
Female...............................	NA	NA	NA	NA	NA	NA	NA
Hispanic or Latino ethnicity[1]	320	219	68.5	204	63.8	15	6.9
Male..................................	161	119	74.1	109	68.1	10	8.1
Female...............................	159	100	62.9	95	59.4	6	5.6
Age							
16 to 19 years.......................	203	77	37.8	69	33.8	8	10.6
20 to 24 years.......................	263	204	77.6	191	72.6	13	6.4
25 to 34 years.......................	575	477	83.0	450	78.2	27	5.7
35 to 44 years.......................	587	482	82.1	459	78.2	23	4.7
45 to 54 years.......................	538	449	83.5	430	80.0	19	4.1
55 to 64 years.......................	482	322	66.8	306	63.5	16	4.9
65 years and over....................	824	149	18.0	142	17.2	7	4.4

NOTE: Data in Table 7 are from the Current Population Survey (CPS) and do not match the estimates in Table 8. See notes and definitions for further information.
[1] May be of any race.
NA = Not available.

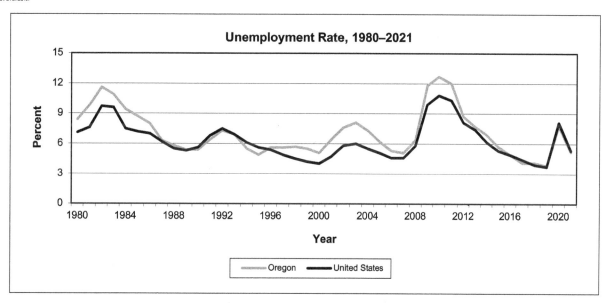

Table OR-8. Employment Status of the Civilian Noninstitutional Population Age 16 Years and Over

(Number, percent.)

Year	Civilian labor force	Civilian participation rate	Employed	Unemployed	Unemployment rate
2010..	1,991,749	65.6	1,778,034	213,715	10.7
2011..	1,995,931	65.1	1,804,257	191,674	9.6
2012..	1,964,662	63.4	1,791,248	173,414	8.8
2013..	1,924,692	61.6	1,775,139	149,553	7.8
2014..	1,950,128	61.6	1,820,202	129,926	6.7
2015..	1,979,475	61.6	1,871,286	108,189	5.5
2016..	2,042,929	62.3	1,946,233	96,696	4.7
2017..	2,075,682	62.4	1,991,503	84,179	4.1
2018..	2,080,199	61.8	1,996,790	83,409	4.0
2019..	2,094,977	61.6	2,017,379	77,598	3.7
2020..	2,104,558	61.3	1,944,845	159,713	7.6
2021..	2,148,333	62.3	2,036,138	112,195	5.2

Table OR-9. Employment and Average Wages by Industry

(Estimates are based on the 2012 North American Industry Classification System [NAICS].)

Industry	2013	2014	2015	2016	2017	2018	2019	2020
	Number of Jobs							
Wage and Salary Employment by Industry........................	1,750,628	1,799,533	1,851,480	1,901,515	1,945,586	1,990,185	2,021,591	1,900,653
Farm Wage and Salary Employment..............................	30,183	29,615	24,152	24,674	30,223	33,263	33,557	25,029
Nonfarm Wage and Salary Employment..........................	1,720,445	1,769,918	1,827,328	1,876,841	1,915,363	1,956,922	1,988,034	1,875,624
Private wage and salary employment.................................	1,444,962	1,492,363	1,544,909	1,590,073	1,627,274	1,663,944	1,691,720	1,589,777
Forestry, fishing, and related activities......................	22,253	22,400	22,938	22,334	22,169	23,188	22,934	22,289
Mining..	1,527	1,546	1,701	1,748	1,832	1,935	1,836	1,773
Utilities..	4,497	4,512	4,485	4,563	4,666	4,802	4,827	4,785
Construction...	75,365	81,274	84,610	91,724	99,193	107,117	111,341	110,357
Manufacturing..	174,834	179,225	185,655	187,821	189,475	194,880	197,773	185,352
Durable goods manufacturing...............................	123,115	125,982	130,082	131,012	131,309	135,420	136,816	128,294
Nondurable goods manufacturing.........................	51,719	53,243	55,573	56,809	58,166	59,460	60,957	57,058
Wholesale trade	71,646	72,583	73,997	75,611	76,785	75,538	76,546	74,376
Retail trade..	192,499	197,116	203,335	206,266	211,664	212,858	210,987	201,975
Transportation and warehousing................................	50,942	53,195	55,346	56,580	59,008	61,379	66,436	70,350
Information	32,343	32,179	33,224	33,370	34,258	34,323	35,063	33,228
Finance and insurance	58,928	59,178	59,596	59,574	61,115	61,115	61,194	61,497
Real estate and rental and leasing.............................	24,258	24,584	25,558	26,266	27,099	28,635	29,798	28,352
Professional, scientific, and technical services	80,477	84,603	88,052	92,517	94,974	98,136	100,582	99,409
Management of companies and enterprises..............	37,980	40,220	42,951	45,352	47,108	48,620	50,542	48,994
Administrative and waste services	91,246	95,308	98,635	101,534	101,967	103,757	104,154	95,581
Educational services	45,139	45,548	45,784	45,379	45,952	43,189	43,456	36,427
Health care and social assistance.............................	222,966	229,829	240,739	250,851	256,215	261,888	268,122	269,101
Arts, entertainment, and recreation...........................	22,627	23,993	24,055	25,974	27,322	27,988	28,327	19,609
Accommodation and food services............................	154,504	159,980	168,344	174,556	179,765	184,285	186,386	143,590
Other services, except public administration........................	80,931	85,090	85,904	88,053	86,707	90,232	91,495	82,732
Government and government enterprises.....................................	275,483	277,555	282,419	286,768	288,089	292,978	296,314	285,847
	Dollars							
Average Wages and Salaries by Industry	45,773	47,258	49,154	50,383	51,951	53,839	55,634	60,649
Average Farm Wages and Salaries	29,778	29,294	30,400	34,450	28,287	27,939	20,006	29,662
Average Nonfarm Wages and Salaries	46,053	47,559	49,402	50,592	52,325	54,280	56,236	61,063
Average private wages and salaries................................	45,546	47,068	48,985	50,101	51,776	53,770	55,679	60,628
Forestry, fishing, and related activities.............................	34,431	36,363	38,506	38,901	39,760	41,842	40,823	46,175
Mining..	50,620	51,229	53,831	57,496	59,248	61,306	63,581	65,261
Utilities..	89,592	93,693	96,245	98,575	103,211	105,180	110,942	119,292
Construction	52,431	54,158	54,434	56,667	58,795	61,341	63,953	67,810
Manufacturing..	63,520	65,742	67,445	69,136	69,853	72,368	73,146	76,856
Durable goods manufacturing...............................	71,840	74,781	76,524	79,015	79,361	82,783	83,677	87,038
Nondurable goods manufacturing.........................	43,713	44,355	46,192	46,354	48,386	48,648	49,509	53,963
Wholesale trade	63,124	65,118	67,518	68,925	72,026	74,732	77,401	82,032
Retail trade..	28,276	29,054	29,890	30,671	31,533	32,494	33,662	36,934
Transportation and warehousing................................	45,414	47,122	47,990	48,429	50,192	52,077	51,915	53,322
Information	69,173	72,606	75,381	77,148	82,084	89,657	91,580	104,100
Finance and insurance	69,661	71,420	76,212	79,047	80,609	83,198	87,514	95,950
Real estate and rental and leasing.............................	36,268	38,275	40,309	42,517	44,844	46,951	50,173	53,369
Professional, scientific, and technical services	67,699	70,558	73,715	75,580	78,992	80,903	84,051	89,855
Management of companies and enterprises..............	107,059	112,297	121,932	117,284	119,523	121,528	126,571	141,879
Administrative and waste services	32,053	33,351	34,852	35,780	37,070	38,596	41,002	45,348
Educational services	25,735	26,176	26,726	27,866	28,259	30,366	31,214	36,620
Health care and social assistance.............................	45,950	47,043	49,070	49,986	51,529	52,750	54,433	56,718
Arts, entertainment, and recreation...........................	27,225	27,511	28,905	29,038	31,107	32,811	34,104	38,642
Accommodation and food services............................	19,829	20,551	21,364	22,123	23,373	25,349	26,391	25,354
Other services, except public administration........................	30,676	31,283	33,102	34,297	36,085	37,271	38,571	42,812
Government and government enterprises.............................	48,712	50,195	51,679	53,316	55,425	57,173	59,415	63,484

Table OR-10. Employment Characteristics by Family Type

(Number, percent.)

Family type and labor force status	2018		2019		2020 [1]	
	Total	Families with own children under 18 years	Total	Families with own children under 18 years	Total	Families with own children under 18 years
All Families..	1,027,648	411,767	1,021,588	400,064	1,034,877	420,914
FAMILY TYPE AND LABOR FORCE STATUS						
Opposite-Sex Married-Couple Families............................	793,537	288,829	780,807	276,756	783,066	291,116
Both husband and wife in labor force.................................	48.6	66.4	48.8	67.0	49.6	66.5
Husband in labor force, wife not in labor force	19.9	26.3	19.2	24.8	20.4	26.9
Wife in labor force, husband not in labor force	8.3	4.6	8.6	5.2	8.4	4.9
Both husband and wife not in labor force...........................	21.7	1.9	21.9	2.0	21.5	1.7
Other Families	234,111	122,938	240,781	123,308	241,299	127,663
Female householder, no spouse present	67.0	70.0	68.7	67.9	68.8	70.0
In labor force...	45.5	56.9	47.8	57.8	48.3	58.6
Not in labor force..	21.5	13.1	20.9	10.1	20.5	11.4
Male householder, no spouse present...........................	33.0	30.0	31.3	32.1	31.2	30.0
In labor force..	25.1	27.8	25.5	29.5	24.7	27.4
Not in labor force..	7.9	2.2	5.7	2.5	6.5	2.6

[1] 2020 ACS 5-Year estimates. 1-Year estimates were not released for 2020 due to the impact of COVID-19 on data collection that year. Data is not comparable to previous years, which are based on 1-year estimates.

Table OR-11. School Enrollment and Educational Attainment, 2020[1]

(Number, percent.)

Item	State	U.S.
Enrollment		
Total population 3 years and over, enrolled in school	948,174	80,497,960
Enrolled in nursery school or preschool (percent)...	5.8	6.1
Enrolled in kindergarten (percent)...	4.8	5.0
Enrolled in elementary school, grades 1-8 (percent)...	40.7	40.4
Enrolled in high school, grades 9-12 (percent)...	20.7	21.0
Enrolled in college or graduate school (percent)...	27.9	27.6
Attainment		
Total population 25 years and over	2,944,830	222,836,834
Less than ninth grade (percent)...	3.4	4.9
9th to 12th grade, no diploma (percent)...	5.4	6.6
High school graduate, including equivalency (percent)...	22.7	26.7
Some college, no degree (percent)...	25	20.3
Associate's degree (percent)...	9.0	8.6
Bachelor's degree (percent)...	21.3	20.2
Graduate or professional degree (percent)...	13.1	12.7
High school graduate or higher (percent)	91.1	88.5
Bachelor's degree or higher (percent)...	34.4	32.9

[1] 2020 ACS 5-Year estimates. 1-Year estimates were not released for 2020 due to the impact of COVID-19 on data collection that year.

Table OR-12. Public School Characteristics and Educational Indicators

(Number, percent; data derived from National Center of Education Statistics.)

Item	State	U.S.
Public Elementary and Secondary Schools		
Number of regular school districts, 2018-19	177	13,452
Number of operational schools, 2019-20...	1,255	98,469
Percent charter schools	10.6	7.7
Total public school enrollment, Fall 2019...	610,648	50,796,445
Percent charter school enrollment	6.7	6.8
Student-teacher ratio, Fall 2019	20.2	15.9
Expenditures per student (unadjusted dollars), 2018-19	12,457	13,187
Four-year adjusted cohort graduation rate (ACGR), 2018-2019[1]...	80.0	85.8
Students eligible for free or reduced-price lunch (percent), 2019-20...	47.9	52.1
English language learners (percent), Fall 2019	9.1	10.4
Students age 3 to 21 served under IDEA, part B (percent), 2020-21	15.0	14.5

Public Schools by Type, 2019-20	Number	Percent of state public schools
Total number of schools...	1,255	100.0
Special education...	1	0.1
Vocational education...	0	-
Alternative education...	35	2.8

[1] Adjusted Cohort Graduation Rates (ACGR) differ from Averaged Freshmen Graduation Rates (AFGR).
- = Zero or rounds to zero.

Table OR-13. Reported Voting and Registration of the Voting-Age Population, November 2020

(Numbers in thousands, percent.)

Item	Total population	Total citizen population	Registered			Voted		
			Total registered	Percent registered (total population)	Percent registered (total citizen population)	Total voted	Percent voted (total population)	Percent voted (total citizen population)
U.S. Total	252,274	231,593	168,308	66.7	72.7	154,628	61.3	66.8
State Total..	3,369	3,242	2,590	76.9	79.9	2,402	71.3	74.1
Sex								
Male	1,645	1,572	1,245	75.7	79.2	1,144	69.5	72.8
Female	1,724	1,670	1,345	78.0	80.5	1,258	73.0	75.3
Race								
White alone..	2,955	2,876	2,345	79.4	81.5	2,191	74.2	76.2
White, non-Hispanic alone	2,712	2,696	2,229	82.2	82.7	2,094	77.2	77.7
Black alone..	82	76	47	57.6	62.2	39	47.5	51.2
Asian alone	143	109	70	49.4	64.8	66	46.2	60.6
Hispanic (of any race)	281	201	122	43.6	60.8	105	37.3	51.9
White alone or in combination	3,064	2,985	2,441	79.7	81.8	2,265	73.9	75.9
Black alone or in combination	93	87	58	62.5	66.8	50	53.5	57.2
Asian alone or in combination.................	179	145	101	56.6	69.8	84	47.3	58.3
Age								
18 to 24 years	388	373	253	65.2	68.0	209	53.8	56.1
25 to 34 years	576	550	439	76.1	79.7	381	66.1	69.2
35 to 44 years	573	539	464	80.9	86.0	418	72.9	77.5
45 to 64 years	1,030	984	785	76.3	79.8	761	73.9	77.4
65 years and over	801	796	649	81.1	81.5	633	79.0	79.5

B = Base is less than 75,000 and therefore too small to show the derived measure.

Table OR-14. Crime

(Number, rate per 100,000. Data are derived from the FBI Uniform Crime Reports.)

Item	State			U.S.		
	2019	2020	Percent change	2019	2020	Percent change
TOTAL POPULATION[1]	4,216,116	4,241,507	0.6	328,329,953	329,484,123	0.4
VIOLENT CRIME						
Number...	12,382	12,380	*	1,250,393	1,313,105	5.0
Rate	293.7	291.9	-0.6	380.8	398.5	4.6
Murder and Nonnegligent Manslaughter						
Number...	117	125	6.8	16,669	21,570	29.4
Rate	2.8	2.9	6.2	5.1	6.5	28.9
Rape[2]						
Number...	1,886	1,565	-17.0	143,224	126,430	-11.7
Rate	44.7	36.9	-17.5	43.6	38.4	-12.0
Robbery						
Number...	2,329	2,180	-6.4	268,483	243,600	-9.3
Rate	55.2	51.4	-7.0	81.8	73.9	-9.6
Aggravated Assault						
Number...	8,050	8,510	5.7	822,017	921,505	12.1
Rate	190.9	200.6	5.1	250.4	279.7	11.7
PROPERTY CRIME						
Number...	117,567	112,782	-4.1	6,995,235	6,452,038	-7.8
Rate	2,788.5	2,659.0	-4.6	2,130.6	1,958.2	-8.1
Burglary						
Number...	15,127	14,386	-4.9	1,118,096	1,035,314	-7.4
Rate	358.8	339.2	-5.5	340.5	314.2	-7.7
Larceny-Theft						
Number...	86,922	81,811	-5.9	5,152,267	4,606,324	-10.6
Rate	2,061.7	1,928.8	-6.4	1,569.2	1,398.0	-10.9
Motor Vehicle Theft						
Number...	15,518	16,585	6.9	724,872	810,400	11.8
Rate	368.1	391.0	6.2	220.8	246.0	11.4

NOTE: Although arson data are included in the trend and clearance tables, sufficient data are not available to estimate totals for this offense. Therefore, no arson data are published in this table.
- = Zero or rounds to zero.
[1] Population figures are U.S. Census Bureau provisional estimates as of July 1, 2020.
[2] The figures shown in the rape (revised definition) column were estimated using the revised Uniform Crime Reporting (UCR) definition of rape.

Table OR-15. State Government Finances, 2020

(Dollar amounts in thousands, percent distribution.)

Item	Dollars	Percent distribution
Total Revenue	43,740,961	100.0
General revenue	35,569,555	81.3
Intergovernmental revenue	13,115,972	30.0
Taxes	12,774,909	29.2
General sales	0	-
Selective sales	1,928,326	4.4
License taxes	1,165,847	2.7
Individual income tax	8635668	19.7
Corporate income tax	892,484	2.0
Other taxes	152,584	0.3
Current charges	6,454,709	14.8
Miscellaneous general revenue	3,223,965	7.4
Utility revenue	922	-
Liquor stores revenue	738064	1.7
Insurance trust revenue[1]	7,432,420	17.0
Total Expenditure	45,418,922	100.0
Intergovernmental expenditure	7,125,885	15.7
Direct expenditure	38,293,037	84.3
Current operation	27,684,971	61.0
Capital outlay	1,961,221	4.3
Insurance benefits and repayments	7,656,740	16.9
Assistance and subsidies	620,052	1.4
Interest on debt	370,053	0.8
Exhibit: Salaries and wages	5,364,794	11.8
Total Expenditure	45,418,922	100.0
General expenditure	37,252,772	82.0
Intergovernmental expenditure	7,125,885	15.7
Direct expenditure	30,126,887	66.3
General expenditure, by function:		
Education	12,254,162	27.0
Public welfare	13,135,976	28.9
Hospitals	2,657,510	5.9
Health	1,097,717	2.4
Highways	1,209,117	2.7
Police protection	249,313	0.5
Correction	1,021,781	2.2
Natural resources	501,090	1.1
Parks and recreation	108,385	0.2
Governmental administration	1,911,930	4.2
Interest on general debt	370,053	0.8
Other and unallocable	2,488,426	5.5
Utility expenditure	172,393	0.4
Liquor stores expenditure	482043	1.1
Insurance trust expenditure	7,656,740	16.9
Debt at End of Fiscal Year	14,600,436	X
Cash and Security Holdings	114,776,636	X

X = Not applicable.

- = Zero or rounds to zero.

[1] Within insurance trust revenue, net earnings of state retirement systems is a calculated statistic (the item code in the data file is X08), and thus can be positive or negative. Net earnings is the sum of earnings on investments plus gains on investments minus losses on investments. The change made in 2002 for asset valuation from book to market value in accordance with Statement 34 of the Governmental Accounting Standards Board is reflected in the calculated statistics.

Table OR-16. State Government Tax Collections, 2021

(Dollars in thousands, percent.)

Item	Dollars	Percent distribution
Total Taxes	17,799,808	100.0
Property taxes	21,310	0.1
Sales and gross receipts	2,386,620	13.4
General sales and gross receipts	X	-
Selective sales and gross receipts	2,386,620	13.4
Alcoholic beverages	18,086	0.1
Amusements	27,122	0.2
Insurance premiums	49,633	0.3
Motor fuels	619,333	3.5
Pari-mutuels	2,336	-
Public utilities	18,564	0.1
Tobacco products	377,921	2.1
Other selective sales	1,273,625	7.2
Licenses	2,483,742	14.0
Alcoholic beverages	5,461	-
Amusements	2,429	-
Corporations in general	1,231,713	6.9
Hunting and fishing	64,021	0.4
Motor vehicle	795,820	4.5
Motor vehicle operators	48,734	0.3
Public utilities	16,902	0.1
Occupation and business, NEC	306,162	1.7
Other licenses	12,500	0.1
Income taxes	12,480,427	70.1
Individual income	11,256,904	63.2
Corporation net income	1,223,523	6.9
Other taxes	427,709	2.4
Death and gift	410,270	2.3
Documentary and stock transfer	1,957	-
Severance	15,482	0.1
Taxes, NEC	0	-

X = Not applicable.
- = Zero or rounds to zero.

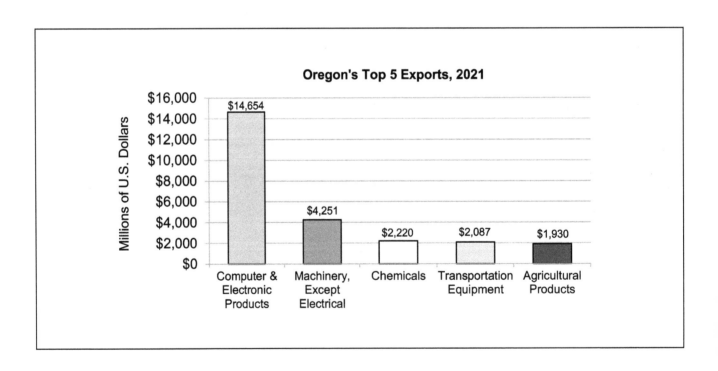

PENNSYLVANIA

Facts and Figures

Location: Northeastern United States; bordered on the N by Lake Erie and New York, on the E by New York and New Jersey, on the S by Delaware, Maryland, and West Virginia, and on the W by West Virginia and Ohio

Area: 46,055 sq. mi. (119,283 sq. km.); rank—33rd

Population: 12,964,056 (2021 est.); rank—5th

Principal Cities: capital—Harrisburg; largest—Philadelphia

Statehood: December 12, 1787; 2nd state

U.S. Congress: 2 senators, 18 representatives

State Motto: Virtue, Liberty, and Independence

State Song: "Pennsylvania"

State Nicknames: The Keystone State; The Quaker State

Abbreviations: PA; Penn.

State Symbols: flower—mountain laurel; tree—Eastern hemlock; bird—ruffed grouse

At a Glance

- With an increase in population of 2.1 percent, Pennsylvania ranked 44th among the states in growth from 2010 to 2021.

- Pennsylvania's median household income in 2021 was $63,627, and 12.0 percent of the population lived below the poverty level.

- Approximately 5.6 percent of Pennsylvanians did not have health insurance in 2020, compared to the national rate of 8.7 percent.

- Pennsylvania's violent crime rate in 2020 was 389.5 per 100,000 population, compared to 398.5 for the entire nation.

- The unemployment rate in Pennsylvania was 6.3 percent in 2020, compared to the national unemployment rate of 5.3 percent.

Table PA-1. Population by Age, Sex, Race, and Hispanic Origin

(Number, percent, except where noted.)

Sex, age, race, and Hispanic origin	2000	2010	2021	Percent change, 2010–2021
Total Population...	12,281,054	12,702,379	12,964,056	2.1
Percent of total U.S. population	4.4	4.1	3.9	X
Sex				
Male...	5,929,663	6,190,363	6,399,810	3.4
Female...	6,351,391	6,512,016	6,564,246	0.8
Age				
Under 5 years..	727,804	729,538	681,354	-6.6
5 to 19 years..	2,542,780	2,449,852	2,333,507	-4.7
20 to 64 years...	7,091,305	7,563,682	7,484,741	-1.0
65 years and over..	1,919,165	1,959,307	2,464,454	25.8
Median age (years)	38.0	40.1	40.9	2.0
Race and Hispanic Origin				
One race				
White..	10,484,203	10,663,774	10,502,382	-1.5
Black..	1,224,612	1,431,826	1,586,231	10.8
American Indian and Alaska Native	18,348	39,735	55,873	40.6
Asian..	219,813	358,195	512,050	43.0
Native Hawaiian or Other Pacific Islander	3,417	7,115	11,476	61.3
Two or more races..	142,224	201,734	296,044	46.7
Hispanic (of any race)...	394,088	758,058	1,084,634	43.1

NOTE: Population figures for 2021 are July 1 estimates. The 2000 and 2010 estimates are taken from the respective censuses.
- = Zero or rounds to zero.
X = Not applicable.

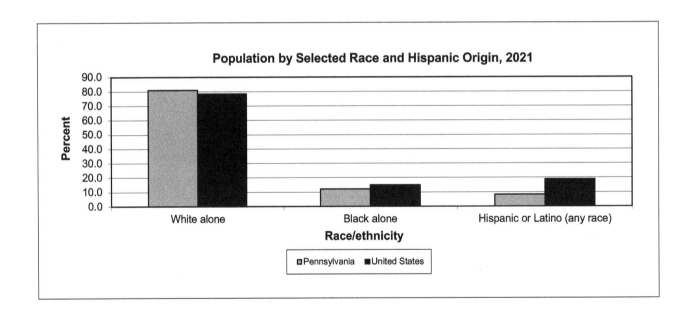

Population by Selected Race and Hispanic Origin, 2021

☐ Pennsylvania ■ United States

Table PA-2. Marital Status

(Number, percent distribution.)

Sex, age, race, and Hispanic origin	2000	2010	2020 [1]
Males, 15 Years and Over	4,686,277	5,031,761	5,152,460
Never married	30.1	35.9	36.5
Now married, except separated...	57.4	50.6	50.1
Separated...	1.9	2.0	1.7
Widowed...	3.3	3.1	3.0
Divorced..	7.3	8.5	8.6
Females, 15 Years and Over	5,175,436	5,406,494	5,459,826
Never married	24.6	29.8	30.6
Now married, except separated...	51.5	46.2	46.6
Separated...	2.4	2.7	2.2
Widowed...	12.7	11.2	10.0
Divorced..	8.8	10.2	10.6

[1] 2020 ACS 5-Year estimates. 1-Year estimates were not released for 2020 due to the impact of COVID-19 on data collection that year.

Table PA-3. Households and Housing Characteristics

(Number, percent, dollars.)

Item	2000	2010	2020 [1]	Average annual percent change, 2010–2020
Total Households..	4,777,003	4,936,030	5,106,601	0.5
Family households..	3,208,388	3,197,710	3,254,545	0.3
Married-couple family................................	2,467,673	2,381,094	2,423,060	0.3
Other family..	740,715	816,616	831,485	0.3
Male householder, no wife present................	186,022	215,082	232,419	1.2
Female householder, no husband present............	554,693	601,534	599,066	-0.1
Nonfamily households...................................	1,568,615	1,738,320	1,852,056	0.9
Householder living alone..............................	1,320,941	1,458,055	1,521,428	0.6
Householder not living alone.........................	247,674	280,265	330,628	2.6
Housing Characteristics				
Total housing units......................................	5,249,750	5,568,820	5,713,345	0.4
Occupied housing units.................................	4,777,003	4,936,030	5,106,601	0.5
Owner occupied...	3,406,337	3,461,678	3,522,269	0.3
Renter occupied...	1,370,666	1,474,352	1,584,332	1.1
Average household size.................................	2.48	2.49	2.42	-0.4
Financial Characteristics				
Median gross rent of renter-occupied housing........	531	763	958	3.7
Median monthly owner costs for housing units with a mortgage..........	1,010	1,390	1,505	1.2
Median value of owner-occupied housing units........	97,000	165,500	187,500	1.9

[1] 2020 ACS 5-Year estimates. 1-Year estimates were not released for 2020 due to the impact of COVID-19 on data collection that year.

Table PA-4. Migration, Origin, and Language

(Number, percent.)

Characteristic	State 2016-2020 [1]	U.S. 2016-2020 [1]
Residence 1 Year Ago		
Population 1 year and over..	12,661,101	322,943,283
Same house..	87.8	86.2
Different house in the U.S..	11.8	13.2
Same county..	7.0	7.7
Different county..	4.8	5.5
Same state..	2.8	3.2
Different state..	2.0	2.3
Abroad..	0.4	0.6
Place of Birth		
Native born..	11,898,032	282,443,680
Male..	49.0	49.4
Female..	51.0	50.6
Foreign born..	896,853	44,125,628
Male..	48.9	48.6
Female..	51.1	51.4
Foreign born; naturalized U.S. citizen..	486,000	22,456,684
Male..	46.6	46.1
Female..	53.4	53.9
Foreign born; not a U.S. citizen..	410,853	21,668,944
Male..	51.7	51.1
Female..	48.3	48.9
Entered 2010 or later..	28.5	22.8
Entered 2000 to 2009..	26.6	25.1
Entered before 2000..	45.0	52.1
World Region of Birth, Foreign		
Foreign-born population, excluding population born at sea........	896,853	44,125,628
Europe..	18.5	10.8
Asia..	39.2	31.3
Africa..	9.1	5.4
Oceania..	0.4	0.6
Latin America..	31.0	50.0
North America..	1.8	1.9
Language Spoken at Home and Ability to Speak English		
Population 5 years and over..	12,092,654	306,919,116
English only..	88.5	78.5
Language other than English..	11.5	21.5
Speaks English less than "very well"..	4.4	8.2

[1] 2020 ACS 5-Year estimates. 1-Year estimates were not released for 2020 due to the impact of COVID-19 on data collection that year.
NA = Not available.
X = Not applicable.
- = Zero or rounds to zero.

Table PA-5. Median Income and Poverty Status, 2020[1]

(Number, percent, except as noted.)

Characteristic	State		U.S.	
	Number	Percent	Number	Percent
Median Income				
Households (dollars)..	63,627	X	64,994	X
Families (dollars)	80,996	X	80,069	X
Below Poverty Level (All People)	1,480,430	12.0	40,910,326	12.8
Sex				
Male	653,231	10.8	18,171,512	11.6
Female	827,199	13.0	22,738,814	14.0
Age				
Under 18 years...	434,413	16.7	12,598,699	17.5
Related children under 18 years......................	424,592	16.4	12,306,532	17.2
18 to 64 years...	860,604	11.4	23,554,920	12.1
65 years and over	185,413	8.2	4,756,707	9.3

X = Not applicable.

[1] 2020 ACS 5-Year estimates. 1-Year estimates were not released for 2020 due to the impact of COVID-19 on data collection that year.

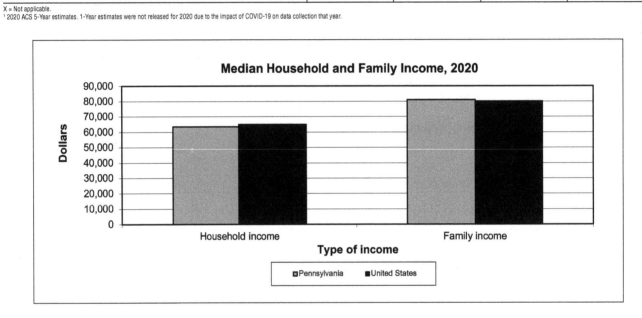

Median Household and Family Income, 2020

Table PA-6. Health Insurance Coverage Status for the Civilian Noninstitutionalized Population and Children Under 19 Years of Age

(Number, percent.)

Item	2011	2012	2013	2014	2015	2016	2017	2018	2019	2020[2]
Civilian Noninstitutionalized Population	12,539,757	12,559,315	12,569,375	12,582,815	12,599,417	12,579,422	12,602,472	12,604,311	12,593,136	12,590,644
Covered by Private or Public Insurance										
Number..	11,275,209	11,334,666	11,346,970	11,518,238	11,797,490	11,870,945	11,910,269	11,904,935	11,866,688	11,884,753
Percent..	89.9	90.2	90.3	91.5	93.6	94.4	94.5	94.5	94.2	94.4
Uninsured										
Number..	1,264,548	1,224,649	1,222,405	1,064,577	801,927	708,477	692,203	699,376	726,448	705,891
Percent..	10.1	9.8	9.7	8.5	6.4	5.6	5.5	5.5	5.8	5.6
Percent in the U.S. not covered...........................	15.1	14.8	14.5	11.7	9.4	8.6	8.7	8.9	9.2	8.7
Children Under 19 Years of Age[1]	2,754,741	2,730,989	2,708,843	2,693,074	2,685,304	2,666,701	2,834,916	2,820,785	2,803,506	2,818,899
Covered by Private or Public Insurance										
Number..	2,605,514	2,592,035	2,561,540	2,553,957	2,573,940	2,550,327	2,709,999	2,697,004	2,675,599	2,690,074
Percent..	94.6	94.9	94.6	94.8	95.9	95.6	95.6	95.6	95.4	95.4
Uninsured										
Number..	149,227	138,954	147,303	139,117	111,364	116,374	124,917	123,781	127,907	128,825
Percent..	5.4	5.1	5.4	5.2	4.1	4.4	4.4	4.4	4.6	4.6
Percent in the U.S. not covered...........................	7.5	7.2	7.1	6.0	4.8	4.5	5.0	5.2	5.7	5.2

[1] Data for years prior to 2017 are for individuals under 18 years of age.

[2] 2020 ACS 5-Year estimates. 1-Year estimates were not released for 2020 due to the impact of COVID-19 on data collection that year. Data is not comparable to previous years, which are based on 1-year estimates.

Table PA-7. Employment Status by Demographic Group, 2021

(Numbers in thousands, percent.)

Characteristic	Civilian noninstitutional population	Civilian labor force		Employed		Unemployed	
		Number	Percent of population	Number	Percent of population	Number	Percent of population
Total..	10,272	6,292	61.3	5,883	57.3	409	6.5
Sex							
Male..	4,961	3,281	66.1	3,050	61.5	231	7.0
Female...	5,312	3,012	56.7	2,833	53.3	178	5.9
Race, Sex, and Hispanic Origin							
White..	8,616	5,268	61.1	4,965	57.6	303	5.8
Male..	4,181	2,761	66.0	2,591	62.0	170	6.2
Female...	4,436	2,507	56.5	2,374	53.5	134	5.3
Black or African American.......................	1,144	680	59.5	595	52.1	85	12.5
Male..	523	327	62.6	278	53.3	49	14.9
Female...	621	353	56.9	317	51.0	36	10.2
Hispanic or Latino ethnicity[1].................	695	425	61.1	373	53.7	52	12.2
Male..	350	234	66.9	205	58.5	29	12.6
Female...	346	191	55.3	169	48.8	22	11.7
Age							
16 to 19 years....................................	637	287	45.1	261	40.9	27	9.3
20 to 24 years....................................	779	583	74.8	527	67.6	56	9.6
25 to 34 years....................................	1,671	1,402	83.9	1,295	77.5	107	7.6
35 to 44 years....................................	1,497	1,245	83.2	1,168	78.0	77	6.2
45 to 54 years....................................	1,450	1,171	80.7	1,107	76.3	64	5.4
55 to 64 years....................................	1,733	1,145	66.1	1,096	63.2	49	4.3
65 years and over................................	2,505	460	18.3	430	17.2	29	6.4

NOTE: Data in Table 7 are from the Current Population Survey (CPS) and do not match the estimates in Table 8. See notes and definitions for further information.
[1] May be of any race.

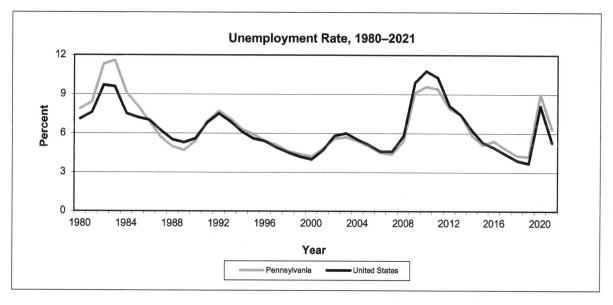

Table PA-8. Employment Status of the Civilian Noninstitutional Population Age 16 Years and Over

(Number, percent.)

Year	Civilian labor force	Civilian participation rate	Employed	Unemployed	Unemployment rate
2010..	6,360,605	63.3	5,838,498	522,107	8.2
2011..	6,381,749	63.1	5,886,748	495,001	7.8
2012..	6,449,023	63.5	5,955,409	493,614	7.7
2013..	6,419,837	63.1	5,962,130	457,707	7.1
2014..	6,389,059	62.6	6,010,075	378,984	5.9
2015..	6,423,155	62.9	6,076,402	346,753	5.4
2016..	6,458,891	63.1	6,114,644	344,247	5.3
2017..	6,485,253	62.6	6,161,913	323,340	5.0
2018..	6,500,149	62.6	6,210,098	290,051	4.5
2019..	6,560,773	63	6,266,508	294,265	4.5
2020..	6,482,770	62.2	5,893,583	589,187	9.1
2021..	6,406,185	61.5	5,999,442	406,743	6.3

Table PA-9. Employment and Average Wages by Industry

(Estimates are based on the 2012 North American Industry Classification System [NAICS].)

Industry	2013	2014	2015	2016	2017	2018	2019	2020
	Number of Jobs							
Wage and Salary Employment by Industry	5,933,931	5,987,610	6,037,780	6,086,529	6,144,339	6,219,072	6,279,312	5,826,487
Farm Wage and Salary Employment	22,320	21,096	23,223	28,025	27,002	22,230	20,404	17,198
Nonfarm Wage and Salary Employment	5,911,611	5,966,514	6,014,557	6,058,504	6,117,337	6,196,842	6,258,908	5,809,289
Private wage and salary employment	5,122,503	5,184,742	5,239,185	5,284,777	5,344,216	5,426,935	5,486,645	5,054,400
Forestry, fishing, and related activities	7,983	8,024	7,826	7,953	7,900	8,083	8,011	7,633
Mining	35,017	36,747	32,872	24,196	25,676	27,834	27,956	22,390
Utilities	22,007	21,466	24,200	23,961	23,749	23,728	23,171	22,662
Construction	231,742	236,823	241,359	245,041	254,827	262,048	267,104	247,580
Manufacturing	564,247	567,886	567,973	559,081	562,315	570,234	575,171	537,897
Durable goods manufacturing	346,410	346,580	346,136	335,559	335,999	342,596	345,888	319,086
Nondurable goods manufacturing	217,837	221,306	221,837	223,522	226,316	227,638	229,283	218,811
Wholesale trade	226,462	226,870	225,646	220,519	219,699	217,966	218,073	205,029
Retail trade	636,957	637,105	637,471	637,434	629,364	624,315	613,766	569,133
Transportation and warehousing	223,734	231,137	242,041	251,164	259,495	267,782	278,192	273,149
Information	88,568	85,327	85,144	84,513	83,462	85,972	87,107	82,883
Finance and insurance	263,434	266,776	266,531	264,978	270,081	272,992	278,992	279,488
Real estate and rental and leasing	60,217	61,758	63,333	63,907	64,526	66,433	67,085	63,662
Professional, scientific, and technical services	326,834	331,310	338,512	350,700	353,765	358,194	364,857	358,867
Management of companies and enterprises	133,362	132,872	132,518	135,026	136,171	136,949	136,177	126,850
Administrative and waste services	294,086	300,887	311,803	313,640	314,754	316,819	320,387	285,147
Educational services	245,970	249,647	252,468	259,240	263,081	270,238	272,155	256,903
Health care and social assistance	936,745	952,147	964,511	988,061	1,011,187	1,040,734	1,062,802	1,023,383
Arts, entertainment, and recreation	93,038	94,463	93,504	96,401	99,026	99,702	102,229	69,054
Accommodation and food services	442,440	447,976	455,122	464,703	471,716	476,066	479,595	358,747
Other services, except public administration	289,660	295,521	296,351	294,259	293,422	300,846	303,815	263,943
Government and government enterprises	789,108	781,772	775,372	773,727	773,121	769,907	772,263	754,889
	Dollars							
Average Wages and Salaries by Industry	48,064	49,495	51,062	51,337	52,865	54,542	56,347	60,612
Average Farm Wages and Salaries	25,011	26,710	21,053	20,021	18,858	23,838	19,945	23,546
Average Nonfarm Wages and Salaries	48,151	49,576	51,178	51,482	53,015	54,652	56,465	60,722
Average private wages and salaries	48,312	49,789	51,351	51,616	53,193	54,802	56,684	61,187
Forestry, fishing, and related activities	28,146	29,173	30,631	32,097	32,815	34,011	34,998	37,413
Mining	77,728	82,934	81,304	80,062	89,379	86,482	90,109	88,397
Utilities	103,325	109,277	109,587	110,850	113,855	119,115	117,255	120,050
Construction	56,823	58,765	60,153	61,596	64,759	66,844	68,602	70,615
Manufacturing	56,671	58,546	59,552	59,789	61,084	62,570	64,234	66,934
Durable goods manufacturing	57,293	59,320	60,099	60,042	62,072	63,762	65,026	66,906
Nondurable goods manufacturing	55,682	57,335	58,698	59,408	59,618	60,775	63,040	66,974
Wholesale trade	72,471	76,288	77,303	77,528	79,577	80,043	82,074	86,580
Retail trade	25,797	26,242	27,322	27,810	28,281	29,150	30,260	33,175
Transportation and warehousing	42,942	44,447	45,863	45,493	47,070	48,311	49,221	51,448
Information	69,087	70,632	73,526	75,193	78,915	87,093	94,858	107,322
Finance and insurance	80,538	84,384	87,424	87,911	91,652	95,281	97,151	103,389
Real estate and rental and leasing	51,230	54,089	56,581	57,730	58,280	60,961	62,614	68,175
Professional, scientific, and technical services	82,781	84,902	87,760	89,048	92,312	94,902	99,357	103,941
Management of companies and enterprises	115,056	120,870	130,137	122,988	127,088	129,265	135,631	138,924
Administrative and waste services	32,324	32,854	33,735	34,241	35,472	36,796	38,413	42,079
Educational services	42,235	42,842	43,982	44,613	45,166	46,310	47,331	50,713
Health care and social assistance	44,916	45,846	47,487	47,958	49,031	50,281	51,833	55,496
Arts, entertainment, and recreation	32,573	33,314	34,629	34,798	34,043	35,377	37,123	42,479
Accommodation and food services	18,274	18,783	19,401	19,874	20,411	21,470	22,163	21,274
Other services, except public administration	30,231	31,094	32,331	32,977	34,013	35,318	36,429	40,409
Government and government enterprises	47,107	48,162	50,006	50,568	51,783	53,597	54,910	57,609

Table PA-10. Employment Characteristics by Family Type

(Number, percent.)

Family type and labor force status	2018		2019		2020[1]	
	Total	Families with own children under 18 years	Total	Families with own children under 18 years	Total	Families with own children under 18 years
All Families...	3,235,257	1,254,628	3,228,224	1,240,704	3,254,545	1,278,062
FAMILY TYPE AND LABOR FORCE STATUS						
Opposite-Sex Married-Couple Families.............................	2,411,269	839,255	2,373,352	816,678	2,403,552	858,717
Both husband and wife in labor force....................................	52.9	72.3	52.3	71.8	53.1	71.5
Husband in labor force, wife not in labor force	18.7	22.3	19.0	22.5	19.3	23.3
Wife in labor force, husband not in labor force	8.1	3.5	8.1	3.8	8.1	3.7
Both husband and wife not in labor force.................	19.5	1.4	19.9	1.4	19.5	1.4
Other Families	823,988	415,373	854,872	424,026	831,485	415,946
Female householder, no spouse present	71.3	72.4	70.9	72.7	72.0	73.6
In labor force..	48.9	59.5	47.8	58.9	49.6	61.0
Not in labor force	22.5	12.9	23.1	13.8	22.5	12.6
Male householder, no spouse present...........................	28.7	27.6	29.1	27.3	28.0	26.4
In labor force..	22.1	24.9	22.6	24.5	21.4	23.6
Not in labor force	6.6	2.6	6.6	2.8	6.5	2.8

[1] 2020 ACS 5-Year estimates. 1-Year estimates were not released for 2020 due to the impact of COVID-19 on data collection that year. Data is not comparable to previous years, which are based on 1-year estimates.

Table PA-11. School Enrollment and Educational Attainment, 2020[1]

(Number, percent.)

Item	State	U.S.
Enrollment		
Total population 3 years and over, enrolled in school	2,908,512	80,497,960
Enrolled in nursery school or preschool (percent)..........................	6.2	6.1
Enrolled in kindergarten (percent)..........................	4.7	5.0
Enrolled in elementary school, grades 1-8 (percent)........................	40.2	40.4
Enrolled in high school, grades 9-12 (percent)........................	21.2	21.0
Enrolled in college or graduate school (percent)........................	27.7	27.6
Attainment		
Total population 25 years and over	8,989,998	222,836,834
Less than ninth grade (percent)	3.1	4.9
9th to 12th grade, no diploma (percent)	5.9	6.6
High school graduate, including equivalency (percent)................	34.2	26.7
Some college, no degree (percent)	15.9	20.3
Associate's degree (percent)	8.6	8.6
Bachelor's degree (percent)	19.5	20.2
Graduate or professional degree (percent)...........................	12.8	12.7
High school graduate or higher (percent)	91	88.5
Bachelor's degree or higher (percent)....................................	32.3	32.9

[1] 2020 ACS 5-Year estimates. 1-Year estimates were not released for 2020 due to the impact of COVID-19 on data collection that year.

Table PA-12. Public School Characteristics and Educational Indicators

(Number, percent; data derived from National Center of Education Statistics.)

Item	State	U.S.
Public Elementary and Secondary Schools		
Number of regular school districts, 2018-19	500	13,452
Number of operational schools, 2019-20................................	2,958	98,469
Percent charter schools	6.1	7.7
Total public school enrollment, Fall 2019...........................	1,732,449	50,796,445
Percent charter school enrollment	8.6	6.8
Student-teacher ratio, Fall 2019...........................	13.9	15.9
Expenditures per student (unadjusted dollars), 2018-19	16,892	13,187
Four-year adjusted cohort graduation rate (ACGR), 2018-2019[1]............	86.5	85.8
Students eligible for free or reduced-price lunch (percent), 2019-20.........	50.7	52.1
English language learners (percent), Fall 2019	4.2	10.4
Students age 3 to 21 served under IDEA, part B (percent), 2020-21	19.9	14.5

Public Schools by Type, 2019-20	Number	Percent of state public schools
Total number of schools.................................	2,958	100.0
Special education	4	0.1
Vocational education	84	2.8
Alternative education.......................................	6	0.2

[1] Adjusted Cohort Graduation Rates (ACGR) differ from Averaged Freshmen Graduation Rates (AFGR).
- = Zero or rounds to zero.

Table PA-13. Reported Voting and Registration of the Voting-Age Population, November 2020

(Numbers in thousands, percent.)

Item	Total population	Total citizen population	Registered			Voted		
			Total registered	Percent registered (total population)	Percent registered (total citizen population)	Total voted	Percent voted (total population)	Percent voted (total citizen population)
U.S. Total	252,274	231,593	168,308	66.7	72.7	154,628	61.3	66.8
State Total......................................	9,902	9,621	7,337	74.1	76.3	6,756	68.2	70.2
Sex								
Male	4,787	4,638	3,489	72.9	75.2	3,192	66.7	68.8
Female	5,115	4,983	3,848	75.2	77.2	3,564	69.7	71.5
Race								
White alone......................................	8,485	8,324	6,390	75.3	76.8	5,875	69.2	70.6
White, non-Hispanic alone	7,910	7,862	6,115	77.3	77.8	5,634	71.2	71.7
Black alone......................................	1,042	981	751	72.0	76.5	694	66.6	70.8
Asian alone	231	171	88	38.0	51.4	84	36.3	49.1
Hispanic (of any race)	618	497	305	49.3	61.4	270	43.6	54.3
White alone or in combination	8,613	8,453	6,486	75.3	76.7	5,965	69.3	70.6
Black alone or in combination	1,139	1,078	824	72.3	76.4	761	66.9	70.6
Asian alone or in combination..................	246	186	103	41.8	55.4	99	40.3	53.2
Age								
18 to 24 years..................................	1,049	1,017	601	57.3	59.1	519	49.4	51.0
25 to 34 years..................................	1,789	1,747	1,354	75.7	77.5	1,207	67.4	69.0
35 to 44 years..................................	1,360	1,281	948	69.7	74.0	866	63.6	67.6
45 to 64 years..................................	3,212	3,122	2,491	77.6	79.8	2,315	72.1	74.1
65 years and over	2,492	2,453	1,943	78.0	79.2	1,850	74.2	75.4

Table PA-14. Crime

(Number, rate per 100,000. Data are derived from the FBI Uniform Crime Reports.)

Item	State [3]			U.S.		
	2019	2020	Percent change	2019	2020	Percent change
TOTAL POPULATION[1]	12,798,883	12,783,254	-0.1	328,329,953	329,484,123	0.4
VIOLENT CRIME						
Number..	39,160	49,793	27.2	1,250,393	1,313,105	5.0
Rate	306.0	389.5	27.3	380.8	398.5	4.6
Murder and Nonnegligent Manslaughter						
Number..	676	1,009	49.3	16,669	21,570	29.4
Rate	5.3	7.9	49.4	5.1	6.5	28.9
Rape[2]						
Number..	4,345	4,228	-2.7	143,224	126,430	-11.7
Rate	33.9	33.1	-2.6	43.6	38.4	-12.0
Robbery						
Number..	9,749	10,728	10.0	268,483	243,600	-9.3
Rate	76.2	83.9	10.2	81.8	73.9	-9.6
Aggravated Assault						
Number..	24,390	33,828	38.7	822,017	921,505	12.1
Rate	190.6	264.6	38.9	250.4	279.7	11.7
PROPERTY CRIME						
Number..	179,670	210,167	17.0	6,995,235	6,452,038	-7.8
Rate	1,403.8	1,644.1	17.1	2,130.6	1,958.2	-8.1
Burglary						
Number..	23,324	31,774	36.2	1,118,096	1,035,314	-7.4
Rate	182.2	248.6	36.4	340.5	314.2	-7.7
Larceny-Theft						
Number..	143,937	162,919	13.2	5,152,267	4,606,324	-10.6
Rate	1,124.6	1,274.5	13.3	1,569.2	1,398.0	-10.9
Motor Vehicle Theft						
Number..	12,409	15,474	24.7	724,872	810,400	11.8
Rate	97.0	121.0	24.9	220.8	246.0	11.4

NOTE: Although arson data are included in the trend and clearance tables, sufficient data are not available to estimate totals for this offense. Therefore, no arson data are published in this table.
- = Zero or rounds to zero.
[1] Population figures are U.S. Census Bureau provisional estimates as of July 1, 2020.
[2] The figures shown in the rape (revised definition) column were estimated using the revised Uniform Crime Reporting (UCR) definition of rape.
[3] Limited data for 2020 were available for Alabama, Maryland and Pennsylvania.

Table PA-15. State Government Finances, 2020

(Dollar amounts in thousands, percent distribution.)

Item	Dollars	Percent distribution
Total Revenue	118,039,146	100.0
General revenue	96,756,922	82.0
Intergovernmental revenue	37,778,820	32.0
Taxes	40,684,520	34.5
General sales	11630402	9.9
Selective sales	9,814,661	8.3
License taxes	2,594,319	2.2
Individual income tax	12372183	10.5
Corporate income tax	2,510,056	2.1
Other taxes	1,762,899	1.5
Current charges	13,082,597	11.1
Miscellaneous general revenue	5,210,985	4.4
Utility revenue	0	-
Liquor stores revenue	2039324	1.7
Insurance trust revenue[1]	19,242,900	16.3
Total Expenditure	122,554,436	100.0
Intergovernmental expenditure	24,373,098	19.9
Direct expenditure	98,181,338	80.1
Current operation	66,550,723	54.3
Capital outlay	9,711,332	7.9
Insurance benefits and repayments	18,247,962	14.9
Assistance and subsidies	2,003,136	1.6
Interest on debt	1,668,185	1.4
Exhibit: Salaries and wages	11,305,570	9.2
Total Expenditure	122,554,436	100.0
General expenditure	102,465,625	83.6
Intergovernmental expenditure	24,373,098	19.9
Direct expenditure	78,092,527	63.7
General expenditure, by function:		
Education	28,750,329	23.5
Public welfare	39,927,502	32.6
Hospitals	5,998,995	4.9
Health	4,062,176	3.3
Highways	9,169,129	7.5
Police protection	1,236,939	1.0
Correction	2,630,519	2.1
Natural resources	823,033	0.7
Parks and recreation	317,235	0.3
Governmental administration	3,252,270	2.7
Interest on general debt	1,668,185	1.4
Other and unallocable	2,890,078	2.4
Utility expenditure	1,678,373	1.4
Liquor stores expenditure	1840849	1.5
Insurance trust expenditure	18,247,962	14.9
Debt at End of Fiscal Year	51,734,691	X
Cash and Security Holdings	140,855,805	X

X = Not applicable.
- = Zero or rounds to zero.
[1] Within insurance trust revenue, net earnings of state retirement systems is a calculated statistic (the item code in the data file is X08), and thus can be positive or negative. Net earnings is the sum of earnings on investments plus gains on investments minus losses on investments. The change made in 2002 for asset valuation from book to market value in accordance with Statement 34 of the Governmental Accounting Standards Board is reflected in the calculated statistics.

Table PA-16. State Government Tax Collections, 2021

(Dollars in thousands, percent.)

Item	Dollars	Percent distribution
Total Taxes	49,571,347	100.0
Property taxes	40,395	0.1
Sales and gross receipts	24,412,646	49.2
General sales and gross receipts	13,717,681	27.7
Selective sales and gross receipts	10,694,965	21.6
Alcoholic beverages	445,401	0.9
Amusements	1,754,340	3.5
Insurance premiums	852,301	1.7
Motor fuels	3,031,113	6.1
Pari-mutuels	10,367	-
Public utilities	994,326	2.0
Tobacco products	1,292,064	2.6
Other selective sales	2,315,053	4.7
Licenses	2,955,413	6.0
Alcoholic beverages	23,511	-
Amusements	48,133	0.1
Corporations in general	15,125	-
Hunting and fishing	86,559	0.2
Motor vehicle	1,307,236	2.6
Motor vehicle operators	94,891	0.2
Public utilities	72,725	0.1
Occupation and business, NEC	1,284,008	2.6
Other licenses	23,225	-
Income taxes	20,023,246	40.4
Individual income	15,977,933	32.2
Corporation net income	4,045,313	8.2
Other taxes	2,139,647	4.3
Death and gift	1,302,914	2.6
Documentary and stock transfer	787,842	1.6
Severance	0	-
Taxes, NEC	48,891	0.1

X = Not applicable.
- = Zero or rounds to zero.

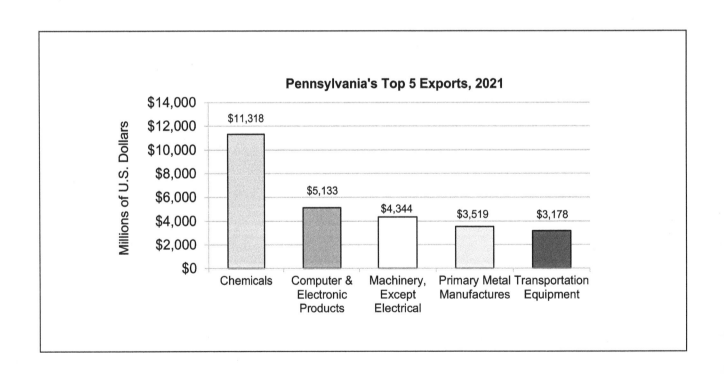

Pennsylvania's Top 5 Exports, 2021

RHODE ISLAND

Facts and Figures

Location: Eastern United States; bordered on the N by Massachusetts, on the E by Massachusetts and the Atlantic Ocean, on the S by Block Island Sound and the Atlantic Ocean, and on the W by Connecticut

Area: 1,545 sq. mi. (4,002 sq. km.); rank—50th

Population: 1,095,610 (2021 est.); rank—44th

Principal Cities: capital—Providence; largest—Providence

Statehood: May 29, 1790; 13th state

U.S. Congress: 2 senators, 2 representatives

State Motto: Hope

State Song: "Rhode Island"

State Nickname: The Ocean State

Abbreviations: RI; R.I.

State Symbols: flower—violet; tree—red maple; bird—Rhode Island red

At a Glance

- With an increase in population of 4.1 percent, Rhode Island ranked 32nd among the states in growth from 2010 to 2021.

- In 2020, 4.3 percent of Rhode Islanders did not have health insurance, the 5th lowest percentage in the country.

- Rhode Island's violent crime rate in 2020 was 230.8 per 100,000 population, compared to 398.5 for the entire nation.

- The median income of Rhode Islanders in 2020 was $70,305, and 11.6 percent of its residents lived below the poverty level.

- In 2021, 19.1 percent of Rhode Island's population was under 18 years old, and 18.1 percent of its population was 65 years or older, compared to the national averages of 22.2 percent and 16.8 percent respectively.

Table RI-1. Population by Age, Sex, Race, and Hispanic Origin

(Number, percent, except where noted.)

Sex, age, race, and Hispanic origin	2000	2010	2021	Percent change, 2010–2021
Total Population..	1,048,319	1,052,567	1,095,610	4.1
Percent of total U.S. population	0.4	0.3	0.3	X
Sex				
Male..	503,635	508,400	536,961	5.6
Female	544,684	544,167	558,649	2.7
Age				
Under 5 years..	63,896	57,448	53,550	-6.8
5 to 19 years..	218,720	204,310	190,150	-6.9
20 to 64 years.......................................	613,301	638,928	653,119	2.2
65 years and over	152,402	151,881	198,791	30.9
Median age (years)	36.7	39.4	40.3	2.3
Race and Hispanic Origin				
One race				
White	891,191	910,253	910,242	-
Black	46,908	75,073	96,864	29.0
American Indian and Alaska Native	5,121	9,173	12,780	39.3
Asian	23,665	31,768	40,493	27.5
Native Hawaiian or Other Pacific Islander	567	1,602	2,325	45.1
Two or more races	28,251	24,698	32,906	33.2
Hispanic (of any race)...............................	90,820	137,169	187,776	36.9

NOTE: Population figures for 2021 are July 1 estimates. The 2000 and 2010 estimates are taken from the respective censuses.
- = Zero or rounds to zero.
X = Not applicable.

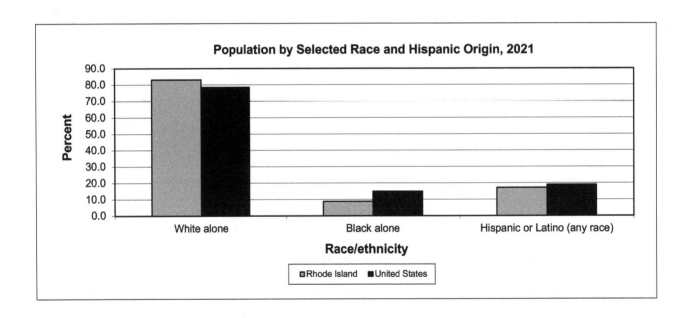

Table RI-2. Marital Status

(Number, percent distribution.)

Sex, age, race, and Hispanic origin	2000	2010	2020 [1]
Males, 15 Years and Over	396,396	414,628	428,146
Never married	32.5	39.8	39.8
Now married, except separated......................................	54.9	45.2	47.0
Separated..	1.5	1.6	1.0
Widowed..	3.0	3.1	2.6
Divorced..	8.0	10.3	9.6
Females, 15 Years and Over	445,107	456,425	461,075
Never married	27.1	32.4	34.4
Now married, except separated......................................	48.5	41.8	42.4
Separated..	2.3	2.4	1.6
Widowed..	11.5	10.4	9.2
Divorced..	10.7	13.0	12.4

[1] 2020 ACS 5-Year estimates. 1-Year estimates were not released for 2020 due to the impact of COVID-19 on data collection that year.

Table RI-3. Households and Housing Characteristics

(Number, percent, dollars.)

Item	2000	2010	2020 [1]	Average annual percent change, 2010–2020
Total Households..	408,424	402,295	414,730	0.4
Family households	265,398	246,028	257,849	0.7
Married-couple family	196,757	173,848	184,719	0.9
Other family	68,641	72,180	73,130	0.2
Male householder, no wife present..............	16,032	17,525	19,320	1.5
Female householder, no husband present......	52,609	54,655	53,810	-0.2
Nonfamily households	143,026	156,267	156,881	0.1
Householder living alone...............................	116,678	125,371	126,890	0.2
Householder not living alone..........................	26,348	30,896	29,991	-0.4
Housing Characteristics				
Total housing units	439,837	463,416	469,289	0.2
Occupied housing units	408,424	402,295	414,730	0.4
Owner occupied	245,156	244,516	255,450	0.6
Renter occupied	163,268	157,779	159,280	0.1
Average household size.................................	2.47	2.51	2.45	-0.3
Financial Characteristics				
Median gross rent of renter-occupied housing	553	868	1,031	2.7
Median monthly owner costs for housing units with a mortgage	1,205	1,837	1,879	0.3
Median value of owner-occupied housing units....	133,000	254,500	276,600	1.2

[1] 2020 ACS 5-Year estimates. 1-Year estimates were not released for 2020 due to the impact of COVID-19 on data collection that year.

Table RI-4. Migration, Origin, and Language

(Number, percent.)

Characteristic	State 2016-2020 [1]	U.S. 2016-2020 [1]
Residence 1 Year Ago		
Population 1 year and over	1,047,800	322,943,283
Same house	88.1	86.2
Different house in the U.S.	11.3	13.2
Same county	6.3	7.7
Different county	5.0	5.5
Same state	1.7	3.2
Different state	3.3	2.3
Abroad	0.7	0.6
Place of Birth		
Native born	909,493	282,443,680
Male	48.5	49.4
Female	51.5	50.6
Foreign born	148,305	44,125,628
Male	49.5	48.6
Female	50.5	51.4
Foreign born; naturalized U.S. citizen...............................	84,023	22,456,684
Male	47.2	46.1
Female	52.8	53.9
Foreign born; not a U.S. citizen.......................................	64,282	21,668,944
Male	52.5	51.1
Female	47.5	48.9
Entered 2010 or later	23.5	22.8
Entered 2000 to 2009	22.6	25.1
Entered before 2000..	53.9	52.1
World Region of Birth, Foreign		
Foreign-born population, excluding population born at sea	148,305	44,125,628
Europe	21.3	10.8
Asia	19.0	31.3
Africa	12.6	5.4
Oceania	0.2	0.6
Latin America..	45.2	50.0
North America	1.7	1.9
Language Spoken at Home and Ability to Speak English		
Population 5 years and over..	1,003,110	306,919,116
English only	77.6	78.5
Language other than English..	22.4	21.5
Speaks English less than "very well"...................................	8.4	8.2

[1] 2020 ACS 5-Year estimates. 1-Year estimates were not released for 2020 due to the impact of COVID-19 on data collection that year.
NA = Not available.
X = Not applicable.
- = Zero or rounds to zero.

Table RI-5. Median Income and Poverty Status, 2020[1]

(Number, percent, except as noted.)

Characteristic	State Number	State Percent	U.S. Number	U.S. Percent
Median Income				
Households (dollars)...	70,305	X	64,994	X
Families (dollars)	89,330	X	80,069	X
Below Poverty Level (All People)	117,785	11.6	40,910,326	12.8
Sex				
Male	52,293	10.5	18,171,512	11.6
Female	65,492	12.6	22,738,814	14.0
Age				
Under 18 years...	31,629	15.6	12,598,699	17.5
Related children under 18 years...	30,732	15.3	12,306,532	17.2
18 to 64 years	69,731	10.9	23,554,920	12.1
65 years and over	16,425	9.3	4,756,707	9.3

X = Not applicable.
[1] 2020 ACS 5-Year estimates. 1-Year estimates were not released for 2020 due to the impact of COVID-19 on data collection that year.

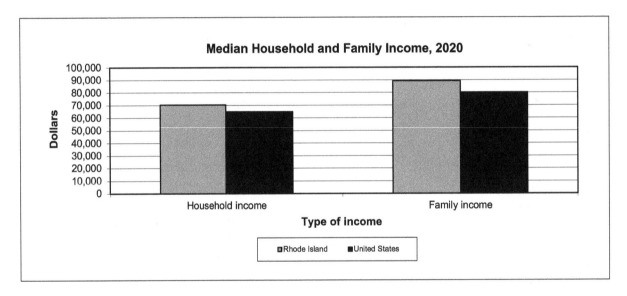

Table RI-6. Health Insurance Coverage Status for the Civilian Noninstitutionalized Population and Children Under 19 Years of Age

(Number, percent.)

Item	2011	2012	2013	2014	2015	2016	2017	2018	2019	2020 [2]
Civilian Noninstitutionalized Population	1,035,117	1,034,895	1,036,046	1,039,789	1,041,268	1,040,259	1,044,111	1,041,309	1,043,753	1,041,644
Covered by Private or Public Insurance										
Number..	923,283	920,030	915,586	962,670	981,858	995,293	995,921	998,828	1,001,033	997,069
Percent...	89.2	88.9	88.4	92.6	94.3	95.7	95.4	95.9	95.9	95.7
Uninsured										
Number..	111,834	114,865	120,460	77,119	59,410	44,966	48,190	42,481	42,720	44,575
Percent...	10.8	11.1	11.6	7.4	5.7	4.3	4.6	4.1	4.1	4.3
Percent in the U.S. not covered.......................................	15.1	14.8	14.5	11.7	9.4	8.6	8.7	8.9	9.2	8.7
Children Under 19 Years of Age[1]	218,624	216,675	212,430	212,271	211,397	208,268	224,008	219,314	220,276	221,949
Covered by Private or Public Insurance										
Number..	209,952	206,885	200,866	205,164	204,137	204,269	219,375	214,529	216,095	216,529
Percent...	96.0	95.5	94.6	96.7	96.6	98.1	97.9	97.8	98.1	97.6
Uninsured										
Number..	8,672	9,790	11,564	7,107	7,260	3,999	4,633	4,785	4,181	5,420
Percent...	4.0	4.5	5.4	3.3	3.4	1.9	2.1	2.2	1.9	2.4
Percent in the U.S. not covered.......................................	7.5	7.2	7.1	6.0	4.8	4.5	5.0	5.2	5.7	5.2

[1] Data for years prior to 2017 are for individuals under 18 years of age.
[2] 2020 ACS 5-Year estimates. 1-Year estimates were not released for 2020 due to the impact of COVID-19 on data collection that year. Data is not comparable to previous years, which are based on 1-year estimates.

Table RI-7. Employment Status by Demographic Group, 2021

(Numbers in thousands, percent.)

Characteristic	Civilian noninstitutional population	Civilian labor force		Employed		Unemployed	
		Number	Percent of population	Number	Percent of population	Number	Percent of population
Total	864	550	63.6	520	60.2	30	5.5
Sex							
Male	415	279	67.3	262	63.2	17	6.0
Female	450	271	60.3	258	57.3	13	4.9
Race, Sex, and Hispanic Origin							
White	760	480	63.1	456	60.0	24	5.0
Male	365	242	66.3	228	62.7	13	5.5
Female	395	238	60.2	227	57.5	11	4.6
Black or African American	63	43	67.4	39	61.1	4	9.4
Male	31	23	75.8	21	68.4	2	10.1
Female	NA	NA	NA	NA	NA	NA	NA
Hispanic or Latino ethnicity[1]	93	60	64.5	54	58.0	6	10.1
Male	45	30	66.9	27	59.9	3	10.7
Female	48	30	62.1	27	56.3	3	9.5
Age							
16 to 19 years	NA	NA	NA	NA	NA	NA	NA
20 to 24 years	62	49	78.4	44	70.5	5	10.3
25 to 34 years	152	129	84.6	122	79.9	7	5.6
35 to 44 years	136	114	83.7	108	79.5	6	5.0
45 to 54 years	123	102	82.9	99	79.9	4	3.5
55 to 64 years	141	91	64.4	87	61.7	4	4.2
65 years and over	201	46	23.0	43	21.6	3	5.8

NOTE: Data in Table 7 are from the Current Population Survey (CPS) and do not match the estimates in Table 8. See notes and definitions for further information.
[1] May be of any race.

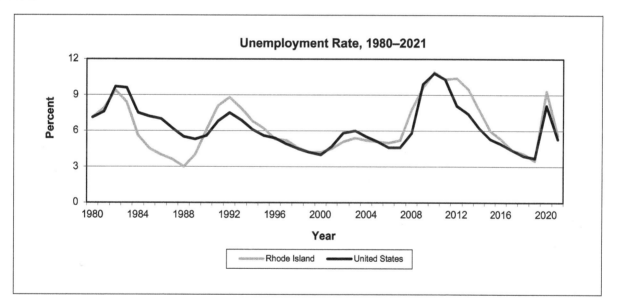

Table RI-8. Employment Status of the Civilian Noninstitutional Population Age 16 Years and Over

(Number, percent.)

Year	Civilian labor force	Civilian participation rate	Employed	Unemployed	Unemployment rate
2010	571,505	67.8	504,957	66,548	11.6
2011	562,061	66.6	500,109	61,952	11.0
2012	560,204	66.1	502,897	57,307	10.2
2013	558,747	65.7	505,776	52,971	9.5
2014	556,635	65.2	513,406	43,229	7.8
2015	555,272	64.9	521,767	33,505	6.0
2016	553,231	64.5	524,438	28,793	5.2
2017	568,144	64.4	542,552	25,592	4.5
2018	571,152	64.3	547,994	23,158	4.1
2019	572,382	64.2	552,057	20,325	3.6
2020	567,055	63.3	514,911	52,144	9.2
2021	571,034	63.6	538,969	32,065	5.6

Table RI-9. Employment and Average Wages by Industry

(Estimates are based on the 2012 North American Industry Classification System [NAICS].)

Industry	2013	2014	2015	2016	2017	2018	2019	2020
	Number of Jobs							
Wage and Salary Employment by Industry........................	483,908	491,596	499,350	502,469	506,216	512,429	516,468	475,325
Farm Wage and Salary Employment..............................	613	615	614	572	571	481	485	463
Nonfarm Wage and Salary Employment..........................	483,295	490,981	498,736	501,897	505,645	511,948	515,983	474,862
Private wage and salary employment...	411,564	419,162	426,862	429,804	433,213	439,088	441,727	401,416
Forestry, fishing, and related activities	(D)	(D)	(D)	(D)	(D)	(D)	(D)	(D)
Mining..	(D)	(D)	(D)	(D)	(D)	(D)	(D)	(D)
Utilities...	1,060	1,057	1,082	1,080	1,093	1,141	1,114	1,100
Construction...	16,545	16,898	17,441	18,578	(D)	19,683	20,451	19,394
Manufacturing...	40,130	40,940	41,195	40,449	40,419	40,380	39,773	37,443
Durable goods manufacturing...............................	25,597	26,138	26,015	25,228	25,133	25,820	25,508	23,419
Nondurable goods manufacturing.........................	14,533	14,802	15,180	15,221	15,286	14,560	14,265	14,024
Wholesale trade	16,763	16,900	17,025	16,730	16,615	16,561	16,646	14,969
Retail trade...	46,892	47,480	48,376	48,511	48,852	49,014	48,370	44,402
Transportation and warehousing................................	9,727	9,934	10,255	10,350	10,587	10,908	11,300	11,086
Information...	9,096	8,867	8,644	8,075	6,136	5,930	5,883	5,241
Finance and insurance	24,717	25,060	25,568	25,531	27,640	27,071	27,117	27,062
Real estate and rental and leasing............................	6,038	6,024	6,129	6,219	6,309	6,527	6,610	5,859
Professional, scientific, and technical services	22,162	23,001	24,074	24,568	25,256	25,745	25,893	25,820
Management of companies and enterprises.....................	11,343	12,013	12,572	13,394	13,509	13,330	13,236	12,634
Administrative and waste services	25,550	26,262	27,347	28,055	28,980	29,803	29,538	27,200
Educational services	24,341	25,402	26,690	26,558	26,866	29,594	29,983	28,155
Health care and social assistance.............................	81,417	81,178	81,252	81,141	80,921	81,029	82,464	76,381
Arts, entertainment, and recreation...........................	8,481	9,098	9,040	9,463	9,557	9,233	8,013	5,784
Accommodation and food services............................	45,401	46,572	47,514	48,458	49,150	50,331	52,342	39,206
Other services, except public administration..........................	21,189	21,718	21,838	21,839	21,739	22,069	22,219	18,894
Government and government enterprises..................................	71,731	71,819	71,874	72,093	72,432	72,860	74,256	73,446
	Dollars							
Average Wages and Salaries by Industry	48,459	49,989	51,271	51,962	53,408	54,327	55,508	60,892
Average Farm Wages and Salaries	27,290	28,821	23,581	29,051	26,410	25,220	19,862	20,205
Average Nonfarm Wages and Salaries	48,485	50,016	51,306	51,989	53,438	54,354	55,542	60,932
Average private wages and salaries............................	47,065	48,768	50,019	50,767	52,210	52,959	54,171	59,966
Forestry, fishing, and related activities	(D)	(D)	(D)	(D)	(D)	(D)	(D)	(D)
Mining..	(D)	(D)	(D)	(D)	(D)	(D)	(D)	(D)
Utilities...	96,739	97,868	98,678	104,545	109,432	118,575	116,879	118,731
Construction	55,199	56,100	57,771	59,346	(D)	62,694	64,476	68,168
Manufacturing...	55,330	56,772	57,995	58,276	59,848	60,788	62,668	66,178
Durable goods manufacturing...............................	56,989	58,117	59,026	59,576	61,935	62,737	64,761	68,426
Nondurable goods manufacturing.........................	52,407	54,397	56,228	56,122	56,416	57,330	58,927	62,425
Wholesale trade	69,412	70,479	70,989	72,725	76,171	76,911	79,311	87,883
Retail trade...	28,639	29,840	31,142	31,663	32,297	33,533	34,673	38,607
Transportation and warehousing................................	41,352	42,414	43,100	43,608	43,781	45,511	45,863	47,850
Information...	67,771	70,540	71,966	74,904	73,152	76,855	78,913	90,462
Finance and insurance	86,567	93,725	93,749	96,726	101,774	100,390	104,088	112,374
Real estate and rental and leasing............................	42,636	44,268	46,486	47,093	48,113	49,290	52,070	56,716
Professional, scientific, and technical services	69,314	72,371	74,492	75,048	77,387	79,616	83,182	87,977
Management of companies and enterprises.....................	116,746	122,500	124,259	122,815	124,079	125,143	111,917	128,623
Administrative and waste services	34,539	35,370	36,138	36,604	37,603	39,225	40,765	45,063
Educational services	42,356	42,729	42,446	41,207	42,624	40,920	41,726	45,692
Health care and social assistance.............................	44,108	45,198	46,935	47,374	48,182	49,341	51,188	55,702
Arts, entertainment, and recreation...........................	29,438	31,215	33,989	35,686	37,031	35,180	34,381	37,405
Accommodation and food services............................	19,985	20,673	21,570	22,672	23,529	25,146	26,497	26,310
Other services, except public administration..........................	31,010	32,009	33,320	34,205	35,062	36,063	37,264	41,264
Government and government enterprises..................................	56,635	57,301	58,947	59,271	60,785	62,767	63,699	66,213

D = Not shown to avoid disclosure of confidential information, but the estimates for this item are included in the total.

Table RI-10. Employment Characteristics by Family Type

(Number, percent.)

Family type and labor force status	2018 Total	2018 Families with own children under 18 years	2019 Total	2019 Families with own children under 18 years	2020[1] Total	2020[1] Families with own children under 18 years
All Families..	247,476	99,772	249,987	96,879	257,849	105,380
FAMILY TYPE AND LABOR FORCE STATUS						
Opposite-Sex Married-Couple Families............................	174,713	63,545	179,776	61,595	182,632	67,004
Both husband and wife in labor force..............................	55.6	74.6	56.5	77.2	57.0	75.1
Husband in labor force, wife not in labor force	18.5	20.5	16.7	17.6	18.1	20.0
Wife in labor force, husband not in labor force	6.6	2.3	8.0	3.9	8.1	3.8
Both husband and wife not in labor force........................	18.1	1.7	18.1	1.1	16.8	1.1
Other Families	72,763	36,227	70,211	35,284	73,130	38,016
Female householder, no spouse present	72.9	76.0	68.9	71.0	73.6	75.7
In labor force..	50.0	60.3	48.1	57.8	51.6	61.5
Not in labor force..	22.9	15.7	20.8	13.2	22.0	14.2
Male householder, no spouse present..........................	27.1	24.0	31.1	29.0	26.4	24.3
In labor force..	19.7	20.2	25.0	26.5	21.0	21.6
Not in labor force..	7.4	3.8	6.1	2.5	5.4	2.7

[1] 2020 ACS 5-Year estimates. 1-Year estimates were not released for 2020 due to the impact of COVID-19 on data collection that year. Data is not comparable to previous years, which are based on 1-year estimates.

Table RI-11. School Enrollment and Educational Attainment, 2020[1]

(Number, percent.)

Item	State	U.S.
Enrollment		
Total population 3 years and over, enrolled in school	255,231	80,497,960
Enrolled in nursery school or preschool (percent).................................	5.4	6.1
Enrolled in kindergarten (percent)..	4.3	5.0
Enrolled in elementary school, grades 1-8 (percent).............................	35.3	40.4
Enrolled in high school, grades 9-12 (percent)...................................	19.0	21.0
Enrolled in college or graduate school (percent).................................	36	27.6
Attainment		
Total population 25 years and over	741,370	222,836,834
Less than ninth grade (percent)..	4.7	4.9
9th to 12th grade, no diploma (percent)	6.1	6.6
High school graduate, including equivalency (percent)............................	28.0	26.7
Some college, no degree (percent)...	18.0	20.3
Associate's degree (percent)...	8.2	8.6
Bachelor's degree (percent)..	21.0	20.2
Graduate or professional degree (percent)..	14.0	12.7
High school graduate or higher (percent)...	89.2	88.5
Bachelor's degree or higher (percent)..	35.0	32.9

[1] 2020 ACS 5-Year estimates. 1-Year estimates were not released for 2020 due to the impact of COVID-19 on data collection that year.

Table RI-12. Public School Characteristics and Educational Indicators

(Number, percent; data derived from National Center of Education Statistics.)

Item	State	U.S.
Public Elementary and Secondary Schools		
Number of regular school districts, 2018-19	36	13,452
Number of operational schools, 2019-20..	316	98,469
Percent charter schools	11.7	7.7
Total public school enrollment, Fall 2019..	143,557	50,796,445
Percent charter school enrollment	7.1	6.8
Student-teacher ratio, Fall 2019..	13.4	15.9
Expenditures per student (unadjusted dollars), 2018-19	17,539	13,187
Four-year adjusted cohort graduation rate (ACGR), 2018-2019[1].....................	83.9	85.8
Students eligible for free or reduced-price lunch (percent), 2019-20................	47.7	52.1
English language learners (percent), Fall 2019.....................................	12.2	10.4
Students age 3 to 21 served under IDEA, part B (percent), 2020-21	17.2	14.5

Public Schools by Type, 2019-20	Number	Percent of state public schools
Total number of schools..	316	100.0
Special education..	1	0.3
Vocational education...	10	3.2
Alternative education..	3	0.9

[1] Adjusted Cohort Graduation Rates (ACGR) differ from Averaged Freshmen Graduation Rates (AFGR).

Table RI-13. Reported Voting and Registration of the Voting-Age Population, November 2020

(Numbers in thousands, percent.)

Item	Total population	Total citizen population	Registered			Voted		
			Total registered	Percent registered (total population)	Percent registered (total citizen population)	Total voted	Percent voted (total population)	Percent voted (total citizen population)
U.S. Total	252,274	231,593	168,308	66.7	72.7	154,628	61.3	66.8
State Total..	840	776	575	68.5	74.1	515	61.3	66.3
Sex								
Male	402	377	273	68.0	72.5	246	61.3	65.3
Female	438	399	302	69.1	75.7	269	61.4	67.2
Race								
White alone.......................................	742	698	519	69.9	74.3	462	62.2	66.1
White, non-Hispanic alone	659	642	484	73.4	75.4	429	65.1	66.8
Black alone..	61	53	39	B	B	37	B	B
Asian alone	25	15	10	B	B	10	B	B
Hispanic (of any race)	88	60	38	B	B	36	B	B
White alone or in combination	750	706	525	70.0	74.4	466	62.2	66.0
Black alone or in combination	68	60	45	B	B	41	B	B
Asian alone or in combination.........	25	15	10	B	B	10	B	B
Age								
18 to 24 years	101	96	59	58.1	61.1	50	49.0	51.6
25 to 34 years	143	135	96	66.8	70.9	80	56.1	59.5
35 to 44 years	130	111	79	60.6	71.1	71	54.5	63.9
45 to 64 years	291	268	207	71.4	77.4	187	64.5	69.9
65 years and over	174	166	135	77.3	81.0	126	72.6	76.1

B = Base is less than 75,000 and therefore too small to show the derived measure.

Table RI-14. Crime

(Number, rate per 100,000. Data are derived from the FBI Uniform Crime Reports.)

Item	State			U.S.		
	2019	2020	Percent change	2019	2020	Percent change
TOTAL POPULATION[1]	1,058,158	1,057,125	-0.1	328,329,953	329,484,123	0.4
VIOLENT CRIME						
Number...	2,357	2,440	3.5	1,250,393	1,313,105	5.0
Rate	222.7	230.8	3.6	380.8	398.5	4.6
Murder and Nonnegligent Manslaughter						
Number...	26	32	23.1	16,669	21,570	29.4
Rate	2.5	3.0	23.2	5.1	6.5	28.9
Rape[2]						
Number...	498	407	-18.3	143,224	126,430	-11.7
Rate	47.1	38.5	-18.2	43.6	38.4	-12.0
Robbery						
Number...	421	336	-20.2	268,483	243,600	-9.3
Rate	39.8	31.8	-20.1	81.8	73.9	-9.6
Aggravated Assault						
Number...	1,412	1,665	17.9	822,017	921,505	12.1
Rate	133.4	157.5	18.0	250.4	279.7	11.7
PROPERTY CRIME						
Number...	16,312	13,166	-19.3	6,995,235	6,452,038	-7.8
Rate	1,541.5	1,245.5	-19.2	2,130.6	1,958.2	-8.1
Burglary						
Number...	2,321	1,763	-24.0	1,118,096	1,035,314	-7.4
Rate	219.3	166.8	-24.0	340.5	314.2	-7.7
Larceny-Theft						
Number...	12,628	9,894	-21.7	5,152,267	4,606,324	-10.6
Rate	1,193.4	935.9	-21.6	1,569.2	1,398.0	-10.9
Motor Vehicle Theft						
Number...	1,363	1,509	10.7	724,872	810,400	11.8
Rate	128.8	142.7	10.8	220.8	246.0	11.4

NOTE: Although arson data are included in the trend and clearance tables, sufficient data are not available to estimate totals for this offense. Therefore, no arson data are published in this table.
- = Zero or rounds to zero.
[1] Population figures are U.S. Census Bureau provisional estimates as of July 1, 2020.
[2] The figures shown in the rape (revised definition) column were estimated using the revised Uniform Crime Reporting (UCR) definition of rape.

Table RI-15. State Government Finances, 2020

(Dollar amounts in thousands, percent distribution.)

Item	Dollars	Percent distribution
Total Revenue	11,331,785	100.0
General revenue	9,808,113	86.6
Intergovernmental revenue	4,288,536	37.8
Taxes	3,526,786	31.1
General sales	1157312	10.2
Selective sales	720,777	6.4
License taxes	120,821	1.1
Individual income tax	1241856	11.0
Corporate income tax	213,303	1.9
Other taxes	72,717	0.6
Current charges	1,138,894	10.1
Miscellaneous general revenue	853,897	7.5
Utility revenue	22,396	0.2
Liquor stores revenue	0	-
Insurance trust revenue[1]	1,501,276	13.2
Total Expenditure	10,548,793	100.0
Intergovernmental expenditure	1,430,784	13.6
Direct expenditure	9,118,009	86.4
Current operation	6,286,086	59.6
Capital outlay	661,828	6.3
Insurance benefits and repayments	1,573,503	14.9
Assistance and subsidies	185,346	1.8
Interest on debt	411,246	3.9
Exhibit: Salaries and wages	1,653,999	15.7
Total Expenditure	10,548,793	100.0
General expenditure	8,844,184	83.8
Intergovernmental expenditure	1,430,784	13.6
Direct expenditure	7,413,400	70.3
General expenditure, by function:		
Education	2,238,744	21.2
Public welfare	3,285,043	31.1
Hospitals	52,196	0.5
Health	382,933	3.6
Highways	595,942	5.6
Police protection	101,754	1.0
Correction	235,830	2.2
Natural resources	76,687	0.7
Parks and recreation	31,855	0.3
Governmental administration	738,930	7.0
Interest on general debt	411,246	3.9
Other and unallocable	676,010	6.4
Utility expenditure	131,106	1.2
Liquor stores expenditure	0	-
Insurance trust expenditure	1,573,503	14.9
Debt at End of Fiscal Year	9,371,823	X
Cash and Security Holdings	19,822,968	X

X = Not applicable.
- = Zero or rounds to zero.
[1] Within insurance trust revenue, net earnings of state retirement systems is a calculated statistic (the item code in the data file is X08), and thus can be positive or negative. Net earnings is the sum of earnings on investments plus gains on investments minus losses on investments. The change made in 2002 for asset valuation from book to market value in accordance with Statement 34 of the Governmental Accounting Standards Board is reflected in the calculated statistics.

Table RI-16. State Government Tax Collections, 2021

(Dollars in thousands, percent.)

Item	Dollars	Percent distribution
Total Taxes	4,344,340	100.0
Property taxes	3,864	0.1
Sales and gross receipts	2,131,988	49.1
General sales and gross receipts	1,334,931	30.7
Selective sales and gross receipts	797,057	18.3
Alcoholic beverages	22,112	0.5
Amusements	16,586	0.4
Insurance premiums	146,288	3.4
Motor fuels	130,104	3.0
Pari-mutuels	393	-
Public utilities	93,449	2.2
Tobacco products	158,682	3.7
Other selective sales	229,443	5.3
Licenses	137,010	3.2
Alcoholic beverages	1,242	-
Amusements	182	-
Corporations in general	7,034	0.2
Hunting and fishing	2,213	0.1
Motor vehicle	28,168	0.6
Motor vehicle operators	8,049	0.2
Public utilities	2,624	0.1
Occupation and business, NEC	80,859	1.9
Other licenses	6,639	0.2
Income taxes	2,015,621	46.4
Individual income	1,757,678	40.5
Corporation net income	257,943	5.9
Other taxes	55,857	1.3
Death and gift	38,141	0.9
Documentary and stock transfer	17,716	0.4
Severance	X	-
Taxes, NEC	0	-

X = Not applicable.
- = Zero or rounds to zero.

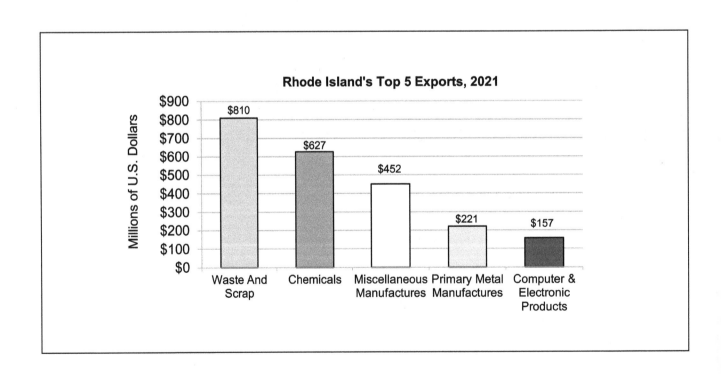

SOUTH CAROLINA

Facts and Figures

Location: Southeastern United States; bordered on the N by North Carolina, on the E by the Atlantic Ocean, on the S by the Atlantic Ocean and Georgia, and on the W by Georgia

Area: 32,020 sq. mi. (82,932 sq. km.); rank—40th

Population: 5,190,705 (2021 est.); rank—23rd

Principal Cities: capital—Columbia; largest—Columbia

Statehood: May 23, 1788; 8th state

U.S. Congress: 2 senators, 7 representatives

State Mottoes: *Animis opibusque parati* ("Prepared in mind and resources"); *Dum spiro, spero* ("While I breathe, I hope")

State Songs: "Carolina"; "South Carolina on My Mind"

State Nickname: The Palmetto State

Abbreviations: SC; S.C.

State Symbols: flower—yellow jessamine; tree—cabbage palmetto; bird—Carolina wren

At a Glance

- With an increase in population of 12.2 percent, South Carolina ranked 10th among the states in growth from 2010 to 2021.

- South Carolina's median household income in 2020 was $54,864, and 14.7 percent of the population lived below the poverty level.

- South Carolina's violent crime rate in 2020 was 530.7 incidents per 100,000 population, which ranked 8th in the nation.

- In 2020, 10.4 percent of South Carolinians did not have health insurance, compared to 8.7 percent of the total U.S. population.

- South Carolina had the 2nd lowest drug overdose death rate in 2020, with 10.3 deaths per 100,000 population.

Table SC-1. Population by Age, Sex, Race, and Hispanic Origin

(Number, percent, except where noted.)

Sex, age, race, and Hispanic origin	2000	2010	2021	Percent change, 2010–2021
Total Population...	4,012,013	4,625,364	5,190,705	12.2
Percent of total U.S. population	1.4	1.5	1.6	X
Sex				
Male..	1,948,929	2,250,101	2,523,715	12.2
Female...	2,063,083	2,375,263	2,666,990	12.3
Age				
Under 5 years..	264,679	302,297	282,964	-6.4
5 to 19 years..	871,099	922,128	968,473	5.0
20 to 64 years...	2,390,901	2,769,065	2,972,869	7.4
65 years and over..	485,333	631,874	966,399	52.9
Median age (years)	35.4	37.9	40.2	6.1
Race and Hispanic Origin				
One race				
White...	2,695,560	3,164,143	3,561,602	12.6
Black...	1,185,216	1,302,865	1,383,427	6.2
American Indian and Alaska Native	13,718	24,665	29,675	20.3
Asian...	36,014	61,247	100,216	63.6
Native Hawaiian or Other Pacific Islander	1,628	3,957	5,399	36.4
Two or more races..	39,950	68,487	110,386	61.2
Hispanic (of any race)..	95,076	243,923	330,096	35.3

NOTE: Population figures for 2021 are July 1 estimates. The 2000 and 2010 estimates are taken from the respective censuses.
- = Zero or rounds to zero.
X = Not applicable.

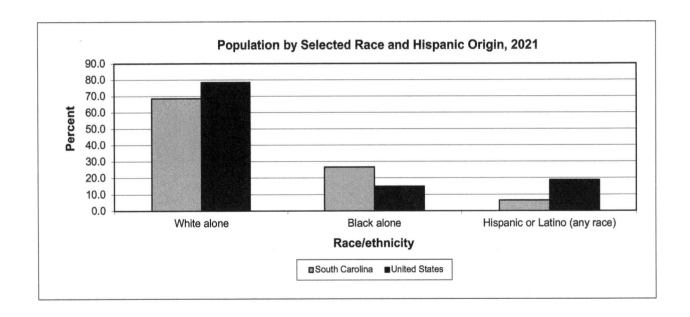

Table SC-2. Marital Status

(Number, percent distribution.)

Sex, age, race, and Hispanic origin	2000	2010	2020 [1]
Males, 15 Years and Over	1,516,125	1,797,441	1,999,660
Never married	28.8	35.2	35.4
Now married, except separated...	57.3	49.4	49.6
Separated...	2.8	3.0	2.3
Widowed..	2.7	2.8	3.2
Divorced..	8.3	9.5	9.5
Females, 15 Years and Over	1,652,793	1,939,054	2,172,887
Never married	23.4	29.1	29.9
Now married, except separated...	51.4	45.2	45.3
Separated...	3.8	3.9	3.0
Widowed..	11.5	10.6	9.9
Divorced..	9.9	11.2	11.8

[1] 2020 ACS 5-Year estimates. 1-Year estimates were not released for 2020 due to the impact of COVID-19 on data collection that year.

Table SC-3. Households and Housing Characteristics

(Number, percent, dollars.)

Item	2000	2010	2020 [1]	Average annual percent change, 2010–2020
Total Households...	1,533,854	1,761,393	1,961,481	1.6
Family households	1,072,822	1,180,687	1,280,623	1.2
Married-couple family	783,142	827,387	923,300	1.7
Other family	289,680	353,300	357,323	0.2
Male householder, no wife present................	62,722	77,062	84,567	1.4
Female householder, no husband present........	226,958	276,238	272,756	-0.2
Nonfamily households	461,032	580,706	680,858	2.5
Householder living alone..............................	383,142	489,995	571,147	2.4
Householder not living alone.........................	77,890	90,711	109,711	3.0
Housing Characteristics				
Total housing units...	1,753,670	2,140,337	2,319,112	1.2
Occupied housing units	1,533,854	1,761,393	1,961,481	1.6
Owner occupied	1,107,617	1,210,160	1,375,391	2.0
Renter occupied	426,237	551,233	586,090	0.9
Average household size...................................	2.53	2.55	2.53	-0.1
Financial Characteristics				
Median gross rent of renter-occupied housing	510	728	918	3.7
Median monthly owner costs for housing units with a mortgage	894	1,177	1,265	1.1
Median value of owner-occupied housing units	94,900	138,100	170,100	3.3

[1] 2020 ACS 5-Year estimates. 1-Year estimates were not released for 2020 due to the impact of COVID-19 on data collection that year.

Table SC-4. Migration, Origin, and Language

(Number, percent.)

Characteristic	State 2016-2020 [1]	U.S. 2016-2020 [1]
Family households		
Married-couple family	5,029,930	322,943,283
Other family	86.2	86.2
Male householder, no wife present.................................	13.4	13.2
Female householder, no husband present........................	6.7	7.7
	6.7	5.5
Nonfamily households	3.3	3.2
Householder living alone...	3.4	2.3
Householder not living alone..	0.4	0.6
Housing Characteristics		
Total housing units..	4,828,314	282,443,680
Occupied housing units	48.4	49.4
Owner occupied	51.6	50.6
Renter occupied		
Average household size...	263,203	44,125,628
Male	50.5	48.6
Female	49.5	51.4
Foreign born; naturalized U.S. citizen...............................	114,347	22,456,684
Male	46.7	46.1
Female	53.3	53.9
Foreign born; not a U.S. citizen..	148,856	21,668,944
Male	53.5	51.1
Female	46.5	48.9
Entered 2010 or later	27.2	22.8
Entered 2000 to 2009	29.7	25.1
Entered before 2000..	43.1	52.1
World Region of Birth, Foreign		
Foreign-born population, excluding population born at sea	263,203	44,125,628
Europe	17.6	10.8
Asia..	25.0	31.3
Africa..	3.6	5.4
Oceania...	0.6	0.6
Latin America...	50.0	50.0
North America...	3.2	1.9
Language Spoken at Home and Ability to Speak English		
Population 5 years and over...	4,799,866	306,919,116
English only	92.6	78.5
Language other than English..	7.4	21.5
Speaks English less than "very well"...............................	2.7	8.2

[1] 2020 ACS 5-Year estimates. 1-Year estimates were not released for 2020 due to the impact of COVID-19 on data collection that year.
NA = Not available.
X = Not applicable.
- = Zero or rounds to zero.

Table SC-5. Median Income and Poverty Status, 2020[1]

(Number, percent, except as noted.)

Characteristic	State		U.S.	
	Number	Percent	Number	Percent
Median Income				
Households (dollars)...	54,864	X	64,994	X
Families (dollars)	68,813	X	80,069	X
Below Poverty Level (All People)	726,470	14.7	40,910,326	12.8
Sex				
Male	313,618	13.2	18,171,512	11.6
Female	412,852	16.1	22,738,814	14.0
Age				
Under 18 years...	231,061	21.2	12,598,699	17.5
Related children under 18 years...	227,005	20.9	12,306,532	17.2
18 to 64 years	410,346	13.8	23,554,920	12.1
65 years and over	85,063	9.6	4,756,707	9.3

X = Not applicable.
[1] 2020 ACS 5-Year estimates. 1-Year estimates were not released for 2020 due to the impact of COVID-19 on data collection that year.

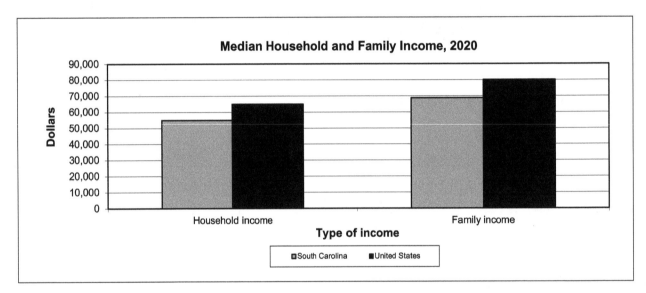

Table SC-6. Health Insurance Coverage Status for the Civilian Noninstitutionalized Population and Children Under 19 Years of Age

(Number, percent.)

Item	2011	2012	2013	2014	2015	2016	2017	2018	2019	2020 [2]
Civilian Noninstitutionalized Population	4,579,231	4,623,171	4,678,122	4,733,742	4,801,301	4,861,188	4,928,260	4,990,240	5,048,513	4,990,992
Covered by Private or Public Insurance										
Number..	3,812,927	3,844,990	3,939,270	4,092,185	4,278,073	4,375,282	4,386,727	4,467,781	4,500,847	4,472,269
Percent...	83.3	83.2	84.2	86.4	89.1	90.0	89.0	89.5	89.2	89.6
Uninsured										
Number..	766,304	778,181	738,852	641,557	523,228	485,906	541,533	522,459	547,666	518,723
Percent...	16.7	16.8	15.8	13.6	10.9	10.0	11.0	10.5	10.8	10.4
Percent in the U.S. not covered...........................	15.1	14.8	14.5	11.7	9.4	8.6	8.7	8.9	9.2	8.7
Children Under 19 Years of Age[1]	1,079,476	1,078,022	1,076,621	1,080,779	1,086,607	1,097,385	1,169,363	1,177,426	1,181,973	1,172,091
Covered by Private or Public Insurance										
Number..	988,285	988,908	1,004,026	1,020,796	1,042,427	1,053,682	1,109,164	1,121,750	1,113,143	1,113,499
Percent...	91.6	91.7	93.3	94.5	95.9	96.0	94.9	95.3	94.2	95.0
Uninsured										
Number..	91,191	89,114	72,595	59,983	44,180	43,703	60,199	55,676	68,830	58,592
Percent...	8.4	8.3	6.7	5.5	4.1	4.0	5.1	4.7	5.8	5.0
Percent in the U.S. not covered...........................	7.5	7.2	7.1	6.0	4.8	4.5	5.0	5.2	5.7	5.2

[1] Data for years prior to 2017 are for individuals under 18 years of age.
[2] 2020 ACS 5-Year estimates. 1-Year estimates were not released for 2020 due to the impact of COVID-19 on data collection that year. Data is not comparable to previous years, which are based on 1-year estimates.

Table SC-7. Employment Status by Demographic Group, 2021

(Numbers in thousands, percent.)

Characteristic	Civilian noninstitutional population	Civilian labor force		Employed		Unemployed	
		Number	Percent of population	Number	Percent of population	Number	Percent of population
Total..	4,192	2,392	57.1	2,295	54.7	97	4.1
Sex							
Male..	1,978	1,229	62.1	1,181	59.7	48	3.9
Female...	2,214	1,163	52.5	1,114	50.3	49	4.2
Race, Sex, and Hispanic Origin							
White..	2,929	1,663	56.8	1,609	54.9	54	3.2
Male..	1,417	890	62.8	861	60.8	30	3.3
Female...	1,512	772	51.1	748	49.5	24	3.1
Black or African American............................	1,076	611	56.8	570	53.0	41	6.7
Male..	478	276	57.8	259	54.2	17	6.2
Female...	598	334	55.9	311	52.0	23	7.0
Hispanic or Latino ethnicity[1].......................	283	197	69.5	192	67.7	5	2.6
Male..	134	115	86	113	85	2	1.5
Female...	NA	NA	NA	NA	NA	NA	NA
Age							
16 to 19 years..	248	96	39	87	35	9	8.9
20 to 24 years..	316	217	68.6	202	63.8	15	7.0
25 to 34 years..	676	551	81.6	523	77.5	28	5.0
35 to 44 years..	630	510	80.8	493	78.3	16	3.2
45 to 54 years..	634	490	77.2	477	75.3	12	2.5
55 to 64 years..	655	384	58.7	372	56.9	12	3.1
65 years and over....................................	1,033	145	14.0	140	13.5	5	3.5

NOTE: Data in Table 7 are from the Current Population Survey (CPS) and do not match the estimates in Table 8. See notes and definitions for further information.
[1] May be of any race.

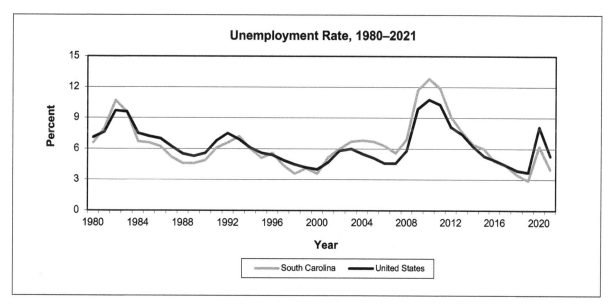

Unemployment Rate, 1980–2021

Table SC-8. Employment Status of the Civilian Noninstitutional Population Age 16 Years and Over

(Number, percent.)

Year	Civilian labor force	Civilian participation rate	Employed	Unemployed	Unemployment rate
2010..	2,174,535	61.0	1,928,442	246,093	11.3
2011..	2,185,171	60.5	1,957,493	227,678	10.4
2012..	2,190,203	59.9	1,992,957	197,246	9.0
2013..	2,197,876	59.3	2,034,404	163,472	7.4
2014..	2,222,426	59.1	2,082,941	139,485	6.3
2015..	2,267,837	59.3	2,134,087	133,750	5.9
2016..	2,286,054	58.8	2,174,301	111,753	4.9
2017..	2,261,766	58.0	2,166,708	95,058	4.2
2018..	2,279,431	57.7	2,202,377	77,054	3.4
2019..	2,321,189	58	2,256,313	64,876	2.8
2020..	2,330,863	57.4	2,191,331	139,532	6.0
2021..	2,364,366	57.4	2,269,813	94,553	4.0

Table SC-9. Employment and Average Wages by Industry

(Estimates are based on the 2012 North American Industry Classification System [NAICS].)

Industry	2013	2014	2015	2016	2017	2018	2019	2020
	Number of Jobs							
Wage and Salary Employment by Industry.........................	1,985,126	2,032,855	2,090,400	2,133,752	2,173,815	2,231,951	2,268,283	2,164,308
Farm Wage and Salary Employment..............................	7,775	6,085	7,511	7,270	9,290	6,389	6,340	5,854
Nonfarm Wage and Salary Employment...........................	1,977,351	2,026,770	2,082,889	2,126,482	2,164,525	2,225,562	2,261,943	2,158,454
Private wage and salary employment.......................................	1,578,018	1,626,266	1,676,940	1,719,909	1,754,938	1,814,653	1,844,856	1,748,033
Forestry, fishing, and related activities............................	6,963	7,073	7,269	7,296	7,231	7,542	7,524	7,298
Mining..	1,141	1,157	1,236	1,467	1,684	1,729	1,851	1,922
Utilities..	12,212	12,349	12,347	12,370	12,356	12,003	11,494	11,241
Construction..	82,074	84,712	89,164	96,912	103,350	106,822	109,211	106,162
Manufacturing...	225,172	230,774	236,121	238,259	240,799	249,716	258,182	244,489
Durable goods manufacturing..	129,356	133,704	137,653	139,580	139,909	146,201	152,566	145,156
Nondurable goods manufacturing..................................	95,816	97,070	98,468	98,679	100,890	103,515	105,616	99,333
Wholesale trade	66,719	68,411	71,193	72,027	72,740	72,178	73,310	72,774
Retail trade...	232,665	238,473	243,263	248,285	248,446	253,400	253,165	247,594
Transportation and warehousing.......................................	52,595	56,594	60,728	63,234	66,165	68,691	71,945	72,434
Information..	26,431	26,472	27,057	27,045	27,471	28,050	26,886	24,725
Finance and insurance	70,580	70,386	70,804	72,039	73,543	74,454	75,343	77,356
Real estate and rental and leasing.....................................	26,757	27,629	28,691	29,800	30,250	31,799	32,478	30,992
Professional, scientific, and technical services......................	82,461	85,612	89,242	94,241	97,522	103,219	103,833	102,786
Management of companies and enterprises.........................	16,489	17,039	16,699	17,946	20,250	21,416	25,019	24,297
Administrative and waste services.....................................	144,898	153,318	158,396	159,475	162,543	171,148	171,193	156,858
Educational services	30,855	32,184	33,170	33,487	33,254	33,508	33,750	31,332
Health care and social assistance.....................................	181,077	185,814	192,677	198,671	203,217	210,804	213,089	207,761
Arts, entertainment, and recreation...................................	27,442	28,739	29,145	29,861	30,772	32,245	33,755	26,303
Accommodation and food services....................................	196,678	201,982	210,983	218,999	224,939	233,147	238,032	202,512
Other services, except public administration........................	94,809	97,548	98,755	98,495	98,406	102,782	104,796	99,197
Government and government enterprises.................................	399,333	400,504	405,949	406,573	409,587	410,909	417,087	410,421
	Dollars							
Average Wages and Salaries by Industry	41,033	42,033	43,277	44,189	45,499	46,285	47,880	50,819
Average Farm Wages and Salaries	19,034	23,408	22,974	19,459	14,836	19,581	14,572	14,509
Average Nonfarm Wages and Salaries	41,119	42,089	43,351	44,273	45,630	46,362	47,974	50,917
Average private wages and salaries.....................................	40,332	41,361	42,638	43,575	45,045	45,673	47,311	50,644
Forestry, fishing, and related activities............................	33,395	35,127	36,259	37,588	39,874	39,532	40,820	43,278
Mining..	55,275	57,682	69,443	66,378	66,306	68,905	81,519	72,864
Utilities..	84,784	87,453	92,420	95,116	97,384	94,413	102,768	104,378
Construction	45,392	47,210	48,886	51,066	54,422	53,649	56,280	59,044
Manufacturing...	54,938	56,963	58,534	59,583	60,831	61,697	62,968	64,135
Durable goods manufacturing..	57,298	59,814	60,997	62,306	63,452	64,161	64,986	65,546
Nondurable goods manufacturing..................................	51,752	53,035	55,089	55,733	57,195	58,217	60,053	62,072
Wholesale trade	61,244	63,914	65,509	66,490	68,936	70,591	73,510	76,576
Retail trade...	26,209	26,478	27,267	27,855	28,497	29,005	29,997	32,829
Transportation and warehousing.......................................	41,924	42,431	43,757	43,476	44,851	45,932	47,143	48,856
Information..	55,517	57,901	59,157	60,341	63,639	64,358	68,503	76,438
Finance and insurance	60,478	61,840	65,044	66,814	69,284	71,940	74,777	82,019
Real estate and rental and leasing.....................................	39,112	40,796	42,450	43,302	45,502	46,953	49,630	53,752
Professional, scientific, and technical services......................	64,092	65,683	67,653	69,305	71,343	72,238	75,045	80,133
Management of companies and enterprises.........................	71,579	71,921	74,614	77,300	81,919	85,116	87,997	92,932
Administrative and waste services.....................................	32,873	33,520	34,140	34,698	35,755	35,770	36,652	39,488
Educational services	30,038	30,636	31,100	32,161	32,303	33,831	33,647	37,487
Health care and social assistance.....................................	43,665	44,826	46,284	46,855	48,142	48,705	50,136	53,072
Arts, entertainment, and recreation...................................	21,030	21,323	22,522	22,773	23,018	23,172	24,051	27,007
Accommodation and food services....................................	18,290	18,572	19,138	19,794	20,350	20,894	21,735	21,472
Other services, except public administration........................	29,631	30,313	31,571	32,583	33,753	34,222	35,339	38,917
Government and government enterprises.................................	44,230	45,041	46,296	47,227	48,139	49,403	50,907	52,084

Table SC-10. Employment Characteristics by Family Type

(Number, percent.)

Family type and labor force status	2018		2019		2020 [1]	
	Total	Families with own children under 18 years	Total	Families with own children under 18 years	Total	Families with own children under 18 years
All Families..	1,258,273	479,098	1,286,326	474,527	1,280,623	491,337
FAMILY TYPE AND LABOR FORCE STATUS						
Opposite-Sex Married-Couple Families..........................	895,552	303,018	928,870	306,409	916,570	313,457
Both husband and wife in labor force................................	47.2	69.0	47.0	69.4	47.0	67.5
Husband in labor force, wife not in labor force	20.4	25.5	20.8	25.0	21.4	27.1
Wife in labor force, husband not in labor force	8.6	3.8	8.3	4.1	8.6	3.8
Both husband and wife not in labor force............................	23.1	1.4	23.4	1.1	23.0	1.6
Other Families	362,721	176,080	357,456	168,118	357,323	176,956
Female householder, no spouse present	76.0	77.2	75.6	79.2	76.3	78.7
In labor force..	51.1	63.8	50.0	65.8	52.1	66.4
Not in labor force	24.9	13.4	25.6	13.5	24.3	12.3
Male householder, no spouse present...........................	24.0	22.8	24.4	20.8	23.7	21.3
In labor force..	17.6	20.6	17.6	18.7	17.4	18.8
Not in labor force	6.3	2.2	6.7	2.1	6.3	2.5

[1] 2020 ACS 5-Year estimates. 1-Year estimates were not released for 2020 due to the impact of COVID-19 on data collection that year. Data is not comparable to previous years, which are based on 1-year estimates.

Table SC-11. School Enrollment and Educational Attainment, 2020[1]

(Number, percent.)

Item	State	U.S.
Enrollment		
Total population 3 years and over, enrolled in school	1,187,922	80,497,960
Enrolled in nursery school or preschool (percent)...	5.1	6.1
Enrolled in kindergarten (percent)...	5.6	5.0
Enrolled in elementary school, grades 1-8 (percent)...	42.3	40.4
Enrolled in high school, grades 9-12 (percent)...	21.0	21.0
Enrolled in college or graduate school (percent)...	26	27.6
Attainment		
Total population 25 years and over	3,512,626	222,836,834
Less than ninth grade (percent)...	3.7	4.9
9th to 12th grade, no diploma (percent)...	8.0	6.6
High school graduate, including equivalency (percent)...	28.9	26.7
Some college, no degree (percent)...	20.6	20.3
Associate's degree (percent)...	9.9	8.6
Bachelor's degree (percent)...	18.2	20.2
Graduate or professional degree (percent)...	10.8	12.7
High school graduate or higher (percent)	88.3	88.5
Bachelor's degree or higher (percent)...	29.0	32.9

[1] 2020 ACS 5-Year estimates. 1-Year estimates were not released for 2020 due to the impact of COVID-19 on data collection that year.

Table SC-12. Public School Characteristics and Educational Indicators

(Number, percent; data derived from National Center of Education Statistics.)

Item	State	U.S.
Public Elementary and Secondary Schools		
Number of regular school districts, 2018-19	84	13,452
Number of operational schools, 2019-20...	1,265	98,469
Percent charter schools	6.3	7.7
Total public school enrollment, Fall 2019...	786,879	50,796,445
Percent charter school enrollment	5.0	6.8
Student-teacher ratio, Fall 2019...	14.7	15.9
Expenditures per student (unadjusted dollars), 2018-19	10,994	13,187
Four-year adjusted cohort graduation rate (ACGR), 2018-2019[1]...	81.1	85.8
Students eligible for free or reduced-price lunch (percent), 2019-20...	63.2	52.1
English language learners (percent), Fall 2019...	6.0	10.4
Students age 3 to 21 served under IDEA, part B (percent), 2020-21	13.9	14.5

Public Schools by Type, 2019-20	Number	Percent of state public schools
Total number of schools...	1,265	100.0
Special education...	8	0.6
Vocational education...	44	3.5
Alternative education...	15	1.2

[1] Adjusted Cohort Graduation Rates (ACGR) differ from Averaged Freshmen Graduation Rates (AFGR).

Table SC-13. Reported Voting and Registration of the Voting-Age Population, November 2020

(Numbers in thousands, percent.)

Item	Total population	Total citizen population	Registered			Voted		
			Total registered	Percent registered (total population)	Percent registered (total citizen population)	Total voted	Percent voted (total population)	Percent voted (total citizen population)
U.S. Total	252,274	231,593	168,308	66.7	72.7	154,628	61.3	66.8
State Total....................	4,010	3,878	2,713	67.7	70.0	2,459	61.3	63.4
Sex								
Male	1,887	1,820	1,266	67.1	69.5	1,158	61.3	63.6
Female	2,123	2,058	1,447	68.2	70.3	1,302	61.3	63.3
Race								
White alone......................	2,840	2,739	2,013	70.9	73.5	1,845	64.9	67.4
White, non-Hispanic alone	2,605	2,590	1,945	74.7	75.1	1,789	68.7	69.0
Black alone.....................	1,032	1,012	613	59.4	60.5	546	52.9	53.9
Asian alone	50	40	37	B	B	34	B	B
Hispanic (of any race)	257	163	77	30.1	47.5	62	24.3	38.3
White alone or in combination	2,888	2,786	2,049	71.0	73.6	1,871	64.8	67.1
Black alone or in combination	1,047	1,026	618	59.1	60.2	551	52.7	53.7
Asian alone or in combination....................	70	59	53	B	B	51	B	B
Age								
18 to 24 years.....................	438	421	269	61.4	63.9	225	51.4	53.4
25 to 34 years.....................	697	673	390	56.0	58.0	329	47.2	49.0
35 to 44 years.....................	577	543	375	65.1	69.1	326	56.6	60.1
45 to 64 years.....................	1,277	1,227	892	69.9	72.8	844	66.1	68.8
65 years and over	1,022	1,015	786	76.9	77.5	735	71.9	72.4

B = Base is less than 75,000 and therefore too small to show the derived measure.

Table SC-14. Crime

(Number, rate per 100,000. Data are derived from the FBI Uniform Crime Reports.)

Item	State			U.S.		
	2019	2020	Percent change	2019	2020	Percent change
TOTAL POPULATION[1]	5,157,702	5,218,040	1.2	328,329,953	329,484,123	0.4
VIOLENT CRIME						
Number......................................	26,307	27,691	5.3	1,250,393	1,313,105	5.0
Rate......................................	510.1	530.7	4.0	380.8	398.5	4.6
Murder and Nonnegligent Manslaughter						
Number......................................	455	549	20.7	16,669	21,570	29.4
Rate......................................	8.8	10.5	19.3	5.1	6.5	28.9
Rape[2]						
Number......................................	2,528	2,086	-17.5	143,224	126,430	-11.7
Rate......................................	49.0	40.0	-18.4	43.6	38.4	-12.0
Robbery						
Number......................................	3,325	3,122	-6.1	268,483	243,600	-9.3
Rate......................................	64.5	59.8	-7.2	81.8	73.9	-9.6
Aggravated Assault						
Number......................................	19,999	21,934	9.7	822,017	921,505	12.1
Rate......................................	387.8	420.3	8.4	250.4	279.7	11.7
PROPERTY CRIME						
Number......................................	151,970	141,987	-6.6	6,995,235	6,452,038	-7.8
Rate......................................	2,946.5	2,721.1	-7.6	2,130.6	1,958.2	-8.1
Burglary						
Number......................................	27,439	23,377	-14.8	1,118,096	1,035,314	-7.4
Rate......................................	532.0	448.0	-15.8	340.5	314.2	-7.7
Larceny-Theft						
Number......................................	109,366	103,892	-5.0	5,152,267	4,606,324	-10.6
Rate......................................	2,120.4	1,991.0	-6.1	1,569.2	1,398.0	-10.9
Motor Vehicle Theft						
Number......................................	15,165	14,718	-2.9	724,872	810,400	11.8
Rate......................................	294.0	282.1	-4.1	220.8	246.0	11.4

NOTE: Although arson data are included in the trend and clearance tables, sufficient data are not available to estimate totals for this offense. Therefore, no arson data are published in this table.
- = Zero or rounds to zero.
[1] Population figures are U.S. Census Bureau provisional estimates as of July 1, 2020.
[2] The figures shown in the rape (revised definition) column were estimated using the revised Uniform Crime Reporting (UCR) definition of rape.

Table SC-15. State Government Finances, 2020

(Dollar amounts in thousands, percent distribution.)

Item	Dollars	Percent distribution
Total Revenue	37,277,585	100.0
General revenue	32,407,457	86.9
Intergovernmental revenue	12,511,074	33.6
Taxes	11,794,684	31.6
General sales	3565480	9.6
Selective sales	1,816,378	4.9
License taxes	633,783	1.7
Individual income tax	5095531	13.7
Corporate income tax	505,025	1.4
Other taxes	178,487	0.5
Current charges	5,809,591	15.6
Miscellaneous general revenue	2,292,108	6.1
Utility revenue	1,703,699	4.6
Liquor stores revenue	0	-
Insurance trust revenue[1]	3,166,429	8.5
Total Expenditure	36,903,182	100.0
Intergovernmental expenditure	6,554,951	17.8
Direct expenditure	30,348,231	82.2
Current operation	21,691,232	58.8
Capital outlay	2,184,169	5.9
Insurance benefits and repayments	4,408,872	11.9
Assistance and subsidies	1,438,575	3.9
Interest on debt	625,383	1.7
Exhibit: Salaries and wages	4,442,915	12.0
Total Expenditure	36,903,182	100.0
General expenditure	31,027,577	84.1
Intergovernmental expenditure	6,554,951	17.8
Direct expenditure	24,472,626	66.3
General expenditure, by function:		
Education	12,051,520	32.7
Public welfare	8,629,441	23.4
Hospitals	2,457,770	6.7
Health	1,309,166	3.5
Highways	2,071,984	5.6
Police protection	189,523	0.5
Correction	528,209	1.4
Natural resources	240,605	0.7
Parks and recreation	176,816	0.5
Governmental administration	863,298	2.3
Interest on general debt	278,269	0.8
Other and unallocable	2,205,834	6.0
Utility expenditure	1,466,733	3.9
Liquor stores expenditure	0	-
Insurance trust expenditure	4,408,872	11.9
Debt at End of Fiscal Year	12,896,315	X
Cash and Security Holdings	52,970,762	X

X = Not applicable.
- = Zero or rounds to zero.

[1] Within insurance trust revenue, net earnings of state retirement systems is a calculated statistic (the item code in the data file is X08), and thus can be positive or negative. Net earnings is the sum of earnings on investments plus gains on investments minus losses on investments. The change made in 2002 for asset valuation from book to market value in accordance with Statement 34 of the Governmental Accounting Standards Board is reflected in the calculated statistics.

Table SC-16. State Government Tax Collections, 2021

(Dollars in thousands, percent.)

Item	Dollars	Percent distribution
Total Taxes	13,286,248	100.0
Property taxes	78,975	0.6
Sales and gross receipts	6,119,790	46.1
General sales and gross receipts	4,154,363	31.3
Selective sales and gross receipts	1,965,427	14.8
Alcoholic beverages	208,490	1.6
Amusements	36,213	0.3
Insurance premiums	273,744	2.1
Motor fuels	838,264	6.3
Pari-mutuels	X	-
Public utilities	28,258	0.2
Tobacco products	28,306	0.2
Other selective sales	552,152	4.2
Licenses	707,027	5.3
Alcoholic beverages	15,414	0.1
Amusements	6,925	0.1
Corporations in general	148,137	1.1
Hunting and fishing	21,855	0.2
Motor vehicle	302,509	2.3
Motor vehicle operators	4,915	-
Public utilities	14,015	0.1
Occupation and business, NEC	171,008	1.3
Other licenses	22,249	0.2
Income taxes	6,196,557	46.6
Individual income	5,456,360	41.1
Corporation net income	740,197	5.6
Other taxes	183,899	1.4
Death and gift	X	-
Documentary and stock transfer	183,899	1.4
Severance	X	-
Taxes, NEC	0	-

X = Not applicable.
- = Zero or rounds to zero.

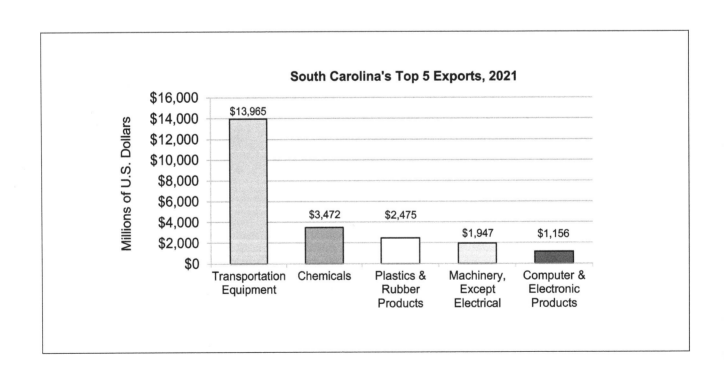

South Carolina's Top 5 Exports, 2021

SOUTH DAKOTA

Facts and Figures

Location: North central United States; bordered on the N by North Dakota, on the E by Minnesota and Iowa, on the S by Nebraska, and on the W by Wyoming and Montana

Area: 77,117 sq. mi. (199,731 sq. km.); rank—17th

Population: 895,376 (2021 est.); rank—46th

Principal Cities: capital—Pierre; largest—Sioux Falls

Statehood: November 2, 1889; 40th state

U.S. Congress: 2 senators, 1 representative

State Motto: Under God the People Rule

State Song: "Hail, South Dakota"

State Nickname: The Mount Rushmore State

Abbreviations: SD; S.D.; S. Dak.

State Symbols: flower—pasqueflower; tree—Black Hills spruce; bird—ring-necked pheasant

At a Glance

- With an increase in population of 10.0 percent, South Dakota ranked 17th among the states in growth from 2010 to 2021.

- In 2020, 9.6 percent of South Dakotans did not have health insurance, compared to 8.7 percent of the total U.S. population.

- South Dakota's violent crime rate in 2020 was 501.4 incidents per 100,000 population, which ranked 9th in the nation.

- South Dakota's median household income in 2020 was $59,896, and 12.8 percent of its residents lived below the poverty level.

- In 2021, South Dakota's unemployment rate was 3.1 percent, which was the 3rd lowest unemployment rate in the country. The national unemployment rate was 5.3 percent.

Table SD-1. Population by Age, Sex, Race, and Hispanic Origin

(Number, percent, except where noted.)

Sex, age, race, and Hispanic origin	2000	2010	2021	Percent change, 2010–2021
Total Population...	754,844	814,180	895,376	10.0
Percent of total U.S. population	0.4	0.3	0.3	X
Sex				
Male..	374,558	407,381	454,842	11.7
Female..	380,286	406,799	440,534	8.3
Age				
Under 5 years..	51,069	59,621	58,668	-1.6
5 to 19 years..	176,412	167,119	185,679	11.1
20 to 64 years...	419,232	470,859	494,611	5.0
65 years and over..	108,131	116,581	156,418	34.2
Median age (years)	35.6	36.9	37.7	2.2
Race and Hispanic Origin				
One race				
White	669,404	706,690	753,542	6.6
Black...	4,685	10,533	22,058	109.4
American Indian and Alaska Native	62,283	72,782	80,491	10.6
Asian...	4,378	7,775	15,057	93.7
Native Hawaiian or Other Pacific Islander	261	517	934	80.7
Two or more races..	10,156	15,883	23,294	46.7
Hispanic (of any race)...	10,903	23,699	41,288	74.2

NOTE: Population figures for 2021 are July 1 estimates. The 2000 and 2010 estimates are taken from the respective censuses.
- = Zero or rounds to zero.
X = Not applicable.

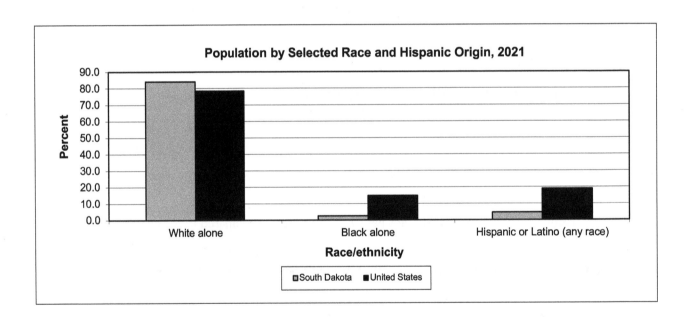

Table SD-2. Marital Status

(Number, percent distribution.)

Sex, age, race, and Hispanic origin	2000	2010	2020 [1]
Males, 15 Years and Over	289,858	322,689	350,626
Never married	29.8	33.5	34.4
Now married, except separated..	58.2	52.5	51.6
Separated...	1.0	0.9	0.9
Widowed...	2.4	2.8	2.6
Divorced..	8.5	10.3	10.5
Females, 15 Years and Over	299,754	325,640	347,195
Never married	22.5	26.0	27.6
Now married, except separated..	55.9	52.1	51.2
Separated...	1.1	1.0	1.1
Widowed...	11.4	9.5	9.0
Divorced..	9.0	11.4	11.1

[1] 2020 ACS 5-Year estimates. 1-Year estimates were not released for 2020 due to the impact of COVID-19 on data collection that year.

Table SD-3. Households and Housing Characteristics

(Number, percent, dollars.)

Item	2000	2010	2020 [1]	Average annual percent change, 2010–2020
Total Households..	290,245	318,955	347,878	1.3
Family households	194,330	204,029	218,705	1.0
Married-couple family	157,391	161,534	171,918	0.9
Other family	36,939	42,495	46,787	1.4
Male householder, no wife present..............	10,734	12,526	15,628	3.5
Female householder, no husband present.....	26,205	29,969	31,159	0.6
Nonfamily households	95,915	114,926	129,173	1.8
Householder living alone...............................	80,040	95,610	106,325	1.6
Householder not living alone..........................	15,875	19,316	22,848	2.6
Housing Characteristics				
Total housing units	323,208	364,031	396,817	1.3
Occupied housing units	290,245	318,955	347,878	1.3
Owner occupied	197,940	216,821	236,495	1.3
Renter occupied	92,305	102,134	111,383	1.3
Average household size...................................	2.50	2.45	2.43	-0.1
Financial Characteristics				
Median gross rent of renter-occupied housing	426	591	761	4.1
Median monthly owner costs for housing units with a mortgage	828	1,151	1,367	2.7
Median value of owner-occupied housing units............	79,600	129,700	174,600	4.9

[1] 2020 ACS 5-Year estimates. 1-Year estimates were not released for 2020 due to the impact of COVID-19 on data collection that year.

Table SD-4. Migration, Origin, and Language

(Number, percent.)

Characteristic	State 2016-2020 [1]	U.S. 2016-2020 [1]
Residence 1 Year Ago		
Population 1 year and over	868,493	322,943,283
Same house	84.9	86.2
Different house in the U.S.	14.6	13.2
Same county	7.0	7.7
Different county	7.6	5.5
Same state	4.4	3.2
Different state	3.2	2.3
Abroad	0.5	0.6
Place of Birth		
Native born	844,425	282,443,680
Male	50.3	49.4
Female	49.7	50.6
Foreign born	34,911	44,125,628
Male	52.9	48.6
Female	47.1	51.4
Foreign born; naturalized U.S. citizen..................................	13,187	22,456,684
Male	48.8	46.1
Female	51.2	53.9
Foreign born; not a U.S. citizen.......................................	21,724	21,668,944
Male	55.4	51.1
Female	44.6	48.9
Entered 2010 or later	42.8	22.8
Entered 2000 to 2009	30.6	25.1
Entered before 2000..	26.6	52.1
World Region of Birth, Foreign		
Foreign-born population, excluding population born at sea	34,911	44,125,628
Europe	13.4	10.8
Asia	30.2	31.3
Africa	25.6	5.4
Oceania	0.7	0.6
Latin America..	26.8	50.0
North America..	3.4	1.9
Language Spoken at Home and Ability to Speak English		
Population 5 years and over..	819,317	306,919,116
English only	93.5	78.5
Language other than English...	6.5	21.5
Speaks English less than "very well"...............................	2.1	8.2

[1] 2020 ACS 5-Year estimates. 1-Year estimates were not released for 2020 due to the impact of COVID-19 on data collection that year.
NA = Not available.
X = Not applicable.
- = Zero or rounds to zero.

Table SD-5. Median Income and Poverty Status, 2020[1]

(Number, percent, except as noted.)

Characteristic	State		U.S.	
	Number	Percent	Number	Percent
Median Income				
Households (dollars)..	59,896	X	64,994	X
Families (dollars)	77,042	X	80,069	X
Below Poverty Level (All People)	108,863	12.8	40,910,326	12.8
Sex				
Male	49,372	11.6	18,171,512	11.6
Female	59,491	14.1	22,738,814	14.0
Age				
Under 18 years..	33,852	16.1	12,598,699	17.5
Related children under 18 years.......................................	32,822	15.7	12,306,532	17.2
18 to 64 years...	62,364	12.5	23,554,920	12.1
65 years and over	12,647	9.0	4,756,707	9.3

X = Not applicable.
[1] 2020 ACS 5-Year estimates. 1-Year estimates were not released for 2020 due to the impact of COVID-19 on data collection that year.

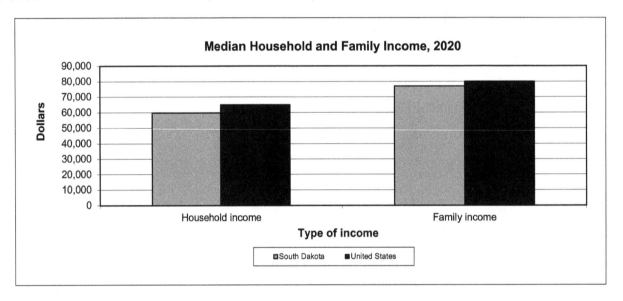

Table SD-6. Health Insurance Coverage Status for the Civilian Noninstitutionalized Population and Children Under 19 Years of Age

(Number, percent.)

Item	2011	2012	2013	2014	2015	2016	2017	2018	2019	2020 [2]
Civilian Noninstitutionalized Population	805,505	816,425	827,039	835,403	841,363	848,774	851,826	864,598	867,305	861,933
Covered by Private or Public Insurance										
Number...	709,597	722,292	733,713	753,472	755,448	774,556	774,488	779,891	778,968	779,526
Percent..	88.1	88.5	88.7	90.2	89.8	91.3	90.9	90.2	89.8	90.4
Uninsured										
Number...	95,908	94,133	93,326	81,931	85,915	74,218	77,338	84,707	88,337	82,407
Percent..	11.9	11.5	11.3	9.8	10.2	8.7	9.1	9.8	10.2	9.6
Percent in the U.S. not covered...	15.1	14.8	14.5	11.7	9.4	8.6	8.7	8.9	9.2	8.7
Children Under 19 Years of Age[1]	200,704	203,033	207,264	209,586	208,580	212,981	224,414	225,191	226,171	226,065
Covered by Private or Public Insurance										
Number...	188,665	191,198	194,142	197,674	194,544	203,436	210,566	211,880	208,534	211,880
Percent..	94.0	94.2	93.7	94.3	93.3	95.5	93.8	94.1	92.2	93.7
Uninsured										
Number...	12,039	11,835	13,122	11,912	14,036	9,545	13,848	13,311	17,637	14,185
Percent..	6.0	5.8	6.3	5.7	6.7	4.5	6.2	5.9	7.8	6.3
Percent in the U.S. not covered...	7.5	7.2	7.1	6.0	4.8	4.5	5.0	5.2	5.7	5.2

[1] Data for years prior to 2017 are for individuals under 18 years of age.
[2] 2020 ACS 5-Year estimates. 1-Year estimates were not released for 2020 due to the impact of COVID-19 on data collection that year. Data is not comparable to previous years, which are based on 1-year estimates.

Table SD-7. Employment Status by Demographic Group, 2021

(Numbers in thousands, percent.)

Characteristic	Civilian noninstitutional population	Civilian labor force		Employed		Unemployed	
		Number	Percent of population	Number	Percent of population	Number	Percent of population
Total..	685	473	69.1	461	67.3	13	2.6
Sex							
Male..	343	258	75.2	251	73.1	7	2.8
Female....................................	342	216	63.0	210	61.4	5	2.5
Race, Sex, and Hispanic Origin							
White......................................	605	422	69.8	414	68.5	8	1.9
Male....................................	305	233	76.3	228	74.7	5	2.1
Female................................	299	189	63.2	186	62.2	3	1.6
Black or African American...............	NA	NA	NA	NA	NA	NA	NA
Male....................................	NA	NA	NA	NA	NA	NA	NA
Female................................	NA	NA	NA	NA	NA	NA	NA
Hispanic or Latino ethnicity[1]	NA	NA	NA	NA	NA	NA	NA
Male....................................	NA	NA	NA	NA	NA	NA	NA
Female................................	NA	NA	NA	NA	NA	NA	NA
Age							
16 to 19 years............................	NA	NA	NA	NA	NA	NA	NA
20 to 24 years............................	NA	NA	NA	NA	NA	NA	NA
25 to 34 years............................	115	98	85.3	95	82.2	4	3.6
35 to 44 years............................	106	94	88.1	92	86.2	2	2.2
45 to 54 years............................	96	84	87.6	83	85.8	2	2.1
55 to 64 years............................	117	88	75.5	87	74.7	1	1.2
65 years and over........................	NA	NA	NA	NA	NA	NA	NA

NOTE: Data in Table 7 are from the Current Population Survey (CPS) and do not match the estimates in Table 8. See notes and definitions for further information.
[1] May be of any race.
NA = Not available.

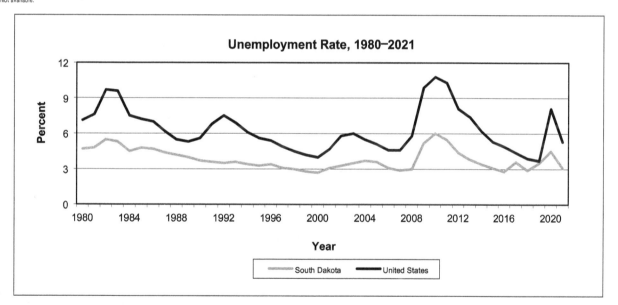

Unemployment Rate, 1980–2021

Table SD-8. Employment Status of the Civilian Noninstitutional Population Age 16 Years and Over

(Number, percent.)

Year	Civilian labor force	Civilian participation rate	Employed	Unemployed	Unemployment rate
2010..	443,618	71.6	421,815	21,803	4.9
2011..	445,866	71.5	425,367	20,499	4.6
2012..	447,056	70.8	428,943	18,113	4.1
2013..	447,479	70.1	430,834	16,645	3.7
2014..	450,769	70.0	435,733	15,036	3.3
2015..	453,091	69.9	439,293	13,798	3.0
2016..	455,133	69.5	441,418	13,715	3.0
2017..	455,339	69.2	441,450	13,889	3.1
2018..	457,328	68.9	444,569	12,759	2.8
2019..	461,610	68.9	448,619	12,991	2.8
2020..	461,624	68.4	441,550	20,074	4.3
2021..	468,015	68.5	453,511	14,504	3.1

Table SD-9. Employment and Average Wages by Industry

(Estimates are based on the 2012 North American Industry Classification System [NAICS].)

Industry	2013	2014	2015	2016	2017	2018	2019	2020
					Number of Jobs			
Wage and Salary Employment by Industry.........................	438,191	444,468	447,390	450,749	453,399	458,271	461,941	448,972
Farm Wage and Salary Employment.............................	6,290	6,366	4,908	4,622	4,979	5,611	5,625	6,899
Nonfarm Wage and Salary Employment..........................	431,901	438,102	442,482	446,127	448,420	452,660	456,316	442,073
Private wage and salary employment...	347,829	353,666	358,339	361,171	362,636	366,517	369,233	357,645
Forestry, fishing, and related activities..............................	2,466	2,426	2,442	2,463	2,458	2,501	2,585	2,514
Mining...	846	816	837	849	872	883	907	911
Utilities...	1,950	1,967	1,996	2,019	1,994	1,980	1,949	1,925
Construction...	21,039	21,790	22,773	23,381	22,894	23,522	24,178	25,013
Manufacturing..	41,573	42,466	42,641	42,196	43,137	44,477	45,015	43,180
Durable goods manufacturing..	27,514	28,506	28,528	27,569	27,597	28,676	28,735	26,970
Nondurable goods manufacturing...................................	14,059	13,960	14,113	14,627	15,540	15,801	16,280	16,210
Wholesale trade	19,971	20,877	21,209	21,267	21,082	20,924	21,194	20,996
Retail trade...	51,594	52,151	53,247	54,108	53,333	52,654	51,584	50,039
Transportation and warehousing..	10,480	11,221	11,500	11,260	11,276	11,457	11,633	11,409
Information	6,025	6,063	5,895	5,771	5,724	5,585	5,501	5,071
Finance and insurance	27,131	27,131	26,920	26,482	26,582	26,488	26,252	25,766
Real estate and rental and leasing.....................................	3,619	3,700	3,805	3,855	3,859	3,980	4,161	4,049
Professional, scientific, and technical services	12,537	12,477	12,623	13,001	13,454	14,187	14,672	14,994
Management of companies and enterprises........................	4,235	4,572	4,936	5,079	4,907	5,270	5,332	5,147
Administrative and waste services	13,092	13,371	13,330	13,378	13,107	13,124	13,333	12,855
Educational services	8,072	8,081	8,131	8,020	8,079	7,710	7,773	7,275
Health care and social assistance......................................	59,928	60,004	60,849	62,349	63,848	64,973	65,984	66,345
Arts, entertainment, and recreation....................................	6,184	6,526	6,604	6,614	6,830	6,956	7,034	6,296
Accommodation and food services.....................................	38,687	39,253	39,793	40,408	40,455	40,665	40,680	35,034
Other services, except public administration........................	18,400	18,774	18,808	18,671	18,745	19,181	19,466	18,826
Government and government enterprises.................................	84,072	84,436	84,143	84,956	85,784	86,143	87,083	84,428
					Dollars			
Average Wages and Salaries by Industry	36,824	38,249	39,630	40,695	41,912	43,181	44,702	48,367
Average Farm Wages and Salaries	38,995	40,036	33,787	38,756	38,114	35,994	45,304	33,902
Average Nonfarm Wages and Salaries	36,792	38,223	39,695	40,715	41,954	43,270	44,695	48,592
Average private wages and salaries....................................	36,969	38,521	40,069	41,043	42,276	43,689	45,312	49,396
Forestry, fishing, and related activities...............................	26,659	25,863	27,417	29,010	29,831	30,699	32,244	35,505
Mining...	55,962	58,757	60,718	58,178	60,280	63,360	63,972	67,336
Utilities...	73,253	74,705	76,281	78,359	80,303	84,378	87,278	91,066
Construction	40,943	42,883	44,987	47,666	47,374	48,975	50,981	54,008
Manufacturing..	42,444	44,506	45,447	45,993	47,888	49,333	50,220	53,293
Durable goods manufacturing..	43,532	45,245	45,994	46,511	48,724	50,047	51,107	53,984
Nondurable goods manufacturing...................................	40,314	42,997	44,343	45,018	46,402	48,037	48,654	52,145
Wholesale trade	52,920	54,998	56,251	57,027	58,393	60,773	62,146	66,279
Retail trade...	25,168	26,194	27,036	27,349	27,803	28,609	29,674	32,282
Transportation and warehousing..	42,816	43,893	44,983	45,476	46,137	47,301	48,033	50,629
Information	43,366	44,812	45,729	46,647	47,159	49,309	51,466	58,032
Finance and insurance	50,335	52,973	56,369	58,717	60,904	63,886	67,496	73,271
Real estate and rental and leasing.....................................	30,640	32,335	34,794	33,888	35,580	36,636	39,225	42,639
Professional, scientific, and technical services	49,917	52,696	56,409	57,467	59,363	60,935	63,086	68,129
Management of companies and enterprises........................	91,577	92,717	93,532	96,695	102,847	99,656	104,001	112,108
Administrative and waste services	27,163	29,191	29,978	31,147	33,208	33,947	35,377	38,991
Educational services	24,891	25,068	25,598	26,422	25,859	27,382	26,658	31,656
Health care and social assistance......................................	44,284	45,830	47,788	48,943	50,473	51,441	53,607	58,295
Arts, entertainment, and recreation....................................	18,294	18,802	19,711	19,414	19,851	20,391	20,875	22,736
Accommodation and food services.....................................	15,533	16,083	17,171	17,874	18,341	19,209	19,782	20,032
Other services, except public administration........................	27,010	28,123	29,445	30,037	31,284	32,418	33,566	37,502
Government and government enterprises.................................	36,063	36,973	38,099	39,319	40,593	41,490	42,076	45,190

Table SD-10. Employment Characteristics by Family Type

(Number, percent.)

Family type and labor force status	2018		2019		2020 [1]	
	Total	Families with own children under 18 years	Total	Families with own children under 18 years	Total	Families with own children under 18 years
All Families...	219,707	92,618	223,964	94,330	218,705	94,515
FAMILY TYPE AND LABOR FORCE STATUS						
Opposite-Sex Married-Couple Families............................	171,939	63,150	177,534	67,439	171,022	66,190
Both husband and wife in labor force..........................	60.0	80.4	59.0	76.5	60.5	79.7
Husband in labor force, wife not in labor force	15.2	15.6	16.4	19.2	15.3	16.0
Wife in labor force, husband not in labor force	7.5	2.7	8.2	3.3	7.6	3.2
Both husband and wife not in labor force......................	16.6	1.0	15.9	0.6	16.6	1.0
Other Families	47,768	29,468	46,430	26,891	46,787	28,146
Female householder, no spouse present..........................	69.0	73.0	66.4	70.0	66.6	68.9
In labor force...	51.0	61.4	48.7	61.3	49.6	58.7
Not in labor force..	18.0	11.6	17.7	8.7	17.0	10.2
Male householder, no spouse present..........................	31.0	27.0	33.6	30.0	33.4	31.1
In labor force...	24.7	26.0	28.1	28.4	27.3	28.9
Not in labor force..	6.3	1.0	5.5	1.6	6.1	2.2

[1] 2020 ACS 5-Year estimates. 1-Year estimates were not released for 2020 due to the impact of COVID-19 on data collection that year. Data is not comparable to previous years, which are based on 1-year estimates.

Table SD-11. School Enrollment and Educational Attainment, 2020[1]

(Number, percent.)

Item	State	U.S.
Enrollment		
Total population 3 years and over, enrolled in school	216,402	80,497,960
Enrolled in nursery school or preschool (percent)...........................	7.1	6.1
Enrolled in kindergarten (percent)...........................	5.8	5.0
Enrolled in elementary school, grades 1-8 (percent)...........................	43.4	40.4
Enrolled in high school, grades 9-12 (percent)...........................	20.7	21.0
Enrolled in college or graduate school (percent)...........................	23.0	27.6
Attainment		
Total population 25 years and over	580,244	222,836,834
Less than ninth grade (percent)...........................	2.8	4.9
9th to 12th grade, no diploma (percent)...........................	5.0	6.6
High school graduate, including equivalency (percent)...........................	30.2	26.7
Some college, no degree (percent)	21.1	20.3
Associate's degree (percent)...........................	11.6	8.6
Bachelor's degree (percent)	20.1	20.2
Graduate or professional degree (percent)...........................	9.2	12.7
High school graduate or higher (percent)	92.2	88.5
Bachelor's degree or higher (percent)...........................	29.3	32.9

[1] 2020 ACS 5-Year estimates. 1-Year estimates were not released for 2020 due to the impact of COVID-19 on data collection that year.

Table SD-12. Public School Characteristics and Educational Indicators

(Number, percent; data derived from National Center of Education Statistics.)

Item	State	U.S.
Public Elementary and Secondary Schools		
Number of regular school districts, 2018-19	149	13,452
Number of operational schools, 2019-20....................................	700	98,469
Percent charter schools	0.0	7.7
Total public school enrollment, Fall 2019....................................	139,949	50,796,445
Percent charter school enrollment	0.0	6.8
Student-teacher ratio, Fall 2019....................................	14.1	15.9
Expenditures per student (unadjusted dollars), 2018-19	10,325	13,187
Four-year adjusted cohort graduation rate (ACGR), 2018-2019[1]....................................	84.1	85.8
Students eligible for free or reduced-price lunch (percent), 2019-20....................................	36.3	52.1
English language learners (percent), Fall 2019	4.8	10.4
Students age 3 to 21 served under IDEA, part B (percent), 2020-21	15.6	14.5

Public Schools by Type, 2019-20	Number	Percent of state public schools
Total number of schools....................................	700	100.0
Special education....................................	13	1.9
Vocational education....................................	1	0.1
Alternative education....................................	30	4.3

[1] Adjusted Cohort Graduation Rates (ACGR) differ from Averaged Freshmen Graduation Rates (AFGR).
NA = Not available.

Table SD-13. Reported Voting and Registration of the Voting-Age Population, November 2020

(Numbers in thousands, percent.)

Item	Total population	Total citizen population	Registered			Voted		
			Total registered	Percent registered (total population)	Percent registered (total citizen population)	Total voted	Percent voted (total population)	Percent voted (total citizen population)
U.S. Total	252,274	231,593	168,308	66.7	72.7	154,628	61.3	66.8
State Total	659	649	437	66.3	67.4	380	57.7	58.5
Sex								
Male	330	326	217	65.6	66.5	189	57.2	57.9
Female	329	323	221	67.0	68.2	191	58.1	59.2
Race								
White alone.....................	587	585	401	68.3	68.5	351	59.7	59.9
White, non-Hispanic alone	577	577	397	68.8	68.8	348	60.3	60.3
Black alone.....................	18	13	5	B	B	4	B	B
Asian alone	12	9	4	B	B	4	B	B
Hispanic (of any race)	13	10	6	B	B	5	B	B
White alone or in combination	600	598	411	68.5	68.7	360	60.0	60.2
Black alone or in combination	18	13	5	B	B	4	B	B
Asian alone or in combination.....................	18	15	8	B	B	8	B	B
Age								
18 to 24 years.....................	79	77	40	50.5	52.0	34	42.7	43.9
25 to 34 years.....................	120	117	67	56.2	57.4	53	44.3	45.2
35 to 44 years.....................	99	95	59	59.8	62.4	50	50.7	52.9
45 to 64 years.....................	210	208	155	73.7	74.2	138	65.6	66.0
65 years and over	152	152	116	76.5	76.5	106	69.5	69.5

B = Base is less than 75,000 and therefore too small to show the derived measure.

Table SD-14. Crime

(Number, rate per 100,000. Data are derived from the FBI Uniform Crime Reports.)

Item	State			U.S.		
	2019	2020	Percent change	2019	2020	Percent change
TOTAL POPULATION[1]	887,127	892,717	0.6	328,329,953	329,484,123	0.4
VIOLENT CRIME						
Number.....................	3,523	4,476	27.1	1,250,393	1,313,105	5.0
Rate	397.1	501.4	26.3	380.8	398.5	4.6
Murder and Nonnegligent Manslaughter						
Number.....................	16	40	150.0	16,669	21,570	29.4
Rate	1.8	4.5	148.4	5.1	6.5	28.9
Rape[2]						
Number.....................	647	599	-7.4	143,224	126,430	-11.7
Rate	72.9	67.1	-8.0	43.6	38.4	-12.0
Robbery						
Number.....................	190	274	44.2	268,483	243,600	-9.3
Rate	21.4	30.7	43.3	81.8	73.9	-9.6
Aggravated Assault						
Number.....................	2,670	3,563	33.4	822,017	921,505	12.1
Rate	301.0	399.1	32.6	250.4	279.7	11.7
PROPERTY CRIME						
Number.....................	15,686	17,468	11.4	6,995,235	6,452,038	-7.8
Rate	1,768.2	1,956.7	10.7	2,130.6	1,958.2	-8.1
Burglary						
Number.....................	2,662	3,036	14.0	1,118,096	1,035,314	-7.4
Rate	300.1	340.1	13.3	340.5	314.2	-7.7
Larceny-Theft						
Number.....................	11,265	12,117	7.6	5,152,267	4,606,324	-10.6
Rate	1,269.8	1,357.3	6.9	1,569.2	1,398.0	-10.9
Motor Vehicle Theft						
Number.....................	1,759	2,315	31.6	724,872	810,400	11.8
Rate	198.3	259.3	30.8	220.8	246.0	11.4

NOTE: Although arson data are included in the trend and clearance tables, sufficient data are not available to estimate totals for this offense. Therefore, no arson data are published in this table.
- = Zero or rounds to zero.
[1] Population figures are U.S. Census Bureau provisional estimates as of July 1, 2020.
[2] The figures shown in the rape (revised definition) column were estimated using the revised Uniform Crime Reporting (UCR) definition of rape.

Table SD-15. State Government Finances, 2020

(Dollar amounts in thousands, percent distribution.)

Item	Dollars	Percent distribution
Total Revenue	6,648,344	100.0
General revenue	6,060,266	91.2
Intergovernmental revenue	3,086,682	46.4
Taxes	2,017,608	30.3
General sales	1204351	18.1
Selective sales	474,358	7.1
License taxes	295,378	4.4
Individual income tax	0	-
Corporate income tax	37,459	0.6
Other taxes	6,062	0.1
Current charges	378,819	5.7
Miscellaneous general revenue	577,157	8.7
Utility revenue	1,373	-
Liquor stores revenue	0	-
Insurance trust revenue[1]	586,705	8.8
Total Expenditure	5,716,059	100.0
Intergovernmental expenditure	922,752	16.1
Direct expenditure	4,793,307	83.9
Current operation	3,003,129	52.5
Capital outlay	829,915	14.5
Insurance benefits and repayments	688,078	12.0
Assistance and subsidies	144,806	2.5
Interest on debt	127,379	2.2
Exhibit: Salaries and wages	799,889	14.0
Total Expenditure	5,716,059	100.0
General expenditure	5,027,981	88.0
Intergovernmental expenditure	922,752	16.1
Direct expenditure	4,105,229	71.8
General expenditure, by function:		
Education	1,671,549	29.2
Public welfare	1,220,042	21.3
Hospitals	23,821	0.4
Health	174,864	3.1
Highways	819,978	14.3
Police protection	54,424	1.0
Correction	128,739	2.3
Natural resources	160,471	2.8
Parks and recreation	42,326	0.7
Governmental administration	225,960	4.0
Interest on general debt	127,379	2.2
Other and unallocable	356,253	6.2
Utility expenditure	0	-
Liquor stores expenditure	0	-
Insurance trust expenditure	688,078	12.0
Debt at End of Fiscal Year	3,855,938	X
Cash and Security Holdings	18,550,686	X

X = Not applicable.
- = Zero or rounds to zero.
[1] Within insurance trust revenue, net earnings of state retirement systems is a calculated statistic (the item code in the data file is X08), and thus can be positive or negative. Net earnings is the sum of earnings on investments plus gains on investments minus losses on investments. The change made in 2002 for asset valuation from book to market value in accordance with Statement 34 of the Governmental Accounting Standards Board is reflected in the calculated statistics.

Table SD-16. State Government Tax Collections, 2021

(Dollars in thousands, percent.)

Item	Dollars	Percent distribution
Total Taxes	2,149,543	100.0
Property taxes	X	-
Sales and gross receipts	1,783,982	83.0
General sales and gross receipts	1,273,575	59.2
Selective sales and gross receipts	510,407	23.7
Alcoholic beverages	20,021	0.9
Amusements	11,045	0.5
Insurance premiums	90,063	4.2
Motor fuels	189,881	8.8
Pari-mutuels	120	-
Public utilities	3,236	0.2
Tobacco products	52,328	2.4
Other selective sales	143,713	6.7
Licenses	300,687	14.0
Alcoholic beverages	1,409	0.1
Amusements	5,210	0.2
Corporations in general	7,398	0.3
Hunting and fishing	32,117	1.5
Motor vehicle	89,194	4.1
Motor vehicle operators	5,942	0.3
Public utilities	X	-
Occupation and business, NEC	136,919	6.4
Other licenses	22,498	1.0
Income taxes	53,960	2.5
Individual income	X	-
Corporation net income	53,960	2.5
Other taxes	10,914	0.5
Death and gift	X	-
Documentary and stock transfer	199	-
Severance	9,811	0.5
Taxes, NEC	904	-

X = Not applicable.
- = Zero or rounds to zero.

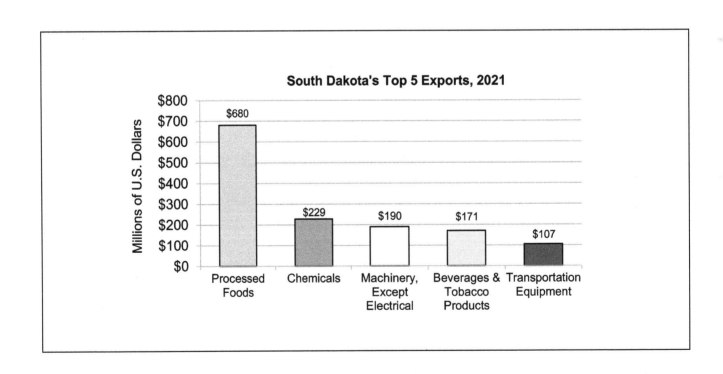

South Dakota's Top 5 Exports, 2021

Export	Millions of U.S. Dollars
Processed Foods	$680
Chemicals	$229
Machinery, Except Electrical	$190
Beverages & Tobacco Products	$171
Transportation Equipment	$107

TENNESSEE

Facts and Figures

Location: South central United States; bordered on the N by Kentucky and Virginia, on the E by North Carolina, on the S by Georgia, Alabama, and Mississippi, and on the W by Arkansas and Missouri

Area: 42,143 sq. mi. (109,151 sq. km.); rank—36th

Population: 6,975,218 (2021 est.); rank—16th

Principal Cities: capital—Nashville; largest—Nashville

Statehood: June 1, 1796; 16th state

U.S. Congress: 2 senators, 9 representatives

State Motto: Agriculture and Commerce

State Song: "The Tennessee Waltz"

State Nickname: The Volunteer State

Abbreviations: TN; Tenn.

State Symbols: flower—iris; tree—yellow poplar (tulip poplar); bird—mockingbird

At a Glance

- With an increase in population of 9.9 percent, Tennessee ranked 18th among the states in growth from 2010 to 2021.

- Tennessee's median household income in 2020 was $54,833, and 14.6 percent of the population lived below the poverty level.

- In 2020, 9.7 percent of Tennesseans did not have health insurance, compared to 8.7 percent of the total U.S. population.

- Tennessee's violent crime rate in 2020 was 672.7 per 100,000 population, the 4th highest rate in the country, and the property crime rate was 2,492.8 per 100,000 population, which ranked 11th in the country.

- Tennessee's unemployment rate of 4.3 percent ranked 32nd among the states in 2021 and was below the national unemployment rate of 5.3 percent.

Table TN-1. Population by Age, Sex, Race, and Hispanic Origin

(Number, percent, except where noted.)

Sex, age, race, and Hispanic origin	2000	2010	2021	Percent change, 2010–2021
Total Population.....................................	5,689,283	6,346,105	6,975,218	9.9
Percent of total U.S. population	2.0	2.1	2.1	X
Sex				
Male..	2,770,275	3,093,504	3,420,001	10.6
Female..	2,919,008	3,252,601	3,555,217	9.3
Age				
Under 5 years...	374,880	407,813	402,350	-1.3
5 to 19 years...	1,186,152	1,268,308	1,305,959	3.0
20 to 64 years..	3,424,940	3,816,522	4,081,637	6.9
65 years and over.....................................	703,311	853,462	1,185,272	38.9
Median age (years)	35.9	38.0	39.1	2.9
Race and Hispanic Origin				
One race				
White	4,563,310	5,056,311	5,457,887	7.9
Black	932,809	1,068,010	1,184,041	10.9
American Indian and Alaska Native	15,152	26,256	35,117	33.7
Asian	56,662	93,897	140,701	49.8
Native Hawaiian or Other Pacific Islander	2,205	5,426	7,423	36.8
Two or more races	63,109	96,205	150,049	56.0
Hispanic (of any race)...............................	123,838	301,090	425,839	41.4

NOTE: Population figures for 2021 are July 1 estimates. The 2000 and 2010 estimates are taken from the respective censuses.
- = Zero or rounds to zero.
X = Not applicable.

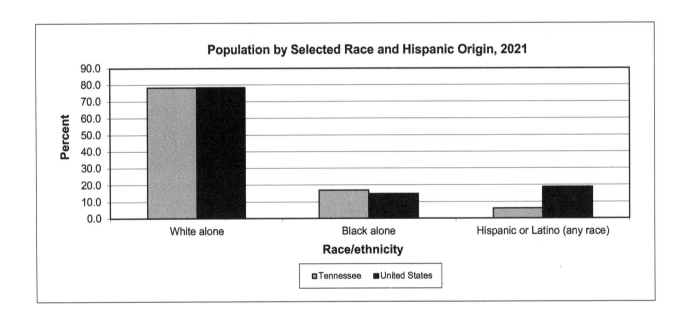

Table TN-2. Marital Status

(Number, percent distribution.)

Sex, age, race, and Hispanic origin	2000	2010	2020 [1]
Males, 15 Years and Over	2,169,327	2,461,573	2,665,244
Never married	26.6	31.4	33.2
Now married, except separated.......................................	58.9	52.2	51.0
Separated..	1.7	2.1	1.8
Widowed..	2.5	2.7	3.0
Divorced...	10.4	11.7	11.0
Females, 15 Years and Over	2,353,303	2,652,823	2,856,879
Never married	20.7	25.3	27.6
Now married, except separated.......................................	53.6	47.9	47.4
Separated..	2.3	2.7	2.1
Widowed..	11.2	10.3	9.4
Divorced...	12.2	13.7	13.4

[1] 2020 ACS 5-Year estimates. 1-Year estimates were not released for 2020 due to the impact of COVID-19 on data collection that year.

Table TN-3. Households and Housing Characteristics

(Number, percent, dollars.)

Item	2000	2010	2020 [1]	Average annual percent change, 2010–2020
Total Households...	2,232,905	2,440,663	2,639,455	1.2
Family households..	1,547,835	1,644,896	1,726,939	0.7
Married-couple family...................................	1,173,960	1,195,406	1,270,962	0.9
Other family..	373,875	449,490	455,977	0.2
Male householder, no wife present.................	85,976	106,616	121,689	2.0
Female householder, no husband present........	287,899	342,874	334,288	-0.4
Nonfamily households.......................................	685,070	795,767	912,516	2.1
Householder living alone.................................	576,401	675,565	754,164	1.7
Householder not living alone...........................	108,669	120,202	158,352	4.5
Housing Characteristics				
Total housing units...	2,439,443	2,815,087	2,996,127	0.9
Occupied housing units.....................................	2,232,905	2,440,663	2,639,455	1.2
Owner occupied...	1,561,363	1,662,768	1,756,534	0.8
Renter occupied..	671,542	777,895	882,921	1.9
Average household size......................................	2.48	2.54	2.51	-0.2
Financial Characteristics				
Median gross rent of renter-occupied housing	505	697	897	4.1
Median monthly owner costs for housing units with a mortgage	882	1,161	1,272	1.4
Median value of owner-occupied housing units.................	93,000	139,000	177,600	4.0

[1] 2020 ACS 5-Year estimates. 1-Year estimates were not released for 2020 due to the impact of COVID-19 on data collection that year.

Table TN-4. Migration, Origin, and Language

(Number, percent.)

Characteristic	State 2016-2020 [1]	U.S. 2016-2020 [1]
Residence 1 Year Ago		
Population 1 year and over	6,699,065	322,943,283
Same house	85.8	86.2
Different house in the U.S.	13.9	13.2
Same county	7.8	7.7
Different county	6.1	5.5
Same state	3.2	3.2
Different state	2.9	2.3
Abroad	0.3	0.6
Place of Birth		
Native born	6,424,882	282,443,680
Male	48.7	49.4
Female	51.3	50.6
Foreign born	347,386	44,125,628
Male	50.7	48.6
Female	49.3	51.4
Foreign born; naturalized U.S. citizen....................................	140,562	22,456,684
Male	46.6	46.1
Female	53.4	53.9
Foreign born; not a U.S. citizen...	206,824	21,668,944
Male	53.5	51.1
Female	46.5	48.9
Entered 2010 or later	30.9	22.8
Entered 2000 to 2009	31.9	25.1
Entered before 2000...	37.2	52.1
World Region of Birth, Foreign		
Foreign-born population, excluding population born at sea	347,386	44,125,628
Europe	10.7	10.8
Asia	31.0	31.3
Africa	10.6	5.4
Oceania	0.5	0.6
Latin America..	44.9	50.0
North America...	2.3	1.9
Language Spoken at Home and Ability to Speak English		
Population 5 years and over..	6,365,282	306,919,116
English only	92.8	78.5
Language other than English...	7.2	21.5
Speaks English less than "very well"................................	2.9	8.2

[1] 2020 ACS 5-Year estimates. 1-Year estimates were not released for 2020 due to the impact of COVID-19 on data collection that year.
NA = Not available.
X = Not applicable.
- = Zero or rounds to zero.

Table TN-5. Median Income and Poverty Status, 2020[1]

(Number, percent, except as noted.)

Characteristic	State		U.S.	
	Number	Percent	Number	Percent
Median Income				
Households (dollars)..	54,833	X	64,994	X
Families (dollars)	68,793	X	80,069	X
Below Poverty Level (All People)	965,213	14.6	40,910,326	12.8
Sex				
Male	425,554	13.3	18,171,512	11.6
Female	539,659	15.9	22,738,814	14.0
Age				
Under 18 years...	308,226	20.8	12,598,699	17.5
Related children under 18 years...	302,832	20.5	12,306,532	17.2
18 to 64 years..	556,149	13.8	23,554,920	12.1
65 years and over...	100,838	9.3	4,756,707	9.3

X = Not applicable.
[1] 2020 ACS 5-Year estimates. 1-Year estimates were not released for 2020 due to the impact of COVID-19 on data collection that year.

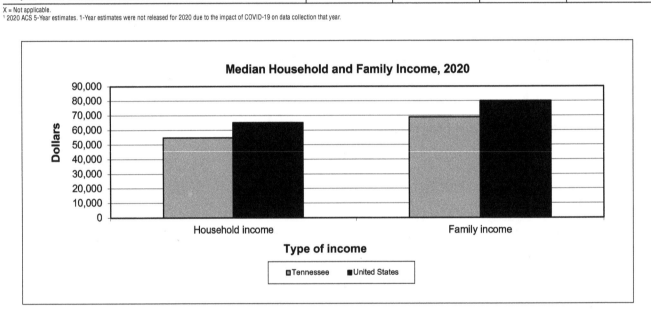

Table TN-6. Health Insurance Coverage Status for the Civilian Noninstitutionalized Population and Children Under 19 Years of Age

(Number, percent.)

Item	2011	2012	2013	2014	2015	2016	2017	2018	2019	2020 [2]
Civilian Noninstitutionalized Population	6,302,351	6,354,629	6,394,644	6,448,737	6,496,300	6,546,914	6,612,552	6,667,784	6,719,315	6,664,134
Covered by Private or Public Insurance										
Number..	5,379,701	5,472,509	5,507,982	5,672,418	5,828,883	5,954,604	5,983,410	5,992,919	6,037,668	6,014,822
Percent..	85.4	86.1	86.1	88.0	89.7	91.0	90.5	89.9	89.9	90.3
Uninsured										
Number..	922,650	882,120	886,662	776,319	667,417	592,310	629,142	674,865	681,647	649,312
Percent..	14.6	13.9	13.9	12.0	10.3	9.0	9.5	10.1	10.1	9.7
Percent in the U.S. not covered..........................	15.1	14.8	14.5	11.7	9.4	8.6	8.7	8.9	9.2	8.7
Children Under 19 Years of Age[1]	1,487,779	1,490,249	1,489,574	1,489,620	1,490,949	1,500,902	1,600,422	1,598,672	1,600,213	1,591,799
Covered by Private or Public Insurance										
Number..	1,402,852	1,405,719	1,404,287	1,412,007	1,428,845	1,447,865	1,529,643	1,515,748	1,519,741	1,513,221
Percent..	94.3	94.3	94.3	94.8	95.8	96.5	95.6	94.8	95.0	95.1
Uninsured										
Number..	84,927	84,530	85,287	77,613	62,104	53,037	70,779	82,924	80,472	78,578
Percent..	5.7	5.7	5.7	5.2	4.2	3.5	4.4	5.2	5.0	4.9
Percent in the U.S. not covered..........................	7.5	7.2	7.1	6.0	4.8	4.5	5.0	5.2	5.7	5.2

[1] Data for years prior to 2017 are for individuals under 18 years of age.
[2] 2020 ACS 5-Year estimates. 1-Year estimates were not released for 2020 due to the impact of COVID-19 on data collection that year. Data is not comparable to previous years, which are based on 1-year estimates.

Table TN-7. Employment Status by Demographic Group, 2021

(Numbers in thousands, percent.)

Characteristic	Civilian noninstitutional population	Civilian labor force		Employed		Unemployed	
		Number	Percent of population	Number	Percent of population	Number	Percent of population
Total...	5,496	3,315	60.3	3,180	57.9	135	4.1
Sex							
Male...	2,624	1,725	65.7	1,662	63.3	63	3.7
Female..	2,872	1,590	55.4	1,518	52.9	72	4.5
Race, Sex, and Hispanic Origin							
White..	4,424	2,683	60.6	2,590	58.5	93	3.5
Male..	2,144	1,430	66.7	1,385	64.6	44	3.1
Female..	2,281	1,253	54.9	1,205	52.8	48	3.9
Black or African American....................	887	522	58.8	485	54.7	37	7.1
Male..	401	243	60.7	228	57.0	15	6.1
Female..	486	278	57.2	256	52.7	22	7.9
Hispanic or Latino ethnicity[1]..............	373	255	68.4	242	64.9	13	5.1
Male..	204	167	81.8	160	78.4	7	4.2
Female..	NA	NA	NA	NA	NA	NA	NA
Age							
16 to 19 years................................	325	143	43.9	127	38.9	16	11.5
20 to 24 years................................	436	317	72.6	295	67.6	22	6.8
25 to 34 years................................	903	743	82.3	715	79.1	28	3.8
35 to 44 years................................	890	718	80.7	690	77.5	28	3.9
45 to 54 years................................	825	651	78.9	634	76.9	16	2.5
55 to 64 years................................	906	550	60.8	533	58.8	17	3.2
65 years and over............................	1,211	193	16.0	187	15.4	7	3.5

NOTE: Data in Table 7 are from the Current Population Survey (CPS) and do not match the estimates in Table 8. See notes and definitions for further information.
[1] May be of any race.

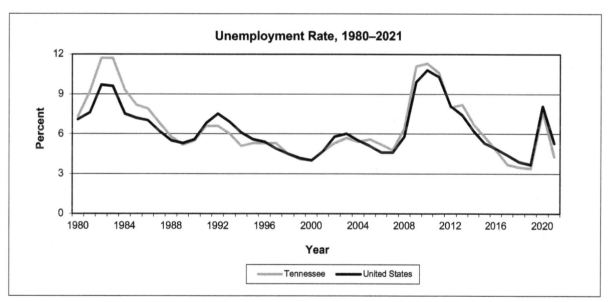

Unemployment Rate, 1980–2021

Table TN-8. Employment Status of the Civilian Noninstitutional Population Age 16 Years and Over

(Number, percent.)

Year	Civilian labor force	Civilian participation rate	Employed	Unemployed	Unemployment rate
2010..........	3,093,118	62.8	2,789,056	304,062	9.8
2011..........	3,117,492	62.7	2,833,278	284,214	9.1
2012..........	3,096,322	61.7	2,849,727	246,595	8.0
2013..........	3,078,892	60.8	2,840,127	238,765	7.8
2014..........	3,043,573	59.6	2,842,540	201,033	6.6
2015..........	3,074,216	59.6	2,902,684	171,532	5.6
2016..........	3,136,399	60.2	2,987,679	148,720	4.7
2017..........	3,197,032	60.5	3,077,515	119,517	3.7
2018..........	3,260,862	61	3,147,030	113,832	3.5
2019..........	3,339,543	61.9	3,226,045	113,498	3.4
2020..........	3,299,424	60.5	3,055,830	243,594	7.4
2021..........	3,327,966	60.4	3,185,263	142,703	4.3

Table TN-9. Employment and Average Wages by Industry

(Estimates are based on the 2012 North American Industry Classification System [NAICS].)

Industry	2013	2014	2015	2016	2017	2018	2019	2020
	Number of Jobs							
Wage and Salary Employment by Industry	2,846,413	2,903,868	2,974,822	3,039,254	3,081,388	3,132,827	3,190,477	3,075,014
Farm Wage and Salary Employment	9,138	9,927	11,141	9,177	10,626	10,796	10,587	10,586
Nonfarm Wage and Salary Employment	2,837,275	2,893,941	2,963,681	3,030,077	3,070,762	3,122,031	3,179,890	3,064,428
Private wage and salary employment	2,389,213	2,448,513	2,521,355	2,585,872	2,624,991	2,670,469	2,725,842	2,612,998
Forestry, fishing, and related activities	4,865	5,030	5,112	4,999	4,971	5,120	5,079	4,782
Mining	3,425	3,430	3,457	3,061	3,276	3,511	3,631	3,378
Utilities	3,342	3,380	3,366	3,395	3,577	3,546	3,633	3,652
Construction	106,545	109,155	115,688	117,844	123,092	127,456	133,276	133,248
Manufacturing	318,901	325,377	332,659	343,890	348,777	351,241	355,242	335,227
Durable goods manufacturing	198,982	205,524	210,630	219,138	221,877	224,894	227,581	211,076
Nondurable goods manufacturing	119,919	119,853	122,029	124,752	126,900	126,347	127,661	124,151
Wholesale trade	122,839	123,636	121,540	120,376	121,808	119,982	121,608	118,687
Retail trade	317,119	322,890	327,928	335,900	337,984	339,531	336,320	327,044
Transportation and warehousing	143,839	147,365	155,367	162,474	163,404	168,892	180,897	185,620
Information	43,474	43,349	43,622	44,961	45,507	44,859	45,120	42,967
Finance and insurance	106,827	109,194	111,288	113,290	116,054	117,866	123,999	125,808
Real estate and rental and leasing	33,547	34,943	37,129	38,776	40,319	41,606	43,175	40,889
Professional, scientific, and technical services	114,996	120,908	129,122	132,943	137,237	141,945	147,459	148,441
Management of companies and enterprises	35,228	37,306	41,468	44,066	44,796	50,104	50,955	49,338
Administrative and waste services	204,851	216,801	224,740	229,108	226,877	227,724	230,050	219,143
Educational services	56,458	57,792	59,145	61,407	62,058	63,324	64,649	63,430
Health care and social assistance	347,800	350,288	360,644	367,745	372,876	377,007	382,003	377,570
Arts, entertainment, and recreation	31,634	33,449	34,795	36,235	38,471	40,402	42,952	34,316
Accommodation and food services	255,997	265,117	274,868	285,354	292,753	299,675	306,749	260,801
Other services, except public administration	137,526	139,103	139,417	140,048	141,154	146,678	149,045	138,657
Government and government enterprises	448,062	445,428	442,326	444,205	445,771	451,562	454,048	451,430
	Dollars							
Average Wages and Salaries by Industry	43,575	44,706	46,191	46,929	48,322	50,004	51,206	54,427
Average Farm Wages and Salaries	23,255	22,681	16,509	23,000	18,027	19,354	15,599	15,152
Average Nonfarm Wages and Salaries	43,640	44,782	46,303	47,002	48,427	50,110	51,324	54,563
Average private wages and salaries	44,117	45,222	46,852	47,538	48,935	50,676	51,913	55,385
Forestry, fishing, and related activities	24,946	25,861	26,648	28,616	29,113	30,341	32,161	34,130
Mining	63,465	67,845	68,194	67,512	67,586	72,357	73,060	75,426
Utilities	65,515	67,995	70,785	71,788	72,503	76,245	79,591	84,608
Construction	47,569	49,910	52,845	54,488	56,584	57,045	58,765	62,272
Manufacturing	54,664	56,296	57,344	58,104	59,531	59,519	60,318	63,136
Durable goods manufacturing	53,199	55,124	56,268	57,331	58,767	59,844	60,740	63,372
Nondurable goods manufacturing	57,094	58,307	59,201	59,463	60,865	58,941	59,566	62,735
Wholesale trade	61,563	64,271	67,297	70,120	70,828	72,531	74,262	77,953
Retail trade	27,881	28,629	29,532	29,994	30,746	31,738	32,132	34,799
Transportation and warehousing	50,677	51,231	52,646	53,035	54,950	56,894	56,903	59,572
Information	58,955	61,755	62,689	64,380	68,480	73,855	75,557	81,367
Finance and insurance	72,250	74,945	75,997	77,912	79,722	86,608	86,270	93,946
Real estate and rental and leasing	42,656	44,661	46,732	48,664	48,975	51,116	53,740	57,739
Professional, scientific, and technical services	70,548	72,042	75,858	75,701	75,515	80,010	82,949	87,427
Management of companies and enterprises	98,318	97,031	100,547	98,574	101,866	109,629	116,460	117,061
Administrative and waste services	33,172	32,317	33,088	33,827	35,421	36,321	38,305	40,816
Educational services	35,986	36,349	36,903	37,476	38,365	39,020	40,339	43,198
Health care and social assistance	46,673	47,796	49,708	49,865	51,450	52,617	53,575	56,826
Arts, entertainment, and recreation	44,134	47,047	53,613	50,397	53,822	55,741	52,504	51,110
Accommodation and food services	18,345	18,869	19,417	20,214	20,947	22,396	23,046	22,103
Other services, except public administration	30,633	32,008	33,331	34,266	35,619	36,434	37,534	41,484
Government and government enterprises	41,097	42,358	43,173	43,882	45,437	46,764	47,791	49,806

Table TN-10. Employment Characteristics by Family Type

(Number, percent.)

Family type and labor force status	2018		2019		2020 [1]	
	Total	Families with own children under 18 years	Total	Families with own children under 18 years	Total	Families with own children under 18 years
All Families...	1,708,168	681,517	1,727,895	678,657	1,726,939	694,368
FAMILY TYPE AND LABOR FORCE STATUS						
Opposite-Sex Married-Couple Families............................	1,245,738	446,721	1,274,887	445,998	1,261,822	456,864
Both husband and wife in labor force..............................	48.0	64.5	48.6	66.7	49.2	66.4
Husband in labor force, wife not in labor force	22.0	28.2	21.6	26.4	22.0	27.3
Wife in labor force, husband not in labor force	8.5	4.4	8.7	4.2	8.5	4.2
Both husband and wife not in labor force.................	20.8	2.4	20.3	2.1	20.3	2.0
Other Families	462,430	234,796	453,008	232,659	455,977	235,461
Female householder, no spouse present	72.5	74.8	72.0	73.5	73.3	74.8
In labor force..	49.0	61.1	49.0	61.3	49.5	61.4
Not in labor force	23.5	13.7	23.0	12.2	23.9	13.4
Male householder, no spouse present...........................	27.5	25.2	28.0	26.5	26.7	25.2
In labor force...	20.0	22.1	21.6	24.4	19.9	22.7
Not in labor force	7.5	3.2	6.5	2.1	6.8	2.5

[1] 2020 ACS 5-Year estimates. 1-Year estimates were not released for 2020 due to the impact of COVID-19 on data collection that year. Data is not comparable to previous years, which are based on 1-year estimates.

Table TN-11. School Enrollment and Educational Attainment, 2020[1]

(Number, percent.)

Item	State	U.S.
Enrollment		
Total population 3 years and over, enrolled in school	1,560,968	80,497,960
Enrolled in nursery school or preschool (percent)...	5.6	6.1
Enrolled in kindergarten (percent)..	5.1	5.0
Enrolled in elementary school, grades 1-8 (percent)..	42.4	40.4
Enrolled in high school, grades 9-12 (percent)..	21.8	21.0
Enrolled in college or graduate school (percent)...	25.1	27.6
Attainment		
Total population 25 years and over	4,649,847	222,836,834
Less than ninth grade (percent)..	4.2	4.9
9th to 12th grade, no diploma (percent)..	7.6	6.6
High school graduate, including equivalency (percent)..	31.8	26.7
Some college, no degree (percent)..	20.7	20.3
Associate's degree (percent)..	7.5	8.6
Bachelor's degree (percent)..	17.8	20.2
Graduate or professional degree (percent)...	10.4	12.7
High school graduate or higher (percent)	88.2	88.5
Bachelor's degree or higher (percent)..	28.2	32.9

[1] 2020 ACS 5-Year estimates. 1-Year estimates were not released for 2020 due to the impact of COVID-19 on data collection that year.

Table TN-12. Public School Characteristics and Educational Indicators

(Number, percent; data derived from National Center of Education Statistics.)

Item	State	U.S.
Public Elementary and Secondary Schools		
Number of regular school districts, 2018-19..	147	13,452
Number of operational schools, 2019-20..	1,878	98,469
Percent charter schools	6.3	7.7
Total public school enrollment, Fall 2019..	1,014,744	50,796,445
Percent charter school enrollment	4.3	6.8
Student-teacher ratio, Fall 2019..	15.7	15.9
Expenditures per student (unadjusted dollars), 2018-19..	9,941	13,187
Four-year adjusted cohort graduation rate (ACGR), 2018-2019[1]..	90.5	85.8
Students eligible for free or reduced-price lunch (percent), 2019-20..	58.8	52.1
English language learners (percent), Fall 2019	5.1	10.4
Students age 3 to 21 served under IDEA, part B (percent), 2020-21	12.7	14.5

Public Schools by Type, 2019-20	Number	Percent of state public schools
Total number of schools..	1,878	100.0
Special education..	16	0.9
Vocational education..	11	0.6
Alternative education...	21	1.1

[1] Adjusted Cohort Graduation Rates (ACGR) differ from Averaged Freshmen Graduation Rates (AFGR).

Table TN-13. Reported Voting and Registration of the Voting-Age Population, November 2020

(Numbers in thousands, percent.)

Item	Total population	Total citizen population	Registered			Voted		
			Total registered	Percent registered (total population)	Percent registered (total citizen population)	Total voted	Percent voted (total population)	Percent voted (total citizen population)
U.S. Total	252,274	231,593	168,308	66.7	72.7	154,628	61.3	66.8
State Total................................	5,283	5,038	3,742	70.8	74.3	3,346	63.3	66.4
Sex								
Male	2,544	2,409	1,766	69.4	73.3	1,563	61.4	64.9
Female	2,738	2,629	1,976	72.2	75.2	1,783	65.1	67.8
Race								
White alone................................	4,212	4,014	2,992	71.0	74.5	2,677	63.6	66.7
White, non-Hispanic alone	3,918	3,890	2,924	74.6	75.2	2,619	66.8	67.3
Black alone.................................	866	853	658	76.0	77.1	592	68.3	69.4
Asian alone	99	65	37	B	B	34	B	B
Hispanic (of any race)	329	152	72	22.0	47.6	63	19.1	41.4
White alone or in combination	4,298	4,101	3,032	70.5	73.9	2,708	63.0	66.0
Black alone or in combination	895	882	671	75.0	76.1	602	67.2	68.2
Asian alone or in combination	111	76	49	43.9	63.7	46	41.3	59.9
Age								
18 to 24 years	641	611	372	58.1	60.9	300	46.9	49.1
25 to 34 years	818	761	521	63.7	68.5	428	52.3	56.3
35 to 44 years	911	829	618	67.9	74.5	549	60.3	66.3
45 to 64 years	1,765	1,699	1,340	75.9	78.9	1,247	70.6	73.4
65 years and over	1,148	1,138	891	77.6	78.2	822	71.6	72.2

Table TN-14. Crime

(Number, rate per 100,000. Data are derived from the FBI Uniform Crime Reports.)

Item	State			U.S.		
	2019	2020	Percent change	2019	2020	Percent change
TOTAL POPULATION[1]	6,830,325	6,886,834	0.8	328,329,953	329,484,123	0.4
VIOLENT CRIME						
Number...	40,908	46,328	13.2	1,250,393	1,313,105	5.0
Rate..	598.9	672.7	12.3	380.8	398.5	4.6
Murder and Nonnegligent Manslaughter						
Number...	515	663	28.7	16,669	21,570	29.4
Rate..	7.5	9.6	27.7	5.1	6.5	28.9
Rape[2]						
Number...	2,943	2,678	-9.0	143,224	126,430	-11.7
Rate..	43.1	38.9	-9.8	43.6	38.4	-12.0
Robbery						
Number...	6,164	5,575	-9.6	268,483	243,600	-9.3
Rate..	90.2	81.0	-10.3	81.8	73.9	-9.6
Aggravated Assault						
Number...	31,286	37,412	19.6	822,017	921,505	12.1
Rate..	458.0	543.2	18.6	250.4	279.7	11.7
PROPERTY CRIME						
Number...	181,801	171,675	-5.6	6,995,235	6,452,038	-7.8
Rate..	2,661.7	2,492.8	-6.3	2,130.6	1,958.2	-8.1
Burglary						
Number...	29,969	26,479	-11.6	1,118,096	1,035,314	-7.4
Rate..	438.8	384.5	-12.4	340.5	314.2	-7.7
Larceny-Theft						
Number...	132,540	124,098	-6.4	5,152,267	4,606,324	-10.6
Rate..	1,940.5	1,802.0	-7.1	1,569.2	1,398.0	-10.9
Motor Vehicle Theft						
Number...	19,292	21,098	9.4	724,872	810,400	11.8
Rate..	282.4	306.4	8.5	220.8	246.0	11.4

NOTE: Although arson data are included in the trend and clearance tables, sufficient data are not available to estimate totals for this offense. Therefore, no arson data are published in this table.

- = Zero or rounds to zero.

[1] Population figures are U.S. Census Bureau provisional estimates as of July 1, 2020.

[2] The figures shown in the rape (revised definition) column were estimated using the revised Uniform Crime Reporting (UCR) definition of rape.

Table TN-15. State Government Finances, 2020

(Dollar amounts in thousands, percent distribution.)

Item	Dollars	Percent distribution
Total Revenue	41,306,618	100.0
General revenue	35,315,871	85.5
Intergovernmental revenue	14,225,935	34.4
Taxes	16,775,270	40.6
General sales	9708042	23.5
Selective sales	3,511,711	8.5
License taxes	1,672,204	4.0
Individual income tax	57642	0.1
Corporate income tax	1,504,881	3.6
Other taxes	320,790	0.8
Current charges	2,122,152	5.1
Miscellaneous general revenue	2,192,514	5.3
Utility revenue	0	-
Liquor stores revenue	0	-
Insurance trust revenue[1]	5,990,747	14.5
Total Expenditure	35,866,341	100.0
Intergovernmental expenditure	7,773,839	21.7
Direct expenditure	28,092,502	78.3
Current operation	21,788,869	60.8
Capital outlay	2,225,966	6.2
Insurance benefits and repayments	1,957,426	5.5
Assistance and subsidies	1,750,677	4.9
Interest on debt	369,564	1.0
Exhibit: Salaries and wages	4,548,206	12.7
Total Expenditure	35,866,341	100.0
General expenditure	33,908,377	94.5
Intergovernmental expenditure	7,773,839	21.7
Direct expenditure	26,134,538	72.9
General expenditure, by function:		
Education	11,310,035	31.5
Public welfare	13,724,733	38.3
Hospitals	402,410	1.1
Health	906,929	2.5
Highways	2,038,289	5.7
Police protection	253,383	0.7
Correction	999,906	2.8
Natural resources	499,047	1.4
Parks and recreation	96,534	0.3
Governmental administration	1,416,469	3.9
Interest on general debt	369,564	1.0
Other and unallocable	1,870,446	5.2
		0.0
Utility expenditure	552	-
Liquor stores expenditure	0	-
Insurance trust expenditure	1,957,426	5.5
Debt at End of Fiscal Year	6,858,341	X
Cash and Security Holdings	78,677,497	X

X = Not applicable.
- = Zero or rounds to zero.
[1] Within insurance trust revenue, net earnings of state retirement systems is a calculated statistic (the item code in the data file is X08), and thus can be positive or negative. Net earnings is the sum of earnings on investments plus gains on investments minus losses on investments. The change made in 2002 for asset valuation from book to market value in accordance with Statement 34 of the Governmental Accounting Standards Board is reflected in the calculated statistics.

Table TN-16. State Government Tax Collections, 2021

(Dollars in thousands, percent.)

Item	Dollars	Percent distribution
Total Taxes	19,977,968	100.0
Property taxes	X	-
Sales and gross receipts	14,492,861	72.5
General sales and gross receipts	11,060,457	55.4
Selective sales and gross receipts	3,432,404	17.2
Alcoholic beverages	210,708	1.1
Amusements	24,503	0.1
Insurance premiums	1,108,673	5.5
Motor fuels	1,210,808	6.1
Pari-mutuels	X	-
Public utilities	8,894	-
Tobacco products	242,926	1.2
Other selective sales	625,892	3.1
Licenses	2,333,130	11.7
Alcoholic beverages	1,669	-
Amusements	380	-
Corporations in general	1,381,686	6.9
Hunting and fishing	44,538	0.2
Motor vehicle	387,781	1.9
Motor vehicle operators	48,880	0.2
Public utilities	4,900	-
Occupation and business, NEC	453,191	2.3
Other licenses	10,105	0.1
Income taxes	2,743,837	13.7
Individual income	179,379	0.9
Corporation net income	2,564,458	12.8
Other taxes	408,140	2.0
Death and gift	1,434	-
Documentary and stock transfer	392,898	2.0
Severance	381	-
Taxes, NEC	13,427	0.1

X = Not applicable.
- = Zero or rounds to zero.

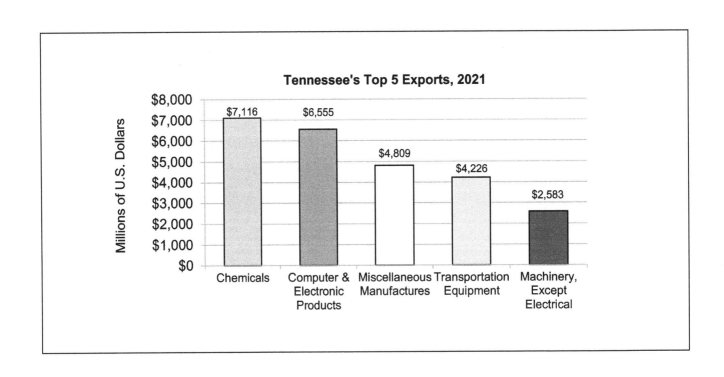

Tennessee's Top 5 Exports, 2021

(Bar chart, Millions of U.S. Dollars)

- Chemicals: $7,116
- Computer & Electronic Products: $6,555
- Miscellaneous Manufactures: $4,809
- Transportation Equipment: $4,226
- Machinery, Except Electrical: $2,583

TEXAS

Facts and Figures

Location: West South Central United States; bordered on the N by Oklahoma, on the E by Arkansas and Louisiana, on the S by Mexico and the Gulf of Mexico, and on the W by Mexico and New Mexico

Area: 268,581 sq. mi. (695,621 sq. km.); rank—2nd

Population: 29,527,941 (2021 est.); rank—2nd

Principal Cities: capital—Austin; largest—Houston

Statehood: December 29, 1845; 28th state

U.S. Congress: 2 senators, 36 representatives

State Motto: Friendship

State Song: "Texas, Our Texas"

State Nickname: The Lone Star State

Abbreviations: TX; Tex.

State Symbols: flower—bluebonnet; tree—pecan; bird—mockingbird

At a Glance

- With an increase in population of 17.4 percent, Texas ranked 3rd among the states in growth from 2010 to 2021.

- In 2021, Texas ranked 2nd for the highest percent of its population under 18 years old (25.3 percent).

- Texas's median household income in 2020 was $63,826, and 14.2 percent of the population lived below the poverty level.

- Texas was the state with the highest percent of uninsured residents in 2020, with 17.3 percent of Texans not having health insurance.

- In 2020, Texas ranked 16th among states for its violent crime rate (446.5 incidences per 100,000 population) and 15th for its property crime rate (2,245.0 incidences per 100,000 population).

Table TX-1. Population by Age, Sex, Race, and Hispanic Origin

(Number, percent, except where noted.)

Sex, age, race, and Hispanic origin	2000	2010	2021	Percent change, 2010–2021
Total Population...	20,851,820	25,145,561	29,527,941	17.4
Percent of total U.S. population	7.4	8.1	8.9	X
Sex				
Male...	10,352,910	12,472,280	14,735,970	18.1
Female...	10,498,910	12,673,281	14,791,971	16.7
Age				
Under 5 years..	1,625,628	1,928,473	1,905,442	-1.2
5 to 19 years...	4,291,608	5,693,241	6,389,970	12.2
20 to 64 years...	12,233,052	14,921,961	17,356,545	16.3
65 years and over	2,072,532	2,601,886	3,875,984	49.0
Median age (years)	32.3	33.6	35.4	5.4
Race and Hispanic Origin				
One race				
White	14,799,505	20,389,793	23,012,250	12.9
Black	2,404,566	3,070,440	3,894,860	26.9
American Indian and Alaska Native	118,362	251,209	314,130	25.0
Asian	562,319	1,000,473	1,616,815	61.6
Native Hawaiian or Other Pacific Islander	14,434	31,242	46,266	48.1
Two or more races...	514,633	402,404	643,620	59.9
Hispanic (of any race)..	6,699,666	9,578,505	11,857,401	23.8

NOTE: Population figures for 2021 are July 1 estimates. The 2000 and 2010 estimates are taken from the respective censuses.
- = Zero or rounds to zero.
X = Not applicable.

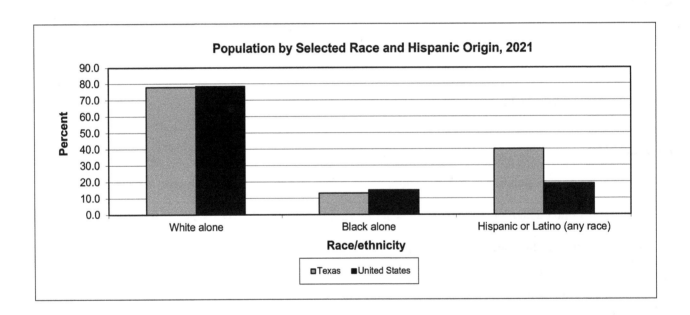

Population by Selected Race and Hispanic Origin, 2021

Legend: Texas, United States

Race/ethnicity: White alone, Black alone, Hispanic or Latino (any race)

Table TX-2. Marital Status

(Number, percent distribution.)

Sex, age, race, and Hispanic origin	2000	2010	2020 [1]
Males, 15 Years and Over	7,820,248	9,587,343	11,086,192
Never married	28.6	34.6	36.3
Now married, except separated..	58.8	51.6	50.5
Separated...	2.0	2.3	1.8
Widowed...	2.1	2.2	2.3
Divorced...	8.5	9.4	9.1
Females, 15 Years and Over	8,117,395	9,903,147	11,404,873
Never married	22.6	27.6	30.4
Now married, except separated..	54.3	48.5	47.4
Separated...	2.9	3.3	2.7
Widowed...	9.1	8.1	7.7
Divorced...	11.0	12.5	11.9

[1] 2020 ACS 5-Year estimates. 1-Year estimates were not released for 2020 due to the impact of COVID-19 on data collection that year.

Table TX-3. Households and Housing Characteristics

(Number, percent, dollars.)

Item	2000	2010	2020 [1]	Average annual percent change, 2010–2020
Total Households..	7,393,354	8,738,664	9,906,070	1.9
Family households	5,247,794	6,091,590	6,838,900	1.8
Married-couple family	3,989,741	4,386,996	4,974,588	1.9
Other family	1,258,053	1,704,594	1,864,312	1.3
Male householder, no wife present...................	320,464	436,727	504,190	2.2
Female householder, no husband present..........	937,489	1,267,867	1,360,122	1.0
Nonfamily households	2,145,560	2,647,074	3,067,170	2.3
Householder living alone..................................	1,752,141	2,166,469	2,507,455	2.2
Householder not living alone............................	393,419	480,605	559,715	2.4
Housing Characteristics				
Total housing units...	8,157,575	9,996,209	11,112,975	1.6
Occupied housing units	7,393,354	8,738,664	9,906,070	1.9
Owner occupied	4,716,959	5,555,903	6,168,808	1.6
Renter occupied	2,676,395	3,182,761	3,737,262	2.5
Average household size.....................................	2.74	2.82	2.83	0.1
Financial Characteristics				
Median gross rent of renter-occupied housing	574	801	1,082	5.0
Median monthly owner costs for housing units with a mortgage	986	1,402	1,654	2.6
Median value of owner-occupied housing units............	82,500	128,100	187,200	6.6

[1] 2020 ACS 5-Year estimates. 1-Year estimates were not released for 2020 due to the impact of COVID-19 on data collection that year.

Table TX-4. Migration, Origin, and Language

(Number, percent.)

Characteristic	State 2016-2020 [1]	U.S. 2016-2020 [1]
Residence 1 Year Ago		
Population 1 year and over	28,277,640	322,943,283
Same house	84.8	86.2
Different house in the U.S.	14.5	13.2
Same county	8.7	7.7
Different county	5.8	5.5
Same state	3.9	3.2
Different state	1.9	2.3
Abroad	0.7	0.6
Place of Birth		
Native born	23,812,490	282,443,680
Male	49.6	49.4
Female	50.4	50.6
Foreign born	4,822,952	44,125,628
Male	50.0	48.6
Female	50.0	51.4
Foreign born; naturalized U.S. citizen...	1,887,584	22,456,684
Male	47.6	46.1
Female	52.4	53.9
Foreign born; not a U.S. citizen..	2,935,368	21,668,944
Male	51.5	51.1
Female	48.5	48.9
Entered 2010 or later	24.2	22.8
Entered 2000 to 2009	26.4	25.1
Entered before 2000..	49.3	52.1
World Region of Birth, Foreign		
Foreign-born population, excluding population born at sea	4,822,952	44,125,628
Europe	4.2	10.8
Asia...	22.6	31.3
Africa	5.4	5.4
Oceania	0.3	0.6
Latin America...	66.4	50.0
North America	1.1	1.9
Language Spoken at Home and Ability to Speak English		
Population 5 years and over...	26,638,435	306,919,116
English only	64.9	78.5
Language other than English...	35.1	21.5
Speaks English less than "very well"..	13.3	8.2

[1] 2020 ACS 5-Year estimates. 1-Year estimates were not released for 2020 due to the impact of COVID-19 on data collection that year.
NA = Not available.
X = Not applicable.
- = Zero or rounds to zero.

Table TX-5. Median Income and Poverty Status, 2020[1]

(Number, percent, except as noted.)

Characteristic	State		U.S.	
	Number	Percent	Number	Percent
Median Income				
Households (dollars)...	63,826	X	64,994	X
Families (dollars)	76,073	X	80,069	X
Below Poverty Level (All People)	3,984,260	14.2	40,910,326	12.8
Sex				
Male	1,775,491	12.9	18,171,512	11.6
Female	2,208,769	15.5	22,738,814	14.0
Age				
Under 18 years..	1,462,277	20.0	12,598,699	17.5
Related children under 18 years...	1,439,337	19.8	12,306,532	17.2
18 to 64 years...	2,144,673	12.5	23,554,920	12.1
65 years and over	377,310	10.7	4,756,707	9.3

X = Not applicable.
[1] 2020 ACS 5-Year estimates. 1-Year estimates were not released for 2020 due to the impact of COVID-19 on data collection that year.

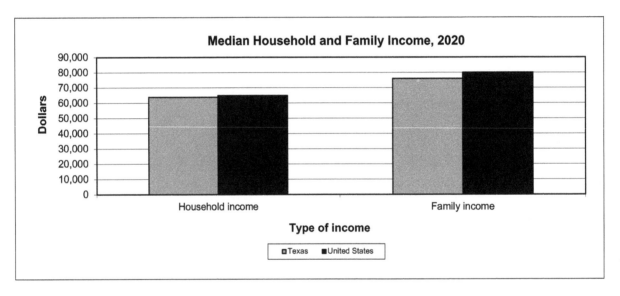

Table TX-6. Health Insurance Coverage Status for the Civilian Noninstitutionalized Population and Children Under 19 Years of Age

(Number, percent.)

Item	2011	2012	2013	2014	2015	2016	2017	2018	2019	2020 [2]
Civilian Noninstitutionalized Population	25,197,453	25,584,499	25,976,562	26,485,838	26,990,435	27,386,023	27,836,924	28,243,191	28,514,428	28,169,961
Covered by Private or Public Insurance										
Number..	19,407,607	19,822,141	20,228,395	21,438,361	22,375,210	22,840,643	23,019,956	23,240,298	23,280,468	23,292,892
Percent..	77.0	77.5	77.9	80.9	82.9	83.4	82.7	82.3	81.6	82.7
Uninsured										
Number..	5,789,846	5,762,358	5,748,167	5,047,477	4,615,225	4,545,380	4,816,968	5,002,893	5,233,960	4,877,069
Percent..	23.0	22.5	22.1	19.1	17.1	16.6	17.3	17.7	18.4	17.3
Percent in the U.S. not covered..	15.1	14.8	14.5	11.7	9.4	8.6	8.7	8.9	9.2	8.7
Children Under 19 Years of Age[1]	6,946,969	6,971,878	7,028,782	7,106,727	7,197,853	7,282,033	7,781,845	7,825,350	7,808,139	7,787,420
Covered by Private or Public Insurance										
Number..	6,030,447	6,108,588	6,140,477	6,322,789	6,515,730	6,611,211	6,947,175	6,952,556	6,812,815	6,918,831
Percent..	86.8	87.6	87.4	89.0	90.5	90.8	89.3	88.8	87.3	88.8
Uninsured										
Number..	916,522	863,290	888,305	783,938	682,123	670,822	834,670	872,794	995,324	868,589
Percent..	13.2	12.4	12.6	11.0	9.5	9.2	10.7	11.2	12.7	11.2
Percent in the U.S. not covered..	7.5	7.2	7.1	6.0	4.8	4.5	5.0	5.2	5.7	5.2

[1] Data for years prior to 2017 are for individuals under 18 years of age.
[2] 2020 ACS 5-Year estimates. 1-Year estimates were not released for 2020 due to the impact of COVID-19 on data collection that year. Data is not comparable to previous years, which are based on 1-year estimates.

Table TX-7. Employment Status by Demographic Group, 2021

(Numbers in thousands, percent.)

Characteristic	Civilian noninstitutional population	Civilian labor force		Employed		Unemployed	
		Number	Percent of population	Number	Percent of population	Number	Percent of population
Total..	22,630	14,271	63.1	13,453	59.4	818	5.7
Sex							
Male..	11,015	7,845	71.2	7,387	67.1	458	5.8
Female..	11,616	6,426	55.3	6,066	52.2	360	5.6
Race, Sex, and Hispanic Origin							
White...	17,806	11,103	62.4	10,519	59.1	584	5.3
Male..	8,764	6,237	71.2	5,903	67.4	334	5.4
Female..	9,043	4,866	53.8	4,616	51.0	250	5.1
Black or African American....................	2,901	1,886	65.0	1,716	59.2	170	9.0
Male..	1,338	919	68.7	829	62.0	90	9.8
Female..	1,563	967	61.9	887	56.7	80	8.3
Hispanic or Latino ethnicity[1]	8,173	5,276	64.6	4,911	60.1	365	6.9
Male..	4,085	3,099	75.9	2,888	70.7	211	6.8
Female..	4,088	2,177	53.3	2,023	49.5	154	7.1
Age							
16 to 19 years...................................	1,701	505	29.7	436	25.6	69	13.6
20 to 24 years...................................	2,042	1,437	70.4	1,294	63.3	143	10.0
25 to 34 years...................................	4,124	3,338	80.9	3,147	76.3	192	5.7
35 to 44 years...................................	3,952	3,215	81.3	3,050	77.2	165	5.1
45 to 54 years...................................	3,638	2,936	80.7	2,807	77.1	130	4.4
55 to 64 years...................................	3,179	2,046	64.4	1,959	61.6	87	4.2
65 years and over..............................	3,993	795	19.9	762	19.1	33	4.2

NOTE: Data in Table 7 are from the Current Population Survey (CPS) and do not match the estimates in Table 8. See notes and definitions for further information.
[1] May be of any race.

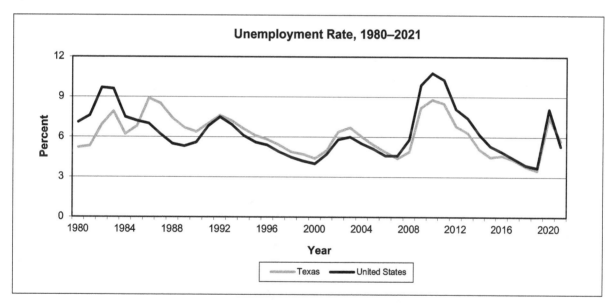

Unemployment Rate, 1980–2021

Table TX-8. Employment Status of the Civilian Noninstitutional Population Age 16 Years and Over

(Number, percent.)

Year	Civilian labor force	Civilian participation rate	Employed	Unemployed	Unemployment rate
2010..	12,260,100	66.0	11,255,444	1,004,656	8.2
2011..	12,499,595	65.9	11,498,869	1,000,726	8.0
2012..	12,639,465	65.4	11,794,975	844,490	6.7
2013..	12,832,035	65.2	12,022,272	809,763	6.3
2014..	13,006,202	64.8	12,333,076	673,126	5.2
2015..	13,090,961	63.8	12,503,464	587,497	4.5
2016..	13,346,836	63.8	12,728,898	617,938	4.6
2017..	13,473,991	63.8	12,888,025	585,966	4.3
2018..	13,684,009	63.8	13,149,672	534,337	3.9
2019..	13,871,780	63.7	13,381,020	490,760	3.5
2020..	13,870,874	62.7	12,808,616	1,062,258	7.7
2021..	14,220,446	63.3	13,413,036	807,410	5.7

Table TX-9. Employment and Average Wages by Industry

(Estimates are based on the 2012 North American Industry Classification System [NAICS].)

Industry	2013	2014	2015	2016	2017	2018	2019	2020
	Number of Jobs							
Wage and Salary Employment by Industry..........................	11,664,195	12,019,579	12,306,014	12,448,418	12,644,682	12,973,344	13,269,719	12,730,770
Farm Wage and Salary Employment.................................	47,444	47,110	49,030	50,698	47,860	49,847	45,619	51,650
Nonfarm Wage and Salary Employment............................	11,616,751	11,972,469	12,256,984	12,397,720	12,596,822	12,923,497	13,224,100	12,679,120
Private wage and salary employment....................................	9,641,641	9,987,530	10,245,568	10,357,353	10,538,306	10,853,274	11,128,829	10,597,042
Forestry, fishing, and related activities................................	32,238	32,901	33,700	33,794	33,672	33,851	34,279	32,715
Mining..	288,452	307,690	271,697	218,710	219,594	243,205	246,894	189,282
Utilities..	48,981	49,026	49,508	49,806	50,333	51,769	52,660	51,586
Construction..	630,241	668,106	701,741	718,755	728,768	758,213	793,456	755,892
Manufacturing...	875,085	888,655	879,061	846,192	853,261	881,465	907,251	869,007
Durable goods manufacturing..	578,574	590,171	577,587	541,233	542,591	563,964	582,612	552,264
Nondurable goods manufacturing..................................	296,511	298,484	301,474	304,959	310,670	317,501	324,639	316,743
Wholesale trade..	564,503	576,387	590,924	583,155	590,939	598,175	611,387	592,505
Retail trade...	1,226,715	1,261,716	1,305,301	1,330,491	1,334,880	1,339,918	1,331,416	1,291,873
Transportation and warehousing.......................................	416,151	436,143	458,604	470,286	491,252	511,591	534,202	549,633
Information..	201,252	203,226	201,364	202,421	202,359	204,029	208,816	198,516
Finance and insurance...	507,022	517,251	534,354	545,239	561,632	572,251	591,172	605,903
Real estate and rental and leasing...................................	192,042	199,652	205,198	208,164	217,434	226,935	235,548	225,746
Professional, scientific, and technical services.....................	652,772	683,593	714,562	732,190	749,697	791,102	831,521	838,280
Management of companies and enterprises........................	93,917	111,922	116,858	119,357	128,420	142,215	147,831	141,058
Administrative and waste services.....................................	727,401	760,783	775,344	786,004	800,972	817,985	826,963	792,744
Educational services	166,288	170,156	176,442	185,294	188,601	198,133	204,996	196,670
Health care and social assistance.....................................	1,294,699	1,324,471	1,377,347	1,426,207	1,457,934	1,489,463	1,522,324	1,489,724
Arts, entertainment, and recreation..................................	118,518	128,047	131,235	137,691	142,018	147,298	152,313	117,934
Accommodation and food services....................................	1,027,754	1,069,189	1,117,193	1,159,908	1,185,162	1,217,465	1,251,745	1,070,846
Other services, except public administration........................	577,610	598,616	605,135	603,689	601,378	628,211	644,055	587,128
Government and government enterprises..............................	1,975,110	1,984,939	2,011,416	2,040,367	2,058,516	2,070,223	2,095,271	2,082,078
	Dollars							
Average Wages and Salaries by Industry	50,668	52,666	53,751	53,847	55,374	57,280	59,285	62,141
Average Farm Wages and Salaries	25,688	30,935	33,207	27,607	30,452	30,581	30,140	17,321
Average Nonfarm Wages and Salaries	50,770	52,751	53,833	53,955	55,468	57,383	59,386	62,324
Average private wages and salaries....................................	51,706	53,784	54,792	54,750	56,314	58,324	60,409	63,421
Forestry, fishing, and related activities................................	26,238	27,553	28,642	30,331	31,860	33,052	34,455	36,596
Mining..	119,583	126,238	128,051	131,123	127,017	127,212	133,111	141,348
Utilities..	97,638	100,433	104,041	105,098	111,521	111,879	115,285	115,213
Construction..	55,705	58,586	60,509	61,677	63,176	65,506	67,517	68,887
Manufacturing...	68,520	71,104	72,813	73,125	75,746	77,627	79,732	81,173
Durable goods manufacturing..	70,288	73,097	74,119	75,480	78,583	80,489	82,830	84,311
Nondurable goods manufacturing..................................	65,069	67,163	70,312	68,945	70,791	72,544	74,173	75,703
Wholesale trade..	74,138	75,833	77,269	78,022	79,901	83,355	86,418	89,715
Retail trade...	29,083	29,987	30,702	30,891	31,608	32,813	34,052	36,879
Transportation and warehousing.......................................	58,338	59,899	61,336	59,605	61,249	62,903	64,001	62,796
Information..	75,296	76,634	79,628	81,189	84,286	87,060	90,847	102,848
Finance and insurance...	75,762	79,588	82,456	83,654	87,273	90,549	94,088	100,669
Real estate and rental and leasing...................................	53,967	57,272	58,248	58,868	61,355	64,060	66,762	68,567
Professional, scientific, and technical services.....................	83,822	86,534	88,389	89,313	91,117	94,431	97,001	100,510
Management of companies and enterprises........................	113,568	123,337	123,876	123,032	131,917	132,870	136,130	139,218
Administrative and waste services.....................................	38,962	40,649	41,809	42,169	43,380	44,822	46,673	50,136
Educational services	38,766	39,125	39,983	40,761	41,227	42,234	42,892	47,758
Health care and social assistance.....................................	42,568	43,925	45,415	45,964	46,991	47,901	49,178	51,600
Arts, entertainment, and recreation..................................	32,988	33,555	35,508	36,479	37,484	37,622	39,671	42,752
Accommodation and food services....................................	19,896	20,546	21,055	21,497	22,115	23,284	24,021	22,736
Other services, except public administration........................	31,108	32,316	33,461	34,291	35,718	36,717	37,924	40,999
Government and government enterprises..............................	46,196	47,553	48,947	49,918	51,138	52,454	53,952	56,741

Table TX-10. Employment Characteristics by Family Type

(Number, percent.)

Family type and labor force status	2018		2019		2020 [1]	
	Total	Families with own children under 18 years	Total	Families with own children under 18 years	Total	Families with own children under 18 years
All Families................................	6,730,268	3,085,438	6,857,641	3,142,131	6,838,900	3,190,138
FAMILY TYPE AND LABOR FORCE STATUS						
Opposite-Sex Married-Couple Families............................	4,871,974	2,115,608	4,954,566	2,153,548	4,932,575	2,199,935
Both husband and wife in labor force................................	49.5	60.1	50.5	61.8	51.0	61.4
Husband in labor force, wife not in labor force	27.6	34.7	27.0	33.2	27.4	33.8
Wife in labor force, husband not in labor force	6.8	3.2	6.5	3.0	6.7	3.3
Both husband and wife not in labor force................................	15.2	1.5	15.2	1.6	14.9	1.5
Other Families	1,858,294	969,830	1,903,075	988,583	1,864,312	980,993
Female householder, no spouse present	72.8	76.7	71.9	75.1	73.0	76.7
In labor force................................	52.5	63.6	51.4	61.8	53.0	64.1
Not in labor force................................	20.3	13.0	20.4	13.3	20.0	12.5
Male householder, no spouse present..........................	27.2	23.3	28.1	24.9	27.0	23.3
In labor force................................	22.1	21.7	23.0	23.4	22.0	21.7
Not in labor force................................	5.1	1.6	5.2	1.6	5.1	1.7

[1] 2020 ACS 5-Year estimates. 1-Year estimates were not released for 2020 due to the impact of COVID-19 on data collection that year. Data is not comparable to previous years, which are based on 1-year estimates.

Table TX-11. School Enrollment and Educational Attainment, 2020[1]

(Number, percent.)

Item	State	U.S.
Enrollment		
Total population 3 years and over, enrolled in school	7,719,304	80,497,960
Enrolled in nursery school or preschool (percent).........................	5.9	6.1
Enrolled in kindergarten (percent)................................	5.3	5.0
Enrolled in elementary school, grades 1-8 (percent).........................	42.9	40.4
Enrolled in high school, grades 9-12 (percent).........................	21.4	21.0
Enrolled in college or graduate school (percent).........................	24.5	27.6
Attainment		
Total population 25 years and over	18,449,851	222,836,834
Less than ninth grade (percent)..........................	7.8	4.9
9th to 12th grade, no diploma (percent)..........................	7.8	6.6
High school graduate, including equivalency (percent)..........................	24.7	26.7
Some college, no degree (percent)..........................	21.5	20.3
Associate's degree (percent)..........................	7.4	8.6
Bachelor's degree (percent)..........................	19.9	20.2
Graduate or professional degree (percent)..........................	10.8	12.7
High school graduate or higher (percent)..........................	84.4	88.5
Bachelor's degree or higher (percent)..........................	30.7	32.9

[1] 2020 ACS 5-Year estimates. 1-Year estimates were not released for 2020 due to the impact of COVID-19 on data collection that year.

Table TX-12. Public School Characteristics and Educational Indicators

(Number, percent; data derived from National Center of Education Statistics.)

Item	State	U.S.
Public Elementary and Secondary Schools		
Number of regular school districts, 2018-19	1,024	13,452
Number of operational schools, 2019-20..........................	8,987	98,469
Percent charter schools	10.1	7.7
Total public school enrollment, Fall 2019..........................	5,495,398	50,796,445
Percent charter school enrollment	7.1	6.8
Student-teacher ratio, Fall 2019..........................	15.1	15.9
Expenditures per student (unadjusted dollars), 2018-19	9,868	13,187
Four-year adjusted cohort graduation rate (ACGR), 2018-2019[1]..........................	90.0	85.8
Students eligible for free or reduced-price lunch (percent), 2019-20..........................	60.2	52.1
English language learners (percent), Fall 2019	19.6	10.4
Students age 3 to 21 served under IDEA, part B (percent), 2020-21	11.3	14.5

Public Schools by Type, 2019-20	Number	Percent of state public schools
Total number of schools..........................	8,987	100.0
Special education..........................	12	0.1
Vocational education..........................	0	-
Alternative education..........................	866	9.6

[1] Adjusted Cohort Graduation Rates (ACGR) differ from Averaged Freshmen Graduation Rates (AFGR).
- = Zero or rounds to zero.

Table TX-13. Reported Voting and Registration of the Voting-Age Population, November 2020

(Numbers in thousands, percent.)

Item	Total population	Total citizen population	Registered			Voted		
			Total registered	Percent registered (total population)	Percent registered (total citizen population)	Total voted	Percent voted (total population)	Percent voted (total citizen population)
U.S. Total	252,274	231,593	168,308	66.7	72.7	154,628	61.3	66.8
State Total	21,485	18,581	13,343	62.1	71.8	11,874	55.3	63.9
Sex								
Male	10,513	9,082	6,338	60.3	69.8	5,580	53.1	61.4
Female	10,972	9,500	7,005	63.8	73.7	6,295	57.4	66.3
Race								
White alone	17,042	14,760	10,734	63.0	72.7	9,612	56.4	65.1
White, non-Hispanic alone	9,615	9,423	7,396	76.9	78.5	6,785	70.6	72.0
Black alone	2,700	2,502	1,759	65.1	70.3	1,521	56.3	60.8
Asian alone	1,239	821	521	42.1	63.5	482	38.9	58.7
Hispanic (of any race)	7,730	5,599	3,538	45.8	63.2	2,972	38.4	53.1
White alone or in combination	17,361	15,079	10,928	62.9	72.5	9,762	56.2	64.7
Black alone or in combination	2,890	2,692	1,882	65.1	69.9	1,636	56.6	60.8
Asian alone or in combination	1,355	937	601	44.4	64.2	546	40.3	58.3
Age								
18 to 24 years	2,617	2,366	1,311	50.1	55.4	1,024	39.1	43.3
25 to 34 years	4,189	3,491	2,275	54.3	65.2	1,912	45.6	54.8
35 to 44 years	3,989	3,124	2,249	56.4	72.0	1,983	49.7	63.5
45 to 64 years	6,827	5,988	4,585	67.2	76.6	4,201	61.5	70.2
65 years and over	3,862	3,613	2,923	75.7	80.9	2,755	71.3	76.3

Table TX-14. Crime

(Number, rate per 100,000. Data are derived from the FBI Uniform Crime Reports.)

Item	State			U.S.		
	2019	2020	Percent change	2019	2020	Percent change
TOTAL POPULATION[1]	28,986,794	29,360,759	1.3	328,329,953	329,484,123	0.4
VIOLENT CRIME						
Number	122,263	131,084	7.2	1,250,393	1,313,105	5.0
Rate	421.8	446.5	5.8	380.8	398.5	4.6
Murder and Nonnegligent Manslaughter						
Number	1,432	1,931	34.8	16,669	21,570	29.4
Rate	4.9	6.6	33.1	5.1	6.5	28.9
Rape[2]						
Number	15,303	13,509	-11.7	143,224	126,430	-11.7
Rate	52.8	46.0	-12.8	43.6	38.4	-12.0
Robbery						
Number	29,126	26,834	-7.9	268,483	243,600	-9.3
Rate	100.5	91.4	-9.0	81.8	73.9	-9.6
Aggravated Assault						
Number	76,402	88,810	16.2	822,017	921,505	12.1
Rate	263.6	302.5	14.8	250.4	279.7	11.7
PROPERTY CRIME						
Number	697,305	659,160	-5.5	6,995,235	6,452,038	-7.8
Rate	2,405.6	2,245.0	-6.7	2,130.6	1,958.2	-8.1
Burglary						
Number	114,494	108,851	-4.9	1,118,096	1,035,314	-7.4
Rate	395.0	370.7	-6.1	340.5	314.2	-7.7
Larceny-Theft						
Number	504,461	466,033	-7.6	5,152,267	4,606,324	-10.6
Rate	1,740.3	1,587.3	-8.8	1,569.2	1,398.0	-10.9
Motor Vehicle Theft						
Number	78,350	84,276	7.6	724,872	810,400	11.8
Rate	270.3	287.0	6.2	220.8	246.0	11.4

NOTE: Although arson data are included in the trend and clearance tables, sufficient data are not available to estimate totals for this offense. Therefore, no arson data are published in this table.
- = Zero or rounds to zero.
[1] Population figures are U.S. Census Bureau provisional estimates as of July 1, 2020.
[2] The figures shown in the rape (revised definition) column were estimated using the revised Uniform Crime Reporting (UCR) definition of rape.

Table TX-15. State Government Finances, 2020

(Dollar amounts in thousands, percent distribution.)

Item	Dollars	Percent distribution
Total Revenue	199,319,560	100.0
General revenue	160,725,548	80.6
Intergovernmental revenue	66,662,596	33.4
Taxes	61,013,294	30.6
General sales	38412349	19.3
Selective sales	14,930,574	7.5
License taxes	3,396,564	1.7
Individual income tax	0	-
Corporate income tax	0	-
Other taxes	4,273,807	2.1
Current charges	17,605,801	8.8
Miscellaneous general revenue	15,443,857	7.7
Utility revenue	0	-
Liquor stores revenue	0	-
Insurance trust revenue[1]	38,594,012	19.4
Total Expenditure	174,210,668	100.0
Intergovernmental expenditure	35,311,864	20.3
Direct expenditure	138,898,804	79.7
Current operation	94,905,723	54.5
Capital outlay	14,114,867	8.1
Insurance benefits and repayments	23,656,436	13.6
Assistance and subsidies	4,258,942	2.4
Interest on debt	1,962,836	1.1
Exhibit: Salaries and wages	21,217,815	12.2
Total Expenditure	174,210,668	100.0
General expenditure	150,479,394	86.4
Intergovernmental expenditure	35,311,864	20.3
Direct expenditure	115,167,530	66.1
General expenditure, by function:		
Education	61,892,565	35.5
Public welfare	44,073,499	25.3
Hospitals	9,377,092	5.4
Health	4,010,562	2.3
Highways	13,074,702	7.5
Police protection	1,263,967	0.7
Correction	4,247,937	2.4
Natural resources	838,092	0.5
Parks and recreation	321,471	0.2
Governmental administration	2,982,209	1.7
Interest on general debt	1,962,836	1.1
Other and unallocable	6,258,323	3.6
Utility expenditure	136,257	0.1
Liquor stores expenditure	0	-
Insurance trust expenditure	23,656,436	13.6
Debt at End of Fiscal Year	57,886,725	X
Cash and Security Holdings	459,751,290	X

X = Not applicable.
- = Zero or rounds to zero.
[1] Within insurance trust revenue, net earnings of state retirement systems is a calculated statistic (the item code in the data file is X08), and thus can be positive or negative. Net earnings is the sum of earnings on investments plus gains on investments minus losses on investments. The change made in 2002 for asset valuation from book to market value in accordance with Statement 34 of the Governmental Accounting Standards Board is reflected in the calculated statistics.

Table TX-16. State Government Tax Collections, 2021

(Dollars in thousands, percent.)

Item	Dollars	Percent distribution
Total Taxes	65,377,430	100.0
Property taxes	X	-
Sales and gross receipts	56,641,560	86.6
General sales and gross receipts	40,413,873	61.8
Selective sales and gross receipts	16,227,687	24.8
Alcoholic beverages	1,262,775	1.9
Amusements	17,514	-
Insurance premiums	2,699,643	4.1
Motor fuels	3,596,892	5.5
Pari-mutuels	4,972	-
Public utilities	725,767	1.1
Tobacco products	1,397,304	2.1
Other selective sales	6,522,820	10.0
Licenses	3,646,437	5.6
Alcoholic beverages	77,839	0.1
Amusements	12,801	-
Corporations in general	259,538	0.4
Hunting and fishing	123,727	0.2
Motor vehicle	2,220,914	3.4
Motor vehicle operators	187,285	0.3
Public utilities	19,383	-
Occupation and business, NEC	585,928	0.9
Other licenses	159,022	0.2
Income taxes	X	-
Individual income	X	-
Corporation net income	X	-
Other taxes	5,089,433	7.8
Death and gift	X	-
Documentary and stock transfer	X	-
Severance	5,089,433	7.8
Taxes, NEC	0	-

X = Not applicable.
- = Zero or rounds to zero.

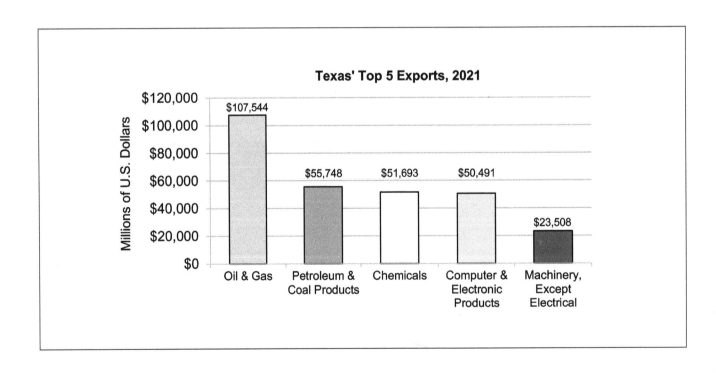

Texas' Top 5 Exports, 2021

Export	Millions of U.S. Dollars
Oil & Gas	$107,544
Petroleum & Coal Products	$55,748
Chemicals	$51,693
Computer & Electronic Products	$50,491
Machinery, Except Electrical	$23,508

UTAH

Facts and Figures

Location: Western United States; bordered on the N by Idaho and Wyoming, on the E by Colorado, on the S by Arizona, and on the W by Nevada; Utah is one of the Four Corner states—at its SE corner it touches Arizona, Colorado, and New Mexico

Area: 84,899 sq. mi. (219,887 sq. km.); rank—13th

Population: 3,337,975 (2021 est.); rank—30th

Principal Cities: capital—Salt Lake City; largest—Salt Lake City

Statehood: January 4, 1896; 45th state

U.S. Congress: 2 senators, 4 representatives

State Motto: Industry

State Song: "Utah, We Love Thee"

State Nickname: The Beehive State

Abbreviations: UT

State Symbols: flower—sego lily; tree—blue spruce; bird—California seagull

At a Glance

- With an increase in population of 20.8 percent, Utah ranked 2nd among the states in growth from 2010 to 2021.

- Utah's violent crime rate in 2020 was 260.7 per 100,000 population, compared to 398.5 for the entire nation.

- Of all the states, Utah had the highest percent of children in 2021, with 28.4 percent of its population under age 18.

- Utah also has the highest birth rate among states in 2020, at a rate of 14.1 births per 1,000 population.

- In 2020, 9.0 percent of Utahns did not have health insurance, compared to 8.7 percent of the total U.S. population.

Table UT-1. Population by Age, Sex, Race, and Hispanic Origin

(Number, percent, except where noted.)

Sex, age, race, and Hispanic origin	2000	2010	2021	Percent change, 2010–2021
Total Population...	2,233,169	2,763,885	3,337,975	20.8
Percent of total U.S. population	0.8	0.9	1.0	X
Sex				
Male..	1,119,031	1,388,317	1,690,069	21.7
Female	1,114,138	1,375,568	1,647,906	19.8
Age				
Under 5 years..	209,378	263,924	237,234	-10.1
5 to 19 years..	601,599	698,613	812,100	16.2
20 to 64 years...	1,231,970	1,551,886	1,899,493	22.4
65 years and over..	190,222	249,462	389,148	56.0
Median age (years)	27.1	29.2	31.8	8.9
Race and Hispanic Origin				
One race				
White	1,992,975	2,547,328	3,013,038	18.3
Black	17,657	33,864	50,597	49.4
American Indian and Alaska Native	29,684	40,729	52,657	29.3
Asian	37,108	57,800	89,680	55.2
Native Hawaiian or Other Pacific Islander	15,145	26,049	38,207	46.7
Two or more races...	47,185	58,114	93,796	61.4
Hispanic (of any race)...	201,559	370,870	493,636	33.1

NOTE: Population figures for 2021 are July 1 estimates. The 2000 and 2010 estimates are taken from the respective censuses.
- = Zero or rounds to zero.
X = Not applicable.

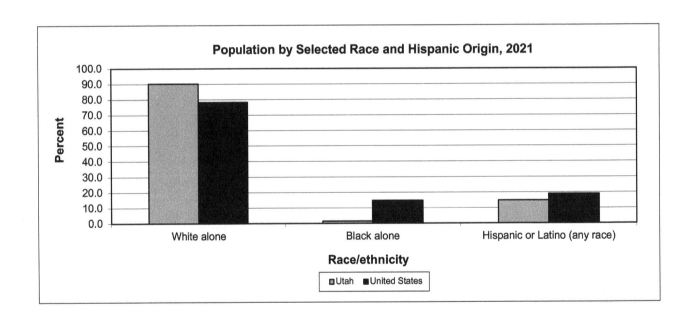

Table UT-2. Marital Status

(Number, percent distribution.)

Sex, age, race, and Hispanic origin	2000	2010	2020 [1]
Males, 15 Years and Over	813,693	1,014,706	1,189,511
Never married	30.6	31.3	33.2
Now married, except separated......................................	59.5	58.0	56.1
Separated...	1.1	1.3	1.1
Widowed..	1.6	1.8	1.7
Divorced..	7.3	7.6	7.9
Females, 15 Years and Over	852,995	1,019,010	1,187,792
Never married	25.2	25.8	27.5
Now married, except separated......................................	58.0	56.6	55.4
Separated...	1.4	1.6	1.5
Widowed..	6.6	5.8	5.5
Divorced..	8.8	10.1	10.2

[1] 2020 ACS 5-Year estimates. 1-Year estimates were not released for 2020 due to the impact of COVID-19 on data collection that year.

Table UT-3. Households and Housing Characteristics

(Number, percent, dollars.)

Item	2000	2010	2020 [1]	Average annual percent change, 2010–2020
Total Households..	701,281	880,025	1,003,345	2.0
Family households..	535,294	665,964	746,286	1.7
Married-couple family......................................	442,931	543,212	611,370	1.8
Other family...	92,363	122,752	134,916	1.4
Male householder, no wife present.................	26,422	37,258	44,672	2.8
Female householder, no husband present........	65,941	85,494	90,244	0.8
Nonfamily households..	165,987	214,061	257,059	2.9
Householder living alone..................................	124,756	164,863	195,917	2.7
Householder not living alone............................	41,231	49,198	61,142	3.5
Housing Characteristics				
Total housing units...	768,594	981,821	1,110,369	1.9
Occupied housing units.....................................	701,281	880,025	1,003,345	2.0
Owner occupied...	501,547	615,142	707,663	2.1
Renter occupied..	188,734	264,883	295,682	1.7
Average household size......................................	3.13	3.1	3.09	-
Financial Characteristics				
Median gross rent of renter-occupied housing........	597	796	1,090	5.3
Median monthly owner costs for housing units with a mortgage.........	1,102	1,433	1,597	1.6
Median value of owner-occupied housing units........	146,100	217,200	305,400	5.8

- = Zero or rounds to zero
[1] 2020 ACS 5-Year estimates. 1-Year estimates were not released for 2020 due to the impact of COVID-19 on data collection that year.

Table UT-4. Migration, Origin, and Language

(Number, percent.)

Characteristic	State 2016-2020 [1]	U.S. 2016-2020 [1]
Residence 1 Year Ago		
Population 1 year and over	3,104,255	322,943,283
Same house..	83.8	86.2
Different house in the U.S...	15.6	13.2
Same county..	9.3	7.7
Different county...	6.3	5.5
Same state...	3.2	3.2
Different state..	3.1	2.3
Abroad...	0.6	0.6
Place of Birth		
Native born..	2,886,701	282,443,680
Male..	50.5	49.4
Female...	49.5	50.6
Foreign born..	264,538	44,125,628
Male..	48.8	48.6
Female...	51.2	51.4
Foreign born; naturalized U.S. citizen...................................	109,703	22,456,684
Male..	46.5	46.1
Female...	53.5	53.9
Foreign born; not a U.S. citizen..	154,835	21,668,944
Male..	50.5	51.1
Female...	49.5	48.9
Entered 2010 or later...	25.0	22.8
Entered 2000 to 2009...	29.0	25.1
Entered before 2000...	46.1	52.1
World Region of Birth, Foreign		
Foreign-born population, excluding population born at sea............	264,538	44,125,628
Europe..	10.0	10.8
Asia..	21.2	31.3
Africa...	3.4	5.4
Oceania...	4.1	0.6
Latin America..	58.0	50.0
North America..	3.2	1.9
Language Spoken at Home and Ability to Speak English		
Population 5 years and over..	2,902,637	306,919,116
English only...	84.7	78.5
Language other than English..	15.3	21.5
Speaks English less than "very well"....................................	4.7	8.2

[1] 2020 ACS 5-Year estimates. 1-Year estimates were not released for 2020 due to the impact of COVID-19 on data collection that year.
NA = Not available.
X = Not applicable.
- = Zero or rounds to zero.

Table UT-5. Median Income and Poverty Status, 2020[1]

(Number, percent, except as noted.)

Characteristic	State Number	State Percent	U.S. Number	U.S. Percent
Median Income				
Households (dollars)	74,197	X	64,994	X
Families (dollars)	84,590	X	80,069	X
Below Poverty Level (All People)	283,360	9.1	40,910,326	12.8
Sex				
Male	129,497	8.3	18,171,512	11.6
Female	153,863	10.0	22,738,814	14.0
Age				
Under 18 years	91,046	9.9	12,598,699	17.5
Related children under 18 years	87,855	9.6	12,306,532	17.2
18 to 64 years	170,935	9.3	23,554,920	12.1
65 years and over	21,379	6.2	4,756,707	9.3

X = Not applicable.
[1] 2020 ACS 5-Year estimates. 1-Year estimates were not released for 2020 due to the impact of COVID-19 on data collection that year.

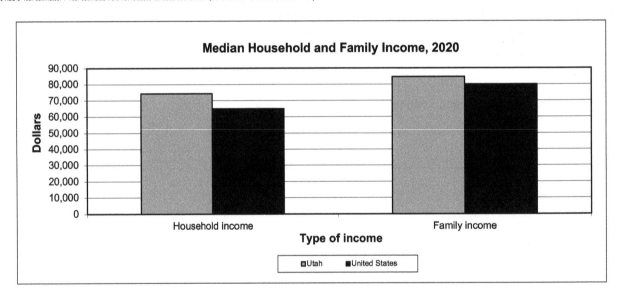

Table UT-6. Health Insurance Coverage Status for the Civilian Noninstitutionalized Population and Children Under 19 Years of Age

(Number, percent.)

Item	2011	2012	2013	2014	2015	2016	2017	2018	2019	2020[2]
Civilian Noninstitutionalized Population	2,789,648	2,829,001	2,874,213	2,916,303	2,971,003	3,024,767	3,076,318	3,135,573	3,178,394	3,124,563
Covered by Private or Public Insurance										
Number	2,363,584	2,419,830	2,472,089	2,550,780	2,659,662	2,759,960	2,794,565	2,840,209	2,871,538	2,844,130
Percent	84.7	85.5	86.0	87.5	89.5	91.2	90.8	90.6	90.3	91.0
Uninsured										
Number	426,064	409,171	402,124	365,523	311,341	264,807	281,753	295,364	306,856	280,433
Percent	15.3	14.5	14.0	12.5	10.5	8.8	9.2	9.4	9.7	9.0
Percent in the U.S. not covered	15.1	14.8	14.5	11.7	9.4	8.6	8.7	8.9	9.2	8.7
Children Under 19 Years of Age[1]	877,812	884,012	893,685	902,311	909,285	918,971	972,601	982,994	982,566	977,347
Covered by Private or Public Insurance										
Number	780,570	794,321	808,794	817,543	844,090	865,371	901,414	910,736	900,949	909,622
Percent	88.9	89.9	90.5	90.6	92.8	94.2	92.7	92.6	91.7	93.1
Uninsured										
Number	97,242	89,691	84,891	84,768	65,195	53,600	71,187	72,258	81,617	67,725
Percent	11.1	10.1	9.5	9.4	7.2	5.8	7.3	7.4	8.3	6.9
Percent in the U.S. not covered	7.5	7.2	7.1	6.0	4.8	4.5	5.0	5.2	5.7	5.2

[1] Data for years prior to 2017 are for individuals under 18 years of age.
[2] 2020 ACS 5-Year estimates. 1-Year estimates were not released for 2020 due to the impact of COVID-19 on data collection that year. Data is not comparable to previous years, which are based on 1-year estimates.

Table UT-7. Employment Status by Demographic Group, 2021

(Numbers in thousands, percent.)

Characteristic	Civilian noninstitutional population	Civilian labor force		Employed		Unemployed	
		Number	Percent of population	Number	Percent of population	Number	Percent of population
Total..	2,449	1,667	68.1	1,618	66.1	49	2.9
Sex							
Male..	1,221	912	74.7	885	72.5	27	3.0
Female	1,228	755	61.5	733	59.7	22	2.9
Race, Sex, and Hispanic Origin							
White..	2,248	1,520	67.6	1,478	65.7	42	2.8
Male..	1,116	830	74.3	808	72.4	22	2.6
Female	1,132	691	61.0	670	59.2	20	2.9
Black or African American........................	NA	NA	NA	NA	NA	NA	NA
Male..	NA	NA	NA	NA	NA	NA	NA
Female	NA	NA	NA	NA	NA	NA	NA
Hispanic or Latino ethnicity[1]	338	237	70.2	229	67.7	8	3.5
Male..	169	134	79.1	130	77.1	3	2.4
Female	169	103	61.3	98	58.3	5	4.9
Age							
16 to 19 years..................................	212	117	55.1	109	51.4	8	6.7
20 to 24 years..................................	301	232	77.2	224	74.4	9	3.7
25 to 34 years..................................	482	388	80.6	378	78.5	10	2.6
35 to 44 years..................................	411	337	82.0	329	80.0	8	2.3
45 to 54 years..................................	358	300	83.6	293	81.7	7	2.3
55 to 64 years..................................	310	215	69.4	209	67.4	6	2.8
65 years and over...............................	NA	NA	NA	NA	NA	NA	NA

NOTE: Data in Table 7 are from the Current Population Survey (CPS) and do not match the estimates in Table 8. See notes and definitions for further information.
[1] May be of any race.
NA = Not available.

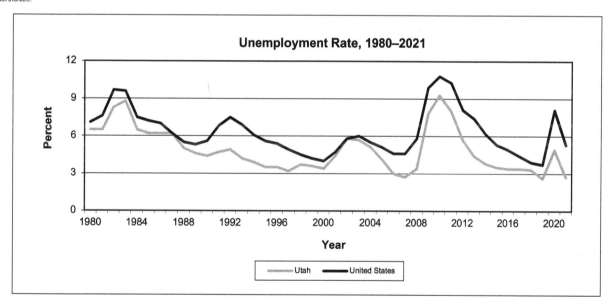

Unemployment Rate, 1980–2021

Table UT-8. Employment Status of the Civilian Noninstitutional Population Age 16 Years and Over

(Number, percent.)

Year	Civilian labor force	Civilian participation rate	Employed	Unemployed	Unemployment rate
2010..	1,350,173	68.5	1,242,907	107,266	7.9
2011..	1,341,427	67.4	1,246,797	94,630	7.1
2012..	1,348,557	66.6	1,284,149	64,408	4.8
2013..	1,385,908	67.2	1,327,560	58,348	4.2
2014..	1,415,779	67.4	1,364,353	51,426	3.6
2015..	1,453,457	67.9	1,401,945	51,512	3.5
2016..	1,500,137	68.4	1,449,981	50,156	3.3
2017..	1,554,352	68.8	1,505,413	48,939	3.1
2018..	1,583,703	68.5	1,537,389	46,314	2.9
2019..	1,618,055	68.4	1,576,421	41,634	2.6
2020..	1,640,426	67.9	1,562,799	77,627	4.7
2021..	1,681,494	67.9	1,636,150	45,344	2.7

Table UT-9. Employment and Average Wages by Industry

(Estimates are based on the 2012 North American Industry Classification System [NAICS].)

Industry	2013	2014	2015	2016	2017	2018	2019	2020
	Number of Jobs							
Wage and Salary Employment by Industry	1,342,353	1,381,561	1,428,802	1,480,533	1,524,228	1,577,719	1,622,060	1,605,868
Farm Wage and Salary Employment	4,792	4,501	4,373	4,619	5,557	4,963	4,975	5,257
Nonfarm Wage and Salary Employment	1,337,561	1,377,060	1,424,429	1,475,914	1,518,671	1,572,756	1,617,085	1,600,611
Private wage and salary employment	1,096,532	1,134,425	1,179,882	1,225,591	1,263,387	1,313,165	1,351,711	1,335,415
Forestry, fishing, and related activities	1,451	1,513	1,573	1,621	1,582	1,619	1,667	1,680
Mining	12,138	12,183	10,321	8,461	8,595	9,443	9,335	8,627
Utilities	3,908	3,888	3,915	3,857	3,917	3,918	3,829	3,700
Construction	75,452	80,601	86,833	93,815	99,788	106,791	112,064	118,253
Manufacturing	118,061	120,068	122,991	125,143	128,499	132,253	136,238	135,724
Durable goods manufacturing	77,827	79,085	81,595	82,418	84,489	86,919	89,340	88,178
Nondurable goods manufacturing	40,234	40,983	41,396	42,725	44,010	45,334	46,898	47,546
Wholesale trade	48,464	48,816	50,198	50,087	51,017	51,103	52,499	53,308
Retail trade	148,790	152,529	159,094	165,764	169,104	173,800	174,665	171,513
Transportation and warehousing	47,119	48,755	51,413	53,183	55,984	59,060	61,663	63,479
Information	31,306	32,163	33,343	35,708	37,287	36,809	38,345	37,275
Finance and insurance	57,632	59,435	63,203	65,413	67,606	70,142	71,980	76,044
Real estate and rental and leasing	18,028	18,486	18,987	19,493	20,019	21,262	22,402	22,614
Professional, scientific, and technical services	78,975	83,585	88,787	92,619	96,767	105,595	110,379	113,883
Management of companies and enterprises	17,408	18,134	18,334	18,469	18,192	17,970	18,546	19,042
Administrative and waste services	80,315	82,572	86,584	90,535	91,474	93,592	94,522	91,985
Educational services	42,911	44,232	46,313	49,619	52,075	55,789	57,922	56,574
Health care and social assistance	130,113	132,587	138,703	145,168	149,665	154,147	159,165	159,197
Arts, entertainment, and recreation	19,664	20,624	21,322	23,333	24,651	25,311	26,335	21,323
Accommodation and food services	104,575	108,525	113,088	115,991	119,395	124,157	128,124	113,236
Other services, except public administration	60,222	65,729	64,880	67,312	67,770	70,404	72,031	67,958
Government and government enterprises	241,029	242,635	244,547	250,323	255,284	259,591	265,374	265,196
	Dollars							
Average Wages and Salaries by Industry	42,723	43,839	45,234	46,124	47,447	49,440	51,586	55,669
Average Farm Wages and Salaries	39,762	40,861	35,594	39,013	32,614	38,973	27,835	35,088
Average Nonfarm Wages and Salaries	42,734	43,849	45,263	46,146	47,502	49,473	51,659	55,736
Average private wages and salaries	43,180	44,377	45,804	46,662	48,062	50,055	52,373	56,704
Forestry, fishing, and related activities	30,164	31,914	31,907	33,722	35,690	38,056	39,197	42,226
Mining	77,998	79,239	80,530	81,677	77,946	78,991	82,501	87,188
Utilities	88,992	90,935	93,348	94,582	99,443	106,246	112,146	112,545
Construction	44,269	45,693	47,341	48,319	49,962	51,976	54,318	58,445
Manufacturing	53,216	54,549	56,323	56,929	58,471	59,930	61,302	63,840
Durable goods manufacturing	56,336	57,764	59,238	59,770	62,236	63,563	65,207	67,355
Nondurable goods manufacturing	47,181	48,344	50,576	51,450	51,242	52,965	53,863	57,321
Wholesale trade	62,389	62,847	64,068	65,730	67,940	70,863	73,102	76,821
Retail trade	28,797	29,770	31,252	32,223	33,030	34,614	35,872	39,916
Transportation and warehousing	46,509	47,501	48,822	50,465	51,170	52,973	54,258	56,095
Information	61,447	65,095	69,302	72,179	73,134	80,544	86,841	99,384
Finance and insurance	63,491	66,148	69,967	70,161	71,762	75,725	79,298	88,946
Real estate and rental and leasing	40,692	42,836	46,302	47,182	49,825	51,857	53,592	57,502
Professional, scientific, and technical services	63,515	66,889	67,988	68,578	71,711	75,332	82,554	86,211
Management of companies and enterprises	85,400	84,988	86,742	90,523	93,593	98,537	98,924	101,935
Administrative and waste services	31,384	32,155	33,000	34,958	36,761	37,645	40,433	43,127
Educational services	28,997	29,904	30,281	29,741	30,410	31,218	32,690	36,261
Health care and social assistance	40,560	41,403	42,042	43,537	44,204	45,462	46,565	49,245
Arts, entertainment, and recreation	26,531	26,754	27,719	28,667	30,691	31,643	32,577	35,486
Accommodation and food services	17,752	18,387	19,258	19,873	20,597	21,674	22,497	21,903
Other services, except public administration	43,959	43,432	45,644	45,436	47,132	48,231	49,806	55,659
Government and government enterprises	40,705	41,377	42,655	43,621	44,728	46,526	48,024	50,866

Table UT-10. Employment Characteristics by Family Type

(Number, percent.)

Family type and labor force status	2018		2019		2020 [1]	
	Total	Families with own children under 18 years	Total	Families with own children under 18 years	Total	Families with own children under 18 years
All Families...	743,767	367,477	760,968	368,068	746,286	368,294
FAMILY TYPE AND LABOR FORCE STATUS						
Opposite-Sex Married-Couple Families...........................	608,407	297,394	619,250	297,203	606,066	296,795
Both husband and wife in labor force........................	51.5	58.8	52.9	60.5	52.8	59.4
Husband in labor force, wife not in labor force	27.8	37.3	26.9	35.3	27.9	37.0
Wife in labor force, husband not in labor force	5.4	2.5	5.5	2.6	5.3	2.4
Both husband and wife not in labor force........................	14.6	1.1	13.8	1.1	13.9	1.1
Other Families	135,360	70,083	141,718	70,865	134,916	70,166
Female householder, no spouse present	66.9	70.0	65.9	67.9	66.9	68.1
In labor force..	48.9	59.6	49.5	58.5	50.0	58.8
Not in labor force	18.0	10.4	16.3	9.4	16.9	9.2
Male householder, no spouse present........................	33.1	30.0	34.1	32.1	33.1	31.9
In labor force..	27.6	29.1	28.8	30.4	28.1	30.4
Not in labor force	5.5	0.9	5.4	1.7	5.1	1.6

[1] 2020 ACS 5-Year estimates. 1-Year estimates were not released for 2020 due to the impact of COVID-19 on data collection that year. Data is not comparable to previous years, which are based on 1-year estimates.

Table UT-11. School Enrollment and Educational Attainment, 2020[1]

(Number, percent.)

Item	State	U.S.
Enrollment		
Total population 3 years and over, enrolled in school	992,124	80,497,960
Enrolled in nursery school or preschool (percent)........................	5.8	6.1
Enrolled in kindergarten (percent)..	5.1	5.0
Enrolled in elementary school, grades 1-8 (percent)........................	41.8	40.4
Enrolled in high school, grades 9-12 (percent)	21.0	21.0
Enrolled in college or graduate school (percent)........................	26.2	27.6
Attainment		
Total population 25 years and over	1,868,472	222,836,834
Less than ninth grade (percent)..	2.4	4.9
9th to 12th grade, no diploma (percent)........................	4.6	6.6
High school graduate, including equivalency (percent)........................	22.8	26.7
Some college, no degree (percent)..	25.5	20.3
Associate's degree (percent)..	10.0	8.6
Bachelor's degree (percent)..	23.0	20.2
Graduate or professional degree (percent)........................	11.7	12.7
High school graduate or higher (percent)	93.0	88.5
Bachelor's degree or higher (percent)........................	34.7	32.9

[1] 2020 ACS 5-Year estimates. 1-Year estimates were not released for 2020 due to the impact of COVID-19 on data collection that year.

Table UT-12. Public School Characteristics and Educational Indicators

(Number, percent; data derived from National Center of Education Statistics.)

Item	State	U.S.
Public Elementary and Secondary Schools		
Number of regular school districts, 2018-19	41	13,452
Number of operational schools, 2019-20..	1,071	98,469
Percent charter schools	12.3	7.7
Total public school enrollment, Fall 2019..	684,694	50,796,445
Percent charter school enrollment	11.3	6.8
Student-teacher ratio, Fall 2019..	22.6	15.9
Expenditures per student (unadjusted dollars), 2018-19	7,950	13,187
Four-year adjusted cohort graduation rate (ACGR), 2018-2019[1]........................	87.4	85.8
Students eligible for free or reduced-price lunch (percent), 2019-20........................	32.7	52.1
English language learners (percent), Fall 2019	8.1	10.4
Students age 3 to 21 served under IDEA, part B (percent), 2020-21	12.6	14.5

Public Schools by Type, 2019-20	Number	Percent of state public schools
Total number of schools..	1,071	100.0
Special education..	60	5.6
Vocational education..	7	0.7
Alternative education..	28	2.6

[1] Adjusted Cohort Graduation Rates (ACGR) differ from Averaged Freshmen Graduation Rates (AFGR).

Table UT-13. Reported Voting and Registration of the Voting-Age Population, November 2020

(Numbers in thousands, percent.)

Item	Total population	Total citizen population	Registered				Voted		
			Total registered	Percent registered (total population)	Percent registered (total citizen population)		Total voted	Percent voted (total population)	Percent voted (total citizen population)
U.S. Total	252,274	231,593	168,308	66.7	72.7		154,628	61.3	66.8
State Total..	2,320	2,178	1,468	63.3	67.4		1,386	59.7	63.6
Sex									
Male	1,146	1,068	699	61.0	65.5		647	56.5	60.6
Female	1,174	1,110	769	65.5	69.3		739	62.9	66.6
Race									
White alone................................	2,096	2,000	1,368	65.3	68.4		1,293	61.7	64.7
White, non-Hispanic alone	1,860	1,832	1,268	68.2	69.2		1,203	64.7	65.7
Black alone.................................	40	33	9	B	B		9	B	B
Asian alone	51	18	10	B	B		10	B	B
Hispanic (of any race).....................	253	180	100	39.4	55.4		89	35.3	49.6
White alone or in combination	2,118	2,019	1,378	65.1	68.2		1,303	61.5	64.5
Black alone or in combination.............	48	41	11	B	B		11	B	B
Asian alone or in combination............	55	20	13	B	B		13	B	B
Age									
18 to 24 years.............................	425	401	225	52.9	56.2		201	47.3	50.1
25 to 34 years.............................	459	416	273	59.4	65.5		247	53.8	59.3
35 to 44 years.............................	407	382	252	61.9	66.0		236	57.9	61.8
45 to 64 years.............................	661	622	444	67.1	71.3		432	65.4	69.5
65 years and over	367	357	274	74.6	76.9		269	73.3	75.6

B = Base is less than 75,000 and therefore too small to show the derived measure.

Table UT-14. Crime

(Number, rate per 100,000. Data are derived from the FBI Uniform Crime Reports.)

Item	State			U.S.		
	2019	2020	Percent change	2019	2020	Percent change
TOTAL POPULATION[1]	3,203,383	3,249,879	1.5	328,329,953	329,484,123	0.4
VIOLENT CRIME						
Number...	7,588	8,471	11.6	1,250,393	1,313,105	5.0
Rate	236.9	260.7	10.0	380.8	398.5	4.6
Murder and Nonnegligent Manslaughter						
Number...	77	102	32.5	16,669	21,570	29.4
Rate	2.4	3.1	30.6	5.1	6.5	28.9
Rape[2]						
Number...	1,865	1,809	-3.0	143,224	126,430	-11.7
Rate	58.2	55.7	-4.4	43.6	38.4	-12.0
Robbery						
Number...	1,130	1,362	20.5	268,483	243,600	-9.3
Rate	35.3	41.9	18.8	81.8	73.9	-9.6
Aggravated Assault						
Number...	4,516	5,198	15.1	822,017	921,505	12.1
Rate	141.0	159.9	13.5	250.4	279.7	11.7
PROPERTY CRIME						
Number...	69,469	80,091	15.3	6,995,235	6,452,038	-7.8
Rate	2,168.6	2,464.4	13.6	2,130.6	1,958.2	-8.1
Burglary						
Number...	8,658	9,444	9.1	1,118,096	1,035,314	-7.4
Rate	270.3	290.6	7.5	340.5	314.2	-7.7
Larceny-Theft						
Number...	54,078	60,359	11.6	5,152,267	4,606,324	-10.6
Rate	1,688.2	1,857.3	10.0	1,569.2	1,398.0	-10.9
Motor Vehicle Theft						
Number...	6,733	10,288	52.8	724,872	810,400	11.8
Rate	210.2	316.6	50.6	220.8	246.0	11.4

NOTE: Although arson data are included in the trend and clearance tables, sufficient data are not available to estimate totals for this offense. Therefore, no arson data are published in this table.
* = Less than one-tenth of 1 percent.
[1] Population figures are U.S. Census Bureau provisional estimates as of July 1, 2020.
[2] The figures shown in the rape (revised definition) column were estimated using the revised Uniform Crime Reporting (UCR) definition of rape.

Table UT-15. State Government Finances, 2020

(Dollar amounts in thousands, percent distribution.)

Item	Dollars	Percent distribution
Total Revenue	27,780,619	100.0
General revenue	21,270,131	76.6
Intergovernmental revenue	5,801,212	20.9
Taxes	8,731,266	31.4
General sales	3105441	11.2
Selective sales	1,121,119	4.0
License taxes	356,811	1.3
Individual income tax	3734504	13.4
Corporate income tax	360,203	1.3
Other taxes	53,188	0.2
Current charges	5,249,524	18.9
Miscellaneous general revenue	1,488,129	5.4
Utility revenue	0	-
Liquor stores revenue	445208	1.6
Insurance trust revenue[1]	6,065,280	21.8
Total Expenditure	25,252,128	100.0
Intergovernmental expenditure	4,624,121	18.3
Direct expenditure	20,628,007	81.7
Current operation	14,638,134	58.0
Capital outlay	2,724,644	10.8
Insurance benefits and repayments	2,213,887	8.8
Assistance and subsidies	846,642	3.4
Interest on debt	204,700	0.8
Exhibit: Salaries and wages	4,234,850	16.8
Total Expenditure	25,252,128	100.0
General expenditure	22,717,732	90.0
Intergovernmental expenditure	4,624,121	18.3
Direct expenditure	18,093,611	71.7
General expenditure, by function:		
Education	9,911,536	39.3
Public welfare	4,647,377	18.4
Hospitals	2,763,214	10.9
Health	474,844	1.9
Highways	1,810,676	7.2
Police protection	196,455	0.8
Correction	375,548	1.5
Natural resources	281,240	1.1
Parks and recreation	64,542	0.3
Governmental administration	1,231,381	4.9
Interest on general debt	204,700	0.8
Other and unallocable	701,021	2.8
Utility expenditure	0	-
Liquor stores expenditure	320,509	1.3
Insurance trust expenditure	2,213,887	8.8
Debt at End of Fiscal Year	7,593,692	X
Cash and Security Holdings	48,015,001	X

X = Not applicable.
- = Zero or rounds to zero.

[1] Within insurance trust revenue, net earnings of state retirement systems is a calculated statistic (the item code in the data file is X08), and thus can be positive or negative. Net earnings is the sum of earnings on investments plus gains on investments minus losses on investments. The change made in 2002 for asset valuation from book to market value in accordance with Statement 34 of the Governmental Accounting Standards Board is reflected in the calculated statistics.

Table UT-16. State Government Tax Collections, 2021

(Dollars in thousands, percent.)

Item	Dollars	Percent distribution
Total Taxes	12,631,617	100.0
Property taxes	X	-
Sales and gross receipts	4,803,232	38.0
General sales and gross receipts	3,628,512	28.7
Selective sales and gross receipts	1,174,720	9.3
Alcoholic beverages	17,880	0.1
Amusements	X	-
Insurance premiums	165,995	1.3
Motor fuels	534,738	4.2
Pari-mutuels	X	-
Public utilities	54,890	0.4
Tobacco products	106,633	0.8
Other selective sales	294,584	2.3
Licenses	371,684	2.9
Alcoholic beverages	0	-
Amusements	X	-
Corporations in general	465	-
Hunting and fishing	32,623	0.3
Motor vehicle	242,790	1.9
Motor vehicle operators	29,576	0.2
Public utilities	X	-
Occupation and business, NEC	59,270	0.5
Other licenses	6,960	0.1
Income taxes	7,418,368	58.7
Individual income	6,672,695	52.8
Corporation net income	745,673	5.9
Other taxes	38,333	0.3
Death and gift	X	-
Documentary and stock transfer	X	-
Severance	37,985	0.3
Taxes, NEC	348	-

X = Not applicable.
- = Zero or rounds to zero.

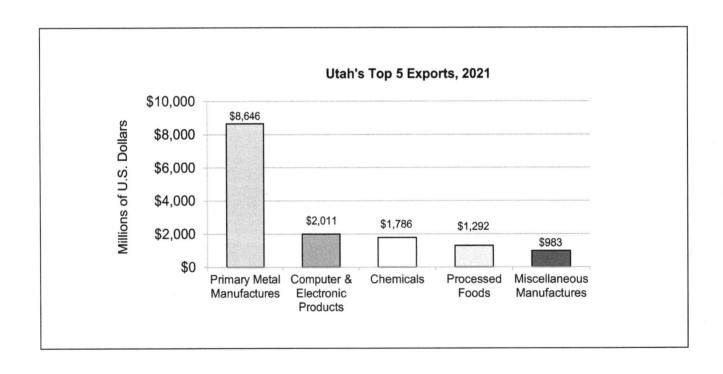

VERMONT

Facts and Figures

Location: Northeastern United States; bordered on the N by Canada (Quebec), on the E by New Hampshire, on the S by Massachusetts, and on the W by New York

Area: 9,614 sq. mi. (24,901 sq. km.); rank—45th

Population: 645,570 (2021 est.); rank—50th

Principal Cities: capital—Montpelier; largest—Burlington

Statehood: March 4, 1791; the 14th state

U.S. Congress: 2 senators, 1 representative

State Motto: Freedom and Unity

State Song: "These Green Mountains"

State Nickname: The Green Mountain State

Abbreviations: VT; Vt.

State Symbols: flower—red clover; tree—sugar maple; bird—hermit thrush

At a Glance

- Vermont experienced an increase in population of 3.2 percent between 2010 and 2021, which ranked 37th in the country.

- Vermont's median household income in 2020 was $63,477, and 10.8 percent of the population lived below the poverty level.

- Vermont's violent crime rate in 2020 was the 3rd lowest in the nation at 173.4 incidences per 100,000 population.

- In 2020, 4.0 percent of Vermonters did not have health insurance, which was the 4th lowest percent in the country.

- Vermont had the lowest percent of its population under 18 years old in 2021, with 18.1 percent of its residents in this age group. It also had the lowest birth rate in 2020, with 8.2 births per 100,000 population.

Table VT-1. Population by Age, Sex, Race, and Hispanic Origin

(Number, percent, except where noted.)

Sex, age, race, and Hispanic origin	2000	2010	2021	Percent change, 2010–2021
Total Population...	608,827	625,741	645,570	3.2
Percent of total U.S. population	0.2	0.2	0.2	X
Sex				
Male..	298,337	308,206	320,850	4.1
Female	310,490	317,535	324,720	2.3
Age				
Under 5 years..	33,989	31,952	28,249	-11.6
5 to 19 years..	132,268	118,323	109,561	-7.4
20 to 64 years...	365,060	384,388	374,502	-2.6
65 years and over..	77,510	91,078	133,258	46.3
Median age (years)..	37.7	41.5	42.9	3.4
Race and Hispanic Origin				
One race				
White	589,208	598,592	607,082	1.4
Black..	3,063	6,456	9,393	45.5
American Indian and Alaska Native	2,420	2,308	2,529	9.6
Asian..	5,217	8,069	12,962	60.6
Native Hawaiian or Other Pacific Islander	141	175	245	40.0
Two or more races	7,335	10,141	13,359	31.7
Hispanic (of any race)..	5,504	9,962	14,384	44.4

NOTE: Population figures for 2021 are July 1 estimates. The 2000 and 2010 estimates are taken from the respective censuses.
- = Zero or rounds to zero.
X = Not applicable.

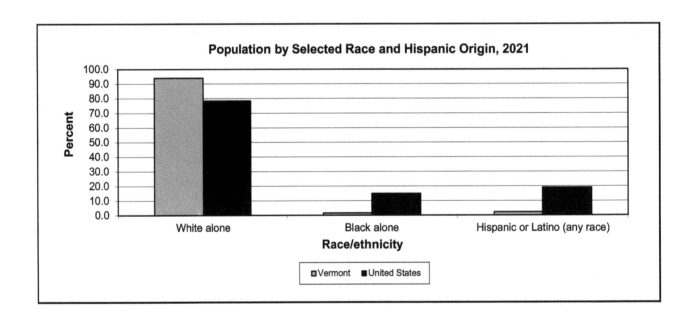

Table VT-2. Marital Status

(Number, percent distribution.)

Sex, age, race, and Hispanic origin	2000	2010	2020 [1]
Males, 15 Years and Over	236,517	254,288	259,548
Never married	29.7	34.2	35.2
Now married, except separated...	57.1	51.3	49.4
Separated..	1.2	1.3	1.1
Widowed...	2.4	2.5	2.9
Divorced...	9.6	10.7	11.4
Females, 15 Years and Over	251,764	266,860	270,488
Never married	23.9	27.7	28.6
Now married, except separated...	53.3	49.7	48.2
Separated..	1.4	1.4	1.0
Widowed...	10.0	8.2	8.6
Divorced...	11.5	13.0	13.6

[1] 2020 ACS 5-Year estimates. 1-Year estimates were not released for 2020 due to the impact of COVID-19 on data collection that year.

Table VT-3. Households and Housing Characteristics

(Number, percent, dollars.)

Item	2000	2010	2020 [1]	Average annual percent change, 2010–2020
Total Households..	240,634	256,922	262,852	0.3
Family households..	157,763	159,846	157,105	-0.2
Married-couple family..............................	126,413	125,678	124,107	-0.2
Other family..	31,350	34,168	32,998	-0.5
Male householder, no wife present.................	9,078	10,887	10,443	-0.6
Female householder, no husband present...........	22,272	23,281	22,555	-0.4
Nonfamily households...................................	82,871	97,076	105,747	1.3
Householder living alone...........................	63,112	75,243	80,826	1.1
Householder not living alone......................	19,759	21,833	24,921	2.0
Housing Characteristics				
Total housing units....................................	294,382	322,698	337,214	0.6
Occupied housing units................................	240,634	256,922	262,852	0.3
Owner occupied....................................	169,784	180,847	187,374	0.5
Renter occupied...................................	70,850	76,075	75,478	-0.1
Average household size................................	2.44	2.34	2.28	-0.4
Financial Characteristics				
Median gross rent of renter-occupied housing.........	553	823	999	3.1
Median monthly owner costs for housing units with a mortgage	1,021	1,445	1,630	1.8
Median value of owner-occupied housing units........	111,500	216,800	230,900	0.9

[1] 2020 ACS 5-Year estimates. 1-Year estimates were not released for 2020 due to the impact of COVID-19 on data collection that year.

Table VT-4. Migration, Origin, and Language

(Number, percent.)

Characteristic	State 2016-2020 [1]	U.S. 2016-2020 [1]
Residence 1 Year Ago		
Population 1 year and over..	619,059	322,943,283
Same house..	86.7	86.2
Different house in the U.S..	12.9	13.2
Same county..	6.9	7.7
Different county..	6.1	5.5
Same state..	2.3	3.2
Different state..	3.8	2.3
Abroad..	0.4	0.6
Place of Birth		
Native born..	595,872	282,443,680
Male..	49.6	49.4
Female..	50.4	50.6
Foreign born..	28,468	44,125,628
Male..	45.6	48.6
Female..	54.4	51.4
Foreign born; naturalized U.S. citizen..	15,803	22,456,684
Male..	42.5	46.1
Female..	57.5	53.9
Foreign born; not a U.S. citizen..	12,665	21,668,944
Male..	49.6	51.1
Female..	50.4	48.9
Entered 2010 or later..	30.7	22.8
Entered 2000 to 2009..	20.9	25.1
Entered before 2000..	48.4	52.1
World Region of Birth, Foreign		
Foreign-born population, excluding population born at sea........	28,468	44,125,628
Europe..	29.0	10.8
Asia..	31.8	31.3
Africa..	9.8	5.4
Oceania..	1.3	0.6
Latin America..	10.4	50.0
North America..	17.7	1.9
Language Spoken at Home and Ability to Speak English		
Population 5 years and over..	595,302	306,919,116
English only..	94.4	78.5
Language other than English..	5.6	21.5
Speaks English less than "very well"........................	1.4	8.2

[1] 2020 ACS 5-Year estimates. 1-Year estimates were not released for 2020 due to the impact of COVID-19 on data collection that year.
NA = Not available.
X = Not applicable.
- = Zero or rounds to zero.

Table VT-5. Median Income and Poverty Status, 2020[1]

(Number, percent, except as noted.)

Characteristic	State		U.S.	
	Number	Percent	Number	Percent
Median Income				
Households (dollars)..	63,477	X	64,994	X
Families (dollars)	83,023	X	80,069	X
Below Poverty Level (All People)	64,700	10.8	40,910,326	12.8
Sex				
Male	28,999	9.8	18,171,512	11.6
Female	35,701	11.7	22,738,814	14.0
Age				
Under 18 years..	13,975	12.3	12,598,699	17.5
Related children under 18 years...	13,212	11.7	12,306,532	17.2
18 to 64 years	41,652	11.3	23,554,920	12.1
65 years and over	9,073	7.7	4,756,707	9.3

X = Not applicable.
[1] 2020 ACS 5-Year estimates. 1-Year estimates were not released for 2020 due to the impact of COVID-19 on data collection that year.

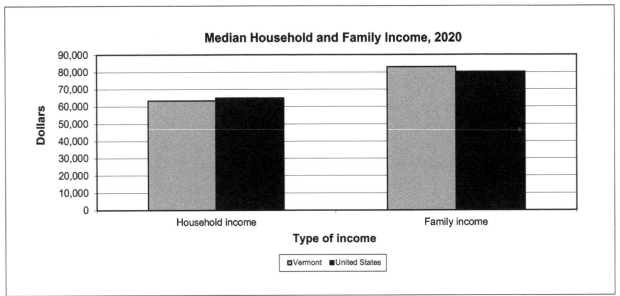

Median Household and Family Income, 2020

Table VT-6. Health Insurance Coverage Status for the Civilian Noninstitutionalized Population and Children Under 19 Years of Age

(Number, percent.)

Item	2011	2012	2013	2014	2015	2016	2017	2018	2019	2020 [2]
Civilian Noninstitutionalized Population	620,159	619,928	620,896	620,453	620,107	618,622	617,556	620,066	618,064	618,184
Covered by Private or Public Insurance										
Number..	578,950	579,875	575,992	589,737	596,431	595,628	589,445	595,078	590,323	593,153
Percent..	93.4	93.5	92.8	95.0	96.2	96.3	95.4	96.0	95.5	96.0
Uninsured										
Number..	41,209	40,053	44,904	30,716	23,676	22,994	28,111	24,988	27,741	25,031
Percent..	6.6	6.5	7.2	5.0	3.8	3.7	4.6	4.0	4.5	4.0
Percent in the U.S. not covered...	15.1	14.8	14.5	11.7	9.4	8.6	8.7	8.9	9.2	8.7
Children Under 19 Years of Age[1]	125,599	123,563	123,812	121,472	119,828	118,351	127,105	124,839	124,542	125,558
Covered by Private or Public Insurance										
Number..	122,580	120,072	119,930	118,832	118,577	116,493	125,077	122,376	121,937	123,491
Percent..	97.6	97.2	96.9	97.8	99.0	98.4	98.4	98.0	97.9	98.4
Uninsured										
Number..	3,019	3,491	3,882	2,640	1,251	1,858	2,028	2,463	2,605	2,067
Percent..	2.4	2.8	3.1	2.2	1.0	1.6	1.6	2.0	2.1	1.6
Percent in the U.S. not covered...	7.5	7.2	7.1	6.0	4.8	4.5	5.0	5.2	5.7	5.2

[1] Data for years prior to 2017 are for individuals under 18 years of age.
[2] 2020 ACS 5-Year estimates. 1-Year estimates were not released for 2020 due to the impact of COVID-19 on data collection that year. Data is not comparable to previous years, which are based on 1-year estimates.

Table VT-7. Employment Status by Demographic Group, 2021

(Numbers in thousands, percent.)

Characteristic	Civilian noninstitutional population	Civilian labor force		Employed		Unemployed	
		Number	Percent of population	Number	Percent of population	Number	Percent of population
Total..	519	322	62.1	311	59.8	12	3.6
Sex							
Male..	254	165	64.9	159	62.6	6	3.6
Female..	265	157	59.4	152	57.2	6	3.6
Race, Sex, and Hispanic Origin							
White..	493	306	62.1	296	59.9	11	3.5
Male..	241	156	64.6	151	62.4	5	3.4
Female..	252	150	59.7	145	57.6	5	3.6
Black or African American....................	NA	NA	NA	NA	NA	NA	NA
Male..	NA	NA	NA	NA	NA	NA	NA
Female..	NA	NA	NA	NA	NA	NA	NA
Hispanic or Latino ethnicity[1]..............	NA	NA	NA	NA	NA	NA	NA
Male..	NA	NA	NA	NA	NA	NA	NA
Female..	NA	NA	NA	NA	NA	NA	NA
Age							
16 to 19 years................................	NA	NA	NA	NA	NA	NA	NA
20 to 24 years................................	29	19	66.1	18	61.9	1	6.9
25 to 34 years................................	82	67	81.6	64	78.4	3	3.9
35 to 44 years................................	86	75	87.7	72	84.6	3	3.6
45 to 54 years................................	67	56	83.7	54	81.2	2	3.2
55 to 64 years................................	88	59	67.4	57	65.5	2	2.9
65 years and over............................	140	35	25.1	34	24.3	1	2.6

NOTE: Data in Table 7 are from the Current Population Survey (CPS) and do not match the estimates in Table 8. See notes and definitions for further information.
[1] May be of any race.
NA = Not available.

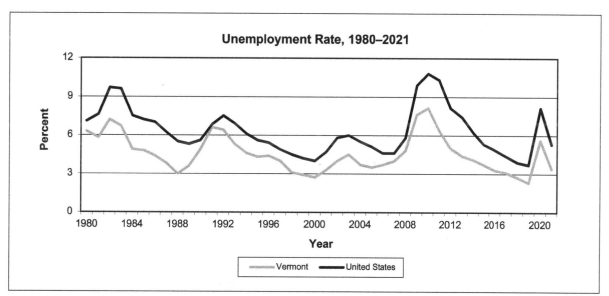

Unemployment Rate, 1980–2021

Table VT-8. Employment Status of the Civilian Noninstitutional Population Age 16 Years and Over

(Number, percent.)

Year	Civilian labor force	Civilian participation rate	Employed	Unemployed	Unemployment rate
2010..	359,692	70.8	336,920	22,772	6.3
2011..	357,676	70.1	337,779	19,897	5.6
2012..	353,947	69.2	336,899	17,048	4.8
2013..	350,175	68.3	334,684	15,491	4.4
2014..	348,697	67.9	334,742	13,955	4.0
2015..	346,512	67.3	334,262	12,250	3.5
2016..	345,851	67.1	335,043	10,808	3.1
2017..	355,385	67.3	344,698	10,687	3.0
2018..	356,456	67.2	347,125	9,331	2.6
2019..	355,950	66.9	347,600	8,350	2.3
2020..	341,137	63.8	322,078	19,059	5.6
2021..	328,216	61	316,941	11,275	3.4

Table VT-9. Employment and Average Wages by Industry

(Estimates are based on the 2012 North American Industry Classification System [NAICS].)

Industry	2013	2014	2015	2016	2017	2018	2019	2020
	Number of Jobs							
Wage and Salary Employment by Industry.......................	320,076	323,339	325,842	326,845	327,624	329,216	329,628	300,757
Farm Wage and Salary Employment.............................	2,949	2,961	2,951	2,754	2,748	2,856	2,877	2,748
Nonfarm Wage and Salary Employment........................	317,127	320,378	322,891	324,091	324,876	326,360	326,751	298,009
Private wage and salary employment...	259,316	261,972	264,746	266,002	266,990	268,458	268,689	242,569
Forestry, fishing, and related activities.............................	880	921	931	902	900	883	916	893
Mining...	621	600	646	639	616	612	623	601
Utilities..	1,790	1,727	1,548	1,342	1,261	1,254	1,237	1,198
Construction...	14,475	15,145	15,562	15,659	15,541	15,625	15,645	14,630
Manufacturing..	31,747	31,238	30,967	30,008	29,569	29,840	30,086	28,246
Durable goods manufacturing..................................	21,225	20,392	19,699	18,771	18,294	18,413	18,660	17,270
Nondurable goods manufacturing............................	10,522	10,846	11,268	11,237	11,275	11,427	11,426	10,976
Wholesale trade	9,254	9,279	9,339	9,518	9,336	9,066	9,111	8,752
Retail trade..	38,011	38,200	38,180	38,400	38,139	37,852	36,961	33,966
Transportation and warehousing.....................................	6,918	6,949	6,834	6,767	6,820	6,913	7,088	6,506
Information..	4,680	4,769	4,643	4,646	4,485	4,284	4,325	3,962
Finance and insurance	9,185	9,247	9,246	9,192	9,296	9,368	9,536	9,439
Real estate and rental and leasing.................................	3,132	3,124	3,016	3,023	3,055	3,125	3,206	2,942
Professional, scientific, and technical services	14,181	13,965	14,334	14,438	14,626	14,781	15,136	15,166
Management of companies and enterprises........................	1,949	2,081	2,219	2,086	2,026	2,018	2,025	2,060
Administrative and waste services	10,477	10,742	11,073	11,440	11,987	12,393	12,466	11,457
Educational services..	14,239	14,571	14,980	15,819	15,811	15,910	15,763	14,245
Health care and social assistance....................................	49,580	49,980	50,794	51,663	52,564	53,093	52,984	49,870
Arts, entertainment, and recreation.................................	4,079	4,341	4,181	4,325	4,483	4,554	4,595	3,259
Accommodation and food services...................................	30,452	31,060	32,087	32,126	33,007	32,849	32,807	22,913
Other services, except public administration......................	13,666	14,033	14,166	14,009	13,468	14,038	14,179	12,464
Government and government enterprises................................	57,811	58,406	58,145	58,089	57,886	57,902	58,062	55,440
								Dollars
Average Wages and Salaries by Industry	41,237	42,190	43,289	44,173	45,314	46,817	48,393	52,832
Average Farm Wages and Salaries	27,297	28,805	23,609	29,033	26,405	25,215	19,876	20,210
Average Nonfarm Wages and Salaries	41,366	42,314	43,469	44,302	45,474	47,006	48,644	53,133
Average private wages and salaries....................................	40,831	41,774	42,909	43,693	44,810	46,304	48,016	52,649
Forestry, fishing, and related activities.............................	29,727	31,160	32,096	33,373	33,358	35,183	35,795	37,161
Mining...	54,473	55,833	57,243	59,197	59,641	61,928	62,490	63,158
Utilities..	98,061	104,380	123,169	105,244	103,795	109,886	103,793	110,937
Construction	45,394	46,235	46,929	48,621	50,118	51,029	52,541	55,050
Manufacturing..	54,653	55,287	55,949	55,797	57,967	59,407	60,751	62,260
Durable goods manufacturing..................................	59,085	59,214	59,890	59,465	62,039	64,453	65,972	66,146
Nondurable goods manufacturing............................	45,712	47,903	49,061	49,669	51,360	51,277	52,224	56,145
Wholesale trade	56,573	56,473	59,043	62,971	61,460	64,990	65,610	70,561
Retail trade..	27,460	28,382	29,432	29,640	30,539	31,758	32,921	36,451
Transportation and warehousing.....................................	38,343	40,032	40,267	40,607	41,505	43,164	44,859	48,794
Information..	51,416	53,754	56,141	56,070	58,287	59,774	62,837	68,537
Finance and insurance	67,666	69,803	73,163	74,453	80,400	81,185	84,260	89,315
Real estate and rental and leasing.................................	37,860	38,498	39,636	41,108	41,977	44,801	45,540	49,688
Professional, scientific, and technical services	68,808	70,921	73,622	75,514	77,731	80,189	83,984	90,701
Management of companies and enterprises........................	81,898	87,230	86,148	92,751	92,827	92,388	108,487	105,731
Administrative and waste services	34,529	36,630	36,129	37,980	40,942	42,173	44,228	47,187
Educational services..	32,442	33,323	32,994	36,115	37,356	38,384	38,853	40,927
Health care and social assistance....................................	41,165	42,055	43,519	44,286	44,433	46,321	48,219	53,118
Arts, entertainment, and recreation.................................	25,264	25,641	25,125	26,246	26,449	27,855	26,934	31,945
Accommodation and food services...................................	21,824	22,636	23,629	24,190	25,142	26,200	27,236	27,959
Other services, except public administration......................	27,768	28,376	29,506	30,551	31,493	32,470	33,208	36,783
Government and government enterprises.............................	43,768	44,733	46,021	47,088	48,540	50,259	51,551	55,247

Table VT-10. Employment Characteristics by Family Type

(Number, percent.)

Family type and labor force status	2018		2019		2020 [1]	
	Total	Families with own children under 18 years	Total	Families with own children under 18 years	Total	Families with own children under 18 years
All Families..............................	155,804	56,530	156,153	57,501	157,105	59,214
FAMILY TYPE AND LABOR FORCE STATUS						
Opposite-Sex Married-Couple Families...........................	122,744	38,930	121,034	37,866	122,168	40,229
Both husband and wife in labor force..............................	56.9	76.6	56.8	81.5	56.8	77.4
Husband in labor force, wife not in labor force	14.2	15.0	14.2	13.6	15.2	16.7
Wife in labor force, husband not in labor force	9.1	4.9	8.7	3.5	9.4	4.5
Both husband and wife not in labor force...........	17.9	2.0	19.2	0.9	18.6	1.5
Other Families	33,060	17,600	35,119	19,635	32,998	18,651
Female householder, no spouse present	63.6	66.8	65.5	67.3	68.4	70.4
In labor force................................	46.3	55.8	48.9	58.8	49.9	58.4
Not in labor force	17.3	10.9	16.6	8.4	18.5	11.9
Male householder, no spouse present...................	36.4	33.3	34.5	32.7	31.6	29.6
In labor force..........................	29.7	30.2	26.7	30.8	25.6	26.3
Not in labor force	6.7	3.0	7.8	2.0	6.0	3.4

[1] 2020 ACS 5-Year estimates. 1-Year estimates were not released for 2020 due to the impact of COVID-19 on data collection that year. Data is not comparable to previous years, which are based on 1-year estimates.

Table VT-11. School Enrollment and Educational Attainment, 2020[1]

(Number, percent.)

Item	State	U.S.
Enrollment		
Total population 3 years and over, enrolled in school	142,422	80,497,960
Enrolled in nursery school or preschool (percent)........................	6.5	6.1
Enrolled in kindergarten (percent)...............................	4.3	5.0
Enrolled in elementary school, grades 1-8 (percent)...........................	35.8	40.4
Enrolled in high school, grades 9-12 (percent)........................	19.6	21.0
Enrolled in college or graduate school (percent).........................	33.8	27.6
Attainment		
Total population 25 years and over	442,089	222,836,834
Less than ninth grade (percent)...........................	2.0	4.9
9th to 12th grade, no diploma (percent).......................	4.5	6.6
High school graduate, including equivalency (percent)........................	28.3	26.7
Some college, no degree (percent)	16.7	20.3
Associate's degree (percent)	8.8	8.6
Bachelor's degree (percent).......................	23.5	20.2
Graduate or professional degree (percent)........................	16.1	12.7
High school graduate or higher (percent)	93.5	88.5
Bachelor's degree or higher (percent)..........................	39.7	32.9

[1] 2020 ACS 5-Year estimates. 1-Year estimates were not released for 2020 due to the impact of COVID-19 on data collection that year.

Table VT-12. Public School Characteristics and Educational Indicators

(Number, percent; data derived from National Center of Education Statistics.)

Item	State	U.S.
Public Elementary and Secondary Schools		
Number of regular school districts, 2018-19	175	13,452
Number of operational schools, 2019-20...........................	308	98,469
Percent charter schools	0.0	7.7
Total public school enrollment, Fall 2019............................	86,759	50,796,445
Percent charter school enrollment	0.0	6.8
Student-teacher ratio, Fall 2019	10.8	15.9
Expenditures per student (unadjusted dollars), 2018-19	21,217	13,187
Four-year adjusted cohort graduation rate (ACGR), 2018-2019[1]...............	84.5	85.8
Students eligible for free or reduced-price lunch (percent), 2019-20..................	35.1	52.1
English language learners (percent), Fall 2019	2.2	10.4
Students age 3 to 21 served under IDEA, part B (percent), 2020-21	18.4	14.5

Public Schools by Type, 2019-20	Number	Percent of state public schools
Total number of schools...............................	308	100.0
Special education.............................	0	-
Vocational education........................	15	4.9
Alternative education........................	1	0.3

[1] Adjusted Cohort Graduation Rates (ACGR) differ from Averaged Freshmen Graduation Rates (AFGR).
NA = Not available.
- = Zero or rounds to zero.

Table VT-13. Reported Voting and Registration of the Voting-Age Population, November 2020

(Numbers in thousands, percent.)

Item	Total population	Total citizen population	Registered			Voted		
			Total registered	Percent registered (total population)	Percent registered (total citizen population)	Total voted	Percent voted (total population)	Percent voted (total citizen population)
U.S. Total	252,274	231,593	168,308	66.7	72.7	154,628	61.3	66.8
State Total	507	500	365	72.0	73.0	342	67.5	68.4
Sex								
Male	250	247	178	71.2	72.1	163	65.5	66.3
Female	257	253	187	72.9	74.0	178	69.4	70.5
Race								
White alone	477	474	354	74.3	74.8	332	69.7	70.2
White, non-Hispanic alone	474	470	351	74.1	74.6	329	69.4	69.9
Black alone........................	8	5	1	B	B	1	B	B
Asian alone	11	11	3	B	B	3	B	B
Hispanic (of any race)	6	6	4	B	B	4	B	B
White alone or in combination	485	482	360	74.1	74.7	337	69.4	69.9
Black alone or in combination	10	7	1	B	B	1	B	B
Asian alone or in combination........................	14	14	6	B	B	6	B	B
Age								
18 to 24 years	54	53	29	B	B	26	B	B
25 to 34 years	81	81	51	62.6	63.1	43	52.3	52.8
35 to 44 years	76	72	54	B	B	49	B	B
45 to 64 years	155	154	117	75.6	76.1	113	72.8	73.4
65 years and over	140	140	114	81.3	81.8	111	79.2	79.6

B = Base is less than 75,000 and therefore too small to show the derived measure.

Table VT-14. Crime

(Number, rate per 100,000. Data are derived from the FBI Uniform Crime Reports.)

Item	State			U.S.		
	2019	2020	Percent change	2019	2020	Percent change
TOTAL POPULATION[1]	624,046	623,347	-0.1	328,329,953	329,484,123	0.4
VIOLENT CRIME						
Number........................	1,293	1,081	-16.4	1,250,393	1,313,105	5.0
Rate	207.2	173.4	-16.3	380.8	398.5	4.6
Murder and Nonnegligent Manslaughter						
Number........................	11	14	27.3	16,669	21,570	29.4
Rate	1.8	2.2	27.4	5.1	6.5	28.9
Rape[2]						
Number........................	298	213	-28.5	143,224	126,430	-11.7
Rate	47.8	34.2	-28.4	43.6	38.4	-12.0
Robbery						
Number........................	71	64	-9.9	268,483	243,600	-9.3
Rate	11.4	10.3	-9.8	81.8	73.9	-9.6
Aggravated Assault						
Number........................	913	790	-13.5	822,017	921,505	12.1
Rate	146.3	126.7	-13.4	250.4	279.7	11.7
PROPERTY CRIME						
Number........................	8,968	7,586	-15.4	6,995,235	6,452,038	-7.8
Rate	1,437.1	1,217.0	-15.3	2,130.6	1,958.2	-8.1
Burglary						
Number........................	1,286	961	-25.3	1,118,096	1,035,314	-7.4
Rate	206.1	154.2	-25.2	340.5	314.2	-7.7
Larceny-Theft						
Number........................	7,378	6,361	-13.8	5,152,267	4,606,324	-10.6
Rate	1,182.3	1,020.5	-13.7	1,569.2	1,398.0	-10.9
Motor Vehicle Theft						
Number........................	304	264	-13.2	724,872	810,400	11.8
Rate	48.7	42.4	-13.1	220.8	246.0	11.4

NOTE: Although arson data are included in the trend and clearance tables, sufficient data are not available to estimate totals for this offense. Therefore, no arson data are published in this table.
- = Zero or rounds to zero.
[1] Population figures are U.S. Census Bureau provisional estimates as of July 1, 2020.
[2] The figures shown in the rape (revised definition) column were estimated using the revised Uniform Crime Reporting (UCR) definition of rape.

Table VT-15. State Government Finances, 2020

(Dollar amounts in thousands, percent distribution.)

Item	Dollars	Percent distribution
Total Revenue	8,595,502	100.0
General revenue	7,858,281	91.4
Intergovernmental revenue	3,422,421	39.8
Taxes	3,419,990	39.8
General sales	431582	5.0
Selective sales	733,070	8.5
License taxes	140,193	1.6
Individual income tax	762641	8.9
Corporate income tax	141,623	1.6
Other taxes	1,210,881	14.1
Current charges	643,290	7.5
Miscellaneous general revenue	372,580	4.3
Utility revenue	4,000	-
Liquor stores revenue	83558	1.0
Insurance trust revenue[1]	649,663	7.6
Total Expenditure	7,591,060	100.0
Intergovernmental expenditure	1,969,208	25.9
Direct expenditure	5,621,852	74.1
Current operation	4,305,906	56.7
Capital outlay	328,996	4.3
Insurance benefits and repayments	687,734	9.1
Assistance and subsidies	195,720	2.6
Interest on debt	103,496	1.4
Exhibit: Salaries and wages	994,763	13.1
Total Expenditure	7,591,060	100.0
General expenditure	6,824,907	89.9
Intergovernmental expenditure	1,969,208	25.9
Direct expenditure	4,855,699	64.0
General expenditure, by function:		
Education	2,934,962	38.7
Public welfare	1,954,918	25.8
Hospitals	23,179	0.3
Health	410,465	5.4
Highways	466,038	6.1
Police protection	103,273	1.4
Correction	149,296	2.0
Natural resources	110,203	1.5
Parks and recreation	23,882	0.3
Governmental administration	209,066	2.8
Interest on general debt	103,496	1.4
Other and unallocable	286,733	3.8
Utility expenditure	44,760	0.6
Liquor stores expenditure	71140	0.9
Insurance trust expenditure	687,734	9.1
Debt at End of Fiscal Year	3,563,173	X
Cash and Security Holdings	10,381,993	X

X = Not applicable.
- = Zero or rounds to zero.
[1] Within insurance trust revenue, net earnings of state retirement systems is a calculated statistic (the item code in the data file is X08), and thus can be positive or negative. Net earnings is the sum of earnings on investments plus gains on investments minus losses on investments. The change made in 2002 for asset valuation from book to market value in accordance with Statement 34 of the Governmental Accounting Standards Board is reflected in the calculated statistics.

Table VT-16. State Government Tax Collections, 2021

(Dollars in thousands, percent.)

Item	Dollars	Percent distribution
Total Taxes	4,102,929	100.0
Property taxes	1,203,059	29.3
Sales and gross receipts	1,247,617	30.4
General sales and gross receipts	507,259	12.4
Selective sales and gross receipts	740,358	18.0
Alcoholic beverages	12,035	0.3
Amusements	X	-
Insurance premiums	63,343	1.5
Motor fuels	109,548	2.7
Pari-mutuels	X	-
Public utilities	9,576	0.2
Tobacco products	77,473	1.9
Other selective sales	468,383	11.4
Licenses	143,501	3.5
Alcoholic beverages	503	-
Amusements	17	-
Corporations in general	3,185	0.1
Hunting and fishing	8,533	0.2
Motor vehicle	75,544	1.8
Motor vehicle operators	14,464	0.4
Public utilities	X	-
Occupation and business, NEC	29,864	0.7
Other licenses	11,391	0.3
Income taxes	1,399,998	34.1
Individual income	1,233,157	30.1
Corporation net income	166,841	4.1
Other taxes	108,754	2.7
Death and gift	26,924	0.7
Documentary and stock transfer	71,421	1.7
Severance	X	-
Taxes, NEC	10,409	0.3

X = Not applicable.
- = Zero or rounds to zero.

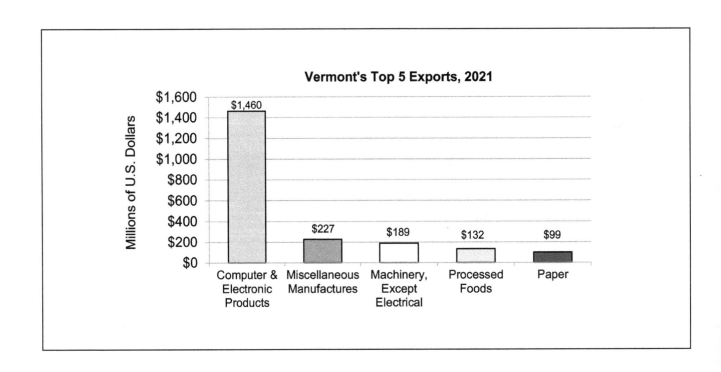

VIRGINIA

Facts and Figures

Location: Eastern United States; bordered on the N and NE by Maryland and the District of Columbia, on the E by the Atlantic Ocean, on the S by North Carolina and Tennessee, and on the W by Kentucky and West Virginia

Area: 42,774 sq. mi. (110,785 sq. km.); rank—35th

Population: 8,642,274 (2021 est.); rank—12th

Principal Cities: capital—Richmond; largest—Virginia Beach

Statehood: June 25, 1788; 10th state

U.S. Congress: 2 senators, 11 representatives

State Motto: *Sic semper tyrannis* ("Thus always to tyrants")

State Song: "Our Great Virginia" and "Sweet Virginia Breeze"

State Nickname: The Old Dominion State

Abbreviations: VA; Va.

State Symbols: flower—flowering dogwood; tree—flowering dogwood; bird—cardinal

At a Glance

- With an increase in population of 8.0 percent, Virginia ranked 19th among the states in growth from 2010 to 2021.

- Virginia's violent crime rate (208.7 incidents per 100,000 population) was the 6th lowest in the country in 2020.

- In 2021, 3.9 percent of Virginians were unemployed, compared to 5.3 percent of the total U.S. population.

- Virginia's median household income in 2020 was $76,398, which ranked 11th in the country. Virginia's poverty rate was 10.0 percent of the population lived below the poverty level, a percent that ranked 42nd among all states.

- Virginia's voter turnout for the November 2020 election ranked 15th in the nation, with 66.0 percent of the population casting votes.

Table VA-1. Population by Age, Sex, Race, and Hispanic Origin

(Number, percent, except where noted.)

Sex, age, race, and Hispanic origin	2000	2010	2021	Percent change, 2010–2021
Total Population.....................................	7,078,515	8,001,024	8,642,274	8.0
Percent of total U.S. population	2.5	2.6	2.6	X
Sex				
Male..	3,471,895	3,925,983	4,277,201	8.9
Female	3,606,620	4,075,041	4,365,073	7.1
Age				
Under 5 years...	461,982	509,625	490,808	-3.7
5 to 19 years..	1,475,104	1,574,060	1,621,428	3.0
20 to 64 years..	4,349,096	4,940,402	5,123,386	3.7
65 years and over	79,233	976,937	1,406,652	44.0
Median age (years)	35.7	37.5	38.8	3.5
Race and Hispanic Origin				
One race				
White...	5,120,110	5,725,432	5,942,209	3.8
Black...	1,390,293	1,579,414	1,729,436	9.5
American Indian and Alaska Native	21,172	41,525	49,207	18.5
Asian...	261,025	449,149	620,996	38.3
Native Hawaiian or Other Pacific Islander	3,946	8,201	10,691	30.4
Two or more races	143,069	197,303	289,735	46.8
Hispanic (of any race)	329,540	660,501	882,402	33.6

NOTE: Population figures for 2021 are July 1 estimates. The 2000 and 2010 estimates are taken from the respective censuses.
- = Zero or rounds to zero.
X = Not applicable.

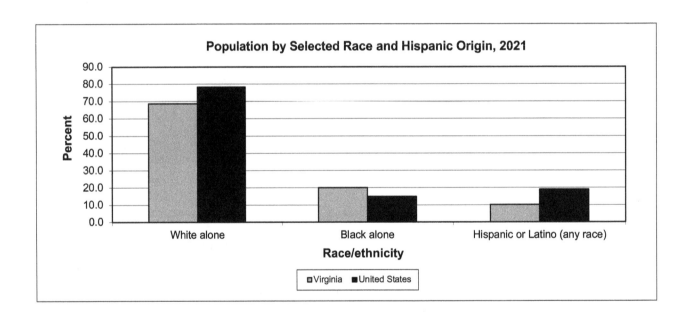

Table VA-2. Marital Status

(Number, percent distribution.)

Sex, age, race, and Hispanic origin	2000	2010	2020 [1]
Males, 15 Years and Over	2,724,334	3,156,115	3,393,138
Never married	29.1	34.2	35.3
Now married, except separated..	58.2	52.6	51.6
Separated..	2.6	2.3	1.9
Widowed..	2.3	2.3	2.6
Divorced..	7.9	8.5	8.6
Females, 15 Years and Over	2,899,294	3,331,264	3,563,921
Never married	23.5	28.0	29.6
Now married, except separated..	53.4	49.0	47.9
Separated..	3.2	2.9	2.3
Widowed..	9.9	8.7	8.6
Divorced..	10.0	11.4	11.5

[1] 2020 ACS 5-Year estimates. 1-Year estimates were not released for 2020 due to the impact of COVID-19 on data collection that year.

Table VA-3. Households and Housing Characteristics

(Number, percent, dollars.)

Item	2000	2010	2020 [1]	Average annual percent change, 2010–2020
Total Households..	2,699,173	2,992,732	3,184,121	0.9
Family households	1,847,796	2,013,520	2,103,100	0.6
Married-couple family	1,426,044	1,517,627	1,598,945	0.8
Other family	421,752	495,893	504,155	0.2
Male householder, no wife present...............	101,462	124,273	137,163	1.5
Female householder, no husband present.......	320,290	371,620	366,992	-0.2
Nonfamily households	851,377	979,212	1,081,021	1.5
Householder living alone............................	676,907	794,535	874,309	1.4
Householder not living alone.......................	174,470	184,677	206,712	1.7
Housing Characteristics				
Total housing units......................................	2,904,192	3,368,674	3,537,788	0.7
Occupied housing units	2,699,173	2,992,732	3,184,121	0.9
Owner occupied	1,837,939	2,025,240	2,123,771	0.7
Renter occupied	861,234	967,492	1,060,350	1.4
Average household size................................	2.54	2.6	2.60	-
Financial Characteristics				
Median gross rent of renter-occupied housing	650	1,019	1,257	3.3
Median monthly owner costs for housing units with a mortgage	1,144	1,728	1,822	0.8
Median value of owner-occupied housing units..........	125,400	249,100	282,800	1.9

- = Zero or rounds to zero.
[1] 2020 ACS 5-Year estimates. 1-Year estimates were not released for 2020 due to the impact of COVID-19 on data collection that year.

Table VA-4. Migration, Origin, and Language

(Number, percent.)

Characteristic	State 2016-2020 [1]	U.S. 2016-2020 [1]
Residence 1 Year Ago		
Population 1 year and over	8,413,940	322,943,283
Same house	85.2	86.2
Different house in the U.S.	14.0	13.2
Same county	6.0	7.7
Different county	8.0	5.5
Same state	4.9	3.2
Different state	3.1	2.3
Abroad	0.8	0.6
Place of Birth		
Native born	7,440,869	282,443,680
Male	49.4	49.4
Female	50.6	50.6
Foreign born	1,068,489	44,125,628
Male	48.1	48.6
Female	51.9	51.4
Foreign born; naturalized U.S. citizen................................	573,073	22,456,684
Male	46.6	46.1
Female	53.4	53.9
Foreign born; not a U.S. citizen......................................	495,416	21,668,944
Male	49.9	51.1
Female	50.1	48.9
Entered 2010 or later	25.5	22.8
Entered 2000 to 2009	29.0	25.1
Entered before 2000...	45.6	52.1
World Region of Birth, Foreign		
Foreign-born population, excluding population born at sea	1,068,489	44,125,628
Europe	10.1	10.8
Asia	42.4	31.3
Africa	10.7	5.4
Oceania	0.3	0.6
Latin America..	35.1	50.0
North America..	1.3	1.9
Language Spoken at Home and Ability to Speak English		
Population 5 years and over..	8,001,236	306,919,116
English only	83.6	78.5
Language other than English...	16.4	21.5
Speaks English less than "very well"..............................	5.8	8.2

[1] 2020 ACS 5-Year estimates. 1-Year estimates were not released for 2020 due to the impact of COVID-19 on data collection that year.
NA = Not available.
X = Not applicable.
- = Zero or rounds to zero.

Table VA-5. Median Income and Poverty Status, 2020[1]

(Number, percent, except as noted.)

Characteristic	State		U.S.	
	Number	Percent	Number	Percent
Median Income				
Households (dollars)..	76,398	X	64,994	X
Families (dollars)	93,284	X	80,069	X
Below Poverty Level (All People)	826,708	10.0	40,910,326	12.8
Sex				
Male	360,440	8.9	18,171,512	11.6
Female	466,268	11.0	22,738,814	14.0
Age				
Under 18 years...	241,637	13.1	12,598,699	17.5
Related children under 18 years..	234,182	12.8	12,306,532	17.2
18 to 64 years..	488,619	9.5	23,554,920	12.1
65 years and over	96,452	7.5	4,756,707	9.3

X = Not applicable.
[1] 2020 ACS 5-Year estimates. 1-Year estimates were not released for 2020 due to the impact of COVID-19 on data collection that year.

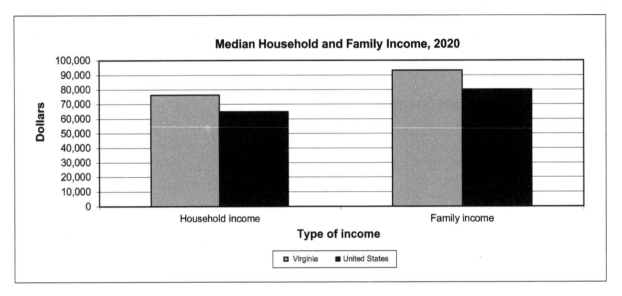

Table VA-6. Health Insurance Coverage Status for the Civilian Noninstitutionalized Population and Children Under 19 Years of Age

(Number, percent.)

Item	2011	2012	2013	2014	2015	2016	2017	2018	2019	2020 [2]
Civilian Noninstitutionalized Population	7,887,164	7,973,466	8,054,191	8,114,884	8,162,517	8,199,576	8,256,810	8,301,038	8,303,671	8,282,997
Covered by Private or Public Insurance										
Number..	6,904,303	6,973,731	7,063,565	7,231,248	7,416,224	7,484,692	7,527,631	7,569,569	7,645,385	7,601,635
Percent...	87.5	87.5	87.7	89.1	90.9	91.3	91.2	91.2	92.1	91.8
Uninsured										
Number..	982,861	999,735	990,626	883,636	746,293	714,884	729,179	731,469	658,286	681,362
Percent...	12.5	12.5	12.3	10.9	9.1	8.7	8.8	8.8	7.9	8.2
Percent in the U.S. not covered..........................	15.1	14.8	14.5	11.7	9.4	8.6	8.7	8.9	9.2	8.7
Children Under 19 Years of Age[1]	1,849,081	1,851,845	1,861,658	1,864,738	1,867,092	1,864,852	1,983,006	1,992,518	1,975,387	1,987,112
Covered by Private or Public Insurance										
Number..	1,740,598	1,747,907	1,760,407	1,757,636	1,776,406	1,775,840	1,881,588	1,890,950	1,878,818	1,887,993
Percent...	94.1	94.4	94.6	94.3	95.1	95.2	94.9	94.9	95.1	95.0
Uninsured										
Number..	108,483	103,938	101,251	107,102	90,686	89,012	101,418	101,568	96,569	99,119
Percent...	5.9	5.6	5.4	5.7	4.9	4.8	5.1	5.1	4.9	5.0
Percent in the U.S. not covered..........................	7.5	7.2	7.1	6.0	4.8	4.5	5.0	5.2	5.7	5.2

[1] Data for years prior to 2017 are for individuals under 18 years of age.
[2] 2020 ACS 5-Year estimates. 1-Year estimates were not released for 2020 due to the impact of COVID-19 on data collection that year. Data is not comparable to previous years, which are based on 1-year estimates.

Table VA-7. Employment Status by Demographic Group, 2021

(Numbers in thousands, percent.)

Characteristic	Civilian noninstitutional population	Civilian labor force		Employed		Unemployed	
		Number	Percent of population	Number	Percent of population	Number	Percent of population
Total..	6,752	4,295	63.6	4,127	61.1	169	3.9
Sex							
Male..	3,232	2,200	68.1	2,109	65.3	90	4.1
Female..	3,520	2,096	59.5	2,018	57.3	78	3.7
Race, Sex, and Hispanic Origin							
White...	4,780	3,007	62.9	2,912	60.9	95	3.2
Male..	2,319	1,589	68.5	1,532	66.0	58	3.6
Female..	2,461	1,418	57.6	1,380	56.1	38	2.7
Black or African American...................	1,302	851	65.4	798	61.3	54	6.3
Male..	598	391	65.4	366	61.1	26	6.5
Female..	704	460	65.3	432	61.4	28	6.1
Hispanic or Latino ethnicity[1]................	682	488	71.5	473	69.2	16	3.2
Male..	342	274	80.2	266	77.7	9	3.1
Female..	341	214	62.8	207	60.8	7	3.3
Age							
16 to 19 years..................................	417	168	40.2	150	36.1	17	10.3
20 to 24 years..................................	548	370	67.5	344	62.8	26	7.0
25 to 34 years..................................	1,089	911	83.7	870	79.9	41	4.4
35 to 44 years..................................	1,118	925	82.8	892	79.7	34	3.6
45 to 54 years..................................	1,087	915	84.2	896	82.5	18	2.0
55 to 64 years..................................	1,091	732	67.1	709	64.9	24	3.2
65 years and over..............................	1,402	275	19.6	266	18.9	10	3.5

NOTE: Data in Table 7 are from the Current Population Survey (CPS) and do not match the estimates in Table 8. See notes and definitions for further information.
[1] May be of any race.

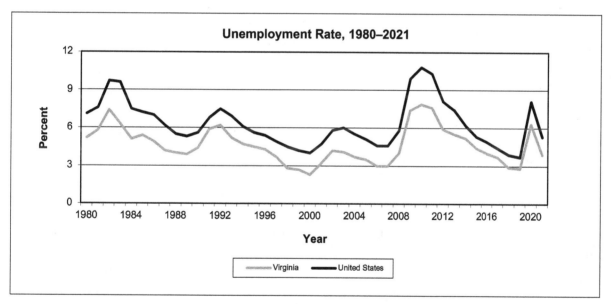

Table VA-8. Employment Status of the Civilian Noninstitutional Population Age 16 Years and Over

(Number, percent.)

Year	Civilian labor force	Civilian participation rate	Employed	Unemployed	Unemployment rate
2010..	4,163,293	67.8	3,858,466	304,827	7.3
2011..	4,205,184	67.4	3,929,008	276,176	6.6
2012..	4,217,529	66.7	3,967,151	250,378	5.9
2013..	4,238,377	66.4	4,002,057	236,320	5.6
2014..	4,258,856	66.1	4,040,908	217,948	5.1
2015..	4,233,981	65.2	4,048,081	185,900	4.4
2016..	4,254,348	65.0	4,084,822	169,526	4.0
2017..	4,352,977	65.7	4,193,290	159,687	3.7
2018..	4,384,657	65.7	4,255,213	129,444	3.0
2019..	4,455,815	66.3	4,332,647	123,168	2.8
2020..	4,368,772	64.6	4,097,860	270,912	6.2
2021..	4,267,656	62.9	4,100,803	166,853	3.9

Table VA-9. Employment and Average Wages by Industry

(Estimates are based on the 2012 North American Industry Classification System [NAICS].)

Industry	2013	2014	2015	2016	2017	2018	2019	2020
	Number of Jobs							
Wage and Salary Employment by Industry.......................	3,947,829	3,972,994	4,049,013	4,100,137	4,138,213	4,199,504	4,257,748	4,036,637
Farm Wage and Salary Employment...............................	11,663	14,301	12,948	11,967	9,671	12,389	13,428	8,195
Nonfarm Wage and Salary Employment..........................	3,936,166	3,958,693	4,036,065	4,088,170	4,128,542	4,187,115	4,244,320	4,028,442
Private wage and salary employment...........................	3,066,711	3,088,877	3,162,460	3,210,985	3,249,618	3,303,338	3,351,424	3,168,846
Forestry, fishing, and related activities.....................	5,950	6,073	6,797	7,001	7,063	6,994	6,544	6,232
Mining...	8,073	7,465	6,840	5,771	5,976	5,939	5,956	5,116
Utilities...	10,536	10,646	10,784	10,857	10,761	10,837	10,804	10,850
Construction..	181,745	182,886	189,681	193,073	198,104	203,098	208,202	207,581
Manufacturing..	231,376	232,106	233,595	232,335	234,535	240,029	243,881	234,337
Durable goods manufacturing.............................	136,594	137,574	138,392	135,300	136,353	140,360	143,751	138,549
Nondurable goods manufacturing........................	94,782	94,532	95,203	97,035	98,182	99,669	100,130	95,788
Wholesale trade	111,792	111,311	111,346	111,529	111,738	110,590	110,666	106,664
Retail trade..	413,745	416,581	421,521	422,544	420,641	416,882	409,960	389,967
Transportation and warehousing............................	105,692	108,481	115,418	119,078	121,844	124,274	131,341	133,104
Information..	71,229	71,686	69,890	68,241	67,993	67,336	68,125	65,352
Finance and insurance	134,028	135,832	139,224	141,973	146,413	148,506	152,061	153,180
Real estate and rental and leasing.........................	52,982	52,364	53,838	53,873	55,121	56,752	58,513	55,726
Professional, scientific, and technical services	397,401	392,536	403,041	413,335	421,166	433,074	440,561	444,933
Management of companies and enterprises...............	75,619	73,973	74,196	73,355	73,939	76,294	81,020	80,653
Administrative and waste services.........................	210,242	216,546	227,201	232,924	238,538	245,910	249,987	236,585
Educational services	73,806	72,542	73,979	75,481	76,626	79,334	80,028	73,036
Health care and social assistance..........................	406,114	410,403	423,026	434,626	439,581	448,220	459,176	441,832
Arts, entertainment, and recreation........................	50,357	51,158	53,503	55,948	55,943	56,635	58,401	44,877
Accommodation and food services.........................	318,053	323,323	334,632	345,633	351,255	354,533	354,833	282,512
Other services, except public administration.............	207,971	212,965	213,948	213,408	212,381	218,101	221,365	196,309
Government and government enterprises...................	869,455	869,816	873,605	877,185	878,924	883,777	892,896	859,596
	Dollars							
Average Wages and Salaries by Industry	53,307	54,334	55,696	56,253	58,022	59,879	61,653	66,523
Average Farm Wages and Salaries	25,271	22,123	19,960	24,784	27,832	22,674	16,611	26,435
Average Nonfarm Wages and Salaries	53,390	54,451	55,810	56,345	58,093	59,989	61,795	66,605
Average private wages and salaries...........................	52,820	53,784	55,172	55,613	57,458	59,456	61,441	66,758
Forestry, fishing, and related activities.....................	30,011	31,634	33,137	34,691	35,588	38,219	40,312	42,347
Mining...	69,165	71,032	69,121	68,091	70,475	75,390	76,406	75,395
Utilities...	101,262	105,902	105,707	105,738	109,278	119,944	120,902	122,048
Construction	49,650	51,003	52,584	54,339	57,182	59,120	61,612	64,678
Manufacturing..	56,293	58,535	59,981	58,740	60,126	62,332	63,701	66,460
Durable goods manufacturing.............................	59,089	61,942	63,605	61,914	64,098	66,273	67,671	69,962
Nondurable goods manufacturing........................	52,264	53,578	54,712	54,313	54,609	56,782	58,001	61,395
Wholesale trade	73,645	75,536	78,168	78,724	81,411	84,546	87,660	91,801
Retail trade..	27,696	28,233	29,041	29,466	30,127	31,060	32,419	35,298
Transportation and warehousing............................	51,128	52,041	52,004	51,807	53,341	54,992	55,081	56,216
Information..	88,031	92,735	97,572	99,388	100,649	103,275	110,493	120,718
Finance and insurance	83,606	86,107	89,737	90,627	95,093	99,594	101,838	111,814
Real estate and rental and leasing.........................	49,594	51,425	53,944	54,540	56,639	58,319	60,768	65,180
Professional, scientific, and technical services	98,127	99,143	100,973	102,208	104,474	107,163	110,615	115,777
Management of companies and enterprises...............	112,749	114,626	121,816	118,025	125,683	130,230	130,072	136,328
Administrative and waste services.........................	38,575	39,273	40,563	41,355	43,100	45,093	46,952	51,309
Educational services	38,935	39,260	39,432	40,035	40,317	40,756	41,260	47,490
Health care and social assistance..........................	47,041	48,040	48,964	49,618	51,001	52,194	53,285	56,591
Arts, entertainment, and recreation........................	27,179	28,178	28,877	28,592	29,859	30,520	31,442	36,675
Accommodation and food services.........................	19,753	20,292	20,889	21,384	22,008	23,141	24,053	23,504
Other services, except public administration.............	36,894	37,793	39,155	40,056	41,424	42,367	43,290	48,286
Government and government enterprises...................	55,400	56,820	58,119	59,023	60,441	61,980	63,126	66,039

Table VA-10. Employment Characteristics by Family Type

(Number, percent.)

Family type and labor force status	2018		2019		2020 [1]	
	Total	Families with own children under 18 years	Total	Families with own children under 18 years	Total	Families with own children under 18 years
All Families	2,094,307	865,834	2,094,763	865,993	2,103,100	888,138
FAMILY TYPE AND LABOR FORCE STATUS						
Opposite-Sex Married-Couple Families	1,579,078	616,946	1,590,659	617,211	1,585,566	635,037
Both husband and wife in labor force	54.4	69.1	53.8	70.9	54.6	69.7
Husband in labor force, wife not in labor force	20.8	26.2	20.4	24.4	21.3	25.5
Wife in labor force, husband not in labor force	7.3	3.0	7.7	3.0	7.5	3.4
Both husband and wife not in labor force	16.6	1.2	17.2	1.3	16.6	1.3
Other Families	515,229	248,888	504,104	248,782	504,155	250,319
Female householder, no spouse present	71.8	73.9	72.3	75.0	72.8	75.2
In labor force	50.3	62.0	52.0	65.4	52.3	64.0
Not in labor force	21.5	11.9	20.3	9.6	20.5	11.2
Male householder, no spouse present	28.2	26.1	27.7	25.0	27.2	24.8
In labor force	22.2	24.5	21.7	23.4	21.6	23.2
Not in labor force	6.0	1.6	5.9	1.6	5.6	1.6

[1] 2020 ACS 5-Year estimates. 1-Year estimates were not released for 2020 due to the impact of COVID-19 on data collection that year. Data is not comparable to previous years, which are based on 1-year estimates.

Table VA-11. School Enrollment and Educational Attainment, 2020[1]

(Number, percent.)

Item	State	U.S.
Enrollment		
Total population 3 years and over, enrolled in school	2,110,795	80,497,960
Enrolled in nursery school or preschool (percent)	5.9	6.1
Enrolled in kindergarten (percent)	4.8	5.0
Enrolled in elementary school, grades 1-8 (percent)	39.1	40.4
Enrolled in high school, grades 9-12 (percent)	20.3	21.0
Enrolled in college or graduate school (percent)	29.9	27.6
Attainment		
Total population 25 years and over	5,831,949	222,836,834
Less than ninth grade (percent)	3.9	4.9
9th to 12th grade, no diploma (percent)	5.8	6.6
High school graduate, including equivalency (percent)	23.9	26.7
Some college, no degree (percent)	19.1	20.3
Associate's degree (percent)	7.9	8.6
Bachelor's degree (percent)	22.4	20.2
Graduate or professional degree (percent)	17.2	12.7
High school graduate or higher (percent)	90.3	88.5
Bachelor's degree or higher (percent)	39.5	32.9

[1] 2020 ACS 5-Year estimates. 1-Year estimates were not released for 2020 due to the impact of COVID-19 on data collection that year.

Table VA-12. Public School Characteristics and Educational Indicators

(Number, percent; data derived from National Center of Education Statistics.)

Item	State	U.S.
Public Elementary and Secondary Schools		
Number of regular school districts, 2018-19	132	13,452
Number of operational schools, 2019-20	2,122	98,469
Percent charter schools	0.4	7.7
Total public school enrollment, Fall 2019	1,297,012	50,796,445
Percent charter school enrollment	0.1	6.8
Student-teacher ratio, Fall 2019	14.9	15.9
Expenditures per student (unadjusted dollars), 2018-19	12,642	13,187
Four-year adjusted cohort graduation rate (ACGR), 2018-2019 [1]	87.5	85.8
Students eligible for free or reduced-price lunch (percent), 2019-20	45.1	52.1
English language learners (percent), Fall 2019	9.2	10.4
Students age 3 to 21 served under IDEA, part B (percent), 2020-21	13.9	14.5

Public Schools by Type, 2019-20	Number	Percent of state public schools
Total number of schools	2,122	100.0
Special education	40	1.9
Vocational education	89	4.2
Alternative education	122	5.7

[1] Adjusted Cohort Graduation Rates (ACGR) differ from Averaged Freshmen Graduation Rates (AFGR).

Table VA-13. Reported Voting and Registration of the Voting-Age Population, November 2020

(Numbers in thousands, percent.)

Item	Total population	Total citizen population	Registered			Voted		
			Total registered	Percent registered (total population)	Percent registered (total citizen population)	Total voted	Percent voted (total population)	Percent voted (total citizen population)
U.S. Total	252,274	231,593	168,308	66.7	72.7	154,628	61.3	66.8
State Total..	6,481	5,974	4,541	70.1	76.0	4,275	66.0	71.5
Sex								
Male	3,084	2,842	2,092	67.8	73.6	1,981	64.2	69.7
Female	3,396	3,132	2,449	72.1	78.2	2,293	67.5	73.2
Race								
White alone......................................	4,526	4,268	3,393	75.0	79.5	3,204	70.8	75.1
White, non-Hispanic alone..................	3,979	3,904	3,160	79.4	80.9	3,018	75.9	77.3
Black alone.......................................	1,237	1,129	764	61.8	67.7	722	58.3	63.9
Asian alone	512	409	271	52.9	66.1	253	49.4	61.8
Hispanic (of any race).......................	678	425	271	39.9	63.8	218	32.1	51.3
White alone or in combination..................	4,620	4,362	3,454	74.8	79.2	3,248	70.3	74.5
Black alone or in combination..............	1,304	1,196	805	61.7	67.3	748	57.4	62.5
Asian alone or in combination.............	535	432	287	53.6	66.4	269	50.3	62.3
Age								
18 to 24 years..................................	730	668	405	55.5	60.6	346	47.4	51.8
25 to 34 years..................................	1,112	956	726	65.3	75.9	666	59.9	69.7
35 to 44 years..................................	1,078	925	732	67.9	79.1	671	62.2	72.5
45 to 64 years..................................	2,176	2,084	1,609	74.0	77.2	1,570	72.2	75.3
65 years and over	1,385	1,341	1,069	77.2	79.7	1,022	73.8	76.2

Table VA-14. Crime

(Number, rate per 100,000. Data are derived from the FBI Uniform Crime Reports.)

Item	State			U.S.		
	2019	2020	Percent change	2019	2020	Percent change
TOTAL POPULATION[1]	8,556,642	8,590,563	0.4	328,329,953	329,484,123	0.4
VIOLENT CRIME						
Number...	17,916	17,925	0.1	1,250,393	1,313,105	5.0
Rate	209.4	208.7	-0.3	380.8	398.5	4.6
Murder and Nonnegligent Manslaughter						
Number..	447	524	17.2	16,669	21,570	29.4
Rate	5.2	6.1	16.8	5.1	6.5	28.9
Rape[2]						
Number..	2,915	2,279	-21.8	143,224	126,430	-11.7
Rate	34.1	26.5	-22.1	43.6	38.4	-12.0
Robbery						
Number..	3,520	2,947	-16.3	268,483	243,600	-9.3
Rate	41.1	34.3	-16.6	81.8	73.9	-9.6
Aggravated Assault						
Number..	11,034	12,175	10.3	822,017	921,505	12.1
Rate	129.0	141.7	9.9	250.4	279.7	11.7
PROPERTY CRIME						
Number..	140,944	125,114	-11.2	6,995,235	6,452,038	-7.8
Rate	1,647.2	1,456.4	-11.6	2,130.6	1,958.2	-8.1
Burglary						
Number..	13,972	11,465	-17.9	1,118,096	1,035,314	-7.4
Rate	163.3	133.5	-18.3	340.5	314.2	-7.7
Larceny-Theft						
Number..	116,656	102,796	-11.9	5,152,267	4,606,324	-10.6
Rate	1,363.3	1,196.6	-12.2	1,569.2	1,398.0	-10.9
Motor Vehicle Theft						
Number..	10,316	10,853	5.2	724,872	810,400	11.8
Rate	120.6	126.3	4.8	220.8	246.0	11.4

NOTE: Although arson data are included in the trend and clearance tables, sufficient data are not available to estimate totals for this offense. Therefore, no arson data are published in this table.
- = Zero or rounds to zero.
[1] Population figures are U.S. Census Bureau provisional estimates as of July 1, 2020.
[2] The figures shown in the rape (revised definition) column were estimated using the revised Uniform Crime Reporting (UCR) definition of rape.

Table VA-15. State Government Finances, 2020

(Dollar amounts in thousands, percent distribution.)

Item	Dollars	Percent distribution
Total Revenue	70,083,028	100.0
General revenue	63,156,784	90.1
Intergovernmental revenue	18,494,271	26.4
Taxes	28,063,901	40.0
General sales	5720715	8.2
Selective sales	4,346,732	6.2
License taxes	972,293	1.4
Individual income tax	14996649	21.4
Corporate income tax	1,362,172	1.9
Other taxes	665,340	0.9
Current charges	11,392,462	16.3
Miscellaneous general revenue	5,206,150	7.4
Utility revenue	0	-
Liquor stores revenue	971169	1.4
Insurance trust revenue[1]	5,955,075	8.5
Total Expenditure	65,338,488	100.0
Intergovernmental expenditure	13,198,424	20.2
Direct expenditure	52,140,064	79.8
Current operation	37,861,895	57.9
Capital outlay	4,607,422	7.1
Insurance benefits and repayments	6,993,032	10.7
Assistance and subsidies	1,518,015	2.3
Interest on debt	1,159,700	1.8
Exhibit: Salaries and wages	8,250,204	12.6
Total Expenditure	65,338,488	100.0
General expenditure	57,363,587	87.8
Intergovernmental expenditure	13,198,424	20.2
Direct expenditure	44,165,163	67.6
General expenditure, by function:		
Education	18,872,998	28.9
Public welfare	15,890,796	24.3
Hospitals	5,992,238	9.2
Health	1,795,306	2.7
Highways	5,318,433	8.1
Police protection	756,391	1.2
Correction	1,679,125	2.6
Natural resources	343,752	0.5
Parks and recreation	167,143	0.3
Governmental administration	1,977,540	3.0
Interest on general debt	1,159,700	1.8
Other and unallocable	2,748,558	4.2
Utility expenditure	650,892	0.9
Liquor stores expenditure	771332	1.2
Insurance trust expenditure	6,993,032	10.7
Debt at End of Fiscal Year	29,340,896	X
Cash and Security Holdings	115,632,239	X

X = Not applicable.
- = Zero or rounds to zero.

[1] Within insurance trust revenue, net earnings of state retirement systems is a calculated statistic (the item code in the data file is X08), and thus can be positive or negative. Net earnings is the sum of earnings on investments plus gains on investments minus losses on investments. The change made in 2002 for asset valuation from book to market value in accordance with Statement 34 of the Governmental Accounting Standards Board is reflected in the calculated statistics.

Table VA-16. State Government Tax Collections, 2021

(Dollars in thousands, percent.)

Item	Dollars	Percent distribution
Total Taxes	32,328,105	100.0
Property taxes	43,332	0.1
Sales and gross receipts	11,719,392	36.3
General sales and gross receipts	6,527,477	20.2
Selective sales and gross receipts	5,191,915	16.1
Alcoholic beverages	295,471	0.9
Amusements	5,557	-
Insurance premiums	551,005	1.7
Motor fuels	1,421,963	4.4
Pari-mutuels	X	-
Public utilities	495,749	1.5
Tobacco products	287,856	0.9
Other selective sales	2,134,314	6.6
Licenses	995,094	3.1
Alcoholic beverages	16,062	-
Amusements	116	-
Corporations in general	76,769	0.2
Hunting and fishing	27,602	0.1
Motor vehicle	504,374	1.6
Motor vehicle operators	80,230	0.2
Public utilities	697	-
Occupation and business, NEC	226,454	0.7
Other licenses	62,790	0.2
Income taxes	18,645,899	57.7
Individual income	17,066,596	52.8
Corporation net income	1,579,303	4.9
Other taxes	924,388	2.9
Death and gift	X	-
Documentary and stock transfer	810,105	2.5
Severance	3,453	-
Taxes, NEC	110,830	0.3

- = Zero or rounds to zero.

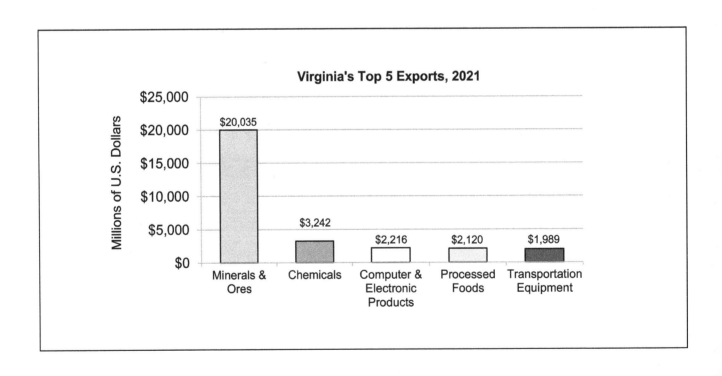

Virginia's Top 5 Exports, 2021

WASHINGTON

Facts and Figures

Location: Northwestern United States; bordered on the N by Canada (British Columbia), on the E by Idaho, on the S by Oregon, and on the W by the Pacific Ocean

Area: 71,300 sq. mi. (184,665 sq. km.); rank—18th

Population: 8,642,274 (2021 est.); rank—13th

Principal Cities: capital—Olympia; largest—Seattle

Statehood: November 11, 1889; 42nd state

U.S. Congress: 2 senators, 10 representatives

State Motto: *Alki* ("By and by")

State Song: "Washington, My Home"

State Nickname: The Evergreen State

Abbreviations: WA; Wash.

State Symbols: flower—coast rhododendron; tree—Western hemlock; bird—willow goldfinch

At a Glance

- With an increase in population of 15.1 percent, Washington ranked 8th among the states in growth from 2010 to 2021.

- Washington's median household income in 2020 was $77,006, and 10.2 percent of the population lived below the poverty level.

- In 2020, 6.2 percent of Washingtonians did not have health insurance, compared to 8.7 percent of the total U.S. population.

- Washington had the 5th highest property crime rate in the country in 2020 (2,732.4 incidences per 100,000 population).

- Washington had the highest drug overdose death rate in the country in 2020, with 81.4 deaths per 100,000 population. The national average was 28.3 drug overdose deaths per 100,000 population.

Table WA-1. Population by Age, Sex, Race, and Hispanic Origin

(Number, percent, except where noted.)

Sex, age, race, and Hispanic origin	2000	2010	2021	Percent change, 2010–2021
Total population..	5,894,121	6,724,540	7,738,692	15.1
Percent of total U.S. population	2.1	2.2	2.3	X
Sex				
Male..	2,934,300	3,349,707	3,898,267	16.4
Female	2,959,821	3,374,833	3,840,425	13.8
Age				
Under 5 years..	394,306	439,657	434,017	-1.3
5 to 19 years..	1,288,713	1,330,238	1,418,064	6.6
20 to 64 years..	3,548,954	4,126,968	4,631,433	12.2
65 years and over	662,148	827,677	1,255,178	51.7
Median age (years)	35.9	37.3	38.2	2.4
Race and Hispanic origin				
One race				
White	4,821,823	5,535,262	5,995,925	8.3
Black..	190,267	252,333	348,170	38.0
American Indian and Alaska Native	93,301	122,649	152,807	24.6
Asian	322,335	491,685	775,470	57.7
Native Hawaiian or Other Pacific Islander	23,953	43,505	63,112	45.1
Two or more races	213,519	279,106	403,208	44.5
Hispanic (of any race)..	441,509	776,539	1,059,156	36.4

NOTE: Population figures for 2021 are July 1 estimates. The 2000 and 2010 estimates are taken from the respective censuses.
- = Zero or rounds to zero.
X = Not applicable.

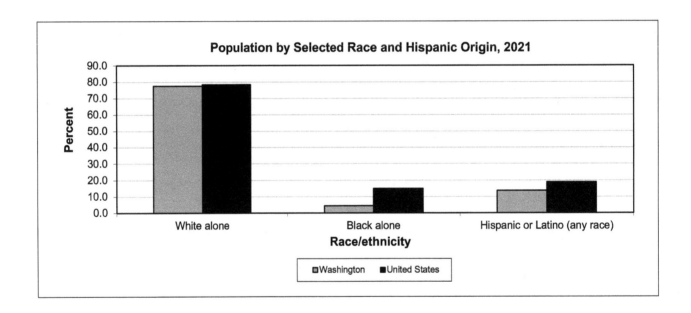

Table WA-2. Marital Status

(Number, percent distribution.)

Sex, age, race, and Hispanic origin	2000	2010	2020 [1]
Males, 15 Years and Over	2,287,431	2,686,801	3,051,503
Never married	29.8	33.8	35.0
Now married, except separated..	56.6	52.0	51.7
Separated..	1.4	1.6	1.3
Widowed..	2.1	2.1	2.2
Divorced..	10.1	10.5	9.8
Females, 15 Years and Over	2,352,091	2,746,158	3,078,254
Never married	22.8	26.4	27.5
Now married, except separated..	54.1	50.6	50.3
Separated..	1.8	2.1	1.6
Widowed..	8.6	7.8	7.3
Divorced..	12.7	13.2	13.2

[1] 2020 ACS 5-Year estimates. 1-Year estimates were not released for 2020 due to the impact of COVID-19 on data collection that year.

Table WA-3. Households and Housing Characteristics

(Number, percent, dollars.)

Item	2000	2010	2020 [1]	Average annual percent change, 2010–2020
Total Households	2,271,398	2,606,863	2,905,822	1.6
Family households	1,499,127	1,681,386	1,874,376	1.6
Married-couple family	1,181,995	1,297,240	1,456,242	1.8
Other family	317,132	384,146	418,134	1.3
Male householder, no wife present	92,514	114,187	136,944	2.8
Female householder, no husband present	224,618	269,959	281,190	0.6
Nonfamily households	772,271	925,477	1,031,446	1.6
Householder living alone	594,325	731,452	775,608	0.9
Householder not living alone	117,946	194,025	255,838	4.6
Housing Characteristics				
Total housing units	2,451,075	2,888,594	3,150,194	1.3
Occupied housing units	2,271,398	2,606,863	2,905,822	1.6
Owner occupied	1,467,009	1,644,939	1,838,059	1.7
Renter occupied	804,389	961,924	1,067,763	1.6
Average household size	2.53	2.53	2.53	-
Financial Characteristics				
Median gross rent of renter-occupied housing	663	908	1,337	6.7
Median monthly owner costs for housing units with a mortgage	1,268	1,736	1,939	1.7
Median value of owner-occupied housing units	168,300	271,800	366,800	5.0

Table WA-4. Migration, Origin, and Language

(Number, percent.)

Characteristic	State 2016-2020 [1]	U.S. 2016-2020 [1]
Residence 1 Year Ago		
Population 1 year and over	7,428,623	322,943,283
Same house	83.0	86.2
Different house in the U.S.	16.2	13.2
Same county	9.8	7.7
Different county	6.4	5.5
Same state	3.1	3.2
Different state	3.3	2.3
Abroad	0.8	0.6
Place of Birth		
Native born	6,422,805	282,443,680
Male	50.3	49.4
Female	49.7	50.6
Foreign born	1,089,660	44,125,628
Male	48.4	48.6
Female	51.6	51.4
Foreign born; naturalized U.S. citizen	522,603	22,456,684
Male	45.6	46.1
Female	54.4	53.9
Foreign born; not a U.S. citizen	567,057	21,668,944
Male	51.0	51.1
Female	49.0	48.9
Entered 2010 or later	26.8	22.8
Entered 2000 to 2009	27.2	25.1
Entered before 2000	46.0	52.1
World Region of Birth, Foreign		
Foreign-born population, excluding population born at sea	1,089,660	44,125,628
Europe	14.5	10.8
Asia	44.0	31.3
Africa	6.4	5.4
Oceania	2.0	0.6
Latin America	28.8	50.0
North America	4.3	1.9
Language Spoken at Home and Ability to Speak English		
Population 5 years and over	7,057,853	306,919,116
English only	80.0	78.5
Language other than English	20.0	21.5
Speaks English less than "very well"	7.6	8.2

[1] 2020 ACS 5-Year estimates. 1-Year estimates were not released for 2020 due to the impact of COVID-19 on data collection that year.
NA = Not available.
X = Not applicable.
- = Zero or rounds to zero.

Table WA-5. Median Income and Poverty Status, 2020[1]

(Number, percent, except as noted.)

Characteristic	State		U.S.	
	Number	Percent	Number	Percent
Median Income				
Households (dollars)...	77,006	X	64,994	X
Families (dollars)	92,422	X	80,069	X
Below Poverty Level (All People)	751,044	10.2	40,910,326	12.8
Sex				
Male	341,490	9.3	18,171,512	11.6
Female	409,554	11.1	22,738,814	14.0
Age				
Under 18 years..	204,059	12.6	12,598,699	17.5
Related children under 18 years...	196,593	12.2	12,306,532	17.2
18 to 64 years...	461,501	10.0	23,554,920	12.1
65 years and over	85,484	7.5	4,756,707	9.3

X = Not applicable.
[1] 2020 ACS 5-Year estimates. 1-Year estimates were not released for 2020 due to the impact of COVID-19 on data collection that year.

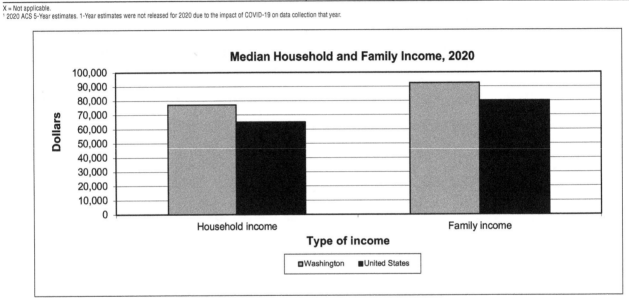

Table WA-6. Health Insurance Coverage Status for the Civilian Noninstitutionalized Population and Children Under 19 Years of Age

(Number, percent.)

Item	2011	2012	2013	2014	2015	2016	2017	2018	2019	2020 [2]
Civilian Noninstitutionalized Population	6,716,822	6,793,078	6,864,149	6,954,806	7,066,812	7,184,110	7,299,812	7,427,599	7,497,453	7,397,932
Covered by Private or Public Insurance										
Number..	5,764,192	5,848,307	5,904,158	6,312,152	6,598,845	6,756,018	6,853,706	6,950,315	7,001,406	6,939,704
Percent..	85.8	86.1	86.0	90.8	93.4	94.0	93.9	93.6	93.4	93.8
Uninsured										
Number..	952,630	944,771	959,991	642,654	467,967	428,092	446,106	477,284	496,047	458,228
Percent..	14.2	13.9	14.0	9.2	6.6	6.0	6.1	6.4	6.6	6.2
Percent in the U.S. not covered...	15.1	14.8	14.5	11.7	9.4	8.6	8.7	8.9	9.2	8.7
Children Under 19 Years of Age[1]	1,578,179	1,583,595	1,594,503	1,601,029	1,610,562	1,627,304	1,739,832	1,755,094	1,757,459	1,745,214
Covered by Private or Public Insurance										
Number..	1,480,971	1,492,516	1,499,708	1,526,102	1,568,043	1,585,868	1,693,734	1,707,612	1,703,314	1,695,768
Percent..	93.8	94.2	94.1	95.3	97.4	97.5	97.4	97.3	96.9	97.2
Uninsured										
Number..	97,208	91,079	94,795	74,927	42,519	41,436	46,098	47,482	54,145	49,446
Percent..	6.2	5.8	5.9	4.7	2.6	2.5	2.6	2.7	3.1	2.8
Percent in the U.S. not covered...	7.5	7.2	7.1	6.0	4.8	4.5	5.0	5.2	5.7	5.2

[1] Data for years prior to 2017 are for individuals under 18 years of age.
[2] 2020 ACS 5-Year estimates. 1-Year estimates were not released for 2020 due to the impact of COVID-19 on data collection that year. Data is not comparable to previous years, which are based on 1-year estimates.

Table WA-7. Employment Status by Demographic Group, 2021

(Numbers in thousands, percent.)

Characteristic	Civilian noninstitutional population	Civilian labor force		Employed		Unemployed	
		Number	Percent of population	Number	Percent of population	Number	Percent of population
Total..	6,167	3,923	63.6	3,706	60.1	217	5.5
Sex							
Male..	3,046	2,098	68.9	1,974	64.8	124	5.9
Female..	3,120	1,825	58.5	1,731	55.5	94	5.1
Race, Sex, and Hispanic Origin							
White...	4,867	3,094	63.6	2,929	60.2	165	5.3
Male..	2,394	1,640	68.5	1,546	64.6	94	5.7
Female..	2,473	1,454	58.8	1,383	55.9	70	4.8
Black or African American................	281	197	69.8	183	64.9	14	7.0
Male..	149	117	78.2	107	71.9	10	8.1
Female..	132	80	60.4	76	57.2	4	5.3
Hispanic or Latino ethnicity[1]............	784	571	72.9	539	68.7	33	5.7
Male..	421	332	78.8	313	74.3	19	5.7
Female..	363	240	66.0	226	62.2	14	5.7
Age							
16 to 19 years...............................	360	126	35.1	103	28.5	24	18.7
20 to 24 years...............................	496	355	71.6	320	64.5	35	10.0
25 to 34 years...............................	1,114	950	85.3	905	81.2	46	4.8
35 to 44 years...............................	1,065	877	82.3	833	78.3	43	5.0
45 to 54 years...............................	978	792	81.0	762	77.9	30	3.7
55 to 64 years...............................	952	609	64.0	575	60.4	35	5.7
65 years and over..........................	1,202	214	17.8	209	17.3	5	2.5

NOTE. Data in Table 7 are from the Current Population Survey (CPS) and do not match the estimates in Table 8. See notes and definitions for further information.
[1] May be of any race.

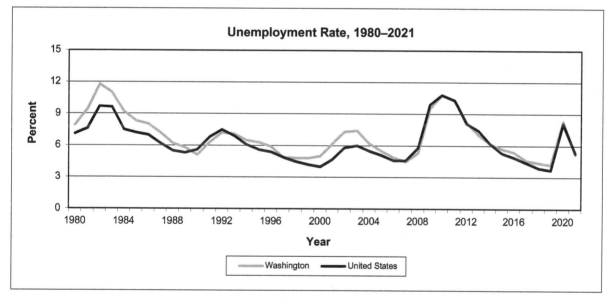

Unemployment Rate, 1980–2021

Table WA-8. Employment Status of the Civilian Noninstitutional Population Age 16 Years and Over

(Number, percent.)

Year	Civilian labor force	Civilian participation rate	Employed	Unemployed	Unemployment rate
2010..	3,458,451	65.9	3,142,109	316,342	9.1
2011..	3,437,871	64.7	3,144,459	293,412	8.5
2012..	3,468,738	64.5	3,203,294	265,444	7.7
2013..	3,460,772	63.6	3,230,947	229,825	6.6
2014..	3,495,153	63.3	3,287,904	207,249	5.9
2015..	3,554,826	63.3	3,361,249	193,577	5.4
2016..	3,648,558	63.7	3,459,527	189,031	5.2
2017..	3,727,683	63.7	3,554,754	172,929	4.6
2018..	3,813,320	64.1	3,644,274	169,046	4.4
2019..	3,933,774	65.2	3,764,634	169,140	4.3
2020..	3,929,477	64.4	3,596,814	332,663	8.5
2021..	3,913,513	63.7	3,708,738	204,775	5.2

Table WA-9. Employment and Average Wages by Industry

(Estimates are based on the 2012 North American Industry Classification System [NAICS].)

Industry	2013	2014	2015	2016	2017	2018	2019	2020
	Number of Jobs							
Wage and Salary Employment by Industry.........................	3,196,913	3,281,417	3,361,935	3,448,656	3,523,477	3,613,897	3,686,545	3,496,277
Farm Wage and Salary Employment...............................	53,313	53,511	51,723	52,493	53,491	53,523	53,994	58,976
Nonfarm Wage and Salary Employment...........................	3,143,600	3,227,906	3,310,212	3,396,163	3,469,986	3,560,374	3,632,551	3,437,301
Private wage and salary employment..............................	2,524,370	2,606,842	2,680,960	2,756,713	2,821,787	2,901,659	2,967,431	2,796,919
Forestry, fishing, and related activities.....................	30,682	31,300	32,341	31,742	31,891	32,607	33,541	32,172
Mining...	2,162	2,245	2,400	2,435	2,562	2,634	2,306	2,116
Utilities...	4,823	4,838	4,943	4,646	4,823	5,120	5,246	5,290
Construction	153,034	164,788	179,299	191,759	204,557	218,279	224,317	217,926
Manufacturing..	286,568	288,634	291,161	289,695	283,889	287,353	293,480	271,618
Durable goods manufacturing...........................	209,185	209,565	211,198	207,338	200,185	201,881	206,681	189,644
Nondurable goods manufacturing......................	77,383	79,069	79,963	82,357	83,704	85,472	86,799	81,974
Wholesale trade...	127,601	130,909	133,520	133,481	134,739	136,337	136,615	131,356
Retail trade..	331,791	345,122	358,633	372,116	387,173	388,696	393,493	388,464
Transportation and warehousing............................	89,979	94,264	98,304	100,601	103,145	110,166	111,937	107,731
Information..	106,435	109,682	114,614	120,859	126,574	133,778	144,742	149,223
Finance and insurance..	96,336	98,130	99,063	99,959	102,082	103,017	104,325	104,814
Real estate and rental and leasing..........................	47,171	48,215	50,404	51,412	53,315	56,606	58,914	56,130
Professional, scientific, and technical services	176,836	184,546	190,534	197,459	202,313	209,391	216,253	217,570
Management of companies and enterprises................	38,894	39,992	41,939	43,177	44,300	44,657	45,083	43,517
Administrative and waste services.........................	147,472	152,139	160,239	164,876	170,082	172,893	176,055	164,982
Educational services	53,694	55,123	55,986	55,722	56,724	56,160	57,220	51,727
Health care and social assistance...........................	392,978	402,147	398,408	411,309	419,621	433,020	444,671	438,872
Arts, entertainment, and recreation.......................	46,917	48,749	48,645	51,180	52,754	54,298	55,262	36,067
Accommodation and food services.........................	242,201	252,062	264,141	274,954	280,824	289,663	294,519	227,081
Other services, except public administration....................	148,796	153,957	156,386	159,331	160,419	166,984	169,452	150,263
Government and government enterprises.....................	619,230	621,064	629,252	639,450	648,199	658,715	665,120	640,382
	Dollars							
Average Wages and Salaries by Industry	53,347	55,329	56,997	58,950	61,893	65,694	68,927	75,550
Average Farm Wages and Salaries	28,769	27,985	29,479	32,384	27,430	27,192	28,673	30,965
Average Nonfarm Wages and Salaries	53,763	55,783	57,427	59,361	62,424	66,273	69,526	76,315
Average private wages and salaries............................	54,106	56,229	57,892	59,906	63,159	67,388	70,728	78,140
Forestry, fishing, and related activities.....................	34,999	35,368	35,427	37,589	38,643	40,194	40,053	42,732
Mining...	63,150	63,998	68,064	67,940	71,680	71,478	75,360	74,123
Utilities...	85,780	87,775	93,335	91,146	94,130	101,022	107,824	116,383
Construction	54,402	55,717	57,726	59,871	62,232	65,288	68,543	70,617
Manufacturing..	71,728	75,435	74,874	75,007	76,408	79,422	81,330	82,066
Durable goods manufacturing...........................	79,332	84,307	83,290	83,516	85,322	89,017	90,934	90,823
Nondurable goods manufacturing......................	51,173	51,921	52,645	53,584	55,091	56,759	58,461	61,809
Wholesale trade...	69,078	71,040	73,204	74,439	77,499	80,617	82,899	87,638
Retail trade..	36,200	38,844	42,090	46,320	52,829	59,036	62,382	71,536
Transportation and warehousing............................	54,340	55,148	56,551	58,115	60,274	62,303	66,650	67,553
Information..	137,008	150,237	150,574	159,038	172,239	194,375	206,778	241,810
Finance and insurance..	79,405	81,936	85,411	87,599	90,555	94,281	100,066	111,979
Real estate and rental and leasing..........................	44,177	46,141	48,009	50,193	52,468	55,806	59,011	63,985
Professional, scientific, and technical services	82,596	85,691	86,061	89,155	92,941	101,271	103,986	112,359
Management of companies and enterprises................	106,965	109,039	108,964	109,700	112,746	118,246	123,439	127,267
Administrative and waste services.........................	43,538	44,639	46,249	47,357	48,797	50,588	53,304	57,224
Educational services	30,579	30,918	31,780	31,883	32,222	33,869	34,473	39,082
Health care and social assistance...........................	43,897	44,888	48,251	49,419	51,378	52,947	54,839	56,725
Arts, entertainment, and recreation.......................	30,573	32,607	33,513	33,826	35,023	35,965	36,484	41,358
Accommodation and food services.........................	22,723	23,035	23,739	24,570	26,874	28,498	29,658	27,349
Other services, except public administration....................	33,818	33,679	34,756	36,634	38,004	38,948	40,309	44,513
Government and government enterprises....................	52,366	53,909	55,447	57,010	59,222	61,357	64,161	68,348

Table WA-10. Employment Characteristics by Family Type

(Number, percent.)

Family type and labor force status	2018		2019		2020 [1]	
	Total	Families with own children under 18 years	Total	Families with own children under 18 years	Total	Families with own children under 18 years
All Families...	1,879,637	791,466	1,882,896	792,196	1,874,376	801,815
FAMILY TYPE AND LABOR FORCE STATUS						
Opposite-Sex Married-Couple Families...........................	1,454,891	566,917	1,448,372	565,882	1,436,613	577,662
Both husband and wife in labor force....................	50.4	63.8	51.1	65.3	51.2	64.1
Husband in labor force, wife not in labor force	22.1	30.1	22.2	29.1	22.7	30.4
Wife in labor force, husband not in labor force	7.7	4.1	7.4	3.7	7.6	4.0
Both husband and wife not in labor force....................	18.3	1.3	17.9	1.1	18.4	1.6
Other Families	424,746	224,549	434,524	226,314	418,134	220,662
Female householder, no spouse present	68.0	69.7	66.8	68.3	67.2	68.8
In labor force....................	49.1	58.5	47.4	56.5	48.5	57.7
Not in labor force	18.9	11.1	19.4	11.8	18.8	11.1
Male householder, no spouse present....................	32.0	30.3	33.2	31.7	32.8	31.2
In labor force....................	25.7	28.1	27.2	28.9	26.5	28.6
Not in labor force	6.3	2.2	6.1	2.8	6.2	2.6

[1] 2020 ACS 5-Year estimates. 1-Year estimates were not released for 2020 due to the impact of COVID-19 on data collection that year. Data is not comparable to previous years, which are based on 1-year estimates.

Table WA-11. School Enrollment and Educational Attainment, 2020[1]

(Number, percent.)

Item	State	U.S.
Enrollment		
Total population 3 years and over, enrolled in school	1,753,707	80,497,960
Enrolled in nursery school or preschool (percent)	6.4	6.1
Enrolled in kindergarten (percent)	5.2	5.0
Enrolled in elementary school, grades 1-8 (percent)	41.5	40.4
Enrolled in high school, grades 9-12 (percent)	20.5	21.0
Enrolled in college or graduate school (percent)	26.4	27.6
Attainment		
Total population 25 years and over	5,199,771	222,836,834
Less than ninth grade (percent)	3.5	4.9
9th to 12th grade, no diploma (percent)	4.8	6.6
High school graduate, including equivalency (percent)	21.8	26.7
Some college, no degree (percent)	23.1	20.3
Associate's degree (percent)	10.1	8.6
Bachelor's degree (percent)	22.8	20.2
Graduate or professional degree (percent)	13.9	12.7
High school graduate or higher (percent)	91.7	88.5
Bachelor's degree or higher (percent)	36.7	32.9

[1] 2020 ACS 5-Year estimates. 1-Year estimates were not released for 2020 due to the impact of COVID-19 on data collection that year.

Table WA-12. Public School Characteristics and Educational Indicators

(Number, percent; data derived from National Center of Education Statistics.)

Item	State	U.S.
Public Elementary and Secondary Schools		
Number of regular school districts, 2018-19	299	13,452
Number of operational schools, 2019-20	2,473	98,469
Percent charter schools	0.4	7.7
Total public school enrollment, Fall 2019	1,142,073	50,796,445
Percent charter school enrollment	0.3	6.8
Student-teacher ratio, Fall 2019	18.4	15.9
Expenditures per student (unadjusted dollars), 2018-19	14,342	13,187
Four-year adjusted cohort graduation rate (ACGR), 2018-2019[1]	81.1	85.8
Students eligible for free or reduced-price lunch (percent), 2019-20	43.9	52.1
English language learners (percent), Fall 2019	11.7	10.4
Students age 3 to 21 served under IDEA, part B (percent), 2020-21	13.5	14.5

Public Schools by Type, 2019-20	Number	Percent of state public schools
Total number of schools....................	2,473	100.0
Special education....................	89	3.6
Vocational education....................	20	0.8
Alternative education....................	319	12.9

[1] Adjusted Cohort Graduation Rates (ACGR) differ from Averaged Freshmen Graduation Rates (AFGR).

Table WA-13. Reported Voting and Registration of the Voting-Age Population, November 2020

(Numbers in thousands, percent.)

Item	Total population	Total citizen population	Registered			Voted		
			Total registered	Percent registered (total population)	Percent registered (total citizen population)	Total voted	Percent voted (total population)	Percent voted (total citizen population)
U.S. Total	252,274	231,593	168,308	66.7	72.7	154,628	61.3	66.8
State Total..............................	5,993	5,389	4,029	67.2	74.8	3,854	64.3	71.5
Sex								
Male	2,947	2,638	1,921	65.2	72.8	1,806	61.3	68.5
Female	3,046	2,751	2,109	69.2	76.7	2,047	67.2	74.4
Race								
White alone............................	4,735	4,413	3,452	72.9	78.2	3,309	69.9	75.0
White, non-Hispanic alone	4,122	3,985	3,177	77.1	79.7	3,070	74.5	77.0
Black alone............................	257	210	136	53.1	64.7	130	50.8	61.9
Asian alone	557	334	213	38.3	63.9	210	37.7	62.8
Hispanic (of any race)...............	680	485	296	43.6	61.0	261	38.4	53.7
White alone or in combination	4,928	4,593	3,573	72.5	77.8	3,426	69.5	74.6
Black alone or in combination	331	285	170	51.2	59.5	164	49.4	57.4
Asian alone or in combination......	590	363	227	38.5	62.5	224	37.9	61.6
Age								
18 to 24 years	556	516	287	51.6	55.6	271	48.6	52.4
25 to 34 years	1,169	989	697	59.6	70.5	654	56.0	66.1
35 to 44 years	1,148	983	739	64.4	75.1	698	60.8	71.0
45 to 64 years	1,828	1,650	1,319	72.2	79.9	1,264	69.1	76.6
65 years and over	1,292	1,250	987	76.4	79.0	967	74.8	77.3

Table WA-14. Crime

(Number, rate per 100,000. Data are derived from the FBI Uniform Crime Reports.)

Item	State			U.S.		
	2019	2020	Percent change	2019	2020	Percent change
TOTAL POPULATION[1]	7,614,024	7,693,612	1.0	328,329,953	329,484,123	0.4
VIOLENT CRIME						
Number...............................	23,095	22,596	-2.2	1,250,393	1,313,105	5.0
Rate	303.3	293.7	-3.2	380.8	398.5	4.6
Murder and Nonnegligent Manslaughter						
Number...............................	205	301	46.8	16,669	21,570	29.4
Rate	2.7	3.9	45.3	5.1	6.5	28.9
Rape[2]						
Number...............................	3,497	2,677	-23.4	143,224	126,430	-11.7
Rate	45.9	34.8	-24.2	43.6	38.4	-12.0
Robbery						
Number...............................	5,356	5,183	-3.2	268,483	243,600	-9.3
Rate	70.3	67.4	-4.2	81.8	73.9	-9.6
Aggravated Assault						
Number...............................	14,037	14,435	2.8	822,017	921,505	12.1
Rate	184.4	187.6	1.8	250.4	279.7	11.7
PROPERTY CRIME						
Number...............................	207,539	210,223	1.3	6,995,235	6,452,038	-7.8
Rate	2,725.7	2,732.4	0.2	2,130.6	1,958.2	-8.1
Burglary						
Number...............................	34,976	40,167	14.8	1,118,096	1,035,314	-7.4
Rate	459.4	522.1	13.7	340.5	314.2	-7.7
Larceny-Theft						
Number...............................	147,778	142,657	-3.5	5,152,267	4,606,324	-10.6
Rate	1,940.9	1,854.2	-4.5	1,569.2	1,398.0	-10.9
Motor Vehicle Theft						
Number...............................	24,785	27,399	10.5	724,872	810,400	11.8
Rate	325.5	356.1	9.4	220.8	246.0	11.4

NOTE: Although arson data are included in the trend and clearance tables, sufficient data are not available to estimate totals for this offense. Therefore, no arson data are published in this table.
- = Zero or rounds to zero.
[1] Population figures are U.S. Census Bureau provisional estimates as of July 1, 2020.
[2] The figures shown in the rape (revised definition) column were estimated using the revised Uniform Crime Reporting (UCR) definition of rape.

Table WA-15. State Government Finances, 2020

(Dollar amounts in thousands, percent distribution.)

Item	Dollars	Percent distribution
Total Revenue	69,823,495	100.0
General revenue	54,977,592	78.7
Intergovernmental revenue	16,189,594	23.2
Taxes	29,013,411	41.6
General sales	16929551	24.2
Selective sales	4,829,876	6.9
License taxes	1,615,374	2.3
Individual income tax	0	-
Corporate income tax	0	-
Other taxes	5,638,610	8.1
Current charges	6,407,434	9.2
Miscellaneous general revenue	3,367,153	4.8
Utility revenue	0	-
Liquor stores revenue	0	-
Insurance trust revenue[1]	14,845,903	21.3
Total Expenditure	69,206,425	100.0
Intergovernmental expenditure	18,305,590	26.5
Direct expenditure	50,900,835	73.5
Current operation	34,932,013	50.5
Capital outlay	2,296,361	3.3
Insurance benefits and repayments	10,781,948	15.6
Assistance and subsidies	1,455,087	2.1
Interest on debt	1,435,426	2.1
Exhibit: Salaries and wages	10,008,812	14.5
Total Expenditure	69,206,425	100.0
General expenditure	58,382,367	84.4
Intergovernmental expenditure	18,305,590	26.5
Direct expenditure	40,076,777	57.9
General expenditure, by function:		
Education	24,358,745	35.2
Public welfare	13,853,312	20.0
Hospitals	4,105,599	5.9
Health	3,819,425	5.5
Highways	3,199,857	4.6
Police protection	498,613	0.7
Correction	1,198,040	1.7
Natural resources	954,325	1.4
Parks and recreation	289,957	0.4
Governmental administration	1,048,744	1.5
Interest on general debt	1,435,426	2.1
Other and unallocable	2,981,665	4.3
Utility expenditure	166,013	0.2
Liquor stores expenditure	0	-
Insurance trust expenditure	10,781,948	15.6
Debt at End of Fiscal Year	29,658,660	X
Cash and Security Holdings	154,379,587	X

X = Not applicable.
- = Zero or rounds to zero.
[1] Within insurance trust revenue, net earnings of state retirement systems is a calculated statistic (the item code in the data file is X08), and thus can be positive or negative. Net earnings is the sum of earnings on investments plus gains on investments minus losses on investments. The change made in 2002 for asset valuation from book to market value in accordance with Statement 34 of the Governmental Accounting Standards Board is reflected in the calculated statistics.

Table WA-16. State Government Tax Collections, 2021

(Dollars in thousands, percent.)

Item	Dollars	Percent distribution
Total Taxes	32,614,091	100.0
Property taxes	4,350,245	13.3
Sales and gross receipts	24,013,256	73.6
General sales and gross receipts	19,056,609	58.4
Selective sales and gross receipts	4,956,647	15.2
Alcoholic beverages	472,949	1.5
Amusements	281	-
Insurance premiums	683,639	2.1
Motor fuels	1,518,342	4.7
Pari-mutuels	883	-
Public utilities	611,339	1.9
Tobacco products	386,660	1.2
Other selective sales	1,282,554	3.9
Licenses	2,072,634	6.4
Alcoholic beverages	213,953	0.7
Amusements	13,791	-
Corporations in general	50,387	0.2
Hunting and fishing	47,739	0.1
Motor vehicle	998,237	3.1
Motor vehicle operators	125,839	0.4
Public utilities	21,114	0.1
Occupation and business, NEC	438,328	1.3
Other licenses	163,246	0.5
Income taxes	X	-
Individual income	X	-
Corporation net income	X	-
Other taxes	2,177,956	6.7
Death and gift	324,421	1.0
Documentary and stock transfer	1,810,495	5.6
Severance	43,020	0.1
Taxes, NEC	20	-

X = Not applicable.
- = Zero or rounds to zero.

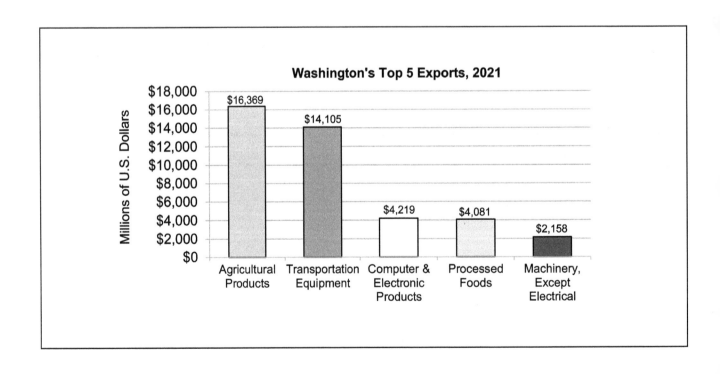

WEST VIRGINIA

Facts and Figures

Location: East central United States; bordered on the N by Ohio and Pennsylvania, on the E by Pennsylvania, Maryland, and Virginia, on the S by Virginia and Kentucky, and on the W by Kentucky and Ohio

Area: 24,230 sq. mi. (62,755 sq. km.); rank—41st

Population: 1,782,959 (2021 est.); rank—39th

Principal Cities: capital—Charleston; largest—Charleston

Statehood: June 20, 1863; 35th state

U.S. Congress: 2 senators, 3 representatives

State Motto: *Montani semper liberi* (Mountaineers are always free)

State Songs: "West Virginia Hills"; "This Is My West Virginia"; "West Virginia, My Home Sweet Home"

State Nickname: The Mountain State

Abbreviations: WV; W. Va.

State Symbols: flower—rhododendron (great laurel); tree—sugar maple; bird—cardinal

At a Glance

- West Virginia experienced the largest population decline among the states from 2010 to 2021, with its population decreasing 3.8 percent.

- West Virginia's median household income was $48,511 in 2020, the 2nd lowest among the states, and 17.1 percent of the state's population lived below the poverty level.

- With 55.3 percent of the voting-age population casting votes, West Virginia had the 2nd lowest voter turnout among the states in the November 2020 election.

- West Virginia had the smallest percent of residents that self-identified as "Hispanic or Latino" in 2021, with 1.9 percent of its population in this category.

- West Virginia had the highest homeownership rate of all the states in 2021, with 79.0 percent of homes being owner-occupied.

Table WV-1. Population by Age, Sex, Race, and Hispanic Origin

(Number, percent, except where noted.)

Sex, age, race, and Hispanic origin	2000	2010	2021	Percent change, 2010–2021
Total Population..	1,808,344	1,852,994	1,782,959	-3.8
Percent of total U.S. population	0.6	0.6	0.5	X
Sex				
Male..	879,170	913,586	889,098	-2.7
Female	929,174	939,408	893,861	-4.8
Age				
Under 5 years..	101,805	104,060	89,407	-14.1
5 to 19 years...	352,910	335,153	312,473	-6.8
20 to 64 years...	1,076,734	1,116,377	1,011,659	-9.4
65 years and over..	276,895	297,404	369,420	24.2
Median age (years)	38.9	41.3	42.8	3.6
Race and Hispanic Origin				
One race				
White...	1,718,777	1,746,513	1,660,372	-4.9
Black...	57,232	63,885	66,240	3.7
American Indian and Alaska Native	3,606	3,975	4,722	18.8
Asian	9,434	12,637	15,746	24.6
Native Hawaiian or Other Pacific Islander	400	485	524	8.0
Two or more races..	15,788	25,499	35,355	38.7
Hispanic (of any race)..	12,279	23,679	33,684	42.3

NOTE: Population figures for 2021 are July 1 estimates. The 2000 and 2010 estimates are taken from the respective censuses.
- = Zero or rounds to zero.
X = Not applicable.

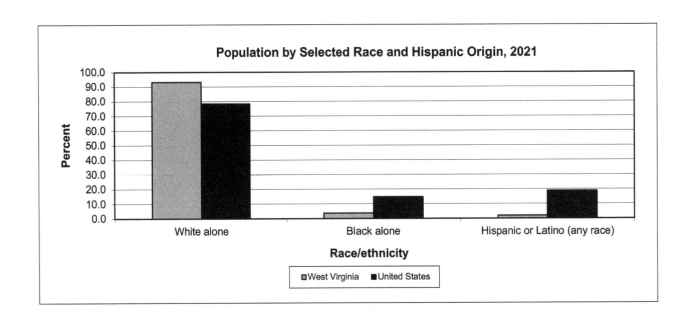

Table WV-2. Marital Status

(Number, percent distribution.)

Sex, age, race, and Hispanic origin	2000	2010	2020 [1]
Males, 15 Years and Over	710,443	750,542	739,470
Never married	25.4	30.3	31.4
Now married, except separated..	59.9	52.1	50.9
Separated...	1.3	1.6	1.3
Widowed...	3.2	3.4	3.7
Divorced...	10.1	12.6	12.7
Females, 15 Years and Over	768,858	785,182	766,505
Never married	19.1	22.6	24.0
Now married, except separated..	54.7	49.7	49.0
Separated...	1.6	1.7	1.5
Widowed...	13.9	12.8	11.7
Divorced...	10.8	13.2	13.7

[1] 2020 ACS 5-Year estimates. 1-Year estimates were not released for 2020 due to the impact of COVID-19 on data collection that year.

Table WV-3. Households and Housing Characteristics

(Number, percent, dollars.)

Item	2000	2010	2020 [1]	Average annual percent change, 2010–2020
Total Households...	736,481	741,940	734,235	-0.1
Family households	504,055	485,652	470,391	-0.4
Married-couple family	397,499	372,301	355,680	-0.6
Other family	106,556	113,351	114,711	0.2
Male householder, no wife present........................	27,436	28,515	35,377	3.4
Female householder, no husband present................	79,120	84,836	79,334	-0.9
Nonfamily households	232,426	256,288	263,844	0.4
Householder living alone	199,587	219,848	221,708	0.1
Householder not living alone	32,839	36,440	42,136	2.2
Housing Characteristics				
Total housing units	844,623	882,213	893,615	0.2
Occupied housing units	736,481	741,940	734,235	-0.1
Owner occupied	553,699	553,429	540,786	-0.3
Renter occupied	182,782	188,511	193,449	0.4
Average household size..	2.40	2.43	2.40	-0.2
Financial Characteristics				
Median gross rent of renter-occupied housing	401	571	732	4.0
Median monthly owner costs for housing units with a mortgage	713	918	1,058	2.2
Median value of owner-occupied housing units............	72,800	95,100	123,200	4.2

[1] 2020 ACS 5-Year estimates. 1-Year estimates were not released for 2020 due to the impact of COVID-19 on data collection that year.

Table WV-4. Migration, Origin, and Language

(Number, percent.)

Characteristic	State 2016-2020 [1]	U.S. 2016-2020 [1]
Residence 1 Year Ago		
Population 1 year and over	1,788,412	322,943,283
Same house...	88.6	86.2
Different house in the U.S.	11.2	13.2
Same county	6.2	7.7
Different county	5.0	5.5
Same state	2.7	3.2
Different state	2.3	2.3
Abroad	0.2	0.6
Place of Birth		
Native born	1,777,842	282,443,680
Male	49.5	49.4
Female	50.5	50.6
Foreign born	29,584	44,125,628
Male	48.0	48.6
Female	52.0	51.4
Foreign born; naturalized U.S. citizen...	14,988	22,456,684
Male	43.6	46.1
Female	56.4	53.9
Foreign born; not a U.S. citizen	14,596	21,668,944
Male	52.5	51.1
Female	47.5	48.9
Entered 2010 or later	30.9	22.8
Entered 2000 to 2009	22.7	25.1
Entered before 2000...	46.4	52.1
World Region of Birth, Foreign		
Foreign-born population, excluding population born at sea	29,584	44,125,628
Europe	18.4	10.8
Asia...	45.5	31.3
Africa	8.1	5.4
Oceania	1.3	0.6
Latin America..	22.3	50.0
North America	4.4	1.9
Language Spoken at Home and Ability to Speak English		
Population 5 years and over..	1,711,734	306,919,116
English only	97.5	78.5
Language other than English..	2.5	21.5
Speaks English less than "very well"..	0.7	8.2

[1] 2020 ACS 5-Year estimates. 1-Year estimates were not released for 2020 due to the impact of COVID-19 on data collection that year.
NA = Not available.
X = Not applicable.
- = Zero or rounds to zero.

Table WV-5. Median Income and Poverty Status, 2020[1]

(Number, percent, except as noted.)

Characteristic	State Number	State Percent	U.S. Number	U.S. Percent
Median Income				
Households (dollars)	48,037	X	64,994	X
Families (dollars)	61,707	X	80,069	X
Below Poverty Level (All People)	300,152	17.1	40,910,326	12.8
Sex				
Male	133,773	15.5	18,171,512	11.6
Female	166,379	18.7	22,738,814	14.0
Age				
Under 18 years	82,218	23.1	12,598,699	17.5
Related children under 18 years	80,352	22.7	12,306,532	17.2
18 to 64 years	183,632	17.5	23,554,920	12.1
65 years and over	34,302	9.8	4,756,707	9.3

X = Not applicable.
[1] 2020 ACS 5-Year estimates. 1-Year estimates were not released for 2020 due to the impact of COVID-19 on data collection that year.

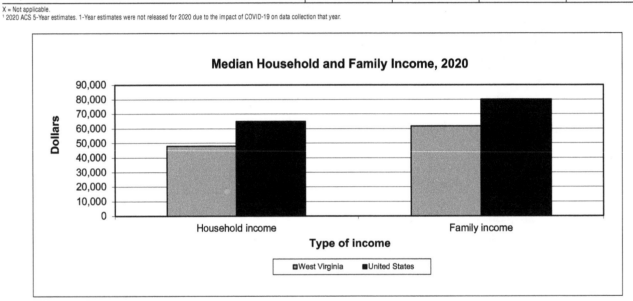

Table WV-6. Health Insurance Coverage Status for the Civilian Noninstitutionalized Population and Children Under 19 Years of Age

(Number, percent.)

Item	2011	2012	2013	2014	2015	2016	2017	2018	2019	2020 [2]
Civilian Noninstitutionalized Population	1,826,485	1,826,512	1,824,821	1,820,836	1,815,505	1,802,572	1,787,126	1,776,965	1,762,052	1,778,080
Covered by Private or Public Insurance										
Number	1,554,198	1,562,703	1,569,752	1,664,746	1,707,423	1,706,690	1,678,237	1,662,859	1,644,408	1,668,236
Percent	85.1	85.6	86.0	91.4	94.0	94.7	93.9	93.6	93.3	93.8
Uninsured										
Number	272,287	263,809	255,069	156,090	108,082	95,882	108,889	114,106	117,644	109,844
Percent	14.9	14.4	14.0	8.6	6.0	5.3	6.1	6.4	6.7	6.2
Percent in the U.S. not covered	15.1	14.8	14.5	11.7	9.4	8.6	8.7	8.9	9.2	8.7
Children Under 19 Years of Age[1]	385,302	382,980	381,156	382,225	378,396	375,790	399,352	388,032	380,871	387,727
Covered by Private or Public Insurance										
Number	368,308	367,957	360,851	370,788	367,613	368,007	388,819	374,932	367,446	376,610
Percent	95.6	96.1	94.7	97.0	97.2	97.9	97.4	96.6	96.5	97.1
Uninsured										
Number	16,994	15,023	20,305	11,437	10,783	7,783	10,533	13,100	13,425	11,117
Percent	4.4	3.9	5.3	3.0	2.8	2.1	2.6	3.4	3.5	2.9
Percent in the U.S. not covered	7.5	7.2	7.1	6.0	4.8	4.5	5.0	5.2	5.7	5.2

[1] Data for years prior to 2017 are for individuals under 18 years of age.
[2] 2020 ACS 5-Year estimates. 1-Year estimates were not released for 2020 due to the impact of COVID-19 on data collection that year. Data is not comparable to previous years, which are based on 1-year estimates.

Table WV-7. Employment Status by Demographic Group, 2021

(Numbers in thousands, percent.)

Characteristic	Civilian noninstitutional population	Civilian labor force		Employed		Unemployed	
		Number	Percent of population	Number	Percent of population	Number	Percent of population
Total..	1,437	783	54.5	746	51.9	37	4.7
Sex							
Male..	703	416	59.2	395	56.2	22	5.2
Female.....................................	734	367	49.9	351	47.8	16	4.3
Race, Sex, and Hispanic Origin							
White.......................................	1,356	729	53.7	696	51.3	33	4.5
Male....................................	662	388	58.6	369	55.7	19	4.9
Female.................................	694	341	49.1	327	47.1	14	4.1
Black or African American...........	NA	NA	NA	NA	NA	NA	NA
Male....................................	NA	NA	NA	NA	NA	NA	NA
Female.................................	NA	NA	NA	NA	NA	NA	NA
Hispanic or Latino ethnicity[1]......	NA	NA	NA	NA	NA	NA	NA
Male....................................	NA	NA	NA	NA	NA	NA	NA
Female.................................	NA	NA	NA	NA	NA	NA	NA
Age							
16 to 19 years..........................	NA	NA	NA	NA	NA	NA	NA
20 to 24 years..........................	98	70	71.3	65	65.8	6	7.8
25 to 34 years..........................	207	166	80.3	157	76.1	9	5.2
35 to 44 years..........................	221	170	76.9	162	73.5	8	4.4
45 to 54 years..........................	218	163	74.9	157	71.9	6	3.9
55 to 64 years..........................	236	129	54.7	125	53.1	4	3.0
65 years and over......................	380	56	14.8	55	14.4	2	2.9

NOTE: Data in Table 7 are from the Current Population Survey (CPS) and do not match the estimates in Table 8. See notes and definitions for further information.
[1] May be of any race.
NA = Not available.

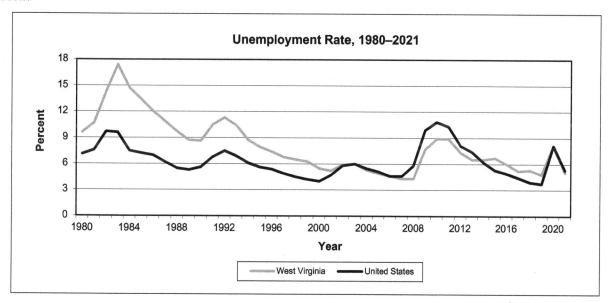

Unemployment Rate, 1980–2021

Table WV-8. Employment Status of the Civilian Noninstitutional Population Age 16 Years and Over

(Number, percent.)

Year	Civilian labor force	Civilian participation rate	Employed	Unemployed	Unemployment rate
2010..	810,101	54.9	739,891	70,210	8.7
2011..	806,568	54.3	743,346	63,222	7.8
2012..	808,022	54.3	749,587	58,435	7.2
2013..	799,481	53.8	745,849	53,632	6.7
2014..	795,733	53.6	743,955	51,778	6.5
2015..	791,526	53.5	739,455	52,071	6.6
2016..	785,104	53.3	737,205	47,899	6.1
2017..	784,744	53.5	743,786	40,958	5.2
2018..	793,715	54.4	752,726	40,989	5.2
2019..	796,776	54.8	757,484	39,292	4.9
2020..	783,027	54.1	719,175	63,852	8.2
2021..	788,826	54.7	749,132	39,694	5.0

Table WV-9. Employment and Average Wages by Industry

(Estimates are based on the 2012 North American Industry Classification System [NAICS].)

Industry	2013	2014	2015	2016	2017	2018	2019	2020
	Number of Jobs							
Wage and Salary Employment by Industry.........................	743,403	740,039	733,992	721,162	720,173	730,807	725,804	679,085
Farm Wage and Salary Employment...............................	1,567	1,703	1,912	1,575	1,823	1,577	1,546	1,546
Nonfarm Wage and Salary Employment...........................	741,836	738,336	732,080	719,587	718,350	729,230	724,258	677,539
Private wage and salary employment...	583,486	581,584	576,322	563,322	563,483	576,464	570,751	527,138
Forestry, fishing, and related activities	1,366	1,412	1,481	1,512	1,486	1,439	1,488	1,268
Mining..	30,889	29,202	25,012	19,344	20,909	21,677	21,516	16,676
Utilities..	5,178	5,204	5,051	5,167	5,299	5,334	5,275	5,033
Construction	35,305	34,632	33,267	30,806	32,334	41,151	36,306	30,333
Manufacturing...	48,468	47,885	47,756	46,878	46,603	46,967	47,001	44,454
Durable goods manufacturing...	29,149	28,942	28,696	28,067	27,999	28,526	28,328	25,945
Nondurable goods manufacturing...................................	19,319	18,943	19,060	18,811	18,604	18,441	18,673	18,509
Wholesale trade	23,015	22,721	22,356	21,225	20,803	20,462	20,288	19,191
Retail trade..	88,212	87,324	87,340	87,425	85,311	83,611	80,944	76,961
Transportation and warehousing..	20,163	20,862	21,468	20,253	20,602	21,574	21,601	19,815
Information...	9,515	9,591	9,646	9,667	8,619	8,278	8,074	7,204
Finance and insurance	19,943	19,646	19,304	19,083	18,974	19,312	19,451	19,511
Real estate and rental and leasing	6,800	6,924	6,951	6,749	6,573	6,722	6,826	6,527
Professional, scientific, and technical services	26,131	26,359	26,116	25,174	25,625	27,124	26,992	25,625
Management of companies and enterprises.........................	6,490	6,381	6,406	6,247	6,469	6,930	7,086	7,656
Administrative and waste services......................................	32,744	34,625	35,067	34,578	34,688	35,437	35,428	32,916
Educational services	8,966	8,912	8,962	9,491	9,461	9,606	9,766	8,158
Health care and social assistance......................................	114,079	113,942	114,846	115,653	115,937	116,875	117,770	117,631
Arts, entertainment, and recreation....................................	7,711	7,919	7,673	7,659	7,933	7,977	8,308	6,783
Accommodation and food services.....................................	67,287	66,900	67,331	66,974	66,908	66,615	67,158	54,938
Other services, except public administration........................	31,224	31,143	30,289	29,437	28,949	29,373	29,473	26,458
Government and government enterprises................................	158,350	156,752	155,758	156,265	154,867	152,766	153,507	150,401
	Dollars							
Average Wages and Salaries by Industry	39,656	40,634	41,195	41,158	42,871	45,537	46,022	47,885
Average Farm Wages and Salaries	23,267	22,682	16,503	22,992	18,027	19,261	15,602	15,152
Average Nonfarm Wages and Salaries	39,690	40,676	41,260	41,198	42,934	45,594	46,087	47,960
Average private wages and salaries	39,587	40,594	41,134	40,952	43,012	45,967	46,207	47,737
Forestry, fishing, and related activities	27,758	28,929	29,738	30,026	30,334	30,896	33,495	35,227
Mining..	80,113	80,803	78,790	75,296	80,779	84,040	84,438	82,501
Utilities..	81,296	85,132	88,951	89,160	91,707	93,303	97,407	101,597
Construction	51,957	53,522	53,331	52,550	57,999	72,158	64,460	60,426
Manufacturing...	53,076	55,058	55,910	56,523	58,657	60,501	61,092	62,378
Durable goods manufacturing...	49,675	51,405	51,693	52,289	54,373	56,835	57,839	58,445
Nondurable goods manufacturing...................................	58,209	60,638	62,259	62,840	65,106	66,172	66,027	67,892
Wholesale trade	52,197	54,980	55,982	56,166	58,694	60,945	63,421	65,822
Retail trade..	24,387	24,633	25,612	26,022	26,583	27,545	28,454	30,322
Transportation and warehousing..	48,752	50,045	50,354	49,873	51,742	51,562	52,504	53,708
Information...	47,609	48,738	51,247	50,706	50,441	52,553	53,247	58,121
Finance and insurance	47,645	49,393	50,858	52,058	54,909	57,317	58,923	61,782
Real estate and rental and leasing	36,538	37,839	37,967	37,454	38,818	42,801	42,996	43,010
Professional, scientific, and technical services	53,746	55,173	56,153	56,925	59,814	63,564	61,997	63,765
Management of companies and enterprises.........................	69,869	72,396	73,968	72,210	77,409	82,066	85,345	80,638
Administrative and waste services......................................	29,576	31,294	31,921	32,173	34,222	36,761	37,973	39,253
Educational services	24,801	24,749	25,205	24,596	25,505	25,266	26,391	30,671
Health care and social assistance......................................	39,623	41,005	42,735	43,911	45,604	47,101	48,823	51,477
Arts, entertainment, and recreation....................................	19,105	19,271	19,999	19,987	19,793	20,573	20,612	22,102
Accommodation and food services.....................................	17,678	18,047	18,729	19,151	19,582	20,546	20,878	20,371
Other services, except public administration........................	27,723	28,221	29,082	29,892	31,243	32,518	33,338	35,620
Government and government enterprises................................	40,069	40,978	41,723	42,086	42,653	44,189	45,642	48,742

Table WV-10. Employment Characteristics by Family Type

(Number, percent.)

Family type and labor force status	2018 Total	2018 Families with own children under 18 years	2019 Total	2019 Families with own children under 18 years	2020 [1] Total	2020 [1] Families with own children under 18 years
All Families...	461,911	164,592	470,472	166,204	470,391	169,583
FAMILY TYPE AND LABOR FORCE STATUS						
Opposite-Sex Married-Couple Families............................	347,271	108,963	352,587	109,336	353,287	113,390
Both husband and wife in labor force...	39.3	59.7	41.2	61.8	41.6	63.5
Husband in labor force, wife not in labor force	21.2	28.4	20.3	26.4	20.2	25.8
Wife in labor force, husband not in labor force	10.6	6.8	12.0	7.6	10.6	6.5
Both husband and wife not in labor force....................................	28.0	4.9	26.2	3.5	27.6	4.2
Other Families	114,640	55,629	117,885	56,868	114,711	55,676
Female householder, no spouse present	70.5	74.1	67.3	69.2	69.2	70.1
In labor force..	40.2	59.6	37.4	50.3	39.7	52.8
Not in labor force	30.3	14.5	29.9	18.8	29.5	17.4
Male householder, no spouse present......................................	29.5	25.9	32.7	30.8	30.8	29.9
In labor force..	18.2	21.4	20.3	25.1	19.6	24.6
Not in labor force	11.3	4.5	12.4	5.7	11.3	5.2

[1] 2020 ACS 5-Year estimates. 1-Year estimates were not released for 2020 due to the impact of COVID-19 on data collection that year. Data is not comparable to previous years, which are based on 1-year estimates.

Table WV-11. School Enrollment and Educational Attainment, 2020[1]

(Number, percent.)

Item	State	U.S.
Enrollment		
Total population 3 years and over, enrolled in school	378,326	80,497,960
Enrolled in nursery school or preschool (percent)..	5.2	6.1
Enrolled in kindergarten (percent)...	4.8	5.0
Enrolled in elementary school, grades 1-8 (percent)...	42.9	40.4
Enrolled in high school, grades 9-12 (percent)..	21.4	21.0
Enrolled in college or graduate school (percent)..	25.6	27.6
Attainment		
Total population 25 years and over	1,283,869	222,836,834
Less than ninth grade (percent)	4.1	4.9
9th to 12th grade, no diploma (percent)	8.3	6.6
High school graduate, including equivalency (percent)...	40.0	26.7
Some college, no degree (percent)...	18.7	20.3
Associate's degree (percent)..	7.6	8.6
Bachelor's degree (percent)	12.7	20.2
Graduate or professional degree (percent)..	8.6	12.7
High school graduate or higher (percent)	87.6	88.5
Bachelor's degree or higher (percent)..	21.3	32.9

[1] 2020 ACS 5-Year estimates. 1-Year estimates were not released for 2020 due to the impact of COVID-19 on data collection that year.

Table WV-12. Public School Characteristics and Educational Indicators

(Number, percent; data derived from National Center of Education Statistics.)

Item	State	U.S.
Public Elementary and Secondary Schools		
Number of regular school districts, 2018-19	55	13,452
Number of operational schools, 2019-20..	725	98,469
Percent charter schools	0.0	7.7
Total public school enrollment, Fall 2019..	263,486	50,796,445
Percent charter school enrollment	0.0	6.8
Student-teacher ratio, Fall 2019	14.0	15.9
Expenditures per student (unadjusted dollars), 2018-19	12,269	13,187
Four-year adjusted cohort graduation rate (ACGR), 2018-2019[1]...........................	91.3	85.8
Students eligible for free or reduced-price lunch (percent), 2019-20....................	51.2	52.1
English language learners (percent), Fall 2019	0.8	10.4
Students age 3 to 21 served under IDEA, part B (percent), 2020-21	18.1	14.5

Public Schools by Type, 2019-20	Number	Percent of state public schools
Total number of schools..	725	100.0
Special education	2	0.3
Vocational education	34	4.7
Alternative education	34	4.7

[1] Adjusted Cohort Graduation Rates (ACGR) differ from Averaged Freshmen Graduation Rates (AFGR).
NA = Not available.

Table WV-13. Reported Voting and Registration of the Voting-Age Population, November 2020

(Numbers in thousands, percent.)

Item	Total population	Total citizen population	Registered			Voted		
			Total registered	Percent registered (total population)	Percent registered (total citizen population)	Total voted	Percent voted (total population)	Percent voted (total citizen population)
U.S. Total	252,274	231,593	168,308	66.7	72.7	154,628	61.3	66.8
State Total................................	1,397	1,379	928	66.4	67.3	773	55.3	56.1
Sex								
Male	684	675	457	66.9	67.7	379	55.4	56.1
Female	714	704	471	65.9	66.8	395	55.3	56.0
Race								
White alone..............................	1,324	1,314	879	66.4	66.9	735	55.5	56.0
White, non-Hispanic alone	1,303	1,301	871	66.9	67.0	729	56.0	56.1
Black alone..............................	45	42	26	B	B	18	B	B
Asian alone	5	1	1	B	B	1	B	B
Hispanic (of any race)...............	23	15	10	B	B	8	B	B
White alone or in combination	1,346	1,336	900	66.9	67.4	754	56.0	56.5
Black alone or in combination...........	54	50	34	B	B	25	B	B
Asian alone or in combination..........	6	2	2	B	B	2	B	B
Age								
18 to 24 years.........................	155	153	71	46.1	46.7	53	34.2	34.6
25 to 34 years.........................	195	191	117	60.1	61.3	79	40.7	41.5
35 to 44 years.........................	213	209	144	67.6	68.7	119	56.2	57.1
45 to 64 years.........................	471	462	319	67.9	69.1	274	58.3	59.3
65 years and over	365	364	276	75.7	75.9	247	67.8	68.0

B = Base is less than 75,000 and therefore too small to show the derived measure.

Table WV-14. Crime

(Number, rate per 100,000. Data are derived from the FBI Uniform Crime Reports.)

Item	State			U.S.		
	2019	2020	Percent change	2019	2020	Percent change
TOTAL POPULATION[1]	1,795,263	1,784,787	-0.6	328,329,953	329,484,123	0.4
VIOLENT CRIME						
Number..	5,725	6,352	11.0	1,250,393	1,313,105	5.0
Rate	318.9	355.9	11.6	380.8	398.5	4.6
Murder and Nonnegligent Manslaughter						
Number..	100	117	17.0	16,669	21,570	29.4
Rate	5.6	6.6	17.7	5.1	6.5	28.9
Rape[2]						
Number..	818	832	1.7	143,224	126,430	-11.7
Rate	45.6	46.6	2.3	43.6	38.4	-12.0
Robbery						
Number..	347	369	6.3	268,483	243,600	-9.3
Rate	19.3	20.7	7.0	81.8	73.9	-9.6
Aggravated Assault						
Number..	4,460	5,034	12.9	822,017	921,505	12.1
Rate	248.4	282.1	13.5	250.4	279.7	11.7
PROPERTY CRIME						
Number..	27,327	24,976	-8.6	6,995,235	6,452,038	-7.8
Rate	1,522.2	1,399.4	-8.1	2,130.6	1,958.2	-8.1
Burglary						
Number..	5,282	4,877	-7.7	1,118,096	1,035,314	-7.4
Rate	294.2	273.3	-7.1	340.5	314.2	-7.7
Larceny-Theft						
Number..	19,825	17,828	-10.1	5,152,267	4,606,324	-10.6
Rate	1,104.3	998.9	-9.5	1,569.2	1,398.0	-10.9
Motor Vehicle Theft						
Number..	2,220	2,271	2.3	724,872	810,400	11.8
Rate	123.7	127.2	2.9	220.8	246.0	11.4

NOTE: Although arson data are included in the trend and clearance tables, sufficient data are not available to estimate totals for this offense. Therefore, no arson data are published in this table.
- = Zero or rounds to zero.
[1] Population figures are U.S. Census Bureau provisional estimates as of July 1, 2020.
[2] The figures shown in the rape (revised definition) column were estimated using the revised Uniform Crime Reporting (UCR) definition of rape.

Table WV-15. State Government Finances, 2020

(Dollar amounts in thousands, percent distribution.)

Item	Dollars	Percent distribution
Total Revenue	16,581,140	100.0
General revenue	14,887,695	89.8
Intergovernmental revenue	6,722,586	40.5
Taxes	5,461,781	32.9
General sales	1386571	8.4
Selective sales	1,432,406	8.6
License taxes	256,240	1.5
Individual income tax	1947946	11.7
Corporate income tax	151,989	0.9
Other taxes	286,629	1.7
Current charges	1,682,062	10.1
Miscellaneous general revenue	1,021,266	6.2
Utility revenue	3,220	-
Liquor stores revenue	116751	0.7
Insurance trust revenue[1]	1,573,474	9.5
Total Expenditure	16,559,564	100.0
Intergovernmental expenditure	2,614,152	15.8
Direct expenditure	13,945,412	84.2
Current operation	10,045,395	60.7
Capital outlay	1,305,936	7.9
Insurance benefits and repayments	1,917,207	11.6
Assistance and subsidies	354,551	2.1
Interest on debt	322,323	1.9
Exhibit: Salaries and wages	2,048,286	12.4
Total Expenditure	16,559,564	100.0
General expenditure	14,536,023	87.8
Intergovernmental expenditure	2,614,152	15.8
Direct expenditure	11,921,871	72.0
General expenditure, by function:		
Education	4,482,487	27.1
Public welfare	5,017,298	30.3
Hospitals	176,515	1.1
Health	332,067	2.0
Highways	1,755,370	10.6
Police protection	94,504	0.6
Correction	373,623	2.3
Natural resources	274,701	1.7
Parks and recreation	71,731	0.4
Governmental administration	695,357	4.2
Interest on general debt	322,323	1.9
Other and unallocable	929,939	5.6
Utility expenditure	23,123	0.1
Liquor stores expenditure	93319	0.6
Insurance trust expenditure	1,917,207	11.6
Debt at End of Fiscal Year	11,625,729	X
Cash and Security Holdings	23,138,406	X

X = Not applicable.
- = Zero or rounds to zero.
[1] Within insurance trust revenue, net earnings of state retirement systems is a calculated statistic (the item code in the data file is X08), and thus can be positive or negative. Net earnings is the sum of earnings on investments plus gains on investments minus losses on investments. The change made in 2002 for asset valuation from book to market value in accordance with Statement 34 of the Governmental Accounting Standards Board is reflected in the calculated statistics.

Table WV-16. State Government Tax Collections, 2021

(Dollars in thousands, percent.)

Item	Dollars	Percent distribution
Total Taxes	6,046,197	100.0
Property taxes	8,122	0.1
Sales and gross receipts	2,968,554	49.1
General sales and gross receipts	1,537,245	25.4
Selective sales and gross receipts	1,431,309	23.7
Alcoholic beverages	17,304	0.3
Amusements	27,584	0.5
Insurance premiums	118,061	2.0
Motor fuels	399,542	6.6
Pari-mutuels	2,850	-
Public utilities	126,206	2.1
Tobacco products	171,187	2.8
Other selective sales	568,575	9.4
Licenses	196,902	3.3
Alcoholic beverages	3,035	0.1
Amusements	4,394	0.1
Corporations in general	756	-
Hunting and fishing	15,302	0.3
Motor vehicle	4,562	0.1
Motor vehicle operators	148,902	2.5
Public utilities	389	-
Occupation and business, NEC	14,521	0.2
Other licenses	5,041	0.1
Income taxes	2,574,275	42.6
Individual income	2,253,788	37.3
Corporation net income	320,487	5.3
Other taxes	298,344	4.9
Death and gift	X	-
Documentary and stock transfer	15,913	0.3
Severance	274,256	4.5
Taxes, NEC	8,175	0.1

- = Zero or rounds to zero.
X = Not applicable.

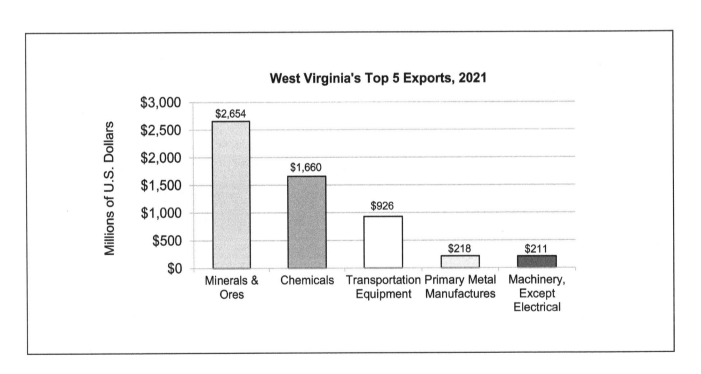

West Virginia's Top 5 Exports, 2021

WISCONSIN

Facts and Figures

Location: North central United States; bordered on the N by Michigan and Lake Superior, on the E by Lake Michigan, on the S by Illinois, and on the W by Iowa and Minnesota

Area: 65,498 sq. mi. (169,639 sq. km.); rank—23rd

Population: 5,895,908 (2021 est.); rank—20th

Principal Cities: capital—Madison; largest—Milwaukee

Statehood: May 29, 1848; 30th state

U.S. Congress: 2 senators, 8 representatives

State Motto: Forward

State Song: "On, Wisconsin!"

State Nickname: The Badger State

Abbreviations: WI; Wis.; Wisc.

State Symbols: flower—wood violet; tree—sugar maple; bird—robin

At a Glance

- With an increase in population of 3.7 percent, Wisconsin ranked 35th among the states in growth from 2010 to 2021.

- Wisconsin's violent crime rate in 2020 was 323.4 per 100,000 population, compared to 398.5 for the entire nation.

- Wisconsin's median household income in 2020 was $63,293, and 11.0 percent of the population lived below the poverty level.

- In the November 2020 election, 71.7 percent of Wisconsin's eligible voters cast ballots, ranking it 5th in the nation for voter turnout.

- The unemployment rate in Wisconsin in 2021 was 3.8 percent, compared to the national rate of 5.3 percent.

Table WI-1. Population by Age, Sex, Race, and Hispanic Origin

(Number, percent, except where noted.)

Sex, age, race, and Hispanic origin	2000	2010	2021	Percent change, 2010–2021
Total Population..	5,363,675	5,686,986	5,895,908	3.7
Percent of total U.S. population	1.9	1.8	1.8	X
Sex				
Male..	2,649,041	2,822,400	2,953,874	4.7
Female..	2,714,634	2,864,586	2,942,034	2.7
Age				
Under 5 years..	342,340	358,443	320,245	-10.7
5 to 19 years...	1,189,753	1,143,753	1,110,757	-2.9
20 to 64 years...	3,129,029	3,407,476	3,407,663	-
65 years and over	702,553	777,314	1,057,243	36.0
Median age (years)..	36.0	38.5	40.1	4.2
Race and Hispanic Origin				
One race				
White	4,769,857	5,036,923	5,106,775	1.4
Black..	304,460	367,021	398,693	8.6
American Indian and Alaska Native	47,228	60,100	71,663	19.2
Asian..	88,763	131,828	186,678	41.6
Native Hawaiian or Other Pacific Islander	1,630	2,505	3,609	44.1
Two or more races..	66,895	88,609	128,490	45.0
Hispanic (of any race)...	192,291	349,366	442,517	26.7

NOTE: Population figures for 2021 are July 1 estimates. The 2000 and 2010 estimates are taken from the respective censuses.
- = Zero or rounds to zero.
X = Not applicable.

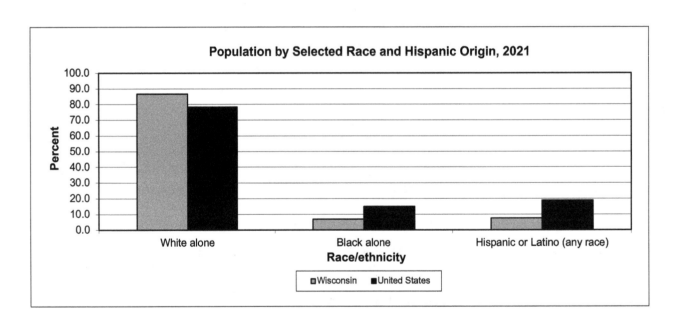

Table WI-2. Marital Status

(Number, percent distribution.)

Sex, age, race, and Hispanic origin	2000	2010	2020 [1]
Males, 15 Years and Over	2,072,397	2,261,022	2,351,501
Never married	30.2	34.1	35.6
Now married, except separated...	57.9	52.1	51.0
Separated..	1.1	1.0	0.8
Widowed...	2.4	2.6	2.5
Divorced...	8.4	10.2	10.0
Females, 15 Years and Over	2,167,164	2,328,733	2,404,783
Never married	24.3	28.1	29.2
Now married, except separated...	54.6	50.1	49.7
Separated..	1.3	1.2	1.0
Widowed...	10.2	9.2	8.4
Divorced...	9.7	11.4	11.7

[1] 2020 ACS 5-Year estimates. 1-Year estimates were not released for 2020 due to the impact of COVID-19 on data collection that year.

Table WI-3. Households and Housing Characteristics

(Number, percent, dollars.)

Item	2000	2010	2020 [1]	Average annual percent change, 2010–2020
Total Households..	2,084,544	2,279,532	2,377,935	0.6
Family households	1,386,815	1,453,332	1,479,364	0.3
Married-couple family	1,108,597	1,125,314	1,148,599	0.3
Other family	278,218	328,018	330,765	0.1
Male householder, no wife present..........................	77,918	96,237	106,274	1.5
Female householder, no husband present...............	200,300	231,781	224,491	-0.4
Nonfamily households	697,729	826,200	898,571	1.3
Householder living alone..	557,875	669,106	715,748	1.0
Householder not living alone.................................	139,854	157,094	182,823	2.3
Housing Characteristics				
Total housing units	2,321,144	2,625,477	2,709,444	0.5
Occupied housing units	2,084,544	2,279,532	2,377,935	0.6
Owner occupied	1,426,361	1,566,039	1,596,500	0.3
Renter occupied	658,183	713,493	781,435	1.4
Average household size..	2.50	2.43	2.38	-0.3
Financial Characteristics				
Median gross rent of renter-occupied housing	540	715	872	3.1
Median monthly owner costs for housing units with a mortgage	1,024	1,404	1,436	0.3
Median value of owner-occupied housing units...........	112,200	169,400	189,200	1.7

[1] 2020 ACS 5-Year estimates. 1-Year estimates were not released for 2020 due to the impact of COVID-19 on data collection that year.

Table WI-4. Migration, Origin, and Language

(Number, percent.)

Characteristic	State 2016-2020 [1]	U.S. 2016-2020 [1]
Residence 1 Year Ago		
Population 1 year and over	5,745,307	322,943,283
Same house	86.4	86.2
Different house in the U.S.	13.3	13.2
Same county	7.9	7.7
Different county	5.4	5.5
Same state	3.5	3.2
Different state	1.9	2.3
Abroad	0.3	0.6
Place of Birth		
Native born	5,515,788	282,443,680
Male	49.7	49.4
Female	50.3	50.6
Foreign born	291,187	44,125,628
Male	50.9	48.6
Female	49.1	51.4
Foreign born; naturalized U.S. citizen................................	137,508	22,456,684
Male	47.7	46.1
Female	52.3	53.9
Foreign born; not a U.S. citizen...	153,679	21,668,944
Male	53.7	51.1
Female	46.3	48.9
Entered 2010 or later	24.8	22.8
Entered 2000 to 2009	28.2	25.1
Entered before 2000...	47.1	52.1
World Region of Birth, Foreign		
Foreign-born population, excluding population born at sea	291,187	44,125,628
Europe	16.4	10.8
Asia	37.1	31.3
Africa	4.8	5.4
Oceania	0.5	0.6
Latin America	38.8	50.0
North America	2.3	1.9
Language Spoken at Home and Ability to Speak English		
Population 5 years and over..	5,475,909	306,919,116
English only	91.3	78.5
Language other than English..	8.7	21.5
Speaks English less than "very well"...............................	3.0	8.2

[1] 2020 ACS 5-Year estimates. 1-Year estimates were not released for 2020 due to the impact of COVID-19 on data collection that year.
NA = Not available.
X = Not applicable.
- = Zero or rounds to zero.

Table WI-5. Median Income and Poverty Status, 2020[1]

(Number, percent, except as noted.)

Characteristic	State		U.S.	
	Number	Percent	Number	Percent
Median Income				
Households (dollars)...	63,293	X	64,994	X
Families (dollars)	80,844	X	80,069	X
Below Poverty Level (All People)	620,947	11.0	40,910,326	12.8
Sex				
Male	277,914	9.9	18,171,512	11.6
Female	343,033	12.0	22,738,814	14.0
Age				
Under 18 years..	177,140	14.2	12,598,699	17.5
Related children under 18 years..............................	171,272	13.8	12,306,532	17.2
18 to 64 years...	369,627	10.7	23,554,920	12.1
65 years and over	74,180	7.8	4,756,707	9.3

X = Not applicable.
[1] 2020 ACS 5-Year estimates. 1-Year estimates were not released for 2020 due to the impact of COVID-19 on data collection that year.

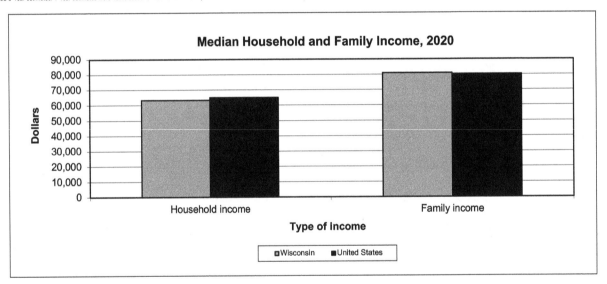

Table WI-6. Health Insurance Coverage Status for the Civilian Noninstitutionalized Population and Children Under 19 Years of Age

(Number, percent.)

Item	2011	2012	2013	2014	2015	2016	2017	2018	2019	2020 [2]
Civilian Noninstitutionalized Population	5,634,063	5,652,085	5,669,266	5,684,725	5,698,995	5,706,681	5,723,963	5,740,669	5,751,404	5,735,703
Covered by Private or Public Insurance										
Number...	5,127,389	5,146,087	5,151,470	5,267,002	5,376,379	5,406,475	5,414,559	5,427,511	5,422,750	5,422,999
Percent..	91.0	91.0	90.9	92.7	94.3	94.7	94.6	94.5	94.3	94.5
Uninsured										
Number...	506,674	505,998	517,796	417,723	322,616	300,206	309,404	313,158	328,654	312,704
Percent..	9.0	9.0	9.1	7.3	5.7	5.3	5.4	5.5	5.7	5.5
Percent in the U.S. not covered..	15.1	14.8	14.5	11.7	9.4	8.6	8.7	8.9	9.2	8.7
Children Under 19 Years of Age[1]	1,322,921	1,315,276	1,304,781	1,297,792	1,290,350	1,283,539	1,361,508	1,350,222	1,344,601	1,354,142
Covered by Private or Public Insurance										
Number...	1,264,685	1,253,719	1,243,493	1,240,181	1,244,122	1,238,131	1,308,778	1,299,125	1,293,888	1,301,866
Percent..	95.6	95.3	95.3	95.6	96.4	96.5	96.1	96.2	96.2	96.1
Uninsured										
Number...	58,236	61,557	61,288	57,611	46,228	45,408	52,730	51,097	50,713	52,276
Percent..	4.4	4.7	4.7	4.4	3.6	3.5	3.9	3.8	3.8	3.9
Percent in the U.S. not covered..	7.5	7.2	7.1	6.0	4.8	4.5	5.0	5.2	5.7	5.2

[1] Data for years prior to 2017 are for individuals under 18 years of age.
[2] 2020 ACS 5-Year estimates. 1-Year estimates were not released for 2020 due to the impact of COVID-19 on data collection that year. Data is not comparable to previous years, which are based on 1-year estimates.

Table WI-7. Employment Status by Demographic Group, 2021

(Numbers in thousands, percent.)

Characteristic	Civilian noninstitutional population	Civilian labor force		Employed		Unemployed	
		Number	Percent of population	Number	Percent of population	Number	Percent of population
Total..	4,673	3,106	66.5	2,990	64.0	116	3.7
Sex							
Male..	2,303	1,645	71.4	1,588	69.0	56	3.4
Female	2,370	1,461	61.7	1,402	59.2	59	4.1
Race, Sex, and Hispanic Origin							
White...	4,196	2,760	65.8	2,673	63.7	87	3.1
Male..	2,085	1,479	70.9	1,433	68.7	46	3.1
Female...	2,111	1,281	60.7	1,239	58.7	41	3.2
Black or African American...........................	257	181	70.6	162	63.0	19	10.7
Male..	NA	NA	NA	NA	NA	NA	NA
Female...	NA	NA	NA	NA	NA	NA	NA
Hispanic or Latino ethnicity[1]	286	197	68.8	186	65.2	10	5.2
Male..	NA	NA	NA	NA	NA	NA	NA
Female...	NA	NA	NA	NA	NA	NA	NA
Age							
16 to 19 years......................................	280	168	59.9	153	54.6	15	8.7
20 to 24 years......................................	340	279	82.2	265	77.9	15	5.2
25 to 34 years......................................	810	692	85.5	664	82.0	28	4.0
35 to 44 years......................................	702	614	87.3	594	84.5	20	3.3
45 to 54 years......................................	671	569	84.8	548	81.7	20	3.6
55 to 64 years......................................	861	582	67.6	568	66.0	13	2.3
65 years and over	1,009	203	20.1	198	19.6	5	2.2

NOTE: Data in Table 7 are from the Current Population Survey (CPS) and do not match the estimates in Table 8. See notes and definitions for further information.
[1] May be of any race.
NA = Not available.

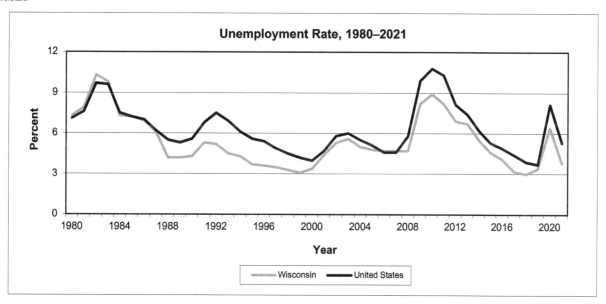

Unemployment Rate, 1980–2021

Table WI-8. Employment Status of the Civilian Noninstitutional Population Age 16 Years and Over

(Number, percent.)

Year	Civilian labor force	Civilian participation rate	Employed	Unemployed	Unemployment rate
2010..	3,082,935	69.5	2,820,620	262,315	8.5
2011..	3,072,157	68.9	2,839,987	232,170	7.6
2012..	3,070,033	68.5	2,857,150	212,883	6.9
2013..	3,077,801	68.3	2,871,988	205,813	6.7
2014..	3,077,981	68.0	2,913,764	164,217	5.3
2015..	3,084,207	67.9	2,947,048	137,159	4.4
2016..	3,110,466	68.1	2,988,744	121,722	3.9
2017..	3,141,757	68.0	3,039,348	102,409	3.3
2018..	3,129,386	67.4	3,036,071	93,315	3.0
2019..	3,120,590	66.8	3,021,491	99,099	3.2
2020..	3,105,882	66.2	2,909,004	196,878	6.3
2021..	3,134,439	66.5	3,016,039	118,400	3.8

Table WI-9. Employment and Average Wages by Industry

(Estimates are based on the 2012 North American Industry Classification System [NAICS].)

Industry	2013	2014	2015	2016	2017	2018	2019	2020
	Number of Jobs							
Wage and Salary Employment by Industry........................	2,874,503	2,912,213	2,945,464	2,980,084	3,000,006	3,032,198	3,044,352	2,879,827
Farm Wage and Salary Employment...............................	25,213	24,495	22,635	22,731	21,672	24,974	26,984	23,015
Nonfarm Wage and Salary Employment..........................	2,849,290	2,887,718	2,922,829	2,957,353	2,978,334	3,007,224	3,017,368	2,856,812
Private wage and salary employment...........................	2,415,066	2,451,523	2,488,641	2,518,437	2,542,669	2,570,541	2,581,648	2,436,393
Forestry, fishing, and related activities......................	5,822	5,890	6,209	6,560	6,568	6,534	6,788	(D)
Mining..	3,009	3,407	3,448	2,999	3,623	3,968	3,474	(D)
Utilities..	10,707	10,418	10,536	9,701	9,549	9,210	8,864	8,499
Construction..	101,212	106,118	112,456	115,418	120,186	125,393	127,430	126,964
Manufacturing..	458,070	465,362	467,976	464,773	467,973	476,008	483,852	459,098
Durable goods manufacturing............................	279,719	283,764	284,907	280,088	281,024	287,308	289,260	269,312
Nondurable goods manufacturing......................	178,351	181,598	183,069	184,685	186,949	188,700	194,592	189,786
Wholesale trade...	119,553	120,908	122,828	124,192	126,488	127,994	124,024	120,059
Retail trade..	300,748	304,680	307,242	311,206	310,405	307,967	300,773	290,329
Transportation and warehousing...........................	91,623	93,660	96,967	99,425	101,178	103,980	106,899	106,371
Information...	47,297	48,073	49,100	49,077	47,808	47,200	47,049	44,916
Finance and insurance	129,009	126,681	127,472	127,522	128,684	128,244	130,120	130,342
Real estate and rental and leasing.......................	25,030	24,852	25,478	25,964	26,831	27,326	27,794	26,713
Professional, scientific, and technical services	100,565	102,141	105,705	108,325	109,993	113,266	116,321	114,968
Management of companies and enterprises.............	55,773	59,397	62,454	68,686	69,129	68,034	66,289	64,630
Administrative and waste services	144,443	147,916	147,260	147,568	147,343	148,790	145,739	132,340
Educational services	55,865	56,059	55,936	55,958	56,554	55,721	56,676	52,824
Health care and social assistance........................	374,338	379,312	384,882	393,796	398,377	403,853	408,952	398,015
Arts, entertainment, and recreation.......................	36,448	37,833	38,317	40,351	41,393	43,044	44,523	32,610
Accommodation and food services........................	226,296	228,394	234,048	237,281	240,818	241,407	242,793	196,992
Other services, except public administration.............	129,258	130,422	130,327	129,635	129,769	132,602	133,288	121,321
Government and government enterprises...................	434,224	436,195	434,188	438,916	435,665	436,683	435,720	420,419
	Dollars							
Average Wages and Salaries by Industry	43,376	44,431	45,878	46,532	47,804	49,544	51,052	54,407
Average Farm Wages and Salaries	31,548	35,368	32,312	39,052	38,048	36,250	33,163	30,390
Average Nonfarm Wages and Salaries	43,480	44,507	45,983	46,589	47,875	49,654	51,212	54,600
Average private wages and salaries...........................	43,907	44,972	46,501	47,200	48,534	50,438	51,991	55,481
Forestry, fishing, and related activities....................	33,130	34,352	36,377	37,456	38,835	40,490	42,177	(D)
Mining..	61,603	67,095	63,674	63,308	64,713	67,271	68,439	(D)
Utilities..	103,594	101,383	103,025	100,327	105,613	108,672	109,682	115,298
Construction	54,210	56,152	58,031	59,588	60,990	62,983	64,778	67,428
Manufacturing..	54,818	56,035	57,114	57,030	58,779	59,987	60,987	63,135
Durable goods manufacturing............................	56,505	57,766	58,403	58,418	60,534	61,552	62,509	64,265
Nondurable goods manufacturing......................	52,174	53,330	55,107	54,925	56,141	57,603	58,726	61,533
Wholesale trade...	60,131	61,723	63,602	64,908	67,229	70,258	72,651	76,461
Retail trade..	24,931	25,527	26,651	26,985	27,754	28,871	29,817	31,942
Transportation and warehousing...........................	42,945	44,622	45,017	44,439	45,565	46,959	47,502	49,681
Information...	61,288	65,528	69,571	71,176	73,947	77,557	84,649	90,787
Finance and insurance	67,041	69,262	72,880	74,665	76,788	79,956	82,535	89,069
Real estate and rental and leasing.......................	35,706	37,087	39,293	41,301	42,187	44,770	46,693	50,479
Professional, scientific, and technical services	64,976	67,288	69,966	71,179	72,513	75,365	78,108	81,720
Management of companies and enterprises.............	91,843	93,747	96,956	98,489	96,710	104,451	107,535	111,183
Administrative and waste services	28,125	28,566	29,805	30,724	32,067	33,423	34,909	37,588
Educational services	35,800	36,096	37,047	38,952	39,066	41,282	42,327	45,913
Health care and social assistance........................	45,325	45,290	46,685	47,161	48,602	50,251	51,993	54,183
Arts, entertainment, and recreation.......................	29,863	30,649	29,953	30,155	31,408	34,954	34,237	37,465
Accommodation and food services........................	15,199	15,750	16,416	17,004	17,687	18,697	19,285	19,108
Other services, except public administration.............	28,442	29,402	30,664	31,647	32,956	34,202	35,380	39,838
Government and government enterprises...................	41,106	41,899	43,011	43,081	44,029	45,041	46,596	49,494

Table WI-10. Employment Characteristics by Family Type

(Number, percent.)

Family type and labor force status	2018 Total	2018 Families with own children under 18 years	2019 Total	2019 Families with own children under 18 years	2020[1] Total	2020[1] Families with own children under 18 years
All Families	1,487,370	610,226	1,470,116	593,666	1,479,364	614,156
FAMILY TYPE AND LABOR FORCE STATUS						
Opposite-Sex Married-Couple Families	1,150,650	414,433	1,140,000	406,282	1,140,756	414,953
Both husband and wife in labor force	55.3	75.2	56.2	77.0	56.4	76.8
Husband in labor force, wife not in labor force	16.4	19.9	15.5	17.9	16.0	18.7
Wife in labor force, husband not in labor force	7.9	3.3	7.9	3.8	7.9	3.5
Both husband and wife not in labor force	19.6	1.2	19.7	0.9	19.7	1.0
Other Families	336,720	195,793	330,116	187,384	330,765	197,859
Female householder, no spouse present	66.4	68.0	67.6	69.4	67.9	69.4
In labor force	50.3	59.5	49.7	59.6	51.4	59.8
Not in labor force	16.1	8.5	17.9	9.8	16.5	9.6
Male householder, no spouse present	33.6	32.0	32.4	30.6	32.1	30.6
In labor force	27.7	29.5	26.3	28.4	26.6	28.4
Not in labor force	5.9	2.5	6.1	2.3	5.6	2.2

[1] 2020 ACS 5-Year estimates. 1-Year estimates were not released for 2020 due to the impact of COVID-19 on data collection that year. Data is not comparable to previous years, which are based on 1-year estimates.

Table WI-11. School Enrollment and Educational Attainment, 2020[1]

(Number, percent.)

Item	State	U.S.
Enrollment		
Total population 3 years and over, enrolled in school	1,393,087	80,497,960
Enrolled in nursery school or preschool (percent)	5.3	6.1
Enrolled in kindergarten (percent)	5.7	5.0
Enrolled in elementary school, grades 1-8 (percent)	40.9	40.4
Enrolled in high school, grades 9-12 (percent)	21.2	21.0
Enrolled in college or graduate school (percent)	26.9	27.6
Attainment		
Total population 25 years and over	3,982,118	222,836,834
Less than ninth grade (percent)	2.5	4.9
9th to 12th grade, no diploma (percent)	4.9	6.6
High school graduate, including equivalency (percent)	30.3	26.7
Some college, no degree (percent)	20.5	20.3
Associate's degree (percent)	11.0	8.6
Bachelor's degree (percent)	20.3	20.2
Graduate or professional degree (percent)	10.5	12.7
High school graduate or higher (percent)	92.6	88.5
Bachelor's degree or higher (percent)	30.8	32.9

[1] 2020 ACS 5-Year estimates. 1-Year estimates were not released for 2020 due to the impact of COVID-19 on data collection that year.

Table WI-12. Public School Characteristics and Educational Indicators

(Number, percent; data derived from National Center of Education Statistics.)

Item	State	U.S.
Public Elementary and Secondary Schools		
Number of regular school districts, 2018-19	420	13,452
Number of operational schools, 2019-20	2,255	98,469
Percent charter schools	10.5	7.7
Total public school enrollment, Fall 2019	855,400	50,796,445
Percent charter school enrollment	5.2	6.8
Student-teacher ratio, Fall 2019	14.3	15.9
Expenditures per student (unadjusted dollars), 2018-19	12,690	13,187
Four-year adjusted cohort graduation rate (ACGR), 2018-2019[1]	90.1	85.8
Students eligible for free or reduced-price lunch (percent), 2019-20	39.7	52.1
English language learners (percent), Fall 2019	6.4	10.4
Students age 3 to 21 served under IDEA, part B (percent), 2020-21	14.5	14.5

Public Schools by Type, 2019-20	Number	Percent of state public schools
Total number of schools	2,255	100.0
Special education	13	0.6
Vocational education	5	0.2
Alternative education	97	4.3

[1] Adjusted Cohort Graduation Rates (ACGR) differ from Averaged Freshmen Graduation Rates (AFGR).
NA = Not available.

Table WI-13. Reported Voting and Registration of the Voting-Age Population, November 2020

(Numbers in thousands, percent.)

Item	Total population	Total citizen population	Registered Total registered	Registered Percent registered (total population)	Registered Percent registered (total citizen population)	Voted Total voted	Voted Percent voted (total population)	Voted Percent voted (total citizen population)
U.S. Total	252,274	231,593	168,308	66.7	72.7	154,628	61.3	66.8
State Total	4,538	4,421	3,391	74.7	76.7	3,253	71.7	73.6
Sex								
Male	2,223	2,158	1,616	72.7	74.9	1,533	68.9	71.0
Female	2,315	2,263	1,775	76.7	78.5	1,720	74.3	76.0
Race								
White alone	4,005	3,931	3,119	77.9	79.3	3,008	75.1	76.5
White, non-Hispanic alone	3,776	3,772	3,020	80.0	80.1	2,914	77.2	77.2
Black alone	263	263	126	47.7	47.7	114	43.5	43.5
Asian alone	117	73	44	B	B	44	B	B
Hispanic (of any race)	242	173	105	43.5	61.0	101	41.7	58.4
White alone or in combination	4,113	4,040	3,192	77.6	79.0	3,081	74.9	76.3
Black alone or in combination	318	318	152	47.8	47.8	141	44.3	44.3
Asian alone or in combination	138	94	59	42.4	62.0	59	42.4	62.0
Age								
18 to 24 years	581	577	333	57.4	57.8	323	55.6	56.0
25 to 34 years	762	714	582	76.4	81.5	557	73.1	78.0
35 to 44 years	650	617	437	67.2	70.8	426	65.5	69.1
45 to 64 years	1,604	1,572	1,241	77.4	79.0	1,171	73.0	74.5
65 years and over	941	941	797	84.8	84.8	776	82.4	82.4

Table WI-14. Crime

(Number, rate per 100,000. Data are derived from the FBI Uniform Crime Reports.)

Item	State 2019	State 2020	State Percent change	U.S. 2019	U.S. 2020	U.S. Percent change
TOTAL POPULATION[1]	5,824,581	5,832,655	0.1	328,329,953	329,484,123	0.4
VIOLENT CRIME						
Number	17,305	18,861	9.0	1,250,393	1,313,105	5.0
Rate	297.1	323.4	8.8	380.8	398.5	4.6
Murder and Nonnegligent Manslaughter						
Number	189	308	63.0	16,669	21,570	29.4
Rate	3.2	5.3	62.7	5.1	6.5	28.9
Rape[2]						
Number	2,358	2,020	-14.3	143,224	126,430	-11.7
Rate	40.5	34.6	-14.5	43.6	38.4	-12.0
Robbery						
Number	2,994	3,081	2.9	268,483	243,600	-9.3
Rate	51.4	52.8	2.8	81.8	73.9	-9.6
Aggravated Assault						
Number	11,764	13,452	14.3	822,017	921,505	12.1
Rate	202.0	230.6	14.2	250.4	279.7	11.7
PROPERTY CRIME						
Number	85,796	86,654	1.0	6,995,235	6,452,038	-7.8
Rate	1,473.0	1,485.7	0.9	2,130.6	1,958.2	-8.1
Burglary						
Number	12,572	12,744	1.4	1,118,096	1,035,314	-7.4
Rate	215.8	218.5	1.2	340.5	314.2	-7.7
Larceny-Theft						
Number	65,687	64,517	-1.8	5,152,267	4,606,324	-10.6
Rate	1,127.8	1,106.1	-1.9	1,569.2	1,398.0	-10.9
Motor Vehicle Theft						
Number	7,537	9,393	24.6	724,872	810,400	11.8
Rate	129.4	161.0	24.5	220.8	246.0	11.4

NOTE: Although arson data are included in the trend and clearance tables, sufficient data are not available to estimate totals for this offense. Therefore, no arson data are published in this table.
- = Zero or rounds to zero.
[1] Population figures are U.S. Census Bureau provisional estimates as of July 1, 2020.
[2] The figures shown in the rape (revised definition) column were estimated using the revised Uniform Crime Reporting (UCR) definition of rape.

Table WI-15. State Government Finances, 2020

(Dollar amounts in thousands, percent distribution.)

Item	Dollars	Percent distribution
Total Revenue	64,984,671	100.0
General revenue	41,731,964	64.2
Intergovernmental revenue	13,304,508	20.5
Taxes	20,114,894	31.0
General sales	5836215	9.0
Selective sales	2,861,597	4.4
License taxes	1,256,103	1.9
Individual income tax	8514409	13.1
Corporate income tax	1,441,416	2.2
Other taxes	205,154	0.3
Current charges	4,907,267	7.6
Miscellaneous general revenue	3,405,295	5.2
Utility revenue	0	-
Liquor stores revenue	0	-
Insurance trust revenue[1]	23,252,707	35.8
Total Expenditure	46,106,704	100.0
Intergovernmental expenditure	11,845,935	25.7
Direct expenditure	34,260,769	74.3
Current operation	23,377,628	50.7
Capital outlay	2,418,115	5.2
Insurance benefits and repayments	6,702,649	14.5
Assistance and subsidies	1,177,053	2.6
Interest on debt	585,324	1.3
Exhibit: Salaries and wages	4,685,998	10.2
Total Expenditure	46,106,704	100.0
General expenditure	39,383,648	85.4
Intergovernmental expenditure	11,845,935	25.7
Direct expenditure	27,537,713	59.7
General expenditure, by function:		
Education	13,331,308	28.9
Public welfare	12,581,854	27.3
Hospitals	2,403,129	5.2
Health	701,310	1.5
Highways	2,854,615	6.2
Police protection	51,781	0.1
Correction	1,084,547	2.4
Natural resources	607,933	1.3
Parks and recreation	49,269	0.1
Governmental administration	1,068,514	2.3
Interest on general debt	585,324	1.3
Other and unallocable	3,991,392	8.7
Utility expenditure	82,259	0.1
Liquor stores expenditure	0	-
Insurance trust expenditure	6,702,649	14.5
Debt at End of Fiscal Year	22,446,313	X
Cash and Security Holdings	156,688,315	X

X = Not applicable.
- = Zero or rounds to zero.
[1] Within insurance trust revenue, net earnings of state retirement systems is a calculated statistic (the item code in the data file is X08), and thus can be positive or negative. Net earnings is the sum of earnings on investments plus gains on investments minus losses on investments. The change made in 2002 for asset valuation from book to market value in accordance with Statement 34 of the Governmental Accounting Standards Board is reflected in the calculated statistics.

Table WI-16. State Government Tax Collections, 2021

(Dollars in thousands, percent.)

Item	Dollars	Percent distribution
Total Taxes	22,300,918	100.0
Property taxes	95,757	0.4
Sales and gross receipts	9,184,622	41.2
General sales and gross receipts	6,373,483	28.6
Selective sales and gross receipts	2,811,139	12.6
Alcoholic beverages	73,778	0.3
Amusements	47	-
Insurance premiums	226,531	1.0
Motor fuels	1,123,970	5.0
Pari-mutuels	0	-
Public utilities	354,279	1.6
Tobacco products	604,097	2.7
Other selective sales	428,437	1.9
Licenses	1,340,711	6.0
Alcoholic beverages	2,327	-
Amusements	36	-
Corporations in general	29,288	0.1
Hunting and fishing	73,772	0.3
Motor vehicle	719,005	3.2
Motor vehicle operators	41,167	0.2
Public utilities	62,868	0.3
Occupation and business, NEC	349,380	1.6
Other licenses	62,868	0.3
Income taxes	11,553,157	51.8
Individual income	9,035,988	40.5
Corporation net income	2,517,169	11.3
Other taxes	126,671	0.6
Death and gift	1	-
Documentary and stock transfer	106,166	0.5
Severance	3,991	-
Taxes, NEC	16,513	0.1

- = Zero or rounds to zero.

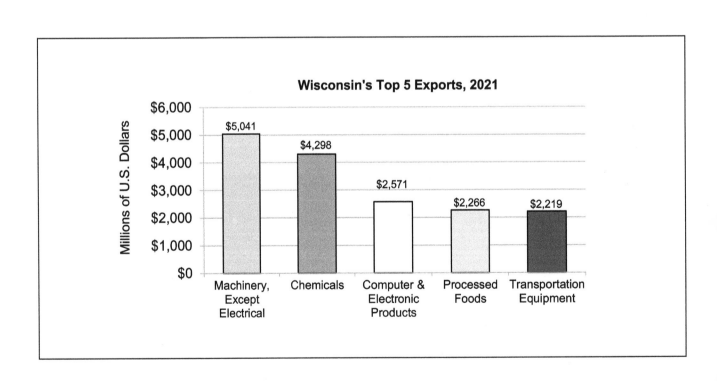

Wisconsin's Top 5 Exports, 2021

WYOMING

Facts and Figures

Location: Western United States; bordered on the N by Montana, on the E by South Dakota and Nebraska, on the S by Colorado and Utah, and on the W by Utah and Idaho

Area: 97,814 sq. mi. (253,336 sq. km.); rank—10th

Population: 578,803 (2021 est.); rank—51st

Principal Cities: capital—Cheyenne; largest—Cheyenne

Statehood: July 10, 1890; 44th state

U.S. Congress: 2 senators, 1 representative

State Motto: Equal Rights

State Song: "Wyoming"

State Nicknames: The Equality State; The Cowboy State

Abbreviations: WY; Wyo.

State Symbols: flower—Indian paintbrush; tree—cottonwood; bird—Western meadowlark

At a Glance

- With an increase in population of 2.7 percent, Wyoming ranked 42nd among the states in growth from 2010 to 2021.

- Wyoming's violent crime rate in 2020 was 234.2 per 100,000 population, compared to the U.S. rate of 398.5 per 100,000 population.

- Wyoming's median household income in 2020 was $65,304, which ranked 21st in the nation.

- In 2020, 10.8 percent of Wyoming residents and 12.3 percent of Wyoming's children lived below the poverty level, compared to the national poverty rates of 12.8 percent and 17.5 percent respectively.

- In 2020, 11.4 percent of Wyoming residents did not have health insurance, compared to 8.7 percent of total U.S. residents.

Table WY-1. Population by Age, Sex, Race, and Hispanic Origin

(Number, percent, except where noted.)

Sex, age, race, and Hispanic origin	2000	2010	2021	Percent change, 2010–2021
Total Population...	493,782	563,626	578,803	2.7
Percent of total U.S. population	0.2	0.2	0.2	X
Sex				
Male...	248,374	287,437	296,214	3.1
Female..	245,408	276,189	282,589	2.3
Age				
Under 5 years..	30,940	40,203	32,291	-19.7
5 to 19 years..	114,406	111,310	114,669	3.0
20 to 64 years..	290,743	342,023	327,966	-4.1
65 years and over..	57,693	70,090	103,877	48.2
Median age (years)	36.2	36.8	38.9	5.7
Race and Hispanic Origin				
One race				
White..	454,670	529,110	534,669	1.1
Black..	3,722	5,135	7,087	38.0
American Indian and Alaska Native	11,133	14,457	16,435	13.7
Asian..	2,771	4,649	6,329	36.1
Native Hawaiian or Other Pacific Islander	302	521	586	12.5
Two or more races	8,883	9,754	13,697	40.4
Hispanic (of any race)..	31,669	52,112	61,087	17.2

NOTE: Population figures for 2021 are July 1 estimates. The 2000 and 2010 estimates are taken from the respective censuses.
- = Zero or rounds to zero.
X = Not applicable.

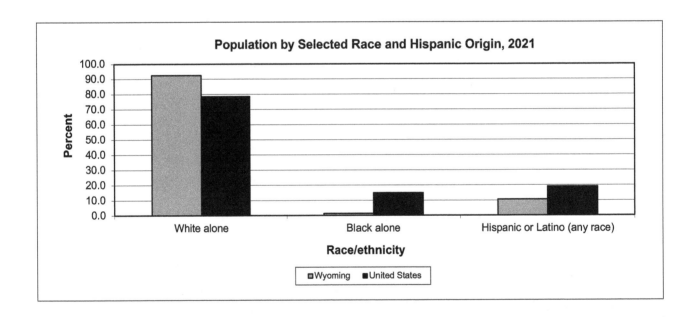

Population by Selected Race and Hispanic Origin, 2021

Legend: Wyoming, United States

X-axis: Race/ethnicity — White alone, Black alone, Hispanic or Latino (any race)
Y-axis: Percent

Table WY-2. Marital Status

(Number, percent distribution.)

Sex, age, race, and Hispanic origin	2000	2010	2020 [1]
Males, 15 Years and Over	195,412	228,725	238,485
Never married	26.6	29.0	30.0
Now married, except separated..	58.8	56.2	54.4
Separated...	1.0	1.3	1.3
Widowed...	2.3	2.4	2.6
Divorced...	11.3	11.2	11.7
Females, 15 Years and Over	195,433	220,169	229,945
Never married	20.0	20.7	23.6
Now married, except separated..	57.5	55.1	54.2
Separated...	1.3	2.0	1.3
Widowed...	9.2	8.6	8.1
Divorced...	12.0	13.6	12.8

[1] 2020 ACS 5-Year estimates. 1-Year estimates were not released for 2020 due to the impact of COVID-19 on data collection that year.

Table WY-3. Households and Housing Characteristics

(Number, percent, dollars.)

Item	2000	2010	2020 [1]	Average annual percent change, 2010–2020
Total Households..	193,608	222,803	233,231	0.7
Family households..	130,497	147,394	149,353	0.2
Married-couple family......................................	106,179	119,756	121,166	0.2
Other family..	24,318	27,638	28,187	0.3
Male householder, no wife present..................	7,481	7,804	9,730	3.5
Female householder, no husband present.........	16,837	19,834	18,457	-1.0
Nonfamily households..	63,111	75,409	83,878	1.6
Householder living alone..................................	50,980	61,775	67,178	1.2
Householder not living alone............................	12,131	13,634	16,700	3.2
Housing Characteristics				
Total housing units...	223,854	262,286	278,495	0.9
Occupied housing units...	193,608	222,803	233,231	0.7
Owner occupied..	135,514	155,278	165,530	0.9
Renter occupied...	58,094	67,525	67,701	-
Average household size..	2.48	2.47	2.43	-0.2
Financial Characteristics				
Median gross rent of renter-occupied housing	437	693	853	3.3
Median monthly owner costs for housing units with a mortgage	825	1,300	1,474	1.9
Median value of owner-occupied housing units..................	96,600	180,100	228,000	3.8

- = Zero or rounds to zero
[1] 2020 ACS 5-Year estimates. 1-Year estimates were not released for 2020 due to the impact of COVID-19 on data collection that year.

Table WY-4. Migration, Origin, and Language

(Number, percent.)

Characteristic	State 2016-2020 [1]	U.S. 2016-2020 [1]
Residence 1 Year Ago		
Population 1 year and over	574,701	322,943,283
Same house..	83.3	86.2
Different house in the U.S.	16.3	13.2
Same county...	9.4	7.7
Different county..	6.9	5.5
Same state..	2.5	3.2
Different state...	4.5	2.3
Abroad...	0.3	0.6
Place of Birth		
Native born...	562,074	282,443,680
Male...	51.1	49.4
Female...	48.9	50.6
Foreign born..	19,274	44,125,628
Male...	48.3	48.6
Female...	51.7	51.4
Foreign born; naturalized U.S. citizen.............................	7,535	22,456,684
Male..	47.9	46.1
Female..	52.1	53.9
Foreign born; not a U.S. citizen......................................	11,739	21,668,944
Male..	48.6	51.1
Female..	51.4	48.9
Entered 2010 or later...	22.3	22.8
Entered 2000 to 2009	35.0	25.1
Entered before 2000...	42.7	52.1
World Region of Birth, Foreign		
Foreign-born population, excluding population born at sea	19,274	44,125,628
Europe	18.7	10.8
Asia..	18.5	31.3
Africa..	3.5	5.4
Oceania..	1.0	0.6
Latin America...	52.3	50.0
North America..	6.0	1.9
Language Spoken at Home and Ability to Speak English		
Population 5 years and over..	545,912	306,919,116
English only	93.0	78.5
Language other than English.......................................	7.0	21.5
Speaks English less than "very well"........................	1.9	8.2

[1] 2020 ACS 5-Year estimates. 1-Year estimates were not released for 2020 due to the impact of COVID-19 on data collection that year.
NA = Not available.
X = Not applicable.
- = Zero or rounds to zero.

Table WY-5. Median Income and Poverty Status, 2020[1]

(Number, percent, except as noted.)

Characteristic	State		U.S.	
	Number	Percent	Number	Percent
Median Income				
Households (dollars)...	65,304	X	64,994	X
Families (dollars)	81,290	X	80,069	X
Below Poverty Level (All People)	61,006	10.8	40,910,326	12.8
Sex				
Male	27,714	9.6	18,171,512	11.6
Female	33,292	11.9	22,738,814	14.0
Age				
Under 18 years...	16,175	12.3	12,598,699	17.5
Related children under 18 years..	15,515	11.8	12,306,532	17.2
18 to 64 years	37,369	10.9	23,554,920	12.1
65 years and over	7,462	8.0	4,756,707	9.3

X = Not applicable.
[1] 2020 ACS 5-Year estimates. 1-Year estimates were not released for 2020 due to the impact of COVID-19 on data collection that year.

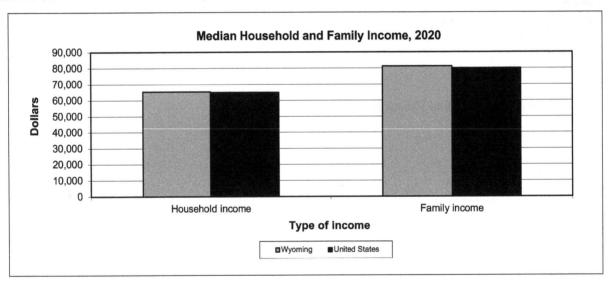

Table WY-6. Health Insurance Coverage Status for the Civilian Noninstitutionalized Population and Children Under 19 Years of Age

(Number, percent.)

Item	2011	2012	2013	2014	2015	2016	2017	2018	2019	2020 [2]
Civilian Noninstitutionalized Population	558,832	567,082	573,210	574,798	576,557	576,027	568,891	567,008	568,859	571,005
Covered by Private or Public Insurance										
Number..	473,001	479,998	496,182	506,050	510,063	509,514	499,176	507,671	498,806	505,708
Percent...	84.6	84.6	86.6	88.0	88.5	88.5	87.7	89.5	87.7	88.6
Uninsured										
Number..	85,831	87,084	77,028	68,748	66,494	66,513	69,715	59,337	70,053	65,297
Percent...	15.4	15.4	13.4	12.0	11.5	11.5	12.3	10.5	12.3	11.4
Percent in the U.S. not covered..............................	15.1	14.8	14.5	11.7	9.4	8.6	8.7	8.9	9.2	8.7
Children Under 19 Years of Age[1]	134,594	136,132	139,291	137,296	138,953	140,464	145,904	142,042	143,312	141,959
Covered by Private or Public Insurance										
Number..	122,956	123,417	131,357	129,159	128,097	128,136	131,974	131,918	128,067	129,376
Percent...	91.4	90.7	94.3	94.1	92.2	91.2	90.5	92.9	89.4	91.1
Uninsured										
Number..	11,638	12,715	7,934	8,137	10,856	12,328	13,930	10,124	15,245	12,583
Percent...	8.6	9.3	5.7	5.9	7.8	8.8	9.5	7.1	10.6	8.9
Percent in the U.S. not covered..............................	7.5	7.2	7.1	6.0	4.8	4.5	5.0	5.2	5.7	5.2

[1] Data for years prior to 2017 are for individuals under 18 years of age.
[2] 2020 ACS 5-Year estimates. 1-Year estimates were not released for 2020 due to the impact of COVID-19 on data collection that year. Data is not comparable to previous years, which are based on 1-year estimates.

Table WY-7. Employment Status by Demographic Group, 2021

(Numbers in thousands, percent.)

Characteristic	Civilian noninstitutional population	Civilian labor force		Employed		Unemployed	
		Number	Percent of population	Number	Percent of population	Number	Percent of population
Total..	458	294	64.2	280	61.3	13	4.5
Sex							
Male..	231	158	68.4	150	64.8	8	5.2
Female.......................................	227	136	59.9	131	57.6	5	3.7
Race, Sex, and Hispanic Origin							
White..	426	274	64.2	262	61.4	12	4.3
Male..	215	147	68.2	139	64.8	7	5.1
Female......................................	212	127	60.1	123	58.0	5	3.5
Black or African American..................	NA	NA	NA	NA	NA	NA	NA
Male..	NA	NA	NA	NA	NA	NA	NA
Female......................................	NA	NA	NA	NA	NA	NA	NA
Hispanic or Latino ethnicity[1]	41	26	63.9	24	58.6	2	8.2
Male..	21	15	70.7	14	63.7	2	10.1
Female......................................	NA	NA	NA	NA	NA	NA	NA
Age							
16 to 19 years..............................	NA	NA	NA	NA	NA	NA	NA
20 to 24 years..............................	34	26	77.3	24	70.8	2	8.4
25 to 34 years..............................	74	62	82.8	59	79.2	3	4.4
35 to 44 years..............................	74	65	87.4	62	84.1	3	3.9
45 to 54 years..............................	59	50	84.2	48	81.6	2	3.0
55 to 64 years..............................	80	54	67.5	52	65.3	2	3.0
65 years and over...........................	106	23	22.1	22	21.1	1	3.8

NOTE: Data in Table 7 are from the Current Population Survey (CPS) and do not match the estimates in Table 8. See notes and definitions for further information.
[1] May be of any race.
NA = Not available.

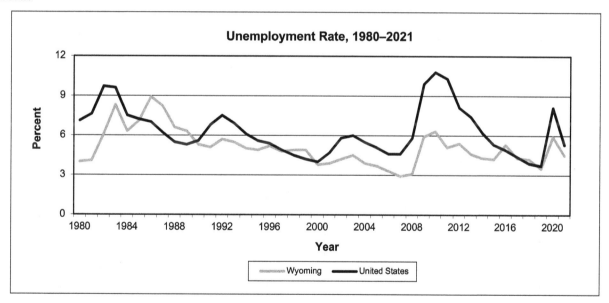

Table WY-8. Employment Status of the Civilian Noninstitutional Population Age 16 Years and Over

(Number, percent.)

Year	Civilian labor force	Civilian participation rate	Employed	Unemployed	Unemployment rate
2010..	301,893	70.1	280,953	20,940	6.9
2011..	302,932	69.3	284,273	18,659	6.2
2012..	303,748	68.4	287,110	16,638	5.5
2013..	302,201	67.4	287,792	14,409	4.8
2014..	302,865	67.3	289,694	13,171	4.3
2015..	301,608	66.8	288,894	12,714	4.2
2016..	300,546	66.6	284,439	16,107	5.4
2017..	293,802	65.9	281,164	12,638	4.3
2018..	292,781	65.7	280,909	11,872	4.1
2019..	294,380	65.8	283,377	11,003	3.7
2020..	293,722	65.3	276,739	16,983	5.8
2021..	290,404	64.1	277,372	13,032	4.5

Table WY-9. Employment and Average Wages by Industry

(Estimates are based on the 2012 North American Industry Classification System [NAICS].)

Industry	2013	2014	2015	2016	2017	2018	2019	2020
	Number of Jobs							
Wage and Salary Employment by Industry	299,508	303,951	302,522	291,463	289,601	291,670	297,577	279,934
Farm Wage and Salary Employment	3,683	3,566	3,822	3,871	4,480	3,906	4,112	3,835
Nonfarm Wage and Salary Employment	295,825	300,385	298,700	287,592	285,121	287,764	293,465	276,099
Private wage and salary employment	220,058	225,017	222,859	211,367	209,803	213,713	218,157	202,878
Forestry, fishing, and related activities	1,134	1,168	1,170	1,171	(D)	1,200	1,228	(D)
Mining	26,482	27,130	23,740	18,703	19,566	20,614	20,638	16,265
Utilities	2,484	2,489	2,535	2,541	2,476	2,510	2,432	(D)
Construction	22,416	24,377	23,865	21,649	20,056	20,749	23,402	21,769
Manufacturing	9,475	9,819	9,767	9,229	(D)	9,729	10,055	9,590
Durable goods manufacturing	4,705	4,875	4,713	4,145	(D)	4,638	5,109	4,794
Nondurable goods manufacturing	4,770	4,944	5,054	5,084	(D)	5,091	4,946	4,796
Wholesale trade	9,288	9,532	9,541	8,532	8,156	8,224	8,420	7,685
Retail trade	29,999	29,979	30,979	30,858	29,871	29,501	29,087	28,900
Transportation and warehousing	12,410	13,238	13,158	11,749	11,648	12,015	12,285	11,641
Information	3,801	3,780	3,782	3,747	3,687	3,552	3,435	3,001
Finance and insurance	7,179	7,195	7,240	7,240	7,306	7,370	7,437	7,559
Real estate and rental and leasing	4,420	4,505	4,366	4,066	4,160	4,311	4,374	4,032
Professional, scientific, and technical services	9,324	9,600	9,465	8,935	8,996	9,387	9,911	9,502
Management of companies and enterprises	1,032	1,014	1,025	901	868	865	857	736
Administrative and waste services	7,911	7,948	8,158	8,090	8,301	8,637	8,549	8,278
Educational services	2,130	2,139	2,208	2,274	2,263	2,146	2,250	2,134
Health care and social assistance	24,382	24,436	24,617	25,161	25,093	25,742	26,007	25,682
Arts, entertainment, and recreation	2,920	3,092	3,174	3,341	3,694	3,673	3,664	3,321
Accommodation and food services	31,856	32,458	33,145	32,703	32,808	32,922	33,556	29,192
Other services, except public administration	11,415	11,118	10,924	10,477	10,320	10,566	10,570	10,024
Government and government enterprises	75,767	75,368	75,841	76,225	75,318	74,051	75,308	73,221
	Dollars							
Average Wages and Salaries by Industry	45,853	47,400	47,182	46,006	47,285	49,252	50,678	52,051
Average Farm Wages and Salaries	38,877	38,757	30,603	34,981	30,400	36,432	24,776	35,386
Average Nonfarm Wages and Salaries	45,940	47,503	47,394	46,154	47,551	49,426	51,041	52,282
Average private wages and salaries	46,263	48,043	47,558	45,696	47,307	49,447	51,509	52,278
Forestry, fishing, and related activities	24,594	25,927	26,729	28,324	(D)	29,803	31,093	(D)
Mining	85,509	88,868	88,770	85,792	89,302	91,876	94,939	93,192
Utilities	85,594	88,876	92,338	92,152	94,797	99,113	102,331	(D)
Construction	51,138	52,318	51,927	51,253	51,753	54,454	58,064	57,629
Manufacturing	58,894	62,391	64,758	66,016	(D)	69,021	70,646	72,406
Durable goods manufacturing	50,898	53,721	54,105	53,216	(D)	58,971	59,180	59,357
Nondurable goods manufacturing	66,782	70,939	74,692	76,452	(D)	78,177	82,489	85,449
Wholesale trade	59,482	64,232	61,196	59,071	62,818	65,749	67,783	67,085
Retail trade	27,857	28,581	29,011	28,766	29,651	30,206	31,251	32,958
Transportation and warehousing	57,008	59,073	58,805	56,770	59,921	61,741	63,880	64,089
Information	44,290	45,939	47,473	47,614	48,615	49,534	51,151	57,009
Finance and insurance	55,109	57,977	60,080	60,113	62,237	64,764	68,997	74,166
Real estate and rental and leasing	46,648	49,020	47,499	44,354	47,083	50,201	51,918	51,212
Professional, scientific, and technical services	59,356	62,523	61,921	60,076	62,164	65,188	69,422	74,910
Management of companies and enterprises	113,451	100,183	103,816	102,041	101,373	106,654	104,286	145,262
Administrative and waste services	31,902	32,613	33,508	33,041	35,175	37,104	39,265	39,234
Educational services	29,581	29,832	28,337	28,521	29,093	33,115	33,667	40,629
Health care and social assistance	41,546	42,603	43,820	43,511	44,141	44,931	46,130	48,204
Arts, entertainment, and recreation	22,100	23,780	23,962	24,498	24,767	26,520	27,441	29,192
Accommodation and food services	20,724	21,224	21,735	22,220	22,844	24,747	25,503	25,525
Other services, except public administration	33,458	33,198	34,095	33,509	34,397	35,953	37,485	39,263
Government and government enterprises	45,000	45,890	46,913	47,426	48,231	49,363	49,684	52,294

(D) = Not shown to avoid disclosure of confidential information; estimates are included in higher-level totals.

Table WY-10. Employment Characteristics by Family Type

(Number, percent.)

Family type and labor force status	2018		2019		2020 [1]	
	Total	Families with own children under 18 years	Total	Families with own children under 18 years	Total	Families with own children under 18 years
All Families..	144,525	58,115	152,859	61,466	149,353	62,804
FAMILY TYPE AND LABOR FORCE STATUS						
Opposite-Sex Married-Couple Families..........................	116,706	41,471	123,545	44,726	120,294	45,360
Both husband and wife in labor force....................................	52.1	69.9	52.7	70.8	53.1	70.1
Husband in labor force, wife not in labor force........................	21.8	26.8	20.4	26.3	21.3	26.6
Wife in labor force, husband not in labor force........................	7.2	2.3	7.6	2.1	7.8	2.5
Both husband and wife not in labor force................................	18.3	0.9	19.0	0.7	17.8	0.8
Other Families	27,819	16,644	29,314	16,740	28,187	17,327
Female householder, no spouse present..................................	69.0	72.5	64.3	64.7	65.5	68.2
In labor force	51.0	60.5	47.7	57.2	48.3	58.5
Not in labor force	18.0	12.0	16.5	7.5	17.2	9.7
Male householder, no spouse present.....................................	31.0	27.5	35.7	35.3	34.5	31.8
In labor force	22.9	26.9	28.7	33.7	28.6	30.5
Not in labor force	8.1	0.6	7.0	1.5	6.0	1.3

[1] 2020 ACS 5-Year estimates. 1-Year estimates were not released for 2020 due to the impact of COVID-19 on data collection that year. Data is not comparable to previous years, which are based on 1-year estimates.

Table WY-11. School Enrollment and Educational Attainment, 2020[1]

(Number, percent.)

Item	State	U.S.
Enrollment		
Total population 3 years and over, enrolled in school	145,076	80,497,960
Enrolled in nursery school or preschool (percent)	6.0	6.1
Enrolled in kindergarten (percent)	4.9	5.0
Enrolled in elementary school, grades 1-8 (percent)	42.4	40.4
Enrolled in high school, grades 9-12 (percent)	20.2	21.0
Enrolled in college or graduate school (percent)	26.5	27.6
Attainment		
Total population 25 years and over	392,819	222,836,834
Less than ninth grade (percent)	1.8	4.9
9th to 12th grade, no diploma (percent)	4.6	6.6
High school graduate, including equivalency (percent)	28.6	26.7
Some college, no degree (percent)	25.4	20.3
Associate's degree (percent)..	11.4	8.6
Bachelor's degree (percent)	17.7	20.2
Graduate or professional degree (percent)	10.5	12.7
High school graduate or higher (percent)	93.6	88.5
Bachelor's degree or higher (percent)	28.2	32.9

[1] 2020 ACS 5-Year estimates. 1-Year estimates were not released for 2020 due to the impact of COVID-19 on data collection that year.

Table WY-12. Public School Characteristics and Educational Indicators

(Number, percent; data derived from National Center of Education Statistics.)

Item	State	U.S.
Public Elementary and Secondary Schools		
Number of regular school districts, 2018-19	48	13,452
Number of operational schools, 2019-20	360	98,469
Percent charter schools	1.4	7.7
Total public school enrollment, Fall 2019	94,616	50,796,445
Percent charter school enrollment	0.7	6.8
Student-teacher ratio, Fall 2019	12.8	15.9
Expenditures per student (unadjusted dollars), 2018-19	16,228	13,187
Four-year adjusted cohort graduation rate (ACGR), 2018-2019[1]	82.1	85.8
Students eligible for free or reduced-price lunch (percent), 2019-20	34.6	52.1
English language learners (percent), Fall 2019	2.9	10.4
Students age 3 to 21 served under IDEA, part B (percent), 2020-21	16.5	14.5

Public Schools by Type, 2019-20	Number	Percent of state public schools
Total number of schools..	360	100.0
Special education	3	0.8
Vocational education	0	-
Alternative education	9	2.5

[1] Adjusted Cohort Graduation Rates (ACGR) differ from Averaged Freshmen Graduation Rates (AFGR).
- = Zero or rounds to zero.

Table WY-13. Reported Voting and Registration of the Voting-Age Population, November 2020

(Numbers in thousands, percent.)

Item	Total population	Total citizen population	Registered				Voted		
			Total registered	Percent registered (total population)	Percent registered (total citizen population)		Total voted	Percent voted (total population)	Percent voted (total citizen population)
U.S. Total	252,274	231,593	168,308	66.7	72.7		154,628	61.3	66.8
State Total..	436	427	296	67.9	69.3		280	64.1	65.5
Sex									
Male	217	212	141	65.0	66.5		132	61.1	62.5
Female	219	215	155	70.8	72.1		147	67.2	68.4
Race									
White alone..	410	405	280	68.3	69.2		265	64.5	65.4
White, non-Hispanic alone	379	376	265	70.0	70.6		251	66.2	66.8
Black alone...	2	2	1	B	B		1	B	B
Asian alone	2	-	-	B	B		-	B	B
Hispanic (of any race)..........................	40	38	23	B	B		21	B	B
White alone or in combination	422	416	290	68.6	69.6		273	64.7	65.7
Black alone or in combination..................	4	3	3	B	B		3	B	B
Asian alone or in combination.................	4	2	2	B	B		2	B	B
Age									
18 to 24 years	52	51	28	B	B		25	B	B
25 to 34 years	74	69	41	B	B		36	B	B
35 to 44 years	70	69	41	B	B		39	B	B
45 to 64 years	145	143	110	75.7	76.8		106	73.0	74.1
65 years and over	96	95	76	79.5	80.1		73	76.0	76.6

- = Zero or rounds to zero.
B = Base is less than 75,000 and therefore too small to show the derived measure.

Table WY-14. Crime

(Number, rate per 100,000. Data are derived from the FBI Uniform Crime Reports.)

Item	State			U.S.		
	2019	2020	Percent change	2019	2020	Percent change
TOTAL POPULATION[1]	580,116	582,328	0.4	328,329,953	329,484,123	0.4
VIOLENT CRIME						
Number...	1,247	1,364	9.4	1,250,393	1,313,105	5.0
Rate	215.0	234.2	9.0	380.8	398.5	4.6
Murder and Nonnegligent Manslaughter						
Number...	13	18	38.5	16,669	21,570	29.4
Rate	2.2	3.1	37.9	5.1	6.5	28.9
Rape[2]						
Number...	323	333	3.1	143,224	126,430	-11.7
Rate	55.7	57.2	2.7	43.6	38.4	-12.0
Robbery						
Number...	67	66	-1.5	268,483	243,600	-9.3
Rate	11.5	11.3	-1.9	81.8	73.9	-9.6
Aggravated Assault						
Number...	844	947	12.2	822,017	921,505	12.1
Rate	145.5	162.6	11.8	250.4	279.7	11.7
PROPERTY CRIME						
Number...	9,097	9,379	3.1	6,995,235	6,452,038	-7.8
Rate	1,568.1	1,610.6	2.7	2,130.6	1,958.2	-8.1
Burglary						
Number...	1,394	1,225	-12.1	1,118,096	1,035,314	-7.4
Rate	240.3	210.4	-12.5	340.5	314.2	-7.7
Larceny-Theft						
Number...	6,981	7,190	3.0	5,152,267	4,606,324	-10.6
Rate	1,203.4	1,234.7	2.6	1,569.2	1,398.0	-10.9
Motor Vehicle Theft						
Number...	722	964	33.5	724,872	810,400	11.8
Rate	124.5	165.5	33.0	220.8	246.0	11.4

NOTE: Although arson data are included in the trend and clearance tables, sufficient data are not available to estimate totals for this offense. Therefore, no arson data are published in this table.
- = Zero or rounds to zero.
[1] Population figures are U.S. Census Bureau provisional estimates as of July 1, 2020.
[2] The figures shown in the rape (revised definition) column were estimated using the revised Uniform Crime Reporting (UCR) definition of rape.

Table WY-15. State Government Finances, 2020

(Dollar amounts in thousands, percent distribution.)

Item	Dollars	Percent distribution
Total Revenue	9,170,744	100.0
General revenue	6,740,388	73.5
Intergovernmental revenue	3,803,816	41.5
Taxes	1,963,461	21.4
General sales	764917	8.3
Selective sales	186,573	2.0
License taxes	204,641	2.2
Individual income tax	0	-
Corporate income tax	0	-
Other taxes	807,330	8.8
Current charges	252,794	2.8
Miscellaneous general revenue	720,317	7.9
Utility revenue	1,399	-
Liquor stores revenue	134409	1.5
Insurance trust revenue[1]	2,294,548	25.0
Total Expenditure	6,355,680	100.0
Intergovernmental expenditure	1,233,962	19.4
Direct expenditure	5,121,718	80.6
Current operation	3,589,087	56.5
Capital outlay	496,092	7.8
Insurance benefits and repayments	964,600	15.2
Assistance and subsidies	44,969	0.7
Interest on debt	26,970	0.4
Exhibit: Salaries and wages	724,076	11.4
Total Expenditure	6,355,680	100.0
General expenditure	5,274,439	83.0
Intergovernmental expenditure	1,233,962	19.4
Direct expenditure	4,040,477	63.6
General expenditure, by function:		
Education	1,940,232	30.5
Public welfare	864,893	13.6
Hospitals	3,768	0.1
Health	315,987	5.0
Highways	589,310	9.3
Police protection	43,539	0.7
Correction	145,716	2.3
Natural resources	208,677	3.3
Parks and recreation	24,346	0.4
Governmental administration	294,843	4.6
Interest on general debt	26,970	0.4
Other and unallocable	703,022	11.1
Utility expenditure	28,786	0.3
Liquor stores expenditure	116630	1.8
Insurance trust expenditure	964,600	15.2
Debt at End of Fiscal Year	949,280	X
Cash and Security Holdings	36,860,605	X

X = Not applicable.
- = Zero or rounds to zero.
[1] Within insurance trust revenue, net earnings of state retirement systems is a calculated statistic (the item code in the data file is X08), and thus can be positive or negative. Net earnings is the sum of earnings on investments plus gains on investments minus losses on investments. The change made in 2002 for asset valuation from book to market value in accordance with Statement 34 of the Governmental Accounting Standards Board is reflected in the calculated statistics.

Table WY-16. State Government Tax Collections, 2021

(Dollars in thousands, percent.)

Item	Dollars	Percent distribution
Total Taxes	1,874,876	100.0
Property taxes	295,925	15.8
Sales and gross receipts	927,089	49.4
General sales and gross receipts	734,785	39.2
Selective sales and gross receipts	192,304	10.3
Alcoholic beverages	2,238	0.1
Amusements	5,018	-
Insurance premiums	36,231	1.9
Motor fuels	111,244	5.9
Pari-mutuels	8,064	0.4
Public utilities	4,592	0.2
Tobacco products	21,553	1.1
Other selective sales	3,364	0.2
Licenses	212,497	11.3
Alcoholic beverages	X	-
Amusements	0	-
Corporations in general	17,751	0.9
Hunting and fishing	42,975	2.3
Motor vehicle	102,438	5.5
Motor vehicle operators	4,675	0.2
Public utilities	X	-
Occupation and business, NEC	44,658	2.4
Other licenses	0	-
Income taxes	X	-
Individual income	X	-
Corporation net income	X	-
Other taxes	439,365	23.4
Death and gift	0	-
Documentary and stock transfer	X	-
Severance	435,314	23.2
Taxes, NEC	4,051	0.2

X = Not applicable.
- = Zero or rounds to zero.

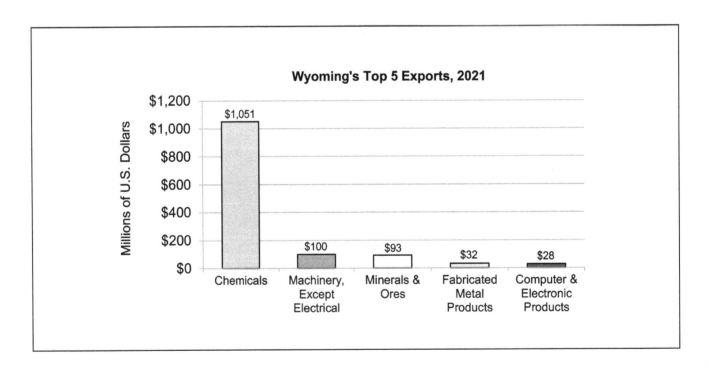

Wyoming's Top 5 Exports, 2021

NOTES AND DEFINITIONS

The state chapters in this book follow a standard plan of organization, and the same data sources are used for the tables and figures found in each chapter. These notes describe the standard data sources, which are presented by topic in the order in which they appear in each chapter. Definitions, brief descriptions of methodology, and sources of additional information are also provided.

Symbols used are included in the footnotes of the tables.

Table 1.
Source: U.S. Department of Commerce, U.S. Census Bureau, 2000 and 2010 Decennial Census, Population Estimates Program, Vintage 2021 Estimates, https:// www.census.gov/programs-surveys/popest.html.

Population estimates data are accessed from the U.S. Census Bureau's website. The data for percent change, 2010–2021, were calculated by the editor.

Population estimates and the decennial census. Population data are estimates produced by the Census Bureau. The Bureau's Population Estimates Program (PEP) produces estimates of the population as of July 1 for each year following the most recently published decennial census (the actual physical count of the population made every ten years, which is described below). Existing data on births, deaths, and domestic and international immigration are used to update the decennial census base. PEP estimates are used to set federal funding allocations, update national surveys, and monitor recent demographic changes.

Noncitizens residing in the United States are included, regardless of their immigration status.

Persons temporarily away from their usual residence on Census Day (April 1), for reasons such as vacation or business trips, were counted as being at their usual residence. People who live at more than one residence during the week, month, or year were counted as being at the place in which they lived most of the year. However, people without a usual residence were counted as being where they were staying on Census Day.

Age, sex, race, and ethnicity. While estimates of the age and sex of the population are straightforward, estimates of race and ethnicity are not. Decennial census data on race and ethnicity are based on self-identification by the respondent, and the same respondent may answer differently on separate occasions. On the 2000 decennial census, respondents could report more than one race; in previous censuses, respondents had to identify themselves as belonging to only one race.

The Census Bureau treats Hispanic or Latino origin as a separate and distinct concept from race. Beginning with the 2000 census, a separate self-identification question was asked regarding Hispanic or Latino origin. Persons of Hispanic or Latino origin are those who classified themselves as belonging to one of the specific categories listed on the questionnaire—Mexican, Puerto Rican, Cuban, or Other Spanish/Hispanic origin (including those whose origins are from Spain, the Spanish-speaking countries of Central and South America, or the Dominican Republic). People who are Hispanic may be of any race, and people in each race group may be Hispanic. The overlap of race and Hispanic origin is a major comparability issue because Hispanic individuals may be of any race. For a further discussion of this issue, see U.S. Census Bureau, *U.S. Census Bureau Guidance on the Presentation and Comparison of Race and Hispanic Origin Data* (June 12, 2003), https:// www.census.gov/topics/population/hispanic-origin/about/ comparing-race-and-hispanic-origin.html.

Table 2.
Source: U.S. Department of Commerce, U.S. Census Bureau, 2000 and 2010 Decennial Census, American Community Survey, 2000, 2010, and 2020 (ACS 5-Year Estimates), https://data.census.gov.

Data on marital status were tabulated for persons 15 years and over. Marital status was reported for each person as either "now married," "widowed," "divorced," "separated," or "never married." Individuals who were living together (unmarried people, people in commonlaw marriages) reported the marital status they considered most appropriate.

Now Married, Except Separated. Includes people whose current marriage has not ended through widowhood, divorce, or separation (regardless of previous marital history). The category may also include couples who live together or people in common-law marriages if they consider this category the most appropriate. In certain tabulations, currently married people are further classified as "spouse present" or "spouse absent."

Separated. Refers to people who were not living with their spouse due to marital discord.

Divorced. Indicates people who reported being divorced and had not remarried.

Widowed. Refers to people whose last marriage ended with the death of their spouse and who had not remarried.

Never married. The term applies to those who had never been legally married or people whose only marriage ended in an annulment.

Table 3.
Source: U.S. Department of Commerce, U.S. Census Bureau, 2000 and 2010 Decennial Census, American Community Survey, 2000, 2010, and 2020 (ACS 5-Year Estimates), https://data.census.gov.

The annual data were obtained from the Census Bureau. The data for average annual percent change, 2010–2020, were calculated by the editor.

Households. A household comprises one or more persons occupying a single housing unit, such as a house, apartment, or a room occupied as separate living quarters. A household may consist of a person living alone, a single family, two or more families living together, or any other group of unrelated individuals sharing a housing unit.

Householder. The person, or one of the people, in whose name the home is owned, being bought, or rented. If there is no such person present, any household member 15 years old and over can serve as the householder for the purposes of the census. Two types of householders are distinguished: a family householder and a nonfamily householder. A family householder is a householder living with one or more people related to him or her by birth, marriage, or adoption. The householder and all people in the household related to him are family members. A nonfamily householder is a householder living alone or with nonrelatives only.

Housing unit. A house, an apartment, a mobile home or trailer, a group of rooms, or a single room occupied as separate living quarters, or if vacant, intended for occupancy as separate living quarters.

Median gross rent. The monthly amount of contract rent plus the estimated average monthly cost of utilities (electricity, gas, water, and sewer) and fuels (oil, coal, kerosene, wood, etc.).

Median monthly owner costs for housing units with a mortgage. The sum of payments for mortgages, deeds of trust, contracts to purchase, or similar debts on the property (including payments for the first mortgage, second mortgages, home equity loans, and other junior mortgages); real estate taxes; fire, hazard, and flood insurance on the property; utilities (electricity, gas, water, and sewer); and fuels (oil, coal, kerosene, wood, etc.). It also includes, where appropriate, the monthly condominium fee for condominiums and mobile home costs (installment loan payments, personal property taxes, site rent, registration fees, and license fees). Selected monthly owner costs were tabulated for all owner-occupied units, and usually are shown separately for units "with a mortgage" and for units "not mortgaged.

Median value of owner-occupied housing units. Data for the median value of owner-occupied housing units are respondents' estimates of how much their property would sell for if it was currently on the market.

Table 4.
Source: U.S. Department of Commerce, U.S. Census Bureau, American Community Survey, 2016–2020 (ACS 5-Year Estimates), https://data.census.gov.

The annual data derives from Census estimates. The data for percent change were calculated by the editor.

Residence 1 year ago. The data on residence 1 year ago were derived from answers to Question 15, which were asked of the population 1 year and older. For the American Community Survey, people who had moved from another residence in the United States or Puerto Rico 1 year earlier were asked to report the exact address (number and street name); the name of the city, town, or post office; the name of the U.S. county; and the ZIP Code where they lived 1 year ago. People living outside the United States and Puerto Rico were asked to report the name of the foreign country or U.S. Island Area where they were living 1 year ago.

Native born. The native population includes anyone who was a U.S. citizen or a U.S. national at birth. This includes respondents who indicated they were born in the United States, Puerto Rico, a U.S. Island Area (such as Guam), or abroad of an American (U.S. citizen) parent or parents.

Foreign born. The foreign-born population includes anyone who was not a U.S. citizen or a U.S. national at birth. This includes respondents who indicated they were a U.S. citizen by naturalization or not a U.S. citizen.

Respondent's ability to speak English. Respondents who reported speaking a language other than English were asked to indicate their English-speaking ability based on one of the following categories: "Very well," "Well," "Not well," or "Not at all." Those who answered "Well," "Not well," or "Not at all" are sometimes referred as "Less than 'very well.'" Respondents were not instructed on how to interpret the response categories in this question. Households in which no one 14 and over speaks English only or speaks a language other than English at home and speaks English "very well" identifies households that may need English language assistance. This arises when no one 14 and over meets either of two conditions: (1) they speak English at home or (2) even though they speak another language, they also report that they speak English "very well".

Table 5.
Source: U.S. Department of Commerce, U.S. Census Bureau, American Community Survey, 2020 (ACS 5-Year Estimates), https://data.census.gov.

Median household income. Includes the income of the householder and all other individuals 15 years old and over in the household, whether they are related to the householder or not. Because many households consist of only one person, average household income is usually less than average family income. Total income is the sum of the amounts reported separately for wage or salary income; net self-employment income; interest, dividends, or net rental or royalty income or income from estates and trusts; Social Security or railroad retirement income; Supplemental Security Income (SSI); public assistance or welfare payments; retirement, survivor, or disability pensions; and all other income. Receipts from the following sources are not included as income: capital gains, money received from the sale of property (unless the recipient was engaged in the business of selling such property); the value of income "in kind" from food stamps, public housing subsidies, medical care, employer contributions for individuals, etc.; withdrawal of bank deposits; money borrowed; tax refunds; exchange of money between relatives living in the same household; gifts; and lump-sum inheritances, insurance payments, and other types of lump-sum receipts.

Median family income. The incomes of all members 15 years old and over related to the householder are summed and treated as a single amount.

Poverty. Following the Office of Management and Budget standards that have been in use since the late 1960s, the Census Bureau uses a set of money income thresholds that vary by family size and composition to determine the proportion of Americans in poverty. If a household's total income is less than the threshold for the applicable family size, age of householder, and number of children present in the family under 18 years of age, every individual in that household is considered to be living in poverty.

Table 6.
Source: U.S. Department of Commerce. U.S. Census Bureau. American Community Survey, 2011-2020 (ACS 5-Year Estimates for 2020), https://data.census.gov.

The data on health insurance coverage were derived from answers to Question 16 in the American Community Survey (ACS), which was asked of all respondents. Respondents were instructed to report their current coverage and to mark "yes" or "no" for each of the eight types of private and public insurance listed. Health insurance coverage in the ACS and other Census Bureau surveys define coverage to include plans and programs that provide comprehensive health coverage. Plans that provide insurance for specific conditions or situations such as cancer and long-term care policies are not considered coverage. Likewise, other types of insurance like dental, vision, life, and disability insurance are not considered health insurance coverage.

Private health insurance. Coverage through an employer or union, a plan purchased by an individual from a private company, or TRICARE or other military health care.

Public health insurance. Coverage includes the federal programs Medicare, Medicaid, and VA Health Care (provided through the Department of Veterans Affairs); the Children's Health Insurance Program (CHIP); and individual state health plans.

Table 7.
Source: U.S. Department of Labor, Bureau of Labor Statistics, Current Population Survey, https://www.bls.gov/cps.

Annual data on the labor force, employment, and unemployment for state and local areas are available from two major sources: the Current Population Survey (CPS) and the Local Area Unemployment Statistics (LAUS) program. In Table 7, the data are obtained from the CPS. The CPS is a monthly survey of approximately 60,000 households conducted by the Census Bureau for the Bureau of Labor Statistics. It provides comprehensive data on topics such as the labor force, employment, unemployment, and persons not in the labor force. The data for 2021 in Table 7 are preliminary, so the data may differ slightly from the final table when it is released.

Civilian noninstitutional population included are persons 16 years of age and older residing in the 50 States and the District of Columbia who are not inmates of institutions (for example, penal and mental facilities, homes for the aged), and who are not on active duty in the Armed Forces.

Civilian labor force includes all persons classified as employed or unemployed who are not inmates of institutions (for example, penal and mental facilities, homes for the aged), and who are not on active duty in the Armed Forces. Civilians 16 years of age and over in the noninstitutional population who are not classified as employed or unemployed are defined as not in the labor force.

Employment includes persons 16 years and over in the civilian noninstitutional population who, during the reference week, (a) did any work at all (at least 1 hour) as paid employees; worked in their own business, profession, or on their own farm, or worked 15 hours or more as unpaid workers in an enterprise operated by a member of the family; and (b) all those who were not working but who had jobs or businesses from which they were temporarily absent because of vacation, illness, bad weather, childcare problems, maternity or paternity leave, labor-management dispute, job training, or other family or personal reasons, whether or not they were paid for the time off or were seeking other jobs.

Unemployed persons. All civilians who were not employed (according to the above definition) during the reference week, but who were available for work—except for temporary illness—and who had made specific efforts to find employment sometime during the previous four weeks. Persons who did not look for work because they were on layoff are also counted as unemployed.

Unemployment rate. The number of unemployed as a percentage of the civilian labor force.

Table 8.
Source: U.S. Department of Labor, Bureau of Labor Statistics, Local Area Unemployment Statistics, https://www.bls.gov/lau/home.htm.

The Local Area Unemployment Statistics (LAUS) program is a Federal-State cooperative effort in which monthly estimates of total employment and unemployment are prepared for approximately 7,300 areas.

The concepts and definitions underlying LAUS data come from the Current Population Survey (CPS), the household survey that is the official measure of the labor force for the nation. State monthly model estimates are controlled in "real time" to sum to national monthly labor force estimates from the CPS. These models combine current and historical data from the CPS, the Current Employment Statistics (CES) program, and State unemployment insurance (UI) systems. Estimates for seven large areas and their respective balances of State are also model-based. Estimates for the remainder of the substate labor market areas are produced through a building-block approach known as the "Handbook method." This procedure also uses data from several sources, including the CPS, the CES program, State UI systems, and the decennial census, to create estimates that are adjusted to the statewide measures of employment and unemployment. Below the labor market area level, estimates are prepared using disaggregation techniques based on inputs from the decennial census, annual population estimates, and current UI data.

Table 9.
Source: U.S. Department of Commerce, Bureau of Economic Analysis, https://www.bea.gov/data/economic-accounts/regional.

In this table, the data by industry reflect the North American Industry Classification System (NAICS), a supply- or production-based system that replaced the Standard Industrial Classification (SIC) system in January 2003. Estimates of state employment and earnings by industry use NAICS. NAICS was adopted to more fully reflect the current composition of U.S. businesses and to establish a standard measure of industry classification throughout the United States, Canada, and Mexico, in accordance with the North American Free Trade Agreement, to enhance cross-border comparisons among these trading partners.

Wage and salary employment, also referred to as wage and salary jobs, measures the average annual number of full-time and part-time jobs in each area by place-of-work. All jobs for which wages and salaries are paid are counted. Full-time and part-time jobs are counted with equal weight. Jury and witness service, as well as paid employment of prisoners, are not counted as wage and salary employment; the payments for these activities are classified as "other labor income" in the personal income measure. Corporate directorships are counted as self-employment. This concept of employment differs from that in the Current Population Survey (CPS), which is the source of the employment data in the table on population and labor force. The CPS is a household survey. It counts each individual only once, no matter how many jobs the person holds, and it includes only civilian employment.

Wages and salaries consist of the monetary remuneration of employees, including corporate officer salaries and bonuses, commissions, pay-in-kind, incentive payments, and tips. It reflects the amount of payments disbursed, but not necessarily earned during the year. Wage and salary disbursements are measured before deductions, such as social security contributions and union dues. In recent years, stock options have become a point of discussion. Wage and salary disbursements include stock options of nonqualified plans at the time that they have been exercised by the individual. Stock options are reported in wage and salary disbursements. The value that is included in wages is the difference between the exercise price and the price that the stock options were granted. Average annual wages and salaries were calculated by the editor by dividing total wages and salaries paid during the year in each sector by total wage and salary employment in that sector.

Table 10.
Source: U.S. Department of Commerce, U.S. Census Bureau, American Community Survey, 2018–2020, https://data.census.gov.

Civilian labor force. (See definition under Table 7.)

Employment. (See definition under Table 7.)

Family. A family consists of a householder and one or more other people living in the same household who are related to the householder by birth, marriage, or adoption. All people in a household who are related to the householder are regarded as members of his or her family. A family household may contain people not related to the householder, but those people are not included as part of the householder's family in tabulations. Thus, the number of family households is equal to the number of families, but family households may include more members than do families. A household can contain only one family for purposes of tabulations. Not all households contain families since a household may be comprised of a group of unrelated people or of one person living alone – these are called nonfamily households. Families are classified by type as either a "married-couple family" or "other family" according to the sex of the householder and the presence of relatives. The data on family type are based on answers to questions on sex and relationship that were asked of all people.

Married-couple family. A family in which the householder and his or her spouse are listed as members of the same household.

Other Family

Male householder, no wife present. A family with a male householder and no spouse of householder present.

Female householder, no husband present. A family with a female householder and no spouse of householder present.

Table 11.
Source: U.S. Department of Commerce, U.S. Census Bureau, American Community Survey, 2020 (ACS 5-Year Estimates), https://www.census.gov/programs-surveys/acs.html.

Data on school enrollment and educational attainment were derived from a sample of the population. Persons were classified as enrolled in school if they reported attending a "regular" public or private school (or college) during the year. The instructions were to "include only nursery school, kindergarten, elementary school, and schooling which would lead to a high school diploma or a college degree" as regular school. The Census Bureau defines a public school as "any school or college controlled and supported by a local, county, state, or federal government." Schools primarily supported and controlled by religious organizations or other private groups are defined as private schools.

Data on educational attainment are tabulated for the population 25 years old and over. The data were derived from a question that asked respondents for the highest level of school completed or the highest degree received. Persons who had passed a high school equivalency examination were considered high school graduates. Schooling received in foreign schools was to be reported as the equivalent grade or years in the regular American school system.

Vocational and technical training, such as barber school training; business, trade, technical, and vocational schools; or other training for a specific trade are specifically excluded.

High school graduate or more. This category includes persons whose highest degree was a high school diploma or its equivalent, and those who reported any level higher than a high school diploma.

Bachelor's degree or more. This category includes persons who have received bachelor's degrees, master's degrees, professional school degrees (such as law school or medical school degrees), and doctoral degrees.

Graduate degree or more. This category includes persons who have a master's degree, including the traditional MA and MS degrees and field-specific degrees, such as MSW, MEd, MBA, MLS, and MEng., or a professional school degree: medicine, dentistry, chiropractic, optometry, osteopathic medicine, pharmacy, podiatry, veterinary medicine, law, and theology.

Table 12.
Source: U.S. Department of Education, National Center for Education Statistics, *Common Core of Data*, https://nces.ed.gov/ccd.

The data are from the Common Core of Data (CCD), which is made up of a set of five surveys sent to state education departments. Most of the data are obtained from administrative records maintained by the state education agencies (SEAs). Statistical information is collected annually from approximately 100,000 public elementary and secondary schools and approximately 18,000 public school districts (including supervisory unions and regional education service agencies) in the 50 states, the District of Columbia, Department of Defense Schools, and the outlying areas. The SEAs compile CCD requested data into prescribed formats and transmit the information to NCES.

A **school district** or Local Education Agency (LEA) is the agency at the local level whose primary responsibility is to operate public schools or to contract for public school services.

The primary grades include pre-kindergarten through grade 4. Middle school grades included grades 5 through 8. High school grades include grades 9 through 12. Ungraded students are included in the total but are not separately listed. Some states have no ungraded students.

The **student-teacher ratio** is calculated by dividing the number of students in all schools by the number of full-time equivalent teachers employed by all schools and agencies.

Current expenditures per student are derived by dividing total current expenditures by the fall student membership count from the CCD. Current expenditures are comprised of expenditures for the day-to-day operation of schools and school districts for public elementary and secondary education, including expenditures for staff salaries and benefits, supplies, and purchased services. They exclude expenditures for construction, equipment, property, debt services, and programs outside of public elementary and secondary education, such as adult education and community services. Student membership consists of the count of students enrolled on or about October 1 and is comparable across all states. Please see the NCES Web site for the exact beginning and ending dates of fiscal years for each state.

The **4-year adjusted cohort graduation rate (ACGR)** is the number of students who graduate in 4 years with a regular high school diploma divided by the number of students who form the adjusted cohort for the graduating class. From the beginning of 9th grade (or the earliest high school grade), students who are entering that grade for the first time form a cohort that is "adjusted" by adding any students who subsequently transfer into the cohort and subtracting any students who subsequently transfer out, emigrate to another country, or die.

Students are eligible for **free and reduced-price lunch** under the National School Lunch Program, which was established by President Truman in 1946. The program is a federally assisted meal program operated in public and private nonprofit schools and residential childcare centers and provides cash subsidies for free or reduced-price meals to students based on family size and income criteria. Participation in the National School Lunch Program depends on income, and eligibility is often used to estimate student needs.

An **English language learner** is an individual who, due to any of the reasons listed below, has enough difficulty speaking, reading, writing, or understanding the English language that it affects their ability to learn in an English-speaking classroom. Such an individual (1) was not born in the United States or has a native language other than English; (2) comes from environments where a language other than English is dominant; or (3) is an American Indian or Alaska Native and comes from environments where a language other than English has had a significant impact on the individual's level of English language proficiency.

Individuals with Disabilities Education Act (IDEA) is a federal law requiring services to children with disabilities throughout the nation. IDEA governs how states and public agencies provide early intervention, special education, and related services to eligible infants, toddlers, children, and youth with disabilities. Infants and toddlers with disabilities (birth–age 2) and their families receive early intervention services under IDEA, Part C. Children and youth (ages 3–21) receive special education and related services under IDEA, Part B.

Public School Types

A **special education school** focuses primarily on special education—including instruction for students with any of the following conditions: autism, deaf-blindness, developmental delay, hearing impairment, mental retardation, multiple disabilities, orthopedic impairment, serious emotional disturbance, specific learning disability, speech or language impairment, traumatic brain injury, visual impairment, and other health impairments—and that adapts curriculum, materials, or instruction for students served.

A **vocational education school** focuses primarily on providing formal preparation for semiskilled, skilled, technical, or professional occupations for high school-age students who have opted to develop or expand their employment opportunities, often in lieu of preparing for college entry.

An **alternative education school** is an elementary/secondary school that (1) addresses needs of students that typically cannot be met in a regular school, (2) provides nontraditional education, (3) serves as an adjunct to a regular school, or (4) falls outside the categories of regular, special education, or vocational education.

Table 13.
Source: U.S. Department of Commerce, U.S. Census Bureau, November Supplement to the Current Population Survey (CPS), *Voting and Registration in the Election of November 2020,* **https://www.census.gov/topics/public-sector/voting/data/tables.html.**

Voter participation data are obtained from additional questions regarding voting and voter registration, which are added to the Current Population Survey each November. Because these data are from a sample of the noninstitutional population, they differ from the "official" tally of voter participation reported by the Clerk of the U.S. House of Representatives.

Voting, people eligible to register. The population of voting age includes a considerable number of people who meet the age requirement but cannot register and vote. People who are not citizens are not eligible to vote. Among citizens of voting age, some people are not permitted to vote because they have been committed to penal institutions, mental hospitals, or other institutions, or because they fail to meet state and local resident requirements for various reasons. The eligibility to register is governed by state laws, which differ in many respects.

Registration is the act of qualifying to vote by formally enrolling on a list of voters. People who have moved to another election district must take steps to have their names placed on the voting rolls in their new place of residence.

In a few states or parts of states, no formal registration is required. Voters merely present themselves at the polling place on Election Day with proof that they are of age and have met the appropriate residence requirements. Therefore, in these areas people who are citizens and of voting age, and who meet the residence requirement, would be considered as being registered.

Voter, reported participation. Voter participation data are derived from replies to the following question asked of people (excluding noncitizens) of voting age: "In any election some people are not able to vote because they are sick or busy, or have some other reason, and others do not want to vote. Did (this person) vote in the election held on November (date varies)?"

Those of voting age were classified as "voted" or "did not vote." In most tables, this "did not vote" class includes those reported as "did not vote," "do not know," noncitizens, and nonrespondents. Nonrespondents and people who reported that they did not know if they voted were included in the "did not vote" class because of the general over-reporting by respondents in the sample.

Voter, reported registration. The data on registration were obtained by tabulating replies to the following question for those people included in the category "did not vote." "Was (this person) registered to vote in the November (date varies) election?"

All people reported as having voted were assumed to have been registered. Therefore, the total registered population is obtained by combining the number of people who voted and people included in the category "did not vote," but who had registered.

Table 14.
Source: U.S. Department of Justice, Federal Bureau of Investigation, Uniform Crime Reports, *Crime in the United States, 2020,* **https://ucr.fbi.gov/crime-in-the-u.s.**

The Uniform Crime Reports (UCR) Program, administered by the Federal Bureau of Investigation (FBI), was created in 1929 and collects information on the following crimes reported to law enforcement authorities: murder and nonnegligent manslaughter, rape, robbery, aggravated assault, burglary, larceny-theft, motor vehicle theft, and arson. Law enforcement agencies also report arrest data for 21 additional crime categories.

The UCR Program compiles data from monthly law enforcement reports and from individual crime incident records transmitted directly to the FBI or to centralized state agencies that report to the FBI. The program thoroughly examines each report it receives for reasonableness, accuracy, and deviations that may indicate errors. Large variations in crime levels may indicate modified records procedures, incomplete reporting, or changes in a jurisdiction's boundaries. To identify any unusual fluctuations in an agency's crime counts, the program compares monthly reports to previous submissions of the agency and to those for similar agencies.

The FBI annually publishes its findings in a preliminary release in the spring of the following calendar year, followed by a detailed annual report, *Crime in the United States*, issued in the fall. (The printed copy of *Crime in the United States* is published by Bernan Press.) In addition to crime counts and trends, this report includes data on crimes cleared, persons arrested (age, sex, and race), law enforcement personnel (including the number of sworn officers killed or assaulted), and the characteristics of homicides (including age, sex, and race of victims and offenders; victim-offender relationships; weapons used; and circumstances surrounding the homicides). Other periodic reports are also available from the UCR Program. Any deviations from UCR standard data are noted in the table.

Note for Users

Since crime is a sociological phenomenon influenced by a variety of factors, the FBI discourages data users from ranking agencies and using the data as a measurement of the effectiveness of law enforcement. Until data users examine all the variables that affect crime in a town, city, county, state, region, or college or university, they can make no meaningful comparisons.

Violent crime is composed of four offenses: murder and nonnegligent manslaughter, rape, robbery, and aggravated assault. According to the UCR Program's definition, violent crimes involve force or threat of force.

Murder and nonnegligent manslaughter is the willful (nonnegligent) killing of one human being by another. Deaths caused by negligence, attempts to kill, assaults to kill, suicides, and accidental deaths are excluded. The program classifies justifiable homicides separately and limits the definition to (1) the killing of a felon by a law enforcement officer in the line of duty; or (2) the killing of a felon, during the commission of a felony, by a private citizen.

Rape is defined as: penetration, no matter how slight, of the vagina or anus with any body part or object, or oral penetration by a sex organ of another person, without the consent of the victim. The FBI UCR Program's definition of rape, formerly "forcible rape," was revised in 2013. Attempts or assaults to commit rape are also included; however, statutory rape (no force used—victim is under the age of consent) and incest are excluded. Due to the revised definition, figures for rape in 2013 and later are not comparable to data from previous years. North Carolina's agencies submitted rape data according to the legacy definition of rape. Use caution when comparing the rape data for North Carolina in this volume to that of other states.

Robbery is the taking or attempted taking of anything of value from the care, custody, or control of a person or persons by force or threat of force or violence and/or by putting the victim in fear.

Aggravated assault is an unlawful attack by one person upon another for the purpose of inflicting severe or aggravated bodily injury. This type of assault usually is accompanied by the use of a weapon or by means likely to produce death or great bodily harm. Attempted aggravated assaults that involve the display of—or threat to use—a gun, knife, or other weapon is included in this crime category because serious personal injury would likely result if the assault were completed. When aggravated assault and larceny-theft occur together, the offense falls under the category of robbery. Simple assaults are excluded.

Property crime includes the offenses of burglary, larceny-theft, motor vehicle theft, and arson. The object of the theft-type offenses is the taking of money or property, but there is no force or threat of force against the victims. The property crime category includes arson because the offense involves the destruction of property; however, arson victims may be subjected to force.

Burglary (breaking or entering) is the unlawful entry of a structure to commit a felony or a theft. The use of force to gain entry need not have occurred. The Program has three subclassifications for burglary: forcible entry, unlawful entry where no force is used, and attempted forcible entry. The UCR definition of "structure" includes, for example, apartment, barn, house trailer or houseboat when used as a permanent dwelling, office, railroad car (but not automobile), stable, and vessel (i.e., ship).

Larceny-theft (except motor vehicle theft) is the unlawful taking, carrying, leading, or riding away of property from the possession or constructive possession of another. Examples are thefts of bicycles or automobile accessories, shoplifting, pocket-picking, or the stealing of any property or article that is not taken by force and violence or by fraud. Attempted larcenies are included. Embezzlement, confidence games, forgery, worthless checks, and the like, are excluded.

Motor vehicle theft is the theft or attempted theft of a motor vehicle. It includes the stealing of automobiles, trucks, buses, motorcycles, snowmobiles, and the like. The taking of a motor vehicle for temporary use by persons having lawful access is excluded from this definition. A motor vehicle is self-propelled and runs on land surface and not on rails. Motorboats, construction equipment, airplanes, and farming equipment are specifically excluded from this category.

Table 15.
Source: U.S. Department of Commerce, U.S. Census Bureau, https://www.census.gov/topics/public-sector/ government-finances.html.

The Census Bureau conducts an annual survey covering a range of government finance activities carried out by all state and local governments in the United States, including revenue, expenditures, debt, and assets. The data in this volume relate to state revenues and expenditures only, with the exception of the District of Columbia, for which local government data was used. Data generally reference state government fiscal year 2020, but data for the District of Columbia is for fiscal year 2019. General revenue comprises all revenue except utilities, liquor store, and insurance trust revenue. Intergovernmental revenue is funds from other governments (mainly the federal government), including general support, grants, shared taxes, and loans or advances. Other data on government finance by state, not shown in this volume, include federal government expenditures, obligations, contract awards, and insurance programs.

Table 16.
Source: U.S. Department of Commerce, U.S. Census Bureau, https://www.census.gov/topics/public-sector/ government-finances.html.

State tax data include all required taxes taken by government for public purposes, except for employer and employee assessments for Social Security and unemployment compensation. The data are shown in this volume are for each state and the District of Columbia for fiscal year 2021.

INDEX

HIGH SCHOOL GRADUATES
HISPANIC OR LATINO ORIGIN, POPULATION BY

HOMEOWNERSHIP RATES
HOUSEHOLDS AND HOUSING CHARACTERISTICS

S

SALARIES

SCHOOL ENROLLMENT AND EDUCATIONAL ATTAINMENT

SEX, POPULATION BY

W

WAGES BY INDUSTRY

WASHINGTON

CPSIA information can be obtained
at www.ICGtesting.com
Printed in the USA
BVHW060006071122
650042BV00005BA/13